AUSTRALIAN DICTIONARY

OF BIOGRAPHY

General Editor
JOHN RITCHIE

AUSTRALIAN
DICTIONARY
OF BIOGRAPHY

VOLUME 12 : 1891-1939

Smy - Z

General Editor
JOHN RITCHIE

Deputy General Editor
CHRISTOPHER CUNNEEN

Section Editors
G. C. BOLTON
K. J. CABLE
R. J. O'NEILL
J. R. POYNTER
HEATHER RADI

MELBOURNE UNIVERSITY PRESS

First published 1990

Typeset by Abb-typesetting Pty Ltd, Collingwood, Victoria
Printed in Australia by Griffin Press Limited
Netley, South Australia, for
Melbourne University Press, Carlton, Victoria 3053
U.S.A. and Canada: International Specialized Book Services, Inc.,
5602 N.E. Hassalo Street, Portland, Oregon 97213-3640
United Kingdom, Ireland and Europe: Europa Publications Limited
18 Bedford Square, London WC1B 3JN

National Library of Australia Cataloguing-in-Publication entry

Australian dictionary of biography. Volume 12, 1891–1939,
  Smy–Z.
  Bibliography
  ISBN 0 522 84437 5.
  ISBN 0 522 84236 4 (set).

  1. Australia—Biography—Dictionaries. 2. Australia
  —History—1891–1901—Biography. 3. Australia—
  History—1901–1945—Biography. I. Ritchie, John,
  1941–   . II Cunneen, Christopher, 1940–
920.094

PREFACE

This volume of the *Australian Dictionary of Biography*, containing 684 entries by 498 authors, is the last of six for the 1891-1939 section. The two volumes of the 1788-1850 section and the four of the 1851-1890 section were published from 1966 to 1976. The late Douglas Pike was general editor for volumes 1 to 5, Bede Nairn for volume 6, Nairn and Geoffrey Serle for volumes 7 to 10, and Serle for volume 11. John Ritchie succeeded Serle on 1 March 1988. The chronological division was designed to simplify production, for 7211 entries have been included in volumes 1-12. (Volumes 1-2, for 1788-1850, had 1116 entries; volumes 3-6, for 1851-1890, 2053; volumes 7-12, for 1891-1939, 4042.) The placing of each individual's name in the appropriate section has been determined by when he/she did his/her most important work (*floruit*). An index will be published in 1991 and four volumes covering those whose *floruit* was after 1939 and who died before 1981 will be published subsequently.

The selection of names for inclusion required prolonged consultation. After quotas were estimated, working parties in each State and the armed services working party prepared provisional lists which were widely circulated and carefully amended. Many of the names were obviously significant and worthy of inclusion as leaders in politics, business, the armed services, the professions, the arts, the labour movement, etc. Others have been included as representatives of ethnic and social minorities and of a wide range of occupations, or as innovators, notorieties or eccentrics. Some had to be omitted through pressure of space or lack of material, and thereby joined the great mass whose members richly deserve a more honoured place, but thousands of these names, and information about them, have accumulated in the biographical register at the *A.D.B.* headquarters in the Australian National University. A selection of 8100 of them was published in 1987 as *A Biographical Register 1788-1939*.

Most authors were nominated by working parties. The burden of writing has been shared almost equally by the staff of universities and other tertiary institutions, and by a variety of other specialists.

The *A.D.B.* is a project based on consultation and co-operation. The Research School of Social Sciences at the Australian National University has borne the cost of the headquarters staff, of much research and of some special contingencies, while other Australian universities have supported the project in various ways. The *A.D.B.*'s policies were originally determined by a national committee, composed mainly of representatives from the departments of history in each Australian university. In Canberra the editorial board has kept in touch with all these representatives, and with the working parties, librarians, archivists and other local experts, as well as overseas correspondents and research assistants in each Australian capital. With such varied support, the *A.D.B.* is truly a national project.

ACKNOWLEDGMENTS

The *Australian Dictionary of Biography* is a programme fully supported by the Research School of Social Sciences at the Australian National University. Special thanks are due to Professor K. S. Inglis for guidance as chairman of the editorial board, and to Professor P. F. Bourke, director of the R.S.S.S., A.N.U., and Mr P. J. Grimshaw, the school's business manager. Those who helped in planning the shape of the work have been mentioned in earlier volumes.

Within Australia the *A.D.B.* is indebted to many librarians and archivists in Canberra and in each State; to the secretaries of historical and genealogical societies; to the Australian War Memorial and the Australian National Gallery in Canberra; to the registrars of probates in the various States, and of the Supreme and Family courts, whose co-operation has solved many problems; to various town and shire clerks; to the Royal Australasian College of Physicians, Sydney; to the Royal Humane Society of Australasia; to the Institution of Engineers, Australia; to the Melbourne Club; and to the Australian Department of Defence for authenticating a host of details. Warm thanks for the free gift of their time and talents are due to contributors, to members of the editorial board and to the working parties. For particular advice, the *A.D.B.* owes much to the late Brigadier M. Austin, Bryan Gandevia, Michael D. de B. Collins Persse, F. B. Smith, the late G. R. Vazenry, Peter Yeend, and to the staff of the Petherick Room, National Library of Australia.

Essential assistance with birth, death and marriage certificates has been provided by the co-operation of registrars in New South Wales, Queensland, South Australia, Tasmania, Victoria, Western Australia, the Northern Territory and the Australian Capital Territory; by the General Register offices in Edinburgh and in London; by Bureaux of Vital Statistics in State Health departments in California, Colorado, Massachusetts, Michigan, Mississippi, New Jersey, Ohio, Pennsylvania and Texas, United States of America; by the Ministry of Health, British Columbia, and the registrars-general, Ontario and New Brunswick, Canada; by the Immigration Department, Hong Kong; by the assistant-archivist, St Paul's Church, Valetta, Malta; by the mayors of Montpellier, Neuilly-sur-Seine, Nice and Reims in France, and of Noumea, New Caledonia; by civil status officers in Arizzo, Como, Ferraro and Milan, Italy; by the state archives in Frankfurt am Main and Aachen, the Evangelische Kirche in Deutschland, Hannover, and the Evangelischer Regionalverband, Frankfurt am Main, Federal Republic of Germany; by the Österreichische Akademie der Wissenschaften, Vienna; and by the South African embassy, Canberra.

For other assistance overseas, thanks are due to Sean Murphy, Dublin, and Betty Iggo, Edinburgh; to Information Systems Consultants Inc., Washington, D.C., U.S.A.; to the archives and libraries of the universities of Cambridge, Durham, Liverpool, London, Manchester and Oxford, the Imperial College of Science and Technology and University College, London, and Sidney Sussex College and Jesus College, Cambridge, England; to the universities of Aberdeen, Edinburgh, Glasgow and Strathclyde, Scotland; to the Queen's University of Belfast, Northern Ireland; to Trinity College, University of Dublin, and University College, Cork, Ireland; to the universities of Auckland and Otago, New Zealand; to the University of Lausanne, Switzerland; to the Free University of Brussels, Belgium; to Friedrich-Schiller Universität, Jena, German Democratic Republic; to Georg-August Universität Göttingen and Philipps-Universität, Marburg, Federal Republic of Germany; and to Columbia

ACKNOWLEDGMENTS

University, Harvard University and the universities of Alaska, Chicago and Montana, U.S.A.

Gratitude is also due to the National Portrait Gallery, London, the Royal College of Physicians, the Royal College of Surgeons of England, the Royal Entomological Society of London, the Royal Geographical Society, the Royal Humane Society, the Royal Institute of Public Health and Hygiene, The Royal Meteorological Society, the Royal Society of Health, the Royal Veterinary College, the Geological Society, the British Psychoanalytical Society, the City of London School and the Institute of Psychoanalysis, all in London, to the Royal Scottish Academy, Edinburgh, to the Department of Justice and the National Archives of Montreal, the *Dictionary of Canadian Biography*, and the parliamentary archives and the chief coroner, British Columbia, Canada; to the *Dictionary of New Zealand Biography*, the reference librarian, Alexander Turnbull Library, and the Ministry of Defence, Wellington, and the Department of Justice, Lower Hutt, New Zealand; to the Archives Cantonales Vaudoises, Chavannes-près-Renens, Switzerland; to the state archivist, Oslo; to the Geological Society of America and St Andrew's Cathedral, Honolulu, and the Historical Services Division, Department of the Army,Washington, D.C., U.S.A.; and to other individuals and institutions who have co-operated with the *A.D.B.*

The *A.D.B.* deeply regrets the death in 1989 of Dr Jim Gibbney, for eighteen years a dedicated and cheerful research editor. The deaths of such notable contributors as F. R. Arnott, Peter Bartlett, Arthur E. E. Bottrell, C. Craven-Sands, W. G. K. Duncan, W. W. Fielder, D. G. Gallon, S. H. Gilbert, A. C. Gray, A. W. Hammett, F. C. Hutley, Phyllis Mander-Jones, John R. Robertson, Mary Turner Shaw, L. A. Simpson, G. R. Vazenry, John M. Ward and Marjorie Wymark are also regretted, as are those of J. A. La Nauze, D. I. McDonald and L. L. Robson who died after the text of this volume was typeset.

Grateful acknowledgment is due to the director and staff of Melbourne University Press; to the editorial and research staff in Canberra: Darryl Bennet, Helen Boxall, Frank Brown, Martha Campbell, Suzanne Edgar, Gillian Fulloon, Helga Griffin, Hilary Kent, Diane Langmore, Margaret Steven and Sheila Tilse; to Susan Hogan in Sydney, Jennifer Harrison in Brisbane, Joyce Gibberd in Adelaide, Wendy Birman in Perth, Anne Rand in Hobart, Geoff Browne and Syd Tregellis-Smith in Melbourne, and Sally O'Neill at Oxford, England; to the administrative staff: Anne-Marie Gaudry, Edna Kauffman and Ivy Meere; thanks are also due to former staff members—Sarah Ferguson, Rachel Hewson, Merrilyn Lincoln, Peter Milthorp and Ann Smith—who worked on Volume 12.

COMMITTEES

When SIR KEITH HANCOCK, the most honoured of Australian historians, died on 13 August 1988 in his ninety-first year, he had seen ten volumes of the *Australian Dictionary of Biography* appear, and launched the tenth with a sunny speech that displayed both pride and modesty: pride in the work, modesty about his own part in creating it. The future of his creation is now so solidly assured that we can confidently expect a long entry on him in a volume as yet unnumbered. In the meantime Volume 12, completing the third stage of the grand enterprise which began under his leadership three decades ago, is a good place for a brief note on what he did for it.

At Oxford in the late 1940s Professor Hancock was on the central committee of the *Dictionary of National Biography*; later, in Australia, he wrote of that work: 'Its patriotic value, if the phrase may be permitted, is rooted in its scholarly value'. The conjunction of *patria* and scholarship is significant, made by a man who entitled his autobiography *Country and Calling*. Writing his life of Smuts in the 1950s, he had good reason to curse the absence of a South African equivalent to the *D.N.B.* which he reckoned could have saved him a year or more.

When he returned to Australia in 1957 as founding director of the Research School of Social Sciences at the Australian National University, the idea of a local *D.N.B.* appealed to him, both as an Australian and as a scholar. He shrewdly saw it as just the sort of initiative that would make people in the State universities value the A.N.U., and one of his first archiepiscopal acts was to summon historians from all over the country to a conference on this and other matters, held at the A.N.U. in August 1957. His A.N.U. colleague Laurie Fitzhardinge had proposed a dictionary of biography at the Australian and New Zealand Association for the Advancement of Science conference of 1951 and had begun to compile a national biographical register. Should this register be continued? More ambitiously, should a biographical dictionary be undertaken? The historians answered 'Yes' to both questions and went home leaving Hancock to begin the planning.

By 1960 the enterprise had an Editorial Board, of A.N.U. people and volume editors, a broadly based National Committee and Working Parties in every State. There was not yet a general editor, or even sufficient agreement around the country on Hancock's plan for having a single person rather than a group of, say, four to do that job. He himself was having to give the project more of his own time than he had expected. By late 1961 he had convinced everybody, and a committee chose Douglas Pike, professor of history at the University of Tasmania, to be general editor from January 1962. Then Hancock had to persuade the A.N.U. Council to create a new chair and to appoint Pike to it in accordance with regular procedures. To a few colleagues he sent a draft of his paper for Council, asking if they thought he had got it right. 'I want to leave Council with the feeling that it is *not* being presented with a *fait accompli*. I also want to leave them with the feeling that they will be awful cads, and the flouters of nationwide academic opinion, if they don't help us to get Douglas Pike on this campus.'

Council approved. Pike moved to Canberra in January 1964, after two years of commuting in which progress was impeded by a conflict between M. H. Ellis, Sydney journalist and historian, and everybody else. 'The good ship *ADB*', Hancock said later, 'nearly became a wreck in Sydney Harbour' until Douglas Pike 'salvaged the sinking ship and set it on course'. The salvage was a joint operation. As chairman of

Editorial Board and National Committee, and as pipe-smoking neighbour, Hancock gave the general editor counsel, blessing and protection while he turned a vulnerable project into what Bede Nairn describes at the beginning of Volume 6 as 'a complex and efficient production system'. The appearance of Volume 1 in 1966 was perhaps the most gratifying event in Hancock's first year of retirement. By the time he launched Volume 10, twenty years later, he was sure that the makers of the *A.D.B.* had not only made good their ambition to produce a work comparable with the British model, but had done better. They had been both more scholarly, he judged, delving deep into primary sources, whereas the *D.N.B.* relied more often than not on published material, and also more adventurous, reaching out beyond the eminent in church and state, commerce and industry, science and literature and art, to include people 'widely representative of endeavour and achievement on *every* front of our experience as an emergent nation'. To prove the point he cited the entry on Eddie Gilbert, Aboriginal cricketer. The comparison was deeply gratifying to Keith Hancock as scholar and as independent Australian Briton.

K.S.I.

AUTHORS

ADAMS, J. D.:
Vogt.
ADRIAN, Colin J.:
Sparks.
ALEXANDER, Alison:
Stevens, J.
ALEXANDER, Fred:
Whitfeld.
ALLEN, B. J.:
Stanley, G.
ALLEN, Stephen:
Whittle.
ANDERSON, Hugh:
Vennard; Williamson.
ANDERSON, John:
Watt, W. A.
APPERLY, Richard E.:
Sulman, Sir J.; Wilson, William Hardy.
ARNOTT, F. R.*:
Wand.
ATCHISON, John:
Thompson, C. V.; Varley; Wearne;
Weingarth.
ATKINSON, H. F.:
Tuckfield.

BAKER, Gwen:
Whitelegge.
BARKER, Anthony:
Timms.
BARRETT, Bernard:
Snowden.
BASSETT, Jan:
Walker, Jean.
BATE, Weston:
Spielvogel; Williams, R. E.
BEHR, John:
Traeger.
BELL, Peter:
Torode.
BENNET, Darryl:
Wynne, A.
BENNETT, J. M.:
Street, Sir P.; Teece; Windeyer, R. & W.
BENNETT, Scott:
Solomon, A.; Stanbury.
BENTLEY, Mollie:
Walsh, J. J.
BENWELL, W. S.:
Triaca; Vigano.
BERTRAND, Ina:
Turnbull, E.
BETTISON, Margaret:
Todd, R.
BIRMAN, Wendy:
Snook; Taylor, G.; Thomson, J.; Wittenoom.

* deceased

BLABER, Ron:
Thwaites, F.
BLACK, David:
Walter; Wilson, F.
BLACKBURN, C. R. B.:
Wade, Sir R.
BLACKMAN, Maurice:
Wenz.
BLUNT, Michael J.:
Woollard.
BODIS, J. P.:
Wallace, A.
BOLTON, G. C.:
Steere; Strange; Venn; Wittenoom.
BOLTON, H. C.:
Stone, W.
BOUGHEN, Robert K.:
Whitehouse.
BOURKE, Helen:
Weaver.
BRADMAN, Donald:
Woodfull.
BRANAGAN, D. F.:
Woolnough.
BRAY, J. J.:
Way.
BREEN, W. J.:
Watson, C. H.
BRIDGE, Carl:
Sowden.
BRIGGS, Mark:
Tickell.
BRINSMEAD, Greg S. J.:
Wilson, A. W.
BROWN, Nicholas:
Wynne, W.
BROWNE, Geoff:
Styles; Weber, I.; Wettenhall, M.; Zeal.
BUCK, A. R.:
Waddell.
BUNNY, Pat:
Wright, J. A.
BURGMANN, Verity:
Winspear.
BURNESS, Peter:
Stapleton; White, A.; Whitham.
BYGOTT, Ursula:
Wallace, R.
BYRNE, Dianne:
Whittingham.

CABENA, Peter:
Treasure.
CABLE, K. J.:
Stephen, R.; Stretch; Talbot, A.; Waddy;
Wentworth-Shields; Woodd.
CAHILL, Peter:
Wilson, Sir L.

xiii

CAIN, Neville:
Theodore.
CALDWELL, Margaret:
Stoddard.
CAMERON, Clyde:
Temple.
CAMPBELL, Keith O.:
Waterhouse, W.; Watt, R.
CAMPBELL, Ruth:
Weigall, T.
CAMPION, Edmund:
Yewen.
CARMODY, John:
Tate, H.; Thompson, G.; Verbrugghen;
Williams, H. J.
CARNELL, Ian:
Thorby; Walters, H.
CARRON, L. T.:
Swain, E.
CARTER, Betty:
Willmott.
CARTER, Ruth:
Tucker, H. & G.
CHAM, Elizabeth:
Stanley, A.
CHAN, Adrian:
Young Wai.
CHAPMAN, Ivan:
Smyth, Sir N.
CHAPMAN, Peter:
Webster, C. & E.
CHAPPELL (SPROTT), Christabel:
Van Raalte.
CHISWELL, Barry:
Steele, B.
CHURCHWARD, M. S.:
Thompson, D.
CLANCHY, John:
Stewart, D.
CLARKE, Patricia:
Tillyard, P.
CLUNE, David:
Spedding.
COBB, Joan E.:
Swain, H.
COLE, Keith:
Warren.
COLLIGAN, Mimi:
Tallis.
COLLINS, Diane:
Spencer, C.
COLTHEART, Lenore:
Tye.
COOPER, Ross:
Stewart, E. T.
COPE, Graeme:
Williams, E.
COSSART, Yvonne:
Welsh.
COULTHARD-CLARK, C. D.:
Steele, A.; Thorpe; Watson, C. V.; Wieck;
Wiltshire.
COWLEY, R. E.:
Tuckett, F. & L.; Tuckett, J.

CRAWFORD, Ian M.:
Woodward, B.; Woodward, H.
CRAWFORD, R. M.:
Wood, G.
CROUCHLEY, Betty:
Tunn; Willmore; Young, W. J., pastoralist.
CROWN, Alan D.:
Thatcher.
CUNNEEN, Chris:
Stace; Steward; Stonehaven; Voigt;
Webb, C.
CURNOW, Ross:
Spence, J.

DALY, Jim:
Virgo.
DANE, P. C.:
Tulloch.
DANIELS, Louis V.:
Whitington.
DE GARIS, B. K.:
Wilsmore.
DEER, A. F.:
Tout.
DENOON, Donald:
Strong, W.
DERKENNE, Warren:
Storkey.
DEXTER, David:
Wray, F.
DICKER, George:
Wallis, W.
DINGLE, Tony:
Thwaites, W.
DONCASTER, E. W.:
Trower.
DONOVAN, Peter:
Solomon, V.
DOOHAN, Noelene:
Watson, W.; Willcock.
DOWNING, H.:
Thomson, H.
DRAFFIN, Nicholas:
Waller.
DRISCOLL, W. P.:
Wilkinson, A. H.
DUKE, Anne:
Southern.
DUNGEY, Peter:
Smyth, C.
DUNSTAN, David:
Stapley; Swanson; Vaude; Wales; Weedon;
Whelan; Wynn.
DUNSTON, A. J.:
Todd, F.

EADEN, Robin:
White, M.
EDGAR, Suzanne:
Stonehouse; Wallis, F.
EDGELOE, V. A.:
Strong, Sir A.
EGAN, Bryan:
Springthorpe.

AUTHORS

ELMSLIE, Ronald:
Watson, A.
ERICKSON, Rica:
Tracey; Truman, J.
EVANS, J. W.:
Waterhouse, G.

FAHEY, Charles:
Sternberg; Williams, H. R.
FAIRWEATHER, D. F.:
Somerset; Wainwright, W.
FANNING, Pauline:
Wadsworth.
FARRELL, Frank:
Tyrrell, T.; West, J. E.; Willis, A.
FARRER, K. T. H.:
Walker, F.; Wilson, D.
FERRALL, R. A.:
Thompson, J. W.; Wardlaw.
FIELDING, Jean P.:
Watson, S.
FINK, Elly:
Young, W. B.
FINN, Paul:
Want.
FINN, Rosslyn:
Williams, M.
FISHER, J. D.:
Stephenson.
FITZHARDINGE, L. F.:
Woodhouse.
FITZPATRICK, Kathleen:
Webb, J.
FORBES, M. Z.:
Symonds.
FOSTER, Leonie:
Taylor, Henry D.
FOX, William E.:
Webb, F.
FRANCES, Raelene:
Solly; Wallis, A.
FRANCIS, Charles:
Winneke.
FRASER, Alan:
Wilson, G. C.
FREEMAN, R. R.:
Young, W. R.
FRENCH, M.:
Tardent; Tolmie.
FULLOON, Gillian:
Westmacott; Wray, L.

GALBALLY, Ann E.:
Streeton.
GAMMAGE, Bill:
Sumsuma; Wanliss, D.; Wanliss, H.
GANDEVIA, Bryan:
Walker, A. S.; Wettenhall, R.
GARDEN, Donald S.:
Throssell, G.; Toutcher.
GARDINER, L. R.:
Stradbroke; Talbot, Sir R.
GARDINER, Lyndsay:
Snowball, W.; Tisdall.

GARRISSON, A. D.:
Williams, Sir R.
GARTON, Stephen:
Stopford, R.; Winn.
GIBBERD, Joyce:
Weber, H.
GIBBS, R. M.:
Ward, J.; Way Lee.
GILBERT, L. A.:
Turner, F.
GILBERT, S. H.*:
Soward.
GILCHRIST, Hugh:
Treloar, G.
GILL, J. C. H.:
Tozer; Wilson, Walter.
GILL, K. E.:
Sterne.
GISTITIN, Carol:
Stopford, J.
GLOVER, C. J. M.:
Waite, E.
GLYN-DANIEL, Charles:
Tunbridge.
GODDEN, Judith:
Ward, E.
GORRELL, Richard:
Towner; Wark.
GOWER, S. N.:
Waite, W.
GRAHAME, Emma:
Swanton.
GRAINGER, G.:
Vaughan, C.
GRANT, Donald:
Stuart, J.
GRAY, A. C.*:
Spence, G.
GRAY, Nancy:
White, H. L.
GREEN, Dorothy:
Watson, E.
GREGORY, Alan:
Somers.
GREVILLE, P. J.:
Wienholt.
GREY, Jeffrey:
Traill, J. C. M.; White, C. B.
GRIFFIN, Helga M.:
Turnbull, G.; Young, F. S.
GRIFFIN, James:
Stevens, H.; Wren, J.
GRIFFITHS, A. R. G.:
Whitford.
GUNSON, Niel:
Waldock; Wheen, J.
GURNER, C. M.:
Thompson, C. W.

HAIG-MUIR, K. M.:
Stewart, P.

* deceased

KIMBER, R. G.:
Stott.
KIRKPATRICK, Peter:
Sorenson.
KIRKPATRICK, Rod:
Sommerlad.
KIRSOP, Wallace:
Spencer, A.
KITSON, W. S.:
Thomson, J. P.
KLEPAC, Lou:
Trenerry.
KLOOT, Tess:
Whittell; Wilson H.
KNIGHT, Stephen:
Upfield; Walsh, J. M.
KNOTT, John:
Spyer.
KRAUSE, Gary:
White, E.
KUNZ, E. F.:
Zimpel.
KWAN, Elizabeth:
Williams, A.

LACK, John:
Snowball, O.; Stewart, Sir A.; Tweddle, J.;
Worrall, H.
LAKE, Marilyn:
Woods, W. A.
LAMONT, Ross:
Thring, W.
LANGMORE, Diane:
Stone-Wigg; Stralia; Townsend, G.;
Turnbull, A.; Wall; Walters, G.;
Watson, J. H.; Wilson, J. P.
LARACY, Hugh:
Watriama.
LAWRIE, Margaret:
Zahel.
LEE, Jack:
Truscott.
LEE, Mary Alice:
Teague; Traill, J. C. A.; Wilson, D. L.
LEE, Stuart:
Stephens, A. G.
LENNARD, Brendan:
Walker, A. C.
LEWIS, Julie:
Woods, J.
LINCOLN, Merrilyn:
Stacy; Statton.
LINDESAY, Vane:
Souter, D.; Vincent, A.
LINDSAY, Frances:
Sutherland, J.
LINN, R. W.:
White, S.
LLOYD, C. J.:
Spooner; Stewart, Sir F.; Wade, L.;
Walsh, H.
LLOYD, D. E.:
Stacy.

LODGE, A. B.:
Squires.
LOGAN, G. N.:
Tryon.
LOMAS, L.:
Yuill.
LOUGHEED, A. L.:
Stewart, Alexander; Stodart.
LOVE, Peter:
Stewart, Archibald; Tunnecliffe.
LOWRY, Jim:
Whitelegge.
LUCAS, Clive:
Wilkinson, L.
LUDLOW, Christa:
Taylor, F.
LUTZ, G. G.:
Stuart, H.
LYONS, Mark:
Wheeler, J.

MACCALLUM, Monica:
Sweet.
MCCALMAN, Janet:
Tudor.
MCCARTHY, Janice:
Sorensen; Wilson, G. M.
MCCARTHY, John:
Ulm.
MCCARTHY, Perditta M.:
White, J. McH.
MCCAUGHAN, J. B. T.:
Vonwiller.
MCCONVILLE, Chris:
Taylor, J.
MACCULLOCH, J.:
Walker, E.
MCDONALD, D. I.:
Templeton; Thomas, W.; Walker, James;
Wollaston, H.
MCDONALD, G. L.:
Walker, A. S.
MCDONALD, Lorna:
Thompson, W. G.; Voss; Wilson, J. L.
MCGRATH, Joyce:
Vale; Wilkie, L.
MCINTYRE, Darryl:
Toft.
MACINTYRE, Stuart:
Somerville, W.
MCKAY, K. J.:
Stawell, F.; Tucker, T. G.
MCKENNA, C. W. F.:
Turner, W.
MACKENZIE, Andrew:
Withers.
MCLENNAN, Graham:
Trevascus; Vincent, J.
MCMINN, W. G.:
Wilks.
MCMULLIN, Ross:
Stewart, J. C.

McNICOLL, Ronald:
Wisdom; Woodward, O.
McQUILLAN, Peter B.:
Thompson, E.
McSHANE, Ian:
Sticht.
MAHONEY, J. C.:
Stable.
MANDLE, W. F.:
Weber, C.
MANSFIELD, Peter:
Thompson, M.
MANTON, Jill:
Wilkin.
MARGINSON, Max:
Young, W. J., biochemist.
MARSH, Ian:
Thomson, D.
MARSHALL, Tony:
Tishler.
MARTIN, F. I. R.:
Stawell, Sir R.
MASLEN, Joan:
Vernon, H.; Young, F. M.
MASON, Keith:
Weigall, C.
MENGHETTI, Diane:
Toll.
MERCER, Peter:
Wiseman.
MEREDITH, John:
Tritton.
MERRALLS, J. D.:
Starke.
MERRETT, D. T.:
Wreford.
MERRITT, John:
Toomey.
MILES, M. A.:
Spence, P.
MILEY, Caroline:
Walker, A. C.
MITCHELL, Ann M.:
Watson, J. F.
MITCHELL, Bruce:
Wade, B.; Wetherspoon; White, H. F.; Woodcock.
MOIGNARD, Kathy:
Ward, F. W.
MOIR, R. J.:
Sutton, G.
MOORE, Andrew:
Waley.
MOORE, John:
Wilton, O.
MORISON, Patricia:
Thompson, J. A.; Wilson, J. T.
MORRIS, Richard:
Swadling.
MORRISSEY, Doug:
Trethowan.
MUIR, Marcie:
Stow.

MULVANEY, D. J.:
Spencer, W. B.; Warner; Willshire.
MUNRO, Craig:
Stephensen.
MURPHY, Greg:
Weston.

NAIRN, Bede:
Spruson; Storey, J.; Thrower; Treflé; Trumper; Watson, J. C.; Webster, E.
NANCE, Susan:
Watson, A.
NASH, Heather:
Watt, W. S.
NELSON, H. N.:
Standley.
NIALL, Brenda:
Turner, E.
NICHOLLS, Bob:
Williams, G.
NORRIS, K. R.:
Tillyard, R.
NORTHEY, R. E.:
Young, Sir F.

OATS, William N.:
Unwin.
O'BRIEN, Anne:
Tenison Woods.
O'BRIEN, Bernard McC.:
Syme, Sir G. A.
O'BYRNE, Valerie J.:
Tait, G.
O'HAGAN, M. D.:
Wheeler, A.
O'NEIL, Bernard:
Wollaston, T.
O'NEIL, W. M.:
Waterhouse, E.
O'NEILL, Sally:
Wheen, A.

PARNABY, Owen:
Sugden.
PASCOE, Robert:
Vaccari; Vanzetti.
PASZKOWSKI, L. K.:
Tarczynski.
PATRICK, Alison:
Swinburne.
PEARCE, Barry:
Wakelin.
PEARCE, Ian:
Wayn.
PEDERSEN, Howard:
Tjangamarra.
PEERS, Juliet:
Tweddle, I.
PENNAY, Bruce:
Thomas, J.
PENNINGS, M. W. H.:
Wheeler, C.

PERRY, Peter W.:
Sturgess.
PHILLIPS, Richard:
Wendt.
PHILPS, R.:
Turner, J. W.
PIERCE, Peter:
Trott; Trumble, H.; Welch; Wolfe.
POTTS, E. Daniel:
Stanford.
POTTS, R. B.:
Wilton, J.
POWELL, J. M.:
Taylor, T.
PRIOR, James:
Wilkinson, A. G.

RADI, Heather:
Taylor, P.; Windeyer, M. & M.
RADIC, Maureen Thérèse:
Zelman.
RAFTERY, Judith:
Weir.
RAMSON, W. S.:
Tyrrell, J.
RANK, Benjamin:
Zwar, T.
READ, Peter:
Wilson, M.
REEKIE, Gail:
Stanley, C.; Wade, J.
REEVES, John H.:
Thurgood.
RENFREY, Lionel E. W.:
Thomas, A.; Wise, P.
REYNOLDS, Peter:
Sulman, Sir J.; Vernon, W.
RICH, Joe:
Tarrant.
RICHARDS, Eric:
Young, Sir W.
RICHARDS, Michael J.:
Vickers, A.
RICKARD, John:
Walpole; Wilkie, A.
RITCHIE, John:
Tauchert; Weathers; Wilson, A. M.;
Worrall, J.
ROBERTS, Alan:
Taylor, Sir A.
ROBINSON, F. M.:
Stone, Sir E.
ROBINSON, Jeffrey:
Wrigley.
ROE, J. I.:
Wildman.
ROE, Michael:
Taylor, G. A.; Thirkell.
RONALD, Heather B.:
Weatherly, M.
ROSIER, Bruce:
Thomas, R.

ROYANS, Jack:
Stewart, E. C.
RUSHWORTH, G. D.:
Truman, E.
RUSSELL, Penny:
Stone, E. & G.
RUTLEDGE, Martha:
Stainforth; Stephen, Sir C.; Stephen, E.;
Storey, Sir D.; Tildesley; Ward, H.; Watt,
E.; Wesché, A. & P.; Willis, W.; Woolley.
RYAN, J. A.:
Wise, B.

ST LEON, Mark Valentine:
Wirth, M.; Wirth, P. & G.
SAUNDERS, Malcolm:
Taylor, Harry; Vardon; Ward, F. F.;
Wilson, R.
SAYERS, Stuart:
Wallace, G.; Yencken.
SCARFE, Janet:
Thornber.
SCATES, Bruce:
Trenwith; Winter, J.
SCHOFIELD, Anne:
Wager.
SCHUMANN, Ruth:
Spence, R.
SELLECK, R. J. W.:
Tate, F.
SEMMENS, Trevor D.:
Thompson, E.
SERLE, Geoffrey:
Syme, Sir G.; Turner, Sir G.; Watt, W. A.;
Wilmot.
SHARKEY, Michael:
Wright, D.
SHARP, M. P.:
Spears.
SHAW, A. G. L.:
Whitton; Williams, H. L.
SHAW, George P.:
Webber.
SHEARMAN, Rodney P.:
Windeyer, J.
SHELDON, Peter:
Stokes.
SHEPHERD, Michael:
Viney.
SHERINGTON, G. E.:
Soubeiran.
SHILLINGSBURG, M.:
Smythe, R.
SIMONS, J. R.:
Steel.
SIMPSON, Caroline:
Wilkinson, D.
SISSONS, D. C. S.:
Takasuka.
SKERMAN, P. J.:
Soutter.
SLOAN, Andrew:
Willis, E.

WARD, John M.*:
Stevens, Sir B.; Wade, Sir C.
WARD, Russel:
Wood, T.
WATERHOUSE, D. F.:
Tillyard, R.
WATERHOUSE, Michael:
Waterhouse, B.
WATERS, Jill:
Waterworth.
WEATHERBURN, A. K.:
Weatherburn.
WELBORN, Suzanne:
Throssell, H.
WHITTLE, Nancy Robinson:
Warnes.
WILCOCK, Arthur A.:
Stillwell.
WILKEY, Don:
Spragg.
WILSON, Janis:
Stoneman.
WILSON, Paul D.:
Wragge.
WINCH, Denis E.:
Wellish.

WINTER, Denis:
Treloar, J.
WISE, Christine:
Webster, W.
WITHYCOMBE, Robert:
Walker, John.
WOOD, R. J.:
Tranter.
WOODS, Carole:
Zwar, A. & H.
WRIGHT, Don:
Stephen, P.; Symon; Taylor, W.
WYMARK, Marjorie*:
Wymark.

YOUNG, J. Atherton:
Stuart, Sir T.
YOUNG, Michael W.:
Williams, F.

ZUBANS, Ruth:
Tucker, T. St G.

* deceased

A NOTE ON SOME PROCEDURES

Among our authors and readers and, indeed, on the editorial board, there is strong disagreement on whether certain facts should normally be included—such as cause of death, burial or cremation details, and value of estate. In this volume our practices have been as follows:

Cause of death: normally included, except in the case of those aged 70 or over.

Burial/cremation: included when details available.

Value of estate: normally included for certain categories such as businessmen, and when the amount is unusually high or low. In recent years, when the practice developed of early distribution of assets in order to avoid estate and probate duties, the sum is not always meaningful; moreover it is not always possible to ascertain the full facts. Hence we have resorted to discretionary use.

Some other procedures require explanation:

Measurements: as the least unsatisfactory solution we have used imperial system measurements (as historically appropriate), followed by the metric equivalent in brackets.

Money: we have retained £ for pounds for references prior to 14 February 1966 (when the conversion rate was A£1 = A$2).

Religion: stated whenever information is available, but often there is no good evidence of actual practice, e.g., the information is confined to marriage and funeral rites.

[q.v.]: the particular volume is given for those included in volumes 1-11 but not for those in this volume. Note that the cross-reference [q.v.] now accompanies the names of all who have separate articles in the *Dictionary*. In volumes 1-6 it was not shown for royal visitors, governors, lieut-governors and those Colonial Office officials who were included.

Small capitals: used for relations and others when they are of substantial import-ance but not included in their own right; these are also q.v.'d.

Five-year rule: a few men and women, whose *floruit* was pre-1940 but who lived to an advanced age, have been excluded on the ground that they died too recently for proper historical consideration. Save for rare exceptions, no one is included who died less than five years before date of publication.

CORRIGENDA

Every effort is made to check every detail in every article, but inevitably a work of the size and complexity of the *Dictionary* includes some errors.

Corrigenda have been published with each volume and a list is included with volume 12 showing corrections made since the publication of volume 11 (1988).

Only corrections are shown; additional information is not included; nor is any reinterpretation attempted. The only exception to this procedure is when new details become available about parents, births, deaths and marriages.

Documented corrections are welcomed. Additional information, with sources, is also invited and will be placed in the appropriate files for future use.

A copy of cumulative corrigenda up to volume 7 and the lists published with volumes 8, 9, 10 and 11 are available from the publishers at cost of postage.

REFERENCES

The following and other standard works of reference have been widely used, though not usually acknowledged in individual biographies:

Australian encyclopaedia, 1-2 (Syd, 1925), 1-10 (1958), 1-12 (1983)

Biographical register for various Australian parliaments: (A. W. Martin & P. Wardle *and* H. Radi, P. Spearritt & E. Hinton *and* C. N. Connolly—New South Wales; G. C. Bolton & A. Mozley—Western Australia; K. Thomson & G. Serle *and* G. Browne—Victoria; D. B. Waterson *and* D. B. Waterson & J. Arnold—Queensland; H. Coxon, J. Playford & R. Reid—South Australia; S. & B. Bennett—Tasmania; and J. Rydon—Commonwealth)

B. Burke, *A genealogical and heraldic history of the colonial gentry*, 1-2 (Lond, 1891,1895)

O'M. Creagh and E. M. Humphris (eds), *The V.C. and D.S.O.: a complete record* . . . 1-3 (Lond, 1934)

Dictionary of national biography (Lond, 1885-1986)

H. M. Green, *A history of Australian literature*, 1-2 (Syd, 1961, 2nd edn 1971), revised by D. Green (Syd, 1984-85)

C. A. Hughes and B. D. Graham, *A handbook of Australian government and politics 1890-1964* (Canb, 1968); *Voting for the Australian House of Representatives 1901-1964*, with corrigenda (Canb, 1975), for *Queensland Legislative Assembly 1890-1964* (Canb, 1974), for *New South Wales* . . . (1975), *Victoria* . . . (1975), and *South Australian, Western Australian and Tasmanian Lower Houses* . . . (1976)

F. Johns, *Johns's notable Australians* (Melb, 1906), *Fred Johns's annual* (Lond, 1914); *An Australian biographical dictionary* (Melb, 1934)

A. McCulloch, *Encyclopedia of Australian art* (Lond, 1968), 1-2 (Melb, 1984)

E. M. Miller, *Australian literature* . . . *to 1935* (Melb, 1940), extended to 1950 by F. T. Macartney (Syd, 1956)

W. Moore, *The story of Australian art*, 1-2 (Syd, 1934), (Syd, 1980)

P. C. Mowle, *A genealogical history of pioneer families in Australia* (Syd, 1939; 5th edn Adel, 1978)

P. Serle, *Dictionary of Australian biography*, 1-2 (Syd, 1949)

Who's who (Lond), and *Who's who in Australia* (Syd, Melb, present and past editions)

W. H. Wilde, J. Hooton & B. Andrews, *The Oxford companion to Australian literature* (Melb, 1985).

ABBREVIATIONS USED IN BIBLIOGRAPHIES

AA	Australian Archives	ed	editor
AAA	*All About Australians*	edn	edition
AAA	Amateur Athletic Association	Edinb	Edinburgh
ABC	Australian Broadcasting Commission/Corporation	Eng	England
ACT	Australian Capital Territory	Fr	Father (priest)
Adel	Adelaide		
Agr	Agriculture, Agricultural	G, Geog	Geographical
AIF	Australian Imperial Force	Govt	Government
AJCP	Australian Joint Copying Project		
		HA	House of Assembly
ALP	Australian Labor Party	Hist	History, Historical
ANU	Australian National University, Canberra	Hob	Hobart
		HSSA	Historical Society of South Australia
ANUABL	ANU Archives of Business and Labour		
ANZAAS	Australian and New Zealand Association for the Advancement of Science	*IAN*	*Illustrated Australian News*
		Inst	Institute, Institution
		introd	introduction, introduced by
A'sian	Australasian	*ISN*	*Illustrated Sydney News*
Assn	Association		
Aust	Australia, Australian	*J*	*Journal*
AWM	Australian War Memorial, Canberra	JCU	James Cook University of North Queensland, Townsville
Basser Lib	Adolph Basser Library, Australian Academy of Science, Canberra	LA	Legislative Assembly
		LaTL	La Trobe Library, Melbourne
		Launc	Launceston
Bd	Board	LC	Legislative Council
BHP	Broken Hill Proprietary Co. Ltd	Lib	Library
		Lond	London
bibliog	bibliography		
biog	biography, biographical	*Mag*	*Magazine*
BL	J. S. Battye Library of West Australian History, Perth	Melb	Melbourne
		MDHC	Melbourne Diocesan Historical Commission (Catholic), Fitzroy
Brisb	Brisbane		
		MJA	*Medical Journal of Australia*
		ML	Mitchell Library, Sydney
c	circa	Mortlock Lib	Mortlock Library of South Australiana
CAE	College of Advanced Education		
Canb	Canberra	MS (or ms)	manuscript
cat	catalogue	mthly	monthly
CO	Colonial Office, London		
co	company	nd	date of publication unknown
C of E	Church of England	NG	New Guinea
Col Sec	Colonial Secretary	NL	National Library of Australia, Canberra
Com	Commission		
comp	compiler	no	number
CSIRO	Commonwealth Scientific and Industrial Research Organization	np	place of publication unknown
		NSW	New South Wales
		NSWA	The Archives Authority of New South Wales, Sydney
cttee	committee		
Cwlth	Commonwealth	NT	Northern Territory
		NY	New York
Dept	Department	NZ	New Zealand
DNB	*Dictionary of National Biography*		
		OL	John Oxley Library, Brisbane

ABBREVIATIONS USED IN BIBLIOGRAPHIES

p, pp	page, pages	SAA	South Australian Archives, Adelaide
pc	photocopy		
PD	*Parliamentary Debates*	Sel	Select
PIM	*Pacific Islands Monthly*	SLNSW	State Library of New South Wales
PP	*Parliamentary Papers*		
PRGSSA	*Proceedings of the Royal Geographical Society of Australasia (South Australian Branch)*	SLSA	State Library of South Australia
		SLT	State Library of Tasmania
priv print	privately printed	SLV	State Library of Victoria
PRO	Public Record Office	*SMH*	*Sydney Morning Herald*
Procs	*Proceedings*	Soc	Society
pt	part, parts	supp	supplement
PTHRA	*Papers and Proceedings of the Tasmanian Historical Research Association*	Syd	Sydney
pub	publication, publication number	TA	Tasmanian State Archives, Hobart
		Tas	Tasmania, Tasmanian
Q	*Quarterly*	*T&CJ*	*Australian Town and Country Journal*
QA	Queensland State Archives, Brisbane	*Trans*	*Transactions*
Qld	Queensland	ts	typescript
RAHS	Royal Australian Historical Society (Sydney)	UK	United Kingdom
		UNSW	University of New South Wales
RG	Registrar General's Office	UNE	University of New England, Armidale
RGS	Royal Geographical Society		
RHSQ	Royal Historical Society of Queensland (Brisbane)	Univ	University
		UPNG	University of Papua New Guinea
RHSV	Royal Historical Society of Victoria (Melbourne)	US	United States of America
RMIT	Royal Melbourne Institute of Technology	*V&P*	*Votes and Proceedings*
Roy	Royal	*VHM(J)*	*Victorian Historical Magazine (Journal)*
RWAHS	Royal Western Australian Historical Society (Perth)		
		v, vol	volume
		Vic	Victoria
1st S	First Session		
2nd S	Second Session	WA	Western Australia
2nd s	second series		
SA	South Australia	*	deceased

Smy

SMYTH, BRIDGETENA (BRETTENA) (1840?-1898), campaigner for women's health reform and women's political rights, was born in Melbourne, second daughter of John Riordan, merchant, and his wife Bridgetena, née Cavanagh. On 28 October 1861 she married storekeeper William Taylor Smyth at St Paul's United Church of England and Ireland, Kyneton. After his death in 1873 she converted the family greengrocery in North Melbourne into a drapery and druggist's business. She had borne five children of whom four were living when she was widowed.

From the age of 43 Brettena was prominent in feminist causes. An active member of the first Australian suffrage organization, the Victorian Women's Suffrage Society (founded 1884), she formed the breakaway Australian Women's Suffrage Society in 1888. In the mid-1890s this group was eclipsed by the temperance-backed Victorian Women's Franchise League and the United Council for Women's Suffrage organized by Annette Bear [q.v.7]. Like a number of the early suffragists, Brettena Smyth was also a freethinker, opposed to orthodox religion and disposed to question other institutions and forms of authority. Her work was supported by the controversial Australasian Secular Association.

Recognizing the liberating potential of birth control for women, Mrs Smyth lectured to large female-only audiences at the North Melbourne Town Hall and other centres, describing various contraceptive techniques and promoting a rubber 'French pessaire preventatif' (sold at her shop) as 'the only article of the kind that can be used without the knowledge of the husband'. Although she was publicly sympathetic to those forced into prostitution and lobbied for reduced gaol sentences for women desperate enough to kill their illegitimate children, she was no champion of sex outside marriage. As did many contemporary women activists, she saw a new kind of family and an enhanced role for motherhood at the heart of social reform. In her lectures and pamphlets she argued that well-matched couples could form a more equal partnership. Planned families would mean fewer children, liberating women from the psychological and financial strains of unwilling pregnancy and motherhood. Such eugenic arguments were not uncommon in the United States of America, providing Smyth with many of her ideas and much of the material she used in well-advertised publications such as *Love, courtship and marriage*

(1892), *The limitation of offspring* (1893) and *The social evil* (1894).

Self-taught but widely read, interested in fringe practices such as electrotherapy and phrenology, she planned to study medicine at the University of Melbourne, but her savings intended for fees vanished in the financial crashes of the 1890s. Her book, *What every woman should know: diseases incidental to women* (1895), albeit somewhat unpolished and derivative, provided women with information that was otherwise relatively inaccessible.

Brettena Smyth enjoyed public speaking; almost six feet (182.9 cm) tall, she had a commanding presence. She became a well-known and respected Melbourne identity, especially in labour circles. Survived by two sons, she died of Bright's disease on 15 February 1898 at Morwell and was buried in the Melbourne general cemetery, with Catholic rites—an ironic end, given her history of support for secularism and birth control.

F. Kelly, 'Mrs Smyth and the body politic', in M. Bevege et al (eds), *Worth her salt* (Syd, 1982); E. Fry (ed), *Rebels and radicals* (Syd, 1983); *Labour Hist*, Nov 1963, no 5; *Table Talk*, 3 Nov 1893; *Nth Melb Gazette*, 18 Feb 1898.   FARLEY KELLY

SMYTH, CHARLES EDWARD OWEN (1851-1925), public servant, was born on 1 January 1851 at Ferrybank, County Kilkenny, Ireland, son of Stephen Smyth, naval architect, and his wife Emma Gaynor, née Owen. Educated at the Erasmus Smith High School, Dublin, he travelled the world as a sailor and house-painter before arriving in Victoria in 1873 where he spent two years as foreman and manager for a builder. He settled in Adelaide in 1876 and on 19 June 1879, in St Peter's Anglican Cathedral, married Bessie Sanderson Davidson. Smyth (who pronounced his name Smith) had joined the civil service in May 1876. As clerk to Edward J. Woods, architect, he copied specifications and attended to correspondence; when Woods became architect-in-chief two years later, Smyth stayed with him as a virtual chief of staff.

In 1886 Smyth was appointed to head the new Works and Buildings Department. He managed to circumvent a policy which required that contracts for all new public buildings costing over £5000 should be awarded to private architects. Despite architects' criticism of his methods, and the 1891 civil service commission report which recommended amalgamation of his department with the engineer-in-chief's, Smyth controlled the design, construction, maintenance, letting and rent of public buildings until he retired in 1920. He supervised such major projects as the Exhibition Building, a wing of the General Post Office, the Museum and Art Gallery of South Australia buildings, Magill Home, Bedford Park Sanatorium, Thebarton Police Barracks, the South Australian School of Mines and Industries, and additions to the Adelaide Hospital (Flinders wing) and Parkside Lunatic Asylum. Although not professionally qualified, Smyth influenced the design of many of the structures which his department built, notably the School of Mines and the hospital additions. He was justifiably proud of his programme which transformed North Terrace and created the Torrens Parade Ground and gardens from a former rubbish tip.

He worked hard in the public interest, even against political pressure; in demanding excellence, he sought value for money. Thickset, with round, passive features, Smyth appeared self-absorbed. While he was admired by some for his rugged outspokenness, the 1888 civil service commission found him vindictive, 'hasty in his temper, impulsive and overbearing'. His conduct was later criticized in parliament and publicity was given to an incident at the Adelaide Hospital in 1900 when he was accused of bullying and insulting the medical superintendent. Following Federation, in 1906 Smyth was South Australian delegate to a Melbourne conference which arranged the transfer of land, buildings and property to the Commonwealth. He was appointed to the Imperial Service Order in 1903 and C.M.G. in 1920. The Royal Agricultural Society of South Australia also awarded him a medal.

An ardent Imperialist and patriot, Smyth was a founder (secretary from 1908) of the Adelaide branch of the Royal Society of St George, and active in the South Australian branches of the League of the Empire and the Navy League; he hung portraits of British monarchs wherever they would be 'educative in loyalty' and insisted on using Australian and British-made materials in public buildings. In World War I he spoke publicly on 'The enemy within our doors'. A Freemason, an Anglican and a collector of walking-sticks, paintings and Aboriginal weapons, Smyth enjoyed field-shooting expeditions throughout the State. He published his reminiscences in the *Register* in 1923-25. Survived by his wife, daughter and younger son (the elder lad was killed at Gallipoli), Smyth died on 1 October 1925 and was buried in North Road cemetery.

Observer (Adel), 21 July 1900, 3 Mar 1923, 26 Mar 1921, 10 Oct 1925; *Advertiser* (Adel) and *Register* (Adel), 2 Oct 1925; Papers of the superintendent of public buildings relating to an inquiry by the Civil Service Commission into complaints against him, 1880-1890 (PRO SA).

PETER DUNGEY

SMYTH, JOHN (1864-1927), educationist, was born on 3 November 1864 at Tollcross, Scotland, son of John Smyth, farmer, and his wife Mary, née Smyth. At an early age he moved with his family to Londonderry, Ireland, where he became a licensed teacher; in 1881 he migrated to Dunedin, New Zealand. He worked as a head teacher in rural schools, then as assistant at an Invercargill school and later at Canterbury High School. He also enrolled at the University of Otago (B.A., 1891; M.A., 1892) and specialized in mathematics and mental science. On Christmas Day 1891 at Christchurch he married Emma Strack; they were to have two sons.

In 1895 Smyth attended the University of Heidelberg; on his return he lectured in mental science at the University of Otago as a replacement for (Sir) John Salmond [q.v.11]. In 1898 Smyth went to the University of Edinburgh (D.Phil., 1900) where he came under the formidable influence of the 'idealist' Simon Laurie; Smyth also studied in Germany with the Herbartian, Wilhelm Rein, at Jena and with the experimental psychologist, Wilhelm Wundt, at Leipzig. In 1900 Smyth took an appointment as chief inspector of the Wanganui school district in New Zealand. His doctoral thesis was published in 1901 as *Truth and reality with special reference to religion*.

In 1902 he was appointed principal of Victoria's Training College (later Melbourne Teachers' College), replacing Frank Tate [q.v.] who had become director of education. Like Tate, Smyth believed that the college should expand as an English-type residential institution, offer a broader range of educational and curricular activities, and become central in the training of all new primary schoolteachers. He quickly enhanced college life by introducing a student magazine, college hymn, motto and crest. As a residential principal until 1919, he governed the college with charm and a paternalistic authority that was tempered only by his wife's intervention.

Smyth attempted to be a progressive innovator of course and staff programmes, but faced constant problems of inflexible staff supply and lack of funds. He was unable to introduce a staff journal or a staff travelling scholarship, as Alexander Mackie [q.v.10] had done at Teachers' College, Sydney, but he did expand the infant and kindergarten training course until 1917 when the Free Kindergarten Union (which he had helped to found) commenced its own training college. As foundation lecturer in the diploma of education in the arts faculty of the University of Melbourne, he influenced the training of teachers in secondary schools. In 1913, bitter at the lack of recognition of his efforts, Smyth declared that he would not continue to teach at the university without salary. A prolonged dispute between the education department and the university was ultimately resolved in 1919 when Smyth was appointed professor of education while remaining college principal. In 1923 he pioneered the introduction of an Australian master of education degree, hoping that it would attract teachers to experimental education.

In his objective of securing pre-service training for all primary teachers at the college, Smyth encountered opposition from the government and the department. This mode of training could not guarantee a steady supply of teachers: apprentice teachers, who had comprised nearly 30 per cent of the primary service in 1903, still made up 27 per cent in 1925. Never a street fighter, Smyth was reluctant to attack this system of training openly, and when he did he was rebuked by Tate.

Smyth realized the obstacles to reform at an early stage in his career in Victoria. He became frustrated and ill. In 1909 he applied unsuccessfully for the position of inspector-general of education for Queensland. Increasingly he delegated the running of his college to the vice-principal. Smyth became more active in university teaching and in the Presbyterian Church where he contributed to the general assembly and to the development of religious instruction programmes.

Smyth's sudden death in Tokyo, on 20 August 1927, came as a shock to Melbourne's Presbyterians and to his former students who eulogized his lifelong dedication to the child. His estate, valued for probate at £4064, endowed the John and Eric Smyth Travelling Scholarship(s) for teachers, named partly in memory of a son who had died accidentally in 1925. Smyth's contribution to Victorian education was later honoured by the Victorian Institute for Educational Research which named a medal after him. His portrait painted by W. B. McInnes [q.v.10] still graces the college walls: its sad, dark eyes suggest Smyth's sense of disappointment as a teacher-educator.

D. H. Rankin, *The spirit that lives* (Melb, 1945); A. D. Spaull and L. A. Mandelson, 'The College principals, J. Smyth and A. Mackie', in C. Turney (ed), *Pioneers of Australian education*, 3 (Syd, 1983); D. S. Garden, *The Melbourne teacher training colleges* (Melb, 1982); Melb Teachers' College, *Trainee*, Nov 1927; *Teachers' J*, 2 Apr 1928; D. E. Edgar, The educational ideas and influence on Victorian education of Dr John Smyth (M.Ed. thesis, Univ Melb, 1968).   ANDREW SPAULL

SMYTH, SIR NEVILL MASKELYNE (1868-1941), soldier, was born on 14 August 1868 in London, son of (Sir) Warington Wilkinson Smyth, mineralogist, and his wife Anna Maria Antonia, née Story-Maskelyne. Educated at Westminster School, he graduated from the Royal Military College, Sandhurst, in 1888 and was posted to the Queen's Bays (2nd Dragoon Guards) in India as a second lieutenant. In 1890 he was attached to the Royal Engineers to assist with a railway survey during the Zhob Valley expedition. By 1896 the Bays were stationed in Cairo at the time General Kitchener was about to launch an offensive against the Khalifa in the Sudan.

With Britain bent on avenging General Gordon's death at Khartoum, Smyth helped to chart some of the Nile cataracts in readiness for the push against Omdurman. In an early battle Lieutenant Smyth had charge of the machine-guns aboard a Royal Navy riverboat which bombarded Metemmeh. On 2 September 1898 Kitchener's Anglo-Egyptian forces assaulted Omdurman. Smyth's role was that of intelligence officer and orderly to Major General Sir Archibald Hunter, commander of the Egyptian division. With the battle ending, a dervish tried to spear two war correspondents; Smyth galloped forward and, though severely speared, shot the man dead. He was awarded the Victoria Cross for this action.

In August 1899 a Mahdist rising on the Blue Nile was suppressed by Captain Smyth who commanded a small force which captured the Khalifa Muhammad al-Sharif and two of the Mahdi's sons. The three were executed following a summary court martial presided over by Smyth who was then acting governor and military commander of the Blue Nile district.

Although Kitchener wanted Smyth to go to the South African War in 1900, he was kept busy charting the Nile cataracts from Wadi Halfa to Abyssinia. After completing a survey up to 200 miles (322 km) west of Khartoum, in 1902 he rejoined the Bays for active service in South Africa. That April the regiment inflicted heavy losses on General Alberts's commandos. Smyth was cut off with five soldiers, all of whom were wounded. He rejected the Boers' call to surrender and escaped on a horse belonging to General Alberts. Promoted major in 1903, Smyth was transferred to the Carabiniers (6th Dragoon Guards) who were then stationed in India but moved to South Africa in 1908. He was commanding officer and lieut-colonel when he took the regiment to England in 1912. Next year he won his aviator's certificate. Although he could have joined the Royal Flying Corps, he went instead to the Egyptian Army. A colonel from

December 1912, he was commandant of the Khartoum district in 1913-14 and active in combating the slave-trade.

In World War I Colonel Smyth was among several senior officers sent by Lord Kitchener to the Dardanelles. He arrived at Gallipoli in May 1915 and supervised the truce of the 24th to allow the Turks to bury their dead. Commanding the 1st Australian Infantry Brigade at the battle of Lone Pine in August, Smyth won the trust and admiration of the diggers. C. E. W. Bean [q.v.7] wrote of Smyth 'directing reinforcements into Lone Pine tunnels as quietly as a ticket collector passing passengers on to a platform'. At the evacuation, Smyth was one of the last officers to leave the peninsula.

Smyth led his brigade in France through the severe fighting for Pozières and Mouquet Farm on the Somme in 1916, and at the end of that year he was given command of the 2nd Australian Division as major general. The pursuit of the Germans to the Hindenburg line and the capture of Bapaume in the spring of 1917 were followed by the battles of Bullecourt and 3rd Ypres. Because of his Sudan experience, Smyth was particularly adept in planning highly successful 'peaceful penetration' raids on the German trenches. When he was transferred back to the British Army in May 1918, Smyth told Lieut-General Sir John Monash [q.v.10]: 'The fortune of war has indeed treated me kindly in enabling me to have the honour of being associated with your historic force'.

In the closing months of the war Smyth briefly commanded the 58th British Division and then the 59th which he handled with characteristic skill at the liberation of Lille. Although the procedure was irregular, he occasionally borrowed an aeroplane to do his own 'spotting' of enemy trenches. After the Armistice he controlled most of the Channel ports and in 1919 was appointed general officer commanding the 47th division of the Territorial Army. He was appointed C.B. in 1916, knighted (K.C.B.) in 1919, and awarded the Belgian Croix de Guerre and the French Légion d'honneur. In his long career he was mentioned in dispatches eleven times. Smyth retired from the British Army in 1924.

While Bean thought that Smyth was sometimes too cautious ('He almost always went to see for himself'), Major General Sir Brudenell White [q.v.] held him in high regard: 'He is so sphinx-like, silent and imperturbable. But there is a quality that stands out in Smyth— his intense thoroughness. That was his great characteristic'. Major General Sir Charles Rosenthal [q.v.11], who succeeded Smyth as G.O.C., 2nd Division, wrote: 'Among the soldiers he was recognized as an officer of wise moderation and calm courage, a strict disciplinarian'. One of his senior officers said that the troops remembered Smyth 'for his ability, fair-mindedness and sterling military qualities'.

On 23 July 1918 at Holy Trinity parish church, Chelsea, London, Smyth had married Evelyn Olwen, daughter of Colonel Sir Osmond Williams, baronet and lord lieutenant of Merionethshire, Wales. Their three children were born in Britain and the family migrated to Australia in 1925, settling on a grazing property at Balmoral, Victoria. Smyth said that he regarded Australians as the finest troops with whom he had ever served, and he wanted to live among them in their country. He took a keen interest in district affairs and in 1931 was an unsuccessful Nationalist Party candidate for the Victorian Senate vacancy caused by the death of Major General H. E. ('Pompey') Elliott [q.v.8].

Survived by his wife, two sons and a daughter, Smyth died at his Balmoral home on 21 July 1941 and was buried in the local cemetery. His portrait by George Coates [q.v.8] is in the Australian War Memorial, Canberra. A son, Dacre Smyth, served in the Royal Australian Navy in 1940-78 and rose to commodore.

C. E. W. Bean, *The story of Anzac*, 2 (Syd, 1924) and *The A.I.F. in France*, 1916-18 (Syd, 1929, 1933, 1937, 1942); L. B. Oatts, *I serve* (Lond, 1966); Westminster School, *Elizabethan*, 1882-85; *Reveille* (Syd), 1 Aug 1932, 1 May 1934; *Daily Graphic* (Lond), 5 Sept 1898; *Daily Mail* (Lond), 31 Aug 1899; *Argus*, 13 May 1931; War diaries, 1st Aust Infantry Brigade, 1915-16 *and* 2nd Aust Division, 1917-18 (AWM) *and* 59th Division, British Army, 1918 (War Office, Lond); Bean papers (AWM); Smyth personal diaries, 1896-1902, 1915-18 held by, and information from Cdre D. Smyth, Toorak, Melb; Wingate papers (School of Oriental Studies, Univ Durham, Eng); information from Mrs O. Hardiman, New Gisborne, Vic.

IVAN CHAPMAN

SMYTHE, ROBERT SPARROW (1833-1917), journalist and entrepreneur, was born in March 1833 at Lambeth, London, son of Robert Smythe and his wife Elizabeth. He served in London as a proofreader for Robson, Levey & Robson, printers, and probably studied law reporting, for he was competent in shorthand. Migrating to Australia in 1855 in search of better health, Smythe became parliamentary reporter on the *Register* in Adelaide and later editor of the *Illustrated Post* (*Illustrated Australian News*), one of the first pictorial papers in Australia. Moving to Melbourne, he wrote for the *Age* and in 1859-80 part-owned and edited the *Chronicle* (St Kilda). After working as a music and drama critic for newspapers in New South

Wales and South Australia, he lived for many years at Deepdene, Melbourne.

In 1862 Smythe turned to theatrical management, accompanying the tenor and soprano duo, the Bianchis. Then followed a five-year tour with French violinists Poussard and Douay in whose musical company he met English-born Amelia Elizabeth Bailey, a popular coloratura soprano, whom he eventually married in Melbourne on 18 October 1881. He also managed the French pianist Boulanger, the magician Robert Heller, the German tragedian Daniel Bandmann and others. During Smythe's 1863 tour of Asia, India and South Africa he claimed to be the first manager to conduct a company into Japan after the 1854 port treaty, and to take professionals to the Himalayas and the Transvaal.

His first Australian 'discovery' was the popular lecturer Rev. Charles Clark [q.v.3]; Smythe piloted him around Australia annually for four years, and eventually on tours of North America and South Africa. After this success, Smythe began about 1872 to specialize in lecture management, taking Australians to Europe and America, and bringing scientists, explorers and literary personalities from there to Australasia. He accompanied English astronomer R. A. Proctor, war correspondent Archibald Forbes, journalist G. Augustus Sala, authors Annie Besant and Professor M. D. Conway, preacher Dr Talmadge and explorer Henry Stanley.

During the 1890s Smythe acted as agent for the French writer Paul Blouet ('Max O'Rell'), baritone Charles Santley, and Sir Charles and Lady Hallé, and was widely respected as one of the best managers in Australasia. In September 1895 he announced tour management as his full-time occupation. His most triumphant 'lion' was Mark Twain who, as a bankrupt in 1895, accepted Smythe's longstanding invitation to tour the world.

Smythe's varied experiences, geniality and excellence as a raconteur made him a popular companion. His short, stocky stature and bushy moustache provided the stuff of caricature for the press. Active in management until 1913, he died at Deepdene on 23 May 1917 and was buried with Anglican rites in Box Hill cemetery. His estate was sworn for probate at £14 956. His wife, two daughters and a son survived him.

The son CARLYLE GREENWOOD SMYTHE (1865-1925), journalist and manager, was born on 16 September 1865 at Ambala, India, while his parents were in the Punjab. He grew up in Melbourne where he was educated at Hawthorn Grammar School and Trinity College, University of·Melbourne (B.A., 1888). During a brief journalistic career, he was for three years editor of the *Belgian Times* in Brussels and author of a history of Belgium.

From the Twain tour of 1895 he became Robert's partner in lecture management. When his father retired, Carlyle conducted Sir Arthur Conan Doyle, Mrs Besant, 'Max O'Rell' and Captain Amundsen, and wrote several magazine pieces about his experiences. On 11 November 1903 he married Elva Dorette Bode at St Barnabas's Anglican Church, Balwyn. After suffering serious burns to his hands, he went to live at Deepdene; he became a music and drama critic as well as a writer on international policy for the *Argus* and other papers. Survived by his wife, he died on 15 December 1925 at Nice, France, where he had undergone surgery. His estate was sworn for probate at £19 825.

Punch (Melb), 24 July 1913; *Age*, 24 May 1917, 18 Dec 1925; *Argus*, 24, 26 May 1917, 18 Dec 1925; *Referee*, 30 May 1917; *Australasian*, 26 Dec 1925.
                                    M. SHILLINGSBURG

SNOOK, CHARLES WILLIAM (1891-1948), aviator, was born on 13 April 1891 at North Fremantle, Western Australia, son of Henry Denis Snook, bank manager, and his wife Lucy Matilda, née Saw. He was educated at the High School, Perth, Sydney Church of England Grammar School (Shore) and Hawkesbury Agricultural College, New South Wales. On 12 March 1912 at Christ Church, Hawthorn, Melbourne, he married Clarice May Adele de Leon. With an impulse that grew from his boyhood passion for model aeroplanes, at 24 Snook learned flying at Hendon Hall in England where he gained his wings; he won a commission in the Royal Flying Corps and was commanding officer at Brooklands aerodrome; flight experts extolled his ability and performances. In 1915 Snook enlisted in the Royal Air Force. Next year he was shot down over Germany and taken prisoner; in 1917 he was exchanged for a German officer and posted to Salisbury.

Returning to Melbourne in 1920, Snook formed Australian Aircraft Pty Ltd. With three aeroplanes bought from R.A.F. disposals, and a maintenance crew, he set up as a commercial pilot in Sydney. Although he was commissioned to chart the Queensland coast, his operational costs exceeded his income. He then took his wife, daughter and son to Western Australia and farmed, unsuccessfully; on 11 December 1928 he was divorced. On 21 February 1929 he married Hilda Burn Kershaw, medical practitioner, at St Mary's Church, South Perth. Having sold his farm, he worked for Winterbottom Motor Co. Ltd, but soon joined the Australian Aero Club, Western Australia section. As an instructor for Western Air Services, he organized joyrides over the wheat belt and Maylands, and performed with parachutist Jimmy Reece.

Snook was a gregarious man, of stocky build and genial expression, who mixed easily; in 1934-36 he was chief pilot on a photographic survey of the eastern goldfields for the Western Mining Corporation; this connexion enabled him and others to form Airlines (W.A.) Ltd. The company operated a twin-engined Monospar and a Spartan on the Perth-Wiluna-Kalgoorlie route, but it was under-capitalized and near collapse when the Monospar was wrecked at Mount Sir Samuel. Overweight and suffering from blood pressure, Snook struggled on with the Spartan, the joyrides and a mail contract. As his finances improved, he added a Stinson Reliant to his outfit and began flights to Rottnest Island, Esperance, Port Hedland, Marble Bar and Meekatharra. The Stinson was destroyed by enemy action at Broome in March 1942, but two Rapides and two Ansons were acquired. With the addition of a Dove aircraft, a concession for the south-west newspaper delivery and charter work for Hoskins Bros (later Vickers Hoskins), Snook's company prospered and he remained managing director until 1948. Although he had attained the rank of wing commander, he was affectionately known as 'Captain'.

In August 1941 Snook had taken honorary command of No.5 Wing Air Training Corps; in 1946-48 he was vice-commander of the Royal Perth Yacht Club and a member of the Western Australia division of the Air Force Association. Survived by his wife and their adopted daughter, he died of heart disease on 23 September 1948. After an Anglican service he was cremated. His estate was sworn for probate at £22 836.

Albany Advertiser, 10 Jan 1931; *West Australian*, 12 Oct 1939; scrap-books and clippings (Aviation Museum, Bullcreek, Perth).   WENDY BIRMAN

SNOW, SIR SYDNEY (1887-1958), retailer, was born on 17 December 1887 at Ballarat, Victoria, third child of Melbourne-born John Snow, draper, and his English wife Emily Lark, née Piper. Leaving Ballarat College, he worked in his father's drapery emporium, John Snow & Co. In 1912 he moved to Sydney; with his father and W. V. Manton, he established Sydney Snow Ltd, a retail softgoods company, which opened a store on the corner of Pitt and Liverpool streets, diagonally opposite Anthony Hordern's [q.v.4]. He returned to Ballarat to marry Ruby Dent Davies at the Lydiard Street Methodist Church on 22 April 1913.

Developing his commercial and business interests, in the 1920s Snow became a director of Yellow Cabs of Australia Ltd and Sun Newspapers Ltd; in 1929-31 he was deputy chairman of Associated Newspapers Ltd which had taken over the *Sun*. With the onset of the Depression he helped to found the All for Australia League and led negotiations for its merger with the National Party: in 1932 he was elected deputy president of the new United Australia Party. He castigated the dismissed premier J. T. Lang [q.v.9] as 'this chief disciple of dishonour and default', and claimed that the U.A.P. offered 'personal security for life and savings' in contrast to the 'sovietised savagery' and 'ruined commerce and industry' of Lang. Snow pursued improved relations with the Country Party and campaigned for Joseph Lyons [q.v.10] in the 1934 Federal election. Chairman of the party's executive and council until he resigned on medical grounds in November 1942, Snow was appointed K.B.E. in 1936.

By then Snow was a member of the Australian Jockey and Victoria Racing clubs; a successful owner, he and A. C. Lewis won the Caulfield Cup with Peshawar in 1953. Snow was 'mad about' his gardens at Kenilworth, Bowral, and at his Wahroonga home, and took his family on fishing holidays. He also belonged to the New South Wales and Australian clubs, Sydney, and the Athenaeum in Melbourne. Big, with blue eyes, Snow was an impressive man, physically and mentally.

With interests in all States by the late 1930s and an office in London, he was a director of Broken Hill South Ltd, General Industries Ltd, H. B. Dickie Ltd, Commonwealth Industrial Gases Ltd and other companies. He was also governing director of his own company and chairman of the local board of the Colonial Mutual Life Assurance Co. Pty Ltd and of Snows Men's Wear Ltd, Melbourne, run by his brother (Sir) Gordon (1898-1954). Active in the Retail Traders' Association of New South Wales, Sir Sydney became president in 1937. He defended youth employment against criticism by the Industrial Commission and argued that its decision to limit females to one-half of the workforce in some shops would displace women workers (who were paid less than men) and increase selling costs. In 1941 he joined the State Recruiting Committee. Next year, at a mass meeting of retail traders, he fought the proposal by John Dedman, minister for war organization of industry, to transfer 40 000 men and women from larger retailing firms to war production, arguing that 'it is one thing to lose our assets through the exigencies of war and another to lose them through the meddling of inexperienced economists'. Snow was an executive member of the Food for Britain fund and vice-president (1948-49) of the Citizens' Reform Association.

Despite rationing, Snow's store had continued to flourish in the war years. He managed to reduce overheads while increasing turnover above pre-war levels. His achievement was considerable, given that his city store (like others in the area) was being overtaken by the concentration of retailers on the Pitt and Market streets axis. By 1951 Snow had opened another store at Camperdown. In failing health, he sold out to Cox Bros (Australia) Ltd in 1954 for over £1 250 000 and lived thereafter at Bowral.

Survived by his wife, son and two daughters, Sir Sydney died on 24 November 1958 in the Scottish Hospital, Paddington, and was cremated after a service at St Columba's Presbyterian Church, Woollahra. He left an estate sworn for probate at some £267 000.

J. Roe (ed), *Twentieth century Sydney* (Syd, 1980); *Draper of A'sia*, Oct 1911, Mar 1912, Feb, Sept 1914; Retail Traders' Assn of NSW, *J*, Oct 1937; *Herald* (Melb), 24 Nov 1958; *SMH*, 26 Feb 1931, 28 May 1932, 11 Sept 1934, 20 Oct 1935, 23 June 1936, 1 July, 17 Sept 1937, 12 Jan 1938, 28 June 1941, 20 Nov 1942, 13 May, 16 July 1948, 5 Mar 1949, 25 Nov 1958; information from Mrs M. Asprey, Warrawee, NSW.   PETER SPEARRITT

SNOWBALL, OSWALD ROBINSON (1859-1928), solicitor and politician, was born on 18 July 1859 at Wolsingham, Durham, England, son of Joseph Snowball, miller, and his wife Sarah, née Fitzgerald. In 1868 Joseph brought his family to Melbourne where Oswald was educated at Carlton College, Fitzroy. After three uncongenial years on the land, he qualified as a barrister and solicitor; admitted to practice in 1883, he went into partnership first with Walter Briggs until 1895 and next with his own brother-in-law, as Snowball & Kaufmann.

In 1884 Snowball was initiated into Freemasonry at Brunswick where he was master in 1888-89. A member of the Loyal Orange Institution of Victoria from 1878, he was district master for Melbourne in 1898. In 1905 he succeeded (Sir) Simon Fraser [q.v.4] as grand master (an office he was to hold for a record twenty-three years) and in 1909-11 he became grand president of the Loyal Orange Council of Australasia. Active in Protestant moral reform crusades of the early 1900s, Snowball opposed gambling and liquor, and advocated Bible reading in State schools, temperance and local option. He was a foundation member of the Victorian Protestant Electors' Committee which supported Orangemen in Victorian elections in 1906-07.

In 1909 Snowball succeeded Sir Thomas Bent [q.v.3] as member for Brighton in the Legislative Assembly. Assiduous in his constituents' interests, he was returned comfortably at seven successive elections. His legal training and independent disposition made him quintessentially a committee man. He was a member of several select committees of inquiry and three royal commissions, and chairman of the royal commission on Victorian outer ports (1923-28).

Snowball's criticisms of the Catholic Church brought him into open conflict with the Catholic Federation, notably in 1912, but his *bête noire* was (Archbishop) Daniel Mannix [q.v.10]. World War I and the conscription issue brought Snowball's Imperial patriotism to a peak and hardened his conviction of Catholic disloyalty, adding fuel to his annual 12 July statements on the Church of Rome in Australia.

Away from the public platform there was a softer and less combative side to the man. Snowball's affable personality and broad sympathies were displayed by his friendships across all parties and creeds, most notably with Labor leader George Prendergast [q.v.11]. In 1924 Snowball was one of five Nationalist rebels who—with the Victorian Farmers' Union—supported Labor's motion of no confidence against the Peacock [q.v.11] administration which resulted in the election of the Prendergast government. Snowball won as an Independent Nationalist in 1927, then rejoined the Nationalist fold.

Despite severe illness, from July 1927 he was an outstanding Speaker for the Hogan [q.v.9] government. Snowball died of obstructive jaundice on 16 March 1928, survived by his wife Ellen Grace, née Anketell (whom he had married with Anglican rites at South Yarra on 16 August 1888), and their daughter and three sons. After a state funeral, he was buried with Presbyterian forms in Brighton cemetery. His estate was sworn for probate at £45 210.

Photographs present Snowball as small, somewhat stern, even pugnacious, but he appears warm and genial in the portrait now held by the Loyal Orange Institution of Victoria. Outside his family, legal practice, the Orange lodge and politics, he was closely associated with the Austin Hospital for Incurables for thirty years and was founder of the Brighton Technical School.

R. H. Croll, *I recall* (Melb, 1939); *PD* (Vic), 22 Aug 1916, p 900, 4 July 1928, p 40; *Aust Sentinel*, 30 Nov 1904, 24 June 1905; *Brighton Southern Cross*, 2, 9 Oct 1909, 18 June, 9 July 1927, 10 Mar 1928; *Age*, 16-30 July 1912, 17, 20 Mar 1928; *Table Talk*, 28 July 1927; *Argus*, 17, 20 Mar 1928; *Bulletin*, 21 Mar 1928; M. Vines, The instability of government and parties in Victoria in the 1920s (M.A. thesis, Univ Melb, 1975); information from Masonic Centre, East Melb, *and* Loyal Orange Inst of Vic *and* Miss M. Snowball, Brighton, Melb.

JOHN LACK

SNOWBALL, WILLIAM (1854?-1902), medical practitioner, was born probably on 7 November 1854 at Carlton, Melbourne, son of John Snowball, builder, and his wife Catharine, née Iley, both from Durham, England. He was educated at Wesley College and Melbourne Church of England Grammar School. Graduating (M.B., 1875; B.S., 1880) from the University of Melbourne, he studied at University College, London (L.S.A., 1876), gained experience at the Great Ormond Street Hospital and in Edinburgh (L.M. et L.R.C.S., 1877), and visited several continental hospitals. Returning to Melbourne, he was appointed resident doctor at the Children's Hospital (1878), becoming an honorary there in 1882 after having commenced his own practice in paediatric medicine at Carlton.

As chairman of the honorary medical staff at the Children's Hospital, Snowball co-operated closely with management to enlarge and improve accommodation. Infection was a constant threat, often introduced by out-patients or their parents and breeding freely among the sick, especially in overcrowded, sunless wards. At his insistence, a new and separate out-patient block was built in 1897 and he helped to plan a new in-patient block. With wide windows, sunny verandahs and facing north, it was to open in 1903. Concern for the welfare of nurses showed in Snowball's constant efforts to have their accommodation improved and in his insistence on prophylactic injections of diphtheria antitoxin to protect them from infection. In the 1890s he introduced hospital lectures by the honorary staff to nurses and medical students.

In 1895 he was president of the Victorian branch of the British Medical Association. Although not noted as a surgeon, as a paediatric physician and clinical teacher he was outstanding. Snowball has been called 'the father of paediatrics in Melbourne': his professional skill, the warmth of his personality and his instant rapport with the young quickly made his a household name. He appreciated that the child, physically, is not a small adult, but a different person with different needs and problems. He devoted his life to children, to their hospital and to those who cared for them. It was said that most doctors could correctly determine nine out of ten children's ailments, but that only Snowball could diagnose and prescribe for the tenth.

Genial, with a kindly, heavily-bearded face and a fine sense of humour, Snowball was a voracious reader and a keen ornithologist. Always a big man who regretted that he had to stoop to reach a flower, he increasingly carried too much weight and his health suffered. At St Philip's Anglican Church, Sydney, on 29 November 1881 he had married Mary Sophia Burton; they lived quietly with their five children on his Narracan property in

the last months before he died of Bright's disease on 22 April 1902. His funeral, at the Melbourne general cemetery, was attended by many professional colleagues and fellow members of the Yorick Club. His contribution as a pioneer paediatrician, would have been greater had he lived more than forty-seven years. His death was fairly recorded as 'a national loss'.

J. Smith (ed), Cyclopedia of Victoria, 1 (Melb, 1903); H. B. Graham, Beacons on our way (Melb, 1953); L. Gardiner, Royal Children's Hospital Melbourne 1870-1970 (Melb, 1970); Intercolonial Medical J of A'sia, 20 May 1902; Australasian, 6 May 1893, 26 Apr 1902; Royal Children's Hospital, Melb, Archives, which include bibliog of Snowball's professional publications comp by Dr U. Shergold, 1970.

LYNDSAY GARDINER

SNOWDEN, SIR ARTHUR (1829-1918), lawyer and politician, was born on 29 July 1829 at Dartford, Kent, England, son of James Snowden, saddler, and his wife Harriet, née Durling. Educated in Dartford and London, he worked for seven years in a law stationery business in London. Migrating to Victoria in the Great Britain in 1852, he spent two years on the Fryers Creek and Bendigo goldfields. In 1854 he went to Melbourne and was a conveyancing clerk for Bennett & Taylor, solicitors, for twelve years. He entered into articles in 1866 and was admitted in 1867 as a practitioner under the Conveyancing Act. After practising alone for ten years, he joined (Sir) Samuel Gillott [q.v.9] in 1877 in a law partnership which in 1886 became Gillott, Croker, Snowden & Co. In 1894 he formed the firm of Snowden, Neave & Demaine.

On 26 June 1856 Snowden had married Elizabeth Jarvis (d. 1900) at St Peter's Anglican Church, Eastern Hill, and in 1858 they settled in a four-roomed cottage beside the Yarra River in St Hellier's Street, Collingwood, a swampy outer suburb. Here he began his involvement in community affairs. In 1864, when Collingwood was dotted with shacks erected for Melbourne's poorest tenants, he participated in establishing St Philip's Anglican Church, a substantial edifice designed to inspire the residents to drain and cleanse the district. Snowden remained an office-bearer of this parish until 1918. In 1868 he was elected to the East Collingwood Borough Council on a reform platform. Concerned about untenanted cottages, the councillors had been encouraging the development of abattoirs, sheep-skin yards, wool-washing works, tanneries, breweries, night-soil dumps and other industries to attract workers to the district. Appalled by council's disregard of health regulations,

Snowden tried to revive the defunct health and sanitation committee; he also supported complaints about local pollution. When the council decided to encourage further industrial development on the River Yarra, he was the only dissentient. His alternative proposal that existing anti-pollution laws be enforced, with compensation for the factory owners, was supported by the Melbourne City Council and the daily press, but, hopelessly outnumbered in the Collingwood council, he resigned after a year.

Snowden became prominent in Melbourne legal and business circles and in 1891 was elected to Melbourne City Council, representing Lonsdale Ward. Immediately popular, he was thrice elected mayor of Melbourne (1892-94) and knighted in 1895. Elected to the Victorian Legislative Council for Melbourne province in 1895 and 1902, he resigned in 1904.

He was regarded as the 'father of the city council' and served it as a vigorous debater until his death. A stickler for propriety, he always insisted that the council should conduct its business 'strictly according to the act' and was quick to seize on any action of which he disapproved. In 1902 he revived the use of the council's Protest Book, a journal enshrined in standing orders but unused since 1876. For the next fifteen years he seemed to make the Protest Book his personal diary, constantly condemning various decisions and procedures. In his late eighties he was still a member of the town hall committee and the baths and parks committee, a council representative on the board of the Melbourne Sailors' Home and one of four managers of the Melbourne general cemetery.

Snowden became a commissioner representing the city council on the Melbourne and Metropolitan Board of Works, the body responsible for sewage and water supply. He was a member of the committee of the Austin Hospital for Incurables and various other community committees, of the Church of England diocesan synod and the diocesan council, and of the executive committee of the Australasian Federation League. A keen gardener, he had many rare plants in the garden of his gracious home, St Helliers, and he occasionally contributed specimens to Melbourne parks. He died at his Collingwood home on 18 June 1918 and was buried in Melbourne general cemetery. Two daughters survived him.

Smith (ed), *Cyclopedia of Victoria*, 1 (Melb, 1903); *Argus*, 14 Sept 1868, 19 June 1918; *Australasian*, 12 Nov 1892; *Weekly Times* (Melb), 12 Nov 1892, 1 June 1895; *IAN*, 1 June 1895; *Age*, 19 June 1918; *Punch* (Melb), 10 Mar 1904; A. H. B. Barrett, The making of an industrial environment, Collingwood, Victoria, 1851-91 (M.A. thesis, Univ Melb, 1970); Protest book, Melb City Council Archives.   BERNARD BARRETT

SODEMAN, ARNOLD KARL (1899-1936), murderer, was born on 12 December 1899 at Hawthorn, Melbourne, son of Karl Sodeman, a German-born engineer, and his native-born wife Violet Esther, née Wood. As a child he was treated severely by his father and frequently witnessed Karl beating Violet. Aged 13, Arnold ran away from home and worked in the coal mines at Wonthaggi, South Gippsland.

In his youth Sodeman was twice brought before the courts to answer criminal charges. At 17 he was convicted of theft and forgery, and sent to a reformatory. Soon after his release, he was convicted in Melbourne in 1920 of attempted robbery under arms and given three years hard labour. Having escaped from French Island, he was apprehended and sentenced to another year. Released in 1926, Sodeman settled down to various labouring jobs, at first in Melbourne and later in Gippsland. To those who knew him he was a hard-working, mild and amiable man with a generous disposition. On 17 July he married Bernice Cecilia Pope at Collingwood with Congregational forms; a daughter was born in 1928. The marriage was a happy one; although Sodeman seemed to suffer from occasional bouts of depression and frequent drunkenness, he was never violent to his family.

On the morning of 2 December 1935 the body of 6-year-old June Rushmer was discovered, lying face-down in a patch of sword-grass, outside the township of Leongatha in Gippsland; she was bound and gagged, and had died from suffocation. The crime resembled three earlier unsolved killings: 12-year-old Mena Griffiths on 8 November 1930, 16-year-old Hazel Wilson on 9 January 1931 (both at Ormond, Melbourne), and 12-year-old Ethel Belshaw at Inverloch, Gippsland, on 1 January 1935. As a result of information received from a suspicious workmate, Sodeman was arrested and questioned about Rushmer's death. At first he denied any involvement with the victim, but after twelve hours interrogation broke down and confessed—to all four murders.

He was tried in February 1936 for the murder of Rushmer. The government medical officer Dr A. J. W. Philpott, his assistant Dr R. T. Allan and a psychiatrist Dr Reginald Ellery all gave evidence that Sodeman was suffering from a disorder of the mind which created an 'obsessional impulse' of such power that—under the influence of alcohol—he was no longer responsible for his behaviour. Since Sodeman was intoxicated on all four occasions, the doctors concluded that he was insane at the times of the murders. Their conclusion was reinforced not only by Sodeman's repetitive behaviour, but also by his family's medical history: both his father and grandfather had died insane.

At the conclusion of the two-day trial, Judge Charles Gavan Duffy [q.v.8] advised the jury to distinguish between opinions given by expert medical witnesses on matters relating to the physical body, which could be proved by surgery, and those concerning the mind. Rejecting Sodeman's defence of insanity, the jury found him guilty of murder. The judge sentenced him to death.

After exhausting all avenues of appeal, Arnold Karl Sodeman was hanged and buried in Pentridge Gaol, Coburg, on 1 June 1936. An autopsy disclosed that he was suffering from leptomeningitis, a degenerative disease which could cause serious congestion of the brain when aggravated by alcohol.

R. S. Ellery, *The cow jumped over the moon* (Melb, 1956); J. P. Bourke and D. S. Sonenberg, *Insanity and injustice* (Melb, 1969); *Vic Law Reports*, 1936; *Cwlth Law Reports*, 1936; *People* (Syd), 31 Jan 1951; *Argus*, 10-13 Nov, 12, 13 Dec 1930, 19 Feb, 20, 21 Mar 1931, 4, 9 Jan, 4, 9, 12 Apr, 16 May, 3, 6 Dec 1935, 1 Jan, 27 Mar, 4 Apr, 30 May, 1 June 1936; transcript of Sodeman's trial, 17, 18 Feb 1936 (Supreme Court, Melb).

GEORGE MARSHALL IRVING

SOLLY, ROBERT HENRY (1859-1932), bootmaker, trade unionist and politician, was born on 9 September 1859 at Ellington, Kent, England, son of Stephen Solly, labourer, and his wife Eliza, née Sage. Aged 7, Bob was employed as a local farm-hand; he next took a job in a rope factory at Ramsgate before being apprenticed to a bootmaker at Newcastle upon Tyne. Having completed his apprenticeship, he migrated with his brother to Adelaide in 1876.

He found employment in Victoria and New South Wales as station-hand and bootmaker before returning to Adelaide where, at St Patrick's Catholic Church, West Terrace, on 12 September 1883 he married Mary Graham. In 1885 he moved to Melbourne and worked at his trade in Collingwood. From the outset 'Fighting Bob' was involved in the affairs of the Victorian Operative Bootmakers' Union and was prominent on its executive during the 1890s struggles with employers over mechanization, subdivision of labour and wage reductions. In 1901-04 he was the union's secretary; he also represented employees on the Victorian Boot Wages Board. Solly was a member of the Eight Hours' Committee and active in the Anti-Sweating

League. In 1901 he was elected president of the Trades Hall Council.

After the defeats of the 1890s, Solly's efforts were increasingly devoted to politics. A founding member of the Richmond branch of the Progressive Political League (later the Australian Labor Party), he was the first Labor member of the Richmond City Council (1903-09). In June 1904 he entered the Victorian Legislative Assembly as special representative of the railway officers and held the position until November 1906. Following a number of unsuccessful bids for parliament—notably for the State seat of Richmond (1902, 1907), the Senate (1903, 1906) and the Federal seat of Batman in 1906—he represented Carlton in the Victorian Legislative Assembly in 1908-32.

During his long term in parliament Solly was distinguished more by diligence and integrity than by brilliance. Seldom delivering prepared speeches, he contributed to debate by his spontaneous declarations on subjects that particularly moved him. He was an active committee member, however, and served as chairman of committees in 1927-29. A member of six royal commissions, he chaired one on metropolitan housing (1917). He sat on the board of trustees of the Exhibition Building (1912-32), and on the councils of the Working Men's College (1899-1932) and the University of Melbourne (1925-32).

Genial but quick-tempered, Solly was respected as a man of sincerity, loyalty and fairness, and admired as a self-educated man if not as a 'Heaven-born genius'. Throughout his career he endeavoured to improve conditions for the working class. Consistent in his principles, he remained on the left of the labour movement. His socialism derived from his youthful experience with the radical politics of Tyneside and from reading writers such as Herbert Spencer, William Morris and Henry George [q.v.4]. Solly was greatly assisted by his wife's support. He died on 5 June 1932 at his Carlton home and was buried in the Melbourne general cemetery; he was survived by his wife, two daughters and two sons, one of whom, Robert Henry, became mayor of Melbourne in 1953.

B. Walker, *Solidarity forever* (Melb, 1972); J. Iremonger et al (eds), *Strikes* (Syd, 1973); *PD* (Vic), 14 June 1932, p 14; *Age, Argus, Sun News-Pictorial* and *Herald* (Melb), 6 June 1932; D. A. Harris, 'Bad neighbourhoods': the inner suburbs and the housing debate: Melbourne 1900-1920 (M.A. thesis, Univ Melb, 1984); B. C. Scates, 'Faddists and extremists': Radicalism and the labour movement in southeastern Australia, 1887-1898 (Ph.D. thesis, Monash Univ, 1987); R. Frances, The politics of work: case studies of three Victorian industries, Victoria 1880-1939 (Ph.D. thesis, Monash Univ, 1988).

RAELENE FRANCES

SOLOMON, ALBERT EDGAR (1876-1914), lawyer and premier, was born on 7 March 1876 at Longford, Tasmania, son of Edward Solomon, clerk, and his wife Mary Anne, née Trebilcock. Educated at Longford State School, Horton College, Ross, and Launceston Church Grammar School, Solomon displayed precocious intellect, securing a State exhibition and matriculating at the University of Melbourne by the age of 13; he gained four degrees from the University of Tasmania (B.A., 1895; LL.B., 1897; M.A., LL.M., 1903). Articled to the firm of Law & Weston in 1893, Solomon was called to the Tasmanian Bar in 1898 and practised with his brother at Launceston and Ulverstone. At Launceston on 13 August 1903 he married Una Alice Hannah Mary Scott.

An active Methodist, the politically ambitious Solomon aligned himself with moral reform and temperance interests at Launceston which helped him top the Bass Anti-Socialist ticket in the 1909 State election. Two months later he became attorney-general and minister for education and mines in Sir Elliott Lewis's [q.v.10] second ministry. As minister for education, he supported the newly appointed W. T. McCoy [q.v.10] as director of education when he swept through the department. Among the more important changes were the improvement of teachers' conditions and pay, the upgrading of teacher education, the establishment of Philip Smith [q.v.2] College and the first state high schools. Wide-reaching syllabus changes were also effected, the inspectorial system became less threatening for teachers and greater provision was made for children from remote areas.

Solomon was respected for his tactical skill in parliament where the increasingly embattled Lewis could always rely on his support. In June 1912 the premier responded to party criticism by resigning his office and Solomon defeated N. K. Ewing [q.v.8] for the position, becoming the youngest Tasmanian premier to that time.

His twenty-one months as premier were demanding. Saddled with the legacy of the Liberal Party unrest that had unseated Lewis, he depended upon the Independent member of the House of Assembly, D. N. Cameron [q.v.7], for a parliamentary majority. Labor tried continually to destabilize the situation with various no-confidence motions and a censure motion over the Mount Lyell disaster. Solomon attempted to secure his position by gaining an early dissolution; in the election of January 1913 Cameron was trounced and the Liberals returned with 52 per cent of the vote and a working majority. This favourable position was soon lost; a by-election defeat, combined with the increasingly erratic behaviour of J. T. H. Whitsitt, saw Solomon lose a no-

confidence motion in April 1914. He advised another dissolution, but John Earle [q.v.8] was invited to form a Labor government and Solomon became leader of the Opposition.

About two years after entering parliament, Solomon had suffered a cut hand. Never a robust man, he did not recover fully from the infection; he was, moreover, exhausted from overwork. Survived by his wife and two sons, he died at his Hobart home on 5 October 1914 of phthisis pulmonalis and was buried in Carr Villa cemetery, Launceston.

C. Turney (ed), *Pioneers of Australian education*, 3 (Syd, 1983); *Daily Telegraph* (Launc), 6 Oct 1914; *Mercury*, 6, 7 Oct 1914. SCOTT BENNETT

SOLOMON, VAIBEN LOUIS (1853-1908), businessman and premier, was born on 13 May 1853 in Adelaide, son of Judah Moss Solomon [q.v.6] and his wife Rachel, née Cohen. He was educated at J. L. Young's [q.v.6] Adelaide Educational Institution and Scotch College, Melbourne. Solomon joined Adelaide merchants Donaldson, Andrews & Sharland, and was their agent in Kapunda before working at the Adelaide Stock Exchange. In early 1873 he joined a prospecting party, largely funded by the Adelaide Jewish community, in the rush to the Northern Territory goldfields. After ten months he returned to Adelaide to find his engagement to a Gentile so strenuously opposed by his father that Vaiben again went to the Northern Territory in August 1874, having also failed to secure appointment as a goldfield warden. He managed the Palmerston business of his elder brother, Moss, until January 1877 when he opened his own store and agency (auctioneers, shipping, mining estate and general commission agents). Next year he formed a partnership with F. P. Stevens and H. H. Adcock. On 6 December 1880, some three months after the death of his father, Vaiben married his early love, Mary Bridgland (d. 1885), née Wigzell, by then a widow with a young son.

Dubbed 'Mr Everything' because there were few pursuits to which he would not turn his hand, Solomon invested in mining and in 1884 promoted the North Australian Pearl Fishing Co. of which he was manager and secretary. He lost heavily on both ventures. Virtually insolvent by 1888, he was able to stave off bankruptcy by taking W. Griffiths as a partner in July 1888. From mid-1885 until mid-1890 Solomon owned and edited the *Northern Territory Times and Gazette*.

Powerfully built, with a heavy, dark beard, Solomon was a dynamic, prominent and popular citizen of Palmerston. His nickname, 'Black Solomon', derived from the occasion when—for a dare—he blackened himself to resemble an Aborigine and walked naked through the town. A foundation member (1874) of Palmerston District Council, he served for several terms. When the Northern Territory was granted parliamentary representation in South Australia's House of Assembly, Solomon was returned at the head of the poll in April 1890. While urging economic development of the Territory, particularly the completion of the transcontinental railway between Adelaide and Palmerston, he advocated total exclusion of Chinese and other Asians. He wound up his affairs at Palmerston. On his way south he gave a number of public lectures opposing Chinese migration to the eastern colonies.

From Adelaide Solomon speculated in Western Australian gold-mining and entered the Adelaide Stock Exchange (1896). Largely because of the forcefulness of his personality, he became a prominent figure in colonial politics. He was government whip for the second Playford [q.v.11] administration in 1890-91 and for the Downer [q.v.8] government in 1893. Forced to resign as an insolvent in March 1891 mainly due to his Territory mining ventures, he was returned at the consequent by-election in May before he had even received his certificate of discharge. In June 1899 he became leader of the conservative Opposition, a motley group of parliamentary factions dubbed the 'Forlorn Hope'; in November, however, he led the attack which brought down the Kingston [q.v.9] administration, and was asked to form a government. Solomon became premier and treasurer on 1 December, but his government faced the House on only two occasions; the first to announce its policy, the second when it was defeated by a simple adjournment motion on 8 December. The sole Jew to have been a colonial or State premier, Solomon also led South Australia's shortest-lived government. It was the last of the factional administrations in what had become essentially a bi-party House after the emergence of the Labor Party during the 1890s. Something of an anachronism in the South Australian parliament, he was always a forceful and witty debater, but never held another ministerial portfolio.

A staunch advocate of intercolonial free trade, Solomon considered it a distinction to have been elected a delegate to the Australasian Federal Convention in 1897 and to have helped draft the Federal Constitution. In 1901, with South Australia voting as a single electorate, he was returned to Federal parliament, but was defeated by E. L. Batchelor [q.v.7] in 1903 for the seat of Boothby. In May 1905 Solomon was again returned as Northern Territory representative to the South Australian Legislative Assembly where, by 1908, he was deputy leader of the Opposition. Ever a determined advocate for the Terri-

tory, he supported its transfer from South Australia to the Commonwealth.

He had compiled successive issues of the *Northern Territory Times almanac and directory* between 1886 and 1890 and later published a *Guide to Western Australia and its goldfields* (Adelaide, 1894). With Thomas Harry, he wrote *Australia at play* (Adelaide, 1908), a pamphlet that guyed the Australian attitude to sport. Solomon died of cancer in Adelaide on 20 October 1908 and was buried in the Adelaide Jewish cemetery. On 22 July 1896 in Melbourne he had married Alice Cohen who survived him with three children and the daughter of his first marriage. His daughter Esther was the first woman elected to the Adelaide City Council: a councillor for twenty-two years and an alderman, she served two terms as deputy mayor.

H. T. Burgess (ed), *Cyclopedia of South Australia*, 1 (Adel, 1907); *Quiz*, 15 Sept 1893, 29 Sept 1898, 8, 15 June 1899; *Aust Jewish Hist Soc, J,* 8 (1977), p 89; *NT Newsletter*, 1, no 1, June-July 1978, p 24; *Observer* (Adel), 20 June 1891, 24 Oct 1908; *Advertiser* (Adel), 21 Oct 1908; D. H. Jaensch, Political representation in colonial South Australia, 1857-1901 (Ph.D. thesis, Univ Adel, 1974); Sth Aust Insolvency Court records, GRG 66/5/6017 (PRO SA).   PETER DONOVAN

SOMERS, ARTHUR HERBERT TENNYSON SOMERS-COCKS, 6TH BARON (1887-1944), governor, was born on 20 March 1887 at Freshwater, Isle of Wight, second child of Herbert Haldane Somers-Cocks, late lieutenant in the Coldstream Guards, and his wife Blanche Margaret Standish, née Clogstoun. Alfred, Lord Tennyson, was his godfather. Arthur and his sister, orphaned by 1896, were brought up by their paternal and maternal relatives who kept them in touch with artistic and literary figures. Succeeding the 5th baron at the age of 12, Arthur was educated at Charterhouse, and New College, Oxford; in 1906 he joined the 1st Life Guards. An all-round athlete who played county cricket, polo, golf and royal tennis, he took leave and farmed in Canada before rejoining his regiment in 1914.

At Ypres he was twice wounded. In 1918 he commanded the 6th Battalion of the New Tank Corps. He was mentioned in dispatches, awarded the Military Cross and Distinguished Service Order, and appointed to the Légion d'honneur. After the war Somers began a lifelong involvement with the scout movement. On 20 April 1921 he married Daisy Finola Meeking at St Paul's Church, Knightsbridge, London.

Inheriting the Eastnor estates from his cousin, Lady Henry Somerset, Somers retired from the army as a lieut-colonel in

1922. A lord-in-waiting and government spokesman in the House of Lords, 1924-26, he was then appointed governor of Victoria and K.C.M.G. Six feet (182.9 cm) tall, with brown hair and a clipped moustache, Somers had charm and natural gaiety which won him popularity. Warm and generous, he had a genuine interest in people, as well as a high sense of duty and leadership. A shrewd and successful governor from 28 June 1926 to 23 June 1931, he was respected by politicians, although he privately lamented their lack of political ability. He administered the Commonwealth as acting governor-general from 3 October 1930 to 22 January 1931.

Somers took special interest in youth, Freemasonry (he was grand master of the United Grand Lodge of Victoria), flora and fauna, music, 'Toc H' and returned servicemen. In 1929, at his own expense, he brought together teenage boys from different backgrounds to what was named Lord Somers' Camp and Power House, a youth organization which continues to this day. Somers revisited Australia and his camp in 1933, and again in 1937 when, as president of the Marylebone Cricket Club, he accompanied the English touring team.

He became chief commissioner of the scouts in 1932, largely running the movement as deputy chief scout in 1935-41. Designated by Lord Baden-Powell as his successor, Somers was appointed chief scout for Great Britain in 1941 and subsequently for the British Commonwealth. Lord-lieutenant of Herefordshire (1933), he was an ardent conservationist and worked to protect the Malvern Hills. In 1940-41 he was Red Cross commissioner in Egypt until debilitated by cancer of the throat. He was a devout Anglican. Survived by his wife and daughter, he died on 14 July 1944 at Eastnor Castle and was cremated. His portraits hang at Lord Somers' Camp, Somers, Victoria, and Dallas Brooks Hall, Melbourne.

L. S. Amery, *My political life*, 2 (Lond, 1953); H. Collis et al, *Baden-Powell's scouts* (Lond, 1961); A. Gregory, *Lord Somers* (Melb, 1987); *The Times*, 15, 18, 25 July 1944, 16 Aug 1966; Letters of Lord Somers, Eastnor papers (held at Eastnor Castle, Hereford, Eng).   ALAN GREGORY

SOMERSET, HENRY ST JOHN (1875-1952), metallurgist, was born on 28 February 1875 at Fortitude Valley, Brisbane, third child of Henry Saint John Somerset, civil service clerk, and his wife Sarah Walker, née Forbes. He attended Brisbane Grammar School where he studied mineralogy and chemistry under J. B. Henderson [q.v.9]. On leaving school, Henry studied in Brisbane for a year with analyst Joseph Fletcher and for a

further sixteen months with analyst and assayer G. K. Irvine. In 1894 Somerset joined the Mount Morgan Gold Mining Co. as assistant assayer and analyst, rising to the position of chief assayer in 1896 and later to chief metallurgist; due to some disagreement with the management, he resigned in 1912 and spent the next two years in Sydney as an investor, living at Hunters Hill.

Great Cobar Ltd, which operated an important copper mine and smelter at Cobar, New South Wales, engaged him as chief metallurgist in 1914, but in 1916 he was attracted to Broken Hill Associated Smelters Pty Ltd at Port Pirie, South Australia. There he became plant superintendent and general superintendent (1917-25). His son recalled their departure when the 'whole town turned out to say farewell, brass band, detonators on the railway line, the lot'. In 1926 Somerset moved to Melbourne as general manager of the Electrolytic Zinc Co. of Australasia Ltd. He was appointed managing director in 1945 and retired in 1947. Somerset held a founding directorship in Associated Pulp & Paper Mills Ltd and was a director of Australian Fertilizers Pty Ltd. A member (1898) and senior member (1949) of the Australasian Institute of Mining and Metallurgy, he was a councillor in 1926-47, vice-president in 1927-30 and president in 1931. He was a member of the Institution of Mining and Metallurgy, London, and fellow of the Australian Chemical Institute. In 1944 he was president of the Australian Mines and Metals Association Inc.

Somerset's contributions to the mining, metallurgical, papermaking and fertilizer industries lay in his inspiring leadership of research, operating and business teams. He was highly respected, in particular by Sir Alexander Stewart [q.v.] and Sir Colin Fraser [q.v.8]. Somerset's short but comfortably ample stature accompanied a strong but pleasant and likeable personality. His clubs included the Australian and Athenaeum in Melbourne, and the Tasmanian; he belonged to the Metropolitan and the Peninsula golf clubs, and lived at Toorak. He died on 30 September 1952 in a private hospital in East Melbourne and was cremated; his estate was sworn for probate at £53 173. On 23 February 1905 at All Saints Anglican Church, Hunters Hill, Sydney, he had married Jessie Bowie, daughter of J. B. Wilson [q.v.6]; she survived her husband with two sons, one of whom (Sir) Henry Beaufort Somerset also had a distinguished career in the papermaking and mining industries.

Argus, 27 May 1947; *Age*, 2 Oct 1952; Associated Pulp and Paper Mills Ltd collection *and* Broken Hill Associated Smelters Pty Ltd collection (Univ Melb Archives); Electrolytic Zinc Co of A'sia Ltd collection, including address of chairman of

directors, Nov 1947, *and* Annual Report, 1947 (TA).
D. F. FAIRWEATHER

SOMERVILLE, GEORGE CATTELL (1877-1959), soldier and administrator, was born on 13 July 1877 at Goulburn, New South Wales, son of John Blakely Somerville, bank officer, and his wife Frances Clara, née Phillips, both Sydney born. The family lived at Morpeth in 1880-84, in Sydney in 1885-89 and then in Brisbane where John became manager of the Woollongabba branch of the Royal Bank of Queensland. George was educated at the Normal School, and at Brisbane Grammar School in 1893-94. His early employment was in insurance (1895-97) and banking (1897-99); he then spent six years with his family on a farm at Millers Forest, New South Wales.

Having joined the Raymond Terrace-Dungog Squadron of the 4th Light Horse as a trooper in 1905, Somerville was commissioned in 1906 and promoted lieutenant in 1908. Appointed to the Australian Military Forces as a lieutenant in 1911, he served on the Administrative and Instructional Staff in Queensland until 1913 when he became adjutant of the 11th Light Horse at Goulburn, New South Wales. With the outbreak of World War I he served briefly as a temporary general staff officer in Queensland before joining the Australian Imperial Force on 20 November 1914 as captain and adjutant of the 6th Light Horse Regiment. The unit embarked for Egypt in December and saw action at Gallipoli (with Somerville as adjutant and temporary major) from May to December 1915. Somerville's career as a staff officer began at Gallipoli with his promotion to major and his appointment as deputy assistant adjutant and quartermaster general, 1st Division, A.I.F., on 1 October. Wounded by shrapnel on 3 December, he was evacuated to Egypt and resumed duty as D.A.A. and Q.M.G. there in March 1916, before sailing for the Western Front in April.

In France, in October, Somerville was promoted lieut-colonel and assistant adjutant and quartermaster general, 2nd Division, A.I.F. From December 1917 to November 1918 he was assistant quartermaster general with Headquarters, 1st Australian Army Corps, and was then a director in the Repatriation and Demobilisation Department, A.I.F., London, until 31 March 1919 when his A.I.F. appointment ended. For his war service he was awarded the Distinguished Service Order and the Belgian Croix de Guerre, appointed C.M.G., and mentioned in dispatches five times. After attending (1919-20) the Staff College, Camberley, England, he returned to Australia and was appointed chief inspector of administration, Inspector General's Branch, Army Headquarters, Melbourne; a year later he was allotted to the Staff Corps as a major with brevet rank of lieut-colonel. In 1921-23 he was a general staff officer, grade 2. His final A.M.F. posting was temporary district commandant and district base commandant in Victoria in 1923-24; he retired in November 1924. During World War II he was deputy director of recruiting, Eastern Command, 2nd A.I.F., in 1940-41.

From 1924 to 1954 Somerville was secretary and chief executive officer of the Royal Agricultural Society of New South Wales and acted as its spokesman on administrative and agricultural matters. He was secretary of many associated breed societies and a judge at rural shows. He was also involved in charitable and civic activities, being a founder of the Legacy movement in New South Wales and its foundation president in 1926-27. Another long-standing connexion was with the National Roads & Motorists Association: a councillor from September 1932 until his death, he was also a member of its board of management, a director of N.R.M.A. Insurance Ltd and a councillor of the Automobile Association of Australia. In the 1930s he was a prominent member of the Old Guard, a conservative paramilitary organization active in New South Wales. Known to his friends as 'Barney', he was 'an easy mixer and well-liked'.

Somerville had married Brenda Elsie Holland at St James's Anglican Church, Sydney, on 4 February 1911. Survived by three daughters, he died in Royal Prince Alfred Hospital, Sydney, on 20 May 1959 and was cremated.

G. L. Berrie, *Under furred hats* (Syd, 1919); B. H. Fletcher, *The grand parade* (Syd, 1988); *Open Road*, 1 July 1959; *Sabretache*, Apr-June 1989, and for bibliog; *SMH*, 22, 23 Oct 1924, 21 May 1959; records (AWM).
J. K. HAKEN

SOMERVILLE, WILLIAM (1869-1954), arbitrator, was born on 24 October 1869 at Merewether, New South Wales, son of Scottish parents, John Somerville, coalminer, and his wife Margaret, née Laird. They lived in a slab cottage and William attended public school before training as a blacksmith at Morrison & Bearby's foundry, Newcastle. Completing his apprenticeship to a boilermaker in 1889, he joined the Amalgamated Society of Engineers. After working in Sydney for about a year, he was laid off and tramped the city streets for months before taking to the road. In the 1890s he humped a swag across New South Wales and Victoria and the experience 'burned deep'. He recalled that when younger and a member of the 'tin gods' (the craft elite of the engineers), he had despised the unemployed until he discovered 'that in our sunny Australia in times of depression if a man has too stiff a back to beg then he can starve like a dog'.

In 1895 Somerville went to Fremantle, Western Australia. On the morning that he landed, he hunted up the union secretary at his breakfast and by starting time had found a job as engine-smith on C. Y. O'Connor's [q.v.11] harbour works. He became a leader of the local labour movement, was active in the 1899 lumpers' strike, and represented the A.S.E. on the new Coastal Trades and Labor Council (president 1901). On 30 March 1899 in Wesley Church, Fremantle, Somerville married Agnes Spunner, schoolteacher; they lived in Mosman Park, a bushland suburb, and Agnes shared her husband's political activity. They had a daughter and three sons.

The elected worker representative on the Western Australian Court of Arbitration from 1905, Somerville was critical of the court's excessive legalism but championed industrial arbitration. 'The law involved is negligible', he insisted. 'There never is—there cannot be —any important argument as to the facts; they are as plain as the nose on one's face'. Mistrustful of lawyers' class sympathies and impatient with arguments from precedent, he saw the court as performing 'the work of a subsidiary legislature'. He supported, and urged his colleagues to award, improved wages (anticipating Henry Higgins's [q.v.9] enunciation of the family wage), shorter hours, enforcement of apprenticeship provisions and other improvements for unionists. While repudiating arbitration's implied circumscription of the claims of labour—'The worker should, without ceasing, constantly struggle toward the goal, "his full share of the wealth he helps to create"'—he upheld the court's authority over unions seeking to overturn awards by direct action. In *Twenty-one years of Arbitration Court work* (1926) he asked 'Has the long grind been worth while? And my answer is sincerely, and I hope not boastfully, "It has!"'

A significant figure in the Australian Labor Party's early history in Western Australia, Somerville stood for State parliament, sought preselection for Federal parliament and was a delegate to pre-war A.L.P. federal conferences. He was an unforgiving anti-conscriptionist in 1916, severing a friendship with (Sir) George Pearce [q.v.11] over the issue. During the secession crisis of 1933-34, the Commonwealth chose him as one of the authors of *The case for union*.

Somerville was an assiduous speaker and newspaper correspondent: on nationalism, the White Australia policy, the tariff, economic development, conservation and educa-

tion. Awarded an honorary LL.D. by the University of Western Australia in 1941, he had been chairman of its adult education committee and a foundation member in 1912 of its senate. Often acting chancellor, he frequently reminded the professors, in blunt and colourful language, of his undertaking to the premier John Scaddan [q.v.11] that he would guard it as a university of the working class; (Sir) Walter Murdoch [q.v.10] was an adversary. Less contentious were his efforts to beautify the grounds and to plant Norfolk Island pines, his 'cathedral of trees', on the university campus. The open-air Somerville Auditorium at Crawley is his memorial. He was also a member of the boards of King's Park and Rottnest Island, where he instigated an ambitious afforestation scheme, and a trustee of the Public Library, Museum and Art Gallery of Western Australia (from 1908).

A cataract of the eye forced Somerville's retirement from the court in 1941, but an operation allowed him to write *Rottnest Island* (1948) and several manuscripts: 'A Blacksmith Looks at a University', 'Western Australia came of Age', and 'An Economic History of Western Australia with Special Reference to Trade Unions and the Influence of Industrial Arbitration'.

Somerville was a pipe-smoking, free-thinking teetotaller. Large-framed and straight-backed, he became bald early. His pleasures were solitary: gardening, fishing, reading and writing in his study, or working in the smithy at his weekend cottage at Chidlow. He disliked idleness or frivolity; his daughter was once instructed to 'stop that knitting and read something'. Humourless, he could be stubborn and dogmatic. As he said, 'There is a good slice of the big-headed Scotchman in me'. He was disdainful of Perth's business and professional elite but sensitive to their slights, and rebuked the governor for backing 'that small section of the community who with insular arrogance arrogate to themselves the title of society'. He cast an equally censorious eye on old comrades whose achievement of ministerial office caused them to succumb to creature comforts. He continued to live in his modest weatherboard house and saw his children pass from government schools to the public university. He was a member of the Australian Round Table. Somerville died at Fremantle on Christmas eve 1954 and was cremated. His children survived him.

F. Alexander, *Campus at Crawley* (Melb, 1963); K. D. Buckley, *The Amalgamated Engineers in Australia, 1852-1920* (Canb, 1970); *Mosman Park Review*, 2, no 7, Feb 1955; A. Clover, Biography of William Somerville, ms, 1958, (BL); B. Latter, Dr William Somerville, ms, 1980, (BL); Somerville papers, (BL) *and* Reid Lib, Univ WA.

STUART MACINTYRE

SOMMERLAD, ERNEST CHRISTIAN (1886-1952), newspaper editor, businessman and politician, was born on 30 January 1886 at Tenterfield, New South Wales, youngest of twelve children of German parents John Henry Sommerlad, farmer, and his wife Louisa Wilhelmina, née Marstella. He left Leechs Gully Public School at 11 to help on the family farm. Restless, he read widely, especially the Bible. Aged 21 he went to Newington College, Sydney, and, overcoming the gibes of his 14-year-old schoolfellows, passed the junior public examination in 1908.

Accepted as a candidate for the Methodist ministry, Sommerlad trained at the Theological Institution, Stanmore. In March 1911 he left for Fiji as a missionary, but after six months returned to Sydney with a throat infection which prevented him from preaching regularly. Nonetheless, he remained closely connected with the Methodist Church as an occasional lay preacher and for ten years was secretary of its young people's department.

Turning to journalism, Sommerlad worked briefly as a reporter on the *Inverell Times* from February 1912. In June he moved to the rival *Inverell Argus* and within three months was editor. At Burwood, Sydney, he married Mildred Alice Vaughan with Baptist forms on 15 March 1913. With a bank loan guaranteed by local businessmen, he bought the *Glen Innes Examiner* in May 1918. 'His paper was his pulpit.' Editorials promoted such advances as a bacon factory, improvements to the town's parks and the local horticultural society (he was president in 1927). From 1924 he organized mergers of rival bi-weeklies at Glen Innes, Inverell and Armidale. He was a founder and managing director of Northern Newspapers Pty Ltd (1926-52) and a State director of Australian United Press Ltd (1939-52).

Sommerlad was a member of the Australian Provincial Press Association, and president (1927-28) and later secretary (1940-45) of the New South Wales Country Press Association. In February 1929 he moved to Sydney to become general manager of the Country Press Co-operative Co. of Australia Ltd (soon Country Press Ltd). An astute businessman, he was the company's managing director (1932-52) and chairman (1948-52). Establishing its advertising arm as a separate company, Gotham (A'sia) Pty Ltd, he became managing director and forged links between country press and radio. He was a director of Northern Broadcasters Ltd and negotiated the issue of licences for radio stations 2LV Inverell and 2AD Armidale.

A founder of the Country Party and State chairman (1950-52), Sommerlad was treasurer of the Northern New State Movement.

He wrote much of the party's publicity material for Federal and State elections from the 1930s, as well as press and radio material for primary industry and referenda campaigns. He also contributed several editorials a week to the northern newspapers. A staunch and uncompromising moralist, he saw issues in black and white. Nominated to the Legislative Council in 1932, he was elected to the reconstituted council in November 1933. In the 1930s he helped the premier (Sir) Bertram Stevens [q.v.] to organize publicity.

Sommerlad published several local histories, including *Inverell* (Sydney, 1917) and *Land of the Beardies* (Glen Innes, 1922), and a handbook on journalism, *Mightier than the sword* (1950). He was a trustee of the Public Library of New South Wales (1930-52), a vice-president of the National Roads and Motorists' Association and chairman of the publicity committee for the sesquicentennial celebrations. He was appointed C.B.E. in 1938.

Gardening was Sommerlad's great recreation—his blooms won many prizes. Yet, he found it hard to relax and worked constantly on his creative writing at his Lindfield home or at his Blue Mountains cottage. At 60 he began playing bowls regularly. He was of middle height, stocky and full-faced; his dark hair receded later in life. Sommerlad died of leukemia at his home on 6 September 1952 and was cremated. His wife, two sons and two daughters survived him.

E. L. Sommerlad, *The migrant shepherd* (Syd, 1986); *Newspaper News* (Syd), 2 Jan 1929, 15 Dec 1945; *JRAHS*, 61, pt 4, Dec 1975, p 225; *Glen Innes Examiner*, 9, 13 May 1918, 13 Dec 1922, 7 Jan 1924, 6 Oct 1925, 5 Oct 1926, 28, 31 Jan 1929, 8, 10 Sept 1952, 22 Oct 1974; *Inverell Times*, 1, 26 Mar, 4 Apr, 7 May, 18 June 1912, 11 Jan, 1 July 1927, 10 June 1938, 8, 10 Sept 1952, 19 Dec 1975; *SMH*, 1 Feb 1929, 8 Sept 1952; NSW Country Press Association, Annual Report, 1927, 1928; information from Mr E. Lloyd Sommerlad, Avalon Beach, and Mr D. J. R. Sommerlad, Richmond, NSW.
                                      ROD KIRKPATRICK

SORENSEN, CHRISTENSE (1885-1958), hospital matron and army nurse, was born on 5 September 1885 at Sandgate, Queensland, second daughter of Danish-born Conrad Emanuel Sorensen, drayman, and his Norwegian wife Hannah Maria Antonetta, née Jacobsen. Conrad, who spoke seven languages, had been a veterinary surgeon in Denmark. Educated at Sandgate State School, Christense took over the household when Hannah became blind after the birth of her eleventh child. In September 1910 Sorensen commenced training at Brisbane Hospital and registered as a nurse on 8 January 1914. She remained on the staff and that year was successively promoted to charge nurse and sister.

Appointed to the Australian Army Nursing Service, Australian Imperial Force, on 10 November as a staff nurse, Sorensen was posted to No.1 Australian General Hospital, Cairo, Egypt. She was seconded to the Middle East Staff in July 1915 and served on the British hospital ship, *Guildford Castle*, which transported wounded soldiers from Gallipoli. Promotion to sister followed in December. Sent to the British Stationary Hospital, Poona, India, in October 1916, she nursed soldiers suffering from cholera, dysentery and plague until January 1917 when she returned to Egypt to work at No.14 A.G.H., Abbassia.

Long and arduous service under trying conditions had taken its toll and she returned to Australia in February 1917. Regaining her strength, she was posted to No.60 British General Hospital, Salonika, in August. The hospital was entirely under canvas, with 2000 patients suffering from malaria, blackwater fever and dysentery. Sorensen was made head nurse and then temporary matron on 22 August 1918. Sent in February 1919 to No.3 Australian Auxiliary Hospital, Dartford, England, she took a six-month course in massage at Guy's Hospital, London, before coming back to Australia in January 1920. Her A.I.F. appointment ended in March. Sorensen's distinguished war service was recognized by a mention in dispatches in 1918 and by the award of the Royal Red Cross (1st class) and the French Médaille des Epidémics in 1919. Her brother Thoralf had also served with the A.I.F.

Resuming civilian nursing in Queensland in April 1921, Christense Sorensen was matron of Rosemount Repatriation Hospital until March 1922 when she became matron of the Brisbane Children's Hospital. In 1925 she undertook her midwifery certificate at Queen Alexandra Hospital for Women, Hobart, as a prerequisite for her appointment as deputy general matron on the integration of the Children's Hospital with Brisbane Hospital. She remained matron of the Children's Hospital until February 1928 when she was appointed matron, General Hospital, a post she held until her retirement on 31 December 1951.

Matron Sorensen was loved and respected for her dedication and compassion, yet feared by student nurses for her strictness. A 'striking figure in her hospital regalia and a smart frocker in mufti', she was active in many nursing organizations, among them the Nurses' Advisory Sub-Committee of Queensland, the Nurses' and Masseurs' Registration Board of Queensland and the Australian Trained Nurses' Association. She was a foundation member of the College of Nursing, Australia,

and became a fellow in 1949. For her services to nursing she was appointed M.B.E. in 1952. In retirement she lived with two of her sisters at Taringa. She read widely, admired paintings and china, and was an avid golfer; she regularly attended Sandgate Baptist Church. After suffering a stroke in 1956, she died on 2 January 1958 in the Repatriation Hospital, Greenslopes, Brisbane, and was cremated. Former colleagues instituted the Christense Sorensen Memorial Fund to assist student nurses and in 1976 a ward for sick nurses at Royal Brisbane Hospital was named in her honour.

A. G. Butler (ed), *Official history of the Australian Army Medical Services in the war of 1914-1918*, 3 (Canb, 1943); D. R. Teague (ed), *Christense Sorensen* (Brisb, 1971); R. Goodman (ed), *Queensland nurses* (Brisb, 1985) and *Our war nurses* (Brisb, 1988); H. Gregory (ed), *A tradition of care* (Brisb, 1988); *London Gazette*, 11 June 1918, 30 June, 21 July 1919; nominal rolls, No.1 A.G.H., and Trained nurses, Roy Brisb Hospital, and official records (AWM).   JANICE MCCARTHY

SORENSON, EDWARD SYLVESTER (1869-1939), writer, was born on 24 September 1869 at Dyraaba, New South Wales, third of eight children of Jacob Sorenson, a Norwegian labourer and miner, and his native-born wife Mary Ann, née Keleher. His early life was an education in itself: from the age of 9 he intermittently attended Casino South (Greenridge) Public School while working at anything from stock-riding, bullock-driving and droving to farming, fencing, dairying and gardening. At 14 he was apprenticed to a carpenter at Casino for two years; at 20 he was a pioneer selector at Myrtle Creek.

He then carried a swag throughout Queensland; he prospected for gold and worked on sheep-stations in north-western New South Wales where he added shearing, woolclassing, engine driving and book-keeping to his skills. By 1900 Sorenson was a teetotalling publican at Tibooburra and secretary of the local jockey club; next year he travelled throughout South Australia, Victoria and New South Wales. Deciding to make writing his profession, he settled in Sydney where he studied at a commercial college as an evening student. On 31 December 1910 he married a widow Alice Newlyn, née Gibbs, at the Congregational Church, Waterloo.

From 1885, as a lonely young farmer, he had contributed to the *Bulletin, Lone Hand, Sydney Morning Herald* and *Catholic Press*; he was encouraged by J. F. Archibald [q.v.3]. Sorenson's *Life in the Australian backblocks* (London, 1911) is a classic account of bush life by a man with first-hand knowledge. In his fiction he remained firmly in the nationalist tradition, although his early novel, *The squatter's ward* (London, 1908), displays incongruous Gothic elements. His collections, *Quinton's rouseabout and other stories* (Melbourne, 1908), *Chips and splinters* (1919) and *Murty Brown* (1925), suggest that his talents were more successfully employed in shorter, notably humorous forms. He also wrote accomplished and witty verse.

Expert descriptions of wildlife are a feature of Sorenson's work. His somewhat anthropomorphized sketches of the lives of native animals, first collected in *Friends and foes in the Australian bush* (London, 1914), distinguish him among his contemporaries. He was a member of the Royal Australasian Ornithologists' Union and the Royal Zoological Society of New South Wales.

A member of the Fellowship of Australian Writers, Sorenson was both a popular and prolific writer. He led a quiet literary life and was no Bohemian. Norman Lindsay [q.v.10] once ungenerously remarked that Sorenson resembled 'a native bear', an image used by David Low [q.v.10] in a caricature. Photographs reveal the gentle, amiable personality behind Sorenson's writing, and something of his Scandinavian inheritance; he had a full moustache, a strong nose and a glint of humour in his eyes.

In the 1930s Sorenson experienced poor health and was granted a Commonwealth Literary Fund pension of £1 a week from 1 December 1934. Survived by a son and daughter, he died of coronary disease at his Marrickville home on 19 December 1939 and was buried in the Anglican section of Rookwood cemetery.

The Bulletin story book, A. G. Stephens ed (Syd, 1901); D. Low, *Caricatures by Low* (Syd, 1915); N. Lindsay, *Bohemians of the Bulletin* (Syd, 1965); *Catholic Press*, 29 Dec 1904; *SMH*, 23 Dec 1939; Cwlth Literary Fund, Minutes of Meetings, 1920-1939, CRS A 3753, 72/2760, part 2 (AA); A. G. Stephens papers (NL).   PETER KIRKPATRICK

SORLIE, GEORGE BROWN (1885-1948), theatrical entrepreneur, was born on 7 February 1885 at Liverpool, England, son of Frederick Sorlie, ship's cook, and his wife Sarah Jane, née Rodick. Migrating with his family to Melbourne, he attended primary school at Williamstown. Following Frederick's death in 1894, George went with Sarah to join relations in Perth. They lived close to poverty until George's rich soprano voice gained him jobs in cheap vaudeville shows. In 1896 mother and son moved to Kalgoorlie, then in the grip of gold-fever. Sorlie sang in bars, halls and in the streets, and was able to support his mother.

Moving to Sydney in 1903, Sorlie obtained work in Harry Clay's Newtown theatre: after a nervous debut, he became an accomplished between-acts singer and soft-shoe dancer. He joined Harry Rickards's [q.v.11] vaudeville circuit in 1905, working in his Tivoli and National theatres as a corner man who led the audience in applause when an act had finished. Having played with James Brennan (1907) and J. C. Bain's Vaudeville Entertainers (1912-14), Sorlie tried his hand at almost anything that fitted a vaudeville programme —acrobatics, dancing, juggling and blackface impersonation. His big break came in September 1914 as the song and dance partner of ad-lib comedian Billy Brown. With Brown in a broad checked suit and Sorlie in top hat and tails, their act proved a resounding success under (Sir) Benjamin Fuller's [q.v.8] management.

In Sydney at St Peter's Anglican Church on 30 December 1915 Sorlie married Grace Florence Stewart. Expert in every aspect of theatre—drama, melodrama, musical accompaniment, even trick cycling—in 1917 he bought out Philip Lytton's travelling tent-theatre and headed for the country circuit. Well-built and dark skinned (his grandfather was Jamaican), Sorlie opened at Wagga Wagga with *Uncle Tom's cabin* and continued with *East Lynne, The forbidden marriage* and *My pal, Ginger* (his own Australian play). By 1922 he had become a theatrical institution, known throughout New South Wales and Queensland. When talking pictures appeared in the 1930s, he survived by embracing vaudeville: a top-line band, the Cleveres acrobatic troupe and a trick cycle act helped to make him one of the nation's wealthiest producers. He claimed to be the only country manager to have gone abroad twice (1927-28, 1936) in search of talent.

At the height of his career (1920-40) Sorlie was known as the 'King of the Road', both as an actor and a producer of drama, pantomime, musical comedy and vaudeville. His cheery smile and devotion to 'clean' entertainment earned him the respect of the theatrical world. Zebra-striped cars heralded a Sorlie show in many a country town. His most famous part was the lead in *Uncle Tom's cabin*: on one occasion a Townsville publican protested at the whipping Tom received from Simon Legree. Helpless on the floor with laughter, Sorlie was unable to reassure his audience that the whipping was theatrical.

Forced to close his show at the outbreak of World War II because of lack of transport, Sorlie put his theatre into storage and lived in Sydney. He belonged to the New South Wales Masonic Club and enjoyed playing golf and bowls. Embarking on a long-cherished project to provide cheap homes for ex-servicemen, in 1945 he established the Sorlie Construction Co. to build a model village at Frenchs Forest.

Situated on the site of the present Arndale shopping mall, the area was once known as Sorlie. Although deposits had been paid to his partners, Twentieth Century Home Service Pty Ltd, a shortage of materials ended the project after less than a dozen homes had been built; considerable litigation ensued and worry is said to have broken Sorlie's health. He died in Sydney on 19 June 1948 following a cerebral thrombosis and was cremated. Theatrical notables such as Fuller and Bert Bailey [q.v.7] attended the funeral. Inheriting her husband's estate, sworn for probate at £12 911, Grace Sorlie revived the tent theatre with Bobby le Brun; it was forced out of business by competition from the clubs in the early l960s. Grace died on 21 December 1962, leaving her estate valued at £212 281 to the Royal Blind Society of New South Wales and the New South Wales Society for Crippled Children.

N. Bridges, *Curtain call* (Syd, 1980); H. Love (ed), *The Australian stage* (Syd, 1984); *Theatre Mag*, 2 Dec 1912, p 37, 1 Oct 1914, p 35; *People* (Syd), 12 Mar 1952; *Outdoor Showman*, July 1957, p 5; *Parade*, July 1961, p 14; *Argus*, 1 May 1915; *SMH*, 6 July 1907, 10 May, 20 Dec 1913, 16 May 1914, 9 Jan, 12 Aug 1947, 21 June 1948, 10 Feb 1949, 14 Mar 1963; *Herald* (Melb), 10 June 1957; *Sun-Herald*, 15 Aug 1954, 30 Dec 1962; *Narrandera Argus*, 16 Nov 1964; *Sun News-Pictorial*, 19 May 1975; *Daily Mirror*, 12 Dec 1977.

PETER SPEARRITT

SOUBEIRAN, AUGUSTINE (1858-1933), headmistress and French patriot, was born on 2 November 1858 in France, daughter of noted French Huguenot educationists. Having been in Paris during the 1870 siege, she attended Madame Trolliet's finishing school at Lausanne, Switzerland, in the mid-1870s. Augustine migrated to Sydney after the death of her parents and worked as a governess. In 1884 she was invited by Louisa Jane Gurney (1852-1937)—sister of T. T. Gurney [q.v.4], professor of mathematics at the University of Sydney—to help in teaching private pupils.

Following her visit to France in 1886, Mlle Soubeiran became one of the first teachers at Fernbank, the school Miss Gurney opened at Edgecliff. In 1891, as co-principals, they moved the school to larger premises at Kambala, Bellevue Hill; it soon became one of the major schools for daughters of the well-to-do. While concentrating on polite behaviour, the school successfully prepared pupils for the university's senior and junior public examinations.

Augustine's knowledge of traditional accomplishments in European finishing schools complemented the more academic, English background of Louisa Gurney. Mlle Soubeiran taught French at Kambala and also at nearby Ascham, Darling Point. In 1895 she was a founder of the Alliance Française which established prizes for French conversation. Kambala old girls long remembered 'Mademoiselle's extraordinarily well-informed mind, her gift of expression, her sense of humour'. She was the school housekeeper as well. An accomplished cook, she presided over the preparation of meals in the boarding house, with French savoury dishes for dinner and her own French salad for lunch. Relations between pupils and teachers were often intimate: the older girls waited upon 'Mademoiselle' and even helped her to lace her corsets —'*Il faut souffrir pour être belle*', she remarked. In her youth she was an elegant, dark-haired woman with brown eyes and a fair complexion; she retained her 'remarkable vivacity', her clear enunciation and her interest in the girls, past and present. In 1911 she was appointed officier de l'Instruction Publique. In 1913 she and Miss Gurney moved Kambala to Rose Bay where they leased Tivoli; next year they handed over the school to Clara and Mary Jane Roseby.

On the outbreak of World War I, with Louisa Gurney's backing Mlle Soubeiran initiated the French-Australian League of Help; as its secretary she assisted in establishing one of the largest patriotic organizations in Australia. At the end of 1917, paying her own expenses, she left for France to distribute the accumulated resources of the league's funds. Based in Paris, she dispensed money and set up a depot for clothes from Australia. In 1918 she came back with the diplomatic mission of General Pau to tell Australians of the 'heartfelt, tearful thanks of my people'. She returned to France again in January 1919 and spent months touring the war-devastated districts, distributing further funds and assisting in reconstruction. About November she was joined by Louisa Gurney.

In December 1920 they returned to New South Wales to live at Bowral. Augustine Soubeiran died, unmarried, on 31 May 1933 at Darlinghurst, Sydney, and was cremated. Awarded the Légion d'honneur posthumously in July, she had bequeathed four special pieces of furniture to the National Art Gallery of New South Wales. Lucy Norman's watercolour sketch of Augustine at Lausanne is held by Kambala.

M. E. David, *Passages of time* (Brisb, 1975); A. Nobbs, *Kambala* (Syd, 1987); *Courrier Australien*, 9 June 1933; *SMH*, 4 Feb, 11 Sept 1918, 3 Jan, 31 Dec 1919, 11 Nov 1920, 1, 2, 3 June, 31 July 1933; Kambala School Archives; French-Australian League papers (ML).   G. E. SHERINGTON

SOUNDY, SIR JOHN (1878-1960), retailer, politician and mayor, was born on 14 November 1878 at Dorchester, England, son of Joshua Tovell Soundy, draper and clothier, and his wife Elizabeth, née Johnson. Arriving in Hobart with his family, John was educated at the Friends' School in 1887-93 and later farmed at Sassafras in north-west Tasmania. He moved to South Africa in 1903, becoming a sanitary inspector in Cape Town and in 1906 a food and dairy inspector at Bloemfontein. Returning to Tasmania, he ran a shop at Queenstown in 1907 and in 1913 moved to Hobart to manage his father's drapery store. When the business was incorporated in 1939 he took over as managing director, a position he held until his death.

His career in public life was long and varied. He was appointed coroner at Queenstown in 1909, a justice of the peace in 1918 and was an alderman of the Hobart City Council in 1917-34 and 1938-50. Mayor of Hobart in 1924, 1929 and 1930-32, he was lord mayor in 1938-46. Soundy sat in the Tasmanian House of Assembly as Liberal member for Denison in 1925-46 and in the Legislative Council in 1946-52. In the Upper House he served as deputy president and chairman of committees.

A deeply committed Christian and a member of the Hobart Baptist Church for over sixty years, he served as secretary for thirty years and as a deacon and life deacon. He was also a serving brother of the Order of St John of Jerusalem and a member of Rotary International. During World War II he chaired the Tasmanian branch of the Australian Comforts Fund. He was, as well, a keen sportsman, fond of fishing, shooting and bowls. As a sporting administrator, he served as president and patron of the Derwent Bowls Club and treasurer of the Southern Hockey Association. He was appointed C.B.E. in 1943 and knighted in 1954.

During the 1930s Depression and World War II, he was influential in the area of economic policy and contributed to the improvement of public health, transport facilities and urban reserves. A champion of the underprivileged, he fought for the provision and upgrading of public housing. As an employer he introduced profit-sharing with his workers: J. T. Soundy Pty Ltd was one of the first Tasmanian firms to offer a superannuation scheme to its staff.

Tall, slim, fair, clean-shaven and bespectacled, Soundy was respected for his sincerity, integrity and serenity. His deep religious convictions influenced his personal and public life. He spoke his mind without fear or favour and his stubborn adherence to his views often infuriated his opponents. He was widely liked by the community and was said never to have lost an election he contested. Quiet, temperate and sober, he was unostentatious and even-tempered, with a good sense of humour.

In Cape Town he had married Edith Wainwright (d. 1958) on 1 April 1907. They had five daughters and two sons, one of whom, John Trevor, was killed in action in World War II while serving with the Royal Australian Air Force. Sir John Soundy died on 25 October 1960 in Hobart and was cremated.

B. G. Murphy, *The parliament of Tasmania 1856-1973* (Hob, 1973); *Mercury*, 15 July, 23 Sept 1919, 19 Oct 1920, 13 May 1929, 1 May 1934, 26 Oct 1960; family papers held by Mr R. Soundy, Hob.

J. SOUNDY

SOUTER, CHARLES HENRY (1864-1944), medical practitioner and writer, was born on 11 October 1864 at Aberdeen, Scotland, eldest son of John Clement Souter, general practitioner, and his wife Helen, née Coutts. John, an accomplished pencil and water-colour artist, collected 'rare classical books and old English china and coins'. The family shifted to Nottingham, England, and in 1872 to Upper Holloway, London. Charles went to Highgate and University College schools, and at 14 was registered as a medical student under his father's tuition at the Royal College of Surgeons.

Sailing in the clipper *City of Corinth* as ship's surgeon, John brought his family to Sydney in March 1879; on the advice of Archbishop Vaughan [q.v.6], they settled inland at Coonabarabran. Charles had enjoyed the sea voyage and gained a lifelong interest in ships and sailors' songs. He worked on the family selection and became an expert horseman.

In August 1882 Souter went to Scotland to study medicine at the University of Aberdeen (M.B., C.M., 1887). He married with Catholic rites Jane Ann Raeburn, daughter of a master baker, on 11 May 1887. Back in New South Wales they moved to Hillston, but, after the birth of a daughter, Jane died in 1889. Souter sailed to Hong Kong as ship's surgeon and then made a number of coastal voyages. In 1891 he went to Balaklava, South Australia, where he practised until 1905. He married Lucy de Neufoille Lucas on 28 April 1896 in Adelaide; she bore him a son. After a year in the city he was at Clarendon (1907-09), Prospect (1910-23), Whyalla (1923-24) and North Adelaide (1925-44). His father and brother also practised medicine in South Australia.

With a wide brow, high cheekbones and a moustache, Charles had a warm smile and dapper appearance. From 1896 he contributed to the *Bulletin*, sometimes using the pseudonyms 'Nil' and 'Dr Nil'. Admired and supported by editors and critics as varied as J. F. Archibald, S. H. Prior, Vance and Nettie Palmer [qq.v.3,11], A. G. Stephens [q.v.] and H. M. Green, he published four collections of verse: *Irish Lords* (Sydney, 1912), *To many ladies* (Adelaide, 1917), *The Mallee fire* (Sydney, 1923) and *The lonely rose* (Adelaide, 1935). His work is characterized by 'a gentle humanity' and belongs with that of other popular balladists such as E. J. Brady, Will Ogilvie [qq.v.7,11] and 'John O'Brien' [q.v.9 Hartigan]. Most of Souter's best verse depicts the daily life of small farmers in the Mallee district of South Australia and is sensitive to the experiences of both men and women. Yet he was influenced by Kipling, Newbolt and Noyes, and his poems of World War I are notable contributions to writing in this field. In 'The dialects of England' and 'The play' he commented on contemporary English and the vernacular. Much of his work reveals the difficulties he encountered in reflecting an authentic Australian diction. His ballads, shanties and poems like 'The Mallee Root', 'Old John Bax', 'Irish Lords' and 'O'Halloran' made a significant contribution to Australian writing.

While serving much of his time as a locum tenens, Souter found the leisure to write and sketch; he also composed and played bush songs, bird calls and shanties on his harmonica and flute. Another of his pastimes was 'manufacturing ornaments, clock stands and jewel boxes from mallee roots'. He belonged to the Adelaide Dual Club and the Australian Society of Authors, and was an expert on 5AD's radio session, 'Information Please'. Survived by his wife, daughter and son, he died at North Adelaide on 20 August 1944 and was buried with Catholic rites in West Terrace cemetery. He was not related to D. H. Souter [q.v.].

P. Depasquale, *A critical history of South Australian literature 1836-1930* (Adel, 1978); *Sth Australiana*, 1, no 1, Mar 1962, p 32; *Adel Chronicle*, 15 Oct 1931; *Advertiser* (Adel), 24 Aug 1944; Souter papers (Mortlock Lib).   VIVIAN SMITH

SOUTER, DAVID HENRY (1862-1935), black-and-white artist and journalist, was born on 30 March 1862 at Aberdeen, Scotland, son of David Henry Souter, engineer, and his wife Ann Smith, née Grant. Apprenticed at 12 to a house-painter and signwriter, he acquired a good grounding in drawing at the local art school under instructors from London and earned five shillings each for anatomical illustrations. He served for a year with the Aberdeenshire Rifle Volunteers and in 1880 joined the staff of the magazine, *Bon Accord*.

Moving in 1881 to Natal, South Africa,

Souter produced drawings and occasional journalism, started a paper which failed, and became colour sergeant in the Prince Alfred Guards. At Port Elizabeth on 17 February 1886 he married Jessie (Janet) Swanson (d. 1931). Deciding against returning to Scotland, they came to Melbourne, but settled in Sydney in 1887. David worked for the printer John Sands [q.v.6] for ten years before joining William Brooks [q.v.7] & Co. Ltd as an illustrator.

Active on the council of the (Royal) Art Society of New South Wales, in 1888 Souter established its Brush Club for members under 26: at monthly meetings Julian Ashton, Albert Fullwood [qq.v.7,8] and other senior artists appraised their work. In 1895 Souter was a founder and council-member of the breakaway Society of Artists, Sydney, and was president (1901-02) when it re-united with the Royal Art Society. After the societies split in 1907, he returned to the Society of Artists with whom he exhibited his watercolours in 1907.

In the 1880s Souter drew cartoons for the weekly *Tribune and News of the Week*. For forty years from 1895 he had at least one cartoon published in every edition of the *Bulletin* and had the distinction of naming his own modest price for a drawing. His graceful penwork showed the early influence of Art Nouveau, a style sinuous and flowing. The drawings were strong on the printed page with large black solid areas complementing fine, firm pen lines. His compositions and groupings were helped by the inclusion of the familiar Souter cat which reputedly originated as a result of the artist furbishing an inkblot on one of his drawings. Some of his cat studies are pictured in *Bush babs* (1933), a collection of nonsense rhymes he wrote for his children and later illustrated for publication. His cats were featured on Royal Doulton chinaware.

Souter illustrated other books, including several for Ethel Turner [q.v.], and co-edited *Art and Architecture* in 1904-11 (to which he contributed a series of articles on Australian painters); he was among the first to draw Australian posters and, with Norman Lindsay [q.v.10], to design bookplates. In September 1907 Souter's operetta, *The grey kimona* (1902), was staged in Adelaide by Clyde Meynell and John Gunn. Involved with Alfred Hill's [q.v.9] Sydney Repertory Theatre Society, Souter produced two plays in 1914 and wrote librettos for light operas including Hill's *Rajah of Shivapore*. A selection of his full-page war cartoons for the *Stock Journal* were reprinted in 1915. Not least of his many triumphs were two comic strips, 'Sharkbait Sam' and 'Weary Willie and the Count de Main', drawn for the Sydney *Sunday Sun* in 1921: frame for frame, their inventiveness

and composition were remarkable. By 1928
Souter was literary editor of *Country Life*.

His *Bulletin* satire, in theme never other
than domiciliary, was always sophisticated,
often wise, with a knowing, gentle cynicism.
A short, thickset and immensely humorous
man who never lost his Scottish burr, Souter
included Jack Brereton [q.v.7] among his
many friends. Survived by three daughters
and two sons, Souter died at his Bondi home
on 22 September 1935 and was cremated
with Presbyterian forms.

Society of Artists, *Spring exhibition* cat (Syd,
1907); M. Muir, *A history of Australian childrens
book illustration* (Melb, 1982); V. Lindesay, *The
inked-in image* (Melb, 1970); *Henslowe's Annual*
(Syd), 1898; *Theatre Mag*, 1 Jan 1918; *B.P. Mag*, 1
Mar 1932; *Scottish A'sian*, Sept 1915; *Art in NZ*,
Mar 1936; *SMH*, 19 Aug 1931, 24 Sept, 5 Oct
1935; J. Le Gay Brereton papers (ML).

                                    VANE LINDESAY

SOUTHERN, CLARA (1862-1940), artist,
was born on 23 July 1862 at Kyneton, Vic-
toria, eighth surviving child of William
Southern, timber merchant, and his wife
Mary, née Bell, both from Northumberland,
England. A boarder at Trentham State
School, Clara attended the Minerva Academy
for girls, Kyneton, where she showed an apti-
tude for drawing and music. She enrolled at
Madame Mouchette's Melbourne studio and
later took lessons from Walter Withers [q.v.].
From 1883 to 1887 she studied at the
National Gallery School, Melbourne, under
G. F. Folingsby and Frederick McCubbin
[qq.v.4,10]. A tall, lithe beauty with reddish
fair hair, she was nicknamed 'Panther' and
became friends with fellow students E. M. 'Jo'
Sweatman and Agnes 'Mama' Kirkwood. In
January 1886 Southern—who was also a violinist—was admitted to the Buonarotti
Society, a sketching club whose members
included writers and musicians. From 1888 to
1900 she shared a studio with Jane Sutherland [q.v.] at fashionable Grosvenor Chambers in Collins Street where she gave painting
lessons. In 1907 her landscapes were
awarded a prize in the fine arts section of the
Australian Exhibition of Women's Work.

On 9 November 1905 she had married John
Arthur Flinn at St John's Anglican Church,
Blackburn. They lived at Blythe Bank,
Warrandyte, along the Yarra valley from Hei-
delberg, where they built a cottage and later a
studio. Southern made the area popular with
other artists, among them Harold Herbert,
Penleigh Boyd [qq.v.9,7], Sweatman, Louis
McCubbin [q.v.10], Frank Crozier and
Charles Wheeler [q.v.], and an artists' camp
was soon established. Her sisters Sarah (also
a painter) and Dora both lived near by. Clara's

subjects were mainly still life and landscapes.
Aiming 'to interpret the message of the Australian bush', she produced work of lyricism
and charm, particularly her paintings of
Warrandyte, that reflected her devotion to
the area where she remained for the rest of
her life.

A councillor (1901-06) of the Victorian
Artists' Society, she showed paintings at its
exhibitions between 1889 and 1917. She was
the first woman to be a member and a committee-member of the Australian Art Association, and exhibited with it in 1914 and
1917-19. Southern also belonged to the Melbourne Society of Women Painters and Sculptors, the Twenty Melbourne Painters and the
Lyceum Club. In March 1914 at the Athenaeum Hall, Collins Street, she held an exhibition of 79 paintings which included 'The Bee
Farm' (purchased in 1942 by the Felton
[q.v.4] bequest for the National Gallery of
Victoria). She held her last one-woman exhibition at the Austral Buildings, Collins Street,
in May 1929.

Southern died on 15 December 1940 at a
convalescent home in Surrey Hills, Melbourne, and was cremated. Her work is held
by the National Gallery of Victoria and the
Ballarat Fine Art Gallery.

J. Burke (ed), *Australian women artists* (Melb,
1980); C. Ambrus, *The ladies' picture show* (Syd,
1984); J. Clark and B. Whitelaw, *Golden summers*
(Syd, 1985); K. Amery, *Hidden women* (Melb,
1986); *Age* and *Argus*, 19 Dec 1940; *Kyneton Guardian*, 21 Dec 1940.   ANNE DUKE

SOUTTER, RICHARD ERNEST (1878-
1955), wheat-breeder and public servant, was
born on 4 September 1878 at Hull, Yorkshire,
England, son of William Soutter, gardener,
and his wife Martha, née Hill. After migrating
with his family to Australia, William became
overseer (1885-98) at the Acclimatization
Gardens, Bowen Park, Brisbane, and taught
his son how to use forceps in crossing plant
varieties. Richard was a foundation student at
Queensland Agricultural College, Gatton, in
1897, but did not stay to qualify. A horticul-
turalist at Westbrook State Farm near
Toowoomba from 1898 to 1902, he transferred to the Maranoa district in 1905 to supervise wheat demonstration plots for 'marginal
areas'. On 7 February 1906 he married
Evelyn Maud Ashburn with Presbyterian
forms in Brisbane.

That year he was appointed manager of the
Roma State Farm: he cleared the prickly
pear, ring-barked the box trees, cultivated
the soil, and supervised the planting of crops
and the breeding of Ayrshire cattle and pigs.
From 1911 wheat-breeding predominated at
the farm and Soutter's varieties had doubled

the average yield per acre of the region. Heavy soils and summer rains created problems for many Queensland wheat-farmers. Soutter therefore encouraged contour cultivation to combat soil erosion, and, to retain moisture, advocated shifts in the pattern of fallow as well as the use of mulch. For the local district, he sought a strain of wheat with a short straw and little flag which would reduce transpiration, mature quickly, have a high gluten content, shed less grain in high winds and be resistant to rust.

Interstate ministers of agriculture in 1913 commended Soutter's experiments in the selection of appropriate wheats for hybridization. Milling tests in the 1920s proved their excellence. Bred from Florence and Bobs and released in 1923, Flora was his first successful commercial variety. He later bred such other varieties as Puora, Puno, Puseas, Warput and Lawrence. Flora's acreage in Queensland increased from 20 (8 ha) in 1928-29 to 55 815 (22 588 ha) in 1939-40. Soutter visited all States to discuss wheat-breeding, contributed papers at conferences and won respect from farmers.

Transferred in 1935 to Brisbane to take charge of wheat and maize-breeding on the Darling Downs, in 1937 Soutter became senior research officer in the division of plant industry of the Queensland Department of Agriculture and Stock. He contributed the chapter on wheat in the *Queensland agricultural and pastoral handbook* (1941), a departmental publication. His retirement in 1948 was accompanied by high tributes. He had produced a wide variety of hybrids which showed virtual field immunity to both species of rust. In 1945-46 eight of Queensland's ten most prolific varieties of wheat had been bred by him.

A photograph of Soutter in his early seventies reveals him, in spectacles and a striped suit, as a man with a high brow, alert eyes and a good-humoured mouth. Survived by his daughter, he died on 12 November 1955 at Brisbane General Hospital and was cremated.

Qld Agr J, 67, 1 July 1948, p 3; Aust Inst of Agr Science, *J*, Dec 1951, p 231; *Courier Mail*, 18 Nov 1955; P. Skerman, History of the Queensland Department of Primary Industry, 11 vols (ms with author, Moggill, Brisb).   P. J. SKERMAN

SOWARD, GEORGE KLEWITZ (1857-1941), architect, was born on 27 August 1857 at Norwood, Adelaide, son of George Soward, timber merchant, ironmonger and later supervisor of public works, and his second wife Bertha, née Klewitz. Having attended the Collegiate School of St Peter in 1867-74, George was articled to Thomas English,

architect; in 1880 they formed English & Soward. A handsome youth with a luxuriant, stylish moustache, Soward married Emmy Lucy Charlotte Beare on 7 April 1880 at St Barnabas's Church, Clare; they lived at Glenelg and were to have two daughters and a son. The architectural partnership ended with English's death in 1884; his son J. W. English joined the firm, as did Soward's son Lewis Douglas from 1921 until his death in 1924. A partnership with H. M. Jackman lasted from 1925 until Soward's retirement in 1936.

Examples of Soward's work in Adelaide included the Beehive Corner (1896), the Widows' Fund Building in Grenfell Street (1888), Ware Chambers in King William Street (1890, since demolished) and Gawler Chambers in North Terrace (1914). Soward also built warehouses and woolstores, but his significant contribution to South Australian architecture endures in his twenty or so fine houses in Adelaide and its suburbs. Of these, Culver House, Walkerville (1881), shows a somewhat confused style in which the Italianate bones are dressed in Tudor detail. By 1884 Soward had designed and built a town house at 64 Pennington Terrace, North Adelaide, exhibiting the Gothic detail for which he had a preference. He built Eothen, East Terrace, 76 Le Fevre Terrace, North Adelaide (1914), and designed the large home at 52 Brougham Place, North Adelaide (demolished 1969); in the mid-1920s he designed a mansion, 19 Palmer Place, North Adelaide, which still stands. In the last three, Soward abandoned his Gothic style.

For the first thirty years his houses were usually constructed of stone, with brick dressings and gabled roofs of unpainted corrugated iron; they were two-storied and frequently had pointed arches in the manner of A. W. Pugin. In an age of cast-iron lacework, Soward was sparing in its use. His love of Gothic detail was usually restricted to his domestic work, but it also surfaced in some commercial sites: Epworth Building (1927), the Bank of Victoria and Alexandra Chambers. He was architect to the South Australian Jockey Club for which he designed a grandstand at Morphettville Racecourse.

A member of the South Australian Institute of Architects and the Adelaide Club, he was a director of City Permanent Building & Investment Society and the Glenelg Railway Co., and chairman of the Charitable Funds Commission. He was a governor of the Public Library, Museum and Art Gallery of South Australia, president of Glenelg Cricket Club and mayor of Glenelg in 1895-98. In 1902-05 he represented Torrens as a conservative in the South Australian House of Assembly.

Soward compiled *Glenelg illustrated* (Adelaide, 1896) and wrote a novel, *The mirthful mutineer*, published in the *Australian Women's Mirror*(Sydney). In 1909-10 he contributed a love story with a local German flavour, 'A Chance Word', and 'Art and Letters in Adam Lindsay Gordon's Country' to the *Lone Hand*: both revealed his sensitivity. Soward died on 21 February 1941 and was buried in the cemetery at St Jude's Anglican Church, Brighton.

E. J. R. Morgan and S. H. Gilbert, *Early Adelaide architecture 1836-1886* (Melb, 1969); *Advertiser* (Adel), 24 Feb 1941; family papers (held by Mr C. E. Soward, Adel).   S. H. GILBERT*

SOWDEN, SIR WILLIAM JOHN (1858-1943), journalist and newspaper editor, was born on 26 April 1858 at Forest Creek, Castlemaine, Victoria, son of Thomas Sowden, miner, and his wife Mary Ann, née Hocking, both from Cornwall. Moving to Kapunda, South Australia, they had returned to Castlemaine by 1867. William attended bush schools and was a pupil-teacher before becoming a printer's devil on the *Castlemaine Representative* and the *Mount Alexander Mail*. In 1874 the family shifted to Moonta, South Australia, where William worked as a reporter on the *Yorke's Peninsula Advertiser* and later was associate editor of the *Port Adelaide News*.

In 1881 he joined the major daily, the *South Australian Register*. Next year he accompanied a parliamentary party to the Northern Territory; his colourful reports, syndicated in the *Argus* (Melbourne) and the *Sydney Morning Herald*, were published as *The Northern Territory as it is*(1882). The *Register*'s leading parliamentary reporter, Sowden wrote a satirical column, 'Echoes from the Smoking Room' by 'A Scribbler', which became an institution in 1882-92: he once described a speech by J. H. Howe [q.v.9] as based on a 'design conceived by the Lord of Misrule for use in Puzzledom'.

Promoted chief leader-writer and associate editor in 1892, Sowden was acting editor in 1897 and editor from 1899 to 1922. In this capacity he exerted strong influence on public opinion. On 28 April 1886 at Richmond, Melbourne, he had married Letitia Grace Adams (d. 1928) with Baptist forms; they were to have two sons.

Politically Sowden was a Liberal, a free trader and an 'avowed anti-Socialist'; while never joining any party, he was consistently anti-Labor. He supported Federation, the South African War, compulsory military training, conscription, state-rights, the unreformed Legislative Council and the formation of the Liberal Union in 1910. *Truth*'s description of Sowden's *Register* as 'the official organ of the Tory party' was barely an exaggeration.

In 1887 he had helped to found a local branch of the Australian Natives' Association; he attended its first intercolonial convention, in Melbourne, which passed pro-Federation resolutions. His pamphlet, *Australia: a native's standpoint* (Ballarat, 1893), 20 000 copies of which were distributed in Victoria to assist the Federal cause, argued for Australian-born governors and promoted things Australian. Sowden suggested that 'Three Cooees' should replace 'Three Cheers'. He was South Australian president of the Australian Wattle Day League and chairman of the Violet Memory Day League.

During the South African War he raised two A.N.A. rifle companies and his *Register* war fund collected one-quarter of a million shillings (£12 500). He was president of the Adelaide branch of the Royal Society of St George and for five years acted as chief scout of the Boy Scouts Association of South Australia. In 1915, with Mrs Seager [q.v.11], he founded the Cheer-Up Society for soldiers; first State president of the Returned Sailors' and Soldiers' Imperial League of Australia, he was knighted in 1918. In that year he visited the Western Front with the Australian press delegation and wrote *The roving editors* (1919).

Sowden was a Freemason, first president of the Discharged Prisoners' Aid Association and a sponsor of Christmas Dinners for the Poor of Adelaide's West End. In 1907 he joined the Adelaide Club. He was president of the Public Library, Museum and Art Gallery of South Australia board from 1908. In 1926 his interference provoked the resignation of the gallery's curator Henri Van Raalte [q.v.]: in the resulting fracas Sowden also resigned. He immediately became president of the Institutes Association of South Australia (1926-37), and of the Australian Library Association (1928-32).

Stocky, ruddy and pugnacious, 'Willie J.' sported a wispy beard in the 1890s and later a clipped military moustache. He smoked, but was a teetotaller. He liked the limelight and his outspokenness made him many enemies, among them Sir Samuel Way [q.v.]. A lively speaker, Sowden gave public lectures, illustrated with lantern slides and curios collected on his five world trips; he published six travel books. Although he had averaged a sixteen-hour day at the *Register*, he found time for bowling and photography, was a keen field naturalist who encouraged forest conservation, and owned a library of 15 000 volumes.

On 2 April 1929 Sowden married, with Presbyterian forms, Margaret Ella Suttie of Mosman, Sydney; they lived at Victor Harbor, South Australia. Survived by his wife, and by a son, he died there on 10 October 1943. After an Anglican service, his ashes were buried in the local cemetery. Sowden's estate was sworn for probate at £75 817.

A. W. Martin (ed), *Essays in Australian Federation* (Melb, 1969); *SA Institutes J*, 30 Nov 1937, 30 Nov 1943, 30 Sept 1944; *Register* (Adel), 7 Sept 1886, 3 June 1918; *Truth* (Adel), 4 Dec 1916, 8 June 1918; *Mail* (Adel), 9 Nov 1912, 2 Sept 1922; *Advertiser* (Adel), 11 Oct 1943; S. J. Way letterbooks, PRG 30/5/9, 2, 30/5/16, 257, 424 (Mortlock Lib).
CARL BRIDGE

SPAIN, ALFRED (1868-1954), architect and army officer, was born on 5 March 1868 at Neutral Bay, Sydney, son of Staunton Spain and his native-born wife Fanny Maria Elizabeth, née Coar. His father, an English-born son of William Spain [q.v.2], was a maritime solicitor. Educated at Robert Horniman's school, Darlinghurst, and the Queen's School, Potts Point, Alfred was articled to the architect Thomas Rowe [q.v.6] in 1885, studied at Sydney Technical College and qualified in 1890; he entered into partnership with Rowe & Wright Campbell in 1893 which became Rowe & Spain (1895), then Spain & Cosh (1904); he was elected a fellow of the Royal Institute of British Architects in 1917. The firm designed office blocks, flats, hotels, fire stations, houses and manufacturing establishments throughout New South Wales. As Spain, Cosh & Minnett (1910-12), it was responsible for the New Zealand Insurance Co.'s offices in Pitt Street and Culwulla Chambers, to then Australia's tallest building —178 ft. (54.25 m)—fronting King and Castlereagh streets. Controversy resulted and led to the Height of Buildings Act, 1912, limiting subsequent structures to 150 ft. (45.72 m). The partnership included Robin Dods [q.v.8] in 1914-20. Its most lucrative clients were Tooth [q.v.6] & Co. Ltd and the Board of Fire Commissioners.

On 31 March 1910 at St Philip's Anglican Church, Sydney, Spain married a widow, Jessie Johnston (d. 1947), née Baikie. A foundation member (1913) of the Town Planning Association of New South Wales, he advocated the cleansing of Sydney Harbour, then polluted by septic tanks and oil from steamers. His mansion, Waione, at Neutral Bay commanded superb views of the harbour. Active in the foundation, design and location of Taronga Zoological Park, which moved to Mosman in 1915-16, he was chairman of trustees in 1928-41.

Spain had been commissioned second lieutenant, 1st Field Company, Engineers, New South Wales Military Forces, in July 1890. Promoted major (Commonwealth Military Forces) in 1903, he was awarded the Volunteer Officers' Decoration in 1910 and retired in 1913 with the honorary rank of lieutcolonel. The work of Spain's engineers was a 'recognised feature of every big camp' in the State before the outbreak of war. In August 1915 he returned to command the Sydney field companies and reinforcement camps. Replaced by A. J. Arnot [q.v.7], Spain enlisted in the Australian Imperial Force in 1916 and served with the Sea Transport Service until May 1917. Retiring in 1919, he was president of the United Service Institution in 1927-29 and 1940-45.

A member of the Board of Fisheries (1903-10), Spain had represented Australia at the 1905 International Fishery Congress in Vienna. His outgoing personality and ability as a publicist brought him many directorships. By the late 1920s he was on the boards of Hetton Bellbird Collieries Ltd, Grenfell Gas Co. Ltd and Katoomba & Leura Gas Co. Ltd (sometime chairman); by the 1930s he had joined (William) Howard Smith [q.v.6] Ltd, the North Coast Steam Navigation Co. Ltd and the Australian Metropolitan Life Assurance Co. He was also a director (1922-51) of Sydney Ferries Ltd which proved the most intractable of his interests as the opening of the harbour bridge halved its trade: Spain failed to persuade the State government to take over the service.

An able yachtsman and a keen fisherman, Spain belonged to the Royal Sydney Yacht Squadron. He was chairman of the Anniversary Day Regatta Committee, and in 1945 president of the State branch of the Royal Empire Society. A member of the board of Sydney Hospital, he won a silver medal from the Royal Shipwreck Relief & Humane Society of New South Wales for rescuing a lad from drowning in 1934. Survived by his stepdaughter, Spain died at Mosman on 9 August 1954 and was buried in South Head cemetery. His estate was sworn for probate at some £137 000. Florence Taylor [q.v.] recalled him as 'Dapper, precise, optimistic', with a love of animals, birds and poetry. The architectural firm still (1989) bears his name.

His brother, STAUNTON WILLIAM, was born on 9 February 1865 at Wallaringa, Neutral Bay, their father's home which Staunton eventually inherited. Educated at Fort Street Model School and Coreen College, he joined the volunteer naval brigade as a cadet in 1880, served with the naval contingent to China in 1900 and became lieut-commander, Royal Australian Naval Reserve, in 1908. He continued with the Royal Australian Naval Brigade, retiring in 1920 as commander. A notary public, he long served as marshal, Admiralty jurisdiction, Supreme Court. He was a member of the local League of Ancient Mariners and in 1925-37 an alderman for North Sydney. Survived by his wife Ella

Jessie, née Sparke, whom he had married in Holy Trinity Anglican Church, Sydney, on 5 July 1905, he died on 8 September 1946 after being struck by a city tram. Spains Wharf Road and a look-out on the tip of Kurraba Point commemorate the family's connexion with Neutral Bay.

Notable citizens of Sydney (Syd, 1940); Building (Syd), 12 Oct 1912, 24 May 1946, 24 Aug 1954; SMH, 1 Aug 1916, 7 July 1921, 12 Aug 1929, 22 July 1932, 6 Jan 1933, 23 Jan 1935; Bulletin, 18 Aug 1954; E. Fayad, The architectural practice of Spain and Cosh, BSc (Arch) paper, Univ NSW, 1986; Spain, Stewart & Lind papers (ML).

PETER SPEARRITT

SPARKS, NICHOLAS GEORGE (1857-1930), fire brigade officer, was born on 27 March 1857 at Portsea, Southampton, England, son of Robert Sparks, naval boatswain, and his wife Ann Maria, née Smith. 'Nico' served in the navy before joining the London Metropolitan Fire Brigade in 1881. At the parish church of St Giles-in-the-Field, Middlesex, he married Emma Thorn on 4 May 1886. Attaining the rank of assistant officer, in 1897 he was recommended to Sydney's Metropolitan Fire Brigades Board.

In June Sparks arrived in Sydney with his wife and two daughters and, as third officer, took up residence in the Castlereagh Street headquarters fire station. On 1 November 1898 he was promoted deputy chief officer at £300 a year. Between 1898 and 1914 he and his chief officer, Alfred Webb, transformed the Sydney fire brigades into a disciplined and professional force equipped with the latest in motorized appliances. Sparks served on a government sub-committee to investigate theatre fire safety in 1904-05.

Committed to improving fire-fighting techniques, he published a Firemen's manual (1907), covering all facets of fire brigade operations, and later Smoke and fire (1911). Rigorous drilling was introduced: trainees and officers aspiring for promotion were henceforward required to pass formal examinations in writing, spelling, composition and drill based on his manual.

On Webb's death in 1913, Sparks became chief officer of the Board of Fire Commissioners which had evolved from the Fire Brigades Board in 1910 and embraced some eighty districts throughout the State. In 1914 he had to put the fire brigades on a 'war footing' and in 1917 'had a strenuous and anxious time when incendiarists started fires in many city buildings'. Sparks and his wife were prominent organizers of art unions and other patriotic fund-raising activities. On 13 December 1921 he directed the unsuccessful fight to save the Pastoral Finance Association Ltd's Kirribilli warehouse—city fire engines had to cross the harbour by punt—but the blaze was contained with the help of the navy. On 31 December he retired to Cronulla on an annual pension of £500.

Described as 'heavy-set, quiet, withdrawn and a strong disciplinarian with a wry sense of humour', Sparks liked the theatre, was a prominent Freemason and kept a close circle of friends; his daughter Gertrude married Arthur Wickham, a district fire officer.

Survived by his wife and two daughters, Sparks died at Cronulla on 4 September 1930. Accorded a full brigade funeral procession, he was buried in the Congregational section of Coogee cemetery. He had been awarded the King's Police medal in 1919 and was dedicated to hard work and to serving the community.

C. Adrian, Fighting fire (Syd, 1984); Fire, Oct-Dec 1961, p 6; T&CJ, 5 Feb 1913; SMH, 2 Jan 1922, 6 Sept 1930.   COLIN J. ADRIAN

SPAULL, GEORGE THOMAS (1876-1965), educationist, was born on 23 January 1876 at Gulgong, New South Wales, second child of Thomas Spaull, London-born miner, and his second wife Sarah, née Barnett, from Sydney. Failing at goldmining, the Spaulls moved to East Sydney and sundry small, unsuccessful businesses. George attended Crown Street Public School, joined the Department of Public Instruction as a pupil-teacher in 1891 and in 1896 won a scholarship to Fort Street Training School. His teaching career (mainly in Sydney) was unremarkable and punctuated by disputes over inspectors' reports and salary anomolies. In 1898 he was acquitted of charges of using physical punishment and abusing a pupil. At St Mary's Cathedral on 6 January 1903 he married a Catholic, Mary Cotter, but he remained an Anglican. They taught at Captains Flat for seven years.

Returning to Sydney in 1910, Spaull achieved 1B classification and enrolled part-time at the University of Sydney (B.A., 1914; M.A., 1920); he came under the spell of the historian G. A. Wood [q.v.] and was active in the Evening Students' Association. Spaull conducted several experiments for the Teachers' College at Darlington Public School, where he taught for many years, and published the results in Schooling and Education and in British history notes in the New South Wales Teacher and Tutorial Guide (1917-18). Under P. R. Cole's [q.v.8] supervision, he completed a thesis on Sir Henry Parkes [q.v.5] and education which was published in 1920. He was active in the Men First Assistants' Group and was council-member of the New South Wales Teachers' Federation

26

(1918-22). Ambitious for recognition, he failed to gain promotion to headmaster or inspector.

His historical research attracted the attention of S. H. Smith [q.v.11] who invited him to expand Smith's earlier *Brief history of education in Australia 1788-1848* (1917). Spaull wrote most of their *History of education in New South Wales 1788-1925* (1925). When the Fuller [q.v.8] government returned textbook publishing to private enterprise, Smith nominated Spaull to his former publisher, William Brooks [q.v.7] & Co. Ltd. Spaull's immediate task was to write a set of graded history and geography texts for the 1922 and 1925 primary syllabuses.

Over some forty years Spaull wrote thirty-five individual titles which were widely used by pupils in history and civics, geography, English, arithmetic and social studies. He became Australia's most prolific school textbook author. He addressed specific changes in the syllabus, often reworking earlier teacher notes or texts. Measured and mannered as most school texts were, Spaull's at least incorporated modern methods, style and aids. His sources were his own notes compiled in the Public Library of New South Wales and from his overseas (1930) and local travels.

Softly spoken, 'with silver voice but iron hand' in the classroom, Spaull led a secluded life after 1924. Increasingly he became obsessed with publishing, which occupied all his spare time, but displayed penchants for silk shirts and a large expensive car—which did not endear him to his colleagues. He retired from teaching in 1940.

Survived by his wife and son, Spaull died at his Gordon home on 30 April 1965 and was buried with Catholic rites in Northern Suburbs cemetery.

A. Spaull, 'The biographical tradition in Australian history of education', *Aust and NZ Hist Education Soc J*, 11, no 2, 1981, and 'The making of an Australian textbook writer', *Vitae Scholasticae*, 4, nos 1 & 2, 1985, and for bibliog.

ANDREW SPAULL

SPEARS, ROBERT ADAM (1893-1950), professional cyclist, was born on 8 August 1893 at Dubbo, New South Wales, second surviving son of John Spears, bricklayer, and his wife Sarah Ann, née McLaughlin, both Irish born. He won his first race at Dubbo at the age of 14 and in 1910 competed in South Australia and Queensland. That season he won the New South Wales half-mile and mile titles and next year the 5-mile Australian championship. Early in 1913 some 25 000 spectators at the Exhibition Ground in Melbourne saw Spears win the final leg of a six-day race and receive his share of the gross gate-takings of about £1000. Relaxing in a hot vinegar bath after his victory, the 6 ft. (182.9 cm) tall Spears told reporters that he had weighed 12 st. (76.2 kg) before the race and lost only 7 lb. (3.2 kg) during the event.

Later that year Spears went to New Jersey, United States of America, where he won the Vailsburg 5-mile championship. In 1914 he took the 3-mile American national championship. He remained in the United States throughout World War I and in 1916 married Marguerite Laggy (d. 1970), a champion figure-skater from Vailsburg, Newark. Spears won twenty-seven races in 1918 and became American all-round champion. Often appearing in a hopeless position 150 yards (137.2 m) from the end, he used his tremendous finish to win by the barest of margins. With broad shoulders and a distinctive cycling style, 'Bob sat on the [specially-made] bicycle . . . his seat several inches behind the centre bracket [and] . . . his long arms pushed against the handlebars like props'.

After the war Spears toured Europe; he won nineteen races in 1919 and was recognized as the world's best sprinter. Having visited Australia, he began the 1920 European season by taking the coveted 2000-metre *Grand Prix de Paris* and went on to win the world sprint championship at Antwerp, Belgium. His European successes included the *grand prix* of Copenhagen, Milan, Paris and Bordeaux (three times each), of Dresden, Amsterdam and the Municipal Towns in France (twice each), and of Leipzig, Turin and Lisbon (once each). Americans claimed Spears as their own: in 1923 doubts over his nationality almost led to his omission from the world championships, but he was eventually allowed to compete as an Australian.

He returned home for a series of international matches in 1924. Although initially overweight, Spears beat the American Willie Spencer and fellow Australian Harris Horder. The Victorian Cyclists' Union boycotted the series in protest at 'the meagre prize money offered for handicap races' compared with the appearance money paid to the 'imported riders'.

Continuing to race in Europe and Australia for the remainder of the decade, Spears never reproduced his earlier form. A heavy drinker even at his peak, he attempted a comeback in Sydney in 1932, but was by then 'only a glimpse of his former self'. When he retired from racing he became track manager at the Sydney Sports Arena, Cleveland Street, the State's only indoor velodrome. While visiting Europe, he died of cancer on 5 July 1950 in Paris.

H. Grivell, *Australian cycling in the golden days* (Adel, 1954); *100 famous Australian lives* (Syd,

1969); *Argus*, 3 Mar 1913, 6 Nov 1914, 12 July 1921, 10 Aug 1923, 14, 20 Feb 1924, 23 Oct 1928; information from Mr D. Spencer, Newcastle, NSW.   M. P. SHARP

SPEDDING, QUENTIN SHADDOCK (1892-1974), journalist, was born on 22 October 1892 at Balmain, Sydney, son of John Spedding, an accountant from Scotland, and his native-born wife Ella, née Plummer. Educated at Sydney Church of England Grammar School (Shore), he began work on the Sydney staff of the *Newcastle Morning Herald* in 1910. Next year he was a foundation member of the Australian Journalists' Association and joined the *Daily Telegraph*; from 1912 he was its Melbourne representative.

Enlisting in the 38th Battalion, Australian Imperial Force, in May 1915, Spedding married Margaret Emma Jones on 17 June at St Peter's Anglican Church, Melbourne. He reached England in August 1916, served in France and was commissioned on 26 June 1917. That year he was wounded in action and thereafter walked with the aid of a stick. In 1919-20, as temporary captain and graves registration staff officer, he organized Australian war graves in France, laid out cemeteries at Villers Bretonneux and on the Somme, and arranged for divisional war memorials: his services were brought to the notice of the secretary of state for war.

Returning to Sydney in mid-1920, Spedding worked for the *Daily Telegraph* in 1921-23. Unable (or unwilling) to pay court costs and £25 compensation awarded against him after a motor cycle accident, he was declared bankrupt in 1923 and discharged in 1929. He edited the *Sunday News* from 1923 until appointed editor of the *Labor Daily* in 1925: he became its managing editor in 1929. Engaged for his practical newspaper experience rather than for any particular Labor affiliation, he was embroiled in the turbulent politics of the J. T. Lang [q.v.9] era. In August 1926 he was questioned by a hostile caucus over stories (later discredited) in the *Labor Daily* which alleged that Labor members had been bribed to cross the floor of the House. Subjected to other intermittent attacks from sections of the labour movement, he was summarily dismissed in 1931 in favour of a more politically committed editor. Under Spedding the *Labor Daily* had increased circulation from 19 000 to 69 000 and occasionally reached 120 000.

After managing *Smith's Weekly* in Melbourne (1931-33), Spedding returned to Sydney and worked on *Truth* in 1935-46. He was an organizer, State council-member and honorary publicity officer of the Returned Sailors' and Soldiers' Imperial League of Australia in the 1920s and 1930s, and compiler and editor of its *Official year book* from 1933.

In 1946 Spedding became press secretary to the New South Wales premier (Sir) William McKell. With his grizzled hair, prominent features, distinct limp and at times formidable manner, 'Sped' became something of an institution in Macquarie Street. A man of strongly held opinions, he was a raconteur who held court in various city pubs. He later served as press secretary and speech writer for premiers McGirr, Cahill, Heffron and Renshaw. Appointed O.B.E. in 1958, Spedding retired in October 1964. Survived by his son, he died in the family home at Bass Hill on 3 June 1974 and was cremated.

R. B. Walker, *Yesterday's news* (Syd, 1980); *Reveille* (Syd), 1 Jan, 1 Sept 1939; *Labour Hist*, May 1976, no 30, p 66; *SMH*, 12 June 1958, 23, 24 Oct 1964; *Daily Telegraph* (Syd), 23 Oct 1964; *Sun* (Syd), 22 Oct 1964, 4 June 1974; bankruptcy file 14/23237 (NSWA); Spedding papers (ML); information from Mr P. Gallagher, Gladesville, and Mr W. Shaddock, Guildford, Syd.   DAVID CLUNE

SPENCE, GEORGE HEYNES (1886-1958), insurance manager, was born on 23 November 1886 at Wallasey, Cheshire, England, son of William Robert Spence, commercial clerk, and his wife Ellen Eliza, née Haycox. He was educated at the Liverpool Institute and School of Art and at a commercial school. Like his father, he joined the staff of the Royal Insurance Co. Ltd at its head office in Liverpool. He migrated to Melbourne in 1913 and was employed there by 'the Royal'. Next year he took over the management of the accident business in Melbourne and Sydney of the Liverpool and London and Globe Insurance Co. Ltd.

In 1917 Spence joined the state insurance branch of the New South Wales Treasury which carried on a form of self-insurance of state property. On 24 December that year he married Nellie Francis Creaton in Melbourne. He was appointed in 1926 deputy manager of the Government Insurance Office of New South Wales which was formed to ensure that compulsory insurance by employers of workers' compensation risks could be implemented. He was promoted general manager in October 1929. A considerable problem of organization was involved and fell heavily on Spence. A more worrying burden was that successive governments made material alterations in the functions of the GIO. As manager and adviser, he trod a difficult path during the second Lang [q.v.9] government and the Depression.

A new general manager was appointed in 1943 when the GIO was reconstituted as a crown corporation: Spence became deputy general manager. Although the office secured a virtual monopoly of the recently introduced compulsory third party (motor-car accident) insurance, its control did not fall directly on Spence who managed a wider business. During World War II he was appointed secretary of the Commonwealth Marine War Risks Insurance Board and was largely responsible for its successful operation.

Spence was deeply religious, with Brethren beliefs, and did not seek self-advancement. His general manager feared that he and Spence might have difficulties, but instead they became firm friends. Spence was meticulous in his work, and did not suffer fools gladly; his hobby was fishing. When he retired to his home at Gordon in 1951, he was spoken of as the 'virtual founder' of the GIO—the insurance branch of the Treasury with a staff of four had grown into the largest general (non-life) insurance office in New South Wales. Survived by his wife, son and two daughters, Spence died of coronary vascular disease in Royal North Shore Hospital on 3 April 1958 and was buried with Brethren forms in Northern Suburbs general cemetery.

NSW Government Insurance Office, *Security*, June 1945, Aug 1947, Jan 1950, Dec 1951, May 1958, and *Annual Report*, 1951; *A'sian Insurance and Banking Record*, 21 Feb 1952, Apr 1958.

A. C. GRAY*

SPENCE, JOHN (1878-1949), public servant, was born on 6 January 1878 at Riccarton, Ayrshire, Scotland, son of John Spence, machinist, and his wife Mary, née Kelly. Migrating with his family, he came to New South Wales when he was aged 11 and was sent to Sydney Boys' High School. He joined the Department of Public Instruction as a pupil-teacher in September 1894 and in June 1897 transferred to the clerical branch of the Department of Public Works.

The period of his initiation in the clerical relieving staff was turbulent due to the methods adopted by the new Public Service Board which were 'vigorous to the point of ruthlessness'. As clerk-in-charge of correspondence and records in the Stores Supply Department (1900-12), Spence took an interest in modern filing systems and office management. In 1901 he enrolled part-time at the University of Sydney (B.A., 1904; LL.B., 1909). President of the Evening Students' Association, he won the (Sir) Wigram Allen [q.v.3] scholarship (1906). He married Ethel May Cooke on 20 January 1909 at the Congregational Church, Woollahra, and was admitted to the Bar on 6 May.

His promotions were rapid. A council-member of the Public Service Association of New South Wales, in 1913 Spence was appointed manager of the building construction branch in the Department of Public Works; in 1915 he was seconded as chief accountant with Norton, Griffiths & Co. until its controversial financial contract with the government was cancelled in 1917. Spence filled various positions in the works department before becoming chief accountant in 1918. Although he joined the Public Service Board as senior inspector in 1919, he retained links with public works and served on numerous public service boards and committees, among them the Stores Supply and Tender Board and the Railway Service Superannuation Board (1922-25). He was made acting government printer in 1922, and promoted to director of finance in the Treasury in 1923 and to the Public Service Board in 1924.

Auditor-general from 1928, Spence was no entrepreneurial administrator: his reports showed painstaking attention to detail; he was prepared to speak plainly, supported by a sense of the moral responsibility of his position; his conduct during the economic and political uncertainties of the Depression secured his reputation for integrity and trustworthiness. He was appointed C.M.G. in 1936. Chairman of the Treasury Insurance Board (1922-25), the State budget (1928) and the taxation investigation (1933-36) committees, he was also a member of the Board of Referees under the War-Time (Company) Tax Assessment Act of 1941.

Retiring in December 1941, Spence practised as a consulting accountant and was a director of various companies, including Nestlé and Anglo Swiss Condensed Milk Co. (Australasia) Ltd, Australia Silknit Ltd and Automatic Totalisators Ltd. He was chairman of Prince Henry Hospital and a trustee of the Australian Museum, Sydney. A good Scots-Australian, he enjoyed both golf and surfing. Survived by his wife and three daughters, Spence died at his Killara home on 26 June 1949 and was cremated with Anglican rites. His estate was valued for probate at £10 028.

A. Eedy (ed), *Official opening of the new school, Moore Park, Sydney, June 9, 1928* (Syd, 1928); H. H. Wiedersehn, *Outline history of the Sydney High School, its records and achievements, 1883-1933* (Syd, 1933); *Public Service J* (NSW), 15 Dec 1924, p 623; *SMH*, 31 May 1922, 17 Mar 1923, 29, 30 Nov 1928, 1 Jan 1936, 17 Nov 1938, 10 June, 2 Oct, 24 Dec 1941, 1 Feb 1943.

ROSS CURNOW

SPENCE, PERCY FREDERICK SEATON (1868-1933), artist, was born on 14 December 1868 at Balmain, Sydney, seventh child of

English parents Francis Spence, civil servant, and his wife Hannah, née Turnbull. Francis held a government appointment in Fiji where Percy spent his youth and painted some competent water-colours.

Back in Sydney by 1888, Spence worked as an illustrator for the *Daily Telegraph, Illustrated Sydney News* and the *Bulletin*. He was an original member of the Brush Club, a group founded by D. H. Souter [q.v.] within the (Royal) Art Society of New South Wales. Spence entered oils and water-colours in the society's annual exhibitions in 1888-94 and became a council-member in the early 1890s. He designed a book-plate for J. L. Mullins [q.v.10] in 1892 and his painting, 'The Ploughman', bought by the National Art Gallery of New South Wales, was hung in the 1893 Chicago exposition.

Sharing a studio with W. Lister Lister [q.v.10] in George Street, Spence gained a reputation as a portraitist. He made two drawings of Robert Louis Stevenson in Sydney in 1893: the first was torn up because it displeased the writer's wife; the second is now in the National Portrait Gallery, London. E. J. Brady [q.v.7], whose stories and poems he illustrated, remembered Spence's 'widebrimmed hat with the folded turban, [and] his handsome, joyous face'.

At Ashfield on 30 January 1894 Spence married Jessie Wright with Congregational forms. They went to England for a year. Two daughters were born in Sydney in 1895 and 1896 before they left again for London in 1898. Able to work with rapidity, Spence contributed to the *Graphic, Sphere, Illustrated London News, Punch* and other journals. He illustrated *Britain's Austral Empire* (1901) and several adventure books. A member of the Chelsea Arts Club, from 1899 he exhibited with the Royal Academy of Arts (twice being 'placed on the line') and the Walker Gallery, Liverpool.

Spence returned to Sydney in 1905-06, and in 1909 to work on a series of water-colours for (Sir) Frank Fox's [q.v.8] *Australia* (London, 1910). These illustrations, however, lack the vitality of his black-and-white work. In 1914 Spence completed a large commissioned painting, 'H. M. Australian Fleet arriving at Sydney Heads', and returned to London to arrange for its presentation, with a water-colour of Rear Admiral George Patey, to King George V; both works are now in Buckingham Palace.

From 1915 until about 1926 Spence had a studio at 4 Edwardes Square, Kensington, which he shared with Phyllis Spence, figure and portrait painter, possibly his daughter. During World War I he served in the Royal Army Medical Corps. He made at least one further visit to Sydney in the early 1920s. Suffering from chronic nephritis and diabetes,

Spence died of uraemia on 3 August 1933 in Middlesex Hospital, London, after an eye operation.

An artist of great versatility, Spence is best remembered for his portraits, many of which were highly praised by his contemporaries, although some were criticized for lack of character. His portraits of Sir George Dibbs, Sir Sydney Jones and Justice Richard O'Connor [qq.v.4,11] are held respectively by the Mitchell [q.v.5] Library, the University of Sydney and the High Court of Australia, Canberra. A. J. Hanson's pencil portrait (1892) of Spence is in the Dixson [q.v.8] Galleries.

(Roy) Art Soc of NSW, *Annual Reports*, 1893-94 and *Annual exhibition cats*, 1888-94, 1905; R. H. Croll, *Tom Roberts, father of Australian landscape painting* (Melb, 1935); *Aust Art Review*, 1 Apr 1899, p 20, 1 Dec 1899, p 30; *All About Australians*, 4, June 1905, p 255; *Catholic Press*, 12 Jan 1905; *SMH*, 14 Sept 1933; Art Gallery of NSW press-cuttings, 1905-06, 1914, 1933; O. B. McCarthy scrap-book *and* E. J. Brady autograph-letters (ML); A. G. Stephens, Australian authors, artists, musicians (ts, NL).   M. A. MILES

SPENCE, ROBERT WILLIAM (1860-1934), Catholic archbishop, was born on 13 January 1860 at Cork, Ireland, son of Robert Spence and his wife Ellen, née Sullivan. Educated at Cork by the Christian Brothers and the Vincentian Fathers, he entered the Dominican novitiate at St Mary's, Tallaght, near Dublin, where he was professed in 1878. In Lisbon he studied at Corpo Santo college where he displayed linguistic and vocal abilities. He was ordained priest on 23 December 1882. Two days later at Bom Sucesso convent he celebrated the first Dominican high mass in Portugal since the suppression of the religious orders in 1833. On his return to Ireland in 1885 he was assigned to St Mary's, Cork, and later St Catherine's, Newry. He gave retreats and missions throughout the country, gaining prominence as a forceful, zealous preacher. From 1892 he was for six years prior of Black Abbey, Kilkenny, where he restored the old church and built a new priory.

In 1898 Spence went to Adelaide as prior (until 1901) of the first house of the Dominican friars in Australia. His photographs show a man of earnest appearance with tiny steel-rimmed glasses and receding hair. At St Laurence's Church and parish, North Adelaide, he built a similar priory to that in Kilkenny. His retreats and missions ministered particularly to other religious. First president of the State branch of the Australian Catholic Federation, he also revived the North Adelaide branch of the Hibernian Australasian Catholic Benefit Society and ran the

Adelaide Catholic Club. During his second priorship at North Adelaide (1908-14), he made additions and alterations to St Laurence's which were completed in 1910. While there, Spence advised Archbishop John O'Reily [q.v.11] and became involved in administering the archdiocese.

On 13 July 1914 Spence was appointed coadjutor archbishop of Adelaide with the right of succession; on 16 August he was consecrated archbishop and next year succeeded to the see. He continued the restructuring of diocesan finances begun by O'Reily, removing the remaining heavy debt; he also carried out extensive and costly building works, among them the transformation and completion of St Francis Xavier's Cathedral. Returning from an *ad limina* visit to Rome (1920-21), he travelled the archdiocese appealing for funds for the cathedral; at the building's opening ceremonies in 1926 only a small debt remained which was a tribute to his initiative and drive. Spence's bearing and manner were impressive, yet he continued to wear the plain robes of his order rather than the episcopal purple soutane. Combining 'urbanity, common sense, business acumen, tact and scholarship', he was an outstanding speaker among contemporary Catholic prelates.

In Ireland on 27 August 1920 Spence received the freedom of the city of Cork. He later spoke in Newry Town Hall where he made a point of saluting 'the flag of Ireland'. His speech alleged that 'soldiers of the British Government were committing atrocities in Ireland'. The incident sparked controversy in Australia. Diplomatic in his approach to the Adelaide community, he obtained from Rome in 1930 a papal blessing for those in his archdiocese, including non-Catholics. Celebrating the golden jubilee of his ordination in 1932, Spence remarked, 'I must be one of the happiest bishops in the world'. In July 1933 he was appointed a count of the Holy Roman Empire, an assistant at the pontifical throne and a companion to Pius XI; in the same month he received a coadjutor, Andrew Killian [q.v.9]. On 5 November 1934 the archbishop died at Glen Osmond; the Adelaide City Council adjourned as a mark of esteem and sympathy. He was buried in West Terrace cemetery.

J. O'Rorke, *St Laurence's Priory, North Adelaide, South Australia* (Melb, 1973); *Southern Cross* (Adel), 18 Sept 1898, 31 July, 16 Aug 1914, 23 Dec 1932, 9 Nov 1934; *Chronicle* (Adel), 22 Dec 1932; *SMH*, 25 Sept 1920, 24 Feb 1921, 19 Dec 1933; *Advertiser* (Adel), 13 Nov 1934; Reminiscences of D'Arcy Woodards, archbishop's secretary, ms, *and* Spence papers (Catholic Archives, Adel); Conventual Archives diary (Archives of Dominican Fathers, Nth Adel).   RUTH SCHUMANN

SPENCER, ALBERT HENRY (1886-1971), bookseller, was born on 8 March 1886 at Balmain, Sydney, younger son of Henry Spencer (formerly Henrik Bertelsen), a labourer from Denmark, and his native-born wife Alice Jane, née Prynne. His father died when Bert was aged 2 and the family's straitened circumstances meant that he had to leave Waverley Superior Public School at 14 to work as a boot-clicker. Eight months later he secured a position as messenger-boy with the booksellers and publishers Angus & Robertson [qq.v.7,11].

Between 1900 and 1922 Spencer learned the trade from its Australian masters, George Robertson himself, and his employees F. V. G. Wymark and J. R. Tyrrell [qq.v.]; he eventually became head of the secondhand department, and the friend and confidant of Sydney collectors such as (Sir) William Dixson [q.v.8] and J. A. Ferguson. On 30 January 1909 Spencer married Eileen Rebecca O'Connor (d. 1964) at Woollahra Presbyterian Church.

Deciding to set up on his own in Melbourne, Spencer had—in addition to a loan of £1000 from H. L. White [q.v.]—the support and encouragement of F. H. Cole [q.v.8] and of Robertson. In 1922 he began trading at the Hill of Content, 86 Bourke Street. For several months in 1928 the business was transferred to the Eastern Market while the shop was rebuilt with an extra storey. Very quickly the new shop emerged as a major outlet for antiquarian, second-hand and fine new books. Spencer's connexions helped him to obtain the privilege in the 1920s of dispersing the spectacular libraries of Robert Sticht [q.v.], Cole and White. He maintained contact with Sydney collectors and successfully attracted the custom of Melbourne's notable citizens and bibliophiles. A limited number of books were published by the business, which formed itself into a private company.

The sudden death in 1946 of his son Gregory, who was planning to join the firm, determined Spencer's sale of the Hill of Content to Angus & Robertson Ltd in 1951. Thereafter he busied himself in superintending the transfer of Dixson's collection to the State Library of New South Wales, working again for his old employers, publishing his memoirs—*The Hill of Content* (1959)—and selling books privately from his Sandringham home. Despite the help of friends and neighbours, Spencer's health was frail and his last years were saddened by the deaths of his wife and daughter. He died at Parkville on 20 February 1971 and was cremated. His estate was valued for probate at $16 034.

Raised in Presbyterian piety, a Freemason and a Rotarian, Spencer shared the prejudices and enthusiasms of his generation. That his bookselling style was far removed from clinical professionalism is suggested by his observation to the editor of his manuscript: 'Emotion is & was my impelling force'. Spencer asserted the strength of English tradition in his approach to the world of books. For all the sentimentalism of his decidedly avuncular stance, he remained an accomplished technician, an astute marketer of his own book, a clever advertiser and an uncompromising stickler for the right of the retailer to set his own prices. In the difficult decades between 1920 and 1950 he helped to give Melbourne and Australia a sense of the mission of antiquarian bookselling.

Aust Booksellers Assn, *The early Australian booksellers* (Adel, 1980); Spencer papers (LaTL).

WALLACE KIRSOP

SPENCER, COSENS (1874-1930), film entrepreneur, was born on 12 February 1874 at Hunston, Sussex, England, and named Spencer, third son of Cornelius Cosens, farmer, and his wife Ellen, née Wheeler. Fired by tales of gold, in 1892 he went with his brother Arthur to British Columbia, Canada. Although well educated, he did whatever came to hand—splitting rails, driving cattle near Vernon and working in a store. Joined by another brother Sidney in 1894, they founded Cosens Bros, universal providers, at Fairview and Camp McKinney; their horsemanship earned them the sobriquet the 'Cayoose Cosens'.

In 1898 Spencer was a clerk at Vernon. Soon after, he began screening moving pictures and reversed his names. He met and married vivacious, Edinburgh-born Mary Stuart Huntly; known professionally as 'Senora Spencer', she became his chief projectionist and business partner. A handsome, dark-haired, dapper man, with a closely trimmed beard and moustache, Spencer was short and stout, and loved jewellery. On 1 July 1905, after exhibiting in New Zealand, the Spencers opened the 'Great American Theatrescope' at the Lyceum Theatre, Sydney. Having made a very profitable tour of Australia, the pair remodelled the Lyceum as a permanent picture theatre from June 1908. That month Spencer established a film production company under Raymond Longford's direction, with Ernest Higgins as photographer [qq.v.10,9]. Their output of narrative, newsreel and scenic films included features such as *The romantic story of Margaret Catchpole* (1911) and *Sweet Nell of Old Drury* (1911). In August 1912 Spencer opened an elaborate new studio at Rushcutters Bay.

The success of the Lyceum enterprise led Spencer to acquire picture theatres across Australia, as well as overseas agencies for film releases, which ensured the continued quality of his programmes. His screenings ranged from footage of the San Francisco earthquake and the Burns-Johnson fight to the American classic, *The great train robbery*, and the Italian epic, *Quo vadis?* The largest importer of films in Australia by 1912, Spencer made the cinema attractive to middle- and working-class audiences by publicity and by providing salubrious premises with ambitious musical and special effects.

In 1911 he had mistakenly placed his diverse interests under the control of a public company, Spencer's Pictures Ltd. Next year, while he was overseas, the board voted to merge with the combine, Australasian Films Ltd, which had no interest in local film-making. Isolated and betrayed, Spencer cajoled Australasian into making a feature, *The shepherd of the Southern Cross*, but its box office failure precluded further productions and he resigned from the board. Legally prohibited by the agreement with Australasian Films from active involvement in exhibition, Spencer maintained links with the industry through his wife who continued to run cinemas at Newcastle and in Brisbane. He lived at Darling Point and contributed generously to war loans. In 1918 the Spencers were sued by Spencer's Pictures Ltd, Australasian Films Ltd and Union Theatres Ltd for an alleged breach of contract; following settlement out of court, Mary sold her exhibition interests to the 'combine'.

The Spencers quit Sydney; by 1923 they had acquired Chilco ranch in British Columbia. Spencer drowned himself in the Chilcotin River after fatally shooting his storeman and wounding another man on 10 September 1930. His wife survived him. His estate was sworn for probate in Canada at $346 059; in Australia his debts exceeded his assets by £8840. He left the residue of his estate to the 'Orphanages of Sydney'.

Spencer's Pictures Ltd, *Souvenir programme . . . August 16, 1912* (Syd, 1912); A. Pike and R. Cooper, *Australian film, 1900-1977* (Melb, 1980); D. Collins, *Hollywood down under* (Syd, 1987); *Theatre* (Syd, Melb), 2 July 1906, 1 Jan 1907, 1 Oct 1910, 1 Jan 1915, 2 Sept 1918; *Lone Hand*, Sept 1918; *Everyone's*, 17 Sept, 22 Oct 1930; M. E. Darling, 'Arthur Cosens, 1872-1949', *Okanagan Hist Soc J*, 1949; *SMH*, 1, 3 July 1905, 30 July, 1 Aug 1918; *Bulletin*, 6 Feb 1906; Coroner's inquest on Cosens Spencer, records (Provincial Archives, Vic, British Columbia, Canada).   DIANE COLLINS

SPENCER, THOMAS EDWARD (1845-1911), building contractor, industrial arbitrator and writer, was born on 30 December 1845 at Hoxton Old Town, London, son of Daniel O'Brien, cabinetmaker, and his wife Ann, née Coulthard. In 1863 Thomas visited the Victorian goldfields with a brother, only to return disappointed to London a year later. He had shed his patronymic by the time he married Jane Harriett Strew on 21 November 1869 in the parish church, Hackney. A stonemason by trade, at 24 he became vice-president of the Stonemasons' Society of London; he helped its president Henry Broadhurst to settle industrial disputes.

Migrating to Sydney in 1875, Spencer set up as a building contractor. As a skilled and reliable craftsman, he won government contracts for work on Goulburn gaol, the University of Sydney's physics laboratory and the sewerage system in Sydney. His wife died in 1880, leaving a 7-year-old son; on 6 April 1882 at Goulburn Spencer married Sarah Ann Christie with Wesleyan forms.

Defeated for the Legislative Assembly seat of Ashburnham in 1894, Spencer entered the tough political arena of industrial arbitration. In 1907 he was appointed employers' representative in the Court of Arbitration under Judge C. G. Heydon [q.v.9] and, after the court's reorganization in 1909, presided over some thirty wages boards. Spencer's services were sought by both sides owing to his 'ever-wakeful instinct for fair play'. An active Freemason and a member of Leinster Marine Lodge, he helped to negotiate the formation of the United Grand Lodge of New South Wales in 1888. Deputy grand master in 1894-96, he was a complimentary past grand master and a leading member of Leinster Marine Royal Arch Chapter of Ireland and of the New South Wales Masonic Club.

In his leisure Spencer 'reeled off a large amount of prose and verse of wildly humorous order'. He began contributing to the Bulletin in 1891. J. F. Archibald [q.v.3] told him: 'Your verses blew into the office like a whiff from the bush. It was a pleasure to read some lines which did not contain wattle and dead men'. Spencer published two collections of verse, How McDougall topped the score (1906) and Budgeree ballads (1908): the ballads were reprinted in 1910 as Why Doherty died because people 'associated the word "Budgeree" with a swear word'. His collections of humorous sketches mostly involved the garrulous Irish-Australian Mrs Bridget McSweeney: The surprising adventures of Mrs. Bridget McSweeney (1906), A spring cleaning and other stories (1908), The haunted shanty (1910) and That droll lady (1911). Spencer's novel, Bindawalla (1912), was published posthumously. All his books appeared in A. C. Rowlandson's [q.v.11] New South Wales Bookstall Co.'s shilling series, went through many impressions and sold extremely well.

In more serious vein he exposed preachers of 'socialistic rot' ('Latter day patriots'), pragmatic politicians ('The political dead-beat')

and dishonest builders ('Suburban Simplicity'). A few of his breezy, rollicking ballads ('How McDougall Topped the Score' and 'O'Toole and McSharry') are still popular school recitation pieces. Spencer died on 6 May 1911 of heart disease and chronic bronchitis at his Glebe Point home and was buried with full Masonic rites in the Anglican section of Rookwood cemetery. His wife and their two sons and two daughters survived him, as did the son of his first marriage.

Daily Telegraph (Syd), 8 May 1911; SMH, 8, 9 May 1911; T&CJ, 10 May 1911; Aust Worker, 11 May 1911; Bulletin, 11, 18, 25 May 1911.

DAVID HEADON

SPENCER, SIR WALTER BALDWIN (1860-1929), university scientist and administrator, anthropologist and connoisseur, was born on 23 June 1860 at Stretford, Lancashire, England, second of eleven children of Reuben Spencer and his wife Martha, née Circuit. Reuben had risen from clerk to managing director of John Rylands and Sons, cotton-spinners and manufacturers; he was a pillar of Manchester Congregationalism; in 1901 he left his children a considerable inheritance. Baldwin was educated at Old Trafford School and at the Manchester School of Art. His interest in art and sketching was lifelong and would reveal itself in his competence as a scientific draftsman and illustrator.

Entering Owens College (Victoria University of Manchester) in 1879, Spencer intended to study medicine. Inspired by Milnes Marshall, a Darwinian disciple, he became a committed evolutionary biologist, soon abandoning conventional religion. After winning a scholarship to Exeter College, he entered the University of Oxford in 1881 to study science under Professor H. N. Moseley who combined enthusiasm for evolutionary biology with ethnological interests and a deep concern for his students. He had visited Australia when a naturalist on the Challenger scientific voyage and later encouraged Spencer to research there. Spencer's own rapport with students owed much to Marshall and Moseley.

Spencer grasped Oxford's diverse opportunities which included lectures by Ruskin and E. B. Tylor. He co-founded the Junior Scientific Club, and excelled in arranging major meetings. Graduating B.A. in 1884 with a first in science, he became a demonstrator in Moseley's laboratory. For a period he shared rooms with (Sir) Halford Mackinder whose example probably inspired Spencer's later biogeographical assessment of Australian faunal distribution and his energetic involvement in Victorian public education.

Spencer's research built upon current

advances in microscopy and histological techniques; studies of the parietal (pineal) eye in reptiles were his major project. Election to a Lincoln College fellowship for 1886 resulted. His colleagues included Melbourne-educated Samuel Alexander [q.v.7] and the distinguished Latinist, W. Warde Fowler, an amateur naturalist who proved a father-figure. They tramped together in the Cotswolds and Fowler broadened Spencer's awareness of the humanities.

Moseley and Tylor obtained Spencer's assistance in transferring the important Pitt-Rivers ethnographic collection from London to its Oxford museum, an experience which taught him the principles of typological classification of artefacts, following technological and dubious presumed evolutionary development. His two mentors proved influential referees when, in 1886, he applied for the foundation chair of biology at the University of Melbourne.

Notified of his appointment on 12 January 1887, Spencer and his wife disembarked in Melbourne on 30 March. On 18 January at Stockport, Chester, he had married with Independent forms Mary Elizabeth ('Lillie') Bowman (1862-1935), the daughter of family friends. They were to have two daughters and a son who died at birth in 1896. Spencer was of medium height and slight build; he camouflaged his youthful appearance behind a moustache which drooped or was trimmed according to fashion's dictates.

With his colleague, Professor (Sir) David Masson [q.v.10], Spencer helped to transform university standards and they co-operated as entrepreneurs of Australian science. The embodiment of controlled energy, Spencer set about designing and funding the biology building which opened within a year, its laboratories providing a model of contemporary planning and lighting. By 1900 it developed into a major centre of research on the Australian biota. His was the first Australian university department to appoint female lecturers and associate professors; by 1919 his departmental colleagues were all women.

Spencer inaugurated undergraduate field excursions, founded a student science society and sponsored the Princess Ida club for women. His sustained involvement in undergraduate sport resulted in the formation of the Sports Union. As its president, he was instrumental in landscaping the university oval and financing its pavilion. He secured the University team's admission to the Victorian Football league in 1908. After its poor performance and its withdrawal from the league in 1914, he transferred his loyalties to the Carlton club. Respected as a statesman of sport, he was president of the V.F.L. in 1919-26.

With Spencer's encouragement, staff and graduate students participated in the vigorous Field Naturalists' Club of Victoria and in the revived Royal Society of Victoria. President of the former in 1891-93 and 1895-97, he edited publications for the latter and was its president in 1904. He and Masson were the Melbourne architects of the British Association for the Advancement of Science meeting in 1914. An exponent of interstate scientific co-operation, he was prominent in the Australasian Association for the Advancement of Science, twice editing Victorian meeting handbooks and serving as 1921 congress president. His versatility extended to co-editorship of the *Australian Critic* in 1890 with the classicist T. G. Tucker [q.v.].

Spencer's administrative skills also resulted in his appointment as honorary director of the National Museum of Victoria in 1899. He supervised the museum's transfer to its present location, master-minded the construction of its Russell Street frontage, personally arranged exhibits by drawing on his English experience of typological classification, and published a *Guide to the Australian ethnographical collection* (1901, 1922). Chairman of the university professorial board in 1903-11, he presided over the recovery of the university's reputation and finances following misappropriations. Despite holding the university's senior executive post, his teaching load remained heavy.

The 1894 Horn [q.v.9] scientific exploring expedition to central Australia recruited Spencer as zoologist and photographer. Because of friction between members and their sponsor, Spencer later combined mediation with editorship of all four volumes of reports. His own seminal contribution included his classic biogeographic interpretation of Australian faunal distribution. This expedition rekindled his anthropological interest when he met F. J. Gillen [q.v.9], the Alice Springs postmaster. What began as his offer to assist in publishing Gillen's ethnological notes matured into an enduring partnership and a landmark in anthropological history.

In 1896 Spencer joined Gillen for the most intensive field-work then attempted in Australia. *The native tribes of Central Australia* (1899) which resulted was to influence contemporary theories on social evolution and interpretations of the origins of art and ceremonial. It impressed (Sir) James Frazer, author of *The golden bough,* who developed a lifelong friendship with Spencer. Selections from their correspondence were published in 1932.

Frazer also raised a petition which obtained from their respective governments the release of the partners for a year. Spencer and Gillen drove a buggy from Oodnadatta to Borroloola in 1901-02, working among Aboriginal groups for several weeks at a time. They pioneered sound recording on wax cylinders and shot movie film under conditions of sheer hardship. Their last joint venture took them briefly to Lake Eyre's Arabana people in 1903. Their research produced *The Northern tribes of Central Australia* (1904); *Across Australia* (2 vols, 1912) was a popular version, originally partly serialized in the *Age* during 1901. These articles provided £1000 towards expedition costs, but all Spencer's other field-work was self-financed.

When the Commonwealth government assumed control of the Northern Territory, Spencer led three other scientists, including J. A. Gilruth [q.v.9], on the 1911 Preliminary Scientific Expedition. Impressed with their findings, the government immediately appointed Spencer to Darwin for a year. As special commissioner and chief protector of Aborigines for some weeks until the arrival of administrator Gilruth, he was the Territory's most senior official. The opposition which his decisions aroused among Darwin's polyglot community anticipated the issues which dominated Gilruth's turbulent era. Spencer's comprehensive but costly blueprint for Aboriginal welfare was tabled in parliament in 1913, and forgotten. His concepts were paternalistic, authoritarian and reflected social Darwinism, yet they were innovative and advocated the creation of extensive reserves.

An infected leg severely restricted Spencer's field-work during 1912. In spite of this permanent source of discomfort, he was hosted by Joe Cooper [q.v.8] on Melville Island and by Paddy Cahill [q.v.7] at Oenpelli and Flora River. *Native Tribes of the Northern Territory of Australia* (1914) described his ethnographic observations and extensive collections. An ethnographic quarry today, it was the source of the term 'Kakadu'. Despite humid conditions, Spencer did more filming. Less fortunate was his trail-blazing 1000-mile (1609 km) drive with Gilruth to Borroloola which achieved little.

Spencer visited Alice Springs and Hermannsburg in 1923, at the government's request, but his recommendations on welfare matters were ignored. He returned there briefly in 1926, stung by criticisms derived from Carl Strehlow [q.v.] that the Spencer-Gillen interpretation of Aranda society was wrong. Gillen had died in 1912, but Spencer had defended their work in *The Arunta: a study of a stone age people* (2 vols, 1927). A popular rewrite of previous books followed—*Wanderings in wild Australia* (2 vols, 1928)—this time under his sole authorship.

While at Oenpelli in 1912, Spencer had initiated the collection of over 200 bark paintings. In a philanthropic gesture, he donated them and his entire ethnographic collection in

1917 to the National Museum of Victoria. Included were his movies, wax cylinders and some 1700 photographic negatives of superb quality.

Among his many friends in literary and artistic circles, Spencer numbered the Lindsay brothers, Heysen and Lambert [qq.v.9]; Streeton [q.v.] initially lodged with him upon his 1906-07 return visit; Spencer commissioned Tom Roberts [q.v.11] to paint his friend A. W. Howitt's [q.v.4] portrait. Several artists acknowledged the importance of his patronage early in their careers. (From such periods he owned about thirty Streeton works and over forty by Norman Lindsay.) He sold over 200 paintings upon his retirement in 1919. S. Ure Smith [q.v.11] claimed this sale as a landmark in the recognition of Australian art. As a trustee (later vice-president) of the National Gallery of Victoria since 1895, Spencer encouraged (not always wisely) the purchase of Australian art. Late in 1916 he voyaged to England to select advisers for the Felton [q.v.4] bequest trustees. Their selections, commencing with the William Blake drawings, enriched the gallery through the 1920s. Spencer's contribution was recognized formally in 1926, with the award of the medal of the Society of Artists', Sydney. His lively portrait by Lambert hangs in the Museum of Victoria; portraits by W. B. McInnes [q.v.10] are owned by the University of Melbourne and Exeter College, Oxford; another by E. Phillips Fox [q.v.8] has not been located.

Spencer retired as emeritus professor in 1919. His nerves and his judgement were impaired from the strain of continuous overwork, the virtual disintegration of his marriage, and concern for his daughters in wartime England. Liquor proved a solace. He was hospitalized in 1921, ostensibly for his old leg injury, but alcoholism was the chief problem.

His health improved and within two years he resumed anthropological activities and rebuilt his art collection. This renaissance evidently coincided with his discreet association with Jean Hamilton, a librarian over thirty years his junior. They lived in London from 1927 and early in 1929 sailed together to Tierra del Fuego to undertake anthropological field-work. After three months under bleak conditions, Spencer died from angina pectoris on 14 July 1929 in a snowbound hut on Navarin Island. Jean Hamilton took his body for burial to Magallanes (Punta Arenas), Chile. His papers were edited as *Spencer's last journey* (1931). His achievements were recognized. Elected fellow of the Royal Society in 1900, he was appointed C.M.G. in 1904 and K.C.M.G. in 1916. Manchester University conferred an honorary doctorate of science, while Melbourne awarded a doctorate of letters. Exeter College, Oxford, elected him to an honorary fellowship in 1907 and stained glass in its hall commemorates his contribution.

Spencer was an approachable, enthusiastic teacher, a brilliant lecturer (in 1902 he packed Melbourne's town hall), a capable and firm administrator, an entrepreneur for national science, one of Victoria's first conservationists (Wilson's Promontory National Park is his monument) and an advocate for Australian artists. People ranging from governors to unlettered frontiersmen called him 'friend'. Yet his significance rests chiefly on his Aboriginal work. He drew upon the assumptions and models of biological evolution and applied them to Aboriginal institutions, beliefs and technology in a mechanistic manner. Although a kindly humanitarian in practice, in theory he saw Aborigines simply as dehumanized 'survivals' from an early stage of social development. His voluminous written and photographic records endure as a priceless Aboriginal archive, despite his unacceptable value judgements on their fossilized society. Sir James Frazer's pompous 1899 pronouncement was prophetic: 'in immortalizing the native tribes of Central Australia, Spencer and Gillen have at the same time immortalised themselves'.

R. R. Marett and T. K. Penniman (eds), *Spencer's last journey* (Oxford, 1931), and *Spencer's scientific correspondence* (Oxford, 1932); D. J. Mulvaney and J. H. Calaby, *'So much that is new'* (Melb, 1985); Roy Anthropological Inst, *J*, 28 (1899), p 281; *Lone Hand*, Mar 1917; Spencer papers (Pitt Rivers Museum, Oxford, *and* ML, *and* Museum of Vic).

D. J. MULVANEY

SPIELVOGEL, NATHAN FREDERICK (1874-1956), teacher, writer and historian, was born on 10 May 1874 at Ballarat, Victoria, son of Newman Frederick Spielvogel, pawnbroker, and his wife Hannah, née Cohen. Newman, an Austrian, and Hannah, a Prussian, were typical of the strong Jewish community on the Ballarat goldfields. Nathan attended Dana Street State School and trained there in 1892-95 as a pupil-teacher. He taught at several schools in the Wimmera, including Dimboola (1897, 1899-1907).

A small man, with sharply chiselled features, a wide forehead, big ears, warm eyes, a jutting chin and a beard that became golden, Spielvogel was adventurous and imaginative. In 1904 he spent his savings of £120 on a six-month journey through Egypt, Italy, Switzerland, Germany and Britain. He had begun his writing career in 1894 with a Christmas story for the *Ballarat Courier*, to which—with the Jewish press, the *Bulletin*, the *Dimboola Ban-*

ner and other newspapers—he contributed regularly under such pen names as 'Genung', 'Eko', 'Ato' and 'Ahaswar'. From the early 1920s he wrote a humorous piece each month for the *Teachers' Journal*, but was probably best known for his first book, *A gumsucker on the tramp* (1906). It sold 20 000 copies. He also published *The cocky farmer* (1914), *A gumsucker at home* (1914), *Old Eko's note-book* (1930) and a volume of poetry called *Our gum trees* (1913).

He loved a beer (not lager) and around 1908 dined every Thursday at Fasoli's café, Melbourne, with writers and artists such as E. J. Brady [q.v.7], Norman Lindsay [q.v.10], Hal Gye [q.v.9], C. J. Dennis and Louis Esson [qq.v.8]. Later he was close to J. K. Moir, Victor Kennedy and R. H. Croll [q.v.8] of the Bread and Cheese Club. Croll thought him 'offensively Australian' yet proudly Jewish, a conjunction that rent Spielvogel in 1901 when his love for a gentile conflicted with a promise to his mother not to marry out of the faith. He remained steadfast and on 6 September 1911 at the Great Synagogue, Hyde Park, Sydney, married Jessie Muriel, daughter of Henry Harris, publisher of the *Hebrew Standard*.

After further postings to other Victorian schools, Spielvogel returned to Ballarat to be headmaster of Dana Street in 1924-39. Inspiring, sympathetic and methodical, he was immensely popular: a phalanx of pupils usually escorted him into the grounds. As president of the revived Ballarat Historical Society (1933-56), he developed a passion for local history. He published vignettes of early Ballarat life and a popular monograph, *The affair at Eureka* (1928). After retirement he was largely responsible for managing the local museum and for placing plaques and monuments at historic sites. His broadcasts and press releases increased historical awareness.

Spielvogel was president of the Ballarat Hebrew Congregation, the Mechanics' Institute, the Teachers' Institute and Dana Street Old Scholars' Association. Strongly patriotic during World War I, he became chairman of the Dads' Association in World War II. A sharp mind lay behind his lifelong interest in chess: he was secretary (1894) and president (1939) of the Ballarat club and represented Victoria in 1921 and 1925. He was instrumental in sustaining the Ballarat synagogue between 1941 and 1953 and wrote Jewish stories with a tenderness and strength that drew from Judah Waten the remark that Jewish literature in Australia began with him. Spielvogel died on 10 September 1956 at Ballarat and was buried in the old cemetery. His wife and their three sons (all of whom had married out of the faith and in his absence) survived him.

Aust Jewish Hist Soc, J, 3, no 2, 1949, 6, no 1, 1964; *Bohemia,* 1 Nov 1956; Education Dept (Vic), *Educational Mag,* July 1971; *Ballarat Courier,* 15 Sept 1956; H. Marks papers (LaTL).

WESTON BATE

SPOONER, ERIC SYDNEY (1891-1952), accountant and politician, was born on 2 March 1891 at Waterloo, Sydney, son of native-born parents William Henry Spooner, printer, and his wife Maud Ann, née Dubois. Aged 14, he left Christ Church St Laurence School to work as a telegraph messenger for 7s. 6d. a week; he gained a diploma in economics and commerce by evening study at the University of Sydney in 1916 and brilliantly passed the Commonwealth Institute of Accountants' examinations. In the Methodist Church, Chatswood, on 9 December 1919 Spooner married Mary Berry, a bank clerk. Having practised as a chartered accountant at Orange from 1919, he returned to Sydney in 1922 to establish the firm of Hungerford, Spooner & Co. with his brother (Sir) William (later a senator and prominent Liberal cabinet minister).

Attracted to politics and encouraged by (Sir) Bertram Stevens [q.v.], Spooner won the Legislative Assembly seat of Ryde for the United Australia Party in June 1932 and joined Stevens' government as an honorary minister. At his first appearance in the House he captured its attention by nodding off to sleep at 9 p.m.: woken by an interjection, he smiled and went back to sleep. Next February Spooner became assistant treasurer and minister for local government; retaining local government in 1935, he also became secretary for public works and deputy leader of the parliamentary party. He implemented unemployment relief and employment-creating capital works, encouraged municipal housing schemes, established the Sydney County Council to provide gas and electricity services, and consolidated Newcastle local government boundaries. In addition, he funded surf clubs, encouraged the meshing of Sydney beaches against sharks and required men to wear full-length bathing costumes. He was rarely out of the news during seven turbulent years as a senior minister.

Spooner's political ambitions made him a central figure in bitter dissensions within the coalition. His portfolios gave him powerful sources of patronage and he was mistrusted by the Country Party leader (Sir) Michael Bruxner [q.v.7]. Increasingly wary of his protégé, in 1938 Stevens bypassed Spooner for Alexander Mair [q.v.10] as treasurer. In mid-1939 Spooner opposed Mair's proposals to cut government spending in order to restrain a growing deficit: at a stormy party meeting on 19 July Spooner did not deny allegations that he had described the State budget as 'faked' and its finances as 'manipulated'. Two days later he resigned from cabinet. On 1 August he moved a parliamentary motion criticizing the government's economic policies. Nine U.A.P. members crossed the floor to defeat the Stevens-Bruxner government. Expecting to succeed Stevens as premier, Spooner failed to form a new coalition with the Country Party (Bruxner refused to join him) and resigned his deputy leadership.

In August 1940 Spooner resigned from the assembly and won the Federal seat of Robertson in October. A vigorous Federal parliamentarian, he rejected deflation and favoured a national government, Australia-wide child endowment and post-war reconstruction. He chaired an inquiry into labour resources, this time clashing with Mair over manpower policy. Despite Spooner's record of independence, even disloyalty, (Sir) Robert Menzies appointed him minister for war organization of industry in June 1941 and to the economic and industrial committee of cabinet. He retained his portfolio under (Sir) Arthur Fadden, but the government was defeated in October. Spooner was a member of a committee which examined uniform taxation in 1942 and supported legislation which he considered constitutional and vital to financing the war effort. He often criticized Menzies' leadership.

Defeated at the elections in August 1943, Spooner returned to commerce and accountancy. He joined Menzies' Liberal Party, but was threatened with expulsion in 1945 for suggesting modification of the White Australia policy. After unsuccessfully challenging Prime Minister Chifley in Macquarie in 1946, Spooner took no further part in politics. In 1950 he served on a committee reviewing Commonwealth tax legislation.

Besides farming at Carcoar and Richmond, Spooner was chairman of Hub Pty Ltd and Western Steel Enterprises Ltd, and a director of Overell's Ltd and Robert Reid [q.v.11] & Co. Ltd. Survived by his wife, three sons and daughter, he died in Sydney on 3 June 1952 of cancer and was buried in the Northern Suburbs cemetery after a state funeral at St Stephen's Anglican Church, Chatswood. Energetic, imaginative and persuasive, Spooner was proud of his achievements and said that 'he had come from the rank and file, of humble parentage, and had fought a battle with life'. His political talents and popular appeal were conceded even by his numerous enemies. Seemingly destined for high political office, he was frustrated by his own impatience and inflexibility, and by the aura of mistrust that he generated among his senior colleagues.

D. Aitkin, *The colonel* (Canb, 1969); C. Hazle-hurst (ed), *Australian conservatism* (Canb, 1979); *PD* (NSW), 18 Aug 1952, p 20; *SMH*, 18 June 1932, 4 June 1952; *Aust National Review*, 28 June 1932; M. Anderson, Notes on Spooner, 24 Aug 1939 (held by ADB, Canb).

C. J. LLOYD

SPRAGG, ALONZO STEPHEN (1879-1904), footballer, was born on 2 October 1879 at Redfern, Sydney, youngest of five children of George Henry Spragg, grocer, and his wife Margaret, née Balser. In 1882 the family moved to Enfield and 'Lonnie' was educated at Druitt Town Public and Sydney Boys' High schools; at Sydney Technical College he studied wool-classing, the trade he entered in 1899.

He began playing Rugby Union football in first-junior grade with the Mercantile club at Burwood in 1897 and attracted attention next year with the Wallaroo senior club. At 18 the youngest senior player in Sydney, Spragg was selected for city against country; later that season, after substituting for Queensland in a match at Newcastle, he made his debut for New South Wales as a winger in both return intercolonial matches in Brisbane. In 1899 he played for his colony against Queensland and Rev. Mullineux's touring British team. His elusiveness and goal-kicking prowess won him a place in Australia's first full international team against Great Britain in Sydney on 24 June. The outstanding local player and top try-scorer in the series, Spragg made the memorable match-winning try in the first Test. That year he helped Wallaroos to the Sydney premiership and represented Strathfield junior (third grade) club on the metropolitan union.

On 2 January 1900 Spragg moved to Rockhampton, Queensland; on 9 May he settled in Brisbane. He was employed by the Queensland Government Savings Bank until 1903, then became a hide and skin merchant. Prominent in many sports, he rowed interstate in Adelaide, was a useful all-rounder, captain and honorary secretary for North Brisbane Cricket Club, and a leading Brisbane table tennis player. Above all, he was the idol of Queensland Rugby for his sportsmanship and the all-round brilliance of his play as an attacking centre three-quarter. His Brisbane football career began with the City team and in 1901-03 he played for North Brisbane. He set new standards in point-scoring: in twenty games in 1901 he scored a total of 195 points, with 26 tries; in a 1902 club match he converted all 10 tries. In 1900-02 he played twelve consecutive matches for Queensland against New South Wales and, aged 22, captained the side in two 1902 Sydney matches. His record total of 70 points scored for Queensland stood for thirty years until bet-tered by Tommy Lawton [q.v.10]. Spragg helped Queensland to five successive wins over New South Wales in Brisbane. In twenty-one international and interstate matches he scored 104 points.

Although only 5 ft. 10 ins. (178 cm) tall and 11 st. 8 lb. (73.5 kg), he was the ideal athlete —strong, unselfish and good-tempered. A staunch teetotaller and non-smoker, noted for his genial personality and cheery smile, he was quick to praise and to assist those in need. At his peak, Spragg injured his knee in a club match in June 1903 which ended his playing career. On 23 January 1904 he played a 'neat' innings of 24 for his cricket club. He then fell ill. Treated for typhoid fever, he died at Brisbane General Hospital on 12 February 1904 after an appendicectomy and was buried with Anglican rites in Toowong cemetery. He was unmarried. A monument over his grave was erected by the 'Athletes of Australia'.

D. B. Ryan, *Fifty years of football* (Brisb, 1932); W. H. Bickley (ed), *Maroon* (Brisb, 1982); J. Pollard, *Australian Rugby Union* (Syd, 1984); *Referee*, 13 July 1898, 17, 20 Feb 1904; *Capricornian*, 28 Apr 1900, 20 Feb 1904; *Evening Observer*, sports ed, 27 July 1901; *Daily Mail* (Brisb), and *Rockhampton Morning Bulletin* and *Saturday Observer*, 13 Feb 1904; *Brisbane Courier*, 13, 15 Feb 1904; *T&CJ*, 17 Feb 1904; *Arrow* (Syd), 15 Aug 1908.

DON WILKEY

SPRINGTHORPE, JOHN WILLIAM (1855-1933), physician, was born on 29 August 1855 at Wolverhampton, Staffordshire, England, second son of John Springthorpe, mercer, and his wife Hannah, née Newell. Brought in infancy to Balmain, Sydney, he was educated at Fort Street Model School, Sydney Grammar School and, from 1872, at Wesley College, Melbourne. He was a brilliant student at the University of Melbourne, winning several exhibitions and graduating M.A., M.B., B.S. in 1879 and M.D. in 1884. After working as a medical officer at Beechworth Asylum, he went to England and became in 1881 the first Australian graduate admitted to membership of the Royal College of Physicians.

Returning to Melbourne in late 1883, Springthorpe obtained posts as pathologist to the Alfred Hospital and out-patient physician to the Melbourne Hospital. His election as an in-patient physician in 1887 caused a storm in medical circles which provided copy for the newsmongers: he was alleged to have breached professional ethics by using an unsuitable election circular, but was vindicated. In 1887 he also became university lecturer in therapeutics, dietetics and hygiene; his Collins Street practice as a physician flourished; he wrote numerous articles for medical and other journals, and published a two-volume textbook, *Therapeutics, dietetics, and hygiene* (1914).

Springthorpe's energies flowed into many areas. He collected paintings and sculpture; he led in setting up a training and registration system in dentistry, and was the first dean of the faculty; he helped to found the Royal Victorian Trained Nurses Association, becoming its first president in 1901 and working with Felix Meyer [q.v.10] in the production of its journal, *Una*; he was first chairman of the Masseurs' Registration Board; ambulance work, child welfare, mothercraft nurses' education and amateur cycling were other fields for his enthusiasm. He was an active member of the Yorick and Wallaby clubs. In medicine, apart from his private practice, his university and hospital work, Springthorpe was frequently an official in congresses, being president of the Victorian branch of the British Medical Association in 1891 and president of the Melbourne Medical Association in 1900.

In 1914 he enlisted in the Australian Army Medical Corps and, with the rank of lieut-colonel, became senior physician to No. 2 Australian General Hospital. He was part of the fierce opposition to (Sir) James Barrett [q.v.7] in Egypt, especially concerning the latter's work for the Australian Red Cross Society. Springthorpe returned to Melbourne in 1916, but was posted again to France and then to England where he worked with soldiers suffering from nervous disorders.

Returning home in 1919 with, he considered, little recognition of his war service, he found that his university and hospital appointments had lapsed; he resumed his post of visitor to metropolitan asylums, recommenced private practice and worked for repatriation and the infant welfare movement. His contributions again became prominent in the press. He enlarged his art collection and gave great care to the grounds of his Murrumbeena home. By this stage he was hampered by deafness.

Short, dynamic, an amusing companion, lively in mind and action, Springthorpe was appropriately known as 'Springy'. He was a distinguished physician whose influence extended beyond medicine through his writings and organizing activities. His energy, however, was accompanied by reflection and introspection: he recorded his deeper currents in notebooks which he kept, with interruptions, from 1883. He had married Annie Constance Marie Inglis with Methodist forms at Richmond, Victoria, on 26 January 1887. After her death in childbirth in 1897, he filled his diary with reflections, prayers, poems and pictures relating to her. These entries, with his plans for her mausoleum in the Kew cemetery executed by Bertram Mackennal

[q.v.10], showed the extremes of his grief. Having gradually recovered, on 15 March 1916, at Hawthorn, Springthorpe married Daisie Evelyn Johnstone, a nurse and daughter of his housekeeper.

Springthorpe died at Richmond on 22 April 1933 and was buried in Boroondara cemetery, Kew, with Methodist forms. He left an estate valued for probate at £8280. His second wife and three of the four children of his first marriage survived him. His youngest son, Guy, became a well-known Melbourne psychiatrist.

B. K. Rank, *Jerry Moore and some of his contemporaries* (Melb, 1975); *Melbourne Hospital Clinical Reports*, 4, no 1, June 1933, p 1; *MJA*, 1 July 1933, p 26; Springthorpe diaries (LaTL).   BRYAN EGAN

SPROGE, PAUL CHRISTIAN JULIUS; *see* REBELL, FRED

SPRUSON, WILFRED JOSEPH (1870–1939), patent attorney, was born on 29 March 1870 at Church Hill, Sydney, son of JOSEPH JOHN SPRUSON (1841–1896) and his wife Lucy Theresa, née Doyle, from County Wicklow, Ireland. Joseph was born at sea when his parents were migrating from Ireland to New South Wales; he became a reader for the government printer and in 1879 was also assistant registrar of copyright; by 1887 he had indexed and classified the colony's confused fifteen volumes of patents, and summarized more than one thousand of the most important items. He gained the diploma of the Institute of Patent Agents, London. Premier Sir Patrick Jennings [q.v.4] promised Joseph the headship of the new office being constituted in place of the Patent Board in 1886, but in April 1887 Sir Henry Parkes's [q.v.5] government appointed A. G. Taylor [q.v.6] to the post.

A member of one of the prominent families of St Patrick's parish, Church Hill, Wilfred was educated at the Marist Brothers' School and became a patent agent. From 1886 he made a special study of electricity as part of his training in science and engineering which included attendance at the University of Sydney in 1887. He told the Public Works Committee in 1891 that it was 'perfectly feasible' to apply electricity to tramway traction.

A dedicated Federationist, Spruson was part of the Catholic group prominent among the fiscal protectionists. In 1894 he failed to gain a seat on the Sydney Municipal Council, but in 1898 won the Legislative Assembly seat of Sydney-Gipps (Millers Point) from George Black [q.v.7]. Spruson's success was a salutary lesson for the Labor Party. Black had taken the voters for granted; Spruson canvassed house-to-house, backed by many supporters who were enthused by his integrity, warm personality and fervent speeches. He was active in the parliament that completed the formalities of Federation for New South Wales. In 1900 he helped the Lyne [q.v.10] government with legislation that involved the demolition of some slums in 'The Rocks' locality of his electorate; little came of it, but Spruson alienated many voters who feared removal from their dwellings. He lost his seat in 1901.

On 29 January 1908 at St Mary's Catholic Church, North Sydney, Spruson married Anne Teresa Loneragan, daughter of the owner of the major retail stores at Mudgee and Gulgong. They moved to Neutral Bay where Wilfred concentrated on his career and became one of Sydney's leading patent attorneys. He exhorted his countrymen not to lag behind other nations in technological training and development. In 1923, with R. G. Ferguson, former Commonwealth commissioner of patents, he founded the firm of Spruson & Ferguson which became among the foremost in Australia in the fields of patents, trade marks and copyright.

Having advised Cardinal Moran [q.v.10] on financial and property matters, in 1902 Spruson was awarded the cross of Leo; in 1929 he was appointed a papal chamberlain. He was a member of the Royal Society of New South Wales and the Australian Institution of Engineers, and a fellow of the Australasian Institute of Patent Attorneys; he was also a foreign member of the Chartered Institute of Patent Agents, London.

Survived by his wife and four daughters, Spruson died of heart disease on 16 August 1939 at Neutral Bay and was buried in Waverley cemetery.

B. Nairn, *Civilising capitalism* (Canb, 1973); J. Hosie, *Challenge* (Syd, 1987); *V&P (LA NSW)*, 1887, 2, 1891-92, 5, 1894-95, 1, 1896, 1; *Freeman's J*, 25 Aug 1900, 24 Aug 1939; *Catholic Press*, 21, 28 July 1904, 23 Mar 1905, 24 Aug 1939; *Daily Telegraph* (Syd), 27 May 1929; *Bulletin*, 21 Mar 1934; *SMH*, 17 Aug 1939; P. McMurrich, Not angels, nor men confirmed in grace: the Society of Mary in Australia, 1892-1938 (M.A. thesis, Univ Syd, 1988); information from Sr J. Spruson, Burradoo, NSW.   BEDE NAIRN

SPYER, HADEN DANIEL (1872-1967), policeman, was born on 2 August 1872 at Acton, London, third child of James Spyer, forwarding agent, and his wife Georgiana Rachel, née Nathan. He grew up in London where he learned watchmaking. Influenced by his reading to migrate, he reached Sydney in 1883, penniless and unable to find work. He tried prospecting for gold, but survived by repairing clocks and watches at farmhouses in exchange for food.

Returning to Sydney, Spyer joined the New South Wales police on 21 September 1893, after attesting that he could swim and ride a bicycle. Physically and temperamentally he was suited for police work: 6 ft. 2½ ins. (189 cm) tall and weighing 15 st. 9 lb. (99.34 kg), he had strong features and an imposing black moustache; his friendly disposition had to it an air of calm authority and in later life baldness only seemed to add to his presence. He began by pounding the beat around Darlinghurst, usually at night.

Following the outbreak of the South African War, Spyer was granted leave to enlist in the New South Wales Army Medical Corps and sailed in the troop-ship *Moravian* on 17 January 1900. The diary he kept in the Transvaal detailed his growing disillusion with the war and his struggles against hunger, the elements and mindless military discipline. His letters to friends were occasionally published in the Sydney *Evening News*. In October he contracted malaria and was invalided home. While visiting his parents in London, he met and married Ada Louise Ebbutt, daughter of a registrar of marriages, at Christ Church, Croydon, on 13 July 1901. Together they came to New South Wales.

In 1903 Spyer received his stripe as constable 1st class. Apart from regular duties, he played the piccolo in the police band. An advocate of lifesaving and resuscitation techniques, he was chief instructor for the Royal Life Saving Society in 1909-10 and at Bondi Surf Bathers' Life Saving Club (1911-15) where he coached championship teams and was later club secretary.

Promoted senior constable and placed in charge of prosecutions at the Water Police Court in 1910, Spyer found his niche. He was elevated to sergeant in 1915 and inspector 1st class in 1921. Transferred to the Central Police Court, he rose to be senior police prosecutor. With his unflappable manner, 'Smiling Sergeant Spyer' was one of the characters of the court, frequently clashing with the solicitor, 'little Ernie' Abigail [q.v.7], yet showing forbearance to the madam, 'Tilly' Devine [q.v.8]; in cross-examination he employed 'a rapier-like method of tearing a witness to pieces, while applying the balm of good humour'.

Given higher duties at police headquarters, Spyer served from 1924 on the new Police Appeal Board, but offended some members of the Police Association. In 1927 he was promoted superintendent 3rd class. As the trusted lieutenant of Police Commissioner James Mitchell, he handled several confidential inquiries and oversaw the establishment of a wireless room at headquarters. Despite Mitchell's recommendation, opposition from the Police Association prevented Spyer from succeeding him as commissioner. In 1929 he was suddenly moved to Bathurst as superintendent 1st class with charge of the Western Police District and unsuccessfully appealed against the transfer. Spyer retired on a full pension on 2 August 1932.

He spent his retirement tending the garden at his Bronte home, playing bowls at Waverley and continuing as an active Freemason (initiated 1895). Predeceased by his wife, he died in Coogee hospital on 26 July 1967 and was cremated with Presbyterian forms. He was survived by two sons.

NSW Police News, 1 Sept 1932; *SMH*, 17 Jan 1965; H. D. Spyer, Diary Transvaal war *and* scrapbook (ML); information from Mr F. G. H. Spyer, Lyons, ACT.   JOHN KNOTT

SQUIRES, ERNEST KER (1882-1940), soldier, was born on 18 December 1882 at Poona, India, son of Robert Alfred Squires, clergyman, and his wife Elizabeth Anne, née Ker. He was educated at Eton, England, and the Royal Military Academy, Woolwich, where he reached the rank of under-officer. Tall and soldierly in bearing, he excelled at sports and was commissioned in the Royal Engineers in January 1903. After two years at the School of Military Engineering, Chatham, he was posted to India early in 1905 as a subaltern in the 3rd Sappers and Miners, and from 1908 commanded the 22nd Field Company. He remained there until 1910 when he was given command of the 23rd Fortress Company at Aden. On 31 July 1912 in the parish church at Westgate-on-Sea, Kent, England, he married Ethel Elsie Sylvia Risley and in June 1913 again went to India.

Promoted captain in January 1914, Squires sailed for France on the outbreak of World War I as assistant field engineer, Lahore Division. Although wounded at Givenchy in December, he continued his sapping operations for four hours before being evacuated. Back in the front line in 1915, he was wounded at Ypres, Belgium, on 25 April. After convalescing in England until August, he returned to France as field engineer, Lahore Division. Sailing with the division to Mesopotamia in December 1915, Squires saw action during the bitter fighting to relieve Kut and in the advance to Baghdad. In 1917 he commanded the field squadron of the Indian Cavalry Division, being promoted major in January 1918. He was awarded the Distinguished Service Order and the Military Cross, and was mentioned in dispatches six times, the last occasion being in 1919 during the Afghan war.

In 1920 Squires attended the Staff College,

Quetta, India, and thereafter held increasingly important staff and instructional appointments; he also attended the Imperial Defence College in 1928. Promoted major general in December 1935, he was appointed director of staff duties in April 1936.

In June 1938 Squires accepted the post of inspector general of the Australian Army (which carried the rank of lieut-general) in preference to that of general officer commanding, Southern Command, India. Some senior officers in Australia questioned the need for such an appointment, but the chief of the General Staff, J. D. Lavarack, foresaw that the Australian Army would benefit from the posting. Squires's first task was to investigate the army's preparedness for war. After reading his report, submitted to the government in December 1938, the chief of the Naval Staff, Sir Ragnar Colvin [q.v.8], threatened to resign because he felt that Squires had proposed too large a role for the army. The government, however, welcomed the report, as did the Military Board. Squires's proposals were sound and wide-ranging: they included raising a permanent force of all-arms, establishing a simplified command arrangement, forming new militia units and increasing the peacetime size of the army.

Under J. A. Lyons [q.v.10], the government began to approve many of the recommendations. Squires was greatly disappointed in 1939 when Lyons's successor, (Sir) Robert Menzies, withdrew approval for the most important proposal: the formation of a permanent force of 3600 troops. Nevertheless, other recommendations designed to increase the army's efficiency were carried out, such as the early retirement (Squires called it a much-needed 'purge') of a number of senior Staff Corps officers and the introduction of an administrative system more suited to active service.

When war broke out in September 1939 Squires, who had been acting C.G.S. since May, was confirmed in the post in time to oversee the formation of the 2nd Australian Imperial Force (so designated at his suggestion), but his health failed early in 1940. Survived by his wife, two daughters and a son, he died on 2 March in St Ives Private Hospital, East Melbourne, following surgery for cancer. His staff officer, Lieut-Colonel (Sir) Sydney Rowell, later wrote: 'Squires did not spare himself. He had a keen, alert mind, he spoke and wrote well and he showed a wide knowledge of all aspects of army life. The reports Squires wrote contained nothing he had not seen for himself, and he was generous in praise and incisive in criticism'. Squires's experience, intelligence, sincerity and amiability, and not least his imperturbable nature, ensured that he had received co-operation and respect from both soldiers and civilians during his time as inspector general and chief of the General Staff.

S. F. Rowell, *Full circle* (Melb, 1974); *Roy Engineers J*, 54, Sept 1940; *Herald* (Melb), 15 Mar 1939; F. Shedden papers (AA); J. Lavarack private collection (held by AWM); Squires papers sighted by author.   A. B. LODGE

STABLE, JEREMIAH JOSEPH (1883-1953), professor of English, was born on 14 May 1883 at Gawler, South Australia, son of Benjamin Stable, seaman, and his wife Mary Ann, née O'Connell. At the age of 4 he was taken to Switzerland where he lived with an aunt; he received his secondary education at the Collège de Genève. In 1902 he entered Emmanuel College, University of Cambridge, and read for the tripos in medieval and modern languages, specializing in English literature (B.A., 1905; M.A., 1909). A fine-featured, sensitive and athletic young man with a good reading voice, Stable tutored in English language and literature at the University of Commerce, Cologne, Germany; he also studied linguistics at Bonn. In 1908 he married Irene Bingham Sheridan and in 1912 took a position as lecturer in English, French and German at the University of Queensland.

In March 1916 Stable was appointed lieutenant, Australian Field Artillery, and in June promoted temporarily to captain for intelligence duties on the district censor's staff. Although tactful, he aroused controversy when—under the direct instructions of Prime Minister W. M. Hughes [q.v.9]—he entered the Queensland printing office on 26 November 1917 and seized all copies of no. 37 *Queensland Parliamentary Debates* because they contained an anti-conscription speech by Premier T. J. Ryan [q.v.11], parts of which Stable had previously censored from the press.

Resuming his full-time university duties in March 1919, Stable was appointed in 1922 to the McCaughey [q.v.5] chair (later Darnell chair) of English language and literature. His lectures were lucid and he was at his best with small groups of honours students. Tall and lean, calm and courteous, he endeared himself to his colleagues and pupils. He encouraged F. W. Robinson [q.v.11] in 1923 to teach Australian literature—the first time such a course was offered at any Australian university. Stable was dean of the faculty of arts (1932-39) and of the faculty of commerce (1932-36).

Stable influenced the intellectual and cultural life of the State. He was president of the Queensland Authors' and Artists' Association (1921-31) and of the English and Modern Languages Association of Queensland (1923-48); with Miss Barbara Sisley and Professor Michie [q.v.10], in 1925 he founded the Brisbane Repertory Theatre Society; in 1930 he became one of the first trustees of the reconstituted Queensland National Art Gallery and was chairman of trustees (1946-48).

A foundation member of the Queensland Historical Society in 1923, with Professor Henry Alcock he edited *The University of Queensland 1910-1922* (1923). For many years Stable contributed articles of literary criticism to the *Brisbane Courier*. His enthusiasm for the study of Australian literature was reflected in his compilation with A. E. M. Kirkwood of the anthology *A book of Queensland verse* (1924) to mark the Brisbane centenary. He insisted on links between Australian and English literature: his anthology for schools, *The bond of poetry* (1924), bore the motto '*Caelum non animum mutant qui trans mare currunt*'. *The high road of Australian verse* (1929) was followed by *The second bond of poetry* (1938) and by *Prose selections* (1947), compiled with A. K. Thomson. From 1936 Stable was general editor of the series, *The Australian students' Shakespeare*, to which he contributed an edition of *Julius Caesar* (1936).

During World War II he rendered service to the Commonwealth government as district censor for the Queensland lines of communication area from 1939 to 1942. He was in charge of the Commonwealth reconstruction training scheme within the university from 1944 and president of the professorial board and a member of the university senate from 1944 to 1952; in 1950 the degree of doctor of laws *honoris causa* was conferred upon him. On his retirement in 1952, Stable became the university's second professor emeritus.

Survived by his wife and three sons, Stable died of a coronary occlusion in his home at Indooroopilly, Brisbane, on 24 December 1953 and was cremated after a funeral service in St Mary's Anglican Church, Kangaroo Point.

E. Scott, *Australia during the war* (Syd, 1936); M. I. Thomis, *A place of light and learning* (Brisb, 1985); H. Gregory, *Vivant professores* (Brisb, 1987); Stable file (Univ Qld Archives); Stable papers (Fryer Lib); information from Justice N. S. Stable, Kenmore, and Prof A. K. Thomson, Taringa, Brisb; personal information.   J. C. MAHONEY

STACE, ARTHUR MALCOLM (1885-1967), pavement scribe, was born on 9 February 1885 at Redfern, Sydney, fifth child of William Wood Stace, a labourer from Mauritius, and his native-born wife Laura, née Lewis. Raised in poverty, Stace later claimed that he became a ward of the state when aged 12, worked for two years in a south-coast coal-mine, was gaoled for drunkenness, lost a succession of jobs and turned to thieving; he also claimed that his two sisters were prostitutes and his two brothers died derelict drunkards. 'Off and on I worked as a grog-runner from a hotel in Surry Hills to two-up schools and houses of ill-fame.' At the time of his enlistment in the Australian Imperial Force on 18 March 1916 he was a labourer, 5 ft. 3 ins. (160 cm) tall, with medium complexion, grey eyes and dark brown hair.

Having served as a private with the 19th Battalion in France, probably as a drummer and stretcher-bearer, and at A.I.F. headquarters in England, he returned to Australia in February 1919 and was discharged medically unfit on 2 May. Falling into old ways, drunk, broke and out of work, in August 1930 Stace was inspired by a preacher at Pyrmont to give up the grog. He helped down-and-out men at R. B. S. Hammond's [q.v.9] hostel, led open-air meetings in the city, and visited the Francis Street Methodist hostel, Callan Park mental hospital and the Lazaret. On 22 January 1942 he married Ellen Esther ('Pearl') Dawson, at St Barnabas's Anglican Church, Sydney, and described himself as a 'missioner'.

In the 1930s he had heard the evangelist John Ridley tell a congregation in Burton Street Baptist Tabernacle that he wished he could 'shout eternity through the streets of Sydney'. Stace was inspired! 'I felt a powerful call from the Lord to write "Eternity". I had a piece of chalk in my pocket, and I bent down right there and wrote it'; 'I've been writing it at least 50 times a day ever since.'

A 'birdlike little man with wispy white hair', Stace became known as 'the Eternity Man', one of the characters of Sydney. For a while he tried writing 'Obey God', but 'it wasn't as good. Eternity makes 'em think'. His cryptic precept in yellow, waterproof chalk, written in copperplate hand, was inscribed on pavements from Martin Place to Parramatta, although he preferred the invitingly black surface of the pavements at King's Cross. 'Some of them concrete paths won't take it', he complained. 'Too light to show up.' It cost him 'six bob a day in chalk' when he was 'running hot'. His one-word message could weather three to six months; one in Surry Hills, he was told, lasted twelve.

Pearl died in 1961 and in 1965 Stace moved from Pyrmont into the Hammondville homes. He died there on 30 July 1967, having bequeathed his body to the University of Sydney medical school and his savings to Baptist missions. In 1977 a brass inscription was unveiled in a paving stone near the Sydney Square waterfall. In the familiar copperplate hand it reads:

Eternity

SMH, 24 May 1958, 28 May 1959, 1, 5 Aug 1967, 23 Aug 1969, 13 July 1977, 12 July 1978; Herald (Melb), 10 July 1963, 16 June 1965.

CHRIS CUNNEEN

STACY, VALENTINE OSBORNE (1882-1929), soldier and medical practitioner, and BERTIE VANDELEUR (1886-1971), soldier and judge, were sons of Beauchamp Stacy, bank manager, and his wife Fannie Augusta Devenish, née Meares, and grandsons of John Edward Stacy [q.v.6]. Both were born at Mudgee, New South Wales, Valentine on 7 March 1882 and Bertie on 7 December 1886, and attended the local grammar school.

Valentine was a schoolboy trumpeter with the district's light horse company and tried to enlist in the Australian Light Horse during the South African War, but his parents insisted that he study medicine at the University of Sydney. He graduated M.B. in 1908 and served for a time as a ship's doctor. By 1911 he was in practice at Boulder, Western Australia. Next year he was commissioned in the Australian Army Medical Corps and allotted to the 1st Battalion, Goldfields Regiment. Appointed to the Australian Imperial Force as a captain with the 2nd Australian Stationary Hospital on 19 October 1914, he embarked for Egypt in December. The hospital was posted to Lemnos and Stacy served on troopships which carried wounded from there, and from Gallipoli, to Egypt. From November 1915 he was officer commanding the 2nd A.S.H., but late that month was invalided to England. Resuming duty in March 1916, he was promoted major in June, evacuated sick in July, and posted to No.1 Australian Casualty Clearing Station in France on 1 November. Promoted temporary lieut-colonel in November 1917, he commanded No.2 A.C.C.S. for the rest of the war and was confirmed in rank in November 1918.

In August 1919 Stacy returned to Western Australia and was demobilized in November. For his war service he was appointed O.B.E. (1919), awarded the French Croix de Guerre and twice mentioned in dispatches. Of his war service, which had seriously impaired his health, a colleague recalled: 'He was a martyr to duty . . . never sparing himself on . . . whatever task was set him. It is related that on one occasion 3000 Australian wounded men passed through his hands . . . within 24 hours'. Stacy resumed medical practice at Kalgoorlie in partnership with Dr Vere Arkle whom he later bought out; he was also A.A.M.C. area medical officer in 1920-26. His genial and generous disposition and his meticulous professionalism made him a popular and prominent goldfields figure. On 15 January 1923 at St James's Anglican Church, Moora, he married Eileen Dorcas O'Brien.

Survived by his wife and two infant sons, Stacy died at Kalgoorlie on 11 May 1929. A coronial inquiry concluded that his death was due to 'an overdose of morphia injected by himself, accidentally'. He was buried with full military honours in Kalgoorlie cemetery after a memorial service in St John the Baptist Anglican Cathedral. The 'large public assemblage of all ranks of citizens of the goldfields' showed the esteem in which he was held. A friend described him simply as 'small in stature and colossal in heart'.

Bertie Stacy began his military career as a sergeant in the School Cadets 4th Rifle Corps at Mudgee. He joined the Commercial Banking Co. of Sydney in 1903 and worked until 1909 at various city and country branches. In 1908-09 he also studied arts at the University of Sydney, becoming a full-time student in 1910 and graduating B.A. in 1911. He was then articled to Dibbs, Parker & Parker; in 1914 he graduated LL.B. and was admitted as a solicitor. On the outbreak of World War I he joined the A.I.F. as a private on 6 August 1914 and was commissioned second lieutenant, 4th Battalion, on 14 September.

The 4th Battalion took part in the Gallipoli landing on 25 April 1915 and Stacy, who was promoted lieutenant on 25 May, was wounded in action on 11 July. Resuming duty, he was promoted temporary captain on 17 October and confirmed in rank in January 1916; promotion to major followed in March. In France he remained with the 4th Battalion through the 1916 fighting on the Somme and until March 1917 when he was promoted lieut-colonel commanding the 1st Battalion, a post he held until the end of the war. On 4 October 1917, at Broodseinde, Belgium, he was wounded by a bomb thrown from a blockhouse and was out of action until early November. In 1915-19 he was mentioned in dispatches six times, awarded the Distinguished Service Order and Bar, and appointed C.M.G. Part of the citation for his Bar illustrateṣ his soldiering style: 'for conspicuous bravery in the attack on Chuignolles and Chuignes on 23 August 1918. He established his head quarters close behind the fighting troops . . . By personal reconnaissance he was able to direct the fire of the heavy artillery on the numerous field-guns and machine-guns which were causing casualties. Owing to his splendid leadership his battalion made an advance of nearly three miles and captured several hundred prisoners'. He returned to Australia in July 1919 and his A.I.F. appointment ended in September. While his apparent austerity and dogged determination to see a task through had sometimes made him unpopular, he was certainly respected by his troops. During World War II he commanded the Sydney University Regiment.

On 31 October 1919 Stacy had been admitted to the New South Wales Bar. On 15 September 1920 at St James's Anglican Church, Sydney, he married Mary Graham Lloyd; they were to have two daughters and a son. He practised as a barrister, mainly in common law, until 1925 when he became a crown prosecutor. Appointed to the District Court bench in 1939, he retired in 1956. As a judge, he was noted for his strictness of procedure and behaviour. A man of vigour and strength, he saw that his court was run with dignity, precision and punctuality. He disliked flowery speech and over-subtle argument, and would tolerate no nonsense. His lithe and agile figure, penetrating voice and piercing eyes gave him a commanding presence. Predeceased by his wife and survived by his children, he died at Darlinghurst, Sydney, on 6 December 1971 and was cremated.

C. E. W. Bean, *The story of Anzac*, 1, 2 (Syd, 1921, 1924), and *The A.I.F. in France 1916-18* (Syd, 1929, 1933, 1937, 1942); A. G. Butler (ed), *Official history of the Australian Army Medical Services in the war of 1914-1918*, 1 (Melb, 1938), 2 (Canb, 1940); G. E. Hall and A. Cousins (eds), *Book of remembrance of the University of Sydney in the war 1914-1918* (Syd, 1939); H. T. E. Holt, *A court rises* (Syd, 1976); *London Gazette*, 5 Nov 1915, 2 Jan, 1 June 1917, 28 May, 6 Nov, 31 Dec 1918, 1 Jan, 1 Feb, 3 June, 11 July 1919; *Listening Post*, 24 May 1929; *SMH*, 13 Aug 1917, 28 Oct 1919, 14 Apr 1938, 23 Mar 1939, 21 Nov, 8 Dec 1956, 7 Dec 1971; *Kalgoorlie Miner*, 13, 14 May 1929; War diaries, 1st *and* 4th Battalions, AIF *and* embarkation roll, 2nd ASH, 1914 (AWM); Lloyd family papers (held by author); Stacy family papers (held by Miss J. Stacy, Rose Bay, Syd).   MERRILYN LINCOLN
                                      D. E. LLOYD

STAINFORTH, MARTIN FRANK (1866-1957), artist, was born on 14 August 1866 at Martley, Worcestershire, England, one of eleven children of Rev. Frederick Stainforth, curate, and his wife Ann, née Shepherd. Taught wood-engraving by Baron Klinkicht, Martin lived in London and exhibited in 1895-99 at the Royal Academy of Arts, mostly producing Madonnas after Italian old masters. His work was chosen for exhibitions in Paris, Berlin and Brussels; it also appeared as illustrations in C. G. B. Allen's *Evolution in Italian art* (London, 1903). When wood-engraving was superseded, Stainforth switched to freelance magazine and book illustrating.

About 1908 he visited a cousin's cattle-station in North Queensland and sketched animals. Persuaded to remain in Australia after the death of the artist Douglas Fry, in 1911 Stainforth settled in Sydney. Leasing a studio in Hunter Street, he studied the moods, 'mannerisms and styles of horses and jockeys';

members of the racing fraternity 'would stop to chat with the slim, little man with the full moustache, who usually wore a tweed suit, bow tie and wide Stetson hat'.

He resolved to 'upset the tradition of race-horse portraiture started by Herring and other old timers [in which] . . . Every animal was shown with a ridiculously small head, tapering legs and tiny feet'. Stainforth's first commissions, Malt King (1911) and Trafalgar (1912), ensured his success. One of his favourite assignments was to visit Melbourne for the spring carnival: he painted many Melbourne Cup winners, including Artilleryman (1919), Poitrel (1920) and Windbag (1925). He carried out commissions for the Australian Jockey and Victoria Amateur Turf clubs, Sir Samuel Hordern [q.v.9], Sir William Cooper, the Falkiner [q.v.8] family and other leading owners.

Expert with oils and water-colour, Stainforth had the gift of detecting a horse's characteristics, the skill to paint a 'coat with such fine detail and beauty of texture that it resembles the work of a painter of miniatures', and the ability to depict speed and movement in his work. He 'was probably the finest painter of the racehorse ever to have worked in Australia'.

With a keen sense of wit, Stainforth liked to paint himself into crowd scenes and to comment on the nature of his subjects (he found Trafalgar 'full of intelligence and dignity'). In 1922 he provided the illustrations for *Racehorses in Australia*, published by S. Ure Smith's [q.v.11] Art in Australia Ltd. Stainforth exhibited with the Royal Art Society of New South Wales and in 1924 was a foundation committee-member of the Australian Water-Colour Institute.

Considering that 'art in Australia is not a gainful profession', he went to New Zealand about 1928 and returned to England in 1930. Stainforth was commissioned to paint Limelight ('a bad-tempered horse') in 1934 by King George V, Lord Derby's Hyperion and two pictures of Carbine (from photographs) for the duke of Portland. Late in 1934 Stainforth went to the United States of America. Known as the 'Hermit of Broadway', he lived at the Hotel Breslin, New York, and occasionally visited studs in Kentucky. He painted many celebrated American horses, among them War Admiral (1937). About 1949 Stainforth went home. He died at Hove, Sussex, on 22 April 1957, leaving an estate valued for probate at £17 967. Examples of his work are held by the Australian Jockey Club and by the National Museum of Racing, Saratoga Springs, New York.

K. Austin et al (eds), *Racehorses in Australia* (Syd, 1922); J. Fairley, *Great racehorses in art* (Oxford, Eng, 1984); B. Lillye, *Backstage of racing*

(Syd, 1985); *N.Z.L. Q Mag*, Sept 1923, p 25; *British Racehorse*, Nov 1960, p 444; *SMH*, 25 Oct 1920, 15 Apr, 19 Dec 1922, 29 Mar, 5 May, 11 July 1923, 10 Jan 1925; *Sun-Herald*, 25 June, 30 July, 13 Aug 1978.   MARTHA RUTLEDGE

STANBURY, JAMES (1868-1945), sculler, was born on 25 February 1868 at Mullet Island, Broken Bay, New South Wales, son of James Stanbury, a farm labourer from Devonshire, and his Sydney-born wife Catherine, née Reilly. Several years later the family shifted to Nowra where young James learned to row on the Shoalhaven. In 1887 he moved to Sydney to join the professional sculling ranks and within a year had stunned onlookers by finishing a close second when Henry Searle [q.v.6] set a Parramatta River record.

Contemporaries described Stanbury's rowing as rough, with most of the drive coming from his arms: Bill Beach [q.v.3] claimed he had never seen so much power gained from such bad rowing. Beach and another former world champion, Peter Kemp, took him in hand; Stanbury confirmed his early promise when he captured John McLean's world title on 28 April 1891. He defended the title successfully in July 1891 and in May next year trounced Tom Sullivan, the New Zealand champion.

With no Australian willing to challenge him, Stanbury left in February 1893 for the United States of America to row against Canadian Jacob Gaudaur, but returned to Australia when terms could not be settled. Following Stanbury's successful defence of his title against Charles Harding, the English champion, in July 1896 in London, Gaudaur agreed to race over the neutral Thames course. In a contest where Stanbury claimed a foul, Gaudaur took the world title on 7 September. The Australian was received coolly in Sydney for having refused to row out the match at racing speed.

After another Australian, George Towns, had wrested the championship from Gaudaur (1901), Stanbury challenged Towns; in July 1905 he surprised the champion by regaining the title, but next year he was easily defeated. The moustachioed Stanbury was well-built, with a 'great development of muscle', which caused one observer to comment that he looked 'ridiculously out of proportion to his little boat'. His racing weight in 1891 was 12 st. 4 lb. (78 kg), his chest was 41½ ins. (105.4 cm) and he stood 5 ft. 11½ ins. (181.6 cm) tall.

Like many other professional scullers, Big Jim Stanbury had made his headquarters at Ryde. He found lodgings at the Royal Hotel where he met the licensee's daughter, Eliza Jane ('Dolly') Jordan, whom he married in

Sydney on 4 January 1893. After living briefly at Waterfall, where he was a (Royal) National Park caretaker, Stanbury bought an orchard at North Ryde and sold peaches, plums and nectarines until handing over active management to his son James in 1940. Survived by his wife, six daughters and a son, he died on 11 December 1945 at Ryde and was buried in the Presbyterian section of the Field of Mars cemetery. At Gladesville, so long the haunt of those whom A. B. Paterson [q.v.11] described as aquatic gladiators, Stanbury Street lies close by Beach, Kemp, Searle and Towns streets.

Referee, 19 July 1888, 29 Apr 1891, 14 July 1896, 19, 22, 26 July 1905, 25, 30 July 1906; *SMH*, 29 Apr 1891, 14 July 1896, 30 July 1906; information from Mrs Clara Allen, Lismore.

SCOTT BENNETT

STANDLEY, IDA (1869-1948), schoolteacher, was born on 19 January 1869 in Adelaide, one of six children of Hanson Woodcock, butcher, and his wife Bertha, née Franklin. Educated at Misses Lucy and Florence Tilley's Hardwicke House Ladies' College, Ida went as governess to the Standley family at Mount Wudinna station on Eyre Peninsula. On 12 August 1887, aged 18, she married George Standley, a 35-year-old farmer. Periodically left to fend for herself, with three daughters and a son to rear, in 1897 Ida became a probationary teacher at the Boothby school, near Cleve, and taught up to twenty-four children. By the time she left Boothby for Gawler River in 1903, her marriage had ended. In 1911 she transferred to Buchfelde. By 1914, after eighteen years in one-teacher schools, her salary had increased from £65 to £100 per annum and her children were old enough to be independent.

In that year the South Australian Education Department advertised for a woman teacher for Alice Springs. No one applied. After local parents agreed to cover the cost of board and washing, Standley took the post and was paid £150. In May she went by train to Oodnadatta whence she was escorted by a constable on a fourteen-day buggy trip to Alice Springs. The school, at the back of the gaol, was formerly a warder's residence, 'a little stone room with a couple of windows and a door'. White parents protested when she suggested that all children attend together, so she taught eleven White children, six mornings a week, and fourteen part-Aborigines on five afternoons. She eventually received an allowance from the Education Department and moved into 'Myrtle Villa', a slab-walled cottage in Wills Terrace.

Under the policy of separating children of mixed descent from their Aboriginal mothers,

the police took them to the 'Bungalow', two galvanized iron sheds with earth floors. Mrs Standley was given charge of the makeshift institution and paid an additional £50. While the number of children at her morning classes declined, the bungalow became so overcrowded that by 1923 sixty children—aged between a few months and 16 years—slept huddled on the floor. Although Professor (Sir) Baldwin Spencer [q.v.] and other visitors condemned the bungalow, plans to build a new institution were postponed. By hard work, efficiency and compassion, Ida Standley gave her Aboriginal children a basic education and increased their self-esteem. A sturdy matron, prim and proper, clothed to neck, wrist and ankle, she still conveyed affection for the children, many of whom called her 'Mum'.

In 1928 the Aboriginal children were shifted to an incomplete new home at Jay Creek, about 30 miles (48 km) west of Alice Springs. Ida delayed her retirement to go with them and spent the summer in a tent. She left the Alice in 1929 and was appointed M.B.E. For fifteen years she had been the only government teacher in Central Australia. Popular and respected, she was described by the press as the 'Beloved Lady'. Retiring to Adelaide, she died at Manly, Sydney, on 29 May 1948 and was buried with Catholic rites at Frenchs Forest. Three daughters survived her. Standley Chasm, near Jay Creek, and the Ida Standley Pre-School, Alice Springs, commemorate her, and a plaque marks the site of her home in Wills Terrace.

School Alice Springs, A518 F241/6/11 *and* Bungalow, A1 27/2982 *and* I. Standley, A1 33/7458 *and* Half-Caste Home, A659 39/1/996 (AA, Canb).

H. N. NELSON

STANFORD, THOMAS WELTON (1832-1918), businessman, spiritualist and philanthropist, was born at Albany, New York State, United States of America, youngest son of Josiah Stanford, public works contractor, and his wife Elizabeth, née Phillips. Educated locally and at Troy Conference Academy, Vermont, in 1852 he abandoned his plans of schoolteaching for the lure of the Californian goldfields which attracted all six Stanford brothers. By 1858 they ran the largest of the western oil companies. Drawn to the Australian colonies by rumours of a strong demand for kerosene, in December 1859 Thomas Welton and his brother De Witt sailed for Melbourne.

Acquiring exclusive Australian marketing rights, Welton—as from 1863 he signed himself—devised innovative ways of promoting the Singer sewing machine, among them time payment. His salesmen travelled through country districts with a model machine mounted on the back of a buggy. Despite stiff competition, they had record sales in 1876-77. Singer policy, however, changed. By the early 1880s the company had taken direct control of Australian distribution.

After De Witt's death in 1862, Stanford had become increasingly lonely. On 12 May 1869 in Melbourne he married Wilhelmina (Minnie) Watt with Wesleyan Methodist forms; she died within a year. He later moved to Clarendon Street, East Melbourne, where he became known for his garden of rare plants, his aviaries of exotic birds, his fine collection of Australian paintings, and, most of all, for his interest in spiritualism.

A 'man of six feet (182.9 cm) or more, dark, with heavy black beard' and 'piercing black eyes', Stanford in 1870 founded the Victorian Association of Progressive Spiritualists with W. H. Terry [q.v.6] and J. B. Motherwell. For many years the 'father of spiritualism in Australia' held exclusive meetings at his home and in his Russell Street office. Concerned for the welfare of her tall, thin, reclusive brother-in-law, Jane Stanford (his brother Leland's widow) visited him in 1903. Disillusioned with seances, she left Australia. Perhaps spurred by her attitude, Stanford gave US$50 000 for psychical research to the Leland Stanford Junior University which had been founded (1885) in California as a memorial to her only son; Welton had previously donated his US$300 000 legacy from Leland who had been a highly successful railroad president.

A member of Stanford University's board of trustees, Welton talked of establishing scholarships for Australian students. He donated his books on Australia and his art collection to be housed in the Thomas Welton Stanford Library which was built, and restored after the 1906 earthquake, with his money. Stanford history students were soon studying 'Australian affairs'.

Although he had threatened to become a British subject during the American Civil War, Stanford remained loyal to the U.S.A. and had served intermittently from 1890 to 1902 as honorary vice consul-general in Melbourne. He died at his home on 28 August 1918 and was buried in the Methodist section of Melbourne general cemetery. The bulk of his personal estate, valued for probate at £130 043, also went to Stanford University, for psychical research.

S. Dickinson, *Catalogue of oil paintings in the collection of T. W. Stanford, Esq., of Melbourne* (Melb, 1882); E. D. and A. Potts, 'Thomas Welton Stanford (1832-1918) and American-Australian business and cultural relations', *Hist Studies*, no 67, Oct 1967, p 193; Stanford papers (Stanford Univ Archives, California, USA); Singer Manufactory Co. papers (State Hist Soc, Wisconsin, USA).

E. DANIEL POTTS

STANG, ELEANOR MARGRETHE (RITA) (1894-1978), medical practitioner, was born on 1 June 1894 at South Yarra, Melbourne, eldest child of Norwegian-born Thomas Newbould Stang, medical practioner and civil servant, and his wife Eleanor Bath, née Eastwood. Educated at Presbyterian Ladies' College from 1905, Rita graduated in medicine from the University of Melbourne in 1918 and completed her Diploma of Public Health (1927). She practised at Port Fairy and was resident medical officer at Melbourne public hospitals. On 10 January 1919 at Hawthorn she married Norman Arthur Albiston, medical practitioner; they had no children and were divorced in 1927.

Replacing Roberta Jull [q.v.9], in 1925 Rita was appointed medical officer of schools in the Western Australian Public Health Department; after a year's experience in London, in 1929 she became supervisor of infant health in Western Australia, holding both positions until she retired in 1955. Dr Stang had, in 1931-46, only one doctor and two nurses to help her; cheerful, energetic and persistent, she saw her staff increase to fourteen by 1951 which made inspection of some kindergartens and Aboriginal missions possible. Her efforts resulted in improved hygiene and the reduction of pediculosis in government schools from a State average of 14.8 per cent in 1925 to 0.69 per cent in 1951. Her nurses visited homes to discuss treatment, especially if parents were negligent. To improve children's diets, the Oslo Lunch was introduced.

Her work was crucial. Infant health centres grew from ten to forty-six, with three hundred sub-centres; by 1955 a special carriage, a mothercraft 'oasis' attached to the 'tea and sugar' train, travelled to remote settlements on the Nullarbor Plain. Infant health sisters received explicit instructions and attended refresher courses, while in 1932 a correspondence sister was appointed to help families in isolated areas. The Eleanor M. Stang Infant Health Centre in Perth became a mecca for country mothers. Dr Stang also gave weekly radio talks and wrote press articles. Her achievements significantly decreased infant mortality.

A member of the National Fitness Council, an examiner for the University of Western Australia and a lecturer in hygiene at the Teachers' Training College, Claremont, Dr Stang broached sex education by inviting students home for a lecture and discussion. By holding a senior position in the predominantly male medical circle and by winning respect for her administrative skill, hard work and professional knowledge, she was a pathmaker in the entry of women to the professions. Concerned with her own status and authority, she fought to raise her salary to that of her male colleagues. In 1948 she was co-founder and first president of the local branch of the Medical Women's Society.

Dr Stang was a strongly built woman who believed in strict control over her sisters and students. Many thought her formidable. She clashed with at least one commissioner of public health whose 1946 report criticized the School Medical Service. Yet, her associates found her fair-minded and generous. After retiring, Rita returned to Victoria where she worked as locum tenens and as ship's doctor, and enjoyed her hobbies of travel and pottery. She died on 18 July 1978 in Melbourne and was cremated. Her estate was sworn for probate at $219 193.

N. A. Stewart, *As I remember them* (Perth, 1987); Commissioner for Public Health, *Annual Report*, 1931-55 (bound copies held in Health Dept of WA, Perth); *West Australian*, 16 Apr, 22 Dec 1932, 19 Feb 1955; *Daily News* (Perth), 23 Nov 1944; Public Health Dept of WA, Infant Health Council, Minute-book, 1932-34, *and* Infant Health Assn, Minute-book, 1924-32, *and* Infant Health Correspondence Scheme, Minute-book, 1934-53 (held by Health Dept of WA, Perth).

M. TAMBLYN

STANLEY, ARTHUR LYULPH, 5TH BARON STANLEY OF ALDERLEY (1875-1931), governor, was born on 14 September 1875 in London, eldest son of Edward Lyulph Stanley, later 4th baron (d. 1925), and his wife Mary Katharine, née Bell, granddaughter of Sir Isaac Lowthian Bell, the millionaire ironmaster of Durham. Belonging to one of England's most famous ruling families, Arthur spent his childhood at the Stanley seats in Cheshire and north Wales. He was educated at Eton (1889-1894) and Balliol College, Oxford (B.A., 1898; M.A., 1902), and served with the militia in the South African War. In 1902 he was called to the Bar at the Inner Temple and two years later was elected to the London County Council. On 29 August 1905 he married Margaret Evelyn Evans Gordon in the parish church at Ightham, Kent. Stanley was Liberal member for Eddisbury division of Cheshire in 1906-10 and parliamentary private secretary to the postmaster-general. A free-thinker, he was exceptionally literate, well-informed and held firm, liberal views. Handsome and charming, with the ease and courtesy of his breeding, he had 'a brisk sense of humour' and a schoolboy appreciation of practical jokes, but was outwardly austere.

In November 1913 Stanley was offered the governorship of Victoria. Appointed K.C.M.G. in January 1914, he arrived in Melbourne on 22 February where his youthful appearance, 'homeliness' and undisguised anxiety to please made a favourable impression. World War I largely determined and dominated his duties: he traversed the State

encouraging donations to patriotic funds, supported recruiting drives and privately agreed with W. M. Hughes's [q.v.9] position on conscription.

Sir Arthur faced a delicate social and political situation. Since Federation no Victorian governor had seen out his full (five-year) term and the governorship had been beset with dissatisfaction, frustration and controversy. There had been agitation to appoint only Australians to the position and some laborites argued for the abolition of the office. Stanley came to agree with these sentiments, albeit for different reasons: he found little work to do; ministers resented any interference in their affairs; and, as both governor and governor-general then resided in the same city, the presence of the State governor was awkward, confusing and superfluous. In August 1917 Stanley offered to resign; when requested by the Colonial Office to remain a further year, he reluctantly agreed. After suffering a duodenal haemorrhage, he left Melbourne on 30 July 1919 on leave of absence and his appointment ended on 30 January 1920.

A director of the National Bank of Australasia and of the Australian Mercantile, Land & Finance Co., Stanley briefly returned to Australia in 1923. That year he failed by 80 votes to win a seat (Knutsford) in the House of Commons. He was chairman (1925-28) of the Royal Colonial Institute and of the East Africa Joint Committee. Stanley died of actinomycosis on 22 August 1931 in London following an operation. His wife, a son and three daughters survived him.

A. Lubbock, *People in glass houses* (Melb, 1977); *Bulletin*, 4 Dec 1913; *Age*, 29 Dec 1913, 23 Feb 1914; *Argus*, 29 Dec 1913, 24 Aug 1931; *Australasian*, 3 Jan 1914; *Punch* (Melb), 19 Mar 1914; *The Times*, 24 Aug 1931; Official Dispatches between Sir A. Stanley and Colonial Office, vols 9, 10, 11 (1914-17) (Govt House Lib, Melb); Stanley papers (LaTL).

ELIZABETH CHAM

STANLEY, CHARLES ROY (1899-1954), advertising executive and publicist, was born on 2 March 1899 at Karangahake, New Zealand, son of Thomas James Stanley, miner, and his wife Julia Elsie, née Robinson, both from Thames, New Zealand. Roy was educated at Te Aroha Public School and Pau College, Auckland, and worked as a draper for G. Court & Sons. Enlisting in the Auckland Regiment, New Zealand Expeditionary Force, on 11 October 1915, he was wounded in Belgium in 1917 and discharged on 2 March 1919. Stanley then went to China as manager of the Chiang-Chow branch of the British American Tobacco Co. Moving to

Sydney in 1921, he was employed in the production department of Parke, Davis & Co. In New Zealand from 1923 he worked for two years as manager of the Dunedin branch of Gordon and Gotch (Australasia) Ltd, advertising agents, and for a year with the country's leading advertising agency, J. Ilott Ltd. On 3 April 1924 he married Gladys Reeve Holme in Wellington.

Settling in Sydney in 1926 as manager of Ilott's Australian operations, Stanley founded (1928) and was secretary (until 1954) of the Australian Association of National Advertisers. Largely due to his efforts the Audit Bureau of Circulation was established in 1931: it required newspaper proprietors to provide reliable and verifiable circulation figures. He contributed numerous articles to trade papers like the *Advertisers' Monthly*, mostly on the association and bureau, but periodically on such subjects as agency contracts, waste and inefficiency in expenditure, and local government restrictions on outdoor advertising.

He served on the committee of the New Zealand and South Seas International Exhibition (Dunedin, 1925-26), managed the Australian Manufacturers' Exhibition (Sydney, 1927), organized the exhibition held concurrently with the sixth Australian Advertising Convention in 1931 and was a member of the construction committee for the Australian pavilions at New York's World's Fair (1939). Stanley was a foundation committeemember of the Sydney Publicity Club from 1929 and honorary foundation secretary of the Outdoor Advertising Association of Australia from 1939 until he retired. President for ten years of the New Zealand sub-branch of the Returned Sailors' and Soldiers' Imperial League of Australia in the 1930s, he was also honorary Australian liaison officer of the New Zealand Returned Services Association and organized the national clothing collection for overseas relief in 1945. He belonged to the New South Wales and Mona Vale golf clubs.

Having been divorced in September 1940, Stanley married Gertrude Alice Pidcock on 23 October at Randwick, where they lived; they had no children. Stanley was killed on 12 September 1954 in a motor car accident at Pymble and was buried with Methodist forms in Botany cemetery. His wife survived him.

E. G. Knox (ed), *The advertisers' and publishers' guide of Australia and New Zealand* (Syd, 1935); Audit Bureau of Circulations, *Twenty-five years* (Syd, 1957); *A'sian Manufacturer,* 17 Dec 1927, p 9, 24 Dec 1927, special exhibition no, p 31; *Newspaper News* (Syd), Dec 1928, p 1, Apr 1931, p i, Sept 1938, p 2, Oct 1954; *SPC,* Nov 1930, p 1, Apr 1931, p 3; *Daily Telegraph* (Syd) and *SMH,* 13 Sept 1954.   GAIL REEKIE

STANLEY, GEORGE ARTHUR VICKERS (1904-1965), geologist and geographer, was born on 26 July 1904 at Little Coogee, Sydney, only child of John Arthur Hall Stanley, estate agent, and his wife Elizabeth, née Moyse, both Australian born. After his mother's death, George was raised from the age of 5 by close relations at Randwick. He attended Sydney Technical College and the University of Sydney (B.Sc., 1926), graduating with first-class honours in geology and geography. Joining a party which surveyed Ontong Java atoll in the Solomon Islands, he later took part in a university survey of the Great Barrier Reef.

In 1927 Stanley was employed by the Anglo-Persian Oil Co. and travelled to Papua and the Mandated Territory of New Guinea where he was to live and work for the rest of his life. In 1930-33 he carried out geological surveys along the coastal ranges between Matapau and Aitape. Appointed by Oil Search Ltd of Sydney in 1934 as leader of a team to carry the survey south of the Torricelli mountains between Maprik and Lumi, he concentrated on an anticlinal structure at Wambara which he was convinced would be worth drilling, but in 1939 the survey was abandoned. That year he investigated possible oil exploration leases near the Dutch border, visited oil fields in the Dutch East Indies and worked for the Australasian Petroleum Co. in Papua.

With the Japanese invasion Stanley left Papua in June 1942. As a lieutenant in the Royal Australian Navy Volunteer Reserve he was attached to the Far Eastern Liaison Organisation, a secret propaganda unit, and returned to Port Moresby. He recruited, trained and supervised local men to act as Australian agents. In 1943 he participated in 'Moss Troop', an unsuccessful attempt to land forces behind Japanese lines on the Upper Sepik, and in 1944 reported on troop movements in the Torricelli foothills. Although the sometimes controversial activities of Stanley and his agents were questioned by other Australians operating in the Sepik, he was awarded the D.S.C. in 1945.

In 1947 Stanley rejoined A.P.C. as a senior geologist. In 1956 he joined the Papuan Apinaipi Oil Co. On 11 November 1961 he married Palu Hehuni of Tupusereia village. Stanley increasingly adopted a studied eccentricity. Although a well-educated and cultured European, president of the Port Moresby Scientific Society, member of the Australian and New Zealand Association for the Advancement of Science, and owner of perhaps the best library of Papua New Guineana, he dressed in a singlet and baggy shorts, and drove about Port Moresby in a battered Landrover, with two or three Papua-New Guineans, collecting empty bottles. In 1962 Stanley joined the Australian Bureau of

Mineral Resources, Canberra. During his last years he was troubled by lack of money and long separations from his family. Suffering from cancer, he returned to Port Moresby where, after receiving Anglican confirmation, he died on 6 October 1965 and was buried in the local cemetery. His wife and daughter survived him. Much of his valuable library went to the University of Papua New Guinea.

A large man, even by the late 1930s Stanley travelled extremely slowly on foot in the bush and was sometimes carried. His scientific contribution was his detailed geological mapping and synthesizing of the exploratory work of others. Stanley was not at home in either colonial European or Papua New Guinean culture. While he disliked the post-war colonial society, he held some of the prejudices towards Papua New Guineans of the pre-war European society.

P. Ryan (ed), *Encyclopaedia of Papua and New Guinea*, 2 (Melb, 1972); D. M. Fenbury papers *and* H. A. J. Fryer papers (NL); G. A. V. Stanley papers (UPNG Lib, Port Moresby).   B. J. ALLEN

STANLEY, MILLICENT FANNY; *see* PRESTON STANLEY

STANSFIELD, WILLIAM (1874-1946), railway officer and soldier, was born on 19 November 1874 at Wadsworth, Yorkshire, England, son of Mitchell Stansfield, master bootmaker, and his wife Margaret Jane, née Forrester. The family migrated to Queensland in 1887, settling in Brisbane where William attended Kelvin Grove State School. He became a printer and, on 13 December 1897, married Amy Louisa Rogers at Ann Street oval with Methodist forms; they were to have three sons and two daughters.

In 1898 Stansfield entered the administration of the Queensland State Railways where he worked until 1914. His career as a soldier had begun in January 1900 when he enlisted in the militia in the Moreton Regiment. Transferred in 1905 to the Australian Army Service Corps, he was promoted warrant officer, class 2, in 1908 and commissioned second lieutenant in 1911.

On 20 August 1914 Stansfield enlisted in the Australian Imperial Force and was posted to the 1st Light Horse Brigade Train. He was appointed brigade supply officer with the rank of captain in October. Landing at Anzac with his brigade on 12 May 1915, he was made officer commanding the beach supply depot of the New Zealand and Australian Division, of which the brigade was part. In August he returned to his brigade and was responsible for its supplies until the eve of the evacuation in December.

When Major General (Sir) Harry Chauvel [q.v.7] formed the Anzac Mounted Division in Egypt in March 1916, he gave his former supply officer command of all the Divisional A.A.S.C. units and promoted him major. In the operations of April 1916-April 1917 that saw the Turkish thrust for the Suez Canal crushed at Romani, Sinai cleared of the enemy and two attempts on Gaza, Stansfield proved himself a master of movement and supply. Consequently, when the Desert Mounted Corps was formed in August 1917, Chauvel made Stansfield—by then a lieut-colonel—his assistant director of supply and transport. The operations that began with the capture of Beersheba on 31 October 1917 placed enormous demands on the logistic services, yet British officers were reported to have remarked: 'the Australians always seemed to have their supplies up with them . . . if resource and energy could work miracles the Australian supply officers deserve the credit for them'. The award (rare in the Army Service Corps) of the Distinguished Service Order in December 1917 crowned Stansfield's achievements.

In 1918 he supplied the Desert Mounted Corps in the malaria-ridden Jordan Valley during static operations which were punctuated by the unsuccessful attempt to capture Es Salt, 1 April-4 May. The battles beginning at Megiddo on 19 September, and the capture of Damascus and Aleppo after advances of some 300 to 500 miles (480-800 km), tested Stansfield's organization to the limit. Not least of his problems was the maintenance of tens of thousands of prisoners. For his 'continuous zeal and ability' and his success in these operations, Stansfield was appointed C.M.G. He was mentioned in dispatches three times in 1917-19.

Returning to Brisbane, he was discharged in October 1919 and slipped quietly back into his old job in the railways. When Sir Harry Chauvel came to Brisbane in December 1919 he praised Stansfield's 'wonderful organization . . . [and] efficient work [which] made the great advance . . . possible'. Disturbed to find Stansfield in such a humble post, Chauvel approached the head of Queensland's railways who appointed Stansfield inspector of passenger rolling stock on 1 January 1920. During the royal visits of 1927 and 1934 Stansfield was State transport officer for Queensland.

He joined the A.A.S.C. of the 1st Division, Australian Military Forces, in 1921, in the rank of captain with the brevet of major. He was promoted lieut-colonel in 1922, commanding Headquarters 5th Divisonal Train and all A.A.S.C. units in the 1st Military District (Queensland) for five years. Placed on the retired list in 1937 as honorary colonel, he returned again as assistant director of remounts, Northern Command, in 1939. His final retirement came in April 1941. Survived by his wife and children, Stansfield died in (Royal) Brisbane Hospital on 19 May 1946 and was cremated.

H. S. Gullett, *The A.I.F. in Sinai and Palestine* (Syd, 1923); A. J. Hill, *Chauvel of the Light Horse* (Melb, 1978); *Courier Mail*, 21 May 1946; A.A.S.C. records for Egypt and Palestine (AWM).

A. J. HILL

STANTON, RICHARD PATRICK JOSEPH (1862-1943), auctioneer and real estate agent, was born on 1 February 1862 probably at Strokestown, Roscommon, Ireland, son of Patrick Stanton, policeman, and his first wife Anne Maria, née Mulvehill. The family reached Sydney as assisted migrants on 29 November in the *Eastern Empire*. Raised as a Catholic, he was educated at St Mary's College, Lyndhurst. In 1882 his father set up as a real estate agent and furniture dealer at Summer Hill; Richard took over Stanton & Son when his father died in 1889. An alderman on Ashfield Municipal Council (1890-1914), he was mayor in 1893-94 and 1906. At Ashfield he had married with Presbyterian forms Florence Beatrice Nicholls, daughter of an accountant, on 1 November 1893; she participated in her husband's property dealings.

The Nicholls became involved in Stanton's business ventures: with them he purchased land north of Parramatta Road at Ashfield in 1901. The Haberfield estate integrated subdivision, controls, house construction and tree-planting in a single development which was marketed as a 'Garden Suburb'. Stanton was influenced by an astute assessment of the real estate market, rather than by attachment to the *rus in urbe* ideal. Rosebery model and industrial suburb followed.

In 1902 Stanton had established a city office in Pitt Street in which the Nicholls were again involved. With H. M. Hawkins [q.v.9] and other agents, in 1908 he formed the Western Suburbs Real Estate Agents Association. Using his personal standing to overcome the animosity between city and suburban real estate agents, he called a meeting in September 1910 which established the Real Estate Auctioneers and Agents' Association of New South Wales (Real Estate Institute from 1921). He long served on its board and was president in 1922-23. Always interested in the latest ideas, Stanton visited North America (1905), Britain (1913 and 1923) and made a world tour (1927-29). In 1916 a timber bungalow of California design had been erected on his estate at Rosebery; the style was widely adopted.

In 1913 he had established Stanton & Son Ltd as a private company with himself the governing director; his two sons later joined the firm. By 1924 he had opened eight suburban branch offices. He invested in country properties and in the 1920s was managing director of Bindebange station, Queensland, Haberfield Pty Ltd, the Town Planning Co. of Australia Ltd and several other real estate companies, and was chairman of the London & Lancashire Insurance Co. Ltd. In 1929 he rebuilt Stanton House, at 133 Pitt Street, but the business encountered difficulties during the Depression. He was a member of the State government's Town Planning Advisory Board, chairman of the Queen Victoria Homes for Consumptives and a fellow of the Auctioneers' and Estate Agents' Institute of the United Kingdom (1913). A valuer to the Sydney Municipal Council, he also advised local, State and Federal governments on resumption schemes.

Stanton had regular features, carefully-waved grey hair and a cleft chin. He lived for many years at Haberfield and liked playing golf, but, professional in outlook, he made business his main hobby. Experienced and astute, he unsuccessfully sought to improve the public perception of property agents and to raise the ethics of the profession. Survived by his wife, two sons and two daughters, Stanton died in debt at his Potts Point home on 11 April 1943 and was cremated with Anglican rites.

J. M. Freeland, *Architecture in Australia* (Melb, 1968); T. Kass, *The sign of the Waratah* (Syd, 1987); *Real Estate Inst of NSW, J*, Jan 1940, May 1943; Cwlth Inst of Valuers, *Valuer*, 1 Jan 1938; Minutes of Bd *and* General Meetings, 1910-43 (Real Estate Inst of NSW, Syd); Companies Office, Company packets, no 5021, Stanton & Sons Ltd (NSWA).

TERRY KASS

STAPLETON, CLAUDE AUGUSTINE (1894-1974), soldier and health inspector, was born on 13 March 1894 at Charters Towers, Queensland, son of William Stapleton, postman, and his wife Mary Ann, née McAuliffe, both native-born. He attended Christian Brothers College and the Charters Towers School of Mines. An accomplished horseman, he worked as a stockman to finance further studies and was a station-hand when he enlisted as a private in the Australian Imperial Force on 27 April 1915.

He joined 'B' Company, 26th Battalion, and embarked for Egypt as a sergeant in May. In September he reached Gallipoli where his battalion served until 12 December; it was transferred to the Western Front in France in March 1916. At Pozières Stapleton twice distinguished himself under fire: on 29 July he led his platoon during an attack; on 4 August, when casualties were heavy, he assumed command of his company. 'He was most energetic and determined throughout in defending his own particular area and was especially prominent in helping to repel counter-attacks.' For his leadership, he received the Distinguished Conduct Medal and the Russian Order of St George. On 16 August 1916 he was commissioned second lieutenant.

While commanding a platoon in the miserable, winter-bound trenches near Flers, Stapleton was promoted lieutenant in December. He was attached to the 2nd Division Reinforcement Depot before rejoining his battalion for the battles of the Hindenburg outpost line in March 1917. During the attack on Lagnicourt on the 26th, he commanded a party which cleared the eastern outskirts of the heavily defended village; with survivors from his platoon, he established a post and—under orders from Captain P. H. Cherry [q.v.7]—held his position during fierce enemy counter-attacks; for two hours the squad repelled assaults from three sides. Stapleton was awarded the Military Cross. Wounded on 28 April, he was later sent to a training battalion.

Rejoining the 26th Battalion in November, Stapleton went with it to the Somme after the opening of the German offensive in 1918. At Morlancourt on 9 June he was again wounded, but remained on duty. On 25 July he was made temporary captain. In the war's closing operations Stapleton again 'showed great courage and able leadership' on the Beaurevoir line when, on 3 October, he cut a path through German entanglements, enabling his men to advance. He then led a party against a machine-gun post and put the gun out of action, for which he won a Bar to his M.C.

Back in Queensland in 1919, Stapleton became a soldier settler, growing pineapples at Glasshouse Mountain and supplementing his income by seasonal cane-cutting. On 5 January 1922 he married Mabel Elizabeth Johnston in Brisbane. He worked as a health inspector for the local shire council at Ayr. In World War II he was appointed an instructor in jungle warfare and held several training appointments until June 1945. He then resumed his post as health inspector. Survived by his wife, three daughters and a son, Stapleton died in Royal Brisbane Hospital on 2 February 1974 and was buried in Redcliffe cemetery with Catholic rites.

C. E. W. Bean, *The A.I.F. in France* 1916-18 (Syd, 1929, 1933, 1937, 1942); information from Mr N. D. Stapleton, Buderim, Qld.

PETER BURNESS

STAPLEY, FRANK (1858-1944), architect and town planner, was born on 24 October 1858 at Hove, Sussex, England, second of three sons of Isaac Stapley, policeman, and his wife Mary Ann, née Hilton. Educated at Hove and trained as an architect, Stapley went to South Africa in 1880 where he practised in Cape Town and on the Kimberley diamond fields. After contracting fever, in 1883 he returned to England. On 5 January 1884 at the parish church, Exeter, he married Eliza Sutherland Dunning (d. 1924) with whom he migrated to Victoria. He joined the office of William Salway, a leading Melbourne architect, worked with the city surveyor's department of the Melbourne City Council in 1887-93, and later practised on his own account and in partnership. Stapley designed domestic, commercial and industrial buildings, including the West Melbourne stadium which had a large interior space without internal roof supports.

As Melbourne's chief advocate of town planning, he was to be influential for more than three decades. The Victorian Town Planning and Parks Association was formed in 1914 and a series of conferences was held throughout Australia in 1917-19. A key figure in this movement, Stapley brought to it the prestige of his presidency of the Royal Victorian Institute of Architects in 1920-21. He was appointed foundation chairman of the nine-member Metropolitan Town Planning Commission in 1922. The commission dealt with many important issues and in its final report (1929) produced a master plan which focused on road transport, land-use zoning and open space. Although well received in professional circles, its recommendations were never comprehensively implemented: with the onset of the Depression, the economic and political climate was unfavourable, and planning at the metropolitan level was inhibited by a plethora of municipalities, much to Stapley's regret.

A member of Melbourne City Council from 1901, Stapley was mayor in 1917-18 and an alderman in 1921-39. He chaired the council's parks and gardens committee, and was also a member of the Melbourne and Metropolitan Board of Works, the Health Commission and the National War Memorial Committee. In 1926 he became the subject of society interest when, following the death of his elder brother Harry, he refused to claim a family title of dubious authenticity, observing that 'it would hardly harmonise with conditions out here'. Tall and handsome, Stapley was a personable reformer. An atypical city councillor of the period, with little in common with his colleagues, he was greatly disappointed by the failure of State and civic authorities to adopt his visionary plan. He was still urging Melburnians in 1935 to prepare for a population of two million within the next fifty years.

Stapley died in Royal Melbourne Hospital on 11 September 1944 and was buried in Brighton cemetery. On 3 September 1924 at St James's Anglican Church, West Melbourne, he had married Edith Ellen Simms who survived him.

G. E. Cokayne, *Complete baronetage*, 3, 1649-64 (Exeter, Eng, 1903); J. Smith (ed), *Cyclopedia of Victoria*, 1 (Melb, 1903); *Argus*, 10 Oct 1917, 13 Sept 1944; *Herald* (Melb), 21 Oct 1926, 2 Feb 1935; *Age*, 12 Sept 1944; D. Vogt, A history of conflict: Melbourne town planning in the 1920s (B.A. Hons thesis, Univ Melb, 1975); W. M. Grubb, A history of town planning in Victoria 1910-44 (M.T.R.P. thesis, Univ Melb, 1976).

DAVID DUNSTAN

STARKE, SIR HAYDEN ERSKINE (1871-1958), judge, was born on 22 February 1871 at Creswick, Victoria, second of four surviving children of Anthony George Hayden Starke, medical practitioner, and his wife Elizabeth Jemima, née Mattingley, both English born. After Dr Starke died of typhoid in 1877, his widow took employment as a postmistress at Sebastopol and Smythesdale. Hayden was educated at local schools and attended Scotch College for six months before being articled to the legal firm of Weigall & Dobson. At the University of Melbourne, where he attended lectures, he was secretary (1891) of the law students' society and won the Supreme Court Judges' prize for articled clerks. A keen competitive rower, Starke was later president of the Victorian Rowing Association. He declined an offer from his firm when admitted to practise in 1892 and went immediately to the Bar. Through industry and force of personality he became a leader at the junior Bar. Having lived with his mother and a sister at Clifton Hill, in 1901 he bought a house in Toorak Road, Malvern, which he named Calembeen. On 1 July 1909 at St Mary's Catholic Church, St Kilda, he married Margaret Mary, only daughter of John Gavan Duffy and granddaughter of Sir Charles Gavan Duffy [qq.v.4]. The loss that year of his mother and sister, passengers to England aboard the *Waratah* which vanished between Durban and Cape Town, was a bitter blow.

Prime Minister Alfred Deakin [q.v.8] invited him to become his personal legal adviser, but Starke declined because the position was to carry no right of private practice. In 1912 he refused silk when it was offered by Chief Justice Sir John Madden [q.v.10] on the grounds that he had married late, had no private means, and preferred the flexibility that allowed him to lead in important cases yet remain free to accept lucrative junior barristers' work. He refused again, in 1919,

because he was unwilling to take advantage of not having served in World War I. In February 1920 the Hughes [q.v.9] government appointed him to the High Court of Australia on the death of Sir Edmund Barton [q.v.7]. Unlike earlier members of the court, Starke had had no political affiliations.

In his first years on the bench Starke often joined in the judgements of others, as in the Engineers' Case (1920) in which he was a party to a judgement largely written by (Sir) Isaac Isaacs [q.v.9] which abandoned the doctrine of the immunity of State and Federal instrumentalities. It was mainly at Starke's instigation that the court embarked in that case upon a root and branch review of its previous decisions. He came to regret the breadth of the statement of some propositions in the Engineers' Case, and in the Uniform Tax Case (1942) and the State Banking Case (1947) sought to confine its reach. Temperamental differences from other judges, especially Isaacs and H. B. Higgins [q.v.9], led Starke to the practice of stating his own reasons for judgement. Though (Sir) Frank Gavan Duffy [q.v.8]—John Gavan Duffy's half-brother—joined in many of his decisions, the work was undoubtedly Starke's. His judgements were lucid, succinct, and emphatic, and he was scornful of the discursive habits of others. His personal isolation within the court became more pronounced after the appointment of H. V. Evatt and (Sir) Edward McTiernan in 1930. At first he co-operated with Evatt, but soon he behaved towards both with an undisguised hostility which was partly personal yet also indicated his inability to work amicably with his colleagues; Starke's adherence to a strict code of honour yielded little to human frailty. During World War II, when the High Court's strength was depleted, he bore a heavy load. Legalistic attempts to escape wartime controls received short shrift from him, though he was concerned that fundamental rights should not be lost to the cause of expedience.

Starke's conduct as a trial judge differed markedly from his behaviour in the Full Court where matters deteriorated after the appointment of his former pupil Sir John Latham [q.v.10] as chief justice in 1935. Starke derided in private the tendency of several judges to follow (Sir) Owen Dixon uncritically. His personal relationship with all but Dixon broke down so badly that he refused to exchange judgements or even to communicate off the bench except by curt, often offensive, notes. Starke resigned in January 1950. His last notable case concerned bank nationalization (1948). Before the hearing he rebuffed a suggestion that he should not sit because his wife had a small shareholding in one of the banks. He never took extended leave and, except for a brief Pacific cruise, never left Australia.

Forceful in personality, dominant in presence, Starke cut an imposing figure. In latter years he refused to wear a wig in court, ostensibly because it irritated his scalp; he also refused to have his portrait painted. With few friends among his contemporaries or elders, he was liked and respected by younger men in the profession whom he helped and guided. He was a member of the Yorick and the Australian clubs, Melbourne. Though appointed K.C.M.G. in 1939, he was never made a privy councillor. Survived by his wife, daughter and son, Starke died on 14 May 1958 at Toorak and was cremated. His estate was sworn for probate at £19 999. Dixon said of him publicly that 'his legal knowledge, his discriminating judgment as to what mattered, his clearness and directness of speech and the strength of his mind and character combined to give him a forensic power as formidable as I have seen'. Starke's son, (Sir) John Erskine Starke, became a judge of the Supreme Court of Victoria.

F. M. Bradshaw, *Selborne Chambers memories* (Melb, 1962); A. Dean, *A multitude of counsellors* (Melb, 1968); R. G. Menzies, *The measure of the years* (Melb, 1970); R. Campbell, *A history of the Melbourne law school 1857 to 1973* (Melb, 1977); *Aust Law J*, 17 Feb 1949, p 468, 16 Feb 1950, p 550, 23 June 1958, p 55; *Cwlth Law Reports*, 97 (1958), p 4; *Melb Univ Law Review*, 2, 1959, p 1; *SMH*, 4, 6 Feb 1920, 13 Aug 1931, 2 Jan 1934, 12 Aug, 23 Oct 1948, 1 Feb 1949, 26 Jan 1950, 16 May 1958; *To-day* (Melb), 1 Sept 1934; *Sun News-Pictorial*, 27 Jan 1950; *Herald* (Melb), 15, 16 May 1958; Latham papers (NL); Dixon papers (held by author, Melb); information from Miss E. M. Starke and Sir J. E. Starke, Melb.   J. D. MERRALLS

STARLING, JOHN HENRY (1883-1966), public servant, was born on 15 January 1883 at Greensborough, Victoria, son of John Henry Starling, carpenter, and his wife Jane, née Gapper, both English born. Educated at the Greensborough State School until aged 15, he won a scholarship to Stott & Hoare's Business College, Melbourne. Having joined the Department of Lands and Survey in 1900, he transferred to the Commonwealth public service in 1902 as a clerk in the Governor-General's Office where he was assistant to (Sir) George Steward [q.v.]. Starling became a licensed shorthand writer (1906) and an accountant and auditor (1908) before being promoted to the Department of External Affairs in 1909. On 15 February 1911 he married Sarah Elizabeth May Price at St Katherine's Anglican Church, Eltham. He transferred to the newly established Prime Minister's Department in February 1912 and was appointed chief clerk in September 1917. As second-in-charge of the department, he took a large part in its organization and development through World War I.

In June 1919 he succeeded Steward as official secretary to the governor-general and secretary to the Federal Executive Council, holding office under Sir Ronald Munro Ferguson, Lord Forster [qq.v.10,8] and Lord Stonehaven [q.v.]. Responsible for the governor-general's correspondence and his establishment's expenditure, Starling also encoded, decoded and dispatched correspondence between governments, and between the governor-general and the secretary of state. He was an associate (1920) of the Chartered Institute of Secretaries and was appointed O.B.E. in 1920 and C.M.G. in 1925. After the Imperial Conference (1926) resolved to alter the existing channel of communication, a system of direct correspondence with the British government was taken over by the Prime Minister's Department in January 1928. (Abolition of the official secretaryship to the governor-general was postponed until parliament transferred to Canberra in 1927.) Starling continued as secretary to the Federal Executive Council until 1933, but in July 1929 was promoted assistant secretary of the department's territories branch. In 1933-35 he was secretary to the Prime Minister's Department and secretary to the Department of External Affairs; he was first assistant Commonwealth Public Service commissioner in 1935-38.

A 'small, neat, grey man who specialised in protocol', Starling was active after his retirement in January 1948 in the Canberra branches of the United Nations Children's Fund, the World Council of Churches and the Royal Institute of International Affairs. His recreations included bowls and golf. In Melbourne he had been a vestryman and member of the Church of England Men's Society; in Canberra he was a church warden and lay reader at St John's, Reid, and a councillor and guarantor of St Paul's, Manuka. A Freemason from 1913, he belonged to Lodge Commonwealth; having been treasurer of the Canberra Rotary Club for ten years, he was made an honorary life member in 1965. Starling died in Canberra Community Hospital on 5 April 1966 and was cremated. Two sons and a daughter survived him.

C. Cunneen, *Kings' men* (Syd, 1983); J. Gibbney, *Canberra 1913-1953* (Canb, 1988); *Canb Times*, 7 Apr 1966; Starling personal papers (AA, Canb); information from Miss J. Starling, Forrest, Canb.
DAVID I. SMITH

STATTON, PERCY CLYDE (1890-1959), soldier and farmer, was born on 19 October 1890 at Beaconsfield, Tasmania, son of Edward Statton, miner, and his wife Maggie

Lavinia, née Hoskins. Educated at Zeehan State School, he became a farm labourer at Tyenna. On 12 September 1907, giving his age as 21, he married with Methodist forms Elsie May Pearce; they were to have two daughters and a son.

Enlisting as a private in the Australian Imperial Force in March 1916, Statton was posted to the 40th Battalion and reached France in November. A temporary sergeant from January 1917, he was confirmed in rank in April. During the battle of Messines, Belgium, on 7-9 June he conducted carrying parties to the front line under heavy artillery and machine-gun fire; he was awarded the Military Medal for his actions. Wounded in October in the 3rd battle of Ypres, he was gassed at Villers-Bretonneux, France, on 10 June 1918.

Early on 12 August the 40th Battalion was assigned an objective south of the Proyart-Chuignes road, requiring an advance of some 1400 yards (1280 m). After covering about 875 yards (800 m), the battalion was halted by an intense artillery barrage. 'A' Company managed to reach Proyart village and with the aid of Statton's Lewis-gun achieved its objective; the rest of the battalion was then able to follow. At dusk the advance of the supporting 37th Battalion was held up by fierce machine-gun fire. Assisting the 37th's progress with two Lewis-guns, Statton saw the attack fail. He took three men with him and got to within 80 yards (73 m) of the first enemy strong-point. Revolver in hand, he then led his men across open ground into the German trench. They destroyed two machine-guns and Statton killed the crews. His party dashed towards the next two gun-posts whose crews fled, only to be killed by the two Lewis-guns which Statton had earlier sited. With one member of his party dead and another wounded, Statton and the third man crawled back to their lines and the 37th moved forward. That night Statton went out and brought in the wounded man and the body of the other. For his valour he was awarded the Victoria Cross.

On 26 November 1919 Statton received a hero's reception in Hobart. He was less certain, however, of a welcome from his wife who had warned the 'strapping, handsome soldier' that if he went off to war she would leave him when he returned. She kept her word and he divorced her on 1 October 1920. After demobilization, Statton found work in a sawmill and then became a farmer at Fitzgerald. On 21 December 1925 at the Registrar General's Office, Hobart, he married a divorcee Eliza Grace Hudson, née Parker (d. 1945); on 16 December 1947 in Hobart he married with Baptist forms Monica Enid Effie Kingston, a teacher. They lived at Ouse where Statton worked as a commercial agent. In the 1950s he was employed by Australian Newsprint Mills.

Survived by his wife and son, Statton died in Hobart of stomach cancer on 5 December 1959 and was cremated with full military honours. His Victoria Cross is in Anglesea Barracks, Hobart.

F. C. Green, *The Fortieth, a record of the 40th Battalion* (Hob, 1922); C. E. W. Bean, *The A.I.F. in France*, 1918 (Syd, 1942); L. Wigmore (ed), *They dared mightily*, second ed revised and condensed by J. Williams and A. Staunton (Canb, 1986); *London Gazette*, 14 Aug 1917, 24 Sept 1918; *Examiner* (Launc) and *Mercury*, 7 Dec 1959; *Sunday Tasmanian*, 11 Aug 1985; information from Mr P. C. Statton junior and Mrs B. Smith, Hob.

MERRILYN LINCOLN

STAWELL, FLORENCE MELIAN (1869-1936), classical scholar and author, was born on 2 May 1869 at Kew, Melbourne, youngest daughter of Sir William Stawell [q.v.6], chief justice of Victoria, and his wife Mary Frances Elizabeth, née Greene. (Sir) Richard [q.v.] was her brother. Her mother recalled her youthful, passionate plea: 'I would rather read Homer in the original than anything else in the world'. Melian spent two distinguished years at the University of Melbourne as an early student at Trinity College Hostel (later Janet Clarke [q.v.3] Hall), gaining first place in classics. In 1889 she went to England, entering Newnham College, University of Cambridge, in the May term. Placed in class 1, division 1, in the classical tripos of 1892 she stayed up a fourth year, but did not take part II of the tripos. In 1894-95 she was a classics tutor at Newnham, but ill health—which was to dog her all her life—forced her resignation. She then embarked on a literary career, generally being based in London.

Her most significant contribution to classical studies was *Homer and the Iliad* (1909) which attacked the conclusions of the scholar Walter Leaf and was pronounced by Gilbert Murray [q.v.10] 'full of fine observation and poetical understanding'. From 1922 the search of the 'analysts' for the 'original *Iliad*' was superseded by new directions of research, but her work within her own generation was impressive. In later years she courageously directed her classical research toward the decipherment of Minoan/Mycenaean scripts which in *A clue to the Cretan scripts* (1931) she identified as Greek. Her book coincided with another finding the solution in Basque, upon which discrepancy reviewers eagerly seized. Later scholarship has confirmed an early form of Greek, although her methodology was unacceptable.

A scholar with wide literary interests,

Melian Stawell published on Aeschylus, Plato, Thucydides and Aristotle, and on Conrad, Shelley and Meredith. Her abilities in translation are evident in works jointly undertaken with G. Lowes Dickinson (*Goethe and Faust: an interpretation,* 1928) and N. Purtscher Wydenbruck (*The practical wisdom of Goethe,* 1933), and in her rendering of Euripides' *Iphigeneia in Aulis* into English verse (1929) for which Murray wrote a preface.

Ardent and idealistic, she held intense convictions which, according to a friend, lit her blue eyes and 'transfigured' her aquiline features. She worked actively for the League of Nations Union, of which Murray was chairman in 1922-38. These interests were reflected in many papers relating to patriotism, democracy, justice and progress, starting with *The price of freedom* (1917). She collaborated with F. S. Marvin in an influential monograph, *The making of the Western mind* (1923), and a small treatise, *The growth of international thought* (1929), was applauded.

Melian Stawell died unmarried at Headington, Oxford, on 9 June 1936. *The Times* pronounced her 'perhaps the most remarkable member of a remarkable family'. Had her physical endurance kept pace with her intellectual vigour and passionate commitment to social issues, she may have been assured of great academic eminence.

M. F. E. Stawell, *My recollections* (Lond, 1911); A. Gardner, *A short history of Newnham College* (Cambridge, UK, 1921); J. A. Grant (ed), *Perspective of a century* (Melb, 1972); L. Gardiner, *Janet Clarke Hall 1886-1986* (Melb, 1986); *Argus,* 13 Sept 1893; *The Times,* 11, 16 June 1936.

K. J. McKay

STAWELL, Sir RICHARD RAWDON (1864-1935), physician, was born on 14 March 1864 at Kew, Melbourne, sixth child of Sir William Foster Stawell [q.v.6] and his wife Mary Frances Elizabeth, née Greene. Florence Melian Stawell [q.v.] was a sister. Educated at Marlborough College, England, Hawthorn Grammar School, Victoria, and the University of Melbourne (M.B., 1887; B.S., 1888; M.D., 1890), Stawell graduated with the scholarship in medicine. He was resident medical officer at (Royal) Melbourne Hospital (1888) and the Hospital for Sick Children (1889) where he was influenced by William Snowball [q.v.].

In 1890-92 Stawell undertook three years postgraduate work in bacteriology, biochemistry and physiology. In London he studied at the National Hospital for Diseases of the Nervous System, Queen's Square, and the Great Ormond Street Hospital for Sick Children. After completing the Diploma of Public Health (London) in 1891, he did further research at Tübingen, Germany, and visited clinics in the United States of America before returning home.

With his hopes of a private income and a career of academic research dashed by the bank crash, he commenced private practice in Collins Street where he lived with his colleagues, Hamilton Russell [q.v.11] and A. Jeffreys Wood. Stawell also formed a firm friendship with (Sir) Charles Martin [q.v.10], then professor of physiology at the university. Honorary physician to the Children's Hospital in 1893-1914 and to out-patients at Melbourne Hospital in 1903-19, Stawell introduced the most recent scientifically-based practice of medicine and raised clinical teaching to the highest level. With his Socratic approach, knowledge and kindly interest in patients and students, he rapidly became pre-eminent as a teacher and a clinician. He demanded high standards and inspired two generations of students. One of them, (Sir) Sidney Sewell [q.v.11], remembered him as 'a tall alert young man with clear-cut delightful enunciation of well-chosen English and a vivid, magnetic personality'. (Sir) Macfarlane Burnet found him 'a man of much wisdom and immense charm', but with 'a waspish intolerance of stupidity'. Stawell published a wide range of scholarly articles and in 1898-1900 edited the *Intercolonial Medical Journal.*

On 12 August 1908 at St Andrew's Anglican Church, Brighton, Stawell married Evelyn Myrrhee Connolly, matron of the Foundling Hospital, East Melbourne. He was elected president of the Victorian branch of the British Medical Association in 1910. In 1915 he enlisted in the Australian Imperial Force, embarking in May as lieut-colonel in charge of the medical section, 3rd Australian General Hospital. He served with distinction in Egypt and at Lemnos until invalided home in June 1916. On his return he became a member of the appeal board of the Repatriation Department. In 1917 Stawell went back to Melbourne Hospital and from 1919 was physician to in-patients. He resigned in 1924 to become a consulting physician. A member of the hospital's board of management in 1905-35, he was president in 1928. He was unanimously elected inaugural president (1930-32) of the Association of Physicians of Australasia (Royal Australasian College of Physicians).

Throughout his career Stawell was concerned with the wider responsibilities of the medical profession in society. As an undergraduate he had supported the admission of women to medical courses. He later attacked the degrading public election of medical staff to Melbourne Hospital and, through the board of management, had it replaced by appointment through an advisory board in 1910. He campaigned against infant mortality linked to gastroenteritis, and successfully advocated closer links between the university and the hospital. In 1930 he chaired a public meeting to establish the Victorian Council of Mental Hygiene which he then served as chairman until his death. A councillor of Trinity College for thirty years and a director of the National Mutual Life Assurance Society, he was knighted in 1929 for his services to medicine and the community.

Wide-ranging in his interests, Stawell had been a tennis champion as an undergraduate; he was later a member of the Royal Melbourne Golf Club. An enthusiastic canoeist and an expert fly-fisher, he belonged to a medico-legal fishing group and was known for his studious approach to the sport. Tall and angular, he had been prominent in undergraduate debates and plays. Maie (Lady) Casey recalled that Dick Stawell could be 'extremely entertaining in his somewhat high-pitched precise voice'. He had a lifelong appreciation of music and painting. A member of the Melbourne Club, he was president in 1920.

After his marriage Stawell lived and practised at 45 Spring Street, Melbourne. He died there on 18 April 1935 and was cremated. His wife, two daughters and son survived him. At the time of his death he was president-elect of the British Medical Association; that year he was posthumously made a fellow of the Royal College of Physicians, England. His Australian colleagues paid tribute to his influence. Professor W. A. Osborne [q.v.11] recalled his 'dominant personality', 'quick and flexible intellect', 'disarming candour', 'lively sense of humour' and 'courtly gesture and address'. Jeffreys Wood described him as 'a figure who has reigned supreme in the history of Australian medicine'; Sewell saw him as 'the greatest of our Australian physicians'. The Sir Richard Stawell Oration, given in Melbourne from 1934 to 1986, commemorates his life and work. Portraits by W. B. McInnes [q.v.10] are held by the Royal Melbourne Hospital and the family.

M. Casey, *Charles S. Ryan* (Melb, 1958); M. Burnet, *Changing patterns* (Lond, 1968); B. K. Rank, *Jerry Moore and some of his contemporaries* (Melb, 1975); R. Winton, *Why the pomegranate?* (Syd, 1988); *MJA*, 18 May 1935, p 629; Roy Melb Hospital, *Clinical Reports*, 6 (1935), p 1; *Argus*, 20 Apr 1935.
F. I. R. MARTIN

STEAD, DAVID GEORGE (1877-1957), naturalist, was born on 6 March 1877 at St Leonards, Sydney, sixth child of English-born Samuel Leonard Stead, house-painter, and his Scottish wife Christina, née Broadfoot. Despite his mother's strictness, he had a happy childhood: the sea, the shoreline and the bush were his early loves. Having attended local public schools, at 12 he was apprenticed to a stampmaker from whom he learned the art of lettering that was his pride. David studied zoology at Sydney Technical College and in 1898 joined the Linnean Society of New South Wales. He was a compositor when he married Ellen Butters on 17 August 1901 at the Sydney registry office. After her death in 1904, he married Ada Gibbins, daughter of an oyster merchant, at Arncliffe with Anglican rites on 1 January 1907.

Appointed a scientific assistant under Harald Dannevig [q.v.8] in the Fisheries Commission in May 1902 at an annual salary of £200, Stead took tireless interest in 'every aspect of nature' and specialized in ichthyology, but acutely felt his lack of academic qualifications all his life. He published *Fishes of Australia* (1906) and *Edible fishes of New South Wales* (1908). In 1914-15, as a special commissioner, he investigated European and American fisheries for the government. From July 1915 to 1920 he was general manager of the State Trawlers Industrial Undertaking which satisfied his socialist leanings but was to end in his dismissal. His controversial and costly management was attacked in parliament and in *Smith's Weekly*. (Sir) George Allard [q.v.7], royal commissioner into the Public Service, appreciated Stead's scientific and practical knowledge, his drive and industry, but regretted his lack of business sense.

Tall, fair and blue-eyed, with thick hair in his youth, Stead was above all an enthusiast, a 'spellbinder', strong and forthright, if somewhat overbearing and self-opinionated at times. When faced—as he often was—with setbacks and criticism of his ideas, he would sing the Moody and Sankey hymn:

> Dare to be a Daniel,
> Dare to stand alone,
> Dare to have a purpose true,
> And dare to make it known.

He went to Malaya in 1921 as fisheries inquiry commissioner and acting director of supplies to the British government; in 1924 he attended the Pan-Pacific Food Conservation Conference in Honolulu. He investigated various methods of rabbit destruction in 1925-26: his solutions were sensible but politically unacceptable. A prolific writer and lecturer, Stead published *Giants and pigmies of the deep* and *The tree book* in 1933, *The rabbit in Australia* in 1935 and *Sharks and rays of Australian seas* posthumously in 1963, besides numerous articles, papers, pamphlets and letters to the press and people in power. He pioneered radio broadcasts on wildlife topics and interested himself in the better treatment of Aborigines; outspoken against war, he was an executive-member of the State branch of the League of Nations Union and in 1936 foundation chairman of the International Peace Campaign.

His great work was as a popular scientific educator and as an advocate of conservation which aroused little enthusiasm in the 1920s and 1930s. In 1909 he had helped to found the Wild Life Preservation Society of Australia, becoming secretary then president. Stead presided over the Aquarium, Naturalists' and Geographical societies of New South Wales, the State branch of the Australian Forest League and the Town Planning Association, and was an executive-member of the Gould [q.v.1] League of Bird Lovers and the Royal Zoological Society of New South Wales, an honorary member of the American Fisheries Society, a fellow of the Linnean Society of London and managing director of the Australian Whaling Co. He often wrote under the pen names 'Physalia' and 'Dinnawan', and edited *Australian Wild Life*, the *Australian Geographer* and *Australian Naturalist*, as well as the Shakespeare Head Press Ltd's nature series.

Delighting in children, he would wait in the street to talk to them, build little red boats as presents for them and amuse them by reciting ditties on the nicknames he gave them all. Stead died on 2 August 1957 at his Watsons Bay home and was cremated. He was survived by his third wife Thistle Yolette, née Harris (a biologist and conservationist whom he had married in his home on 30 June 1951), by three sons and two daughters of his second marriage and by the only child of his first marriage, the novelist Christina Stead. The character Sam Pollit in her novel, *The man who loved children* (New York, 1940), is based on her childhood memories of her father. He is commemorated by the David George Stead Memorial Wildlife Research Foundation of Australia and by Mount Stead in the Blue Mountains.

W. S. Ramson (ed), *The Australian experience* (Canb, 1974); *PP* (NSW), 1916, 5, p 975, 1920, 1st S, 1, p 361; *PD* (NSW), 1918, p 1763, 1919, pp 82, 319; *Aust Wild Life*, 3, Mar 1958; *Wireless Weekly*, 11 Sept 1931; Cwlth Director of Fisheries, Dept of Primary Industry, *Fisheries Newsletter*, 16, no 9, 1957; Linnean Soc NSW, *Procs*, 83 (1958); Roy Zoological Soc NSW, *Procs*, June 1958; *Overland*, no 53, Spring 1972; *SMH*, 6 Dec 1921, 22, 23 Oct 1924, 20 July 1925, 26 Mar, 14 Apr 1927, 7 Nov 1928, 7, 12 Aug, 14 Sept, 8, 10 Oct 1929, 15 Mar, 30 Nov 1933, 29 Oct 1935; Carruthers correspondence (ML); CRS A 1838 (AA); information from Mr G. Stead, Hurstville, Syd.   G. P. WALSH

STEDMAN, JAMES (1840-1913), confectionery manufacturer, was born on 25 December 1840 at Parramatta, New South Wales, son of Henry Stedman (d. 1893), servant, and his wife Catherine, née Murphy. Henry, who came from Surrey, had reached Sydney in the *Mermaid* on 6 May 1830, sentenced to fourteen years for robbing his master. James attended a private school at Brisbane Water, started work in a butcher's shop and at 14 joined William J. Cates, a Sydney confectioner whose business at 436 George Street was taken over by Wright & Smith in the early 1860s. At Christ Church St Laurence, Stedman married Margaret Noble on 14 February 1860. After John Smith sold out, Stedman worked as foreman for John M. Wright for twelve years and bought the business in 1875. Meanwhile Margaret ran a retail confectionery at their Crown Street premises.

About 1888 Stedman moved to new premises, with a shop in George Street and a factory (on which he spent £6000) in Clarence Street, adjacent to the Grand Central Coffee Palace and convenient to the wharves. Stedman (who 'would not sell for £25 000') employed between forty and fifty people in his wholesale and retail business which had an output of over five tons a week in 1889. As well as confectionery, he manufactured a range of pastry products; he also imported confectionery and essences, and advertised purely vegetable 'colouring matters'.

His success was largely due to his innovative outlook and quality control. In 1889 and 1896 Stedman visited England and brought back improved plant. Another feature of the business was close family involvement: two brothers, six sons and two nephews worked for the firm. In March 1900 James Stedman Ltd was incorporated with authorized capital of £60 000; Stedman was managing director and his second son George Albert became secretary. By 1903 popular lines included peppermints, brandy balls and bull's eyes, and Stedman's Imperial Steam Confectionery Works had about 130 staff. His 'Lion' brand sweets—among them 'Butter Scotch', 'Tofflets' and 'Lankee-Bill Toff-E'—were awarded a silver medal and diploma at the 1908 Franco-British Exhibition in London.

Active in community work, Stedman was a director of Sydney Hospital, the Benevolent Society of New South Wales and the Society for Destitute Children's asylum at Randwick; he was also a trustee of the City Night Refuge and Soup Kitchen. In 1890 he had been appointed a justice of the peace. Balding and bearded, with a compact, burly figure, he was a keen patron of sport, especially cricket and athletics. Survived by six of his eight sons, Stedman died on 1 February 1913 in Highbury Hospital, Hobart, after an appendicectomy and was buried in Waverley cemetery, Sydney. His estate was valued for probate at about £150 000.

In June 1920 James Stedman-Henderson's Sweets Ltd was registered as a public company with Stedman's eldest son James Noble (1860-1944) as chairman. It became celebrated as the manufacturer of 'Minties'.

W. F. Morrison, *The Aldine centennial history of New South Wales*, 2 (Syd, 1888); E. Digby (ed), *Australian men of mark*, 2 (Syd, 1889); *Cyclopedia of N.S.W.* (Syd, 1907); *Old Times*, Apr 1903, p 74; *T&CJ*, 5 Feb 1913; *SMH*, 5 Aug 1893, 3 Feb 1913, 8 June 1944.   G. P. WALSH

STEEL, THOMAS (1858-1925), industrial chemist and naturalist, was born on 8 September 1858 at Glasgow, Scotland, son of William Steel, timber merchant, and his wife Marion Currie, née Kyle. The family moved to Greenock, Renfrewshire, where Thomas attended the academy. From about 1874 he acquired some knowledge of chemistry in the laboratory of Patterson & Ogilvie, public analysts, and from about 1876 with J. Walker & Co., sugar refiners.

Recruited by the Colonial Sugar Refining Co., Steel migrated to Sydney in 1882. He worked as a laboratory chemist in their sugarmills at Murwillumbah (1882-84) and Nausori, Fiji (1885-87), and in all three of the company's refineries at Auckland, New Zealand, Pyrmont, Sydney, and Yarraville, Melbourne. On a visit to Greenock he married Mary Sinclair Boag at the White Hart Hotel on 18 August 1892 with Church of Scotland forms. Under T. U. Walton [q.v.] he was a chemist at the company's head office in Sydney from 1892 until he retired in 1918. A fellow of the Chemical Society, London, he was an active member (chairman 1910-11) of the Sydney section of the Society of Chemical Industry.

From boyhood Steel was interested in natural history. Throughout his life he engaged in field-work, giving modest and generous service to other naturalists. A fellow of the Linnean Society of London from 1897, he was a councillor of the Linnean Society of New South Wales (1897-1925) and president in 1905-07; he was also president of the Field Naturalists' Club (later Society) in 1903-04 and edited its journal, the *Australian Naturalist*, in 1911-25. He corresponded for many years with Sir Walter Baldwin Spencer [q.v.], a fellow-member of the Field Naturalists' Club of Victoria.

Steel's significant contribution to Australian biology related to two very inconspicuous groups of fauna: the *Onycophora* and the *Turbellaria*. In two papers in 1896-97 on the onychophoran genus, *Peripatus*, he demonstrated that the slime threads characteristically produced by the creatures were a food snare as well as a defence mechanism;

furthermore, he showed that the geographical distribution of the egg-laying forms extended much farther south than previously thought. The key reference on this subject remains his definitive article in the *Australian encyclopedia* (1925). His main work on turbellarians comprised four papers (1897-1901) of taxonomic importance in which he described and categorized sixteen distinct groups of the creatures. He made many donations to the Australian Museum, Sydney.

Steel died of heart disease at his Killara home on 17 August 1925 and was buried in the Presbyterian section of Northern Suburbs cemetery. He was survived by his wife and three sons of whom the two eldest had served with the Australian Imperial Force.

A. B. Walkom, *The Linnean Society of New South Wales* (Syd, 1925); A. Musgrave, *Bibliography of Australian entomology 1775-1930* (Syd, 1932), p 304; A. G. Lowndes (ed), *South Pacific enterprise* (Syd, 1956); *Aust Museum Mag*, 2, no 8, 1925, p 276; *Aust Naturalist*, 5, no 16, 1925, p 255; Linnean Soc NSW, *Procs*, 51, no 1, 1926, p vii; *SMH*, 18 Aug 1925; W. B. Spencer papers (ML); Mus Corres/S/9/100/1925 (Aust Museum Archives, Syd); CSR Co. staff records and correspondence (ANUABL).   H. G. HOLLAND
                              J. R. SIMONS

STEELE, ALEXANDER (1888-1917), soldier, was born on 20 August 1888 at Mount Gambier, South Australia, son of Dugald Steele, painter, and his wife Elizabeth Burton, née Laywood. Educated at Mount Gambier Grammar School, he worked for a local bootmaker (a member of the volunteer corps) under whose influence Steele began his military career in the ranks of the South Australian Infantry Regiment.

From qualifying school, he was appointed to the Administrative and Instructional Staff of the Permanent Military Forces in August 1910 and posted to Gawler where in January 1911 he was appointed staff sergeant major; next year he qualified at the Permanent Military Force's School of Musketry. Posted in September 1913 to the Royal Military College, Duntroon, as the non-commissioned instructor in infantry and musketry, he passed a course on machine-guns at the School of Musketry and applied for a commission, but withdrew from the examination.

Travelling to Queensland, reputedly to meet a friend who was about to join up, Steele enlisted on 25 August 1914 in the 9th Battalion, Australian Imperial Force. He sailed with the unit's machine-gun section next month and served as machine-gun sergeant during the Gallipoli landing on 25 April 1915. His work in the first ten days ashore earned special mention in Army Corps routine orders. For manning and maintaining his gun in action for several days after the rest of his section had been killed or wounded, he was awarded the Distinguished Conduct Medal; on 28 April he was also commissioned second lieutenant. Wounded on 19 May when an expanding bullet struck his forearm, he was evacuated to hospital in Egypt. He was mentioned in dispatches on 3 August and promoted lieutenant on the 4th; he returned to his battalion a few days later, but was re-admitted to hospital at the end of the month and did not rejoin his unit until December.

Having been made machine-gun officer for the 3rd Brigade, in February 1916 Steele was promoted captain. He raised the brigade machine-gun company and was its commanding officer when the brigade went to France in March. During the period of trench-raids to which the A.I.F. was first exposed on this front, Steele showed himself to be skilled in machine-gun tactics. In the battle of the Somme in the months to October, his services were 'conspicuous and consistent' for displaying 'marked resourcefulness and leadership'. He was promoted major in August, awarded the Distinguished Service Order in December and again mentioned in dispatches in January 1917.

After attending a senior officers' course in early 1917 at Aldershot, England, he resumed command of his machine-gun company on 4 April. On the 27th he was given temporary command of the 10th Battalion and led this unit in the 2nd battle of Bullecourt on 6 May. Transferred to the 11th Battalion on 5 July as second-in-command, he was temporarily commanding this unit at Broodseinde Ridge, Belgium, when, on 7 October, the battalion headquarters were heavily shelled and he was killed; nothing reportedly remained of Steele save his tunic. He had been, as the historian C. E. W. Bean [q.v.7] noted at the time, 'a splendid officer . . . [who] was the makings of the 11th Battalion'.

Steele's rise from non-commissioned rank on the outbreak of war to his first command of a battalion three years later, at the age of 28, was clear evidence of the calibre of the personnel serving in the ranks of Australia's small pre-war permanent forces. The fact that, by his ability, he was so able to rise, was one of the strengths of the A.I.F. He was unmarried.

C. E. W. Bean, *The story of Anzac* (Syd, 1921) and *The A.I.F. in France, 1917* (Syd, 1933); C. B. L. Lock, *The fighting 10th* (Adel, 1936); W. C. Belford, *Legs-eleven* (Perth, 1940); J. E. Lee, *Duntroon* (Canb, 1952); C. M. Wrench, *Campaigning with the fighting 9th* (Brisb, 1985); *London Gazette*, 3 June, 5 Aug 1915, 29 Dec 1916, 2 Jan 1917.

C. D. COULTHARD-CLARK

STEELE, BERTRAM DILLON (1870-1934), professor of chemistry, was born on 30 May 1870 at Plymouth, England, son of Samuel Steele, surgeon, and his wife Hariette Sarah, née Acock. Educated at Plymouth Grammar School, he began an apprenticeship with his father; in 1889 he migrated to Melbourne where he attended the Victorian College of Pharmacy in 1890-91 to complete his training.

Having practised as a pharmacist, in 1896 Steele enrolled in medicine at the University of Melbourne before transferring to science. He graduated (B.Sc., 1898) with the exhibition and first-class honours in chemistry among other awards. Professor D. O. Masson's [q.v.10] recommendations secured Steele a brief acting professorship in chemistry at the University of Adelaide in 1899. On 18 September he married Amy Woodhead at Surrey Hills, Melbourne.

With his wife, Steele travelled to London to work with Professor J. N. Collie, then to Breslau, Germany, for research under Professor R. Abegg. He attracted the admiration of (Sir) William Ramsay at London and Professor F. Haber at Karlsruhe. In 1902 he was granted a D.Sc. *in absentia* by the University of Melbourne. He taught briefly in Dublin, at McGill University, Montreal, and as assistant professor at Heriot-Watt College, Edinburgh.

From 1 March 1906 Steele was successively appointed lecturer and acting professor in chemistry at the University of Melbourne. His research into the reactions of gaseous compounds demanded great skill in making scientific equipment and in glassblowing; his construction of the Steele-(Sir Kerr) Grant [q.v.9] microbalance, which was sensitive to 4×10^{-6} mg (4 ng), won him Ramsay's acclaim; he also published extensively in physical, organic and inorganic chemistry.

Appointed to the foundation chair of chemistry at the University of Queensland from 20 December 1910, Steele instituted courses in the former kitchen and scullery of the old Government House and supervised the design of the university's new chemistry building. Of medium height, with '10% genial smile and 90% sang froid', Steele was a brilliant lecturer who, as president of the board of faculties, exercised academic leadership with strength, thoroughness and tact. He appreciated music and sport and collected *objets d'art*. Immaculately groomed, with starched collar and neat bow-tie, he had a high brow, handsome features and wore spectacles.

In 1915, to help the war effort, Steele returned to University College, London. His work led to a British government invitation to design, build and operate a munitions factory to produce synthetic phenol. He returned to Brisbane in 1919 in which year the Royal Society elected him a fellow—its only fellow then in Queensland. Serving on the University of Queensland's second and third senate (1919-26), in 1923 Steele became chairman of the royal commission to investigate the prickly pear problem and in 1927 undertook a study for the Queensland government of the Roma oil bore.

From 1927 his health declined. Retiring from the university on 28 February 1931, Steele died at Parkerview Hospital, Brisbane, on 12 April 1934. Childless, he was survived by his wife. His remains in Lutwyche cemetery were later cremated.

A. Hardman-Knight, *The life and work of Bertram Dillon Steele* (Brisb, 1941); B. Chiswell, A diamond period (ms, 1986, held by author, Univ Qld); *A'sian J of Pharmacy*, Dec 1910, p 383; *J of Chemical Soc* (Lond), 1934, p 1479; *Obituary Notices of Fellows of the Roy Soc*, 3, Dec 1934, p 345; *Roy Aust Chemical Inst Procs*, 25, 1958, p 413; *Telegraph* (Brisb), 12, 13, 14 Apr 1934.

BARRY CHISWELL

STEERE, SIR JAMES GEORGE LEE (1830-1903), politician, was born on 4 July 1830, third of six sons of Lee Steere of Jayes, near Ockley in Surrey, England, and his wife Anne, née Watson. A fox-hunting Tory squire whose ancestors had held Jayes since before the Norman Conquest, Lee Steere late in life represented the western division of Surrey in the House of Commons, setting an example of paternalistic public service which deeply influenced James. After education at Thames Ditton and Clapham Grammar School, James entered the East India Co.'s mercantile marine in 1845, rising in six years from midshipman to chief mate of the *Sea Park*. In 1852 he took his master's ticket on the *Bombay* and in 1854-58 was captain of the *Devonshire*. In 1855 his younger brother Augustus had migrated to Western Australia. James decided to follow after his marriage on 16 June 1859 at St John's Church, Hampstead, to the belle of Perth, Catherine Anne, sister of George and (Sir) Luke Leake [qq.v.5].

The young couple arrived in Western Australia in 1860. Within a few months Steere was offered a partnership by the merchant and pastoralist, J. H. Monger [q.v.5], in a grazing property on the upper Blackwood River at the edge of settlement in the south-west. There, from brick and local timber, the Steeres built a homestead, naming it Jayes after the ancestral estate, and there they raised their large family in Anglican principles. In this unlikely environment Steere blossomed as a Tory paternalist: created justice of the peace immediately on his arrival, he fell easily into the squire's role. A just and conscientious, if at times self-important, magistrate, he was a spokesman for local public

works, foundation secretary of the Southern Districts Agricultural Society, first chairman of the Blackwood roads board, and in 1865 a leading petitioner for representative government. When in 1868 Governor John Hampton [q.v.1] agreed to nominate six members to the Legislative Council on an informally elected basis, Steere easily defeated two opponents to represent the south district. After the council gained an elected majority in 1870, Steere was returned as member for Wellington. Immediately accepted as spokesman for the non-official members, Steere declined the Speakership in favour of his brother-in-law Luke and began to urge responsible government.

In later life Steere liked to think that around 1870 he was 'looked upon as a kind of anarchist, who was going to upset everything in the colony'. In fact he was always identified with the property-owning elite and expected that its control over Western Australia's development would be strengthened by self-government. In 1874 he sponsored a successful motion calling for a Legislative Assembly, elected on a property franchise, and a Legislative Council confined to nominees and substantial property owners. The Colonial Office, however, refused to hand over nearly a million square miles (2.59 million km^2) to an electorate of under 10 000 White men. Meanwhile, Steere was not subtle enough to reconcile the competing interest-groups in the colony. In 1871 he had taken the lead in the Legislative Council's rejection of state aid for Catholic schools. Although he later spoke in favour of aid, the Catholic vote was alienated. He was perceived as having a rural bias against the urban working class, but in 1876 he served on a tariff commission which recommended that corn imports should remain duty-free, thus provoking a feeling of betrayal among farmers who advocated protection. In 1878 when a group of younger politicians such as (Sir) Edward Stone [q.v.] and (Sir) Stephen Henry Parker [q.v.11] formed a Reform League to renew the struggle for self-government, Steere thought them too democratic and stood aloof, choosing instead to take his family on an extended visit to England. Vexed at his indifference, the voters of Wellington rejected him in February 1880, but he was returned in May at a by-election for Swan.

Once more leader of the unofficial members, Steere took advantage of an unexpectedly large deficit in the colony's finances to push through an audit bill to strengthen the council's influence over budget policy. The Colonial Office vetoed the bill, but allowed it to pass in a modified form in 1881, and Steere became a leading member of the council's finance committee. Yet, he was losing ground. Having bought out Monger's share of

Jayes, he admitted a new partner who proved incompetent, and between 1881 and 1888 Steere was obliged to live on the property and devote energy to its rehabilitation. In the meantime Parker had seized leadership of the responsible government movement, and Steere was among the conservatives who sided with Government House in resisting the pressure. In October 1884 he had declined to contest Swan, and in July 1885 became a nominated member of the Legislative Council. In December Governor Sir Frederick Broome [q.v.3] placed him on the Executive Council as an unofficial representative. In the stormy quarrels between Broome, Chief Justice (Sir) Alexander Onslow [q.v.5], Attorney-General A. P. Hensman [q.v.4] and Surveyor-General (Sir) John Forrest [q.v.8], Steere endeavoured to act as a mediator, but was often seen as a stooge for Government House, and his influence suffered. Nevertheless, when the Speaker died in May 1886, Steere was unanimously chosen as successor.

The position was tailor-made for him. By now Steere looked the elder statesman: tall, with authoritative good looks, well-groomed sideburns and moustache, and a dignified but kindly manner. As Speaker he was firm, courteous and a stickler for proper procedures; members respected him because he was seen as embodying English tradition. He believed that 'no legislature could have very much power in the country unless it had the confidence and respect of the people', and accordingly imposed a high standard of parliamentary decorum. In 1888 he was knighted and came to reside permanently in Perth. When the first parliament under responsible government was elected in November 1890, he chose to enter the Legislative Assembly as member for Nelson. One or two newspapers credited him with a lingering hope of becoming the first premier, but he made no public move and the commission went to Forrest. As a member of the outgoing Executive Council, Steere had considerable influence on the nomination of members for the new Legislative Council. He also held for some months during 1890 and 1891 a dormant commission to act as governor in the event of the incumbent's death or incapacity. Despite early reservations he soon became a steady, though never uncritical, supporter of Forrest and his policies.

Until overshadowed by Forrest, Steere served as Western Australian delegate to several sessions of the Federal Council of Australasia, of which he was a consistent supporter. In 1886 in Hobart he had spoken cogently on defence issues and in 1888-89 was chairman of committees. After supporting the smaller colonies at the 1890 session he was savaged by Sir Henry Parkes [q.v.5], but went imperturbably as a delegate to the 1891 National Australasian Convention. Alfred Deakin [q.v.8] described him as having the 'slowness of the Englishman, uniting a very practical sense of all the issues involved, and a kindness of disposition which made him a general favourite'. Steere was a delegate to the 1897-98 Federal convention. He cooled towards Federation, seeing it as insufficiently protective of Western Australian interests, but accepted Forrest's decision to press ahead.

During the 1890s Steere was regarded as the figure without whom no respectable Perth board of directors would be complete. He was foundation chairman of the Western Australia Trustee Executor & Agency Co., a local director of the board of the Australian Mutual Provident Society and of Dalgety [q.v.4] & Co. Ltd, and a director of Millars' Karri and Jarrah Forests Ltd as well as many more. Naturally, he was president (1893-1901) of Perth's elite Weld [q.v.6] Club. Excluding two breaks totalling five years, he was a governor of the Perth Boys' High School from its foundation in 1876 until his death. He served on the committee of the Victoria Public Library and was its chairman from 1890 to 1903, the year in which the main library building was completed. He was also foundation chairman of trustees (1895-1903) for the Western Australian Museum, again presiding over the erection of a new building. For many years he served on the Anglican synod of the Perth diocese. In 1898 he was appointed K.C.M.G. and with his wife made his final visit to England. It was no longer home. The man whose Western Australian public career was so largely founded on the perfection of his image as an English gentleman returned complaining that London was full of strangers and nobody wanted to know anything about Australia.

With the 1890s gold rush Western Australia was also changing in ways unwelcome to Steere's conservative temper. Although originally a supporter of votes for women on a limited property franchise, Steere had become an opponent before the measure passed in 1899. He disliked the rising influence of the Trades and Labor Council after 1897, but his habitual courtesy did not desert him in 1901 when the first Labor members entered the legislature. In 1902 he was present at the laying of the foundation stone of the new Parliament House in West Perth, and busied himself with the building's planning. With diabetes undermining his health, he resisted the idea of resignation. Survived by his wife, four sons and seven daughters, he died at St George's Terrace, Perth, in the early hours of 1 December 1903. He was given a state funeral and interred in Karrakatta cemetery. He left an estate valued for probate at £39 759. In later life he and his wife were usually known as Sir James and Lady Lee Steere. Most of the family followed this practice including his nephew (Sir) Ernest Lee Steere [q.v.10], one of whose grandsons inherited Jayes in Surrey.

Steere was the epitome of that type of English gentleman for whom character is more important than brains. Methodical and deliberate, he was not without financial ability, but was no master of long-term political strategy. In his active career as a colonial politician during the 1870s and 1880s his manner gained him an ascendancy which he lacked the skill to consolidate. As Speaker and company director in his later years, he gave Western Australia a valuable model of probity at a time when public morality risked succumbing to a get-rich-quick mentality.

F. K. Crowley, *Forrest*, 1 (Brisb, 1971); *JRWAHS*, Dec 1945; *West Australian*, 3 Dec 1903; P. D. Tannock, Sir James George Lee Steere (Ph.D. thesis, Univ WA, 1975).   G. C. BOLTON

STEPHEN, SIR COLIN CAMPBELL (1872-1937), solicitor and horseman, was born on 3 May 1872 at Woodside, South Kingston (Stanmore), Sydney, fourth of seven children of native-born parents Septimus Alfred Stephen [q.v.6], solicitor, and his wife Lucy, daughter of Robert Campbell [1804-1859,q.v.1]; he was also a grandson of Sir Alfred Stephen [q.v.6]. Colin was educated at All Saints' College, Bathurst, and privately tutored in England for three years. Quick of eye and quick of tongue (despite shyness and a slight stammer), he was ambidextrous and good at games.

The only one of his siblings to live in Australia, Stephen returned to Sydney in 1890 and was articled to C. S. de Grey Cowper, a solicitor and partner in (M. C.) Stephen [q.v.6], Jaques & Stephen. Colin was admitted to practice on 30 May 1896 and to a partnership on 1 July. He married Dorothy (d. 1935), daughter of E. W. Knox [q.v.9], on 26 October 1899 with Anglican rites at All Saints' Church, Woollahra; they lived at Llanillo, Bellevue Hill. As a trustee and executor of several large estates, Stephen did much work for 'his personal friends'. In that capacity he was questioned about his father's station by the royal commission into the administration of the Lands Department in 1905.

A noted amateur rider, Stephen first won at Randwick in 1892 on his own horse Pro-Consul. From 152 mounts between 1891 and 1903, he had 58 wins, including the Bong Bong Picnic Race and Tirranna cups. He bred, owned and raced horses: after 1904 they were mainly the progeny of his mare Elvo and were trained by Tom Payten [q.v.11]; carrying his pale blue colours and white cap, Fide-

lity won the Maribyrnong Plate in 1935. A leading polo player, Stephen had been a member of the governor-general Lord Denman's [q.v.8] team which won the [Countess of] Dudley [q.v.8] Cup in 1912. Stephen was president of the New South Wales Polo Association (1929-37) and of the Australasian Polo Council from 1927.

A committee-member of the Australian Jockey Club from 1912, he sat on (Sir) Adrian Knox's [q.v.9] sub-committee which framed the rules of racing that year. As chairman of the A.J.C. from October 1919, Stephen was determined 'to make racing in New South Wales a clean and healthy pastime'. His revised rules were adopted throughout Australia in 1933. After protracted litigation and an appeal to the Privy Council, in 1936 he eventually won the right for the A.J.C. committee to disqualify the bookmaker Rufe Naylor [q.v.10].

A notary public from 1928, Stephen became senior partner of one of the best-known legal firms in Sydney. His clients included the Sydney Morning Herald and Fairfax family [qq.v.8], the Australian Mutual Provident Society, the 'coal baron' John Brown, actress Maud Jeffries [qq.v.7,9] and circus proprietor Philip Wirth [q.v.]. Through his connexion with Brown, Stephen was chairman (1926-37) of Abermain Seaham Collieries Ltd which merged with J. & A. Brown [qq.v.3] in 1932. He was a local director of the National Bank of Australasia, chairman of the Scottish Hospital and a member of the Union Club.

Spare and blue-eyed, with a thin, 'alert and thoughtful face', Stephen had a 'shrewd and analytical mind', a high conception of duty and a capacity to master detail. His versatility, experience and 'formidable strength of character' led many to seek his advice. He was knighted in January 1935. Diagnosed as having suffered from mitral stenosis since his youth, Stephen died of a coronary occlusion at Llanillo on 14 September 1937 and was cremated. His son and two daughters survived him.

Cyclopedia of N.S.W. (Syd, 1907); *PP* (NSW), 1906, 2, p 1 (580); *SMH*, 18 Nov 1922, 14 July 1923, 18 June 1924, 2 Mar 1932, 3 Aug 1934, 1 Jan, 1 Mar 1935, 27 Feb, 15, 16 Sept 1937; *Punch* (Melb), 5 Mar 1925; C. C. Stephen letter-books (held by family); L. C. Stephen, History of Stephen, Jaques & Stephen (ts, held by author); information from Mrs T. L. F. Rutledge, Bellevue Hill, Syd.

MARTHA RUTLEDGE

STEPHEN, EDWARD MILNER (1870-1939), barrister, alderman and judge, was born on 9 July 1870 in Sydney, second of six children of Edward Milner Stephen (d. 1894), mercantile clerk, and his native-born wife Florence Adelaide Mansel (d. 1880), née Smith. His father, fourth son of (Sir) Alfred Stephen [q.v.6], was born in Hobart Town and later became official assignee. Milner was educated at Sydney Grammar School from 1881 (school captain, 1887) and won the junior (1886) and senior Knox [q.v.5] prizes, and the Salting [q.v.2] exhibition (1887).

Resident in St Paul's College, University of Sydney (B.A., 1891), Stephen graduated with first-class honours in classics (University medal) and in logic and mental philosophy. Beginning articles of clerkship in October 1890, he qualified for admission as a solicitor in 1895 but was admitted to the Bar on 24 November 1896.

From Selbourne Chambers Stephen built up a successful practice mainly in common law and became a familiar figure on the southern circuit. On 18 December 1913 at St John's Church, Darlinghurst, he married a masseuse, Mary (Mollie) Stuart Graham, daughter of a Queensland pastoralist. Stephen was a member of the Council of the Bar of New South Wales for thirteen years between 1910 and 1929 and counsel for the Incorporated Law Institute. In the 1920s he appeared in several constitutional cases in the High Court of Australia which involved shipping. He took silk in July 1928.

Inheriting his grandfather's 'sense of civic responsibility', Stephen represented Fitzroy Ward on the Sydney Municipal Council continuously from 1900 until the council was temporarily disbanded in 1927. Deputy mayor in 1912, he was for a time vice-chairman of the finance and electric light committees. He advocated a single municipal wages board before the 1913 royal commission on the constitution of a greater Sydney. For nearly twenty-five years Stephen chaired the Citizens' Reform Association aldermen. In the 1920s he showed 'unfailing urbanity' in dealing with those who impeded administrative reforms, with the disputed resignation of the town clerk T. H. Nesbitt [q.v.11] and, from 1924, with a Labor majority. His supporters presented him with a silver coffee service in 1927.

A council-member of the Town Planning Association of New South Wales, Stephen deplored the piecemeal widening of streets and warned of impending traffic congestion. Visiting Europe and the United States of America in 1923, he was impressed by the open spaces in London and Paris, and by the modern city of Los Angeles. He also toured Egypt and at Luxor saw artefacts being removed from Tutankhamun's tomb.

An acting judge from February 1929, when appointed a puisne judge on 10 June Stephen was the fourth generation of his family to sit on the Supreme Court bench in New South Wales. Able to unravel knotty legal problems, he had a quiet, courteous and dignified manner, but was quick to appreciate amusing situations in court and to rebuff those who tried to mislead him or the jury. A devout Anglican, he was foundation secretary of the Prisoners' Aid Association and belonged to the Economic Research Society and the Australian Club.

Proficient at tennis and golf, Stephen was an original member of Royal Sydney Golf Club from 1894 and its sole handicapper for many years. Of middle height, spare, with a good-humoured countenance, he had wavy brown hair. His gift of mimicry made him a skilful amateur actor. He loved literature, music (especially singing) and the stage. Word perfect in the operas of Gilbert and Sullivan, he often reflected their wit in his own humour. He retained a boyish zest for life, but could be pernickety as when he complained to the local councils about the prevalence of cockroaches near his home in Jersey Road.

Milner Stephen collapsed and died of heart disease in the Supreme Court on 28 April 1939 and was cremated after a service at All Saints Church, Woollahra. His wife survived him but their only child had died in infancy. His estate was valued for probate at £5300.

R. Bedford, *Think of Stephen* (Syd, 1954); F. A. Larcombe, *The advancement of local government in New South Wales, 1906 to the present* (Syd, 1978); *PP*(NSW), 1913, 2, 2S, p 1 (362); *SMH*, 27 Nov 1924, 27 Dec 1927, 14 July 1928, 11 June 1929, 11 Mar 1936, 29 Apr, 1-3 May 1939.

MARTHA RUTLEDGE

STEPHEN, PATRICK JOHN (1864-1938), Methodist minister, was born on 2 February 1864 at Peterhead, Aberdeenshire, Scotland, son of Peter Stephen, shipmaster, and his wife Margaret, née Hay. He was educated at a Scottish national school and Harley College, London. As a youth he took part in a mission at Aberdeen and became interested in social questions and the welfare of the working class.

Arriving in Sydney in 1886, Stephen was accepted for the Wesleyan Methodist ministry. After a years training he was appointed to the Homebush circuit. While serving at Balmain (1888-93), he married Amy Mary Blackmore on 20 March 1890 at Leichhardt; they were to remain childless. In the same year he founded the Balmain mission: he used outdoor services and brass bands to attract an audience and revived the flagging Methodist class meeting system, employing it as the training ground for new converts. An emotional fundamentalist preacher and a good platform speaker, he rapidly transformed a failing cause into one which had difficulty in housing the congregation which flocked to his services in the neutral ground of Balmain Town Hall. He successfully undertook similar work at Leichhardt in 1903-07, having served on the Parramatta (1894-96), Wesley Church (1897-99) and West Maitland (1900-02) circuits.

Stephen presided over the Christian Endeavour Union in 1896 and later the Evangelical Council of New South Wales; he was active in the temperance and Protestant defence movements. He published several pamphlets, including *The morals and manners of Cardinal Moran* [q.v.10] in 1904. Stephen's interest in social issues had led him to support the striking Lucknow goldminers in 1897. He was a strong advocate of trade unionism and argued that strikes would remain the best way of resolving industrial disputes until the state introduced an adequate arbitration system.

A voracious reader, Stephen had a sound knowledge of theological questions. He was a capable teacher at Leigh [q.v.2] College, and at the Sydney Central Methodist Mission from 1908 to 1914: there he spent four years under W. G. Taylor [q.v.] and two as superintendent; he left in 1915 only because of ill health. While serving at Lindfield (1916-19), he was president of the united Australasian Methodist Conference in 1917.

After short terms at Manly, Annandale and Cronulla, in 1924 Stephen was appointed to his last circuit, Ashfield; he became a supernumerary in 1927. In the 1920s he chaired the Leigh College committee and in 1927 was chairman of the New South Wales Council of Churches.

Survived by his wife, he died of hypertensive cerebrovascular disease at Ashfield hospital on 22 July 1938 and was buried in Rookwood cemetery. While Stephen was noted for his sympathy for young people, he did his greatest work at the Balmain and Leichhardt missions. The 'whimsical, mystic, Celtic strain' in his nature, his passion for social reform, his fiery manner and his solidity of character enabled him to reach out to members of the industrial working class.

D. I. Wright, *Mantle of Christ* (Brisb, 1984); Methodist Church of A'sia (NSW) *Conference Minutes*, 1939; *Methodist* (Syd), 25 Apr 1908, 30 July 1938.   DON WRIGHT

STEPHEN, REGINALD (1860-1956), Anglican bishop, was born on 9 December 1860 at Geelong, Victoria, seventh child of George Alexander Stephen, woolbroker, and his wife Emily, née Johnstone, both London born; he was a distant connexion of Sir Alfred Stephen [q.v.6]. Educated at Geelong Church of England Grammar School and at Trinity College, University of Melbourne (B.A., 1882; M.A., 1884), he won exhibitions and graduated with first-class honours in history and political economy, the Cobden Club medal and the Bromby [q.v.3] prize for biblical Greek. Inspired by Bishop Moorhouse and Alexander Leeper [qq.v.5,10] at Trinity, Stephen and J. F. Stretch [q.v.] belonged to the first Victorian-born generation who were to make significant contributions to the Australian Church. Made deacon on 23 December 1883 and ordained priest on 21 December 1884 by Moorhouse, Stephen became curate of Christ Church, St Kilda. There, on 22 July 1885, he married Selina Emma Maude Low (d. 1895), daughter of the vicar.

Gaining his own parish at Balwyn in 1889, Stephen moved in 1894 to the prosperous bayside church of St Andrew, Brighton. Already a university examiner in history, he moved back to Trinity College in 1899 as subwarden and chaplain. Returning briefly in 1904 to parish work at Holy Trinity Church, Balaclava, on 23 January he married Elsie Clarice (d. 1936), daughter of Canon Horace Tucker [q.v.], at Christ Church, South Yarra. A cathedral canon from 1903, Stephen was appointed in 1906 by Archbishop Lowther Clarke [q.v.8] to head the new St John's Theological College at St Kilda. In his 1908 Moorhouse lectures, *Democracy and character*, Stephen tried to provide a theological perspective to current Australian political developments. Two years later, he also became dean of Melbourne.

Stephen was now at the height of his powers: tall and spare, with a cleft chin and classical profile, he preached thoughtful, astringent sermons and supervised non-graduate students. In a diocese where issues of churchmanship were unresolved, St John's became a centre of controversy and, amid some ill will, the Evangelicals set up Ridley College. Stephen was elected bishop of Tasmania on 17 February 1914 and consecrated in Sydney on 21 September.

At first, Stephen found Tasmania a challenge. His predecessor J. E. Mercer [q.v.10], an outspoken Christian Socialist, had not impressed conservative Anglicans. Stephen had always advocated social reform, but was no crusader. His efforts to placate the people were aided by World War I; like most of his leading co-religionists, he took a strongly Imperial line. Nevertheless, he did not feel at ease in Tasmania which offered little scope for his talents and ambitions. With the support of Stretch, he was elected bishop of Newcastle, New South Wales, and was enthroned there on 15 July 1919.

After attending the 1920 Lambeth Conference in London, Stephen settled down to coping with the post-war problems of his part-rural, part-industrial, diocese. A careful and thorough administrator, he chose effective and popular assistants in Henry Woodd [q.v.] as archdeacon and Horace Crotty (later bishop of Bathurst) as dean. In C. A. Brown, he had a registrar who could manage the unusually centralized finances. Stephen's major coup, as befitted a theological teacher, was to arrange for the removal of the inter-diocesan St John's College from Armidale to Morpeth where it came within Newcastle's control. Under the dynamic E. H. Burgmann, St John's developed into an important centre for the supply of clergy and Stephen went on to establish two grammar schools. He was less at home, however, with the industrial section of his diocese. Inexperienced with and uneasy about working-class religion, he lacked the 'common touch'. On another level, Stephen worked conscientiously on constitutional problems and prayer book revision for the Australian Church.

By the end of 1927 he had had enough; he resigned the see on 31 March 1928 and retired to Melbourne. He acted briefly as warden of Trinity College (1930), delivered many sermons and lectures—including the 1935 Moorhouse series, *Ancient laws and modern morals* (1936)—and gave episcopal assistance to successive archbishops. Stephen died at Kew on 7 July 1956 and was cremated. He was survived by his daughter and a son; another son Reginald (1906-1943) had been a Bush Brother.

A. P. Elkin, *The diocese of Newcastle* (Syd, 1955); J. Handfield, *Friends and Brothers* (Melb, 1980); Geelong C of E Grammar School, *Corian*, Aug 1914, p 3, Aug 1956, p 161, Mar 1974, p 161; *Geelong Advertiser*, 19 Feb 1955; *Age*, 9 July 1956; *Anglican*, 13 July 1956; *Aust Church Record*, 2 Aug 1956; Stephen papers (Geelong C of E Grammar School Archives).   K. J. CABLE

STEPHENS, ALFRED GEORGE (1865-1933), literary critic, editor and publisher, was born on 28 August 1865 at Toowoomba, Queensland, eldest of thirteen children of Samuel George Stephens, a storekeeper from Swansea, Wales, and his Scottish wife Euphemia Tweedie, née Russell. Samuel was later a successful businessman and part-owner of the *Darling Downs Gazette* who helped to found Toowoomba Grammar School in 1877; Alfred was the first student enrolled there.

Educated under John Mackintosh, a capable headmaster, Stephens passed the senior public examination of the University of Sydney in 1880. He was apprenticed to W. H. Groom [q.v.4], proprietor of the *Chronicle*, and was soon transferred to A. W. Beard of George Street, Sydney. He completed his course through Sydney Technical College (obtaining certificates of merit in French and German) and was admitted to the New South Wales Typographical Association in 1886. Otherwise Stephens was self-educated; he was well-read in contemporary and classical literatures, political science, moral philosophy and history.

From 1888 to 1893 Stephens was exceptionally busy: he edited two country newspapers, the *Gympie Miner* (1888-90) and the *Cairns Argus* (1891-92); wrote leaders for Gresley Lukin's [q.v.5] Brisbane *Boomerang* (1891), and published two spirited and cogent political pamphlets; and went on a world tour, sending back syndicated articles which became *A Queenslander's travel-notes* (1905). He wrote literary supplements for both the *Miner* and the *Argus* while his column, 'The Magazine Rifle', in the *Boomerang* was a precursor to the 'Red Page'. His pamphlet *The Griffilwraith* (Brisbane, 1893)—about an opportunistic political coalition between Sir Samuel Griffith and Sir Thomas McIlwraith [qq.v.9,5]—described Griffith as 'the prodigal child of Australian politics', spending his nation's substance 'on riotous legislation'. Impressed by his journalistic flair, J. F. Archibald [q.v.3] invited Stephens to join the *Bulletin* as junior sub-editor; he did so in January 1894. At the Sydney Unitarian Church on 19 December Stephens married Constance Ivingsbelle Smith whom he had met at Cairns.

In his creative period, from 1894 to about 1916, Stephens wrote the criticism and produced the books on which his literary reputation now stands. Within two years he had transformed the inside front cover of the red-jacketed *Bulletin* from advertising space for books into the fully-fledged literary column with which his name is now linked. In the process the anonymous 'A.G.S.', described by Joseph Furphy [q.v.8] as 'the three-initialled terror', became the country's most influential, widely read and respected literary critic.

What readers could expect in the 'Red Page' was a potpourri of articles, reviews, extracts, letters, paragraphs, anecdotes and notes, occasionally with photographs or cartoons. The poem of the week, starred to indicate its quality, appeared in a top corner and in the bottom corner might be blunt, cruelly witty advice to rejected contributors. Stephens' common practice was to spark controversy by attacking an established writer, such as Burns, Thackeray, Kipling, or Tennyson, thereby enticing correspondents as varied as Chris Brennan [q.v.7] or George Burns to attack and counter-attack, sometimes over weeks. It was heady stuff.

As literary editor, Stephens broadened the basis of work chosen for initial and subsequent book publication by including writers of serious literary intent, like Bernard O'Dowd [q.v.11] and Furphy, as well as popular bush balladists and comic prose writers like 'Steele Rudd' [q.v.8 A. H. Davis]. Significantly, Stephens persuaded the *Bulletin* management to issue a literary journal which he called the *Bookfellow* (Series 1) and which supplemented and drew on the 'Red Page'. The small, dilettantish magazine did not pay its way and ceased publication after only five monthly issues in 1899.

In October 1906 Stephens left—or was pushed from—the *Bulletin* and his days of security and power were ended, but not his achievement. He devoted much of his remaining time, talent and energy to producing the high-class literary journal which eventually ruined him financially and broke his spirit: the '*Bookfellow* was his dream and our curse', wrote his daughter, Constance [q.v.11 Robertson], a journalist. In all, and almost single-handedly, Stephens brought out 123 issues between 1907 and its demise in 1925, with fifty-one of the best issues between 1911 and 1916. The *Bookfellow* represents an idealistic and courageous attempt to satisfy the need for a quality literary journal, and when it failed there was a cultural gap until the appearance of *Southerly* and *Meanjin* in the 1940s. Although not as lively or provocative as the 'Red Page', and padded with a good deal of non-literary material, the *Bookfellow* is more mature, balanced and reflective. That much of the criticism (especially of overseas writing) is significant in the literary canon was illustrated when Leon Cantrell in selecting seventy-six essays from a life-time's work for preservation in book form—as *A. G. Stephens: selected writings* (Sydney, 1977)—chose twenty-one from the *Bookfellow*. (Dame) Mary Gilmore, Hugh McCrae and John Shaw Neilson [qq.v.9,10] were Stephens' most important protégés; he edited and published Neilson's first four volumes of verse.

Obsessed by the *Bookfellow* and determined to finance the glossy weekly (Series 2) which appeared from January 1907, Stephens went into business as a bookseller from October 1906 until May 1907, but the venture failed, as did a 'giant' two-day sale of stock and valuable books and manuscripts from his library. *Bookfellow* abruptly ceased publication in August; in an attempt to recoup his finances, Stephens went to Wellington, New Zealand, where he worked as leader-writer on Lukin's *Evening Post* until 1909. Back in Sydney next year he negotiated the syndication of a literary feature, 'The Bookfellow Column', which appeared in Sydney in the *Sunday Sun* from 24 July 1910. From this naturally followed the *Bookfellow* (Series 3) which appeared monthly from December 1911 to January 1916, with the financial help of Mary Gilmore from 1913.

The years of comparative decline after 1916 were frustrating and bitter for a man as proud and previously influential as Stephens. In 1919 he revived *Bookfellow* (Series 3), but it had a small audience and little impact, and finally disappeared in 1925 without a seeming ripple. He published over fifty articles in journals and newspapers, though they added little to his reputation, generally being backward-looking, or rehashes of earlier work, or out of touch and sympathy with the vital new writing of younger contemporaries. This is best illustrated in 'Satyrs in slops', a fierce condemnation of 'The alleged new poetry in Sydney' by poets of the calibre of Kenneth Slessor and R. D. FitzGerald. Stephens was invited by the Returned Sailors' and Soldiers' Imperial League of Australia to edit *An Anzac memorial* (Sydney and London, 1916, 1917, 1919); he produced two well-written monographs on Australian writers: *Henry Kendall* [q.v.5] (1928) and *Chris Brennan* (1933). He also published under the *Bookfellow* imprint seven more volumes of verse, three by Neilson. Otherwise he was involved in lecturing on Australian literature for the Workers' Educational Association, in unrealized plans for publishing anthologies and school texts, and in writing inferior potboilers, short stories and verse pamphlets, some of which he published.

Stephens' historical importance in relation to the then emerging Australian literature is widely recognized. Thus T. Inglis Moore has described him as the strongest single force in the shaping of Australian literature, an opinion endorsed by Vance Palmer [q.v.11] who thought his criticism was 'a lucky gift' for the writers of the day and by H. M. Green who wrote that no other critic had 'so strong, so wide, so beneficial an influence'. As a critic Stephens achieved eminence for establishing the 'Red Page' and *Bookfellow* as literary forums; in the process he created a body of criticism that is both substantial and distinguished. His work is marked by a confident pragmatism that enabled him to argue from first principles and to rely on the integrity of his own independent responses. His fervent nationalism led him to respond generously to works redolent of the Australian spirit, but he insisted always that standards must be maintained by measuring the local product against the best being written elsewhere. His critical writings convey a firm impression of native intellect, practical common sense and keen devotion to letters, and are expressed in a mature, flexible, energetic and often picturesque prose style. His essays, taken separately, seem fragmentary: they are characterized by flashes of brilliance and insights eloquently expressed, rather than by construction on the larger scale. In part this bittiness is because of the circumstances under which he worked and published as a hard-pressed columnist, but, significantly, he left no major book. It is also argued that he lacked a coherent rationale or theory of criticism, but this allegation is refuted by his many perceptive comments on the subject, including what he wrote to Kate Baker [q.v.7]:

Criticism is in the nature of a bridge between art and the public. Its function is to set up a standard, and to guide the public to *self-use* of that standard. It demands in its construction minds fully trained to understand and appreciate the aesthetic laws which underlie art, and with a grasp of psychology which enables the critic to know what the public wants and what degree of improvement it will stand in its wants. It suffers from a divorce in these qualities.

Apart from his criticism, Stephens' strength as a writer lay in *belles-lettres*, factual articles and literary biography. He was, as well, a superb journalist who elevated the 'interview' to an art form. His creative writing illustrates his own theory—that the critical and creative faculties are not necessarily complementary—and is best ignored. Stephens' fine achievement as editor was to have published in his lifetime over forty meticulously produced books which are now part of our literary heritage.

His diary and an unpublished biography by Constance Robertson reveal Stephens as a difficult and demanding head of household whose relationship with his wife deteriorated over the years. After leaving the *Bulletin* he was often hard-pressed for money and his 'brood of seven children' placed strains on him as provider. He was said to be aloof and irascible with the children to whom he showed little overt affection. He rarely sat down at the table with the family, but had his meals sent to his room with the meat finely cut so he could eat with a fork one-handed, hardly taking his eyes from the page he was reading. His daughter commented that as 'he walked alone on his literary path so to a great extent he was alone among his children'.

A solidly-built, handsome man with wide-open blue eyes, Stephens had a blond beard and a proud, erect bearing. Some found his manner intimidating, but those who knew him well agree with Norman Lindsay [q.v.10] that 'the head thrown back, the jutting beard, the resolute walk and the expanded chest' concealed a nervous, sensitive and vulnerable nature which was easily moved by evidence of feeling in a poem or story. His dress was distinctive, somewhat like that of a bushman in town: an open-necked Crimean shirt with rolled-up sleeves and an old reefer-jacket with seams much stretched due to frequent chest expansions. His voluminous manuscripts are written in vivid purple ink and in a large, confident, fluent hand that reinforces the imperious effect of the ink. He was anticlerical and an acknowledged free-thinker in youth and middle age; he chose the title, *The red pagan* (1904), for a book based on articles from the 'Red Page'.

Stephens' death in St Luke's Hospital, Darlinghurst, on 15 April 1933 was associated with mitral regurgitation and anaemia; he was cremated. His wife, two sons and four daughters survived him. The eldest son John Gower Stephens graduated brilliantly from the University of Sydney (B.Sc., with first-class honours and the University medal for chemistry, 1919; M.B., 1924; Ch.M., 1925); he became a radiologist and lived mainly overseas. Nettie Palmer [q.v.11] complained about 'the appalling lack of public response' to the news of Stephens' death. Mary Gilmore wrote an obituary tribute, entitled 'The last of the giants', which concluded:

Only those who were intellectually shaped by his hand, only those who stood on the strong steps of his work, know with what a sense of loss the words were uttered, 'A. G. Stephens is gone'.

P. R. Stephensen, *The life and works of A. G. Stephens ('The Bookfellow')* (Syd, 1940); V. Palmer (ed), *A. G. Stephens* (Melb, 1941); J. Barnes, *The writer in Australia* (Melb, 1969); B. Bennett (ed), *Cross currents* (Melb, 1981); W. H. Wilde, *Courage a grace* (Melb, 1988); *Texas Q*, 5, no 2, 1962, p 96; *Aust Literary Studies*, 1, no 4, 1964, p 219, 8, no 1, 1977, p 82; *Southerly*, 8, no 4, 1947, p 246, 24, no 3, 1964, p 161; *Meanjin Q*, 27, no 4, 1968, p 459, 38, no 4, 1979, p 495; C. Maguire, An original reaction from art: an analysis of the criticism of A. G. Stephens in the Red Page of the *Bulletin* (M.A. thesis, ANU, 1973); S. E. Lee, The self-made critic: A. G. Stephens (M.A. thesis, Univ Syd, 1978); J. R. Tyrrell papers *and* C. Robertson papers (ML); L. Hayes papers *and* A. G. Stephens letters (Fryer Lib, Univ Qld); Stephens papers (ML, NL and Alexander Turnbull Lib, Wellington, NZ).

STUART LEE

STEPHENS, ARTHUR AUGUSTUS (1867-1914), educationist, was born on 21 March 1867 at New Town, Hobart, son of William Stephens, bootmaker, and his wife Jane, née Calman. Educated at New Town State School, he won a government exhibition at 11, continued with distinction at the High School, Hobart, and began to study part time for a B.A. degree from the University of London which he completed in 1904.

At 19 Stephens established the New Town Classical and Commercial School which, within four years, merged with Officer College, Hobart. In July 1893 he opened Queen's College in Hobart, its main object being to prepare pupils for university examinations, although special classes were also provided in commercial subjects. Such was Stephens' character that, when he left Officer College, its best students followed him.

Queen's was to be a school over which he ruled absolutely, free from the controls of school councils and committees. Although Stephens was a practising Anglican, his school had no denominational affiliation or external assistance. By 1895 he had made Queen's largely co-educational: while there were 'mixed-classes', there was strict segregation at other times, with separate playgrounds for boys and girls. To Stephens, the co-educational experiment had been a very satisfactory innovation. Nevertheless, as Queen's grew in size and reputation, boys came to predominate in number and in 1908 the Girls' Department was discontinued.

Academic excellence was the hallmark of Queen's. The school motto, *Palme non sine pulvere* (No reward without hard work), summed up Stephens' approach to study. 'He was indefatigable himself, but boys soon learnt that they had more to do than watch him work. He had a wonderful power of impressing upon others a portion at least of his own zeal and enthusiasm.' Stephens' wisdom, liberality and understanding made Queen's the most notable school in Tasmania over a period of nineteen and a half years. Loyalty was another element which he had engendered. Roy Bridges [q.v.7], an ex-student, wrote of Stephens that he was 'good-looking, dark-haired, dark-moustached, fresh-faced and kind of eyes; black of tail coat; grey of trousers, and white of waistcoat and starched linen. From the moment he smiled, offered me his hand and called me by my Christian name, I worshipped Arthur Stephens'.

Around 1911 he began to feel the administrative burdens and saw value in the backing of an institution like the Church of England. Plagued by continued ill health, Stephens was to allow the amalgamation in 1912 of his far larger school with The Hutchins School, of which he became vice-master. By late 1913 his health had so deteriorated that he was persuaded to take three months leave. Stephens died at New Town of pernicious anaemia on 14 May 1914, survived by his wife, Ida Ethel Marion, née Steele, whom he had married at Forcett on 28 June 1905, and two small children. Five hundred people attended his funeral at St John's Anglican Church, New Town, and Queen's old boys carried the coffin to the churchyard cemetery.

R. Bridges, *That yesterday was home* (Syd, 1948); W. N. Oats, *The rose and the waratah* (Hob, 1979);

G. H. Stephens, *The Hutchins School, Macquarie Street years, 1846-1965* (Hob, 1979); M. E. W. Stump, *Early recollections of a west Hobartian* (Melb, 1986); *Walch's Tasmanian Almanack*, 1895; *Hutchins School Mag*, June 1914; *Hutchins School Centenary Mag*, 1946; *Church News* (Hob), May 1913, Jan, June 1914; *Mercury*, 8 July 1893, 19 Dec 1896, 16 May 1914, 10 Jan 1930; *Daily Post* (Hob), 15 May 1914; Hutchins School Archives.

G. H. STEPHENS

STEPHENS, HENRY DOUGLAS (1877-1952), paediatric surgeon, was born on 26 June 1877 at Williamstown, Melbourne, eldest son of John Charles Stephens, newspaper proprietor, and his wife Kate, née Douglas. Educated at Camberwell Grammar School (dux in 1894), he graduated from the University of Melbourne (M.B., 1899; B.S., 1900) with honours in all years and an exhibition in anatomy. While training at St Vincent's and the Melbourne and Children's hospitals, he was influenced by William Snowball [q.v.] and by the surgeon Peter Bennie. Stephens was awarded an M.D. (1903) and M.S. (1905) by the University of Melbourne. On 6 September 1911 he married with Congregational forms Eileen, daughter of the paediatrician Frank Hobill Cole [q.v.8] with whom he was in private practice for some time.

A tireless worker, Stephens became resident medical officer at the Children's Hospital in 1901, clinical assistant to the out-patients' department in 1903 and honorary medical officer attending out-patients in 1909. He also served as honorary pathologist in 1904-14. Appointed honorary surgeon to in-patients in 1920, he retired in 1940 but returned to act in that post during World War II. He was a member of the committee of management in 1946-52. Serving the Children's Hospital for forty-five years, Stephens became recognized as one of Australia's leading paediatric surgeons: colleagues respected his energy, his receptive mind and his devotion to duty. His prime interest was in surgery of the cleft lip and palate. The Henry Douglas Stephens Memorial Operating Theatre was named in his honour. He was also consultant paediatrician to the Women's Hospital, Melbourne, in 1931-45.

Co-founder of the Melbourne Paediatric Society, Stephens was its honorary secretary for twenty years (president 1928 and 1940). He was also president of the British Medical Association (Victoria) in 1926, vice-president of the B.M.A. centenary meeting in London in 1932 and president of the paediatric section of the Australasian Medical Congress, Adelaide, in 1937. He was, as well, president of the Melbourne Medical Association (1920), the Australian Physiotherapists' Association (1945-51) and foundation president of the

Australian Paediatrics Association (Australian College of Paediatrics) in 1950. He served from 1931 to 1940 on the faculty of medicine and lectured at the university on diseases of children; from 1935 to 1940 he was dean of the clinical school, Royal Children's Hospital; and he was a councillor of the Royal Victorian College of Nursing and the Victorian Society for Crippled Children.

A 'kindly, lovable soul', Stephens died in Melbourne on 17 June 1952 and was cremated. He was survived by his wife, three daughters and a son. James Govett's portrait of Stephens is owned by the family.

MJA, 20 Sept 1952, p 419; *VHM*, 33, no 1, Aug 1962; Stephens family papers (held by Mrs H. de Wolf, Sth Yarra, Melb).   F. DOUGLAS STEPHENS

STEPHENSEN, PERCY REGINALD (1901-1965), writer, editor and publisher, was born on 20 November 1901 at Maryborough, Queensland, eldest son of Christian Julius Stephensen, wheelwright, and his Russian-born Swiss wife Marie Louise Aimée, daughter of H. A. Tardent [q.v.]. Percy attended Biggenden State School, then boarded at Maryborough Grammar. At the University of Queensland (B.A., 1922) he acquired the lifelong nickname 'Inky' (from the popular wartime song, *Mademoiselle from Armentières*); he also made friends with two returned servicemen, Fred Paterson, the communist, and Eric Partridge [q.v.11], the lexicographer. Norman Lindsay's [q.v.10] son, Jack, introduced him to Brisbane radicals and intellectuals. Stephensen edited the university magazine, *Galmahra*, in 1921 and caused controversy by including Jack's erotic lyrics. That year Stephensen joined the Communist Party of Australia. After graduating, he taught at Ipswich Grammar School in 1922-23. To everyone's surprise, including his own, he won the 1924 Queensland Rhodes scholarship and left for England in August.

Reading philosophy, politics and economics at The Queen's College, Oxford, Stephensen joined the university branch of the Communist Party with A. J. P. Taylor, Graham Greene and Tom Driberg, an undercover agent for MI5. Threatened with expulsion by the university authorities for his communist agitation, Stephensen was involved in the 1926 general strike and, after it failed, helped to organize the Workers' Theatre Movement in London.

Graduating with second-class honours in 1927, Stephensen joined Jack Lindsay and managed the Fanfrolico Press at Bloomsbury, London. He devoted his energies to literary and fine press publishing, issuing about twenty titles in 1927-29: all lavishly printed

and illustrated limited editions, they included works by the Lindsays and Hugh McCrae [q.v.10], as well as his own translation, *The antichrist of Nietzsche*. He also co-edited with Jack the literary magazine, *London Aphrodite*. Stephensen began living with a former ballerina Winifred Sarah Venus, née Lockyer, with whom he shared the rest of his stormy life. They married, after her husband's death, on 7 November 1947 in Melbourne; Winifred raised a son Jack from her first marriage.

After meeting D. H. Lawrence in December 1928, Stephensen established the Mandrake Press (1929-30)—with backing from a Bloomsbury book-dealer—to publish Lawrence's controversial paintings. As a champion of Lawrence, he took part in a spirited anti-censorship crusade, writing satirical pamphlets and arranging with Lawrence to produce a secret English edition of *Lady Chatterley's lover*. He also published his own collection of Australian stories, *The bushwhackers* (1929), as well as work by Jack McLaren [q.v.10] and others, among them the legendary Aleister Crowley.

Returning to Australia in 1932, Stephensen established the Endeavour Press in Sydney with Norman Lindsay, producing over a dozen titles by such writers as A. B. Paterson and Miles Franklin [qq.v.11,8]. Disagreements with the board led to Stephensen's resignation in 1933. He set up his own undercapitalized firm, P. R. Stephensen & Co., which brought out another dozen Australian books by Franklin, Henry Handel Richardson [q.v.11], Eleanor Dark and others. The company's inevitable demise in 1935 delayed publication of Xavier Herbert's *Capricornia* until 1938.

With the failure of his publishing ventures, Stephensen became active as a polemicist and organizer. The attempted banning of the Czech writer Egon Kisch from Australia in 1934-35 prompted Stephensen to lead a rebellion against George Mackaness [q.v.10] in the Fellowship of Australian Writers; 'Inky' was supported by Frank Clune, for whom he was to ghost-write almost seventy books over the next thirty years. Stephensen expanded a long essay for his short-lived 'national literary magazine', *Australian Mercury*, into *The foundations of culture in Australia* (1936) which was his most significant achievement and one of the most stimulating works of the 1930s. Its influence led to the formation of the Jindyworobak poetry movement.

Publication of the book was financed by a new patron W. J. Miles [q.v.10] who, with Stephensen's assistance, in July 1936 launched the monthly *Publicist*; it had a strongly anti-British, anti-Semitic and anti-democratic flavour by 1938 and was criticized for its overt Fascism. An early champion of Aboriginal rights, Stephensen helped to organize the

'Day of Mourning and Protest' to mark the sesquicentenary on 26 January 1938.

The central puzzle of Stephensen's life was his sudden shift of sympathy from the left to the far right. If his need to rely on the patronage of Miles was one reason, another was his frustration at his own business failures. The widely-publicized Moscow trials of 1936-38 convinced him that communism was no longer a solution. Disillusioned with democracy, he now looked to extreme nationalism, although he idolized Gandhi rather than Hitler. Like conservative Australian politicians, Stephensen showed admiration for Japan.

In October 1941 Stephensen formed the Australia-First Movement, a political pressure group based on the programme advocated by the *Publicist*. Military Intelligence, after failing to have the group banned, used a plot concocted by an *agent provocateur* in Western Australia to implicate Stephensen. He took over as editor of the *Publicist* in January 1942, but was arrested and interned without trial on 10 March, with fifteen other A.F.M. members, on suspicion of collaboration with the Japanese and of planning sabotage and assassination.

There was uproar in Federal parliament and criticism of the Labor government when it became clear that there was no genuine connexion between the Western Australian 'plot' and Stephensen. Yet he was held without trial in various internment camps for the rest of the war. A Commonwealth commission of inquiry found that there were 'substantial reasons' for Stephensen's detention, but this opinion was mainly based on pre-war evidence of his disloyalty to Britain and admiration for Germany and Japan. An official war historian, (Sir) Paul Hasluck, wrote that the detentions were the 'grossest infringement of individual liberty made during the war'.

For ten bitter years after World War II Stephensen lived with Winifred in various parts of Victoria, sustained only by his ghost-writing for Clune. In 1954 their major biography of Jorgen Jorgenson [q.v.2], *The Viking of Van Diemen's Land*, was published by Angus and Robertson [qq.v.7,11] Ltd; Stephensen's memoir of the Fanfrolico Press, *Kookaburras and satyrs*, appeared that year.

Having returned to Sydney with Winifred in 1956, Stephensen lived at Cremorne within sight of the harbour. He ghosted books for retired sea captains and published under his own name the definitive *History and description of Sydney Harbour* (Adelaide, 1966). He wrote or edited many entries in the 1958 *Australian encyclopaedia*, edited four volumes of William Baylebridge's [q.v.7] poetry (1961-64), was a foundation member of the Australian Society of Authors (1963) and worked as a literary agent. On 28 May 1965, after giving an enthusiastic speech to the Sydney

Savage Club, he collapsed and died in the State Ballroom. Walter Stone gave a panegyric at his cremation. Stephensen's wife survived him; they had no issue.

An intellectual and literary adventurer, as well as a political rebel, Stephensen was a talented writer and a brilliant editor. As a publisher he influenced the careers of major writers. In the 1930s he helped to improve the standard of Australian book design and production, and to stimulate more vigorous cultural and intellectual debate. Almost 6 ft. (182.9 cm) tall, Stephensen was of athletic build, with fair to reddish hair and a toothbrush moustache. A portrait of him by Edward Quicke, a fellow-internee at Tatura camp, Victoria, is held by the National Library of Australia, Canberra.

B. Muirden, *The puzzled patriots* (Melb, 1968); P. Hasluck, *The government and the people 1942-1945* (Canb, 1970); E. Stephensen, *Brief biographical memorandum of Percy Reginald ('Inky') Stephensen* and *Bibliography of Percy Reginald Stephensen* (Melb, priv print, 1981); J. Lindsay, *Life rarely tells* (Melb, 1982); C. Munro, *Wild man of letters* (Melb, 1984); *PP*(Cwlth), 1945-46, 4, p 941; R. Fotheringham, The life of P. R. Stephensen, Australian publisher (B.A. Hons thesis, Univ Qld, 1970); R. L. Hall, Notes about P. R. Stephensen 1918-1932 (Fotheringham papers, Fryer Lib); Stephensen papers (ML and Fryer Lib).

CRAIG MUNRO

STEPHENSON, SIR ARTHUR GEORGE (1890-1967), architect, was born on 5 April 1890 at Box Hill, Victoria, one of six children of Arthur Robert Stephenson, schoolmaster and Congregational preacher, and his wife Sarah Ann, sister of Charles Chewings [q.v.7]. Educated at Melbourne Church of England Grammar School where he was an outstanding athlete, Stephenson was apprenticed to a builder and studied construction part time at the Working Men's College, Melbourne. In 1911-13 he was a construction supervisor for Burns, Philp [qq.v.7,11] & Co. Ltd in New Guinea, then an assistant architect with the Western Australian government. He returned to Melbourne as junior architect with Eggleston & Oakley, the builders of Collins House, whose design consultant was W. B. Griffin [q.v.9]. On 9 June 1915 Stephenson married Evelyn May Mackay with Congregational forms at Kew, Melbourne.

In November 1915 he was commissioned lieutenant in the Australian Imperial Force and next May was promoted captain in the 3rd Pioneer Battalion. During his service in France he was twice mentioned in dispatches and in December 1917 was awarded the Military Cross. Discharged in England after the war, he studied at the Architectural Association School, London, and qualified as an associate (1920) of the Royal Institute of British Architects. His family joined him in London where he worked before returning to Eggleston in Melbourne at the urging of his patrons, the Baillieus [qq.v.7]. In 1921 he went into partnership with P. H. Meldrum: starting with a borrowed desk, he built what was described as 'the colossus of Australian architectural practices'.

An instinctive internationalist and a tireless traveller, Stephenson specialized from 1924 in institutional and hospital work. In this most difficult and complex branch of modern architecture he sought solutions adapted to the functions of modern medicine, listening 'with sympathy and acute intelligence' to the men and women who would work in his buildings. He was a controversial reformer whose reputation was established with St Vincent's, the Mercy and Royal Melbourne hospitals, and with the Royal Prince Alfred in Sydney, monuments to his revolution in hospital design. Many of the major hospitals built in Australia from the 1920s to the 1960s reflected Stephenson's influence; in Melbourne they included the Royal Children's Hospital, Queen Victoria, Alfred, Eye and Ear and the Freemasons; in Sydney he was responsible for modifying the Children's Hospital and St Vincent's; he also designed the Royal Newcastle General and Woden Valley (Canberra) hospitals. As well as major buildings in every capital city in Australia, and in New Zealand and Iraq, Stephenson opened offices overseas and managed to nourish talent by a close-knit, 'team' approach. In 1937, with the withdrawal of Meldrum, D. K. Turner became Stephenson's partner.

During World War II Stephenson and Turner built military hospitals and defence projects for the Commonwealth government. They were later responsible for Australia's first atomic energy reactor at Lucas Heights, New South Wales, and for numerous commercial and industrial buildings. The Australian pavilions at the World Fair in Paris (1936) and at the Wellington Exhibition, New Zealand (1939), were built by the firm; New York honoured Stephenson with citizenship for his work on its 1939 World Fair. 'Make no little plans', he once advised, 'they have no magic to stir men's blood'.

A tireless correspondent, he also lectured and wrote widely on aspects of his profession. Innumerable committees, especially those connected with town planning and hospitals, claimed his presence. A member (1930, 1951) of the executive committees of the International Hospitals Federation, he was a foundation member (1952) of the Hospital Advisory Council, Melbourne, and a trustee (1956) of the National Museum of Victoria. A fellow of the British, Australian and New Zealand institutes of architects and an asso-

ciate member of the Town Planning Institute of Great Britain, he held honorary memberships of the American Institute of Architects and the American College of Hospital Administrators. In 1954 he was awarded R.I.B.A.'s royal gold medal and in 1964 received the gold medal of the Australian institute. He was appointed C.M.G. in 1953, knighted in 1954 and appointed K.B.E. in 1964.

Stephenson was sought after but rarely seen outside his own circle of friends, themselves 'a cross section of the heirs of the Melbourne Establishment'. Blue-eyed, mild-mannered, with a square jaw and looking in maturity 'the very model of a double-breasted conservative', he avoided outward show, yet was often unconventional. An individualist 'to whom life itself in all its manifestations was a challenge', in later years he turned with enthusiasm in his cruiser *Jasta* to the solitude and beauty of the ocean. Stephenson died on 20 November 1967 at Prahran and was cremated. His wife, two daughters and a son survived him.

K. S. Inglis, *Hospital and community* (Melb, 1958); J. M. Freeland, *The making of a profession* (Syd, 1971); J. Shaw, *Sir Arthur Stephenson Australian architect* (Syd, 1987); *Aust Builder*, Sept 1952; *Aust Financial Review*, 30 June 1960; Stephenson papers (AA).   J. D. FISHER

STERNBERG, JOSEPH (1852-1928), auctioneer and politician, was born on 3 April 1852 at Whitechapel, London, son of Alexander Sternberg, clothier, and his wife Frederica, née Platt. Migrating to Victoria in the 1850s, Alexander became a storekeeper and timber merchant before moving with his family to Rochester in 1861. There Joseph selected land in 1865. He proved the soil suitable for cereals, planted vines, speculated in livestock and, with his brother, established an auctioneering and stock and station agency. On 3 November 1880 at Sandhurst he married with Jewish rites Selina, daughter of Barnet Lazarus and sister of D. B. Lazarus [q.v.10]. A foundation commissioner of the Campaspe Irrigation Trust, Sternberg was a foundation member of the local agricultural society, president of the racing club and chairman of the Rochester school board of advice.

In 1888 Sternberg Bros amalgamated with a Bendigo firm as L. McPherson, Sternberg & Co. Ltd (capital £150 000) to cater for the rich farming hinterland. A keen speculator in mining scrip, in 1892 Sternberg organized the flotation of the New Prince of Wales mine; he was a director of the Clarence, New Moon Consolidated and Suffolk United mines; he was also a founder of the Sandhurst Trustees and Executors' Co.

In 1889 Sternberg stood for the Victorian

Legislative Council seat of Northern Province: narrowly defeated, he was successful in June 1891 and held the seat until May 1904. Following a redistribution, he represented Bendigo province—practically without opposition—from June 1904 until his death and was known as the 'father' of the chamber. He sat on numerous committees, including royal commissions on old age pensions (1897), the operation of the factories and shops law of Victoria (1900-03), the railway and tramway systems of Melbourne and suburbs (1910-11), and housing conditions in Melbourne and the major centres of the State (1914-18). In 1906 he had opposed adult suffrage, being prepared to extend the franchise only to women who were breadwinners.

As a member of the Bendigo Development League, Sternberg supported rural capital works and development, took a keen interest in mining legislation and saw in the closer settlement Acts a means to decentralize population. As a member of the first council of education in Victoria, he sought the introduction of agricultural high schools. A prominent Freemason, he was associated with friendly societies and many public bodies, among them the Bendigo hospital, benevolent asylum, art gallery and agricultural society. He was president of the Bendigo Athletic and the Sandhurst Rowing clubs.

One of the 'great personalities' of Bendigo, Sternberg died on 13 January 1928 in Mount St Evin's Hospital, Fitzroy; after a service in the Bourke Street Synagogue, he was buried in Melbourne general cemetery. A son and a daughter survived him. His estate was sworn for probate at £23 106.

W. B. Kimberly, *Bendigo and its vicinity* (Ballarat, 1895); *Annals of Bendigo*, 1928; L. M. Goldman, *The Jews in Victoria in the nineteenth century* (Melb, 1954); *Age* and *Argus*, 14 Jan 1928.

CHARLES FAHEY

STERNE, ELIZABETH ANNE VALENTINE (1880-1973), community leader, was born on 14 February 1880 at Emerald, Queensland, fifth surviving child of Irish parents, Michael Hanrahan, labourer, and his wife Elizabeth Anne, née Trant. Having passed the junior public examination at the age of 12, Elizabeth left school to work for a merchant at Townsville and subsequently became assistant clerk of Wambo Shire Council, Dalby. She next taught business subjects at Charters Towers Technical College and was correspondent for the *Townsville Evening Star*.

Moving to Warwick in 1909, Elizabeth taught at the local technical college. On 6 October in Brisbane she married Henry Sterne, a widower and editor of the *Warwick Examiner*. Helping to establish Warwick High School, 'E.V.A.' (as she was called by her peers) remained honorary secretary of the school and technical college for twenty years. The mother of four children and stepmother of three, she nevertheless found time for community service. During World War I she was active in the Red Cross Society and from 1928 to 1968 helped to organize the Anzac Day diggers' lunches; she was one of the first women in Queensland to become a justice of the peace.

Appointed to the governing council of the new Queensland Country Women's Association, Sterne was its first State treasurer from 1924 to 1944. She also became deputations delegate, responsible for bringing matters that concerned the association to the attention of the Queensland government. A gifted public speaker with 'an alert executive brain', she knew 'how to disarm with a jest'. Her talents extended to finding good ideas in others and to presenting them in acceptable form. The State international officer (1944-47, 1951-53 and 1959-62), she represented the Q.C.W.A. at overseas conferences. As the association's State president from 1947 to 1950, and national president in 1950, she entertained many eminent visitors. 'Her deep but unintrusive religious faith' expressed itself in a wide range of charitable works. Noted for her money-raising ability, she was invited to organize the Australian Comforts Fund at the beginning of World War II; she was appointed O.B.E. in 1941.

Known affectionately as 'Chute' by her family, Sterne combined a loving domestic life with public professionalism. She was founding president of the Warwick Business and Professional Womens' Club and for some years a member of the Warwick Hospital board. From the age of 70 to 90 she ran a catering business. Predeceased by her husband, Sterne died in Warwick General Hospital on 17 April 1973 and was buried with Catholic rites in Warwick cemetery. She was survived by one son, two daughters, a stepdaughter and a foster-daughter. An obituary paid tribute to her charm, eloquence and drive.

Qld Country Women's Assn, *Fifty years 1922-72* (Brisb, 1972?); J. McKey, *The Warwick story* (Warwick, 1977); *Qld Countrywoman*, June 1973; *Queenslander*, 23 June 1927; *Warwick Daily News*, 18 Apr 1973; information from Mrs L. A. Wiemers, Atherton, Nth Qld.

K. E. GILL

STEVENS, ARTHUR BORLASE (1880-1965), soldier and railways officer, was born on 26 June 1880 at Erskineville, Sydney, son of William Borlase Stevens, commercial traveller, and his wife Elizabeth Annie, née Merchant. Educated at the College School,

Summer Hill, he joined the clerical division of the New South Wales government railways. On 2 September 1903 at St James's Anglican Church, Wickham, he married Vera Eleanor McIsaac Proctor; they were to remain childless. Stevens joined the Light Horse in 1910 and spent a year in the ranks before appointment as second lieutenant to the New South Wales Lancers. He transferred to the 14th (Hunter River) Infantry and then to the 21st Infantry in 1913.

By 1914 Stevens was a railway telegraphist. Enlisting in the Australian Imperial Force on 27 August, he was one of a select group of officers chosen by its commander, Lieut-Colonel G. F. Braund [q.v.7], for appointment to the 2nd Battalion; on 23 September Stevens was made lieutenant. Promoted captain on 18 October, he embarked that day for Egypt. He landed at Gallipoli on 25 April 1915 and was with his men during the fighting on Walker's Ridge: for three days and nights the 2nd Battalion, largely isolated and under almost constant attack, held the most vital ground in the area. The fighting was so close that at one stage Captain Stevens shot a Turk who had crept near enough to touch his bayonet. Wounded by shell-fire on 9 May, Stevens was back with his unit by 9 July. A few days afterwards he was transferred to 1st Brigade Headquarters as acting staff captain, but returned to his unit on 4 August as second-in-command with the rank of major.

Prominent in the battle of Lone Pine, Stevens led the original battalion attack and commanded it until Colonel Scobie came forward; he then directed the defence and consolidation of the left flank. On 7 August he took temporary command of the battalion when Scobie was killed. As he took charge, a stream of Turks could be seen moving along a sap towards the heart of the battalion's position; Stevens brought up a machine-gun: its fire hampered, then halted, the Turkish advance. All four of the gun's crew were recommended for the Victoria Cross. For his part in the Lone Pine fighting, Stevens was mentioned in dispatches and awarded the Distinguished Service Order. He remained on Gallipoli until the evacuation.

By February 1916, in Egypt, Stevens was the senior officer remaining in the 2nd Battalion. On 12 March he was promoted lieutcolonel in command. In eighteen months he had risen from second lieutenant to lieutcolonel. In March he embarked for France, commanding his battalion at Pozières in July when, in three days, it lost 10 officers and 500 men. The battalion was briefly engaged at Mouquet Farm in August. At Pozières and elsewhere Stevens encouraged his men by example, making himself conspicuous where enemy fire was hottest. For his service in 1916 he was appointed C.M.G.

From November he commanded the 1st Division Training School—a welcome relief from the anxieties of a fighting commander—and in March 1917 he was posted as commander of the 1st Advanced Divisional Base Depot. He resumed command of the 2nd Battalion on 19 December, after the Passchendaele battles; except for two periods totalling eight weeks when he was acting brigade commander, he led it through all but the last of the great battles of 1918. On 18 September he was granted furlough to Australia.

After the war Stevens re-entered the New South Wales railways; from being an inspector in the electrical branch, he rose to chief inspector. He maintained his interest in soldiering and in 1921-26 commanded the 36th Militia Battalion. Posted to the reserve of officers in 1931, he returned in 1940 to full-time service as commanding officer of the 9th Recruit Reception Battalion. In 1941-42 he was area commander at Narellan and then at Ingleburn, one of the State's largest training and transit camps for troops. He was placed on the retired list as an honorary colonel in October 1942. Survived by his wife, he died suddenly on 4 September 1965 at Dee Why Bowling Club, Sydney, and was cremated.

C. E. W. Bean, *The story of Anzac*, 1, 2 (Syd, 1921, 1924) and *The A.I.F. in France*, 1916, 1918 (Syd, 1929, 1937, 1942); F. W. Taylor and T. A. Cusack (eds), *Nulli secundus* (Syd, 1942).

A. J. SWEETING

STEVENS, SIR BERTRAM SYDNEY BARNSDALE (1889-1973), accountant and premier, was born on 2 January 1889 at Redfern, Sydney, seventh surviving child of English-born John Stevens, carpenter, and his Victorian wife Sarah Ann Lucas, née Barnsdale. Educated at Fort Street Model School, Stevens was employed as a clerk with the Sydney Municipal Council in 1905. From 1908 he was deputy town clerk of Manly and from 1912 a clerk in the Department of Local Government. At Annandale on 18 April 1914 he married Edith Lillie Anderson; they were to share a happy family life.

His rise was rapid. By 1920 Stevens was a Public Service Board inspector and in 1924, aged 35, became under-secretary and director of finance at the State Treasury. In his new post Stevens soon clashed with the redoubtable Labor premier and treasurer J. T. Lang [q.v.9] and, although supported by the Public Service Board, resigned in 1925 rather than have his authority diminished by reorganization of duties. Resignation endowed him with an aura of martyrdom and opened the door to politics. In 1927 he became an alderman on Marrickville Municipal Council. With (Sir) Thomas Bavin's [q.v.7] help, he was elected to the Legislative Assembly as a Nationalist representing Croydon. With a reputation for efficiency and probity, Stevens stood for private enterprise and good administration. A strict Methodist (in early life a lay preacher), he was also a teetotaller and never smoked.

By driving Stevens out of the Treasury Lang had made a formidable enemy and given the National Party an energetic and ambitious leader. In Bavin's ministry (formed in October 1927) Stevens was assistant treasurer until April 1929, then treasurer and minister for railways to November 1930. The businessmen who dominated party finances were already grooming him for leadership, but some Nationalists preferred the experienced Bavin—despite his ill health and distrust of the All for Australia League—to the combative newcomer.

Late in March 1932 Stevens became leader of the United Australia Party. On 13 May Governor Sir Philip Game [q.v.8] dismissed Lang and commissioned Stevens to form a ministry, although Stevens had only thirty-five supporters including fifteen Country Party members in a House of ninety. At the elections Stevens campaigned triumphantly in the names of law and order, sound finance and reduced unemployment. He won a record victory with sixty-four seats in coalition with the United Country Party led by Lieut-Colonel (Sir) Michael Bruxner [q.v.7].

Stevens' major problem on taking office was not so much unemployment and the Depression as law and order under the Constitution. In 1933, after Lang's attempts to swamp the Legislative Council, the Stevens-Bruxner ministry secured public and parliamentary approval for the first major reform of the Upper House since 1861. In the name of democracy, the council—consisting of sixty members elected for staggered terms of up to twelve years by members of both Houses voting as one electorate—was made safe against Labor for many years (until 1949). Only the assembly could initiate money bills and council's power to amend appropriation bills was restricted. Disagreements over other bills were to be settled by conference and referendum. The people supported this measure by 716 938 votes to 676 034. Following the report of the royal commissioner H. S. Nicholas [q.v.11], in 1935 the government gratefully allowed the New States proposal to lapse.

Adhering to the Premiers' Plan, Stevens used relief work to mop up the worst extremes of discontent and demoralization. He wanted to demonstrate that government and the economic system could operate in the interests of the majority of the people. The possibility that wages paid to relief workers might retard full economic recovery was less important to him than were the self-respect and political outlook of the 200 000 adult men unemployed in June 1932.

Although Stevens abolished the family endowment tax, the coalition valued the family and absorbed family endowment claims into general revenue. The most public problem was that of landlords and tenants, creditors and debtors. While Lang had been premier, parliament had legislated to protect mortgagors and tenants. Stevens' Moratorium Act of 1932 (extended in 1936 and again in 1939) did not provide a complete moratorium, but it did restore confidence among both creditors and debtors. The building of new houses for rent markedly increased. The Landlord and Tenant (Amendment) Act allowed rents that had been compulsorily reduced to be increased and, on evictions, provided a basis that the courts used to favour the landlord. Stevens was criticized within his own party, especially by Sir Thomas Henley [q.v.9], formerly a supporter of the New Guard, for allowing so much governmental control of private property to continue.

The 1935 electoral campaign was conducted on a basis of continuing to save the state and society from the ravaging attacks of Labor under Lang. There were difficulties in taking this position. Within the U.A.P. voices like that of A. Spencer Watts, past president of the Sydney Chamber of Commerce, complained that industry and commerce were still over-taxed and that free enterprise was not being given its chance to restore prosperity. Why had Stevens not balanced the budget in priority to every other objective? Stevens had his own doubts. More than any other leading Australian politician of his time he valued the advice of economists and of academics. He was among the first political leaders in Australia to be aware of what Keynes was advocating; Keynes's teachings increasingly suited his conviction that public finance was an instrument and a servant, not an altar on which social stability and human happiness should be sacrificed: was a balanced budget really the highest good? Another problem for Stevens was that he never persuaded himself that Labor could, or should, be for ever consigned to the 'howling political wilderness', as some of his party hoped. A practical man, who consulted professional students of politics and economics, Stevens admitted to his friends that New South Wales had a strong natural bent towards Labor. That he did not attempt to shatter Labor was counted against him by some of his own party. So was his growing interest in wider aspects of social and political problems. Like (Sir) Robert Menzies, he did not travel overseas until relatively late in his career. For Stevens 1936 was a year of revelation that he communicated to his colleagues in a series of able reports and letters, both circular and private. He had deepened his understanding of unemployment and the economy, had become a firm believer in Empire development and had had his interests turned towards foreign affairs and the prospect of another world war. Henceforth his hopes—already bent on a wider field of service in Canberra—grew and were encouraged by powerful figures in the U.A.P., especially in Victoria, and from 1939 by Prime Minister Joseph Lyons [q.v.10].

Plagued by an unruly and discontented back-bench, in 1935 Stevens had ruthlessly disposed of the deputy leader, R. W. D. Weaver [q.v.], by reconstructing the ministry without him. Even before Stevens left to go abroad, he had been troubled by the ambitions of his protégé Eric Spooner [q.v.], deputy leader of the U.A.P., who thought that Stevens conceded too much to the Country Party and contrasted Stevens' amicable relations with its members with his stern rule of the U.A.P. Matters simmered during Stevens' absence: Spooner resented Bruxner acting as premier. In 1938 Stevens brought forward the elections and in the ensuing cabinet reconstruction passed over Spooner for the Treasury. Early in 1939 Spooner challenged Stevens' leadership over unemployment relief policies.

Resigning from the ministry in July, Spooner led an attack on Stevens, alleging that the premier was concealing the true state of public finances and bearing harshly on the unemployed; such a stand constituted a call for a new financial policy and appealed to party members who distrusted Stevens' uncertain orthodoxy on balanced budgets. On 3 August a censure motion against Stevens was carried by two votes in the assembly; he immediately resigned the premiership. He possibly expected to be again premier once the party had taken stock. His successor Alexander Mair [q.v.10], together with Bruxner—who had refused to serve under Spooner—and much of the press encouraged Stevens' hopes.

After resigning, Stevens set up in practice as a consulting accountant and remained closely in touch with politics and business. Sleek in appearance, with very short hair and a pronounced widow's peak, Stevens 'worked with almost fanatical energy and dedication' yet was considerate to his personal staff: 'A birth, a sickness of a staff member or wife, would bring him personally to the hospital with a huge bunch of flowers from his own garden'.

With his lively interest in primary and secondary industry, in railways and in shale oil, few premiers had been as energetic as Stevens in promoting development. No other premier, unless it were W. A. Holman [q.v.9], had shown so strong an interest in foreign affairs and in defence. Stevens laid it down that in public works priority should be given to those of defence value. In *Planning for war and peace* (1939), a small book published shortly after resigning the premiership, he set out principles for economic policy during and after the war which had begun within a month of his leaving office. In 1940 he published a pamphlet, *The next year in the Pacific*, outlining the problems of Australian foreign policy. Throughout his public life Stevens produced a steady stream of books, articles, pamphlets and reports, mostly written with the assistance of young graduates and distinguished university staff, but all of them bearing the imprint of his own thinking, literary style and ambition for public service. In 1937 Stevens had the statutory grant for the University of Sydney increased to £100 000 a year; he was also active in founding New England University College.

His hopes of entering Federal politics ended in 1939 with the death of Lyons, who had been willing to have Stevens in his cabinet and even to accept him as his successor. Menzies, the new prime minister, recognized Stevens' abilities, praised him publicly, saw him as a rival, and rebuffed him. Stevens resigned his seat in the Legislative Assembly in August 1940, but was decisively defeated for the Labor electorate of Lang at the Federal elections that year and effectively quit politics.

Appointed K.C.M.G. in 1941, Stevens went to New Delhi as Australian representative on the new Eastern Group Supply Council. There he threw himself into war work with immense efficiency and developed a lifelong sympathy with the Indian people. Returning to Australia in 1942, he resumed his accountancy practice, took an interest in matters of public policy and helped to found the India League of Australia. He came out strongly in public against Dr H. V. Evatt's 'powers' referendum, likening the proposals to Fascism. In 1948, after visiting Britain, Europe, India and Malaya, he again supported Empire migration and investment. In 1958 he advocated modifying the White Australia policy by a quota system. That year he completed an important survey of local government in New South Wales on behalf of the Local Government Association.

A great sadness overshadowed Stevens' later years. His health, previously so robust, declined. Predeceased by his wife, he died in a nursing home at Concord West on 24 March 1973 following a long illness; accorded a state funeral, he was buried with Methodist forms in the Garden of Peace cemetery, Pine Grove. A son and two daughters survived him. Before his death Stevens tasted to the full the ingratitude that sustained public service can engender. He died a poor man, an almost forgotten premier.

In retrospect he has appeared as an outstandingly good administrator with the foresight and vision of a true statesman. He was not, however, so good as a politician. He spent only twelve years in parliament, ten of them in office and seven as premier which was then a record for New South Wales. His political career spanned the struggle against Lang and, when the danger was removed, Stevens could no longer sustain his own ascendancy.

Notable citizens of Sydney (Syd, 1940); D. Aitkin, *The colonel* (Canb, 1969); H. Radi and P. Spearritt (eds), *Jack Lang* (Syd, 1977); C. Hazlehurst (ed), *Australian conservatism* (Canb, 1979); *PD* (NSW), 27 May 1973, pp 3937, 3989; *To-day* (Melb), 16 Apr, 6 Aug 1932; *A'sian*, 18 July 1925; *SMH*, 10 Oct 1927, 4 May, 6 Aug 1932, 26-29 Mar 1973; personal recollections.   JOHN M. WARD*

STEVENS, BERTRAM WILLIAM MATHYSON FRANCIS (1872-1922), literary and art critic, was born on 8 October 1872 at Inverell, New South Wales, eldest child of William Mathyson Stevens, an English-born storekeeper, and his wife Marian, née Cafe, from Queanbeyan. By 1882 the family had moved to Newtown, Sydney; he was educated at public schools. From 1895 to 1910 he worked as a solicitor's clerk for Allen, Allen [qq.v.1,3] & Hemsley, but also immersed himself in books, freelanced as a journalist and mixed with literary people. David Scott Mitchell [q.v.5] gave him access to his library of Australiana. Stevens campaigned for Henry George's [q.v.4] 'land nationalisation', temporarily converted his friend Henry Lawson [q.v.10] to the cause and in 1897 edited several issues of the *Single Tax*. With John Le Gay Brereton [q.v.7] as his best man, on 2 April 1902 at Guildford Stevens married Florence Edith Wogoman with Congregational forms; Bertram shaved off his moustache and 'imperial' beard at Edith's request.

A founding member of the Dawn and Dusk Club in 1899 and of the Casuals Club in 1906, Bert was, as Lawson remarked, 'a Bohemian at heart', but 'didn't look the part, and couldn't speak the lines very well. He could relax with the rest of us, but he couldn't be reckless'. Stevens helped sundry ill and needy writers and their families. In 1903 he advised Bertha Lawson to seek a decree for judicial separation from Henry; he was later a force behind schemes to rehabilitate Henry at Mallacoota and Yanco. After John Farrell's [q.v.4] death Stevens edited Farrell's *My sundowner and other poems* (1904) and arranged government assistance for the family. As Victor Daley's [q.v.8] literary executor, he edited

Daley's verse as *Wine and roses* (1911) and raised £30 for his widow which encouraged Alfred Deakin [q.v.8] to form the Commonwealth Literary Fund.

A proficient, lucid critic, Stevens was preeminently a cultural catalyst and pioneer who perceived needs and lacunae. His *An anthology of Australian verse* (1906), although uneven, was the first seriously edited collection of its kind; improved as *The golden treasury of Australian verse* (1909), it became a standard text. In 1907 he edited the first five issues of the *Native Companion* (Melbourne), but difficulties in working from Sydney forced his resignation. Editor of the *Bulletin*'s 'Red Page' in 1909-10, he was less successful, at a bad time, than its originator A. G. Stephens [q.v.], though he did promote Louis Esson and Bernard O'Dowd [qq.v.8,11]. Stephens in the *Bookfellow* lambasted his 1912-18 editing of the declining *Lone Hand*, without acknowledging wartime problems, poor contributions and competition from the cinema. Stevens' editorials and articles vigorously supported the war effort and conscription; he published C. J. Brennan's 'A Chant of Doom' and Norman Lindsay's [qq.v.7,10] illustrations.

From 1916 Stevens edited *Art in Australia* with Sydney Ure Smith [q.v.11]; his commentaries and experience were essential to this first effective, widespread display of Australian art in periodical form, and to its discussion of established and contemporary influences. Culturally conservative but openminded, Stevens was inaugurating editor of the *Home* in 1920; in it he published W. Somerset Maugham's critique of paintings in *Art in Australia*. Lindsay was appalled, and attacked Stevens' liberal Christian eclecticism, deriding him as 'an epitome of the whole human race, muddled, helpless, moribund and stupid'; he unsuccessfully sought to have *Art in Australia* renamed 'Vision' and to have his son Jack replace Stevens as editor. (Stevens had brought Norman and Jack together after their estrangement, edited Norman's pen drawings in 1918 and encouraged him to write fiction.)

Having left the *Lone Hand*, Stevens edited *Commerce*, produced de luxe publications for Art in Australia Ltd, wrote weekly items for the *Sydney Mail* and freelanced. He included biographical research and uncollected poems in his 1920 edition of Henry Kendall's [q.v.5] verse. Stevens' projected history of Australian literature was never completed. The 'gentle anthologist' died of cerebral haemorrhage and chronic nephritis on 14 February 1922 and was buried in the Anglican section of South Head cemetery. His wife, two sons and a daughter survived him: they were assisted by the Bertram Stevens Memorial Fund and by George Robertson's [q.v.11] purchase of Stevens' papers for the Mitchell Library. Lawson, who had once assaulted Stevens with a walking-stick, wrote a warm confessional tribute in the *Bulletin*; Norman Lindsay avoided the funeral.

D. Prout, *Henry Lawson, the grey dreamer* (Adel, 1963); C. Mann (ed), *The stories of Henry Lawson, third series* (Syd, 1964); R. Lindsay, *Model wife* (Syd, 1967); R. D. FitzGerald (ed), *The letters of Hugh McCrae* (Syd, 1970); K. Taylor, *A history with indexes of the Lone Hand, the Australian monthly* (Melb, 1977); R. G. Howarth and A. W. Barker (eds), *Letters of Norman Lindsay* (Syd, 1979); A. Clark, *Christopher Brennan, a critical biography* (Melb, 1980); *Home*, 1 Mar 1922, p 6; *SMH*, 15 Feb 1922; *Bulletin*, 23 Feb, 2 Mar 1922, 5 Aug 1953; B. Stevens *and* J. Le Gay Brereton (the younger) papers (ML); Lothian Publishing Co. papers (LaTL). KEN STEWART

STEVENS, EDWARD (1858-1930), businessman and philanthropist, was born on 21 July 1858 in London, son of John Jeeves Stevens, solicitor's clerk, and his wife Susannah, née Card. Obliged to leave school at an early age, Edward found employment in minor clerical and accounting positions in city branches of the London and Westminster Bank. Deeply interested all his life in scholarship and learning, he assiduously attended lectures in the extension programme of the University of London and supported the Toynbee Hall movement which was designed to bring education to London's poor.

Attracted by greater opportunities in Australia, Edward and his brothers George and Frederick left England for Melbourne in 1885. Edward immediately found employment with the firm of Henry and Howard Berry [q.v.3], salt merchants and importers. Commencing in a comparatively junior position, he rose rapidly through the ranks and by 1913 was a director. In 1920 he became managing director of its associated companies.

A patriotic supporter of Australia's involvement in World War I, he was a generous donor to public causes and in countless private ways. After the death on active service of his only son, Stevens helped in the foundation of returned servicemen's associations. As chairman of the Prahran repatriation committee, he not only financed the committee's welfare activities to a substantial extent, but also took a personal interest in finding employment for returned servicemen. His generosity extended to war widows and orphans for whom he financed housing. In the 1920s Stevens' opinions were greatly respected by Melbourne's businessmen among whom he was renowned for his courtesy and ready availability. A modest person, he was reluctant to accept positions of office-bearer in most of the organizations in which he participated. Foremost of these was the University of Melbourne where Stevens—a council-member (1926-30) with a particular involvement in the finance and buildings committees—provided a strong link with the business community. With his wife, he gave several benefactions to the university, including the clock in the tower of the Arts building (presented in memory of their son), a stained-glass window designed by Napier Waller [q.v.] in Wilson Hall, and a large donation for landscaping.

Interested in literature, history and the arts, in particular those of the Elizabethan era, Stevens was an active member and president of the Shakespeare Society. He was also a member of the Royal Empire Society, the Royal Society of St George, the Wallaby Club, the Rotary Club of Melbourne, the Athanaeum Club, and the Town and Country Union of which he was first president. His wife Eliza, née Snelgrove (d. 1952)—whom he had married with Anglican forms in the parish church at Woodford, Essex, England, on 2 July 1883—shared his scholarly and literary interests.

Stevens died at Richmond on 4 November 1930 and was buried in Boroondara cemetery. The bulk of his estate, sworn for probate in Victoria at £51 611, was divided between the University of Melbourne and the Royal Melbourne Hospital.

E. Scott, *A history of the University of Melbourne* (Melb, 1936); *Age* and *Argus*, 5 Nov 1930; Council of Univ Melb, Minute-book, 7 Apr, 1 Dec 1930 (Central Registry, Univ Melb). T. A. HAZELL

STEVENS, HORACE ERNEST (1876-1950), bass-baritone, was born on 26 October 1876 at Prahran, Melbourne, son of Horace Stevens, dentist, and his wife Fanny, née Gittins. At All Saints Grammar School and Anglican Church, St Kilda, in 1884 he began singing in a choir which trained voices for the opening of St Paul's Cathedral, Melbourne, in 1891. The 'silver-voiced' soprano (who had previously sung the Youth with (Sir) Frederick Cowen [q.v.3] in Mendelssohn's *Elijah* at the Centennial Exhibition in 1888) then sang beneath the central tower while the walls were 'a mass of scaffolding'. At St Paul's fiftieth anniversary the 'silver-haired' Stevens, a lay clerk since 1898, had temporarily succeeded A. E. Floyd [q.v.8] as choirmaster. Stevens resigned as chorister only in 1949. His treble, which did not break until he was 17, had a remarkably smooth passage to bass-baritone and, for some ensuing years as choirmaster at All Saints, he alternated in both ranges, probably accounting for his 'genuine bass trill' in later stentorian days.

Having been apprenticed to his father,

Stevens practised as a Collins Street dentist for twenty years. On 26 August 1905 he married Nellie Chapman (d. 1931) at St Paul's Cathedral; they were to have four sons. A Victorian champion sculler (1910-11, 1911-12), he also rode, shot and played tennis. Serving as a captain in the dental corps of the 14th Field Ambulance in 1915-18, he was mentioned in dispatches on the Western Front and was invalided to England. On Armistice night, after performing impromptu in a London café, he was offered a retainer and Sir Henry Wood suggested that he make singing his career. Sending his allotment to his wife, Stevens lived off his ten-guinea fee until his début in *Elijah* with the Queen's Hall Orchestra in 1919, after Wood had him locally demobbed. Sir Edward Elgar dubbed Stevens the greatest Elijah of his age. It was an edifying role, suited to his grave demeanour—and to English taste. With meticulously reverent preparation he performed it 500 times. Over fifteen years he sang at major oratorio festivals in Britain and the United States of America, including in his repertoire Brahms's *Requiem* and Bantock's *Omar Khayyam*, as well as standard Bach and Handel.

Moving to opera, Stevens' massive voice and torso 'created' Samuel Coleridge Taylor's *Hiawatha* at its lavish London premiere in 1924. He thundered as Wagner's 'best British' Wotan and rollicked as Verdi's Falstaff and Gounod's Mephistopheles, but he could irk divas like Florence Austral [q.v.7] with his pedantic re-chalking of movement variations on the stage floor. Returning to Australia in 1934 with Sir Benjamin Fuller's [q.v.8] Grand Opera company, on 5 December at Scots Church, Melbourne, Stevens married Ella Elizabeth Hallam, née Davis, 'the only woman builder and contractor practising in Australia'. Looking to encourage music at home, he sang in 1936 in the first Melbourne performance of Alfred Hill's [q.v.9] *Auster*. At the University of Melbourne Conservatorium of Music from 1938 to 1950 he gave sometimes crotchety tuition beneath the unyielding gaze of photogravures of himself as a full-feathered Hiawatha.

Stevens was a hearty Bohemian of the Savage Club in London as well as in Melbourne where, at the fiftieth jubilee in 1944, he sang *Simon the cellarer* never 'with greater vigour and clearer diction'. Survived by his wife and three sons, on 18 November 1950 he died suddenly of a coronary occlusion at his South Yarra home. After choral obsequies at St Paul's Cathedral he was cremated.

D. M. Dow, *Melbourne Savages* (Melb, 1947); I. Moresby, *Australia makes music* (Melb, 1948); B. and F. Mackenzie, *Singers of Australia* (Melb, 1967); *Sun News-Pictorial* (Melb), 15 Feb 1934, 25 May 1935, 3 Oct 1941, 22 Mar 1948, 26 Aug 1949, 20, 21 Nov 1950; *Age*, 25 May 1935, 5, 11 May 1937, 26 Aug 1949, 20 Nov 1950; *Argus*, 5 May 1937, 20 Nov 1950; *Herald* (Melb), 7 Nov 1938, 18, 21 Nov 1950; *Glasgow Herald*, 20 Nov 1950; personal information.   JAMES GRIFFIN

STEVENS, JEMIMA ELIZABETH MARY (1855-1940), educationist and Anglican nun, was born on 20 August 1855 at Aldeburgh, Suffolk, England, daughter of William Stevens, gentleman, and his wife Maria, née Moss. A well-educated woman, she cared for her widowed mother before joining in 1888 an Anglican teaching and charitable order—the Community of the Sisters of the Church—as Sister Phyllis. For four years she worked among the poor in East London. Following requests from Bishop Henry Montgomery [q.v.10] of Hobart for assistance in establishing schools, in 1892 the order sent Sisters Phyllis and Hannah to Tasmania. In October they opened a school in Harrington Street for girls and young boys, naming it the Hobart Higher Grade Elementary School.

In July 1893 Sister Phyllis took charge of the order's mission school for poor children, but by October had returned to the elementary school where she taught the boys. She became headmistress in April 1895. Her pupils included Bernard Montgomery, the bishop's son (later Viscount Montgomery of Alamein). In July, with the bishop's financial assistance, the Sisters moved their school (by then known as Collegiate School) to 'more gracious premises' in Macquarie Street; pupils were taught to matriculation level. That year Sister Phyllis recorded that the senior teachers all held a university certificate. From 1894 the school took boarders; after 1898 boys were no longer accepted.

Collegiate School attracted unwelcome publicity in 1900 when some parents complained about the 'High Church' views allegedly held by Sisters Phyllis and Hannah, and of the teaching of 'false doctrines in their religious classes'. The complaints appear to have arisen over the Sisters' views on confession and the school lost several of its pupils. At Sister Phyllis's urging, Bishop Montgomery examined the texts, teaching notes and the children's exercise books. His inquiry exonerated the Sisters from 'imparting any false doctrine' and a lengthy report to this effect was published in the press. The extent to which Sister Phyllis subscribed to High Church ideas is not clear, although before 1900 she had encouraged confession among her pupils.

By 1914 'Collegiate' was one of Hobart's leading girls' schools. Students were prepared for public examinations and emphasis was placed on academic achievement, but Sister Phyllis also aimed to turn out Christian ladies. The establishment developed along the lines of an English public school, with regular written examinations, compulsory uniform, prefects, a traditional house system and a pro-British spirit. Dignified and gracious, as well as forceful and competent, Sister Phyllis ran the school ably until 1927, inspiring considerable respect among her pupils and the local community. She had been novice mistress at the school from 1920; when the novitiate was moved to Melbourne in 1927, she worked there until her return to Hobart in 1932. She died at Collegiate School on 5 March 1940 and, after a memorial service in St David's Cathedral, was buried in Cornelian Bay cemetery.

Community of the Sisters of the Church, *A valiant Victorian* (Lond, 1964); *Church News* (Hob), Oct 1892, Jan, July, Sept, Oct 1893, Aug 1894, Apr, July, Nov 1895; *Hob Centre J*, 1892-1903; *Collegiate School Mag*, June 1940; *Mercury*, 6, 8 Mar 1940; Hob Higher Grade School, record book, 1892-1905 (held by Collegiate School). ALISON ALEXANDER

STEVENSON, GEORGE INGRAM (1882-1958), soldier and chartered accountant, was born on 8 March 1882 at Kelvinside, Lanarkshire, Scotland, son of George Stevenson, colliery cashier, and his wife Margaret Ann, née Ingram. The family came to Australia in 1888 and George was educated at Brunswick College, Melbourne. He served in the South African War with the Prince of Wales Light Horse and the 4th Battalion, Australian Commonwealth Horse, and was awarded the Queen's Medal with five clasps. Enlisting subsequently in the (volunteer) Garrison Artillery in Victoria, he was commissioned in the Australian Field Artillery on 20 September 1909 and became captain in 1912. He had qualified as a chartered accountant in 1909, went into practice in 1911 and was to establish the accountancy firm of G. I. Stevenson & Co. in Melbourne in 1933.

Shortly after the outbreak of World War I he joined the Australian Imperial Force and was posted to the 2nd Field Artillery Brigade as a captain. He embarked in October 1914 with the 6th Field Battery, landed on Gallipoli on 25 April 1915, and in May was promoted major and appointed battery commander. In an action on 14 November 1915 he directed the fire of one of his guns while its shells just cleared his head. Mentioned in dispatches, he was appointed C.M.G. for his Gallipoli service.

In March 1916 Stevenson was promoted lieut-colonel with command of the 21st Howitzer Brigade; he was mentioned in dispatches for consistent good work as a brigade commander and for meritorious service at Pozières, France. Given charge of the 2nd

Field Artillery Brigade in January 1917, he commanded the group of artillery in the Lagnicourt Valley on 15 April 1917 at the time of the German breakthrough. The guns of all four batteries of the 2nd Field Artillery Brigade had to be abandoned, but their breech-blocks and dial-sights were removed by the retreating Australians. He later commanded the re-equipped brigade at the 3rd battle of Ypres and was again mentioned in dispatches for his skill and coolness.

Appointed in August to command the 3rd (Army) Field Artillery Brigade, by September 1918—during the attack on the Hindenburg outpost line—he had charge of the Left Artillery Group consisting of four artillery brigades. Stevenson was awarded the Distinguished Service Order in September 1918, the citation reading: 'This officer has commanded his brigade in the most able and efficient manner during the whole of the operations carried out by this [Australian] Corps since coming on the Amiens front. His brigade has been continuously in action and has constantly moved from one part of the front to the other. He frequently commanded large groups of brigades of artillery for active offensive operations and on occasions under the most trying conditions . . . His fearless courage under shell fire has been the means of maintaining the high morale that exists in his brigade.'

Embarking for Australia on Anzac leave in October 1918, Stevenson was discharged from the A.I.F. in February 1919; he was reappointed in May as officer commanding troops on transports and returned to Australia in January 1920. In July he temporarily commanded the 8th Field Artillery Brigade, Australian Military Forces, and was then given charge of the 22nd Field Artillery Brigade. In 1922-27 he was Commander Royal Artillery, 3rd Division, A.M.F., with the rank of colonel, and in 1931-35 commanded the 10th Infantry Brigade.

After demobilization Stevenson had resumed work as an accountant. On 30 May 1923 he married Frances Clare Dennis (d. 1931) with Anglican rites at Christ Church, South Yarra, Melbourne. They were to have a son and daughter. On 22 December 1936 he married a widow, Hilda Mabel Kidd, daughter of H. V. McKay [q.v.10], at Toorak Presbyterian Church. Survived by his wife (D.B.E., 1968) and by the children of his first marriage, he died in East Melbourne on 11 July 1958 and was cremated. His son, Major General John Dennis Stevenson, A.O., C.B.E., served in Korea and Vietnam.

Aust Defence Dept, *Official records of the Australian military contingents to the war in South Africa*, P. L. Murray ed (Melb, 1911); C. E. W.

Bean, *The story of Anzac*, 2 (Syd, 1924) and *The A.I.F. in France*, 1917-1918 (Syd, 1933, 1942); W. Perry, *The Naval and Military Club, Melbourne* (Melb, 1981).
E. J. H. HOWARD

STEVENSON, JOHN BRYAN (1876-1957), naval officer, was born on 7 August 1876 at Toxteth Park, Lancashire, England, son of John Stevenson, insurance broker, and his first wife Eleanor Alicia, née Bryan, who died when young John was born. From the Royal Naval College, H.M.S. *Britannia*, he became a midshipman in the Royal Navy in 1892, sub-lieutenant in 1896, lieutenant in 1898 and commander in 1911. He served continuously with the Royal Australian Navy from 1 July 1912, first on loan as commander, then as acting captain from 1 January 1913 and captain from 1 January 1919; he permanently transferred to the R.A.N. on 4 May 1919.

While serving in H.M.S. *Camperdown* in the Mediterranean in January 1893, Stevenson saw her collide with H.M.S. *Victoria* which then sank with the loss of 400 lives, including Admiral Sir George Tryon [q.v.6]. Stevenson later watched the Russian fleet *en route* to its destruction by the Japanese at the battle of Tsushima in 1905.

His service in the R.A.N. in 1911-31 placed him in sea and shore commands, at courses and in liaison duties in Britain, and as a member of the Australian Naval Board. His sea appointments included H.M.A.S. *Encounter* (1912-13), and command of *Berrima* (1914), *Encounter* (1916-18), *Brisbane* (1921-22), *Adelaide* (1923-24) and *Sydney* (briefly in 1928). He took *Berrima* to New Guinea in 1914 and *Adelaide* on a cruise to Britain in 1924 with the R.N. special service squadron led by Vice Admiral Sir Frederick Field in H.M.S. *Hood*.

Second naval member of the Naval Board from 1 September 1927 to 11 June 1929 (except for his brief command of *Sydney* from 10 April to 8 May 1928), Stevenson was acting first naval member from 12 June to 27 October 1929. His other appointments ashore included service at H.M.A.S. *Cerberus*, the naval depot at Williamstown, Victoria, in 1913-14, and then in 1915-16 in command. He was director of naval ordnance at Navy Office in 1918-20. In England he attended the senior officers' war course at the Royal Naval College, Greenwich, in 1920-21 and was Australian naval representative in London from 10 October 1924 to 15 July 1927. On 28 October 1929 he succeeded Captain H. P. Cayley [q.v.7] as captain superintendent Sydney; Captain H. J. Feakes [q.v.8] took over from him when Stevenson retired as rear admiral on 6 August 1931.

At St David's Anglican Cathedral, Hobart,

on 4 June 1914 Stevenson had married Olive Brooke Bailey (1886-1978), a nurse. Their first son, James, a spitfire pilot in the Royal Air Force, was killed over Dunkirk in 1940; their daughter, Noel, was mentioned in dispatches in the Women's Auxiliary Air Force in World War II, and their second son, Captain John Stevenson, served in the R.A.N. in 1935-69.

Standing 5 ft. 9 ins. (175.3 cm) and weighing 12 st. 12 lb. (81.6 kg), Stevenson had fair hair and brown eyes. He was well-spoken and of a retiring disposition. He had a penchant for quoting poetry, knew French, and played cricket in his youth and tennis into his mature years. A devoted family man, a non-drinker and non-smoker, he cloaked a sense of humour beneath a formal personality that earned him the nickname 'Stiffy Steve'. Although conscious of his status, he was not overly ambitious. He was an active member of the United Service Institution, the Returned Sailors', Soldiers' and Airmen's Imperial League of Australia and the Navy League (president 1937). While given more to reading than to public speaking, he did indicate a strong conviction that Australia needed to continue to develop her naval forces and should remain a close naval partner of Britain.

Stevenson was appointed C.M.G. in January 1925. He received the thanks of the Admiralty in 1927 for his work as Australian naval representative. In 1931 the Naval Board sent him their 'deep appreciation' that he had 'played an important part in the successful development of the Australian Navy'. Survived by his wife, son and daughter, he died at Wahroonga, Sydney, on 13 July 1957 and was cremated after a Presbyterian service.

A. W. Jose, *The Royal Australian Navy 1914-1918* (Syd, 1928); *PD* (Cwlth), May 1931, p 2100; *SMH*, 29 Nov 1924, 1 Jan 1925, 2 Sept 1927, 18 July 1929, 11 Apr 1930, 16 July, 24 Sept 1931, 20 Nov 1935, 13 Apr 1939, 15 July 1957; *Bulletin*, 24 July 1957; MT 856, MP 981 (AA, Melb); information from Capt J. P. Stevenson, Inclined Village, Nevada, USA, and Mrs N. Grant, Hawthorn, Melb.
ROBERT HYSLOP

STEWARD, SIR GEORGE CHARLES THOMAS (1865-1920), public servant, was born on 18 March 1865 at St George in the East, London, son of George Steward, labourer, and his wife Susannah, née Barnes. In July 1880 he joined the London Post Office as night messenger and was a sorter of foreign parcels, 1st class, by 1890. A sculler and an amateur middleweight boxer, he was living at Stepney when he married at the parish church Edith Jermyn, a fishmonger's daughter, on 27 December 1885. They came to Tasmania in 1892, but the marriage was unhappy and in 1894 Edith returned to London with their two sons. Steward shot to the top of the colony's civil service. A clerk in the Railway Department (1892), chief clerk and accountant in the Education Department (1893), secretary to the premier and clerk of the Executive Council (1894), he was under secretary for Tasmania in 1896. He also held additional offices, including chief inspector of explosives and supervisor of totalizators, and was briefly town clerk of Hobart (1897).

In January 1901 Steward transferred to the Commonwealth Department of External Affairs, expecting to be its head; when Alfred Deakin [q.v.8] secured that billet for Atlee Hunt [q.v.9], Steward became chief clerk. In January 1902 it was he who conveyed to Brisbane customs officers Barton's [q.v.7] secret instructions for administering the immigration dictation test. Uneasy working under Hunt, in December 1902 Steward became official secretary to the governor-general, Lord Tennyson [q.v.], and secretary of the Executive Council. Except for six weeks in 1910, when he was Victorian land tax commissioner, for seventeen years Steward was right-hand man to five governors-general, responsible for official correspondence, including coded dispatches, and official expenditure. He was appointed C.M.G. (1909) and K.B.E. (1918).

To his rival, Hunt, Steward had 'no knack of getting men to work for him otherwise than by driving them'. Tennyson thought him 'too big for his boots', but his relations were good with other governors-general. Although Sir Ronald Munro Ferguson [q.v.10] described him as an 'exceedingly jealous and domineering character', he also found him 'reliable and very efficient', particularly in the first weeks of World War I when the official secretary was the conduit for secret communications between Australia and Britain. To Melbourne *Punch*, Steward was 'Distingué'. With a 'military bearing, his moustache rampant a la Emperor Wilhelm, and his air of hauteur', he was 'brusque and decisive in manner as in mind'. An enthusiastic citizen soldier, Steward claimed to have joined the Royal Engineers in 1882 and to have been a 'special duty officer'. Commissioned lieutenant, Tasmanian Auxiliary Forces, in March 1898, he had raised and commanded the Tasmanian Mounted Infantry and was captain from March 1900. He joined the 10th Australian Light Horse in 1905; as a major (1908-12), he served in the Australian Intelligence Corps. In 1915-19 he commanded the 50th Infantry (St Kilda) Regiment (as honorary lieutcolonel from 1917).

More shadowy was his other role. In 1916 Steward founded and headed the Counter Espionage Bureau, Australia's first secret service, whose agents pursued International Workers of the World and Sinn Fein activists. Munro Ferguson was as unenthusiastic about these duties of his secretary (whom he dubbed 'Pickle the Spy') and the unsavoury characters who consequently lurked about Government House as he was with the secret political work which Steward sometimes performed for Prime Minister Hughes [q.v.9].

In 1919 Steward became chief commissioner of police in Victoria. The first outsider appointed since 1858, he successfully instituted important reforms, improved systematic police training and expanded the use of fingerprint analysis. Championing better working conditions for his men, he was popular with the force and an efficient administrator, but his health was overtaxed by his new post.

An 'adept' water-colourist and a temperance advocate, Steward enjoyed working on his farm at Cranbourne. He died of heart disease while driving his Cadillac in St Kilda Road on 11 May 1920 and was buried in St Kilda cemetery. He had divorced Edith in 1907 and was survived by their sons, and by his wife Anne Lucas Synnot whom he had married in Holy Trinity Church, East Melbourne, on 20 February 1908. His estate was sworn for probate at £19 071.

R. Norris, *The emergent Commonwealth* (Melb, 1975); C. D. Coulthard-Clark, *The citizen general staff* (Canb, 1976); F. Cain, *The origins of political surveillance in Australia* (Syd, 1983); C. Cunneen, *Kings' men* (Syd, 1983); R. Haldane, *The people's force* (Melb, 1986); *Police J* (Melb), 1 Mar 1919, p 10; *Punch* (Melb), 18 July, 29 Aug 1907, 23 Dec 1910, 18 Dec 1919; *Argus*, 14 Feb 1919; *Herald* (Melb), 17 Feb 1919; *Australasian*, 15 May 1920; Hunt *and* Novar *and* Tennyson papers (NL); Vic Police records, VPRS 3992, unit 2087, file B1940 *and* divorce papers, VPRS 283, unit 159, item 1906/58 (PRO Vic); records, Post Office Archives, Lond.

CHRIS CUNNEEN

STEWART, ALEXANDER (1835-1918), merchant and manufacturer, was born on 4 August 1835 at Caputh, Perthshire, Scotland, second of four children of Charles Stewart, veterinary surgeon, and his wife Elspeth, née Tait; his parents were cousins. Stewart migrated to Brisbane in 1858 and there, with few financial resources, established a small clothing retail business.

With William Hemmant, he set up a general drapery on the corner of Queen and Albert Streets. After their shop was gutted by fire in 1864, the partners re-established themselves on nearby Queen and Adelaide Streets. Their enterprise flourished due to their keen business sense, the central location of their store and Brisbane's increasing population; they even opened a branch in London. The partnership was dissolved when Hemmant entered parliament in 1871. As Alexander Stewart & Sons Ltd, the firm became a limited liability company on 31 July 1903 with a nominal capital of £140 000; Stewart remained manager for most of his life. The company's factory produced clothing such as moleskin trousers under the Manx brand and shirts under the Thistle brand. Retail branches were established in Sydney and Melbourne.

In the mid-1870s Stewart had purchased 250 acres (101.2 ha)—at what became the Brisbane suburb of Ashgrove—on which he built his home, Glenlyon. Constructed from bricks made on the property and covered with plaster to simulate stone, the mansion was erected by Melanesian labourers. When completed in 1877, it boasted imported Corinthian columns, a black-and-white marble verandah floor (which a maid polished with butter milk) and an exquisite interior. A stained-glass window above the first-floor landing incorporated part of a crest —a lion's head—and the motto 'semper fidelis'. With servants' quarters, a billiard and gun room, tennis court, gardens, terraced lawns and an avenue of Bunya pines, the estate had its own dairy herd, fowls, orchard, vegetable garden and a well.

Stewart married three times with Presbyterian forms: on 13 March 1862, in Brisbane, Maria Vine Martin (d. 1865) who bore him a daughter; on 27 February 1866, also in Brisbane, Anne Killough (d. 1905) who bore him seven children; and on 15 January 1907, in Melbourne, Edith Annie Best (d. 1945). A considerate man and a philanthropist, Stewart cherished his Scottish background: he was a staunch Presbyterian, a trustee of St Andrew's Church, Brisbane, a member of the Scottish constitution of Freemasons and a director of the Australian Mutual Provident Society.

Survived by his wife Edith, by the daughter of his first marriage and the six sons and daughter of his second, Stewart died at home on 12 August 1918 after a long illness and was buried in Toowong cemetery. His Queensland estate was sworn for probate at £4232.

M. Truscott, Alexander Stewart, 1868-1918, and Glenlyon House, Ashgrove (ms, 1977, OL); Brisbane Courier, 14 Aug 1918.   A. L. LOUGHEED

STEWART, SIR ALEXANDER ANDERSON (1874-1956), engineer and company director, was born on 31 May 1874 at Aberdeen, Scotland, eldest of nine children of Robert Phillip Stewart, ship carpenter, and his wife Sarah Ann, née Geddes. Educated locally at Robert Gordon College, he served his apprenticeship at a shipyard in Aberdeen.

His father's death in an accident at work left the 19-year-old Alexander responsible for the family. In 1897 he gained his chief engineer's certificate with the Aberdeen White Star Line. On the run from Australia in 1900 he met Grace Mary, daughter of industrialist James Cuming senior [q.v.8]. Stewart took his discharge in Melbourne in 1904 and married her with Anglican rites on 4 January 1905 at Yarraville. He was chief engineer to Michaelis Hallenstein at their Footscray tannery before joining fellow Scot William Fyvie in Fyvie & Stewart (1906-32, later Alex. Stewart & Co.), consulting engineers. After acquiring critical German patents, this enduring and productive partnership was a pioneer of the industrial gas industry in Australia. In 1911, in association with English-based British Oxygen, it formed the Commonwealth Oxygen Co. which merged in 1935 with a Grimwade [q.v.9] family company to form Commonwealth Industrial Gases Ltd, of which Stewart was first chairman.

The death of Cuming senior in 1911 brought Stewart a seat on the board of Cuming Smith & Co. Ltd. Involvement followed with Commonwealth Fertilisers & Chemicals Ltd, Australian Fertilizers Ltd, Industrial Chemicals and Imperial Chemical Industries of Australia & New Zealand Ltd. Likewise, his association with Broken Hill South Ltd as consulting engineer and director carried him into Western New South Wales Electric Power Co. Pty Ltd, Broken Hill Associated Smelters Co., British Australian Lead Manufacturers Pty Ltd (later BALM Paints Ltd), Metal Manufactures Ltd, Australian Bronze Co. and Electrolytic Zinc of Australasia Ltd. Other financial interests and directing responsibilities included Australian Consolidated Industries Ltd, Dunlop Rubber of Australia Ltd, The Trustees Executors & Agency Co. Ltd, Gold Mines of Australia Ltd, North British & Mercantile Insurance Co. Ltd, and Mutual Life and Citizens Association Co. Ltd. Knighted in 1937, Stewart was prominent among the Melbourne-based entrepreneurs known as the 'Collins House group' which dominated Australian finance and industry from the 1920s.

Few Australians outside business circles fully appreciated Stewart's influence. At his death he was chairman of six major Australian companies, including Broken Hill South Ltd and the Trustees Executors & Agency Co., and a director of some fifteen others. A very private person with few interests other than business and his family, he even used a weekly round of golf at the Metropolitan club with his close friend and Collins House associate Sir Colin Fraser [q.v.8] as an opportunity for business discussion. Stewart's membership of the Felton [q.v.4] bequest committee resulted from his association with Trustees Executors

& Agency Co. rather than from any real interest in the arts. The Stewarts lived a measured and retiring life, holidaying at Mount Macedon and periodically travelling to Scotland. His long association with the Alfred Hospital began in 1911 as honorary consulting engineer; his presidency (1935-39, 1942-46) and vice-presidency of the board were interrupted only by his service on government industrial and munitions panels during World War II.

Survived by his wife and two sons, Sir Alexander died on 6 May 1956 at Cliveden Mansions and was buried in Brighton cemetery. Eric Dunshea of Dunlop Rubber paid tribute to his kindly and generous nature and to the 'ability and wise counsel' which made him 'one of the outstanding leaders of Australian industry'. Stewart's estate was sworn for probate at £282 475. His portrait by Max Meldrum [q.v.10], painted late in Sir Alexander's life when his health was failing, is held by the family.

J. R. Poynter, *Russell Grimwade* (Melb, 1967); P. Hasluck, *The government and the people, 1939-1941* (Canb, 1952); A. M. Mitchell, *The hospital south of the Yarra* (Melb, 1977); J. Lack (ed), *James Cuming* (Melb, 1987); *Aust Manufacturer*, 12 May 1956; *Advertiser* (Footscray), 7, 14 Jan 1905; *Age* and *Argus* and *Herald* (Melb) and *Sun News-Pictorial*, 7, 8 May 1956; Cuming Smith & Co. papers (Univ Melb Archives); information from Mrs J. C. and Mr A. W. Stewart, Toorak, Melb.

JOHN LACK

STEWART, ARCHIBALD (1867-1925), trade unionist and political official, was born on 30 December 1867 at Sebastopol, Victoria, seventh surviving child of John Stewart, miner, and his wife Ann, née Erskine, both Scottish born. He grew up in Creswick where his father became caretaker of the botanical gardens. In his early working years Archibald took numerous jobs, from mining in the Creswick district to selling groceries at Ballarat. As an active member of several labour organizations, he faced an employers' blacklist which made it difficult for him to find permanent employment and to support Mary, née Edwards, whom he had married at Fitzroy with Victorian Free Church forms on 25 June 1891. Stewart was an early member of the Australian Workers' Union and, until 1910, its delegate on the Ballarat Trades and Labor Council.

Following a visit by Tom Mann [q.v.10] in 1902, Stewart helped to establish the Ballarat branch of the Political Labor Council, serving as secretary in 1905-06. His considerable organizing skills were obvious to party officials during James Scullin's [q.v.11] unsuccessful campaign against Alfred Deakin [q.v.8] at the 1906 election. Stewart stood as Labor candidate for the Legislative Assembly seat of Ballarat East in 1908, but was defeated by the Liberal R. McGregor; in 1910 he was narrowly beaten for the Federal seat of Grampians by H. W. H. Irvine [q.v.9]. Although he left Ballarat soon after the election, Stewart maintained close contact with the area, tackling Irvine again at the 1913 poll and joining the board of the Ballarat *Evening Echo* in 1914.

After moving to Melbourne, Stewart was elected senior vice-president of the Political Labor Council in 1910 and appointed full-time secretary in 1911, following the resignation of P. R. Heagney [q.v.9] whose stewardship had been severely criticized. The pay was poor, but Stewart worked in a diligent and methodical way to consolidate the Labor Party organization in Victoria and, by 1914, was acknowledged as one of the 'powers behind the throne' of the Fisher [q.v.8] government. His influence was recognized by his appointment as secretary of the newly established Australian Labor Party federal executive in 1915, a post he held until 1925.

Stewart's staunch adherence to Labor principles led him to play a leading role in organizing opposition to W. M. Hughes's [q.v.9] conscriptionist policy in 1916-17. Drawing on the experience of more than twenty State and Federal conferences, he conducted some of the delicate negotiations that helped to keep the industrial and political wings of the labour movement together when they threatened to split over the issue of syndicalism and the socialist objective in 1919-21. A sturdy, kind-faced man, Stewart had a blunt and occasionally gruff manner; his integrity and generous nature made him popular in a movement not noted for brotherly love. He died of tuberculosis at his Sandringham home on 29 May 1925. The sorrow of his wife and three surviving sons was shared by the many mourners at the Coburg general cemetery where Scullin paid him the rarest tribute accorded a political activist: 'He was a man whose word was his bond'.

L. F. Crisp, *The Australian Federal Labour Party 1901-1951* (Lond, 1955); J. Robertson, *J. H. Scullin* (Perth, 1974); D. J. Murphy (ed), *Labor in politics* (Brisb, 1975); P. Weller and B. Lloyd (eds), *Federal executive minutes, 1919-1955* (Melb, 1978); *Aust Worker*, 4 July 1923, 3 June 1925; *Argus*, 30 May 1925; *Age*, 30 May, 1 June 1925; *Creswick Advertiser*, 2 June 1925; *Labor Call*, 4 June 1925.

PETER LOVE

STEWART, DAVID (1883-1954), carpenter and educationist, was born on 11 April 1883 at Leith, Edinburgh, Scotland, eldest son and third of ten children of David Stewart, porter, and his wife Jane (Jean), née

Crawford. His early life was shaped by two powerful influences: the frequent unemployment of his father and the proud, working-class puritanism of his mother who, by dint of careful management, kept her burgeoning family together and out of debt. On leaving school at 12, young David worked as a messenger-boy in a draper's shop; at his mother's insistence, he was then apprenticed to a cabinetmaker.

By the age of 19 Stewart was the family's chief breadwinner. His activities as a unionist and later as an office-holder in the Independent Labour Party made steady work difficult to obtain. For three years he studied economics and sociology at workers' education classes; he discovered in socialism both an explanation and a cure for the ills of his age. In 1908 he worked his passage to New Zealand. Although there were jobs aplenty, he found the cold and isolation of Palmerston North distressing.

Two years later Stewart moved to Sydney where he worked as a carpenter and upholsterer; he was a delegate to the Labor Council of New South Wales from 1911. His passion for reading and for studying society was unabated, and he used his position in the labour movement to press for a programme of workers' education. At the invitation of Albert Mansbridge, founder of the Workers' Educational Association in Britain, Stewart established a branch in Sydney in November 1913 and was elected unopposed as general secretary of the Workers' Educational Association of New South Wales. For the next forty-one years, his life and the progress and vicissitudes of the association were indissolubly linked. He pursued adult education and the workers' cause with missionary zeal; his indefatigable energy, doggedness and considerable powers of advocacy were expended in its service. On 11 November 1916 at Summer Hill he married Lillian May Garth Tevelein, a schoolteacher.

The growth of the W.E.A. was swift. By 1914 there were fifty-five affiliated organizations and Meredith Atkinson [q.v.7] offered the first classes under the joint sponsorship of the W.E.A. and the Department of Tutorial Classes of the University of Sydney. By 1915, largely at the instigation of Mansbridge and Stewart, branches had been established in every State and in New Zealand. A federal council (with Stewart as treasurer) was inaugurated in November 1919 following the launching of the association's journal, *Australian Highway*, to which he was to contribute numerous articles and reviews. From 1927 Stewart was the council's secretary. A residential summer school, built largely by his own hands and posthumously named after him, was established at Newport.

Yet, set-backs to his work were frequent.

The association was continually short of money and, although he never complained of it, Stewart was paid a pittance. Relations with the university were sometimes troubled, most particularly in 1918 and in 1932-33 when divisions arose over the control of tutorial classes. Even more damaging were conflicts within the labour movement itself in 1916 over the conscription issue and in 1942-43 over perceived anti-Russian bias in one of the classes. Against all these pressures, Stewart steadfastly upheld the right of free speech and, through the *Highway* and at union meetings, re-asserted the association's original purpose as a non-partisan, non-sectarian, voluntary workers' educational movement. For his devotion to these ideals he was appointed O.B.E. in 1953.

On 30 April 1948 Stewart, then a widower, married Flora Mary Carmichael Smith at Burwood. She supported him in his many activities. Afflicted with diabetes for twenty years, Stewart died of heart disease on 4 August 1954, at the end of a full day's work for the association, and was cremated after an Anglican service at St James's Church, King Street. He was survived by his wife, and by two daughters and a son of his first marriage. A portrait of Stewart by Mary Abbott is held by W.E.A. House, Sydney.

E. M. Higgins, *David Stewart and the W.E.A.* (Syd, 1957); *Aust Highway*, 36, no 4, Nov 1954, 38, no 1, Feb 1956; *SMH*, 10 Jan 1935, 23 Nov 1946, 24 Oct 1947, 1 Jan 1953, 6 Aug, 7 Sept 1954, 18 Aug 1955; Workers' Educational Assn of NSW, Annual Reports, 1914-55 (held by WEA of NSW, Syd).
                                        JOHN CLANCHY

STEWART, ELEANOR CHARLOTTE (NORA) (1879-1966), dancing teacher, was born on 1 May 1879 at Port Pirie, South Australia, eldest of three children of Robert Walter Stewart, surgeon, and his wife Gertrude Theodora Fydell, née Lindsay, whose forebear Arthur Fydell Lindsay arrived on the *Buffalo* in 1836 and became a member of the House of Assembly in 1857. Nora and her sister Geraldine enjoyed riding and swimming during their childhood; the family moved to Adelaide in 1908 and Dr Stewart later took them to London where Nora studied ballet.

In 1914 they returned home. Suddenly 'required to turn some talent to account', Nora took over Isobel Young's dancing classes. Tall, slender and graceful, Nora had the intelligence and brisk, carrying voice to galvanize and awe her pupils. The visiting dance teacher to most of Adelaide's private colleges, to the Police Force of South Australia and to the Adelaide Hunt Club, she also taught games and callisthenics and schooled debutantes in decorum. She used school premises and hired halls for her own classes: the Trades Hall in the city, the North Adelaide Institute and the Blind Institute in King William Road. Classes often comprised several hundred pupils. Among them were the pianist prodigy Philip Hargraves; Henry Legerton, who was to join Sadler's Wells Ballet Co.; Elizabeth Cameron Wilson, founder and artistic director of the Australian Dance Theatre; Morna Dobbie (Smeaton), a brilliant teacher of the Margaret Morris method of barefoot dancing; Dorothy Slane, another future ballet teacher; and (Sir) Robert Helpmann who said of Nora, 'she taught me to appreciate classical music and to understand what dance meant'.

Miss Stewart's discipline—boys wore white gloves—and her mannerisms made her a loved and legendary figure; 'Going to Nora's' was a catchphrase in Adelaide for nearly fifty years. She proved a shrewd businesswoman. In her prime she employed four pianists and twelve assistants: they commenced the classes; Nora arrived by public transport, took over, then left for another class. She rarely danced herself, but instructed, walked the steps and demonstrated through her assistants. After her father's death, she and her sister supported their mother; the three lived together, with Nora's dogs.

Every second year the elegant Miss Stewart visited London, Paris and the Riviera to buy French hats and underwear, and to keep up with the latest dances (Charleston, quickstep and tango) and teaching techniques; she also assessed such new approaches as Dalcroze eurythmics which she disliked. She worked with Mrs Wordsworth, Madame Vacani, and Edouard and Judith Espinosa. In Adelaide she regularly choreographed ballets about gypsies; to Elizabeth Cameron Wilson, 'she had the gypsy soul— unconventional, romantic, daring and somewhat mysterious'. As Nora aged, she grew wiry, her facial bones becoming more prominent.

Stewart also trained dancers for fund-raising performances in aid of charities like the Fighting Forces Comfort Fund and the Australian Red Cross Society. She taught ballet until she was 79, after which she continued her ballroom classes. She died at her home in Molesworth Street, North Adelaide, on 6 October 1966 and was cremated.

A. Laube, *Settlers around the bay* (Adel, 1985); M. Page (ed), *Greater than their knowing* (Adel, 1986); *Woman's World*, 1 Aug 1925; *Observer* (Adel), 19 Apr 1924; *News* (Adel), 30 June, 16 Dec 1958; *Advertiser* (Adel), 7 Oct 1966; information from Mrs E. Bonython, Glen Osmond, and Mrs M. Howard, Vale Park, Adel.   JACK ROYANS

STEWART, ELEANOR TOWZEY (NELLIE) (1858-1931), actress, was born on 20 November 1858 at Woolloomooloo, Sydney, daughter of Richard Stewart Towzey (c.1826-1902), English-born comedian, and his Irish-born wife Theodosia, née Yates, formerly Guerin. Her mother, a descendant of the famous Drury Lane players Richard and Mary Ann Yates, arrived in Hobart with Mrs Clarke's Opera Company in 1840 and married the actor James Guerin by whom she was to have two daughters. Nellie's father tried gold digging before turning to stage management in 1857 when he married the widow Mrs Guerin and adopted the name 'Stewart'. Shortly after Nellie's birth, the family moved to Melbourne where she was educated at the National Model and Training School and Grandtown House boarding school.

Ancestry and strict parental education combined to make Nellie, at the age of about 5, an early success with Charles Kean in *The stranger*. In 1877, with her family, she sang and danced through seven parts in *Rainbow revels*, an entertainment by Garnet Walch [q.v.6]. The Stewarts toured India, England and the United States of America in 1879; next year George Coppin [q.v.3], manager of Melbourne's Theatre Royal, cabled Nellie in America offering the part of principal boy in the pantomime *Sinbad the sailor*. This engagement marked one of the turning points in her career for, after a fourteen week run, she met George Musgrove [q.v.5] and became the lead in his production of Offenbach's *La fille du tambour major*. Thus began a romantic and professional relationship that was interrupted only by her marriage (dissolved in 1901) to Richard Goldsbrough Row at Scots Church manse, Sydney, on 26 January 1884—'just a girl's mad act to repent of at leisure'. This date, and that on which George Musgrove died, she later described as the two most tragic days of her life.

Between 1883 and 1887 Nellie played continuously in comic opera, taking twenty-one roles (her interpretation of Yum Yum in *The Mikado* gained special praise) and touring with them under the management of J. C. Williamson [q.v.6], Arthur Garner and Musgrove. She appeared in grand opera in 1888 as Marguerite in Gounod's *Faust*, but unwisely strained her voice by singing this demanding role for twenty-four consecutive nights. Eventually she had a repertoire of thirty-five prima donna roles before she was forced to relinquish opera and turn to comedy and drama.

After starring for Musgrove in *Paul Jones* in 1889, Nellie went with him to England where their daughter Nancye was born in 1893. Returning to Australia in September, she headed a comic opera company which toured Australasia until 1895 when she returned to

London. Except for a small part in one unsuccessful play, she did not appear on the stage until Christmas 1898 when she was principal boy in the Drury Lane pantomime *The forty thieves*. In 1900-01 she played in the pantomime *Cinderella* in Australia and in May 1901 she proudly sang the memorial ode 'Australia' at the opening of the first Commonwealth parliament. On 15 February 1902 she began the greatest part of her career as Nell Gwynne in *Sweet Nell of Old Drury* by Paul Kester: for a fortnight the show wavered in Melbourne and then proved a resounding success. Because of her strong personal identification with the role, it became the one for which she was remembered and loved by Australians as 'Sweet Nell'.

In 1905 the company began a tour of the U.S.A. *Sweet Nell* was successful in San Francisco, but the 1906 earthquake shattered plans of reaching New York. The stoic manner in which Nellie and Musgrove took this financial adversity was characteristic of their temperaments; so also was the way she sold her jewellery to help the company to return to Australia. It was not until 1909 that she had another hit—in *Sweet Kitty Bellairs*—which she played in a long season in alternation with *Zaza*, or *As you like it*, or *Sweet Nell*. In March 1910 she played the comedy role of Maggie Wylie in *What every woman knows*, followed by parts in *When knighthood was in flower* and *Trilby*.

Nellie Stewart was one of the first world-class performers to be enshrined in celluloid when she acted in the six-reel Australian film *Sweet Nell of Old Drury* directed by Raymond Longford [q.v.10] and premiered at the Sydney Lyceum on 2 December 1911. A contemporary described her appearance as one of grace and youth in which the inexorable lens could find no trace of time. The film screened for at least six years. Although in her autobiography (*My life's story*, 1923) Nellie stated that 'a copy was held to be produced when I am no more', no print has subsequently been found.

With the outbreak of World War I, a bleak period followed for the theatre. Nellie lived on her savings. When Musgrove died on 21 January 1916, she felt 'like one who had been torn apart from some other world', and it required the tact of Hugh D. McIntosh [q.v.10] to persuade her to tread the boards once again in a version of *Sweet Nell*.

A beautiful woman with expressive eyes, a finely tilted mouth and dimpled smile, Nellie was a talented, considerate and versatile actress. She was fortunate to have had her family's support, to have found her vocation so early and to have met Musgrove so fortuitously. Yet, besides her luck went strenuous, dedicated work and forthright common sense. She had little trace of pettiness or affectation,

but was inspired by a sense of beauty in the world and driven on a quest to better herself. Her greatest attribute was the magnetism that allowed her to reach beyond the footlights to captivate a public for whom she retained loyalty. Commented upon by all, and obvious in her 1931 recording of the coquettish lines from *Sweet Nell*, was her perennial youthfulness. Probably no other woman has played young roles as successfully so late in life.

Nellie made many appearances for charities and was responsible for assisting to raise £3000 in 1910 to buy radium for Sydney Hospital, which named its children's ward after her. When nearly 70 she played in an astonishing revival of her lithe, graceful Sweet Nell. Survived by her daughter, she died in Sydney on 21 June 1931 and was cremated. Her ashes were buried in her family tomb in the Boroondara cemetery, Kew, Melbourne, beneath a kneeling angel bearing her facial likeness. In 1938 the Nellie Stewart Memorial Club erected a monument to their idol in the Botanic Gardens, Sydney.

M. Skill, *Sweet Nell of old Sydney* (Syd, 1973); *Everyone's*, 24 June 1931; Recording of N. Stewart's voice, 1931 (ML).   Ross Cooper

STEWART, SIR FREDERICK HAROLD (1884-1961), businessman, politician and philanthropist, was born on 14 August 1884 at Newcastle, New South Wales, son of native-born parents James Henry Stewart, carter, and his wife Ellen, née Murray. Educated at Newcastle South Public School, he joined the New South Wales railways at 14 as a clerk. On 8 April 1908 he married Lottie May Glover (d. 1943) at the Central Methodist Mission, Newcastle; they were to have six children.

In 1919 Stewart created the basis of a substantial fortune by buying and subdividing 50 acres (20 ha) at rural Chullora on the outskirts of Sydney. When the government refused to extend tram or railway services there, he began his own transport service with one bus. By the mid-1920s he was Sydney's largest private bus proprietor. At its peak, his Metropolitan Omnibus & Transport Co. Ltd had a total capital of £200 000, employed 4000 people and carried 16 million fares over three million miles (4 827 900 km) each year. As chairman of the Motor Transport Association from 1923, he campaigned to extend private bus services and to discourage government transport monopolies. His proposal to buy the State tramways in order to replace trams with buses was rejected. Stewart was defeated in the early 1930s by a combination of government discouragement, high licence fees, and motor and petrol taxes.

In a final flourish he offered his fleet of ninety buses to the government, provided his drivers and conductors kept their jobs; the gesture was declined. In 1937 the State government paid him nominal compensation of £38 600.

In the late 1920s Stewart had diversified his business activities, founding Australian National Airways Ltd with (Sir) Charles Kingsford Smith [q.v.9] and Charles Ulm [q.v.] and establishing New South Wales Woollen & Felt Industries Ltd at Mascot. A director of Associated Newspapers Ltd, he was governing director of 2CH radio which he established for the New South Wales Council of Churches in 1933.

Active, albeit unobtrusively, in church and civic charities, Stewart supported the Methodist Overseas Mission; locally, he provided free transport for blind children and took mothers of poor families on outings. Distressed by the impact of the Depression, he supplied 50 000 free bus tickets in one month to the unemployed. An able publicist, he tried to lease the unoccupied Prime Minister's Lodge in Canberra for a holiday home for overworked city women. Stewart expressed dissatisfaction with an order which imposed so much deprivation and suffering 'in a world so bountifully endowed by its creator'. His interest in public finance was whetted by several years as president of the Taxpayers' Association.

Convinced of the need for industrial reform, shorter working hours and comprehensive social betterment programmes (such as national insurance and workers' housing schemes), Stewart unsuccessfully sought Nationalist pre-selection for the Federal seat of Martin in 1929 and contested Concord in the 1930 State elections. In the December 1931 landslide victory of Joseph Lyons [q.v.10] and the United Australia Party, Stewart won the Federal seat of Parramatta. Vigorous and innovative, he quickly asserted himself in the House of Representatives and served as minister for commerce from October 1932. Given responsibility for Australian trade policy following the Imperial Economic Conference of 1932, Stewart was not overwhelmed by the minutiae of departmental affairs. His political outlook was imbued with the business ethic; his debating style was often fiery: he was suspended from the parliament for saying that the Speaker J. S. Roseveare had a 'larrikin face'.

Retaining his portfolio in September 1934, within a month Stewart stood aside for (Sir) Earle Page [q.v.11]; when Stewart refused a junior ministry, Lyons appointed him parliamentary under-secretary for employment. Knighted in 1935, he renewed his support for a 40-hour week after visiting the International Labour Office in Geneva that year. To set an example, he granted the shorter working week to employees in his own enterprises. He criticized the high dividends paid by companies during the Depression, and resisted pressures within the government to impose more deflationary measures while unemployment remained high. Stewart resigned his post in February 1936 and gave up most of his remaining business associations: he wanted freedom to develop his social betterment programmes.

In 1936-37 he was active within U.A.P. branches, urging the creation of a social betterment wing and threatening to stand against Sir Archdale Parkhill [q.v.11], leader of the conservatives, unless the government introduced social reforms. Re-elected in 1937, the Lyons government announced a modified national insurance scheme, but Stewart refused to rejoin cabinet, preferring the freedom of the back bench. He was not, he reiterated, merely a 'fatuous apologist' for everything the party did. Although Stewart was a perpetual irritant at this time, Lyons was sympathetic to his objectives.

When (Sir) Robert Menzies formed his U.A.P. government in April 1939, Stewart was restored to the ministry with responsibility for health and social services. He continued to push for the implementation of the national insurance scheme and for its extension to a broader range of beneficiaries including the unemployed. Stewart introduced pension payments by cheque, posted in plain envelopes to eliminate any stigma. In November the Navy Department was added to his responsibilities. He became minister for supply and development in March 1940, accepting the onerous responsibility for developing defence industries, and procuring weapons and equipment for the armed services. He was much criticized over defence contracts and shortages, but showed ingenuity in hunting out stocks of essential equipment and adapting them to military needs. He solved one deficiency in army uniforms by locating 15 000 World War I tunics and having them refurbished.

In October 1940 Stewart became minister for social services, health and external affairs. Looking to post-war reconstruction, he urged the ultimate conversion of war industries to domestic needs and coined the slogan 'from guns to mod cons'. As external affairs minister he frequently warned of dangers from growing Japanese militarism, but sought to preserve links for as long as possible. After the defeat of (Sir) Arthur Fadden's coalition government in October 1941, Stewart served as chairman of the Joint Committee on Social Security (1943-44) and maintained a degree of independence: he voted against his party leadership on the 'Uniform Tax Scheme' of 1942. He retired from parliament in 1946 and virtually from public life.

Short and broad-shouldered, with wisps of dark hair above a ruddy complexion, Stewart was bustling but personable, opinionated but without pomposity. At his model farm at Dundas he planted English grasses, bred pigs, merinos, cattle and poultry, and played bowls and a pipe organ for relaxation. For many years he held the car registration plate NSW 1. Stewart had married Hilda Marjorie Evelyn Dixon at Lindfield, Sydney, on 6 October 1945. He established at his own expense a 'preventorium' at Curl Curl for undernourished children, an infants' home at Carlingford and the Methodist Mission's hospital in New Britain. Survived by his wife, and by two sons and three daughters of his first marriage, Stewart died on 30 June 1961 in Royal North Shore Hospital, Sydney, and was cremated after a state funeral. His estate was valued for probate at £168 000.

In many ways Stewart was the antithesis of a professional politician, being prepared to sacrifice political advancement to achieve social reform. He relished his role as a gadfly: he was critical of his party leaders to the brink of disloyalty, but always commanded their respect. More active in social and industrial policy than virtually all Labor politicians of his generation, he was frustrated in his supreme objective of implementing a national insurance scheme. His idealism, administrative talents and disregard for political aggrandizement made him one of the more effective and attractive of Australia's politicians in an era of depression and war.

G. Sawer, *Australian Federal politics and law 1929-49* (Melb, 1963); *Star* (Melb), 4 Jan 1934; *Herald* (Melb), 22 Feb 1936, 1 July 1961; *SMH*, 1 July 1961; *Sun News-Pictorial*, 18 Aug 1936; E. D. Cardner, Sir Frederick Stewart (ts, 1936, *SMH* Lib).   C. J. LLOYD

STEWART, JAMES CAMPBELL (1884-1947), soldier and public servant, was born on 19 January 1884 at Belfast (Port Fairy), Victoria, son of James Stewart, bank manager, and his wife Elizabeth, née Grant, both Victorian born. After attending Terang High School he became a bank officer, but his great love was soldiering. Having moved to Melbourne, in 1901 he joined the Victorian Scottish Regiment, a volunteer unit, was promoted sergeant in 1905 and commissioned in 1909. With the reorganization of Australia's defence forces, the Victorian Scottish emerged as the 52nd (Hobson's Bay) Infantry; in 1912 Captain Stewart became its adjutant.

For a 'king and country' man with a passion for soldiering, there was only one possible response to the outbreak of World War I: Cam Stewart enlisted on 17 August 1914 and was appointed adjutant of the 5th Battalion, Australian Imperial Force. The Gallipoli landing proved a stern test. Amid the chaos and carnage of 25 April 1915 Stewart was soon acting battalion commander, and early that afternoon led the battalion reserve forward 'under the hail of shell fire' to the fighting on 400 Plateau. About 3 p.m. he was hit by shrapnel and later evacuated to Egypt. He returned to Gallipoli on 2 June and remained with the 5th Battalion until the evacuation.

In February 1916 the A.I.F. was enlarged and Stewart was appointed to command the 57th Battalion in the newly created 15th Brigade; he was a lieut-colonel from 12 March. His exacting brigadier, H. E. Elliott [q.v.8], considered that the three other battalion commanders allotted him were obviously unsuitable, but had no qualms about Stewart: he 'is far and away the best man for the job'. On the Western Front Elliott continued to praise Stewart's work, including his stints as acting brigadier when Elliott was on leave. Stewart was of average height and build; his oval face, moustache, probing eyes and expansive forehead lent a certain refinement to his appearance that could be deceptive, for he drove his men hard when necessary. C. E. W. Bean [q.v.7] described him as 'a cool, experienced and trusted officer'.

At the disastrous battle of Fromelles, Stewart was fortunate when a postponement meant that his 57th was placed in reserve instead of being one of the assault battalions that were slaughtered. He performed capably as commander of 'Stewart's Force' in the harassment of the German retreat in March 1917. In September the 15th Brigade's major operation at Polygon Wood was jeopardized when a British unit alongside was forced to retreat. After Elliott sent the 57th forward to rectify the situation, Stewart 'personally reconnoitred the position, in advance of his battalion, under an intense enemy barrage'. In the inferno his battalion filled the gap in the line, enabling the operation to proceed successfully. He was 'simply wonderful', enthused Elliott, 'his own men think the world of Cam Stewart'.

Promoted colonel commanding the 14th Brigade in March 1918, Stewart left the 57th Battalion on the day the Germans launched their great March offensive. He regarded the ensuing months until the Armistice as the pinnacle of his career. In both defence and attack his leadership during the battles of 1918 was characteristically cool and reliable, although he was criticized by Sir John Monash [q.v.10] for 'lack of driving power' at Péronne. Stewart was awarded the Distinguished Service Order and Bar, appointed C.M.G. and mentioned five times in dispatches.

Back in Melbourne in November 1919, Stewart was employed in various positions by the Department of Lands, including chairman of the Farmers' Relief Board and member of the Closer Settlement Board. On Christmas eve 1925 he married a divorcee Annie Edith Pinsent, née Miller (d. 1936), at the Sydney registry office. Living at Elwood, Melbourne, he was a Freemason who enjoyed fishing, gardening and golf. Yet his chief interest continued to be soldiering. In the Australian Military Forces he commanded the 14th Brigade (1920-21), the 10th Brigade (1921-26) and the 15th Brigade (1930-34); he was a well-known figure as chief marshal of Melbourne's Anzac Day march for over two decades. During World War II he was rejected for A.I.F. enlistment on age and medical grounds, but commanded Melbourne Metropolitan Group, Volunteer Defence Corps, in 1942-45. On 12 August 1946 he married Mary Imelda Polan with Catholic rites. Survived by his wife, he died of hypertensive cerebrovascular disease on 2 June 1947 in South Melbourne and was cremated. He had no children.

C. E. W. Bean, *The story of Anzac*, 1 (Syd, 1921), and *The A.I.F. in France* 1916-18 (Syd, 1929, 1933, 1937, 1942); F. W. Speed, *Esprit de corps* (Syd, 1988); *Age* and *Argus*, 3 June 1947; H. E. Elliott papers (AWM).   ROSS McMULLIN

STEWART, JAMES DOUGLAS (1869-1955), veterinary surgeon, was born on 18 August 1869 at Windsor, New South Wales, second son of John Stewart junior [q.v.6], a veterinary surgeon from Edinburgh, and his Parramatta-born wife Jessie, née Walker. James was educated at Sydney Grammar School and then articled to an accountant for three years. Entering the Royal (Dick) Veterinary College, Edinburgh, in 1890, he passed its examinations with three gold medals and was admitted to membership of the Royal College of Veterinary Surgeons, London, in May 1893.

Back in Australia, Stewart assisted his father at Windsor and in 1894 founded the Veterinary Medical Association of New South Wales. Next year he became honorary veterinary surgeon to the New South Wales Zoological Society and in 1896 assistant teacher, later lecturer, in veterinary science, farriery and meat inspection at Sydney Technical College. As veterinary officer in the Department of Agriculture from 1898, he organized the colony's veterinary services, published in the *New South Wales Agricultural Gazette* and initiated measures to control the scourges of tuberculosis and ticks in cattle. He was appointed chief inspector of stock in 1907. On 4 September 1901 at Randwick he had married with Presbyterian forms Edith May Forsyth, daughter of John and niece of Archibald Forsyth [q.v.4].

In 1909 Stewart accepted the foundation chair of veterinary science at the University of Sydney (B.V.Sc., 1911). During World War I student numbers dropped to four; but for Stewart's 'courage and determination', the school might have closed. He lectured on every subject in the curriculum and it was some time before he could devote his attention to the study of veterinary medicine. From being a captain in the Australian Army Veterinary Corps, he was promoted major; he was also director of veterinary services of the Australian Military Forces at Headquarters in Melbourne. With (Sir) Thomas Lyle and (Sir) David Masson [qq.v.10], he served on the executive committee of the Commonwealth Advisory Council of Science and Industry.

President of the Australian Veterinary Association in 1922, he secured the passage of the 1923 Veterinary Surgeons Act and sat on the Veterinary Surgeons Board (president, 1931-34). 'Always insistent that the veterinarian must take his place as the scientific equal of the members of any of the scientific professions', he was president of the veterinary science section of the Australasian Association for the Advancement of Science in 1926 and of the Royal Society of New South Wales in 1927-28.

Retiring in August 1939, Stewart maintained his lifelong interest in horses: he was veterinary surgeon to the Australian Jockey Club (1908-53), and a founder and director of the club's apprentices' school of which he was an honorary instructor from 1940. He was, in addition, a founder and director of the Corps of Commissionaires for ex-servicemen.

The recipient of many honours, Stewart was an honorary life member of the Royal Agricultural Society of New South Wales (1935), a fellow (1936) and honorary associate (1954) of the Royal College of Veterinary Surgeons, London, and fellow of the Australian Veterinary Association (1941) which awarded him the Gilruth [q.v.9] prize in 1953.

Survived by a son and three daughters, Stewart died at Darlinghurst on 17 September 1955 and was cremated. A pioneer in veterinary education in Australia and New Zealand, he was a man of vision, action and achievement. His portrait by Norman Carter [q.v.7] is held by the University of Sydney.

Veterinary J (Lond), 36, 1893, pp 34, 65; *Aust Veterinary J*, Oct 1935, p 173, Oct 1955, p 271, 11 Mar 1988; Univ Syd Veterinary Assn, *Centaur*, 1939, 1955; *SMH*, 31 Mar 1926, 5 May 1927, 7 Jan 1929, 25 Mar 1932, 3 Apr, 5 May, 19 Aug 1936, 25 Aug 1939, 26 Nov 1940, 1 July 1950, 14 May 1954, 18 Sept 1955; *Country Life*, 7 Oct 1955; Aust Veterinary Assn historical collection (AVA Archives, Artarmon, Syd, *and* Harden, NSW); information from Dr D. F. Stewart, Blackheath, NSW.   ROBERT I. TAYLOR

STEWART, JOHN McKELLAR (1878-1953), philosopher, was born on 4 May 1878 at Ballangeich, near Warrnambool, Victoria, son of Alexander Stewart, a farmer from Scotland, and his native-born wife Lillias, née McKellar. John became a pupil teacher at Warrnambool State School and then taught at Charlton and Benalla. He entered Ormond [q.v.5] College at the University of Melbourne in 1903 where he studied under (Sir) John Latham and Henry Laurie [qq.v.10]. In 1906 Stewart topped his final year in philosophy with first-class honours; he won a Hastie scholarship and lectured to Ormond College students in 1907-09, while studying theology and ministering in the Presbyterian Church. On 3 November 1909 at Scots Church, Melbourne, the serious and friendly young man married Margaret Grace Stuart Bothroyd (M.A.) who later wrote for the *Argus* and was active in the League of Women Voters; they were to have a daughter and three sons. Stewart proceeded to the University of Edinburgh, where he wrote a thesis on Bergson's philosophy (D.Phil., 1911), and the Philipps University of Marburg, Germany, noted for its Kantian scholarship. His *A critical exposition of Bergson's philosophy* (London, 1913) portrayed his subject through somewhat Kantian eyes and resisted Bergson's anti-intellectualism.

Having returned to the University of Melbourne in 1912 as lecturer in philosophy, in 1920 Stewart attained the newly established rank of associate professor. He had previously come a close second to W. R. B. Gibson [q.v.8] for the chair. They had a harmonious partnership; both were influenced by Husserl. As vice-president of the university's controversial Public Questions Society, Stewart showed diplomacy in defending contentious students against an outraged professoriate. He was honorary secretary of the university extension board. He was also a champion golfer at club level. His manner, which was warm and dignified, reflected his liberal attitudes and Scottish background.

In 1923-50 he held the (Sir Walter) Hughes [q.v.4] chair of philosophy at the University of Adelaide. He published occasional lectures and journal articles, especially in the *Australasian Journal of Psychology and Philosophy*; although his manuscript for a book on Husserl was destroyed by a fire in 1939, some of Stewart's translations from Husserl have survived. As a teacher, he prepared lectures meticulously. He was active outside academic philosophy as vice-chancellor of the university in 1945-48 and as a member of its council; he was also president of the Kindergarten Union of South Australia and a member of the Australian Round Table. In 1949 he was appointed C.M.G.

At his home at Blackwood in the Adelaide hills Stewart was a keen gardener, with a fondness for raising native plants from seed often brought back from fishing trips on Kangaroo Island. Predeceased by his wife and survived by his four children, the professor died in Calvary Hospital, North Adelaide, on 25 April 1953 and was cremated. A grandson John Finnis is a leading jurist and philosopher of law at the University of Oxford, England.

W. K. Hancock, *Country and calling* (Lond, 1954); S. A. Grave, *History of philosophy in Australia* (Brisb, 1984); *Adel Univ Mag*, 5, no 2 (1923); *A'sian J of Philosophy*, 31 (1953), p 137, 32 (1954), p 169; Univ Adel Archives; information from Mrs M. Finnis, Leabrook, Adel.　　J. J. C. SMART

STEWART, JOHN MITCHELL YOUNG (1865-1940), medical practitioner, was born on 14 December 1865 at Tarland, Aberdeenshire, Scotland, eldest of four children of Robert Stewart, minister of the Free Church of Scotland, and his wife Isabella Henrietta, née Fergusson. Mitchell, as his family called him, was educated at Merchison Castle School and the University of Glasgow (M.B., C.M., 1887).

After practising briefly in Glasgow, he came to Western Australia in 1887; he assisted a doctor at Albany and acted as port medical officer and quarantine officer. Stewart later practised at York where, on 4 June 1890 at Holy Trinity Anglican Church, he married Annie Selina Taylor; they were to have three children. In 1891 he began general practice at Guildford where he was appointed district government medical officer and resident magistrate (1894). There he was joined in partnership by his brother James Edmund Fergusson and sister Roberta Henrietta Margaritta [q.v.9 R. Jull], fellow graduates from the University of Glasgow. All three attended a meeting in Perth in 1898 to form a Western Australian branch of the British Medical Association; Mitchell was later elected to the first council. He moved to Perth in 1906 to practise as a gynaecologist.

In Scotland Stewart had served five years in the Lanarkshire Volunteers. Commissioned second lieutenant in the Guildford Rifles, Western Australian Volunteer Force, in 1894, he was appointed captain on the medical staff in 1899 and served as medical officer with Western Australia's 2nd contingent to the South African War in 1900-01. Promoted major in 1901, he held various medical appointments until resigning in 1912.

In that year Stewart registered as a medical practitioner in New South Wales and practised at Bangalow until his appointment on 14 November 1914 as major in the 2nd Australian General Hospital, Australian Imperial Force. Two weeks later he embarked for Egypt where in early 1915 he transferred to the 12th Battalion as regimental medical officer. During the landing at Gallipoli on 25 April Stewart suffered a displaced cartilage in his right knee, but tended the wounded until he was evacuated to Egypt two days later. Transferred to hospital in England in May, he was discharged on 3 June but re-admitted a day later with enteric fever. He was transferred to the supernumerary list in November and served at convalescent depots until appointed to the 11th Australian Field Ambulance at Larkhill in August 1916. The unit served on the Western Front from November and in May 1917 Stewart was promoted lieutcolonel to command the 15th Australian Field Ambulance. His organizing skills were recognized by the award in December of the Distinguished Service Order. He had previously been mentioned in dispatches for his service in France and Belgium. Stewart's next appointment was as colonel commanding the 1st Australian Dermatological Hospital at Bulford, Wiltshire, England, from January 1918 to December 1919 when he returned to Australia. For this service, he was appointed C.B.E. His A.I.F. appointment ended in 1920 and he was transferred to the retired list in 1923.

Stewart's first marriage had been dissolved on 13 July 1915; fifteen days later he married Australian-born Muriel Fredda Heaverside Meallin at Camberwell, London. After demobilization Stewart practised at Temora, New South Wales; in 1924 he moved to England and bought a practice in Shenley, Hertfordshire. Deteriorating health forced him to sell it in 1925, at considerable financial loss, and from then he was unable to practise. An enteric carrier, Stewart had received a war disability pension since 1920 and was accepted as totally and permanently incapacitated. He went to Canada in 1927, Bermuda in 1930-33 and Jersey, Channel Islands, from 1933 until September 1935 when he was taken to Surrey, England. Described then as a 'big, stout man', he remained hospitalized, except for a few months in 1936, until he died at the Red Cross Hospital for Officers, Brighton, on 24 April 1940 of typhoid fever and cerebral haemorrhage. The Repatriation Commission granted a pension to his widow.

Stewart's brother James (1874-1937) also served as an A.I.F. medical officer in Egypt, France and Belgium.

B. C. Cohen, *A history of medicine in Western Australia to 1900* (Perth, 1965); Aust Defence Dept, *Official records of the Australian military contingents to the war in South Africa*, P. L. Murray ed (Melb, 1911); A. G. Butler (ed), *Official history of the Australian Army Medical Services in the war of*

1914-1918, 1 (Melb, 1938); *London Gazette*, 28 Dec 1917, 1 Jan 1918, 12 Dec 1919; *Reveille* (Syd), 1 Apr 1933; *Western Mail* (Perth), 20 Jan, 3, 10 Feb, 7 Apr, 26 May, 2 June, 7 July, 18 Aug 1900, 16 Feb, 2 Mar 1901; *Temora Independent*, 2, 27 Feb 1924; War diaries, 11th *and* 15th Aust Field Ambulance, *and* 1st Aust Dermatological Hospital, AIF (AWM).

J. B. HOPLEY

STEWART, PERCY GERALD (1885-1931), farmer and politician, was born on 18 October 1885 at Footscray, Melbourne, son of William Stewart, master mariner, and his wife Isabella, née Farrington, both Victorian born. After leaving Yarraville State School, he worked at a bottle factory, then as a 'water-joey' on the Mildura railway line and a shepherd in the southern Mallee. In 1905 he joined a British cargo ship and obtained his master's certificate, but suffered such debilitating malaria that he left the sea and travelled in Europe and Canada before returning to Australia in 1909. Having worked as a farm labourer, in 1913 he selected a 'green' Mallee block at Carwarp in north-west Victoria which he later sold when he moved to Eastern View at Carwarp West. On 17 April 1916, at Yarraville, Stewart married Edith Catherine Roberts with Methodist forms.

During World War I Stewart volunteered three times for active service but was rejected on health grounds. His interest in scientific farming led him to pioneer new cropping techniques for semi-arid regions and to work closely with the Department of Agriculture and other groups in improving yields from light Mallee soils. From the early 1920s until 1931 he wrote a weekly article on Mallee farming for the Mildura *Sunraysia Daily*; in 1924 in partnership with R. C. D. Elliott [q.v.8] and Ethel, wife of (Sir) Earle Page [q.v.11], he bought this newspaper and was its chairman in 1924-31.

Having observed the political power of the Canadian grain growers' associations, Stewart was keen to organize similar groups in Victoria. In May 1916, when president of the Carwarp Progress Association, he invited delegates from kindred organizations to a conference at Ouyen to discuss the formation of a Mallee farmers' union. Learning of a similar project led by Isaac Hart and J. J. Hall [q.v.9], he joined with them to found the Victorian Farmers' Union, forerunner of the Victorian Country Party. At its first annual conference in September 1916 Stewart was appointed to the central council. In November 1917 he won the seat of Swan Hill to become one of four V.F.U. representatives in the Legislative Assembly.

'One of the few genuinely radical leaders of the early Country Party', the thin and lanky Stewart was an ascetic individualist who set great store by his principles. Convinced that the V.F.U. could best serve farmers by remaining independent from other parties, after 1918 he sat next to the Labor opposition and frequently voted with them. Stewart's intransigence, combined with his electoral popularity, created a problem for his own party which was then canvassing coalition with the Nationalists. In October 1919, however, he resigned and won the Federal seat of Wimmera which he was to hold until his death. One of five original members of the Federal parliamentary Country Party, Stewart was also one of the three managers appointed to look after its interests. He took a leading role in negotiations that led to the formation of the Bruce [q.v.7]-Page government in late 1922. Offered a choice of two portfolios in that administration, he chose works and railways (February 1923-August 1924) which included presidency of the River Murray Commission. He was therefore able to accelerate such major national projects as the Hume water storage, while improving roads, postal and telephone facilities in the Wimmera and Mallee. He also helped to establish the dried fruit and citrus industries in the Murray Valley, and he assisted in the provision of domestic water and irrigation in north-west Victoria. Initially opposed to the notion of a Federal capital at Canberra, Stewart was to alter his view and to advocate that it be built quickly and economically. On 28 August 1923 he turned the first sod on the site of Parliament House.

After a bitter quarrel with Page, Stewart resigned his portfolio in August 1924 in protest against a pact between Bruce and Page which gave electoral protection to sitting members. To Stewart, this deal violated fundamental Country Party principles, and unjustly restricted electors' choice of candidates. In March 1926 he and others resigned from the V.F.U. over the issue of (State) composite governments. Stewart and (Sir) A. A. Dunstan [q.v.8] then organized the Victorian Country Progressive Party. A radical group with its power base in Bendigo and the Mallee, it effectively held the balance of power in Victoria during the latter 1920s. Stewart urged compulsory nation-wide wheat pools and guaranteed prices for grain. He publicized his campaign widely in country newspapers, hoping to achieve a growers' organization big enough to combat the influence of banks, grain merchants and fertilizer companies. The first branch of the Victorian Wheatgrowers' Association was formed at Ultima in November 1928: within twelve months a thriving movement existed.

The Victorian split was partly over fundamental party doctrines, but it also involved personal rivalries. The dispute between Page and Stewart was so bitter that Page campaigned against Stewart in the 1928 and 1929 elections. Both times Stewart was easily returned, but he rarely spoke in the House after his argument with Page. As the rural depression deepened, even party conservatives became radicalized; the two factions reunited late in 1930.

Stewart consistently took a radical line and often voted with Labor even after reunification of the V.C.P. The sole Federal representative of the V.C.P.P., he became a close personal friend of W. M. Hughes [q.v.9], despite their political differences. They were the only non-Labor members to oppose the sale of the Commonwealth Shipping Line in 1927. In March 1929 Stewart was the only Country Party member to support Labor's proposal for a Federal wheat marketing scheme; in September he voted against the abolition of the Federal arbitration system, thus helping to bring down the Bruce-Page government. Stewart strongly supported Scullin's [q.v.11] 1930 'Grow More Wheat' campaign and endeavoured to compel him to ratify a guaranteed price for wheat despite overwhelming political and economic difficulties. Nevertheless, Stewart backed the Melbourne Agreement (1930) which split the Labor Party. Apart from local-area issues, he concentrated his political attention on tariff reductions, compulsory wheat pools, 'orderly marketing', guaranteed prices, a rural bank, grain bulk-handling, mortgage relief and lower freight rates for primary produce.

Stewart was an excellent debater with a keen analytical mind. Although often abrupt and aggressive, and at times bitter, he was a highly persuasive speaker. His 'frail figure and sensitive, remarkably intelligent face' stood out among his colleagues. A thorn in Page's side until the last, Stewart was said to have worried about losing his seat in parliament because he always had another waiting on his plough. He had long suffered from poor health and on 15 October 1931 died at Woomelang of pneumonia. He was buried in Carwarp cemetery after a State funeral. His wife survived him. Stewart's memorial at Red Cliffs was unveiled by Hughes in 1937.

E. C. G. Page, *Truant surgeon*, A. Mozley ed (Syd, 1963); U. R. Ellis, *A history of the Australian Country Party* (Melb, 1963); B. D. Graham, *The formation of the Australian Country Parties* (Canb, 1966); *Farmers Advocate*, 20 Nov 1919; *Argus*, 16 Oct 1931; *Sunraysia Daily*, 16, 17 Oct 1931, 13 Aug 1937; *Times* (Donald-Birchip), 12 June 1984; information from Mr H. J. Dowd, Glenroy, and Mrs K. Edwards, Essendon, Melb.

K. M. HAIG-MUIR

STICHT, ROBERT CARL (1856-1922), metallurgist and mining engineer, was born on 8 October 1856 at Hoboken, New Jersey, United States of America, son of German-American parents from Brooklyn. He graduated B.Sc. from the Brooklyn Polytechnic in 1875, then specialized in metallurgy at the Royal School of Mines, Clausthal, Germany, completing his studies in 1880. Appointed chief chemist and assistant metallurgist at a Colorado smelting company, he became interested in smelting techniques and in his fifteen years on the fields of Colorado and Montana became the foremost authority on pyritic smelting in the U.S.A.

In 1893 he was approached by William Knox and William Orr [qq.v.9,11], directors of the newly formed Mount Lyell Mining & Railway Co. Ltd, who offered him the position of metallurgist at the new Queenstown mine, Tasmania. Sticht arrived at Queenstown in 1895 with his wife of six months, Marion Oak, née Staige, from Illinois; he was to become a dominant figure in Tasmanian industry and in the west-coast community.

His first task was to persuade the company principals to abandon their plans of roasting the Mount Lyell ore and smelting it in a blast furnace in favour of the more efficient but fickle process of pyritic smelting. Sticht directed the construction of a reduction works, partly of his own design, and the first two furnaces were fired in 1896. Appointed general manager in 1897, he was not a desk-bound administrator, but spent much time on the works' floor and set about making the remote west-coast mine as self-sufficient as possible.

Although the Economist nominated Mount Lyell as the best-managed mine in Australasia, the ore body proved disappointing, but the efficiency of the Lyell smelters partly offset the poor yield of the ore and in 1902 Sticht announced the first successful purely pyritic smelting in the world. The difficulty of sustaining this process, however, led him to reintroduce up to one per cent coke into the furnace.

As smelting required the correct fusion of air, metal, flux and fire, so Sticht conceived of the Mount Lyell works as a unit within which natural resources, capital and labour should work in concert to achieve maximum productive efficiency. A paternalistic manager, Sticht would not concede that the interests of the company were not fully shared by the workforce. He opposed union organization, holding that the Amalgamated Miners' Association challenged his authority. To counter what he considered to be the displaced loyalty of the miners, he established and became president of a medical union which offered first-rate services.

The years before World War I were the most trying of Sticht's tenure. Labour shortages, industrial disputes and a mining disaster in which forty-two men were killed led the company to improve living conditions for the workforce. Sticht's confrontationist approach to worker organization was not long favoured by the directors who appointed R. M. Murray [q.v.10], a local metallurgist, as deputy manager to take charge of housing and co-operative schemes, and to mediate between Sticht and his workforce.

Sticht had pioneered a metallurgical technique that paid handsome dividends—in one year the company had earned more revenue than the Tasmanian government—but by the 1920s it had been superseded by the flotation method of separating copper. His last years were marked by inefficiency. In 1920, following the collapse of world prices, the company was selling copper at a loss. Sticht's solution was to cut wages and to shorten working hours, but his plan was opposed by the Combined Unions Council and the Commonwealth Court of Conciliation and Arbitration. In 1921 he fell ill and was replaced as general manager next year by Murray who soon abandoned pyritic smelting and returned the mine to profitability.

Sticht was short and stocky, with a bald pate and fair moustache. Abstemious and careful, he urged restraint among his employees, particularly in regard to alcohol. When old or unlucky prospectors approached him for a job, he was usually sympathetic. His house, Penghana, overlooked the reduction works, but within its walls he was cocooned from that environment. He read widely and assembled a fine private library which included items of incunabula, Caxton Bibles, Reformation tracts, early editions of Shakespeare and Australiana. His art collection included Dürer woodcuts and Rembrandt etchings. Some of it is housed in the National Gallery of Victoria, acquired through the Felton [q.v.4] bequest.

Survived by his wife and three sons, Sticht died of renal carcinoma in St Margaret's Hospital, Launceston, on 30 April 1922. His body was taken to Melbourne for cremation at Springvale, but at his request there was no funeral service: he had once described himself as a 'scientific agnostic'. The mineral stichtite commemorates his name.

G. Blainey, The peaks of Lyell (Melb, 1978); Mount Lyell Mining and Railway Co. Ltd papers (TA and Univ Melb Archives); Sticht papers (TA).

IAN McSHANE

STILLWELL, FRANK LESLIE (1888-1963), geologist, was born on 27 June 1888 at Hawthorn, Melbourne, seventh of eight children of London-born Alfred Stillwell, printer, and his Victorian wife Mary Eliza, née Townsend. Alfred had arrived in Victoria with his parents in 1855. His father, John, was by 1868 one of the principals of a printing and publishing business to which, in due course, Frank's father and brother succeeded. Frank was educated at Auburn State School, Hawthorn College and the University of Melbourne (B.Sc., 1911; M.Sc., 1913) where two older sisters, Effie (M.B., B.S., 1901) and Florence (M.Sc., 1903), had preceded him. He graduated with first-class honours, having won in every year the exhibitions and scholarships open to candidates in geology. At the end of 1911 he went as geologist with the Australasian Antarctic Expedition led by (Sir) Douglas Mawson [q.v.10]. Stillwell was a member of the main base party at Commonwealth Bay and leader of two sledging parties which did topographic and geological work to the east for about sixty miles (96.6 km) along the coast. He returned to Australia in March 1913. His study, 'The metamorphic rocks of Adelie Land' published in the expedition's reports, earned him a D.Sc. (1916) from the University of Melbourne.

In 1914-15 Stillwell taught mineralogy at the University of Adelaide. He enlisted in the Australian Imperial Force in 1916, but was withdrawn to assist the Commonwealth Advisory Council of Science and Industry. In 1919-21 he worked as a geologist at Broken Hill, New South Wales, and Bendigo, Victoria. A visit in 1922-23 to the mining fields in Europe, South Africa and North America led him into the emerging field of mineragraphy, the study of polished surfaces of mineral aggregates under a reflecting microscope as a means of determining the identity and relationships of the minerals.

Appointed to a research fellowship at the University of Melbourne under Professor E. W. Skeats [q.v.11], in 1927 Stillwell became research petrologist for the Council for Scientific and Industrial Research and did outstanding work on the Kalgoorlie goldfield, Western Australia. He built no bureaucratic empire: his first assistant, Dr A. B. Edwards, was not appointed until 1935 and they had cramped laboratory space in the geology department at the university until the opening of an adjacent building a decade later. The creation of a mineragraphic section and the conversion of C.S.I.R. to the Commonwealth Scientific and Industrial Research Organization involved changes in title without affecting the character of his work or the respect in which he was held by the mining industry. He retired from the C.S.I.R.O. in 1953. Many honours were conferred upon him. In 1951 the Royal Society of New South Wales awarded him its (W. B.) Clarke [q.v.3] medal. In 1952 he was made correspondent of the Geological Society of America. In 1954 he was appointed O.B.E. and elected fellow of the Australian Academy of Science. In 1958 the Australasian Institute of Mining and Metallurgy, which had awarded him a medal in 1948, honoured his seventieth birthday by publishing the *Stillwell anniversary volume*. Other honours included two of the less usual: Mawson named Stillwell Island in Antarctica after him, and a new mineral was named Stillwellite.

Stillwell's service to science extended beyond his special field, especially in his life-long work for the Royal Society of Victoria which he joined in 1910. From 1929, when he became honorary secretary, until his death he served in various positions including that of president (1953-54), and it was to the society that the largest of his bequests was made.

Stillwell died, unmarried, at Richmond on 8 February 1963 and was cremated. Looking back on Antarctic days, C. F. Laseron [q.v.9], one of Stillwell's sledging companions, remarked that some persons invite nicknames while others do not, and that Stillwell —though a fine chap and popular with everybody—was called Frank and nothing else. That his contemporaries found in Stillwell as a young man a reserve which they respected was no surprise to those who knew him later. He was not cold, simply quiet. With the spoken word, he was economical; with the publicly spoken word, diffident. His silences ranged from the warmly approving to the firmly dissenting. A portrait by Orlando Dutton hangs in the Stillwell Room of the Graduate Union of the University of Melbourne.

Univ Melb Gazette, 19, 1963; *Melbourne Graduate*, 15, no 10, Dec 1964; *Records of the Aust Academy of Science*, 1, no 1, Dec 1966; *Age*, 9 Feb 1963.

ARTHUR A. WILCOCK

STODART, JAMES (1849-1922), merchant and politician, was born on 15 September 1849 in Edinburgh, son of James Dickson Stodart, accountant, and his wife Maria Louisa Margaretha, née Meincke. The family migrated to Melbourne in 1855 and 1856. Educated at Scotch College, James worked with Holmes, White & Co. and then Turnbull, Smith & Co., leading mercantile businesses. He followed Robert Murray Smith [q.v.6] to the New Zealand Loan & Mercantile Agency Co. as its accountant, but left in 1876 to set up his own business as a general merchant in Brisbane. An agent for the sugar refiners and distillers (Robert) Tooth [q.v.6] & Cran [q.v.8], James became one of its directors after it merged with the Millaquin & Yengarie Sugar Co. On 22 October 1878 he married Elizabeth Henrietta Noble Gair at Toorak, Melbourne, with Presbyterian forms.

Winning the seat of Logan in the Queensland Legislative Assembly, Stodart held it from 1896 to 1918: he served in government

(1896-1903 and 1908-15) and in Opposition (1903-08 and 1915-18). Stodart was chairman of committees in 1911-15. He held broad liberal views and favoured Federation, moderate protection, closer settlement and immigration of 'the yeoman class'. He opposed the indiscriminate introduction of Pacific islanders, wanting them restricted to tropical industries and segregated from large population centres. In his electorate, where he owned a sugar mill, he enthusiastically supported the establishment of the co-operative Farmers' Industrial Association.

He helped to establish the Mackay Coffee Estates Co. and was president of the Brisbane Chamber of Commerce (1911-12) and a director of the National Mutual Life Association of Australasia Ltd. A foundation member of the Royal Geographic Society (Queensland branch), he was vice-consul for Sweden (from 1906) and consul (1913-22). He was, as well, grand master of the Grand Lodge of Ancient, Free and Accepted Masons of Queensland. Survived by two sons and a daughter, Stodart died at his Ascot home on 20 June 1922 and was buried in South Brisbane cemetery.

His son ROBERT MACKAY STODART (1879-1956), soldier and businessman, was born on 14 September 1879 in Brisbane. From Brisbane Grammar School, he entered business. In October 1897 he enlisted in the Queensland Mounted Infantry. Promoted lieutenant in 1898, he served in the South African War and was awarded the Queen's medal with three clasps. Robert was a captain in the 13th Light Horse Regiment from 1903 and military adjutant in 1907-11; promoted major in 1908, he commanded the 13th L.H.R. from April 1912. Transferred to the 2nd L.H.R. in July, he was promoted lieut-colonel in 1913 and continued to command this regiment until 1921.

During World War I Stodart had served at Gallipoli from May to September 1915 in charge of the 2nd L.H.R. Although wounded on 6 June, he remained on duty until evacuated on 15 September. From Egypt on 3 March 1916 he embarked for home medically unfit. He commanded troops on sea transports until 15 April 1917 when his appointment in the Australian Imperial Force was terminated.

On the retired list of the Australian Military Forces with the rank of honorary colonel from April 1921, Stodart commanded the 1st Cavalry Brigade in Brisbane and became a full colonel in 1935. He was aide-de-camp to the governors-general Sir Isaac Isaacs and Lord Gowrie [qq.v.9] in 1935-40. Appointed an honorary brigadier on 1 May 1940, Stodart became Queensland member of the Joint State Council, Voluntary Aid Detachments, and chairman of the Compensation Board, Northern Command. During his military car-

eer he was appointed chevalier of the Order of Vasa and commander brother of the Order of St John of Jerusalem.

In the inter-war years Stodart had taken over his father's business and was much involved in public affairs. On 4 July 1912 he had married Adele Madelene Abercrombie at the Anglican Church of St Mary the Virgin, Brisbane. Survived by three daughters, Stodart died at his Coorparoo home on 29 June 1956 and was cremated.

Alcazar Press, *Queensland, 1900* (Brisb, nd); Aust Defence Dept, *Official records of the Australian military contingents to the war in South Africa*, P. L. Murray ed (Melb, 1911); G. H. Bourne, *Nulli secundus, the history of the 2nd Light Horse Regiment, A.I.F.* (Tamworth, NSW, 1926); *Brisb Grammar School Mag*, Nov 1922; *Brisbane Courier*, 21 June 1922.   A. L. LOUGHEED

STODDARD, MARY (1852?-1901), artist, was born probably in Edinburgh, daughter of Peter Devine, portraitist and later a photographer, and his wife Catherine, née Rae. Mary and her sisters Katie and Eliza studied drawing and painting with their father and exhibited landscape and figure studies with the Royal Scottish Academy. On 17 December 1875 in Edinburgh she married with Episcopal forms Frederick Wahab Stoddard, a medical student. About three years later they went to New Zealand to farm, but by 1880 had moved to Sydney where Frederick secured employment in 1886 as a clerk at £299 a year in the Colonial Secretary's Office.

Soon after arriving in Australia Mary Stoddard joined the Art Society of New South Wales and entered two pictures in its 1880 exhibition. Thereafter she regularly exhibited portraits (many painted on commission), some still life paintings and a few seascapes (priced from five guineas to £120). To supplement her income, she taught painting and drawing. She won many competitions, including that for a Christmas card 'of distinctly Australian character' for John Sands [q.v.6] (1881), the design for the 20s. postage stamp (1888), the Hunters Hill prize at the Exhibition of Women's Industries (1888) and 100 guineas for the best design for the Melbourne exhibition award.

Working in oils and water-colour, she painted portraits and miniatures of prominent people, among them Sir Henry Parkes (1891 and 1896), E. C. Merewether (now in the Australian Club), J. T. Toohey, the wives of Governors Carrington and Hampden [qq.v.5,6,3,9], and members of such Sydney families as the Burdekins [q.v.3] and Merivales. Her work was also seen in a coloured Christmas supplement to the *Illustrated Sydney News* in 1886. The National Art Gallery of

New South Wales purchased her still life, 'From Earth and Ocean', in 1889 and included it in the 1898 Exhibition of Australian Art at the Grafton Galleries, London.

There was much favourable comment on her nude study, 'Lorelei', in the Art Society's 1888 exhibition; her 'style was careful and delicately finished and always sympathetic in quality of interpretation'. In May 1891 the *Illustrated Sydney News* praised her for combining 'the qualities of the artist, the woman and the mother' and saw her as 'a brilliant encouragement to her own sex'. Supporting his wife's endeavours, Frederick joined the Art Society and attended its various functions; Mary was a council-member in 1894-1900. She taught her daughters painting and drawing, and they also exhibited with the Art Society.

Mary's wish to return to London—to benefit her health and to further her children's education—was finally fulfilled in 1900. Survived by her husband, three daughters and a son, she died on 10 June 1901 at Kensington, London, after an operation to relieve an intestinal obstruction. Her daughter Florence Enid became a successful miniaturist whose work was hung by the Royal Academy of Arts.

Bulletin, 19 June 1886, 1 Sept 1900; *ISN*, 28 Nov 1889, 9 May 1891; *Table Talk*, 3 Aug 1901; *Cosmos Mag*, 30 Apr 1896; *A'sian Art Review*, Aug and Dec 1899; Art Soc of NSW, *Aust Mag*, Sept 1899 *and* Annual Reports, 1881-1902 *and* Parkes correspondence *and* J. Plummer, Album of newspaper-cuttings *and* G. V. Thompson, Newspaper-cuttings, 1881-1901 (ML).

MARGARET CALDWELL

STOKES, EDWARD SUTHERLAND (1869-1945), public health officer and soldier, was born on 6 March 1869 at Newcastle, New South Wales, second of seven sons of native-born parents Henry Edward Stokes, merchant, and his wife Clara Maude, daughter of J. F. Josephson [q.v.4]. A grandson of F. M. Stokes (an original proprietor of the *Sydney Morning Herald*), Edward was educated at Newcastle Grammar School and lived in St Andrew's College while he studied arts then medicine at the University of Sydney (M.B., Ch.M., 1891). He was resident medical officer in (Royal) Prince Alfred Hospital in 1891. While practising at Port Macquarie, he married Irish-born Kathleen Jane Mary Maher (d. 1944) on 15 May 1893 at St Mary's Catholic Cathedral, Sydney. They lived at Crookwell from 1896.

Like some of his bright contemporaries, Stokes chose to enter the field of public health where progress in engineering linked to advances in medical theory offered a way of making an immediate contribution to disease prevention. Appointed medical officer at Trial Bay gaol in 1900, he went to Britain and obtained a diploma of public health from the Royal College of Surgeons and Physicians in Dublin (1901).

Returning to Sydney, Stokes was assistant medical officer of health for the city's combined sanitary districts and on 30 November 1904 joined the Metropolitan Board of Water Supply and Sewerage as medical officer and bacteriologist. Responsible for testing water quality, sewage wastes and gases from sewer ventshafts, he studied and reported on the incidence of specific diseases arising from poor water or inadequate waste disposal; he made extensive tours of catchment areas to discover sources of contamination; and, as company doctor, he examined sick or injured employees.

While conscientious in regard to public health questions, Stokes was less scrupulous about occupational health. In 1910 sewerage maintenance workers complained that he had neglected their problems and obstructed claims for sick pay; in consequence, they boycotted him in favour of their lodge doctors. Stokes's standpoint combined a lack of sympathy with methodological myopia: as these workers rarely visited him, his records showed that they suffered a lower rate of sickness than any other group which led him to suggest that working in the sewers was healthier than office work or labouring above ground. His attitude did not soften with the years.

Already involved with military sanitation, Stokes enlisted in the Australian Imperial Force on 20 August 1914. Posted as major to the 1st Field Ambulance, he sailed in October. He took part in the Gallipoli landing and was responsible for ensuring that the soldiers received pure water. As temporary colonel and deputy assistant director of medical services, he supervised sanitary facilities when a plague of flies in summer threatened to spread endemic diseases. He was evacuated sick in July 1915 and arrived in Sydney to become principal medical officer for the 2nd Military District, New South Wales.

Although Stokes returned to the water board in January 1918, he remained involved with the Australian Military Forces until transferring to the reserve in 1929. With sewerage extension and major dam-building under way, the risks to Sydney's public health receded and his work lost its urgency. After retiring on 12 July 1935, he practised privately as a water technologist and had a well-equipped private laboratory at his Lindfield home. A director of the New Redhead Estate & Coal Co. Ltd, and a founder (1913) and later president of the Sydney Technical College Chemical Society, he was a member of the Royal and Linnean societies of New South

Wales and read papers at the Australasian Medical congresses in 1905, 1908 and 1911.

During World War II Stokes returned to the water board from January 1942 to April 1943. Both he and his wife were associated with the Edith Cavell Memorial association. Earnest and reserved by nature, he had a brusque manner, but his medical colleagues found his cryptic remarks a joy. Survived by his son and daughter, Stokes died at his home on 12 April 1945 and was cremated.

A. G. Butler (ed), *Official history of the Australian Army Medical Services in the war of 1914-18*, 1 (Melb, 1938), 2, 3 (Canb, 1940, 1943); *MJA*, 9 June 1945, p 599; *SMH*, 14 Apr 1945; Metropolitan Bd of Water Supply and Sewerage, Syd, Personnel report 25094 (Water Board Archives, Syd); Minutes, Metropolitan Water and Sewerage (General Labourers') Wages Board, Jan 1910 (Water and Sewerage Employees Union Archives, Syd); Annual roll 1874-1902, St Andrew's College Archives, Syd.   PETER SHELDON

STONE, SIR EDWARD ALBERT (1844-1920), judge, was born on 9 March 1844 in Perth, Western Australia, third of nine children of George Frederick Stone [q.v.2], lawyer, and his wife Charlotte Maria, née Whitfield. At 11 he was sent to Chigwell Grammar School, Essex, England. After being articled to his father and to E. W. Landor [q.v.2] of Perth, he was admitted to the Western Australian Bar in 1865, a third generation lawyer. On 13 July 1867 in the Wesleyan Chapel, Perth, Edward married Susannah Shenton; they were to have seven daughters and three sons.

Having gone into partnership with his father, in 1876 he joined Septimus Burt [q.v.7] and founded the firm of Stone & Burt. Edward Stone appeared as counsel in many civil and criminal cases, among them the trial of a squatter, Lockier Clere Burges, for murdering an Aborigine, and the dispute over the will of William Henry Vincent: both cases aroused public interest and excited newspaper comment in 1871-72. Despite his plea of self-defence, Burges was sentenced to five years imprisonment for manslaughter. People in Perth were outraged. When Stone petitioned Queen Victoria the sentence was reduced. The Vincent case resulted in the conviction of Stone's opposing counsel (Sir) S. H. Parker [q.v.11] and three newspaper publishers for contempt of court; Parker was fined and the publishers imprisoned. Stone represented two of the publishers and Parker in the contempt proceedings.

Stone was clerk to the Legislative Council in 1870-74 and a nominated member of that body in 1880-82. From 1879 to 1883 he held acting appointments as attorney-general and chief justice. Crown solicitor in 1882-83, he was appointed puisne judge of the Supreme Court in 1883. Turbulent times followed. Disputes between Chief Justice Sir Alexander Onslow [q.v.5] and Governor Sir Frederick Broome [q.v.3] resulted in Onslow's suspension by the governor and his reinstatement, twice, by the Colonial Office. As chief justice of Western Australia in 1901-06, Stone had an uneventful career. Handsome, austere and stately, he showed marked common sense and kindliness, once addressing a man appearing in his own defence: 'You may be poor, but you are still entitled to justice'. Knighted in 1902, Stone was appointed K.C.M.G. in 1912 and was lieut-governor from 1906 to 1920.

In 1874-79 he had been chairman and part-time editor of the *Western Australian Times* and contributed regularly to its columns. A prominent lay reader and warden, he was choirmaster of St George's Cathedral, Perth. He also helped to found the Perth Musical Union, sang in oratorios and was an amateur actor. He was a trustee of the Public Library, Museum and Art Gallery of Western Australia, and a director of the Western Australian Bank and the Perth Building Society; his benevolence extended to Parkerville Children's Home, the Silver Chain Nursing League and the Victoria Institute for the Blind. Fond of cricket, football, boxing, riding and shooting, he organized and trained a roller-skating club in the Perth Town Hall.

Stone was well known and well liked; he revealed facets of his nature in his autobiography, *Some old-time memories* (1918). Survived by his wife and nine of their children, he died on 2 April 1920 and, after a state funeral, was buried in the Anglican section of Karrakatta cemetery.

Truthful Thomas, Through the spy-glass (Perth, 1905); J. S. Battye (ed), *Cyclopedia of Western Australia*, 1 (Adel, 1913); E. Russell, *A history of the law in Western Australia and its development from 1829 to 1979*, eds F. M. Robinson and P. W. Nichols (Perth, 1980); *West Australian*, 20 July 1917, 3, 8 Apr 1920; F. M. and A. W. Robinson, The history of Stone James & Co (ms, held by the authors, Perth); P. U. Henn, Genealogical notes on W.A. pioneer families, Perth 1930s-1973 (ms, Battye Lib).   F. M. ROBINSON

STONE, EMMA CONSTANCE (1856-1902) and GRACE CLARA (1860-1957), medical practitioners, were born on 4 December 1856 and on 12 January 1860 in Hobart Town, daughters of William Stone, builder, and his wife Betsy, née Haydon. William Stone [q.v.] was their brother. The family moved to Melbourne in 1872. Both girls were educated chiefly at home by their mother, a former governess.

Constance early developed an interest in

anatomy, but it was not until 1884 that she went overseas to study medicine, since the University of Melbourne did not then admit women to its medical course. She completed a three-year degree at the Women's Medical College of Pennsylvania, United States of America, and in 1888 graduated M.D., Ch.M. with first-class honours from the University of Trinity College, Toronto, Canada. She then proceeded to London where she worked with Mary Scharlieb at the New Hospital for Women and qualified as licentiate of the Society of Apothecaries. Her experience at the New Hospital was to inspire her ambition to found a hospital 'by women, for women' in Melbourne. This wish was reinforced by her early experience in Melbourne where she returned in 1890 to become the first woman to register with the Medical Board of Victoria. Photographs of the time portray her as a fine-featured woman with a high forehead and a strong, regular profile. She practised one day a week at the free dispensary attached to Dr Singleton's mission in Collingwood and was quickly convinced that work 'as great as their strength could compass' awaited female doctors who ministered to needy women.

By this time her sister Clara was almost ready to join her. In 1887 the university allowed women to enter its medical school and Clara was one of seven whose requests for admission had led to this change. She started her degree that year and in 1891 became one of the first two women to graduate in medicine from the university. She then went into private practice with Constance and joined her at the free dispensary.

EMILY MARY PAGE STONE (1865-1910), cousin of Constance and Clara, was born on 31 May 1865 at Mornington, Victoria, daughter of John Stone, storekeeper, and his wife Laura Matilda, née Reed, both English born. When she was 10 she went to England and stayed for six years with an aunt who kept a ladies' boarding school at Kew where Mary was educated. She trained as a teacher, returned to Melbourne and taught at various private schools. After attending classes at the Athenaeum to prepare herself to matriculate at the University of Melbourne, she commenced her medical studies there in 1889. In 1893 she graduated, having gained honours in each year of her course, and was placed sixth in the final examination. This result should have entitled her to a residency at the Melbourne Hospital, but her application was refused on the pretext that she had carried out her clinical studies entirely at the Alfred Hospital. The Melbourne Hospital did not admit any women to its residencies until 1896. Mary began private practice at Windsor but, after a few months, moved to Hawthorn.

Constance, Clara and Mary were all involved in the early activities and networks of Melbourne's female doctors. Constance's home was the venue for the first meeting in March 1895 of the Victorian Medical Women's Society, formed with the chief object of 'effecting a closer relationship between medical women graduates and undergraduates and to advance the knowledge to further their interests generally'. Clara was the first president and all three women supported the society throughout their lives. At a meeting held on 5 September 1896 eleven women doctors decided to set up a hospital of their own: their vision, and its subsequent achievement, was attributed by the others to Constance's inspired leadership. From its beginnings as an out-patients' dispensary in La Trobe Street (where the three Drs Stone worked on Monday mornings), the Queen Victoria Hospital, funded by a jubilee shilling fund appeal, evolved and was officially opened in July 1899.

By this time Constance Stone was ill; she died of tuberculosis on 29 December 1902. She had married Dr David Egryn Jones in the Congregational Church, St Kilda, on 4 July 1893; he survived her, as did their young daughter who was later also to become a doctor. Clara remained on the honorary staff of the Queen Victoria Hospital until 1919 and, after retiring from this position, continued in private practice in Alma Road, St Kilda. She died, unmarried, at her St Kilda home, on 10 May 1957 and was cremated.

In addition to her work at the hospital, Mary Page Stone maintained a close involvement with the National Council of Women, being honorary secretary of the Victorian branch in 1904-10. At the first congress of the N.C.W. in October 1903 she presented a paper on epileptic colonies, thereby inspiring the Talbot [q.v.] Colony for Epileptics which opened at Clayton in 1907 and with which she was deeply involved. Killed on 19 December 1910, when her bicycle collided with a wagon, she was buried in St Kilda cemetery. The N.C.W. initiated a movement to have an operating theatre for out-patients at the Queen Victoria Hospital (opened 1912) as her memorial.

The contribution of the three Drs Stone to the initial group of medical women and to the health of Melbourne's poor was inestimable. Constance was described by one of her medical colleagues, Janet Lindsay Greig [q.v.9], as 'the real pioneer' who alone deserved the honour of having started the Queen Victoria Hospital; Clara was said to be 'the hard worker', a tiny, bird-like woman of indomitable character who was a loyal friend to the younger generation in the V.M.W.S.; Mary was 'always ready to help in any cause furthering the welfare of women and the community at large, and was much beloved by her private patients'. All three embodied a spirit of service and sacrifice characteristic of the early professional women in this country.

M. H. Neve, *This mad folly* (Syd, 1980); *Southern Sphere*, 1 Jan 1911; Queen Victoria Hospital (Melb), *Annual Report*, 1920; *T&CJ*, 7 Jan 1903; *Herald* (Melb), 13 May 1957; P. A. Russell, Mothers of the race (B.A. Hons thesis, Monash Univ, 1982); M. Wells, 'Gentlemen, the ladies have come to stay' (M.A. thesis, Univ Melb, 1988); Stone papers (LaTL).

PENNY RUSSELL

STONE, LOUIS (1871-1935), novelist and playwright, was born on 21 October 1871 at Leicester, England, and baptized William Lewis, son of William Stone, basketmaker, and his wife Emma, née Tewkes. William senior had served as a Royal Navy marine in the Middle and Far East and, on retiring, migrated with his family to Brisbane in 1884. Next year the Stones moved to the Sydney suburb of Redfern and soon after to nearby Waterloo.

Louis began training in 1888 as a pupil-teacher with the Department of Public Instruction and in 1889 was appointed to Waterloo; in providing his particulars he described himself as an agnostic. In 1893 he won a half-scholarship to Fort Street Training School and matriculated at the University of Sydney where he studied arts until 1895. Qualifying as a primary schoolteacher that year, Stone had temporary appointments in inner city suburbs before a regular posting to Cootamundra in 1900. Transferred next year to South Wagga Wagga, he met (Field Marshall Sir) Thomas Blamey, a pupil-teacher who was influenced by Stone's interest in literature and music.

In 1904 Stone was moved back to Sydney where he remained, mainly at Coogee, between 1913 and 1930; his teaching career was increasingly interrupted by bouts of illness attributed to nervous disorders. He married Abigail Allen, a teacher and an accomplished pianist, probably in 1908. About this time he began writing *Jonah* (London, 1911), a novel based on his memories and on painstaking observation of life at Waterloo. It contrasts the lives of two larrikins—Joe Jones, known as 'Jonah', and his friend 'Chook'—as they graduate from their 'push', marry and make their ways in the world: whereas 'Jonah' becomes a capitalist, but suffers disappointment in his marriage and a love affair, 'Chook' settles into proletarian domestic contentment. While the novel has its share of contrivance and sentimentality, its evocation of Sydney working-class life and of the city itself were to win Stone the reputation of being one of the first Australian writers to present urban existence both realistically and imaginatively.

Apart from an enthusiastic review by A. G. Stephens [q.v.], *Jonah* passed unnoticed, although Norman Lindsay [q.v.10] was impressed by the novel and he and his wife befriended the Stones. Lindsay described Lou as having a withdrawn and obsessive personality and as one who, towards the end of his life, became incapable of communicating with former associates. In *Bohemians of the Bulletin* (1965) Lindsay depicted him as a tallish, but slight, melancholy figure with 'heavy-lidded, haunted eyes', a mane of dark hair and a drooping moustache.

In 1912 Stone published an essay, 'On being fat' in Stephens' *Bookfellow*. Stone's second novel, *Betty Wayside* (London, 1915), a melodramatic study of a musically talented young woman, was set mainly in the Sydney suburbs of Paddington and Woollahra. Rejected by his first English publisher, the manuscript was accepted by another on the condition that Stone delete a scene of low life. The uncut version had been serialized in the *Lone Hand* from July 1913 to August 1914.

During World War I two of Stone's short stories appeared in collections for the troops which were edited by Lindsay and by Ethel Turner and Bertram Stevens [qq.v.]. By this time Stone's interest had turned to drama. From 1914 he worked on a three-act comedy, *The lap of the gods*, which, with other scripts, he took to England in 1920: he claimed that John Galsworthy and others praised them. After Stone returned to Sydney *The lap of the gods* was placed second in a competition run by the *Daily Telegraph* in 1923; published in that paper, it was produced, unsuccessfully, by Gregan McMahon [q.v.10] in 1928. Of some six other plays that Stone wrote, only the brief one-act *The watch that wouldn't go* was published, in *Triad* (November 1926).

Ill health forced Stone to take early retirement in 1931, but he enjoyed belated recognition in the last years of his life: in 1933 *Jonah* was republished by P. R. Stephensen [q.v.] and was also published as *Larrikin* in the United States of America. Suffering from inanition and arteriosclerosis, Stone died on 23 September 1935 and was buried in the Methodist section of Randwick cemetery. *Jonah* was adapted for an Australian Broadcasting Commission television series in 1982 and provided the basis for a musical, *Jonah Jones*, performed by the Sydney Theatre Company in 1985.

N. Lindsay, *Bohemians of the Bulletin* (Syd, 1965); R. Lindsay, *Model wife* (Syd, 1967); H. J. Oliver, *Louis Stone* (Melb, 1968); *Biblionews*, 4, no 14, Dec 1951, p 44; *Aust Literary Studies*, 2, no 1, June 1965, p 15; *Bulletin*, 4 Jan 1912; teachers' records, Dept of Education (NSW) archives, Syd; Lindsay family papers (ML).   BRIAN KIERNAN

STONE, WILLIAM (1858-1949), electrical engineer and physicist, was born on 12 May 1858 in Hobart Town, son of William Stone, builder, and his wife Betsy, née Haydon. Emma Constance and Grace Clara [qq.v.] were his sisters. He came to Victoria as a boy and in 1883 joined the Victorian Railways as an electric foreman. In 1905 he was appointed electrical and lighting engineer in the telegraph branch.

In 1907 the Victorian government commissioned from C. H. Merz of Britain a report which recommended the electrification of Melbourne's suburban railways. After the State government authorized the proposal in 1912, Stone toured Britain, Europe and the United States of America studying electrification. Next year he was promoted to chief electrical engineer in the new electrical engineering branch which had been created to transform the suburban railway system from steam to electric traction and which also expanded the Newport power station. He worked closely with Merz's assistant, F. F. P. Bisacre, who visited Australia in 1912-13. Electrification of the railway began in 1913 and the official opening took place on 28 May 1919.

Stone, who as early as 1893 had sat on a railway committee comparing the use of black and brown coal for steam engines, was appointed in 1917 to the advisory committee on the utilization of brown coal; the other members were H. Herman, H. R. Harper [qq.v.9] and F. W. Clements. The committee recommended the foundation of a state electricity commission, government distribution of electrical energy for industrial development and the establishment of an open-cut mine and power-house at Morwell in the Latrobe Valley. In 1919 Merz, who had first canvassed the possibility in 1908, supported the use of brown coal for electrification.

Retiring from the Victorian Railways in 1920, Stone retained his membership of the engineering faculty of the University of Melbourne (1903-37). A keen amateur scientist, he had a lifelong interest in microscopy. He helped his friend H. J. Grayson [q.v.9] to make his ruling engines for microscope test plates and diffraction gratings. Stone was also a pioneer of X-rays and, from 1896, made at least nineteen focus type tubes. Another friend, A. G. M. Michell [q.v.10], encouraged him to work on lubrication: Stone made an absolute viscometer for lubricating oils and helped Michell with his crankless engine. He maintained a long and fruitful scientific correspondence with Bisacre from 1921 to 1934,

and was assistant to (Sir) Thomas Lyle [q.v.10] on the Grayson engines at the University of Melbourne in 1932-34. Stone's papers reveal him as a practical scientist who sought practical solutions to practical problems with an enthusiasm that elicited from his contemporaries both affection and respect.

A rather gaunt, bearded man with a domed forehead and prominent cheekbones, Stone had married Jane Simpson Massie with Congregational forms at St Kilda on 4 March 1885. He died, a widower, at his Kew home on 25 January 1949 and was cremated. His son and five daughters survived him.

A'sian Radiology, 19, 1975, p 216; H. C. Bolton, 'The development of ruling engines in Melbourne 1890-1940: a link between amateur and professional science', Hist Records of Aust Science, 6, 1987, p 493; R. W. Home, Bibliography of physics in Australia to 1945 (ms, History and Philosophy of Science Dept, Univ Melb); W. Stone papers (Univ Melb Archives).   H. C. BOLTON

STONEHAVEN, JOHN LAWRENCE BAIRD, 1ST VISCOUNT (1874-1941), governor-general, was born on 27 April 1874 at Chelsea, London, elder son of Sir Alexander Baird and his wife Annette Maria, née Palk. The Bairds were of the Scottish gentry. Educated at Eton, and for two terms at Christ Church, Oxford, in 1894 Johnny was aide-de-camp to Sir Robert Duff [q.v.8], governor of New South Wales, before entering the British diplomatic service. On 16 February 1905 at St Paul's Church, Knightsbridge, London, he married Lady Ethel Sydney Keith-Falconer (b. 20 September 1874); they were to have two sons and three daughters. The eldest child of the 9th earl of Kintore [q.v.5], Lady Ethel had also been in Australia during the 1890s.

While serving in the Intelligence Corps in France in 1914-15, Baird was awarded the Distinguished Service Order. Conservative member for Rugby (1910-22), then for Ayr Burghs (1922-24) in the House of Commons, he was under secretary of state for the air ministry (1916-19) and for the home office (1919-22), minister for transport (1922-24) and first commissioner for public works (1924). When selected by S. M. (Viscount) Bruce [q.v.7] from the British short list, Baird was appointed governor-general of Australia in 1925, created Baron Stonehaven of Ury and appointed G.C.M.G.

He was sworn in on 8 October 1925 in Melbourne. A short, sturdy man, with red moustache and florid complexion, Stonehaven smoked a pipe, wore a gold-rimmed monocle and liked riding, yachting and golf. Believing that 'the Representative of the King should live on a different footing and in a different atmosphere from other people', he was an ostentatious viceroy whose lavish entertainments drew criticism from the Labor Opposition.

In May 1927 Parliament House, Canberra, was opened by the duke of York, Stonehaven's guest in the newly renovated Government House, Yarralumla. An additional £2000 a year was provided for the governor-general as a Canberra allowance. At first enthusiastic about 'pretending to be the King', Stonehaven later felt the strains of the 'artificial existence' and constant travelling; he inhabited three official residences (Sydney, Melbourne and Canberra) and visited all States and Papua and New Guinea, using and encouraging the new air services. In the only constitutional issue he had to resolve, he uncontentiously accepted Bruce's advice to dissolve the House of Representatives in September 1929 following the defeat of government legislation.

Stonehaven's term ended on 2 October 1930 in controversy over the selection of Sir Isaac Isaacs [q.v.9] as his replacement. An appropriate social figurehead, Stonehaven had got on well with Bruce, although he was less sympathetic to Scullin's [q.v.11] ministry. During Stonehaven's term the governor-general's role as the symbolic link with Britain had remained, but his quasi-diplomatic role as the channel of communication with the British government ended after the Imperial Conference of 1926.

Back in Britain, Stonehaven was chairman of the Conservative Party in 1931-36. Elevated to viscount in 1938, he died of hypertensive cardiac disease at Ury House, Stonehaven, Scotland, on 20 August 1941. In 1966 his widow, who had succeeded to the earldom of Kintore, entered the House of Lords and was its oldest living member shortly before her death on 21 September 1974.

C. Cunneen, *Kings' men* (Syd, 1983); C. D. Coulthard-Clark (ed), *Gables, ghosts and governors-general* (Syd, 1988).
                                        CHRIS CUNNEEN

STONEHOUSE, ETHEL NHILL VICTORIA (1883-1964), writer, was born on 1 August 1883 at Nhill, Victoria, fourth of twelve children of Robert Stonehouse, blacksmith, and his wife Jane, née Hardingham. Educated until she was 14 at Charlton State School, she claimed to have considered entering a convent. From 1894 Ethel published verse and short stories; she later worked at journalism in Melbourne and joined the Australian Modernist Society of Enlightened Roman Catholics. Her first novel, *Smouldering fires* (Melbourne, 1912), concerned the seduction and desertion of a young Catholic woman by a priest. Its controversial theme was to be repeated so often and so violently in her writing as to seem personal and obsessive; she also published the epistolary *Love letters of a priest* (1912).

In London in 1911 she joined the International Modernist Association and the Jeanne d'Arc League; by 1913 she asserted, 'I have only read three books in my life, and have written five'. Stonehouse used pseudonyms, the most frequent being 'Patricia Lindsay Russell'. Her style was polemical, prolix and clichéd: 'There was a long moment, red with pulsing flame'. But it was popular. *Smouldering fires* sold 100 000 copies in Australia alone; it ran to eight editions. That year she was in Melbourne, announcing a four-figure income and large publishers' advances for her next romance, *Souls in pawn.*

A fair, blue-eyed woman who at 30 still wore long braids that framed her oval face and 'winsome smile', 'Pat' affected a 'child-like simplicity' which could switch to the 'pensive melancholy' evident in her photographs. On 23 September 1914 at St Ninian's Church, Stonehouse, Lanarkshire, Scotland, she married John McNaught Scott with the forms of the Established Church of Scotland. A Harley Street specialist who had treated her consumption, he was then a member of the Australian Army Medical Corps; Web Gilbert [q.v.9] sculpted a bust of him. Mrs Scott spent some of the war years in Ireland writing nine more novels. In 1918 she published *Earthware* in which plot and characterization are more subtle and complex. Much of it again seems autobiographical: a talented authoress, crushed by her insensitive Scottish husband, finally renounces ambition and preserves her marriage. Stonehouse never published another novel.

After the war she and Scott settled at Mortlake, Victoria, a country town in which her early work had been banned. Her last publication was a collection of sentimental poetry, *The caravan of dreams* (1923). People in the district believed that the childless marriage of the Scotts was unhappy. 'Pat' was eccentric: it was said that she fed pet rats and collected chamber pots. After her husband's death in 1942, she lived as a hermit. Seven years later she entered Royal Park psychiatric hospital suffering from 'mental enfeeblement' caused by neglect, a sad outcome for someone who had written, 'O, the trim paths, the prim paths, these are not for me'.

Most of her novels were about women rebelling—against Catholicism, Calvinism, marriage, the English class system—and their settings covered Australia, Britain, India and Indonesia. In her prime, her work had been praised by K. S. Prichard [q.v.11] and by the *Sydney Morning Herald*. While her novels were hastily executed and their reputation did not endure, they had earned her brief fame as 'the Australian Marie Corelli'. Stonehouse died on 1 May 1964 at Mont Park mental hospital and was buried in Footscray cemetery.

P. Hay (ed), *Meeting of sighs* (Warrnambool, Vic, 1981); *British A'sian*, 20 Mar 1913, 29 Oct 1914; *Everylady's J*, 6 July 1913; *Book Lover*, Sept 1913, June 1917; *East Charlton Tribune*, 26 Feb 1898; *Mortlake Dispatch*, 4, 7 June 1913, 23 June, 25 Aug 1920; *Punch* (Melb) and *Table Talk*, 5 June 1913; *Bulletin*, 26 June 1913; *Herald* (Melb), 18 Aug 1914; information from Mr W. McKinnon, Terang, Vic, and from Mont Park Hospital, Melb.

SUZANNE EDGAR

STONEMAN, ETHEL TURNER (1890-1973), psychologist, was born on 10 August 1890 in Perth, Western Australia, second daughter of Charles Edgar Stoneman, coffee importer, and his wife, Minnie Caroline, née Farmer. After her mother's death in 1891, Ethel ('Effie') and her sister were reared by their grandmother, Lydia Farmer. In 1909 Ethel attended the Teachers' Training College, Claremont, and in 1913 entered the University of Western Australia (B.A., 1916) where she began a lifelong commitment to experimental psychology. Independent and adventurous, she left Australia in 1916 to study intelligence testing and abnormal psychology at Stanford University, California, United States of America. She came back two years later to lecture at her old college. In 1924 Stoneman researched in Britain and Europe: at the University of London she worked with leading psychologists and conducted experiments in measuring changes of emotion in patients at the Bethlem Royal Hospital.

Returning to Perth next year, she persuaded Phillip Collier's [q.v.8] government to establish (under her directorship) a State Psychological Clinic which opened at West Perth in 1926. Stoneman also lectured part time at the university, giving courses in experimental and abnormal psychology. Her teaching inspired Norma Parker and Constance Moffat among others to become innovative social workers and Stoneman was significant in establishing the professional status of clinical psychology in Australia.

She concentrated on the application of psychology to education, vocational guidance and criminal correction. Stoneman gave intelligence tests to state school pupils in order to make comparisons with overseas data and to obtain norms for Western Australian children. She tested applicants for printing apprenticeships and applied psychological techniques to crime, many of her clients being boys from the Children's Court and the Child

Welfare Department. She also ran a branch of her clinic in Fremantle Gaol. As State psychologist, her major concern was with the diagnosis of mental deficiency which eugenists then considered to be a major social problem. In 1926 she drafted a bill for state control of the mentally handicapped. Parliament rejected it.

Opposition to Ethel Stoneman's work stemmed from sexual discrimination, from professional rivalry and from ideological antipathy. Men like (Sir) Walter Murdoch [q.v.10] saw psychology as intrusive and scientifically unreliable. The defeat of Labor in Western Australia in 1930 contributed to the abolition of the clinic and to Stoneman's retrenchment. Bitterly disappointed, Ethel travelled to Scotland and did research in the medical department at the University of Edinburgh (Ph.D., 1933); her thesis, an inquiry into attempted suicide, was published as *Halfway to the hereafter* (Perth, 1935). In 1934 she returned to Perth as a consulting psychologist and in 1935 established a practice in Collins Street, Melbourne.

Ethel Stoneman always hoped that scientific psychology would ameliorate mental deficiency, delinquency and crime, and that it would contribute to an 'efficient' society. She was an advanced thinker who found fulfilment in her work. Slightly built, with magnetic eyes, she was an intensely private woman and a devout Anglican. She died, unmarried, in Diamond Valley Community Hospital, Victoria, on 5 July 1973 and was buried in Nillumbik cemetery. Her estate was sworn for probate at $34 000.

West Australian, 8, 28 Nov 1930; biographical index *and* State Psychological Clinic (WA), Annual Report, 1926-39 *and* Chief Secretary (WA), records: Establishment of psychological clinic and appointment of psychologist (Battye Lib); Univ WA Archives.

JANIS WILSON

STONE-WIGG, MONTAGU JOHN (1861-1918), Anglican bishop, was born on 4 October 1861 at Tunbridge Wells, Kent, England, son of John Stone Wigg, gentleman, and his wife Ellen Matilda, née Clements. Montagu's father was stern and forbidding; five of his six children chose to migrate. Educated at Winchester College (1875-80) and University College, Oxford (B.A., 1883; M.A., 1887), Montagu prepared for the Anglican priesthood at Ely Theological College; he was made deacon in 1884 and ordained priest in 1885. He served as curate at St Andrew's, Well Street, London, in 1884-86, and in the mission district of Holy Innocents', Hammersmith, in 1886-89.

Responding to a plea for clergy from Queensland's Bishop Webber [q.v.] who had been his former vicar at St Andrew's, Stone-Wigg became assistant curate (1889-91), vicar (1891) and canon residentiary and sub-dean (1892-98) at St John's Cathedral where he confessed himself less at home among the 'swells' of Brisbane than among the artisans of Hammersmith. A dedicated Anglo-Catholic, he established a sisterhood in 1892.

In 1898 Stone-Wigg was appointed bishop of the newly established see of New Guinea where an impoverished, understaffed mission had struggled for survival since 1891. Conse-crated in St Andrew's Cathedral, Sydney, on 25 January 1898, he was enthroned at Dogura, head-station of the diocese, in May. The Australian Board of Missions transferred responsibility to him for recruiting staff, rais-ing funds and finding his own stipend. He committed his personal inheritance of £10 000 to the diocese.

Stone-Wigg's response to his Papuan flock was scholarly, sympathetic and humane. In 1902 he collaborated with anthropologist A. C. Haddon in a lecture at Cambridge on the similarities between Christianity and Papuan religions, and in 1907 he published *The Papuans, a people of the South Pacific*. When the Papua bill (1906) threatened the security of Papuan land tenure, Stone-Wigg was in the vanguard of a successful missionary effort to have the offending clause removed.

Although he failed to fulfil his Tractarian ideal of a celibate mission committed to life service, Stone-Wigg inculcated discipline in his priests and lay workers. Ascetic, frugal and devout, he had high expectations of oth-ers. If his staff chafed at the uncompromising régime, they relished his humour and admired his outspoken loyalty to the Anglican Church. Tall, handsome and urbane, Stone-Wigg married Elfie Marcia Mort at St John's Church, Gordon, Sydney, on 21 August 1907.

During his episcopacy he extended the mis-sion's traditional activities of preaching, teaching and healing, initiated plantations and industrial work, cleared the mission of debt and gained endowment for the see. These constant demands wrought havoc with a constitution already debilitated by chronic asthma and malaria. Bishop Henry Mont-gomery [q.v.10] remembered Stone-Wigg's 'spare and wasted form' at Anglican synods.

Resigning on medical advice in 1908, Stone-Wigg settled in Sydney, an uncongenial climate for his uncompromising Anglo-Catholicism. There he founded and edited the monthly *Church Standard*, established a chil-dren's home at Burwood and served on the Australian Board of Missions. Increasingly incapacitated, he died at his Burwood home on 16 October 1918 and was buried in St

Thomas's churchyard, Enfield. His wife and two young daughters survived him.

D. Langmore, *Missionary lives* (Honolulu, 1989); *Aust Christian World* (Syd), 25 Oct 1918; Aust Bd of Missions, *ABM Review*, 1 Nov 1918; *The Times*, 7 Nov 1918; *SMH*, 26 Jan 1898, 17 Oct 1918; Stone-Wigg diaries (New Guinea Collection, UPNG); Stone-Wigg papers (held by Mrs E. Beat-tie, Frenchs Forest, Syd).   DIANE LANGMORE

STOPFORD, JAMES (1878-1936), trade unionist and politician, was born on 22 July 1878 at Rockhampton, Queensland, son of John Joshua Stopford, butcher, and his wife Elizabeth, née Wilson, both Irish born. As a child he moved with his family to Mount Mor-gan where his father was a miner. After attending state schools, James worked at the mine, qualified as an engine driver and became active in the union movement. On 24 April 1901 in the Church of the Sacred Heart, Mount Morgan, he married Ellen Williams with Catholic rites.

As Fitzroy delegate to the 1910 Labor-in-Politics convention at Townsville, Stopford secured the adoption of his proposals for com-pensation to miners afflicted with phthisis. At Mount Morgan he organized the General Workers' Union and the southern central dis-trict of the Australian Workers' Association which succeeded it. In 1912 he made an unsuccessful bid as Labor candidate for Mount Morgan, but won the seat in the Legis-lative Assembly in 1915 when Labor came to office under T. J. Ryan [q.v.11]; after his elec-torate was abolished in 1932 by the Moore [q.v.10] government's redistribution, Stop-ford won and held Maryborough until his death. In 1916-24 he served as second branch vice-president of the Australian Workers' Union and in 1918 was elected a delegate to its national convention; he also represented the union on the Queensland Central Execu-tive of the Australian Labor Party.

Jimmy Stopford's parliamentary career included appointment in 1917 to the public works committee (chairman 1918). He was minister without portfolio in 1922, home secretary in 1923-29 and secretary for mines in the Forgan Smith [q.v.11] cabinet in 1932-36. The welfare of miners was always Stop-ford's principal concern. During the 1917 strike on the issue of compulsory unionism, he had appeared for the A.W.U. and won its case before Justice McCawley [q.v.10]; in 1921 and 1925 Stopford supported miners who struck against Mount Morgan Co. which had earlier sacked him for his union activities. When an underground fire followed the 1925 strike, he played an important role in quelling extremists and negotiating a new agreement in the hope that underground mining would be replaced by open-cut operations. In parliament Stopford supported the amendment to the Workers' Compensation Act of 1916 which had it incorporate provisions for industrial and mining diseases; furthermore, he helped to establish a sanitarium for pulmonary sufferers at Westwood, near Rockhampton. As secretary for mines during much of the Depression, he increased gold production by encouraging small companies and individuals who battled on isolated fields.

Solidly built, with a facial resemblance to Napoleon Bonaparte, 'Stoppy' was a kindhearted man, staunch in principles and friendships. He was a spontaneous and witty phrasemaker, a good teller of tales, imperturbable in the hottest debate and was never heard to say an unkind word in the House of any of his political opponents, even of W. M. Hughes [q.v.9] whose conscription campaigns he resisted. Predeceased by his wife and five children, Stopford died of heart disease and cirrhosis of the liver on 30 November 1936 at Mater Misericordiae Hospital, Brisbane. After a state funeral he was buried in Toowong cemetery.

The Labour government of Queensland (Brisb, 1915); C. A. Bernays, *Queensland politics during sixty (1859-1919) years* (Brisb, nd, 1919?); C. Lack (ed), *Three decades of Queensland political history, 1929-1960* (Brisb, 1962); *Qld Government Mining J*, 33, no 386, 15 July 1932, p 200, 37, no 439, Dec 1936, p 418; *Maryborough Chronicle*, 1 Dec 1936; *Daily Record* (Rockhampton), 7 Sept 1916; *Morning Bulletin*, 21 Sept 1925, 1 Dec 1936; Aust Workers Union records (ANUABL).   CAROL GISTITIN

STOPFORD, ROBERT (1862-1926), medical practitioner and politician, was born on 20 February 1862 at Upholland, Lancashire, England, son of John Stopford, property owner, and his wife Jane Elizabeth, née Yates. He studied medicine at University College, Liverpool, and qualified as licentiate of King and Queen's College of Physicians, Ireland, in 1885.

Setting up in private practice at Southport, Lancashire, Stopford developed an interest in homoeopathy. He married Elizabeth Ann Johnson at Rivington on 21 September 1889, joined the Liberal Party and was a volunteer in the King's Liverpool Regiment. In 1902 he and his family migrated to Wellington, New Zealand. There he became involved in the infant welfare movement organized by Lady Plunkett. Moving to Auckland by 1905, he ran the hydropath institute and served as a Labour alderman (1907-08) on Auckland City Council. To Stopford, politics was a means of advancing infant welfare.

In May 1911 he arrived in Sydney. For eight years he ran a clinic for slum children at Balmain, where he lived, and then established himself as a consultant in children's diseases: in 1925 Stopford claimed to have attended the delivery of over 30 000 babies in Sydney. Deploring the medical profession's 'pecuniary interest in disease', he treated soldiers' dependants without charge and advocated the introduction of a state medical service. He did not join the State branch of the British Medical Association and, when criticized, was protected by (Sir) David Storey [q.v.], the minister for public health.

Actively involved in Labor politics until the split over conscription in 1916, Stopford joined the National Party and unsuccessfully contested the traditional Labor stronghold of Balmain in 1917 and 1920. He was a councillor (1917-26) and vice-president (1920-21 and 1925-26) of the National Association of New South Wales. Benefiting from support for his prominent local role, he won the seat of Balmain in 1922. While in the Legislative Assembly, where he was known as a 'straighthitter', he chaired the 1922 select committee into Sydney's milk supply and served on the 1923 royal commission into lunacy law and administration. As president of the Balmain Amateur Radio Club, he asked the Speaker to arrange for the broadcasting of members' speeches. He was defeated in the 1925 election.

A heavily built, bald and generous-faced man, with a clipped moustache and thin-rimmed glasses, Stopford was a Freemason, a member of the New South Wales Protestant Federation and president of the Poultry and Pigeon Club of New South Wales. In 1925 Balmain's citizens made a public presentation to him for his contribution to the community.

When Stopford died on 28 January 1926 in St Luke's Hospital, the *Bulletin* concluded that he had led 'a more than ordinarily useful life'. He was buried in the Anglican section of South Head cemetery. His wife, son and two daughters survived him. His estate was valued for probate at £5685.

PD (NSW), 30 Jan 1924, p 638; *SMH*, 29 May 1916, 28 Feb 1918, 23 Mar 1920, 24 Apr 1923, 26 Sept 1925, 28 Jan 1926; *Bulletin*, 4 Feb 1926.
                                        STEPHEN GARTON

STOREY, SIR DAVID (1856-1924), businessman and politician, was born on 18 August 1856 at Aughagaw, Tydavnet, Monaghan, Ireland, son of Robert Storey, farmer, and his wife Margaret, née Colvin. Educated at Wattsbridge Academy, at 14 he was apprenticed for five years to James Hartley, woollen draper at Cavan, and later worked for Robert Lindsay & Co., Belfast. Attracted by the Sydney International Exhibition, Storey reached Sydney in November 1879 and was employed by Ross, Morgan & Robertson, warehousemen. In mid-1881 he set up his own premises with £10 000 credit and supplies from James Lindsay of Belfast. On the dissolution of their partnership in 1883, he established David Storey & Co., softgoods warehousemen and importers of hats, shirts and mercery, in Barrack Street. He married Rachel Agnes Doig (d. 1940) on 4 July 1883 with Presbyterian forms in Sydney.

Having been his own commercial traveller in the early 1880s, he became president of the Commercial Travellers' Association of New South Wales in 1893. In 1896 he acquired a large building in York Street, next year he established an agency in London and by 1907 he had opened a branch in Brisbane. The firm also manufactured several varieties of popular hats. Believing in co-operation between capital and labour, he was fair and generous to his employees.

Although a political novice, he challenged (Sir) Edmund Barton [q.v.7] for the Legislative Assembly seat of Randwick in July 1894. Campaigning for free trade and against Federation, Storey won Randwick and held it until 1920. In the 1890s he was honorary secretary of the Freetrade, Land and Reform League and later treasurer of the Liberal Party; he refused office in the Lyne and Carruthers [qq.v.10,7] ministries in 1899 and 1904 for party and business reasons. A picturesque and colourful speaker with flashes of 'twinkling humour', he was known as 'King David' or 'the Duke of York-street'.

Independent-minded, Storey preferred the cross benches: he disliked (Sir) Charles Wade's [q.v.] 'one-man government', deploring his tactics in the elections of October 1910 as well as the 'machine politics' of Labor. He held Randwick as an Independent and led a group of seven rebels. When Labor began introducing what he termed 'offensive legislation', Storey rejoined the Liberals. During World War I he addressed recruiting meetings and later campaigned for conscription: three of his four sons were serving with the Australian Imperial Force.

After Labor split over conscription Storey helped to form the National Party (claiming to have named it) and in November 1916 accepted office under W. A. Holman [q.v.9] as an honorary minister. Storey acted as minister for public health from July to December 1917. Next February with (Sir) George Beeby [q.v.7] he resigned over Teesdale Smith's [q.v.11] wheat silo contract, but relented when agreed safeguards were included. As minister for public health from 18 July 1919, Storey did much to put the hospitals on a sounder footing. Late in January 1920 he resigned his portfolio and seat; he had refused to accept any ministerial salary. Nominated to

the Legislative Council on 4 February 1920, he was knighted in 1923.

After the war Storey believed in the importance of Empire preference and implacably refused to trade with Germany. He was chairman of the Insurance Office of Australia Ltd, and with his sons invested in pastoral property near Yass and in Queensland. A Freemason, he was president and a 'leading spirit' of the Ulster Association of New South Wales and a council-member of the Millions Club and the British Empire League. He belonged to the Athenaeum, New South Wales, Masonic and Australian Jockey clubs.

From the 1880s the Storeys lived at Sherbrooke House, Randwick. A devoted family man, David was an elder of the local Presbyterian Church and foundation president of the Bronte Surf Bathing Association (1907); he played bowls and regularly attended the annual Rifle Club dinner; as a director of the Society for the Relief of Destitute Children from 1903, he took a keen interest in its Randwick asylum. He was 5 ft. 8½ ins. (174 cm) tall, with blue eyes and a square chin, and habitually covered his bald pate with a top hat. Dubbed 'the smiling Irishman' by George Black [q.v.7], he 'had a helping hand for everyone'. His wife was a foundation executive-member of the State division British Red Cross Society in 1914 and foundation president of the Randwick branch for fifteen years; she started home nursing classes, was president of the Forum Club and worked for the Royal Empire Society and Victoria League.

Sir David died of pneumonia at his Randwick home on 27 July 1924 and was buried in South Head cemetery; the cortège was followed by 111 cars. His wife, daughter and four sons survived him and inherited his estate, valued for probate at £59 106. The Bulletin concluded that Storey 'was no statesman, but he was a great hand at making friends and keeping them'.

Cyclopedia of N.S.W. (Syd, 1907); H. V. Evatt, *Australian Labour leader* (Syd, 1945); *PD* (NSW), 1924, p 636; *Fighting Line*, 19 July 1913; *Aust National Review*, 18 Jan 1923, 18 Aug 1924; *Bulletin*, 21 Jan 1924; *Daily Telegraph* (Syd), 23 June 1894, 11 July, 21 Oct 1910, 1 Nov 1911, 6 July 1914, 11 Dec 1918, 15 Apr 1921, 28 July 1924; *SMH*, 30 Nov 1910, 27 June 1911, 6 June, 23 Dec 1912, 10 Nov 1915, 19 Aug, 16 Oct 1916, 18 Jan, 3 Dec 1917, 18 July, 28 Oct 1919, 30 Jan, 11 Mar, 25 May 1920, 1 Jan 1923, 28, 29 July 1924, 29 Apr 1940; *Evening News* (Syd), 28 July 1924; information from Dr David M. Storey, Strathfield, Syd.

MARTHA RUTLEDGE

STOREY, JOHN (1869-1921), boilermaker and premier, was born on 15 May 1869 at Currambene Creek, Shoalhaven,

New South Wales, son of William Storey, shipbuilder, and his wife Elizabeth, née Graham, both English born. At the age of 6 he moved with his family to Balmain, Sydney. Educated at St Mary's Church of England School, Adolphus Street, he later attended night-school. Apprenticed at 14 as a boiler-maker to Perdriau & West, he worked as a journeyman at Mort's [q.v.5] Dock & Engineering Co. Ltd where his political instinct was aroused by dangerous working conditions. On 14 May 1891 in Christ Church St Laurence, Sydney, he married Elizabeth Merton Turnbull.

He played minor grade Rugby and, with his brothers, was active in the foundation of Balmain Cricket Club in 1897. Left-handed, stocky and strong, he was a leading all-rounder in the top grade team. Later, he was a trustee of the Birchgrove Reserve which had become the club's headquarters. Prominent in the United Society of Boilermakers and Iron Ship Builders of New South Wales, he joined the Labor Party in 1891.

Genial and gregarious, though a teetotaller, Storey was a Balmain identity when—with some reluctance—he sought and gained Labor's nomination for the seat of Balmain North which he won in 1901. In parliament he mastered his public shyness and became an entertaining speaker, popular with all members. Appointed a justice of the peace in 1902, he studied politics closely and was on the executive of the party in 1903 and 1907. But he was neither thrustful nor sectarian and, following a redistribution, was beaten in 1904 for the new seat of Balmain by Walter Anderson who was backed in an unsavoury campaign by the Loyal Orange Institution and the Australian Protestant Defence Association. Although Storey faced some employers' discrimination, he found work at his trade until he defeated Anderson in 1907. He held the seat until his death.

Labor won the 1910 general elections. Storey did not nominate for the party's first cabinet, but became chairman of the Parliamentary Standing Committee on Public Works. He was a confidant of the premier J. S. T. McGowen [q.v.10], another ex-boiler-maker, but the deputy premier W. A. Holman [q.v.9] thought that Storey talked too much and overdid the common touch. When Holman replaced McGowen in 1913, Storey lost his public works post and failed to make the new cabinet, although he was elected deputy chairman of committees.

Holman's conflicts with Labor's non-parliamentary section came to a head when his government was censured on 26 April at the 1916 party conference. Storey was caught up in the tactical manoeuvrings and next day told the conference that the ministry had resigned to caucus. The censure was confirmed and a

new cabinet elected, headed by Storey. But the *status quo ante* was restored, and on 4 May Storey resigned with relief. The incident reflected a deep fissure in the party, and in August-November it was widened by a great debate over conscription which culminated in the expulsion of Holman, Prime Minister W. M. Hughes [q.v.9] and many others. Holman formed a National (pro-conscription) government on 15 November. With Storey again reluctant, Ernest Durack [q.v.8] became the leader of the truncated Labor Party; when he resigned on 21 February 1917, Storey had no choice but to take over. Although opposed to conscription, Storey supported voluntary war service. Two of his three sons, Eric (at 16) and (Sir) John enlisted in the Australian Imperial Force; his eldest son Tasman served as an engineer with the United States of America's submarine construction project.

Storey's close links to the trade unions had buoyed him during the 1916 troubles, and they assisted him in keeping Labor's structures intact in the turbulent years from 1917 to 1920 when overlapping industrial (union) and socialist groups threatened to alter the nature of the party. Leadership stimulated him to disclose qualities of political skill and determination previously hidden by the style that had attracted many friends at cricket and football matches, on the racecourse and at sailing races on Sydney Harbour. His genial oratory now proved an asset and helped to ensure that Labor's defeat at the 1917 elections was not a rout.

Rejecting the revolutionary Industrial Workers of the World as 'the bitterest opponents that the party had got', he nonetheless insisted during the election campaign in February 1917 that, if the twelve I.W.W. members gaoled in 1916 had been unfairly convicted, there was a democratic duty to obtain justice for them. In June at the annual conference he declared himself opposed to all secret factions in the party. He astutely encouraged the Australian Workers' Union and other unions to combat extremist groups, headed by J. S. Garden [q.v.8] and A. C. Willis [q.v.], which were trying to absorb the Labor Party into the 'One Big Union'. The success of the moderates at the 1919 conference confirmed Storey's policy. Labor, he said, was not associated with the Bolsheviks of Russia, or the Spartacists of Germany, or the I.W.W. of the U.S.A.: he might have added the Sinn Feiners of Ireland.

By the 1920 elections Storey had achieved wide popularity as an honest and down-to-earth political leader. He faithfully reflected Labor's pragmatism. 'What was the use', he had asked in 1919, 'of putting on the [party] platform planks which are shibboleths?' As an 'evolutionary socialist', he invited 'imported agitators' to leave Australia: Holman compared him with the vicar of Bray. Storey's 1920 policy speech included promises for child endowment, the electrification of suburban railways and the completion of the city underground railway. Electors warmed to his buttonholes which displayed his fondness for flowers. Beneath his unfeigned amiability now lay an experienced politician's finesse, illustrated by his formation of a government after the March elections had given him an uncertain majority of one, with a non-Labor Speaker, (Sir) Daniel Levy [q.v.10]. Storey called it 'half a mandate'.

On 15 June, after negotiating from April, Storey had Justice N. K. Ewing [q.v.8] appointed a royal commissioner into the gaoling of the 'I.W.W. twelve'; his report was accepted on 2 August; on the 4th ten were released. Storey soon found that his reforming legislative programme was crippled by his insecure control of the Legislative Assembly, coupled with Labor's small representation in the Legislative Council: after he had sixteen nominees appointed in 1921 the party was outnumbered there by forty-four to twenty-nine. Trade unions and electoral branches impatiently demanded implementation of industrial and social policy. In January, in the Town Hall, a large meeting of women called for motherhood endowment, but Storey pointed to financial stringency as well as parliamentary problems and looked to a state lottery to fund family allowances. The pressures on him were exacerbating a painful kidney disease (nephritis) which had caused his periodic physical collapses since 1919.

Storey found agreeable diversion in the visit of the prince of Wales (later King Edward VIII) in mid-1920. His enjoyment of the prince's company reflected majority Labor and national opinion, though Garden and other minority radicals objected. At a grand function in the Town Hall the prince confided to Storey that he had no notes for his speech; the premier replied that he had lost his at Randwick racecourse that afternoon.

At a special meeting of the Labor Party executive on 13 January 1921 Storey was rebuked for what was considered inadequate performance by the parliamentarians. The executive also complained about his plan to prorogue parliament for six months during his forthcoming trip to England. Storey explained that the Opposition would not provide a pair and that financial imperatives demanded his presence in London. Of equal, personal, importance was the need to consult a Harley Street specialist about his illness. He left Sydney on 22 January. The doctor's prognosis was alarming, but Storey undertook a heavy official programme and renewed his acquaintance with the prince of Wales. On his return on 20 July Storey was welcomed by a large crowd and by the band of the Professional Musicians' Association, but he looked gaunt and tired. On 9 September he was admitted to Clermont Private Hospital, Darlinghurst. He died there on 5 October 1921, survived by his wife, three sons and two of his three daughters. He was buried in the Anglican section of the Field of Mars cemetery.

Storey's leadership after the conscription split was a vital reason for the survival and rehabilitation of the Labor Party. His integrity, fortitude, friendliness and democratic instinct complemented his political skills to maintain the accepted pragmatism of the party at a time when it might have been loosened from its traditional base by foreign ideologies. His brother Thomas (1871-1953) was a Labor member of the Legislative Council in 1921-34. His nephew Sydney Albert Dawson Storey (1890-1966) was a non-Labor member for Hornsby in the Legislative Assembly in 1941-62.

H. V. Evatt, *Australian labour leader* (Syd, 1940); T. Stephens and A. O'Neill, *Larrikin days* (Syd, 1983); B. Nairn, *The 'Big Fella'* (Melb, 1986); *T&CJ*, 4 Dec 1907; *Daily Telegraph* (Syd), 17 Jan 1914; *SMH*, 29 Apr, 5 May 1916, 23 Feb 1917, 7, 23 Mar, 12 June 1919, 18 Feb, 9 Apr, 12 May, 27 Aug 1920, 3, 14, 21 Jan, 8 Apr, 15, 21 July, 6 Oct 1921; *Freeman's J* (Syd), 7 Aug 1919, 15 Apr 1920, 13 Oct 1921; *Sun* (Syd), 5 Oct 1921; information from Mr C. M. Winning, Drummoyne, Syd.

BEDE NAIRN

STORKEY, PERCY VALENTINE (1893-1969), soldier and judge, was born on 9 September 1893 at Napier, New Zealand, son of English-born Samuel James Storkey, printer, and his wife Sarah Edith, née Dean, from Auckland. Educated at Napier Boys' Grammar School and Victoria College, Wellington, he reached Sydney in 1911 where he worked as a clerk for the Orient Steamship Co. and then for the Teachers' College, Blackfriars. In 1912 he joined the administrative staff of the University of Sydney and next year enrolled as a law student.

Having had five years service with the Wellington Infantry, he enlisted in the Australian Imperial Force as a private on 10 May 1915 and was commissioned second lieutenant in September. A 'well-knit figure [5 ft. 7½ ins. (172 cm) tall] with dark hair and eyes . . . a laughing face and dare-devil, happy-go-lucky ways', he embarked for England in December with reinforcements for the 19th Battalion. On 14 November 1916 he joined his unit in France; five days later, while the 19th was attacking Gird Trenches north of Flers, he was wounded. Promoted lieutenant in January 1917, he was again wounded on 10 October during the 3rd battle of Ypres.

On 7 April 1918 the 5th Brigade, of which

the 19th Battalion formed part, was assigned to clear the area north of Hangard Wood, near Villers-Bretonneux. Intelligence had inaccurately reported that the wood was 'lightly held'. The attacking company of the 19th, whose men were tired, lay down at the starting line at dawn. Storkey, who was second-in-command, fell asleep and his company left without him; it had advanced about eighty yards (73 m) when he woke. He caught up with his men only to go through heavy machine-gun fire which had hit 25 per cent of them even before the company's leading groups reached the edge of the wood. Captain Wallach, the company commander, was shot in both knees and Storkey took over, leading six men through head-high saplings to get behind the German machine-gun force. Together with another officer and four men, they broke into a clearing behind several trenches from where the Germans were firing at the rest of Storkey's company. One of the Australians yelled when he saw the enemy, some of whom looked around. For both sides it was attack or perish. Storkey instantly headed the charge, engaging the nearest Germans before they had fully reacted. His party killed or wounded thirty of them and the survivors —comprising over fifty men—surrendered. Storkey's confident and determined leadership had given the impression that he led a larger force than the handful visible to the Germans. He was awarded the Victoria Cross. He was later again wounded in action and in May promoted captain; he returned to Australia in November and his A.I.F. appointment ended in January 1919.

Resuming his studies at the university, he graduated LL.B. in 1921 (while holding an appointment as associate to Justice Sir Charles Wade [q.v.]). Admitted to the Bar on 8 June, Storkey practised in common law before being appointed to the New South Wales Department of Justice as crown prosecutor for the south-western circuit. He held this post for eighteen years. On 15 April 1922 he married an English-born divorcee Minnie Mary Gordon, née Burnett, at St Stephen's Presbyterian Church, Sydney; they made their home at Vaucluse. At the Bar Storkey was 'practical and realistic', his outlook being tempered by humour and compassion. In May 1939 he became district court judge and chairman of quarter sessions in the northern district of New South Wales. There he became an identity, making many friends and being recognized for his quick assessment of character and for his sound common sense. He was 'good looking, with dark hair and a shortish, well-built figure, always well dressed'. In 1955 he retired and went to England with his wife to live at Teddington, Middlesex, where he died without issue on 3 October 1969. His wife survived him. Storkey

bequeathed his Victoria Cross to his old school at Napier. His portrait by Max Meldrum [q.v.10] hangs in the Archives Building, Wellington.

C. E. W. Bean, *The A.I.F. in France*, 1918 (Syd, 1937); H. T. E. Holt, *A court rises* (Syd, 1976); L. Wigmore (ed), *They dared mightily*, second ed revised and condensed by J. Williams and A. Staunton (Canb, 1986); Syd Univ Students' Representative Council, *Hermes*, June 1918; *Reveille* (Syd), 1 Dec 1935, Feb 1970; *Who was who*, 1961-70; *Bulletin*, 13, 20 June 1918; *SMH*, 1 Feb 1924, 2 July 1934, 25, 27 Apr, 25 May 1939, 25 Oct 1949, 22 May 1954, 10 May 1955.　WARREN DERKENNE

STORY, ANN FAWCETT (1846-1911), cookery instructor, was born on 25 September 1846 at St Mary-in-the-Castle, Hastings, Sussex, England, daughter of William Morris, agricultural labourer and later gentleman, and his wife Jane, née Cramp. Having completed a years full-time course at the National Training School for Cookery, South Kensington, and gained a first-class certificate, she was employed by a leading firm of London caterers. On 1 May 1867 Annie married Wilson Fawcett Story, son of a tanner, in the parish church of Stoke Newington, Middlesex. With her husband (by then a hidebroker) and their seven children, she arrived in Sydney in the *Forfarshire* on 16 January 1882.

Following the birth and death of her youngest child in 1883, Mrs Story was appointed by the Board of Technical Education to teach cookery to women of all ages. She also demonstrated the preparation of meals for invalids at (Royal) Prince Alfred Hospital. When shortage of funds caused the cancellation of her popular classes in 1886, she joined the Department of Public Instruction as a lecturer in domestic economy at Hurlstone Training College.

Given encouragement and the freedom to follow her own ideas, Annie set about reviving the teaching of cookery in New South Wales public schools. She began the experiment at Fort Street Model School in 1889. Next year she was appointed instructress of cookery; in 1891 she was made directress, responsible for organizing classes, writing curricula and generally overseeing the scheme. At her suggestion, the training of specialist cooking teachers began in 1892 and portable kitchens were bought to extend the classes to country areas. Mrs Story travelled to twelve centres throughout the colony to examine students and award certificates. After a disagreement in 1896 she left the school service and returned to Sydney Technical College; while the department did not replace her, the system she had initiated was continued under district inspectors.

In 1898 Mrs Story accepted the challenge to establish Victoria's first cookery centre at Queensberry Street State School where she impressed members of the royal commission on technical education chaired by Theodore Fink [q.v.8]. Her clear-eyed, pleasant face revealed her self-assurance, directness and determination. Firmly opposed to the idea that her curriculum was intended to train domestic servants, Mrs Story stated in an article in the *Education Gazette and Teachers' Aid* (July 1900): 'Teach women to make homes healthy, happy and prosperous, and the streets will gradually lose much of their charm' for young people. That year she began lecturing at the Victorian teachers' training college and campaigned vigorously for a school of domestic economy; although approved in 1901, the plan was delayed by financial problems.

In 1904 Annie Fawcett Story resigned and went to live with a daughter in Cape Town, South Africa; she was a widow when she died of tuberculosis at Sea Point on 11 February 1911; she was buried in nearby Maitland cemetery.

J. Docherty, *The Emily Mac* (Melb, 1981); J. I. Peacock, *A history of home economics in New South Wales* (Syd, 1982); *Education Gazette and Teachers' Aid*, 25 July 1911, p 230.

SHEILA TILSE

STORY, JOHN DOUGLAS (1869-1966), public servant and university vice-chancellor, was born on 7 August 1869 at Jedburgh, Roxburghshire, Scotland, son of John Douglas Story, grocer, and his wife Frances, née Davidson. His parents migrated to Queensland, arriving in Brisbane on 15 September 1877 with their five children. John senior's article 'Voyage from Glasgow to Queensland (by a Jedburgh man)', later published in a Scottish newspaper, described his and the children's daily study of the birds and fish they saw and the lands they sailed past.

Beyond the birth of two more children, little is known of the family's early years in Brisbane. The father ran a grocer's shop (until becoming insolvent in 1892) while young John attended Brisbane Boys' Normal School which—under James Kerr [q.v.9]—was a major pupil-teacher training establishment, renowned for its rote teaching which assured many pupils of scholarships to the state-endowed grammar schools then providing Queensland's only secondary education. In 1883 John won the right to three years at Brisbane Grammar School. Under the headmastership of Reginald Roe [q.v.11], the school provided discipline without resort to punishment and offered a classical yet practical education. In 1885 Roe recommended

Story as the bright junior clerk requested by J. G. Anderson [q.v.3], director of education; Story's application was subsequently minuted: 'Nice intelligent look—rather small and lean and does not look robust. Brain . . . stronger than body'. He began work on 23 March.

Quick and efficient, Story soon mastered the department's operations. He also continued to study with a private tutor and at Brisbane Technical College. His rise was rapid: assistant correspondence clerk (1886), record clerk (1888), acting chief clerk (1902), chief clerk and acting under secretary (1904) and, on Anderson's retirement, under secretary (1906). Anderson and David Ewart [q.v.4], the chief inspector, had been censured by the 1888-89 royal commission into the civil service for their failure to plan and initiate reforms. Education in Queensland had suffered from a centralized bureaucratic system, stultified curricula, poorly trained teachers, no state secondary schools and the lack of a university. Co-operating with ministers Andrew Barlow and (Sir) James Blair [qq.v.7], and later with a Labor government eager for change, Story presided over a fruitful period in Queensland's education which paralleled developments in other States. He married Mary Lamont Campbell with Presbyterian forms on 9 September 1904 at Albion, Brisbane.

From 1909 he was supported by Roe as chief inspector. While Story was under secretary his department assumed full establishment costs for new schools, took over and expanded the technical colleges, opened the first State high schools in six towns without grammar schools (1912) and set up a teachers' college (1914). An apprenticeship scheme and rural schools were introduced, pupils received medical and dental treatment, the school leaving age was raised to 14, and opportunities for secondary education were dramatically widened by the extension of scholarships to all who passed the examination. Under the auspices of Story's department, the University of Queensland was founded (1910), with Roe as vice-chancellor and Story a government representative on the senate. He chaired the senate's vital administrative and financial committees, the management committee for a local Workers' Education Association branch, and select committees on agricultural education (1917) and university organization and expansion (1919).

After public service unions had rejected a new classification scheme, on 19 September 1918 the Ryan [q.v.11] Labor government made Story a royal commissioner to examine the classification of Queensland public service officers and the allowances payable to them. Between October 1918 and May 1919 the commission travelled 5500 miles (8851 km) and interviewed 273 witnesses. Story's approach was incisive yet humane, showing concern for employees' working conditions. His report, a classic of its type and influential beyond Queensland, recommended a new and fairer classification scheme which the government adopted. Story was appointed sole public service commissioner (1920-39), replacing a board whose members had known little of inner departmental workings.

Although he left public instruction reluctantly, Story reorganized the public service enthusiastically. A recognized procedure for advertising vacancies was instituted; public servants were permitted to challenge appointments through appeal boards, to reply to charges and to appeal against penalties; codes of conduct and discipline were formulated; their unions gained access to the State Industrial Commission on issues affecting salaries and conditions, and to the commissioner on grievances previously ignored. To increase efficiency, modern office methods and mechanization were introduced, and university staff gave advice on professional and technical procedures. The commissioner and departmental heads conferred regularly and there was frequent inspection of departments.

On the Public Service Superannuation Board (1913-42) Story advised ways to maximize benefits to contributors. As chief crown advocate before the Industrial Commission on public service matters, he was just and equitable. He acted firmly to ensure wage reductions during the Depression, but in 1938 was able to organize restoration of full-time employment at award rates for many previously on relief payments. As public service commissioner, Story had interests which encompassed wider aspects of Queensland's economic development. Having visited California, United States of America, he inspired the formation and became founding chairman of the Council of Agriculture (1922) which brought primary producers into closer touch with government. He was prominent in the establishment of organized marketing boards for primary products. Through his membership of the Bureau of Industry—established by the Moore [q.v.10] government and continued by its Labor successor—Story assisted post-Depression job creation through large public works. He served on boards which constructed the new university at St Lucia, built Somerset Dam to assure Brisbane's water supply and reduce flooding, and erected a badly-needed bridge from Kangaroo Point to Fortitude Valley: the bridge was named in his honour in 1940. ,

As a public servant, Story smoothed the way for many new politicians. He was courteous, rising to greet visitors and to put them at ease: 'They go in pretty glum, but they all come out smiling', said one of his observers. He was straightforward, believing that most good ministers expected 'sound administrative advice and honest opinion . . . [not] opinion and advice to order'. His motives were not pecuniary: in his subsequent twenty-one years as vice-chancellor he received only his public service superannuation. Sharing his family's dislike of publicity, he refused a knighthood and honorary degrees, but treasured his I.S.O. (1923) as a proper reward.

A gifted administrator and a good judge of character, Story chose his subordinates well. 'More work, less argument' was a typical maxim. He thought logically and analytically with due attention to detail: considering anticipation as 'one of the main keys to successful administration', he was discerning and far-sighted. Outmanoeuvred by his planning, some saw him as authoritarian: at meetings to propound projects or review matters, he advised, 'go fully prepared and with something to suggest. The man with the scheme is usually the man who wins through'. He had a streak of canniness, and knew that initiative and daring were necessary in administration. He deplored 'petty meannesses', but demanded frugality, the best possible value for money. As senate finance committee chairman, he was proud that the university had 'neither overdraft nor loan; it owes not any man'. He set new standards of honesty and integrity. Story was apolitical and served both Labor and non-Labor governments diligently. He appreciated the conservative leanings of the Queensland Labor governments whose liberal reforms were more concerned with giving workers, small businessmen and farmers the means to survive through education, security and a basic standard of living than with destroying capitalism.

Story's retirement in 1939 was illusory. Having exerted considerable influence on the University of Queensland since 1910 and having been its elected part-time vice-chancellor in 1938, he now became honorary full-time vice-chancellor. His links with government, while criticized by some academics, had been crucial in gaining Premier William Forgan Smith's [q.v.11] promise to build a permanent home for the university. Story presided over the building, albeit interrupted by the exigencies of war. He was involved in drafting the university Act amendment and national education co-ordination bills (1941), envisaging an integrated education system from kindergarten to university, a concept always dear to his heart. The bills which provided for a majority of government nominees on the senate, thereby strengthening links between the university and the education department, created suspicion in university circles; when enacted, however, they widened senate representation, led to a doubling of government endowment and instituted boards of adult education and post-primary studies.

The university weathered a post-war explosion of enrolments from 1400 (1938) to 10 000 (1960), while annual budgets climbed from £40 000 to £2 million. Despite the vice-chancellor's insistence on administrative efficiency and economy, and his efforts to elicit private benefactions by publicizing the university's role in the community, Commonwealth money became necessary. Story saw university centres established throughout Queensland for the benefit of external students and the beginnings of the University College of Townsville; with Professor Fred Schonell, he organized (1955) a conference of university administrators, academics and state and private school principals to discuss the relationship between secondary and tertiary education. Succeeded by Schonell as Queensland's first salaried vice-chancellor, Story retired in 1960, but remained on the senate until 1963. He was honoured by the naming of the new J. D. Story Administration Building.

Education was his greatest interest. He saw it as a democratic tool giving those with will and ability the chance to progress, and proudly wrote in his *State education in Queensland* (1915): 'secondary education in Queensland is free to those who prove their fitness ... it is just as possible for the son of the wharf-labourer, the sugar-worker or the shearer to enjoy a full course of secondary education as for the son of the shipowner, the sugar-planter or the station-owner'. Like Peter Board [q.v.7] in New South Wales and Frank Tate [q.v.] in Victoria, he believed education was crucial: 'National efficiency is the concern of the State and as education is one of the main contributors towards national efficiency, the State is interested deeply in making every part of the education system as good as possible'. He supported vocational alongside academic education, in the practical Scottish tradition. Like many of his contemporaries in late-nineteenth-century Queensland, Story finished his full-time education at 15, but was a lifelong student.

In his youth J. D. Story was a keen debater and played in the department of public instruction's football team. He enjoyed weekly golf until his eighties, but his work remained his greatest interest, reading his chief relaxation. Photographs in his thirties reveal a keen expression, dark hair and moustache, while those of later years show a craggy and determined, even forbidding, face. He was called 'the old eagle' or 'J.D.' in public service and university circles. His personality appeared dour and unemotional, but his sense of humour was wry and lively. Typists and secretaries remembered his birthday years after they had left him. He treasured close friends: Reginald Roe, the university administrators Cecil Page-Hanify and Cyril Connell, James Blair, Archbishop Sir James Duhig [q.v.8], Inigo Jones, the long-range weather forecaster whom he visited at Crohamhurst Observatory and whose work he persuaded Professor Harry Priestley [q.v.11] to examine, and William Forgan Smith with whom he shared a 'tough tongue at times' and the ability to recognize good work. A widower since 1944, Story died on 2 February 1966 at The Chateau, a convalescent home at New Farm, Brisbane, and was cremated. He was survived by two sons and a daughter; his estate was sworn for probate at $74 388; his portrait by William Dargie hangs in the University of Queensland's Darnell Art Gallery.

M. I. Thomis, *A place of light and learning* (Brisb, 1985); K. Wiltshire (ed), *Administrative history in Queensland* (Brisb, 1986); *Univ Qld Gazette*, May 1960, p 2, Dec 1961, p 3; SCT/CA 168 no 999, 1982 (QA); Story personal papers (held by Mr J. D. Story, St Lucia, Brisb).   GEORGINA STORY

STOTT, ROBERT (1858-1928), police commissioner, was born on 13 July 1858 in the blacksmith's croft at Nigg, Kincardineshire, Scotland, son of James Stott, fishery overseer, and his wife Catharine, née Cruickshank. Of his early life nothing is known, save that his correspondence shows that he had a good education. He served with the Lancashire constabulary and migrated with three friends to Australia in 1882. In August he joined the South Australian Police Force as a foot constable, 3rd class, but in December 1883 transferred to the Northern Territory Police, becoming a mounted constable who often went on long patrols. For a decade he was posted at Burrundie, Roper River, where the 'blacks were wild and the "cattle-duffer" had free scope', but he also spent time at the Victoria River. At Palmerston (Darwin) on 27 November 1899 he married English-born Mary Duggan at the Wesleyan Church; after her death, on 21 April 1902 at Darwin he married Agnes Heaslop of Cooktown.

From 1908 Stott was a 1st class mounted constable at Borroloola. In 1911 he transferred to Alice Springs as sergeant in charge of the vast central Australian region of some 200 000 square miles (518 000 km²). A month's journey from his immediate superiors, he was head of police, and also by proxy mining warden, lands department official, stock inspector and protector of Aborigines. He was firm yet humane in his attitude toward the Aborigines, encouraging his children to befriend them and to respect Aboriginal customs and beliefs: they gained fluency in the local Aranda language. Short and burly, with his own codes of conduct, Stott was known by all station managers and hands, and respected wherever he went. He ruled with only a riding crop and the force of his remarkable character. When the surveyor-explorer, Captain H. V. Barclay, made complaints against the Hermannsburg Mission, Stott held an inquiry in 1912 and played an ameliorating role, acknowledging some criticisms but generally giving support to the missionaries. Accepting people on their merit, his family was hospitable to the roughest of bushmen as well as to touring dignitaries among whom was Lord Stradbroke [q.v.]. In 1914 Stott saw that the family of a dead goldminer was housed, found a job for the eldest son and ensured that the children attended school. He was chairman (1918-26) of the committee that led to the establishment of Adelaide House, Central Australia's first hospital.

By the late 1920s he had become a legendary figure, careering about in one of the earliest motor cars in Central Australia and widely known to enjoy a whisky. When the local school children were paraded for the benefit of a visiting official who asked them to name the King, they replied: 'Sergeant Stott'. In 1927-31 the Territory was divided into northern and central districts, each with its own resident and commissioner of police. Stott was first commissioner of the Central Australian Police Force until his retirement in 1928 when the office reverted to the government resident.

Stott died on 5 May 1928 in Adelaide Hospital after having been struck by a train. He was buried in West Terrace cemetery. His wife, four sons and two daughters survived him. Stott Terrace, Alice Springs, and a mountain, north-east of the Alice, are named after him.

P. Bridges, *A walk-about in Australia* (Lond, nd, 1925?); C. T. Madigan, *Central Australia* (Melb, 1944); R. G. Kimber, *Man from Arltunga* (Perth, 1986); P. Donovan, *Alice Springs* (Alice Springs, 1988); *Citation*, Dec 1965; *Advertiser* (Adel), 7 May 1928; *Observer* (Adel), 12 May 1928; *SMH*, 31 Dec 1965; *Centralian Advocate*, 27 Sept 1985; CRS A659, item 42/1/2696 (AA); information from the National Trust, Alice Springs.   R. G. KIMBER

STOW, CATHERINE ELIZA SOMER-VILLE (1856-1940), collector of Aboriginal legends, was born on 1 May 1856 at Encounter Bay, South Australia, daughter of Henry Field, pastoralist, and his wife Sophia, daughter of Rev. R. W. Newland [q.v.2]. Henry had migrated to South Australia in 1837; with James and Andrew Chisholm of Goulburn, he established Marra station on the Darling in New South Wales.

An Aboriginal girl saved Katie's life, when two of her sisters drowned in the Darling, and later shared the lessons Mrs Field gave to her children. The family moved to Adelaide in 1872; that year Sophia died after the birth of her eighth child. Katie and her sister Rosina (b. 1863) attended a girls' school.

At St Peter's Church, Glenelg, on 12 January 1875 Catherine married Langloh Parker (b. 1840), a well-known pastoralist who served as a model for Lal Parklands in *A colonial reformer* by 'Rolf Boldrewood' [q.v.3 T. A. Browne]. In 1879 Parker acquired Bangate station on the Narran River, near Walgett, New South Wales. Katie wrote a description of her journey there and some reminiscences of her outback life, posthumously published as *My bush book* (1982).

Childless, she studied her surroundings, taking a particular interest in the Aborigines. She respected their culture and traditions, so gaining their trust, and began to collect their myths and legends. Although she had learned some of their languages, she checked and rechecked the tales with interpreters, and was scrupulous in recording them as they were told to her.

Writing as K. Langloh Parker, she published *Australian legendary tales* with an introduction by Andrew Lang (London, 1896) in David Nutt's folklore series for children; the tales were widely praised and went into a second edition. *More Australian legendary tales* appeared in 1898. Lang also wrote an introduction to *The Euahlayi tribe* (London, 1905), her serious anthropological study of the Narran River Aborigines. In addition, she wrote for the *Bulletin, Lone Hand, Pastoralists' Review* and other journals.

Bad seasons and the depression of the 1890s forced the Parkers off their station; Langloh died in Sydney in 1903. While visiting London in 1905, Catherine Parker met Percival Randolph Stow (d. 1937), a lawyer and son of R. I. Stow [q.v.6]; they married in St Margaret's Church, Westminster, on 7 November. Returning to Adelaide, they lived at Glenelg and took an active part in the cultural and social life of the city. Their collection of paintings included landscapes by Hans Heysen [q.v.9].

When young, Katie had determined that, as she was not conventionally beautiful, she would be clever: she was known for her sharp wit and forceful character, yet her thick, throaty voice could be caressing. A founder of the Victoria League of South Australia, she was a vice-president until 1939 and chaired the executive committee for many years. During World War I she ran Victoria League committees to help the Red Cross and supported other fund-raising activities. She contributed to the *Lady Galway Belgium book* (1916) and compiled *A gardening calendar* in

1917; she had tried to revive the Adelaide (Women) Writers' Club in 1915, and published two small collections of Aboriginal legends in 1918 and 1930.

Catherine Stow died on 27 March 1940 and was buried in St Jude's Anglican cemetery, Brighton. In search of a field of intellectual endeavour, she turned to preserving traditional Aboriginal tales and made one of the earliest attempts to bring Aboriginal culture to the attention of White Australians in a serious and sympathetic manner. An ambitious selection of her work was published in 1953 (reprinted nine times by 1973, with American and Russian editions); the two original collections were republished complete in 1978.

M. Muir (ed), *My bush book* (Adel, 1982); *A'sian Anthropological J*, Apr 1897; *Lone Hand*, 2 Dec 1912; *Bulletin*, 9 Jan 1896, 10 Apr 1940; *SMH*, 28 Nov 1896; *Australasian*, 4, 11 Sept 1915, 8, 15 July, 28 Oct 1916; Vic League in SA, Annual Report, 1938-39, p 8, 1939-40, p 6 (Mortlock Lib); Stow papers (ML).   MARCIE MUIR

STRACHAN, HUGH MURRAY (1851-1933), woolbroker, company director and pastoralist, was born on 5 February 1851 at Geelong, Victoria, seventh child of James Ford Strachan [q.v.2], merchant, and his wife Lillias, daughter of Hugh Murray [q.v.2]. Educated at the local National Grammar School, Geelong College and Melbourne Church of England Grammar School (1867-69) which he represented as an oarsman, Strachan then worked briefly as a clerk for Turnbull Smith & Co., Melbourne importers, before spending a year in western Victoria and two years in Europe to broaden his education. In 1874, in partnership with James and Lewis Howatson, he purchased Boondarra, on the Lachlan in New South Wales, and later acquired adjoining Tarrawonga, and Marlbed, north of St Arnaud, Victoria.

On his father's death in 1875, Strachan took over the Geelong and Melbourne merchant firm of Strachan & Co. and merged with John Wilson & Co. to become Strachan, Murray, Shannon & Co. On 3 February 1876 Strachan married with Presbyterian forms English-born Elizabeth Campbell Shannon at Hampden. Through Charles Shannon and William Murray, there were interlocking partnerships with Sanderson, Murray & Co., London, and John Sanderson [q.v.11] & Co., Melbourne. In due course Strachan also became a partner in John Sanderson & Co. In 1882 Strachan sold his pastoral holdings and invested in the Mackay sugar industry, but by 1888 had lost virtually all he possessed. His financial exposure and what his partners interpreted as a deterioration in his business judgement, brought on by pressure and anxiety, forced him to resign from John Sanderson & Co. in 1887, although he continued for a while on a salary. The partnership of Strachan, Murray, Shannon & Co. was dissolved.

In 1889 Strachan took into partnership T. E. Bostock whose intelligence and energy amply compensated for his lack of capital. Strachan, Bostock & Co. was fortunate in concentrating on woolbroking at Geelong precisely when local wool sales were beginning to develop at the expense of the London auctions. In 1897-98 the business merged with Shannon, Murray & Co. Incorporated as Strachan, Murray & Shannon, its issued capital was £50 000. Strachan, who succeeded Shannon in 1911, remained chairman until his death. The business became a public company in 1919, was listed on the Melbourne Stock Exchange in 1926 and shortened its name to Strachan & Co. in 1931. By this time it handled one-quarter of the wool auctioned at Geelong.

A director of the Union Trustee Co. of Australia (1905-33), the National Bank of Australasia (1912-33) and the Australian Mutual Provident Society, Victoria (1915-33), he possessed a wide knowledge of rural affairs, and contributed letters and articles to the Melbourne *Argus* and to the *Pastoral Review*. In *Some notes and recollections* (Melbourne, 1927) he traced his family's part in Victoria's early pastoral and mercantile development; he also published privately *A short account of the settlement in Victoria in the early days by the Murray family* (1932).

Strachan died at home in Toorak on 17 December 1933 and was buried in Boroondara cemetery, Kew. The Melbourne wool auction room observed a silence for the passing of the oldest woolbroker in Australia. A daughter survived him.

G. L. Strachan, *Strachan & Co. Limited, Geelong* (Geelong, 1965); *Geelong Advertiser* and *SMH*, 19 Dec 1933; *Argus*, 20 Dec 1933; *Australasian*, 23 Dec 1933; Strachan & Co. Ltd records (Univ Melb Archives); information from Mr J. F. Strachan, Geelong, and Mr R. R. Aitken, Melb.

R. J. SOUTHEY

STRADBROKE, GEORGE EDWARD JOHN MOWBRAY ROUS, 3RD EARL OF (1862-1947), governor, was born on 19 November 1862 in London, only son of John Edward Cornwallis Rous, second earl, and his wife Augusta, née Musgrave. Educated at Harrow School and Trinity College, Cambridge (B.A., 1884; M.A., 1890), he succeeded his father in 1886. On 23 July 1898 at St Paul's Church, Knightsbridge, he married Helena Violet Alice Keith Fraser. Stradbroke was aide-de-camp to successive sovereigns in 1902-29 and Queen Alexandra stood sponsor to his first son. Vice-admiral of the Suffolk coast and chairman of the East Suffolk County Council, he was an honorary colonel in the Territorial Army. In World War I he commanded a number of Royal Field Artillery brigades in France, Egypt and Palestine, and was awarded the Territorial Decoration in 1918. He was appointed C.B. (1904), C.V.O. (1906), C.B.E. (Military) 1919, Knight of grace of the Order of St John of Jerusalem (1920) and K.C.M.G. (1920).

As governor of Victoria from 24 February 1921 to 7 April 1926, he spanned five changes of ministry. Arriving after a period of staid local deputizing, the dutiful and outgoing Stradbroke and his volatile wife met their moment brilliantly. The States-wide clamour in 1925 for Australian-born governors failed in Victoria which wore its 'Lang Syne' with a difference. Yet only reluctantly (mainly over money differences with the Colonial Office) did Stradbroke extend his term to three, then to five years. Knowledgeable about farming, ex-servicemen, education, youth (scouting and guiding), immigration, economic development, horse-racing and yachting, Stradbroke effectively managed the appropriate word. A Freemason, he was grand master of the United Orange Lodge of Victoria (1922-26).

His Victorian visits read like map references to the entire State. In 1921 he travelled in New South Wales and Queensland, and next year in Western Australia, 'Gaining Fresh Ideas'. While in Central Australia in 1924 he was anxiously reported overdue, and 'Lord Stradbroke's Plight' was headlined. In 1925 he visited New Zealand via Tasmania, '3000 miles in Three Weeks'. 'Do something for somebody', he advised at St Mark's, Camberwell, that September. He exemplified the family motto, 'I live in hope'.

Lady Stradbroke, D.B.E., mother of five sons and three daughters, was regal in appearance and, where possible, informal in manner. Despite her brush with Lady Forster (two vice-regal ladies cramped in one city), she was a good mixer at all levels. Her philanthropy was evinced in her dedication to her 'newsboys', and in the farewell to her at St Kilda in 1926 enthusiastically attended by a wide representation of women.

A cheery-faced man of medium height and build, in 1928-29 Stradbroke was parliamentary secretary to the Ministry of Agriculture and Fisheries, which befitted his amphibious interests, landholdings and practical knowledge of stock-breeding. From 1935 he was lord-lieutenant of Suffolk, the county in which he farmed 10 000 acres (4047 ha). He died on 20 December 1947 at Henham Hall, Suffolk, where he was buried.

J. Lindsay, *Time without clocks* (Melb, 1962); *Woman's World*, 1 Apr 1926; *Punch* (Melb), 28 May 1925; *Argus*, 23 Aug 1922, 1, 2 Aug 1924, 24 Aug, 21 Sept 1925, 23 Feb, 1 Apr 1926, 23 Dec 1947; *Australasian*, 3 Apr 1926; *The Times*, 22, 23 Dec 1947; Lady Stradbroke papers (LaTL); AJCP microfilms: Governor's Dispatches and CO notes, 1922, CO 418/220, 1923, CO 532/234, 1924, CO 532/273, 1925, CO 532/307-8; *and* Stradbroke diary of journey to central Australia, 1924, A 15/13 *and* Rous family papers *and* Presentation address from Lord Mayor, 25 Mar 1926, A 15/9.

L. R. GARDINER

STRALIA, ELSA (1881-1945), soprano, was born on 1 March 1881 in Adelaide and named Elsie Mary, daughter of Hugo Fischer, tobacconist, and his wife Annie, née Clausen. Hugo, a well-known baritone, was secretary of the Adelaide Liedertafel. In 1889 the family moved to Melbourne where Elsie was convent-educated. After the death of her parents she auditioned at Marshall-Hall's [q.v.10] conservatorium and was awarded two annual scholarships to study with Mme Elise Wiedermann [q.v.11 Pinschof]. Completing her studies, Elsie travelled with the J. C. Williamson [q.v.6] Comic Opera Co. to Sydney where she studied with Gustave Slapoffski [q.v.11]; he was impressed by the 'unusual breadth, power and feeling' of her singing, and presented her in 1909 at a concert of the Sydney Philharmonic Society.

On 24 December 1908 Elsie Fischer married William Mountford Moses at St Stephen's Presbyterian Church, Sydney. They travelled to Europe in 1910 where Elsie studied at Milan and in London. Invited to audition for the Royal Opera Company, she made her début at Covent Garden as Donna Elvira in *Don Giovanni* on 10 July 1913. While recognizing her inexperience and nervousness, critics praised the range and power of her voice. For her operatic début, she adopted the professional name 'Elsa Stralia'.

Following a two-month contract at the Carlo Felice Opera House, Milan, she sang at Covent Garden until the outbreak of World War I. During the war years she took leading roles in Sir Thomas Beecham's opera seasons at Drury Lane Theatre, went with a concert party to South Africa, was soloist with the Royal Philharmonic Society and toured with violinist Eugene Ysaye, pianist Vladimir de Pachmann and with (Dame) Clara Butt. Many of her appearances raised funds for the war effort; two of her brothers were killed in action.

In 1919 Elsa Stralia was engaged for the grand opera season at Covent Garden; next year she sang with the Lamoureux Orchestra in Paris. In 1921-22 she was soloist for twelve concerts with the New York Symphony

Orchestra under Walter Damrosch who wrote: 'The big voice soars and swells; her top notes can be a clarion or have the soft beauty of a woodwind'. Having toured a number of larger American cities and once sung *The star-spangled banner* while dressed as the Statue of Liberty, she visited London to record with the Columbia Gramophone Co.

In 1925 Elsa made a successful Australasian tour. She returned to London and New York, mainly for radio work, and again toured the antipodes for the Australian Broadcasting Commission in 1934. Obtaining a divorce from her husband on the ground of desertion, she married Adolph Theodor Christensen on 14 November 1935 at St Stephen's Presbyterian Church, Sydney. They lived at Patea, New Zealand, until his death in 1943 when she moved to Melbourne. Suffering from diabetes and heart disease, she died childless at Belgrave, Victoria, on 31 August 1945 and was buried in Melbourne general cemetery. Her estate, valued for probate at £3936, established a scholarship for young Australasian female singers.

Strong featured, dark and handsome, though stout in later years, Elsa Stralia looked 'every inch the prima donna'. She had a fine stage presence and 'a temperament of southern warmth'. Likened to Melba's [q.v.10], her voice was 'clear, pure, ringing and sweet', at her peak 'the most powerful in England'. Followers of her Australian concerts found that, despite her American accent and international success, she was still 'simple, warm-hearted and sincere'.

H. D. Rosenthal, *Two centuries of opera at Covent Garden* (Lond, 1958); B. & F. MacKenzie, *Singers of Australia* (Melb, 1967); *Footlight Star*, May 1919; *Woman's World*, 1 Mar 1925; *Wireless Weekly*, 1 June 1934; *Aust Musical News and Musical Digest*, 1 Oct 1945; *The Times*, 11 July 1913, 3 July 1914, 6 Dec 1915, 1 Sept 1945; *SMH*, 22 Oct 1920, 6 Sept 1924, 25, 26 Mar, 11 Apr 1925, 31 Mar, 22 May 1934, 1 Sept 1945; *Punch* (Melb), 14 May 1925; *Advertiser* (Adel), 14 Mar, 1 May 1934.

DIANE LANGMORE

STRANGE, BENJAMIN EDWARD (1868-1930), cartoonist, was born on 10 May 1868 at the cavalry barracks, Newbridge, County Kildare, Ireland, son of Benjamin Strange, private in the 10th Hussars, and his French wife Augustine, née Menefoz. After serving in India, his father retired and Ben attended a London board school. He learned drawing and painting at evening art classes and from a family friend who illustrated weekly journals.

Migrating to Western Australia in 1885, he went a few years later to the Yilgarn goldfields as a dryblower and while there contributed cartoons to the Sydney *Bulletin*. He joined the staff of the *Coolgardie Miner* and *Coolgardie Pictorial* in 1894. Next year the Coolgardie *Goldfields Courier*, owned by James MacCallum Smith [q.v.11], retained him to provide a weekly page of humorous sketches. Because his drawings had to be mailed via Fremantle to Melbourne or Sydney for engraving and then back to the West, he generally depicted the foibles of local characters rather than attempting contemporary political comment. He transferred to the *Coolgardie Pioneer* in 1897 and in April 1898 began a page of topical 'cartoonlets' for (Sir) Winthrop Hackett's [q.v.9] Perth weekly, the *Western Mail*. Except for a period in 1899-1900 when he served in the South African War with Lord Roberts's Horse, he stayed with the *Mail* for the rest of his life.

Strange was a skilled draughtsman with vivid powers of characterization and his heyday extended from the latter years of Sir John Forrest's [q.v.8] premiership to World War I. Among his favourite subjects were Sir John and Alexander Forrest, (Sir) Walter James and John Scaddan [qq.v.8,9,11]. His cartoons were 'never gross and never such as to give needless pain or offence to their subjects'. Their satire was of the gentler Gilbertian sort'. A staunch Western Australian and an Imperial patriot, he turned his sharpest thrusts against radicals and Labor politicians. His most celebrated cartoon, 'East is East, and West is West', appeared after the rejection of conscription at the 1916 referendum: his outline map of Australia showed Western Australia as a British lion and the 'No'-voting eastern States as a timid rabbit.

Short and stocky, with a waddle in his walk, Strange was good humoured and kindly; a bachelor and at times a loner, he was fond of a drop and lived at the edge of suburban Perth near the Canning Bridge. In the 1920s his cartoons lost much of their local appeal and were reduced from their full-page spread, but his work appeared regularly in the *Western Mail* until he died suddenly of heart disease on 16 August 1930. He was buried in the Anglican section of Karrakatta cemetery.

In artistic merit and humorous imagination Strange at his best was the peer of any *Bulletin* cartoonist. By remaining in Perth he missed wider recognition and stimulus; although it was frequently reproduced in the English *Review of Reviews*, his work has been unduly neglected. A collection of his cartoons may be seen at History House, Armadale.

M. Mahood, *The loaded line* (Melb, 1973); R. L. Wallace, *The Australians at the Boer War* (Canb, 1976); *Western Mail* (Perth), 21 Aug 1930; information from Sir P. Hasluck, Perth.

G. C. BOLTON

STREET, GEOFFREY AUSTIN (1894-1940), soldier, grazier, politician and cricket devotee, was born on 21 January 1894 at Woollahra, Sydney, son of John William Street, solicitor, and his wife Mary Veronica, née Austin. His great-grandfather John Street had come to New South Wales with merinos from the Henty [q.v.1] flock in 1822. At Sydney Grammar School, Street was a prefect and represented the school as a cricketer, swimmer, athlete and Rugby footballer. He later excelled at hockey and golf, but cricket remained his first love: he bowled right arm googlies to great effect for the University of Sydney and the Melbourne Cricket Club; his remarkable memory for statistics was underpinned by a well-read library of nearly 600 cricket books.

While studying law at the University of Sydney he enlisted in August 1914 as a private in the Australian Naval, Military and Expeditionary Force. Persuaded that Europe rather than New Guinea would be the focal theatre of war, he transferred to the 1st Battalion of the 1st Infantry Brigade, Australian Imperial Force. Commissioned in September, he sailed with the 1st Division in October. He was wounded at the Gallipoli landing, and later served in a variety of combat and staff appointments until he was shot in the right wrist in September 1918. After three years in the Middle East, France and Belgium, Street admitted to being 'a little "war worn"', but told his parents that he was 'still in love with soldiering'. Although he had impressed (Sir) Brudenell White [q.v.], served as brigade major, 15th Infantry Brigade under H. E. ('Pompey') Elliott [q.v.8] from July 1917 to April 1918, and was awarded the Military Cross in December 1917, a post-war military career held little promise.

Street married Victorian-born Evora Francis Currie with Church of Scotland forms in St Columba's, London, on 29 June 1918. Purchasing a portion of his father-in-law's property, he established a prize-winning Polwarth flock and quickly became prominent in Western District pastoral circles as well as in local government. A member of Hampden Shire Council from 1924, he was president in 1931-32. He held office in the Lismore Agricultural and Pastoral Society, the Australian Sheep Breeders' Association, and the Returned Sailors' and Soldiers' Imperial League of Australia. He had resumed army (militia) service as a major in the 4th Light Horse in 1931, and was promoted to lieut-colonel and regimental commander in December 1932.

Brought to wider notice as a member of the Transport Regulation Board set up by the Victorian government in 1933, he was recognized by (Sir) Robert Menzies as the principal author of its 'masterly report'. A reluctant recruit to Federal parliamentary politics when internal divisions loosened the Country Party's hold on his local electorate, he was successful as the United Australia Party candidate for Corangamite at the 1934 general election.

In Canberra, Street's qualities were soon discerned by his colleagues and by a press which delighted in his mobility (60 000 miles [96 558 km] travelled in his electorate, 1934-37) and integrity (he twice declined restoration of his parliamentary salary to its pre-Depression level because it had not been canvassed at the previous elections). He was a fluent debater, speaking with a particular authority on military matters that was further enhanced when he was given command of the 3rd Cavalry Brigade in 1935 and promoted to temporary brigadier in 1938. While carefully distancing himself from Labor's schemes for banking reform and rural rehabilitation, Street argued that defence should be 'above party politics'. In 1937 he advocated a small standing army and the inclusion of the leader of the Opposition in a reconstructed council of defence. He renewed his plea for a standing army in May 1938, questioning the wisdom of relying on the diversion of British naval strength to Singapore in wartime. Notwithstanding his critical stance, Street was invited by J. A. Lyons [q.v.10] to become parliamentary secretary to the Department of Defence in July 1938. In this unsalaried post Street's brief embraced routine administration and parliamentary liaison, assistance in preparation of legislation, and answering questions on notice.

Beset with controversy over defence policy and H. V. C. Thorby's [q.v.] administration of the portfolio, but unwilling to yield to Menzies' preference for compulsory service, Lyons installed Street as minister for defence in November 1938. The new minister was also designated a member of a 'senior Cabinet group', replacing T. W. White who complained with scant credibility about the creation of a 'coterie' controlling government policy. Street had, as his U.A.P. colleague Sir Henry Gullett [q.v.9] wrote, 'advanced himself neither by intrigue nor by making himself a conspicuous nuisance'.

Elevation to cabinet rank entailed relinquishing his militia command and, as it turned out, his ambition to lead the cavalry in battle. As defence minister he presided effectively over an expansion of the militia, air force and navy, as well as increased munitions production and shipbuilding. He steered the unpopular National Registration Act (1939) through parliament, unexpectedly accepting a suggestion to include a census of wealth.

On the creation of the Menzies U.A.P. government in April 1939, Street kept defence portfolio, rising to fourth place in ministerial seniority after W. M. Hughes [q.v.9] and R. G. (Lord) Casey. Menzies' commitment to accelerated defence preparations and his focus on the 'Near North' made Street's role pivotal. Closely allied with his friend J. V. Fairbairn [q.v.8] who became minister for civil aviation and minister assisting the minister for defence, Street oversaw the final preparation of the Commonwealth War Book.

At the outbreak of war his personal knowledge of Australia's military leaders gave him a crucial voice in the allocation of army and headquarters commands. In November 1939 Menzies detached the ministries of air and navy from defence, and left Street with diminished but still formidable responsibilities as minister for the army and for repatriation. When the U.A.P. and United Country Party formed a coalition government in March 1940, Street retained his portfolios and cabinet seniority.

In his capacity as defence and army minister, Street's informality but obviously professional inspection of naval, military and air force establishments in every State made him a favourite with servicemen. The press reported an awesome régime of travel and deskwork, punctuated by well-publicized three-mile morning runs, frequent riding and skating with his children Tony and Veronica ('Tim'), and occasional cricket matches. Relying on action rather than oratory, Street issued no major appeal for recruits until May 1940 when he announced the formation of the 8th Division.

Unaffected geniality and political intelligence made the manifestly unambitious Street a key member of the Menzies ministry. His death—with Fairbairn, Gullett, Brudenell White and others—in an aircrash in Canberra on 13 August 1940 was a severe blow to the war government. It also robbed post-war Australia of a mature and popular political leader with rare consensual gifts. Survived by his wife and two children, Street was buried at Lismore, Victoria.

C. E. W. Bean, *The story of Anzac*, 1 (Syd, 1921), and *The A.I.F. in France*, 1916, 1918 (Syd, 1929, 1942); P. Hasluck, *The government and the people, 1939-1941* (Canb, 1952); C. Hazlehurst, *Menzies observed* (Syd, 1979); D. M. Horner, *High command* (Canb, 1982); J. Robertson and J. McCarthy, *Australian war strategy 1939-1945* (Brisb, 1985); *Sydneian*, 1910-18; Street papers and press-cuttings (NL); records (AWM); G. Armstrong recollections (ts, held by author, Canb).   CAMERON HAZLEHURST

STREET, SIR PHILIP WHISTLER (1863-1938), chief justice and lieutenant-governor, was born on 9 August 1863 at Victoria Street, Sydney, second son of Bathurst-born parents John Rendell Street, merchant and later pastoralist, and his wife Susanna(h) Caroline, née Lawson, granddaughter of William Lawson [q.v.2]. His father had been first managing director of the Perpetual Trustee Executor & Agency Co. Ltd and represented East Sydney in the Legislative Assembly (1887-91). Philip was educated at Waverley Hall, Sydney Grammar School and St Paul's College, University of Sydney (B.A., 1883). His zest for study was not hampered by deteriorating vision and ultimate blindness in his left eye. Although completing divinity, he turned to law, read with Cecil Bedford Stephen and was admitted to the Bar on 25 August 1886. He married Belinda Maud Poolman at St John's Anglican Church, Toorak, Melbourne, on 1 February 1888. Returning to Sydney, they lived at Woollahra, at Meadowbank and from 1906 at Liverynga, Elizabeth Bay.

After a struggle, Street entered the Equity Bar's 'closed shop'. By 1900 he had a good practice, but, before he could take silk, he accepted an acting judicial appointment in 1906. A vacancy led to his swearing in as judge of the Supreme Court on 11 February 1907. Attorney-General (Sir) Charles Wade [q.v.] commended the elevation of one with qualifications earned at home, not overseas. Street became judge in bankruptcy and in probate, often sitting at common law in Sydney and on circuit. As deputy president of the Court of Arbitration he heard many industrial disputes. By 1918, when appointed chief judge in Equity, he had sat in or presided over every jurisdiction of the Supreme Court and in the Vice-Admiralty Court. From 1909 he had served on many royal commissions, notably into the case against the Industrial Workers of the World in 1918.

Succeeding Sir William Cullen [q.v.8] as chief justice, Street was sworn in on 28 January 1925. Although his judgements lacked the intellectual sparkle of Cullen's and the enduring brilliance of (Sir) Frederick Jordan's [q.v.9], Street was an able judicial lawyer in all departments and a capable adminstrator. He brought 'fine dignity and decorum' to the court, adopting an appropriate reserve. Friends knew him as 'a delightful companion and a witty conversationalist'. Espousing law reform when it was unpopular, he struck down technicalities and refused to permit 'surface complexity to hinder the discovery of the real issue'.

Appointed K.C.M.G. in 1928, Street visited England with his wife in 1929. 'Much taken' by their passage in the *Orsova*, albeit with 'nobody of any particular distinction aboard', they delighted in London, attending a royal garden party and dining at Lincoln's Inn hall. Returning to increased burdens, in 1930 he was commissioned lieut-governor and administered the State government three times between 1934 and 1937. As the economy worsened, Premier J. T. Lang [q.v.9] tried to swamp and to abolish the Legislative Council, as well as to abrogate State financial obligations. In December 1930 Street presided at the hearing of *Trethowan* [q.v.] v. *Peden* [q.v.11] when the Full Bench ordered the government not to present for royal assent, unless ratified by the electors, bills to abolish the council. Controversially, but with ample historical precedent, as adviser to Governor Sir Philip Game [q.v.8] Street was drawn into the constitutional imbroglio that led to the dismissal of Lang in May 1932 and, according to Sir John Harvey [q.v.9], did not depart 'a hair's breadth from the highest standard of judicial conduct'. Sir Philip Street retired on 22 July 1933 after a term exceeded only by Sir Alfred Stephen [q.v.6].

Street took pleasure in his home, his significant collection of etchings and his extensive library. With Lady Street, he had many philanthropic and public interests. He was a member of the senate (1915-34) and deputy chancellor (1926-27) of the University of Sydney, a council-member of Women's College, chairman of trustees of Sydney Grammar School, a trustee from 1923 of the National Art Gallery of New South Wales (chairman, 1934-38) and of the Australian Museum, Sydney, and patron in New South Wales of the Victoria League, English-Speaking Union, Japan-Australia Society and the Royal Zoological Society. A member of the Union Club and of numerous other bodies, he was also president of the Institute of Public Affairs, the St John Ambulance Association (invested knight of grace of St John of Jerusalem in London in 1929), the Boy Scouts' Association and the Boys' Brigade.

Sir Philip died on 11 September 1938 at Liverynga, leaving an estate sworn for probate at £29 162. He was buried in South Head cemetery after a state funeral at St Andrew's Cathedral. His wife and two sons survived him; another son Laurence Whistler had been killed in action at Gallipoli in 1915. Street's eldest son (Sir) Kenneth and grandson (Sir) Laurence also held office as chief justice and lieut-governor of New South Wales. William McInnes's [q.v.10] portrait of Sir Philip is held by the Supreme Court House, Sydney.

K. W. Street, *Annals of the Street family of Birtley* (Syd, 1941); J. M. Bennett, *Portraits of the chief justices of New South Wales 1824-1977* (Syd, 1977); L. Foster, *High hopes* (Melb, 1986); *State Reports* (NSW), 6, 1906, 25, 1925, 33, 1933, 38, 1938; *Aust Law J*, 7, 1933, p 132, 12, 1938, p 168; *SMH*, 12 Sept 1938; Street family papers (ML); information from the Hon. Sir L. Street (Syd).

J. M. BENNETT

STREETON, SIR ARTHUR ERNEST (1867-1943), artist, was born on 8 April 1867 at Duneed, Victoria, fourth of five children of Charles Henry Streeton, schoolteacher, and his wife Mary, née Johnson, whom Charles had met on his voyage from England in 1854 and married in 1857 on his appointment to Queenscliff. The family moved to Melbourne in 1874 when Charles joined the administrative staff of the Education Department. They settled at Richmond and Arthur attended the Punt Road State School until 1880 when he became a junior clerk in the office of Rolfe & Co., importers, of Bourke Street.

As a child Arthur liked to draw and sketch in water-colour. He enrolled in night classes at the National Gallery of Victoria School of Design in 1882-87 and in 1886 his skill at sketching led to his being apprenticed as a lithographer to Charles Troedel [q.v.6] & Co., of Collins Street. Streeton's first independently published black-and-white work, 'His First Snake', appeared in the *Australasian Sketcher* of 24 January 1889. He had no formal instruction in painting; his earliest extant oils date from 1884 and at this stage he was largely self-taught; he used such manuals as William Morris Hunt's *Talks about art* (1877) which urged the emulation of *plein air* French painters Jean Millet and Camille Corot. Inspired by his reading, Streeton wrote to the compiler of Hunt's book for photographs of Corot's work.

In the summer of 1886 Streeton met Tom Roberts [q.v.11] at Mentone. Seeing his work 'full of light and air', Roberts asked him to join a painting group which included Frederick McCubbin [q.v.10] and Louis Abrahams. In their company Streeton continued to work on the problems of light and heat and space and distance which had already absorbed him. With the sale of 'Settler's Camp' and 'Pastoral', both exhibited with the Victorian Artists' Society in 1888, he was able to paint full time: for the next two years he worked at Box Hill and Heidelberg with his artist friends who now included Charles Conder [q.v.3], and also in the city where he did portraits and studies of the Yarra River and its bridges. A camp established at an old house at Eaglemont, overlooking the Yarra valley near Heidelberg, became the focus of their artistic fellowship. Streeton and Conder supplemented their income by giving painting lessons to young women; at weekends artists and students visited to paint and picnic beneath the pines.

On 17 August 1889 the Heidelberg painters opened their 9 x 5 (inches) Exhibition of Impressions at Buxton's Art Gallery, Melbourne. The exhibition was a statement of rebellion by young artists, influenced by international trends, against the prevailing academic tradition of Victorian painting. The

182 exhibits included forty by Streeton. Mostly painted on cedar cigar-box lids and hung among silks, they were Impressionist in the direct manner of painting and the study of momentary effects, while retaining the *plein-airist* tonal use of colour. The catalogue stated: 'An effect is only momentary: so an impressionist tries to find his place . . . So in these works, it has been the object of the artists to render faithfully, and thus obtain first records of effects widely differing, and often of very fleeting character'. The exhibition won popular success, but provoked critical scorn, expressed most virulently by the influential *Argus* critic James Smith [q.v.6]. Streeton, Roberts and Conder responded in a letter to the *Argus*, asserting: 'Any form of nature which moves us strongly by its beauty, whether strong or vague in its drawing, defined or undefinite in its light, rare or ordinary in its colour, is worthy of our best efforts'.

The camp broke up in January 1890; three months later Conder left Australia for Paris, taking with him Streeton's 'Golden Summer' (1889) which was exhibited at the Royal Academy of Arts in London in 1891, and hung on the line and awarded an honorable mention at the Salon de la Société des Artistes Français, Paris, in 1892. Streeton, whose 'Still Glides the Stream and Shall for Ever Glide' (1890) had been acquired by the National Art Gallery of New South Wales, moved to Sydney. Julian Ashton [q.v.7] saw him then as 'a slim, debonair young man . . . with a little gold pointed beard and fair complexion', who, when he was not painting, 'was quoting Keats and Shelley'. Streeton lived at 'Curlew Camp', Little Sirius Cove, Mosman, with Roberts and other impecunious artists, and painted a variety of harbour views, Coogee beach scenes, *art-nouveau*-inspired nudes and in 1893 two urban masterpieces, 'Circular Quay' and 'The Railway Station'. With Roberts he opened a teaching studio in Pitt Street.

In 1891 Streeton wrote to Roberts of his yearning to 'try something entirely new': 'to translate some of the great hidden poetry of the immense, elemental outback. He travelled inland in New South Wales and painted directly in front of his subject, striving to capture—as he told Roberts—the 'great, gold plains', the 'hot, trying winds' and the 'slow, immense summer'. The paintings of this period, including 'Fire's On' (1891), are heroic landscapes which successfully balance bravura technique with real inspiration and feeling. His Hawkesbury River series (1896) is remarkable for the rendering of light, heat and distance. On the recommendation of John Mather [q.v.10] the National Gallery of Victoria bought one, 'The Purple Noon's Transparent Might', shown at Streeton's first one-man Melbourne exhibition in December 1896.

After this success Streeton sailed for England, spending five months painting in Cairo *en route*. The early years in London were hard; he had few friends and felt none of the intuitive affinity with the English landscape that had inspired his Australian paintings. Homesick and nostalgic for his youth, he seems also to have suffered a time of artistic confusion. There was little interest in his work and little success at the major exhibiting venues, the Royal Academy and the New English Art Club. In 1906-07 he spent a year in Australia and had considerable acclaim with sales of his English and recent Australian work. G. W. Marshall-Hall [q.v.10] and (Sir) Walter Baldwin Spencer [q.v.] were early patrons who became friends.

Returning to London, Streeton married Esther Leonora Clench, a Canadian violinist, on 11 January 1908 in the Marylebone register office. Apart from a visit home in 1913-14, he spent the years before World War I based in London whence he sent works for exhibition in Australia. During this period Streeton's art began to win recognition in England, France and at the international exhibitions held in the United States of America. His wife's extensive social contacts helped with commissions and Streeton's formerly rather reclusive personality had to respond to *de rigueur* 'country-house' weekends.

On 24 April 1915 Streeton enlisted as a private in the Australian Army Medical Corps and was posted to Wandsworth where he worked as an orderly for the next two years. Commissioned honorary lieutenant and appointed official war artist in 1918, he spent two periods in France documenting the Western Front for the Commonwealth government. In contrast to the Middle East paintings of George Lambert [q.v.9], Streeton concentrated on the landscape of war; his paintings show the desolation of the terrain, but none of the tragedy or drama of human suffering. As throughout his career, landscape views rather than figure-painting remained the core of his art. In July 1919 at the Alpine Club, London, he showed a series of war paintings entitled 'With Australians on the Somme'. His best water-colours recall his early work in their immediacy and delicate portrayal of light.

After the war Streeton and his family visited Australia. In 1922 they returned to London, via St Mary's, Ontario, Canada, where Nora Streeton's mother lived. Streeton's paintings of Canada were exhibited at the Montross Gallery, New York, in January 1923, but they aroused little interest in spite of a warm press reception. That year he returned to Victoria where he bought a home at Toorak and built a cottage at Olinda in the

Dandenong Ranges. He made painting trips to many Australian sites and in 1928 was awarded the Wynne prize for landscape for 'Afternoon Light: the Goulburn Valley'.

In his later years Streeton became a national institution. He continued to paint sunny, pastoral landscapes, but many were mannered, fluent and facile, and devoid of the inspiration of his radical early work. Leading critics, particularly J. S. MacDonald and Lionel Lindsay [qq.v.10], extolled his art which—with that of Roberts and McCubbin—was to some extent appropriated by the art establishment in the cause of a conservative, isolationist nationalism. Most responded to the optimism of Streeton's romantic blue and gold vision of a pastoral Australia. William Blamire Young [q.v.] was one of the few to contrast unfavourably Streeton's later canvases with the small 'gem-like' pictures of his early years. Reviewing a retrospective exhibition in 1933, he wrote that 'in many cases the poet has been over-powered by the technician'. As art critic for the *Argus* from 1929, Streeton himself became a tastemaker; although an early supporter of Hans Heysen and Norman Lindsay [qq.v.9,10], he was not receptive to modern art. He frequently wrote in the press on art, the environment and public affairs. At the same time he embellished and consolidated the Streeton legend, writing his interpretation of the history of Australian painting, organizing his own numerous exhibitions and producing the *Arthur Streeton catalogue* (1935). In 1937 he was appointed K.B.E.

After his wife's death in 1938, Streeton retired to Olinda and devoted much of his time to his garden. He died there on 1 September 1943, having been received into the Catholic faith during his last long illness, and was buried in Ferntree Gully cemetery. His son survived him.

Widely read in English literature and poetry, Streeton was a Romantic. His love of music formed a great bond with his wife. Artistically he always preferred the tonal landscapes of the French *plein air* movement of the 1870s and late-Victorian Romantic landscapists like Alfred East. In the twentieth century he showed little interest in *avant-garde* art, believing to the end in the values of sound drawing and tonally orchestrated colour. He was of medium height and slightly built. Roberts's portrait, 'Smike Streeton, age 24' (1891), shows a fine-featured profile, wide, expressive, dark eyes, brown hair, a gold-tinged moustache and beard, and an eager, boyish expression. It is in the Art Gallery of New South Wales, as is a self-portrait, presented in 1924.

Smike to Bulldog—letters from Sir Arthur Streeton to Tom Roberts, R. H. Croll ed (Syd, 1946);

B. Smith, *Australian painting 1788-1960* (Melb, 1962); A. Galbally, *Arthur Streeton* (Melb, 1979); G. Serle, *From deserts the prophets come* (Melb, 1973); *Art in Aust*, no 2, 1915, no 16, 1926; *Meanjin Q*, 10, no 2, 1951; Streeton papers (AWM); Roberts papers (ML).   ANN E. GALBALLY

STREHLOW, CARL FRIEDRICH THEODOR (1871-1922), missionary, was born on 23 December 1871 at Fredersdorf, Uckermark, Germany, seventh child of Carl Strehlow, teacher, and his wife Friederike, née Schneider. Carl's education began at his father's Free Lutheran Church school. In 1888 he entered the seminary at Neuendettelsau and graduated in 1891. At the request of the Immanuel Synod in South Australia, he went there to serve the German migrants of his faith. He was ordained in 1892 and worked for the missionary J. G. Reuther of the Bethesda Mission at Killalpaninna among the Dieri Aborigines near Cooper's Creek, South Australia; he helped Reuther to translate the New Testament into the Dieri language.

In September 1894 the Immanuel Synod bought the dilapidated Finke River Mission at Hermannsburg (later Ntaria) and appointed Strehlow to head the mission to the Western Aranda and Loritja (Kukatja) of Central Australia. He took charge on 12 October. Except for his travels among the Aborigines as far as Alice Springs, Strehlow left Hermannsburg only four times during his twenty-eight years of service. He went to South Australia where he married his German fiancée Frieda Johanna Henrietta Keysser at Point Pass on 25 September 1895. They returned to the financially troubled mission and continued working, their meagre salary subsidized by the Strehlow family in Germany. In 1903-04 Strehlow, with his wife and their four children, spent leave in Adelaide. After two more sons were born, the family visited Germany in 1910-12. Although Strehlow had been naturalized shortly after arriving in Australia, he was investigated by the Federal government during World War I for allegedly 'lecturing to aborigines regarding the present crisis on the European Continent'. He was exonerated.

Some colleagues found Carl Strehlow strong-willed, with a high opinion of his own ability; his rigid self-discipline made him a stern pedagogue and a strict parent. He was a dedicated missionary who placed his obligations to God above all else. A handsome, full-bearded man, stocky and robust, Strehlow strained his health by a relentless schedule which included pastoral, teaching, accounting and administrative duties, tending the sick and management of the mission farm. He devoted his leisure to linguistic and ethnological field-work and to preparing the results for publication in Germany.

In addition to protecting them from squatters and policemen, he acknowledged the Aborigines' spiritual heritage. Despite his paternalism and refusal to attend traditional Aboriginal ceremonies, Strehlow recognized the need to understand the culture of those to whom he wished to bring his own, and grew to be a great philologist of Aboriginal languages, one of the most important anthropologists in the tradition of the continental European schools and an authority on Central Australian Aborigines. To them Strehlow became 'ingkata', a trusted leader and teacher. As he published mostly in German, his anthropological work was not fully recognized in Australia. He added to Dieri a fluency in the cognate Aranda and Loritja languages, and started to compile an Aranda dictionary. In 1904 he printed an Aranda school primer with translations of hymns by his assistant H. A. Heinrich; in 1919 he completed translating extracts from the Old Testament into Aranda which was published in 1928. His greatest achievement was his work on the myths, legends, material culture and customs of the Aranda and Loritja, in seven volumes, edited first by Moritz von Leonhardi and then by Bernhard Hagen (Städtisches Völker-Museum, Frankfurt, Germany, 1907-20). Two of Strehlow's letters to von Leonhardi were published and aroused interest among European anthropologists who were divided over the questions of spirituality in 'primitive' societies and whether a researcher should speak native languages.

In 1922 the desperately ill Strehlow left Hermannsburg for a fourth and final time. He set out for Adelaide to receive medical treatment; the trip was arduous and protracted, and his faith in God was sorely tried; completing less than 150 miles (241 km) of the journey, he died of dropsy on 20 October at Horseshoe Bend and was buried there. He was survived by his wife, five sons and a daughter.

Strehlow's findings on totemism were accepted by many contemporary European scholars, among them Durkheim, Malinowski, Freud and Roheim; more recently, Worms, Lommel and Petri have used his work; Lévi-Strauss's *Les structures élémentaires de la parenté* (Paris, 1949) and Eliade's *Australian religions* (Cornell, 1973) also drew substantially on his research. British social anthropologists, however, have placed more reliance on Sir Walter Baldwin Spencer [q.v.] and his collaborator Francis Gillen [q.v.9]. Spencer considered Strehlow an unreliable scientist and persuaded Sir James Frazer to expunge references to him from the *Golden bough*. The rivalry between Spencer and Strehlow—who never wrote to each other and never met—is dealt with in *'So much that is new'*, a book which also recognizes Strehlow's 'significant studies of Aranda religion'. Otherwise, Australian anthropology has largely neglected one of its greatest scholars, although Strehlow's work remains one of the best nineteenth-century published sources for Aranda and Loritja legends and languages. *Journey to Horseshoe Bend* (Sydney, 1969) is a moving memorial by his son Theodor, professor of Australian linguistics at the University of Adelaide (1970-73). In 1960 the Carl Strehlow Memorial Hospital was opened at Hermannsburg.

C. T. Madigan, *Central Australia* (Lond, 1936); E. Leske (ed), *Hermannsburg* (Adel, 1977); W. McNally, *Aborigines, artefacts and anguish* (Adel, 1981); D. J. Mulvaney and J. H. Calaby, *'So much that is new'* (Melb, 1985); D. J. Mulvaney, *Encounters in place* (Brisb, 1989); *Auricht's book almanac* (Aust Lutheran Almanac) (Adel), 1924; *Year book of the Lutheran Church in Australia*, 1974; *Observer* (Adel), 28 Oct 1922; Aborigines' Friends' Assn, Annual Report, 1957 (Mortlock Lib); CRS A3 item NT/15/2274 (AA, Canb).   WALTER F. VEIT

STRETCH, JOHN FRANCIS (1855-1919), Anglican bishop, was born on 28 January 1855 at Geelong, Victoria, eldest son of Rev. John Cliffe Theodore Stretch and his wife Frances, née Heath, both English born. John senior, himself a clergyman's son, had reached Victoria in the *Blackwall* in 1853 and joined his elder brother Rev. Theodore Stretch [q.v.6]. John Francis belonged to an important clerical family and was influenced by his energetic uncle, a founder of the diocese of Ballarat.

Educated at Geelong Church of England Grammar School, Stretch proceeded to Trinity College, University of Melbourne (B.A., 1874; LL.B., 1887), and worked in the Office of Titles. Abandoning ideas of the Bar, he was made deacon on 22 December 1878 and ordained priest on 21 December 1879 by Bishop Moorhouse [q.v.5] of Melbourne. Stretch was one of several young Australians who responded to the new bishop's liberal theology and constructive approach to the problems of colonial society; they were to become the first generation of locally-trained Church leaders.

After serving as curate and locum tenens at Geelong, St Kilda and Brighton, Stretch was incumbent of Maldon (1883-85). Ethel ('Henry Handel') Richardson [q.v.11] in *Myself when young* (1948) described the tall and slender Jack Stretch: 'the features were classic and exquisitely modelled, but redeemed from severity by a pair of laughing dark-blue eyes and a fascinatingly cleft chin'. Knowledgeable about horses, at Maldon he 'was mostly to be seen flying about in his light, two-wheeled buggy'. On 7 January 1885 at

St Paul's Church, Geelong, Stretch married Amelia Margaret Weekes (d. 1914).

After incumbencies at Fitzroy (1885-92) and Brighton (1892-94), in 1894 he moved to the diocese of Ballarat as dean. Next year he was made assistant bishop (from 1896 co-adjutor) of Brisbane. With Henry Cooper, Stretch was consecrated by the primate, Bishop Saumarez Smith [q.v.11], on 1 November 1895; Cooper's appointment to a similar position at Ballarat would have overshadowed Stretch's continuation there as dean.

The 'first Australian, born and bred, to become a member of the episcopal bench in Australia', Stretch was proud of his achievement. He aided Bishop Webber [q.v.] in a vigorous expansion programme in Brisbane; in 1897 he visited Britain for the Pan-Anglican Congress and was awarded an honorary D.D. by the University of Oxford. As rector of Roma, archdeacon of the Western Downs and residentiary canon of the cathedral, he played a key role in the diocese, but the failure of the Peattie fund to provide an adequate stipend led him to move to Newcastle, New South Wales, as suffragan bishop and dean in 1900.

Bishop Stanton [q.v.6], scholarly and retiring, lived at Morpeth, leaving Stretch to attend to the industrial region around the see city. He did so with energy. It was almost a matter of course that (despite some conservative opposition) he was elected bishop on 21 February 1906 after Stanton's death. Stretch made the diocese Newcastle-centred: he moved his official residence and the registry from Morpeth and pushed on with the construction of Christ Church Cathedral, a process long impeded by architectural problems and by the personal animosities generated by Horbury Hunt and Dean Arthur Selwyn [qq.v.4,6]. Parish life in the rapidly expanding Newcastle area received a major impetus, the number of clergy increased from forty-five to seventy and the bishop organized the diocesan finances on a sound basis. Bishop Wentworth-Sheilds [q.v.] of Armidale found Stretch 'deliciously human and deliciously humorous', 'the most genial and entertaining of hosts'.

As much an Imperialist as his episcopal colleagues, Stretch nevertheless maintained an independent attitude to the industrial disputes that plagued his diocese and to the issues raised by the conscription referenda (three of his sons, of whom Thomas was killed in action, served with the Australian Imperial Force). Stretch published little, but his short, pungent, practical addresses received widespread recognition. Believing that there was a model for an Australian bishop—a socially conscious leader who would be pragmatic and yet expound a clear spiritual message—he did his best to realize this role.

In failing health Stretch resigned his see early in 1919 and died of a cerebral haemorrhage at Killara, Sydney, on 19 April; he was buried in Sandgate cemetery, Newcastle; two daughters and four sons survived him. Two of his sons, John Carlos William (1885-1967) and Cliffe Maurice Osmond (1889-1939), were Anglican clergymen.

A. P. Elkin, *The diocese of Newcastle* (Syd, 1955); Geelong C of E Grammar School, *Grammar School Q*, Dec 1895, p 24, and *Corian*, May 1919, p 38; *SMH* and *Newcastle Sun*, 21 Apr 1919; *Newcastle Morning Herald*, 21, 22 Apr 1919, 19 Dec 1939; *Church Standard*, 25 Apr 1919, 22 Dec 1939; *Aust Church Record*, 4 Jan 1940; Stretch papers (Univ of Newcastle Archives).   K. J. CABLE

STRICKLAND, SIR GERALD, 1ST BARON STRICKLAND OF SIZERGH CASTLE (1861-1940), governor and politician, was born on 24 May 1861 at Valletta, Malta, eldest son of Captain Walter Strickland, R.N., and his wife Maria Aloysia (Louisa), née Bonnici, niece and heiress of Sir Nicholas Sceberras Bologna, fifth Count della Catena in Malta, whom Gerald succeeded in 1875; he was also a nephew of (Sir) Edward Strickland [q.v.6]. Educated at St Mary's College, Oscott, and Trinity College, Cambridge (B.A., LL.B., 1887), he was called to the Bar at the Inner Temple. During a world tour in 1883-84 he had visited Maltese settlers in Queensland and in Sydney discussed with the premier (Sir) Alexander Stuart [q.v.6] the possibility of bringing Maltese orange- and olive-growers to New South Wales.

Elected in 1886 to the council of the government of Malta, Strickland represented the island at the first Colonial Conference and helped to frame its constitution in 1887. As chief secretary (1889-92) he initiated many reforms and public works. Although he showed a sound knowledge of public finance and administrative techniques, his tactlessness caused some uneasiness in the Colonial Office. On 26 August 1890 Strickland married Lady Edeline Sackville (d. 1918), daughter of the seventh Earl De La Warr, in Our Lady of Victories Church, Kensington, London.

Appointed K.C.M.G. in 1897, he governed the Leeward Islands from 1902 and was transferred to Tasmania in October 1904. Belonging to an ancient English Catholic family, he was only the third Catholic to govern any Australian colony or State. In May 1909 Strickland became governor of Western Australia. In the early days of Federation he was involved in the delicate matter of State rights and the appointment, role and salaries of governors. He strongly supported Federation (as opposed to unification), as well as Imperial federation, and restrained his ministers from expressing secessionist views. A stickler for formalities and constitutional propriety, he also endeavoured to persuade members of cabinet not to recommend expenditure without parliamentary sanction. He did, however, quarrel privately with Governor-General Lord Dudley [q.v.8] over the dormant commission and the channels of communication with the secretary of state.

Strickland was appointed G.C.M.G. in 1913 and advanced to New South Wales where he noted 'there was some religious friction'; he was confident that 'an *English* Roman Catholic Governor' would be the best person to control it. Yet, it was politics and not religion that was to bring about his downfall. He roused the antipathy of the governor-general Sir Ronald Munro Ferguson [q.v.10] who told Bonar Law that 'I find him altogether too machiavellian for ordinary intercourse'.

Handsome, solidly built and of middle height, Strickland triumphantly entered Government House, Sydney, in 1915. He was 'a genial host and brilliant controversialist'. Soldiering in his young years (he served with the Cambridge University Rifles) and mechanical engineering were his main hobbies; his spinning wheel and combination tool were exhibited at an industrial and models exhibition in Sydney.

In May 1916 Strickland criticized Premier Holman's [q.v.9] manoeuvre of pretending to resign his commission to avoid a vote of censure at the Political Labor Conference; he reminded Holman that 'resignation' from office meant resignation to the governor, not to a conference or caucus. While Strickland's interventions had been tolerated in Tasmania and Western Australia, they were resented in New South Wales. Later that year, after a renewal of the channel of communications dispute, Strickland and Holman came into open collision. When Holman—deposed as leader of the Labor Party—was negotiating a coalition government with (Sir) Charles Wade [q.v.], Strickland intimated that he could 'no longer transact business' with him. By demanding in substance the return of Holman's commission, Strickland aroused indignation among Holman's supporters:

The political split in the Labour arena
Was *delicatessen* to della Catena
Who, snug in an ambush, for some time had laid
Intent on the scalps of the Holman brigade.

While Strickland's object had been to safeguard the electors against a government which had never received popular endorsement, appeals to Downing Street resulted in the governor receiving a stinging rebuke. Directed by the Colonial Office to assent to the National government's bill prolonging the life of the parliament, he did so, albeit most unwillingly. Strickland was recalled and left Australia on 30 April 1917.

Retiring from the colonial service, he divided his time between his Maltese and English estates (having acquired Sizergh in Westmorland from a cousin in 1896). Strickland was elected to the House of Commons as a Conservative for Lancaster in 1924; he married Margaret Hulton (D.B.E., 1937) on 31 August 1926 in the same church as his earlier wedding; in 1928 he was raised to the peerage. Having entered the Maltese Legislative Assembly in 1921, he helped to draft the Milner-Avery constitution. He formed the Anglo-Maltese (later Constitutional) party and was involved in bitter battles against Fascist, Italian and Church interference in politics. Prime minister in 1927-32, he narrowly escaped assassination in May 1930. In 1932 he became leader of the Opposition against a pro-Italian government; he founded the *Times of Malta* (daily and weekly) and *Il Berka*, the first vernacular newspaper in Malta.

Strickland died in Malta on 22 August 1940 and was buried in the family vault of St Cajetanus's Cathedral. His wife survived him, as did five daughters of his first marriage; his two sons and a daughter had died in infancy. The combination of his English and Maltese inheritance accounted for the strength of his dual patriotism, but it brought out a pugnacity which often antagonized would-be sympathizers and obscured the worth of his policies. A portrait of Strickland by E. Caruana Dingli is in Malta and a statue by Anton Sciortina stands in upper Barracoa Gardens, Valletta.

H. Hornyold, *Genealogical memoirs of the family of Strickland of Sizergh* (Kendal, Westmorland, Eng, 1928); *DNB*, 1931-40; H. V. Evatt, *The king and his dominion governors* (Lond, 1936), and *Australian Labour leader* (Syd, 1942); E. Dobie, *Malta's road to independence* (Norman, Oklahoma, USA, 1967); H. Smith, *Lord Strickland* (Amsterdam, Netherlands, 1983); *SMH*, 24, 26 Jan 1884, 11, 13 Nov 1916, 23 Aug 1940; *Catholic Press*, 25 Aug 1904; *Punch* (Melb), 16 Nov 1915; *Freeman's J*, 1 Mar 1917; *The Times*, 18, 20, 24, 28 Sept 1917, 23 Aug 1940; Deakin *and* Novar papers (NL); CO 418/74/f367, 55/f24, 147/f350, 148/f164, 160/ff20, 82, 111 (PRO, Lond, microfilm NL); personal information.
                                              G. P. WALSH

STRONG, SIR ARCHIBALD THOMAS (1876-1930), scholar, teacher and man of letters, was born on 30 December 1876 at South Yarra, Melbourne, son of Herbert Augustus Strong [q.v.6], professor of classics in the University of Melbourne, and his wife Helen Campbell, née Edmiston. The family moved to Liverpool, England, in 1883 when Herbert was appointed professor of Latin at University College.

From Sedbergh School, Archibald went in 1893 to read classics at University College, Liverpool, graduating B.A. in 1896; then as a classical exhibitioner he proceeded to Magdalen College, Oxford, where he graduated in *literae humaniores* in 1900. As an undergraduate at Liverpool he was active in sport, a member of the Students' Representative Council and an editor of the *Sphinx*. In vacations he acquired an extensive knowledge of the literatures and a competence in the languages of France and Germany; he was later to add Italian to his store.

In 1901 ill health compelled him to abandon reading for the Bar under F. E. Smith (Lord Birkenhead); in search of a more congenial climate, Strong returned to Melbourne. There he became influential in educational, literary and dramatic communities: teaching and examining at secondary level, giving extension lectures for the university, serving as president of the Melbourne Literature (1910), Melbourne Shakespeare (1913) and Mermaid societies. He was chief Commonwealth censor of 'cinematograph films' (1919-22), an advocate of a national theatre, and with Gregan McMahon [q.v.10] a founding member and trustee of the Melbourne Repertory Theatre. He was, as well, the editor of a relatively short-lived literary journal, the *Trident*, and for fifteen years literary critic for the Melbourne *Herald*.

Rejected on medical grounds from active service in World War I, Strong gave unstinted civilian service in support of the allied cause. He spoke regularly at recruiting rallies, drafted material to raise war loans and to campaign for compulsory service, wrote numerous press articles and constantly emphasized Imperial ties. He also served on the executive of the Commonwealth Directorate of Education Propaganda on War and Peace Issues. Nettie Palmer [q.v.11] regarded his occasional denigration of some contemporary German men of letters as unrepresentative of the general Australian literary community. During the war Strong published *Australia and the war* (1915) and *Story of the Anzacs* (1917).

From 1912 to 1921 he taught at the university, being acting professor and head of the department of English in 1916-19 while (Sir) Robert Wallace [q.v.] was absent on war service. Yet it was as the first Jury professor of English language and literature (1922-30) in the University of Adelaide that Strong made his original and lasting contribution to academic education in his special field by introducing in 1923 a four-year course for an honours degree. Thickset, bull-necked, but with refined features, he had commanding

presence as a lecturer and displayed extensive and profound scholarship, especially of the Elizabethan and Romantic periods. His publications included small volumes of original verse in traditional form and style in 1905, 1916 and 1918; volumes of literary criticism in 1910, 1911, 1921 and (posthumously) 1932; translations into modern English verse of the ballads of Theodore de Banville in 1913 and of *Beowulf* in 1925; and, with Wallace, a short history of English literature (1921) and an anthology of English verse and prose (1923).

Strong's international standing was attested by his articles on Australia for the *Liverpool Daily Post* in 1903, on literature for the *Australian encyclopaedia* in 1925 and on Australian poetry for *The Times* in 1927; he also published his address to the International Conference on Education at Vancouver, Canada, in 1929, an article on cultural development in Australia in the *Cambridge history of the British Empire* and eleven sonnets in the second edition of the *Oxford book of Australasian verse*. Recognition of his academic stature was accorded by the award in 1920 of a Litt.D. by the University of Melbourne, and of his extensive contributions to the literary and dramatic arts by a knighthood in 1925. He was described as Australia's 'most highly cultured' and 'most widely-read' man.

Strong never married. He died in Adelaide on 2 September 1930 of cerebral thrombosis and was buried in the North Road cemetery. The library of the University of Adelaide acquired his valuable collection of more than 5000 books.

All About Books, Oct 1930; *Aust Q*, Dec 1930; *Observer* (Adel), 25 Mar 1922, 6 June 1925; *Chronicle* (Adel), 4, 11 Sept 1930; *Argus*, 3 Sept 1930; records of Univ Adel *and* Univ Liverpool *and* Magdalen College, Oxford; Directorate of War Propaganda file (NL); newspaper cuttings (Univ Adel Archives).   V. A. EDGELOE

STRONG, WALTER MERSH (1873-1946), medical administrator, was born on 24 September 1873 at Camberwell, Surrey, England, son of Richard Strong, gentleman, and his wife Ellen Emma, née Mersh. Educated at Alleyn's College of God's Gift (Dulwich College), London, in 1892 he went to Trinity College, Cambridge (B.A., 1895; M.A., 1899; B.Ch. and M.B., 1903). His university career included first-class honours in the natural sciences tripos and election as a scholar in 1895. At St Thomas's Hospital, London, he earned his membership of the Royal College of Surgeons and a licentiate of the Royal College of Physicians (1903). In 1914 he gained the diploma of Tropical Health and Medicine.

At the age of 30 Strong joined the Daniells anthropological expedition to British New Guinea (later Papua) to investigate cancer. Although deployed as a doctor, he was attracted to ethnographic research and contributed to C. G. Seligman's *The Melanesians of British New Guinea* (1910). Disenchanted with the expedition, he resigned in Port Moresby in 1904 to become assistant resident magistrate at Kairuku, Central Division. His ethnographic interests persisted and his next publication, in the 1910-11 Papua *Annual Report*, was a note on languages of the North Eastern Division of Papua where he had been promoted resident magistrate in 1908.

In 1912 Strong was drawn back into medicine when Lieut-Governor (Sir) Hubert Murray [q.v.10] deputed him to investigate and control dysentery among Papuan labourers. The heavy attrition of administration doctors accelerated Strong's promotion to chief medical health and quarantine officer after World War I. He presided over a small staff and a budget which was inadequate at best (£18 175 in 1928) and dangerously so during the depressed 1930s when the allocation shrank to £13 758. Strong stretched minimal resources to maximum effect.

When he arrived in Papua the medical priority was to preserve the health of expatriates and to minister to indentured labourers, while guarding the quarantine chain. Papuans outside the formal workforce seldom troubled medical officers until the 1920s when the introduction of arsenical injections to treat yaws gave Western medicine a sudden popularity and imposed new demands on services. Mission personnel were taught to give these injections. Strong's pamphlets on dysentery and nutrition encouraged plantation managers to intervene in health matters. His most widely consulted pamphlet was the *Handbook on the treatment and prevention of disease in Papua when medical advice is unobtainable* (which is to say, most of the time). Medical resources were also supplemented by a Rockefeller Foundation grant to fund hookworm control.

During the Depression Strong proposed a programme for training Papuans as medical assistants. In 1933-35 he taught basic science to small groups, then dispatched them to the University of Sydney for several months in a course specially tailored by Dr F. W. Clements. Strong entrusted wide responsibilities to Papuans as extension workers and dispensers, thereby enlarging the reach of the department without bursting its slender budget. Resources were also husbanded by an implicit policy of disregarding women: Strong did not inquire into women's health issues from his ethnographic research of 1904 until he noticed mission medical work in the 1930s.

In the era before antibiotics, when Western medicine offered little to tropical populations, Strong was probably wise to insist upon quarantine and segregation as preventive tactics, since he had only Epsom salts and other purgatives for therapy. Political imperatives required disproportionate resources for the health of expatriates, but, by astute use of mission workers and Papuan medical assistants, he redirected effort and personnel to extension work among villagers.

Strong married Mary Gwendolen Evans, an English journalist, at Samarai on 5 February 1927, though she is not mentioned in his 1941 will. Tall, lean, bespectacled and aloof, he impressed and puzzled his Australian colleagues and Papuan subordinates. He was Murray's kind of man: not a narrow technician, but animated by wide-ranging curiosity. He doubled as government anthropologist until F. E. Williams [q.v.] was appointed in 1928. Strong's ethnographic work is now disregarded, but the Rockefeller Foundation representative Dr Sam Lambert (who criticized most other doctors) thought well of his medical abilities, and Murray (who admired his administrative skills) made him a member of Papua's Executive and Legislative councils from 1920. He retired in 1938 to a plantation near Rigo which he had acquired from Beatrice Grimshaw [q.v.9]. His expertise became redundant in an era of miracle drugs and bottomless budgets; even his Papuan medical assistants gradually leached out of medical work. In his own time, however, he embodied the most humane and effective approaches—as well as the narrow focus—of Western medicine. Strong died at his home near Port Moresby on 4 October 1946 and was buried in the local cemetery. Much of his estate, sworn for probate at £6669, was bequeathed to the University of Sydney for the education of Papuans and for medical research.

S. M. Lambert, *A doctor in paradise* (Lond, 1942); F. West (ed), *Selected letters of Hubert Murray* (Melb, 1970); V. H. Wallace, *The Wallace story* (Melb, 1973); E. Kettle, *That they might live* (priv pub, Syd, 1979); D. Denoon, *Public health in Papua New Guinea* (Cambridge, Eng, 1989) *and* 'Walter Mersh Strong', in B. G. Burton-Bradley (ed), The medical history of Papua New Guinea (ms held by author, Canb).   DONALD DENOON

STUART, ATHOL HUGH (1893-1954), journalist and general manager, was born on 19 May 1893 at Louth, Lincolnshire, England, elder son of Alexander Kedslie Stuart, chemist's assistant, and his wife Julia, née Gresswell. Educated at James Gillespie's Schools for Boys and Girls, Edinburgh, Hugh contributed articles to local newspapers from the age of 15. After being employed by the *Louth and North Lincolnshire News*, he migrated to Australia in 1913. He worked as a reporter for three years on the Lismore *Northern Star*, then, with a reference declaring him possessed of '*savoir faire* beyond his years', gained a similar position on the *Sydney Morning Herald*, published by John Fairfax & Sons [qq.v.4,8] Ltd.

During the next ten years Stuart distinguished himself as a graceful descriptive writer, sub-editor and occasional leader-writer. In 1926-28 he managed the Fairfax office in London; in 1930 he became the firm's assistant manager and in 1933 its general manager, responsible to the managing director, (Sir) Warwick Fairfax. That year he became a council-member of the Sydney Chamber of Commerce. Although Stuart's term as chief executive lasted only five years, it was notable for certain initiatives both inside and outside the firm. In 1933 the *Herald* responded to the challenge of the new *Australian Women's Weekly* by incorporating a weekly 24-page tabloid women's supplement; next year the company purchased S. Ure Smith's [q.v.11] magazines, *Art in Australia* and the *Home*.

After negotiations in which Sir Keith Murdoch [q.v.10] of the Herald and Weekly Times Ltd took the leading part and Stuart was closely involved, the two main organizations sending cable news from London—the Australian Press Association and the Sun-Herald Cable Service—were amalgamated in 1935 to form a non-profitmaking co-operative, Australian Associated Press Pty Ltd. In 1934 Stuart had suggested to Murdoch a merger between Paper Makers Pty Ltd, in which John Fairfax was the largest shareholder, and Derwent Valley Paper Pty Ltd. From that overture came Australian Newsprint Mills Ltd.

Stuart had sleek hair parted in the centre, widely spaced eyes and a plump face. He enjoyed golf and motoring and belonged to the Australian Club. His career ended abruptly in August 1938 when he was requested to resign on medical grounds. Diabetes may have contributed to the sudden and alarming change in his behaviour which finally obliged him to step down. In September he led a government-backed expedition to the Northern Territory to collect material for an exhibition in Sydney and was impressed by the potential for irrigation in the north. During the rest of his life Stuart, who was unmarried, caused his mother and brother such concern that in January 1942, on the brother's written request, he was declared insane and confined at Bayview, a licensed psychiatric hospital in Sydney. Nine months later the minister for health ordered Stuart's release. His period of con-

finement later provided material for the canard (spread in one notorious instance under parliamentary privilege on 23 March 1954 by a State attorney-general, W. F. Sheahan) that the Fairfax organization had 'incarcerated its former manager in a mental institution'. John Fairfax & Sons denied the allegation.

Stuart died of arteriosclerosis on 10 April 1954 in Winchester Private Hospital, Darlinghurst, and was cremated with Anglican rites.

G. Souter, *Company of Heralds* (Melb, 1981); *PD* (NSW), 23 Mar 1954; *Newspaper News* (Syd), 1 May 1954; *SMH*, 10 Oct 1942.   GAVIN SOUTER

STUART, FRANCIS (1844-1910), manufacturer and politician, was born on 21 May 1844 at Penrith, New South Wales, son of Robert Stuart, estate manager to Sir John Jamison [q.v.2], and his wife Elizabeth, née Matthews. At 13 Frank was apprenticed to a Sydney draper.

He next worked for a Penrith storekeeper and at 22 eloped with his employer's daughter, Matilda Coulter. They married in Sydney on 24 March 1866 and sailed for Melbourne where Stuart joined the fashionable Collins Street mercery store of Alston & Brown. After being employed by Dixon Bros, warehousemen of Flinders Lane, in 1871 he entered another 'Lane' softgoods firm, L. Stevenson & Sons. In 1884 he joined McIvor & Lincoln; on the death of the senior partner, Lincoln Stuart & Co., clothiers, was registered as a limited company in February 1889; when Lincoln retired, Stuart was sole proprietor. A prosperous business, among its early successes was a contract in 1885 to supply uniforms within seventeen days for the hastily raised New South Wales Sudan contingent. Alert to new opportunities, Stuart recognized possibilities in the rubber industry and joined with Barnet Glass & Sons Co. to manufacture waterproof clothing; he became a director of the company which was later taken over by Dunlop. Stuart was president (1885) of the Victorian Chamber of Manufactures and chairman (1887) of the Clothing and Manufacturers' Association.

In April 1889 he was elected with the free-trader, E. L. Zox [q.v.6], to the two-member seat of East Melbourne in the Victorian Legislative Assembly. When the Munro [q.v.10] ministry was formed on 5 November 1890 Stuart, with (Sir) Simon Fraser and (Sir) Alexander Peacock [qq.v.4,11], was appointed minister without portfolio. He resigned from the ministry in April 1891 and remained a private member until he lost his seat at the next election. Although a protectionist, he argued persistently for the duty-free import of goods which could not be produced locally. When he contested East Melbourne in 1894 the *Argus* described him as an advocate of tariff reform, while the protectionist *Age* denounced him for having stood on the Liberal ticket to become 'a mere Tory tool . . . a political prostitute of the worst sort. No Liberal can tolerate his return to the House with anything but loathing'.

A vigorous and long-standing advocate of intercolonial free trade, Stuart campaigned for Federation, particularly through the Australian Natives' Association. In June 1904 he was returned to the Legislative Council as member for North Melbourne. His parliamentary energies were concentrated on the improvement of education, public health and military training; he denounced dependence on London's money market, politically-motivated railway development, and French imperialism in the New Hebrides; and he opposed plural voting, property qualification, income tax and female suffrage. He resigned in May 1907 to have more time for business.

Stuart had speculated in real estate, registering 51 land titles in 1870-90, mostly in Hawthorn and at the Gippsland Lakes. He had retired from these ventures before the land boom reached its peak, but reduced his fortune by re-entering the market (in 1891-1910 he acquired 14 titles) and by guaranteeing colleagues who emerged bankrupt. Deciding in 1910 that 'land and shares is not our business', he liquidated all except two country properties to finance an imaginative walkway from Collins Street to Flinders Street railway station which was to be engineered by (Sir) John Monash [q.v.10].

'A stalwart man of average height' with a clean-shaven, square-set face and jaunty air, Stuart held a commission in the Victorian militia. He achieved acclaim as an oarsman, cyclist and marksman; he was founding captain of the Victoria Golf Club and a pioneer motorist who drove in the 1905 Sydney to Melbourne Dunlop Reliability Trial. A voracious reader, he founded the Melbourne Beefsteak Club, patronized the arts and funded Bertram Mackennal's [q.v.10] move to Paris. Stuart was an ardent Australian nationalist and proud of being country-born. Although an enthusiastic subject of Queen Victoria, he criticized Imperial strategy in the Pacific and declared that Switzerland had shown that republicanism was 'the right form of government'.

Returning from a world tour, Frank Stuart died of a cerebral haemorrhage on 16 October 1910 in the *Otranto* and was buried at sea off Aden. His wife and three sons survived him. His property Nyerimilang, Lakes Entrance, Victoria, became a national park.

J. F. Deegan, *The chronicles of the Melbourne Beefsteak Club 1886-89* (Melb, 1890); J. Smith (ed), *Cyclopedia of Victoria*, 1 (Melb, 1903); *Table Talk*, 7 Aug 1891, 18 Mar 1892; *Argus*, 21 Oct 1910; *Australasian*, 22 Oct 1910; Stuart correspondence (held by author, Canb).   FRANCIS STUART

STUART, HERBERT AKROYD (1864-1927), mechanical engineer, was born on 28 January 1864 at Halifax, Yorkshire, England, son of Charles Stuart, machinists' model-maker, and his wife Ann, née Akroyd. He attended Newbury Grammar School, Berkshire, and the City and Guilds Technical College, Finsbury, where he assisted in the mechanical engineering department, and later worked in his father's Bletchley Iron and Tinplate Works which he managed after Charles's death.

Various experiments in engineering led Stuart to take out several patents. One day in 1885 he accidentally spilt oil from a paraffin lamp into a pot of molten tin. The oil vaporized, rose to the lamp and burst into flame. In his words, 'that lucky incident . . . gave me a clear insight . . . as to what happens when oil vapour is commingled with air and ignited. Straightaway, I began to think out a scheme . . . to design an engine to work on oil vapour'.

After further tests, in 1890 he and Charles Binney patented their 'Improvements in engines operated by the explosion of mixtures of combustible vapour or gas and air'. What followed was the Hornsby-Akroyd hot-bulb heavy-oil engine, constructed by Richard Hornsby & Sons who gained production rights next year. Their engine drew only air into the cylinder and compressed it, with the oil being injected at the end of the compression stroke. The first of its type, the engine proved a success: some operated for over sixty years. Manufactured under the Hornsby-Akroyd name, an oil engine for use in a military tractor earned Stuart a prize of £1180 from the British War Office in 1903. *Strand* magazine was to describe it in 1917 as 'the first definite proposal for a fighting machine on the lines of the existing tank'.

Having migrated to Western Australia in 1900, he joined his brother Charles who helped to form the engineering firm Saunders & Stuart; interested in gas producers, Herbert designed a highly successful unit operating on the downdraft system, using wood as fuel.

He maintained that he was the inventor of the compression ignition oil engine, ahead of Dr Rudolf Diesel whose German patents were taken out two years after Stuart's and who produced a successful engine some seven years after the Hornsby-Akroyd. Stuart's claim was supported by many, including his friend Professor William Robinson who tested several original Akroyd oil engines. To help establish his claim, Stuart made substantial bequests to the universities of Western Australia and Nottingham, and to the Institution of Mechanical Engineers, the Royal Aeronautical Society and the Institute of Marine Engineers, England. Income from the bequests is used for the Herbert Akroyd Stuart lectures on the origin and development of heavy oil engines. Modern oil engines use Stuart's method of oil-pump spray injection with constant volume burning in preference to the Diesel method of air-blast injection with constant pressure burning.

A courteous and gentle man who never married, Stuart was somewhat embittered by lack of recognition of his work. He died of throat cancer on 19 February 1927 at his home Akroydon, Claremont, Perth, and was buried in the cemetery of All Souls Anglican Church, Akroydon, Halifax, England. His will directed that his papers, drawings and models be burnt. In 1964 the local archaelogical and historical society unveiled a stone tablet at Bletchley to mark the centenary of his birth.

West Australian, 23 Feb 1927; H. A. Stuart files *and* correspondence *and* reports of Dr A. T. Bowden (held by Dept of Mechanical Engineering, Univ WA.   G. G. LUTZ

STUART, JOHN (JULIAN) ALEXANDER SALMON (1866-1929), trade unionist, journalist, poet and politician, was born on 18 December 1866 at Eagleton, New South Wales, seventh of ten children of Scottish-born parents, Donald Stuart, farmer, and his wife Amelia, née McPherson. Christened John, he was to change his name to Julian, thinking it more fitting for a poet. The family moved to small farms on the Hunter and Clarence rivers. In Sydney in 1884-87 Julian trained as a teacher, but resigned after two years. Influenced by William Lane [q.v.9] and by an Irish-American striker, Stuart took a fencing contract and belonged to the Queensland Labourers' Union in 1889 when three of his fellows at Burenda were charged with rioting. At the Blackall union meeting in 1890 he proposed 'a scheme for better organising, which the failure of the watersiders had proved necessary'.

Next year Stuart was chairman of the shearers' camp at Clermont. Arrested on a charge of conspiracy, he was tried with other union leaders at Rockhampton in May. Twelve of them, including Stuart, were sentenced to three years imprisonment with hard labour. He described the judge, George Harding [q.v.4], as 'venomous and vindictive and bloodthirsty'. Released in 1894, Stuart married Rhoda Florence Collings (d. 1932), a singer and sister of J. S. Collings [q.v.8], on 4 September 1895 in the General Registry Office, Brisbane. After a brief period organizing for the Labor Electoral League, Stuart went to the goldfields of Western Australia where he prospected and held offices in the Australian Workers' Association. He was secretary, manager and editor of the *Westralian Worker* (Kalgoorlie) in 1903-06 and represented Leonora in the Legislative Assembly in 1906-08: the newspaper referred to his 'caustic criticism of the Parliamentary Labor Party's methods and policy'. In 1908 the *Worker*'s board accused him of misappropriating £16. Protesting that he was guilty only of carelessness, Stuart continued campaigning for his seat at that year's election, but his nomination was invalidated because he had not lodged the deposit.

He became a timberworker: an accident in 1919 blinded him in one eye; another in 1923 paralysed his right hand. He then wrote for such newspapers as the *Brisbane Worker* and the *Western Mail*. His earlier prose and poetry had appeared in a range of publications, among them the *Bulletin* and the *Coolgardie Miner,* sometimes under the pseudonyms of 'Curlew' and 'Saladin'. Much of it reflected his lifelong interest in working men and women:

> I am deformed by labor
> I am the working man
> Cursing the fate that holds me
> A dull-browed Caliban

Another poem, 'A brand of shame' (1905), condemned the way in which Aborigines had been treated.

Stuart's wife also wrote for the *Worker,* as 'Hypatia' and 'Adohr'; their six children included the writers Lyndall Hadow and Donald Stuart. Handsome and strong in his heyday, Julian Stuart was about six feet (182.9 cm) tall. He died of 'hemiplegia and asthma' on 3 July 1929 in Perth and was buried in Karrakatta cemetery. Frank Spruhan described him as 'the strongest character we had. He never let up . . . even the staunchest of them Labor MPs were too mild for Julian'.

J. Stuart, *Part of the glory* (Syd, 1967); D. Grant, 'Literary journalism', in B. Bennett (ed), *The literature of Western Australia* (Perth, 1979); *PD* (WA), 29 July 1908; *Westerly,* Mar 1977, no 1, p 80; *West Australian,* 18 Aug 1908, 5 July 1929; *Sun* (Kalgoorlie), 27 Sept 1908; *Westralian Worker,* 26 Oct 1906, 28 Aug 1908, 5 Dec 1919, 12 July 1929; *Daily Standard,* 21 July 1923; *Kalgoorlie Miner,* 4 Sept 1929; *Aust Worker,* 10 July 1929.
                                        DONALD GRANT

STUART, SIR THOMAS PETER ANDERSON (1856-1920), professor of physiology and medical administrator, was born on 20 June 1856 at Dumfries, Scotland, son of Alexander Stuart, master clothier and tailor, and his wife Jane, née Anderson. The only child of Alexander's second marriage, Thomas had one surviving half-sister, Annie, whose mother and three brothers had died of tuberculosis. His father was a member of the town council and a local magistrate.

Educated at Dumfries Academy until aged 14, Anderson Stuart was apprenticed to a pharmacist. He passed his preliminary examinations at 16, but was prevented by regulations from sitting for his finals until he reached the age of 21. In 1874 he passed the preliminary examinations for entry into medicine at the University of Edinburgh (M.B., C.M., 1880; M.D., 1882). He spent a year at a gymnasium at Wolfenbüttel, Germany, improving his French and German, and late in 1875 returned to Edinburgh. He did brilliantly, winning ten medals in various subjects, and topped his final year in 1880 with first-class honours and a gold medal. Thereafter he spent a year at Strassburg, studying biochemistry and pharmacology under the celebrated Felix Hoppe-Seyler and Oswald Schmiedeberg. In Schmiedeberg's laboratory he studied the physiological properties of the salts of nickel and cobalt, work that he later wrote up as his doctoral thesis which won him another gold medal. Becoming chief demonstrator in 1881 to William Rutherford, professor of physiology at Edinburgh, in mid-1882 he accepted the chair of anatomy and physiology at the University of Sydney.

In Edinburgh on 21 November Anderson Stuart married Elizabeth (Lizza) Ainslie with Church of Scotland forms; they embarked in the *Parramatta*, arriving in Sydney in March 1883. He began work in a four-room, stuccoed-brick cottage (on the site of what is now called the Old Geology Building) which he shared with W. J. Stephens [q.v.6], professor of natural history. Within a year he had displaced Stephens and had had constructed an annexe containing a lecture room, mortuary and dissecting theatre. Beginning with a standard of excellence that he wished to see maintained, he failed the six students in the first intake (one eventually graduated), but six of the ten students who enrolled in 1884 managed to graduate. In his teaching he was assisted by Stephens, Archibald Liversidge, professor of chemistry, W. A. Haswell and (Sir) Alexander MacCormick [qq.v.5,9,10], a former classmate whom he engaged as demonstrator in 1883.

As early as March that year Anderson Stuart had asked the university senate to approach the government for funds for a better building; in June 1884 the university agreed to build a permanent medical school. Plans drawn up by James Barnet [q.v.3], the government architect, were approved in November and the government granted £15 000 towards construction in 1885. Anderson Stuart claimed to have used the original allocation to lay the foundations of a much larger and grander building than the senate and government had envisaged. By April 1889, at a cost of £65 000, it was substantially complete, although interior fitting out continued until 1892 and cost a further £15 000. Barnet's structure, forming the south range of the old medical school as it now stands, is a masterpiece of Victorian Gothic Revival.

The years 1883-1912 were ones of extraordinary activity for Anderson Stuart, dean of medicine from 1891 and fellow of the senate (1883-1920): the undergraduate enrolment in medicine rose from 6 to 604 and staff also increased substantially. Drawing heavily on Edinburgh, his appointments—among whom were the foundation professors of anatomy (J. T. Wilson [q.v.] in 1890) and pathology (D. A. Welsh [q.v.] in 1902)—included several highly talented scientists: Wilson, (Sir) Almroth Wright and (Sir) Charles Martin [q.v.10], all of whom became fellows of the Royal Society (London). Anderson Stuart, known to the undergraduates as 'Andy', was an illuminating lecturer, 'plain, direct, concise', who took infinite pains preparing his blackboard diagrams and founded the Sydney University Medical Society to assist students. He even managed some modest research activity of his own (on the structure of the eye and on the function of the epiglottis and larynx), although his colleagues disparaged his efforts and considered him to be antipathetic to research.

In 1901, in succession to Sir Alfred Roberts [q.v.6] and Wilson, he was appointed honorary secretary, soon chairman, of (Royal) Prince Alfred Hospital, with William Epps (who was destined to become his biographer) as paid secretary. Henceforward, Anderson Stuart's attention was focused on the development of the hospital and he increasingly came to rely on H. G. Chapman [q.v.7] for the administration of the medical school. In the 1900s Anderson Stuart devoted himself to a massive building programme: in 1904 the Victoria and Albert pavilions were built to flank G. A. Mansfield's central block. Anderson Stuart had given the country another important institution, as well as an architectural monument of elegance and grandeur.

In addition to his university posts, from 1893 to 1896 he was medical advisor to the government, emigration officer for Port Jackson and president of the Board of Health; after 1896, when he was displaced as president, he remained a member of the board until his death. An 'obsessive, even compulsive, organizer', at various times he was president of such community organizations as the Highland Society, the Royal and (Royal) Zoological societies of New South Wales, the Civil Ambulance and Transport Brigade, the British Seaman's Guild and the local branch of the British Immigration League of Australia; he was, as well, a founding executive-member of the State division of the British Red Cross Society (1914). A Freemason, he was deputy grand master of United Grand Lodge of New South Wales. He belonged to the Union and Australian clubs, and was even patron of the Double Bay Pastime Cricket Club! Within the university he was largely responsible for the establishment of the school of dentistry (1901) and in 1905 became the first president of the United Dental Hospital of Sydney, having overcome the opposition of American-trained dentists led by Henry Peach [q.v.11]. Anderson Stuart was also to the fore in establishing the department of veterinary science (1909).

His private life was less successful. Anderson Stuart's marriage, which remained childless, was a failure from the start. On 28 February 1886 his wife died from an overdose of morphia in their home at 10 Toxteth Road, Glebe. At the time Anderson Stuart had left her and was staying at the house of Robert Scot Skirving [q.v.11] to whom he had spoken of his plans for divorce. Although Anderson Stuart was not directly involved in his wife's death, it was evident that many people, including the coroner's jury who returned an open verdict, felt that he was morally responsible. On 18 September 1894 at St James's Anglican Church, Toowoomba, Queensland, he married 19-year-old Dorothy Primrose, a granddaughter of Bouviere Primrose who was an uncle of Lord Rosebery [q.v.5 Primrose]. The newlyweds lived in Lincludin, a fine house in Fairfax Road, Double Bay.

With the 'profile of an imperious Roman and an enormous fund of self-confidence', Anderson Stuart was a man of drive, energy and vision who made many enemies. He was involved in dissension with Frances Holden [q.v.9], lady superintendent of the Hospital for Sick Children, and in 1887 was cleared of her allegation that he had neglected a patient. His support for the acceptance of women into medicine on a basis of equality with men, and for the award of bursaries to deserving but impoverished students, brought him only obloquy. His vision and sense of social justice must be weighed against his arrogance, ruthlessness and determination always to prevail over opposition. Anderson Stuart's 'long-standing dislike of and antagonism to' Thomas Storie Dixson [q.v.8] led him into complicated manoeuvres that resulted in the unceremonious abolition of Dixson's materia medica lectureship in December 1917 and in the appointment of his own protégé Chapman to the chair of pharmacology.

Not all with whom Anderson Stuart worked were his enemies: his career at the university was also aided by allies of whom the greatest was his fellow Edinburgh graduate, Sir Normand MacLaurin [q.v.10], chancellor of the university in 1896-1913. With his unswerving support, Anderson Stuart became the virtual dictator of things medical in Sydney. He received honorary doctorates from the universities of Edinburgh (LL.D., 1900) and Durham (D.Sc., 1912), and was knighted in 1914.

Although Sir Thomas destroyed his personal papers, on his death-bed he dictated lengthy biographical memoirs to Epps. Anderson Stuart died at his Double Bay home on 29 February 1920, eleven months after the diagnosis of an inoperable abdominal cancer, attended by MacCormick and Scot Skirving. He was buried in the Presbyterian section of South Head cemetery. His wife and their four sons, two of whom became medical practitioners, survived him.

While he did little to further the discipline of physiology, Anderson Stuart did much for medicine in Sydney. He created one of the most important medical schools in the Empire outside Britain. The Victoria and Albert pavilions at R.P.A.H. and the old medical school building at the university are appropriate monuments to his greatness. Marble busts of Anderson Stuart by James White [q.v.] are held by R.P.A.H. and by the University of Sydney which also holds a fine portrait by John Longstaff [q.v.10]. Anderson Stuart is also remembered by various details on the medical school building which was formally named after him in January 1960: his arms surmount the eastern portal; his crest is on a gable on the north-west range and rendered in stained glass beside the south portal. Most curious of all, he is represented as a stone crow, sculptured by Tomaso Sani [q.v.6], high above the eastern portal, commemorating his student nickname ('Coracoid', from the Latin *corax*, a crow) earned because of his prominent nose and somewhat priggish personality.

W. Epps, *Anderson Stuart M.D.* (Syd, 1922); H. M. Moran, *Viewless winds* (Lond, 1939); A. R. Chisholm, *Men were my milestones* (Melb, 1958); J. A. Young et al (eds), *Centenary book of the University of Sydney faculty of medicine* (Syd, 1984); A. Macintosh, *Memories of Dr Robert Scot Skirving 1859-1956* (Syd, 1988); *Syd Univ Medical J*, Mar 1920, p 186; Syd Univ Students' Representative Council, *Hermes*, May 1920, p 31; Syd Univ Post-graduate Cttee of Medicine, *Bulletin*, 1948, no 4, p 105; *SMH*, 6 Mar 1886; T. P. Anderson Stuart, Common place book (Academy of Science Lib, Canb) *and* Undergraduate lecture-notes (Roy A'sian College of Physicians, Syd); J. Shewan, Note-book of Anderson Stuart's lectures (Fisher Lib).

J. ATHERTON YOUNG

STUART, WILLIAM (1860-1940), builder, was born on 13 December 1860 at Lumsden, Aberdeenshire, Scotland, son of Alexander Stuart, carpenter, and his wife Ann, née Grant. Educated at the Mechanics' School of Arts, Aberdeen, he came to Sydney in 1882. After working briefly as a joiner for Smith & Bennett he went to western New South Wales. On 6 November 1883 he married Sarah Jane Whittaker at Blayney. Back in Sydney, in 1886 with his brother James he founded Stuart Bros, builders.

Their first job was altering the Sydney Mechanics' School of Arts. The firm went on to build numerous woolstores, offices for the *Sydney Morning Herald, Evening News,* Colonial Sugar Refining Co. and Commercial Banking Co. of Sydney, stores, theatres and two pavilions at the showground. In undertaking such projects Stuart Bros made itself as independent as possible with its own quarries and joinery works; it oversaw all parts of the building process; at one time it claimed to employ 1000 men. After the death of James in 1914, two of William's sons joined the business.

Despite his Scottish ancestry, William looked to North America for models and often visited there to keep abreast of developments. The introduction of 'modern stone facings' for buildings and the early use of welding in structural steel were among his innovations: the offices of Union Steamship Co. of New Zealand in George Street were claimed to be the first large concrete structure in Sydney (c. 1912).

Deeply involved in his business, Stuart shunned politics. He strongly supported the Master Builders' Association (president, 1896) and, as a founder and vice-president of the Employers' Federation of New South Wales, actively promoted a viable arbitration system with the building workforce. He was a founder of the Sun Newspaper Ltd, Sydney Steel Co. Ltd and New South Wales Brick Co. Ltd. He also endowed a ward at the Royal Alexandra Hospital for Children, was a trustee of the Sydney Cricket Ground and represented the city commissioners on the Metropolitan Water, Sewerage and Drainage Board (1928-31).

A short, slightly stooped man, with a drooping moustache, Stuart projected a quiet and thoughtful air. His main interests were boating and motoring, although he never learned to drive a car. He belonged to the (Royal) Automobile Club of Australia and the Highland Society of New South Wales. Retiring from active involvement with Stuart Bros in 1930, he died on 7 December 1940 at his home, Glenhurst, Yarranabbe Road, Darling Point, and was buried in the Presbyterian section of South Head cemetery. His wife, one of his three sons, and three daughters survived him.

Home, June 1925; *Building* (Syd), Dec 1940; *SMH,* 22 June 1914, 9 Dec 1940; Stuart Bros, Plans (Faculty of Architecture, Univ Syd).

TERRY KASS

STURGESS, REGINALD WARD (1892-1932), artist, was born on 18 June 1892 at Newport, Melbourne, third surviving child of Edward Richard Sturgess, cabinetmaker, and his wife Emma, née Ward, both from Bath, England. Aged 12, he left Williamstown State School and later enrolled (1905) in the National Gallery schools, Melbourne, where he studied drawing under Fred McCubbin [q.v.10] and was nicknamed 'Stodgy'. In 1909 Sturgess moved upstairs to the painting school under L. Bernard Hall [q.v.9], winning prizes for still life and landscape painting in oils. Penleigh Boyd, Louis McCubbin, Percy Leason, W. B. McInnes, John Rowell [qq.v.7,10,11] and A. E. Newbury were among his fellow students.

An admirer of the works of R. P. Bonington, J. S. Cotman and the Maris brothers, Sturgess was also influenced by the illustrations of Edmund Dulac and Harry Rountree and by the Art Nouveau movement. When he left the gallery schools in 1912 he painted in every spare moment, often working late at night and striving for perfection in fluency of wash and colour harmony. During this period he produced decorative lampshades, for which he had a constant and lucrative market until the outbreak of World War I. He also assisted his father with his seedsman's business at Williamstown; after his father's death in 1916, Sturgess managed alone until 1926 when he closed the shop. Only then was he able to concentrate entirely on his painting. On 30 July 1917 at St John's Anglican Church, Malmsbury, he had married Meta Townsend, a prizewinning student at the gallery schools (1909-14).

Modest about his work, Sturgess had been persuaded to show a few examples at the Victorian Artists' Society. While these attracted considerable attention, it was not until July 1922, at the Athenaeum Gallery, that he held his first one-man exhibition. Encouraged by the response, he then exhibited regularly, mostly at the Fine Art Society's gallery, Melbourne, but also in Adelaide (1926-27) and Sydney (1928-29). He lived in close retirement and worked prodigiously. Concerned with effects of nature rather than localities, he had little need of travel to find subject matter: his favourite haunts were the Malmsbury district, the You Yangs region and his native Williamstown. His work was romantic, delicate and lyrical, and had an affinity with that of J. J. Hilder [q.v.9].

A 'rare spirit' of 'strong individuality and charm', Sturgess was intense and a free-thinker. Tall, broad shouldered and very thin, he had great energy and allowed himself little rest. He shared a deep love of music with his close friend Frank Homewood. In 1926 Sturgess was injured in a motor accident and his jaw was broken; although he recovered, his health deteriorated; his fading eyesight finally forced him to put away his brushes and paints in 1930. He died at his Williamstown home on 2 July 1932 of a cerebral tumour and was buried in the local cemetery. His wife and daughter survived him. He is represented in State galleries in Victoria, South Australia and Queensland, as well as in various regional galleries in Victoria.

R. H. Croll, *The life and work of R. W. Sturgess* (Melb, 1938); P. Perry and B. Sinclair, *R. W. Sturgess, water-colourist 1892-1932* (Castlemaine, Vic, 1986); *Herald* (Melb), 5, 6 July 1932; *Bulletin*, 20 July 1932.
PETER W. PERRY

STYLES, JAMES (1841-1913), contractor, civil engineer and politician, was born on 3 July 1841 at Croydon, Surrey, England, son of William Styles, labourer, and his wife Harriet, née Friend. In 1849 the family arrived in Melbourne where James was educated at St James's Church of England Grammar School and the Protestant Hall. He then worked for a railway contractor. In 1861 he joined his father in Brisbane where they took jobs as contractors for municipal street and sewerage works. Styles was next employed by the English firm of Peto, Brassey & Betts on the construction of the Ipswich-Toowoomba railway and subsequently by Styles, Murray & Co. on the Toowoomba-Dalby line. On 23 February 1865 he married Irish-born Teresa Dignam at Rockhampton with Presbyterian forms.

Returning to Victoria in 1869 Styles undertook contracting and engineering work on the Seymour-Benalla and Oakleigh-Bunyip railways. In 1877-78 he was employed by the South Australian government as resident engineer and agent on the Burra-Hallett extension. He later carried out contracts for government water-supply works and major portions of the Adelaide sewerage system. By 1883 Styles was again in Victoria, living at Williamstown, and carrying out reclamation contracts for the Melbourne Harbour Trust and the Department of Public Works. In 1889 he gave up contracting, but continued to work as a consulting engineer and arbitrator.

In 1885-88 and 1890-1901 Styles was a member of the Williamstown Municipal Council and represented it in 1891 on the new Melbourne and Metropolitan Board of Works; in the same year he applied unsuccessfully for the post of chairman of the board. He remained on the board until 1901 and, in 1891-94, chaired its sewerage committee. His pamphlet, *A lecture on sanitary reform for greater Melbourne* (1888), anticipated James Mansergh's [q.v.5] suggestions for constructing a sewerage system. In 1890 he criticized elements of Mansergh's scheme; over the next decade he clashed frequently with the board's chairman, E. G. FitzGibbon [q.v.4], and the chief engineer, William Thwaites [q.v.], and condemned their extravagance. He, in turn, was accused of being a mere 'amateur'. Styles served on the Melbourne Harbour Trust in 1891-94 and the Board of Health in 1896-1912. He was a life member of the Society of Engineers, London.

After contesting the Legislative Assembly seat of Williamstown unsuccessfully in 1889 and 1892, Styles won it in 1894. He served on the standing committee on railways in 1897-1900. Defeated in 1900, he was elected next year to the Commonwealth Senate as a protectionist. He was a member of the select committee on tobacco monopoly (1905) and of the select committee (1904) and royal commission (1906-07) into old-age pensions. Defeated again in 1906, he took no further part in politics. Having supported the Labor Party in the assembly, he remained strongly sympathetic to Labor in the Senate. Styles was partially crippled. Melbourne *Punch* described him as having 'no exceptional endowments'; his strengths were industry, perseverance and 'a passion for details'. As a speaker he was 'lucid though long-winded' and often 'serenely self-satisfied'. Survived by his wife, son and a daughter, Styles died at his Hawthorn home on 4 February 1913 and was buried in Boroondara cemetery with Anglican rites.

Daily Telegraph (Melb), 30 Sept, 1, 2, 6 Oct 1890; *Table Talk*, 3 Nov 1894, 18 Apr 1901; *Punch* (Melb), 16 Aug 1906; Melb and Metropolitan Bd of Works records (held by Bd of Works, Melb).
GEOFF BROWNE

SUGDEN, EDWARD HOLDSWORTH (1854-1935), clergyman and educationist, was born on 19 June 1854 at Ecclesfield, Yorkshire, England, eldest son of Rev. James Sugden, Wesleyan minister, and his wife Sarah, née Holdsworth. Edward was educated at Woodhouse Grove, a boarding school between Bradford and Leeds for the sons of Wesleyan Methodist ministers. Life was spartan and discipline severe, but the teaching sound and thorough, and in his final year in

1870 he won the Gilchrist scholarship to Owens College, Manchester, where he read for University of London degrees (B.A., 1872; B.Sc., 1876). In 1874 he was accepted for training as a Wesleyan Methodist minister at Headingley Theological College, Leeds, where he was also tutor in classics, an appointment rare for one so young. After seven years at Headingley he served as a minister in two circuits in the Bradford area. In 1887 Sugden was appointed master of the new Queen's College at the University of Melbourne.

Some Methodists feared that, by combining their theological institution with a university college, the religious zeal of their theological students might be dissipated by secular learning. That these fears proved groundless and that this first Methodist theological institution was to become the most influential in Australia, were due in a large measure to Sugden in whose personality the evangelical zeal of Wesley and the humanism of the university tradition were in accord. He came to hold the two highest offices of Australian Methodism: president of the Victorian and Tasmanian conference in 1906 and president general of the Methodist Church of Australasia in 1923-26. On the other hand he was equally at home and accepted in the university and among his friends in the Melbourne Beefsteak Club. A fellow member wrote, 'No one has ever been found to suggest that he was a bad parson or a bad Methodist. At the same time, he is a man of the world, a man of science, a musical enthusiast and a universal favourite'. Ecumenical in outlook, he initiated joint theological teaching with the Baptists from 1895 and with the Congregationalists from 1902. He encouraged the theological students of different denominations to form a combined theological students' association and to participate in the Student Christian Union. He was a liberal in the British political sense and brought to Melbourne the spirit which had made the nonconformist conscience so influential in British politics. Soon after his arrival, Sugden began a Sunday evening Peoples' Service at Wesley Church, Lonsdale Street, which became a centre for evangelism, fellowship and social welfare on the model of similar centres in British cities. It led to the founding of the Wesley Central Mission in 1893.

Sugden stamped his personality on the college of which he was master for forty years. From his closest friend and mentor, Benjamin Hellier, governor of Headingley College, he adopted the precept of trying to find something in every person that he could respect, and to build on that. Sugden expected the best from those in his charge, yet he was tolerant and understanding of their failures. For him the college was a family wherein the older members provided a supportive environment in which the younger could develop their talents and sense of social responsibility. To successive generations of Queen's students, tutors and masters, this characteristic was accepted and upheld as the Sugden tradition. Sugden gathered around him distinguished scholars and involved them in the life of the college. The first honorary fellows included three anthropologists of world stature, Lorimer Fison, William Howitt [qq.v.4], and (Sir) Baldwin Spencer [q.v.]. Among professors newly appointed to the university from overseas whom he welcomed as resident members were William Ralph Boyce Gibson [q.v.8], Harold Woodruff, (Sir) Robert Wallace [qq.v.] and (Sir) Samuel Wadham.

An influential figure in university affairs, in 1891 Sugden was appointed a founding member of the University Extension Board. In 1900 he refused to join his fellow heads of church schools and university colleges when, under the leadership of Dr Leeper [q.v.10] of Trinity, they petitioned the university council not to renew G. W. Marshall-Hall's [q.v.10] appointment on the grounds that he was unacceptable as a teacher of the young—especially young women—because he had published a book of love lyrics which paraphrased *Hymns Ancient and Modern*. On the day the petition was to be presented, Sugden published a letter in the *Argus* stating that, as a member of Marshall-Hall's conservatorium orchestra and father of a daughter who took his classes, he had never heard anything objectionable or immoral in the professor's conduct. Two months later Sugden's stand was vindicated when he defeated Judge Molesworth [q.v.5] in an election to the university council which reflected the division on the Marshall-Hall question. He remained a member of the council until 1925.

A Liberal Imperialist, at the age of sixty Sugden offered his services on the outbreak of World War I. He was appointed chaplain with the rank of captain and throughout the war spent half of each working day ministering to the troops in training at Royal Park. He was not a jingoist, but his students had no doubt that he thought they should enlist. Sugden was chairman of the committee of the University Conservatorium of Music and a member of the university council when, in the fever that followed the first casualty lists from Gallipoli, Leeper moved for the immediate dismissal of two German nationals from the university staff, one of them, Edward Scharf, a teacher at the conservatorium. While MacFarland, Masson [qq.v.10] and others opposed this motion, Sugden supported L. A. Adamson's [q.v.7] motion that the appointments be not renewed when they expired in December 1915. When that time came, as chairman of the conservatorium committee Sugden moved the termination of Scharf's appointment, though he would have preferred it to be deferred.

Apart from his vocation as a preacher and pastor, Sugden had three passions: literature, the theatre and music. His tutorials in literature at Queen's were legendary, attracting students from the other colleges and non-residents from the university. Twice Sugden took charge of teaching in the English department. From his youth he had been an avid book-collector and his library of first editions of John Wesley's works, which he donated to the college, was among the best in the world. He was a trustee of the Public Library, museums and National Gallery of Victoria from 1902 and its president in 1933-35, and he was the first chairman of Melbourne University Press in 1922-25. His own publications included translations from the classics, a metrical edition of the Psalms, an edition of Wesley's sermons, and, with (Sir) Frederic Eggleston [q.v.8], a biography of George Swinburne [q.v.] (1931). His major book, for which he was awarded a Litt.D. (1918) from the University of Melbourne, was *A topographical dictionary of the works of Shakespeare and his fellow dramatists* (1925), a standard reference, but one that did not offer scope for those qualities for which he was most admired —wisdom, humour and literary expression. In 1911 he was president of the educational and mental science section of the Australasian Association for the Advancement of Science meeting in Sydney. He was president of the Melbourne Shakespeare Society in 1914-15.

On the college foundation day each year he directed the students in the production of a play, usually Shakespearean, which gained the college a reputation for the quality of its productions. It was in music, however, that he excelled. As a student at Owens College he had been a pupil of (Sir) John Frederick Bridge, organist of Manchester Cathedral and later of Westminster Abbey. Sugden had sung in the Leeds Festival Choir and conducted combined choirs in Bradford and Melbourne. He played the viola in Marshall-Hall's orchestra and in informal string quartets. In 1904-12 he was music critic for the *Argus* and *Australasian*, and from 1915 enjoyed a close association with Dr A. E. Floyd [q.v.8], organist and choir master of St Paul's Cathedral, Melbourne.

Sugden retired from Queen's in 1928 and visited England to deliver the Fernley Lecture to the British Methodist Conference, published as *Israel's debt to Egypt* (1928). He died at his Hawthorn home on 22 July 1935 and was buried in Melbourne general cemetery. Sugden married twice. His first wife, Mary Florence, née Brooke, whom he had married at Stockport, Cheshire, England, on

22 August 1878, died in childbirth in 1883. On 27 October 1886 he had married Ruth Hannah Thompson at Bradford, Yorkshire, England. She predeceased him in 1932. Three daughters of each marriage survived him.

Sugden was a big man, fair, fresh complexioned, with a charming smile. In later life he suffered arthritis of the hips and was confined to a wheel-chair. A member of the Metropolitan Golf Club, he was a keen follower of other sports, especially cricket. There are two portraits of him by Charles Wheeler [q.v.], one at Queen's College painted in 1910, the other in the National Gallery of Victoria.

M. F. Sugden, *Edward H. Sugden* (Melb, 1941); *Methodist Mag* (Lond), 145, Oct 1922, p 727; *Age* and *Argus*, 23 July 1935; Sugden papers (Queen's College Archives, Melb).   OWEN PARNABY

SULLIVAN, ARTHUR PERCY (1896-1937), soldier and banker, was born on 27 November 1896 at Prospect, Adelaide, son of Arthur Monks Sullivan, storekeeper, and his wife Eliza, née Dobbs. Educated at Crystal Brook Public School and Gladstone High School, he joined the National Bank of Australasia at Gladstone in 1913 and was transferred to Broken Hill, New South Wales, and then to Maitland, South Australia.

Sullivan enlisted as a private in the Australian Imperial Force on 27 April 1918 and embarked in July as a general reinforcement. He transferred on 5 October to the artillery, but the war was over before he was allotted to a unit in France. Promoted acting corporal on 23 May 1919, he joined the British North Russia Relief Force five days later and was officially discharged from the A.I.F. on 12 June. The relief force landed at Archangel in June and July, and relieved most of the original 1918 expeditionary force which included nine A.I.F. members. Sullivan was with the 45th Battalion, Royal Fusiliers, in L. W. de V. Sadleir-Jackson's brigade which moved 150 miles (241 km) down the Dvina River.

On 10 August the British attacked on the Dvina front in order to demoralize and disorganize the Bolsheviks and so give time for an unhindered evacuation of North Russia. During the attack, which was a complete success with minimal British casualties, Sullivan won the Victoria Cross. His unit was cut off and, while fighting their way back to their lines, an officer and three men fell from a narrow plank into a deep swamp on the Sheika River. Without hesitation and under intense fire, Sullivan jumped into the water and rescued all four, bringing them out singly. The evacuation was completed by late September and the relief force was demobilized in England.

Sullivan left for Australia on 1 November without waiting to be decorated by the King. He was presented with the V.C. in Adelaide in April 1920 during the tour of the Prince of Wales who smiled and said to Sullivan: 'Aren't you the man who ran away from father?'

Known as the 'Shy V.C.', Sullivan was a popular personality. At Fairfield, Melbourne, he married Dorothy Frances Veale with Anglican rites on 5 December 1928; they were to have three children, including twins. After the war Sullivan had rejoined the National Bank and in 1929 moved to its Sydney office; in July 1934 he was appointed manager of the Casino branch. He joined the Australian contingent to the coronation of King George VI and took with him the ashes of British V.C. winner Sergeant Arthur Evans who had died in Australia. On 9 April 1937, eleven days after handing over these remains, Sullivan died when he accidentally slipped and struck his head against a kerb in Birdcage Walk near Wellington Barracks, London. After a military funeral, his ashes were returned to Australia and placed in the Northern Suburbs crematorium, Sydney. In 1939 a memorial plaque was erected on the gates of Wellington Barracks. His wife died in 1980, leaving his V.C. to the Australian War Memorial where it is displayed in the Hall of Valour.

L. Wigmore (ed), *They dared mightily*, second ed revised and condensed by J. Williams and A. Staunton (Canb, 1986); *Reveille* (Syd), July 1966, p 11; *Defence Force J*, no 22, May-June 1980, p 31; *Advertiser* (Adel), 1, 2 Oct 1919; *The Times*, 10, 12, 14 Apr 1937; *Age*, 30 July 1980; *Canb Times*, 13 Feb 1980; *News* (Adel), 4 May 1988; Lummis, V.C. and G.C. files (Military Hist Soc, Lond).

ANTHONY STAUNTON

SULMAN, FLORENCE (1876-1965), author and benefactor, was born on 13 January 1876 at Bromley, Kent, England, eldest child of (Sir) John Sulman [q.v.], architect, and his first wife Sarah Clark (d. 1888), née Redgate. Florence attended Miss Wheeler's school at Bromley and in 1886, with her sister, joined her parents and brother in New South Wales where she was educated in the Blue Mountains and at Abbotsleigh, a 'good girls' school conducted by Miss Clarke' [q.v.8] at Parramatta. Florence shared an intellectually stimulating and happy family life with her siblings at Ingleholme, Turramurra, and spent summer holidays with them in the Blue Mountains and at Mittagong where they went bushwalking with their father.

A woman of diverse talents and enormous energy, she was an active member of the Society of Arts and Crafts of New South Wales from 1910 and a lifelong supporter of Australian design. In 1916 she accompanied her brother Geoffrey to England and cared for him until his death in an aircraft accident in 1917. While there she taught craft to convalescing soldiers. Returning to Sydney in 1917, Florence took up her pre-war activities, serving as president (1928-36) of the Arts and Crafts Society. In 1933 she described crafts as a 'bulwark of national sanity and an antidote for unemployment'. A frequent traveller to Europe, she lectured on new trends and in 1936-37 sent home samples from the Englishwoman Exhibition of Arts and Handicrafts: some were purchased by the Technological Museum, Sydney.

Throughout her life Florence encouraged the study, appreciation and preservation of native plants. Her *Popular guide to the wild flowers of New South Wales* (2 vols, 1914), illustrated by Eirene Mort [q.v.10], revealed the depth and detail of her knowledge. They continued their partnership over many years, producing a painting book, postcards and other material aimed at educating children.

Miss Sulman had begun her long association with the Kindergarten Union of New South Wales in 1914 and was vice-president of the Surry Hills Free Kindergarten which was to be named after her. As president of the Kindergarten Union, she was a generous benefactor, equipping a tea-room, establishing Playways Kindergarten Toy Shop, lecturing on overseas developments in pre-school education and donating the proceeds of her painting book of wildflowers. She created jobs for unemployed kindergarten teachers during the Depression and established a bursary at Sydney Kindergarten and Preparatory Teachers' College. Elected an honorary life-member in 1952, she was appointed M.B.E. in 1958 for her services to child welfare. She also found time to work with her stepmother for the Rachel Forster Hospital for Women and Children and for the State branch of the Australian Red Cross Society.

Her letters written from England in 1916-17 reveal her as intelligent, good-humoured, enterprising and affectionate. Friends paid tribute to her courage and to her 'concern for everybody's needs but her own'. She did not marry. Florence Sulman died on 15 June 1965 at Mona Vale and was cremated with Anglican rites. Her will shows the breadth of her interests and the generosity of her spirit.

SMH, 25 July 1929, 29 Jan 1931, 26 Oct 1933, 7 Nov 1950, 12 June 1958, 1 July 1965; Annual Reports, 1895-1971, Kindergarten Union of NSW, Syd; Letters from England and France by Florence and Geoffrey Sulman during wartime, 1916-1917 *and* Sulman papers (ML); Historical sketch of the Society of Arts and Crafts of NSW, 1906-56 (ML).

MARGARET HENRY

SULMAN, SIR JOHN (1849-1934), architect, was born on 29 August 1849 at Greenwich, Kent, England, third son of John Sulman, jeweller, and his wife Martha, née Quinton. He was educated at Greenwich Proprietary School and in 1863 passed the Oxford junior examination. After his family moved to Croydon next year, he was articled to Thomas Allom, a London architect; he learned the use of oils and water-colour, and executed perspective drawings for Sir Giles Gilbert Scott.

Following illness, Sulman resumed work in London in 1868. While articled to H. R. Newton, he attended classes at the Architectural Association and at the Royal Academy of Arts, winning the Pugin travelling scholarship in 1871. An associate of the Royal Institute of British Architects in 1872 (fellow, 1883), Sulman designed the Congregational Church at Caterham, Surrey: the first wedding there was his own, to Sarah Clark Redgate (d. 1888) on 15 April 1875. They moved to Bromley, Kent. He lectured on applied art and formed the Nineteenth Century Art Society.

In Italy in 1882 he contracted typhoid at Naples; two years later Sarah showed signs of tuberculosis. Although president elect of the Architectural Association, Sulman sold his practice (which had produced over seventy churches and other buildings) and left with his wife and son for Australia. Reaching Sydney on 13 August 1885, he paid £3000 next year to enter partnership with C. H. E. Blackmann in Sydney. Some months later Blackmann fled the country with a Sydney barmaid, leaving Sulman liable for his debts. From 1889 to 1908 Sulman practised with Joseph Porter Power. Sulman's commissions included The Armidale School (1889), Women's College, University of Sydney (1890-94), and Presbyterian churches at Woollahra (1889), Manly (1889-92) and Randwick (1890). His most important work was the Thomas Walker [q.v.2] Convalescent Hospital at Concord, designed in Federation free classical style.

Always ready to discuss art and architecture, Sulman founded the Palladian Club in 1887 and became an honorary corresponding secretary of the R.I.B.A. He was asked by Aston Webb to 'clean up' the Institute of Architects of New South Wales: Sulman had joined the institute in 1887 and been elected vice-president, but J. Horbury Hunt [q.v.4] foiled his attempt to become president; Sulman resigned in 1892 and did not rejoin until 1912 when he was again vice-president. In 1887-1912 he also lectured part time in architecture in the faculty of engineering at the University of Sydney; he visited Britain and the United States of America in 1892 to report on architectural schools.

In 1890 A. B. Smith [q.v.11], minister for public works, had convened a 'secret committee' of six architects (including Hunt, W. L. Vernon [q.v.] and Sulman) to investigate complaints that the colonial architect James Barnet [q.v.3] had a monopoly on the design of large, and therefore lucrative, public buildings. They recommended that such work be open to competition. As Barnet was to retire, Smith sought to replace him with Sulman, who declined. In October Sulman formed the Parramatta half-squadron of lancers, but resigned his commission as first lieutenant four years later.

At St Luke's Anglican Church, Burwood, on 27 April 1893 he married Annie Elizabeth Masefield, the childhood companion of (Dame) Eadith Walker [q.v.]. Annie took up photography and published collections of her studies of Australian wildflowers. Sulman again became seriously ill in 1896 and took his family to Europe. Returning next year, he made the cottage he had begun for his parents at Turramurra into a rambling family house, Ingleholme.

A visit to Paris in 1873 had impressed on Sulman the need for town planning. In 1890 his paper, 'The laying-out of towns', delivered to the Australasian Association for the Advancement of Science, advocated the 'spider's web' plan in preference to the grid; he used the motto 'convenience, utility and beauty'; his paper marked the beginning of town planning in Australia as a formal discipline. In 1907 the Daily Telegraph published his series of articles on the need for a plan for Sydney; on eleven occasions he gave evidence before the royal commission for the improvement of the city of Sydney and its suburbs (1908-09). Many of his proposals are evident in Sydney today: the extension of Martin Place, the location of Circular Quay railway station and the widening of Elizabeth, Oxford and William streets (with a tunnel under King's Cross). A bill authorizing Sulman to construct an underground railway connecting Milsons Point and the city had lapsed in 1895. He considered Australia's architectural heritage insignificant and at various times recommended the demolition of Hyde Park Barracks, St James's Church, Darlinghurst gaol, Victoria Barracks and Sydney Hospital.

After retiring from practice in 1908, Sulman held influential positions as director of the Daily Telegraph Newspaper Co. Ltd from 1902 (chairman 1922-25), president of the Town Planning Association of New South Wales (1913-25) and chairman of the Town Planning Advisory Board to the Department of Local Government (1918). At the University of Sydney he endowed a lectureship in aeronautics (in memory of his son Geoffrey killed with the Royal Flying Corps in 1917), and gave the Anzac memorial bursary (1922) and £2500 to encourage the teaching of town planning (1926). He was Vernon memorial lecturer in town planning at the university in 1919-26.

A supporter of Walter Burley Griffin's [q.v.9] plan for Canberra, Sulman gave evidence at the Parliamentary Standing Committee on Public Works in 1915. As chairman of the Federal Capital Advisory Committee (1921-24), he nonetheless advocated departures from the Griffin plan wherever he saw fit. Serving without fee, and making repeated journeys to Melbourne and Canberra, Sulman opposed the building of a permanent parliament house (because of lack of funds) and its siting on Capital Hill. Lasting monuments to him in Canberra are his Mediterranean style Civic Centre buildings.

On behalf of the Commonwealth and New South Wales governments, in 1924 Sulman visited Europe and the United States of America to study city plans and systems of local government. He attended the British Empire Exhibition, Wembley, and the International Garden Cities and Town Planning Federation conference at Amsterdam. In July he was appointed K.B.E. A trustee from 1899 (president from 1919) of the National Art Gallery of New South Wales, he purchased items for it while overseas and organized London representatives. In 1927 he commissioned (for £1000) and donated to the gallery the fourth bas-relief bronze panel for its exterior. He again travelled to Europe in 1930. That year he established the annual Sir John Sulman award for architectural merit in New South Wales.

Sulman died at North Sydney on 18 August 1934 and was cremated with Presbyterian forms. His wife, their daughter and two of their sons survived him, as did the son and a daughter Florence [q.v.] of his first marriage. They endowed the Sir John Sulman prize for genre painting or mural decoration. His estate was sworn for probate at £171 615.

Versatile, gifted and energetic, Sulman was forceful and decisive in action and in speech. By turns polished and aggressive, he was seldom deflected from any task. Driven by ambition and a virile ego, he was politically adroit, able to cultivate useful acquaintances to become the central figure of any organization with which he was connected. His taste was essentially conservative (he considered much modern art to be 'awful rubbish'), but his interests ranged from painting to town planning: 'the former seeks art in small framed spaces, the latter in wide, prettily and properly-planned places'. His portrait by John Longstaff [q.v.10] was commissioned by the National Art Gallery of New South Wales and won the Archibald [q.v.3] prize for 1931.

J. M. Freeland, *The making of the profession* (Syd, 1971); *PP* (NSW), 1909, 5, p 379; *A'sian Builder and Contractor's News*, 24 Mar, 31 July 1888; *Build-ing, Engineering and Mining*, 23, 30 July, 17, 24 Sept 1892, 2 Dec 1893; *Cwlth Home*, 17 July 1925; *Salon* (Syd), Sept 1916, p 55; Trustees of National Art Gallery of NSW, *Annual Report*, 1931; *Art in Aust*, Nov 1934; *Cumberland Argus*, 23 Oct 1890; Sulman papers, 1868-1972, *and* J. H. Hunt papers (ML); Reconstruction of the Architect's Branch of the Dept of Public Works (NSWA); Federal Capital Advisory Cttee, Minutes, 1921-24 (AA).

RICHARD E. APPERLY
PETER REYNOLDS

SUMMONS, WALTER ERNEST ISAAC (1881-1970), medical practitioner, was born on 7 July 1881 at Ballarat, Victoria, second son of Samuel Summons, school inspector, and his wife Elizabeth Ann, née Edwards, both Victorian born. Walter was educated at Scotch College and the University of Melbourne (M.B., 1903; B.S., 1904; M.D., 1907; D.P.H., 1908). His Diploma of Public Health was the first awarded in Victoria. Stringy and sandy throughout his life, while at university Summons represented Victoria at lacrosse.

In 1906 he was chosen by (Sir) Richard Stawell [q.v.] to investigate miners' phthisis at Bendigo. Summons linked the increase in respiratory disease mortality (from 77 per 10 000 in the late 1870s to 130 per 10 000 in 1906) to the spread of percussion rock drills which intensified silica dust, and to the bad ventilation of mines which had become the world's deepest. Bendigo miners died from lung ailments at six times the rate of Victorian adult males; related females and non-miner males had tuberculosis death-rates above their respective Victorian averages. Summons's reports on ventilation in 1906 and on the epidemiology of lung disease in 1907 were founded on detailed study of work practices and exact clinical observation. He recommended higher, mandatory standards of air quality and use of water jets with drills; employment underground of phthisics was to be prohibited and mine sanitation rules enforced; invalid miners and advanced tuberculosis cases were to receive additional state relief. His proposals were coolly received in Bendigo. Neither owners nor miners had supported his research: the former feared further state intervention with higher costs; the latter resented curbs on work habits. Moreover, the reports coincided with a downturn in mining productivity and profits. The government tacked Summons's recommendations to the Mines Act of 1907. Practice improved and lives were saved.

At university Summons had joined the Officers' Corps and begun a lifelong association with the army. In December 1914 he embarked for No. 1 Australian General Hospital at Heliopolis, Egypt, moving with that hospital to Rouen, France, in 1916. At the war's end he commanded the largest of the Australian hospitals, at Abbassia, Egypt. The youngest colonel commanding a military hospital in 1918, he was the oldest in July 1940 when he took charge of the 2/7th Australian General Hospital in the Middle East. Recalled in 1942 to Caulfield Military Hospital, he made a notable investigation of the persistence of bilharziasis. He was appointed O.B.E. in 1919, and mentioned in dispatches in both wars.

From 1919 Summons built a large private practice in Camberwell. An honorary physician and tutor at the Alfred Hospital in 1920-35, he was elected president of the Victorian branch of the British Medical Association in 1936. He held high ideals of medical service and was conciliatory to government proposals to redistribute the costs of medical attention. Between 1919 and 1968 he served on the Victorian Public Health Commission.

A devoted Anglican, Summons was vicar's warden for thirty years at St Mark's Church, Camberwell. He and his wife Viva St George, née Sproule (M.B., B.S., 1907), whom he had married at Holy Trinity Anglican Church, Kew, on 2 June 1909, were stalwarts of Camberwell Grammar School. Predeceased by his wife in 1956, he died on 10 May 1970 and was cremated. His three sons and one daughter survived him. A distinguished medical-military colleague, Sir Geoffrey Newman-Morris, remembered Summons for his skill and for his 'capacity for friendship and command'.

History of Scotch College, Melbourne, 1851-1925 (Melb, 1926); I. V. Hansen, *By their deeds* (Melb, 1986); *MJA*, 16 Jan 1937, p 77, 5 Sept 1970, p 476; *Medical History*, 17, 1973, p 372.

F. B. SMITH

SUMSUMA (1903?-1965), boat captain and New Guinea patriot, was born about 1903 at Sasa village on Boang Island, New Ireland, son of Tamapuat, of Ansingsing village on Tefa island, and Tarapat of Sasa. His parents were not influential and his prospects therefore few, but at age 10 he entered the foreigner's world: his mother beat him and he ran away to sea. By 1927 he was captain of the Melanesian Co.'s motor schooner, *Edith*, a coastal trader out of Rabaul, and was probably the highest-paid New Guinean in the Mandated Territory, earning, with bonuses, up to £12 a month when most New Guineans working for cash received five shillings.

During December 1928 Sumsuma organized a strike by almost all Rabaul's 3000 New Guinean workers to win them £12 a month. He united in common purpose men from around coastal New Guinea, many recently hostile to one another; he kept their plans secret from every European; and he gained

the vital co-operation of another remarkable leader, N'Dramei of Pitylu island off Manus, the senior sergeant-major of police. Led by the police and the 'boss boys' (foremen), workers began quitting Rabaul after dusk on 2 January 1929 and by late that night had gathered at the Catholic or Methodist missions on the Kokopo road. Sumsuma had expected the missionaries to mediate, but they would not, and Rabaul's employers would not negotiate. Although some strikers held firm for two or three days, and a few never went back to work, by mid-morning on 3 January the strike had collapsed.

Nonetheless, most of Rabaul's Europeans, especially the planters and business people, reacted with fear and fury. The government dismissed 190 police, sentencing most to six months hard labour as carriers. Sumsuma, N'Dramei and nineteen others were imprisoned for three years: Sumsuma served his sentence at Aitape and Kavieng, where warders beat him so severely that he bore the scars for the rest of his life and never forgot the cruelties he suffered.

On being released, he went home to Boang and for the next thirty years searched for the road of progress. Both before and after World War II he organized copra marketing co-operatives, but they failed or were suppressed. When the Japanese came he collaborated, learning from them as he had from Europeans. When they left, his people were ready to elect him king, but the Australians returned and put him in prison again, for cargo cult activities. He toiled on, resourceful, innovative, determined to lead. With the local Catholic mission he established a bank, a power-house, a school and other projects. He was still looking ahead when he died of asthma on 20 August 1965 in the Boang mission hospital. From obscurity he had become a leader of his people, and one of the first—Black or White—to consider seriously the place of New Guineans in a rapidly changing world. His death stilled a great vision, a restless spirit, a friend of the people, and a true man.

D. Denoon and R. Lacey (eds), *Oral tradition in Melanesia* (Port Moresby, 1981); *J of Pacific Hist*, 10, pt 3, 1975, p 3.　　BILL GAMMAGE

SÜSSMILCH, ADOLPH CARL VON DE HEYDE (1875-1946), geologist and educationist, was born on 12 February 1875 in Sydney, third son of Christian Bernhard Süssmilch, a music teacher from Hamburg, and his German wife Anna Emilie, née Merkle. Educated at William Street Public School, he became an indent clerk in a warehouse and attended science classes at Sydney Technical College in his spare time.

Joining the Department of Public Instruction in 1899, Süssmilch next year became an assistant at Sydney Technical College. He studied at Fort Street Training School and, as an unmatriculated student, attended lectures in the faculty of engineering at the University of Sydney in 1901-03. He taught geology, mineralogy and mining at the college from 1903, and visited the United States of America in 1912 to study methods of technical education.

Appointed principal of the Newcastle branch Technical College in 1914, Süssmilch was president of the Newcastle division of the Institution of Engineers, Australia, in 1920. In an address to the local chamber of commerce in 1922, he publicly criticized unscientific mining methods on the northern coalfields and the great waste in the south coast coke industry; he also called for scientific research to be carried out to enable the recovery of more coal and better use of the industry's by-products. In 1927 he was president of the Rotary Club of Newcastle. That year he was appointed assistant superintendent and principal of East Sydney Technical College. After a world tour, in August 1935 he praised the New South Wales education system, but pointed out that its technical branch urgently required more buildings and equipment. From 1934 until he retired in June 1936, he was acting superintendent of technical education.

A painstaking teacher, Süssmilch took elocution lessons to perfect his presentation. His friend and colleague E. C. Andrews [q.v.7] wrote that 'he sought to inspire his students and the public with a love for geology and a robust spirit of comradeship and citizenship', and that his lectures were models of lucidity, delivered with conviction. Süssmilch's popular, annual field-excursions (meticulously organized with railway timetable precision) attracted numerous special visitors as well as the students. With receding hair and rimless spectacles, he had a round face and 'beaming smile'; his chief enjoyment was music, in which he was well-versed.

Chairman of directors of the New South Wales Society for Crippled Children, Süssmilch sat on its educational and vocational guidance committee from April 1931 until February 1940 when he became honorary secretary. His interest in the young, his knowledge of educational facilities and his experience in the manual arts helped him to make a significant contribution to the rehabilitation of physically handicapped children. He retired from the society through ill health in September 1943.

While better known to the public for his work with crippled children and for his pioneering efforts in technical education, Süssmilch was predominantly a scientist. In 1905 his first scientific paper—on basic plutonic rocks near Kiama—appeared in the journal of the Royal Society of New South Wales; in 1911 he published *An introduction to the geology of New South Wales* (new editions 1914 and 1922) which was widely used as a textbook. Between 1905 and 1941 he published nineteen papers, some with H. I. Jensen [q.v.9], H. S. Jevons and T. G. Taylor [q.v], on various aspects of geology and the State's physical geography, especially the mountains and tablelands; they mainly appeared in the *Technical Gazette of New South Wales* and in the proceedings of the local Royal and Linnean societies. His later papers, largely in the fields of geomorphology and palaeozoic stratigraphy, included two with (Sir) Edgeworth David [q.v.8] in 1919 and 1931 on the vexed question of the plane of separation between the Permian and Carboniferous periods in Australia.

Having attended the Pan Pacific Scientific Conference in Honolulu in 1920, Süssmilch went to subsequent Pan Pacific congresses in the 1920s and 1930s, firmly believing that they were a force for tolerance without which there could be no real peace. To visiting scientists, he was a generous host and friend. He was a councillor of the Royal (1910-38; president, 1922) and Linnean (1933-46; president, 1936-37) societies; chairman of section C (geology) in 1935 and a trustee and fellow of the Australian and New Zealand Association for the Advancement of Science; a member of the Australian National Research Council and a trustee of the Australian Museum, Sydney, (1943-46); and he also promoted the Science House project which opened in Sydney in 1931.

A fellow of Sydney Technical College (1914) and of the Geological societies of London (1905) and America, he was honoured by the local Royal Society's (W. B.) Clarke [q.v.3] medal in 1939 and was its Clarke memorial lecturer in 1941. He belonged to the University Club, Sydney. Süssmilch died at his Burwood home on 6 December 1946 and was cremated with Anglican rites. He was unmarried.

Geological Soc of Lond, *QJ*, 103 (1947), p 61; Roy Soc of NSW, *J*, 81 (1947), p 4; Linnean Soc NSW, *Procs*, 73 (1948), p 242; *SMH*, 4 May 1922, 17, 30 Aug, 26 Oct 1923, 26 Feb 1929, 10 Aug 1933, 9 Aug 1935, 24 Sept 1941, 10 Dec 1946.

G. P. WALSH

SUTHERLAND, JANE (1853-1928), painter and teacher, was born on 26 December 1853 in New York, eldest daughter of George Sutherland, woodcarver, and his wife Jane, née Smith, both Scottish born. The family arrived in Sydney in 1864 and moved to

Melbourne in 1870 where George became a drawing instructor with the Department of Education and exhibited with the Victorian Academy of Arts (1875-78). He was joined by his brothers, Alexander and John, and the Sutherlands played a distinguished role in science, education and the arts; Alexander, George [qq.v.6] and William [q.v.] were Jane's brothers.

At the National Gallery School of Design Jane studied under Thomas Clark in 1871-75, O. R. Campbell in 1877-81 and Frederick McCubbin [qq.v.3,10] in 1886. She attended the school of painting in 1877 under Eugen von Guerard and in 1882-85 under George Folingsby [qq.v.4]. In October 1883 she was awarded the Robert Wallen [q.v.6] prize of five guineas at the annual students' exhibition. She exhibited in 1878 with the Victorian Academy of Arts, then with the Australian Artists' Association, and with the Victorian Artists' Society (formed 1888) until 1911. From 1888 she shared a studio with Clara Southern [q.v.] in Grosvenor Chambers, Collins Street, where Tom Roberts [q.v.11] also had a studio. One of the first women elected (1894) to the Buonarotti Society, she was a councillor (1900) of the V.A.S. In 1899, 1903 and 1906 she sent paintings to the federal exhibitions at the South Australian Society of Arts, and in 1907 to the Australian Exhibition of Women's Work in Melbourne.

Sutherland was the leading female artist in the group of Melbourne painters who broke with the nineteenth-century tradition of studio art by sketching and painting directly from nature. She accompanied artists such as Roberts, McCubbin and Walter Withers [q.v.] on *plein-air* sketching trips to the outlying rural districts of Alphington, Templestowe and Box Hill. Her lyrical landscapes—such as 'The Mushroom Gatherers' (c.1895) and 'Field Naturalists' (c.1896)—are often the setting for women engaged in rural activities, or for children at play.

About 1904 Jeannie Sutherland suffered a mild stroke. Thereafter her younger brother William helped her to move around and she continued to produce small works in oils and pastel, including a number of landscape views of the Yarra River at Kew and Abbotsford. Assisted by her cousin and fellow artist Jean Goodlet Sutherland, she also exhibited and gave art lessons. William's death in 1911 brought an end to her mobility and to her career. She died on 25 July 1928 at her Kew home and was buried in the Presbyterian section of Box Hill cemetery. Her estate was sworn for probate at £223.

S. Rosewarne and F. Lindsay, *Sutherland*, exhibition cat (Melb, 1977); J. Clark and B. Whitelaw, *Golden summers: Heidelberg and beyond*, exhibition cat (Syd, 1985); *Lip*, 1978-79; *Argus*, 26 July 1928.   FRANCES LINDSAY

SUTHERLAND, WILLIAM (1859-1911), theoretical physicist and physical chemist, was born on 24 August 1859 at Glasgow, Scotland, son of George Sutherland, woodcarver, and his wife Jane, née Smith. The family, which migrated to Sydney in 1864 and settled in Melbourne in 1870, was close-knit and encouraged intellectual and artistic pursuits. Alexander and George [qq.v.6] were William's brothers and Jane [q.v.] his sister.

Having attended Wesley College, in 1876 Sutherland enrolled at the University of Melbourne; he graduated (B.A., 1879; M.A., 1883) with first-class honours in natural science, and also completed course-work for the university's certificate of engineering. Instead of undertaking the year of supervised practical engineering required to complete the certificate, he proceeded to England to take up the Gilchrist scholarship which he had been awarded for further study in science at University College, London. He completed a B.Sc. in 1881 with first-class honours and the scholarship in experimental physics. During his course the professor of physics at University College, George Carey Foster, gave him his first experience of research.

Early in 1882 Sutherland, who had not enjoyed his time in Europe, returned to Melbourne. Seemingly without ambition for wealth or success, he devoted his life to reading and research. To support his modest needs, he did some private coaching and served as an examiner at the university. He was an unsuccessful applicant for the chairs of chemistry (1884) and physics (1885) at the University of Adelaide. When Melbourne's professor of natural philosophy, H. M. Andrew [q.v.3] fell ill and died in 1888, Sutherland acted as lecturer until (Sir) Thomas Lyle [q.v.10] arrived to take up the chair. Sutherland had also applied for this chair, but his application is reported to have been misfiled in London and thus not considered by the selection committee. In 1898 the chair of physics at the University of Sydney fell vacant, but Sutherland was deemed ineligible on account of age. When Lyle took leave in 1899 Sutherland was appointed acting professor. He augmented his income by writing for newspapers and from 1901 contributed regularly to the Melbourne *Age*, especially on scientific topics.

In 1885 Sutherland sent his first scientific paper to London for publication in one of the world's leading physics journals, the *Philosophical Magazine*, to which he subsequently became a prolific contributor. In all, he published seventy-eight scientific papers, mostly in major international journals. Because he had no access to laboratory facilities, his research was almost entirely confined to theoretical investigations, chiefly in the field of molecular dynamics. His approach was founded on the assumption that the particles of which matter is composed exert an attractive force on each other in addition to gravity. Although his theory contrasted with that of Ludwig Boltzmann and other contemporaries who adopted a purely kinematical outlook, it is now widely accepted. Indeed, in introducing the idea, modern texts usually refer to the 'Sutherland model' and characterize the force in terms of the 'Sutherland potential'. In his early papers Sutherland supposed that the complete law of force between particles is a power series in $1/r^2$ of which gravity is but the first term; he believed he had uncovered the second, $1/r^4$ term, in his own investigations into the behaviour of matter at the molecular level. (Nowadays this force is usually taken to be $1/r^7$ in form.) Sutherland's general approach enabled him in 1893 to account successfully for one of the more striking difficulties confronting molecular theory at the time, the discrepancy between theory and experiment in regard to the dependence of the viscosity of a gas on its temperature. He showed that the existence of an attractive force between the molecules of the gas would increase the effective diameter of the molecules in the theory that had been worked out for forceless molecules. This research led him to include an extra term C/T in the formula linking viscosity and temperature, T being the absolute temperature and C a constant for any particular gas that is now called Sutherland's Constant. Sutherland later came to regard his new inter-molecular force as quite separate from gravity and attributable to the existence within all ordinary molecules of polarized electric doublets. Working out the consequences of this notion became a major part of his subsequent research.

Sutherland's principal concern was to understand the properties of matter in bulk in terms of its behaviour at the microscopic level. He worked very much on his own, although he enjoyed cordial relations with the few other physicists working in Australia. He wrote for an international audience, attacking such questions as the surface tension of liquids, diffusion, the rigidity of solids, the properties of solutions (including an influential analysis of the structure of water), the origin of spectra and the source of the earth's magnetic field. His ideas were invariably treated with respect, even when they did not win wide acceptance.

While modest and unassuming, Sutherland defended his views vigorously. A widely cultured man with a passion for music as well as science, he liked nothing more than long tramps through the bush. Somewhat shy, but held in deep affection by those who knew him, he never married. He died of a ruptured heart on 5 October 1911 at his family's Kew home and was buried in Melbourne general cemetery.

W. A. Osborne, *William Sutherland* (Melb, 1920); *Contemporary Physics*, 1, 1960, p 191; newspaper cutting-books, 1901-11 (NL and LaTL); correspondence with W. H. Bragg (Roy Inst, Lond), and W. A. Osborne (Aust Academy of Science, Canb).
                                                        R. W. HOME

SUTTON, GEORGE LOWE (1872-1964), agricultural scientist, was born on 23 October 1872 at Everton, Lancashire, England, son of Henry Hall Sutton, shipping agent, and his wife Ellen, née Lowe. George's widowed mother took him to New South Wales in 1882 where he attended Fort Street Model and Sydney Boys' High schools, on scholarships, and Sydney Technical College. He then went dairy-farming at Moorebank and worked in Queensland. In 1900 he was appointed experimentalist and later lecturer in agronomy at Hawkesbury Agricultural College where he became a friend of William Farrer [q.v.8]. At Glenfield on 22 April 1896 Sutton had married English-born Ada Alice Everington; they were to have four daughters and two sons.

In 1905 Sutton opened and managed an experimental farm at Cowra to further the wheat-breeding work of the Department of Agriculture. After Farrer's death in 1906, Sutton took charge of wheat-breeding in New South Wales and of the experimental farms at Cowra and Coolabah. His developmental work in low rainfall areas led (Sir) James Mitchell [q.v.10], State minister for lands and agriculture, to appoint him agricultural commissioner for the Western Australian wheat belt. Sutton began duties in Perth in 1911. Bespectacled and serious, if at times a long-winded speaker, he was a dedicated administrator whose ideas had influence in political, industrial and community circles. He developed morale in his department, although his dominant personality and the government's periods of financial austerity caused some friction. The demand for advice and technical resources increased and Sutton was hard pressed to meet it. While needing highly qualified staff, it was not until 1921 when he became director of agriculture that he could implement a policy of government cadetships for undergraduates in agriculture at the University of Western Australia.

Severe droughts after 1911 had reduced seed wheat to critical levels and the responsibility for overcoming the situation fell upon

Sutton. He converted State 'model' farms into experimental ones with the task of supplying commercial quantities of pure variety seed wheat and other crops to farmers; field days and public demonstrations were also held. Sutton continued his breeding work, using early generation crossbred material from New South Wales and emphasizing baking and milling quality, yield, resistance to disease and environmental suitability. In 1918 he released the Nabawa variety. Its qualities, particularly rust resistance, made it Australia's premier wheat until the 1930s when it was replaced by Bencubbin. Although Sutton's insistence on quality was not always appreciated because of inverse yield considerations, it eventually led to the formation of a national register of wheat varieties in 1927.

He endeavoured to modify the wheat selling system. The 'Fair Average Quality' standard used in Australia was based on samples from each State which were incorporated into a mixed bushel under supervision by State chambers of commerce. Sutton 'struck' the standard in Western Australia for many years. The commercial hiatus between harvest and striking of the yearly F.A.Q. standard was overcome by Western Australian legislation in 1935 which established the grade, 'W.A. Standard White'; it went further than the single bushel weight attribute of F.A.Q.

As early as 1914 Sutton had chaired a committee which reported on bulk handling of grain at farm, rail and port depots: it recommended that a standards board be established and that wheat be graded for export. A subsequent report in 1932 saw the formation of the Grain Pool of Western Australia and Co-operative Bulk Handling Ltd.

Sutton wrote on a wide variety of topics: many of his seventy papers in the *Agricultural Gazette of New South Wales* also appeared in the country press; he published over 110 papers in the *Journal of the Department of Agriculture of Western Australia* and in departmental bulletins; he conducted a large correspondence with farmers and spoke on radio. In 1952 he published *Comes the harvest*.

A firm yet gentle father who managed his income frugally, Sutton was raised as a Wesleyan; he ceased being a churchgoer, but remained a teetotaller. Reading, carpentry, gardening, photography, walking and vinegar-making occupied his leisure. He belonged to the State committee of the Council for Scientific and Industrial Research, presided over the Royal Society of Western Australia, and was a fellow of the Australasian Association for the Advancement of Science and a member of the Australian Institute of Agricultural Science.

In 1937, the year of his retirement, Sutton received an honorary doctorate of science in agriculture from the University of Western Australia; in 1951 he was appointed C.M.G.; in 1959 the flour millers and bakers of Western Australia gave him £815 for 'championing the improvement of Australian wheat, flour and bread'. Predeceased by his wife (d. 1960), he died on 11 January 1964 in Royal Perth Hospital and was buried in the Methodist section of Karrakatta cemetery.

Bulk Handling of Grain Advisory Bd (WA), *Report* (Perth, 1914); Dept of Works and Labour (WA), *Bulk handling of wheat: Reports* (Perth, 1932); A. R. Callaghan and A. J. Millington, *The wheat industry in Australia* (Syd, 1956); L. Hunt (ed), *Westralian portraits* (Perth, 1979); *Sunday Times* (Perth), 21 Jan 1962; *West Australian*, 23 Feb 1963; *Countryman* (Perth), 5 Feb 1959, 16 Jan 1964; Bibliography of G. L. Sutton (Lib of WA Dept of Agr); family papers held by Miss E. Sutton, Bentley, Perth.

R. J. MOIR

SUTTON, HARVEY VINCENT (1882–1963), professor of medicine, was born on 18 February 1882 at Jail Hill, Castlemaine, Victoria, eighth child of William Sutton, head warder, and his wife Hannah, née Howe, each of whom had migrated from Ireland in the 1850s. Harvey attended school at Castlemaine, and St Andrew's College, Bendigo. Resident in Trinity College from 1898, he studied medicine at the University of Melbourne (M.B., 1902; Ch.B., 1903; M.D., 1905), receiving his clinical training at Melbourne Hospital; J. H. L. Cumpston [q.v.8] was among his fellow students. Sutton gained a string of honours, including the Beaney [q.v.3] scholarship in pathology; he represented the university in lacrosse, athletics and cricket, and his college in rowing and football. At various times he held the Victorian and Australasian half-mile records and the Victorian record for the mile.

While resident and senior resident medical officer at the Children's Hospital, Sutton was awarded the Rhodes scholarship for Victoria. In 1905 he entered New College, Oxford (B.Sc., 1908); working for two years under J. S. Haldane, he completed a research degree on the effects of increasing body temperature on the metabolic rate. He represented Oxford against Cambridge in athletics and lacrosse, and in 1908 competed for Australia in the 800 metres at the Olympic Games in London. Sutton served as resident medical officer at Charing Cross Hospital and the Lister Institute of Preventive Medicine before returning to Melbourne where he was medical officer with the Victorian Department of Public Instruction from September 1909 until World War I.

As a captain in the Australian Army Medical Corps, from March 1916 Sutton served with the Australian Imperial Force in Egypt, Sinai, Palestine and Syria. With Major Eustace Ferguson [q.v.8], he commanded No.7 Sanitary Section, Anzac Mounted Division, and Anzac Field Laboratory: epidemic dysentery and malaria were particular problems. On leave in London, Sutton married Frances Beatrice Davis on 23 October 1917 at St Philip's Church, Kensington. Returning to Egypt in January 1918, he survived the sinking of the hospital ship, *Aragon*. He worked in several hospitals and, as a temporary major from February 1918, became deputy assistant director of medical services at Headquarters. He was twice mentioned in dispatches (1918 and 1920) and appointed O.B.E. in 1919. Sutton became interested in archaeology and remained fascinated by the ancient civilizations of the Middle East. He brought back to Australia a bottle of water from the River Jordan which was later used to baptize his children.

Returning to Melbourne in 1919, Sutton completed a diploma in public health. Next year he joined the New South Wales Department of Public Instruction as principal medical officer. For much of the 1920s he also lectured part time in public health and preventive medicine at the University of Sydney. When the Commonwealth government and the university established the School of Public Health and Tropical Medicine in 1930, Sutton was appointed to the chair of preventive medicine and became the school's first director. During World War II his school was involved in advising and training the armed services on all aspects of tropical health. Sutton also became inspector of army camps in New South Wales with the rank of lieutcolonel. He retired from the university in 1947.

Sport had remained a passion: Sutton attended the inaugural meeting of the Australian Universities' Sports Association in 1920 and was to be active in its organization throughout his life. He would often appear at the university oval with stethoscope and stopwatch, eager to assess sporting performances. His talent extended to boomerang and spear throwing. A great all-rounder, he was a tall, athletic, family man, embodying many of the contemporary ideals of citizenship and public service. He promoted the public health movement, which he viewed in triumphalist terms, and physical education, particularly of school children. Sutton warned that Fascist states had done more than the democracies to create efficient populations. 'God', he once wrote, 'marches on the side of the fittest battalions'. He attributed nervous breakdowns, delinquency and divorce to unfitness, and argued that 'Vitamins, sunshine, open-air life and exercise remove the cause of mental instability'.

With Dr J. S. Purdy [q.v.11], he inaugurated Health Week in 1921 and was for many years president of the Sydney Health Week Council. Sutton helped to organize the Father and Son Welfare Movement of Australia (established in Sydney in 1926), and regularly spoke in support of family values and sex education; he was also involved in the Recreation and Leadership Movement, the Surf Life Saving Association of Australia, the Family Planning Association, the Sydney University Settlement, Legacy, the Royal Society of New South Wales, the Fairbridge [q.v.8] Farm Schools of New South Wales and the local branch of the Royal Sanitary Institute. He served, as well, on the National Fitness Council of New South Wales and the Child Welfare Advisory Council.

In sundry papers—many delivered to the Australasian Association for the Advancement of Science and the Australasian Medical Congress—Sutton examined some of his central concerns: the prophylactic and diagnostic aspects of malaria, delinquency, feeblemindedness, sanitation and the health needs of school children. A regular contributor to the *Medical Journal of Australia* and the *Sydney University Medical Journal*, he published his 1941 Livingstone lectures (sponsored by Camden College) as *Mental health in peace and war* (1942) and a textbook, *Lectures on preventive medicine*, in 1944. Given his proclivity for collecting books, Sutton's room at the university grew wonderfully crowded. Yet, he was never a bookworm and practised what he preached when it came to lecturing and research, insisting on rest, good diet and regular exercise. For the tropical medicine school, he designed a sunken garden where he sometimes took classes, or encouraged performances of Greek and Elizabethan drama. He was convinced that the inhabitants of modern, industrial cities needed to rediscover a Greek sense of the unity of mind and body, and was fond of observing that the 'greatest Teacher of all time taught His disciples chiefly in the open air'.

Survived by his wife, three sons and four daughters, Harvey Sutton died at his Rose Bay home on 21 June 1963 and was buried in Waverley cemetery. His portrait by Joshua Smith is held by the University of Sydney.

A. G. Butler (ed), *Official history of the Australian Army Medical Services in the war 1914-18*, 1 (Melb, 1938); M. Roe, *Nine Australian progressives* (Brisb, 1984); J. A. Young et al (eds), *Centenary book of the University of Sydney faculty of medicine* (Syd, 1984); *Syd Univ Medical J*, June 1930, Sept 1931; *Aust Rhodes Review*, 1934, 1939; Univ Syd Union, *Union Recorder*, 28 Nov 1963; *MJA*, 28 Mar 1964.

D. R. WALKER

SUTTON, ROBERT; *see* SIEVIER

SWADLING, WILLIAM THOMAS (1882-1964), trade unionist, was born on 5 October 1882 in Sydney, sixth child of Edward Swadling, native-born publican, and his Welsh wife Mary Ann, née Davis. He was a sailor when he married Margaret Elizabeth Wright (d. 1919) on 12 December 1906 at St Paul's Anglican Church, Sydney; they were to have five children. After the birth of his second child in 1909, Swadling left the sea and lived at Balmain. He was employed by the Sydney Harbour Trust and did general labouring (1913) before working on the docks.

Elected vice-president of the Ship Painters and Dockers' Union of Port Jackson in 1915, Swadling was soon recognized as a diplomatic negotiator in waterfront demarcation disputes. In 1916 he was a trade union delegate to the Naval Dockyards Demarcations Board. Having enlisted as a private in the Australian Imperial Force on 20 February, he embarked for England in August. Blue-eyed and brown-haired, he was 5 ft. 5 ins. (165 cm) tall. In December 1917 he was posted to the Australian Army Medical Corps Details and on 6 February 1918 to the Australian Base Depot Staff in France.

Returning home a widower in September 1919, Swadling was elected State president in 1921 (vice-president in 1923, 1929 and 1931) of the Federated Ship Painters and Dockers' Union of Australia. He regularly represented the union on the Labor Council of New South Wales and at Labor Party conferences. Lobbying on a range of industrial and political issues, he favoured union amalgamations to solve demarcation problems and work rationing to remedy unemployment during trade recessions. In 1922 he condemned Labor's expulsion of Communist Party members. At Labor conferences he identified his union with the support of widows' benefits, motherhood endowments and the 'Hands off China Policy'. On 7 February 1923 he married a widow Margaret Camarsh, née Spalding, at Balmain.

After the death of John McDonald, in 1933 Swadling became secretary of the F.S.P.D.U., the sole salaried official in the State branch. His office was in the Union Hall, Mort Street, Balmain, where the Federal secretary was also located. During the Depression Swadling coped with lean times and the inability of members to pay their dues. In 1937 he reported that financial membership had fallen from 1500 to 700. By the outbreak of World War II numbers had begun to increase; in 1940 'Old Bill' received his first rise to £6 10s. and in 1943 he was paid £10 per week.

The war brought comparative prosperity to Swadling and to his members, about half of whom—according to Justice Sir George Beeby [q.v.7]—had been paid 'a long way below the basic wage' in 1939. Swadling encouraged campaigns for better hiring practices for the largely casual ship-painter and docker workforce. Occasionally in conflict with his colleagues, he retired as branch secretary in 1944, but continued as a Federal councillor.

On 16 April 1964 Swadling died in Concord Repatriation General Hospital and was cremated with Anglican rites. Three sons and two daughters of his first marriage and a son of his second survived him.

Cwlth Arbitration Reports, 42, 1940, p 241; *F.S.P.D.U. Bulletin*, 13, no 2, 1964; FSPDU minutes (ML); information from Mr I. Wyner, Balmain, Syd.
                                            RICHARD MORRIS

SWAIN, EDWARD HAROLD FULCHER (1883-1970), forester, was born on 6 April 1883 at Glebe, Sydney, third child of English-born Edward Plant Swain, flour merchant, and his Tasmanian wife Annie Maria, née Dodd. Educated at Parramatta South Public and Fort Street Model schools, he was appointed the first cadet forester in the forestry branch, Department of Lands, on 18 June 1900. He attended the University of Sydney in 1901, Sydney Technical College in 1902 and studied eucalypts under J. H. Maiden [q.v.10] at the National Herbarium of New South Wales in 1904. During a series of country appointments, mainly on the north coast, he undertook pioneering forest surveys and resource assessments before becoming assistant district forester at Fernmount in 1910. Next year he published *Reafforestation and the hardwood supply in relation to North Coast forests* and was appointed district forester for the north-west, based at Narrabri. He visited New Zealand in 1912.

On 28 April 1915 Swain married Margaret Milroy Hewetson with Presbyterian forms at St Andrew's Church, Glen Innes. Taking long service leave, he completed a six-month forestry course at the University of Montana, United States of America, and wrote *An Australian study of American forestry* (1918). He moved to Queensland in 1916 as district forest inspector at Gympie and Nanango. Having succeeded N. W. Jolly [q.v.9] as director of forests in 1918, he became chairman of the Provisional Forestry Board in 1924. In this post he created a professional staff training scheme and combined the national parks with the State forests under the board's supervision. Believing that silviculture—the pivot of forestry—depended on effective, economic harvesting and utilization, he established a forest products division to investigate the properties and uses of local woods; the resulting *Timbers and forest products of Queensland* (1928) became a standard reference work.

Amid conflict over the allocation of land, a royal commission was appointed in 1931 to inquire into the development of North Queensland. Mounting strong opposition to settlement of the rainforests, Swain was accused by the commission of making 'false statements on oath', but was subsequently exonerated by the auditor-general. In September 1932 the Provisional Forestry Board was abolished by the new Labor government and his services terminated.

Setting up as a private consultant, Swain conducted several inquiries, including a comprehensive survey in 1934 for the South Australian government and Australian Paper Manufacturers Ltd on various aspects of a long-standing and publicly sensitive proposal to thin the State's radiata pine plantations for wood pulp. His voluminous report received close consideration by the 1935 royal commission on coniferous afforestation, although many of his findings and recommendations were disputed by other foresters.

Appointed sole commissioner for forestry in New South Wales in August 1935, Swain created a professional staff training scheme and a division of wood technology which became the commission's major centre for research. His conviction of the need for the mutual understanding and co-operation of foresters, sawmillers and timber merchants had prompted his fervent sponsorship of equitable royalty (stumpage) systems, and led him to found the Eastern States (Australian) Timber Industry Stabilisation conferences in 1943. In 1947 he attended the British Empire Forestry Conference in London. Following continual disagreements involving the government and the Public Service Board, he retired in April 1948. He was employed by the United Nations as forestry adviser to the Emperor of Ethiopia in 1950-55 and awarded the N. W. Jolly medal by the Institute of Foresters of Australia in 1963 for his contributions to Australian forestry.

Although at odds on occasions with his more academically qualified contemporaries, Swain had an extensive self-taught knowledge of forests and forestry, an enormous capacity for work and a strong rapport with the bush and its people. Confident in his abilities and judgements, he was impatient with those whose ideas differed from his own. As a writer, he was prodigious and colourful: his work ranged from tender, lyrical poetry to impassioned speeches and polemics on the value of forests and forestry. He was also a confirmed diarist. He had an interest in climatology, especially in the value of homoclimatic indexes for tree introduction, and bel-

onged to the Royal societies of New South Wales and Queensland. Golf, landscape gardening and literature provided his recreation. In retirement he lived in the Blue Mountains until moving to Brisbane where he died at Indooroopilly on 3 July 1970. He was survived by his son and daughter.

E.H.F.S. [Swain papers], (NSW Forestry Commission, Syd, 1971); *Aust Forestry*, 12, no 1, 1948, p 3, 27, no 2, 1963, p 152; *Land Annual*, 6 Nov 1968, p 25; *Hist Records of Aust Science*, 5, no 1, 1980; *Brisb Courier*, 30 Sept 1932.   L. T. CARRON

SWAIN, HERBERT JOHN (1882-1959), engineer and educationist, was born on 28 April 1882 at Lambeth, London, son of Frederick Ashton Swain, carpenter, and his wife Florinda, née Johnston. Brought to Australia as a child, he was educated at Sydney Boys' High School. While serving an apprenticeship in mechanical and electrical engineering at the New South Wales railway workshops, he attended classes at Sydney Technical College; he became a journeyman fitter and later transferred to the General Post Office instrument shop. In 1905 he won a Sir Peter Russell [q.v.6] scholarship to the University of Sydney (B.E., 1908; B.Sc., 1910). Graduating with first-class honours, Swain was awarded an Exhibition of 1851 scholarship in 1909. At Emmanuel College, Cambridge (B.A. [Research], 1911), he studied the internal combustion engine under Professor B. Hopkinson.

Returning to Sydney, Swain was awarded the Russell gold medal for research (1912), lectured (until the late 1940s) at the university on combustion engines and was asked to design a petrol and hydraulics laboratory. On 9 January 1914 he married Clarice Kate Mitchell at St Philip's Anglican Church; they were to have two sons and a daughter.

As lecturer-in-charge of mechanical engineering at Sydney Technical College from 1913, Swain administered a growing department which was responsible for engineering courses in branch colleges. Following Peter Board's [q.v.7] 1913 reforms, Swain was involved in redesigning diploma and trade courses, and setting up advisory committees. In 1916 he was asked to direct the pilot training school at Richmond: after the war its aircraft mechanics section was transferred to the college's new East Sydney annexe where Swain established the bases of later schools of aircraft and automotive engineering.

Despite shortage of funds, the department of engineering expanded in the 1920s and recovered quickly from the Depression. Between 1935 and 1940 enrolments in all engineering courses in the State rose from 1250 to 3800; technical education received greater government attention after the 1933 commission of inquiry set up by D. H. Drummond [q.v.8]. Swain was appointed principal of Sydney Technical College in 1936.

After 1939 he adapted to the demands of a wartime college which operated on a 24-hour basis and was expected to fulfil normal training functions; its inadequate facilities were stretched to provide accommodation and training for defence services, munition factory workers and military personnel, and to conduct the vastly increased range of correspondence courses required by allied troops. By 1944 the first Commonwealth Reconstruction Training Scheme students were also accommodated. Swain prepared, as well, for the introduction of daylight training for apprentices.

A founder of the Technical Teachers' Association, Swain was an executive-member of the Engineering Association of New South Wales and the Sydney University Engineering Society, and a foundation associate of the Institution of Engineers, Australia; he served on various government committees and chaired the royal commission into administrative matters under the Metropolitan Water, Sewerage and Drainage Board (1932-33).

Nicknamed 'Bunny', he was a large, uncoordinated man who was known for bursts of colourful, inventive language. Rumour had it that he could be heard in Melbourne without a telephone. His colleagues found him generally good-humoured and good-hearted. Swain retired in 1947. Survived by his wife and one son, he died at his Gordon home on 8 August 1959 and was cremated.

Engineering Assn of NSW, *Minutes*, 1913-14, p 161; *Technical Gazette of NSW*, 3, pt 3, 1913, p 43, 8, pt 1, 1918, p 56, and pt 2, p 65; Dept of Technical Education files, 1913-47 (NSWA).

JOAN E. COBB

SWANSON, DONALD ALEXANDER (1859-1940) and SIR JOHN WARREN (1865-1924), builders, were born on 20 December 1859 and 12 May 1865 at Sandhurst, Victoria, sons of Scottish-born William Swanson (d. 1892), carpenter, and his English wife Mary, née Shields. The family moved to Melbourne about 1870 where Donald was educated at St Paul's Grammar School. He served his indentures with his father and took over the business when William retired in 1889; one of William's last works was the west block of the Newport railway workshops. John was educated at Walker's School, West Melbourne; after a sojourn in Tasmania with an unsuccessful theatrical company, he joined the family firm with which another brother Alexander also had a brief involve-

ment. On 5 June 1890, at Albert Park, John was married to Alice Comins by Rev. Charles Strong [q.v.6].

During the 1890s Melbourne's building industry slumped and Donald moved briefly to Queensland where he carried out railway work and constructed a major bridge over the Burdekin River. John was left in charge of the Melbourne office. When activity resumed, Swanson Bros became one of Melbourne's leading builders, specializing in contracts requiring extensive masonry work; at one stage 150 stonemasons were employed at their William Street yards. The firm built the Crown Law offices, the Collins Street Assembly Hall, the dining-room wing of Parliament House, the city baths, the Commonwealth Bank, the Arts and other buildings at the University of Melbourne, the city court, the New Zealand Loan Co. building, Scotch College and the Athenaeum Club. After much controversy, Swanson Bros was chosen in 1911 to construct the reinforced concrete dome of the Melbourne Public Library. Both Donald and John were presidents of the Master Builders' Association of Melbourne and the Federation of Master Builders of Australia.

Completely absorbed by his work as a building contractor, Donald was the driving force in the business while John became the public figure. A prominent Freemason, John was a Melbourne City councillor (1914-23) for Bourke ward, chairman (1919) of the council's public works committee and mayor (1920-23). Knighted in 1923, he inaugurated the Lord Mayor's Metropolitan Hospitals Fund and was president of the National War Memorial Committee. Survived by his wife and five daughters, he died at St Kilda of cirrhosis of the liver on 4 February 1924 and was buried in the local cemetery. His estate was sworn for probate at £31 757.

Donald continued to manage the business even after his total loss of sight in 1931. Blindness did not deter him from being driven in a motor car to building sites where he could discuss projects with his foremen. He died at his St Kilda home on 11 September 1940 and was buried in Brighton cemetery. His estate was sworn for probate at £18 891. On 26 March 1903 at East Melbourne he had married with Presbyterian forms Charlotte Baillie Luff who survived him with their two daughters and a son. Swanson Bros remained a family business until 1983.

J. Smith (ed), *Cyclopedia of Victoria*, 2 (Melb, 1904); *Architectural Science Review*, 2, no 1, Mar 1959, p 39; *Table Talk*, 7 Dec 1911; *Argus*, 9 Oct 1920, 5 Feb 1924, 13 Sept 1940; information from Mr D. C. Swanson, Toorak, Melb.

DAVID DUNSTAN

SWANTON, MARY HYNES ('MAMIE')
(1861-1940), trade unionist, was born on 22
June 1861 in West Melbourne, second child of
James Swanton, car proprietor, and his wife
Sarah Marie, née Connelly, both Irish born.
Educated by Benedictine nuns, 'Mamie' later
became a committed atheist. About 1889 she
arrived in Western Australia as a tailoress. In
1896 she attended a Perth public meeting
which called for women's suffrage, and for
women municipal and parliamentary representatives. Having joined the Australian
Natives' Association, in 1900 she was the
first woman to be awarded honorary life
membership. That year she helped to found
the Australian Women's Association (Perth)
and was its first secretary.

Foundation president (1900-05) of the
Perth Tailoresses' Union until its amalgamation with the Tailors' Union, Swanton was a
delegate to the coastal Trades and Labour
Council. She maintained a tireless campaign
to expose and investigate 'sweating' and child
labour in the Perth clothing trades, and wrote
to newspapers and to State and Federal governments. Familiar with the health risks and
the exploitation to which girls of 11 and 12
were exposed, she gave evidence before
numerous inquiries. Her efforts ensured that
the State government and the trade union
movement could not ignore the issue. In 1907
she was elected first woman president of the
Tailors and Tailoresses' Union of Western
Australia. In the same year, after spending
time in Perth Public Hospital, she was so horrified by nurses' hours and conditions that she
crusaded on health issues, advocating the
establishment of a foundlings' home and a
maternity hospital. She also became a prominent member of the Children's Protection
Society.

Possibly because her agitation made it difficult for her to find work in Perth, Swanton
went in 1913 to keep house for her brother at
Kalgoorlie. Intelligent, articulate and a voracious reader, she was active in the local
branch of the A.N.A. and wrote frequently to
newspapers about such issues as conscription
which she vehemently opposed. By 1920 she
had returned to Subiaco. In 1927, when she
officially opened the Perth Working Girls'
Club, a complimentary social was held in her
honour. A lifelong commitment to the cause
of labour did not limit her trenchant criticism
of the movement when it ignored women's
working conditions. Her photograph,
presented in 1927 by the West Australian
Association of Labour Women, shows a
round-faced woman with short bobbed hair
and pince-nez. Swanton was a foundation
member of the Karrakatta Club, and a friend
and associate of the reformers Katharine
Susannah Prichard [q.v.11] and Cecilia
Shelley.

In 1933, after engaging in a controversy
over cremation (which she supported),
'Mamie' visited Britain and her relations in
the United States of America. Returning to
live in Sydney, she confessed to being 'lonely
for my kindred spirits in the West where my
heart is'. They had not forgotten her and sent
telegrams on her birthday. She died in Sydney
on 25 November 1940 and was buried in the
Catholic section of Rookwood cemetery.

J. Williams, *The first furrow* (Perth, 1976);
Westralian Worker, 30 Dec 1940; Swanton papers
(ML).
                                                    EMMA GRAHAME

SWAYNE, EDWARD BOWDICH (1857-
1946), cane-farmer and politician, was born
on 4 December 1857 at Erith, Kent, England,
son of Herbert Wigan Swayne, surgeon, and
his wife Eugenia Keir, née Bowdich. The family moved to New Zealand in 1864, to New
South Wales in 1868 and to the Peak Downs
district in central Queensland in 1876.
Swayne worked as a drover and horse-
breaker on his father's stations, then went to
Plane Creek in the Mackay district where he
engaged in sawmilling and cane-farming; by
1884 he was the proprietor of the Alligator
Creek sawmill and by 1906 owned a cane-
farm of 580 acres (235 ha). On 11 June 1890
he had married Margaret Ellen Thompson (d.
1915) with Anglican rites at Holy Trinity
Church, Mackay.

When the advent of the central mill system
made it necessary for small cane-growers to
organize, Swayne was a leading spirit in
founding the Pioneer River Farmer's Association in 1892. For fourteen years the secretary of what subsequently became the most
powerful farmers' organization in Queensland, in 1906 Swayne took over the presidency of the P.R.F.A. which later merged
with the United Cane Growers' Association.

After a brief stint with the Pioneer Shire
Council, he stood for the seat of Mackay as an
Independent in 1902 and won it in 1907 as a
farmers' candidate supporting (Sir) Robert
Philp [q.v.11]. Swayne convened a meeting of
rural parliamentarians in December 1909 to
form the Farmers' Parliamentary Union, a
group within the government founded 'to discuss measures relating to agricultural pursuits, and if necessary to arrange concerted
action thereon'. He was appointed secretary
of this body, from which the Country and Progressive National Party later developed. The
F.P.U. facilitated the passage of several
measures beneficial to agriculture, especially
the sugar industry. Its effectiveness was neutralized with the Labor victory of 1915.
Swayne was to remain his party's secretary
until he retired from politics in May 1935.
When the conservative Moore [q.v.10] gov-

ernment was formed in 1929 Swayne did not receive a portfolio, possibly because it was thought that he would allow his staunch rural regionalism to take priority over cabinet policy. In 1931 he successfully introduced a private member's bill—a simple but effective amendment to the Courts of Conciliation Act —allowing justices of the peace and police magistrates to undertake some of the work previously done by qualified lawyers.

Swayne died in Brisbane on 15 June 1946 and was cremated; he was survived by his wife Olive Lilian, née Kay, whom he had married on 16 June 1925 at St Stephen's Anglican Church, Coorparoo, and by three sons and two daughters of his first marriage. Although 'quiet' and 'unobtrusive', Swayne had been able to mould the farmers in his district and their representatives in parliament into strong rural lobbies. He had swum flooded creeks, when necessary, to keep appointments and had lived to see fulfilled his 1899 prediction that farmers would achieve their legislative requirements through their own unity.

C. A. Bernays, *Queensland politics during sixty (1859-1919) years* (Brisb, nd, 1919?); *Qld Agr J*, 1 Aug 1899, p 154; *Illustrated souvenir of the city and district of Mackay* (Mackay, 1937); *Pugh's Almanac*, 1912; *Daily Mercury*, 17 June 1946.

BRIAN F. STEVENSON

SWEET, GEORGINA (1875-1946), zoologist, academic and philanthropist, was born on 22 January 1875 in Brunswick, Melbourne, elder of two daughters of GEORGE SWEET (1844-1920), then a plasterer, and his wife Fanny, née Dudman, both English born. George, a fellow of the Geological Society, ran the Brunswick Brick, Tile & Pottery Co. An amateur geologist, he built up an extensive fossil collection, now in the Museum of Victoria, corresponded widely with Australian geologists and was president of the Royal Society of Victoria (1905). In 1888-95 he investigated fossils in the Mansfield district for (Sir) Frederick McCoy [q.v.5], and was second-in-command to (Sir) Edgeworth David [q.v.8] on the Funafuti expedition in 1897. As a girl, Georgina played the organ in the local Methodist church where her father was steward and lay-preacher. She acted as assistant in his geological work and learned sound business principles from him. He encouraged her to take up a career in science.

Georgina was educated at Parkville Ladies' College and the University of Melbourne (B.Sc., 1896; M.Sc., 1898; D.Sc., 1904), winning awards such as the university's Mac-Bain [q.v.5] scholarship (1898). Her research was carried out in the biology department—

initially under Professor (Sir) Baldwin Spencer [q.v.] to whom she was devoted and who counted her one of his best students—and later in the veterinary school. At first she worked on the zoology of Australian native animals. She had a paper on Australian earthworms read before the Linnean Society of London in 1900 and her doctorate was awarded for a detailed study of *Notoryctes*, the Australian marsupial 'mole'. Later she became interested in the parasites infesting Australian stock and native fauna and this work won her the David Syme [q.v.6] research prize (1911). She published widely and came to be judged the country's foremost parasitologist. On overseas leave in 1913-14 she investigated worm-nodules in cattle for the Federal government, and during a 1925-27 journey in Asia gathered information on the buffalo fly for the Council for Scientific and Industrial Research. She was for many years a member of the Australian National Research Council.

Her family apart, Sweet's life became centred in the university. In 1896-1907 she also taught in several of Melbourne's leading secondary schools and served on the council of the Association of Secondary Teachers (1905-12). She began her university teaching career in 1898, demonstrating in biology to medical and science students. From 1901 she was lecturer in biology at Queen's College until December 1908 when she was appointed lecturer and demonstrator in biology in the university. From 1909 she was also lecturer in parasitology in the new veterinary school and research institute under Professor J. A. Gilruth [q.v.9] and, later, Professor H. A. Woodruff [q.v.]. Keenly interested in her students' welfare, she could transfer to them her own enthusiasm, and won a high reputation for teaching and organizational skills; but, despite her great energy, she was to find the dual appointment a source of strain. From 1911 to 1919 her workload was frequently increased by the often prolonged absences of both her professors and, during the war years, by the concentration of the veterinary course to allow for earlier qualification. On the death of T. S. Hall [q.v.9] in 1915, Sweet became second-in-command of the biology school, and during Spencer's absence from November 1916 to March 1917 she was Australia's first female acting professor. In 1919, when Spencer was due to retire, Sweet was persuaded to apply for the chair (now zoology), despite exhaustion from overwork and distress due to the recent deaths of her mother and her sister, Elizabeth Mary Sweet, M.D., and the uncertain health of her father. She had enthusiastic support from academics at home and abroad, but the chair went to W. E. Agar [q.v.7]. In 1920 Sweet became the university's first woman associate-professor.

By 1921, however, she had to apply for sick-leave. At the end of 1924, she retired from zoology, remaining part-time lecturer in the veterinary school. Two years later she resigned altogether, but, as an honorary lecturer, still did some teaching.

Sweet took an active part in many sides of university life. She served on the science, veterinary and agriculture faculties, and in 1924 was acting dean of the veterinary faculty. On the council of the Graduates' Association and the executive committees of the Science Club and the women students' club, she gave popular public lectures on scientific subjects and was honorary secretary of the University Union in 1912. Moderately wealthy after her father's death, Sweet gave generously to university and other appeals. Although she did not see herself as one of the 'new women' and never felt disadvantaged by her sex, she was always a vigorous supporter of women's rights. She pushed to have women admitted to the university senate, and for seventeen years was president of the provisional council, working to establish the University Women's College which she served for the rest of her life. In 1936 fellow graduates elected her the first woman member of the university council.

Equally energetic outside the university, Sweet became involved in national and international affairs and professional bodies. She was an active member of the Australasian Association for the Advancement of Science, the Royal Society of Victoria, the Field Naturalists' Club and the Lyceum Club. Australian president of the Young Women's Christian Association in 1927-34, she was a vice-president of the world Y.W.C.A. from 1934. She was a foundation member of the Victorian Women Graduates' Association and its representative on the national and international bodies. In 1930 she became first president of the Pan-Pacific Women's Association. When she was appointed O.B.E. in 1935, representatives of over twenty organizations in which she was involved gathered to congratulate her.

Late in her life Sweet's eyesight deteriorated; she wore blue-tinted spectacles, walked with a stick and appeared somewhat formidable to young students; but her straightforward and generous nature was appreciated by a wide and varied circle of friends. Her greatest recreational delight was travelling. Her journeys usually combined business with pleasure and included a trek through Africa from the Cape to Cairo (1922) with Jessie Webb [q.v.], and extensive travel in Asia. Having a keen sense of fun, she was amused when students dubbed her 'Spencer's Faerie Queene'. She had deeply-held religious beliefs, belonged to the Methodist Church and, like her father, served for many years on the council of Queen's College. She died at her Canterbury home on 1 January 1946 and was cremated. Her estate, valued for probate at £98 263, included considerable sums for the university, her Church and various charitable bodies.

Principal women of the Empire, 1 (Lond, 1940); D. J. Mulvaney and J. H. Calaby, 'So much that is new' (Melb, 1985); *Aust Women's Digest*, May 1946; *Argus*, 10 June 1914, 24 Sept 1934, 9 Dec 1936; *Star* (Melb), 15 Oct 1934; *Sun News-Pictorial*, 4 July 1935; *Spectator* (Melb), 9 Jan 1946; J. R. Rapke, Papers on various Australian women: Georgina Sweet (ms, NL); Univ Melb Archives; information from Dr H. E. Albiston, Nth Balwyn, Melb.

MONICA MACCALLUM

SWINBURNE, GEORGE (1861-1928), businessman, politician and philanthropist, was born on 3 February 1861 at Paradise, near Newcastle-upon-Tyne, England, eldest of three sons and a daughter of Mark William Swinburne, patternmaker, and his wife Jane, née Coates. After his formal education at the Royal Grammar School, Newcastle, ended at 13, George was apprenticed to J. Williamson & Co., chemical merchants. Although his commercial training proved useful, he wanted to be an engineer like his maternal uncles and, while working as a clerk (1880-82), took himself to night-classes. His spare time was occupied with music lessons (he had a fine voice), political debates, lectures, omnivorous reading, Methodist Sunday School teaching and, before work, the study of shorthand and German. He also went walking and fishing, but took hard work for granted.

In September 1882 Swinburne left home for London, where his uncle John Coates was a gas and hydraulic engineer, and found employment to supply the practical experience he needed. In May 1884 R. Dempster & Sons sent him to Vienna, in charge of seven English workmen, to install a gas-holder and plant. He had self-taught German, night-class engineering theory and eighteen-months experience to support his innate energy, intelligence and tact in enabling him to avert an impending strike, to handle a 'leisurely' workforce of mixed nationalities and to complete his job to Dempsters' satisfaction. In April 1885 he put £300 savings into a partnership with his uncle; when Coates went to Australia in December to start a business there, Swinburne was left in charge in London. In 1886 he joined his uncle in Melbourne.

The first initiative was the Melbourne Hydraulic Power Co. (1887), supplying power to city buildings. Swinburne developed the gas-engineering side of the business into the

Colonial Gas Association, linking small municipal gasmakers scattered around Australia into a network with access to the necessary capital and expertise. Prospering through the difficult 1890s, the association launched him on a successful business career. He became superintendent, managing director and finally chairman of directors (Australasia) of Colonial Gas; other directorships included those with Johns [q.v.4] & Waygood (1891-1905, 1908-13), the Broken Hill Water Supply Co. (from 1898), the Metropolitan Gas Co. (1898-1911), the National Mutual Life Assurance Society Ltd (1910-13, 1924-28; chairman 1928), and the Mount Lyell Mining & Railway Co. (1913, 1918-28; chairman 1924-28). Along the way he gained formal qualifications, becoming a member of the Institution of Mechanical Engineers (1897) and of the Institution of Civil Engineers (1914).

These engagements mostly reflected Swinburne's original professional bent, but most of them had also some innovative aspect; it was an interest in innovation, allied with concern for the social aspects of engineering, which took him beyond the business world. Interest in electric power development, dating from an 1897 visit to Germany, led him in 1898 to stand for the Hawthorn City Council. By 1902 he was mayor. Thenceforward his public career limited his business activities; directorships were periodically sacrificed to public obligations.

After standing unsuccessfully for the Legislative Assembly in 1900, Swinburne entered it as member for Hawthorn in 1902 on an 'economy and reform' ticket. Under (Sir) Thomas Bent [q.v.3], he was minister for water supply (1904-08) and agriculture (1905-08). He left the ministry in 1908, with Sir Alexander Peacock and Donald Mackinnon [qq.v.11,10], having found Bent an impossible leader. Swinburne might have become premier in 1908 and again in 1913, but he had no taste for factional politics and was never again a minister, although he made major contributions to debate, such as his speech on the 1910 Education Act. He resigned his seat in 1913. In 1922 he ran unsuccessfully for the Commonwealth Senate on the Nationalist ticket. In 1928 he was elected to the Legislative Council, defeating the young (Sir) Robert Menzies.

Swinburne's short political career included some important achievements. He was appointed minister of water supply in 1904 because the 1901-02 drought had focused attention on irrigation policy for which he had a recognized concern. His Water Act of 1904 placed all State water-supplies under the control of a new statutory authority—publicly-funded and in principle independent of political control—the State Rivers and Water

Supply Commission. He thought that the public, and not the private landowner, should own running water, that irrigation policy should be a State rather than a local responsibility, that farmers given water rights should be rated accordingly whether they used them or not, and that, in setting up a new system, the State should take over debts accumulated by existing small-scale enterprises. Swinburne had a good analytical mind, he listened to comment and his integrity was absolute. In getting his Act through, he spent much time winning over the country electorate and his speech to the Legislative Council, made by special permission, overcame the council's original opposition. On the closely-allied question of the interstate sharing of Murray River water, he made little progress because New South Wales and South Australia were still havering and Commonwealth participation was also needed, but his draft agreement of 1906 was remarkably close to that finally accepted in 1915. Characteristically, he saw his other portfolio, agriculture, as primarily concerned with educating the Victorian farmer; to this end, he did his best to promote practical agencies—agricultural colleges and high schools, demonstration farms, departmental publications—backing them with support for university chairs in agriculture and veterinary science. Here, too, he set valuable precedents.

After he left the assembly, Swinburne spent more than ten years in government posts, nearly all Federal. In 1913, abandoning all other commitments, he became chairman of the Inter-State Commission which had been planned as a permanent organization investigating and resolving economic conflicts between the States. Under his chairmanship it produced valuable reports, but when a High Court of Australia decision of 1915 invalidated its quasi-judicial powers, Swinburne saw it as an ineffectual body and resigned in 1917. However, he valued its creation of the Advisory Council of Science and Industry, the germ of the future Commonwealth Scientific and Industrial Research Organization. By the time he withdrew, he was deeply involved in war work: he was 1917-18 controller of capital issues, and became chairman of the Defence Department's business administration board, civil and finance member of the Military Board and a member of the Australian Imperial Force Canteens trust.

In 1919-25 Swinburne was a foundation member of the State Electricity Commission. This involvement was significant. He disclaimed any interest in the theory of 'state socialism', but as an engineer he accepted that in the public utility area there were some tasks which, if they were to be done at all, would have to be in public rather than in private hands, and that the supply of electricity from Victoria's brown-coal reserves was one such task. The model for the S.E.C. was his own water supply commission.

As background to these activities—and to others such as membership of the council of the University of Melbourne (1908-13, 1918-28), the Queen's College council and the board of trustees of the Public Library, museums and National Gallery (1910-28), and as League of Nations delegate (1925)—there lay a lifelong interest in education. Swinburne believed that, although basic education should be funded by the state, it could not flourish without maximum local involvement. When in 1907 he followed up the Fink [q.v.8] report by giving £3000 to found an Eastern Suburbs Technical College, he persuaded the Kew, Hawthorn and Boroondara municipalities to underwrite it. The future Swinburne Technical College (so named against its founder's wishes) opened in 1909 and became a 'selfish hobby' to which he gave upward of £20 000; he chaired its council until he died. In his eyes the education needed for economic progress should also open intellectual windows; his student plumbers learned architectural history as background to the technique of their craft. He was concerned for the mass of adolescents drifting into dead-end, unskilled, 'uneducative' occupations, and urged the provision of compulsory part-time 'continuation' classes: 'I see no other method of giving equal opportunity than by increasing the facilities of education'. Interestingly, (Sir) William McPherson and H. V. McKay [qq.v.10] were close friends. All were Nonconformists; all were wealthy self-made engineers; all were convinced that private wealth should be used for public benefit, and that some of it should be channelled into education.

In private and public life, and in his many benefactions, Swinburne had the unswerving support of his wife Ethel, née Hamer, whom he had married at the Collins Street Independent Church on 17 February 1890. The support was mutual, for his confidence in her innate abilities launched her on a considerable independent career of charitable activity. He backed women's suffrage, and he and his wife insisted that their daughters be well-educated, able to support themselves if necessary. There was one persistent shadow. In 1901 a daughter developed osteomyelitis of the jaw. Almost all of Swinburne's public life had a background of acute domestic anxiety, ending only in 1925 when a London surgeon operated on his daughter with triumphant success.

Swinburne collapsed and died in the chamber of the Legislative Council, in which he had only served for three months, on 4 September 1928. Survived by his wife and four daughters

he was cremated. His estate was valued for probate at £64 321.

The Gladstonian liberalism of Swinburne's youth had stayed with him, expanded by wide reading and generous imagination. His political assets were intelligence, integrity, prodigious energy which taxed his long, thin frame, and instinctive tact and humour. He had a good eye for people: he knew the worth of Elwood Mead, (Sir) Harold Clapp and Tom Cherry [qq.v.10,8,7], and the university owed him gratitude for his selection of (Sir) Samuel Wadham as its new professor of agriculture in 1925. Nevertheless, Swinburne was no natural politician. He had felt obliged to work with Bent, without apparently realizing that the personal association might have persuaded a suspicious Age that Swinburne could not be as honest as he seemed. The resultant libel in 1908—which cost the Age £3250 in damages—was peculiarly outrageous in that, far from profiting from office, Swinburne served the State for nothing: his whole parliamentary income went unobtrusively to charity. He was a modest man, uninterested in public honours, and a lifelong Methodist with strong, sometimes rigid, principles. At his home, Shenton, no games were played on Sundays. Yet, he was not intimidating. What everyone remembered was his great infectious shout of laughter.

E. H. Sugden and F. W. Eggleston, *George Swinburne* (Syd, 1931); F. W. Eggleston, *State socialism in Victoria* (Syd, 1932); G. Serle, *John Monash* (Melb, 1982); C. W. Coates, *Coates, the first one hundred years* (Syd, 1985); W. Osmond, *Frederic Eggleston, an intellectual in Australian politics* (Syd, 1985); *PD* (Vic), 1908, p 699; *Age*, 15 July, 8, 9 Sept 1908, 5 Sept 1928; *Argus*, 16, 17, 19 Sept 1908, 26 Aug 1909, 16 Mar 1910, 5 Sept 1928; S. Murray-Smith, A history of technical education in Australia (Ph.D. thesis, Univ Melb, 1966); Swinburne Inst of Technology Archives *and* Uniting Church, Collins St, Melb, Archives (LaTL); Univ Melb Archives; personal information.

ALISON PATRICK

SYKES, ALFRED DEPLEDGE (1871-1940), clergyman, was born on 20 March 1871 at Lepton, Yorkshire, only son of Samuel Sykes, fancy weaver, and his wife Annie, née Depledge; although baptized Abraham, he later took the name Alfred. Having been raised an Anglican, as a young man he joined Queen Street Wesleyan Chapel, Huddersfield, and in 1893 transferred membership to Moldgreen Congregational Church. In 1894-96 he studied at the Congregational Institute, Nottingham, then trained for the ministry at Western College, Plymouth. On 15 May 1902 in St Helier, Jersey, he married Julia Agnes Hooper. In

1900 he had been ordained at Romford Road Congregational Church, Forest Gate, London, where he ministered until 1904; that year he took the pastorate of Stow [q.v.2] Memorial Church, Adelaide, the 'cathedral church' of South Australian Congregationalism.

A well-known exponent of liberal Christianity who believed in the need for 'a theology which reckons with the dominant intellectual conceptions of the twentieth century', he introduced his congregation to the ideas of Adolf von Harnack and the 'New Theology' of R. J. Campbell. Sykes taught that religion's primary function was to 'specialise on the spiritual life' and to 'foster the worshipful spirit'. To this end, he altered the church's interior to emphasize the sanctuary and persuaded his congregation to adopt a semi-liturgical form of service with a robed choir.

Because of his wife's tuberculosis, Sykes resigned in 1906 to take her to the Channel Islands. There she died. He resumed his pastorate in 1907-13 and in 1911 was chairman of the Congregational Union of South Australia. At Unley Park on 9 January 1912 he married Dorothy Grace Bakewell, daughter of a wealthy deacon of Stow Church. Having visited England, he accepted appointment in 1915 to Collins Street Independent Church, Melbourne. After two years he resigned and moved to Strathfield-Homebush Congregational Church, Sydney, where he became prominent in New South Wales Congregationalism.

Tall and red-headed, Sykes thrived on debate and had a restless, inquiring mind. Although he remained liberal in theology, he embraced the view that Christianity required a corporate expression through dogma, sacraments and the 'historic episcopate'. In 1922 he joined the Church of England and was ordained priest next year in Adelaide where he was assistant curate of St John's, Halifax Street, and priest-in-charge of St Cyprian's, North Adelaide (1923-35). He frequently wrote on topical and religious subjects for Adelaide newspapers, including a weekly column in the *News* as 'Mark Western'. He retained an interest in scholarly theology and in 1924, with Congregationalist E. S. Kiek [q.v.9], founded the interdenominational Adelaide Theological Circle.

In the early 1930s Sykes became involved in the Oxford Group movement and grew dissatisfied with Anglican ecclesiasticism. Following nine months in Perth in 1936 as locum tenens at Christ Church, Claremont, he returned to Adelaide and withdrew from the Anglican ministry. In 1937 he rejoined Stow Church which appointed him associate pastor. Survived by his wife and two sons, Sykes died of heart disease in Adelaide on 31 July 1940 and was buried in Mitcham cemetery.

E. S. Kiek, *Our first hundred years* (Adel, 1950); *SA Congregationalist*, Dec 1907; *Stow Church Mag*, 1909-11; *Congregationalist* (Syd), Aug 1922; *Observer* (Adel), 30 Mar 1907; *Register* (Adel), 23 June 1922; *Advertiser* (Adel), 1 Aug 1940; Stow Memorial Church records (held by Pilgrim Uniting Church, Adel); Congregational Union of SA records (Mortlock Lib); Sykes sermons and addresses (held by Mr M. Sykes, Bordertown, SA).

DAVID HILLIARD

SYME, DAVID YORK (1876-1963), businessman, was born on 24 November 1876 at Williamstown, Melbourne, fourth child of David Yorke Syme, clerk and later shipowner, and his wife Mary Eliza, sister of (Sir) George Reid [q.v.11]. Educated locally and at Scotch College, Melbourne, David worked in 1893 as a junior clerk in his father's Melbourne Steamship Co. and then gained experience with other firms. Appointed manager of M.S.Co. in Perth, Western Australia, in 1904, he returned to Melbourne as joint manager in 1909. On 10 December 1912 he married Jessie Mary Laycock with Presbyterian forms at Trinity Church, Camberwell.

During World War I Syme was chairman (1917-18) of the Australian Steamship Owners' Federation. He became general manager of M.S.Co. in 1918 and managing director in 1919. That year, as a member of the Commonwealth Shipping Board, he was appointed deputy controller of shipping and was later a member of the board's interstate central committee. When Prime Minister Hughes [q.v.9] intervened in the marine engineers' strike of 1920, he summoned Syme and hastened the referral of the dispute to a tribunal. Syme was an Australian delegate to the International Conference of Shipowners (1921) which did the ensuing work of such previous maritime law conferences as the International London Convention (1914) and the Hague Rules (1921). Concentrating its effort on deck cargoes, load-lines and shipowners' liability, the conference succeeded in having regulations approved in these areas.

In 1932 Syme succeeded his father as chairman of the M.S.Co. In the same year he was appointed honorary consul for Japan in Melbourne, a position in which he took pride and from which he drew satisfaction. In October 1937, while visiting the Far East with his wife and daughters, he was granted an audience with the Emperor of Japan and met the Emperor's brother, Prince Chichibu. Both showed interest in Australia and Syme found them well informed. In November the Emperor conferred on Syme the Imperial Order of the Sacred Treasure (fourth class). Having ensured that an agreement for the purchase of that season's wool clip (500 000 bales) would be honoured, Syme went to Manchukuo (Manchuria) where he was impressed by development projects. On his return to Australia he became an apologist for the puppet state. Together with Japanese consulate officials in Melbourne, Syme received menacing letters and death threats after Japan's pact with Germany in October 1940.

From 1939 to 1945 Syme was a member of the Commonwealth Shipping Control Board which had wide-ranging powers over water transport. In 1942-45 he was appointed chairman of the New South Wales Cargo Control Committee. He was equally occupied with other problems of the industry, such as the change to diesel motors (which he had advocated since 1934), cargo pillaging and the shortage of skilled labour. After 1945 Syme helped to address issues like the shortfall in shipowners' wartime earnings, the effect of continuing pillaging on rising cargo-handling costs, and the slow shipping turnaround due to the shortage of wharf labourers.

A commissioner (1929-52) of the Melbourne Harbour Trust, Syme was an associate member (1936) of the Institute of Naval Architects (Great Britain). He sat on the board of several companies, including the National Bank of Australasia, the Mount Lyell Mining & Railway Co. Ltd and the Metropolitan Gas Co. Syme was also active in charitable and philanthropic work. For forty-four years a member of the board of management of the Royal Melbourne Hospital, he was an executive member of several other organizations and a benefactor of the Mission to Seamen. He belonged, as well, to Melbourne Rotary Club.

Predeceased by his wife, Syme died at his Kew home on 8 May 1963 and was cremated; two sons and two daughters survived him; his estate was sworn for probate at £165 188. With his death the shipping industry lost an autocratic financial magnate of 'acumen, rigid honesty and soundness', and an outstanding personality.

History of Scotch College, Melbourne, 1851-1925 (Melb, 1926); *SMH*, 30 Jan 1920, 26 Nov 1921, 20 Nov, 6 Dec 1937, 16 Feb, 5 Sept 1939, 14 Oct 1940, 3 Sept 1942, 25 Feb 1943, 28 Aug 1947, 24 Feb 1949, 30, 31 Aug 1951, 9 May 1963; *Sun News-Pictorial*, 26 Oct 1932, 10 Dec 1937; *Herald* (Melb), 1 Oct 1934, 15 Aug 1936; *Age*, 9 May 1963.
                                        G. R. HENNING

SYME, SIR GEOFFREY (1873-1942), newspaper proprietor, was born on 3 March 1873 in South Melbourne, fourth son of David Syme [q.v.6], newspaper proprietor, and his wife Annabella, née Johnson. He attended Kew High School (1883-89) and the University of Melbourne (1891-92) where he took

two years to complete first-year arts, being primarily interested in football. He then joined the *Age* and from 1898 was trained in management by his father who had chosen him as his successor. In 1901 Geoffrey worked briefly on the London *Observer* and on 15 January 1902 at Waddington, Yorkshire, married 18-year-old Violet Addison Garnett; intelligent and widely read, she discussed current events daily with him. In 1902 he began editing *Every Saturday*, forerunner of the *Age*'s literary supplement.

Under the terms of his father's will, in 1908 Geoffrey was given editorial control of the *Age* and the *Leader*. His elder brother John Herbert (1859-1939), the business manager, objected, but Sir Samuel Gillott's [q.v.9] legal opinion confirmed Geoffrey's position. For thirty-four years, assisted by editors G. F. H. Schuler, L. V. Biggs [qq.v.11,7] and (Sir) Harold Campbell, he dictated the *Age*'s policy.

Idealistic and earnest, Syme determinedly attempted to carry on his father's radical protectionist if idiosyncratic policies, immediately identifying himself with the Deakin-Brookes [qq.v.8,7] Liberal grouping but opposing the Fusion of 1909 and providing much less than entire support at the 1910 election. Journalist Roy Bridges [q.v.7] described Syme as 'keen of eyes, dark, dry, quiet and incisive'; his reputation for hardness and grimness may have masked shyness and reticence. A later *Age* man Herbert Mishael recalled Geoffrey's graciousness toward the staff he respected and how he upheld the ideal of 'a responsible, reliable, and well-written' paper not simply directed to money-making.

Under Geoffrey Syme the *Age* was sometimes characterized as 'the yacht', twisting and tacking on major issues. It strongly supported a Greater Melbourne Council and the exploitation of Victoria's coal resources by the state, but constantly attacked the State Electricity Commission and the Victorian Railways, often on flimsy grounds. The *Age* reviled the Bruce-Page [qq.v.7,11] government for abandoning the arbitration system, supported Labor at the 1929 and 1931 elections and Theodore's [q.v.] economic policies, but backed the Premiers' Plan. It constantly criticized rural subsidies and the University of Melbourne, but broadly supported Dunstan's [q.v.8] State government.

Although Syme competed aggressively with rival proprietors, (Sir) Keith Murdoch's [q.v.10] lively *Sun News-Pictorial* captured the popular market. By 1940 the *Age*'s circulation was slightly less than in 1900. David Syme's complicated will made it difficult to modernize the paper, but in the late 1930s a new press was installed and the front page at last featured the news.

Syme took an interest in rubber and coconut-planting in Papua and established Dorset Horn sheep on his inherited Pendleside estate. His home, Blythswood, was at Kew. A golfer and racing man, he was a member of the Australian and Athenaeum clubs. In 1941 he was appointed K.C.M.G. Survived by his wife and four daughters, he died at the Mercy Private Hospital, East Melbourne, on 30 July 1942 and was buried in Booroondara cemetery, Kew, with Anglican rites. His estate was sworn for probate at £177 450. His younger brother Oswald Julian (1878-1967), a cattle-breeder and dairy-farmer at Macedon, took control of the *Age*. In 1948 it was converted to a public company in which the family retained a majority interest. Numerous takeover offers were resisted until 1972 when, following a partnership arrangement in 1966, Fairfax interests took control.

H. H. Peck, *Memoirs of a stockman* (Melb, 1942); R. Bridges, *That yesterday was home* (Syd, 1948); C. E. Sayers, *David Syme* (Melb, 1965); *Age*, 16 Oct 1954, centenary supp; Syme family papers *and* V. Condon mss *and* H. Mishael, Lend me your ears, ms (LaTL); R. Priestley diary, 30 June 1937 (Univ Melb Archives). GEOFFREY SERLE

SYME, SIR GEORGE ADLINGTON (1859-1929), surgeon, was born on 13 July 1859 at Sherwood, Nottinghamshire, England, son of George Alexander Syme, Baptist minister, and his wife Susanna, née Goodier. In 1863 his father brought the family to Melbourne, where his brothers David and Ebenezer [qq.v.6] had founded the *Age*, and worked as a journalist and editor of the *Leader* newspaper.

Educated at Wesley College and the University of Melbourne (M.B., 1881; B.Ch., 1882; M.S., 1888), George Adlington graduated with first-class honours and an exhibition, and became a resident medical officer at the Melbourne Hospital. After studying at King's College Hospital, London, he was made a fellow of the Royal College of Surgeons of England in 1885. He held appointments at the Royal London Ophthalmic Hospital, the Central London Throat and Ear Hospital and the Soho Hospital, receiving excellent testimonials from senior London surgeons.

In 1887 Syme returned to Melbourne and was appointed demonstrator and examiner in anatomy at the university, honorary pathologist to the Women's Hospital, editor of the *Intercolonial Medical Journal* and honorary surgeon to out-patients at the Melbourne Hospital. In 1889 he became surgeon to the Victorian police force and in 1890 acting professor of anatomy. In 1891 he was appointed honorary consultant surgeon to the Mel-

bourne Dental Hospital and in 1893 honorary surgeon to in-patients at St Vincent's Hospital where, that year, he carried out the first successful removal of an intra-cranial meningioma in Australia.

On 10 May 1899 at St John's Anglican Church, Camberwell, Syme married English-born Mabel Berry (d. 1931). He established his home and practice at 19 Collins Street, Melbourne. In 1903 Syme resigned from St Vincent's when he was appointed in-patient surgeon to the Melbourne Hospital. There he practised general surgery: his interests included abdominal surgery, ophthalmology, otolaryngology, neurosurgery and orthopaedics. The Melbourne was his first love: he was a student, resident, surgeon, consultant surgeon and finally president of that hospital.

A man of few words, he was known as 'Silent Syme'. Short and thickset, he was highly intelligent, but of dour expression. He spoke slowly, and precisely. Though not a humorous man, he appreciated humour in others. A member of the Repertory, Beefsteak and Wallaby clubs, he was interested in classics, theatre and bushwalking. Above all, he was a man of honesty and integrity, with a profound respect for ethics.

In 1914 Syme enlisted in the Australian Imperial Force with the rank of lieut-colonel and served with the 1st Australian General Hospital in Egypt. He was appointed surgeon consultant to the hospital ship *Gascon* which anchored off Gallipoli. Invalided back to Australia in 1916, after contracting septicaemia through operating, he was an active consultant to the Repatriation Commission and a member of the university council (1912-29). He retired from the Melbourne Hospital in 1919. In 1924 he chaired the Commonwealth royal commission on health.

Twice president of the Victorian branch of the British Medical Association (1908, 1919), chairman of the federal council (1922-29) and a vice-president of the parent body, Syme was knighted in 1924 on retirement from practice. He was president of the Australasian Medical Congress (British Medical Association) in 1924-27. His crowning achievement came with the formation of the College of Surgeons of Australasia (Royal Australasian College of Surgeons) of which he became first president in 1927. His stability, judicial approach and wisdom made him a natural leader. In 1928 he was awarded an honorary LL.D. by the University of Wales and an honorary fellowship of the American College of Surgeons. Syme died of a cerebral haemorrhage at his Malvern home on 19 April 1929 and was buried in Brighton cemetery. His wife, three daughters and son survived him. A portrait by John Longstaff [q.v.10] is held by the Royal Australasian College of Surgeons, Melbourne.

In memoriam. George Adlington Syme 1859-1929 (Melb, nd, 1929?); B. K. Rank, *Jerry Moore and some of his contemporaries* (Melb, 1975); P. Kennedy (ed), *The founders of the Royal Australasian College of Surgeons* (Melb, 1984); *MJA*, 7 July 1956.

BERNARD McC. O'BRIEN

SYMON, SIR JOSIAH HENRY (1846-1934), lawyer and politician, was born on 27 September 1846 at Wick, Caithness, Scotland, son of James Symon, cabinetmaker, and his wife Elizabeth, née Sutherland. Educated at the Stirling High School (dux, 1862) and the Free Church Training College, Edinburgh, Symon migrated to South Australia in 1866. He settled at Mount Gambier and was articled to his cousin J. D. Sutherland. At the invitation of the advocate (Sir) Samuel Way [q.v.], Symon transferred his articles to the Adelaide firm of Way and Brook in 1870. Called to the South Australian Bar in November 1871, Symon entered into partnership with Way on Brook's death in 1872. In 1876 Way became chief justice and, at 29, Symon assumed responsibility for one of Adelaide's finest legal practices. On 8 December 1881 at St Peter's Anglican Cathedral, Adelaide, he married Mary Eleanor Cowle. Appointed Queen's Counsel in 1881, he declined elevation to the Supreme Court Bench in 1884.

On 10 March 1881 he had become attorney general in (Sir) William Morgan's [q.v.5] ministry and won the seat of Sturt in April. After the government fell in June, Symon remained in the Legislative Assembly until 1887 when he contested the south-eastern seat of Victoria and was defeated because of his opposition to protection and the payment of members. In parliament Symon had supported free trade (he was president of the South Australian Free Trade League and an honorary member of the Cobden Club), the independence of the judiciary, liberal pastoral legislation, and the abolition of oaths in courts of law (a policy he continued to press as late as 1929). Despite invitations, he never returned to the colonial parliament. He also declined the offer of a safe Conservative seat in the House of Commons while on a visit to England in 1886.

His major contribution to Australian politics related to Federation. Symon opposed the Federal council bill in 1884, arguing that it would delay or prevent the attainment of a real Federation and endanger responsible government. Already in touch with (Sir) Edmund Barton [q.v.7] and inclined to question the Federal commitment of South Australia's premier Charles Kingston [q.v.9], Symon became president of the Australasian Federation league of South Australia in 1895, and later of the Commonwealth league. He brought the popular Federal movement to life

in the colony. His sense of Australia's destiny rivalled Barton's, and his vision of the possibility of combining nationalism with Imperialism was no less than Alfred Deakin's [q.v.8]. Symon's nationalism was not contradicted or limited by his insistence on the maintenance of certain State rights, although this stand made him a Federalist rather than a unificationist. He aimed, as well, to win the support of newly enfranchised women in South Australia for the Federal movement.

A prominent member of the 1897-98 Australasian Federal Convention, he chaired its judiciary committee. Colonial premiers and Edmund Barton apart, no one spoke more often than Symon and few were listened to with more care. The questions which interested him above all others were those major issues which gave the convention trouble: equal representation of the States in the Senate, equality of power between the Senate and the House of Representatives (even over money bills), the solution of deadlocks between the two Houses of the Federal parliament, the Murray waters question, and the establishment of a Federal supreme court of appeal to replace the anachronistic system of appeal to the Privy Council (about which he changed his mind many years after Federation). Such issues came naturally to an eminent lawyer and a representative of one of the smaller States. Deakin estimated Symon's influence as falling into the second level, a consequence of Symon's inexperience in backroom politicking rather than of his public performances in the convention chamber.

As president of the Federation League, as a speaker and as a pamphleteer, Symon was active in the referendum campaign in his colony. His argument for Federation was based on economics (especially free trade between the States), defence, political advantage, and strongly-felt national sentiment. Along with Kingston and Patrick Glynn [q.v.9], he also made a significant contribution in Western Australia (especially on the goldfields) after the so-called 'apostasy' of Premier Sir John Forrest [q.v.8] and helped to ensure its participation as an original State. When the Commonwealth bill was before the Imperial parliament, Symon co-operated with the delegates in London to prevent re-insertion of the right of appeal to the Privy Council in constitutional cases; at home he tried to stiffen the resolve of colonial governments to counter the machinations of Sir Samuel Way and Sir Samuel Griffith [q.v.9]. In January 1901 Symon was appointed K.C.M.G. for services to the cause of Federation.

In the 1901 Commonwealth elections Symon topped the Senate poll in South Australia; he became leader of the Opposition in that chamber, but remained more interested in improving than opposing nation-building legislation. His greatest interest was in the judiciary bill (1903). He saw the High Court of Australia as 'the keystone of the federal arch' and wished to give it the dignity and usefulness of the Supreme Court of the United States of America. Symon was attorney-general in the Reid-McLean [qq.v.11,10] government of 1904-05; his term in office was notable for the vehemence of his struggle with Chief Justice Griffith over the costs and status of the court. Symon's cause was just, but he spoiled it by the violence of his argument. Perhaps he was partly motivated by the events of 1900 and even by envy of Griffith's appointment. Having again topped the poll at the 1906 election, which he fought on a strong anti-socialist platform, Symon stood aside from the Fusion arrangements of 1910 and refused to sign the Liberal Union's manifesto at the 1913 election. Standing as an Independent, he failed to gain a place and retired to a lucrative practice which he had never really abandoned. While in the Senate he had tried to establish that chamber as a genuine States' House, and as an active House of review.

Symon campaigned vigorously for the war effort and in 1917 became vice-president of the Royal Empire Society (he was already president of the Adelaide branch) and of the Anglo-Saxon Club. In 1928 he gave evidence before the royal commission on the Constitution (1927-29); in 1931 he opposed the appointment of Chief Justice Sir Isaac Isaacs [q.v.9] as governor-general on the ground that it tended to break down the separation of the judiciary, a principle Symon had defended for at least fifty years.

In his understanding of the law and in his skill as an advocate, Symon towered over his contemporaries. He was the acknowledged leader of the South Australian Bar for over thirty years. His ability to marshal arguments and to lead the Bench imperceptibly towards the conclusion he wanted was effective in civil cases. His attention to detail, ability to break down a hostile witness without bullying or harassment, and eloquent pleading to the jury in criminal cases made the death penalty largely obsolete for more than a generation. Such famous cases as the Australian Mutual Provident Society conspiracy case, and those of Bonney (1889), Schippan (1902), Joseph Vardon [q.v.] (1907) and Gillett (1923), marked high points in a distinguished career. Symon was president (1898-1903, 1905-19) of the Law Society of South Australia; a member of the Society of Comparative Legislation and International Law, he occasionally contributed to its journal. He retired from court practice in 1923, but continued to work in chambers almost until his death.

Regarded as one of the finest orators of his day, it was he who was called upon to address the packed Adelaide Town Hall on Queen Victoria's diamond jubilee (1897). The two-hour oration ('Tis Sixty Years Since') was long remembered in the city. Symon filled halls for his speeches on Federation, and in 1900 drew an unprecedented audience to the Democratic Club to hear him speak on abolition of appeals to the Privy Council. He had all the necessary physical attributes. Over six feet (182.9 cm) tall, with a spare and muscular frame, Symon had a broad forehead and a face 'full of power and character'; he bore himself with dignity. His eyes might 'gleam like cold steel' or 'glow with merriment' as he conveyed the range of emotions in a clear and resonant voice. Clearly marshalled, his arguments were unfolded in a manner that was 'winning, gracious and sympathetic'.

A man of broad scholarship, whom some thought 'one of the best informed Shakespearean scholars in Australia', Symon lectured on literary subjects and wrote *Shakespeare the Englishman* (Adelaide, 1929). He was president (1897-98) of the Literary Societies' Union, a patron of the Poetry Recital Society, and a member of the Adelaide University Shakespeare Society and of the Home Reading Union. Sidney Webb described Symon as 'The most considerable person in Adelaide, from an intellectual standpoint' and 'the only man we have met in Australia who can lay claim to the indescribable quality of "distinction" as understood by a fastidious society'. When Symon arrived in South Australia he brought two boxes of books. The library at his Upper Sturt estate, Manoah, grew to be one of the best in the country: consisting of some ten thousand volumes, of which one-quarter related to his legal interests, it was an excellent example of a 'gentleman's library'. He bequeathed his legal books to the university and the remainder (especially rich in English literature) was given to the Public Library of South Australia where it is retained as a separate collection.

Symon's wide-ranging interests included education and scholarship. He was a councillor of the university and in the 1920s sought to establish a residential college for women. Unable to achieve this object, he donated £10 000 for a Women's Union (the Lady Symon Building) and insisted that it be managed by university women. In 1922 he gave £1000 to the University of Sydney for a literary scholarship; in 1924 he donated a bell for the carillon; next year he represented the university at the Congress of the Universities of the Empire. He also established the Sir Josiah Symon Scholarship to send a pupil from Stirling High School to university, and in 1930 gave £1000 to Scotch College, Adelaide, for an English literature scholarship.

His philanthropy extended further.

Symon's financial and managerial interest in the Minda Home for intellectually handicapped children spanned many years. In 1927 he gave £1500 to the Australian Inland Mission to establish the Eleanor Symon Hospital at Innamincka. He also helped to establish the Northcote Rest Home for mothers and babies. In his father's memory, he donated a stained-glass window and funds to the Stirling Baptist Church in 1927. Symon died on 29 March 1934 in North Adelaide, survived by his wife, five sons and five daughters. Given a state funeral, he was buried in North Road cemetery. His estate was valued at £230 330. A court ordered that certain words in his will, 'scandalous, offensive, and defamatory to the persons about whom they were written', be omitted from probate.

J. J. Pascoe (ed), *History of Adelaide and vicinity* (Adel, 1901); H. T. Burgess (ed), *Cyclopedia of South Australia* (Adel, 1907); *To-day* (Melb), 1 May 1934; D. I. Wright, 'Sir Josiah Symon, Federation and the High Court', *JRAHS*, 64, pt 2, Sept 1978; *Advertiser* (Adel) and *Register* (Adel), 30 Mar 1934; *Observer* (Adel), 7 Feb 1903, 27 Nov 1920, 21 Feb 1925; Symon papers (NL).   DON WRIGHT

SYMONDS, SAUL (1894-1952), barrister and Jewish leader, was born on 23 March 1894 in Sydney, second son of Morris Symonds, a Russian-born furniture dealer, and his wife Celia, née Goldstein, a Londoner. He was educated at Sydney Grammar School where he won the junior Knox [q.v.5] prize (1908), excelled at languages and was school captain (1911), and at the University of Sydney (B.A., 1915; LL.B., 1921) where he took first-class honours in French and German (1914). In 1916 he returned to his old school as an assistant master while studying law. On 12 September 1917 he married Lorna Doris Trenn at her Bronte home. He was admitted to the Bar on 16 May 1921 and practised until 1939 when he entered the family business, Symonds Furnishing Ltd. During World War II he worked for the Anzac Buffet and Australian Comforts Fund.

From the 1920s Symonds took an active role in various Jewish organizations and strove to promote Zionism. For many years a councillor, he was president of the New South Wales Board of Jewish Education (1928-30). Like his father, Saul also became a leader of the Great Synagogue, serving on its board from 1933 and holding the positions of treasurer (1936-39, 1945 and 1950-52) and president (1940-44 and 1946-50). He was prominent in the affairs of the New South Wales Jewish Advisory Board and a founder in 1945 of its democratic successor, the New South Wales Jewish Board of Deputies (president 1945-52).

Honorary treasurer for many years of the Sydney Jewish Aid Society, Symonds gave vigorous leadership to the Australian Jewish Welfare Society as treasurer (1938-48) and president (1948-52). He strongly supported Jewish immigration and helped many European refugees to establish themselves within the Australian community. Although regarded by some as a 'patrician' by background, he was sympathetic to newcomers and a forceful negotiator with the government. He markedly exerted himself as president of the Executive Council of Australian Jewry for two terms in 1946-48 when the character of the Jewish community was changing due to the influx of increased numbers of migrants from central Europe.

With cropped dark hair that receded in middle age, Symonds possessed a keen intellect, a sharp wit and a decisive nature. He was a noted patron of art and was thought to have influenced the work of Elioth Gruner [q.v.9] whose paintings he collected. The garden at his Wahroonga home was known for its orchids and admired for its beauty. Survived by his wife, daughter and two sons, Symonds died of a cerebral haemorrhage on 9 April 1952 at Wahroonga and was buried in Rookwood cemetery. He had served the Jewish community with unflagging devotion, gaining the respect and allegiance of those who worked with him.

I. Porush, *The house of Israel* (Melb, 1977); S. D. Rutland, *Edge of the diaspora* (Syd, 1988); *Great Synagogue Congregational J*, May 1952; *Aust Jewish Hist Soc, J*, 3, pt 8, Mar 1953.   M. Z. FORBES

SYMONS, WILLIAM JOHN (1889-1948), soldier and businessman, was born on 12 July 1889 at Eaglehawk, Victoria, son of William Samson Symons (d. 1904), miner, and his wife Mary Emma, née Manning. Educated at Eaglehawk State School, in 1906 he moved with his family to Brunswick, Melbourne, and worked as a commercial traveller. He served for eight years in the militia (5th and 60th battalions) before enlisting in the Australian Imperial Force on 17 August 1914. Posted to the 7th Battalion as colour sergeant, he embarked for Egypt on 18 October, was promoted acting regimental quartermaster sergeant on 9 April 1915 and landed with his battalion at Gallipoli on 25 April. He was commissioned second lieutenant next day and promoted lieutenant on 2 July.

About 5 a.m. on 9 August the Turks made a series of determined attacks on Jacob's Trench at Lone Pine where six Australian officers were killed or severely wounded. Learning that the position had been overrun, Lieut-Colonel H. E. Elliott [q.v.8] ordered Symons to retake the trench. 'I don't expect to see you again', he said, 'but we must not lose that post'. Symons led the charge that drove off the Turks, but the enemy continued attacking from the front and both flanks. Symons received Elliott's permission to abandon fifteen yards (13.7 m) of open trench and to establish a new barricade. Although the Turks set fire to the overhead woodwork, Symons extinguished the flames, kept the barricade in place and finally forced the enemy to discontinue their attacks. One of seven Australians to win the Victoria Cross at Lone Pine, Symons was cited for his conspicuous gallantry and received his V.C. from King George V at Buckingham Palace on 4 December.

Returning to Australia in March 1916, 'Curly' Symons was fêted at civic receptions at Bendigo and Brunswick. He re-embarked for the Western Front as a captain commanding a company in the 37th Battalion. Wounded in the 10th Brigade's raid on 27 February 1917, he was subsequently gassed during the battle of Messines, Belgium, on 7 June. He rejoined his unit in January 1918 and fought at Dernancourt, France, in March. On 15 August he married Isabel Annie Hockley at St Mary's Church, Hayling Island, Hampshire, England; they left next day for Australia, arriving a month before the Armistice. His A.I.F. appointment terminated on 7 December.

In 1918 he adopted the surname of Pen Symons. With his family he later settled at Kenton, Hampshire, where he became a director of several engineering and construction companies. He served as a lieut-colonel in the home guard in 1941-44. Survived by his wife and three daughters, he died of a brain tumour on 24 June 1948 in London. His V.C. and medals are in the Hall of Valour at the Australian War Memorial, Canberra.

C. E. W. Bean, *1, 2 (Syd, 1921, 1924) and The A.I.F. in France,* 1917-18 (Syd, 1937, 1942); L. Wigmore (ed), *They dared mightily,* second ed revised and condensed by J. Williams and A. Staunton (Canb, 1986); *Sabretache,* 23, no 4, Oct/Dec 1982, p 28; *Bendigo Advertiser,* 18, 21 Oct 1915, 14, 17, 21 July 1982; *The Times,* 6 Dec 1915, 26 June 1948; *Argus,* 23 Mar 1916; *Canb Times,* 4 Oct 1967; Lummis, V.C. and G.C. files (Military Hist Soc, Lond); 7th Battalion, item 2, 1st Aust Division, AWM28 collection 2 (AWM); information from Mr D. Pillinger, Maidenhead, Berkshire, Eng.

ANTHONY STAUNTON

SYNAN, MARY (1837-1915), Brigidine nun, was born on 26 January 1837 in Limerick, Ireland, daughter of John Synan, grocer and draper, and his wife Mary, née Sullivan. Of Jewish origin, the Synans had settled in Cork before moving to Limerick as farmers. At age 16, having completed her schooling at the Brigidine Convent, Mountrath, Queen's County, Mary joined the Sisters of St Brigid (founded in 1807); two of her sisters joined the same order. She was professed on 17 January 1857, taking the religious name Mary John.

In 1882 Bishop James Murray [q.v.5] of Maitland, New South Wales, invited the Brigidine Sisters to take charge of the school at Coonamble. A woman of vision, with leadership qualities and administrative ability, Mother John was chosen as superior of the six Sisters who had volunteered to work in Australia. They left London on 20 April 1883 in the *Chimborazo* and arrived in Sydney on 7 June; after a further journey by boat and coach, the Sisters reached the presbytery at Coonamble on the 21st. They took charge of the school, housed in the church and previously staffed by lay teachers, on 9 July. According to custom, the school was divided into classes for young ladies and the poor. In 1884 Mother John supervised the building of a convent, which contained a dormitory for boarders, and a school building was erected.

Named Australian provincial superior of the Brigidine Sisters in New South Wales and Victoria in 1893, Mother John became provincial superior of New South Wales next year when the Victorian Sisters formed a separate province. Under her leadership (until 1907) the Brigidines opened schools at Cooma (1887), Cowra (1894), Cundletown (1899) and Randwick, Sydney (1901), and in New Zealand at Masterton (1898), Foxton (1901) and Pahiatua (1906). The convent at Randwick became the provincial house and novitiate. Cultured and intelligent, Mother John played an important part in developing the high standard of education which characterizes the Brigidine convents. Her 'gifts, poetical and literary, were known, in spite of all precautions, outside the convent walls'.

Strict, upright, blunt, yet with a warmth of personality, she was described as 'a combination of Queen Victoria and Saint Thérèse of Lisieux'. Her compassion and common sense enabled her to compromise between the strictures of Irish monastic life and the different customs, needs and climate of Australia. The superior of Mount St Brigid Convent, Randwick, Mother John died on 6 March 1915 and was buried in the local cemetery.

Freeman's J, 7 Feb 1907, 11 Mar 1915; *Catholic Press,* 11 Mar 1915; Brigidine Sisters Archives (Brigidine convents at Mountrath, Ireland, and St Ives, Syd).

NAOMI TURNER

T

TAAM SZE-PUI; *see* SEE POY, TOM

TAIT, CHARLES (1868-1933), JOHN HENRY (1871-1955), JAMES NEVIN (1876-1961), EDWARD JOSEPH (1878-1947) and SIR FRANK SAMUEL (1883-1965), concert, film and theatrical entrepreneurs, were five of the nine children of John Turnbull Tait (1830-1902), a tailor from Scalloway, Shetland Islands, Scotland, and his English wife Sarah, née Leeming. Tait migrated to Victoria in 1862 and settled at Castlemaine where he married Sarah. Charles, John, Nevin and Edward were born there and educated at Castlemaine State School. About 1879 the family moved to Richmond, Melbourne, where Frank was born. Edward and Frank attended Richmond State School; Frank later studied at Melbourne Church of England Grammar School.

Charles, born on 15 November 1868, left school aged 11 and earned pocket money as an usher at Saturday-night concerts in the Exhibition Building, the Athenaeum Hall and the Melbourne Town Hall. In 1884 he started work as a messenger-boy at Allan [q.v.3] & Co.'s musical warehouse. His brilliance as an organizer ensured a series of promotions. He travelled overseas with George Clark Allan in 1893 and became manager of Allan's store in 1896. On 21 June 1899 Charles married Elizabeth Jane Veitch at St John's Anglican Church, Heidelberg; they were to have two daughters and two sons.

John was born on 21 August 1871. Ambitious to study law, he started his working life as a lawyer's clerk. On 16 February 1898 at Armadale he married Catherine Victoria Scott with Victorian Free Church forms; they were to have six daughters and one son. He forsook the law for theatrical work and in 1902 was engaged by George Musgrove to manage (Dame) Nellie Melba's [qq.v.5,10] triumphal return tour.

Nevin, who was born on 27 June 1876, started work with a sharebroker. On 27 July 1908 at St Peter's parish church, Cranley Gardens, London, he married ELIZABETH MAY NORRISS (1878-1939). Edward, born on 21 August 1878, found employment with a financier, but in 1900 joined J. C. Williamson's [q.v.6] theatrical enterprise, becoming treasurer two years later. He married Anita Jessie Coutie on 26 April 1905 at Scots Church, Melbourne; they were to have three children. Frank, born on 12 November 1883, found

work with a tea merchant. He was married twice: on 29 November 1913 at St Peter's Anglican Church, Melbourne, to Iris Olga Field Barnard (d. 1938); on 16 August 1941 at Toorak Presbyterian Church to Viola Wilson Hogg.

In 1902 John, Nevin and Frank founded J. & N. Tait, concert promoters. Charles, while remaining with Allan's, guided the business, and Edward, still with Williamson, watched from the sidelines. Nevin made his first trip to London in 1903 and engaged a number of celebrity artists to tour Australia, including the Welsh Male Choir, soprano Madame Albani, violinists Haydn Wood and Marie Hall, and (Dame) Clara Butt with her husband Kennerley Rumford. Nevin's further forays resulted in tours by the Royal Besses o' th' Barn Band, Emma Calvé, the Cherniavsky Trio, John McCormack and Harry Lauder.

The brothers' earliest presentations centred on the Athenaeum Hall in Collins Street. Their concerts often included popular, short, film screenings and this interest led them to join with Millard Johnson and William Gibson [q.v.8] in the production of *The story of the Kelly gang* which premièred on 26 December 1906. Running for more than an hour, it was the longest narrative film yet seen in Australia, and possibly the world. It was directed by Charles Tait and much of the film was shot on his wife's family's property at Heidelberg; his wife (who played the role of Kate Kelly), children and brothers all took part. The film, which cost £1000, was extremely successful, and was said to have returned at least £25 000 to its producers.

The Taits, Johnson and Gibson merged their film interests in 1911 to form Amalgamated Pictures which continued to produce features and newsreels. Amalgamated combined with its main opposition, Australasian Films, in 1912, and the Taits then concentrated their energies on concert presentation and occasional film exhibition.

In 1913 J. & N. Tait took a twenty-year lease on a prominent site in Collins Street and constructed a large, luxurious concert-hall, the Auditorium, which opened in May with a gala concert by Butt and Rumford. It was used by the Taits as their principal concert venue until 1934 when it was remodelled and leased to Metro-Goldwyn-Mayer.

Edward—'E.J.'—had maintained his involvement with J. C. Williamson Ltd (affectionately known as 'the Firm'). He became business manager in 1911 and general manager in 1913, following Williamson's death.

Strained relations with (Sir) George Tallis [q.v.] and Edward's continuing close association with his brothers' activities made his position difficult: he left Williamson's in 1916 and joined J. & N. Tait, looking after their affairs in Sydney. A few months later Nevin moved permanently to London to act as their overseas 'anchor'. J. & N. Tait now expanded to include theatrical presentations and challenged Williamson's domination of Australian live theatre. The Taits' first production was *Peg o' my heart*, a comedy romance which proved highly popular. Other plays, pantomimes and musicals followed.

In 1920 the J. & N. Tait and J. C. Williamson interests combined, with J. & N. Tait continuing as a separate company to promote celebrity artists. Over the next two decades many of the world's greatest concert and stage stars appeared in Australia under the Williamson/Tait aegis, among them Melba, Galli-Curci, dal Monte, Chaliapin, Brownlee [q.v.7], Heifetz, Grainger [q.v.9], Paderewski, Menuhin and Pavlova.

Alert to the early possibilities of wireless, the Taits in 1924 formed on behalf of J. C. Williamson Ltd the Broadcasting Co. of Australia Pty Ltd which was granted the licence for 3LO radio in Melbourne. When 3LO came under the control of the government-franchised Australian Broadcasting Co., Williamson's, with Allan's and the *Age* newspaper, were granted a licence to operate 3AW which went on air in 1932 from studios in His Majesty's Theatre, Melbourne. Later, a modern studio complex was built in La Trobe Street.

'The Firm's' theatrical headquarters were located in the Comedy Theatre, Melbourne, from where they controlled a network of theatres across Australia and New Zealand. An attempt to extend their theatrical production activity to London in 1928-29 failed, but their pre-eminence in the theatrical and concert field in Australia and New Zealand remained unchallenged.

The Depression brought hard times for the Taits. Both the Theatre Royal, Melbourne, and His Majesty's, Sydney, were sold for redevelopment; His Majesty's, Melbourne, partly burnt out in 1929, did not reopen until 1934. Charles died in Sydney on 27 June 1933 of hydronephrosis and was buried with Anglican rites in Springvale cemetery, Melbourne. His estate was sworn for probate at £19 404. 'The Firm' survived both the Depression and a short period in 1938-39 when the Taits temporarily lost control of the business to New Zealand-based interests. They kept their theatres open through the war years by staging revivals of past successes and sending their evergreen Gilbert and Sullivan Co. on tour.

Although the Australian Broadcasting Commission began its own programme of celebrity concert artists, many continued to appear for J. & N. Tait, including Gracie Fields, Marjorie Lawrence [q.v.10], Jan Peerce, David Oistrakh and Marian Anderson. Williamson theatres hosted tours of companies led by Cicely Courtneidge, Anthony Quayle, Vivien Leigh and (Sir) Robert Helpmann. Among the major musicals presented by 'the Firm' after World War II were *Annie get your gun, Oklahoma!, Camelot, My fair lady* and *Oliver!*

Two of the brothers died in the post-war decade: Edward of cancer at Point Piper, Sydney, on 12 July 1947 and John—'the grand old gent of the theatre'—at his Malvern home in Melbourne on 23 September 1955. Both were cremated. Their estates were sworn for probate in Victoria at £22 427 and £66 979 respectively.

On 7 March 1961 Nevin died in London, leaving an estate valued at £72 886. His wife Bess Norriss had won a reputation as a miniature portraitist. Born in Melbourne, she had studied at the National Gallery of Victoria School of Art before setting up a studio in London. In 1907 she was made a member of the Royal Society of Miniature Painters. She exhibited at the Royal Academy, the Paris Salon and on return visits to Australia. Examples of her work are in the galleries of New South Wales and Victoria, and in the Royal Collection.

The last of the brothers, Frank, was knighted in 1956. His dream to present Joan Sutherland in her homeland was fulfilled. At the close of her triumphant season, he died at Portsea on 23 August 1965. Survived by his wife and three daughters from each of his marriages, he was cremated. His estate was valued for probate at £121 743. Following his death, 'the Firm's' fortunes faded. Production ceased in 1976, and its theatres were sold.

For over seventy years the Taits had combined to bring to Australians some of the best of the world's musical and theatrical attractions. While their philosophy of quality entertainment, well presented, rarely failed to win audiences, they sometimes resorted to jaded revivals of popular musical comedies. Although they were criticized for not encouraging local talent, they did provide—without any form of government subsidy—employment and experience for thousands of singers, musicians, actors and backstage personnel, and lifted the standard of Australian theatre.

C. Kingston, *It don't seem a day too much* (Melb, 1971); V. Tait, *A family of brothers* (Melb, 1971); J. West, *Theatre in Australia* (Syd, 1978); A. Pike and R. Cooper, *Australian film, 1900-1977* (Melb, 1980).   F. VAN STRATEN

TAIT, GEORGE (1844-1934), Presbyterian minister and administrator, was born on 12 April 1844 at Parramatta, New South Wales, fourth child of Rev. John Tait and his wife Elizabeth, née Blair, both of whom had emigrated from Scotland in 1837 in response to an appeal for clergy to assist the colonial Presbyterian Church.

Educated at Scotch College, Melbourne, George excelled academically and in sport. He matriculated and entered the University of Melbourne (B.A., 1865; M.A., 1878) where he won second-year exhibitions in Greek and Latin, English and logic. He also played football (for Melbourne and Geelong) and intercolonial cricket. Proceeding to New College, Edinburgh, he studied theology and was licensed in 1869 as a preacher by the Free Presbytery of Edinburgh. On 22 June 1869 he married Mary Agnes (d. 1933), daughter of Rev. John Sym with whom he was associated at Greyfriars Church.

Returning to Victoria, in 1870 Tait was ordained and inducted into the widely scattered rural pastorate of Donald which he traversed on horseback. His next ministry (South Yarra) was interrupted by the Victorian Presbyterian Assembly which appointed him principal of the newly established Ladies' College (later Presbyterian Ladies' College) in 1875. Tait brought impressive qualities to this task. As well as possessing intellectual stature and having a commitment to Christian principles, he combined practical common sense with administrative skill. Although inexperienced in the field of education, he insisted on the right to appoint the best talent available to staff the college and stamped it with high standards of academic excellence. In 1879 he caused widespread dismay by resigning. The reasons for his action are not known, but it followed the controversy surrounding the dismissal of his headmaster C. H. Pearson [q.v.5] in 1877.

Tait accepted a call to Warrnambool where his ten years service was marked by an increased Church membership and an extensive building programme. Active in civic affairs, he also became involved in theological controversy with the Baptist community. Never one to shirk an issue, in Sermons on Christian baptism (1881) he argued for the scriptural basis of infant baptism by sprinkling. He also contributed to the atonement debate sparked by discussion of Rev. Charles Strong's [q.v.6] ministry. On public questions, he supported the shorter working week and the placing of Bibles in State schools. These activities and his increasing involvement in assembly affairs brought him prominence within the Church.

In rapid succession Tait was appointed junior clerk of the Church's Victorian Assembly, convenor of the business committee (1883), home mission superintendent (1889), then senior clerk (1891-1933). Meanwhile, in 1891 he returned to South Yarra where he remained until his retirement in 1914. In his capacity as moderator of the Victorian Assembly (1900-01) he attended the inaugural General Assembly of Australia, and served as its clerk until 1933.

In retirement Tait continued to espouse causes through his publications which included *Church union* (1917), *The case against prohibition of the liquor traffic* (1932) and *The Bible, how to think of it* (1919). His assembly speeches were lucid and persuasive. Tall, erect and serious, with a high forehead and white beard, he was the epitome of a scholarly clergyman of his time. Quiet and reserved, he possessed a sense of humour, but did not suffer fools gladly. His family regarded him with affection, tinged with awe, and selflessly met his material needs. He enjoyed reading widely and watching cricket from the members' stand at the Melbourne Cricket Ground.

Born into and nurtured by the Presbyterian Church, George Tait served it with honour and devotion as an administrator whose historical knowledge and judicial mind skilfully guided business through Church courts. In the parish he was esteemed for his evangelical preaching and innovative pastoral work. His theological writings, while not extensive, showed a willingness to confront issues and argue from first principles. Unusually for his time, he was an ecumenist.

Survived by five daughters and three sons, Tait died on 21 December 1934 at East Malvern and was buried in Kew cemetery. His portrait by W. B. McInnes [q.v.10], commissioned in 1930 to commemorate sixty years in the ministry, hangs in the Assembly Hall, Melbourne.

T. W. H. Leavitt (ed), *Australian representative men*, 2 (Melb, 1887); K. Fitzpatrick, *PLC Melbourne* (Melb, 1975); *Centenary history of South Yarra Presbyterian Church, 1854-1954* (np, nd); Presbyterian Church of Vic, *Procs of the Commission of Assembly*, May 1901, May 1902, Nov 1914, May, Nov 1933, May 1934, May 1935; *Procs of the General Assembly of the Presbyterian Church of Aust*, July 1901; *Sth Yarra Presbyterian Church Chronicle*, May 1911; *Messenger* (Presbyterian, Vic & Tas), 11 Jan 1935; information from Mrs J. Drew, 'Chihuahua', Glenthompson, *and* Mrs E. Tait, Warrnambool, Vic, *and* Miss M. Tait, East Brighton, Melb.   VALERIE J. O'BYRNE

TAIT, SIR THOMAS JAMES (1864-1940), railway commissioner, was born on 24 July 1864 at Melbourne, Quebec, Canada, son of (Sir) Melbourne McTaggart Tait, advocate and later chief justice of the Superior Court, Montreal, and his wife Monica Blanche Louisa, née Holmes. Educated at Montreal High School and McGill University, Thomas entered the service of the Grand Trunk Railway in 1880. Between 1882 and 1886 he was private secretary to Sir William Van Horne and subsequently filled a variety of administrative positions with the Grand Trunk and Canadian Pacific railway companies. On 10 December 1890 Tait married Emily St Aubert Cockburn. His railway career continued to prosper and by 1903 he was manager of transportation with Canadian Pacific.

In March 1903 the premier of Victoria, (Sir) William Irvine [q.v.9], announced that Tait had been appointed chairman of commissioners of the Victorian Railways with a salary of £3000 per annum. W. F. Fitzpatrick and C. Hudson were appointed additional commissioners on £1500 per annum. Tait's appointment occurred against the background of continued efforts by the State government to reduce public expenditure following the 1890s depression and was followed by an engine drivers' strike in May 1903. A major feature of the Tait years was the investigation by C. H. Merz into the electrification of Melbourne's suburban railways. In 1908 Merz submitted a plan for the electrification of 124 miles (200 km) of track, a scheme which was estimated to cost £2 227 000 and to take four years to complete. Believing that Merz's proposal was premature, Tait opposed electrification, arguing that money would be better spent on the further development of the State's resources.

Heavily built (13 stone, 82.6 kg) and frequently flourishing a thick cigar, Tait was a strong man who spoke his mind and brooked no interference. He looked upon the railways 'as a great public trust which he was commissioned to administer on sound lines'. His resignation in 1910 caused 'surprise and regret' among those who appreciated his work. During seven years in Victoria he had turned a 'ruinous' annual deficit into a profit, improved and increased the railways' rolling stock, and—as an economy measure—reduced the frequency of trains. Knighted in 1911, he left Victoria with his wife and daughter amid expressions of appreciation and goodwill. Electrification work began in 1913, but was interrupted by World War I: the red carriages of Melbourne's new electric trains were known as 'Tait cars'.

Appointed director-general of national service for Canada in 1916, Tait resigned from this post within a few weeks of accepting it and retired to private life. He died at his summer home at St Andrews, New Brunswick, on 25 July 1940.

L. J. Harrigan, *Victorian Railways to '62* (Melb, nd, 1962?); J. Iremonger et al (eds), *Strikes* (Syd, 1973); *Punch* (Melb), 14 May 1908; *Argus*, 30 Nov, 1 Dec 1910; *Australasian*, 14 Jan 1911; *Herald* (Melb), 1 Nov 1940.   SUSAN JOHNSTON

TAKASUKA, JŌ (1865-1940), farmer, was born on 13 February 1865 at Matsuyama, Japan, only son of Kahei Takasuka and his wife Katsu, née Tamura. He enrolled in the economics faculty of Keiō University, Tokyo, in 1892, but shortly afterwards went to study in the United States of America where he gained his B.A. at Westminster College, Pennsylvania, in 1896.

As a candidate of the Liberal Party, he was returned to the Japanese House of Representatives in March 1898 and retained his seat in the election that followed the government's peremptory dissolution of the House in May. The cost of two campaigns within five months strained the family's financial resources and he did not contest the next election in 1902.

Accompanied by his wife Ichi (1874-1956), daughter of a district court judge Michimoto Maejima, and their two infant children, Takasuka arrived in Melbourne in 1905 and was admitted on a twelve months 'certificate of exemption from the dictation test' granted to enable him to engage in the export and import trade. He set up in business as Takasuka, Dight & Co., Japanese indentors, at 136 Queen Street. As a part-time activity he also taught the Japanese language at Stott & Hoare's Business College. Within eighteen months, however, Takasuka had moved to Nyah, sowed 35 acres (14.2 ha) of rice on land rented from a local farmer, and entered into negotiations with the Victorian government to acquire a suitable allotment of crown land subject to annual flooding on which to cultivate rice. He was granted permissive occupancy of 200 acres (80.9 ha) of such land at Tyntynder West from January 1908 at an annual rent of 6d. per acre (0.4 ha), convertible to a perpetual lease at 3d. per acre after five years and the expenditure of £500 on improvements. The Federal government no less than its State counterpart was impressed by departmental advice that the land was typical of hundreds of acres along the River Murray, 'of little use for other purposes', and indicated that annual extensions of their certificate of exemption were likely for the duration of his experiments. In this manner Takasuka embarked upon a twenty-year battle against the elements in what was then the only sustained attempt to grow rice in Victoria. Yet, he lacked the £700-£800 capital required to build in a single season the levee bank necessary to control the floods, and his attempts to construct it in stages were swept away each year.

His first success was in 1911 when test-plots on his property were harvested. Using these seeds, he grew rice successfully on small parcels of rented land for the next three seasons. At that time the total value of his improvements was only £119. Sales to commercial seedsmen in 1915 enabled him to add another £230 and, although the total still fell short of the required £500, a perpetual lease was issued to him.

Seasonal conditions were such that he was unable to sow rice again until 1919 and then the seed was so old that the crop failed. In 1921 and 1922 he had good harvests on his own property. In the course of his experiments he had developed methods of cultivation appropriate to Australian conditions. Instead of transplanting the seedlings by hand as was done in Japan, he sowed the seed in its permanent position by drill in the manner of Australian wheat-farmers. He was able to show that, by using from two to four feet (61 cm-122 cm) of water per acre, yields of more than one ton could be obtained. But it was a blind alley. Tests of his best variety conducted over four seasons at Yanco Experiment Farm, New South Wales, were not favourable. In 1927 he abandoned rice cultivation, moved elsewhere in the district and tried to grow, in succession, vines, tomatoes and bamboo-shoots, with little success. By disposition he was a theorist rather than a practical man: at Nyah the story is still current that the first time he set a rabbit-trap he baited it.

In July 1939 Takasuka returned alone to Japan with the intention of re-entering trade. He had just set up an office in Kobe as Australia Barter Trade & Co. when he died of heart disease on 15 February 1940 at Matsuyama. He was survived by his wife, daughter Aiko Watters (1903-1970)—a state schoolteacher—and two sons: Sho (1900-1972), tomato-grower and president (1966-67) of Huntly Shire, and Mario (b. 1910), orchardist, who served in Crete and New Guinea with the Australian Imperial Force.

D. C. S. Sissons, 'A selector and his family', *Hemisphere*, 25, no 3, Nov-Dec 1980, p 168; 05075/204 (Lands Dept, Vic); A1 25/27797 (AA).

D. C. S. SISSONS

TALBOT, ALBERT EDWARD (1877-1936), Anglican clergyman, was born on 18 August 1877 at Salford, Lancashire, England, son of Edward Talbot, milk dealer, and his wife Elizabeth, née Rothwell. Educated at Manchester Grammar School, he worked as an estate agent before winning a scholarship to Emmanuel College, Cambridge (B.A.,

1904; M.A., 1908). Awarded several prizes and the Tyrwhitt Hebrew scholarship, he obtained a double first in the theology tripos. Made deacon in 1905, he was ordained priest by the bishop of Manchester on 10 June 1906. Despite tutoring at the conservative Church Missionary Society's training college, Islington (1907-09), he held liberal views and, as rector of Stowell memorial church, Salford (1909-12), joined the 'Group Brotherhood' (Anglican Evangelical Group Movement).

In 1912 Talbot was appointed dean and archdeacon of Sydney by a fellow brotherhood member, Archbishop J. C. Wright [q.v.], who expected him to make St Andrew's Cathedral the centre for an Evangelical social gospel. Talbot responded vigorously. A powerful preacher with a reformist message, he joined the Anglican Church League which stood for a general low churchmanship; he later became its president and wrote for the *Australian Church Record*. Synod and its social questions committee became an important forum. His growing interest in Labor politics, stimulated by his association with Premier James McGowen [q.v.10], set him apart from his colleagues.

Having enlisted in the Australian Imperial Force as senior Anglican chaplain, Colonel Talbot married Adrienne Elizabeth Vert in St Andrew's Cathedral on 5 September 1914. Next month he embarked for Egypt with the 3rd Battalion. On Gallipoli he developed a strong rapport with the troops and demonstrated his ecumenism. Wounded at Lone Pine in August 1915, he returned to Australia next February. Demobilized in March, he retained his connexion with the Australian Military Forces until 1933. He succeeded H. D. McIntosh [q.v.10] in 1916 as president of the Returned Soldiers' Association.

Dismayed at the polarization of the conscription referenda, Talbot refused to advocate a 'Yes' vote. His opposition to government policy during the 1917 strikes and his co-operation with the Catholic priest M. J. O'Reilly [q.v.11] fuelled Protestant suspicion. Talbot, however, was no firebrand: he saw the Church as the mediator in a disjointed society and the advocate of a better Australia. He helped to form the short-lived Australian Christian Social Union and supported the Industrial Christian Fellowship founded by A. C. Willis [q.v.] in an attempt to bring Christian values into Labor politics.

Tall, athletic and impulsive, Talbot generally agreed with Wright's moderate policies and promoted the call for a new constitution for an autonomous Australian Church and a revised prayer book. Yet, his pugnacity and his support for a fellow-member of the Heretics' Club, Rev. Samuel Angus [q.v.7], alienated many conservative Evangelicals. With Wright's death and the election of his conservative successor Howard Mowll in 1933, Talbot left the Anglican Church League to form the Anglican Fellowship. In November he delivered the Moorhouse [q.v.5] lectures, published as *Church of England divines and the Anglican tradition* (1934), but his influence waned. In 1935 he visited England. Survived by his wife, he died of pleurisy in St Luke's Hospital, Darlinghurst, on 9 July 1936. His ashes were placed in front of the dean's stall in the cathedral.

M. McKernan, *Australian churches at war* (Syd, 1980); S. Judd and K. Cable, *Sydney Anglicans* (Syd, 1987); C of E, *Procs of General Synod* (Syd Diocese), 1912-36 and (NSW Province), 1917; *Drover*, 1 Aug 1936; *Labor Daily*, 10, 11 July 1936; *Aust Worker*, 15 July 1936; *Aust Church Record*, 16 July 1936; *Church Standard*, 17 July 1936; R. V. L. Russell, The search for social justice: the Protestant churches and the labour movement in N.S.W., 1914-1919 (M.A. thesis, Univ Syd, 1987).

K. J. CABLE

TALBOT, SIR REGINALD ARTHUR JAMES (1841-1929), governor, was born on 11 July 1841 in London, third son of Henry John Chetwynd Talbot, later the 18th earl of Shrewsbury, and his wife Lady Sarah Elizabeth, née Beresford, daughter of the 2nd marquess of Waterford. Educated at Harrow School, he entered the army and was sublieutenant, 1st Life Guards, in 1859, colonel in 1885 and commanded the unit in 1885-86. As Conservative member for Stafford in the House of Commons (1869-74), he spanned Gladstone's Liberal reform ministry, speaking infrequently but knowledgeably in support of army interests. He delineated the characteristics of 'so-called Army reformers since they had sprung into notoriety' as 'great carelessness', 'great inaccuracy', frequent 'want of knowledge', and 'great bitterness of expression'. On 8 May 1877 he married Margaret Jane Stuart-Wortley, granddaughter of the 1st baron Wharncliffe.

Talbot saw active service in the Zulu War (1879), Egypt (1882) and the Nile expedition which did not rescue General Gordon (1884-85). Military attaché in Paris during 1889-95, he returned to command the Cavalry Brigade in 1896. A major-general from 1898, he led the British army of occupation in Egypt, 1899-1902. He appeared 'the noblest figure of a man of war ever seen' and 'the highest type of Guards' Brigade Officer, haughty, distinguished, yet very human'. Talbot was appointed C.B. (1885) and K.C.B. (1902). He was governor of Victoria from 25 April 1904 to 6 July 1908, taking eight months leave in England in 1907.

Strongly practical, Talbot quickly appreciated (Sir) Thomas Bent [q.v.3], his constant premier, whose unpolished efforts Talbot

recognized as directed to the thrifty improvement of Victoria. Visible improvement mattered for Talbot. His last despatch favourably compared the statistics of Victoria in 1907 with 1903. Perhaps echoing his acquaintance Frank Tate [q.v.], he deplored backward technical and secondary education. A valedictory report commended his then unusual energy in travelling around Victoria and getting to know its people.

Lady Talbot (1855-1937), far from being that governor's wife, the woman behind the man behind the times, actively promoted advanced social welfare projects. First president of the subsidized charitable institution the Talbot Colony for Epileptics, opened at Clayton in 1907, she had 'ensured the success of the new venture'. From 1908 the Lady Talbot Milk Institute dispensed wholesome, 'pure' but unpasteurized milk to approved needy recipients. In March 1907 she officially opened the College of Domestic Economy for which she had fought. Premier Bent sighed in her presence, 'I am getting frightened of Lady Talbot now. She is in so many things that are making demands on the Treasury'.

Retirement was not oblivion for Talbot. He welcomed Victorian visitors and worked for disabled World War I servicemen. His name recurred amongst 'Distinguished Invalids' in *The Times* during the weeks before he died, respected, on 15 January 1929 in London. He was buried at Medenham, Buckinghamshire. To the end he remained the model of a major-general.

J. Docherty, *The Emily Mac* (Melb, 1981); R. J. W Selleck, *Frank Tate* (Melb, 1982); *PD* (GB), 23 Mar, col 539, 9 June 1871, col 1803, 6 June 1873, col 552; *Leader* (Melb), 13 Feb 1904; *Weekly Times* (Melb), 13 Feb, 30 Apr, 7 May, 4, 6 June, 26 Nov 1904, 3 June 1905, 15 Sept 1906, 13 June, 4, 11 July 1908; *Australasian*, 19 Mar, 30 Apr 1904; *Argus*, 19, 20 Nov 1907; *The Times*, 21 Jan, 1 Apr 1929, 7, 9 Oct 1937; Colonial Office: Governor's Despatches and CO notes, CO 418/33, f343, 418/48, f384-86, 418/55, f239, 318, 418/64, f365-71, 379-85 (AJCP); information from Mrs L. Gardiner, Port Melbourne, and Mr S. S. Steele, Kew, Melb.

L. R. GARDINER

TALLIS, SIR GEORGE (1869-1948), theatrical entrepreneur, was born on 28 October 1869 at Callan, Kilkenny, Ireland, son of John Tallis, shopkeeper, and his wife Sarah, née Nicholson. From the age of 16 Tallis worked for a local newspaper, the *Kilkenny Moderator*. Armed with letters of introduction to J. C. Williamson [q.v.6] and the chief of staff of the *Argus*, he arrived in Melbourne in 1886 and was employed as an office-boy by the theatre-managers, Williamson, Garner and Musgrove [q.v.5]. When Williamson found that Tallis could write shorthand, he made him his private secretary. Soon afterwards Tallis became treasurer at the Theatre Royal and the Princess Theatre. On 8 September 1898 he married Amelia Young (d. 1933), daughter of an hotelier, at St Peter's Anglican Church, Melbourne. A sister of Florence Young [q.v.], she had sung in Williamson's comic opera productions.

Surrendering his journalistic ambitions, Tallis was closely associated with the J. C. Williamson firm for over fifty years. In 1896 he bought a quarter share in the company; in 1904 Williamson accepted him and Gustave Ramaciotti [q.v.11] as partners. As Williamson gradually relinquished his active role, Tallis took over 'the Firm' in Melbourne. While concentrating on the business side, he learned every aspect of theatrical management, from choosing costumes to handling temperamental stars. Sarah Bernhardt's tour of Australia in 1891 marked a high point in his early career and in 1911 he was involved in planning (Dame) Nellie Melba's [q.v.10] opera season.

On Williamson's death in 1913, Tallis became a managing director of 'the Firm'. He was knighted in 1922 for services to the theatre and for wartime fund-raising. In 1926 he gave £2700 to the Melbourne University Conservatorium of Music for an additional wing which was named after him. His diverse interests during the 1920s included a directorship of radio station 3LO and an association with the film-maker F. W. Thring [q.v.]. Hoping to open an English outlet for 'the Firm', in 1928 Tallis leased the Apollo theatre in London for J.C.W.

Having retired in 1931 through ill health, he returned four years later to the board of directors. In 1937, with Arthur Wigram Allen, he sold a controlling interest in J. C. Williamson's to Sir John McKenzie, a New Zealand-based businessman who had little knowledge of the theatre. This impulsive action, the outcome of a long-standing feud with E. J. Tait [q.v.], J.C.W.'s Sydney manager, weakened 'the Firm'. In partnership with the Taits since 1920, Tallis respected their concert management, but doubted their theatrical acumen.

After retirement, Tallis travelled widely and bred Ayrshires at his property, Beleura, on the Mornington Peninsula, Victoria. Immaculately groomed, he was undemonstrative in business, yet warm and impulsive within his family circle. He was a born manager whose talents blended creative perception, visual imagination, good taste, intuition and courage. He died at Wagga Wagga, New South Wales, on 15 August 1948 and was cremated. A daughter and three sons survived him. His estate was sworn for probate at £163 460.

C. Kingston, *It don't seem a day too much* (Adel, 1971); V. Tait, *A family of brothers* (Melb, 1971); J. Tallis et al, *In search of the sun* (Adel, 1988); *Punch* (Melb), 2 Apr 1908, 27 May 1913; *Herald* (Melb), 17 Mar 1923; *Age*, 24 Dec 1926; information from Mr J. Tallis, Mornington, Vic.   MIMI COLLIGAN

TANNER, ALFRED JOHN (1887-1955), livestock expert, was born on 9 May 1887 at Shrawardine, Shropshire, England, son of Alfred Tanner, farmer, and his wife Priscilla, née Craig. He was educated at Wellingborough Grammar School and his long association with the livestock trade began with his family's Herefords.

Shortly before World War I Tanner brought a shipment of Lincoln and Shropshire sheep to Australia. Impressed by the country's prospects, he decided to stay. He first worked for the Weston family of Kadlunga, South Australia. Moving to Blacktown, Sydney, he began sheep-breeding and dealing in the County of Cumberland before joining George and Henry Badgery's [q.v.3] stud-stock auctioneering firm. He married 34-year-old Jean Way Weston of Kadlunga on 24 February 1914 at St James's Anglican Church, Sydney. When Badgery Bros was taken over by Goldsbrough, Mort [qq.v.4,5] & Co. Ltd, Tanner stayed on for about five years; he then joined the Commonwealth Wool & Produce Co. Ltd in January 1932 and managed the stock department. In 1942-46 he was mainly responsible for stud beef cattle shows and sales.

By shrewd judgement and dedication, Jack Tanner quickly built up an Australian and world-wide reputation as a livestock authority who specialized in beef cattle. Firmly convinced that Britain was the hub of the industry, he regarded British breeds as more suitable for Australia than those of North America (with the exception of Canadian Aberdeen Angus) and made numerous trips abroad to buy stock and to keep abreast of recent trends. He judged at shows in New Zealand and in Australia; in 1949 he judged the Hereford section at the Royal Agricultural Society's show at Shrewsbury, England. Tanner classed many studs and herds throughout eastern Australia and helped to found studs at Milton Park near Bowral for Anthony Hordern [q.v.9], at Hobartville, Richmond, New South Wales, and at Netherby, Warwick, Queensland. He was perhaps best known for the stud he founded for John Biddlecombe at Golf Hill, Shelford, Victoria, which was based on Herefords from the Tocal dispersal sale.

From January 1949 Tanner was the highly respected stud-stock expert for Dalgety [q.v.4] & Co. Ltd until he retired in 1954. Honorary secretary of the Aberdeen-Angus

Society and publicity officer of the Shorthorn Society, he wrote clearly and incisively about beef cattle in the *Sydney Morning Herald*, *Pastoral Review* and *Australasian*. He helped to establish stud cattle sales in the Northern Territory at Brunette Downs in 1953 and in Queensland at Cloncurry next year. A council-member from August 1932, he was made an honorary life-member of the Royal Agricultural Society of New South Wales in 1953.

The genial, bespectacled, pipe-smoking Tanner sailed in the *Orcades* for Britain and the United States of America in May 1955, carrying retainers from several cattle breeders to select and buy stock on their behalf. He also hoped to see his aged mother, but died of heart disease on 21 May at sea between Colombo and Aden. His wife survived him; they had no issue.

Pastoral Review, 16 May, 16 June 1955; *SMH*, 1 Sept 1925, 21 Mar, 27 Aug 1932, 25 Feb 1938, 10 Nov, 8 Dec 1950, 9 Mar 1951, 6 Feb, 27 Mar, 22 May 1953, 18 Mar 1954, 21 Jan, 4, 29 Apr, 24 May 1955; *A'sian*, 28 Mar 1936; *Bulletin*, 1 June 1955.
G. P. WALSH

TARCZYNSKI, STANISLAW VICTOR DE (1882-1952), violinist, was born on 7 April 1882 in Warsaw, son of Jozef de Tarczynski, professor of the Warsaw Conservatorium, and his wife Bronislawa, née Bobinska. Brought up a Catholic, he was educated at a local high school and the Warsaw Conservatorium where he received his diploma with distinction and a gold medal. At the age of 20 he was engaged for a year as leading violinist with the Moscow Grand Opera. Returning to Poland, he joined the staff of a musical and literary periodical, *Mloda Muzyka (Young Music)*. He later studied in Berlin and gave concerts in Dresden and Prague before being elected to lead the famous Ysaÿe Symphony Orchestra in Brussels.

When he was approaching international fame, one finger of Tarczynski's left hand became paralysed. Broken in health and spirit, he went to Egypt where he slowly recovered under the care of his sister and a Polish friend, Jadwiga Kilbach (d. 1950), who accompanied him on a visit to Australia. Arriving in 1912, they were married on 16 March 1913 at the Lutheran Church, East Melbourne. Prevented by the outbreak of war from returning to Europe, Tarczynski reluctantly changed his status from tourist to immigrant and began playing the violin in Melbourne theatres. His wife taught languages in several private girls' schools and at the university; she was later a foundation member of the International Club of Victoria and a national vice-president.

Although Tarczynski's fingers never regained their previous flexibility, his achievements in Australia were remarkable. His composition *Mazourka melancolique* was published in 1915 and he edited *Kayser studies for violin*, opus 20. In 1922-36 he taught at the Melbourne University Conservatorium of Music and at the Albert Street Conservatorium. He was regarded as one of the best teachers in Australia: many of his pupils were to achieve distinguished positions in the world of music. Tarczynski became the leader of the Melbourne Symphony Orchestra and virtually permanent leader of all touring opera companies in Australia and New Zealand which were associated with J. C. Williamson [q.v.6] Ltd. For five years from 1936 he was leader of the Adelaide Symphony Orchestra. He was naturalized in 1940.

At his Mont Albert home, which he had designed in the style of a Polish landed gentleman's residence, with a spacious music room, Tarczynski entertained musicians, writers and painters. He had ability in drawing and his closest friend was Max Meldrum [q.v.10]. Tarczynski loved to tell a story—clean and otherwise—and was well-known for his sense of humour and practical jokes. In his prime he had striking, blonde, shoulder-length hair, blue eyes, classical features and refined manners. He was 5 ft. 4 ins. (162.6 cm) tall, but stood erect and was well-proportioned. His English pronunciation was never perfect.

Survived by two sons and a daughter, Tarczynski died in Melbourne on 18 June 1952 and was cremated with Unitarian forms. A portrait by Max Meldrum is held by the family; another, by Norma Bull, is held by the artist. Meldrum's portrait of Jadwiga is in the Australian National Gallery, Canberra.

L. Paszkowski, *Polacy w Australii i Oceanii 1790-1940* (Lond, 1962), published in English (Syd, 1987); *Aust Musical News*, 5, no 3, Sept 1915, pp 1, 69, 86, and 43, no 1, July 1952, p 5; Univ Melb, *Calendar*, 1926, p 60, 1935, p 88, 1936, p 89; *Argus* and *Advertiser* (Adel) and *Sun News-Pictorial*, 19 June 1952; *Age*, 19 June 1952, 1 Oct 1966; *Polish Weekly*, 24 Aug 1963, 18 Mar 1978.
L. K. PASZKOWSKI

TARDENT, HENRY ALEXIS (1853-1929), journalist and horticulturist, was born on 1 March 1853 at Le Sépey, Vaud, Switzerland, son of Louis Marc Samuel Tardent, vintner, and his wife Marie Louise, née Perrod. Educated in local schools until the age of 10, Tardent travelled and studied privately from 1869 in Galicia, the Ukraine and Bessarabia; he learned Polish, German, Russian and Latin, and made a living by tutoring. He matriculated at the university at Odessa and in 1875 became a language teacher. On

30 June 1876 he married a distant relative, Hortense Tardent, in the Reformed Church at Chabag, Bessarabia; she bore him twelve children.

Troubled by delicate health, worried by instability in Russia, and impressed by accounts of Queensland, Tardent arrived with his family in Brisbane on 12 December 1887. For the next decade he established and operated a farm and co-operative winery at Roma. He was naturalized on 5 March 1890. Struggling to support his family, on 19 April 1897 Tardent took employment as first manager of Westbrook State Farm, near Toowoomba. He turned an unpromising site into a fine experimental farm and blamed petty bureaucracy for his transfer to Biggenden State Farm on 1 August 1898. He resigned in April 1901 after the government had objected to his 'community involvement', principally to his public support of farming and labour organizations.

Tardent unsuccessfully contested the seat of Burnett for Labor in March 1902; from 1904 to 1908 he published the *Toowoomba Democrat and Downs Agriculturist* while operating an insurance business at Toowoomba. Out of work and drawn to Atherton, he became managing editor of the *Tableland Examiner* (1909-10), agricultural editor of the pro-Labor *Daily Standard* (1913-29) and a contributor to the *Worker* (Brisbane). In 1911 he helped to settle Russian migrants at Wallumbilla.

While he was keen in promoting scientific agriculture, Tardent also suggested to Sir Samuel Griffith and Andrew Fisher [qq.v.9,8] how Swiss federalism and military conscription might be introduced into Australia. Wherever he lived, he helped to establish societies with musical, literary, scientific or agricultural interests. His prolific publications included *Science as applied to agriculture* (1907), *The life and poetry of George Essex Evans* (1913), *The life and works of Richard John Randall, Australia's greatest artist* (1916), *In freedom's cause: Australia's contribution to the World War* (1923) and *Mrs. Ellis Rowan and her contributions to Australian art and science* (1927). A founding member in Brisbane of Les Causeries Françaises in 1922 (Alliance Française from 1926), he promoted Australia extensively in French and Swiss publications overseas. His ambition to end life as a 'sage and philosopher' was rewarded when the French government appointed him officier d' Académie in March 1929.

Tardent 'adored children' and found recreation in 'purposeful, tireless walking, cycling and, above all, gardening and horticulture'. He died at Wynnum West on 5 September 1929 and, a Huguenot, was buried in Bulimba cemetery with Presbyterian forms.

His wife, three sons and four daughters survived him.

J. L. Tardent, *The Swiss-Australian Tardent family history and genealogy* (Southport, Qld, 1982); *Qld Agr J*, Oct 1929; *Worker* (Brisb), 8 Mar 1902; *Queenslander*, 28 Mar, 12 Sept 1929; *Brisbane Courier*, 7 Sept 1929.   M. FRENCH

TARRANT, HARLEY (1860-1949), businessman, was born on 6 April 1860 at Clunes, Victoria, son of Joseph Tarrant, miner, and his wife Caroline, née Brownlow, both from Oxford, England. His father owned the *Clunes Gazette* and, later, the *St Kilda Chronicle* and *Prahran Chronicle*. After attending Clunes Grammar School, Harley was articled to a firm of civil engineers; he worked as a surveyor on the Nullarbor Plain and from 1884 for the New South Wales Department of Lands. In 1888 he set up his own surveying business in Melbourne and undertook commissions for the Melbourne and Metropolitan Board of Works.

His interest in motoring began in this period. In 1897-98, basing his account primarily on overseas journals, he helped to publicize the new motor car in the cycling monthly *Austral Wheel*. His rural background and surveying experience had made him aware of its potential value in a country of immense distances and relatively few railway lines. In August 1897 he patented an engine powered by kerosene, a fuel which he declared to be safe, cheap and readily available, whereas electric motors needed recharging stations, and steam-driven machines were dangerous and 'too heavy for rough country roads'. Although his first car was a failure, its kerosene motor proved suitable for such stationary work as pumping water to farm houses. By 1899 he sold his engines as far afield as Western Australia. With larger premises, he also imported cars, beginning in February 1900 with a Benz.

Business boomed and the profits enabled Tarrant and his partner in Tarrant Motor & Engineering Co., W. H. H. Lewis [q.v.10], to build one of the earliest Australian-made petrol-driven cars: completed in 1901, it had an imported Benz engine. Two years later their next machine was 90 per cent locally made, including the engine, and became the prototype for at least eight others, all built—to suit Australian conditions—for endurance rather than speed. Tarrant's victory in the two Dunlop reliability trials of 1905 and the success of a Tarrant car in 1906 helped to develop confidence in local manufacturing, but he could not compete with imports produced in larger numbers for a bigger market, especially after Tarrant Motors Pty Ltd acquired the Victorian franchise for Ford in 1907. Nevertheless, the firm made three aero engines for the military in 1915 and continued to manufacture motor bodies which, being bulky, were expensive to import. During World War I the company began assembling chassis from imported components; by this time it also had a thriving spare parts, accessories and repair business.

Tarrant played an important role in local motoring affairs. He lobbied on behalf of the Motor Importers' Association for better traffic regulations and served in 1906-10 on the governing committee of the Automobile Club of Victoria, helping to demonstrate the capabilities of the motor car by organizing and participating in the club's competitions and tours. In 1904 he had won his event in the club's first motor race meeting, averaging 26 miles (42 km) per hour.

In 1908 Tarrant had become first commanding officer of the Victorian branch of the part-time Australian Volunteer Automobile Corps and from September 1914, with the rank of colonel, was in charge of Commonwealth military motor transport. The magnitude and urgency of wartime needs made mistakes inevitable. A 1918 royal commission report charged his administration with inefficiency and waste, alleging that the public had been misled by the extent to which Tarrant Motors was favoured with repair contracts. Harley accepted responsibility by resigning, but in 1920 was appointed M.B.E.

After the war Tarrant retired from the business, complaining of physical exhaustion and a skin rash. Sufficiently wealthy not to need to work, he freely indulged his passion for camping and overseas travel. In 1932 he came out of retirement to take over production supervision at Ruskin Motor Bodies Pty Ltd, an affiliate of the Tarrant company. A tall, dignified man with a bushy moustache, he had done much to pioneer and consolidate the first phase of the Australian motor industry. His wife Charlotte Jane, née Gill, whom he had married on 20 March 1901 at Balaclava with Australian Church forms, died in 1945. Survived by a daughter, Tarrant died on 25 February 1949 at his Toorak home and was cremated with Anglican rites. The company was sold in 1950 to the Austin Motor Co. (British Motor Corporation).

N. Darwin, *The history of Ford in Australia* (Newstead, Vic, 1986); G. Easdown, *Ford* (Syd, 1987); *Austral Wheel*, Mar 1898; *Aust Motorist*, 1 Oct 1913, 1 Jan 1919, 1 June 1925; *Radiator* (Melb), 16 Mar 1949; *Royalauto*, Oct 1961; *Business Archives and History*, 3, no 2, Aug 1963; *Argus*, 26 Feb 1949; Particulars of the career of Colonel Harley Tarrant, as dictated to his daughter, Doreen Holmes (held by Mrs D. Holmes, Canterbury, Melb).   JOE RICH

TATE, FRANK (1864-1939), educationist, was born on 18 June 1864 at Mopoke Gully, near Castlemaine, Victoria, son of Aristides Franklin (usually called Henry) Tate and his wife Mary Bessy, née Lomas, both English born. For nine years after Frank's birth Henry Tate moved his family around goldfields in the Castlemaine area. In his best days he established and managed mining companies and helped to found the Castlemaine Mining and Stock Exchange; in less successful days he kept a shop at Fryerstown. His failure to make a fortune left his son with an abiding concern for financial security. In 1873 Henry moved to Melbourne where his family continued to live while he returned—intermittently and usually unsuccessfully—to the mining districts.

Frank spent most of his school-days at the Old Model School, Spring Street, Melbourne, where he was influenced by the independence and intellectual power of its headmaster Patrick Whyte [q.v.6]. Having completed his elementary schooling, Tate enrolled in 1877 as a pupil-teacher at the school; ironically for one who was to become a brilliant teacher, he twice failed the annual examination in the art of teaching. The gruelling four-year schedule of a pupil-teacher did not kill his enthusiasm: unlike nearly all of his contemporaries, he enrolled for a further two-year course at the Training Institution which brought him into contact with stimulating members of staff such as the brave and eccentric intellectual, John Robertson [q.v.11], and the superintendent Frederick Gladman [q.v.4].

Contemporaries remembered Tate as a tall young man with dark curly hair, a powerful and attractive personality, marked skill as a raconteur, an agile wit, a passion for literature and an overwhelming determination to succeed. He began his teaching career in 1884 at Panton Hill State School, having completed at the Training Institution a course which the *Australasian Schoolmaster* described as being of 'an exceptional brilliancy'. Although a successful teacher, he grew more critical of the narrow curriculum offered in state schools, their stern and sometimes brutal discipline, and the pupil-teacher system which produced defectively educated drudges trained to follow the ways of their elders. Above all, he attacked the system of payment by results which reduced education to a self-protective grind and undermined such professional pride as had survived the rigidities of pupil-teacherdom.

Advancing rapidly through the teaching ranks at schools on the outskirts of Melbourne at Koonung Koonung and Box Hill, Tate showed that he was adept at satisfying the demands of the payment by results system. Nevertheless, he grew impatient with the Education Department's bureaucracy and with the niggardly attitudes of governments towards teachers' salaries. With Gladman's former trainees, such as Charles Long [q.v.10], he helped to found the State Schools Teachers' Union of Victoria which struggled, often ineffectually, to improve the lot of teachers. Tate's anger did not restrict his ambition; in 1885 he began part-time study at the University of Melbourne (B.A., 1888; M.A., 1894), becoming one of the first pupil-teachers to complete a tertiary qualification and confirming his promise as a rising young man in the Education Department.

On 2 October 1888 at Christ Church, South Yarra, Tate married with Anglican rites a former pupil, Ada Victoria Hodgkiss. That month he was appointed to the Central Training Institution (by then known as the Training College). Tate was a stimulating lecturer; he spoke publicly on educational issues, joined the Shakespeare Society and—displaying his own intellectual interests and a wish to improve his fellow teachers—established in 1892 the State School Teachers' Literary Society. In 1893, as part of savage retrenchment measures forced by the depression, the college was closed and he was placed in charge of pupil-teacher classes. Disillusioned, in 1894 he applied unsuccessfully for the chief inspectorship of the Auckland Education Board.

In 1895, after some unexpected reshuffling in the Education Department, Tate was appointed inspector at Charlton. From there he administered a district which contained 136 schools and spread over 5400 square miles (13 986 km^2) mainly in the Mallee of north-western Victoria. While a professional triumph in such lean times, the appointment entailed personal sacrifice: Tate was often away from Charlton for six weeks at a time as he toured his domain, and was separated for much longer periods from his wife and two young children who had remained in Melbourne.

Performing his inspectorial tasks efficiently, Tate was not content to be a routine inspector and embarked on a personal crusade to revive Victorian state education. He sped through his huge district, winning the loyalty of teachers by his gift for humour, anecdote and epigram, and by his seemingly inexhaustible flow of quotations from English literature, especially Shakespeare. He offered them a vision of a liberal curriculum, imaginative and realistic methods, and a gentler and more constructive discipline; he introduced them to the ideas of the 'new education', a loosely organized reform movement which was gaining popularity in Britain. He showed teachers, as they toiled for meagre salaries in century heat in their tin-roofed schools, that their task, although grossly undervalued by society, was one of importance and dignity. Through them, state-school children, previously offered a narrow and unappealing fare dominated by the three Rs taught rigidly and by rote, could be introduced to the richness and variety of a great culture. As for many of his generation that culture was best exemplified by English literature and history.

Seeking an audience beyond the Mallee through his published annual reports, through public addresses given under the auspices of the Literary Society and the Teachers' Union, and through letters to the *Age*, Tate attacked the administration of state education. He expressed indignation at its neglect of the country schoolteachers, at the closing of the Training College, at the failure of administrators to keep up with overseas developments, at the block to teacher promotion which followed from the retrenchment measures, and at payment by results. He spoke at considerable risk to himself. At least one of his reports was amended—he accepted the amendment and restated his criticism the following year—as his outspokenness made his superior officers suspicious. His, however, was the voice of the future.

When criticism of government education by Alfred Deakin [q.v.8] was supported by the *Age*, the minister for public instruction (Sir) Alexander Peacock [q.v.11] appointed a royal commission on technical education (1899-1901) under the chairmanship of Theodore Fink [q.v.8]. He boldly turned the inquiry into an analysis of Victorian state education and produced a series of reports which exposed previous governments and provided a programme for reform. Tate gave impressive evidence to the Fink commission and, by contrast with some senior departmental officials whom Fink attacked mercilessly for conservatism and incompetence, appeared as an exciting reformer. As a result of pressure from the commission, the Melbourne Training College was re-opened in February 1900 and Tate was appointed principal. He held this position for only a short time, but made a striking impression. The Fink commission, wishing to overcome a crippling division of authority in the Education Department, had recommended that its permanent head (to be called the director of education) should have a professional knowledge of education and be given undisputed control. Tate began his duties as director on 26 February 1902.

In the following years Tate pursued vigorous reforms which drew on the recommendations of the Fink commission. He abolished payment by results and modified the pupil-teacher system. In 1902 he introduced a new course of study, much of which he wrote himself, embodying the educational ideas he had espoused at Charlton, and he mounted a campaign to explain those ideas to teachers and the public. From both came the cry that the basics were being neglected for 'fads' and 'frills'. Detecting in this response an attempt to bestow a spurious intellectual value upon the rigidities of the past, Tate pushed ahead with his plans.

Using his membership (1903-39) of the council of the University of Melbourne, as well as the university's dependence on government when a fraud left it financially crippled, Tate forced through the introduction of a diploma of education in 1903 and thus prepared the ground for the better educated teacher about whom he had often spoken. In 1905 he persuaded the government to introduce a Teachers and Schools Registration Act which gave government its first vestige of control over private schools. In 1911—in accordance with a Fink commission recommendation—the Council of Public Education was established, but, as Tate appointed himself chairman, it never fulfilled the role of independent critic which Fink, and Tate in earlier statements, had intended. In 1913, after protracted negotiations with the university, Tate helped to establish a Schools Board which secured increased influence for government schools.

In the first decade of his directorship the introduction of state high schools provided Tate with his greatest challenge. Governments were unwilling to incur additional expense; some church groups were dubious about extending secular education beyond the elementary school; and the private schools, recognizing the threat to their own livelihood, fought bitterly against Tate's plans. When legislation failed, Tate resorted to subterfuge and in 1905, at his persuasion, the Bent [q.v.3] government established the Melbourne Continuation School which he defended as a means of providing an improved education for students intending to be teachers. In fact it immediately placed itself in competition with the private secondary schools, offering the same or a wider range of subjects and publicizing its matriculation results with similar pride. Defenders of the private schools like W. H. Fitchett [q.v.8] denounced this state intrusion into education as 'simply Socialism', arguing that scholarships could provide for the bright child of poor parents. Tate gradually developed the argument that the state should enter secondary education to ensure that it was equally available to all children.

In 1907 Tate went abroad and next year produced his *Preliminary report of the director of education upon observations made during an official visit to Europe and America*. Departing from the convention of a neutral civil servant, Tate used the report to argue a passionate case for state secondary schooling, basing his claim on the educational benefits it con-

ferred on individuals and on Australia's need for a skilled and educated workforce if it were to become a modern industrial democracy. In 1909 Tate persuaded the government to introduce a bill which allowed the open establishment of state high schools. It was redrafted and eventually passed as the 1910 Education Act. By late 1914 Tate presided over forty-three state schools, offering either a complete or a partial secondary education.

He paid a price for his invocation of the needs of industry when it became obvious that students from the new high schools preferred professional employment to industrial and technical occupations. He conceded the need for junior technical schools to cater for children who had finished elementary (or, as it was increasingly called, primary) school but who were too young to enter the technical colleges. There thus developed a dual system of post-primary education. An advocate of liberal education for all students, Tate was ensnared in a web of his own weaving: having invoked economic needs in support of his plans for state high schools, he could not disregard them when they took him in a direction he had not envisaged.

In 1914 Tate's expansionary plans were curtailed. He flung himself into the war effort, using the departmental machine to assist patriotic causes. The Education Department's *School Paper* brought news of the war into every classroom, state school children raised large sums of money and honour rolls began to record their frightening message. Although aggressively Australian when faced with English condescension, Tate was convinced of the rightness of the Imperial cause and regarded Daniel Mannix's [q.v.10] campaign against conscription with horror and anger.

After the war Tate strove to expand the State's secondary schools, making some improvements in teacher education and fighting a series of political battles with governments bent on economy. In the last years of his directorship Victoria stumbled towards another depression. If no longer at the forefront of educational thinking, he kept in touch with modern ideas and encouraged the efforts of younger colleagues. His political toughness, administrative shrewdness, personal charm and wit, and his longevity—during his directorship he served sixteen ministries and nineteen ministers—won him respect in Australian educational circles. He also earned a reputation overseas. His eloquence, experience and intense commitment to education made him a leading figure at Imperial Education conferences in London in 1923 and 1927, and he was invited to conduct commissions of inquiry in New Zealand in 1925, Fiji in 1926 and Southern

Rhodesia in 1929. For so ardent a servant of Empire, this was sweet recognition. He was appointed C.M.G. in 1919 and a chevalier of the Légion d'honneur in 1927.

Tate retired as director in 1928. His wife, to whom he was deeply devoted, died in 1932 and three of their six children predeceased him. Throughout these personal griefs Tate continued to work for educational causes. He played an important part in the establishment of the Australian Council for Educational Research (president, 1930-39), attracting money from the Carnegie Foundation and using his persuasive abilities and reputation as the elder statesman of Australian education to overcome the interstate jealousies which surrounded this venture. Again with the assistance of Carnegie money, he created the opportunity for Ralph Munn, director of the Carnegie Library in Pittsburgh, and Ernest Pitt [q.v.11] to produce their influential report, *Australian libraries* (1935). He added to these activities an extraordinary amount of voluntary work for social, artistic and cultural causes. Tate died at Caulfield on 28 June 1939 and was buried in Box Hill cemetery. His estate was valued for probate at £5582. A portrait by W. B. McInnes [q.v.10] is held by the University of Melbourne.

J. O. Anchen, *Frank Tate and his work for education* (Melb, 1956); R. J. W. Selleck, *Frank Tate* (Melb, 1982); Tate papers (Univ Melb Archives).

R. J. W. SELLECK

TATE, HENRY (1873-1926), musicologist, was born on 27 October 1873 at Prahran, Melbourne, son of Henry Tate, a London-born accountant, and his Tasmanian wife Eliza Ann, née Mathews. Educated at St Kilda State School, he later attended night-school while working as an office clerk. His interest in music began as an Anglican choir-boy at Christ Church, St Kilda; when the University of Melbourne opened its Conservatorium of Music in 1895, he enrolled as a student under G. W. L. Marshall-Hall [q.v.10].

Although Tate was to become a poet, essayist, teacher, composer and critic, his importance was as a thinker and writer about the essential character of Australian music. Some of his ideas have yet to be fully assimilated by contemporary composers: he collected Aboriginal music and bird calls (of which he had a catalogue exceeding one hundred); long before Olivier Messiaen drew so productively on birdsongs, Tate indicated their importance as raw material for composers. In the pamphlet, *Australian musical resources* (1917), he wrote: 'Contrapuntal methods seem in accord with the mystery of

the bush with its hidden past . . . Effort to incorporate our bird calls . . . in contrapuntal combinations of all degrees of intricacy should reap a rich reward'. His extended essay was received with hostility by Melbourne's musical establishment, but was favourably reviewed in the United States of America. He also devised a 'deflected scale' (a major scale with second and sixth notes flattened) and in 1924 elaborated upon his ideas in *Australian musical possibilities*. That year he became music critic for the *Age* and, until his death, repeatedly stressed the importance of indigenous inspiration in music, while championing the causes of Australian musicians and musical craftsmen.

As an active member of the Australian Institute of Arts and Literature, Tate collaborated with his friends Louis Esson, William Moore and Bernard O'Dowd [qq.v.8,10,11]. Typical of the lectures he gave for the institute was the series on 'The romance of music and life'; several of his musical works premièred there, including a sixteen-part piano cycle, *The Australian*, first performed in 1915. He also wrote 'The Dreams of Diaz', a musical play about a mythological Portuguese discovery of Australia; his *Songs of reverie* were settings of poems by Furnley Maurice [q.v. Wilmot]. Joining Moore and Dora Wilcox [q.v.10 Moore] in an elaboration of their play, *The dangerous moonlight*, Tate declared: 'It will be the first production of its kind here, that is, in which drama, music, poetry, art, acting, singing and dancing will be blended in one production'. In 1926 his rhapsody, *Dawn*, based on Australian bird calls, was performed by the university symphony orchestra. His music, however, was less interesting and accomplished than his theories.

Tate wrote a significant quantity of poetry and literary criticism. His slim volume, *The rune of the bunyip*, appeared in 1910. He published short stories in the *Bulletin* and the Sydney *Sun*, as well as in Melbourne papers. A prolific writer on chess for the *Australasian* (1914-15), *Weekly Times* (1913-14) and *Leader* (1912-15), he corresponded with international authorities, devised more than sixty original problems and represented Victoria in interstate competition. He was also a leading bowls player at the Hawthorn and Camberwell clubs.

Katharine Susannah Prichard [q.v.11], who thought highly of Tate's poetry, described him as 'a slight, cadaverous man with great luminous eyes'. Another contemporary saw him as 'one of the well-beloved, whose failures spelt sorrow and whose successes brought elation to his friends. He was a gentle and kindly soul . . . a patriot in the truest and finest sense of that word'. That patriotism made him hostile to the attitudes and presence of visiting English music examiners and made the 'job he had set himself nothing less than the creation of an Australian school of music'.

Survived by his wife Violet Eleanor, née Mercer—an accomplished violinist whom he had married with Presbyterian forms at Malvern on 1 September 1919—Tate died of streptococcal septicaemia complicating tonsillitis on 6 June 1926 at South Yarra and was buried in Brighton cemetery. His estate was valued for probate at £41. He had no children. A posthumous volume, *The poems of Henry Tate*, was published in 1928.

Spinner, July 1926; *Manuscripts*, Nov 1932; *Age*, 7 June 1926; *Argus*, 8 June 1926; *Bulletin*, 17 June 1926; *Herald* (Melb), 22 July 1927; *SMH*, 3 Sept 1932; H. Tate papers (LaTL *and* ML *and* Grainger Museum, Univ Melb); Hince *and* Palmer papers (NL).   JOHN CARMODY

TAUBMAN, GEORGE HENRY (1862-1938) and NATHANIEL JAMES (1864-1931), manufacturers, were born on 5 May 1862 and 5 February 1864 in Sydney, sons of John Taubman, a fireman from the Isle of Man, and his wife Sarah, née Pearson, a Londoner. George became a signwriter and married Isabella Scott on 20 August 1884 in St David's Anglican Church, Surry Hills. Educated at Cleveland Street Public School, Nathaniel was apprenticed to a plumber and wed Mary Elizabeth Higgs (d. 1953) on 25 March 1885 in the same church. In September 1887 the patent office granted him a certificate of provisional protection for 'The Taubman bath heater and hot shower machine'.

By 1898 George was an importer and distributor of painters' and signwriters' supplies, with a shop on the corner of Park and Castlereagh streets; at one time he held the agency for Berger Lewis & Sons Ltd's paints. Reasoning that Federation would result in customs duties on his imports, he and Nathaniel experimented in making varnish. In 1901 they set up paint and varnish works at St Peters; in February 1912 it became Taubman's Ltd with authorized capital of £6000.

Selling out to his brother in 1914, Nathaniel and his son Claude Percival founded the Sterling Varnish Co. in Huntley Street, Alexandria. Nathaniel took a keen interest in the Church of England and was a warden at St Matthew's, Ashbury. He died of heart disease on 21 December 1931 at Croydon, survived by his wife, son and daughter, and was buried in Rookwood cemetery. Probate of his estate was sworn at £12 778.

During World War I Taubmans Ltd established selling branches in all mainland States and a factory in Wellington, New Zealand. George retired as managing director in 1916, but remained as chairman. In 1928 Taubmans became associated with the world-wide group, Pinchin, Johnson & Co. Ltd of London. Popular with his employees, George showed interest in their welfare. For many years he was president of Manly Bowling Club. He died on 3 September 1938 at Balgowlah, survived by his wife, two sons and two daughters. Probate of his estate was sworn at £38 500.

His son HENRY GEORGE (1886-1959) was born on 1 September 1886 at Glebe and educated at Arncliffe Public School with his brother Walter Scott (1890-1981). Henry was a notable athlete and swimmer in his youth, and one of the first to gain the bronze medallion for lifesaving. He became Taubmans company secretary in 1912, managing director in 1916 and was chairman in 1938-52. At Haberfield on 15 July 1916 he had married with Presbyterian forms Marjorie Naomi Carita Crowley; they were divorced in 1931. He was also a director of Cereal Foods Ltd and managing director of Arthur H. Pearce Pty Ltd, indent merchants of Sydney and Melbourne. He died on 23 August 1959 at Mosman, survived by his wife Lucy Violet, née Craig, and by a son and a daughter of his first marriage. Following expansion during World War II, the firm established new factories in all States in the 1950s. By 1964 Taubmans Industries Ltd was one of Australia's biggest companies.

Taubmans News, no 8, June 1965; *SMH*, 21 Dec 1928, 22 Dec 1931, 16 Dec 1936, 25 Aug 1959, 13 Feb 1981.   G. P. WALSH

TAUCHERT, ARTHUR MICHAEL (1877-1933), vaudevillian and film actor, was born on 21 August 1877 at Waterloo, Sydney, seventh child of German-born Frederick William Tauchert, cabby, and his Irish wife Nora, née McNamara. Educated at Crown Street Public School and the Sacred Heart School, Darlinghurst, he found intermittent employment in nondescript jobs before serving an apprenticeship to Woods & Spinks, carriagebuilders. Arthur's flair for entertaining led him from South Sydney 'smokos' to one-night engagements as a parody singer with Bert Howard's and Harry Rickards's [q.v.11] vaudeville circuits. He then joined Harry Clay's troupe as a funny man in minstrel items. Billed as a 'live wire' comedian, he appeared in Sydney and Melbourne with James Brennan's National Vaudeville Entertainers. On 14 September 1909 at St Andrew's Cathedral, Sydney, Tauchert married Elizabeth (Lizzie) Le Bean, a signwriter's daughter: she was aged 22, Arthur declared himself to be 28. He toured Australasia with the Brennan-Fuller [q.v.8] circuit, bringing his humorous patter to a wider public; by 1913 he was with J. C. Bain's Vaudeville Entertainers; he later took his brother-in-law Jack Kearns as a partner.

In 1918 Raymond Longford [q.v.10] won the backing of Southern Cross Feature Film Co. Ltd for a screen adaptation of C. J. Dennis's [q.v.8] *The songs of a sentimental bloke* (1915). Deciding to turn 'Bill' into a larrikin from Woolloomooloo, Longford and Lottie Lyell [q.v.10] met Tauchert and found their 'Bloke'. The film was released next year. It was a masterpiece. Distributed in Australia and Britain by E. J. and Dan Carroll [qq.v.7], it proved an instant, popular and critical success. Tauchert's star reached its zenith. He was engaged to make personal appearances and to recite verses before screenings of the film. In 1920-28 he went on to play major roles in Longford's and Lyell's *Ginger Mick* (with his son Jack as young 'Bill') and *The dinkum bloke*, in Beaumont Smith's *The digger earl* and *Joe*, and in Arthur Higgins's [q.v.9] *Odds on*; he took lesser parts in films directed by Wilfred Lucas, Charles Chauvel [q.v.7] and Norman Dawn. Tauchert also did fund-raisers for charitable and religious bodies, and coached children for school concerts.

With the advent of 'talkies', he starred as 'Roughie' in *Fellers* (1930) and as 'Hap' in *Showgirl's luck* (1931). The collapse of local film production due to the Depression and to the block-booking system adopted by American-dominated theatre chains obliged Tauchert to turn to radio: he gave recitations from *The sentimental bloke* and crooned comic lyrics. Illness halted his new career. He was admitted to the Sacred Heart Hospice, Darlinghurst, and died of cancer on 27 November 1933. Survived by his wife, two sons and daughter, he was buried with Anglican rites in the Catholic section of Waverley cemetery.

Tauchert's reputation rested on his 'Bloke'. While age and podginess did little to enhance his resemblance to the larrikin, he won the affection of film-goers and of Dennis who was 'more than pleased' with the portrayal of 'Bill'. The key to Arthur's success lay in the plainness of his performance, and in its blend of sentiment and satire. Rough-hewn but romantic, able to cope with life's ups and downs, he was very much the character he acted.

A. Pike and R. Cooper, *Australian film, 1900-1977* (Melb, 1980); *SMH*, 22 June, 21 Sept 1907, 15, 17 Mar 1913, 28 Nov 1933; *Argus*, 9 Nov 1907, 25 July, 1 Aug 1908; *Rugby League News*, 8 May 1920; *Herald* (Melb), 27 Nov 1933; *Aust Worker*, 6 Dec 1933; C. J. Dennis to A. Tauchert, 13 Sept 1919 (copy on Tauchert file, ADB, Canb); information from Mr J. Tauchert, Randwick, Syd, and Mr M. Wasson, Armidale, NSW.   JOHN RITCHIE

TAVERNER, SIR JOHN WILLIAM (1853-1923), politician, was born on 20 November 1853 in Melbourne, son of Henry Taverner, police sergeant, and his wife Margaret Sarah, née Large, both Irish born. Educated at Scots Grammar School, Williamstown, he went in 1864 to Kerang where his family had selected land. Taverner began his working career cutting thistles for five shillings a day and then held a surveyor's chain for seven shillings a day; he later drove for Cobb [q.v.3] & Co. and kept an hotel. On 23 May 1879 at Kerang he married Elizabeth Ann Bassett Luxton with Anglican rites. In 1882-96 he was the senior partner in two firms and then the principal of a limited liability company of stock and station agents at Kerang.

At Swan Hill Taverner became involved in local government. He was president of the shire council in 1881-83, justice of the peace (1882) and for three years chairman of the Water Trust, representing the Swan Hill shire; he was also a vice-president of the North Western Municipal Association of Victoria, a president of the mechanics' institute and twice president of the Kerang branch of the Australian Natives' Association. He strongly supported the Kerang-Koondrook Tramway, the first to be constructed by a local body: this initiative was made possible by £200 000 granted by the O'Loghlen [q.v.5] government.

Entering the Legislative Assembly in April 1889 as member for Donald and Swan Hill, Taverner quickly made his mark as a spokesman for previously neglected Mallee settlers. In the 1890s legislation was amended to give improved security of tenure which enabled farmers to obtain greater financial help. Taverner was appointed a member of the first Railways Standing Committee in 1889 and then chairman of the Light Railways Committee. In 1894-99 he was vice-president of the Board of Land and Works, commissioner for public works and minister for agriculture in (Sir) George Turner's [q.v.] government; in 1895 he was also minister for health. Taverner was president of the royal commission for the Greater Britain Exhibition of 1899 and represented Victoria during the currency of that exposition. Throughout the South African War he encouraged rural exports to the Cape by arrangements with the British War Office.

In forming his second ministry (1900-01), Turner ignored Taverner's claims. Personal ambition and a growing distrust of Turner's Liberals (who were supposedly dominated by city and Trades Hall interests) led Taverner, as leader of a 'Country' faction, to intrigue with Opposition groups in the assembly. The success of two conservative pressure groups —the Kyabram Movement and the National Citizens Reform League—helped in 1902 to defeat the Peacock [q.v.11] government which had succeeded the Turner ministry. Taverner was commissioner for public works, vice-president (1902-03) then president (1903-04) of the Board of Land and Works, commissioner for crown lands and survey, and minister for agriculture in the Irvine [q.v.9] government (1902-04). In helping to draw up land regulations, Taverner kept in touch with the problems of the early Mallee settlers.

In 1904, when Irvine resigned, Taverner fancied his chances of succession, but lacked the influence of (Sir) Thomas Bent [q.v.3] who became the new premier. Taverner was appointed Victorian agent-general in London. He was no sooner overseas when charges were made that he had used his office as minister for agriculture for his personal benefit. A royal commission was set up to investigate the allegations, most of which were dismissed by the commissioner, (Sir) Thomas à Beckett [q.v.3], who found, however, that Taverner had exerted improper influence to gain preferment. Bent took no action and Taverner again repaired to London where he was knighted in 1909 and retained his agent-generalship until 1913. He stayed in London until 1922. On returning home, he became a member of the State Fruit Advisory Board and chairman of the Victorian directorate of the Primary Producers' Bank. On 17 December 1923, while attending a meeting at Doncaster, Melbourne, to open a branch of the bank, he collapsed and died of apoplexy after speaking a few words. Survived by his wife, he was buried in Brighton cemetery.

Thickset and genial, with a walrus moustache, Taverner was a loyal propagandist for Mallee settlers and an ardent advocate of adequate water storage systems and railway facilities in remote parts of Victoria. He anticipated coming generations of Country Party politicians.

E. H. Sugden and F. W. Eggleston, *George Swinburne* (Syd, 1931); B. D. Graham, *The formation of the Australian Country parties* (Canb, 1966); K. Rollison, Groups and attitudes in the Victorian Legislative Assembly, 1900-1909 (Ph.D. thesis, La Trobe Univ, 1972); *Kerang New Times*, 21 Dec 1923.
S. M. INGHAM

TAYLOR, SIR ALLEN ARTHUR (1864-1940), timber merchant, ship-owner and politician, was born on 13 May 1864 at Wagga Wagga, New South Wales, fourth child of John Bate, a bricklayer from Worcestershire, and his native-born wife Martha Jane, née King. From the age of 12 Allen was employed for two years as a railway 'nipper'. Moving to Sydney about 1882, he attended night-school while working for railway contractors. He was a clerk when he married Adela Mary Elliott, daughter of a coach proprietor, on 19 June 1886 with Presbyterian forms at Annandale. He claimed to have tried his fortune in Western Australia before becoming a road and bridge contractor in 1888. For reasons that remain obscure, he changed his surname to Taylor some time between 1890 and 1895.

Moving into the field of hardwood timber supply, he founded the firm of Allen Taylor & Co. Ltd of which he was managing director. In the 1890s he also became chairman of the Illawarra and South Coast Steam Navigation Co. Ltd and the North Coast Steam Navigation Co. Ltd. He was in partnership with (Sir) Robert Anderson [q.v.7] in the early 1900s. Through the shipping companies, he promoted the economic development of the north and south coast districts, providing finance for building silos and improving dairy herds. He was also a local director of the London Bank of Australia, a director of the Insurance Office of Australia Ltd and the Auburn Brick Co. Ltd, and a trustee of the Savings Bank of New South Wales.

He felt sufficiently secure in business by 1895 to stand for the Borough Council of Annandale, where he lived, an inner western suburb of Sydney at the centre of the timber-milling and shipping trade. Elected, Taylor became chairman of the works committee in 1896 and was mayor in 1897-1902; he visited Britain and Europe 'mainly to get a practical knowledge of municipal methods and requirement in the older lands'.

An alderman on the Sydney Municipal Council, he represented Pyrmont Ward (1902-12) and Bourke Ward (1915-24). Persuading parliament to grant the council additional powers of resumption and borrowing money, as lord mayor in 1905-06 and 1909-12 Taylor embarked on a vigorous programme of civic improvement. Like a child with building blocks, 'he arranges, alters, amends, improves, develops'. His most notable achievements were the clearing of a notorious slum known as Wexford Street to create Wentworth Avenue, the widening of Oxford Street and the creation of the square that bears his name at Darlinghurst. Taylor supported a Greater Sydney through territorial expansion (incorporating Camperdown and the University of Sydney) and promoted the extension of the council's electric power to the suburbs. A member of the Board of Health and a commissioner for the Franco-British Exhibition, London, in 1908, he was knighted on the occasion of King George V's coronation in 1911 and resigned from council next year owing to the strains of office.

Efficient urban transport remained an abiding interest. Taylor returned from another overseas visit in 1924, satisfied that the

Taylor

remedy for London's traffic problems (removing the trams) would be followed in Sydney and convinced of the importance of motor cars in 'solving' traffic problems in the United States of America. He continued proposing various street widenings and extensions, and was a member of the Citizens' Reform Association which defeated the Labor domination of the council in 1921.

Conservative in politics, Taylor was nominated to the Legislative Council in 1912; when it was reconstituted in 1933, he was elected for a six-year term and re-elected in 1940. He was successively a member of the Liberal, National and United Australia parties and of the shadowy Consultative Council, the fund-raising organization behind the National Party. In 1922 he was guest of honour at a banquet held by Sydney's business community and was praised by the former premier, W. A. Holman, and the governor of the Reserve Bank, Sir Denison Miller [qq.v.9,10].

A director of the Benevolent Society of New South Wales (1909-13) and of Royal Prince Alfred Hospital (1916-36), Taylor helped to found the Dreadnought Fund (to add a warship to the Royal Navy) and was chairman of the Dreadnought Trust Fund (1926-31): the £90 000 it had raised was partly used to sponsor the immigration of British boys to be trained for rural work in New South Wales. He was also a member of Taronga Zoological Park Trust and a supporter of many charitable institutions. A 'rough, bluff man of action', Taylor was portly, with a drooping moustache and jowls that gave the impression of a receding chin; his partial baldness was accentuated by his cropped hair.

Lady Taylor died on 4 May 1924. On 29 December 1926 Sir Allen married a widow Linda Turner Hawkes, née Carter, at St Matthias's Anglican Church, Paddington. Predeceased by his wife and by the son of his first marriage, Taylor died at his home in Lang Road, Centennial Park, on 30 September 1940 and was buried with Anglican rites in South Head cemetery. His estate was sworn for probate at £49 517.

A self-made man, Taylor was widely respected for his entrepreneurial and managerial skills in business, skills which he brought to bear on civic administration with notable success. He was a New South Wales patriot, always keen to promote the 'expansion and importance of our magnificent city and State'. His portrait by Norman Carter [q.v.7] is held by Sydney Municipal Council.

F. A. Larcombe, *The advancement of local government in New South Wales, 1906 to the present* (Syd, 1978); *PD* (NSW), 8 Oct 1940; *Lone Hand*, 1 Feb 1912; *Arrow* and *Bulletin*, 28 Apr 1906; *Daily Telegraph* (Syd), 21 June 1911; *Punch* (Melb), 21 Mar 1912; *SMH*, 16 Apr 1912, 8 Feb 1922, 9 Jan 1923, 8 Sept 1924, 1 Dec 1926, 2 Nov 1937, 1 Mar 1939, 1 Oct 1940; Allen Taylor & Co Ltd papers (ANUABL); information (Syd Municipal Council Archives).
ALAN ROBERTS

TAYLOR, FLORENCE MARY (1879-1969), architect and publisher, was born on 29 December 1879 at Bedminster, Somerset, England, eldest daughter of John Parsons, labourer, and his wife Eliza, née Brooks. The family migrated to Sydney in 1884 where John worked in the sewerage construction branch of the Department of Public Works. Educated at Presbyterian Ladies' College, Croydon, Florence assisted her father with his engineering calculations. After his death in 1899, she had to find work to support her two sisters. She decided to become a draftsman. While articled to the architect Edmund Skelton Garton, she attended night-classes at Sydney Technical College. The only woman among some 200 men, she failed all her subjects in her first year, but persevered and completed the course in eight years. She also attended the University of Sydney (B.A., 1906).

She had meanwhile been promoted chief draftsman in Garton's office. Having completed her articles, she went as chief draftsman to J. B. Clamp [q.v.8] who nominated her in 1907 for associate membership of the Institute of Architects of New South Wales. Despite his defence of her talent (she 'could design a place while an ordinary draftsman would be sharpening his pencil'), the nomination was defeated, notwithstanding which she built up a thriving practice designing homes.

On 3 April 1907 at St Stephen's Presbyterian Church, Sydney, Florence married George Augustine Taylor [q.v.]. Sharing many of his interests, on 5 December 1909 she reputedly became the first Australian woman to fly—in a glider built in his workshop at Redfern. With George, she was a founding member (1913) of the Town Planning Association of New South Wales and its secretary for many years. Together they started the Building Publishing Co. Ltd which produced trade journals, three of which Florence edited: *Harmony*, *Young Australia* and the *Australian* (later *Commonwealth*) *Home*. Through their journals they campaigned for urban planning, improved construction methods and better materials; through them, they also promoted the interests of engineers, architects and builders. In 1920 Florence was eventually invited to join the Institute of Architects. She accepted.

When George Taylor died suddenly in 1928 he left his estate, valued for probate at £10 147, to his wife. Florence was determined to carry on their business. Although forced to cease publishing eight of their eleven journals, she maintained *Building* (later *Building, Lighting and Engineering*) (1907-72), *Construction* (1908-74) and the *Australasian Engineer* (1915-73), editing them herself. She continued to produce town planning schemes, but relied on others to draw them as she was unable to spare time from publishing. She visited Europe, the Americas and Asia, bringing back ideas on urban and rural planning which informed her writings and speeches.

An 'indefatigable founder and joiner', Mrs Taylor was closely involved in the Arts Club, (Royal) Aero Club of New South Wales, Society of Women Writers, New South Wales branch of the Australian Forest League, Australian-American Association, Royal Empire Society and the Bush Book Club, among others. She was widely respected, even if her questions and criticism irritated some of her professional colleagues. Her energy, determination and outspokenness earned her the title, 'The Grand Old Lady of Publishing'. Remembered by her contemporaries for dressing (even in the 1930s) in long sweeping skirts and a picture hat decorated with ostrich feathers, she was a tall, striking woman, with blue eyes and blonde hair, and a fine singing voice. She retired at the age of 81. Appointed O.B.E. in 1939 and C.B.E. in 1961, she was an honorary member of the Australian Institute of Builders and a fellow of the Royal Society of Arts, London.

Her ideas on the responsibilities of women were fixed: for 'a woman to marry, get into the confines of the home and never be articulate in public affairs is a disgrace'. Her achievements and the publicity they received did much to advance the public acceptance of women in the professions. In declining health she sequestered herself at her Potts Point home with her sister Annis Parsons. Florence Taylor died there on 13 February 1969 and was cremated with Anglican rites. Her estate was valued for probate at $226 281. She had no children. A portrait by Jerrold Nathan is held by the Mitchell [q.v.5] Library, Sydney.

J. M. Giles, *Some chapters in the life of George Augustine Taylor* (Syd, 1957) and *50 years of town planning with Florence M. Taylor* (Syd, 1959); J. M. Freeland, *The making of a profession* (Syd, 1971); M. Roe, *Nine Australian progressives* (Brisb, 1976); *People*, 30 Dec 1953, p 423; *Building* (Syd), Mar 1969, p 9; F. M. *and* G. A. Taylor papers *and* K. Maegraith papers (ML).   CHRISTA LUDLOW

TAYLOR, GEORGE (1861-1935), shearer, prospector and politician, was born on 30 May 1861 at Balgonie, New South Wales, second son of Robert Taylor, farmer and carpenter, and his wife Margaret, née Burke, both native-born. George left school at Wollongong at the age of 12, joined a shearing team, drifted to Queensland and became part of the embryonic labour movement. Known as 'The Native', Taylor helped to form the Queensland Shearers' Union and to organize the Australian Labour Federation. During the 1891 shearers' strike, with J. A. Stuart [q.v.] and others, he was convicted for conspiracy by Judge Harding [q.v.4] at Rockhampton and imprisoned for three years. Released early for good conduct, and sporting a black, bushy beard, Taylor went prospecting at Coolgardie, Western Australia.

His reputation had preceded him. He worked at the Mulga Queen Mine near Erliston and afterwards at Mount Sir Samuel; he was also a founder of the North Coolgardie branch of the Amalgamated Workers' Association (Union). In 1901 the 'big, brainy ... man from Darlot' was the successful Labor candidate for the vast Mount Margaret electorate. Taylor proved formidable on the hustings against his affluent opponent J. W. Hall and held the Legislative Assembly seat until its abolition in 1929.

In parliament he was a confrontationist: he attacked much of (Sir) Walter James's [q.v.9] legislation and the appointment of W. J. George [q.v.8] as commissioner of railways, and fell out with his colleagues T. H. Bath and W. D. Johnson [qq.v.7,9]. After being expelled from caucus for crossing the floor on the appointment of (Sir) Cornthwaite Rason [q.v.11] to the ministry, Taylor attacked the parliamentary Labor Party's leader, Robert Hastie. Despite such rows, in 1904 Taylor's constituents at Kookynie gave him a purse of sovereigns and in August he was made colonial secretary. In this portfolio he administered the gaol and prison department, but resigned in June 1905 over Premier Daglish's [q.v.8] vacillating administration. Taylor was Speaker of the Legislative Assembly in 1917-24; in 1910-11 he had been chairman of committees during Frank Wilson's [q.v.] Liberal government, to the displeasure of his Labor colleagues.

Taylor's favourite pastime was attending the vaudeville. On 12 December 1910 he married a widow, Neta Hannah Stanley Whalan, née Oughton, manageress of the Follies Co. His bushman's image was replaced by that of 'a gentleman with ... red necktie, red buttonhole, beard closely cropped à la Française, moustache waxed'. His speeches may also have changed from their 'straight-out rude, loud' form, but 'Mulga' never lost his punch. He split with the Labor Party in 1917 over his support for conscription; although he sat thereafter on the front bench as a Nationalist, he remained essentially a labour man and his electors on the goldfields stayed loyal.

Chairman of the board of the Perth Public Hospital and a member of the licensing bench in 1930-35, Taylor was a keen fan of trotting. Predeceased by his wife in 1933, he died on 24 September 1935 and was buried in the Anglican section of Karrakatta cemetery. Three stepchildren survived him.

B. Fitzpatrick, *A short history of the Australian Labor movement* (Melb, 1940); G. C. Bolton and P. Joske, *History of Royal Perth Public Hospital* (Perth, 1982); *Westralian Worker*, 12 Apr, 10 May 1901, 8, 21 Mar 1902, 4, 11, 18, 25 Mar, 22 Apr, 20 May, 3, 22 June, 26 Aug 1904, 9 June 1905, 11 Jan 1917; *Kookynie Press*, 7, 10, 17 June 1905; *Morning Herald* (Fremantle), 10, 14, 17, 21 June, 1 July, 26 Aug, 4, 25 Oct, 26 Nov 1905; *West Australian*, 25 Sept 1935; *Worker* (Brisb), 14th anniversary special ed, 1940.
WENDY BIRMAN

TAYLOR, GEORGE AUGUSTINE (1872-1928), craftsman and journalist, was born on 1 August 1872 in Sydney, second son of George Faulty Taylor, native-born fruiterer, and his Irish wife Annie Maria, née McFadden. Educated at the Marist Brothers' St Mary's High School and Sydney Technical College, he learned a trade in building. Through the 1890s Taylor lived chiefly by cartooning, especially for the *Bulletin* and *Punch* (London); he mixed with various artistic-literary sets, belonged to the Dawn and Dusk Club and was a council-member of the (Royal) Art Society of New South Wales. Around 1900 Taylor's interests shifted. Fascinated by technology, he saw in wireless and telephony evidence for his deepening faith in spiritualism. As a businessman, he manufactured 'bagasse', a cement-plaster which he used to present motifs of Australian fauna and flora. Nationalism suffused all his doing.

On 3 April 1907 Taylor married Florence Mary Parsons [q.v. Taylor]. He published the *Construction and Local Government Journal*, *Australasian Engineer* and *Radio Journal of Australia*. Pre-eminent among his publications was *Building* which upheld 'The New Journalism'—not only to 'write' things, but to 'do' things—and fostered modernism in architecture and town planning. The journal greeted the building of a national capital in Canberra with enthusiasm, welcoming W. B. Griffin [q.v.9] and publishing important articles by him (1912-14). Taylor helped to found the Institute of Local Government Engineers of Australasia in 1909 and the Town Planning Association of New South Wales in 1913.

He became a disciple of martial technology. From at least 1908 he showed interest in aviation: he established a factory to make light craft, flew gliders and extolled Lawrence

Hargrave [q.v.9]. In 1909 Taylor promoted the Aerial League of Australia and urged the Federal government to establish an airforce. As an inventor, he applied himself to machine flight and, more successfully, to military uses of radio and telephony. He founded the Wireless Institute of New South Wales (1910), and was elected to the Royal Geographical Society of London for his military maps and to the Royal Astronomical Society for his theory of moon-life. His pen produced weird science fictions which presented technology as alone capable of saving Australia from Germany and Japan.

In 1914 George and Florence travelled abroad, notably to the United States of America; he had long admired Theodore Roosevelt's progressivism. An honorary lieutenant in the Australian Intelligence Corps from December 1909, he was commissioned in January 1912. With World War I, he joined the 7th Light Horse in October 1914, was seconded to the Intelligence Section General Staff for the duration and became an ardent patriot. His next science fiction depicted a Europe torn between 'scientific militants' and humanistic pacifists who were sympathetic to Germany: Taylor's advocacy of the former bespoke a fascist strain in his thinking.

On 30 May 1916 Taylor issued a new weekly, *Soldier*, dedicated 'to preserve and extend the spirit of National Devotion and the faith of Imperial Duty'. *Soldier* argued for effective repatriation of Australian troops, urging them to organize in civil politics under some war-tested hero like A. C. Carmichael, (Sir) John Monash or (Sir) Charles Rosenthal [qq.v.7,10,11]. In 1918 Taylor published *Those were the days*, an account of Sydney's cultural world of the 1890s. With the Armistice, he urged the building of war memorials to honour and inspire. His town planning advocacy now gave greater emphasis to preserving historic buildings.

Yet, technology remained Taylor's passion. In 1919 he helped to found the Institution of Engineers, Australia, and in 1922 the Australian Inventions Encouragement Board; the Association for Developing Wireless in Australia (1923) was his own creation. He insisted that broadcasting should serve community ends and not those of such vested interests as the Amalgamated Wireless (Australasia) Ltd. Still an experimenter, he continued his pre-war work on proto-television, reportedly achieving colour transmission in the mid-1920s.

He had meanwhile become an advocate of pacificism and domesticity. Going overseas in 1922, he proclaimed Australia as the ideal site for a city dedicated to peace; he also upheld the League of Nations. Keen to improve the ordinary home, particularly through labour-saving devices, the Taylors attended the British Empire Exhibition of 1924 as Australian experts in this field. *Soldier* ceased publication and *Australian Home* began in January 1925.

Intensifying his broadcasting crusade, Taylor did much to prompt the 1927 Federal royal commission into wireless. His propaganda urged the establishment of a 'Communications Commission' and exhorted government to pursue radio research; his side comments forecast the development of atomic energy and reaffirmed his spiritualism.

An epileptic, Taylor drowned in the bath in his Sydney home on 20 January 1928. He was cremated with Anglican rites. His nature had been sweet, generous and upright. A committee intending to honour his memory included C. E. W. Bean, Mary Booth, W. Lister Lister, J. S. Purdy [qq.v.7,10,11], David Stead [q.v.] and Rosenthal. Taylor had bridged arts and science, craft and technology, war and peace, radicalism and fascism, earth and infinity.

J. M. Giles, *Some chapters in the life of George Augustine Taylor* (Syd, 1957); C. D. Coulthard-Clark, *The citizen general staff* (Canb, 1984); M. Roe, *Nine Australian progressives* (Brisb, 1976); Inst of Engineers, Aust, *Trans*, 9, 1928, p 279; Taylor papers (ML).   MICHAEL ROE

TAYLOR, HARRY SAMUEL (1873-1932), newspaper-owner, was born on 13 January 1873 in North Adelaide, eldest son of William Henry Taylor, warehouseman, and his wife Mary Jane, daughter of Samuel Smith [q.v.6]. Having attended various primary schools, he won a scholarship to Prince Alfred College where from 1887 he spent four years as student and teacher. He enjoyed natural history, gymnastics and Australian Rules football; he also pursued social and political issues, partly through Rev. Hugh Gilmore's [q.v.4] inspiration. Harry abandoned teaching and a university course, and at 18 made a lecture tour of South Australia to preach the theory of Henry George [q.v.4]. He became secretary of the South Australian Single Tax League and edited its journal, the *Pioneer*.

He was perhaps most changed by William Lane [q.v.9] and his plan for a 'New Australia' in South America where people could live in 'a communal paradise' free from capitalist evils. In July 1893 Taylor sailed with the first party of Christian-Socialists to Paraguay. Within months, back in Adelaide, he helped to organize the next group of migrants. By the time he returned to Paraguay bitter divisions had undermined 'New Australia'. In 1894 he followed Lane to form a neighbouring settlement, Cosme, where for two years the idealists endured hard labour, primitive conditions and hunger.

At Cosme (Dame) Mary Gilmore [q.v.9]

found that Taylor had 'the most forgiving nature of any man she ever knew'. On his second voyage across the Pacific he had produced a hand-written weekly, the *Porpoise*; in South America he wrote and read to the community each night his *Cosme Evening Notes* which were imbued with cheerful optimism and faith in the commune's leader. Taylor later reflected that the settlers failed because the only real bond between them was their worship of Lane.

Taylor's family asked him to come home after his father died in 1895. Reluctantly he complied, working his passage via England where he met H. G. Wells. Next year Taylor briefly worked at Murtho on the upper Murray River, but fell ill and went to Warrakoo sheep-station near Cal Lal. He was living at Angaston, South Australia, when he married Sarah Helen Smith on 28 July 1898; they were to have one son.

Finding their life lonely at Four Corners, on Warrakoo, Harry joined his brother in buying a fruit-growing property at Mildura, Victoria. His lemons and figs failed, so he bought a milk run. In time he became president of the local branch of the Australian Natives' Association and secretary of the Mildura Dried Fruit Trust; as 'the Rambler', he edited the farming page of the *Mildura Cultivator*. In 1905 he bought the weekly *Renmark Pioneer*; as managing editor, he transformed it into a major influence in the region from Wentworth, New South Wales, to Karoonda, north of Murray Bridge in South Australia. With his lucid and vigorous style, Taylor pushed the riverland's interest through his paper; he also led deputations to premiers and government ministers. The causes he espoused included irrigation, locks for the Murray, closer settlement, organized marketing for grapes and dried fruits, and co-operation among primary producers. Regarded as one of the best horticultural papers in Australia, the renamed *Murray Pioneer* drew wide praise.

While sympathetic to the underdog, Taylor managed to win the confidence and friendship of many conservative readers. He initially supported the Labor Party, but advocated conscription in World War I and believed that the party had ensured its 'moral destruction' by opposing the measure. Having sent free copies of his newspaper to volunteers from the riverland who served overseas, he agitated for post-war soldier settlement in the district, and his pamphlets and manuals about horticulture were regarded as the soldier settlers' 'fruitgrowing guide and bible'. The *Murray Pioneer* stood for freedom, equal rights and brotherhood, and Australia for White Australians.

After the Armistice he broke convention by arguing that Germany alone was not responsible for the war, and that Russia and Austria-Hungary were more to blame; furthermore, he condemned the Treaty of Versailles. Taylor was riverland representative on the advisory board of the Agricultural Bureau of South Australia and president of the Renmark Show Society. From 1919 he sat on the board of the Renmark District Hospital and was several times elected to the local council. A lay preacher at the Congregational church, he was a Freemason and a supporter of the Salvation Army. Among other projects, he championed the extension of the railway to Paringa and Renmark, the Paringa bridge and an agricultural high school for Renmark.

He had a wiry physique, wore a beard when it was no longer fashionable and dressed eccentrically: in summer his immaculate tussore suits clashed with his old sandshoes with the laces trailing. In no way materialistic, he was generous to a fault. Taylor read in several European languages and maintained an interest in foreign affairs, politics and religion. His vast collection of books, covering history, religion and English literature, was often culled to benefit the local institute and libraries. He enjoyed walking, cycling and gardening; on his block he cultivated rare plants and tried to breed koalas. Apart from his geniality and intelligence, Taylor impressed his contemporaries by the courage with which he expressed his idealism. He died of cancer on 13 February 1932 at Renmark and was buried in the cemetery there.

S. Grahame, *Where socialism failed* (Lond, 1912); G. Souter, *A peculiar people* (Syd, 1968); *Pictorial Australian*, Nov-Dec 1893; *Advertiser* (Adel), 15 Feb 1932; *SMH*, 16 Feb 1932; *Murray Pioneer*, 19 Feb 1932; W. R. Crocker, 'Harry Taylor of the "Murray Pioneer"', *and* M. Howie, 'Harry Taylor', Personalities remembered (Mortlock Lib); Taylor papers (held by Mr D. Taylor, Renmark, SA).   MALCOLM SAUNDERS

TAYLOR, HEADLIE SHIPARD (1883-1957), agricultural machinery designer, was born on 7 July 1883 at Bungowannah, New South Wales, son of native-born parents Phillip Culling Taylor, farmer, and his wife Mary Jane, née Shipard. Headlie attended school at Henty, but left aged 14 to work on his parents' wheat and sheep farm at Emerald Hill.

Convinced that farm machinery could be improved, in 1910 Taylor lodged his first patent, an improvement for stripper harvesters. Next year he set out to design a harvester which would handle storm-damaged crops better than the stripper harvester. With family support, working long shifts and teaching himself engineering, he produced his first machine for the 1911-12 harvest. Dis-

appointed with it, he constructed a successful second machine and patented his design in October 1913. Its key features were a long-fingered comb which combined with a reciprocating knife and twin spirals to convey the cut crop from the comb to the elevators. In 1914 Taylor demonstrated a third machine at the Henty show. Interested farmers offered capital to produce it, but he preferred that an existing Australian manufacturer undertake its production.

At Taylor's invitation, the agricultural machinery manufacturer H. V. McKay [q.v.10] saw the header in action and was so impressed that he negotiated for the patent rights and engaged Taylor to supervise production of the header at his works from 6 April 1916. Output grew rapidly: 6 machines in 1916, 143 in 1917, 325 in 1918. During 1920, when widespread storms flattened crops, the factory worked day and night to produce 1024 machines equipped with special 'crop lifters'. By the end of the decade, headers outsold stripper harvesters. The first commercial harvester to combine the reciprocating knife with the Australian stripping-comb, Taylor's header provided the harvesting capacity needed in the broadacre dry farms of the wheat belt.

He also produced a string of other innovations: crop lifters (1917), pick-up attachments enabling the header to harvest field peas (1919), the 'Sunshine' engine-functioned header (1922), the 'Sunshine' auto-header (1924), a pick-up front for the auto-header (1929), the 'Sunshine' TD stripper harvester (1934), the 'Sunprong' pasture renovator (1936), power take-off mechanisms for the header (1938), a comb cleaner for the header and for stripper harvesters (1943), a cutter bar for pick-up fronts (1943) and a redesigned auto-header (1953). In World War II he designed three machines to meet the pressing need for equipment to harvest flax.

The 'Sunshine' auto-header—the first self-propelled harvester to be manufactured in large numbers—stood out as Taylor's second major achievement. Capable of harvesting at 3.5 miles (5.6 km) per hour, it had a capacity of 4 acres (1.6 ha) per hour or more. In 1929 Taylor set up a factory in Canada to make auto-headers for the North American market. Production proceeded until the merger of McKay and Massey Harris interests in 1930. In all, 932 auto-headers were produced for Australian and overseas markets.

On 26 March 1918 Headlie Taylor had married Ruby Maud Howard in the Baptist Church at Goombarganah, New South Wales. In 1954 he retired from his position as superintendent of agricultural machinery works at H. V. McKay Massey Harris Pty Ltd. Widely respected in the Henty and Sunshine communities, he was a director of the Sunshine Employees' Trust Ltd and a member of the council of the Sunshine Technical School. Survived by his wife, three sons and two daughters, he died at Sunshine on 22 March 1957 and was cremated. His estate was valued for probate at £54 649.

From early beginnings, Henty, N.S.W., home of the header (Henty, NSW, 1986); F. Wheelhouse, *Digging stick to rotary hoe* (Adel, 1972); M. Newton, *Ancestry from 1590* (priv pub, Henty, NSW, 1974); *A'sian Manufacturer*, 19 Jan 1929, p 29; *Implement and Machinery Review*, 1 Mar 1929, p 1163; *Sunshine Review*, 5, no 3, Dec 1948, p 11; *Massey-Ferguson Review*, no 86, Dec 1956, p 8; *Wimmera Star*, 5 Feb 1925; Aust patent and patent application record 4394/05, 17021/10, 10989/13, 2208/16, 15959/24, 21123/24 (Patents Office, Canb); information from Mr H. H. Taylor, Ocean Grove, and Mr J. Taylor, Portarlington, Vic.

M. L. HALLETT

TAYLOR, HENRY D'ESTERRE (1853-1909), Federationist and banker, was born on 11 January 1853 at Richmond barracks, Melbourne, eldest child of Robert Crofton Taylor, mounted police cadet, and his wife Mary Jane, née D'Esterre. In 1870 he commenced work with the Melbourne Savings Bank (State Savings Bank of Victoria).

A free trader, Taylor became a member of the Victorian branch of the Imperial Federation League in 1885; largely through his efforts it survived the collapse of the London parent organization in 1893. The league promoted closer union of the British Empire and advocated the establishment of an Imperial parliament to be composed of Britain and the self-governing members of the Empire. Taylor was honorary secretary of the Victorian branch (1895-1907) and its honorary corresponding secretary until his death.

A proponent of Australian Federation as a preliminary means to a greater end, Taylor joined the Melbourne branch of the Australian Natives' Association, hoping to gain converts. Inevitably, he clashed with republicans over his I.F.L. prize-winning essay, *The advantages of Imperial Federation* (Melbourne, 1888). His address, *Three great federations: Australasian, national and racial* (London, 1890), delivered to the A.N.A. at Ballarat, met with approval in so far as he urged Australian Federation; but his advocacy of Imperial Federation and, ultimately, a federation of the British races (two causes later espoused by Lionel Curtis of the Round Table) aroused heated opposition. Although Taylor held that trade, defence and financial advantage would flow from Imperial Federation, others feared that in such an organization Australia's voice would be submerged. The conservative

Melbourne *Argus* supported Taylor; the radical *Age* opposed him.

Taylor was an I.F.L. delegate to the 1893 Corowa conference of the A.N.A. He claimed, with some bitterness, that it was he, rather than (Sir) John Quick [q.v.11], who originated the famous proposal for an enabling bill; Taylor maintained that he had privately suggested the idea to Quick before having to leave the conference for another meeting. Taylor was deeply disappointed that Prime Minister (Sir) Edmund Barton [q.v.7] and Victorian Premier (Sir) Alexander Peacock [q.v.11] would not recognize that he and Quick had an equal claim to a knighthood. Later attempts to have the matter taken up in London also failed, but in 1900 the Prahran A.N.A. and in 1909 the Victorian I.F.L. acknowledged the justice of Taylor's claim.

An outstanding mathematician, Taylor had been inspector of branches, accountant, assistant auditor and manager of city branches of the Melbourne Savings Bank until ill health forced him to retire in March 1908. Although once castigated by an opponent as an 'Australian imbecile', Taylor was a graceful public speaker, an articulate debater and a discerning art critic. A pamphleteer for the I.F.L., he also wrote for other periodicals. He was a foundation member (1886-1906) of the Bankers' Institute of Australasia and contributed articles to its *Journal*. Tall and fair-haired, with a beard and moustache, in later years he resembled King George V. Taylor never married, but had a wide circle of friends. He died of cerebral sclerosis on 28 April 1909 at East Melbourne and was buried in Melbourne general cemetery.

Imperial Federation League Victorian branch (Melb, 1909); H. L. Hall, *Victoria's part in the Federation movement* (Lond, 1931); *Herald* (Melb), 1 May 1909; L. Foster, The Imperial Federation League in Victoria after Australian Federation (B.A. Hons thesis, Monash Univ, 1979); Imperial Federation League of Australia, Letter-book (NL); information from documentation archivist, State Bank of Victoria.   LEONIE FOSTER

TAYLOR, HENRY JOSEPH STIRLING (1874-1948), farmer, businessman and public servant, was born on 22 October 1874 in North Melbourne, eleventh child of Scottish migrants Alexander Taylor, labourer, and his wife Jane, née Scoles. Educated in Victoria, he joined the Western Australian postal service in the 1890s and in 1900 was postmaster at Port Hedland. He operated pearling luggers out of Broome from about 1901 and in 1910 bought a wheat farm at Kellerberrin. Finding that drought, taxes, rail freights and protective tariffs made wheat-growing unprofitable, he became convinced of the need for marketing co-operatives. In February 1915 Stirling Taylor was appointed managing secretary of Westralian Farmers Ltd, Perth, established in 1914 by the Farmers and Settlers' Association as a marketing and farm supply co-operative. Taylor built up the company rapidly and he also encouraged the establishment of some seventy local co-operatives.

In March 1919 Taylor became director of the recently established Commonwealth Bureau of Commerce and Industry. His objective was to modernize and diversify Australian primary and secondary industry. Enthusiastically gathering and disseminating information and advice, he gave particular attention to encouraging exports and pressed for the establishment of an Australian trade commissioner service; he also played a significant role in stimulating the rapid development of the Australian woollen manufacturing industry in the early 1920s. From 1923 he undertook Prime Minister Bruce's [q.v.7] 'national stocktaking' of Australian resources.

On 10 November 1922 Taylor was appointed part-time secretary and executive member of the British Empire Exhibition Commission—housed with the bureau in Melbourne—to organize meetings, correspondence and research. Public controversy over the selection of a Federal executive officer affected Taylor's position when he opposed the appointment of Victor Ryan on administrative grounds. Taylor believed that the affair had damaged his relationship with the commission chairman, Senator (Sir) Reginald Wilson [q.v.]. Ryan was appointed in May 1923; in June Taylor resigned, citing the need for a full-time secretary. In that month he was appointed to the reconstituted bureau which became the Commercial and Industrial Bureau of the Commonwealth Board of Trade. Although the bureau had supporters in industry and parliament, it was seen as too small and visionary; in 1925 it was absorbed into Wilson's new Department of Markets and Migration. While conceding that Taylor himself was 'affable' and 'picturesque', the *Bulletin* gave the bureau a vituperative obituary as 'One of Hughes's many contributions to the towering pyramid of over-government'. The *Countryman*, however, defended the bureau's 'inspiring and helpful influence', a monument to Taylor's enterprise and ability. Taylor's appointment was terminated on 31 May 1925.

In 1928 he became manager in Adelaide of the newly established South Australian wheat pool co-operative. From 1933 he farmed and developed vineyards at Happy Valley. Retiring to North Adelaide about 1947, Taylor died of heart disease at his home on 9 July 1948 and was buried in Centennial Park cemetery. On 16 June 1915 at St George's Anglican Church, Boyanup, Western Australia, he had married Caroline Evelyn Duce, who, with their son and daughter, survived him.

J. Sandford, *Walter Harper and the farmers* (Perth, 1955); *PP* (WA), 1917-18, 2, p 564; *PD* (Cwlth), 11, 12 June 1925, pp 68, 135; *Punch* (Melb), 13 Mar 1919; Bureau of Commerce and Industry (Cwlth), *Annual Report*, 1919-22; *Countryman* (Melb), 6 Mar 1925; *Bulletin*, 12 Mar 1925; CRS A458, H154/17, pt 1, *and* CP211/2, bundle 11, pt 1, CP374/1, bundle 1, covers 1-7 (AA); information from Mr D. S. Taylor, St Georges, Adel, and Wesfarmers Ltd, Perth.

H. J. W. STOKES

TAYLOR, IRENE FRANCES (1890-1933), journalist and feminist, was born on 17 December 1890 at St Kilda, Melbourne, daughter of Rev. Edward Taylor, Congregational minister, and his wife Alice, née Mumford, both English born. During her childhood the family moved to New Zealand, but returned to Melbourne where she completed her education at Presbyterian Ladies' College.

Frances served her apprenticeship in journalism at Mildura on the *Sunraysia*, working as secretary to the manager and editor. In 1916 she rode a horse from Mildura to Melbourne in twelve days and kept a brief diary outlining her adventures. Determined to earn her living by writing, she edited the trade journal of the Grocers' Association of Victoria and, in the 1920s, the *Gum Tree*, the journal of the Forest League in Australia. A woman journalist saw her as a 'slim, boyish figure', with 'vivid blue eyes'. She wore a well-cut, tailor-made suit and felt hat. Her manner was casual, her mode of speech brusque, but she was generous and warm-hearted.

In 1921 she founded the monthly magazine, *Woman's World*. Her motives were similar to those of Louisa Lawson [q.v.10] when founding the *Dawn* in 1888. Its ideal was to 'provide the intelligent Australian woman with an up-to-date paper dealing with the latest developments in the world of women'. Like Louisa Lawson, Frances Taylor personally solicited advertisements for her first issue which appeared on 1 December. Forty pages long and excellently illustrated, it covered a range of subjects: child-care, housework, fashion, sports, music, social service and interviews with prominent women.

As managing editor, she continued to improve the quality of the magazine's paper, print and layout, and to extend the scope and variety of the topics it covered. Eager to broaden her own horizons, she travelled up the east coast of Australia and visited Papua.

By 1926 she had twelve thousand readers. That year Taylor spent six months abroad, attending—as *Woman's World* delegate—the Empire Conference of Women in London, the Victorian Women's Society for Equal Citizenship and the conference of the International Suffrage Alliance at the Sorbonne in Paris. In London she forged links with the editors of *Time and Tide* magazine who saw her position of founder, editor and business manager of a magazine as unique. For some years she also made daily radio broadcasts on 3UZ, giving 'morning tea talks' on issues of interest to women. In the Depression she dedicated her magazine and her broadcasts to helping women to economize. She was a member of Melbourne's Lyceum Club and a lively conversationalist at its Press Gang table.

Independent and vital, Frances Taylor had an intense love of the Australian bush. She owned a holiday cottage at Kangaroo Ground, Victoria, where 'clad in breeches and riding boots, soft shirt and slouch hat', she was a 'different being' from the tailored city journalist. She died of cancer on 26 December 1933 in Melbourne and was buried in Kangaroo Ground cemetery. The *Argus* continued to publish her magazine until its own demise in 1957.

F. Fraser and N. Palmer (eds), *Centenary gift book* (Melb, 1934); J. M. Gillison, *A history of the Lyceum Club* (Melb, 1975); M. O. Reid, *The ladies came to stay* (Melb, 1960); *Woman's World*, 1 May 1926, 1 Feb 1934; *Argus*, 27 Dec 1933.

MAYA V. TUCKER

TAYLOR, JOSEPH LESLIE THEODORE, 'SQUIZZY' (1888-1927), criminal, was born on 29 June 1888 at Brighton, Victoria, son of Benjamin Isaiah Taylor, coachmaker, and his wife Rosina, née Jones, both Victorian born. The family moved to Richmond and Leslie tried to make a career as a jockey on the inner city pony circuit where he came to the notice of the police. At 18 he was convicted of assault. Other convictions followed, mainly on minor charges of theft.

Between 1913 and 1916 Taylor was linked to several more violent crimes including the murder and robbery of Arthur Trotter, a commercial traveller, the burglary of the Melbourne Trades Hall, in which a police constable was killed, and the murder of William Patrick Haines, a driver who refused to participate in the hold-up of a bank manager at Bulleen. Taylor was tried for the murder of Haines and found not guilty. Although rarely convicted after 1917, Taylor remained a key figure in an increasingly violent and wealthy underworld. His income came from armed robbery, prostitution, the sale of illegal liquor and drugs, as well as from race-fixing and protection rackets. With Paddy Boardman, he conducted an efficient and lucrative business in rigging juries, a service of which he made regular use.

Disputes between rival racketeers resulted in the 'Fitzroy vendetta' of 1919 in which several men were shot. Taylor was among the principal figures in these gangland shootings. Charged under warrant in 1921 with theft from a city bond store, he eluded the police for twelve months but gave himself up in 1922. He was acquitted. In 1923 the bank-manager Thomas Berriman was robbed and murdered at Glenferrie railway station. Angus Murray and Richard Buckley were charged with the murder. Taylor faced charges of aiding and abetting the crime, and of assisting Murray's escape from Pentridge prison. On both counts he again escaped conviction. He was eventually found guilty of harbouring Murray and sentenced to six months imprisonment.

Taylor had married Irene Lorna Kelly at the manse of St James's Congregational Church, Fitzroy, on 19 May 1920. On 6 May 1924 they were divorced. On 27 May again at St James's he married Ida Muriel Pender, the woman with whom he had shared much of his adult life. In 1923 they had co-starred in a film about Taylor's life, *Riding to win*; banned by the Victorian censor, it was released in Brisbane in 1925 as *Bound to win*.

On his release from prison Taylor continued thieving, but concentrated his efforts on race-tracks. Involved in selling cocaine, he came into conflict with several Sydney gangsters. He was wounded in a gunfight with one of them, John 'Snowy' Cutmore, at a house in Barkly Street, Carlton, and died in St Vincent's Hospital, Fitzroy, on 27 October 1927. Survived by his wife and by a daughter of his first marriage, Taylor was buried with Anglican rites in Brighton cemetery.

'Squizzy' was a colourful figure in the drinking and gambling clubs of Fitzroy, Richmond and Carlton. A dapper little man who dressed loudly, he strutted through the courts, race-courses and theatres. While hiding from the police, he wrote letters and verse to the press. Yet he had few redeeming qualities. Taylor won lasting notoriety by imitating the style of American bootleggers; he never matched their influence or immunity from the law, and at the time of his death could no longer command fear or loyalty from the underworld.

H. Anderson, *Larrikin crook* (Brisb, 1971); E. H. Buggy, *The real John Wren* (Melb, 1977); *People* (Syd), 26 Apr 1950; *Vic Police Gazette*, 1906-28; *Argus* and *Sun News-Pictorial*, 28 Oct 1927; Chief Commissioner of Police (Vic), Correspondence, 1906-23 (PRO, Vic).

CHRIS McCONVILLE

TAYLOR, SIR PATRICK GORDON (1896-1966), aviator and writer, was born on 21 October 1896 at Mosman, Sydney, third son of Patrick Thomson Taylor [q.v.], manufacturer's agent, and his wife Alice Maud(e), née Sayers. As a child he so disliked his Christian names that he called himself 'Bill'. In his dinghy, *Query*, on Pittwater, he adventured to uninhabited Lion Island and acquired a lifelong love of the sea.

Soon after leaving The Armidale School, where he was senior prefect, Taylor was rejected by the Australian Flying Corps and went to Britain. Commissioned in the Royal Flying Corps on 12 August 1916, he joined No.66 Squadron which was equipped with Sopwith Pup scouts. Awarded the Military Cross in July 1917, he was promoted captain and served with Nos.94 and 88 Squadrons. He later wrote: 'I deplored the killing and all the other evils of war'.

In 1919 Taylor returned to Australia. During the 1920s he flew as a private pilot, worked for De Havilland Aircraft Co. in England, completed an engineering course and studied aerial navigation. He operated a Gipsy Moth seaplane from Sydney Harbour (1928-32) and also flew as a captain with Australian National Airlines Ltd (1930-31). He was second pilot and navigator in the Fokker *Southern Cross* on Sir Charles Kingsford Smith's [q.v.9] 1933 and 1934 flights (Australia-New Zealand-Australia) and navigator aboard Charles Ulm's [q.v.] Avro Ten *Faith in Australia* for two flights in 1933 (Australia-England-Australia). Disappointed at missing the Victorian Centenary Air Race, 'Smithy' and Taylor completed the first Australia-United States of America flight, via Suva and Hawaii (21 October-4 November 1934) in the Lockheed Altair, *Lady Southern Cross*.

On 15 May 1935 Taylor was Kingsford Smith's navigator in the *Southern Cross* for the King George V jubilee airmail flight (Australia-New Zealand). After flying for six hours, the heavily-laden aircraft had almost reached half-way when part of the centre engine's exhaust manifold broke off and severely damaged the starboard propeller. 'Smithy' closed down the vibrating starboard engine, applied full power to the other two, turned back to Australia and jettisoned the cargo. The oil pressure on the port engine began to fall alarmingly. The flight appeared doomed.

Taylor reacted heroically. Climbing out of the fuselage, he edged his way against the strong slipstream along the engine connecting strut and collected oil from the disabled starboard engine in the casing of a thermos flask. He then transferred it to the port engine. With assistance from the wireless operator, John Stannage, he carried out this procedure six times before the aircraft landed safely at Mascot some nine hours later. For his resourcefulness and courage, Taylor was awarded the Empire Gallantry Medal, gazetted on 9 July 1937; it was superseded by the George Cross (instituted in May 1941). Taylor portrayed his exploit in the 1946 film, *Smithy*.

From 1935 Taylor operated a succession of Percival Gull Four and Gull Six aircraft on private and charter flying; having visited Britain in 1938, he became agent for Percival Aircraft Ltd in Australia. His marriage on 29 December 1924 in St James's Anglican Church, Sydney, to Yolande Bede Dalley, niece of J. B. Dalley and granddaughter of W. B. Dalley [qq.v.8,4], had quickly proved disastrous; she eventually divorced him in March 1938. On 10 May he married Eileen Joan Broadwood (d. 1950) in the Methodist Church, Mosman. He made the first flight across the Indian Ocean from Port Hedland, Western Australia, to Mombasa, Kenya, in the Consolidated flying-boat *Guba II* on 4-21 June 1939.

Taylor ferried flying-boats from U.S.A. to Australia in 1941. On 9 June 1943 he was commissioned flying officer in the Royal Australian Air Force. Transferring to the Royal Air Force in 1944 as a civilian captain, he ferried aircraft from Canada across the Atlantic Ocean. At his own request, he commanded the R.A.F. Catalina *Frigate Bird* in September-October 1944 on a pioneer Pacific Ocean survey flight from Bermuda to Mexico, Clipperton Island, New Zealand and Sydney. In March 1951 he flew across the South Pacific from Australia to Chile, via Tahiti and Easter Island, in the Catalina *Frigate Bird II*.

A writer of distinction, subtle and realistic, Taylor published eight books: *Pacific flight* (1935), *VH-UXX* (1937), *Call to the winds* (1939), *Forgotten island* (1948), *Frigate Bird* (1953), *The sky beyond* (Melbourne, 1963), *Bird of the islands* (Melbourne, 1964), and *Sopwith scout 7309* (London, 1968). In 1963 he took part in the Australian Broadcasting Commission's television film, *An airman remembers*. Taylor lived at Bayview on Pittwater, where he sailed a 35-ft. (10.7 m) sloop and in 1947 established Loquat Valley School for his daughters. On 4 May 1951 he married Joyce Agnes Kennington at St Mark's Anglican Church, Darling Point. Chairman of the family firm, P. T. Taylor Pty Ltd, and a director of Trans Oceanic Airways Pty Ltd, 'P.G.' operated the Sandringham 7 flying-boat *Frigate Bird III* from Sydney on Pacific island cruises in 1954-58. A wiry man, greying at the temples, with crowsfeet edging his blue eyes, he belonged to the Union Club and Royal Aero Club of New South Wales.

Awarded the 1951 Oswald Watt [q.v.] gold medal for his Australia-South America flight and the Johnson memorial trophy of the Guild of Air Pilots and Air Navigators, London (1951 and 1952), Taylor was knighted in 1954 (and known as Sir Gordon). He died in Queen's Hospital, Honolulu, on 15 December 1966. His ashes were scattered over Lion Island where the dreams of his adventurous life were conceived. His wife, their son and two daughters survived him, as did the two daughters of his second marriage. Norman Carter's [q.v.7] portrait of Taylor is held by the Art Gallery of New South Wales. *Frigate Bird II* is held by the Powerhouse Museum, Sydney, and *Frigate Bird III* by the Musée de L'Air, Le Bourget, France.

As a pilot and navigator, Taylor was a perfectionist, fastidious, demanding, sharp and candid. Yet, his character was complex. Those 'with the patience to come to know him discovered a man of immense sensitivity, intelligence and courage'.

C. E. K. Smith, *My flying life* (Lond, 1937); A. J. Hughes, *History of air navigation* (Lond, 1946); J. Stannage, *Smithy* (Lond, 1950); L. A. Triebel, *The literature of flying and fliers* (Syd, 1955); N. Ellison, *Flying Matilda* (Syd, 1957); O. Tapper, *The world's great pioneer flights* (Lond, 1975); *London Gazette*, 26 July 1917; *Sea, Land, and Air*, May 1919; *People* (Syd), 9 May 1951; *Walkabout*, Aug 1967; *SMH*, 17 Dec 1966; information from Lady Taylor, Elanora, Qld.   KEITH ISAACS

TAYLOR, PATRICK THOMSON (1862-1922), businessman and politician, was born on 22 May 1862 at Newstead, near Govan, Lanarkshire, Scotland, son of William Taylor, grain merchant, and his wife Jane, née Wilson. After education at home and at the High School, Glasgow, he was apprenticed to an accountant, but came to New South Wales before finishing his articles. A year of station life restored his health and, about 1882, he entered the office of Alfred Lamb & Co., Sydney. He then went to the Australian Kerosene Oil & Mineral Co. Ltd's shale works at Joadja Creek and soon afterwards began his own business as an accountant in Sydney. At Milsons Point he married Alice Maud(e) Sayers on 29 November 1883.

A shareholder in the North Shore Steam Ferry Co. from 1892, Taylor was a director from 1899 when the company was reconstructed as Sydney Ferries Ltd. From this basis in local shipping, he acquired interlocking directorships in steamships, gas companies (purchasing coke for his vessels), iceworks (using a gas works' residual product, ammonia) and insurance. His business interests benefited from urban growth on the north shore and from financial management involving share-splitting. An original alderman on Mosman Municipal Council (1893-98), Taylor was mayor in 1896. In time he became chairman of Sydney Ferries Ltd, North Shore Gas Co. Ltd and New South Wales Fresh Food and Ice Co. Ltd, deputy-chairman of the Australian Gas Light Co., and a director of the Newcastle and Hunter River Steamship Co., Norwich Union Fire Insurance Society Ltd and Toohey's [q.v.6] Ltd.

His accounting skills and command of technology earned Taylor respect in business circles: when he acted for the gas company in arbitration proceedings arising from the resumption of the Kent Street gas works, the sum awarded was substantially more than the government's initial offer.

Two of his three sons served in World War I: Kenneth was killed in action in France and (Sir) Gordon [q.v.] served in the Royal Flying Corps. After the gas works had become involved in the 1917 strike, Taylor arranged evening entertainments for the volunteers who replaced the strikers. He was one of the negotiators when W. A. Holman [q.v.9] and his followers joined the Liberals to form the National Party. Taylor remained influential in the new party and raised funds for it. He was nominated to the Legislative Council in 1917. His gas company was allowed a remission of £14 000 for losses incurred in the 1917 strike and shortly afterwards was permitted to increase the price of gas. Next year Taylor replaced J. Chalmers on the Commonwealth royal commission on defence and signed its report on naval administration.

A backroom politician, Taylor was irregular in his attendance at the council and never spoke. On leave of absence for health reasons in 1919, he visited Vancouver and San Francisco and later advised on trade prospects with North America. Sailing on Pittwater (where he once owned Scotland Island) and farming at Hartley were his main recreations. Taylor died of a cerebral haemorrhage on 17 November 1922 at his Edgecliff residence and was buried in the Presbyterian section of South Head cemetery. His wife, two sons and a daughter survived him. His estate was sworn for probate at £90 762.

H. V. Evatt, *Australian Labour leader* (Syd, 1945); *PD* (NSW), 1912, pp 886, 958, 1936, and 1917, pp 2507, 2711; *PP* (Cwlth), 1917-19, 4, p 175; *SMH*, 7 May, 10 Sept 1917, 10 Nov 1919, 16 Nov 1922, 23 Feb 1923; Sydney Ferries Ltd, Annual Report, 1899 (ML).   HEATHER RADI

TAYLOR, THOMAS GRIFFITH (1880-1963), geographer, was born on 1 December 1880 at Walthamstow, Essex, England, son of James Taylor, metallurgical chemist, and his wife Lily Agnes, née Griffiths. He attended a modest private school until 1893 when the family migrated to New South Wales where James secured a position as government metallurgist. Educated at Sydney Grammar School, briefly, and The King's School, Parramatta, in 1898 Griffith was employed as a clerk in the Treasury. Resigning next year, he enrolled in arts (later transferring to science) at the University of Sydney (B.Sc., 1904; B.E. [mining and metallurgy], 1905).

He excelled in science and mining engineering under Professor (Sir) Edgeworth David [q.v.8] who nurtured his interest in palaeontology. Taylor contributed to David's demanding field programme, worked as a demonstrator in geology, lectured in commercial geography, collaborated in the production of an elementary geographical text on New South Wales and began corresponding with internationally-known geographers. Awarded an 1851 Exhibition scholarship in 1907 to Emmanuel College, Cambridge (B.A. [Research], 1909), Taylor was elected a fellow of the Geological Society, London, in 1909 and in 1910 completed *Australia in its physiographic and economic aspects* (Oxford, 1911). He established strong friendships with (Sir) Raymond Priestley [q.v.11], Canada's Charles Wright, the Australian Frank Debenham and others who shared his passion for Antarctic exploration. David arranged for Taylor to join the new Commonwealth Weather Service as physiographer on his return from England.

When Robert Falcon Scott contracted to take the Cambridge group on the *Terra Nova* expedition (1910-13), it was agreed that Taylor would act as the Weather Service's official representative since Antarctica was known to exercise a powerful influence on Australia's climates. Taylor's youthful energy and irrepressible humour made an indelible mark on the historic, ill-fated expedition. During the long winter confinement, he was a popular participant in the lecture series and made lively contributions to the *South Polar Times.* As leader of the successful western geological party, he supervised the first significant topographical and glaciological interpretations of extensive areas, and his own physiographical and geomorphological research was rewarded in 1916 with a doctorate from the University of Sydney. The 'race' for the pole between Scott and Amundsen, and the deaths of Scott and his companions, attracted wide interest throughout the British Empire and accentuated the powerful aura surrounding every Antarctic adventurer. In 1913 Taylor was awarded the King's Polar medal and elected a fellow of the Royal Geographical Society of London. His *With Scott: the silver lining* (London, 1916) was well received, and he lectured on the subject in several countries. The mystique of the *Terra Nova* episode assisted his early professional career and, quite as importantly, the arduous field experiences on

the frozen continent left a deep and lasting impression on him.

At Queen's College, University of Melbourne, Taylor married Priestley's sister, Doris Marjorie, on 8 July 1914 with Methodist forms; the bride was given away by the wife of his revered mentor, David. Between 1912 and 1920, confident and ambitious, Taylor rapidly consolidated and extended his reputation in physical geography and related fields. In his senior research position with the Weather Service he busily produced some of his most famous work on Australian meteorological conditions and 'climatic controls' in agriculture and settlement expansion.

World War I brought new demands and opportunities: the Weather Service was linked with the Intelligence Branch under the control of the Department of Home Affairs, and the character of much of the work undertaken was dictated by considerations of defence. Taylor also lectured in meteorology at the Commonwealth Flying School (1914-18) and in physiology at the University of Melbourne (1917-18). His early pronouncements on resource limitations and the inadvisability of tropical settlement have to be seen in this context; he established an independent viewpoint on these matters and refused to give way to political and military arguments. For similar reasons, he proposed the compilation of a national resources atlas (the idea was taken up after World War II) and served as a founder member of the Australian National Research Council in 1919. His 'pessimistic' and 'unpatriotic' forecasts for Australia's development infuriated the settlement boosters, notably in Western Australia and Queensland; Taylor was embroiled in bitter controversy at home and abroad. Undaunted, he accepted David's advice and in 1920 was appointed associate professor and foundation head of Australia's first university geography department, in Sydney.

The 'Australia Unlimited' catchcry won considerable support. Daisy Bates, W. C. Grasby [qq.v.7,9] and respected scholars holding Imperialist views, including Professor J. W. Gregory [q.v.9], publicly challenged Taylor's efforts to dilute the appeal of Australia as the Empire's major field for White immigration. Naive and mischievous speculations on future population capacities of between 100 and 500 million abounded, but Taylor steadfastly insisted that the environmental factors would be sufficiently strong to restrict the total to about 19 or 20 million by the turn of the century. His influential opponents labelled him an 'environmental determinist'; at one point they arranged for Canada's noted 'possibilist', Vilhjalmur Stefansson, to inspect Australia's deserts and marginal regions and to expound on their potential in the metropolitan newspapers.

Taylor's writings were savaged across the country; at one extreme, Western Australia's education authorities and university senate banned his text on Australia because of his temerity in employing the terms 'arid' and 'desert'. Taylor never gave quarter in his frequent battles with the optimists in the daily press: his serious technical and academic approach was sometimes carelessly laced with obscure literary references and pedagogical rebukes which his enemies considered arrogant and offensive.

The adoption of a 'national issues' orientation attracted students to the new Sydney department, but Taylor's denunciation of the White Australia policy, of the extension of continental railways through the interior and of the development of the tropical north was scarcely calculated to build a secure foundation for a young academic subject in a severely provincial milieu. Taylor attempted to expand his Australian interests into broad global generalizations and *Environment and race* (London, 1927) established his name on the international scene. In 1923 he had been awarded the Livingstone Centenary medal of the American Geographical Society and his works were regularly cited in Britain and North America. On the domestic front, he belonged to the Royal Society of New South Wales and the Sydney group of the Round Table, and was founding president in 1927 of the Geographical Society of New South Wales and joint editor of the *Australian Geographer*.

Repeatedly denied the rank of full professor while he was being aggressively courted by prominent American universities, Taylor lost patience with the Sydney authorities and accepted a chair of geography at the University of Chicago, United States of America. He resigned his Sydney post in 1928, still unrepentant at the time of his departure. At a farewell luncheon given by the university in his honour, he indulged another hobby-horse, the need to strip the classics of their high status in secondary and tertiary curricula in order to accommodate more useful courses in geography and the sciences: he made a barbed allusion to his university's motto, *Sidere mens eadem mutato* ('The same spirit under a different sky'), which he rendered 'Though the heavens fall I am of the same mind as my great-great-grandfather!'

Although he remained at Chicago until 1935, Taylor was seldom at ease and never attempted to stake a personal claim to controversial geographical analyses of the United States. In 1935 he became professor of geography at the University of Toronto, Canada, and built a highly respected department. As in Australia, his idiosyncratic approaches delivered fresh statements on major national concerns: climatic limitations to the further development of the cold deserts

were vigorously outlined as Taylor reclaimed his old niche, but in the case of Canada his generalizations were comparatively optimistic and corrected a much gloomier political and popular perspective. His views were well illustrated in his textbook, *Canada* (London, 1947).

On the broader front, he continued writing on environmental influences in cultural and urban development, notably in *Environment and nation* (Toronto, 1936) and *Urban geography* (London, 1949). He was president of the geography section of the British Association for the Advancement of Science in 1938, and elected first non-American president of the Association of American Geographers in 1940 and a fellow of the Royal Society of Canada in 1942, but remained bitterly disappointed that he was never elected a fellow of the Royal Society, London, an honour he had unashamedly coveted in his most productive years.

In 1948 Taylor accepted an invitation from the interim council of the Australian National University to join a team of consultants advising on the establishment of research schools. He spent three months touring Australia and delighted in his unusually warm reception. Sponsored by the British Council, he also made a lecture tour of British universities with Priestley, then vice-chancellor of the University of Birmingham. Retiring from Toronto in 1951, Taylor decided to settle in Sydney. Before leaving, he was elected president of the new Canadian Association of Geographers which he had been promoting for several years. In 1954 he was made a fellow of the Australian Academy of Science, the sole geographer in that fraternity; in 1959 he became the first president of the Institute of Australian Geographers and was awarded an honorary D.Litt. by the University of Sydney. He was still publishing, on Antarctica and on the contribution of geographical studies to world peace, in the year of his death.

In his self-image Taylor was the enterprising frontiersman, pushing out one ragged and remote outer boundary after another, leaving the mundane in-filling to more timid types. He also made use of other workers' ideas when it suited him. His theories on racial origins, distributions and migrations attracted attention outside geography: *Environment and race* provided anthropology students with useful elementary geographical information and demonstrated the importance of mapping; it was widely read, sold well and was translated into Japanese and Chinese. On the other hand, neither his vague reply to the Germans' *Geopolitik* in his notions of 'Geopacifics', nor his efforts in urban geography, was deemed worthy of lasting academic attention.

Taylor was never so brazenly or completely deterministic as some authors have claimed. Prior to his Sydney appointment he derived some amusement from the label, but he moved rapidly to safeguard his considerable ego as the debate intensified, and declared that possibilism might be preferable in the study of small, better-favoured areas. Though he maintained his view of himself as an *enfant terrible*, an anachronistic tone could be identified in several aspects of his work. It might be said, somewhat unkindly, that his deterministic stance mainly provided a convenient model for his broad attacks on themes which interested him.

He believed that academics had a duty to be professionally concerned with the great controversies of their day. In Australia in the 1920s Taylor's views on racial origins and dispersals, and on tropical development, were taken to imply either depopulation or support for Asian peasant settlement in Queensland and the Northern Territory; the powerful supporters of the White Australia policy howled him down. His remarkably accurate prediction of Australia's future population capacity remains highly regarded in political, administrative and academic spheres.

Survived by his wife and two sons, Griffith Taylor died at Manly, Sydney, on 5 November 1963 and was cremated. His portrait by Doris Toovey is held by the University of Sydney; topographical maps of Antarctica commemorate his pioneering achievements.

J. M. Powell, *An historical geography of modern Australia* (Cambridge, Eng, 1988); M. Sanderson, *Griffith Taylor* (Ottawa, Canada, 1988); *Geographical Review*, 53 (1964), p 427; *Aust Geographer*, 12, 1972, p 115; *Geographers, Biobibliographical Studies*, 3, 1978, p 141; *JRAHS*, 66, 1980, p 163; G. S. Tomkins, Griffith Taylor and Canadian geography (Ph.D. thesis, Univ Washington, USA, 1966); Taylor papers (NL).   J. M. POWELL

TAYLOR, WILLIAM GEORGE (1845-1934), Methodist minister, was born on 18 January 1845 at Knayton, Yorkshire, England, son of John Shemelds Taylor, grocer and later mill-owner, and his wife Mary Ann, née Morton. From Preston Grammar School, Stokesley, in 1859 William was apprenticed to an accountant with Gilkes, Wilson, Pease & Co., local 'iron kings'. Converted at the age of 12 in a Wesleyan class meeting, Taylor began his own evangelical preaching career in 1861, winning his first convert in July. He was received as a candidate for the Wesleyan ministry in 1868 and trained at Richmond College, London.

In answer to a call for preachers in Australia, Taylor reached Sydney in the *Patriarch* on 18 January 1871. He was appointed second minister at Albert Street, Brisbane, then served at Warwick (1872-75) and Toowoomba (1876-78). Soon after her arrival from England, he married Ann Sarah Robey on 25 February 1874 at Kinellan, near Brisbane.

Appointed in 1879 to the Manning River, New South Wales, Taylor transferred to Glebe, Sydney, in 1882. In the midst of a successful ministry, he was removed in 1884 against his will to the failing York Street Church in the hope that he could save Wesleyan Methodism from the embarrassment of a near empty church in the inner city. To the consternation of many, Taylor resolved to employ unorthodox methods: street preaching, brass bands and the use of 'shocking pink' posters and handbills to advertise services. A singer of some ability, he also made imaginative use of choral and solo music in his services and after-meetings. He stressed the place of prayer and once held a ten-day prayer meeting. He also founded the 'United Methodist Holiness Association' to emphasize the Wesleyan teaching of 'entire satisfaction' or 'scriptural holiness'.

Worn out by 1887, Taylor visited Britain for his health. Back in Sydney he spent a year at William Street before returning in 1888 to York Street (Sydney Central Methodist Mission) where he remained, save for five years, until 1913. On special assignment he raised funds in Britain and the United States of America in 1893-94 and spent three years at Bathurst (1895-97). He was president of the New South Wales Wesleyan Methodist Conference in 1896 and of the New South Wales Council of Churches in 1899. Chaplain to the military forces (1900-06), he was also Methodist naval chaplain on the Australian Station until 1915.

Taylor gradually introduced a panoply of service organizations around his church; these included a mission to seamen (1886), a training college for evangelists (1889), a boys' brigade, Dalmar Children's Homes (1893), a shelter for 'fallen' women (1902), together with general philanthropic assistance. Most innovative of all, if a little provocative, since some thought it involved a step toward Rome, was his creation in 1890 of the Home for 'Sisters of the People', essentially the beginning of the Methodist deaconess movement in Australia. While many of these steps were taken in imitation of his English friends Charles Garrett of Liverpool and Hugh Price Hughes of London, the name Central Methodist Mission was probably first used in Sydney by Taylor.

A product of the fervent Methodism characteristic of Yorkshire, Taylor was essentially an evangelist and regarded any preaching that did not aim at winning converts as opportunity wasted. He possessed a fine voice, a commanding presence and a vigorous and picturesque preaching style. Revival followed him wherever he went and ailing Methodist causes were renewed in spiritual power, as well as in numbers and financial security. Taylor was a man of vision with the executive and administrative ability to implement his ideals. Able to inspire extraordinary loyalty in others who willingly co-operated in his plans, he combined the traditional spiritual life of the Church with Christian humanitarianism.

Becoming a supernumerary in 1913, Taylor published his autobiography, *The life story of an Australian evangelist* (London, 1920), a lively account of Methodism in Australia. In 1924 he gave a collection of books to the Fisher [q.v.4] Library and continued to take a vital interest in the work of the Church. Survived by his wife, three sons and five daughters, he died at his Lindfield home on 24 September 1934 and was buried in the Methodist section of Gore Hill cemetery.

D. I. Wright, *Mantle of Christ* (Brisb, 1984); Methodist Church of A'sia, *NSW Conference Minutes*, 1935, p 86; D. Wright, 'W. G. Taylor and the foundation of the Central Methodist Mission', *Church Heritage*, 3, no 3, Mar 1984, p 226; *SMH*, 13 Mar 1920, 6 Feb 1924, 25 Sept 1934; *Sun* (Syd), 25 Sept 1934; *Methodist* (Syd), 29 Sept 1934.

DON WRIGHT

TAZEWELL, EVELYN RUTH (1893-1983), sportswoman, was born on 19 August 1893 at Newtown, Hobart, only daughter of George Webber Tazewell, shopkeeper and champion cyclist, and his wife Florence, née Hawkins, both English born. In 1914 the family moved to Adelaide where Eva embarked on a career in hockey, playing in both the full-back and goalkeeper positions. She joined the Aroha (now Adelaide) Hockey Club and the South Australian Women's Hockey Association. Having captained the State team against Western Australia in Adelaide in 1918, she remained its captain from 1920 to 1936. During a career that spanned four decades to the 1960s, she was a member of the South Australian executive, selection and umpires committees.

President of the All-Australian Women's Hockey Association in 1920 and State delegate in 1920-65, Miss Tazewell was selected in the Australian team in 1925, 1928, 1929 and in 1930-36. In 1930 the team entered the Empire Tournament in South Africa, and toured Britain and Europe; in 1935 she captained the side against New Zealand in Melbourne. Next year she was vice-captain when Australia played at the International Federation of Women's Hockey Associations tournament in the United States of America. After World War II she helped to convert an almond and orange orchard into the Women's Memorial Playing Fields at St Mary's, Adelaide; the grounds were dedicated to Australian nurses who had perished in Banka Strait, off Sumatra, in 1942.

A lean, long-limbed woman, with a tanned complexion, she dressed in tweed sportsclothes. She was independent and reticent, with high standards, but her brief words of praise meant much to her fellows. After the death of her parents, from the late 1930s she shared her family's Forestville home for thirty years with another hockey player Agnes Magarey. Miss Tazewell's interests included stamp collecting, handicrafts, gardening and bridge. She retired from playing hockey in 1940, but continued coaching Aroha, Woodlands Church of England Girls' Grammar School (who became champions under her guidance), Adelaide Girls' High School and the South Australian team (1946-51). In retirement she and Agnes visited their hockey contacts throughout the world.

'Taz' was a delegate to the International Federation of Women's Hockey Associations in 1953 and 1959. In 1972 she retired as an umpire and spent her last years in a unit, cared for by her close friend Lyndall Morris. Evelyn Tazewell died on 29 December 1983 and was cremated. Her Australian blazer and hockey stick are to be displayed at The Pines, the State hockey centre in Adelaide, and her name is inscribed in the Sport Australia Hall of Fame, Melbourne.

Cyclopaedia of Tasmania, 1 (Hob, 1900); *Woodlands Mag*, 1984; *Observer* (Adel), 21 Aug 1920; *Advertiser* (Adel), 30 Dec 1983; information from Mrs R. Magarey, Coromandel Valley, Adel; records of SAWHA *and* Aust Women's Hockey Assn, comp by author, Adel.

LORNA M. JOLLY

TEAGUE, VIOLET HELEN EVANGELINE (1872-1951), artist, was born on 21 February 1872 in Melbourne, daughter of James Pascoe Teague, a medical practitioner from Cornwall, and his Canadian wife Eliza Jane, née Miller. Violet was educated by a French governess and at the Presbyterian Ladies' College, Melbourne. In the 1890s she roamed the art galleries of Europe, and studied in Brussels at the studio of Ernest Blanc Garin and in England with (Sir) Hubert von Herkomer where she probably learned to make woodcuts. In 1897 she joined the National Gallery schools, Melbourne, studying with L. Bernard Hall [q.v.9]; while at the Melbourne School of Art run by E. Phillips Fox [q.v.8] and Tudor St George Tucker [q.v.], she joined the Charterisville group.

She had already begun to paint portraits of Melburnians: her picture of Colonel Rede [q.v.6] was hung at the Salon de la Société des

Artistes Français, Paris. In 1902 she was appointed to the council of the Victorian Artists' Society which that year published her poem 'A Cloud Fantasy' in its journal. Two illustrated books, *Birds in the sunny south* and *Night fall in the ti-tree* (which she produced in collaboration with Geraldine Rede) were published in 1905. During 1905-14 she produced many Japanese-style woodcuts and lectured on the technique at the Victorian Arts and Crafts Society.

In 1915 her portrait of Mrs Otway Falkiner [q.v.8] won a bronze medal at the Panama-Pacific International Exposition, San Francisco. In 1911 Violet had painted 'Boy with a Palette'; submitted to the Old Salon, Paris, the painting won a silver medal when hung in 1920; next year it was allotted pride of place at the Royal Academy of Arts, London. An admirer of Gainsborough and the English school of portraiture, Teague often introduced eighteenth-century mannerisms in her pictures. Her portraits are among the best Australia has produced. She occasionally painted genre scenes: her picture 'Welcome News From the Front' commemorates the South African War.

While she exhibited infrequently in the 1920s and 1930s, she turned to making altarpieces. For the Kinglake (War) Memorial Church, Victoria, she made one in which the adoring shepherds were replaced by portraits of Australian light-horsemen; when commissioned in 1938 to execute the altarpiece of the Arctic Cathedral at Alkavic, Canada, she again chose a contemporary and regional setting, dressing the madonna and child in furs. She made other panels and, at the Church of St James the Less, Mt Eliza, collaborated with her friend Jessie Traill [q.v.].

Less than five feet (152.4 cm) tall, with grey-blue eyes and masses of light brown hair, Teague was described in 1949 as being: 'a small frail person . . . quiet of manner, yet with a surprising vitality and a more surprising sense of whimsy . . . she comes out direct in a mannered way and her eyes twinkle humorously'. She 'can talk on any subject from racehorses to the decline of Western Culture exactly and wittily'. Teague died on 30 September 1951 at Mt Eliza, Victoria, and was cremated. A member of several leading Australian art societies, she is represented in the Australian National Gallery, Canberra, and the National Gallery of Victoria.

C. Deutsher and R. Butler, *A survey of Australian relief prints 1900-1950*, cat (Melb, 1978); R. Butler, *Melbourne woodcuts and linocuts of the 1920's and 1930's*, cat (Melb, 1981); *Art and Architecture*, 5, no 5, Sept-Oct 1908, p 180, 8, no 5, Sept-Oct 1911, p 337; *Table Talk*, 25 July 1901; *Woman's World*, 1 Dec 1922, 1 May 1933; *Argus*, 29 Nov 1921, 31 June 1922, 17 Nov 1931, 18 Nov 1938.

MARY ALICE LEE

TEECE, RICHARD (1847-1928), actuary, and **RICHARD CLIVE** (1877-1965), barrister, were father and son. Richard was born on 29 April 1847 at Paihia, New Zealand, second son of William Teece, a gold prospector from Wales, and his English-born wife Catherine, née Hassett. The family moved in 1854 to the 'Snowy Mountain diggings' in New South Wales, then to Lambing Flat (Young) before settling at Goulburn. Richard was educated at Goulburn Grammar School and the University of Sydney (1865-67). An accomplished sportsman, he was secretary of the University Boat Club and played in early intervarsity cricket matches and later with the Albert and I Zingari clubs. On 10 February 1876 at Pitt Street Congregational Church he married with Methodist forms Helena (d. 1914), daughter of Benjamin Palmer, mayor of Sydney.

Leaving the university without a degree, at the age of 19 Teece had joined the Australian Mutual Provident Society as an actuarial clerk, advancing to chief clerk at 25. Qualified as an actuary, he soon had a leading position and became a fellow of the Institute of Actuaries, London, the Faculty of Actuaries of Scotland and the Actuarial Society of America. He was successively secretary, general manager and actuary (from 1890) and a director (1917-27) of the A.M.P. Society, and was described as the 'master-mind behind [its] stupendous growth'.

A Freemason, Teece was deputy grand master of United Grand Lodge (1897-98). He was president of the Australian Economic Association, Actuarial Society of New South Wales, Insurance Institute of New South Wales, Sydney Mechanics' School of Arts, Free Trade and Liberal Association, and the New South Wales Club (1914-19), vice-president of the Sydney Philharmonic Society and honorary secretary of the New South Wales Cricket Association. A fellow of the university senate (1889-1919), he was a founder and council-member of Women's College (1892-1902).

While temporarily deranged, Teece shot himself at his Point Piper home on 13 December 1928; he was buried in the Anglican section of Gore Hill cemetery. Four sons and three daughters, including Linda Littlejohn [q.v.10], survived him.

His eldest son, known as Clive, was born on 24 September 1877 at Woolloomooloo. Educated at Sydney Grammar School and St Andrew's College, University of Sydney (B.A., 1899; M.A., 1901; LL.B., 1903), he thrice graduated with first-class honours and won the University medal (for classics, modern history and law). His many prizes included the 1902 Beauchamp [q.v.7] prize for his essay, 'A Comparison of the Federal Constitution of Canada with that of Australia'.

Having read in the chambers of Dr Richard Sly and (Sir) Adrian Knox [qq.v.11,9], he was admitted to the Bar on 29 October 1903.

Tempted by academic life, Teece became acting professor of law at the University of Tasmania (1905), but returned to professional practice in Denman Chambers, Sydney. Family connexions marked out a career in commercial and property law, equity and appellate work. He served in 1910 as vice-principal of his old college. On 6 July 1911 he was married by H. L. Clarke [q.v.8], the Anglican archbishop of Melbourne, to Fanny Frederica (d. 1950), daughter of F. S. Grimwade [q.v.4], at Holy Trinity Church, Balaclava; they were to have a son and three daughters. The family lived in Sydney at Bellevue Hill and later at Vaucluse, and had a country retreat at Leura.

Teece's practice thrived: he became King's Counsel in December 1922, being reciprocally admitted to the Victorian Bar in 1932. He described his recreations as 'golf, with occasional irruptions into political controversies' on the conservative side. Much of his time outside the law was devoted to the Church of England: Teece was chancellor of the diocese of Bathurst (1928-36) and a member of the Sydney diocesan synod; as chairman of committees of the general synod, he was principal draftsman of a proposed new constitution for the Australian Church. When senior counsel for the informants in the 'Red Book Case' in the Supreme and High courts (1944-48), Teece succeeded in having the bishop of Bathurst restrained from making major liturgical changes. About the same time he was retained to advise private banks on the Federal government's proposed legislation to nationalize banking.

From 1940, when war service depleted the Sydney University Law School staff, Teece lectured in legal ethics for over twenty years. His lectures were published as *Law and conduct of the legal profession in New South Wales*, in 1949 with W. N. Harrison and in 1963 on his own account. A strict disciplinarian as lecturer, Teece cut a sartorial figure with rosebud buttonhole and distinctive monocle. In 1946 the majority of the practising barristers on the faculty—still simmering at the senate's refusal to delay filling vacant chairs in law until after the war—took their revenge by electing Teece 'caretaker' dean, thereby blocking the immediate aspirations of the few full-time academic members.

A proponent of the corporate organization of the legal profession, Teece was a member of the Council of the Bar, and foundation president of the New South Wales Bar Association (1936-44) and of the Law Council of Australia (1934-35, 1937-38). He had practised for just over fifty years on his retirement in October 1953. Continuing to lecture for over a decade, he regularly dined at the Union, University and Australasian Pioneers' clubs. Survived by his four children, Teece died at Randwick on 6 November 1965 and was cremated after a service at St Mark's Anglican Church, Darling Point.

T. C. Hammond (ed), *The Bathurst ritual case* (Syd, nd); *Cyclopedia of N.S.W.* (Syd, 1907); *Fifty years of service* (Syd, 1916); J. M. Bennett (ed), *A history of the New South Wales Bar* (Syd, 1969); R. A. Littlejohn, *Richard Teece, 1847-1924* (Syd, 1979); *Univ Syd News*, 27 Mar 1974; *SMH*, 14 Dec 1928, 8, 9 Nov 1965; *Anglican*, 18 Nov 1965; Reminiscences of Clive Teece Q.C. (held by NSW Bar Assn, Syd); information from Mrs H. Davidson, Vaucluse, Syd.

J. M. BENNETT

TEMPLE, DAVID (1862-1921), trade unionist, was born on 4 July 1862 at Bald Hills, Creswick, Victoria, one of six children of David Temple, a Scottish-born miner, and his English wife Ellen, née Ogle. Little is known of his early life except that he became a miner and part-time shearer. In April 1886 shearing rates were cut. Provoked by the forfeiture of his earnings, Temple placed notices in the *Ballarat Courier* and the *Star*, at his own expense, calling a meeting of shearers on 12 June at Fern's Hotel, Ballarat. He invited W. G. Spence [q.v.6] to take the chair, but other meetings were abandoned and Temple's office was closed. Left to his own resources, Temple canvassed shearers on foot from house to house. He wrote regularly to local newspapers and, when shearing began, set off by train for Echuca. From there he carried his swag to Nyang station, owned by (Sir) Simon Fraser [q.v.4] who did nothing to impede Temple's efforts to unionize his shed. Within five weeks Temple enrolled 1500 members; he engaged other organizers and, before shearing ended, the union had 8000 members.

In January 1887 the small shearers' unions of Wagga Wagga and Bourke, both in New South Wales, joined with Temple's union to become the Amalgamated Shearers' Union of Australasia (forerunner of the Australian Workers' Union). Temple was elected general secretary and Spence president. Within three years the union was the largest and most effective labour organization in Australia. Temple refused a £50 bonus voted him by a grateful membership in 1889.

Much against Spence's initial wishes, Temple threw the weight of the union behind the 1890 maritime strike. When it failed, he recognized the need for labour to establish its own newspapers and to form a political party. At the 1891 annual conference in Adelaide he moved the historic motion providing for union organization to return Labor candidates at the next general elections. In a call for a 'union of unions', not achieved until 1927, Temple used the example of the Roman *fasces* to explain the advantages of affiliation with the Victorian Trades and Labor Council.

He resigned the secretaryship in 1897. In 1900 Spence accused him of misappropriating union funds, but, when challenged by Temple, Spence admitted publicly that 'no shortage was ever found in Mr. Temple's account'.

With a deep understanding of the class struggle, Temple followed the endeavours of the Knights of Labor and other American activists. An avid reader of the classic social writers, from Henry George [q.v.4] to Karl Marx, he owned a large library and—according to his daughter—occupied most of his spare time in reading. He was 6 ft. 2 ins. (188 cm) tall with a commanding presence. In retirement he kept a grocery business, but spent the last years of his life clearing postal boxes at Footscray. He regularly gave sweets to poor children in his locality.

Temple died of heart and kidney disease on 27 September 1921 and was buried in the Anglican section of Fawkner cemetery. On 8 April 1891 he had married Jane Bickley Dunn at Creswick. Two daughters survived him. The headquarters of the A.W.U.'s South Australian and New South Wales branches were named after him in 1986.

J. Merritt, *The making of the AWU* (Melb, 1986); *Shearers' Record*, 8 Mar 1889, 16 Feb 1891; *Australasian*, 12 Jan 1884, 3 Apr 1886; *Daily Telegraph* (Launc), 23 Feb 1886; *Tocsin*, 17 Oct, 7, 21 Nov, 12 Dec 1901; *Labor Call*, 10 Nov 1910; Cameron-Fraser correspondence, 14 July 1980 (held by author, Tennyson, Adel); personal information.

CLYDE CAMERON

TEMPLE-POOLE, GEORGE THOMAS; *see* POOLE

TEMPLETON, HENRY BARKLEY (1868-1943), public servant, was born on 28 May 1868 at Windsor, New South Wales, son of Henry Templeton, bootmaker, and his wife Margaret Jane, née Hissken, both Sydney born. Educated at St Barnabas's Church of England School, Sydney, he later trained as an accountant and worked with a Sydney solicitor before entering the office of R. Goldsbrough [q.v.4] & Co.'s wool stores, Pyrmont.

In January 1885 he joined the Postmaster-General's Department as a clerk in the accounts branch, General Post Office, Sydney. In 1893, although a comparatively junior officer when he was appointed clerk-in-charge, intercolonial and international postal affairs, he was judged by the deputy postmas-

ter-general, S. H. Lambton, to be 'the most efficient and only competent officer for the position'. On 12 June 1895 at St John's Anglican Church, Darlinghurst, Templeton married Eva Charlotte, daughter of W. S. Dowel, a former member of the Legislative Assembly.

In 1900-01 Templeton acted as secretary to the intercolonial conference of permanent heads making preparations for the transfer of post and telegraph departments to the Commonwealth. He joined the staff of the Commonwealth Postmaster-General's Office in July 1901, was accountant and senior clerk at Melbourne (1902-06) and became chief clerk in January 1907. In order to protect his department's financial interests, Templeton chaired a board set up in 1907 to report on the best method of issuing Commonwealth postage stamps. On 1 November 1908 he was appointed Queensland deputy postmaster-general.

In his evidence before the royal commission on postal services (1908-10) Templeton defended his permanent head, (Sir) Robert Scott [q.v.11], against his detractors, and explained those problems which had arisen under Commonwealth control. While defining the role of deputy postmasters-general, he expressed concern that insignificant administrative tasks so often distracted officers from important duties. Supporting the appointment of women as telephonists because they did not seek promotion, he defined the role of staff associations as one of 'social and even protective purposes' which should not 'be permitted to go beyond proper and reasonable bounds'. Furthermore, he did not hesitate to criticize incompetent senior officers or any who had resisted central office control. He later gave evidence before a parliamentary standing committee on public works which investigated the remodelling of the General Post Office, Sydney (1920).

In July 1922 Templeton was appointed assistant commissioner of Federal taxation and in 1929-35 was second commissioner. He was, as well, a fellow of the Institute of Chartered Accountants. He died on 10 September 1943 at Royal Park, Melbourne, and was buried in Brighton cemetery. Two daughters survived him.

Roy Com on postal services, *PP* (Cwlth), 1910, 4, 5 (50); Parliamentary Standing Cttee on public works, *PP* (Cwlth), 1920-21, 5 (172); *Argus*, 11 Sept 1943; information from PMG's Dept, Brisb.

D. I. McDONALD

TENISON WOODS, MARY CECIL (1893-1971), lawyer, was born on 9 December 1893 in Adelaide, daughter of John Kitson, police detective, and his wife Mary Agnes, née

McClure. Educated at St Aloysius's College by the Sisters of Mercy and at the University of Adelaide (LL.B., 1916), she was the first woman to graduate in law in South Australia and to be admitted to the Bar (20 October 1917). She practised as a barrister with the firm of (T. S.) Poole [q.v.11] & Johnstone with whom she had served her articles, becoming a partner in the reconstituted firm of Johnstone, Ronald & Kitson in 1919. Much of her early work was in the Children's Court and laid the basis for her later commitment to the cause of child welfare reform. Her application to become a public notary in 1921 led to a change in the law: the existing Act did not include women as 'persons'.

At St Lawrence's Catholic Church, North Adelaide, on 13 December 1924 Mary Kitson married Julian Gordon Tenison Woods, a lawyer who was two years her junior. A member of one of Adelaide's best known Catholic families and a cousin of Julian Tenison-Woods [q.v.6], he was described as 'widely popular, of taking manners, and fluent in speech'.

As her partners preferred not to work with a married woman, Mary Tenison Woods left the firm and with Dorothy Somerville formed what may have been the first female legal practice in Australia in 1925. Her son, also named Julian but known as 'Mac', was born on 8 April 1927, slightly disabled. Two months later she left her husband after his name was removed from the roll for misuse of trust funds. She was divorced in 1933 and never remarried. As the sole supporter of her son, she took a more lucrative position with the firm of Bennett, Campbell, Browne & Atkinson in 1928.

Her failed marriage may have sharpened her dedication to improving the status of women, although in 1950 she claimed that she had 'personally never . . . come up against sex discrimination in any walk of life, although it definitely does exist'. Certainly the care of her son kept her in the workforce all her life and his disability stimulated her public role in child welfare reform. She was to say later that 'After Mac was born [child welfare] became the love of my life. I came to feel that any child could become a delinquent, even, but for the grace of God, my own red-haired son'.

By the mid-1930s she and Mac had moved to Sydney where she worked as a legal editor with Butterworth & Co. Australia Ltd. The job provided her with a modest, steady income and left her enough time to look after Mac and pursue her other interests: she wrote or co-authored several legal textbooks on subjects ranging from landlords and tenants legislation to prices regulation; she contributed a chapter on 'Reforms and Law Affecting Women and Children' to *A book of South Australia* (Adelaide, 1936); with Marjorie Robertson, she pseudonymously pub-

lished *Leaves from a woman lawyer's casebook* (Sydney, 1947), a humorous collection of legal anecdotes.

Before leaving Adelaide she had received grants from the Carnegie Corporation of New York to research into delinquency and published her findings in a book, *Juvenile delinquency* (Melbourne, 1937), which argued for greater emphasis on rehabilitation and a larger role for psychiatrists, psychologists and social workers in the sentencing of offenders. From 1941 she was a member of the Child Welfare Advisory Council (New South Wales); in 1942 she was sponsored by that council—as well as by the Australian Council for Educational Research, the Walter and Eliza Hall [qq.v.9] Trust and the Australian Association of Social Workers—to study child welfare in England.

Her belief in the centrality of social workers in the rehabilitation process led to further honorary positions: she served on the Board of Social Study and Training of New South Wales (1935-40) and its successor, the University of Sydney's Board of Social Studies (1941-49); in 1940-50 she also lectured part time at the university on legal aspects of social work; in 1947 she was guest speaker at the first Australian Conference of Social Work, held in Sydney. During World War II she had sat on the board of the Women's Australian National Services.

While chairing the Child Welfare Advisory Council's delinquency committee, Mary Tenison Woods played a major role in creating a separate Child Welfare Department. In 1943 the committee reported that the Girls' Industrial School at Parramatta emphasized detention rather than rehabilitation, that its inmates were inadequately classified and that its staff was untrained. Rather than allowing the critical report to be shelved—as had been the fate of an earlier report of the pre-school child committee—Mary wrote two articles for the *Sydney Morning Herald* in 1944 which highlighted problems at Parramatta and at the Gosford Farm Home for Boys. A vigorous debate in the press followed. Her criticisms were endorsed by professional and women's organizations, and—with an election pending—a public service judicial inquiry was ordered which led to the creation of a Department of Child Welfare separate from the Department of Education and to the appointment of a new director of child welfare.

Tenison Woods gained companionship and direction from her involvement in Catholic laywomen's organizations. Although a committed Catholic, she criticized ecclesiastical attitudes and practices regarding women. In 1946 she was a founder of the New South Wales branch of St Joan's Social and Political Alliance, a small but vigorous group of educated Catholic laywomen. Despite its small numbers and opposition from the Church (membership was proscribed and reporting of its activities censored in the Catholic press), the alliance was a powerful lobby group. Strongly anti-communist, it joined the International Liaison Committee of Women's Organisations which was hastily formed in 1947 to prevent Jessie Street from representing Australia for a second term on the United Nations' Commission on the Status of Women. Tenison Woods's nomination in 1948 was not accepted, but in 1950 she was appointed chief of the office of the status of women in the division of human rights, United Nations Secretariat, New York.

During her term two major conventions were adopted: the Convention of the Political Rights of Women (1952), the first international law aimed at the granting and protection of women's full political rights, and the Convention of the Nationality of Married Women (1957) which decreed that marriage should not affect the nationality of a wife. When she left the United Nations in 1958 Tenison Woods was commended by delegates for her dedication to the cause of women, her ability to inspire teamwork, her competence and her sincerity. Professor R. J. Lawrence, of the University of New South Wales, remembered her as a 'guide, philosopher and friend for many years'.

Appointed O.B.E. (1950) and C.B.E. (1959), Tenison Woods retired to Sydney. Survived by her son, she died on 18 October 1971 in Mount St Margaret Hospital, Ryde, and was cremated.

Delinquency Cttee, Child Welfare Advisory Council, *A report on the Girls' Industrial School, Parramatta* (Melb, 1945); S. Kennedy, *Faith and feminism* (Syd, 1985); *Women's Weekly*, 10 June 1950; *SMH*, 2-5, 7, 11 Feb, 2 Mar 1944, 19 May 1950, 21 Oct 1971.   ANNE O'BRIEN

TENNYSON, HALLAM, 2ND BARON (1852-1928), author and governor-general, was born on 11 August 1852 at Twickenham, Middlesex, England, eldest son of the poet laureate Alfred (later 1st baron) Tennyson and his wife Emily Sarah, née Sellwood. Educated at Marlborough College and at Trinity College, Cambridge, he trained as a barrister at Inner Temple but never practised. In 1883 he became a councillor of the Imperial Federation League. At Westminster Abbey on 25 June 1884 he married Audrey Georgiana Florence Boyle (d. 1916). Hallam acted as his father's amanuensis and companion until he succeeded to the title on Alfred's death in 1892. He had already published a children's book, *Jack and the beanstalk* (London, 1886), which was followed by the two-volume *Alfred*

Lord Tennyson: a memoir by his son (London, 1897).

He had initially sought the governorship of South Australia, but hesitated when it was offered to him in January 1899: Tennyson was influenced by speculation that after Federation the post might be subordinated to that of the governor-general, or even abolished. He arrived in Adelaide in April and proved popular: the press and the people saw him as hardworking, competent, dignified and frugal. His association with premiers Charles Kingston and (Sir) Frederick Holder [qq.v.9] was less cordial: Tennyson's refusal to dissolve parliament in December caused Kingston's resignation, and he earned Holder's displeasure by his association with Chief Justice Sir Samuel Way's [q.v.] campaign supporting provision for unrestricted right of appeal to the Privy Council in the Constitution bill. He led the action against the diminution of gubernatorial salaries and battled against the centralizing of official correspondence through the governor-general. Tennyson also organized a boycott by governors of the Commonwealth inauguration ceremony, although they attended the opening of the Federal parliament. He promoted the dispatch of H.M.C.S. *Protector* to China during the Boxer rebellion (1899) and his patriotism was roused by the South African War. He helped to design the South Australian seal and flag, and provided a Tennyson medal for students.

Appointed acting governor-general on 4 July 1902 after Lord Hopetoun's [q.v.9] unexpected resignation, Tennyson was confirmed in this position in January 1903, at his own request for one year only. If some of Barton's [q.v.7] government suspected him of vigorous provincialism, as governor-general he appeared to become more centralist. He resigned at the end of 1903.

On his return to England he was made a privy counsellor and in 1905 refused the governorship of Madras. He edited collections of his father's poems and published *Tennyson and his friends* (London, 1911). He was president of the Royal Literary Fund and the Folk Lore Society. From 1913 he was deputy governor and steward of the Isle of Wight. On 27 July 1918 he married the widowed Mary Emily Hichens, née Prinsep. He died on 2 December 1928 at Farringford, Freshwater, Isle of Wight. His wife and one of the three sons of his first marriage survived him, the two youngest having been killed in World War I.

L. H. Tennyson, *From verse to worse* (Lond, 1933); N. Campbell (comp), *Tennyson in Lincoln*, 1, 2 (Lincoln, 1971, 1973); A. Hasluck (ed), *Audrey Tennyson's vice-regal days* (Canb, 1978); C. Cunneen, *Kings' men* (Syd, 1983); *The Times*, 3 Dec 1928; R. D. Hodgkinson, Lord Tennyson: the role of the State governors at the time of Federation (B.A. Hons thesis, Flinders Univ, 1985); GRG 2/19, vol 3, 11 Mar 1903 (PRO, SA); Tennyson papers (NL).   ROMA D. HODGKINSON

TEWKSBURY, WILLIAM PEARSON (1869-1953), businessman, was born on 7 February 1869 at Yackandandah, Victoria, youngest of four children of John Edward Tewksbury, carpenter and goldminer, and his wife Sarah Edith, née Croft, both English born. Pearson was delicate and in his youth prone to more accidents than average. What education he got was 'fugitive and patchy', though he claimed to have spent a period at Fort Street Model School after his family moved to Sydney. At 14 he was apprenticed to a Sydney watchmaker, but later speculatively explored several other occupations, including that of country salesman for tea merchants Atcherley & Dawson. 'Tewks' returned to his trade at Muswellbrook, New South Wales, after seizing the opportunity to buy a failing watchmaker's business with a borrowed £5. He added a bicycle agency to his storekeeping and sold so many penny-farthings that he became a travelling representative of a cycle agency. On 5 December 1893 in Sydney he married Juanita Blunt with Methodist forms; they were divorced in 1924.

While recuperating at Porepunkah, Victoria, from an eye problem that threatened his sight and his future, Tewksbury became interested in gold prospecting. Attracted by the idea of alluvial dredging as then practised in New Zealand, he took up 100 acres (40.5 ha) at Bright and managed to form a syndicate to begin bucket-dredging. When the syndicate ran into critical difficulties, Tewksbury bought out its liabilities and its expensive dredge, and prospected with a New Zealand crew as director of the Ovens Valley Gold Dredging Co. Desperately dependent on that 'seventh sense which creates the bridge between desire and achievement', he was eventually able to cover his risk. He then formed eight companies, known as the Tewksbury Group, employing dredges in the Bright district, Victoria, and at the Shoalhaven and the Araluen Valley, New South Wales. He also cannily kept control of all smelting and was reputed to have banked gold worth £1 million. He set up headquarters in the Equitable Buildings, Collins Street, Melbourne. 'Slim, upright, of middle build' with 'a touch of friendly shyness', in 1910 he bought the Oriental Hotel in Collins Street where he subsequently lived.

A child of his time, Tewksbury enthusiastically embraced the technology of the day—bicycles, cars (he owned a de Dion in 1903) aeroplanes and films—and rather prided himself on 'thinking today what other people would be thinking next week'. About 1910 he founded the City Motor Service, one of the first hire services that revolutionized motor passenger transport. In Melbourne, and later Sydney, a 'high chugging four cylinder Fiat' with a smartly uniformed driver could be hired for a minimum of 3s. 6d. In America Tewksbury saw meter-operated taxi-cabs for the first time and returned to promote Yellow Cabs of Australia Ltd and Yellow Express Carriers Ltd with a capital of £1 million in 1922. One hundred of these cabs imported to Melbourne carried 200 000 passengers within three months. As a prelude to their appearance in Sydney, Tewksbury held personal negotiations with J. T. Lang [q.v.9] to persuade him to amend local regulations. In 1926 Tewksbury founded Drive Yourself cars and in the following year resigned as chairman of Yellow Cabs.

A visit to Hollywood inspired him to produce a commercial film of Rolf Boldrewood's [q.v.3 T. A. Browne] Robbery under arms, which he shot in the Araluen Valley in 1922 and in which he acted. Next year he made a pioneering journey by car from Bourke to the Gulf of Carpentaria. An avid traveller, he joined several flights in the early 1930s, including the first west-east crossing of the United States of America and another from London to Alexandria. For recreation he went big-game hunting in Africa in a collar and tie, and with a camera more often than a rifle, frequently travelling with his favourite niece.

During World War I Tewksbury had raised £20 000 for disabled servicemen by raffling a 'Kitchener Flag' signed by leading war personalities. In World War II he repeated the pattern with his 'Churchill Flag', this time raising £28 000. He published an account of his life and struggles, donating the proceeds to the Australian Red Cross Society. As one of Melbourne's wealthy men, he made public gifts to charities.

Somewhat of an outsider, Tewksbury all his life had to manufacture his own publicity. In later years, monocled, natty, vain, and coy about his age, he wandered in 'a sober blue suit with a dark silk handkerchief flowing out of his breast pocket'. He was appointed O.B.E. in 1920. Survived by a son and daughter, he died on 12 July 1953 at the Oriental Hotel and was cremated. His estate was sworn for probate at £119 546.

His elder brother ALPHONSO REED TEWKSBURY (1864-1959) was born on 17 October 1864 at Yackandandah and educated at Fort Street, Sydney. He, too, began his business career early and by 1888 was able to enter into partnership in a brewery at Wagga Wagga. He later opened a brewery at Temora—which then had no water-supply—and was that city's mayor for three successive years.

An owner-trainer of trotters and a leading authority in the sport, he established his Delavan Stock Farm at Temora where he bred such major winners as Countess Chimes, Delavan's Guest and Delavan Bill. In 1923 he transferred the stud to Windsor. That year he joined Yellow Express Carriers as managing director and was chairman in 1938-46. Vice-chairman (1938-52) of Yellow Cabs of Australia, he was a foundation director (1936) and chairman of Australian Motorists Petrol Co. (Ampol Petroleum Ltd from 1949). In his youth an outstanding amateur cyclist, 'Alf' was an expert marksman and car enthusiast. He was also a founder and chairman (1943-55) of the Veteran Motorists Association of Australia. Survived by his wife Santina Isabel, née Moglia, and by three daughters and a son, he died on 3 May 1959 at Strathfield, Sydney, and was cremated with Anglican rites.

C. A. Grant, *500 Victorians* (Melb, 1934); V. Kelly, *Achieving a vision* (Syd, 1950); G. Blainey, *The rush that never ended* (Melb, 1963); J. Reynolds, *Men and mines* (Melb, 1974); *People* (Syd), 14 Mar 1951, 16 Dec 1953; *Parade*, June 1959; *Punch* (Melb), 29 May 1913; *Sun News-Pictorial*, 18 May 1929; *SMH*, 17 Sept 1926, 11 Aug, 12 Nov 1927, 12 Aug 1943, 13 July 1953; *Herald* (Melb), 24 Jan 1948, 25 Jan 1956; *Age*, 13 July 1953.

MARGARET STEVEN

THATCHER, GRIFFITHES WHEELER (1863-1950), Congregational minister and linguist, was born on 6 August 1863 at Collingwood, Melbourne, eldest child of Richard Henry Thatcher, stationer, and his wife Sarah Anne, née Smith, both English born. He regularly attended Sunday school at the Brighton Congregational Church and was influenced by its minister Rev. John Legge. Educated at Brighton College and the University of Melbourne (B.A., 1883), Griffithes gained his M.A. in 1885 with first-class honours in natural sciences. His interest in geology was lifelong.

Assisted by a Congregational College of Victoria bursary, he was granted a certificate in mid-1885 which permitted him to enter a divinity course at the University of Edinburgh (B.D., 1886). He completed his studies within a year and also found time to study music. Late in 1887 Thatcher returned to Melbourne to teach Biblical languages and literature at the Congregational College. Ordained in 1888 (although he was never to exercise his ministry in a pastorate), he visited Egypt, Palestine, Syria and then went on to Leipzig in 1889. While living at Mansfield College, he attended the University of Oxford (B.A., 1892; M.A., 1896).

Graduating in the honours school of oriental studies, Thatcher lectured in Hebrew and Old Testament languages and literature at his college, and in 1900 became senior tutor. Some of his pupils, like Arthur Sadler [q.v.11], became prominent in Arabic or Semitic studies. At Mansfield College Thatcher worked with eminent scholars and was clearly of their ilk. His most enduring work, *Arabic grammar of the written language* (1911), won him international acclaim. He also contributed to Hastings's *Dictionary of the Bible* (1900) and *Dictionary of Christ and the Gospels* (1906), and to *Encyclopaedia Britannica*; he edited the volume, *Judges and Ruth*, in the Century Bible and wrote numerous articles, but his major glossary of South Arabian remained unpublished.

Guided by his evangelical convictions and by a belief that he was doing God's work, in 1909 Thatcher accepted the wardenship of Camden College (the Congregational training institution in Sydney) and thereby sacrificed his chances of being offered chairs in Britain or Europe. Arriving in Sydney with fifty-three cases of books, he was inducted on 17 March 1910. He devoted himself to building the non-residential college into a first-rate institution, both through his stature and through his teaching and administrative skills. He persuaded the council to provide residential facilities and in 1915 a new building at Glebe opened with six students. It was run on Oxford lines, with gowns, address by surnames, senior and junior common rooms, and a high table.

During World War I many of its men enlisted; Thatcher made the college a bastion of patriotism; he served as a censor and adviser to the Australian government. The shortage of staff encouraged him to invite the Presbyterian, Methodist and Congregational colleges to pool their resources and to give joint lectures, except on matters relating directly to their own church history.

With Rev. Samuel Angus, Canon Garnsey [qq.v.7,8] and Dean Talbot [q.v.], Thatcher had founded and was first president of the Heretics' Club in 1916. As acting professor of oriental studies at the University of Sydney in 1921, he lectured in and on Japanese. He was awarded an honorary D.D. by McGill University, Canada, in 1926. His unchallengeable academic credentials and his friendships with senior university academics (many of whom lectured at Camden College on subjects ranging from evolution to geography) made it possible for him to press persistently for the recognition of theological studies as suitable subjects for study at the university. After his retirement as warden in December 1932, the university was given authority to confer degrees in divinity and the Board of Studies in Divinity was established in 1937.

As a foundation member of the board, Thatcher taught its early syllabus in Old Testament studies and Hebrew, and drafted its administrative regulations for teachers and students. He also fought zealously to maintain teaching standards and to introduce research work in the field of divinity. Although he had hoped to cease teaching in 1941, circumstances obliged him to continue until October 1943; next March he resigned from the board due to illness.

All who knew Thatcher spoke of his facility with languages: after his retirement he undertook to learn a language a year, and he had a solid knowledge of thirty-seven tongues. Once, when a lecturer forgot verbal paradigms in Russian, Thatcher filled the lacunae promptly, from memory. His celibate status allowed him untrammelled freedom to study. A 'singularly modest man', he 'was lean and lantern-jawed'.

Skilled in Church politics and adroit in side-stepping controversy, Thatcher was chairman of the Congregational Union of New South Wales in 1910-11 and 1935-36: his annual addresses showed that he favoured church unity. He died on 11 March 1950 at Chatswood, Sydney, and was cremated. His estate was sworn for probate at £7955. Sydney University Press published a volume in Thatcher's honour in 1967, edited by one of his pupils Evan MacLaurin.

A. R. Chisholm, *Men were my milestones* (Melb, 1958); J. A. Garrett and L. W. Farr, *Camden College, a centenary history* (Syd, 1964); E. C. B. MacLaurin (ed), *Essays in honour of Griffithes Wheeler Thatcher 1863-1950* (Syd, 1967); Congregational Union of NSW, *Year Book*, 1910-11, 1935-36, 1951; *SMH*, 21 Apr 1932, 8 Apr 1933, 23 Oct 1935, 14 Mar 1950; Uniting Church Archives, Parramatta; Bd of Studies in Divinity, Minutes (Univ Syd Archives).   ALAN D. CROWN

THEODORE, EDWARD GRANVILLE (1884-1950), premier, Federal treasurer and company director, was born on 29 December 1884 at Port Adelaide, South Australia, second of six children of Basil Theodore, labourer, and his wife Annie, née Tanner, poor immigrants who had met on board ship. Basil, originally surnamed Teodorescu, was Rumanian; Annie, Liverpool-born, had an Irish mother and an English father. Working around the wharves and on the tugboats of Port Adelaide, Basil also cultivated a small, unrewarding orchard at Aldgate in the hills. Educated to the age of 12 at Le Fevre's Peninsula Catholic and Aldgate State schools, Edward found jobs as gardener, farm-hand and timber-getter, before heading in 1900 for Murchison on the Western Australian goldfields.

Moving east in 1903, he worked in South Australia then took employment—and an apprenticeship in labour politics—in the mines at Broken Hill, New South Wales. In 1906 he departed for the Chillagoe-Irvinebank hinterland of Cairns, Queensland, where, mixing mine labouring with prospecting for wolfram and tin, he perceived and set about repairing a lack of effective organization among the district's workers. With others he formed in 1907 the Amalgamated Workers Association of North Queensland, becoming at 22 its first secretary. Helped by William McCormack [q.v.10], who was to remain a close friend, he built the union into a broad-based and militant organization whose major achievements included the absorption of the sugar workers in 1910, victory in the sugar strike of 1911 and amalgamation in 1913 with the Australian Workers' Union, of which Theodore became State president. When he relinquished this post in 1916 his union career—marked by aggression, administrative cleverness, centralizing tendencies and clear-sighted pragmatism—came to a close.

Believing that workers' interests—conceived as improvement in job opportunities, wages and hours, and the exclusion of 'alien' labour—could not be served effectively by industrial action alone, Theodore had early affiliated the A.W.A. with the Labor Party, had subsequently thrown the resources of the A.W.U. behind that organization, and had embarked upon a political career. In October 1909 he won the Queensland Legislative Assembly seat of Woothakata (from 1912 Chillagoe) for Labor. On 20 December 1909 in St Stephen's Catholic Cathedral, Brisbane, he married Toowoomba-born Esther Mahoney, a contractor's daughter; while remaining privately ambivalent toward Catholicism, he would be well served in Queensland Labor politics by a resulting ambience of faith and domestic stability.

Theodore's rise was swift. In 1912, when T. J. Ryan [q.v.11] was elected leader of the parliamentary party, he became deputy leader, and, on Labor taking office in June 1915, deputy premier, treasurer and secretary for public works. In October 1919, when Ryan resigned to enter Federal politics, Theodore became premier. Nearing 35, he cut an impressive figure. Wide-shouldered, deep-chested, thick-necked and almost six feet (182.9 cm) tall, he might have been a rugby front-rower. His hair was dark, his eyes piercing and set well apart, his face broad, with thick lips and a strong, cleft chin. Speech lessons, intensive use of the parliamentary library and careful attention to his appearance had transformed the somewhat untidy, anti-intellectual and ill-informed parvenu of 1909 into a politician of presence. Adroit in debate and knowledgeable in financial as well as industrial matters, he was already revealing a preference for the company of books to that of his political colleagues.

Among the dramatic episodes of his 'Queensland period' were the anti-conscription campaigns of 1916-17, the associated referenda and a conspiracy charge arising from attempts to avoid the censorship of Theodore's pamphlets—in all of which he and Ryan vigorously opposed Prime Minister Hughes [q.v.9]. Just as turbulent were Theodore's hard-nosed confrontations with strikers and radical elements in the labour movement brought obstreperously to life by the divisions of war and events in Russia. Of more lasting interest was government intervention in the Queensland economy, embracing labour market regulation, business enterprises, and the level and structure of taxation. The philosophy of development—of 'opening up' Queensland's resources for closer settlement—was accommodated by railway, road and irrigation outlays, and by the creation or improvement of services (educative, marketing, financial) for the small farmer who was cosseted as natural ally of the working man. In the labour market, union ideals were honoured by the Trade Unions (1915) and Industrial Arbitration (1916) Acts, and by legislation covering compensation, unemployment and workplace safety. Restriction of competition among workers was matched by an enthusiasm to promote it elsewhere: with the intention of curbing private monopoly while enhancing revenue, various state enterprises were established—cattle stations and butcher shops, timber and sugar mills, banking and insurance services, even an hotel. In other cases, such as the purchase of the Chillagoe and Mungana mines in 1918 and 1922, the maintenance of regional production and employment was a consideration. While Theodore's approach to the budget was orthodox, he sought—in keeping with emerging if contested principles of public finance—to meet mounting expenditure from taxation based upon 'ability to pay'.

Although there was (within the constraints imposed by war and post-war dislocation) a flurry of intervention under Ryan and Theodore, its novelty diminishes in comparison with the policies of other Labor—and even conservative—governments during the first quarter-century of Federation. The question of its effectiveness is complex, subject to intersecting political and economic considerations: politically, the strength of conservative resistance (in legislature, courts and the business community) which delayed or modified where it did not reject government initiatives; and economically, the degree to which policies as finally implemented were matched by their market outcomes. It is likely that historians will be impressed less by the intervention than by the vigour with which Theodore met opposition to it, by the brusqueness he displayed toward a laborite constituency unsettled by his stewardship, and by evidence that 'Red Ted' had himself begun to measure the gap between Labor idealism and the realities of a mixed and fluctuating economy.

Perhaps the most dramatic of several encounters between Theodore and the Queensland establishment began in 1920 with yet another rejection by the Legislative Council of a bill to increase pastoral rents. After appointing a complaisant lieutenant-governor (William Lennon [q.v.10]), Theodore augmented Labor's numbers in the council in order to pass the legislation. He then set off for London to negotiate overseas borrowing which had been interrupted by war. A delegation of three under Sir Robert Philp [q.v.11] representing pastoral and banking interests with English connexions preceded him, determined to compromise his dealings with the City. Theodore came away empty-handed and during 1921-22 was obliged to borrow more expensively in New York.

Meanwhile, a substantial reduction in Labor's majority after the 1920 State election led to such harassment in the assembly that Theodore resorted first to proxy-voting to circumvent Opposition 'misbehaviour' over pairs, and then to legislation to abolish the council which was passed in 1922. His 1921 Act governing the retirement age of judges would also change the composition of the Supreme Court. At the 1923 election Labor's parliamentary position improved, and early next year in London Theodore sought the conversion of loans due to mature in 1924-25. There followed a *rapprochement* which, despite Theodore's protest that he had yielded no more than a promise to freeze pastoral rents, drew strong criticism from radical laborites. Long unimpressed by his pragmatic, 'within system' approach to reform, they were now prepared to believe that a Labor government had succumbed to the English 'money power'.

That a man of the temper of Theodore should, during Federal A.L.P. conferences in the early 1920s, engage in bruising conflict with ideologues bent upon the destruction of capitalism is hardly surprising; indeed, he led the move to banish Communists from the party. The radicals, however, were able to exploit a misgiving among Labor supporters that Theodore's once ardent commitment to the party's economic objectives had weakened. The truth was that he had awakened to the potential for conflict between these objectives, especially in difficult times, and to the costs as well as the benefits of government intervention in economic life. There was also a matter of personal style: increasingly autocratic in his handling of government business and exuding a conviction that large affairs were best left in his keeping, Theodore resisted the unions with a no-nonsense frankness that aggravated their hurt. Incisively intelligent but lacking in urbanity, he evidently presumed that in politics logic should suffice, when too frequently it is not even necessary.

Pre-selected for the Federal seat of Herbert in July 1924, Theodore surrendered the premiership in February 1925 and in September resigned as member for Chillagoe to contest the Federal election. He had, in political terms, accomplished much in a relatively small State; and as an able, ambitious, young, yet immensely experienced politician who had come to see the advantages (for himself as for the party) of pursuing Labor policies from the centre, he could only have been tempted by an obvious weakness in the Federal leadership. But in November his bid for Herbert failed. While his subsequent decision to seek a seat in New South Wales was guided chiefly by the need for a more credible political base from which to challenge for leadership, it was strengthened by a realization that in Queensland his appeal had waned. Striving to extend his influence, he had agreed in late 1924 to adjudge a running dispute between the New South Wales executive and the A.W.U.—the notorious case of ballot-boxes with sliding-panels—and had found against John Bailey [q.v.7], the A.W.U. official involved. During 1926 he spent time in Sydney broking among the party's factions. Such tactics, risky at any time, were especially so in the State where the wily manipulator J. T. Lang [q.v.9] had become premier in 1925.

Theodore's accession to the Federal seat of Dalley in January 1927, after the sitting Labor member obligingly withdrew, was clouded by his relationship with John Wren [q.v.] and by allegations of bribery which were made the subject of a Commonwealth royal commission. Although Theodore emerged formally unscathed, it was a 'characteristic beginning for [a] federal career in which his great ability, strength of will and capacity for resolute leadership, which the Labor Party so badly needed, were effectively neutralized by the association of his name with transactions of a questionable nature'. His parliamentary speeches, robustly eloquent rather than rhetorical, and directed mainly to economic matters, drew large and respectful audiences. He badgered the treasurer (Sir) Earle Page [q.v.11] over financial policy, accused the government of a weakening commitment to tariff protection, and vehemently supported the unions—timber workers, coal miners and stevedores—in their militant defence of wages and hours. In this latter respect his performance smacked of opportunism, but in that of protection it rang with industrial patriotism.

By February 1928 Theodore had reached the Opposition front-bench, but in March, when J. H. Scullin succeeded Matthew Charlton [qq.v.11,7] as leader, even the deputy leadership eluded him. At the November Federal election Labor's position improved, and in February 1929 he became deputy leader with an unenviable brief to mediate in the great industrial disputes of that time. When Prime Minister (Viscount) Bruce [q.v.7] went to the people in October over the industrial issue, Labor won handsomely and Theodore became deputy prime minister and treasurer. As campaign director for New South Wales in both elections, he had displayed his usual industry and cleverness, though obliged to deal with a State executive from which Lang —decanted from government in 1927—was trying to isolate him.

Carefully attired, aloof, grave and measured in manner, the new treasurer stood out in a parliament where his air of brooding strength and confident grasp of the world at large intimidated colleague and foe alike. Incapable of small talk or *bonhomie*, and preferring to spend what little leisure he had in reading or fly-fishing, Theodore was a solitary man. In the comfortable library of his Kirribilli home were gathered works ranging from economics and history to philosophy and literature. Proud and relentlessly self-improving, already prospering from investments and multiplying his contacts in the business world, he had moved far in style and circumstance from the working man he once was; and the feelings he aroused in others— of admiration, of enmity, of simple envy— were, as ever, strong.

The 1929 Federal election coincided broadly with the onset of economic depression and political manoeuvring against Theodore from either side: in Queensland the conservative Moore [q.v.10] government set up a royal commission into allegations of corruption over Mungana, and questions were asked in parliament about Theodore's Mt Isa shareholding; in New South Wales the Langites worked to ensure that Theodore would not supplant Lang in control of the State machine, and to extend their influence over local members of the Federal caucus.

Australia's Depression problem was formidable. How was a small, primary-producing, debtor country, which was determined to meet its international obligations, to deal with a massive external deficit inflicted by collapsing terms of trade and the abrupt cessation of capital inflow? Such were the character and severity of the crisis, and Australia's political circumstances in 1930-31, that little was possible by way of compensatory monetary and fiscal policy. Even had Theodore (rightly regarded as enlightened for his day) been able to implement reflationary measures, it remains an open question how much they might have achieved—the more especially in a world which was not behaving similarly.

Scullin inherited a hostile Senate, a deeply orthodox chairman of the Commonwealth Bank, Sir Robert Gibson [q.v.8], and an electorate resistant to novelty in economic policy. The suspension of assisted immigration and the sharp raising of tariffs in 1929-30 were characteristic Labor responses to mounting unemployment. These reactions, together with the countercyclical timing of public works financed in the normal way, were elements of Theodore's own thinking. So, too, was the manipulation of credit; but not, as some laborites were urging, by tinkering with the note issue or requiring the Commonwealth Bank to finance large capital projects when the loan market was quiescent. He offered, instead, his central reserve bank bill of April 1930, embracing the philosophy of price stabilization by monetary management which reformers like J. M. Keynes had been advocating in the 1920s when Theodore had read upon the subject. At this early stage, then, Theodore was of the liberal, rather than radical, monetary persuasion. Despite a wide sympathy for central banking ideas, the bill— at first delayed in committee and later rejected by the Senate—failed for political reasons. In April, too, the Mungana commission exposed McCormack's secret half-share in the mines before their sale to the Queensland government, and Lang finally secured control of the State executive, putting Theodore's pre-selection for Dalley at hazard.

Worse was to come. On 4 July the commission found Theodore and McCormack guilty of 'fraud and dishonesty' and abuse of ministerial position. The case against Theodore hinged upon McCormack's regular payment to him of sums equal to one-half of McCormack's receipts from the Mungana mines. On 5 July Theodore resigned from cabinet; on the 8th he vehemently defended himself in parliament. He also learned that the Queensland government intended to take civil action to retrieve the large difference between the price of the mines and their estimated worth. It was to be another year, however, before this action began.

For about four months, as the Depression deepened, Theodore absented himself from parliament and caucus, denying the Mungana charges, monitoring the policy debate and manoeuvring to recapture his position within the party. On 18 August Sir Otto Niemeyer, representing the Bank of England, delivered the chastening orthodox advice—vigorous cost cutting and swift budget balancing—

which was to be embraced by Australian governments in the notorious 'Melbourne Agreement' of November. Scullin departed for London on the 25th, leaving J. E. Fenton as acting prime minister and J. A. Lyons [qq.v.8,10] as acting treasurer to conduct policy in his absence. Making effective use of the Niemeyer bogey, Lang won the New South Wales election of 25 October. Apparently stung, Theodore returned to caucus as sponsor of the 'Gibbons resolution'. Its most striking feature was a proposal that the Commonwealth Bank should in effect cover the shortfall between government tax-loan revenues and planned expenditures (including domestic loan conversions and a public works programme of up to £20 million). The exchange rate was to be flexible and the price level was to be monitored. Now aligned with the laborites he had once rebuffed, he was thought to be preparing a challenge to Scullin. But, after Scullin's return in mid-January 1931, Theodore changed tack and supported Scullin's suggestion that Commonwealth Bank lending be directed more to the private than the government sector. A target for the price level— that of the later 1920s—was also set. At the caucus meeting of 26 January, despite opposition from Lyons and others on the right, Scullin restored Theodore to his former cabinet positions.

During the premiers' conference of February 1931 various under-treasurers aired severely deflationary ideas which lent urgency to Theodore's espousal of reflation. He approached the banks with proposals informed by a memorandum which Melbourne economists E. C. Dyason, L. F. Giblin [qq.v.8] and (Sir) Douglas Copland had submitted to Lyons in September. In the course of the conference he and Scullin, accepting that a cut in real wages was unavoidable, pressed the advantages of achieving it within a policy which focused upon prices more than costs. Thus credit creation and exchange depreciation would ease the pressure upon money wages and deprive local bondholders of the bonus which a subsiding price level had brought them. A special tax would ensure that they shared in the reduction of living standards imposed by world events. If the banks co-operated in this scheme, governments would rein in their expenditures. Throughout these discussions Theodore drew upon Giblin in various ways and, when C. H. Wickens [q.v.] fell ill, made Giblin acting statistician and effectively the government's official adviser.

As bargaining with the banks proceeded, Lang, with an eye on Federal office, declared that not only should local bondholders suffer (by a statutory reduction of interest rather than taxation), but that payments to British bondholders should be suspended altogether.

By easing government budgets and the balance of payments, this course would have given more room for manoeuvre in economic policy, but it was condemned by the conference. Theodore's own scheme, presented now as a 'middle way' between repudiation and deflation, was rejected by the bankers who insisted upon fiscal discipline as the prerequisite to any assistance they might offer. He was accordingly impelled to his renowned 'fiduciary' expedient by which £18 million of unemployment relief works and farm assistance was to be financed by an expansion of the unbacked note-issue. As the fiduciary notes and associated bills went to their fate in the Senate, he persisted in a belief—buttressed by Keynesian and other authority—that reason was sufficient to the occasion. This same faith found expression in his abortive attempt to release gold for shipment on government account, not by modifying the note-issue reserve requirement, but by abolishing it altogether.

In February-March Lang's plan became the catalyst for an open split between the New South Wales and Federal executives. Federal caucus expelled the Langites who, with the defection of Lyons and his followers from the A.L.P., had the government at their mercy. Theodore, expelled with others from the State A.L.P., was also rebuffed by his Dalley electoral council which endorsed the Lang solution. In early April Lang's defaults began, but were made good by the Federal government. In this month, too, Gibson delivered his 'ultimatum' on government finance which led to the establishment of the Copland committee to devise a scheme of deficit reduction. Its proposals, delivered to the premiers late in May, underpinned the deflationary Premiers' Plan of June.

The Plan was not as great a defeat for Theodore as commonly supposed. Its retrenchment programme was less severe than earlier proposals, and in an unprecedented Lang-like breach of contract, a statutory reduction of interest on internally held bonds was applied which—unlike contemporary wage cuts—would not be reversed as conditions improved. Moreover, during the protracted stand off over budgetary policy, the Commonwealth Bank had been obliged to expand credit significantly. Believing that the rest of the world would soon reflate, Theodore was even able to comfort himself that the Plan itself had uses within a strategy of delay, or so he maintained to Curtin in 1932. But his hopes of softening its impact with projects to relieve unemployment foundered upon banking intransigence.

On 22 July 1931 civil proceedings began over Mungana. A 'not guilty' verdict was handed down on 24 August, yet Theodore's failure to testify before either the commission or the court left his enemies with ammunition. In the electoral débâcle of December precipitated by the J. A. Beasley group, Theodore was Labor's most conspicuous casualty: opposed by a Langite, he saw his 78 per cent of Dalley's formal vote (1929) plummet to 20. Bitterly contemptuous of what he construed as the treachery of Lang and the banks, and the unintelligence of Labor's traditional constituency—'the fool workers'—he resisted importunings to return. The man whom conservative (Sir) Bertram Stevens [q.v.] described as 'the coolest, best and most experienced financial brain in the southern hemisphere' had abandoned politics for ever.

Theodore's subsequent career embraced publishing, gold-mining and wartime public service. In 1932 he was asked by the A.W.U. to report on the operations and prospects of its struggling newspaper, the World. Finding his recommendations for its rescue uncongenial, the union offered Theodore an option on the paper. With a youthful (Sir) Frank Packer and others, he formed a company which in November 1932 exercised the option. Subsequently the Australian Women's Weekly (1933), a revitalized Daily Telegraph (1936) and the Sunday Telegraph (1939) appeared; by World War II Consolidated Press Ltd, with Theodore as chairman of directors, was well launched upon its impressive career.

Meanwhile, the prospect of high returns, as well as the test of nerve and skill associated with gold, had lured him to Fiji. There, in partnership with Wren, Packer and P. F. Cody, Theodore backed his own judgement against an unfavourable survey which had rattled his colleagues, and triumphed. By July 1935 the syndicate had opened the Emperor, Loloma and Dolphin mines, of which the first two were later floated on the Melbourne stock exchange. Living near Suva as managing director of all three, Theodore involved himself in local matters and made fewer trips to Sydney. From 1937 he ranged farther afield, seeking gold in Borneo and then on Guadalcanal, Solomon Islands, which he left just before the Japanese invasion.

Mindful of his abilities, men from both sides of politics sought to draw him into the war effort. (Sir) Percy Spender's attempt in May 1940 was foiled by Country Party objections which led (Sir) Robert Menzies to remonstrate: 'Give up this deplorable habit of throwing stones at great men'. John Curtin later secured Theodore's appointment as director general (February 1942-October 1944) of the Allied Works Council. As organizer of resources for war-related projects, he showed his usual force and skill, but his return to public service brought controversy. In September 1942, protesting political interference, he threatened resignation over clashes with his old antagonists Beasley and E. J.

Ward; his secondment of Packer from the army to be his director of personnel attracted criticism; and his willingness to invoke punitive labour regulations did not endear him to the unions.

After World War II Theodore occupied himself with mining and newspaper business, and talked of settling in Fiji. In 1946 he was a delegate to the Imperial Press Conference in London. Aware of his serious heart condition, he carried on with increasing difficulty; after joining the board of Great Boulder Mines Ltd, he suffered a major heart attack in 1948. He resigned the chairmanship of Consolidated Press in January 1949 and made his last trip to Fiji. On 9 February 1950 at Edgecliff, Sydney, he died of hypertensive cardiovascular disease; after a state funeral he was buried in South Head cemetery. His wife, two sons and two daughters survived him. His estate in Victoria, New South Wales and Queensland alone was sworn for probate at £629 915. In a panegyric Archbishop (Sir) James Duhig [q.v.8] traced the way in which Theodore's intellect, character and industry had overcome his lack of formal education, but spoke of how the envy of others had brought him down in public life.

L. F. Giblin, *The growth of a central bank* (Melb, 1951); G. Sawer, *Australian Federal politics and law 1901-1929* (Melb, 1956), and . . . *1929-49* (Melb, 1963); C. B. Schedvin, *Australia and the great Depression* (Syd, 1970); I. Young, *Theodore* (Syd, 1971); K. H. Kennedy, *The Mungana affair* (Brisb, 1978); D. J. Murphy and R. B. Joyce (eds), *Queensland political portraits 1859-1952*, ch 11 (Brisb, 1978); B. Nairn, *The 'Big Fella'* (Melb, 1986); R. T. Appleyard and C. B. Schedvin (eds), *Australian financiers*, ch 13 (Melb, 1988); *Politics* (Syd), Dec 1971, p 26; Theodore papers (NL); N. Cain, 'The Australian economists and controversy over Depression policy, 1930-early 1931', Working Papers in Economic Hist, ANU, no 79, May 1987.   NEVILLE CAIN

THESIGER, FREDERICK JOHN NAPIER; see CHELMSFORD

THIRKELL, ANGELA MARGARET (1890-1961), author, was born on 30 January 1890 at Kensington, London, daughter of John William Mackail, civil servant and later professor of poetry at the University of Oxford, and his wife Margaret, née Burne-Jones. Angela's grandfather was the artist Edward Burne-Jones and her kin included Rudyard Kipling and Stanley Baldwin. As a child she gave evidence of a strong and wilful personality; her many cousins regarded her as bossy. She was educated at the Froebel Institute, Kensington, and St Paul's School, Hammersmith, then spent some months in

Paris and Gotha, Germany. Five ft. 10 ins. (177.8 cm) tall, with 'a small, shapely head', fine features, blue eyes and a 'swan-neck', she was an acknowledged beauty. On 5 May 1911 at the parish church of St Philip, Kensington, London, she married James Campbell McInnes, a Lancashire-born professional singer. Bi-sexual and alcoholic, McInnes fathered two sons (Graham and Colin), but in 1917 Angela won a divorce.

In September 1917 she met Captain George Lancelot Allnutt Thirkell. Born in 1891 to a Tasmanian landed family, 'Thirk' was a graduate in engineering who had joined the Australian Imperial Force in August 1914 and served in Egypt, Gallipoli and France. On leave he mixed with high society; while convalescing at Glamis Castle he was befriended by Elizabeth Bowes-Lyon (the future consort of King George VI). A good, brave and kind man, Thirkell had little of Angela's culture. Her marriage to him at the Register Office, Kensington, on 13 December 1918 further bespoke her passion-fed defiance of common sense, altogether contrary to her later image.

Early in 1920 the Thirkells returned to Australia aboard the *Friedrichsruh*, a horrendous voyage when rank-and-file diggers became increasingly assertive. After a sojourn at Hobart, the family settled in suburban Melbourne. In January 1921 a son, Lancelot George, was born. Thirkell's business activities as a director of a small engineering firm won only modest rewards. Although she mixed with Melbourne's cultured élites, Angela always felt homesick. Prompted by financial need, as Graham McInnes has told, 'she began the satirical essays and short stories which ultimately led to the great flow of novels that poured out in the last thirty years of her life'. Her radio broadcasts for children also enjoyed success.

Angela's alienation from husband and Australia increased. She returned to England for over a year from mid-1927 and permanently in November 1929. Before 1935 she published six books, including *Trooper to the Southern Cross* 'by Leslie Parker'. It told of the *Friedrichsruh* voyage through the eyes of Major Bowen, in effect George Thirkell. It is witty and shrewd.

Angela's thirty subsequent 'middle-brow' novels presented English 'county' society in sympathetic and often penetrating style. They sold well, notably in the United States of America. Angela became ever narrower in her sympathies, being especially caustic about post-1945 Labour governments. She kept little or no contact with George, yet always insisted on being *Mrs* Thirkell; at his death in 1959 she claimed an Australian widow's pension. She died at Bramley, Surrey, on 29 January 1961, leaving an estate estimated at £74 656. The National Gallery of Victoria holds her portrait by John Collier.

DNB, 1961-1970; M. Strickland, *Angela Thirkell* (Lond, 1977); G. McInnes, *The road to Gundagai* (Lond, 1965); M. Roe, 'Thirk', *Meanjin Q*, 28 (1969); *The Times*, 18 Mar 1961; L. Thirkell, *Assassination of an authoress* (SLT); personal information.   MICHAEL ROE

THOMAS, ARTHUR NUTTER (1869-1954), Anglican bishop, was born on 11 December 1869 at Hackney, London, second child and first son of Charles James Thomas, feather merchant, and his wife Mary Matilda, née Nutter. Arthur was educated at St John's Grammar School, Hackney, and Oundle school (1884-88). At Pembroke College, University of Cambridge (B.A., 1893; M.A., 1895; D.D., 1906), he gained a first in the classical tripos (1891) and won the Jeremie Septuagint (1892) and Carus Greek Testament (1893) prizes; he was also an active sportsman. After a year in Wells Theological College, he was made deacon in 1894 by the bishop of Wakefield and ordained priest on 9 June 1895. Thomas was domestic chaplain to the archbishop of York in 1895-99, assistant curate at Leeds in 1899-1901 and rector of Guisborough in 1901-06. He married Mary Theodora Lewis (d. 1941) at the parish church of St Peter, Upper Gornal, Staffordshire, on 1 June 1904.

Elected bishop of Adelaide (in succession to J. R. Harmer [q.v.9]) by a panel of selectors in England, Thomas was consecrated in Westminster Abbey on 2 February 1906. He arrived with his wife in South Australia on 2 April and was enthroned in St Peter's Cathedral two days later; his episcopate was to span 34 years and 179 days, the longest, to then, of any Anglican in Australia. The diocese covered the whole State so that, in addition to the tasks of administration in Adelaide, the bishop had to do much travelling. He had a strong frame and tackled his work with vigour. Although he appeared reserved and undemonstrative to many, none doubted his unsparing devotion to duty. After assessing his diocese, Thomas recognized the need for more episcopal oversight. At first he hoped for an assistant bishop, but synod pressed for dividing the area of his responsibility: the diocese of Willochra, covering the vast northern area of the State, was founded in 1915.

The years 1911-22 were marked by Thomas's attempts to deal with a ritual controversy. Canon P. W. C. Wise [q.v.] of Goodwood, who had been his contemporary at Cambridge, was the central figure in the catholic revival in South Australia. Thomas issued a public admonition to Wise in 1919 and charged him in the ecclesiastical courts with breach of ritual. The case came to nothing and Wise continued at Goodwood, but there remained considerable bitterness in the diocese and Thomas was saddened by his inability to heal the breach.

Deeply interested in education, Thomas played a leading part in founding Woodlands Church of England Girls' Grammar School at Glenelg in 1923 and St Mark's College, affiliated with the University of Adelaide, in 1925. On political and social issues his outlook was conservative. In the Depression his public statements on unemployment and economic policy created controversy and aroused the indignation of members of the labour movement. In religious matters he was cautiously innovative, administering his diocese fairly and resolutely. He was a clear rather than an eloquent preacher, and presided over the synod with patience, skill and occasional flashes of humour. During his episcopate St Peter's Cathedral was completed by the addition in 1927 of the choir stalls and bishop's throne, and improvements were made in the grounds. In the 1920s he advocated a wider role for women in church affairs and supported the movement for Christian reunion.

Thomas was tall and stately, with an English manner. His three children were born at Bishop's Court. Both daughters married clergymen, and his son Christopher, a chaplain in the Royal Navy in World War II, became a canon in the diocese of Melbourne. Retiring on 30 September 1940, Thomas lived in North Adelaide. He died there on 10 April 1954 and was cremated; his estate was sworn for probate in South Australia at £20 003. There is a memorial panel in St Peter's Cathedral under his coat of arms, and his portrait by Ivor Hele hangs in Bishop's Court, North Adelaide.

G. W. Halcombe, *The birth of the diocese of Willochra* (Adel, 1918); P. W. C. Wise, *An appeal of an Australian priest* (Adel, 1920); D. Hilliard, *Godliness and good order* (Adel, 1986); L. E. W. Renfrey, *Arthur Nutter Thomas* (Adel, 1988); *Year Book of the C of E in the diocese of Adelaide*, 1906-40; scrap-books of A. N. Thomas (held by Rev Malcolm C. N. Thomas, Nth Frankston, Vic).   LIONEL E. W. RENFREY

THOMAS, JOSIAH (1863-1933), miner and politician, was born on 28 April 1863 at Camborne, Cornwall, England, son of Josiah Thomas, mine agent, and his wife Ann, née Rablin. As a child he went with his father to Mexico, then worked in Cornish mines before coming to Australia in the mid-1880s. He worked at the Barrier Range, was a member of a royal commission on collieries in 1886, and was a mining captain and assayer at Broken Hill South in 1890. On 27 July 1889 at

Broken Hill he had married Henrietta Lee Ingleby (d. 1901).

Elected to the executive of the Amalgamated Miners' Association in July 1891, Thomas became president of the Broken Hill branch in 1892. A member of the all-union Labour Defence Committee formed during a prolonged strike in 1892, he was sent to Adelaide and Queensland to raise funds. While he was absent, eight other committee-members were arrested on conspiracy charges. On his return he made a speech reflecting on the integrity of the magistracy; his commission as a justice of the peace was withdrawn. Blackballed by the mining companies, after the strike he was reduced to labouring. As president of the A.M.A., however, he sat on a New South Wales Legislative Assembly board of inquiry (1892) into lead poisoning at Broken Hill mines.

In 1894 Thomas won the Legislative Assembly seat of Alma for Labor and held it until 1901. In the assembly he took a particular interest in workers' safety and health; he campaigned against the Federation bills on the grounds that they made inadequate provision for national referenda. From 1901 to 1917 Thomas held the Federal seat for the Barrier. In Andrew Fisher's [q.v.8] administrations he was postmaster-general in 1908-09 and 1910-11, and on the death of E. L. Batchelor [q.v.7] became minister for external affairs (1911-13). As postmaster-general he favoured measures such as penny postage and scaled telephone charges, and constantly endeavoured to secure the resources of the state from exploitation by commercial interests. While he held the external affairs portfolio, immigration from Britain increased rapidly. He showed particular interest in establishing an Australia House in London and in the development of northern Australia. He served on a select committee (1905) and a royal commission (1906) on the ocean shipping service. In 1916 he visited England as a member of the Imperial Parliamentary Association.

Absent during the conscription split, Thomas—whose son was killed in action in France—followed W. M. Hughes [q.v.9] into the National Party. In 1917 Thomas was elected to the Senate. Defeated in 1922, he was re-elected in 1925 but again defeated in 1928. Under the Constitution he sat until June 1929, in which year he chaired the select committee into beam wireless charges.

After he left parliament Thomas devoted himself to the British Empire League. An enthusiastic Methodist of 'cheerful disposition and moral enthusiasm', he was active in establishing 2CH as a radio station for the Council of Churches. He was a circuit steward at the Broken Hill Wesleyan Church and a popular lay preacher who urged congregations to improve the conditions of their fellows. Opposed to gambling, smoking and drinking, he pursued prohibition energetically and persistently. Always a 'robust speaker' in parliament, Thomas corrected Biblical allusions, spoke against the adjournment of the House for the Melbourne Cup and insisted on Canberra's hotels being 'dry'.

Although an able administrator, whom the *Bulletin* found 'offensively erudite' in 1904, Thomas has been criticized for having a more limited conception of external affairs than did his predecessor; more radical contemporaries regarded this 'least combative of men' as timid and easygoing early in his political career. He was, nonetheless, respected as a man of principle. Thomas had taken the unusual step of giving up a mine-managership to become union president. He retained his interest in working conditions and even as postmaster-general marched at the head of a procession in the 1909 Broken Hill strike. His presence on the platform lent particular distinction to Rechabite meetings when he attained cabinet rank.

Thomas died of heart disease at Croydon Park on 5 February 1933 and was buried in Rookwood cemetery. At Adelaide on 20 February 1909 he had married Clara Ingleby. She survived him, as did a son by each of the sisters he had married.

B. Kennedy, *Silver, sin and sixpenny ale* (Melb, 1978); P. G. Edwards, *Prime ministers and diplomats* (Melb, 1983); *V&P* (LA NSW), 1892-93, 3, p 315; *Southern Sphere*, 1 July 1910; *Rechabite and Temperance News*, 15 Sept 1910; *SMH*, 9, 16 Mar, 9 Apr 1901, 6 Feb 1933; *Australasian*, 14 Feb, 6 Mar 1910; *Barrier Miner*, 6 Feb 1933; B. Pennay, Industrial disputes at Broken Hill up to 1909 (M.A. thesis, Univ Syd, 1968).   BRUCE PENNAY

THOMAS, RICHARD (1880-1958), Anglican bishop, was born on 24 October 1880 at Lydney, Gloucestershire, England, son of Daniel Thomas, railway clerk, and his wife Jane, née Griffiths. Baptized in 1888 at Glendower Street Congregational Church, Monmouth, Wales, Richard was educated at the Monmouth Grammar School. After working as a railway clerk, he trained for the Anglican ministry at the Society of the Sacred Mission, Kelham, Nottinghamshire, and was placed in the first class in the 1908 universities preliminary theological examination.

Made deacon on 14 June 1908 and ordained priest on 6 June 1909 in Worcester Cathedral, Thomas was assistant curate of St John the Baptist, Coventry, from 1908. He came to Australia in 1914 to serve as a Bush Brother in northern Queensland. A good rider and bushman, he travelled widely in his pastoral role. He was made sub-warden of the Community of St Barnabas in 1923 and arch-deacon of North Queensland. Elected second bishop of the outback South Australian diocese of Willochra in succession to Gilbert White [q.v.], Thomas was consecrated on 6 April 1926 in St Andrew's Cathedral, Sydney, and enthroned at Port Pirie on 21 April.

In constant need of clergy and money, Thomas proposed forming a local Bush Brotherhood in 1926; next year he announced the establishment of the Willochran Association as a British base. He went to Britain regularly, seeking support and recruiting clergy. With rural Australia deep in Depression and Willochra suffering dry years during the 1930s, the Bush Brotherhood of St Stephen (centred at Quorn) closed in 1939. Thomas's failure to appreciate that all business had to be transacted through the synod led to difficulties with his standing committee over clerical appointments and grant payments; it took the committee some years to convince him that he was not free to act without their advice and consent.

He kept the diocese in touch with the wider Church, attended general synod and bishops' meetings, and was awarded a Lambeth D.D. in 1928. A fine, strong preacher, he modelled his style on that of the celebrated English Baptist, C. H. Spurgeon. Thomas was an early exponent of tree-planting and advocated the conservation of native plants and animals. He wrote vigorously to Adelaide newspapers and his regular letters in the *Willochran* gave vivid accounts of his ministry and teaching.

Although he was loved by people in the bush, Thomas seemed too remote to a number of his clergy. His wide outback pastoral experience and high standards led him to assume that others would cope as well as he did: when they turned to him for support, they could find him distant and unhelpful. In 1954 Bishop Robin of Adelaide notified his intention to resume the Eyre Peninsula; the decision disappointed Thomas who had not been consulted.

Thomas did not marry. *En route* to Lambeth Conference, he died on 16 April 1958 at Grays Thurrock, Essex, England, and was buried at Cowbridge, Glamorgan, Wales. His estate was sworn for probate at £16 187.

J. O. Feetham and W. V. Rymer (eds), *North Queensland jubilee book 1878-1928* (Townsville, 1929); R. A. F. Webb, *Brothers in the sun* (Adel, 1978); H. A. J. Witt, *Bush bishop* (Adel, 1979); D. Hilliard, *Godliness and good order* (Adel, 1986); *Willochran*, 55, 1 Jan 1926, 183, 1 July 1958.

BRUCE ROSIER

THOMAS, WILLIAM CHARLES (1890-1957), public servant, was born on 27 June 1890 at Sebastopol, near Ballarat, Victoria, son of native-born parents William Charles Thomas, farmer, and his wife Rosina, née Stevens. He was educated at state schools, the Working Men's College, Melbourne, and the University of Melbourne (B.Com., 1934). In July 1903 he joined the Victorian branch of the Postmaster-General's Department as a telegraph messenger, becoming a telegraphist at St Arnaud, Clifton Hill (1908) and the Melbourne General Post Office (1909). He was promoted to the note issue branch of the Treasury in March 1913. A private in the Victorian Rangers and two years a signaller in the Signal Corps, Thomas enlisted in the Australian Imperial Force in June 1915. On 2 October he married Mary Isidore Lowther Graves. After training he was commissioned lieutenant in the 14th Battalion. He fought in the French-Belgian war zone where he was twice wounded and badly gassed.

Discharged in September 1919, Thomas returned to the Treasury, transferring in March 1920 to the accounts branch. From 1925 he was temporarily employed on duties relating to the Expropriation Board of the Mandated Territory of New Guinea; in 1927 he was appointed its chairman and executive member. For a short time he also acted as New Guinea trade agent, an office of Treasury based in Sydney which was responsible for buying stores and selling products for the Mandated Territories. In 1929-46 Thomas was custodian of expropriated property, serving a board which was instituted to liquidate German commercial interests under the reparations provisions of the Treaty of Versailles.

Thomas moved to Canberra in 1931 while a sub-accountant in the Treasury. He was subsequently loans officer (1936), accountant (1943) and assistant secretary (1946). From being secretary to the Loan Council and the National Debt Commission, in May 1952 he was appointed first assistant secretary, budget and accounting branch. He retired in June 1955. His subordinates regarded him as a hard taskmaster, but never doubted his professional abilities.

Unlike a number of his colleagues, Thomas was not deeply involved in the developing Canberra community. Treasurer (1936-37) of the Royal Canberra Golf Club, he was an indifferent player. A member of the parish of St John the Baptist, he was involved in the church community in which he had a wide circle of friends.

Thomas died of heart disease on 14 September 1957 after a long illness and was buried in Canberra cemetery with Anglican rites. His wife and one son of their six children survived him.

Argus, 19 Jan 1927, 24 July 1929; *Canb Times*, 26-28 Aug 1935, 18 Aug, 14 Sept 1936, 12 Aug

1937, 16 Sept 1957; War diary of the 14th Battalion, AIF (AWM); information from Mr G. Temperley, Campbell, Canb.   D. I. McDONALD

THOMPSON, CHARLES VICTOR (1885-1968), journalist and politician, was born on 10 September 1885 in Sydney, son of Charles Thompson, carpenter, and his wife Mary Annie, née Lewis, both native-born. Educated at Cleveland Street and other public schools, he became a journalist. After experience in 1903-10 at Narrabri, Murwillumbah and Albury, he joined the *Tamworth Daily Observer* in 1911 as senior reporter and, within months, was appointed editor. Over the next decade Thompson emerged as a skilled advocate of rural development. He transformed the *Observer* into the regional morning *Northern Daily Leader*, the principal newspaper of north-west New South Wales.

From 1919 Thompson was chief inspirer and organizer of the Northern New State Movement in New South Wales; he was secretary of the New State League and of its provisional executive committee. He launched the movement at Tamworth in 1920 and, in the tide of secessionist fervour, organized the first convention at Armidale in April 1921. General secretary of the All-Australia New State Movement and influential at its Albury convention, he also edited the *New State Magazine*. With (Sir) Earle Page [q.v.11], Thompson was significant in tying provincial newspaper support to the emerging Country Party.

In December 1922 he won the Federal seat of New England for the Country Party. He was chairman of the party's parliamentary propaganda committee and edited its *Journal*. A member (1926-27) of the joint select committee on Commonwealth electoral law and procedure, while president of the Australian Tobacco Growers Association he chaired the 1929-30 select committee on the tobacco growing industry. In 1934-37 he was party whip and parliamentary secretary; in 1937-40 he was minister without portfolio, variously assisting the treasurer and the ministers for repatriation, the interior, and commerce.

Compromise with the strong vested interests controlling political processes troubled Thompson; as secretary of the Federal Parliamentary New States Committee, he believed that there was 'no party flavour about this great national project'. In 1936 he had attacked the divisional organization of the Country Party and felt that the self-government movements should not have merged with it. He was unseated at the 1940 election by J. P. Abbott, former president of the Graziers' Association of New South Wales, who had Country Party endorsement.

Thompson returned to Tamworth to edit the *Leader*. A director and one of its largest shareholders, he moved in 1953 to Strathfield, Sydney, from where he wrote leading articles, not only on the New State movement for which his passion never abated, but also on the border rivers and Darling basin schemes. He retired from the *Leader*'s board in 1965. During a fifty-seven-year association with the paper, he contributed over 15 000 articles.

On 24 June 1907 at Campbelltown Methodist parsonage, New South Wales, Thompson had married Emma Minnie Elizabeth Bell. Survived by their daughter, he died at Ashfield on 11 May 1968 and was cremated with Anglican rites.

R. Milliss, *City on the Peel* (Syd, 1980); U. Ellis, *The Country Party* (Melb, 1958) and *A history of the Australian Country Party* (Melb, 1963); Armidale Hist Soc, *J and Procs*, 28 (1985); *SMH*, 15 Dec 1922, 13 May 1968; *Armidale Express*, 15 Dec 1922; *Northern Daily Leader*, 13 May 1968.

JOHN ATCHISON

THOMPSON, CLIVE WENTWORTH (1882-1941), medical practitioner and soldier, was born on 21 September 1882 at Bathurst, New South Wales, the seventh of eleven children of native-born parents William Gilbert Thompson, postmaster, and his wife Jane Amelia, née Fraser. Educated locally at All Saints' College, in 1902 he entered the University of Sydney medical school, but spent his time on sport and humorous escapades, and in 1905 went on the land. He later resumed his course (B.Sc., 1911; M.B., 1913), becoming a junior resident at Royal Prince Alfred Hospital, Sydney, and a captain in the Australian Army Medical Corps in 1913.

When war was declared in 1914 he immediately joined the A.A.M.C., Australian Imperial Force, as regimental medical officer to the 1st Battalion. His war service was outstanding. He landed with his battalion on the first day at Gallipoli and, apart from one short rest period, remained there throughout the Anzac campaign. Best remembered as the medical officer who warned Major General Sir William Throsby Bridges [q.v.7] to be careful, and who then skilfully treated and evacuated the mortally wounded general, he repeatedly undertook many dangerous tasks and was awarded the Military Cross for his Gallipoli service. A non-commissioned officer wrote: 'I never saw a man go about his work so coolly as he did . . . helping wounded men under a withering shrapnel fire'.

Thompson was promoted and served as a medical staff major in Egypt and France. As lieut-colonel commanding the 14th Field Ambulance, a post he held for two years, he participated in the battles of Ypres and the Somme and the attack on the Hindenburg line. He was awarded the Distinguished Service Order, part of the citation stating: 'He showed great gallantry, initiative and organizing ability throughout this trying period. He regularly visited all advanced medical posts, and by his tact and courage and experience was instrumental in coordinating the medical arrangements of his own (Division) and the American Division operating with us'.

The 'initiative and organizing ability' were always evident. At Gallipoli he had retained—rather than dispersed—his medical personnel and, with his colleagues from the 3rd Battalion, established an important medical post. Early in 1918, in France, he conducted an 'admirable Australian Corps Medical School where . . . medical officers and N.C.O.s were given up-to-date training'; this was the predecessor of World War II A.A.M.C. schools and the Regular Army School of Army Health. In May-July 1918 Thompson developed a standardized advanced dressing station of three wooden huts, built in sections, transportable on three lorries, and capable of 'leap-frogging'. Estimating that 2 per cent of casualties held in forward posts could not undertake the long evacuation to surgical facilities, he introduced anaesthetic and resuscitation equipment to the field ambulance so that these men could be stabilized before evacuation; he further recommended that an operating team be provided at a divisional location for deployment forward as necessary. An Australian 'first', the concept was developed by the A.A.M.C. and then by the Royal Army Medical Corps.

Thompson's service distinctions included the Medaille de la Reconnaissance Française and four mentions in dispatches. He was twice wounded. A modest, humorous but determined man, 'always straight and game . . . unswerving in his affections and his friendships . . . Thompson was an excellent doctor and a better soldier'. Over six feet (182.9 cm) tall and lightly built, he was an all-round sportsman in his youth.

After returning to Sydney in late 1918, Thompson held resident appointments at the Royal Alexandra Children's and Crown Street Women's hospitals, and gained the degree of Master of Surgery from the University of Sydney in 1919. In 1919-23 he practised at Bathurst and in 1926 moved to Hamilton, New South Wales, where he was a general practitioner and assistant honorary surgeon to the Royal Newcastle Hospital until illness forced his retirement. A dedicated doctor who never spared himself, he treated many of his poorer patients without charge.

Thompson had married May Davis at St John's Anglican Church, Parramatta, on 17 April 1928. Survived by his wife, son and daughter, he died from mitral valve disease on 26 March 1941 in the Masonic Hospital, Ashfield, Sydney, and was cremated at Rookwood with Presbyterian forms.

C. E. W. Bean, *The story of Anzac* (Syd, 1921, 1924) and *The A.I.F. in France*, 5 (Syd, 1937); A. G. Butler (ed), *Official history of the Australian Army Medical Services in the war of 1914-1918*, 1-3 (Melb, 1938, Canb, 1940, 1943); C. D. Coulthard-Clark, *A heritage of spirit* (Melb, 1979); *London Gazette*, 28 Jan, 1 Feb, 11 July 1916, 1 June 1917, 3 June, 11 July 1919; *British A'sian*, 10 Feb 1916; *Prince Alfred Hospital Gazette*, 30 Dec 1916; *Cwlth of Aust Gazette*, 15 Oct 1931; *MJA*, 12 Apr 1941; family papers held by Mr W. W. Thompson, Kelso, NSW; information from Mrs C. W. Thompson, Syd.

C. M. GURNER

THOMPSON, DAVID (1865-1916), engineer and manufacturer, was born on 5 December 1865 at Castlemaine, Victoria, eldest of six children of DAVID THOMPSON (1828-1889), miller and later engineer, and his wife Bessie, née Caldwell, both Irish born. Within a year of his arrival in Victoria in 1852, Thompson senior and his brother James had set up as contractors, erecting iron houses in Melbourne and Collingwood. In 1855 they moved to the Castlemaine goldfields as quartz miners, machinery erectors and battery operators. Their local flour-mill, established in 1863, won an award at the 1867 Paris Exhibition. In 1875 the brothers opened an engineering works at Castlemaine to repair and manufacture gold-mining machinery; by 1888 they employed some 250 workmen in the production of a wide range of steam-engines, boilers, mining machinery, railway equipment and centrifugal pumps. After Thompson's death his partner James managed the business until 1891 when another brother John took over.

Educated locally, David Thompson junior served his apprenticeship in the family's engineering works. He assisted his father and uncles in the management of the business, but also spent much of his time supervising installation of the firm's machinery throughout Victoria. On 23 June 1896 he married Elizabeth Florence Whitehead at St Thomas's Anglican Church, Moonee Ponds, Melbourne. Between 1889 and 1908 the firm diversified into the production of heavy-duty pumping plants for the Metropolitan Board of Works and the State Rivers and Water Supply Commission; it also began production of hydraulic-sluicing and dredging equipment. By 1910 there were fifty Thompson-made sluicing and dredging plants in the Castlemaine district alone. Effectively head of the company since 1908, David became general manager when John died in 1910. Under David's direction the firm expanded into the manufacture of high-speed force-lubricated steam-engines, water-tube boilers and steam superheaters. Awarded a contract to supply twenty DD class locomotives for the Victorian Railways, Thompson & Co. (Castlemaine) Pty Ltd was floated in April 1913 with a paid-up capital of £88 333. Thompson inspected production at engineering and locomotive works in England and Germany; after his return the firm spent £63 000 extending and re-equipping the Castlemaine workshops. By 1919 sixty locomotives had been built for the Victorian Railways and another twenty-two were later made for the Commonwealth.

A member of the Chamber of Manufacturers, the Victorian Institute of Engineeers and the American Society of Mechanical Engineers, Thompson served for many years on the Engineering Wages Board which met in Melbourne. He was an outspoken critic of excessive railway freight charges and an advocate of protective import tariffs; in 1914 he had appeared before the Inter-State Commission. Thompson took a warm interest in the welfare of his employees: he encouraged apprentices to attend classes at the local technical school, supported employees' sporting clubs, organized an annual picnic for the firm's workers, and was a playing member and president of the Thompson Foundry Band from its inception in 1886.

On 4 February 1916 Thompson died at his Castlemaine home from injuries received in an accident at the foundry. He was buried with Presbyterian forms in the local cemetery. His wife survived him. They had no children. David Thompson had developed the business into one of the largest and best equipped non-government engineering works in Australia with a maximum workforce of over 600. The family connexion ended in 1925 when the company was restructured as Thompsons Engineering & Pipe Co. Ltd. In 1974 it became a subsidiary of Borg-Warner (Australia) Ltd.

The Thompsons-Byron Jackson centennial (Castlemaine, Vic, 1975); A. F. Johnston, Thompsons' Engineering Works of Castlemaine (ms, 1975, Univ Melb Archives).   M. S. CHURCHWARD

THOMPSON, DUNCAN FULTON (1895-1980), footballer, was born on 14 March 1895 at Warwick, Queensland, fourth of nine children of Charles Thompson, carpenter, and his wife Jane Elizabeth, née McLeod, both Queensland born. Educated at local schools, he worked at the Warwick Post Office, then joined the Australian Bank of Commerce in 1911 and was transferred to Ipswich. There he played Rugby League football with St Paul's Church of England and the

Starlights clubs; he also played cricket and ran in competitive sprints. Thompson's sporting prowess was most evident as a half-back in Rugby League: he represented Combined Country in 1913 and Queensland in 1915; when the bank transferred him to Sydney, he played for Norths.

As his parents would not allow him to volunteer at the outbreak of World War I, Thompson went to Queensland and enlisted in the Australian Imperial Force on 20 September 1916. He sailed to England as a reinforcement for the 49th Infantry Battalion, trained at Salisbury Plain and joined his unit at Ypres, Belgium. Shot through the chest at Dernancourt on 5 April 1918, he was repatriated and discharged in January 1919 with the edict that he could never play sport again.

Joining the Commonwealth Bank, he was sent to Ipswich where he played social cricket. Known as 'One Lung' and 'the Wizard', in 1919 Thompson played Rugby League for the Starlights, for Queensland (as captain) and for Australia against New Zealand. He was in the Valley (Brisbane) side in the 1919-20 cricket season when they won a premiership. On 12 October 1920 he married Dorothy Agnes Easton at St Paul's Anglican Church, Ipswich. Through his bank, Thompson initiated a move to New South Wales where he played for Wests in Newcastle, then rejoined North Sydney which won league premierships in 1921 and 1922. Having been a member in 1920 of the Australian team in the second and third Tests against Harold Wagstaff's Englishmen, in 1921-22 Thompson toured England, scoring 107 points from 49 goals and 3 tries. In 1920-23 he captained New South Wales.

In March 1923 Thompson resigned from the bank to set up a sports store. He represented Australia in two Tests in 1924, and played for Queensland (1924-25) and for Toowoomba for three years (at £400 a year) when that city was known as the Rugby League capital of the world. In this period Toowoomba's 'Galloping Clydesdales' defeated England, New South Wales, Victoria, South Sydney, Ipswich and Brisbane. Not a noted tackler, though one of the finest running half-backs in the history of the game, Thompson was lightly built and 'played with his eyes and brain'.

Retiring from football at the end of 1925, he represented Queensland in tennis, had a handicap of three in golf and played bowls for Toowoomba in later life. During World War II he served in the A.I.F. as amenities officer at Townsville and in Papua New Guinea. In the early 1950s Thompson (the 'Downs Fox') coached Toowoomba to six State victories. A great theorist of the game, he became an administrator, Australian selector and patron of the Queensland Rugby League. He was appointed M.B.E. on 1 January 1960. Survived by his wife, son and daughter, Thompson died at Wesley Private Hospital, Auchenflower, on 17 May 1980 and was cremated.

J. Sweeney, *The gentle Clydesdale* (Toowoomba, Qld, 1975); *Qld Rugby League Annual*, 1926; *Sunday Truth* (Brisb), 20 June 1971; *Courier Mail*, 20 May 1980; D. Thompson, Rugby League: the game (ms, 1978, held by Mr I. Thompson, Brisb).

M. L. HOWELL
R. A. HOWELL

THOMPSON, EDWARD HENRY (1851-1928), entomologist and Anglican clergyman, was born on 16 May 1851 at Newcastle upon Tyne, Northumberland, England, son of Edward Pett Thompson, merchant, and his wife Elizabeth, née Man. Privately educated, he arrived in Australia in 1870 and for five years served as a stipendiary licensed reader in the Anglican dioceses of Melbourne and Ballarat. Having been invited to Tasmania in 1875 by Bishop Charles Bromby [q.v.3], Thompson was made deacon and sent to Fiji as locum tenens for the mission at Levuka. When he returned to Tasmania in 1876, he was appointed to Port Cygnet as curate of D'Entrecasteaux. Ordained a priest in 1878, he became rector of the Huon district and made his base at Franklin, a place famous for its orchards. That year, on 27 November, he married Lucy Harrietta Grove at Long Bay.

His fascination with biology rested in the tradition of the nineteenth-century clergyman-naturalist and was fostered by his father, a respected natural historian. The Franklin region gave Thompson ample opportunity to indulge his interests in horticulture and entomology; he soon became a valued source of practical information for local orchardists. As British and mainland markets developed in the late 1880s, the increase in Tasmania's apple production was threatened by the incidence of insects (notably codlin moth) and fungus diseases, and further exacerbated by the depression of the early 1890s. To counter the crisis, Thompson was entomologist and scientific adviser to the Council (later Department) of Agriculture in 1891-96 and was credited with restoring prosperity to the orchard industry during those years. A member of the American Association of Economic Entomologists, he incorporated the latest ideas into his experiments with insecticides (oils and arsenicals) and fungicides (mainly metallic salts), and into methods for their application. Anti-pest spraying was rapidly adopted by growers which, together with improved cultural and hygienic practices, led to reliable control.

Thompson discovered many new agricultural pests and made original observations on their biology. He recruited farmers to assist him. His extensive activities included lecturing throughout Tasmania to agriculturalists and writing various information bulletins. He also published two books: *A handbook to the insect pests of farm and orchard* (1892) and *Insect and fungus pests of the field, farm and garden* (1895). In addition, he served on various agricultural bodies such as the rust in wheat commission and the fruit nomenclature committee.

Although he left government employment in 1896, Thompson gave freely of his advice until a new entomologist, Arthur Lea [q.v.10], was appointed in 1899. In 1908 Thompson moved to Hobart as rector of St John the Baptist Church where he remained active in diocesan affairs until his retirement in 1924 when he shifted to Moonah. In poor health, Thompson left Tasmania in December 1927. Survived by his wife, son and three daughters, he died in Sydney on 6 January 1928.

J of the Council of Agr, 1892-96; *Tas Mail*, 23 Apr 1904; *Mercury*, 7 Jan 1928.

PETER B. MCQUILLAN
TREVOR D. SEMMENS

THOMPSON, MRS F. LINDSAY; *see* TURNER, LILIAN

THOMPSON, GERALD MARR (1856-1938), journalist, was born on 11 September 1856 at Paddington, London, son of John Thompson, solicitor, and his wife Emma, née Hitchcock. Brought up in a family atmosphere of music and literature, he was educated at York Gate House, Broadstairs, Kent, and University College School, London. After working in the London and County Bank, he followed his two medical brothers John Ashburton [q.v.] and Charles to Australia, reaching Adelaide on 10 June 1881.

While employed there (1881-82) by the Bank of Australasia, Thompson wrote on music and drama for the *Advertiser*. He spent three months on the *Western Grazier* at Wilcannia, New South Wales, then joined the *Daily Telegraph* in Sydney in 1883 as critic of art, music and drama. Having travelled to Britain and the United States of America in 1886, he married English-born Eleanor Lucy Cole on 7 April 1887 at St Philip's Anglican Church, Sydney.

In 1891 Thompson succeeded Austin Brereton as drama and music critic for the *Sydney Morning Herald* and soon added art to his responsibilities. Meeting the considerable demands of the Sarah Bernhardt season, he thereafter contributed a weekly column, 'Music and Drama', as well as commenting on a wide range of Sydney's cultural life. He also wrote occasionally on travel: in 1896 he contributed an extended series, 'From old worlds to new', to the *Daily Telegraph*. Among the principal artists he interviewed were the Boucicaults, Amy Sherwin, Oscar Asche, Ada Crossley, Percy Grainger, (Dame) Nellie Melba [qq.v.3,6,7,8,9,10], Nellie Stewart, Hugh Ward [qq.v.] and John MacCormack.

As a critic Marr Thompson was, with his contemporary Griffen Foley [q.v.9], revered by the professions. His judgements, particularly of vocal and dramatic technique, were well-based, he was well-informed on Shakespeare and he was extremely diligent. He strove for originality in his writing and was forthright in his opinions. A contemporary wrote, 'He thunders his criticisms . . . and his word has been waited for shiveringly'. Thompson's critiques contained a good deal of information about the audiences and their dress, especially when vice-regal personages were in attendance. Conservative in his tastes, he found Elgar's work to be 'always of the most advanced musical idiom', thought that the *Dream of Gerontius* 'will soon be forgotten' and dismissed Schönberg on the basis of second-hand reports. He did, however, profess an interest in the development of an Australian 'school' of theatre.

Retiring in 1925, Thompson visited England; there he contributed articles on music in Australia to the London *Daily Telegraph* and sent pieces back to the *Herald* for which he continued to write occasionally. He was a small man, bald in middle age, with an austere face, ample moustache and pince-nez. Predeceased by their daughter, his wife died in 1927. At St Andrew's Cathedral on 20 December 1932 Thompson married French-born Mathilde Pognon who lectured at Teachers' College, Sydney. Survived by her, he died at his Double Bay home on 28 February 1938 and was cremated. His estate was sworn for probate at £2784.

J. Fairfax Ltd, *Century of journalism* (Syd, 1931); W. A. Orchard, *The distant view* (Syd, 1943); G. Souter, *Company of Heralds* (Melb, 1981); *Theatre Mag* (Syd and Melb), 1 Nov 1912, p 5; *Observer* (Adel), 18 June 1881; *SMH*, 26 Jan 1916, 11, 26 Mar 1925, 30 July 1927, 1-3 Mar 1938; *Bulletin*, 26 Mar 1925; G. M. Thompson, newspaper-cuttings (ML).

JOHN CARMODY

THOMPSON, JAMES (1863-1945), engineer, was born on 22 August 1863 at Drogheda, County Louth, Ireland, son of Thomas Thompson, supervisor, and his wife Mary Henderson, née Logan. The family moved in 1870 to Cork where young James was educated at Carmichael's School and Queen's College (Royal University of Ireland, B.E.,

1882). In 1882 he was appointed assistant to Dr Stoney, engineer to the Dublin Docks and Harbours Board, and worked on railway and harbour projects. On 22 December 1888 Thompson married Sarah Highet (d. 1900) with Presbyterian forms at Trinity Church, Cork; they were to have one son.

They migrated in 1889 to Melbourne where James was employed in the survey branch of the Victorian Railways. He joined the Public Works Department of Western Australia in 1891 and assisted C. Y. O'Connor [q.v.11] in preparing documents for railways. In 1894 Thompson became resident engineer on the Northam-Southern Cross-Kalgoorlie railway and in 1896 engineer in charge of the harbours and rivers branch. After six months acting in the position, he was appointed engineer-in-chief of the department in September 1904. During his term, work was completed on metropolitan water supply and sewerage and drainage projects (1904-12), Fremantle harbour and extensions to Victoria Quay (1908), extensions to North Quay and consequent dredging (1914-15), harbours and rivers improvements at Albany, Bunbury, Hopetoun and Geraldton, roads and bridges, clearing and construction of main and feeder roads in the wheat belt, town water supplies, and drainage and irrigation. He directed all railway construction until 1911: of 4095 miles (6590 km) of government railways built in Western Australia before World War II, 2914 miles (4690 km) of main track were constructed while he controlled the department. In 1909 and 1910 he had also been consulting engineer to the Fremantle Harbour Trust and the Bunbury Harbour Board.

In 1913 Thompson visited Berlin and reported on trials of the Mueller road trains. He inspected the Giovi electric railway near Genoa, and river works in Britain and Europe. In Canada he studied the wheat handling system. He had been elected a member of the Institution of Civil Engineers, London, in 1899 and became founding president of the Western Australian Institution of Engineers in 1910. A handsome man who kept his full head of hair and luxuriant moustache, he retired in 1925.

On 6 March 1920 at Christ Church, Claremont, Perth, Thompson had married with Anglican rites a divorcee, Constanza Georgina Hardwicke, née Staszewski, who predeceased him. Survived by his son and stepson, he died on 2 January 1945 and was buried in the Presbyterian section of Karrakatta cemetery.

J. S. Battye (ed), *Cyclopedia of Western Australia*, 1 (Adel, 1912); J. S. H. Le Page, *Building a State* (Perth, 1986); *West Australian*, 4 Jan 1945; information from Inst of Civil Engineers, Lond.

R. M. STRICKLAND

THOMPSON, JOHN ASHBURTON (1846-1915), medical officer and epidemiologist, was born on 31 July 1846 at Kensington, London, eldest child of John Thompson, solicitor, and his wife Emma, née Hitchcock. He was educated at St Paul's and University College schools, Guy's and Middlesex hospitals, London (L.R.C.P., M.R.C.S., L.M., L.S.A., 1868), and the Free University of Brussels (M.D., 1876). From 1872 he combined an appointment with the Great Northern Railway Co. with private practice and in 1877 was elected councillor, Obstetrical Society, London. In poor health, he visited New Zealand and several Australian colonies, doing insurance work.

Obtaining a diploma in public health (Cambridge, 1882), Thompson migrated next year to Australia. Early in 1884 he served briefly as resident surgeon of the Hospital for Pacific Islanders, Mackay, Queensland, during a dengue outbreak. Confronting appalling conditions, he peppered the government with telegrams and submitted a report proposing radical remedies. In Sydney he witnessed a smallpox epidemic and in July was appointed a temporary medical officer by (Sir) Charles Mackellar [q.v.10], president of the Board of Health. Promoted deputy medical adviser and chief medical inspector to the board in August, Thompson was the only trained epidemiologist in the colony. He became the board's driving force.

Pressure for a public health Act failed in 1885, but Thompson's exhaustive report tracing a typhoid outbreak to a polluted dairy well in Leichhardt resulted in the Dairies Supervision Act (1886). With few legal powers to support him, he publicized the problems: in evidence to commissions of inquiry; in papers read before medical congresses, the Australasian Association for the Advancement of Science and the Royal Society of New South Wales; and, helped by his brother Gerald [q.v.], anonymously in the press. Ashburton's first-hand reports on outbreaks of infectious disease and insanitary 'nuisances' established him as an authority. In 1884 he was special delegate to the Australasian Sanitary Conference of Sydney, in 1887 a member of the Government Asylums Inquiry Board and in 1891 official delegate to the International Congress of Hygiene and Demography, London. He chaired the inquiry into lead poisoning at Broken Hill (1892-93) which resulted in effective safeguards. He was also an examiner at the University of Sydney (1892-99).

Appointed chief medical officer and president of the Board of Health in 1896, Thompson helped (Sir) George Reid [q.v.11] to draft the 'comparatively incomplete' public health bill which was passed in November. With a sure hand, he built a small but effective service, although its legal powers remained scattered in many Acts. He appointed the microbiologist Frank Tidswell and two medical officers of health: William Armstrong [q.v.7] in Sydney and Robert Dick in Newcastle. A fellow (1905) of the Royal Sanitary Institute, London, Thompson helped to establish a local board of examiners to supply trained sanitary inspectors; as chairman (1900-13), he examined 367 candidates. His policies stressed disease prevention by environmental control, sanitary reform and education. Insistent that State rather than local government should control public health, he was to have national influence in areas such as quarantine and food laws.

An able, if irascible, administrator, Thompson was a better epidemiologist and published many articles on the subject. His skill in smallpox diagnosis was 'unerring' and his prize-winning study of leprosy in Australia (1897) won him a world-wide reputation. His observation and analysis of the 1900 bubonic plague and its recurrences endorsed the unfavoured theory of the French scientist P. L. Simond that the flea was the transmitter of the plague bacillus. Thompson's reports were 'models of cogent reasoning' and his conclusions—verified by the second Indian Plague Commission (1905)—were of prime practical importance in combating the disease; he showed that plague is primarily a disease of rats, transmitted only by the flea to rats and humans, and could best be prevented by making occupied buildings rat-proof. Saluted by his peers overseas, he addressed the 1906 meeting of the American Medical Association, Boston, and the Royal Society of Medicine, London, of which he was a fellow. In Australia he passed unhonoured.

At St Mark's Anglican Church, Darling Point, on 21 August 1902 Thompson had married a widow Lilian Simpson, daughter of Sir Julian Salomons [q.v.6]; they lived at Woollahra. Energetic and hard-working, he was reticent and quietly spoken. His recreations were music and theatre. While not always popular among his colleagues, he commanded their respect. Thompson was a member of the Australian Club and the Thatched House Club, London. Retiring in 1913, he died of a cerebrovascular disease on 16 September 1915 at South Kensington, London. His wife, a stepson and stepdaughter survived him.

C. E. Cook, The epidemiology of leprosy in Australia (Canb, 1927); L. F. Hirst, The conquest of plague (Oxford, Eng, 1953); C. R. Boughton, A coast chronicle (Syd, 1963); E. Ford, Bibliography of Australian medicine 1790-1900 (Syd, 1976); C. J. Cummins, A history of medical administration in New South Wales 1788-1973 (Syd, 1979); MJA, 25 Sept 1915; J of Roy Sanitary Inst, 36 (1915), p 435, 70 (1950), p 73; Health, 3, no 4, 1925; G. Marr Thompson, newspaper-cuttings (ML).

PATRICIA MORISON

THOMPSON, JOHN WILLIS (1860-1934), publican and transport pioneer, was born on 3 December 1860 in Hobart Town, son of John Thompson, shipwright, and his wife Eliza, née Kelly. He had virtually no education and was first employed driving the mail-coach from Bellerive to Sorell. Later, and in partnership with his brothers, he bought the local coaching firm which then became known as Thompson Bros. The business ended abruptly with the coming of the railway to the eastern coast. On 15 October 1884 at St David's Anglican Cathedral, Hobart, Thompson married Mary Ann Dixon, née Jackson, a widow with three children; they were to have five sons and two daughters.

In 1892 he moved to St Helens, leasing and later buying the Telegraph Hotel. Thompson pioneered the development of transport services on the east coast: he soon managed mail contracts, freight, passenger conveyance, boat hiring, and fishing and tourist excursions. He kept his teams of horses, coaches and equipment in immaculate condition. About 1912 Thompson bought a number of motor cars, including two 'Noiseless Napiers', one of which travelled close to half a million miles (804 650 km) before it was taken out of service. The need for reliable operatives for his undertakings was largely filled by the members of his family.

At the age of 50 Thompson passed some of his responsibilities to his sons. By this time the St Helens Hotel, as it had become known, was one of the biggest seaside hotels in Tasmania. Though he remained active, Thompson began to be regarded as somewhat eccentric: he wandered around his domain with his eyes half-closed, seldom removing his hat or revealing his thoughts. When he did speak, it was slowly, and with deliberation. His chubby, red, weather-beaten face and deadpan expression, together with an apparent guilelessness, concealed an agile brain. Nicknamed 'Gimlet', he was a generous family man who sought to give his patrons the best value possible; he took delight in preserving his 'closeness' in everyday affairs.

Survived by his seven children and three stepchildren, Thompson died on 4 May 1934 at St Helens and was buried in the local cemetery. His estate was sworn for probate at £11 023.

Cyclopedia of Tasmania, 1 (Hob, 1900); R. A. Ferrall, *Partly personal* (Hob, 1974); *Mercury*, 5 May 1934; *Examiner*, 5, 7 May 1934; information from St Helens history room, St Helens, *and* Mr B. Haley, Scamander, *and* Mrs L. Johnson, Underwood, Tas.

R. A. FERRALL

THOMPSON, MATILDA LOUISE (1871-1959), businesswoman and philanthropist, was born on 28 April 1871 at Ballarat, Victoria, fifth child of English-born John Clennell, engine driver, and his Scottish wife Matilda, née McIntosh. Having migrated to Melbourne in the early 1850s, her parents moved to Ballarat in 1870 where they quickly became respected members of the Jubilee Wesleyan Church. Both at home and at Sunday School, Tilly was taught to be self-sufficient and helpful: this philosophy was to remain with her.

Tilly left Wendouree State School aged 13 and commenced work at a local drapery store. A woman of 'boundless and terrifying energy', in 1905 she was offered the post of principal sales representative with E. Lucas & Co. Pty Ltd, a firm which designed and manufactured women's clothing. After obtaining a driver's licence and a motor car, she became a 'travelling sales lady'. Her task was to display new fashion designs and to take orders throughout southern Australia. She then moved into a senior managerial position at Lucas's, taking charge of production and a staff of 250 women. In 1913-14 she visited Europe to evaluate new machinery and fashion trends.

World War I brought Tilly greater public prominence. She and the 'Lucas Girls' threw themselves into charitable works, collecting thousands of pounds for patriotic funds. Tilly decided that more should be done. She encouraged the Lucas staff and numerous other charitable bodies to build a suitable memorial to the local volunteers: it took the form of Ballarat's Avenue of Honour (3912 trees) and the Arch of Victory which was unveiled by the prince of Wales in June 1920.

On 6 August 1914 at Ballarat Tilly had married with Methodist forms William Daniel Thompson, a wealthy mining speculator and a widower with six children. When he died in 1927 she retired and spent five years in Europe. Returning to Ballarat in 1933, she launched immediately into other projects with typical zest. On the shore of Lake Wendouree she built a large house, Sunways, which became a temporary refuge for any ex-serviceman who was down on his luck. Over two decades hundreds of men and women enjoyed Mrs Thompson's assistance: she gave financial support to numerous local charities, ran women's self-help, callisthenics and dietary classes, and travelled throughout Victoria speaking to women's groups.

A vibrant woman who never lost her ability to promote unconventional ideas, she was awarded the gold medal of the Returned Sailors' and Soldiers' Imperial League of Australia in 1939 and appointed M.B.E. in 1941. Still upright, alert and bright-eyed in old age, she died at Ballarat on 7 April 1959 and was buried in the old cemetery. Her estate was valued for probate at £12 559.

M. White, *The golden thread* (np, nd, 1963?); *Ballarat Courier*, 17 May 1929, 2 Jan 1941, 8 Apr 1959.   PETER MANSFIELD

THOMPSON, WILLIAM BETHEL (1906-1945), racing motorist, was born on 28 December 1906 at Summer Hill, Sydney, second child of William Ernest Thompson, customs clerk, and his wife Gladys Macdonald, née Bethel, both native-born. On completing his education at Sydney Grammar School in 1923, William worked in the motor trade. He married Jean Mavis Anderson at St Stephen's Presbyterian Church, Sydney, on 26 September 1929.

Of moderate means, he was helped by Arthur Burkitt, professor of anatomy at the University of Sydney, who owned several of the cars that Thompson raced. He retired from his first Australian Grand Prix at Phillip Island, Victoria, in 1929, but won the 1930 race in a new, supercharged Type 37A Bugatti owned by Burkitt who travelled as riding mechanic. Starting from scratch, Thompson won again in the same car in 1932 and won for a third time in a Brooklands Riley in 1933. He finished second (by 14 seconds) driving a supercharged MG Magnette in 1934 and was again second (by 27 seconds) in 1935.

Despite his youth, Thompson approached his driving with a thoroughness that was uncommon in Australian motor racing, then in its infancy. Observers commented on the clean and efficient presentation of his cars, and on the lack of last-minute work they needed. Behind the wheel he was very fast and exceptionally consistent; his lap times on the 6.569-mile (10.571 km) rectangle of rough and dusty Phillip Island roads often varied by no more than a second. An outstanding finishing record was an essential part of his success. While he made occasional driving errors, he took exceptional care of his cars. He did some of his own mechanical work, but had expert helpers, among them the skilled engineer Bill Balgarnie who was often his riding mechanic.

Strongly built and about 5 ft. 11 ins. (180.3 cm) tall, Thompson parted his dark hair in the centre. Contemporaries recall him as well-tailored, confident—almost calculating—but also impulsive and given to practical joking at post-race parties. His Riley and MG drives were for Melbourne motor traders and he moved to that city in 1934 to head the MG department of Lane's Motors Pty Ltd; he later transferred to the Shell Co. of Australia Ltd. He was briefly involved with midget speedcars in Melbourne and Sydney in 1934-

35, but from 1936 his racing career faded. Divorced in 1938, Thompson married Millicent Francklyn Ironside, née King, a widow with two children, on 10 June 1942 at the government statist's office, Melbourne.

Joining the Royal Australian Air Force as flying officer in 1940, Thompson was based in Melbourne from 1941 where he organized the manufacture and supply of engine spares for rescue boats. He held the rank of squadron leader when he was drowned in an aircraft accident on 12 February 1945 in the Marshall Islands, Pacific Ocean. His wife survived him, as did the two sons of his first marriage.

Aust Motorist, Apr 1929, p 460, Apr 1930, p 439, Apr 1932, p 395, Apr 1934, p 418; *Car*, Apr 1929, p 10, Apr 1930, p 15, May 1934, p 10, July 1934, p 17, Apr 1935, p 9, Sept 1935, pp 2, 5; *Motor Life*, Apr 1929, p 9, Apr 1930, p 17; *Motor in Aust and Flying*, Apr 1932, p 15, Dec 1933, p 40; *Midget Car Broadsider* (Wentworth Park Speedway programme), 9 Nov 1935; *Argus*, 19 Mar 1929; *Age*, 25 Mar 1930; *SMH*, 21 Mar 1932, 2 Jan, 12, 14, 20 Mar 1934; information from Mrs F. Thompson, Toorak, Mr T. P. Dooley, Hawthorn, Melb, and Mr K. McKinney, Foster, Vic.   GRAHAM HOWARD

THOMPSON, WILLIAM GEORGE (1863-1953), merchant, soldier and politician, was born on 2 March 1863 at Lurgan, Armagh, Ireland, son of William Thompson, building contractor, and his wife Isabella, née Campbell. The family arrived at Keppel Bay, Queensland, in 1864. William left North Rockhampton State School at 11 and joined a mercantile firm as office-boy; his sister—determined that he should receive further education—worked as a dressmaker to pay his night-school fees. A founding member (1881) of the North Rockhampton Protestant Alliance Friendly Society, in 1886 he set up the bonded warehouse of W. G. Thompson & Co. Paid secretaryships of the local hospital and jockey club, together with auditing and general commission work, added to his income and good repute. A youthful alderman of the North Rockhampton Borough Council, he was mayor in 1890. On 17 August 1901 he married Mary Ellen Bancroft with Presbyterian forms at Rockhampton.

With a keen interest in soldiering, Thompson had enlisted in the militia in 1889; as a captain in the 2nd Queensland Mounted Infantry he had charge of troops at Clermont during the shearers' strike of 1891; he went in 1897 with the Australian contingent to Queen Victoria's diamond jubilee. Second-in-command of Queensland's 1899 contingent to the South African War, he saw repeated action and—as a magistrate of the High Court of Pretoria—administered martial law. As lieut-colonel, in 1908 Thompson commanded the 15th Regiment, Australian Light Horse, and next year helped to revise its manual. In 1910-16 he was in charge of training camps in Queensland. Promoted colonel, Australian Imperial Force (sea transport service), he then spent eighteen months in charge of troops on convoy work. Holding standard campaign decorations, he retired a brigadier general in 1921.

Having unsuccessfully contested the Queensland Legislative Assembly seat of Keppel in 1918, Thompson was elected to the Senate as a Nationalist in December 1922. In parliament he fought a losing battle to gain Federal support for the development of the Great Bowen Basin coal resources in central Queensland. A member of a parliamentary mission to Canada in 1928, he became its leader when General Sir William Glasgow [q.v.9] was recalled. Next year Thompson served on the joint committee on public accounts. Like many conservative Queensland politicians, he was defeated in the Depression, losing his seat in June 1932.

Although he retired from his own business in 1925, Thompson was president of the Rockhampton Chamber of Commerce (1933-43) and of the Employers' Association of central Queensland; he also chaired the Bluff Colliery Co. and the Central Queensland Coal Board. Vice-consul for Sweden in central Queensland for thirty-two years, in 1940 he received a Swedish knighthood (Royal Order of Vasa). He performed in an amateur orchestra and enjoyed polo, rowing, tennis and later bowls.

Thompson retired to Sydney several years before his death at Petersham on 7 March 1953. He was cremated and his ashes interred in General Thompson Park, North Rockhampton, on 24 March 1961. A daughter survived him.

L. McDonald, *Rockhampton* (Brisb, 1981); *Morning Bulletin*, 23 Oct 1896, 7 Apr 1897, 2 May 1908, 14 Aug 1909, 23 Apr 1921, 16 Dec 1922, 30 June 1932, 19 Jan 1940, 10 Mar 1953; information from Mrs L. Twigg, Rockhampton, Qld.

LORNA McDONALD

THOMSON, DUGALD (1849-1922), merchant and politician, was born on 28 December 1849 at Camberwell, London, son of John Thomson, insurance broker, and his wife Jane, née Duncan. Migrating to South Australia in 1850, the family later moved to Victoria. Dugald was sent to England to complete his schooling and to be trained in his uncle's Liverpool business. He spent two years at sea before returning, aged 19, to Melbourne where he joined Robert Harper [q.v.9] & Co. for whose firm he set up a branch in Sydney in 1877. Thomson was managing partner until an accident forced him to withdraw from the

business in 1892. In the late 1870s, with J. P. Garvan [q.v.4], he had established the co-operative North Shore Steam Ferry Co. Ltd.

In 1894, as a free trader, Thomson won the Legislative Assembly seat of Warringah; he retained it in 1895 and 1898. He supported the premier, (Sir) George Reid [q.v.11], though objecting to measures (such as an eight-hour day for coalminers and the application to all adults of factory and shop regulations) which derived from the tacit alliance between Reid's Free-Trade ministry and Labor. Thomson also opposed the idea of a referendum to settle any deadlock between the Houses and disagreed with proposals to make government contracts conditional upon payment of union wages. He was an early advocate of bridging Sydney Harbour, preferably by a private firm.

Unwavering in support of Federation, Thomson campaigned actively against his Free-Trade colleagues in the Constitution bill referenda. He was elected to the House of Representatives for the seat of North Sydney in 1901, holding it unopposed until he retired in 1910. He was minister for home affairs (August 1904-July 1905) in the Reid-McLean [q.v.10] government. A member of the select committee on decimal coinage (1901-02), he sat on royal commissions on the S.S. *Drayton Grange* (1902) and the navigation bill (1906). In 1907 he represented Australia at a merchant shipping conference in London. Holding a leading position in the Opposition, Thomson represented Reid during some of his numerous absences and remained loyal to Reid's position on the major Federal issues of conciliation and arbitration, pensions, bounties and White Australia. A common-sense, rather than eloquent, debater who was principally concerned with Australia's maritime potential, Thomson spoke frequently on navigation and customs issues, performing inexhaustibly in the tariff debates of 1902 and 1908. Respected for his 'strong convictions and eminent fairness', he was too goodnatured and straightforward to seek or exploit political advantage. When urged to nominate for the Speakership, he modestly declined.

Involved in Scottish community organizations, he was a veteran member (1887) and senior office-holder in the Highland Society. Philanthropic, and active on behalf of veterans, he was a founder of the Graythwaite Convalescent Home of Oversea Military Forces, and chairman of the North Sydney War Memorial Committee and of the King Edward Memorial Fund. Thomson died on 27 November 1922 at Kirribilli, Sydney, and was buried in the Presbyterian section of Gore Hill cemetery. He was unmarried.

Aust Mag (Syd), 1 Nov 1909; *SMH*, 30 May 1911, 28, 29 Nov 1922; *Daily Telegraph* (Syd), 17

Oct 1911, 5 July 1915, 27 Jan 1917; *Australasian*, 21 Dec 1922; Crouch memoirs (LaTL).

IAN MARSH

THOMSON, HERBERT (1870-1947), car manufacturer and engineer, was born on 13 July 1870 at Prahran, Melbourne, ninth child and seventh son of Henry Thomson, wheelwright and later contractor, and his wife Isabella, née Walker, both Scottish born. The Walkers, with their two eldest children, had arrived in Melbourne in April 1853. Herbert worked for his father as a boy and helped him to install coal-producing bores at Yallourn and Altona. At 19 Herbert constructed a steam-engine which was used in a launch on the Yarra River. After early training as an engineer, in 1897 he set up as a manufacturer of steam-engines and boilers near his father's business in High Street, Armadale. There he began making a steam car, one of the first self-propelled road vehicles in Australia. Operational by July 1899, the car had its initial public run at a suburban cricket ground; it was exhibited at Melbourne, Sydney and other agricultural shows, and demonstrations were given in Victoria and New South Wales.

Quiet and smooth-running, the 'six-seat Phaeton of fiddle-back ash and silky oak' had an engine with two cylinders in tandem. In April 1900 Thomson and his cousin Edward Holmes set out in it from Bathurst, New South Wales, for Melbourne. The trying journey of 493¼ miles (793.8 km) on difficult roads was completed in 56 hours and 36 minutes of driving time, at an average speed of 8.72 miles (14 km) per hour, which was attributed by Holmes to Thomson's intention 'to err on the side of safety'; on one section, however, they reached 15 miles (24.1 km) per hour and on another raced and won against a pair of horses over 12 miles (19.3 km).

Before that journey Thomson had patented his innovations in Victoria, New South Wales and Queensland, while Holmes set up a syndicate to manufacture cars. The Thomson Motor Car Co. Ltd, incorporated on 18 June 1900, bought Thomson's patent for one hundred and fifty £10 shares and produced approximately twelve improved vehicles: they had two parallel cylinders and a top speed of 25 miles (40.2 km) per hour. A Thomson car raced successfully against a Benz imported to Melbourne by Harley Tarrant [q.v.]. By 1902 Thomson's catalogue listed a variety of vehicles from seven different overseas manufacturers. The company moved from Flinders Lane to Thomson's works at 835 High Street, Armadale, but went out of business in 1912. By this time Thomson had produced a motor vehicle for

the metropolitan fire brigade and some steam-engines for merry-go-rounds: the best-known, at St Kilda beach, was later purchased by the Commonwealth government and moved to Canberra.

Thompson became a consulting engineer. He died on 26 October 1947 at Richmond and was cremated. His native-born wife Mary Ethel, née Clague, whom he had married with Presbyterian forms at Malvern on 19 April 1905, survived him, as did their daughter. His 1899 car is in the Museum of Victoria and an early Thomson engine is in the Powerhouse Museum, Sydney.

A'sian Coachbuilder and Saddler, 15 Sept 1899; *Bulletin of the Business Archives Council of Aust*, 1, no 6, 1959; *Walkabout*, 31, Feb 1965; *Leader* (Melb), 1 July 1899; *Prahran Telegraph*, 29 July 1899; *Australasian*, 28 Apr 1900; *Age*, 27 Oct 1947; *Chronicle* (Adel), 30 Oct 1947.

H. DOWNING

THOMSON, JAMES (1852-1934), journalist, commissioner and newspaper editor, was born on 1 September 1852 at Cullycapple, Londonderry, Ireland, son of Alexander Thomson, contractor, and his wife Martha, née Gilmor. The family arrived in Victoria in 1853. James attended Geelong Presbyterian School and the National Grammar School, Castlemaine. With his schoolmates he formed a 15 shillings paid-up mining syndicate and successfully panned gold at Wattle Flat until a disastrous explosion ended the enterprise. Later he was a mine manager.

Having been a runner for the *Mount Alexander Mail*, at the age of 16 Thomson was apprenticed at the *Australasian*. Successively, he edited the *Kyneton Observer*, worked as a journalist on Melbourne's *Daily Telegraph* and was secretary to parliamentary boards of inquiry and royal commissions. He married Alice Leyland on 1 June 1878 at Trinity Church, Melbourne. As Victorian secretary to the commissioners for the Melbourne International Exhibition (1880), and for the Calcutta and the Colonial and Indian exhibitions (1886), he travelled in India and via Venice to London. There, due to his appearance, he was often mistaken for the explorer, (Sir) Henry Stanley. In 1888 Thomson was a commissioner for the Melbourne Centennial International Exhibition.

Appointed to the *Argus* in the early 1880s, Thomson resigned in 1889 to become founder-manager of the *Evening Standard* which he left in 1894 when it amalgamated with the *Herald*. Commissioned that year by the Melbourne *Age* to write about Western Australia, he embarked in the *Innamincka* for Fremantle.

At Perth and Geraldton Thomson mixed with everyone, especially those with Victorian connexions. Sir John Forrest, J. M. A. Despeissis and W. H. J. Carr-Boyd [qq.v.8,3] were among his friends. A witty raconteur, whose penchant was dropping names of people and places, Jimmy had a rubicund appearance, 'with geniality bubbling from every pore and wrinkle', and became widely known in the city and on the Murchison goldfields. He ate 'diminutive' crayfish, frequented country race meetings, travelled his magisterial circuits by train when wildflowers were in bloom, and was unperturbed when a bearded prospector dropped 900 oz. (25.5 kg) of gold on his bedroom floor.

Thomson's racy articles and his publication, *Nor-west of west* (1904), gained attention in Melbourne. Meanwhile, he drove in his 'pegs' at Cue, imported a Wharfdale printing machine and set up the *Murchison Times and Day Dawn Gazette*. A widower, he married Blanche White on 26 February 1908 at the Congregational Church, Fremantle. He retired to Queen's Park, but continued to write articles based on his own experience and local legend. Survived by the two sons of his first marriage, he died in Perth on 4 August 1934 and was buried with Anglican rites in Karrakatta cemetery. His estate was sworn for probate at £244.

Truthful Thomas, *Through the spy-glass* (Perth, 1905); *Western Mail* (Perth), 12 June 1924, 19 Mar 1933; *West Australian*, 4 Aug 1934.

WENDY BIRMAN

THOMSON, JAMES PARK (1854-1941), geographer and public servant, was born on 20 June 1854 and baptized on 23 July at Unst, Shetland Islands, Scotland, eldest son of Lawrence Thomson, farmer, and his wife Joan, née Park. Educated at the local parish school, at the age of 18 he took up seafaring, visited the United States and South America between 1872 and 1874 and then learned the rudiments of marine engineering at Glasgow. In 1876 Thomson visited New Zealand and from 1877 spent two years working with surveyors in New South Wales. Securing an appointment in Fiji, he was registered as a land surveyor in March 1880: his work was comprehensive, thorough and accurate. In 1882 he also supervised observations of the transit of Venus; his fascination with astronomy was to continue into his retirement when he established a private observatory in Brisbane.

Leaving Fiji in 1884, Thomson travelled the South Pacific before joining the Queensland Department of Public Lands as a draftsman in 1885. From his base in Brisbane he computed the trigonometrical survey of the colony. In 1885 he founded the Queensland branch of the (Royal) Geographical Society of Australasia; he was its honorary secretary, president (1894-97) and edited its *Journal*. He was involved in discussions that led to the formation of the Australasian Association for the Advancement of Science. Thomson wrote well over two hundred scientific papers and was instrumental in the adoption of the zonal system for reckoning time. In 1900 the Queensland branch of the R.G.S.A. named its foundation medal after him and he was its first recipient in 1901. Other honours included the Peek award from the R.G.S., London (1902), and an honorary LL.D. from Queen's University at Kingston, Ontario, Canada (1903).

In 1909 Thomson successfully identified and astronomically determined the position of R. O'H. Burke's [q.v.3] and W. J. Wills's [q.v.6] most northerly camp on the Bynoe River. By then he considered that most Queenslanders lacked a proper appreciation of their physical environment. He was further censorious about civil servants with British citizenship who earned Queensland salaries and then returned home. Appointed C.B.E. in 1920, he retired from the public service in 1922, but continued to work tirelessly for the R.G.S.A.'s Queensland branch. Always a keen traveller with wide connexions, Thomson lectured at such towns as Charleville, Roma, Longreach, Blackall and on Thursday Island. He raised locals' awareness of their specific environments, while giving them a sense of union with a wider world.

He married twice in Sydney with Anglican rites: on 20 December 1880 Grace Winter, and, a widower, on 29 June 1887 Ada Gannon. An accomplished horsewoman, Ada was also involved with the R.G.S.A. She and their three sons and daughter survived Thomson who died at Kilcoy, Queensland, on 10 May 1941 and was cremated. Distinguished men wrote laudatory and affectionate tributes, among them Sir Douglas Mawson [q.v.10] who extolled Thomson's 'energy and enthusiasm'.

Qld Geographical J, 16, 1900-01, p 91, 17, 1901-02, pp 1, 144, 33, 1941-42, p 8, 44, 1957-59, p 48; *Brisbane Courier*, 16 Sept 1906; *Queenslander*, 14 Aug 1930, 5 July 1934; J. P. Thomson box, RGSA, Qld; Thomson cutting-book (OL). W. S. KITSON

THORBY, HAROLD VICTOR CAMPBELL (1888-1973), farmer and politician, was born on 2 October 1888 at Annandale, Sydney, third son of English-born Frederick James Thorby, builder, and his Irish wife Elizabeth, née Campbell. He assisted his maternal grandparents on their farm at Geurie and was educated locally before attending Sydney Grammar School.

Later, while working his own property at Geurie, Thorby studied woolclassing, veterinary science and architecture through the Sydney Technical College. He also acted as foreman for his father's building projects in Sydney and Newcastle. On 6 September 1916 at All Saints Anglican Church, Wongarbon, he married Vera Lynda Morley (d. 1958). An active member of the Farmers and Settlers' Association (State president 1925-27), Thorby was secretary of the Western Railway League and the Macquarie Valley Water Conservation League. From 1922 to 1940 he was to represent the Country Party in State and Federal parliaments.

Having been member for Wammerawa from 1922 in the Legislative Assembly, in 1927 he won the seat of Castlereagh. In the Bavin-Buttenshaw [qq.v.7] government he was minister for agriculture and chairman of the Water Conservation and Irrigation Commission in 1927-30. Using his portfolio 'almost as a junior public works department', Thorby saw Wyangala Dam commenced, Burrinjuck Dam finished, Hawkesbury Agricultural College enlarged and numerous wheat silos built. He also established the Rice Marketing Board of New South Wales, and pushed through the Swine Compensation Act (1928) and the Advances to Settlers (Government Guarantee) Act (1929). With his architectural and building background, Thorby achieved efficiencies in such government construction projects as the new building for his department and the Royal North Shore Hospital nurses' block.

After his defeat in Castlereagh in 1930, he won the Federal seat of Calare the following year. Thorby clashed with Prime Minister Lyons [q.v.10], but became assistant minister for repatriation (1934-35) in Lyons's coalition government. Their relations improved and in 1935 he accompanied Lyons to England to negotiate a meat agreement. Thorby also attended an international wool conference in Berlin. He was minister in charge of War Service Homes (1935-36) and assistant minister for commerce (1935-37), acting occasionally as minister for commerce and minister for defence. In cabinet his knowledge of architecture and building was often called on, and he supervised extensions to the Caulfield Military Hospital, Melbourne. His sympathetic approach to the problems of repatriation widows was well-known. In 1937-40 he was deputy leader of his party.

When Thorby became minister for defence in November 1937 he began a three-year expansion programme and developed a valuable system of war annexes attached to existing factories. In retrospect, however, the programme proved too modest and failed to absorb even planned levels of expenditure. In November 1938 Thorby was appointed minister for works, chairman of the Murray Valley Water Commission and minister for civil aviation. He was subsequently post-master-general and minister for health (March-October 1940).

Defeated in the 1940 election, Thorby unsuccessfully contested Dubbo in 1941, and Calare in 1943 and 1946. He then took up the property of his wife's parents at Wongarbon. A councillor (1952-55) of the Graziers' Association, he continued to be active in the Country Party and in 1957 was made an honorary life member. On 14 May 1960 he married Alfreda Elizabeth Rogers at the Presbyterian Church, Toowong, Brisbane. He then ran a property at Quirindi and later one at Tamworth, New South Wales.

Robust, rugged and 'built like a policeman', Thorby could be pugnacious and aggressive, but was recognized as a 'gentle giant'. He was an accomplished horseman and rifle-shot, and also a fine tenor, flautist and clarinet player. He belonged to the Presbyterian Church. Quickly able to absorb information, he knew what he wanted politically and usually 'preferred to drive over obstacles to achievement rather than circumvent them'. Thorby died on 1 January 1973 at Wahroonga, Sydney, and was cremated. Two daughters of his first marriage survived him.

U. R. Ellis, *The Country Party* (Melb, 1958) and *A history of the Australian Country Party* (Melb, 1963); D. Aitkin, *The colonel* (Canb, 1969); P. Hasluck, *The government and the people, 1939 1941* (Canb, 1952); *Country Party J*, Apr-Nov 1938; *Country Life*, 3 Aug 1934, *SMH*, 4 Jan 1973; information from Mrs S. Beeman, Roseville, Syd.

IAN CARNELL

THORNBER, CATHERINE MARIA (1812?-1894) and her daughters CATHERINE MARIA (1837-1924), RACHEL ANN (1839-1930) and ELLEN (1851-1947) were schoolmistresses. Mrs Thornber, daughter of Charles Rowland, was born at Rodd, Herefordshire, England. She married Robert Thornber, hosier, and in 1839 they migrated with their six children to Adelaide where Robert prospered; in 1848 he donated land for the Anglican Church of St Michael, Mitcham. After his suicide on 29 December 1854, the stately Mrs Thornber opened a school at Mitcham in 1855. Relocated at Unley Park, it became one of the city's best-known academies for young ladies. Its pupils were the daughters of the middle class, especially of professional men and Anglican clergy who provided patronage to support the Thornbers' goal of a broad, liberal, secondary education.

Athough Unley Park School's reputation was quickly established, its zenith occurred under Miss Catherine, born on 17 November 1837 at Harpurhey, near Manchester, Lancashire. A music governess in private homes, she became the school's headmistress after her mother's death in Adelaide on 14 May 1894. Ellen, born on 7 September 1851 at Mitcham, was then in England, attending conferences, visiting leading girls' schools and assessing educational trends. Catherine made a similar trip six years later. In its methods and curricula the Thornbers' school was among South Australia's most progressive: it offered chemistry, physiology, geology and botany, taught by university-educated women. By 1898 it had an enrolment of 125 pupils. Preparation for the university was emphasized, but the school's successes there did not prevent the sisters from deploring the university's restrictive entrance requirements.

With buildings and equipment worth £4000, Unley Park School had an imposing appearance. Its teaching reflected the owners' interest in method: geological excursions, lantern-slides acquired by Miss Ellen in England and a skeleton (kept behind a satin curtain) enlivened senior lessons; in 1894 pupils had studied history, geography and literature by following Miss Ellen's journey overseas. German was taught and French was popular: one teacher was sent to Paris to study for a year as a means to 'keep us in touch with the old land and its modern systems'. Some of Adelaide's leaders in art, music and elocution taught at the school, while club-swinging, drill, tennis, cricket and swimming were also provided.

Because the Thornbers espoused 'the glorious principles of Froebel', in the kindergarten (which included boys) time was devoted to structured play; the sisters supported Lillian De Lissa [q.v.8], an advocate of Montessori's system, who stayed with them on her return from England. With her, Miss Catherine was a promoter of the Kindergarten Union of South Australia.

The sisters' personalities differed. The devout Rachel, born on 3 March 1839 at Harpurhey, was afflicted with a stutter; overshadowed by the others, she ran the boarding-house. She died at home on 4 February 1930. Catherine was noted for 'the sweetness of her disposition': small, dainty and precise, she generally wore black, corded silk, and often supervised the lessons of gentlemen teachers. The youngest, Ellen, was an awe-inspiring figure. Absorbed by educational theory and practice, she had attended the university in 1880 and 1885-86, and the (teachers') Training College. She taught (1880-86) and was acting headmistress in 1885 at the Advanced School for Girls. She died at home on 18 March 1947. The family were well-known in Adelaide as hostesses to governors,

bishops and clergy. Embodying their period's refinement and values, they were conscious of the challenges and difficulties imposed by distance from England.

The school began to fail with the spread of government secondary education and the sisters' increasing age. In 1907 they handed over to a former staff member, Caroline Jacob [q.v.9], then headmistress of Tormore House; she remained in charge until Unley Park School closed in 1911. Its unusual longevity, its quality and, above all, the personalities of the Thornbers had made it a leading school, although it did not make the owners rich. All four lived to advanced years in their home at 39 Thornber Street, Unley Park. The Thornber bursary for women at the University of Adelaide commemorates Miss Catherine who died at home on 30 September 1924.

H. Jones, *Nothing seemed impossible* (Brisb, 1985); *Register* (Adel), 16, 17 May 1894; *Observer* (Adel), 19 May, 29 Dec 1894, 24 Dec 1898, 23 Dec 1899, 6 Dec 1924; *Advertiser* (Adel), 4 Oct 1924.

JANET SCARFE

THORPE, HARRY (1886-1918), soldier, was born on 7 October 1886 at Lake Tyers Mission Station, Victoria, fourth surviving child of William Thorpe, a labourer and an Aborigine of the Brabuwooloong tribe, and his wife Lilian, née Wilson, who was to die in 1889. Raised on his father's ten-acre (4 ha) farm at Lakes Entrance, he helped to cultivate beans and potatoes and to plant fruit trees, and often supplemented the family food supply by hunting kangaroos and wallabies. He also worked as a labourer; at times he and his father dug graves, at others they stripped wattle bark for sale to tanneries. On 3 August 1905 at Lake Tyers he married with Anglican rites Julia Scott, a domestic servant; they lived on the family farm in a house built from bark and palings. They had two sons, the younger of whom died in childhood. Thorpe trained as a hurdler on a track near his house, coached by his brother-in-law Percy Pepper.

On 12 February 1916 Thorpe enlisted in the Australian Imperial Force at Sale. He embarked for overseas service in April, joining the 7th Battalion in France in July. He was wounded in action at Pozières on 19 August and did not rejoin his unit until November. Promoted lance corporal in January 1917, he was again wounded at Bullecourt on 29 April, but a month later returned to duty. Well regarded in his unit as a footballer and athlete at brigade or divisional sports, he was also noted as a scout.

On 4-5 October Thorpe was conspicuous for his courage and leadership during operations at Broodseinde, near Ypres, Belgium. In mopping up enemy resistance in dug-outs and pillboxes, he displayed initiative and disregard of all danger which inspired the men he commanded. For his 'splendid example', he was promoted corporal on 5 October. He was also awarded the Military Medal, although the recommendation originally sent from his unit had been for the Distinguished Conduct Medal.

During an advance on 9 August 1918 at Lihons Wood, south-west of Vauvillers, France, a stretcher-bearer found Thorpe shot in the stomach. He died shortly after being taken to a dressing station near Bayonvillers and was buried in Heath military cemetery, Harbonnières. His friend, William Rawlings [q.v.11], another Aborigine who had won the M.M., was killed in action the same day.

P. Pepper, *You are what you make yourself to be* (Melb, 1980); *London Gazette*, 14 Dec 1917; *Sabretache*, Oct 1977; *Argus*, 10 Sept 1918; information from Mr W. Jamieson, 7th Battalion AIF Assn, Melb.   C. D. COULTHARD-CLARK

THOW, WILLIAM (1842-1926), railway engineer, was born on 29 June 1842 at West Derby, Lancashire, England, son of John Thow, engineer, and his wife Mary Nicholson, née Milne. After attending schools at Carlisle, he worked under his father on the Lancaster and Carlisle Railway. William was a pupil of Alexander Allan on the Scottish Central Railway before being employed as a draftsman with Dübs Locomotive Works, Glasgow. When Allan was made general manager of the Worcester Engine Works Co., Thow joined him, became chief draftsman and worked at Crewe under John Ramsbottom. In London on 28 March 1871 Thow married a widow Agnes Noble (d. 1897), née Forrester, then went to Egypt as inspector and mechanical assistant to (Sir) John Fowler.

Appointed locomotive engineer for the South Australian Railways in 1876, Thow was hampered in that colony by insufficient funds, gauge problems and political interference. He attempted to modernize and rationalize obsolete and diverse locomotive stock. On the narrow gauge he introduced, in 1878, thirty-five 'W' class, and, in 1886, 134 'Y' class engines. He was less successful on the broad gauge, but his engines included twenty-two 'Q' class of 1885 and thirty 4-6-0 'R' class of 1886; the latter formed the basis of continuing South Australian locomotive development until the 1920s.

In 1888 Thow was asked by the New South Wales government to report on its locomotives and rolling-stock. He criticized previous policy and condemned a situation which mirrored his early experience in South Australia. There were a large number of classes, often with few locomotives, and many were obsolete. Thow was appointed locomotive engineer on the New South Wales Government Railways in 1889 and embarked on a massive programme of modernization and standardization. In 1892 the first of 161 advanced P6 (C32) class passenger locomotives was introduced. The standard goods T524 (D50) class was introduced in 1896 and eventually totalled 280. The S636 (C30) class suburban tank-engines followed in 1903 and 145 were built. All three classes continued in use until the State gradually abandoned railway steam-engines after World War II. The P6 class, well to the forefront of passenger locomotives when introduced, became world famous.

The growth of the system and of traffic did not allow Thow to achieve his objectives. Far too many of the earlier locomotives remained, and twenty goods engines and twelve passenger engines were purchased from the Baldwin Co. while Thow was overseas. In 1892 he was involved in two royal commissions. The first, which inquired into alleged defects of the American locomotives, saw him in the role of expert witness rather than culprit; the second investigated charges by W. F. Schey against E. M. G. Eddy [qq.v.11,8] in which Thow was accused of belonging to a 'ring' with Eddy, Fowler and the English locomotive manufacturers, Beyer, Peacock & Co. The charges, largely political, were dismissed.

For the rest of his career Thow built up his locomotive stud, improving and standardizing the carriage and wagon stock, and creating the facilities to operate and maintain them. He gave the railways a look and character which lasted until the 1950s. The dogbox carriages, introduced for express trains, were eventually seen throughout the network and were only retired from branch lines in the 1970s. On 21 January 1901 Thow married a widow with four children, Margaret Elphinstone Simpson, née Monteith, at Elsternwick, Victoria. He retired on 13 June 1911. A member of the institutions of Civil and Mechanical engineers, London, he also belonged to the American Railway Master Mechanics' Association.

Survived by his wife, and by a daughter of his first marriage, Thow died on 10 March 1926 at his Warrawee home, Sydney, and was buried in the Anglican section of Waverley cemetery; his estate was sworn for probate at £15 962. His influence on Australian locomotive development was enormous. When the trans-continental railway was completed in 1917, it was operated by a variant of his P6 class. Until the introduction of diesels, Thow's designs operated on five Australian systems.

Cyclopedia of N.S.W. (Syd, 1907); Aust Railway Hist Soc, *A century plus of locomotives* (Syd, 1965); O. S. Nock, *Great steam locomotives of all time* (NY,

1977); J. Westwood, *Locomotive designers in the age of steam* (Lond, 1978); R. G. Preston, *Standards in steam* (Syd, 1985 *and* 1987); R. E. Fluck et al, *Steam locomotives and railcars of the South Australian Railways* (Roseworth, SA, 1986); *V&P* (LA NSW), 1892-93, 5, pp 149, 543; *NSW Railway and Tramway Mag*, 1 Dec 1920, p 768.

J. D. WALKER

THRELFALL, SIR RICHARD (1861-1932), physicist and chemical engineer, was born on 14 August 1861 at Hollowforth, near Preston, Lancashire, England, eldest son of Richard Threlfall, a small landholder, wine merchant and sometime mayor of Preston, and his second wife Sarah Jane, née Mason. Richard was educated at Clifton College, Bristol, where he shared a study with (Field Marshal Lord) Haig, and at Gonville and Caius College, Cambridge (B.A., 1884; M.A., 1888). He also read mathematics privately with W. J. Ibbetson and, midway through his course, studied at the University of Strasbourg under August Kundt and Rudolph Fittig. On graduating with first-class honours in the natural sciences tripos, he lectured at his college and worked as a demonstrator in the Cavendish Laboratory under his friend J. J. Thomson.

In 1886 Threlfall was appointed to the chair of physics at the University of Sydney. He was exactly the right person to bring its somewhat moribund teaching into line with the best modern practice, for his training had instilled in him the latest vision of the subject: a body of knowledge expressed in the language of mathematics, but grounded upon laboratory practice characterized by ever-increasing precision of measurement. Despite having lost several fingers while experimenting with explosives, Threlfall was an outstanding manipulator of apparatus whom Thomson regarded as 'one of the best experimenters I ever met'.

Fired with a passion for research and a determination to create in Sydney a major centre of physical inquiry, immediately upon his arrival Threlfall launched an extensive series of projects using equipment he had bought, without authorization, in Europe. By sheer force of personality, he soon prevailed upon the university and the colonial government to provide him with a splendid new building (completed in 1888) in which to house it. Threlfall's research developed along three separate lines. One, on explosives and the propagation of explosions, led to his being used as a consultant by the local military authorities. Another involved the electrical properties of dielectric materials such as sulphur and selenium. Finally, Threlfall and his student and friend J. A. Pollock [q.v.11] developed a quartz thread torsion balance for use

as a gravity meter, and then used this to make measurements in a wide range of eastern Australian localities.

Threlfall's success in developing a programme of research inspired his fellow physics professors (Sir) Thomas Lyle in Melbourne and (Sir) William Bragg [qq.v.10,7] in Adelaide to do likewise. The emergence of new technologies, especially electrical power technology, was giving physics an increasingly utilitarian aspect. Threlfall established a lucrative business in the early 1890s as a consultant to municipal authorities and private companies. He also sought to establish a course in electrical engineering at the university, but was frustrated in this aim, as well as in his larger ambitions for his department, by the bank crash of 1893 and its aftermath.

A born leader, Threlfall was short, with a powerful physique and vigorous personality, and could sway a crowd with his oratory. He was a formidable Rugby blue who claimed that 'only an aversion from treading on a man's face had prevented him from playing for England'; in Sydney he turned out with the university team. He loved shooting, fishing and the outdoors, belonged to the Union Club and was 'one of the most sociable and "clubbable" of men', a quality that stood him in good stead when it came to extracting from the New South Wales government the money he needed for his new laboratory. Threlfall advised the government on sewage disposal and chaired two royal commissions (1896-98) inquiring into the causes of spontaneous combustion of coal cargoes in ships. His mastery of technique is amply displayed in his book, *On laboratory arts* (London, 1898), illustrated by his wife. On 18 January 1890 Threlfall had married English-born Evelyn Agnes Baird (d. 1929) at St John's Anglican Church, Hobart. They had met while she was visiting her sister Lillian, wife of Bernhard Wise [q.v.]. Evelyn published two books of poetry and was also a talented artist.

Secretary of section A at the inaugural (1888) meeting of the Australasian Association for the Advancement of Science, Threlfall presided over the section in 1890. He was president of the Royal Society of New South Wales (1894-95) and one of the few consistent supporters of Lawrence Hargrave [q.v.9] in his efforts to design a heavier-than-air flying machine. Threlfall's 'wild prophecy' that Hertz's newly discovered electromagnetic radiation might be useful in communication affected the wording of section 51 (v) in the Australian Constitution.

Through scientific correspondents in Europe and North America, of whom Thomson was by far the most important to him, Threlfall kept abreast of developments in his field. Leaving Australia in 1898, he found a congenial position as director of research with Albright & Wilson, chemical manufacturers, at Oldbury, England. Shortly afterwards he joined their board and was elected a fellow of the Royal Society, London, in 1899.

He was responsible for major improvements in his company's production methods. With the outbreak of hostilities in 1914, Threlfall was completely occupied in important war-related work, especially on the use of phosphorus in smoke-screens and in tracer ammunition. He served on the Admiralty's Board of Invention and Research (working closely with Admiral Lord Fisher), the Advisory Council on Scientific and Industrial Research and numerous other wartime science-related committees. He was also part-time director of the Chemical Research Laboratory, Teddington. Appointed K.B.E. in 1917 (G.B.E., 1927), he was awarded the Society of Chemical Industry's gold medal in 1929.

Following World War I, Threlfall remained active in public life while maintaining his position at Albright & Wilson. In poor health after a stroke in 1929, he died at his home at Edgbaston, Birmingham, on 10 July 1932. Four sons and two daughters survived him.

DNB, 1931-40; R. E. Threlfall, *100 years of phosphorus making, 1851-1951* (Birmingham, Eng, 1951); *Nature* (Lond), 130 (1932), p 228; *Obituary notices of fellows of the Roy Soc*, 1 (1932), p 45; *J of the Chemical Soc* (Lond), 1937, p 186; *Notes and Records of Roy Soc of London*, 16 (1961), p 234; *Records of the Aust Academy of Science*, 1, no 3, 1968, p 36; *Hist Records of Aust Science*, 6, no 3, 1986, p 333; Rayleigh papers (Rayleigh Archive, Hanscomb Air Force Base, Massachusetts, USA); Threlfall papers and correspondence, 1870-1932 (City of Birmingham Reference Lib, Eng) *and* 1887-98 (Univ Syd Archives); H. Hartley, *Sir Richard Threlfall, G.B.E., F.R.S.* (ts, Threlfall papers, Univ Syd Archives); J. J. Thomson papers (Cambridge Univ Lib, Eng).   R. W. HOME

THRING, FRANCIS WILLIAM (1882-1936), entrepreneur, was born on 2 December 1882 at Wentworth, New South Wales, son of William Francis Thring, labourer, and his wife Angelina, née McDonald, both native-born. Little is known of his early years; he became a conjurer in the outback before starting Biograph Pictures in Tasmania. He worked as a bootmaker at Gawler, South Australia, where, on 26 December 1904, he married Grace Wight (d. 1920) with Presbyterian forms.

About 1911 Thring began his Melbourne theatrical career as a projectionist at Kreitmayer's Waxworks. He opened the Paramount Theatre in 1915 and in 1918 became managing director of J. C. Williamson [q.v.6] Films Ltd. After this company merged in 1926 with Hoyts Pty Ltd to form Hoyts Theatres Ltd, Thring became its dynamic managing director.

In 1930 he sold his large holdings in Hoyts to Fox Film Corporation and announced his intention to establish the talking film industry in Australia under the trade name (from his initials) Efftee Film Productions. The versatile showman Tom Holt (father of Prime Minister Harold Holt) became his manager. Using the derelict His Majesty's Theatre as a studio, Thring imported the latest RCA sound equipment and made his first feature, *Diggers*, starring Pat Hanna [q.v.9] in 1931. It was well received. However, Thring's *The sentimental bloke* (1932) was, according to Ken Hall, a 'pale shadow of the original' Longford [q.v.10] version. *His royal highness* (1932), Australia's first musical film to star Thring's protégé George Wallace [q.v.], succeeded at home and abroad.

Visiting Britain in 1932-33, Thring sold Efftee's entire output: seven features, nine shorts and a series about the Great Barrier Reef made with Noel Monkman. On his return, Thring moved his studio to the Wattle Path Dance Palais, St Kilda. In 1933-35 he also promoted Australian theatre; amongst other plays, he successfully staged the Australian musical, *Collits' Inn*, starring Gladys Moncrieff [q.v.10], in Melbourne and Sydney. In March 1935 he purchased the operating rights to 3XY radio in Melbourne.

From 1932 Thring had been the leader of a campaign for a quota for Australian films. Two years later he suspended Efftee's operations, announcing that resumption would depend upon the introduction of an effective quota system in Victoria. After New South Wales passed its Cinematograph Films (Australian Quota) Act in September 1935, Thring resumed production in February 1936, in Sydney, becoming chairman of directors of Mastercraft Film Corporation Ltd while remaining managing director of Efftee Film Productions. In March he sailed for Hollywood in search of scriptwriters and actors. Returning in June, he died of cancer on 1 July 1936 in East Melbourne and was buried in Burwood cemetery. He was survived by a daughter of his first marriage, by his second wife and helpmate Olive, née Kreitmayer, whom he had married with Anglican rites at Christ Church, South Yarra, on 25 April 1921, and by their 10-year-old son, the actor Frank Thring.

Contemporaries lamented the loss to theatre and the film industry through Thring's early death. Gladys Moncrieff recalled him as 'a gentle and exceptionally kind man' who 'knew the theatre and what he wanted he eventually got'. Ken Hall considered him the first Australian to 'make professional sound feature films'. If some doubted his artistic ability, all praised his skills as a producer. He was, said Monkman, a man 'whose big body was matched by his courage, vision and ambition'.

J. Baxter, *Australian cinema* (Syd, 1970); E. Reade, *Australian silent films* (Melb, 1970), and *The talkies era* (Melb, 1972); G. Moncrieff, *My life of song* (Syd, 1971); E. Samuels, *If the cap fits* (Syd, 1972); K. G. Hall, *Directed by Ken G. Hall* (Melb, 1977); A. Pike and R. Cooper, *Australian film, 1900-1977* (Melb, 1980); G. Shirley and B. Adams, *Australian cinema* (Syd, 1983); *Woman's World*, 1 May 1932; *SMH*, 26 Aug 1978.

J. P. HOLROYD

THRING, WALTER HUGH CHARLES SAMUEL (1873-1949), naval officer, was born on 30 May 1873 at Bradford, Wiltshire, England, son of Rev. John Charles Thring, and his wife Lydia Eliza Dyer, née Meredith. In 1886 Thring entered H.M.S. *Britannia*, passing out two years later as midshipman. After heading the examination lists, he served from 1893 as gunnery lieutenant in the Channel, Pacific and China squadrons and the Mediterranean Fleet. He was promoted commander in 1903, became flag commander to Admiral Lord Charles Beresford in 1908 and shared in the admiral's eclipse in 1909. Thring's lines for Dumaresq's [q.v.8] rate of change of bearing instrument were adopted by the Royal Navy's gunnery. He chose early retirement in February 1911.

Next year the Australian Naval Board was looking for a gunnery expert as assistant to the first naval member, Rear Admiral Sir William Creswell [q.v.8], and in December Thring accepted the appointment to the Royal Australian Navy. On 11 January 1913 at St Mary's Church, Kilburn, London, he married Dorothy Wooldridge and on the 28th they left England; their three children were born in Australia. Shortly after Thring's arrival in Melbourne the Naval Board required him to accompany the second naval member and the chief of the general staff, Brigadier General J. M. Gordon [q.v.9], to northern Australia and Papua. Seeing the futility of such a mission without a strategy for the naval defence of Australia, Thring advocated an early form of forward defence against Japan. He proposed naval bases at Bynoe Harbour, Northern Territory, and at the southeastern tip of New Guinea. He appreciated the necessity for an Australian naval staff, developed a system of naval intelligence and produced a comprehensive war book which was completed only a few weeks before August 1914. His foresight meant that Australia entered World War I with a high degree of naval preparedness.

Insisting on the priority of eliminating German warships in the Pacific, Thring had successfully pressed the Naval Board to take precautionary steps on the eve of war; on 4 August he secured his minister's support for a request to the Admiralty to change the war orders of the battle-cruiser H.M.A.S. *Australia*. The result was the speedy appearance of Australian warships in Rabaul harbour. Frustrated by orders from London to seize Germany's Pacific possessions, Thring never understood or excused British disregard of the Australian navy's wish to act with maximum strategic orthodoxy.

Acting second naval member for three months from October 1914, Thring was promoted captain and appointed director of (naval) ordnance from January 1915. As director of war staff he became the genius of whatever wartime autonomy the Naval Board preserved. In the Navy Office A. W. Jose [q.v.9] was required to analyse the history of the R.A.N.'s wartime operations. He and Thring prepared for Prime Minister W. M. Hughes [q.v.9] the navy's views on post-war naval policy in the Pacific.

The collection of Pacific naval intelligence continued and an expansion of naval censorship and counter-intelligence work led to conflicts with other surveillance organizations. In March 1918 the head of the Counter Espionage Bureau, (Sir) George Steward [q.v.], complained that—according to Admiral Creswell —'practically the whole of the administrative work of the Commonwealth Navy had been and was being carried out by Captain Thring'. Before Lord Jellicoe arrived in Australia, Thring's health broke down, but Jellicoe's reports reflected much of Thring's strategy.

Routine tasks were found for him in England and Australia until his appointment in early 1920 as Australia's naval liaison officer with the Admiralty in London. In 1922 his wife died. Soon afterwards Thring was eased out of his post and he resigned from the R.A.N. He had been appointed C.B.E. in 1920. Left with his young children, for a short time Thring farmed in Gloucestershire and then established a school at Leiston, Suffolk, in which village on 11 July 1927 he married a widow Syria Elmslie Pearson, née Horwood. Survived by his wife, and by two daughters and a son of his first marriage, he died on 17 January 1949 at Bristol.

A. W. Jose, *The Royal Australian Navy, 1914-1918* (Syd, 1928); E. T. Patterson (ed), *The Jellicoe papers vol II 1916-1935* (Lond, 1968); F. Cain, *The origins of political surveillance in Australia* (Syd, 1983); Hughes *and* Latham *and* Piesse papers (NL); Jose papers (AWM); MP 1049/1, 15/054, 18/0238, 18/0736, 21/0614 (AA, Melb); information from Cdr A. W. Grazebrook, Mansfield, Vic, and Prof M. W. Thring, Brundish, Suffolk, Eng.

ROSS LAMONT

THROSSELL, GEORGE (1840-1910), merchant and premier, was born on 24 May 1840 at Fermoy, County Cork, Ireland, eldest son of Michael Throssell, mail clerk, and his wife Jane. As a guard in the convict transport *Scindian*, Michael brought his family to Western Australia in 1850 and became a sergeant of police in Perth. George was sent to school. With the death of both his parents in 1854-55, he found himself rearing a younger brother and sister. He sailed to Adelaide, sent them on to Sydney to be raised by a relation, and returned alone and poor to Perth. Having joined Walter Padbury's [q.v.5] mercantile firm, he spent evenings at the Swan River Literary and Debating Society where Joseph Reilly [q.v.11] extended his education. About 1860, while manager of the firm's premises at Guildford, Throssell met Anne Morrell, daughter of an early settler and farmer in the Northam district; George married Anne on 6 June 1861 in St George's Cathedral, Perth.

Next year Throssell opened his own store in Northam's main street. Combining financial expertise, hard work and drive, he became the region's most successful businessman. He gave credit to small-farmers, bought and sold stock, crops and sandalwood, speculated in land and was a building contractor. As the dominating personality in the community life of the district he loved, he dreamed of opening the country to small-farmers. An active Anglican, he was a foundation member of Northam Mechanics' Institute and of the local temperance movement and lodges. He sat on the School Board, Road Board, Farmers' Club and Settlers' Association. A founder of Northam Municipal Council in 1879, he was mayor in 1887-94. Partly due to Throssell, Northam gained a branch of the Avon Valley railway in 1886.

From 1890 he represented Northam in the new Legislative Assembly, holding the seat until 1904 and only once being opposed in five elections. He supported (Sir) John Forrest's [q.v.8] government and influenced the decision in 1892 to choose Northam as the starting point of the railway to the eastern goldfields. The town grew to be the principal centre of the Avon Valley and that made Throssell wealthy; his enterprises expanded into pastoral and metropolitan ventures. In parliament he advocated land reform, supporting the 1893 Homesteads Act and the 1894 Agricultural Bank Act. As commissioner for crown lands from March 1897, he used the 1896 Homesteads Land Purchase Act to enable the government to acquire and subdivide a number of large estates.

'The lion of Northam' had the luxuriant silver hair of a patriarch, a buoyant and assertive optimism and 'a habit of placing a hand on your shoulder when speaking'. He kept a shrewd eye on the main chance. Deafness led him to construct a large cardboard 'sounding-board' which he held against his chest with one corner of it in his mouth: he rid himself of tedious deputations by removing it to terminate the interview. He succeeded Forrest as premier on 15 February 1901, but Throssell's government was short-lived. Although a competent administrator, he was not a strong political leader and his deafness imposed limitations. The factions supporting his party drifted apart and Throssell lost his majority. At the April election many of his followers lost their seats. On 27 May he resigned and returned to the back-bench.

Three years later he retired to Fermoy, his mansion on the hill overlooking Northam. His wife died in 1906. Next year Throssell won the Legislative Council seat of East Province and in 1909 was appointed C.M.G. He fell down a staircase at his home, jarring his spine, died four days later on 30 August 1910 and was buried in Northam cemetery. His estate was sworn for probate at £50 879. He was survived by six daughters and five sons of his fourteen children, the most famous of whom was Hugo Throssell [q.v.].

W. B. Kimberly, *History of West Australia* (Melb, 1897); Truthful Thomas, *Through the spy-glass* (Perth, 1905); O. L. B., *George Throssell, an appreciation* (Northam, WA, 1910); J. S. Battye (ed), *Cyclopedia of Western Australia*, 2 (Perth, 1913); J. Kirwan, *My life's adventure* (Lond, 1936); D. S. Garden, *Northam, an Avon Valley history* (Melb, 1979); *WA Bulletin*, 9 June 1888; *Northam Advertiser*, 19 Aug 1905, 23 May 1906, 17 Aug 1907, 31 Aug, 17 Sept 1910; *Western Mail* (Perth), 10 Sept 1910; E. Bartlett-Day, Reminiscences *and* G. Throssell estate papers (mss, BL).

DONALD S. GARDEN

THROSSELL, HUGO VIVIAN HOPE (1884-1933), soldier and farmer, was born on 26 October 1884 at Northam, Western Australia, youngest son of George Throssell [q.v.], storekeeper and later premier, and his wife Anne, née Morrell. One of fourteen children, Hugo was educated at Prince Alfred College, Adelaide, where he captained the football team and became a champion athlete and boxer. He then worked as a jackeroo on cattle stations in the north of the State. In 1912 he and his brother, Frank Erick (Ric) Cottrell (b. 1881), took up land at Cowcowing in the Western Australian wheatbelt. Severe drought during the next two years strengthened the bond between them; they were later described as 'David and Jonathan' in their devotion to one another. Hugo was tall, with a long face and strong features.

With the outbreak of war Hugo and Ric joined the 10th Light Horse Regiment, formed in October 1914. Hugo was commissioned as second lieutenant and remained in

Egypt when the 10th was sent to Gallipoli in May 1915. He landed on Gallipoli on 4 August, three days before the charge at the Nek—'that FOOL charge' as he described it —when 9 officers and 73 men of his regiment were killed within minutes. Throssell was one of the leaders of the fourth and last line of attacking troops which was recalled after having advanced only a few yards. This experience increased his eagerness to prove himself in battle. He wanted to avenge the 10th L.H.R. which, like so many of the Anzac troops, was battle-worn, sick and depleted. His chance came later that month at Hill 60 during a postponed attempt by British and Anzac troops to widen the strip of foreshore between the two bridgeheads at Anzac and Suvla by capturing the hills near Anafarta. Hill 60, a low knoll, lay about half a mile (0.8 km) from the beach. Hampered by confusion and lack of communication between the various flanks, the battle had been raging for a week with heavy losses.

At 1 a.m. by moonlight on 29 August the 10th Light Horse was brought into action to take a long trench, 100 yards (91 m) of which was held by Turkish troops on the summit of Hill 60. As a guard, Throssell killed five Turks while his men constructed a barricade across their part of the trench. When a fierce bomb fight began, 'a kind of tennis over the traverse and sandbags', Throssell and his soldiers held their bombs on short fuse until the last possible moment before hurling them at the enemy on the other side of the barricade. Throughout the remainder of the night both sides threw more than 3000 bombs, the Western Australians picking up the bombs thrown at them by the Turks and hurling them back. Towards dawn the Turks made three rushes at the Australian trench, but were stopped by showers of bombs and heavy rifle-fire. Throssell, who at one stage was in sole command, was wounded twice. His face covered in blood from bomb splinters in his forehead, he repeatedly yelled encouragement to his men. For his part in the battle Hugo Throssell was awarded the Victoria Cross. It was the first V.C. to be won by a Western Australian in the war.

Evacuated to hospital in England, Throssell was promoted captain and joined his regiment in Egypt. He was wounded in April 1917 at the 2nd battle of Gaza where his brother Ric was killed. On the night that Ric disappeared, Hugo crawled across the battlefield under enemy fire, searching in vain for his brother among the dead and dying, and whistling for him with the same signal as they had used when boys. Hugo returned to his regiment for the final offensives in Palestine and led the 10th Light Horse guard of honour at the fall of Jerusalem.

On 28 January 1919 in the Collins Street registry office, Melbourne, Throssell married the Australian author Katharine Susannah Prichard [q.v.11] whom he had met in England. They settled on a 40-acre (16 ha) mixed farm at Greenmount, near Perth. His wife wrote that those early years of marriage with Hugo, whom she called Jim, were her happiest. When she became a foundation member of the Communist Party of Australia in 1920, Hugo joined her as a speaker supporting unemployed and striking workers. He claimed that the war had made him a socialist and a pacifist. The combination of her award-winning novels and Communism, and his Victoria Cross, brought them fame and notoriety. Hugo acted as soldiers' representative on the Returned Soldiers' Land Settlement Board, became a real estate agent and worked temporarily in the Department of Agriculture in Western Australia.

Hard times came in the Depression. Katharine believed that her political activities lost Hugo his job with the settlement board, and that his passion to own land led him to borrow recklessly from the banks. He joined the search for gold at Larkinville in the early 1930s. When that proved unsuccessful, he devised a scheme which he hoped would prove a money-spinner. While Katharine was on a six-month visit to Russia, he organized a rodeo on his Greenmount property on a Sunday, not knowing that it was illegal to charge entry fees on the sabbath. The only money Hugo raised from the 2000 people who attended was a meagre silver collection for charity. The episode plunged him further into debt and shattered his optimism.

Imagining that he could better provide for his wife and 11-year-old son if he left them a war service pension, he shot himself on 19 November 1933 at Greenmount. Friends blamed his melancholy on an attack of meningitis at Gallipoli and saw it as the cause of his suicide. He was buried with full military honours in the Anglican section of Karrakatta cemetery, Perth.

In 1954 a memorial to him was unveiled at Greenmount, opposite his home. In 1983 his son Ric presented Hugo's Victoria Cross to the People for Nuclear Disarmament. The Returned Services League of Australia bought the medal and presented it to the Australian War Memorial, Canberra. A pencil portrait of Hugo Throssell by the Australian war artist, George Lambert [q.v.9], is also held there.

A. C. N. Olden, *Westralian cavalry in the war* (Melb, 1921); H. S. Gullett, *The A.I.F. in Sinai and Palestine* (Syd, 1923); C. E. W. Bean, *The story of Anzac*, 2 (Syd, 1924); K. S. Prichard, *Child of the hurricane* (Syd, 1963); R. Throssell, *My father's son* (Melb, 1989); *West Australian*, 29 May 1916, 21 Nov 1933, 20 Feb 1954; information from Mr R. Throssell, Canb, ACT.   SUZANNE WELBORN

THROWER, THOMAS HENRY (1870-1917), upholsterer and politician, was born on 28 June 1870 at Surry Hills, Sydney, son of Frederick Thrower, a bootmaker from London, and his native-born wife Mary Anne, née Comerford. Thomas attended Shoalhaven Public School and at 15 went to Sydney with his family; he hoped to study law, but was apprenticed to a cabinetmaker. W. A. Holman [q.v.9] was a workmate: they formed a lasting friendship.

A keen debater, Thrower honed his skills in the Catholic Young Men's Debating Club at St Peter's Church, Surry Hills. In the late 1880s he was involved in the amalgamation of several associated trades into the United Furniture Trade Society which faced strong competition from Chinese working more than the standard forty-eight hours a week at less than the union's pay rates. Thrower joined the Labor Party in 1891 and was a delegate on the Trades and Labor Council of New South Wales.

By 1900 he had been secretary and president of his union, vice-president and secretary of the Eight Hour (Day) Committee, and had become one of the leading unionists of the colony. When the T.L.C. was re-formed in February 1900 as the Sydney Labor Council, he became its first president and was secretary in 1901-04. On 30 January 1901 at St Peter's Church he married Catherine Newman. That year he told the royal commission investigating the operation of the factories and workshop law of Victoria that furniture workers in Sydney were still 'considerably' affected by Chinese who outnumbered 'European' cabinetmakers and worked about '60 hours' a week.

Thrower widened his Labor Party experience by membership of the central executive committee in 1900; he was also a member in 1902-06, 1908 and 1914-15. With political ambitions, he ran unsuccessfully for the Legislative Assembly at a by-election for Tamworth in April 1903 and for East Sydney against (Sir) George Reid [q.v.11] at the Federal general election in December. Thrower won the State seat of Macquarie next year; defeated in 1907, he regained it in 1910 and held it until his death.

As a country member who had vacated his city power base, Thrower could not rally sufficient support to enter the Labor cabinet; but he was chairman of committees in 1914-17, and was adept in the procedures and rules of the assembly. Generous and circumspect, he played an important role in consolidating his party's general electoral appeal in New South Wales. He bridged country and trade union interests, helping to ensure that rural issues were not overlooked and that contacts with the Labor Council were maintained. In addition, he stressed the significance of the Federal branch.

Opposed to conscription, Thrower did not follow Holman in 1916 when he was expelled and formed a National government. Holman, however, resisted pressure to campaign against him in Macquarie at the March 1917 elections. Thrower suffered severely from chronic nephritis from late 1915. He died at Redfern on 21 June 1917, survived by his wife, three sons and a daughter, and was buried in Waverley cemetery.

B. Nairn, *The 'Big Fella'* (Melb, 1986); *PP* (Vic), 1902-03, 2 (31); *Aust Worker*, 20 Aug 1904; *SMH*, 24 Feb 1913, 9 Jan 1914, 22 June 1917; *Freeman's J* (Syd), 28 June 1917.

BEDE NAIRN

THURGOOD, ALBERT JOHN (1874-1927), Australian Rules footballer, was born on 11 January 1874 in North Melbourne, son of John Joseph Thurgood, builder, and his wife Amelia Mary, née Buckland, both London born. He was educated at Brighton Grammar School.

In 1892 Thurgood joined the Essendon Australian Rules Football Club, winner of the Victorian Football Association premiership in 1891-94. He immediately became a key player in the side. Six feet (182.9 cm) tall and weighing twelve stone (76.2 kg), he usually played at centre-half-forward, but his versatility enabled him to be switched to any position on the ground. In an era of long kicking Thurgood became famous as the longest kick of all: he could regularly punt-kick over 80 yards (73.15 m) and drop-kick over 90 yards (82.3 m). One of his place-kicks (1899, with slight wind assistance) was measured at 107 yards 2 ft. 1 in. (98.48 m) and is still regarded as the record. For Essendon, in the three seasons from 1892 to 1894 in premiership matches he kicked 56, 64 and 63 goals from centre-half-forward.

To the consternation of supporters, Thurgood did not turn out with Essendon for four years from 1895 when he left Victoria for Western Australia to seek work. Having played for Fremantle, he returned to Melbourne in 1898 and next year resumed with Essendon which had become a member of the recently formed Victorian Football League. On 26 April 1899 he married with Methodist forms Ida Alma Mary Thomas at Fairfield. In the Essendon side he again became the dominant player. Three times champion of the colony (1893, 1894 and 1901), he was one of the greatest footballers the game has produced. He headed the goal-kicking list with 26 goals in 1900 and co-headed it in 1902 with 33. These levels were only half his goal tallies of association days: the more equal quality of sides in the league was revealed in more effective opposition.

The peak of Thurgood's career came with the 1901 grand final against Collingwood, played on 7 September at the South Melbourne ground before a crowd of some 30 000. In one of his finest performances he kicked three of his side's six goals and was a major contributor to Essendon's victory. Next year Thurgood was suspended for three matches for striking opposition players. He played in the grand final, but only scored one goal in the match won by Collingwood. After three non-playing years, Thurgood came back for a few games in 1906; he was not particularly successful and retired permanently from football.

A better than average cricketer and golfer, after his retirement Thurgood became active in horse-racing, for some years as a bookmaker and subsequently as an owner. He ran a number of successful horses, including Amazonia which won the Bagot Handicap in 1921 and was placed third in the Melbourne Cup that year. Thurgood died in the Alfred Hospital, Prahran, on 8 May 1927, as a result of a motor car collision, and was buried with Anglican rites in Brighton cemetery. His wife and two daughters survived him.

G. Atkinson (comp), *The Courage book of VFL finals, 1897-1972* (Melb, 1973) and *Everything you've ever wanted to know about Australian Rules football* (Melb, 1982); M. Maplestone, *Flying high* (Melb, 1983); *Age,* 9 Sept 1901, 22 Sept 1902, 9 May 1927; *Argus,* 9 Sept 1901, 22 Sept 1902, 14 May, 3, 28, 29 June 1927; *Herald* (Melb), 9 May 1927.   JOHN H. REEVES

THURSTON, FREDERICK ARTHUR (1893-1918), clerk and soldier, was born on 24 September 1893 at Summer Hill, Sydney, second child of James Thurston, monumental mason, and his wife Sophia, née Ashworth, both English born. Employed as a clerk, Thurston enlisted in the Australian Imperial Force on 10 April 1916 and was posted as a reinforcement to the 33rd Battalion. He arrived in England on 11 October and joined his battalion, part of the newly formed 3rd Division. The 33rd reached France on 22 November and entered the line in the quiet sector at Chappelle d'Armentières. For the next few months it took part in raids on German positions and maintained its defences against determined counter-attacks. The trenches in the Armentières area were long established, but winter service was still harsh.

In June 1917 the battalion fought in the battle of Messines, Belgium. Thurston won the Military Medal for conspicuous bravery at Messines Ridge on 19 June during operations which cost his battalion 11 officers and 357 men. Soon after the battle he was appointed temporary corporal and on 4 July this rank was confirmed. On the 28th he was wounded in action near Messines and sent to hospital. He rejoined his unit, then at Campagne Lez Boulonnais, on 8 November and took part in the winter operations on the Somme, France. On 4-5 March 1918 he was a member of a party which raided trenches near Warneton. Thurston had charge of a Lewis-gun covering the deepest point of penetration of the German trench system. The enemy counter-attacked fiercely during the night; with carefully and coolly directed Lewis-gun fire, supported by rifle grenades and rifle fire, Thurston broke up the German attack, thus ensuring the safety of the raiding Australians. He was awarded a Bar to his M.M. for his gallantry during this operation.

A second Bar followed on 30 March during the counter-attack by the 33rd Battalion on the Marcelcave-Aubercourt line. Although badly wounded in the thigh, Thurston led his men forward through heavy machine-gun and rifle fire, refusing to be evacuated until his company had consolidated on recaptured ground. He resumed duty on 16 May and in July-August attended a course at an officer cadet unit. On 30 August 1918 he was killed in operations near Mont St Quentin. He was unmarried.

Thurston was a cheerful and optimistic leader whose steadfast qualities were an inspiration to his mates. In a few months of active campaigning he had been thrice decorated (with a rare combination of medals) and twice wounded. Death intervened to deny him the advancement in rank which his achievements would have warranted.

C. E. W. Bean, *The A.I.F. in France,* 1917-18, (Syd, 1933, 1937, 1942); War diary, 33rd Battalion, AIF (AWM).   A. J. SWEETING

THWAITES, FREDERICK JOSEPH (1908-1979), novelist, was born on 23 May 1908 at Balmain, Sydney, fifth child of Walter William Alfred Thwaites, compositor, and his wife Emily Victoria, née Savage, both native-born. Frederick was a great-grandson of Francis Jenkins of Buckingbong station, Narrandera, where he spent holidays. Leaving school at 13 to support the family, he worked as a cutter and next as a clothing designer, and studied at night at a technical college.

Claiming to have written his first novel, *The broken melody,* at the age of 17, he published it himself in 1930; he acted as his own commercial traveller and began to sell it in the Riverina. His sales boomed after his *Hell's doorway* (London, 1932) was read on 2UE radio. In June 1934 the Melbourne *Herald* set out in two columns the passages from his latest novel, *Flames of convention* (1933), which it claimed bore 'a remarkable resemblance' to D. G. Phillips's *Susan Lenox* (New York, 1922). *Smith's Weekly* alleged in 1936 that Thwaites had incorporated 'slices of a story' from the American crime magazine, the *Master Detective*, in his latest book, *The defender* (1936).

Following the success in Australia of his first novels, he visited England and the United States of America in 1934. When *The mad doctor* appeared in 1935 Thwaites took to wearing a sola topi like the figure on the dustjacket. In 1936 he formed the F. J. Thwaites Publishing Co. and later set up another company to make radio transcriptions of his books. He drove a racing car and in 1938 competed in the South Australian Grand Prix in a Ford V8.

On 28 February that year at St John's Anglican Church, Toorak, Melbourne, Thwaites married Jessica Edna Harcourt, a mannequin and cosmetician who had played Sarah Purfoy in the film version of *For the term of his natural life* (1927). Later in 1938 Ken Hall made a film of *The broken melody* with music composed by Alfred Hill [q.v.9]. Settling in Sydney, during World War II Thwaites worked in the Department of Information, but retained his business interests which by 1950 included four dress shops. That year he moved to Bowral, naming his house Buckingbong.

Small, with dark, wavy hair and a pencil-thin moustache, Thwaites was an old-fashioned, professional writer who penned 2500 words a day. Although seen by critics as romantic and sentimental, his thirty-one adventure novels—characterized by themes of struggle and redemption—were immensely popular, particularly with lending libraries, and sold more than four million copies. Written in 'tempestuous prose', they were crammed with incident and swung between Australian and exotic settings. *Whispers in Tahiti* (1940) was translated into French and *They lived that spring* (1946) into Spanish.

Roaming widely in search of authentic settings, Thwaites embarked on a series of journeys from London to Sydney in 1955 and through Europe and the Americas in 1958-59 which he recalled in three travel books, *Husky be my guide* (1956), *Press on regardless* (1960) and *Destination Spain* (1962). Survived by his wife and two sons, he died of cancer on 13 August 1979 at Manly and was cremated.

P. Spearritt and D. Walker (eds), *Australian popular culture* (Syd, 1979); *People* (Syd), 29 Mar 1950; *Herald* (Melb), 28 Feb, 4 Mar 1933, 21 June 1934, 11 July 1955; *Smith's Weekly*, 31 Oct 1936; *SMH*, 9 Apr 1933, 22 July 1955, 15 Aug 1979; *Sun-Herald*, 8 Jan 1956, 4 Jan 1959; *Canb Times*, 19 Aug 1979.   RON BLABER

THWAITES, WILLIAM (1853-1907), civil engineer and public servant, was born on 13 August 1853 in Melbourne, son of Thomas Thwaites, cabinetmaker, and his wife Eliza, née Raven, both English born. Educated at the Victorian Grammar School, Collins Street, and the Model School, Spring Street, he passed the civil service examination in 1868, but went to the University of Melbourne (Certificate of Engineering, 1873; B.A., 1874; M.A., 1876; M.C.E., 1901). An outstanding student, he won numerous prizes and scholarships.

Commencing his professional career as a pupil-draftsman with the Victorian Department of Railways in 1874, he transferred in 1876 to the South Australian department as an assistant draftsman. In 1879 he returned to the Victorian Department of Public Works and completed engineering surveys for Sir John Coode's [q.v.3] reports on Portland Harbour, Lakes Entrance and the Sale navigation, as well as a survey for defence purposes of Swan Island in Port Phillip Bay. Transferring to the water supply branch, he designed the Toorourrong reservoir, the Essendon and Caulfield service reservoirs, and other facilities. Thwaites was appointed engineer of roads, bridges and reclamation works in 1883. Here he made his mark on Melbourne's landscape through the Dight's Falls scheme (which directed salt-free water to the lakes in the Botanic Gardens and in Albert Park), and by draining Elwood swamp and Port Melbourne lagoon. He also began drainage works at the Condah, Moe and Koo-wee-rup swamps.

Elected a member of the Victorian Institute of Engineers (1881) and a councillor of the Institute of Surveyors (1887), Thwaites became a member of the Institution of Civil Engineers, London, in 1889, and Australasian representative on its council in 1899-1901. He was appointed co-examiner in engineering at the University of Melbourne and in 1890 was elected to the university council. In 1889 he gave evidence before the royal commission into Melbourne's sanitary conditions and provided the most detailed and comprehensive scheme for underground sewers put before the commission. Next year he became engineer in charge of the water supply branch. In 1891 he was appointed engineer-in-chief of the Melbourne and Metropolitan Board of Works which had been established to build the sewerage system urgently recommended by the royal commission. There were a few critics of his appointment, but Melbourne's engineers held a banquet to honour the local achievement.

While James Mansergh [q.v.5] is commonly regarded as the architect of Melbourne's sewerage system, Thwaites deserves credit both for its design and construction. He modified Mansergh's preferred scheme so that what was built owed more to the plans Thwaites had earlier put before the royal comission. Construction began in 1892. It was by far the largest building project in Melbourne during the depression, providing work for several thousand men and contracts for local businesses. An innovative administrator, Thwaites managed all aspects of the work, making use of the recently introduced telephone to check on progress. He worked well with contractors who trusted him and respected his expertise. Despite problems in raising loan finance, difficulties in tunnelling, and accidents, the sewerage system quickly became operational: house connexions were made during 1897. Thwaites personally answered the many criticisms of the M.M.B.W. and of his work, appearing before parliamentary committees of inquiry in 1896 and 1900, at public meetings and in print. He gave evidence before royal commissions on tariffs and on technical education, and also maintained a massive output of memoranda and reports. Robust in build and seemingly inexhaustible, he had few interests outside his work.

Although he never travelled abroad, Thwaites had one of the best engineering libraries in Victoria and was well informed on overseas engineering practice. His knowledge of the physical and climatic characteristics of the metropolitan area amazed his colleagues. He 'had a genius for statistics' and carried out most of the M.M.B.W.'s statistical projections, in the engineering area and in relation to finance. Behind his schemes lay a firm belief in the ability of the engineer to improve the natural world for the benefit of humanity. One of his more interesting proposals was for fuller use of the Yarra River to provide water, electricity and recreational areas.

Thwaites was twice married, with Congregational forms: on 18 October 1879 in Melbourne to Elizabeth Ferres (d. 1905), daughter of the government printer; on 16 December 1905 at Balwyn to Margaret Barton. There were no children. He died of uraemia and pneumonia on 19 November 1907 at San Remo. Survived by his wife, he was buried in Melbourne general cemetery.

Melbourne and Metropolitan Board of Works sewerage scheme (Melb, 1900); J. Smith (ed), *Cyclopedia of Victoria*, 1 (Melb, 1903); *PP* (LA Vic), 1895-96, 2, (3), p 351, 1901, 2, (7), p 361; *Building and Engineering J*, 25 July 1891; *Age*, 30, 31 Jan, 20 Nov 1907; *Argus*, 20 Nov 1907. TONY DINGLE

THYNNE, ANDREW JOSEPH (1847-1927), solicitor and politician, was born on 30 October 1847 at Ennistymon, Clare, Ireland,

third son of Edward Thynne, farmer, and his wife Bridget Stuart, née Fitzgerald. Educated at the local Christian Brothers' school and by a private tutor, he matriculated at Queen's College, Galway, in 1861 and entered its faculty of arts. Andrew arrived in Queensland with his parents in 1864 and joined the public service as a clerk. Resigning within the year, he was articled to Graham Hart and was admitted as a solicitor in December 1873. 'A brainy and industrious lawyer', he formed a partnership with (Sir) Edward Macartney [q.v.10] and represented some of Queensland's largest corporations.

In January 1882 Thynne was appointed to the Legislative Council, remaining a member until its abolition in 1922. He was the only councillor in cabinet in 1888-90 when he served as minister of justice in the McIlwraith and Morehead [qq.v.5] governments. In subsequent cabinets he was minister without portfolio (1893-94), postmaster-general (1894-97) and secretary for agriculture (1896-98); he helped to establish the Queensland Agricultural College at Gatton. Thynne represented his colony at the National Australasian Convention in Sydney in 1891, at a colonial conference held in Ottawa, Canada, in 1894 and at a postal conference in Hobart in 1895. In March 1898 he resigned his portfolio in order to give more time to his other professional interests.

As leader of the government in the Legislative Council and principal of the firm handling the Chillagoe Pty Co.'s legal interests, Thynne argued successfully for government assistance to his corporate client. In late 1916 he clashed acrimoniously with Premier T. J. Ryan [q.v.11] over the attempted transformation of the company into a state-owned mining enterprise. He accused Ryan of forcing his clients to sell 'at a wrecker's price'. The bill associated with the sale was defeated in the council.

Thynne was president of the City (later Queensland) Ambulance Transport Brigade from 1892 until his death. A founder of the Rifle Association, he captained Queensland shooting teams in intercolonial competitions and won the local Queen's prize in 1882 and 1884. Having joined the volunteers as a private in 1867, he rose to the rank of lieutcolonel and command of the Volunteer Corps, Queensland Defence Force. In 1892 Colonel (Sir) George French [q.v.8], the retiring commandant of the Q.D.F., publicly stated that the volunteers were not providing an adequate return for taxpayers' money. Thynne was affronted. During the ensuing dispute with French's successor, Major General (Sir) John Owen, Thynne submitted his resignation. The premier, Sir Samuel Griffith [q.v.9], intervened and Thynne retained his command until 1896. On the outbreak of

World War I, despite his age, he worked sixteen hours a day as chairman of the State Recruiting Committee.

Appointed to the first senate of the University of Queensland in April 1910, Thynne was elected vice-chancellor in 1916 and chancellor in 1925. A traditionalist to the core, he argued successfully against fellow senate member A. H. Barlow [q.v.7] who advocated that criteria other than matriculation be used for university entry. As vice-chancellor, Thynne reaffirmed the position of the original senate that university professors should not be involved in politics.

Thynne had married Mary Williamina Cairncross (d. 1918) on 3 June 1869 in St Stephen's Catholic Church, Brisbane. On 11 October 1922 he married a widow Christina Jane Corrie, née Macpherson, in the vestry of St Patrick's Catholic Church, Sydney. At 50 Thynne might readily have been taken for 40: he was 'still as straight as a gun-barrel, and as nimble as a possum'. Throughout his adult life he kept himself fit by rifle-shooting, bowls and gardening. As a speaker, his debating skill, command of language, personal charm and persuasiveness compensated for his soft voice and his tendency to touchiness.

With his friend Archbishop (Sir) James Duhig [q.v.8] by his bedside, Thynne died on 27 February 1927 at Thoonbah, his home in Highgate Hill. After a requiem Mass he was buried in South Brisbane cemetery. He was survived by his wife, and five daughters and three of the four sons of his first marriage. His estate was sworn for probate at £21 264. Notions of duty and obligation had propelled Thynne to become an extraordinarily energetic and versatile public man who made many influential friends. In his panegyric Duhig praised him as 'an ideal adviser in the many weighty matters of state and private interest with which he was called to deal'.

C. A. Bernays, *Queensland politics during sixty (1859-1919) years* (Brisb, 1920); D. H. Johnson, *Volunteers at heart* (Brisb, 1974); D. J. Murphy, *T. J. Ryan* (Brisb, 1975); M. I. Thomis, *A place of light and learning* (Brisb, 1985); *Queenslander*, 6 Feb 1897, 5 Feb 1898, 5 Mar 1927; *Daily Mail* (Brisb), 16 Apr 1918, 28 Feb 1927; *Brisbane Courier*, 28 Feb 1927.   BRIAN F. STEVENSON

TICKELL, FREDERICK (1857-1919), naval officer, was born on 7 March 1857 at Amoy Harbour, China, son of Captain George Tickell, mariner and member of the Royal Naval Reserve, and his wife Charlotte, née Crabbe. The early part of Frederick's life was spent on his father's ship, but in 1869 the family settled in Melbourne. Educated at Scotch College in 1870-75, Tickell went to sea and later joined the Union Steamship Co.

in New Zealand, gaining a master's certificate; in 1888 he became a sub-lieutenant with the Victorian Naval Brigade. He had married Mary Elizabeth Figg on 18 December 1886 with Presbyterian forms at Williamstown, Victoria.

Promoted lieutenant in 1889, Tickell spent six months in 1890 attached to the Royal Navy's Australian Squadron, serving aboard H.M.S. *Rapid*. In 1893 he was selected for instruction in England where he gained first-class certificates in gunnery and torpedo, and completed a course in ordnance at Woolwich Arsenal. During his time in England he served as a lieutenant in the protected cruiser H.M.S. *Royal Arthur* and joined in manoeuvres aboard H.M.S. *Northampton* and the battleship H.M.S. *Majestic*.

On his return to Australia in 1897 Tickell was promoted commander and in November became commandant of the Victorian Naval Forces, a position he was to hold until 1904. In 1900 the Victorian government offered assistance to Britain in putting down the Boxer rebellion in China. With her navy all but defunct after a decade of neglect, Victoria could provide no warships, merely a naval brigade. Under Tickell's command two hundred men left for Hong Kong aboard the requisitioned liner S.S. *Salamis* in August 1900. Sent initially to occupy the captured forts at Taku, the Victorians were employed as troops but saw little action. Tickell was mentioned in dispatches and was subsequently appointed C.M.G. for his services in China.

In December 1900 he was promoted captain and after Federation became third in seniority in the Commonwealth Naval Forces behind (Sir) William Creswell and Captain C. J. Clare [qq.v.8]. In the reorganization which followed the creation of the C.N.F. Tickell served as naval commandant in Queensland in 1904-07 before resuming his former position as naval commandant in Victoria. He was acting naval director while Creswell attended the 1909 Imperial Defence Conference in London. Together with his fellow officers in the C.N.F., Tickell was an advocate of a local naval force and a supporter of Creswell in his calls for a national Australian navy. In 1910 Tickell brought the recently completed destroyers *Yarra* and *Parramatta* from England.

Like other former colonial naval officers who did not have backgrounds in the Royal Navy, Tickell was transferred to an administrative position when the Royal Australian Navy was formed in 1911. He became director of naval reserves, subsequently renamed auxiliary forces, a post which he held for the rest of his life. In 1912 he was appointed an aide-de-camp to the governor-general. Promoted commodore in 1916, he was raised to rear admiral in March 1919 in recognition of his war work and length of service. Tickell died of a cerebro-vascular disease on 19 September 1919. Survived by his wife and three daughters (his son having been lost at sea in 1904), he was buried in Boroondara cemetery, Kew.

History of Scotch College, Melbourne, 1851-1925 (Melb, 1926); H. J. Feakes, *White ensign—Southern Cross* (Syd, 1951); B. Nicholls, *Bluejackets and Boxers* (Syd, 1986); *Argus*, 17 Mar, 22 Sept 1919; MP472/1/S19/2000 (AA, Melb).   MARK BRIGGS

TILDESLEY, EVELYN MARY (1882-1976) and BEATRICE MAUDE (1886-1977), teachers and women of letters, were born on 8 March 1882 and 27 September 1886 at Willenhall, Staffordshire, England, daughters of William Henry Tildesley, curry-comb manufacturer, and his wife Rebecca, née Fisher. They attended King Edward VI High School, Birmingham, and the University of Cambridge. At Newnham College from 1902, Evelyn completed the classical tripos in 1905 and the medieval and modern languages tripos in English in 1906. The university did not then confer degrees on women and it was not until 1926 that she was accorded her M.A. She taught at Priorsfield School (run by Mrs Leonard Huxley at Godalming) in 1906-09 and mixed in a circle that included Aldous and Julian Huxley. After spending 1909-10 in Vienna, she took temporary teaching posts in England. At Girton (1906-09), Beatrice also completed the classical tripos, then taught at Burton-on-Trent High School (1910-12) and Redland High School for Girls, Bristol (1912-15).

Following the trail of Robert Louis Stevenson, Evelyn arrived in Sydney in 1913, intending to go on to Samoa. Instead, she joined the staff at Normanhurst, a girls' school at Ashfield, and in June next year became headmistress; Beatrice arrived in 1915 and taught classics. Although their pupils achieved academic success, Evelyn—who had 'a first-class mind, illumined by a lively imagination'—believed in a well-rounded education and encouraged classes in drama and physical training. Both sisters were swordswomen and gave displays for the Sydney Fencing Club. In 1918 Evelyn donated a shield for a tennis competition between girls' schools; largely due to Daphne Akhurst [q.v.7], Normanhurst won the first Tildesley shield. The sisters visited Britain in 1923 and, obtaining the means of independence, returned to Sydney but not to Normanhurst.

At the behest of Susan Williams [q.v.], Evelyn was acting principal of Women's College, University of Sydney, in 1925. Beatrice was a committee-member of the Classical Association of New South Wales and belonged to the Friends of the Nicholson [q.v.2] Museum of Antiquities at the university, to which she gave a fifth-century Etruscan bronze mirror. In 1923-35 she was art, theatre and film critic for magazines such as *Beckitt's Budget* and the *Australian Women's Weekly*.

An executive-member of the National Council of Women of New South Wales, Evelyn was honorary interstate secretary and became a life vice-president. She was also a foundation member of the Repatriation Department's Soldiers' Children Education Board in 1921-67 (deputy chairman from 1945): taking a deep personal interest in its activities, she encouraged some young people to pursue distinctive careers, as in ballet.

Sharing a love of the theatre, the Tildesleys belonged to Gregan McMahon's [q.v.10] Sydney Repertory Theatre Society in 1920-28; Beatrice played Margaret Orme in *Loyalties* (1922) and continued to appear in productions until her eighties. In the late 1920s they were involved with the Turret Theatre; despite Evelyn's differences with (Dame) Doris Fitton, in 1930 Beatrice helped to form the Independent Theatre Ltd where in 1964 she took a leading part in *The Aspern papers*. Beatrice was a member of the Playwrights' Advisory Board (which had been established to encourage Australian drama) and was honorary secretary of the Good Film League of New South Wales. Evelyn was a founder, honorary secretary and a director (1937-67) of the British Drama League; she regularly contributed to its journal, *Drama*. Acquainted with Hugh Hunt, from the 1950s the Tildesleys supported the Australian Elizabethan Theatre Trust.

Both sisters contributed articles and book reviews to the *Sydney Morning Herald, Bulletin, Australian Quarterly* and other journals. They gave many talks, often on the radio. They could cap almost any quotation. Their favourite authors were Shakespeare, Boswell, Miss Austen and W. S. Landor. In the 1920s the Tildesleys had befriended the artists Margaret Preston, Thea Proctor and Grace Cossington Smith [qq.v.11] whose work they bought. Beatrice was a life member of the Australian Institute of International Affairs and during World War II was honorary secretary of the Women's Voluntary Service. Evelyn worked for the Australian Red Cross Society and later for the State branch of the National Trust of Australia. Appointed M.B.E. in 1950, she belonged to the Queen's Club and published its history in 1970.

Widely travelled but proud of being 'Mercians', the sisters knew an astonishing number of people; Evelyn enjoyed a discreet love affair. Dinner parties at their home, 1 The Grove, off Queen Street, Woollahra, were famous for the food, wine and company that ranged from cabinet ministers to artists. They both sailed in Richard Windeyer's [q.v.] *Bluebird*. Evelyn was 'naturally an optimist' who tried 'to find silver linings', while Beatrice was apt to curse politicians and prognosticate the worst. At home Evelyn did the garden and Bea saw to domestic matters. As in temperament, they differed in appearance: Evelyn was short, even dumpy, but very pretty and red-haired in youth, with 'luminous grey eyes' glinting with 'impish amusement' and a 'sudden, almost raucous chuckle'; Beatrice, tall, fair and distinguished-looking in a Burne-Jones manner, held deeper currents.

Evelyn died on 6 June 1976 in the Scottish Hospital, Paddington, and Beatrice on 26 January 1977 at Rose Bay; following respective services at St James's Anglican Church, Sydney, they were cremated.

S. E. Napier, *Sydney Theatre Repertory Society, its history and significance* (Syd, 1925); H. Wyndham, *Miss Evelyn Tildesley* (priv print, Syd, 1976); C. Badger, *In memoriam Beatrice Tildesley 1886-1977* (priv print, Syd, 1977); P. Spearritt and D. Walker (eds), *Australian popular culture* (Syd, 1979); J. Milburn and K. Grose, *The Tildesley shield* (priv print, Armidale, NSW, 1988); *Normanhurst School Mag*, June 1915, p 2, June 1923, p 2, June 1924, p 4, June 1932, p 32, May 1942, p 7; Aust Federation of Uni Women (NSW), *Newsletter*, 1976 and 1977; *Australasian*, 8 Apr 1916; *SMH*, 4 June 1924, 22 July 1926, 16 June 1927, 10 Dec 1930, 7 May 1931, 17 Jan 1936, 7 Apr, 3 Nov 1945, 8 June 1950; Tildesley papers *and* Pennington papers (ML); information from Mrs D. Stretton, Double Bay, Syd, *and* Mr C. Badger, Kensington, Melb.

MARTHA RUTLEDGE

TILLY, WILLIAM HENRY (1860-1935), linguist, was born on 29 November 1860 at Petersham, Sydney, third son of Charles Tilley, a gardener from Hampshire, and his Irish wife Elizabeth, née Edgerton. Educated in Sydney, William became a pupil-teacher at Devonshire Street Public School, moving to Paddington (1876) and Fort Street Model School in 1877. In July that year he resigned; he studied at the University of Sydney in 1879-80, then returned to Fort Street as a temporary second-assistant.

On 12 August 1881, at Waverley, Tilley married Frances Rachel Sanders with Congregational forms. He taught in country schools at Ironbarks and Wellington before being transferred in 1884 to Dubbo. His wife died in 1888, leaving three children; on 3 January 1889 at Wallgrove, near Penrith, Tilley married with Presbyterian forms Mary Jane Bathune Shand, mistress of the Dubbo infants' school. Already a disciplinarian, he was censured and warned to run his school with less caning.

Resigning in April 1890 to study in Europe, Tilley went to Germany. In 1892 he became

lektor in English at the University of Marburg under the renowned phonetician, Professor Wilhelm Viëtor. At this time Tilly adopted the Germanic spelling of his name by dropping the 'e'. He took part in Viëtor's phonetic experiments, acting as an English-speaking subject for vowel duration measurements, and learned his revolutionary 'direct method' of foreign language study. He established his own school, the Institut Tilly, at Marburg, and from 1902 at Lichterfelde, Berlin. He could accommodate one hundred students, who came from all parts of the world to undertake six months intensive tuition in German. Some of his nine surviving children, brought up as German native speakers, were among the teachers in his school. The course was rigorous: students had to agree not to speak, hear or read their native tongue for the duration of their stay. German was used in all situations, social and pedagogic, inside and outside the institute.

Portly, with a clipped moustache, Tilly 'looked extraordinarily clean and healthy'. He was an opinionated Germanophile who had a particular affinity for Prussian meticulousness and efficiency; the classicist bias in his profound if rigid admiration of German culture led him to deify Goethe and to detest Wagner.

Within the institute, Prussian discipline was the order of the day. A combination of the newest innovations in language teaching and a close attention to minute detail, especially in the area of pronunciation, produced excellent results. Tilly insisted that his students speak absolutely accent-free German for he despised all regional pronunciations, including that of Berlin. His students included academics, diplomats and businessmen, as well as younger people completing an education; among them were Margaret Bailey [q.v.7], headmistress, E. G. Waterhouse [q.v.] and A. R. Chisholm, professors of German and French at the universities of Sydney and Melbourne, the English phonetician Daniel Jones and a chief justice of Victoria, (Sir) Edmund Herring.

One measure of the efficacy of Tilly's methods was that after six months his better students were able to pass the examination for the German diploma of the International Phonetic Association, conducted under stringent conditions by Viëtor. A member of the Phonetic Association since 1892 and a council-member from 1900, Tilly was a considerable force in foreign language teaching and in the field of speech training generally.

On the outbreak of war in 1914 Tilly and his sons were interned and his property confiscated. In 1916 he was permitted to go to Switzerland and later to England. From 1917 until 1934 he alternately taught English and phonetics at summer session and extension at

Columbia University, New York. In America, as in Germany, he was indefatigable in developing linguistic excellence in his students by a programme of frequent, exacting tests. His disciples established the William Tilly Phonetic Association. It became one of his eccentricities that he professed to abhor everything associated with America. He died at Tenafly, New Jersey, on 29 September 1935. His sister Hannah had married W. J. Clunies Ross [q.v.8].

A. R. Chisholm, *Men were my milestones* (Melb, 1958); *British A'sian*, 31 Dec 1914; *Aumla*, 45 (1976), p 91; *SMH*, 9 Oct 1935; teachers' records, Dept of Education (NSW) archives, Syd; information from Columbia Univ, NY.

PHILIP THOMSON

TILLYARD, PATTIE (1880-1971), community leader, was born on 30 August 1880 at Borstal, Kent, England, daughter of William Robert Craske, commercial clerk, and his wife Fanny, née Downing. From Rochester Girls Grammar School she went in 1900 to Newnham College, Cambridge, where she completed her natural sciences (botany) tripos with second-class honours at a time before the university granted degrees to women. One of ten similarly situated women on whom Trinity College, Dublin, conferred an honorary B.A. (1905), she was awarded a belated M.A. (Cantab.) when Cambridge changed its policy in 1921.

Tall, with dark hair and deep blue eyes, Pattie became a science mistress at Hitchin Girls Grammar School, Hertfordshire. After studying for a diploma in public health, she spent three months at the Nile delta with her brother before travelling to Australia in 1909 to join her persistent suitor Robin John Tillyard [q.v.] whom she married at St Michael's Anglican Church, Vaucluse, Sydney, on 23 June 1909. While raising their four daughters, she was a member of the educational committee of the Australasian Trained Nurses' Association (New South Wales). In 1919 the family moved to New Zealand and she was appointed to the Nelson Colleges board: when protests were made about a female appointee to Governor-General Lord Jellicoe, he merely inquired 'What is wrong with her qualifications?' During these years the colour and monochrome illustrations she provided lent distinction to her husband's published works. After arriving in 1928 in isolated Canberra, she became noted for her widespread hospitality. Her visitor's book remains an evocative record of early Canberra social life. 'My nature', she once said, 'is akin to that of a homeless cat, so adjustment was not difficult for me'.

A councillor (1929-32) and frequent vice-president of the University Association of Canberra, Pattie represented it on the Canberra University College Council (1942-45). She was a member of the Canberra Community Hospital Board (1935-37), standing for election because she felt that 'there ought to be women on every governing body'. As a former suffragist, she regarded the right to vote as a 'privilege and a duty' which was 'to a great extent neglected' by Australian women. She was commissioner of the Girl Guides Association (A.C.T.), and president (1929-33) of the Young Women's Christian Association, the Association of Women Graduates, Canberra, the Victoria League and the Women's Hockey Association. She retained the supreme confidence of a 'Newnhamite' in her ability to chair a meeting, take charge of an organization, or entertain the highest in the land. During World War II she was chairman of commandants of the Lady Gowrie Services Canteen which, after the war, staffed Canberra Community Hospital canteen. In 1951 she was appointed M.B.E.

A striking figure on her old-fashioned Cambridge bicycle, in her later years she became the 'grande dame' of Canberra; at 89 she reluctantly relinquished her driving licence. Survived by her daughters, she died on 10 March 1971 and was buried in St John the Baptist churchyard, Canberra. The Australian Federation of University Women (A.C.T.) erected a memorial to her at the Australian National University in 1976.

ANU Reporter, 9 Apr 1976; *Canb Hist J*, no 24, Sept 1989; *Canb Times*, 24, 30 Sept 1935, 1 Jan 1951, 13 Mar, 28 May, 13 Nov 1964, 11 Mar 1971, 29 Mar 1976; *SMH*, 22 Aug 1970; *Canb News*, 1 Sept 1970; P. Tillyard's Visitor's book, 1928-71, held by Mrs P. Wardle, Canb, who also provided information.

PATRICIA CLARKE

TILLYARD, ROBIN JOHN (1881-1937), naturalist and entomologist, was born on 31 January 1881 at Norwich, Norfolk, England, and named Robert, son of John Joseph Tillyard, solicitor, and his wife Mary Ann Frances, née Wilson. Educated at Dover College, he took up a scholarship to Queens' College, Cambridge (B.A., 1903; M.A., 1907), being placed senior optime in the mathematics tripos. After reading oriental languages and theology, in 1904 Robin abandoned ideas of joining the Church, but a search for health took him to Australia where he taught mathematics and science at Sydney Grammar School in 1904-13. Progressively more absorbed with studies on insects, he resigned to study zoology at the University of Sydney (B.Sc., 1914).

The Linnean Macleay [q.v.5] fellowship (1915-20) in zoology allowed him full time for research: his broadening interests were reflected in publications on dragonflies, lacewings and scorpionflies. He became particularly interested in the phylogeny of a group of higher insect orders which he called the panorpoid complex. The year after he published his classic work, *The biology of dragonflies* (Cambridge, 1917), he was awarded a D.Sc. (1918) by the University of Sydney; he also received a Sc.D. (1920) from the University of Cambridge. His knowledge of aquatic insects led the New Zealand government to invite him in 1919 to investigate diminishing trout numbers. He was chief of the biology department of the Cawthron Institute at Nelson, New Zealand, in 1921-28. Following the biological control in France of the woolly aphis apple pest with a parasite introduced from North America, Tillyard established the same parasite so successfully in New Zealand that he was encouraged to advocate biological control of other pests. During 1921-24, largely single-handed and despite severe ill health, he wrote *The insects of Australia and New Zealand* (Sydney, 1926), a book which gave enormous impetus to the study of entomology. In England in 1926 he canvassed the advantages of biological control and obtained valuable financial support. There was little success, however, at that time from campaigns against further insect pests and weeds in New Zealand.

Tillyard's reputation prompted the newly created Council for Scientific and Industrial Research in Australia to offer him the position of Chief of the Division of Economic Entomology in Canberra. At first reluctant, he eventually accepted in 1928. He maintained what was then a far-sighted advocacy of biological control, but in the absence of any early successes the council became disillusioned. Its attitude, combined with some of Tillyard's not very felicitous interactions with staff members and his increasing restiveness with administrative matters, made the early 1930s an unfulfilling time for him. Primarily a systematist with a broad interest in the natural history of insects, Tillyard was neither an applied entomologist nor an ecologist; surprisingly, he made no use of his mathematical talents in his research. One of his achievements was to establish insect taxonomy within the division. He also made important contributions to insect palaeontology.

He received many honours and was a member of many scientific bodies. A fellow (1925) of the Royal Society, London, and honorary fellow (1928) of Queens' College, Cambridge, Tillyard received the Crisp prize and medal (1917) of the Linnean Society, London, the (W. B.) Clarke [q.v.3] medal (1931) of the Royal Society of New South Wales, and the Mueller [q.v.5] medal (1935). His scientific

publications (over 200) are listed in Anthony Musgrave's [q.v.10] *Bibliography of Australian entomology, 1775-1930* (Sydney, 1932) and in an unpublished supplement.

Throughout his life Tillyard was plagued by pain, ill health and accidents; a railway crash in 1914 was responsible for his badly bent back. Following a nervous breakdown after the Pan-Pacific Science Congress in Chicago in 1933, he resigned in February 1934. Despite his physical frailty, he had an intense vitality and the 'enthusiasm of a delighted schoolboy'. His forehead was high and his keen brown eyes gave shrewd appraisal through his large spectacles. Egocentric, with a mercurial disposition, he was a convincing and dramatic lecturer whose conversation reflected alertness, wit and 'puckish humour'. While spiritualism absorbed him in his later years, he took a keen interest in civic affairs and higher education; he was a councillor of Canberra University College and joint editor of the *Australian National Review*.

He died on 13 January 1937 in Goulburn District Hospital from injuries received in a car accident, and was buried in the churchyard of the Anglican Church of St John the Baptist, Canberra. On 23 June 1909 in Sydney he had married Pattie Craske [q.v. Tillyard], a loyal and stabilizing influence in his life. With four daughters, she survived him.

A. Musgrave, *Bibliography of Australian entomology 1775-1930* (Syd, 1932); J. W. Evans, *John Murtagh Macrossan lecture* (Brisb, 1962), and *The life and work of R J Tillyard 1881-1937* (Brisb, 1963); Linnean Soc NSW, *Procs*, 71 (1946), p 252; *NZ Entomologist*, 6, no 3, 1977, p 305; *SMH*, 27 Aug 1970; CSIRO Archives, Canb, Series 3, PH/TIL/2 and Series 67.　　　　　　D. F. WATERHOUSE
　　　　　　　　　　　　　　　　　　K. R. NORRIS

TIMMS, EDWARD VIVIAN (1895-1960), novelist and scriptwriter, was born on 7 April 1895 at Charters Towers, Queensland, son of William Henry Timms (d. 1898), a chemist from Worcester, England, and his Victorian-born wife Bertha, née Bawden. Bertha moved to Western Australia where she married a Presbyterian minister, Rev. Angus King, who served at Coolgardie and Fremantle before settling in Sydney in 1906. Taught at Fremantle Boys' School by (Field Marshal Sir) Thomas Blamey, Edward attended public schools in Sydney, then studied electrical engineering. Using his stepfather's surname, he was commissioned in the 1st Battalion, Australian Imperial Force, on 27 August 1914 and promoted lieutenant on 15 March 1915. He took part in the landing on Gallipoli on 25 April, was wounded and invalided home.

Reverting to his patronymic, Timms married Alma McRobert in his stepfather's church, St David's, Haberfield, on 19 August 1916. With another couple, they took up a soldier-settler block on the Richmond River, but inexperience and drought forced them to quit. Back in Sydney, Timms published his first novel, *The hills of hate*, in 1925; there followed two adventure stories, a humorous novel (*James! don't be a fool*) and *Lawrence, prince of Mecca* (1927) under the pseudonym 'David Roseler'; *The cripple in black* (1930), set in the seventeenth century, was the first of his historical romances.

In addition to twenty-two novels, Timms wrote many short stories and innumerable plays, serials, scripts and adaptations of novels for the cinema and radio. Having adapted *The hills of hate* for Raymond Longford's [q.v.10] film in 1926, he wrote the scripts for *The grey glove* (1928) and *The squatter's daughter* (1933), and collaborated with Charles Chauvel [q.v.7] on *Uncivilised* (1936) and *Forty thousand horsemen* (1940). In January 1938 Timms began conducting 'The diggers' session' for the Australian Broadcasting Commission and wrote a serial for it until 1940.

During World War II he served in Australian Garrison battalions from June 1940. With the rank of temporary major, from October 1943 Timms was in charge of Italians as commandant of C Camp, No.12 Prisoner of War Compound, Cowra. On the night of the mass Japanese break-out (5 August 1944), he led C company in fending off a rear attack by the Japanese and gave the order to fire. He later testified at the military court of inquiry and published a description, 'Bloodbath at Cowra', in *As You Were* (Canberra, 1946). In 1945-46 he was inspection officer for prisoner-of-war camps.

Tall and strongly built, with brown hair and a ruddy complexion, Timms was essentially a family man. He had no illusions about his writing and considered himself simply a good story-teller. His novels were popular and some were translated into Spanish, German, French, Dutch and Norwegian; *Forever to remain* was adapted as a stage musical.

After the war Timms embarked on his 'Australian saga', a twelve-volume sequence of historical novels that began with *Forever to remain* (1948) and portrayed the lives of an English immigrant family, the Gubbys. In 1954 he went into semi-retirement at Budgewoi, near Gosford, where he enjoyed gardening, walking and fishing. Survived by his wife, daughter and two sons, he died there on 14 June 1960 of hypertensive heart disease and was buried in Northern Suburbs cemetery, Sydney. His widow completed *The big country* (1962) and wrote the final volume of the 'Australian saga', *Time and chance*

(1971). F. L. Tregear's portrait of Timms is held by a son.

C. Carr-Gregg, *Japanese prisoners of war in revolt* (Brisb, 1978); A. Pike and R. Cooper, *Australian film 1900-1977* (Melb, 1980); *Wireless Weekly*, 15-21 Jan 1938, 17 Feb 1939; *SMH*, 16 Aug 1934, 21 Sept 1939, 25 Sept 1954, 16 June 1960; *Courier Mail*, 21 July 1934; *Daily Telegraph* (Syd), 29 Dec 1951; *Sun-Herald*, 27 May 1962; Report on visit to Cowra, AWW 54, items 780/3/2,4 (AWM); Court of Inquiry on mutiny at Cowra, AA 1977-461-2, Ser A1608/1, item Ax 20/1/1 (AA); information from, and Timms scrap-books held by, Mrs J. M. Scotford, Mosman, Syd; Angus & Robertson correspondence (ML); ML printed cat for publications.

ANTHONY BARKER

TISDALL, ALICE CONSTANCE (1877-1968), educationist, was born on 17 August 1877 at Walhalla, Gippsland, Victoria, seventh child of HENRY THOMAS TISDALL, teacher, and his wife Lucy, née Weekes. Henry (1836-1905), originally from Waterford, Ireland, had migrated to Victoria in 1858. He and his English-born wife had arrived at Walhalla in 1868 to become head teacher and work mistress at Stringer's Creek State School. Four of Lucy's sisters were also teachers and three taught with them there. An amateur botanist, Henry collected, identified and illustrated Gippsland wildflowers and fungi. Sponsored by Baron von Mueller [q.v.5], he was elected a fellow of the Linnean Society, London, in 1883.

Constance, as she was known, attended Walhalla School as a small child; after the family moved to Melbourne in 1886 she went briefly to Montague Street State School and later to a dame's school at Toorak. Her serious education in the humanities occurred at home under her parents' guidance. Matriculating in 1897, she lacked grounding in classics and mathematics and failed first year arts at the University of Melbourne. A resident bursary to Trinity College enabled her to try again: in 1899 she won the first year logic exhibition. She graduated (B.A., 1903; M.A., 1906) and accepted a teaching post at Alexandra College, Hamilton, where she reaffirmed her childhood conviction that she was 'born to teach'.

The principal, successively, of Rosbercon College (1906-33) (her family's school at Brighton), St Anne's Church of England Girls' Grammar School at Sale (1934-43) and St Christopher's Training College for Women, East Malvern (1945-47), she became president of both the Women Graduates' Association of Victoria and the Victorian Headmistresses' Association. In 1961 she was appointed O.B.E. That year she published *Forerunners*, the story of the teaching experiences of the Tisdall and Weekes families.

She had little interest in administration. Her rejection in 1911 of Archbishop Lowther Clarke's [q.v.8] offer to take over Rosbercon as a nucleus of an Anglican girls' school for the southern suburbs led ultimately to its eclipse by Firbank Church of England Girls' Grammar School; small family schools like Rosbercon were unable financially to meet demands for increased mathematics and science teaching, as well as for better facilities. St Anne's and St Christopher's, with institutional backing, benefited from Constance's stimulating teaching without suffering unduly from her lack of business acumen.

A deeply Christian woman, Constance kept diaries which reveal stern spiritual self-examination and a constant awareness of the presence of God. Her ideal of education was essentially a person-to-person relationship, based on exchange of ideas, mutual trust, firm discipline (as in a well-ordered family), and above all on love. At Rosbercon she adopted a modified version of the Dalton Plan, taught English literature and Scripture, and imbued the school with a Christian ethos. St Anne's, when Constance arrived, had some thirty-five pupils, all primary; teaching took place in the parish hall, a mile (1.6 km) from the boarding hostel; when she left, the school with ninety pupils was on one site and had secondary registration. At St Christopher's she guided a group of young women interested in teaching religious education and in youth leadership.

On retirement, Constance continued teaching English literature, mainly to migrants. Still bright-eyed and owlish, she read voraciously, and enjoyed visits and reunions with 'old girls'. Small and spry, she was remembered by former pupils as an affectionate teacher, with a capacity for pepperiness. She died, unmarried, on 24 August 1968 and was cremated after an Anglican service at St James's Church, Glen Iris.

Sprogs-News from St. Anne's, no 1, Mar 1964, 5, no 2, Oct 1968; *Argus*, 13 July 1905; *Herald* (Melb), 31 Oct 1931, 2 Dec 1933, 13 Dec 1944, 8 Dec 1959, 3 Oct 1961, 12 Aug 1967, 4 June 1969; *Sun News-Pictorial*, 13 Dec 1944, 10 June, 9 Nov 1961, 17 Aug 1967; *Age*, 23 May 1947, 10, 21 June, 11 Nov 1961, 11 Dec 1963, 26 Aug 1968; Tisdall family papers (LaTL).   LYNDSAY GARDINER

TISHLER, JOSEPH (1871–1956), poet, was born on 18 March 1871 at Dunedin, New Zealand, son of Aaron Tishler, builder, and his wife Maria, née Simpson. The family moved to Melbourne and settled at St Kilda where Joseph attended primary school. He took work as a strolling minstrel (playing the accordion), stage-hand, woodchopper, wagoner, carpet-beater and salesman. In 1898, having failed as a second-hand dealer, he spent an unsuccessful period in Tasmania. Returning to Melbourne, he continued to pursue his 'up and down varied career', finally establishing himself as a dealer in fancy goods at the Queen Victoria Market.

Although Tishler had long recognized his gift for verse, it was not until 1908 that he first contributed to the *Bulletin*. Under the pseudonym of 'The Wasp' his poem, 'Found Dead in the Street', was published in the 'Answers to Correspondents' column on 4 June. It began:

> An unfortunate woman was
> Found dead in the street
> By an officer of Justice
> While on his early morn beat.
> Conveyed to the Morgue
> For a doleful inquest.
> From the wages of sin
> Her soul was at rest.

The work of most aspiring contributors was simply rejected; Tishler's was so strikingly bad that his contributions were printed in full. Often on topical themes or recording his observations of street life in Melbourne, his poems became a regular and popular feature in the magazine. In 1910 he began to use the pseudonym 'Bellerive' by which he was to be widely known. Described by the *Bulletin* as 'the Poet Laureate of the Perpetually Rejected', he continued to contribute until 1953: not only poems (including extensive autobiographical verse), but also a small three-act melodrama (published in the 'Red Page' on 13 December 1913) and an entry in the magazine's 1928 fiction competition.

'Bellerive' was shy, with a deep fear of being made a laughing-stock. He was encouraged and supported in his writing by the *Bulletin*'s W. E. Fitzhenry, the poet Edward Harrington and the literary patron J. K. Moir who initiated a project to publish a selection of 'Bellerive's' verse. His aim was eventually achieved in Douglas Stewart's *The book of Bellerive* (1961).

For most of the last thirty years of his life Tishler lived in North Melbourne with his wife Jane, née Pantille, whom he had married about 1918. There 'Bellerive' was a familiar figure wheeling an old handcart around the streets; when their house was destroyed by storms in 1952, they moved to Carlton. Harry Pearce described Tishler in 1950 as 'somewhat of a stooping build, but when younger and erect must have been fully six feet [182.9 cm], and built in proportion. He had a twinkle in his eyes and a sort of fleeting smile that seemed a permanent part of his expression'.

Despite the affectionate ridicule to which the *Bulletin* and the Australian public subjected him, 'Bellerive' never lost faith in himself as a serious poet. He continued to assure his supporters that he was 'breaking new ground'. Stewart concluded that he did so only in his naivety, although 'given another turn of the wheel, we would have had a minor lyrist of genuine quality in Bellerive'. Tishler died at Parkville on 7 August 1956 and was buried with Anglican rites in Melbourne general cemetery. His wife survived him; they had no children.

People (Syd), 30 Aug 1950; *Bulletin*, 4 June 1908, 19 Sept 1912, 9, 16 Dec 1926, 10 May 1950; Tishler papers *and* J. K. Moir collection *and* H. H. Pearce reminiscences (LaTL). TONY MARSHALL

TIVEY, EDWIN (1866-1947), soldier and stockbroker, was born on 19 September 1866 at Inglewood, Victoria, fourth surviving child of Joseph Tivey, an English-born storekeeper who had arrived in Australia in 1848 at the age of 14, and his wife Margaret, née Hayes, from Tasmania. Edwin was educated at All Saints Grammar School, St Kilda, and at Wesley College, Melbourne, where he rowed bow in the second crew of 1882. 'No scholastic genius', he eschewed university to return to Inglewood as an accountant. He was commissioned lieutenant in the Inglewood detachment of the Victorian Rangers in 1889 and promoted captain in 1891. Townsfolk elected him to the Inglewood Borough Council on which he served for five years from 1894. In 1899 he became a founder and first president of the local branch of the Australian Natives' Association.

In May 1900 Tivey embarked for South Africa as a captain in the Victorian 4th (Imperial) Contingent. Serving in widespread operations, he was mentioned in dispatches. He was also awarded the Distinguished Service Order for leading forty troops on a forced march to Philipstown on 11 February 1901. His men drove back over 300 opponents, occupied the adjacent kopjes and held them until reinforcements arrived.

In 1903 Tivey became a member of the Melbourne Stock Exchange. On 26 September 1906 he married Annie Bird Robb (d. 1921) at the Presbyterian Church, Toorak. A captain in the new 9th Light Horse Regiment of the Victorian militia, in 1906 Tivey was appointed brigade major in the Victorian 3rd Light Horse Brigade and in 1911 as lieutcolonel became its commander. He received the Volunteer Officer's Decoration in 1910.

By the commencement of World War I Tivey was a successful stockbroker and temporary colonel commanding the Victorian 5th L.H.B. He was promoted colonel in January 1915 and was commandant of the officers' school at Broadmeadows. 'Of neat build,

middle height, crisp appearance, he looks every inch a soldier', observed Melbourne *Punch*.

In July Tivey was appointed commander of the Australian Imperial Force's 8th Infantry Brigade which he personally helped to recruit. He quickly endeared himself to men of all ranks with his sincerity and his concern for their interests. In December the brigade disembarked in Egypt where it held a sector of the Suez Canal defences. Its men were soon dubbed 'chocolate soldiers' because, to relieve Moascar, they travelled by train from Tel-el-Kebir while supporting troops marched for two days through heat and sand. Thenceforth the brigade was known as 'Tivey's Chocs'.

Tivey was appointed temporary brigadier general in February 1916 and in June his brigade left with the Australian 5th Division for France. It went into action at the battle of Fromelles and continued to fight on the Western Front until the war's end. In December 1916 Tivey was wounded in action but remained on duty. For brief periods in 1917 and 1918 he temporarily commanded the 5th Division when Major General (Sir) Talbot Hobbs [q.v.9] was absent. Tivey was again wounded at Westhoek Ridge, Belgium, in October 1917 and was gassed in May 1918. In the great allied offensive of 8 August 1918 his brigade captured 831 prisoners and 85 machine-guns. During the war he was mentioned in dispatches six times; he was appointed C.B. in 1917 and C.M.G. in January 1919.

From late November 1918 to May 1919 Tivey was temporary major general, again temporarily commanding the 5th Division. In July 1919 he embarked for Australia where, in the reserve of officers, Australian Military Forces, he was promoted major general in June 1920. In 1921-26 he commanded the 2nd Cavalry Division of the Citizen Military Forces. Governor-General Lord Forster [q.v.8] undervalued Tivey in 1925 by describing him as 'a nice little man who fancies himself a bit'. Having resumed trading as a respected and well-known member of the Melbourne Stock Exchange, from 1920 Tivey lived in a small mansion, Nauroy, Kooyong Road, Toorak, and worshipped at nearby St John's Anglican Church. He was an honorary colonel in the Victorian mounted rifles from 1928 and, from 1932, in the Victorian 32nd Battalion. On his eightieth birthday he was described as a 'silver haired dapper sharebroker [who] retains his soldierly bearing' and 'attends his office every day'.

Tivey died at his Toorak home on 19 May 1947 and was buried with full military honours by the bishop of Geelong in Brighton cemetery, Melbourne. His estate was sworn for probate at £75 303, the principal beneficiary being his daughter Violet. His son Major Edwin Peter Tivey had died as an Italian prisoner of war in 1943.

A. E. Ellis, *The story of the Fifth Australian Division* (Lond, 1920); G. Blainey et al, *Wesley College* (Melb, 1967); *London Gazette*, 22, 25 Mar, 7 May 1901; *Inglewood Advertiser*, 10, 21 Aug 1894, 25 Apr, 2, 19 May 1899; *Advance Aust*, 15 May 1900; *Punch* (Melb), 5 Aug 1915; *Herald* (Melb), 30 Jan, 19 Sept 1946, 20 May 1947; Tivey papers (AWM); Stonehaven papers (NL); St John's Anglican Church, Toorak, records.   ROGER C. THOMPSON

TJANGAMARRA (1870?-1897), Aboriginal leader, was born about 1870 into the Bunuba tribe which occupied mountainous country in the Kimberley district of Western Australia. The Napier and Oscar Ranges presented a barrier which had prevented the pastoral frontier from encroaching on Bunuba territory. As a youth Tjangamarra learned to ride horses, shear sheep and use fire-arms on William Lukin's neighbouring Lennard River station and won repute as the district's finest Black stockman. He spoke English confidently. Lukin named him 'Pigeon' because he was small, fleet-footed and had a cheeky but endearing personality.

At 15 he returned to his traditional land for initiation and became a skilful hunter. Late in 1889 he and a fellow tribesman, Ellemarra, were captured by police at Windjina Gorge, chained together and marched to Derby gaol; charges of killing sheep were dropped when Tjangamarra agreed to serve the police by taking care of their horses. He won popularity and trust at Derby. A year later he went to Lennard River as a stockman, and then to his mountain home where it is alleged that he violated Bunuba law.

Avoiding retribution by the tribe, he went to live at Lillimooloora station where he formed a close friendship with Bill Richardson, a stockman. In 1894 Richardson joined the police force and Tjangamarra was recruited as a tracker. With another Aborigine called 'Captain', he was assigned to Constable Richardson at the abandoned Lillimooloora homestead, seventy miles (113 km) from Derby, which had been taken over by the police as an outpost. The three formed a mutually dependent unit. Although it was not official policy to use tribal members against their own people, Tjangamarra helped to locate and capture Bunuba warriors. He once saved Richardson's life during an attack by Aborigines.

In a dramatic defection Tjangamarra subsequently shot and killed Richardson as he slept, then released sixteen Aboriginal prisoners, among them Ellemarra. The sixteen—who included some of his blood relations—

had told him that he was obligated to them for having waived tribal punishment for his offences; they had described a new policeman at Fitzroy Crossing who was murdering Aborigines; and they had announced the imminent invasion of Bunuba country by the Europeans.

Together they formed a gang and with captured guns ambushed a stock party, killing two of its members. Tjangamarra planned a military defence of his country by using fire-arms and held a vision of an Aboriginal uprising which would transcend tribal boundaries. Panic engulfed the small White settler community, scattered as it was over an area of nearly 11 500 square miles (29 785 km^2). The police gained sweeping powers to crush the uprising and killed many Aborigines.

Fifty ochre-painted warriors fought the Whites in the major battle of Windjina Gorge on 16 November 1894. Ellemarra was killed and Tjangamarra was severely wounded, but recovered and spent two years hiding in caves to the south. Although his strategies had caused them great suffering, the Bunuba credited him with supernatural powers.

In November 1895 he raided Lillimooloora police station, shocking the Whites who had thought him dead. Late in 1896 he again humiliated the police at Lillimooloora. By this stage many of his gang had been captured and others killed. In March Tjangamarra and twenty others attacked Oscar Range homestead; a number of his party were killed and wounded, but their leader escaped through a tunnel and was succoured by Terrawarra. He was finally shot dead at Tunnel Creek on 1 April 1897 by Aboriginal trooper Minko Mick.

Leopold Downs pastoral station was established in the heart of Bunuba territory and within two years most of the tribe's land was similarly occupied. Tjangamarra has become the subject of such writing as Colin Johnson's novel, *Long live Sandawara* (Melbourne, 1979). In 1988 a heritage trail was constructed for people to visit Tjangamarra's country.

A. Shoemaker, *Black words, white page* (Brisb, 1989); *Studies in WA Hist*, 8, Dec 1984; *Aboriginal Hist*, 9, pt 1, 1985.   HOWARD PEDERSEN

TODD, FREDERICK AUGUSTUS (1880-1944), professor of Latin, was born on 14 March 1880 at Alexandria, Sydney, fourth child of native-born parents, William Alexander Neil Todd, bootmaker, and his wife Margaret Ann, née Lappin. Educated at Sydney Boys' High School, he won the James Aitken scholarship for general proficiency at matriculation and the Cooper [q.v.3] scholarship for classics (*proxime accessit*). At the University of Sydney he studied Latin and Greek under Thomas Butler and Walter Scott [qq.v.7,11], and won the Cooper scholarship in 1899 and 1900. He graduated B.A. in 1901, with first-class honours in Latin and Greek, the University medal for classics and the Woolley [q.v.6] travelling scholarship.

Enabled to study at Leipzig and the University of Jena, Germany, in 1902 Todd was admitted to the classical seminar of two of the most distinguished Latinists in Europe, Professors G. Goetz and R. Hirzel. He graduated Ph.D. in classics *magna cum laude* in December 1903; his thesis, *De musis in carminibus poetarum Romanorum commemoratis*, was published at Jena that year.

Earlier in 1903 Todd was appointed assistant lecturer in Latin at the University of Sydney. He was acting professor of Greek in 1908 and of Latin in 1909. Assistant professor of Latin (1913) and acting professor (1920), he succeeded Butler in the chair in 1922. He was a stern upholder and defender of what he saw as the university's traditions and responsibilities. With E. R. Garnsey, he founded the Classical Association of New South Wales in 1909; secretary of the University Extension Board (1912-21), for over twenty-five years he was a member of the Board of Examiners (later Board of Secondary School Studies). In these capacities he made his influence and that of his discipline felt in the general education and intellectual life of city and country alike. In 1924 he was unsuccessfully sued for alleged defamation by a schoolteacher whose competence he had questioned at a meeting of examiners; Todd was defended at public expense. Engaging in all the university union's activities, he was its president in 1914. While on leave in 1924 he represented the university at the Imperial Education Conference in London. He was dean of the faculty of arts and a fellow of senate in 1930-37.

Duties of this nature exacted a heavy toll from Todd and the major original work in classics predicted by Goetz did not materialize. However, his philological notes and papers in the *Classical Review* and *Classical Quarterly* provide ample evidence of scholarship and an extensive reading of classical literature. His book, *Some ancient novels* (Oxford, 1940), based on a series of Extension Board lectures, was a pioneering introduction to the subject: Oxford University Press suggested that he undertake a much larger study, but Todd did not do so, perhaps because he planned a work on Pompeian metrical inscriptions. His greatest contribution to scholarship was his teaching and the imposing array of former pupils who carried on the classical tradition in universities and schools.

Todd's personality aroused strong reactions both of affection and of antipathy, the latter possibly because he 'sometimes identified the opinions he disliked with the men who held them'. On occasions he struck his colleagues as being acerbic: the historian G. A. Wood [q.v.] called him 'the Metternich of the University'.

From August 1914 Todd was a military interpreter, termed an assistant censor from 1916. On 16 October 1918 he enlisted in the Australian Imperial Force, but did not go overseas. At Holy Trinity Church, Marrickville, on 4 February 1919 he married Florence Helen Grahame Glover who graduated in arts later that year; they lived at Mosman. For his children's enjoyment, he compiled a collection which he entitled *Nugarum liber*. This scrapbook, mainly hand-written, includes copies of his translations from and into classical verse, the subjects ranging from Sappho to nursery rhymes; it also contains letters and press-cuttings of events and controversies in which he had participated: the volume reveals the congenial side of his nature.

Survived by his wife, three daughters and two sons, Todd died of coronary occlusion at the university on 13 June 1944 and was cremated with Anglican rites. The university war memorial hymn for the carillon, *Campanarum canticum*, for which he had composed the inspiring words, was played when the quadrangle was stilled concurrently with his funeral service at St Augustine's Anglican Church, Neutral Bay.

H. E. Barff, *A short historical account of the University of Sydney* (Syd, 1902); A. R. Chisholm, *Men were my milestones* (Melb, 1958); R. M. Crawford, *'A bit of a rebel'* (Syd, 1975); H. D. Jocelyn, 'Australia-New Zealand: Greek and Latin philology', in *La filologia greca e latina nel secolo xx*, 1 (Pisa, Italy, 1989); Univ Syd Union, *Union Recorder*, 13 July 1944; Todd papers (Univ Syd Archives).

A. J. DUNSTON

TODD, ROBERT HENRY (1859-1931), medical administrator, and ELLEN JOY (1860-1948), journalist, were husband and wife. Robert was born on 10 July 1859 in Old Burlington Street, London, son of Armstrong Todd, surgeon, and his wife Frances Alicia, née Kinahan. Educated at Christ's Hospital school, Hertford College, Oxford (B.A., 1882) and Trinity College, Dublin (M.B., Ch.B., M.D., 1886), he gained a diploma in state medicine and in 1887 was elected a fellow of the Royal College of Surgeons in Ireland.

Ellen was born on 16 May 1860 at Woolwich Arsenal, Greenwich, Kent, daughter of Captain Andrew Orr, Royal Artillery, and his wife Lucy Erskine, née Acworth. After Andrew's death in 1870, Lucy and her seven children lived with her father, an

Anglican clergyman, at Wimborne and Stoke. The girls were educated at home and learned Italian.

In Monkstown parish church, Dublin, Robert and Ellen were married by her grandfather with Church of Ireland rites on 14 June 1887. Robert sailed as ship's surgeon in the *Hawkesbury*, reaching Sydney with his bride in October. He practised in the suburbs and was honorary anaesthetist at (Royal) Prince Alfred Hospital; she was a founder of the Ladies' Club in 1889. Moving to Maclean on the Northern Rivers in 1889, Todd was government medical officer at Grafton and Ellen secretary of the local St John Ambulance Association.

When an infection permanently weakened his wrist, Todd returned to Sydney in 1892 and studied law; he was admitted to the Bar on 23 February 1894 and practised until 1926. He was deputy city coroner in 1899-1904 and chaired several industrial boards. Intensely musical, he was honorary secretary of the Sydney Amateur Orchestral Society and played the clarinet in its orchestra under Roberto Hazon [q.v.9]. As associate to (Sir) Charles Mackellar [q.v.10], in 1903-04 Todd was largely responsible for drawing up the report of the royal commission into the decline of the birth-rate. He was a member of the Medical Board of New South Wales in 1907-28 and lectured in medical jurisprudence (1910-31) and in ethics of medical practice (1922-31) at the University of Sydney.

Meanwhile Ellen contributed to the *Echo*, *Illustrated Sydney News* and to Louisa Lawson's [q.v.10] *Dawn*. Joining the staff of the *Australian Town and Country Journal* under the editorship of Walter Jeffery [q.v.9], she supplied book reviews and theatrical and musical critiques, as well as the obligatory social notes. From January 1906 until 1923 she was foundation editor of the weekly *Woman's Budget*, published by S. Bennett [q.v.3] Ltd. In the first issue it claimed to be 'WRITTEN by WOMEN for WOMEN'. Although the magazine featured items on cookery, dressmaking and fashion, it also included articles of wider interest and provided an outlet for women writers. Circulation under her editorship was estimated to have reached 150 000 weekly.

A council-member of the New South Wales branch of the British Medical Association from 1896, Todd was its honorary secretary in 1908-31. He helped to found the Federal Council in Australia of the B.M.A. in 1912, drafted its constitution and was secretary from 1918. As company secretary he also set up the Australasian Medical Publishing Co. Ltd in 1913 to produce the *Medical Journal of Australia*. Unstinting with his time, he was consulted by council-members and State branches. He was elected a vice-president of

the B.M.A. in England (1922), was awarded the Federal Council's gold medal (1923) and served on the Commonwealth royal commission on health in 1925.

A trustee of Taronga Zoological Park, Todd personally conducted the elephant, Jessie, from Moore Park to her new home. With classical features and silver hair, Robert was dapper in appearance. The Todds' large and comfortable home at Double Bay was filled with books. Ellen enjoyed playing contract bridge. Whenever the maid left, she persuaded a neighbour's daughter to cook for her. A small-boned, bustling woman with patrician manners and old-fashioned black clothes, Ellen 'almost ran with quick little steps' rather than walking.

Robert died at his home on 14 December 1931 and was cremated with Anglican rites. From 1933 until 1940 Mrs Todd worked in an honorary capacity for the *Empire Gazette*, edited by Adela Pankhurst Walsh [q.v.]. *Looking back*, Ellen's recollections of social and artistic life in Sydney, was published in 1938. Her *Rhymes at random* had appeared in 1917. She died on 24 February 1948 at Double Bay and was cremated with Anglican rites; her estate was valued for probate at £20 030. The Todds were childless.

R. B. Walker, *The newspaper press in New South Wales, 1803-1920* (Syd, 1976); *Woman's Budget*, no 1, 30 Jan 1906, p 11; *A'sian Journalist*, 10, no 7, July 1922, p 148; *Newspaper News*, 4, no 9, Jan 1932, p 10; *MJA*, 12 Mar 1932, p 379; *Empire Gazette*, no 42, Nov 1933, p 13; *ISN*, 26 Sept 1891; *Clarence and Richmond Examiner*, 21 Mar, 11 July, 12 Dec 1891, 2 July 1892; *SMH*, 15 Dec 1931, 26 Feb 1948; information from Ms L. Thornton and Mrs E. Wolfe, Braddon, ACT.

MARGARET BETTISON

TOFT, JOHN PERCY GILBERT (1894-1985), public servant and soldier, was born on 11 November 1894 at Bundaberg, Queensland, son of John Toft, an English-born storekeeper, and his native-born wife Lenorah Kate, née Ball. Educated at Maryborough Grammar School, he developed a lifelong interest in reading, music and sport. Toft worked as a probationary teacher and then as a clerk in the Queensland Lands Department; he also served with the senior cadets and for two years with the 4th Infantry Battalion, Australian Military Forces, before enlisting as a private in the 15th Battalion, Australian Imperial Force, on 25 October 1914.

Embarking from Melbourne on the troopship *Ceramic* in December, Toft's battalion sailed for Egypt. He landed at Gallipoli on the evening of 25 April 1915. The 15th Battalion was at Quinn's Post where sniping was heavy. Serving as a runner, Toft was wounded on 26 May; he was evacuated and did not rejoin his unit until 2 August. While at Gallipoli he was promoted corporal and later sergeant. He left Anzac in September.

The 15th Battalion reached France in June 1916 and went into reserve at Bois Grenier. Between 5 and 10 August it saw action near Pozières during the advance on Mouquet Farm. Toft commanded a platoon of 'C' Company and was awarded a Military Medal for his work, especially during the attack against Circular Trench. During this action the battalion's officers suffered heavy casualties and Toft was commissioned second lieutenant on 19 August. He was appointed battalion, and subsequently 4th Brigade, intelligence officer.

Toft did not see action again until June 1917 when, having returned to the 15th, he fought in the battle of Messines, Belgium. After a period in reserve at Neuve Eglise, the battalion went into the front line on the night of 10 June, its primary objective being to establish whether Gapaard Farm and Les Quatre Rois Cabaret were occupied by the enemy. Toft commanded two parties on the nights of 11-12 and 12-13 June to investigate these positions. He killed the German snipers who had been harassing the Australians, then occupied their positions and directed the mopping-up and consolidation of six small posts stretching from Gapaard Farm to Les Quatre Rois Cabaret. For outstanding bravery and leadership, which did much to maintain the morale of his men, he was awarded the Military Cross.

In late August he was transferred to the 4th and then to the 12th Training Battalion. Promoted captain on 15 October, he returned to the 15th Battalion in February 1918. In command of 'C' Company, between 26 March and 5 April Toft took part in the capture of Hébuterne, France, and succeeding operations. He again displayed bravery and determination on 28 March near Fonquevillers where, under intense bombardment, his company beat off an enemy raid and prevented the establishment of machine-gun posts. His exemplary performance earned him a Bar to his M.C.

After the battle of Hamel, in which Toft acted as liaison officer between the 15th and 43rd Battalions, he was appointed assistant instructor at the 4th Army Infantry School from August 1918 to January 1919. On 18 March 1919 he married with Church of Scotland forms Grace McFarlane Stewart at Crieff, near Perth, Scotland. His wife had served as a nurse in France. They returned to Australia in April 1919 and Toft was discharged in August. During the 1920s he served with the 47th Battalion (militia), reaching the rank of major.

He resumed his public service career in Queensland, principally as an inspector in the Agricultural Bank organizing loans to farmers. Toft also worked as a clerk with the Australian Army prior to his retirement in 1959. Although not actively involved with the returned servicemen's movement in the inter-war period, he wrote about the 'Anzac spirit' in a series of articles, 'Playing a man's game', which were published in *The Queensland Digger* in 1935-41.

A man of integrity, with a cheerful, energetic and generous nature, Toft died on 9 February 1985. Survived by a daughter and two sons, he was buried with Uniting Church forms in Redcliffe cemetery, Brisbane.

C. E. W. Bean, *The story of Anzac* (Syd, 1921, 1924), and *The A.I.F. in France* 1916-18 (Syd, 1929, 1933, 1937, 1942); T. P. Chataway, *History of the 15th Battalion A.I.F.* (Brisb, 1948); *Qld Digger*, 1935-41; War diary, 4th Infantry Brigade, AIF *and* records (AWM); information from Dr H. I. Toft, Armidale, NSW.   DARRYL McINTYRE

TOLL, FREDERICK WILLIAM (1872-1955), army officer and accountant, was born on 18 January 1872 at Bowen, Queensland, eldest son of Benjamin Toll, carpenter, and his wife Annie, née Richards, both English born. The family soon moved to Charters Towers where Frederick was educated at the Normal School; at Brisbane Grammar School in 1888 he joined the army cadets. Back at Charters Towers, he became an accountant, was commissioned in the Kennedy Regiment on 2 February 1892 and promoted captain in 1897. On 22 September 1894 he had married English-born Emma Bone (d. 1901), a shop assistant, at St Peter's Anglican Church, Townsville.

Volunteering for service in the South African War, Toll sailed with the 2nd Queensland contingent as a special service officer in January 1900. From Cape Town, he joined Lord Roberts's army in the occupation of Bloemfontein, commanding an infantry company of the (44th) Essex Regiment; he was next a field-aide and acting aide-de-camp on the 18th Brigade staff. Toll saw action during the advance to Kroonstad, Johannesburg, Pretoria and Belfast. After the capture of Nellspruit he was appointed provost-marshal and commanded troops who returned to Brisbane in December.

As second-in-command of the 5th (Queensland Imperial Bushmen) contingent, Toll returned to South Africa in March 1901. He was promoted major in April, commanded the contingent from 1 August in actions in the Cape and Orange River colonies and the Transvaal, and was captured briefly by Boers in January 1902. He reached Brisbane in April; his appointment terminated in July. At Charters Towers, Toll's enthusiastic letters to his father had received wide press coverage and the return of the town's 'favourite son' was fêted. He had been mentioned in dispatches and awarded the Queen's South Africa medal (with five clasps) and the King's (with two).

On 31 October 1904 at Charters Towers-Baptist Church Toll married English-born Maria Louisa Berry; abandoning plans to settle in South Africa, they returned to Queensland. In 1906 he became manager of Mt Molloy sawmill. For various periods he served in the militia and cadets, and in 1913 was awarded the Volunteer Officers' Decoration. Enlisting again for overseas service on 7 November 1914, he embarked for New Guinea in January 1915, leading the 3rd Battalion, Australian Naval and Military Expeditionary Force, with the rank of major (lieut-colonel from 1 March). As officer commanding the troops in Rabaul, he was twice acting administrator of New Guinea in the absence of Colonel (Sir) Samuel Pethebridge [q.v.11]. With the formation of the 8th Infantry Brigade, Australian Imperial Force, Toll was given command of the 31st Battalion and posted to Egypt in November. He served in the Middle East for six months and embarked for France in June 1916. The battalion fought under Toll at Fromelles in July (for which action he was awarded the Distinguished Service Order), Bapaume (March 1917) and Polygon Wood (September). Between 28 October and 14 November he temporarily led the brigade and in November was awarded a Bar to his D.S.O. Seriously injured and gassed at Polygon Wood, he was evacuated to Britain in January 1918. Having served with the A.I.F. Administrative Headquarters in London, he returned to Australia in March 1919 and his appointment terminated in May. He had twice been mentioned in dispatches by General Haig. Toll became commissioner for war service homes, then managed timber businesses in Brisbane and at Mackay. On 18 February 1932 he retired with the rank of honorary colonel.

Despite his prowess as a marksman, athlete and Rugby footballer, early photographs depict Toll as slightly built, with fine eyes, a generous mouth and even more generous ears. He was a foundation member of the Returned Sailors' and Soldiers' Imperial League of Australia, its Brisbane vice-president in 1924-27 and Mackay president in 1928-30. In poor health, he returned to Brisbane in 1930 for medical attention and settled at Woody Point. He was appointed M.B.E. in 1939. During World War II he was district manpower officer, then services liaison officer. Late in life he collected material for a book on the Boer War. Toll died on 6 November 1955 at Greenslopes repatriation hospital, Brisbane, and was cremated. He was predeceased by his wife, and by the son and daughter of his first marriage: the son had been killed at Gallipoli.

Aust Defence Dept, *Official records of the Australian military contingents to the war in South Africa*, P. L. Murray ed (Melb, 1911); C. E. W. Bean, *The A.I.F. in France*, 1916-17 (Syd, 1929, 1933); S. S. Mackenzie, *The Australians at Rabaul* (Syd, 1927); D. H. Johnson, *Volunteers at heart* (Brisb, 1974); *Northern Miner*, 21 Oct 1899, 15 May-4 July 1900, 17 Mar 1901, 17 Mar 1902; *Queenslander*, 16 Mar 1901; *Charters Towers Mining Standard*, 7 Apr 1902; J. Neal, Charters Towers and the Boer War (B.A. Hons thesis, JCU, 1980); D. Menghetti, Charters Towers (Ph.D. thesis, JCU, 1984); R. Burla, Portrait of a citizen soldier: Lt-Col Frederick William Toll (ts, held by Mrs R. Gibson, Ingham, Qld); War diary, 31st Battalion, AIF (AWM); Charters Towers City Council, Minutebooks (QA).

DIANE MENGHETTI

TOLMIE, JAMES (1862-1939), newspaper proprietor and politician, was born on 25 July 1862 on board the *Rajasthan, en route* from Liverpool to Brisbane, eldest son of Scottish parents Roderick Tolmie, farmer, and his wife Helen, née Macrae. Arriving on 4 November 1862, Roderick secured employment as an overseer on Wallan station, near Miles. About 1870 the family moved to Toowoomba, ostensibly to take advantage of better schooling opportunities.

Educated at Toowoomba South Boys' School until aged 13, James worked as a grocer's assistant before training as a pupil-teacher in his old school from 1877 to 1880. He served at Toowoomba South Boys' (twice), Fortitude Valley and Emu Creek schools, then became head teacher at Gowrie Creek near Toowoomba in 1884. After his wife's death in 1881, Roderick deserted their nine children, leaving James to support the family.

Regarded as an earnest and conscientious employee, with a reputation for efficiency and integrity, Tolmie 'threw himself body and soul into the execution of his duty', but was hampered by his own moderate scholastic achievements; in 1890 he barely scraped a pass in the examination for promotion to second division of the teaching service. Confronted with poor prospects of advancement, he resigned on 31 August 1894 to become editor and half-owner (with S. C. W. Robinson) of the conservative Toowoomba newspaper, the *Darling Downs Gazette*. When it merged in 1922 with its rival, the *Toowoomba Chronicle*, Tolmie remained as chief leader-writer, specializing in international affairs, until 1939.

In 1899 he had unsuccessfully contested the seat of Drayton and Toowoomba as a (Sir)

James Dickson [q.v.8] Ministerialist, but at the 1901 by-election—consequent upon W. H. Groom's [q.v.4] transfer to Federal politics—he succeeded as an independent supporter of (Sir) Robert Philp [q.v.11]. Tolmie subsequently became leader of the 'new Darling Downs Bunch' which defended the established agricultural interests of southern Queensland. Quarrelling with Philp over railway policy, he switched allegiance to (Sir) Arthur Morgan and then to William Kidston [qq.v.10,9] before disagreement over land taxation, trades disputes and the lack of cabinet consultation forced a return to Philp. In the 1907 election Tolmie was defeated by the Kidstonites. Having failed to regain his seat as a farmers' candidate in 1908, he succeeded next year as a Kidston-Philp co-alitionist. In 1911 he was appointed secretary for agriculture and stock in the Liberal ministry of D. F. Denham [q.v.8], allegedly to appease the agricultural interest, and served as secretary for public lands from 1912 to June 1915 when he became leader of the Opposition. Shortly before the election in 1918 he resigned as leader due to illness and lost his seat. He never regained it, despite attempts in 1920 and 1923. He served one term (1924-27) as a Toowoomba City Council alderman.

Although a 'keen and clever electioneer', Tolmie had an agrarian base that was gradually undermined by Toowoomba's industrial development. He may also have contributed to his loss of support by his arrogance, his absences on crucial parliamentary votes and his lukewarm stand on conscription. As a minister, he had devised an expensive, 'utopian and impracticable' farm policy which envisaged 'ready made farms . . . fenced, house erected, and crops growing for new settlers'. As party leader, he readily delegated tasks to specialists, but was 'a poor performer' on the floor of the House, being a dogmatic and platitudinous speaker, inclined to bully rather than persuade. His great achievement was to give fervent backing to the formation of the University of Queensland along 'democratic' lines.

A genial, bulky man with a huge laugh and a larger appetite, he held no grudges and was personally popular. He was an active sportsman and represented Queensland in its last intercolonial Australian Rules football match in 1884. He also had an extensive reference library and was active in the local School of Arts. In 1903 he published an authoritative article, 'Drayton and Toowoomba: their early history', in the Queensland Geographical Journal. He also helped to establish the Darling Downs Building Society. Tolmie had served nine years with the Queensland Volunteer Defence Force before enlisting in the Australian Imperial Force in February 1916; he commanded troops in transports travelling to and from Egypt.

An active Presbyterian and Freemason, he died on 5 April 1939 and was buried in Toowoomba cemetery, leaving an estate sworn for probate at £4343. He had not married.

C. A. Bernays, *Queensland politics during sixty (1859-1919) years* (Brisb, nd, 1919?) and *Queensland—our seventh political decade 1920-1930* (Syd, 1931); D. J. Murphy, *T. J. Ryan* (Brisb, 1975); N. Yeates, *Stone on stone* (Coffs Harbour, NSW, 1979); *Courier Mail*, 20 Mar 1907, 6 Apr 1939; *Toowoomba Chronicle*, 6 Apr, 2 Sept 1939; register of male teachers, 1860-1903 (QA).

M. FRENCH

TOMHOLT, SYDNEY JOHN (1884-1974), playwright and critic, was born on 6 January 1884 at Fitzroy, Melbourne, eldest of three children of Daniel John Tomholt, a Dutch-born waiter, and his Tasmanian wife Louisa, née Whelan (d. 1898). After a limited education at state schools, he joined a firm of chartered accountants, but left about 1911 to join the Gloria (gas) Light Co.

Encouraged by Gregan McMahon and W. G. Moore [qq.v.10], in the early 1900s Tomholt began writing, chiefly one-act plays. On 2 November 1912 at All Saints Anglican Church, St Kilda, he married a pianist Hilda Merle Cotham; they were to have one daughter; late in 1914 he moved to Sydney to open an office for his firm. On 28 December 1915 Tomholt enlisted in the Australian Imperial Force and next year went to France with reinforcements for the 24th Battalion. Evacuated sick in November, he was attached to the Pay Corps in London from March to September 1917. Through Charles Charrington, he met such leading writers as J. M. Barrie and G. K. Chesterton. G. B. Shaw wrote several times to Tomholt whom he recognized as 'a serious dramatist with a flair for atmosphere and emotional and dramatic intensity'. In December he was sent to No. 2 Command Depot, Weymouth, but John Drinkwater arranged six months leave without pay for him to study drama from September 1918. Between May and October 1919 Tomholt attended the University of London as a playwright before embarking for home.

Unsettled after divorcing his wife in 1921, Tomholt left Australia in 1922 for Mongolia and China. He engaged in transport work in the Gobi Desert and was granted a rare interview with the Panchen Lama in Tibet. At Shanghai, by 1924 he was financial editor of the *China Press* and *Shanghai Times*. He married a White Russian refugee, Mary, née Kouptzova, who bore him a daughter in 1925.

From the late 1920s he worked for the American firm, Pacific Commercial Co., in Manila where he met Tom Inglis Moore who became a lifelong friend.

Settling in Sydney in 1933, Tomholt joined 2GB radio as chief dramatic script writer. His serial, 'The Dreyfus case' and several of his dramas were broadcast; *Anoli the blind* was placed in a *Bulletin* competition and included in *The best one act plays of 1936* (London, 1937). He published *Bleak dawn and other plays* in 1936. Written in a period when Australian dramatists encountered difficulties with unsympathetic theatre managements, his plays were rarely performed: in general they emphasized 'the anguish of life'.

From 1937 Tomholt was film, music and dramatic critic for the *Sydney Morning Herald*. He joined the Allied Works Council during World War II, held Commonwealth Literary Fund fellowships in the mid-1940s and later ran a literary agency. Known to his friends as 'Tommy', he 'thought and spoke so rapidly that he often uttered delicious malapropisms'. Living in the inner city, he made his flat (always called 'The Room') into an informal meeting place for poets, theatre people and academics, among them Hugh McCrae [q.v.10], R. D. FitzGerald, (Dame) Doris Fitton and May Hollinworth; his friend Maxine Poynton-Baker, née Murray-Jones, helped him at these gatherings. Survived by his wife and daughters, Tomholt died at Darlinghurst on 23 April 1974 and was cremated.

N. Keesing, *Riding the elephant* (Syd, 1988); *SMH*, 18 Nov 1933, 19 June 1936, 13 May 1947, 26 Apr 1974, Divorce file, 1920, no 468 (Prothonotary's Office, Supreme Court, Melb); information from Mrs M. Poynton-Baker, Potts Point, Syd.

NANCY KEESING

TOOMEY, JAMES MORTON (1862-1920), trade unionist and Labor Party organizer, was born on 28 November 1862 at Gribbin station, Wagga Wagga, New South Wales, son of native-born parents James Henry Toomey, superintendent, and his wife Sarah Jane, née Morton. He grew up in the Riverina and in 1886 helped to found the Wagga Wagga Shearers' Union. Moving to Young in March 1888, he was elected secretary of a new branch of the Amalgamated Shearers' Union of Australasia. Soon after, he established a branch of the Amalgamated Miners' Association and the Young District Carriers' Union, becoming secretary of both. He then formed a trades and labour council of which his three unions were the only members. Although his lone drive to mobilize labour at Young failed, Toomey was enthusiastic and energetic; he was also a forceful public speaker whose letters to newspapers were clearly argued.

In June 1888 he arranged a conference between the Young branch of the A.S.U. and the Young and Lachlan Districts Sheepowners' Association; W. G. Spence [q.v.6] was present and G. H. Greene [q.v.9] of Iandra station led the pastoralists. The result was a formal agreement which specified shearing rates and working conditions for local sheds. Toomey and Greene were given most of the credit for negotiating the first such agreement between the union and a pastoralists' association: it was to serve as a model for the four-colony agreement negotiated by the A.S.U. and the Pastoralists' Federal Council of Australia in 1891.

When it seemed that Queensland's bitterly fought shearers' strike would spread into New South Wales in June that year, Toomey approached Whiteley King, secretary of the Pastoralists' Union of New South Wales, and helped to bring the P.F.C.A. to the conference table in August 1891. Spence and David Temple [q.v.], secretary of the A.S.U., alleged that Toomey had weakened their bargaining position by defying an executive ruling to leave negotiations to senior officials. Temple, however, had allowed himself no room for manoeuvre through his unyielding statements; a conference became possible only after Toomey had shown willingness to compromise.

Although he described himself as a socialist, Toomey was at heart a pragmatic reformer. His strengths were his ability to reconcile differences and his indefatigable pursuit of those objectives he considered worthwhile. That the fledgling Labor Party—prone to urban and rural factionalism, and divided over policy and the candidates' solidarity pledge—managed a united effort at the 1894 elections was largely attributable to his exertions. Toomey was tireless in his attempts to organize a Labor vote in country electorates. At several party conferences and on the executive of the shearers' union (forerunner of the Australian Workers' Union), he put the case for unity with verve and courage. The work he did in these years helped Labor to develop a strong rural base in New South Wales. Defeated for the Legislative Assembly seat of Boorowa in 1894 by the adroit Protectionist organizer T. M. Slattery [q.v.11], Toomey might have won if he had contested Young, but in the interests of unity he had persuaded J. C. Watson [q.v.] to stand for that seat.

The decision to make way for Watson marked a change in Toomey's fortunes. He never again won pre-selection for the Labor Party and in 1896 the A.W.U. abolished the Young branch to cut administrative costs. Bitter at being deserted by Watson, Toomey drifted in and out of jobs. He represented the Creswick (Victoria) branch of the A.W.U. at Federal conferences in 1898 and 1899, before returning to Young where he was declared bankrupt in 1905. At St Patrick's Catholic Church, Sydney, on 26 December 1906 he married Elizabeth Mary Post, a dressmaker from Maitland. He later became an accountant and paymaster on the northern coalfields, only to lose his job when he supported striking miners. He was working as a commercial traveller when he died of chronic nephritis at his Lambton home on 1 April 1920; he was buried in Sandgate cemetery, Newcastle; his wife and 12-year-old daughter survived him.

B. Nairn, *Civilising capitalism* (Canb, 1973); J. Merritt, *The making of the AWU* (Melb, 1986); *Newcastle Morning Herald*, 3 Apr 1920; bankruptcy file 16399 (NSWA); Watson papers (NL).

JOHN MERRITT

TORODE, WALTER CHARLES (1858-1937), master builder, was born on 17 September 1858 in North Adelaide, son of Henry Kaines Torode, storeman, and his wife Sarah, née Sperring. Henry, who had migrated from Guernsey, was a cabinetmaker and Walter's uncle was a brickmaker. In 1873-79 Torode trained as a carpenter at William King & Co.'s steam sawmill, North Adelaide. On 12 May 1881 he married Sophia Minnie Gellentien; they were to have six children. Torode seized opportunities offered by the new hills railway which converted Aldgate and Stirling villages into fashionable resorts for Adelaide's leading families. Leasing several quarries, he specialized in contracts for architect-designed mansions; he avoided sub-contracts, employing day-labour exclusively.

By 1900 Torode's self-sufficiency, entrepreneurial flair and building skill had won him a number of large contracts, among them the Allan Campbell [q.v.7] Building at Adelaide Children's Hospital, the Elder [q.v.4] Conservatorium, the Adelaide Stock Exchange, the Lady Chapel and western spires of St Peter's Cathedral (his favourite achievement), several suburban churches, extensions to Unley Town Hall, Ruthven Mansions and additions to Pulteney Street School.

Among the first Australian builders to grasp the structural potential of reinforced concrete, he used it as early as 1907. Next year he built himself a concrete house at Unley, employing cavity walls cast *in situ* with perforated steel sheet reinforcement; he also constructed a substantial concrete bridge and buildings at Anlaby station, near Kapunda. By 1909 he had adopted imported asbestos-cement sheeting for linings and stucco render over external cast-concrete surfaces. He built many concrete houses in Adelaide over the next two decades and the South Australian Railways adopted his method for their low-cost cottages. While he was not an innovator in concrete construction and took out no patents, he skilfully rode the wave of modern building techniques.

Torode's designs favoured the picturesque and arts-and-crafts motifs, as if to temper his mechanistic technology. His own homes, which also served as display houses, revealed an eclectic mind that ranged across techniques and styles. Torode's most remarkable home was Amphi Cosma (Wayville, 1914) which was inspired by the work of American architect Orson Fowler. Daring in its reinforced concrete structure and octagonal plan, for all its impracticality it was a minor landmark in Australian domestic architecture. A tall, broad-shouldered man of jocular ways whose fame owed much to self-promotion, Torode published *How to build* (1904) and *At home* (1917). His achievement commands respect for his technical mastery, his success at vertical integration of the building industry, and his fine craftsmanship.

After his wife's death in 1913, Torode married Ida Edith Lower (d. 1928) on 4 April 1914 at North Adelaide. He was active in the Brougham Place Congregational Church and the Sunday School movement within the Congregationalist, Baptist and Presbyterian churches. He played cricket when young and later bowls. Buying a motor cycle in 1902, he became patron of the Motor Cycle Club of South Australia; he relished anecdotes about his one-day round trip from Adelaide to Murray Bridge in that year. Torode moved in 1928 to Melbourne and in 1935 to Sydney where he died on 28 January 1937 and was cremated. Three daughters and two sons survived him.

J. Smillie, *Descriptive Australia and Federal guide* (Adel, 1890); *Architecture in Australia*, 77, no 4, June 1988, p 65; *Mail* (Adel), 13 Sept 1913; *Advertiser* (Adel), 29 Jan 1937; J. Ashton, Personalities remembered: Walter C. Torode (ABC radio script, 18 Oct 1970) *and* Recollections of incidents combined with the career of Walter Torode from boyhood until he became master builder (ts, 1931) *and* Torode papers (Mortlock Lib); Miscellaneous Torode papers and memorabilia (held by Mr N. Torode, Lower Mitcham, Adel).

PETER BELL

TORR, WILLIAM GEORGE (1853-1939), headmaster, was born on 26 May 1853 at Tavistock, Devon, England, fourth son of illiterate parents John Torr, miner, and his wife Ann, née Green. The family migrated to South Australia in 1855 and settled at Burra. Educated locally and at Stanley Grammar School, Watervale, at 17 William worked on a sheep-station in Tasmania. Returning to

South Australia, in 1875 he trained as a teacher and was appointed to the one-teacher Ulooloo Public School, to the Model School at Grote Street, Adelaide, and—as headmaster —to Moonta Mines Public School where he gained his first-class certificate. On 30 March 1877 at Mintaro he married Charlotte Chewings; they were to have a daughter and son who survived infancy. In 1884 he took his family to Europe.

A Bible Christian, Torr became a lay preacher. In 1885 when his Church proposed to establish Way College, a boys' school in Adelaide, he undertook to accept the position of headmaster; having attended the University of Adelaide, he planned to go to Britain to acquire further qualifications. On 10 August Charlotte died, leaving him ample means. He attended the universities of Oxford, where he was a member of St John's College (B.A., 1889; B.C.L., 1891; M.A., 1892), Cambridge, where he entered Downing College, and Trinity College, Dublin (LL.B., 1891; LL.D., 1892). Called to the Bar at the Inner Temple in 1891, he never practised law. Back in Adelaide, on 20 December 1892 he married an English widow Albertina Santo, née Kidner. Way College opened that year. The school had three divisions: the 'University' course prepared students for the public service, commerce and tertiary study; the 'Practical' section supplemented basic education with instruction in areas such as carpentry and horticulture; the 'Theological' course trained older students for the ministry. In 1899 Torr reported to the government on educational trends he had observed in Britain and other countries. With Methodist union in 1900, Way College was made redundant by the Wesleyans' Prince Alfred College. Way, which had seen 1100 boys pass through it, closed in 1903.

The headmaster became an evangelist, conducting missions throughout Australia and in New Zealand. In 1909, the year of Albertina's death, he set up and was governor (until 1920) of the Methodist Training Home at Brighton, Adelaide; here he prepared some young men for the ministry and others as lay workers and preachers. When the institution was given to the Methodist Church in 1922, Torr continued as an honorary tutor. Interviewed that year, he reclined on a lounge in his study, wearing an emerald-green smoking-cap, while clouds from his pipe curled through his thin, pale whiskers. He admitted to having been a martinet in his college days, but claimed that he had produced men who could stick at things; his students seem to have remembered him fondly.

For nearly forty years from 1902, as 'Old Oxford', he wrote 'Talks To Young Men' for the Methodist weekly, the *Australian Christian Commonwealth*. His wide-ranging homilies swayed thousands of Methodist men and women. Torr endorsed a non-fundamentalist view of Christian scripture; he was essentially a popularizer whose colloquial, down-to-earth articles (correspondents were 'chums') expressed his modernist views of the Bible. By influencing lay preachers and future ministers, he helped to liberalize local Methodist attitudes.

Interested in harmonizing religion and science, he became a considerable collector of chiton shells, overseas, along Australia's coastline and with (Sir) Joseph Verco's [q.v.] dredging expeditions. Even when elderly, Torr delighted in wading through rock pools collecting loricates. He published four scientific papers and three shells were named after him. Torr also enjoyed bowls, poetry and sketching. His devoted wife Mary Frances Buchan, née Walter—a widow whom he had married on 6 February 1912 at the Catholic Apostolic Church, Melbourne—died in 1937. Survived by a daughter, Torr died at his Brighton home on 13 September 1939 and was buried in North Brighton cemetery. The council named an avenue after him and there is a memorial window in Brighton Uniting Church.

T. Piper, *Way College* (Adel, 1891); J. J. Pascoe (ed), *History of Adelaide and vicinity* (Adel, 1901); P. M. T. Tilbrook, *The life and times of Dr. William George Torr* (Adel, 1972); A. D. Hunt, *This side of heaven* (Adel, 1985); *Aust Christian Cwlth*, 15 Apr 1932, 22 Sept 1939; *SA Methodist Hist Soc J*, 1, Oct 1967; *Mail* (Adel), 22 July 1922; *Advertiser* (Adel), 14 Sept 1939; Torr correspondence in S. J. Way letter-book (Mortlock Lib); information from former students.   ARNOLD D. HUNT

TOUT, SIR FREDERICK HENRY (1873–1950), solicitor, pastoralist, businessman and politician, was born on 13 January 1873 at Calabash, near Young, New South Wales, sixth child of English parents, Samuel Tout, grazier, and his wife Sarah, née Kelly; twice widowed, Sarah had four other children. After education at Fort Street Model School and Newington College, where he played Rugby, he was articled to Sir Joseph Abbott [q.v.3]. On 21 August 1897 Tout was admitted as a solicitor and on 8 September in the Congregational Church, Glebe, married Minnie Agnes, daughter of Francis Abigail [q.v.3]. Entering into partnership with Macartney Abbott, Tout practised in Sydney and Burrowa until 1907 and retained an interest in the firm to 1933.

Taking over part of his father's estate near Young, Tout developed Wambanumba into a highly productive sheep- and wheat-station, and established a successful Aberdeen Angus stud. He later owned Uah (near Forbes) and other properties. Prominent in local affairs, he was chairman of the Young Pastures Protection Board and repatriation committee, president of the local branch of the Graziers' Association of New South Wales (1918-33), a member of the Burrangong Shire Council and long-time president of the hospital board.

In January 1928 Tout was appointed to the three-member Federal valuation board, formed to review land tax assessments. A council-member (1913-41) of the Graziers' Association, in 1928 he became president and served for an extended term of five years during the Depression. Conspicuous in negotiations about primary industry, he was a member of many of the association's special committees, a delegate to the Australian Woolgrowers' Council, the Employers' Federation of New South Wales and other organizations, and a State representative on the association's federal council. A founding member (1929) and chairman (1933-34) of the Australian Oversea Transport Association, he was involved in schemes to promote wool and to regulate meat exports.

Fiercely opposed to the policies of J. T. Lang [q.v.9], in October 1931 Tout chaired a conference of the National Party, Country Party and the All for Australia League in an attempt to co-ordinate opposition to the Federal and State Labor governments. Next year he attended the Imperial Economic Conference, Ottawa, as an adviser; returning via England, he criticized marketing in that country of Australian primary products. In 1933 he became president of the Australian Economic Advisory Council, an influential group which included Sir George Allard, (Sir) Philip Goldfinch and H. S. Nicholas [qq.v.7,9,11]; they opposed socialism and wanted the rehabilitation of industry to continue, regardless of political changes. Tout was knighted in 1935.

In 1922 he had unsuccessfully contested the Legislative Assembly seat of Cootamundra. As a member of the Country Party, he was president of the local electorate council, and trustee and vice-chairman (1933) of the State central council. Nominated to the Legislative Council in September 1932, Tout was elected in November 1933 to the reconstituted council for twelve years. He did not seek re-election in 1946.

From the late 1920s Tout's advice was sought by several important companies: he was a director of the Australian Mutual Provident Society, Goldsbrough, Mort [qq.v.4,5] & Co. Ltd, the Graziers' Co-operative Shearing Co. Ltd (Grazcos), Associated Newspapers Ltd, Expeditionary Films (1933) Ltd and the McGarvie Smith [q.v.11] Institute. He was a local director of the Commercial Union Assurance Co. Ltd. As president (1945-50) of the Bank of New South Wales, he was concerned with post-war reconstruction and fought nationalization of the trading banks. He was a director (1938-41) of Sydney Hospital and a fellow (1939-49) of the senate of the University of Sydney.

Short and plump, Sir Frederick considered himself a '"pure merino" bushman'. Untiring in his efforts to promote primary industry, he remained courteous and never appeared hurried. He was a member of the Australian and Union clubs. His wife died in 1942 and on 28 September 1945 at St Michael's Anglican Church, Rose Bay, he married Marie Gwendoline Glennie. Survived by her, and by two sons and a daughter of his first marriage, he died in a private hospital at Darlinghurst on 4 July 1950 and was cremated with Anglican rites. His estate was sworn for probate at £127 610.

L. E. Gent, *The Fort Street centenary book* (Syd, 1949); *NSW Graziers' Annual*, 1925-33; *Pastoral Review*, 16 Feb 1932, 15 July 1950; Bank of NSW, *Annual Report*, 1945-49; *Syd Univ Gazette*, Sept 1950; *SMH*, 31 Mar 1928, 15, 18, 20 Nov 1931, 13 Jan, 14 Sept 1932, 3 Feb, 6 Nov 1933, 31 Jan, 3 June 1935, 6 July 1950; *Smith's Weekly*, 5 Mar 1932; *Sun News-Pictorial*, 18 Apr 1932; G. S. Harman, Graziers in politics: the pressure group behaviour of the Graziers' Association of New South Wales (Ph.D. thesis, ANU, 1968). A. F. DEER

TOUTCHER, RICHARD FREDERICK (1861-1941), politician and nationalist, was born on 27 May 1861 at Maryborough, Victoria, son of Charles Toutcher, architect, and his wife Ellen, née Finnen, both Irish born. Charles was a prominent citizen in Maryborough from the late 1850s and designed many of its buildings; in 1866-75 he was town clerk and then engineer and valuer of the shire of Huntly; he was town clerk at Ararat in 1877, but died suddenly in 1878, leaving a widow and eight children.

Richard, generally known as Dick, attended Maryborough Grammar School. After moving to Ararat, he entered the civil service in July 1877 as a letter carrier in the Postal Department. He became an enthusiastic nationalist and joined the local branch of the Australian Natives' Association, serving as president for three terms. On 20 April 1883 at Ararat he married with Anglican rites Marion Theresa Ryan; they were to have seven children. Shifting to Melbourne in 1888, he worked briefly as a mail sorter before transferring to the Trade and Customs Department.

Toutcher became increasingly involved in nationalist and liberal movements at the highest level in Melbourne. He joined the Richmond branch of the A.N.A. and served as its president. In 1894 he was one of a group of radical young members elected to the central board of directors and next year was elected vice-president. When the directors initiated the moves which led to the formation of the Australasian Federation League of Victoria in 1895, he became its secretary and held the position throughout its existence. Apparently indefatigable, he also became a member of the Anti-Sweating League.

Despite these activities, Toutcher was content with his humble occupation. Transferred in 1896 to the Income Tax Office, he protested, claiming that the move caused his health to deteriorate. He took sick-leave next year and, after an application for a return to the Customs Department on the grounds of ill health was rejected, obtained a medical certificate recommending that he be transferred to outdoor work. The Public Service Board responded by retiring him.

In 1897 Toutcher was elected chief president of the A.N.A. At the election in October, he stood for the Legislative Assembly seat of Ararat as a Liberal supporter of Sir George Turner [q.v.]. The campaign was hard fought, marked by criticism of Toutcher's struggle with the Public Service Board, but he was returned comfortably. He held the seat until 1904 and then the combined Stawell and Ararat seat until 1935. In that time he won fifteen elections.

The years between his 1897 election and the achievement of Federation were the most active in Toutcher's career. One of a group of young A.N.A. politicians who defied the *Age's* opposition to the Constitution bill and prodded the Turner government into supporting it, he chaired the A.N.A. conference of March 1898 which decided to support the bill. He gained a reputation for seizing every opportunity to make a pro-Federation speech. Contemporary photographs show him as slightly balding, with a handlebar moustache.

After Federation, as a back-bencher Toutcher was less prominent. He continued to fight for liberal causes such as female suffrage and factory legislation, but the passage of time and the advent of Labor pushed him with other Liberals towards conservatism. In the course of his long career he served on most parliamentary committees and for several years chaired the Railways Standing Committee. He was minister of public instruction and forests in the Peacock [q.v.11] government in April-July 1924.

A director of the A.N.A. until 1913, Toutcher continued to be active in the branch at Elsternwick, the suburb where he lived. He served as a trustee of the Exhibition Building and as a member of the board of control of the Boy Scouts' Association, Victorian section. On retirement from parliament through ill health in February 1935, he was described as a 'cheerful, kindly soul' with a gentle disposition. He died on 6 September 1941 at Caulfield. Survived by his wife, a daughter and a son, he was buried in Ararat cemetery.

J. E. Menadue, *A centenary history of the Australian Natives' Association 1871-1971* (Melb, 1971); *PD* (Vic), 1934, p 2540; *IAN*, 1 May 1895; *Ararat Advertiser*, 5 Oct 1897, 9 Sept 1941; *Age* and *Argus* and *Sun News-Pictorial*, 8 Sept 1941; M. Aveling, A history of the Australian Natives' Association, 1871-1900 (Ph.D. thesis, Monash Univ, 1970).
                                    DONALD S. GARDEN

TOWNER, EDGAR THOMAS (1890-1972), soldier and grazier, was born on 19 April 1890 at Glencoe station, near Blackall, Queensland, son of Tasmanian-born Edgar Thomas Towner, grazier, and his second wife Greta, née Herley, from Ireland. His parents were among the first settlers on the Barcoo River. Edgar was educated at home, at Blackall State School and at Rockhampton. In 1912 he took up his own selection which he optimistically named Valparaiso; before developing it, he enlisted on 4 January 1915 as a private in the Australian Imperial Force. By March 1916 he was on the battlefields of Belgium and France, a sergeant in the 25th Battalion. In the year that followed he was commissioned lieutenant and twice mentioned in dispatches for 'devotion to duty and consistent good work'.

At Morlancourt, France, on 10-11 June 1918 he won the Military Cross while fighting with the 2nd Machine-Gun Battalion. One of the first to reach his objective near the town of Albert, he quickly brought his section into action, thereby assisting troops from the 7th Infantry Brigade to advance and consolidate; he also made use of captured enemy machine-guns. On the morning of 11 June he capped his gallantry with a feat of daring in daylight, helping to re-establish a post under heavy attack 'at great personal risk'. On 1 September he again distinguished himself at Péronne during the assault on Mont St Quentin. In the early stages of the advance Towner single-handedly captured an enemy machine-gun, then brought his men forward to produce 'such effective fire that the Germans suffered heavy losses'. He later took twenty-five prisoners before capturing another machine-gun 'which, in full view of the Germans, he mounted and fired so effectively that the enemy retired, thus enabling the Australians to advance'. Even when wounded, Towner continued to fight and to inspire his men. His bravery won him the Victoria Cross which was gazetted on 14 December 1918.

The hero returned to Australia in April 1919, but was unable to raise sufficient funds to stock his property. He gave up Valparaiso, went jackerooing and did itinerant work for three years from 1922. Entering into a partnership in Kaloola station (near Longreach) in 1925, Towner thenceforward made the pastures and lands of central Queensland the focus of his life and successfully built up Russleigh Pastoral Co., Isisford.

He took on the bush just as he had accepted the challenges of battle and stuck it out through hard times, preserving his stock as best he could. Towner made himself an expert on the frontier environments of western Queensland and Central Australia, as well as on the exploits of Sir Thomas Mitchell [q.v.2] who had mapped and named parts of the country. By 1946 Towner had successfully lobbied the Commonwealth government for a postage stamp to commemorate Mitchell. In 1955 he crowned his lifelong geographical work with an address to the Royal Geographical Society of Australasia in Brisbane; his efforts were rewarded with the James Park Thomson [q.v.] gold medal and a fellowship of the society; next year his address was published as a booklet entitled *Lake Eyre and its tributaries.*

Edgar Towner was a big man with an imposing personality. In military kit he was burly and tough-looking, but out of it he was shy and distant, engrossed in thought. Without wife or children, he was deemed a loner. A younger generation regarded him as eccentric: always to be seen wearing a suit and frequently disappearing into the outback for long periods of study or exploration. Towner died at Longreach on 18 August 1972 and was buried in the local cemetery with Anglican rites and full military honours.

K. R. Cramp, *Australian winners of the Victoria Cross* (Syd, 1919); B. Hannant, *What price valour* (film, 1985, held by Aust Film Com, Lindfield, Syd); L. Wigmore (ed), *They dared mightily*, second ed revised and condensed by J. Williams and A. Staunton (Canb, 1986); *Longreach Leader*, 25 Aug 1972; War diary, 25th Battalion, AIF (AWM); letters and family papers (held by Mrs D. Watts, El Arish, Qld).   RICHARD GORRELL

TOWNSEND, ALFRED RICHARD (1893-1984), soldier and farmer, was born on 11 October 1893 at Leckhampton, Gloucestershire, England, son of George Townsend, master baker, and his wife Eliza Jane, née Spiers. The family migrated to Australia and, after learning his father's trade, Alfred worked as a farm labourer in western New South Wales where he became a proficient horseman. He enlisted in the Australian Imperial Force on 14 January 1915 and embarked for Egypt with the 12th Light Horse Regiment.

Sent to Anzac as a reinforcement for the 7th L.H.R., he was promoted corporal in December and sergeant when the 12th L.H.R. was re-formed in Egypt in February 1916. At the 2nd battle of Gaza, Townsend—now squadron quartermaster sergeant—was wounded on 19 April 1917, but returned to the firing-line. He was awarded the Distinguished Conduct Medal. On 31 October he rode with 'B' Squadron, 12th L.H.R., in the charge at Beersheba. When a Turkish redoubt on the left flank directed heavy fire at the Australians, he and a fellow sergeant attacked the position, killing ten of the enemy, capturing two and scattering the remainder. For his action Townsend was awarded a Bar to his D.C.M., a distinction gained by only two Australian lighthorsemen during the war. Two days after the charge, he was commissioned second lieutenant. He was mentioned in dispatches in January 1918 and promoted lieutenant next month.

Townsend returned to Australia in November 1919 and next year was allocated a soldier-settler block of 640 acres (259 ha) in the red-soil country of the New South Wales central Riverina at Billabong (later Rand). Naming his property Ramleh after a town in Palestine, he worked with eight- and ten-horse teams to grow wheat, bought more paddocks to graze sheep and share-farmed with a neighbour. Despite floods, droughts, pests and the Depression, he eventually farmed nearly 2000 acres (809 ha). He also undertook a range of community service, becoming a councillor of Urana Shire in 1928, president in 1937 and in 1939-50. On 17 July 1929 Townsend had married Eleanor Mary Jobson with Catholic rites at Culcairn; she died in 1944, leaving him with two young daughters. He married her sister Amabel Alice Jobson on 26 February 1945 at the Presbyterian church, Culcairn.

President of the Shires' Association of New South Wales in 1947 and of the Australian Council of the Local Government Association in 1948, Townsend was disturbed by the increasing influence of party politics in the local arena. The trend so disheartened him that he retired from his shire presidency in 1950, sold his farm and moved to Sydney where he worked as merchandise manager of the Farmers & Graziers' Co-operative Grain, Insurance & Agency Co. Ltd. In 1953 Townsend was appointed M.B.E. for his services to local government. He retired in 1958.

Survived by his wife, a daughter of his first marriage, and a son and daughter of his second, he died at West Ryde, Sydney, on 13 October 1984 and was cremated. He is commemorated by the Townsend Bridge over Billabong Creek at Rand, a modest memorial for an extraordinarily modest man whose military and civilian lives were equally characterized by courage, determination and concern for others.

H. S. Gullett, *The A.I.F. in Sinai and Palestine* (Syd, 1923); W. A. Bayley, *Billabidgee* (Urana, NSW, 1959); *Back to Rand 1926-1976* (Rand, NSW, 1976); *London Gazette*, 12 Jan, 14 Feb, 26 Mar 1918; *SMH*, 1 Jan 1953; War diary, 12th Light Horse Regiment, AIF *and* records (AWM); taped interview with Townsend, 1976 (held by Rand Public School); information from Mrs A. Townsend, Carlingford, Mr T. L. Bray, Eugowra, Mr and Mrs S. Webster and Mrs E. Fagan, Rand, NSW, and Mr W. Carey, Syd.   IAN JONES

TOWNSEND, GEORGE WILFRED LAMBERT (1896-1962), district officer, was born on 5 April 1896 at Sandgate, Brisbane, son of George Townsend, engineer, and his wife Annie, née Evans, both English born. Moving to Melbourne in 1904 when his father was appointed Commonwealth commissioner of patents, he was educated at Trinity Grammar School, Kew.

After twelve months service in the Australian Military Forces, George enlisted on 7 June 1915 in the Australian Imperial Force and on 10 August embarked with the 7th Reinforcements, 2nd Field Artillery Brigade, for Egypt and Gallipoli. From March 1916 he served in France and Belgium. Having trained from November at the Royal Artillery Cadet School, St John's Wood, London, he was commissioned second lieutenant on 23 April 1917 and posted to the 3rd Brigade, Australian Field Artillery. On 1 August he was promoted lieutenant. His A.I.F. appointment terminated in September 1919.

A chance meeting in February 1921 with Brigadier General Wisdom [q.v.], administrator of the new Mandated Territory of New Guinea, led Townsend to accept an invitation to become a patrol officer. On arrival at Rabaul he found himself acting as clerk and cashier for the Expropriation Board whence he acquired his lifelong, German-derived nickname, 'Kassa'. After some reluctant months at his desk, he was appointed patrol officer in the Aitape district. Then followed postings to every region of the mandate. He threw himself into the myriad tasks of a *kiap*, supervising police, labourers and prisoners, signing on labour recruits, collecting taxes and census data, patrolling, exploring, settling disputes and arresting offenders. At Ambunti he hanged men who had violated the prohibition on head-hunting.

On 25 July 1927 at Rabaul he married Mary Lynette Tonge, daughter of an A.I.F. padre. Promoted district officer in 1931, Townsend took charge of the new Sepik district, his favourite region, in 1933. Apart from his routine duties, he led a long exploratory and mapping patrol, planned and supervised the building of the district headquarters and airstrip at Wewak, together with a sub-station at Maprik, and initiated an agricultural policy. He published articles on New Guinea in *Blackwood's Magazine* and in the journal of the Royal Geographical Society of which body he was made a fellow. In 1940 Townsend was posted to Salamaua from where he supervised the upgrading of Lae airstrip which was completed, ironically, in time for Japanese bombers to use it in 1942.

Refused permission to enlist because he was needed for the 'efficient administration' of the territory, Townsend resigned in October 1941; he was reappointed by the army to set up the Australian New Guinea Administrative Unit in which he was promoted captain, then major. In October 1942 he transferred to the propaganda-disseminating Far Eastern Liaison Office. He was renowned for his pidgin broadcasts which concluded, 'Goodbye all-a-boy. Me, Townsend'. Mentioned in dispatches, he retired with the rank of lieutcolonel in October 1945 and was appointed O.B.E.

As one who considered the United Nations to be 'the best hope for a peaceful world', he accepted an invitation in 1946 to work for the secretariat in New York as area specialist for the south-west Pacific in the Department of Trusteeship and Information from Non-Self-Governing Territories. He retired in 1956 to Montville, Queensland. Survived by his wife, son and daughter, he died at Nambour on 9 February 1962 and was cremated with Anglican rites. His autobiography, *District officer*, was published posthumously in 1968.

Short and fair, curt in speech, Townsend was remembered by his fellow *kiaps* as a 'loner' who courted neither popularity nor approval. He loathed red tape and exploited his remoteness from headquarters to take unapproved initiatives. A strong sense of justice governed his actions from his first months in New Guinea, when he deplored the ruthless looting of expropriated German property, to his last, when he saw his World War II service as 'expiation' for the administrative bungling that led to unnecessary casualties during the Japanese invasion. The coast-watcher Eric Feldt wrote that no one doubted Townsend's integrity or his devotion to duty. In his dealings with New Guineans, 'Kassa' was a benevolent paternalist, tough and fair.

PIM, Feb, Mar 1962; *Herald* (Melb), 14 Jan, 17, 18 Oct 1946; Townsend papers (NL); information from Mrs J. McGinty, Coolum Beach, Qld, and Mr G. A. B. Townsend, Birdwood, SA.
                                   DIANE LANGMORE

TOZER, SIR HORACE (1844-1916), solicitor and politician, was born on 23 April 1844 and baptized Horatio at Port Macquarie, New South Wales, son of Horatio Thomas Norris Tozer, chemist, and his wife Charlotte Winifred Amelia, née Croft. Educated at Newcastle and at Rev. W. H. Savigny's Collegiate School, Sydney, he was articled to James Malbon Thomson in Brisbane in 1862 and admitted as a solicitor of the Supreme Court of Queensland on 7 December 1867. The practice he established next year at Gympie soon flourished. A joint owner of mining leases, Tozer became an authority on mining law and was a member of the Gympie Mining Court; he conducted two mining appeals before the Privy Council, in London.

After election to the Legislative Assembly as member for Wide Bay on 13 July 1871, he retired on 23 September, by prior arrangement, to make way for H. E. King who won the seat in the ensuing October by-election. With experience from 1880 as an alderman in the first Gympie Municipal Council, in 1888 Tozer again accepted nomination for Wide Bay and was returned as a Ministerialist on 17 May; he held the seat until 5 March 1898. In 1886 he had taken Anthony Conwell (d. 1897) into legal partnership. Tozer was twice married with Anglican rites: on 12 February 1868 at Ipswich to Mary Hoyles Wilson (d. 1878) and on 10 August 1880 at Gympie to a widow Louisa Lord, née Lister.

In C. A. Bernays's [q.v.3] parliamentary pen-portraits Tozer appeared as a versatile, popular politician whose knowledge of mining laws was much respected and used. He had a fine physique, a 'hail-fellow-well-met disposition' and magnificent pomposity; his astonishingly large voice gave vent to garbled sentences that were 'an outrage upon the English language'; J. M. Macrossan [q.v.5] coined the term 'Tozerisms' for 'something which might be true but probably was not'. Such judgements, however, did not concur with those of other contemporaries who saw that there was more to Tozer than his shell.

From 12 August 1890 until his retirement from parliament Tozer was never out of ministerial office. He was colonial secretary and secretary for public works until March 1893 in the Griffith-McIlwraith [qq.v.9,5] government, colonial secretary in the McIlwraith ministry from March to October 1893 and in the Nelson [q.v.10] ministry from October 1893 to August 1896, and home secretary from then until 2 March 1898. From March to November 1897 he acted as premier in the absence of Sir Hugh Nelson. In that year Tozer was appointed K.C.M.G.

Tozer introduced important legislation which included a Public Service Act (1896), a Factories and Shops Act (1896)—the first Queensland Act regulating hours and conditions—an Election Act (1897) and the subsequently controversial Aboriginals Protection and the Sale of Opium Act (1897). Tozer was noted for his efforts to ameliorate the condition of Queensland Aborigines: he wanted them to regain 'freedom of life and action' and he viewed reservations as places of protection which Aborigines should enter by choice rather than coercion. W. E. Roth [q.v.11] dedicated his *Ethnological studies among the north-west central Queensland Aborigines* to Tozer. In his ministerial capacity Tozer was responsible for founding in 1895 the Free Public Library and the National Art Gallery of Queensland.

Queensland's agent-general in London from 1898 to 1909, Tozer retired because of indifferent health. Survived by two sons and two daughters of his first marriage, he died on 20 August 1916 at his South Brisbane home and was buried in Toowong cemetery.

C. A. Bernays, *Queensland politics during sixty (1859-1919) years* (Brisb, nd, 1919?); *Pugh's Almanac*, 1889; *Brisbane Courier*, 21 Aug 1916; *Gympie Times*, 12 July 1871, 22 Aug 1916; Qld Law Soc Archives, Brisb; roll of attorneys, solicitors and proctors, 1857-1953 *and* Mines Office, Gold mining leases, 1871-76 (QA).   J. C. H. GILL

TRACEY, ELIZA (1842?-1917), litigant, was born in India, daughter of an Irish soldier named Kearns. As an assisted immigrant from Ireland, she came to Western Australia in 1859 and on 12 January 1860 at Guildford married James Tracey, an illiterate labourer and ex-convict. They ran an inn, but failed to pay their debts. When refused credit in 1873, she twice sued the merchant, unsuccessfully. In 1870 the Traceys were charged with stealing sheep; James was imprisoned and thereafter disappeared from Eliza's life.

She became housekeeper to the widower Richard Edmunds, an ageing blacksmith at Guildford who owned two cottages and a farm. Mrs Tracey managed his business and reared his two resentful grandchildren. With the help of a lawyer, John Horgan [q.v.9], she induced Edmunds to bequeath her a life interest in his properties. After his death in 1886 she received rent from the cottages and farm, but the grandson claimed the farm rents since the titles were in his mother's name. Horgan advised Eliza to contest the three resulting lawsuits. She lost them all.

Eliza quarrelled with a tenant of one of the cottages and sued him for abusive language; he refused to pay rent, so she put his scant possessions on the street. The tenant won a suit for trespass with £30 damages. On the advice of Horgan, she refused to pay; to her indignation, she was imprisoned. Horgan asked for £250 in fees; Eliza gave him the titles to her cottage—as security—and transferred her legal business to R. S. Haynes [q.v.9]. When a sheriff arranged to sell her cottage to raise the £30, Eliza thought that no one would bid for property in which she held only life interest. Haynes then paid £17 and acquired her property which was worth £600. Horgan protested and received £250 from Haynes for the titles. Evicted from her cottage, Eliza petitioned parliament for redress. In 1889 a select committee uncovered her shady past and her reputation as a 'virago and scold', and concluded that she had compounded her loss by greed and deceit; while Horgan and Haynes had employed 'adroit' practices, they were within the law.

Perturbed by these events, other lawyers offered their aid. To raise £130 to bring her case to court, Eliza went begging in the settlements of the Swan and Avon valleys. The Full Court ruled that there were insufficient grounds for charges. Further appeals were refused in 1893. She again petitioned the government in 1901 when she appeared dressed as a lawyer; eventually, in 1904, parliament granted her a compassionate allowance. Determined to 'fight so long as I have life in my body', she saw the attorney-general in 1907 who concluded that no case existed for reviewing the original decision.

Waging a vendetta against the legal fraternity, Eliza published a pamphlet, *Robbed by malice and corruption by our judges and lawyers*; she also placed a notice in the *Sunday Times* stating that brothels in Roe Street flourished because judges patronized them. From her soap box at the Esplanade on Sundays, she harangued the men of Perth about topical issues and thieving lawyers. The butt of ribald interjections, she responded with coarse wit. Towards the end of her life she conducted a labour bureau. Mrs Tracey died on 24 February 1917 at Victoria Park and was buried in the Anglican section of Karrakatta cemetery. Her estate was sworn for probate at £134.

R. Erickson, 'Eliza Tracey, a woman with a grievance', *JRWAHS (Early Days)*, 1983.

RICA ERICKSON

TRAEGER, ALFRED HERMANN (1895-1980), engineer, was born on 2 August 1895 at Glenlee, Dimboola, Victoria, eldest son of Johann Hermann Traeger, farmer, and his wife Louisa, née Zerna, both South Australian born. His German grandparents had migrated to South Australia in 1848 and his father returned there with his family in 1902. A curious, patient, precise child, at 12 Alfred made a telephone receiver and transmitted between the toolshed and his house. He attended Balaklava Public School and the Martin Luther School before spending two years at technical high school. From 1912 he studied mechanical and electrical engineering at the South Australian School of Mines and Industries (associate diploma, 1915). He worked for the Metropolitan Tramways Trust and the Postmaster-General's Department. In World War I he was angered that his application to join the Australian Flying Corps was refused, even though his grandparents had been naturalized. About 1923 Traeger joined Hannan Bros Ltd in Adelaide, handling their car generator and electrical repairs. Intrigued by radio, he obtained an amateur operator's licence and built his first pedal transmitter-receiver, later forming Traeger Transceivers Pty Ltd.

John Flynn [q.v.8] was planning his Australian Inland Mission Aerial Medical Service for remote communities and from 1926 Traeger worked for him, at £500 a year, on Northern Territory radio experiments. After an outback tour of duty, Traeger began work in Adelaide on a transceiver for the flying doctor network. The sets had to be cheap, durable, small and easy to operate. Using bicycle pedals to drive the generator, he found that a person could comfortably achieve 20 watts at a pressure of about 300 volts. He enclosed the generator's fly-wheel and gears in cylindrical metal housing, with pedals outside and a cast base to be screwed on to the floor beneath a table. Traeger built the transceiver into a box, employing a master switch to separate the crystal controller transmitter from the receiver. His famous pedal wireless was actually a pedal-operated generator which provided power for a transceiver. Traeger's time was divided between his workshop and the field where he taught radio operating and Morse code; despite the heat, he wore a dark suit and braces.

Once the first pedal sets had been introduced in Queensland in 1929, the invention created a communications revolution by diminishing the loneliness of the inland world. In 1933 Alf invented a typewriter Morse keyboard, an accessory to the pedal sets which was widely used until the advent of radio telephony. In 1939 Traeger's set dispensed with pedals and adopted a vibrator unit. Emergency call systems linked inlanders with hospitals, and sets were used by the School of the Air, doctors, ambulances, councils, taxis, airways and ships.

In 1944 Traeger was appointed O.B.E. A stocky, dark-haired man, with spectacles and a scar on his left cheek, he was friendly, but shunned publicity: his work was his life. He was a member of the Institution of Radio Engineers, Australia. He had married Olga Emilie Schodde (d. 1948) in Adelaide on 11 November 1937. On 2 August 1956 he married a 29-year-old widow, Joyce Edna Mibus, née Traeger (no relation).

In 1962 pedal sets were sold to Nigeria; in 1970 Traeger's firm provided an educational radio network for Canada. Traeger continued inventing: he designed a turbine-driven car and used solar power to convert salt water to fresh water. Survived by his wife, their son and two daughters, and by two daughters of his first marriage, he died on 31 July 1980 at Rosslyn Park, Adelaide, and was buried in Centennial Park cemetery. At Alice Springs a sports field, a plaque and the Royal Flying Doctor Service aeroplane commemorate him.

Lutheran, 14, no 15, 15 Sept 1980; *Advertiser* (Adel), 7 Jan, 23 Dec 1965, 27 Sept 1972; *News* (Adel), 28 Sept 1972; *SMH*, 23 Aug 1980; Royal Flying Doctor Service radio history 1928-85 (RFDS Federal Council Archives, Syd, *and* ML *and* NL); Traeger papers *and* information from Rev. F. McKay, RFDS Federal Council, Syd; information from Mrs J. Traeger, Panorama, Adel.

JOHN BEHR

TRAILL, JESSIE CONSTANCE ALICIA (1881-1967), artist, was born on 29 July 1881 at Brighton, Victoria, youngest of four daughters of George Hamilton Traill, a banker from Scotland, and his Tasmanian wife Jessie Frances Montague, née Neilley. She was educated privately and in Switzerland, her two lifetime occupations—art and travel —being fostered at an early age. Tom Roberts [q.v.11] encouraged her to paint and remained a friend and mentor for much of her career. Inheriting sufficient income to ensure her independence, in 1900 Jessie enrolled in John Mather's [q.v.10] Austral Art School, Melbourne. She was one of the first women to practise etching in Australia; by 1905 her work was exhibited alongside that of Mather and John Shirlow [q.v.11].

Having attended the National Gallery schools (1902-06) under Frederick McCubbin and Bernard Hall [qq.v.10,9], Traill went to London where she studied etching with Frank Brangwyn and visited Belgium and Holland (1907-08) with his summer classes. She enrolled in the Académie Colarossi in Paris for a term, and in 1909 her etchings were hung at the Salon de la Société des Artistes Français, Paris, and the Royal Academy, London. That year she held her first one-woman show in Melbourne. Her style of painting was broad, fluid and neo-impressionist, in both oil and water-colour. In 1914 her entries at the Panama Pacific International Exposition won a gold and a bronze medal. After the outbreak of World War I she went to England, joined the Voluntary Aid Detachment and nursed in military hospitals near Rouen, France.

In 1921 Traill joined the Australian Painter-Etchers' Society and regularly entered her etchings and aquatints in its annual exhibitions. Her preferred subjects— the trees and moods of the landscape—were influenced by Japanese woodcuts and Art Nouveau, and she experimented with unusual decorative formats including the frieze. Using Brangwyn's radical methods, she worked with the largest plates that the press would take and achieved dramatic chiaroscuro. As subjects, she also chose mines, factories and buildings under scaffolding, and, in 1927-32, the Sydney Harbour Bridge. Her prints blended Whistler's sensitivity to design with sound knowledge of engineering and architectural detail.

In 1928 she pinned her water-colours of Central Australia to blankets at the police station for her exhibition at Alice Springs. Sometimes encountered lying in the bush gazing upward to get a 'worm's eye' view, Traill also obtained the opposite outlook from the windows of a flying boat and made several flights in the 1940s. She was generous with knowledge, resources and patronage. Shy and softly spoken, with clear, penetrating blue eyes and graceful hands, she became an eccentric figure, wearing the same old tweed suit and black 'Monty' beret, smoking heavily and carrying her paints in a cereal box tied with string. She spent her later years at her cottage near Berwick, Victoria, on country properties, and in England and France. Traill died on 15 May 1967 at Emerald, Victoria, and was cremated.

In certain stylistic traits, such as the manipulation of space and distance, her work anticipated modernism and has been compared with that of Fred Williams. Reappraised during the 1970s, it is now prized. Traill exhibited with the Society of Graphic Arts, London, the Melbourne Society of Women Painters and Sculptors, the Victorian Artists' Society, the A.P.E.S., the Yarra Sculptors' Society and a number of private galleries. Occasionally she hung her work in country barns. She is represented in all State and many regional galleries, and the Australian War Memorial, Canberra. Her pastel portrait by Janet Cumbrae Stewart [q.v.8] is in the National Gallery of Victoria.

Herald (Melb), 17 July, 29 Nov 1928; *Age*, 29 June 1929; M. A. Lee, Jessie C. A. Traill 1881-1967 (M.A. thesis, Univ Melb, 1983); Traill pâpers (LaTL).
                                   MARY ALICE LEE

TRAILL, JOHN CHARLES MERRIMAN (1880-1942), soldier and grazier, was born on 24 January 1880 in Edinburgh, son of George William Traill, book-keeper, and his wife Phoebe Marshall, née Trew. Educated at

George Watson's College, Edinburgh, he served in the British Army with the Royal Scots and Paget's Horse during the South African War and was wounded at Zeerust. He claimed to have joined the Bechuanaland Mounted Police after the war, and then apparently worked in Mexico and Argentina as a station-manager before migrating to Victoria where he became a grazier at Stawell.

Enlisting in the 8th Battalion, Australian Imperial Force, on 18 August 1914, Traill sailed for Egypt where he was promoted sergeant on 3 April 1915. His battalion landed at Gallipoli on the 25th. He was allotted to the machine-gun section and, with the battalion's two leading companies, pushed forward until he reached the Turkish positions on Pine Ridge. This small force remained forward of the rest of the Anzacs for most of that day and many of Traill's section were killed. The battalion was then ordered to secure a position on the top of Bolton's Hill from where it resisted Turkish counter-attacks for the next two days. Traill served through the Gallipoli campaign, being commissioned second lieutenant on 9 May after the attack on Krithia. He was battalion machine-gun officer thereafter. Awarded the Military Cross and mentioned in dispatches for service at Gallipoli, he was promoted lieutenant on 17 October.

Proceeding to France with his unit in March 1916, Traill was promoted captain on 26 May. He commanded 'A' Company in the fighting at Pozières on 23-24 July when his men cleared two trenches of Germans and captured a machine-gun. Although his company avoided the worst of the enemy bombardment that followed, Traill was wounded in the left arm and evacuated to England. After convalescing, he married Georgina Pearson on 12 February 1917 at St Mary's Cathedral, Edinburgh. They were to have two children. On rejoining his battalion he was appointed second-in-command. He participated in the 3rd battle of Ypres, Belgium, and, during the attack on Broodseinde on 4 October, took command of the assault-line, led his men in successive attacks upon the German defences and destroyed several machine-guns. He and one other man worked forward and killed the crew of a field-gun which was holding up the advance, thus allowing the assault to continue and 'saving a very critical situation'. Traill was awarded the Distinguished Service Order and promoted major on 14 December. On 28 October 1918 he was promoted temporary lieut-colonel with command of the 5th Battalion. During 1917-18 he was twice mentioned in dispatches.

He embarked for Australia in May 1919 and his A.I.F. appointment ended on 10 September. Traill and his wife settled on a farm near Flinders, Victoria, but in 1923 she returned to Scotland, taking the children with her. Divorced on 24 July 1928, Traill married English-born Mollie Helen Roche at the Melbourne registry office on 8 November that year; they were to have two sons. By 1928 Traill lived at Warracknabeal as a wool-buyer and was the New Zealand Loan & Mercantile Agency Co.'s representative for Charlton and Wimmera. On the outbreak of World War II he was appointed manpower officer for these districts and group commander of the Volunteer Defence Corps for north-western Victoria. Survived by his wife and children, he died of 'myocardial degeneration' on 12 June 1942 at Wangaratta and was buried with Anglican rites in the local cemetery.

A. W. Keown, *Forward with the Fifth* (Melb, 1921); C. E. W. Bean, *The story of Anzac* (Syd, 1921), and *The A.I.F. in France*, 1916-18 (Syd, 1929, 1933, 1937); *Reveille* (Syd), July 1933, Apr 1936; *Argus*, 13 June 1942; Bean papers *and* diaries *and* notebook *and* Traill biog file (AWM).

JEFFREY GREY

TRANTER, CHARLES HERBERT (1868-1935), banker, was born on 2 October 1868 at Little River, Victoria, son of Charles Evenden Tranter, schoolteacher, and his wife Mary Ann, née Roberts, both English born. Joining the Geelong branch of the Commercial Bank of Australia as a junior clerk in 1884, three years later Charles was appointed accountant at Murchison in the Goulburn Valley where the bank had financed much of the district's agricultural development. In 1889 he was transferred to the inspector's office, Melbourne, where he shortly became securities clerk, supervising loan documents. At 24 Tranter was appointed inspector's accountant, responsible for the weekly returns from over one hundred branches. He had charge of the branch network routine during the traumatic period of the bank's suspension and reconstruction in 1893, and its subsequent painful recovery. On 29 November 1893 at Carlton he married Ada Alice Cary (d. 1931) with Congregational forms.

In March 1900 Tranter was promoted assistant inspector and in July 1906, as inspector, was one of the triumvirate controlling the bank's branches. In 1913, during eight months paid leave, he travelled in Europe and in 1917 was sent to conduct a detailed inspection of the London branch and to relieve the manager for five months. In 1924-29 Tranter managed the Melbourne office, overseeing much of the bank's lending for the development of secondary industry in Victoria. He was appointed general manager on the death of H. L. Heron in September 1929. A more public man than Heron, with a mind open to fresh ideas and with a close involvement in the Rotary movement, he was eminently suited to lead the bank through the Depression. Courteous and kindly, he was seen in 1930 as 'a dark star in the banking firmament'. As chairman of the Melbourne Associated Banks, he represented their views to the Senate committee on the Labor government's controversial Central Reserve Bank bill (1930). Although not opposed to the establishment of a genuine central bank, Tranter objected to the potential risk of political control which might result from the compulsory deposit of trading bank funds.

A ready public speaker, Tranter expressed intelligently the conservative viewpoint of the time. As the Depression intensified, he pointed out the folly of parrot cries for 'release of credit' to solve difficulties: 'if we mortgage the future we have to pay for it', he warned. Though he accepted the need for currency depreciation due to the adverse balance of payments, he counselled cautious action to prevent a loss of confidence.

A man of simple tastes, he enjoyed bowls, billiards and photography. By May 1934 his health had deteriorated. He took six months leave, then retired in October. Tranter died of a coronary occlusion on 3 October 1935 at his Oakleigh home and was buried in Springvale cemetery. On 28 November 1932 at Flemington he had married with Baptist forms Jessie Isabel May, his 25-year-old housekeeper, who survived him with their 2-year-old daughter. His Victorian estate was sworn for probate at £37 174.

Select cttee of the Senate appointed to consider and report upon the Central Reserve Bank bill, Reports, *PP* (Cwlth Senate), 1929-31, p 465; *A'sian Insurance and Banking Record*, Apr 1913, Jan, May, Oct 1934, Oct 1935; *Argus*, 10 Feb 1930; *Age*, 4 May 1934, 4 Oct 1935; CBA archives (Westpac Banking Corp, Syd). R. J. WOOD

TREASURE, HARRY LOUIS (1877-1961), cattleman, was born on 20 July 1877 at Wandiligong, Victoria, son of Emmanuel George Treasure, miner, and his wife Emily, née Langford, both English born. In April 1878 George moved his family—the children strapped to chairs on the sides of pack-horses —to King's Spur, on the eastern slopes of the Dargo High Plains. Their home, a two-roomed, bark-roofed log hut, was situated at the winter snow-line. The family, with its nine boys and two girls, made a living in the bush by milking cows, growing vegetables, packing goods for the nearby gold-mines, fossicking, and by operating a small store, hotel and post office.

In 1888 George acquired a one-third share in the Dargo High Plains cattle-run; when local mining activity began to decline, the family turned to cattle for a livelihood. All the children assisted with farm work, but Harry and his brothers were given an elementary education by a teacher employed by his parents. In 1888 Harry attended the Dargo school, receiving board with the local policeman in return for odd jobs, but returned next year to work on the family property.

On 4 March 1903 at College Church, Parkville, Treasure married with Presbyterian forms Clare Victoria Gamel, a schoolteacher from Beechworth. Over the following half-century they and their five children became the principal, and finally the only, cattle graziers on the Dargo High Plains. When rabbits ravaged the bush pastures in the immediate vicinity, Treasure bought a property at Castleburn, south of Dargo, as the family's winter abode. Each summer, when the snows melted, they returned with their stock to the high plains where Harry and his sons eventually built a substantial weatherboard homestead from local timber.

A renowned bushman, axeman, buckjump rider and horse-breaker, Treasure could cope with a multitude of tasks, including housebuilding, storekeeping and butchering. He was a councillor of the Avon Shire for over thirty years from 1918 and a supporter of the Bush Nursing Centre at Dargo. He took his children into the family business, among them his daughter Freda who could ride and work cattle as well as any man. Harry died on the Dargo High Plains on 28 December 1961; survived by his wife, daughter and three sons, he was buried with Anglican rites in Dargo cemetery. His estate was sworn for probate at £49 678.

H. Stephenson, *Cattlemen and huts of the high plains* (Melb, 1988); *The Gap*, 1963; *Herald* (Melb), 9 Nov 1951; *Bairnsdale Advertiser*, 18 Jan 1962; P. Cabena, Grazing the high country, Victoria, 1835-1935 (M.A. thesis, Univ Melb, 1980); information from Mr J. Treasure, Lindenow, Vic.

PETER CABENA

TREFLÉ, JOHN LOUIS (1865-1915), politician, farmer and newspaper proprietor, was born on 4 December 1865 at Penshurst, near Hamilton, Victoria, son of John Treflé, sheepfarmer, and his Scottish-born wife Mary, formerly Tyrer, née McKenzie. The father was a French Canadian whose original name was John Treflé Etue; in 1876 he was one of the first to select land at Temora, New South Wales. John Louis was educated at a convent at Hamilton and in 1876-79 as a boarder at St Patrick's College, Goulburn. Failing to realize his hopes of becoming a priest, in the 1880s he worked with his father and brother Charles on their Temora farm. He became an expert ploughman; in 1888-95 he was undefeated in triple-furrow matches and lost only one double-furrow contest—to his brother.

Combining his practical experience with organizing and public-speaking skills, Treflé was responsive to the needs of farmers as agriculture grew in importance in the rural economy in the late 1880s and 1890s. A chief founder of the Farmers and Settlers' Association in 1893, he was its secretary (1893-98) and vice-president (1902-04 and 1905-06). He toured the colony and became known as an articulate, informed and radical publicist for country people. He was a member of the Cootamundra land boards and influenced the drafting of the Reid [q.v.11] government's Crown Lands Act of 1895.

In 1895 Treflé bought the *Temora Independent* and edited it; in 1906 he took J. H. Bradley as a partner and passed control of the paper to him. Treflé became a versatile and accomplished newspaper man. In 1902 he helped to form the New South Wales Country Press Co-operative Co. Ltd, and was president of the New South Wales Country Press Association in 1902-04 and 1910-12. He was director of the Independent Cable Association of Australasia Ltd in 1910-15.

Devout and upright, Treflé reflected his family background in his abhorrence of sectarianism. Dark-complexioned, he was austerely handsome and dressed well. On 23 April 1902 in Manly Catholic Church he married Kathleen Shelly of County Kilkenny, Ireland; they made their home at Waverley. His marriage brought him closer to the majority Irish-Australian Catholics and he became a supporter of Home Rule. He helped P. J. Minahan [q.v.10] to found the Catholic Club in Sydney in 1910; chairman of its building fund, he promoted the erection of a fine club building in Castlereagh Street. Treflé's denominational impartiality was unaffected, and in 1914 he was rebuked by the zealous P. S. Cleary [q.v.8] for his coolness toward the Catholic Federation.

Politics had attracted Treflé from the early 1890s. He became a friend of W. A. Holman [q.v.9] who in 1895 contested the seat of Grenfell (which included Temora) for the Labor Party. Treflé was sympathetic to Labor's agricultural policy and to its plan for a national bank. He hoped that the F.A.S.A. would form a radical country political group, but he failed in his attempt to link the association with the Labor Party. His mother and brother Charles joined Labor in the 1890s and became prominent in the party. Treflé, however, stayed with the F.A.S.A. and in 1904 ran for the Legislative Assembly seat of Upper Hunter with its support: his defeat finally influenced him to join the Labor Party. As its candidate in 1906 he won Castlereagh, a north-west country electorate. With N. R. W. Nielsen [q.v.11], he promoted the revision of Labor's land policy, refining its emphasis on land taxation and leaseholding.

When Labor won government under J. S. T. McGowen [q.v.10] in 1910, Treflé became a minister without portfolio. On 11 September 1911, during the illness of Donald Macdonell [q.v.10], he took over the department of agriculture and became minister on 7 November. He immediately initiated important reforms, stressing the need to combine the experience of farmers with the knowledge of experts: farming methods were improved and a new system of keeping farm accounts was introduced. Treflé retained the agriculture portfolio with the secretaryship of land from 10 December 1912 until 29 January 1914; he continued in the lands portfolio until his death.

Treflé's ministerial work helped to consolidate Labor's strong support in rural electorates. His wide range of experience and skills was complemented by his reforming zeal and rapport with country people. Without a trace of condescension or pomposity, he tempered popularity with personal integrity. His repute was an important factor in showing that the Labor Party could produce efficient and progressive managers of economic growth and social improvement. At the height of his powers, he died suddenly of acute appendicitis and its complications on 11 January 1915 in St Vincent's Hospital, Sydney. Survived by his wife, daughter and son, he was buried in Waverley cemetery.

B. D. Graham, *The formation of the Australian Country parties* (Canb, 1966); *Agr Gazette of NSW*, 2 Feb 1915; *Catholic Press*, 3 Aug 1901, 19 Dec 1918; *T&CJ*, 27 May 1908, 13 Oct 1915; *Daily Telegraph* (Syd), 15 July, 23 Aug 1910, 17 June 1914, 12 Jan 1915; *SMH*, 7 Mar, 18 Apr 1911, 31 May 1912, 24 June 1913, 22 Jan 1914, 11 Jan 1915; *Temora Star*, 11 Jan 1915; *Warren Herald*, 16 Jan 1915; *Freeman's J*, 14 Jan 1918; Treflé papers (held by ADB, Canb).   BEDE NAIRN

TRELOAR, GEORGE DEVINE (1884-1980), gentleman of fortune, was born on 23 April 1884 at Ballarat, Victoria, son of Thomas Reid Treloar, chemist, and his wife Jane, née Devine, both Victorian born. Educated at Ballarat's St Patrick's College, he was a bank clerk at Ballarat for five years, then a jackeroo in western Victoria before he farmed in Western Australia. While travelling by ship to Adelaide, he was recruited by actor-manager Julius Knight and toured Australia with his troup, playing in romantic dramas. Oscar Asche [q.v.7] took Treloar to South Africa and England where he was acting when war broke out in 1914.

Having previously served at Ballarat as a lieutenant in the 3rd Victorian Rifles, Treloar immediately volunteered. Although rejected because of defective eyesight, he wangled his way into the 20th Middlesex (Artists) Rifle Volunteers in 1915 as a private and secured a transfer to the Coldstream Guards. He served in France, was commissioned and ultimately promoted to major, second-in-command of the 3rd Battalion. Buried twice by shellbursts on the Somme and almost bullet-riddled at Ypres, he was awarded the Distinguished Service Order and the Military Cross. In 1918 he commanded the Brigade of Guards Officers' School of Instruction and, following the Armistice, served with his battalion in the Rhineland Occupation Force.

After commanding the post-war Royal Military, Naval and Air Force Tournament at Olympia, London, in 1919, Treloar joined the British Mission to the White Russian armies as assistant military secretary to Major-General Holman. At Constantinople after the withdrawal of the mission, Treloar served with the Tsarist army as a colonel under Baron Wrangel. When the White Russians were defeated Treloar commanded a British camp for Russian refugees at Tousla on the Sea of Marmora. His attempt to set up as a timber concessions trader in Constantinople was frustrated by the Turks. He then became a representative of the League of Nations High Commissariat for Refugees in northern Greece.

In 1922-26 Treloar was engaged in the resettlement of Greek refugees from Asia Minor; at first he worked at Gumuldjina (Komotini) in Thrace and later in Salonika; by 1923 his mission was handling over 108 000 refugees. His efforts to organize food, shelter, medical care and resettlement precipitated disputes with indifferent league officials in Geneva and with a senior Greek official. Treloar was appointed to the Order of the Saviour (gold cross) and a refugee village (Thrilorion) near Komotini was named after him.

In Constantinople on 27 December 1923 Treloar married Kathleen May Douch whose father was an engineering consultant to the Turkish government. When the league's resettlement operation ended, Treloar suffered severe financial loss in a fraudulent mining investment and in 1927 returned to Australia to seek work. Eight years later his family rejoined him. He sold insurance and sought business opportunities in Queensland before unsuccessfully contesting the New South Wales Legislative Assembly seat of Ashfield for the United Australia Party in 1930. In that year Colonel Eric Campbell [q.v.7] appointed him second-in-command of the New Guard. In 1931, however, Treloar denounced Campbell as a Fascist and militarist, and founded his own short-lived movement, the Civic Legion.

In 1935 the Treloars moved to Western Australia where George prospected and managed several mining enterprises. As 'The Archer', he became known for his trenchant radio commentaries on foreign affairs and for his programme, 'Perth Speaks'. A handsome man of commanding presence, forthright speech and strongly-held conservative views, 'the Major' stood unsuccessfully for the Legislative Council seat of West Province in 1950 and worked for the Liberal and Country League until 1956. Treloar died on 29 November 1980 at Dalkeith and was buried in the Anglican section of Karrakatta cemetery, Perth. His wife and two sons survived him.

Australasian, 26 Mar 1921; *Herald* (Melb), 5 May 1927; *SMH*, 10 May 1927; *Smith's Weekly* (Syd), 17 Sept 1927; *Broadcaster*, 12 June 1946, 6 Nov 1948; *West Australian*, 3 Dec 1980.

HUGH GILCHRIST

TRELOAR, JOHN LINTON (1894-1952), public servant, was born on 10 December 1894 at Port Melbourne, Victoria, son of William Henry Treloar, grocer, and his wife Jane Freeman, née Caddy, both Victorian born. Educated at Albert Park State School where he was an outstanding athlete, in 1911 he was appointed a military staff clerk in the Commonwealth Department of Defence. In August 1914 he enlisted in the 1st Division, Australian Imperial Force, and served as a staff sergeant at Gallipoli from April to September 1915 when he was evacuated with enteric fever and later invalided to Australia. In February 1916 he resumed duty as a lieutenant (equipment officer) in No.1 Squadron, Australian Flying Corps, went to Egypt and then in July to France as confidential clerk to Brigadier General (Sir) Brudenell White [q.v.] at 1st Anzac Corps Headquarters.

In May 1917 Treloar was selected to organize the Australian War Records Section. 'Treloar works enormously hard', Charles Bean [q.v.7] observed, the 'Section is simply his creation. He tries to read and criticise every unit war diary'. A 'fair-haired, pink-cheeked youngster . . . with very new captain's stars on his shoulder straps', Treloar represented Australia on the Imperial War Trophies Committee. On 5 November 1918 at the Wesleyan Chapel, Lancaster Road, London, he married Clarissa Maud Weir Aldridge. In the same month he was promoted major. Next year he was appointed O.B.E. After the Armistice, with the aid of a vast staff of ex-diggers, Treloar classified war documents under thirty-six subjects, each further divided into five sections. The result of his work, which concluded in 1932, was an archival record of remarkable detail and accessibility.

His second great contribution was to establish on a firm footing the Australian War Memorial of which he was director (1920-52). Treloar worked a six-day week and, when moved from Melbourne to Canberra, lived in rooms next to his office: only his strict observance of a Methodist Sunday and his passion for watching cricket interrupted this régime. Treloar's 'boyish ingenuous face and simple direct address' gave little indication of his shrewdness and alertness of mind. Shy and reserved, he pursued his goals with inflexible purpose. In a period of uncertainty during the Depression, a trust fund provided crucial financial support: Bean recorded in 1929 that the fund was 'entirely due to Treloar's brain and effort'. When Bean's multi-volume *Official history of Australia in the war* encountered difficulties in the 1930s, the war memorial took over publication and distributed it through a government order scheme, another of Treloar's innovations.

Appointed head of the new Department of Information in September 1939, Treloar became officer-in-charge of the military history section at Army Headquarters, Melbourne, in October 1941 and began to lay the foundations for the collection of World War II records and relics. As a lieut-colonel and liaison officer, he worked with the Department of Information, the War Memorial Board and the 2nd A.I.F. in the Middle East. With the section absorbed by army public relations, record gathering was a shadow of that done for World War I.

Treloar died suddenly after an intestinal haemorrhage on 28 January 1952 in Canberra Community Hospital and was buried in Canberra cemetery. His wife, two daughters and a son survived him; another son had been killed in action with the Royal Air Force in 1943.

Reveille (Syd), 1 Oct 1939; *Canb Times*, 29, 31 Jan 1952; *Bulletin*, 6 Feb 1952; C. E. W. Bean papers (AWM); Letter from J. Treloar to G. M. Long on the military history section, World War II, 7 June 1949 (AWM registry files); information from Mrs D. Shilling, Melb, Mr A. Treloar, Armidale, NSW, and Miss E. Southern, Canb.   DENIS WINTER

TRENERRY, HORACE HURTLE (1899-1958), artist, was born on 5 December 1899 in Adelaide, second of five children of Horace Trenerry, butcher, and his wife Florence Mary, née Pridmore. Having left school, he lived with an aunt who encouraged his artistic interests and provided his first studio. He worked for F. H. Faulding & Co. [q.v.4], bottling cough mixture, but studied drawing at night-classes and went sketching on the weekends; he then joined a group who met at Arthur Milbank's studio where he learned the rudiments of painting. After being employed in a drapery at Kadina where he was remembered as 'artistic, slightly effeminate and quiet', he returned to Adelaide about 1918 and joined Archibald Collins's studio at the Royal Exchange Building. He probably gained a feeling for paint quality here, before leaving to join James Ashton's [q.v.7] Academy of Arts; his 'Hay Stooks', sent by Ashton to the Royal Drawing Society, London, received a gold star medal in 1920. Horace had first exhibited at the Federal Exhibition of the (Royal) South Australian Society of Arts in 1918, showing four still-life paintings.

Winning a scholarship to the South Australian School of Arts and Crafts, he worked under Fred Britton. When Britton became principal of the School of Fine Arts at North Adelaide in 1921, Trenerry went with him, although often unable to pay the fees. Next year he attended Julian Ashton's [q.v.7] Sydney Art School for a few months and met Elioth Gruner [q.v.9] who influenced him; Trenerry painted several fine views of Sydney at this time. Back in Adelaide, he re-established himself in the hills and shared a studio with d'Auvergne Boxall [q.v.7] in town. Trenerry's first one-man exhibition at the Society of Arts gallery in 1924 included sixty-four works; almost everything sold and he received excellent reviews. This pattern was repeated over succeeding years during which the artist revelled in the good life: parties, dancing and distinguished friends. A gifted pianist, he was at once generous, witty and charming, and reckless, eccentric and temperamental. In the late 1920s he was encouraged by Hans Heysen [q.v.9] whose pencil portrait of Trenerry (1931) is in the Art Gallery of South Australia. In 1930, inspired by Heysen's example, he visited the Flinders Ranges and was profoundly affected. It marked the beginning of his individual style.

Trenerry's fortunes plummeted in the Depression; whereas his previous solo exhibitions had sold out with prices as high as £52, by 1933 they dropped to a few guineas. He sold as many possessions as he could, paid some debts and in late 1934 moved to Willunga on the south coast where he occupied a deserted two-storey building. Friends sent food which helped him to survive. The work he now produced was remarkable, with a delicate sense of colour and strong design; he evolved into a unique painter having greater affinities—in his choice of colour and use of pigment—with English contemporaries such as Gwen John than any Australian. Trenerry's exhibition in 1938 at the Riddell Galleries, Little Collins Street, Melbourne, was reviewed favourably by Basil Burdett [q.v.7], but was criticized by Harold Herbert [q.v.9] for a 'monochromatic muddiness of colour'. Only one painting sold.

In 1940 Trenerry enlisted in the Australian Imperial Force; he was soon discharged as medically unfit. After a short period as a mess steward in the Royal Australian Air Force, he returned to the south coast. This crucial period of his life coincided with the onset of the inherited disease, Huntington's chorea. As his work grew bold and characterized by chalky paint and lyrical colour, his health deteriorated. He neglected himself, ate irregularly and became testy. His poverty, his loss of co-ordinated movement and his inability to paint saddened the years before he entered the Home for Incurables, Adelaide, in 1951. In September 1953 a retrospective exhibition was organized at John Martin & Co. Ltd's gallery. The artist attended in a wheelchair. Trenerry died, unmarried, on 10 January 1958 and was buried in West Terrace cemetery. Two of his works were included in the Tate gallery's exhibition of Australian painting in 1962-63.

L. Klepac, *Horace Trenerry* (Adel, 1970); *Art in Aust*, 8, Dec 1970; E. Harry, 'H. H. Trenerry', Personalities remembered (Radio talk, 12 Sept 1971, ms, Mortlock Lib); personal information.

LOU KLEPAC

TRENWITH, WILLIAM ARTHUR (1846-1925), bootmaker, trade unionist and politician, was born probably on 15 July 1846 at Launceston, Tasmania, second son of convict parents William Trenwith, shoemaker, and his wife Beatrice McBarrett. Aged 7, William followed his father's trade, toiling with his hands for a living; when he was 13 his mother died. Unschooled and scarcely literate, Trenwith began his education in 1864 when he joined the provisional committee of the Launceston Working Man's Club. There he developed a flair for debating and made his first appearance in the boxing ring: by 19, Billy was the lightweight champion of Hobart Town and an equally formidable orator. He married Susannah Page (d. 1896) at St John's Church, Launceston, on 2 November 1868 and left for Victoria.

After a time on the track, Trenwith set up in the boot trade at Carlton. He quickly became embroiled in local politics. His vigour and ability earned him an appointment as lecturer and organizer for the National Reform League, a loose coalition of selectors, miners, manufacturers and trade unionists, which aimed for a high protective tariff on local industries, a land tax and reform of the Legislative Council. Pragmatic and patriotic, Trenwith made these three issues central to his early political philosophy. He was involved in the great reform agitation of 1878 and fiercely defended (Sir) Graham Berry's [q.v.3] assault on the Legislative Council. In 1879 Trenwith contested the seat of Villiers and Heytesbury, styling himself a 'radical candidate', but was defeated. He then turned his energies elsewhere and in May 1879 chaired the founding meeting of the Victorian Operative Bootmakers' Union in Collingwood. In 1883 he became its secretary; his salary of £3 a week won him instant notoriety as a 'paid agitator'.

He fought for the abolition of outwork in the bootmaking industry, hoping to eliminate cheap labour and to encourage unionization. The lock-out in 1884 testified to his ability as an organizer: Trenwith co-ordinated the strike effort from Trades Hall, imposing a levy on all bootmakers still at work and soliciting support from affiliated unions; he also sought assistance outside Victoria and outside the labour movement. Given his prominence in the dispute, many employers blamed him for their troubles. His 'objectionable and dictatorial manner' led them to expel him from negotiations and his 'well directed blow' at a non-unionist prompted efforts to have him imprisoned. To add insult to injury, Trenwith seemed to have stepped beyond his station: one employer complained that he dressed like a gentleman and drove from one factory to another in a buggy.

By 1885 the strike had become a crusade against sweated labour and secured Trenwith's place as a leader of the labour movement. Its termination reaffirmed his faith in the benefits of conciliation and in the fair and reasonable employer. By 1886 Trenwith had moved through a series of executive posts to presidency of the Trades Hall Council. His influence soon extended to the affairs of other unions: he became president of the Australian Journeyman's Butchers Association, secretary of the Railway Employees' Union, and helped to establish a boot trades conciliation board in Adelaide. Even so, Trenwith's rise in the labour movement was not without opposition. In 1887 he was appointed lifelong trustee of the Trades Hall, ending a protracted legal battle with the council's founding father, Benjamin Douglass [q.v.4]. The appointment represented a triumph of the new guard over the old which had opposed Trenwith's militant political leadership. His relationship with the rank and file proved equally stormy. Meetings of the V.O.B.U. frequently censured him for his threatening and abusive language; when Trenwith offered to resign, applause and testimonials effected an uneasy reconciliation.

Trenwith, however, had his sights set on higher office. Throughout the 1880s he had been a consistent advocate of labour's political representation. By 1886 he was president of the Trades Hall parliamentary committee and, despite opposition from conservative sections of the council, stood for Richmond as a National Liberal League candidate. To advocate labour representation and to run for the Liberal party was no contradiction. It was in the Victorian radical tradition of an alliance of capitalist and worker against the squatters and in support of the tariff. Trenwith was no advocate of 'class legislation'. He held that the workers' presence in parliament was in the community's interest and scorned any suggestion of a Trades Hall party. Such assurances notwithstanding, he was again beaten.

In 1886-89 Trenwith prepared for parliament in a dozen lesser forums, assuming executive positions on the Workingman's Club, the Democratic Society, the Sunday Liberation Society and the Secularist Society. Despite his avowed atheism, he edged his way into respectable circles. In 1886 he was appointed a commissioner on the Adelaide Jubilee Exhibition and took a similar post on Melbourne's International Exhibition of 1888. He also sat on the provisional committee of the Workingman's College.

Trenwith's election to the Legislative Assembly as member for Richmond (1889-1903) was cheered in the Trades Hall Council. For a time, at least, 'Trenny' justified such confidence. Working-class education, unemployment and protection formed the staple of his initial speeches. In 1889 he moved the first of many resolutions for an eight-hour bill; it was easily defeated. Trenwith remained an active member of the T.H.C. which, in 1890, chose him to debate against Henry George [q.v.4], a fervent opponent of protection. In August Trenwith assumed *de facto* leadership of the maritime strike in Melbourne. A shrewd strategist, he urged an end to the strike and opposed moves to extend it to the shearing industry. The strike's defeat in November confirmed his belief in compulsory arbitration. As for many labour leaders, the strike marked the most radical period of his career. Alfred Deakin's [q.v.8] 'dastardly' decision to call out the militia compelled Trenwith to attack his former political patrons. In November 1891 at the 4th Intercolonial Trades Union Congress he moved for independent labour representation in parliament. In April 1892 Trenwith was joined in the assembly by several new labour members and promptly—albeit unofficially—assumed leadership of the party. Labor was numerically weak and many of its policies were indistinguishable from those of the Liberals. Jealous of his independence as a parliamentarian, Trenwith refused to pledge himself to a party or platform.

He worked to secure Labor's partnership with the Liberals. At his insistence the name 'United Labor and Liberal Party' was adopted and from 1894 members gave consistent backing to (Sir) George Turner's [q.v.] Liberal ministry. Trenwith became a vocal supporter of such liberal initiatives as direct taxation, electoral reform and industrial legislation, and served on royal commissions on constitutional reform (1894) and factory legislation (1900). Protection remained his abiding obsession. With the free trade revival of 1893-94, he defended the tariff inside and outside parliament. In espousing such policies, he sometimes styled himself a socialist. Well-read in radical literature, he saw the state as the 'aggregate parent' of its citizens; its 'highest duty' was to provide for their well-being. His 'socialism' was practical and palliative.

Trenwith's concessions to the Liberals raised the ire of radicals. In June 1892 a procession of unemployed marched to his Richmond home, declared him to be 'a traitor to the trust . . . reposed in him' and demanded his resignation. As the depression deepened, disaffection spread. Ignoring Trenwith's plea that they had 'nothing but their cause in their favour', in 1894 the V.O.B.U. struck against mechanization and wage reductions. Militants endeavoured to have Trenwith dismissed from the union: despite his annual salary of £300 he had not paid his union dues. He was, moreover, losing touch with his party. In May 1896 the United Labor Party succeeded the U.L.L.P. It demanded a pledge from its parliamentarians and censured the Liberals for failing to achieve social reform. Trenwith repudiated both these resolutions. At Fitzroy on 7 April he had married with Victorian Free Church forms a widow, Elizabeth Bright (d. 1923), and sailed with her to England. On his return he faced two successive challenges to his leadership, both sponsored by the radical wing of the party.

Despairing of labour politics, Trenwith threw himself behind the Federation movement. In 1897 he was the only Labor member to be elected to the Australasian Federal Convention; there he argued the benefits of protection, adult suffrage, proportional representation and referendum. His decision to support the bill, despite 'its many objectionable features', provoked a furore in labour circles: the *Tocsin* damned him as a 'political blackleg'. Trenwith then drifted from the party he had founded and relinquished his position as leader. From November 1900 to February 1901 he served as minister for railways, commissioner for public works and vice-president of the board of land and works in the Peacock [q.v.11] Liberal ministry, and also as chief secretary in 1901-02. His support for the South African War and for Ted Findley's [q.v.8] expulsion from the Legislative Assembly for seditious libel alienated many of those who still believed in him.

Trenwith also came under attack from older political allies: in 1902 the *Age* accused him of snobbery and extravagance for travelling in a state carriage while minister for railways.

Retaining sufficient influence to win election to the Senate in 1903, Trenwith continued to support much of Labor's policy, particularly in the sphere of industrial legislation. He did so as an Independent member, his faith in protection and practical reforms overriding sectional loyalties. He further distanced himself from the labour movement by leaving his home and business premises at Richmond for a comfortable villa at Camberwell. His final rift with Labor came in 1909 when he withdrew his support from Fisher's [q.v.8] government and backed the Fusion under Deakin in the hope of securing protection, the single political objective he was never willing to compromise. The people 'took their political revenge' when he was defeated by a Labor candidate in 1910.

Having unsuccessfully contested the State seat of North Gippsland in 1911 and the Federal seat of Denison (Tasmania) in 1913, Trenwith was defeated for the Senate in 1914. He then retired from public life. On 1 October 1924 he married Helen Florence Sinclair at Echuca with Presbyterian forms. He died on 26 July 1925 and was buried in Brighton cemetery. His wife, three sons and a daughter of his first marriage, and two sons and a daughter of his second, survived him. Obituaries in the labour press stressed the apostasy of his later years at the expense of his earlier achievements, deeming him to be 'unwept, unhonoured and unsung'.

J. Norton (ed), *The history of capital and labour in all lands and ages* (Melb, 1888); H. G. Turner, *The first decade of the Australian Commonwealth* (Melb, 1911); B. R. Wise, *The Commonwealth of Australia* (Lond, 1913); A. Deakin, *The Federal story* (Melb, 1944); G. Serle, *The rush to be rich* (Melb, 1971); D. J. Murphy (ed), *Labor in politics* (Brisb, 1975); G. Davison, *The rise and fall of marvellous Melbourne* (Melb, 1978).   BRUCE SCATES

TRETHOWAN, SIR ARTHUR KING (1863-1937), grazier and politician, was born on 14 September 1863 at Spring Hill, Victoria, second son of Samuel Trethowan, a Cornish-born auctioneer, and his wife Charlotte Dyer, née King, from the Isle of Wight. Baptized an Anglican, he was educated at Creswick Grammar School. At 14 he took his first job, driving a bullock team; he soon joined his father as an auctioneer at Numurkah. During his youth Arthur was recognized as a crack shot and a good cricketer. On 9 November 1886 at Nathalia he married a blacksmith's daughter, Jane Alice Manifold, with Wesleyan forms.

Engaged in wheat and sheep farming in the Goulburn Valley from the 1880s, Trethowan selected land at Berrigan, New South Wales, in 1898 and later bought Clear Hills station, Oaklands, and several grazing properties in the Upper Hunter and Dubbo districts. His reputation as a scientific wheat farmer and fine-wool producer was recognized throughout the Riverina. He was secretary of the local branch of the Farmers and Settlers' Association of New South Wales and a founder of the railway league. A member of Urana Shire Council (1907-15), he was president in 1908, 1912 and 1915; a foundation member (1908) of the Shires Association of New South Wales, he served as vice-president (1910-12) and president (1915). He was also president of the Farmers and Settlers' Association of New South Wales in 1916-20 (and treasurer in 1930-37).

Trethowan had been defeated as a Farmers and Settlers' candidate for the Legislative Assembly seats of Deniliquin (1910) and Burrangong (1913). He was endorsed in the anti-Labor Senate team in 1914, but not elected. Nominated to the Legislative Council in December 1916, he was elected for six years to the reconstituted council in December 1933.

During the strikes of 1917 Trethowan commanded the country loyalists' camp at the Sydney Cricket Ground. That year he founded and was managing director (until 1937) of the Farmers & Graziers' Co-operative Grain, Insurance & Agency Co. Ltd, set up to assist farmers in the transport and sale of produce. Governing director and chairman of the Land Newspaper Ltd, he was a director of the Producers & Citizens Co-operative Assurance Co. of Australia Ltd and Amalgamated Textiles (Australia) Ltd. A colleague recalled his 'alertness and firm decision when great problems came before the board'. In 1930, with Sir Henry Braddon and A. E. Heath [qq.v.7,9], he served on the Council for the Prevention and Relief of Unemployment.

In parliament Trethowan 'illuminated debates by relating his experiences' and liked reminding his colleagues of his humble beginnings as a selector. A founder of the Country Party, he served as chairman of the State central council in 1919-21 and 1925-37. He strongly opposed J. T. Lang's [q.v.9] attempt in 1930 to abolish the Legislative Council without a referendum; with (Sir) David Maughan [q.v.10] as counsel, Trethowan, T. A. J. Playfair [q.v.11] and others successfully defended the council in appeals to the High Court of Australia and Privy Council.

Trethowan was a 'big man, physically and mentally, and his determined face was a mirror of his strong character'. Warm-hearted and kindly, with a 'rugged simplicity of character', he was a devoted family man and always tried to get home for weekends. He was knighted in 1936. Sir Arthur died at Dubbo on 26 November 1937 and was buried in the local cemetery with Anglican rites. His wife, eight sons and two daughters survived him. His estate was valued for probate at £17 629.

His younger brother HUBERT CHARLES (1868-1934) was born on 4 April 1868 at Plymstock, Devonshire, England. Brought to Victoria, he was educated at Creswick Grammar School and in 1889 entered the Bank of Australasia in Melbourne. After he was transferred to Perth in 1896, he joined the harbours and rivers branch of the Department of Public Works as a clerk. In 1898 he became involved with the goldfields water-supply and served from 1903 as the division's accountant. He had married Eliza Josephine Graham at the registrar's office, Subiaco, on 29 March 1900. Qualifying as an associate of the Institute of Accountants and Auditors of Western Australia, in 1909 he became secretary of the Goldfields Water Supply Administration. He was under secretary for water-supply, sewerage and drainage (1912-18), for agriculture (1918-20), and for the Chief Secretary's Department and comptroller-general for prisons (1920-31). Survived by a son and daughter, he died on 30 October 1934 at Subiaco and was buried in the Anglican section of Karrakatta cemetery.

E. G. Knox (ed), *The advertisers' and publishers' guide to Australia and New Zealand* (Syd, 1935); *PD* (NSW), 1937, p 2044; *SMH*, 5 June 1914, 27 Nov 1937.   DOUG MORRISSEY

TREVASCUS, WILLIAM CHARLES (1880-1956), soldier and carpenter, was born on 2 December 1880 at Shepparton, Victoria, second child of Abraham Trevascus, bricklayer, and his wife Elizabeth, née Sibley, both English born. Nothing is known of his schooling. Said to be a bushman when he volunteered for service in the South African War, he left Melbourne on 15 February 1901 as one of 250 men selected for the marquis of Tullibardine's Scottish Horse. He returned to Melbourne in October and in 1902 joined the 2nd Battalion, Australian Commonwealth Horse, which left in February, took part in a 'drive' from Noitverwacht in May and embarked for home in July. Trevascus was awarded the Queen's South Africa Medal with five clasps. He worked as a labourer and on 16 September 1903 at Kew married with Baptist forms Mary Matilda Key, an 18-year-old waitress.

Describing himself as a builder, Trevascus

enlisted in the 21st Battalion, Australian Imperial Force, on 26 March 1915. He embarked for Egypt with 'A' Company on 9 May, was promoted sergeant next month and fought at Gallipoli from early September until the evacuation in December. After operations in Egypt, the battalion reached France in March 1916, went into the line at Fleurbaix on 7 April, and saw action at Pozières in July and Mouquet Farm in August. That month Trevascus was temporary company sergeant major before becoming company quartermaster sergeant. Following the second battle of Bullecourt, in May 1917 he was promoted C.S.M.

In August Trevascus was posted to the 6th Training Battalion. Rejoining his unit in March 1918, he was wounded in action on 23 July, but was back in the line within six weeks. He was awarded the Distinguished Conduct Medal for his heroism in the allied advance on Mont St Quentin in September: attacking an enemy machine-gun post with bombs, he enabled his men to reach their objective. On 5 October, during operations at Montbrehain, he won a Bar to his D.C.M. when he established and held two posts, and captured an enemy machine-gun and six prisoners. He was transferred briefly to the 24th Battalion before being posted to No.5 Officer Cadet Battalion at Cambridge, England, on 8 November. Commissioned provisional second lieutenant in January 1919, he rejoined the 24th Battalion, was promoted lieutenant on 6 April and returned to Australia in August. His A.I.F. appointment ended a year later.

A smallish, burly man, with brown hair and eyes, Trevascus was quietly spoken and energetic. He resumed work as a carpenter and, after being divorced, on 10 January 1922 married Mary Elizabeth Masters at Richmond with Congregational forms. Having visited France in 1924, he later took a job in New Zealand. Back in Melbourne, on 20 December 1939 he was appointed an area officer at Westgarth with the temporary rank of captain; he transferred to the reserve of officers on 5 April 1941. Survived by his wife and their son, and by a son and two daughters of his first marriage, he died at his Coburg home on 2 August 1956 by accidentally inhaling carbon monoxide. He was buried in Coburg cemetery.

Aust Defence Dept, *Official records of the Australian military contingents to the war in South Africa*, P. L. Murray ed (Melb, 1911); C. E. W. Bean, *The A.I.F. in France*, 1916-18 (Syd, 1929, 1933, 1937, 1942); W. Calder, *Heroes and gentlemen* (Melb, 1985); War diary *and* embarkation roll, 21st Battalion, AIF (AWM); transcript of citations (held by Mr J. Trevascus, Epping, Melb); information from Mr J. Price, Cheltenham, Melb.   GRAHAM MCLENNAN

TRIACA, CAMILLO (1887-1972), restaurateur and sculptor, was born on 16 April 1887 at Lucignana, Tuscany, Italy, son of Gesualdo Triaca, shoemaker, and his wife Palmira, née Dinelli. Educated at local schools, Camillo cultivated a natural talent for sculpture which he put to commercial use by making religious objects and figurines. His business prospered and he took his work to sell in the United States of America. Coming to Melbourne in 1909, he practised his craft at Richmond, but went back in 1914 to serve with the Italian Army. Having married Brasilina Damiani, Triaca returned alone to Melbourne in 1923; three years later his wife and family joined him. He continued his decorative sculpture at his Richmond home and then at Fitzroy. He was naturalized in 1928.

In 1925 Triaca and Rinaldo Massoni had taken a lease of an Australian wineshop, the Café Bella, at 206 Exhibition Street, Melbourne; when it was sold, the two parted. In 1930 Triaca leased the same property: the wine bar operated at street level; upstairs he opened a restaurant, the Café Latin, which would be known simply as 'the Latin'.

With its plain, narrow room providing about fifty covers, the restaurant soon proved popular. The cuisine was 'casalinga' (Italian home-style) of excellent quality. Initially patronized by theatre people, artists, writers and musicians, 'the Latin' came to attract lawyers, doctors, publishers and certain clergymen. A Bohemian character was established early, and remained.

Known as 'Cam' to his regulars, Triaca had considerable presence: 6 ft. 3 ins. (190.5 cm) tall, strongly built, well tonsured and with a trim moustache, he was quietly spoken, dignified, gentle and considerate. By habit, he sat at his own small table at the top of the stairs, the better to make greeting or farewell, the easier to see and take pleasure in his clientele. Brasilina did not often appear in the restaurant, but she made excellent cheese which was served at the tables. There was a good wine list, especially in the later years.

In 1955 the restaurant freehold was purchased by Mario Vigano [q.v.], 'the Latin' closed and Triaca retired. His son David carried the restaurant's name to 55 Lonsdale Street and opened the 'new' Latin. With a similar clientele, his establishment flourished. When David retired in 1984 the business passed to other hands. The site of the 'old' Latin is now overbuilt. Camillo died at Fitzroy on 2 July 1972 and was buried with Catholic rites in Boroondara cemetery. His wife, two sons and daughter survived him. Two portraits are held by the family.

Age, 3 July 1972; *Australian*, 5 July 1972; *Sun News-Pictorial*, 16, 18 July 1966, 3 July 1972, 31 Jan 1984; naturalization papers (AA); information from Mr D. G. Triaca and Mrs E. Martinoli, Kew, and Mr G. Leckie, Eaglemont, Melb.
W. S. BENWELL

TRICKETT, OLIVER (1847-1934), surveyor and spelaeologist, was born on 29 May 1847 at Bridlington, Yorkshire, England, son of Rev. Edward Trickett, Baptist minister, and his wife Henrietta, née Young. Arriving in Victoria aged about 15, Oliver was appointed clerk in the Office of Mines, Melbourne, on 28 August 1865. He qualified as a mineral surveyor in 1870 and by 1875 was acting secretary of the Board of Examiners (Mines) in Collins Street. Moving to New South Wales next year, he was licensed as a surveyor by the Department of Lands.

After completing surveys in various parts of the colony, in March 1880 Trickett joined the Department of Mines. By the late 1880s he had begun private practice as a mining surveyor, broker and agent at 114 Pitt Street, Sydney, and was also associated with R. W. Harvey in a Sydney general auctioning business. Trickett's agency managed mines in New South Wales (mainly around Broken Hill) and some in Queensland and the Northern Territory. With Harvey, he published the *Handy register of mining companies* (1889). Trickett became agent for Chaffey [q.v.7] Bros Ltd's 'Irrigation Colonies'; with four others, he ran the East Lambton Colliery Co. which went bankrupt in 1892.

Rejoining the Department of Mines in June as a draftsman and surveyor in the geological survey branch, Trickett developed an interest in the limestone caves of New South Wales. To assist in surveying them, he designed an adaptation of the plane table to be used in conjunction with the theodolite. In addition, he gave advice on protecting the caves' formations and on improving them for tourists. On 8 June 1893 at the Catholic presbytery, Miller Street, North Sydney, he married Melbourne-born Elizabeth Anne Collins (d. 1933).

He published *Notes on the limestone caves of New South Wales* (1898) and guides to the Jenolan (1899), Wombeyan, Wellington and Yarrangobilly (1906) caves. Other works included a large-scale tourist map of the Blue Mountains (1909), a *Bibliography of the economic minerals of New South Wales* (1919) for prospectors, and an article on limestone caves in the *Australian encyclopaedia* (1925).

Eventually chief draftsman in the branch, Trickett prepared numerous maps, sections, diagrams and models. Among his most notable achievements were (Sir) Edgeworth David's [q.v.8] maps of the Maitland coalfield, a model of Sydney Harbour, a geological map of the State (1915) and a model of the Broken

Hill lode which won a gold medal at the Panama Pacific International Exposition (1915). His limestone cave models, many executed in his spare time, were popular exhibits in the Mining and Geological Museum, Sydney.

An untiring worker in both field and office, Trickett—though of a retiring disposition—was well-known to tourists all over the State as the genial 'cave man'; his spelaeological work was fundamental to the scientific study of Australian karst topography. Survived by two sons and four daughters, he died on 31 March 1934 at his Crows Nest home and was buried with Presbyterian forms in the Catholic section of Northern Suburbs cemetery.

Dept of Mines (NSW), Annual Report, 1896-1918; *Bulletin*, 12 Sept 1907; *SMH*, 3 Apr 1934.
　　　　　　　　　　　　　　G. P. WALSH

TRIGGS, ARTHUR BRYANT (1868-1936), grazier and collector, was born on 30 January 1868 at Chelsea, London, son of James Triggs, carpet agent, and his wife Celia Anne, née Bryant. His younger brother H. Inigo Triggs became a well-known architect and garden designer; the architect Inigo Jones was a family connexion. Educated at Chiswick College, London, and Dr Harris's school at Worthing, Sussex, Arthur arrived in Sydney in 1887.

In May he joined the Bank of New South Wales; following a number of temporary appointments, in November 1888 he became accountant at the Yass branch. On 29 June 1892 Triggs married Maria Sophia Ritchie (d. 1897) at St Andrew's Presbyterian Church, Yass. In July 1896 he took six months leave and, with Abraham Wade, bought 8000 wethers; acquiring Wade's interest, he sold them at a profit and in February 1897 resigned from the bank. On 6 March 1901 in the same church he married Mary Maria McBean (d. 1945).

Operating on a definite plan, Triggs realized that stock could always be bought at profitable rates as long as he had the land to receive them. He bought and leased a string of stations from Bourke to Kiandra—including Fort Bourke, Wirchilleba, Tara, Merri Merrigal, Wollogorang, Douro, Willie Ploma, Wee Jasper and Talbingo—so that his travelling stock were never far from his next property. He gave close attention to subdivision and rabbit destruction, and usually ran from 250 000 to 500 000 sheep, as well as some cattle.

Using an elaborate system of book-keeping, Triggs operated from bank-like premises in Cooma Street, Yass, before moving his office to Sydney in 1915. Attributing his success to loyal staff, he recruited good men (like his chief inspector Hugh Stewart and secretary John Fraser), paid them well and trusted them implicitly. He often bought without inspection and was able to sell large mobs solely on his own report, or that of his staff, thereby building up a trusted clientele. He started many men on the land through financial assistance.

His scale of operations was important in maintaining sheep values in parts of New South Wales through his ready purchase of surplus stock. It was said that 'when Mr Triggs was prosperous, Yass was prosperous'. Drought, financial stringency and the outbreak of World War I forced him into bankruptcy in 1915 with debts of about £1.5 million. After wool prices rose, he was marketing 12 000 bales; by 1921 he had paid off all his creditors with 5 per cent interest which earned him a public testimonial from the citizens of Yass.

A Greek, Biblical and Shakespearian student, Triggs had an informed appreciation of literature and art. On visits to London he took advice at the British Museum and frequented William Spencer's bookshop. He collected valuable medieval manuscripts, Bibles, *incunabula*, autographs, Dickensiana, ancient coins, pictures and other *objets d'art*, mainly in Britain and Europe. His wife collected laces made for royalty. Triggs published a *Catalogue of the collection of historical documents and autograph letters* (1924), but his cherished intention to establish a small Dickens [q.v.4] museum at Yass went unrealized. Reading and numismatics were his main recreations; he belonged to the Australian and Warrigal clubs (Sydney) and the Junior Carlton (London); despite his friendship with Sir George Reid [q.v.11], he took little interest in politics.

Slightly built and of middle height, with a receding hairline from his thirties, Triggs was very much the cultivated and courteous Englishman, beloved by many for his quiet and genial nature. He was especially generous to the Yass hospital (of which he was president), to various local social works and to sporting bodies. He provided a holiday house at Manly for his managers and their families, and each Christmas entertained state wards and their guardians.

Triggs died of a coronary occlusion on 9 September 1936 at his residence, Linton, Yass, survived by a daughter of his first marriage, by his wife and by their two sons and two daughters. He was buried in the local cemetery. Probate of his estate was sworn at £21 460. In 1938 his rare collection of about 2500 coins was given by his widow to the Nicholson [q.v.2] Museum of Antiquities, University of Sydney. An impressive gateway, paid for by public subscription, was erected in his memory at the entrance to Victoria Park, Yass, in August 1939. The contents of Linton were disposed of in a notable three-day auction conducted by J. R. Lawson [q.v.10] in September 1945. Next year the house was acquired by the Commonwealth government as a war veterans' home.

W. T. Spencer, *Forty years in my bookshop* (Lond, 1923); J. R. Lawson [auctioneers], *Catalogue of the valuable period furniture* [etc of] Linton, Yass, N.S.W. (Syd, 1945); J. R. Tyrrell, *Old books, old friends, old Sydney* (Syd, 1952); K. V. Sinclair, *Descriptive catalogue of medieval and renaissance western manuscripts in Australia* (Syd, 1969); *Pastoral Review*, 15 Nov 1907, 15 July 1911, 16 Oct 1936; *Home*, June 1921, Mar 1922; *SMH*, 26 June 1922, 19 July 1927, 11, 12 Sept, 4, 11 Nov 1936, 13 Dec 1937, 12 May 1938, 17 Aug 1939, 27, 28 Nov 1945; *Argus*, 11 Sept 1936; *Bulletin*, 16 Sept 1936.
G. P. WALSH

TRITTON, HAROLD PERCY CROYDON ('DUKE') (1886-1965), shearer and folksinger, was born on 3 October 1886 at Five Dock, Sydney, second son of Edgar Joseph Tritton, labourer, and his wife Frances, née Lane, both Sydney born. Educated at Waterloo and Belmore (Lakemba) public schools, he left at 13 and found work, first with a fisherman, then as a newsboy, a factory worker, an apprentice and a builder's labourer. With his mate, 'Dutchy' Holland, Tritton decided in 1905 to try his hand at shearing.

For the next four years they went 'on the track' through inland New South Wales, carrying swags and occasionally 'jumping the rattler'. They were employed as shearers by J. C. & C. Young. Between seasons Tritton worked as fencer, timbercutter, coach driver, roadworker, fossicker, rabbiter and a boxer with a travelling troupe. During one boxing match he was given the nickname 'Duke'. In country towns 'Duke' and 'Dutchy' earned extra money by singing in the streets.

On 1 December 1909 Tritton married Caroline Goodman with Anglican rites at Buckaroo, near Mudgee. After some months in Sydney in 1910, they returned to Mudgee where Tritton took various bush and station jobs. Rejected by the army in 1914 for flat feet—despite his proven record 'on the wallaby'—he spent time on odd jobs around Cullenbone. He was finally accepted by the army in 1918, but the war ended before he was posted.

Moving to Sydney in 1919, Tritton built a house at Punchbowl and found work delivering timber for H. McKenzie Ltd. When he lost his job in the 1927 timber strike he returned to Mudgee and went prospecting at Mount Knowles. In 1933 with his wife and ten children he moved to his 38-acre (15.4 ha) selection at Cullenbone. Too small for grain crops, it was used to fatten lambs while Tritton took extra casual work. In 1936 he became a powder monkey on the Sandy Hollow-Maryvale railway. A loyal union man, he was the Australian Workers' Union delegate for Jackson's gang.

In 1938 'Duke' sold his selection. He shifted with his family to Sydney, resumed work at McKenzie's and tried unsuccessfully to enlist. After the war he formed a syndicate to mine Mount Knowles, then moved back on to the selection which his son had repurchased; in 1957 he retired to Sydney.

Encouraged by Nancy Keesing, Tritton wrote an account of his early outback experiences, *Time means tucker* (1959), which was published by the *Bulletin*. In Sydney at Bush Music Club workshops he became a popular performer of bush songs, both the traditional and those of his own composition. In 1957 two of his songs were recorded on the Wattle label and issued on a vinyl long-playing disc, *Australian traditional singers and musicians*. Tritton later toured Australian capital cities with a group of folk-singers. 'Tall and tough as ironbark', with intense blue eyes and a mop of snowy hair, he had presence and a strong, clear voice. ('You should always put a bit of venom into it', he used to say.) Sincere and strong-minded, he was sardonic, unpretentious and believed in mateship.

'Duke' Tritton died in Sydney, at the peak of his singing career, on 17 May 1965 and was cremated. His wife and nine of their children survived him. The National Library of Australia holds recordings of his folk-songs.

L. McLean, *Pumpkin pie and faded sandshoes* (Syd, 1981); J. Meredith, *Duke of the outback* (Melb, 1983); *SMH*, 22 May 1965.
JOHN MEREDITH

TROMPF, PERCIVAL ALBERT (1902-1964), commercial artist, was born on 30 May 1902 at Beaufort, Victoria, ninth child of Henry Alexander Trompf, fruiterer, and his wife Catherine Amelia, née Elliott, both Victorian born. Educated at Sebastapol State School and the Ballarat Technical Art School, in 1923 Percival joined Giles & Richards, commercial artists in Melbourne, and designed chocolate boxes and wrappings for the confectioners A. W. Allen Pty Ltd. Later, from his studio at Little Collins Street, he painted and designed thousands of advertising posters commissioned by such prominent companies as Bryant & May Pty Ltd and Palmolive Co. Ltd, and by the magazine, *Walkabout*. His posters for the Australian National Travel Association and the Victorian Government Railways received widespread recognition for their images from nature (sea-gulls at the beach and crystal creeks at Mount Buffalo), but his most popular posters drew upon historical events (Captain Cook's [q.v.1] landing at Botany Bay and the building of the Sydney Harbour Bridge).

His bright, colourful, optimistic pictures had wide appeal, especially during the Depression. Trompf supervised all stages of production, including the printing; most of his posters were 25 ins. by 40 ins. (64 cm by 102 cm), but large advertising hoardings required 24 sheets connected in jigsaw fashion. On 14 May 1932 he married Vera Johns at the Methodist Church, Armadale. His modest income was augmented by taking life-classes and teaching briefly at the National Gallery schools.

In the 1930s his posters attracted attention overseas: the Royal Society of Arts, London, awarded him first prize in an annual industrial poster competition; his design for a bunch of apples—captioned 'Best Under the Sun'—won the Ideal Label Contest in 1934 from over 700 entries; in 1938 the Canadian Pacific Railway commissioned him to design a poster of Banff. Trompf shifted his studio in 1939 to Queen Street, from where he designed posters for the National Safety Council of Australia. On 4 May 1942 he enlisted in the Royal Australian Air Force and was commissioned as a pilot in June; he served mostly at Milne Bay, Papua, and also worked as a camouflage officer; he was demobilized in February 1948 with the rank of flying officer.

In 1946 Trompf's poster of the Jamieson Valley had won first prize (£100) in the Blue Mountains Council's nation-wide competition, but after World War II, as photographs gradually replaced graphic imagery, the demand for poster art fell. In his late fifties Trompf was a graphic designer for books issued by the Australian Publicity Council. While president (1961-62) of Camberwell Rotary, he helped to inaugurate its art show. Slimly built, he combined a keen sense of humour with a warm humanity and was an avid follower of cricket.

Survived by his wife and two daughters, Trompf died of a renal infection on 17 July 1964 at Heidelberg and was cremated. His national and regional images captured the imagination of his contemporaries and found a renewed appreciation in the 1980s.

Art Training Institute, prospectus (Melb, c1950); G. Caban, *A fine line* (Syd, 1983); *Sun News-Pictorial*, 31 Aug 1946; *Ballarat Courier*, 18 May 1923; *Brisbane Courier*, 19 Jan 1929; *Herald* (Melb), 8 Feb 1934; *Argus*, 8 May 1938; *Age*, 12 May 1981; information from and thesis held by Mrs B. Gill, Mornington, Vic.

KATIE SPEARRITT
PETER SPEARRITT

TROTT, GEORGE HENRY STEVENS (1866-1917) and **ALBERT EDWIN** (1873-1914), cricketers, were born on 5 August 1866 and 6 February 1873 at Collingwood, Melbourne, sons of Adolphus Henry Trott, West Indies-born accountant, and his English wife Mary Ann, née Stephens. Both boys began with the local Capulet junior club.

Harry, a postman, first played for Victoria in 1885-86 and captained his colony intermittently from the mid-1890s. An elegant right-hand batsman, a useful leg-break bowler and a fine fieldsman at point, he was selected for Australia's tours of England in 1888, 1890 and 1893. The brothers first played together for Australia in the Adelaide Test of the 1894-95 series when Albert made a remarkable début: twice not out (38 and 72), he took 8 wickets for 43 runs in the second innings and 'hounded England to abject defeat'. In his three Tests for Australia he averaged 102.5 runs.

Soon the brothers' careers diverged. Harry captained the 1896 team to England and presided over such a renaissance of Australia's cricketing fortunes that the home Tests of 1897-98 would see a four-to-one triumph. Albert had been perplexingly omitted from the 1896 tour, but sailed in the same ship as his brother to further his career in England. While Harry made his highest Test score of 143 at Lord's, Albert had begun work with its ground staff as he waited to qualify for Middlesex.

'Alberto's' county career began in 1898. At once he blossomed as an all-rounder. In 1899 he made 1175 runs and took 239 wickets; next year he again completed the double with 1337 runs and 211 wickets. He bowled with low delivery, imparting vigorous spin, but commanded a fine variety of pace, including a quick yorker. Jack Pollard wrote that his batting was 'sprinkled with blows that remain part of cricket legend'. Albert is the only man known to have hit a ball over the pavilion at Lord's, a feat accomplished in 1899 off the bowling of M. A. Noble [q.v.11]. Albert developed a taste for slogging, to the detriment of his batsmanship. In two Tests for England (1898-99) in South Africa he made 23 runs at 5.75 and took 17 wickets at 11.64. Although his county career declined as he put on weight, he had one great bowling spell left: in his benefit game in 1907 he destroyed Somerset's second innings with four wickets in four balls and then took another hat-trick, an unprecedented feat which shortened the match and, in his words, bowled him 'into the workhouse'.

Retiring as a county player in 1910, Albert became an umpire. A tall, heavily-moustached man with huge hands, he had earlier been a convivial spirit. Melancholic and suffering from dropsy, he shot himself in his lodgings in north-west London on 30 July 1914, leaving his landlady £4 and his wardrobe.

The career of the imperturbable, good-humoured Harry was less spectacular, but few Australian captains have been better liked and respected. He played twenty-four Tests, scoring 921 runs at 21.92 and taking 29 wickets. After the 1897-98 victories he suffered a breakdown and was committed to a mental institution. When he recovered he played for Victoria until 1907. He died of Hodgkin's disease at his Albert Park home on 9 November 1917 and was buried in Brighton cemetery. His wife Violet Priscilla, née Hodson, whom he had married at Fitzroy on 17 February 1890, and their son survived him.

A. G. Moyes, *Australian cricket* (Syd, 1959); C. Martin-Jenkins, *The complete who's who of Test cricketers* (Adel, 1980); J. Pollard, *Australian cricket* (Syd, 1982); *Wisden Cricketers' Almanack*, 1915, 1918; *Australasian*, 8 Aug 1914, 17 Nov 1917.

PETER PIERCE

TROWER, GERARD (1860-1928), Church of England bishop, was born on 3 December 1860 at Hook, Yorkshire, England, son of Arthur Trower, Church of England priest, and his wife Jane, née Lawford. From Merchant Taylors' School, London, he proceeded to Keble College, Oxford (B.A., 1885; M.A., 1888), and to Ely Theological College. Made deacon in 1888 and ordained priest in 1889, he was curate at St Mary's, Redcliffe, and at St Alban's, Birmingham. From 1895 he was rector of Christ Church St Laurence, Sydney. His High Church leanings provoked some controversy: he introduced altar lights and costly vestments, and responded to a 'Reformation Festival' by preaching on ritualism, auricular confession and sacerdotalism. A tall, strong man, he usually hurried, dressed in an overcoat, with a flat clerical hat perched on the back of his head, and a book or umbrella tucked under his arm. Though a stern rector, he was a sound administrator and a witty preacher. His parishioners sent him a pectoral cross of gold set with amethysts when he left in 1901 to become bishop of Likoma, Nyasaland, Africa.

He was consecrated in Westminster Abbey next year. At Likoma he undertook a massive building programme: there were 68 schools when he arrived and over 150 when he departed; a hospital, a cathedral and a theological college were established. A corresponding spiritual growth reflected the bishop's energy and devotion. He doubled the indigenous ministry and supported the Universities' Mission to Central Africa.

Regarded by the local people with affection, Trower proved himself a popular prelate who thrived on toil. He left Africa reluctantly to become the first bishop of North-West Australia, being enthroned by Bishop C. O. L. Riley [q.v.11] in St George's Church, Carnarvon, Western Australia, on 4 July 1910.

The bishop's new task was twofold: to establish a diocese and to found an Anglican mission to the Aborigines. He had many difficulties with which to contend: he rented rooms to live in for the first four years; there was an inadequate number of priests; the little church at Broome had to serve as a pro-cathedral; there was no synod and little money. These problems were compounded by a decline in the pearling and pastoral industries, and by the travails caused by cyclones and remoteness. With five others, he set off in 1913 to establish a mission at Forrest River (west of Wyndham); it survived, but did not flourish. Trower's attempts to form a brotherhood pattern of ministry and to erect a cathedral also failed. His only ordination was that of the first Aboriginal deacon, Rev. James Noble [q.v.11], in 1925. Bishop Trower was seldom happy in the North-West where he had been an outspoken critic of those with whom he disagreed and those whose views he did not understand. He resigned in 1927.

Trower returned to the Isle of Wight, England, where he was rector of Chale. He died on 25 August 1928 at Ryde.

A. E. M. Anderson, *The history of the Universities' Mission to Central Africa 1859-1909* (Lond, 1909); L. M. Allen, *A history of Christ Church, S.Laurence* (Syd, 1939); C. L. M. Hawtrey, *The availing struggle* (Perth, 1949); E. W. Doncaster, *Spinifex saints* (Perth, 1985); *Anglican Messenger* (Diocese of North-West Australia), May 1980; *WA Church News*, 1 Sept 1928; H. W. Boake, In memoriam (transcript of sermon preached at Broome, WA, on 16 Sept 1928, held by Archdeacon E. Doncaster, Port Lincoln, SA).

E. W. DONCASTER

TRUMAN, ERNEST EDWIN PHILIP (1869-1948), musician, was born on 29 December 1869 at Weston-super-Mare, Somerset, England, son of Edwin Philip Truman, fish, game and poultry dealer, and his wife Elizabeth Robinson Cranford, née Smith. About 1875 the family migrated to Melbourne and soon after to New Zealand. Ernest was taught music by his father and began formal studies at 13 with A. J. Bath of Dunedin. Moving to Sydney in 1885, he studied piano with Julius Buddee.

In 1888 Truman enrolled at the Royal Conservatorium of Music, Leipzig, Germany, to study under Salomon Jadassohn and Karl Reinecke (composition), Bruno Zwintscher (piano) and Paul Homeyer (organ); Alfred

Hill [q.v.9] was a fellow-pupil. Several of Truman's compositions were performed at concerts by the Ossian Society and Gewand-haus Orchestra. He visited London and qual-ified as associate of the Royal College of Organists and licentiate of the Royal College of Music. In 1893 he received a diploma from the Leipzig conservatorium.

Returning to Sydney that year, Truman was successively an occasional organist at St Mary's Cathedral, Christ Church St Laurence and St Patrick's, Church Hill. On 30 June 1894 at the registrar's office, Glebe, he married a divorcee Nellie Edith Bettye, née Maxey; she often accompanied him at recitals. He hoped to become a successful composer: his works include a Mass per-formed in St Mary's Cathedral in 1899, an operetta (*Club life*), chamber music, a Mag-nificat setting, a book of songs and a cantata (*The pied piper of Hamelin*), based on Robert Browning's poem and first performed in Adelaide on 25 September 1913. Although well received at the time (three were broad-cast in the 1930s), his works are now mostly forgotten.

Appointed city organist in 1909, Truman presided at the Sydney Town Hall organ for twenty-six years. His programmes at over 3000 concerts were probably designed to appeal rather than to educate, although he generally included more genuine organ music than had his predecessors. A gifted musician, he was also a respected teacher of piano and organ. He accompanied many distinguished artists including Melba, Florence Austral, Peter Dawson [qq.v.10,7,8], Dame Clara Butt, Laurence Tibbett and Richard Crooks.

From 1912 Truman's fondness for opera was displayed in 'Grand Operatic Organ Re-citals' at Sydney Town Hall; in 1925 he included his transcriptions of *Cavalleria rus-ticana* and *Pagliacci* and the first Australian performances of Puccini's *Gianni Schicchi* and *Il tabarra*. He devised concerts devoted to transcriptions of music from Gilbert's and Sullivan's operas in the 1930s. His retirement in 1935 marked the end of an era of free weekly organ concerts. He was rarely heard again.

Of medium build, Truman had dark, wavy hair and a handlebar moustache. He was des-cribed by W. A. Orchard [q.v.11] as 'cheerful' and 'much-liked . . . not only for his musical ability, but because of his dry humour'. Tru-man's wife died in 1917; on 8 November 1923 he married a 27-year-old musician, (Marie) Millicent Anglés, at St John's Anglican Church, Darlinghurst. Survived by his wife, Truman died in St Vincent's Hospital on 6 October 1948 and was cremated with Angli-can rites. He was predeceased by the son of his first marriage.

W. A. Orchard, *The distant view* (Syd, 1943) and *Music in Australia* (Melb, 1952); G. D. Rushworth, *Historic organs of New South Wales* (Syd, 1988); *All about Australians*, 29 May 1901; *SMH*, 7 Mar, 29 Aug 1891, 18 Nov 1892, 30 Apr 1932, 23 Mar, 6 Apr 1935, 8 Jan 1942, 9 Oct 1948; *Syd Mail*, 14 July 1894, 24 Nov 1900; *T&CJ*, 4 Aug 1909; *Adver-tiser* (Adel), 26 Sept 1913; Truman organ concert programmes, 1910-25 (ML).

G. D. RUSHWORTH

TRUMAN, JOHN (1884-1965), barley-grower, was born on 25 October 1884 at Combe Fields, Warwickshire, England, son of James Truman, farm labourer, and his wife Elizabeth, née Over. John left school at the age of 9 to work in a coal-mine, but later joined the British Army, serving in India and France, and attaining the rank of sergeant major. He won the Belgian Croix de Guerre in World War I. On 1 May 1906 he had married Eva Dow, tailoress, in the register office, Col-chester. With his wife and daughter, he migrated to Western Australia and in 1923 bought land at Calingiri in the Victoria Plains district where he established a flourishing farm. He became active in local organiz-ations.

Short, stout and rosy-cheeked, with an authoritative military bearing, Truman was respected for his integrity, but was consi-dered biased at times. He was well-known as an ardent member of the Primary Producers' Association and, through it, as a promoter of the Country Party. Early in the Depression a coalition between the Country and Nationalist parties was mooted in an effort to win a better deal for farmers. Country Party members with Labor leanings favoured withholding grain from sale and broke from the P.P.A. to form the Wheatgrowers' Union. There were fiery debates at conference where Truman was dubbed 'Dynamite Jack' for supporting the P.P.A.; differences were finally resolved in 1944 when the two bodies united as the Farmers' Union of Western Australia. Tru-man had grown barley from the early 1930s and promoted it in the State. He conducted trial plots and in 1934 inaugurated a local barley-growing competition. After three consecutively successful years as an exhibi-tor, in 1936 he won the Swan Cup at Perth's Royal Agricultural Show for his barley. By criticizing the Australian Barley Board in 1942-46 for policies that favoured maltsters and growers in eastern Australia, Truman eventually won greater representation for growers on that board.

During World War II he had been a recruit-ing officer for the 2nd Australian Imperial Force and for the Volunteer Defence Corps;

he subsequently served on the local rehabilitation committee which settled soldiers on the land. Truman endeavoured to revive the Victoria Plains Agricultural Show: having established Kanoona stud in 1949, he successfully exhibited his wool. He also reconstituted the local football association: as its president, he donated the Truman Shield and enjoyed its repeated presentation to his own Calingiri club. He helped, as well, to organize the Victoria Plains Junior Football Association and his barracking for Calingiri teams became legendary.

Failing health led Truman to resign from the Farmers' Union in 1953, with a record of having attended every one of its conferences (and those of the P.P.A.) and every zone council meeting; he had also served for twenty-five years on the wool executive. Survived by his wife and daughter, he died at Subiaco on 5 January 1965 and was buried in the Anglican section of Toodyay cemetery. His estate was sworn for probate at $40 089.

R. Erickson, *The Victoria Plains* (Perth, 1971); *Countryman* (Perth), 21 Jan 1965.

RICA ERICKSON

TRUMBLE, HUGH (1867-1938), cricketer and administrator, was born on 19 May 1867 at Collingwood, Melbourne, son of Irish-born William Trumble, warder, and his Scottish wife Elizabeth, née Clark. Thomas [q.v.] and John William, who became a Test cricketer, were his brothers. Educated at Hawthorn Grammar School, Hugh played grade matches with the Melbourne Cricket Club. He joined the National Bank of Australasia in 1887, and rose to be accountant at Richmond in 1903 and manager at Kew from 1908. On 12 March 1902 at St George's Anglican Church, Malvern, he had married Queensland-born Florence Christian.

In 1887-88 Trumble first played for Victoria, taking 7 for 52 against New South Wales with his medium-paced off breaks. He made five tours of England, the first in 1890: according to Wisden, he improved 'almost beyond belief' each time. In 1896 he took 18 wickets in three Tests, including 12 for 89 in a losing side at The Oval. A fine slips fieldsman (45 Test catches) as well as an accomplished batsman, Trumble shared with Clem Hill [q.v.9] the long-standing record for a seventh wicket partnership (165) in the fourth Test of 1897-98. Trumble made the double (1183 runs and 142 wickets) on the 1899 tour of England; it was then that W. G. Grace called him 'the best bowler Australia has sent us'.

In the 1901-02 series against England Trumble was victorious in two Tests as captain, taking 28 wickets for the series and a hat-trick at Melbourne. In 1902, in two of the closest Test matches of all time, he took 10 for 128 at Old Trafford (where Australia won by three runs), and at The Oval made 64 not out and 7 not out, while taking 12 for 173 (England won by one wicket). Trumble's Test career finished spectacularly on the Melbourne ground in the 1903-04 series when he took 7 for 28 in England's second innings which he ended with another hat-trick to ensure Australia's victory by 218 runs. In 31 Tests against England he took 141 wickets at 21.78, a record aggregate for either side until beaten in 1981 by D. K. Lillee. Trumble scored 851 runs in Test matches at 19.78 and made three first-class centuries.

An English opponent, C. B. Fry, called Trumble 'one of the greatest bowlers of all time', and saw him as a 'cunning and long-headed adversary, who knew every move of the game'. Trumble made the most of his height (6 ft. 4 ins., 193 cm), kept an impeccable length, turned the ball sharply on helpful pitches and varied pace deceivingly. 'Where most bowlers attacked weakness, Trumble fed the opposition's strength, challenging the batsman's ambition', wrote A. G. Moyes who ranked this imperturbable and resourceful bowler as one of the immortals of the art. M. A. Noble [q.v.11] described Trumble's approach to the wicket as 'sidelong and insinuating, with his neck craned like a gigantic bird'.

Lanky, with long bones, a prominent nose and large ears, Trumble was affectionately described by (Sir) Pelham Warner as 'that great camel'. A life member of the Melbourne Cricket Club and secretary from 1911 until his death, Trumble was a shrewd, genial and popular administrator. While secretary, he oversaw the building of two new grandstands at the Melbourne Cricket Ground. He was a renowned story-teller, generous in his time with the press and encouraging to young players.

Survived by his wife, six sons and two daughters, Trumble died at his Hawthorn home on 14 August 1938 and was cremated. Memorabilia held by the Melbourne Cricket Club include his pipe, one of his imported stetsons, a caricature by Hal Gye [q.v.9] and a portrait by A. E. Newbury.

A. G. Moyes, *Australian bowlers from Spofforth to Lindwall* (Syd, 1953) and *Australian cricket* (Syd, 1959); K. Dunstan, *The paddock that grew* (Melb, 1962); C. Martin-Jenkins, *The complete who's who of Test cricketers* (Adel, 1980); J. Pollard, *Australian cricket* (Syd, 1982); B. M. Crowley, *A history of Australian bowling and wicket-keeping, 1850-1986* (Melb, 1986); *Wisden Cricketers' Almanack*, 1938; *Age* and *Argus*, 15 Aug 1938; *Australasian*, 20 Aug 1938.

PETER PIERCE

TRUMBLE, THOMAS (1872-1954), public servant, was born on 9 April 1872 at Ararat, Victoria, fifth child of Irish-born William Trumble, lunatic asylum superintendent, and his Scottish wife Elizabeth, née Clarke. The cricketer Hugh Trumble [q.v.] was his brother. Educated at Yarra Park State School and at Wesley College, Melbourne, Thomas was appointed clerk in the Victorian Public Service in September 1888. From 1891 he served in the defence department under (Sir) R. H. M. Collins [q.v.8], for a time as private secretary to the minister. On 5 April 1899 Trumble married Katherine Helen Hutchinson at St Columb's Anglican Church, Hawthorn.

In July 1901 Trumble transferred to the Commonwealth Department of Defence when his Victorian chief, Collins, became its secretary. From June 1910 as chief clerk he worked with the secretary (Sir) Samuel Pethebridge [q.v.11] in putting into effect the policies of (Sir) George Pearce [q.v.11], especially on naval expansion and compulsory military training. Trumble was appointed acting secretary in November 1914. He was secretary of the department from February 1918 to July 1927. His career was dramatic. As a comparatively young acting head in 1914, he had come through the civil service, whereas his predecessors had both been naval officers. Trumble had new ground to break. World War I brought an extraordinary expansion of his official burdens, particularly in wartime army administration and in the difficult post-war years when the Navy Office was returned to his jurisdiction. During the war some administrative errors were revealed by a royal commission, but Trumble was not personally criticized. Newspapers wrote of him in the highest terms and in 1915 and 1918 Melbourne *Punch* saw him as a hard worker who said little, did a great deal and who knew his department thoroughly. The demands upon Trumble were severe. They called for intense application over long hours, and required a detailed understanding of the defence system and personal knowledge of the qualifications of men to be selected for important work. In his official history of the war (Sir) Ernest Scott [q.v.11] observed:

The part played in war by the chief of a secretariat can never be so spectacular as that of field officer, but the administrative work of Trumble . . . was marked by steady efficiency and a capacity for smooth collaboration with other departments and their administrators which was grounded in a considerate and unselfish disposition.

Pearce recorded that 'courteous and patient, self-sacrificing and zealous, [Trumble] has perhaps borne more of the heat and burden of the day than any other officer, civil or military'. Trumble was appointed C.B.E. in 1918 and C.M.G. in 1923.

In July 1927 he became official secretary to the high commission for Australia in London and travelled to Britain with Sir Granville Ryrie [q.v.11], the new high commissioner. Trumble exchanged positions with M. L. Shepherd [q.v.11]. The transfer was the subject of public comment; questions were raised in parliament about the expense involved and why the change was necessary. In 1931 Trumble relinquished the secretaryship to become Australian Defence Liaison Officer in London, a move that was not welcomed by armed services personnel in Australia who saw it as displacing their senior liaison officers. Criticism of the appointment again put Trumble in the public eye, and Prime Minister Scullin [q.v.11] had to reply to questions in the House. As a product of the Westminster system, Trumble did not relish such publicity. He retained the post, assisted by a junior officer from each of the services, until his retirement, at his own request, in December 1932.

Still remembered in 1940 for his warmth and friendliness when he had been departmental secretary, he was welcomed when he returned to Victoria Barracks, Melbourne, during World War II as director of voluntary services, Department of Defence Co-ordination in July 1940. He left the service in September 1943. Trumble was 'long of limb and lean of flank'; he had blue eyes, a 'perennial smile' and spoke with a disarming drawl. A good golfer, and in his younger days a fair cricketer, he had a 'legion' of friends. Survived by his wife and daughter, he died at Caulfield, Melbourne, on 2 July 1954 and was cremated.

E. Scott, *Australia during the war* (Syd, 1936); R. Trumble, *The golden age of cricket* (Melb, 1968); *PD* (Cwlth), 11 Mar 1931, p 48; *London Gazette*, 4 Oct 1918, 2 June 1923; *Reveille* (Syd), 1 Nov 1937; *Punch* (Melb), 15 July 1915, 28 Feb 1918; *T&CJ*, 27 Feb 1918; *Herald* (Melb), 13, 17, 31 May 1927; *SMH*, 13, 14, 17 May 1927, 17 Nov 1930, 14 Feb, 7 Mar 1931, 31 Dec 1932, 13 Jan 1933; *Argus*, 31 May, 8 June 1927; *Age* and *Sun News-Pictorial*, 5 July 1954; *Bulletin*, 14 July 1954; A664/1, A1567/1, MP124/4, MP1162/3 (AA); letter from Mrs G. Walker to Mr W. Perry, 3 June 1972 (held by Mr W. Perry, Eaglemont, Melb).

ROBERT HYSLOP

TRUMPER, VICTOR THOMAS (1877-1915), cricketer, was born probably on 2 November 1877 in Sydney. He was probably a great-grandson of Charles Trumper, hatter, and his wife Jane, née Samson, who were married in London in 1834 and migrated to Sydney in the *Resource* in 1837. Victor's putative parents were Charles Thomas Trumper and his wife Louise, née Coghlan, who were married on 15 May 1883 at Ultimo with Primitive Methodist forms. Charles Thomas, a boot clicker, became a footwear manufacturer; he lived at Surry Hills and later at Paddington. He was sufficiently well-off to keep Victor at Crown Street Superior Public School until he passed the junior public examination in 1893. Victor became a junior clerk in the Treasury; in 1904, when a clerk in the Probate and Intestate Estates Office, he resigned from the public service.

Victor's juvenile cricket talent was happily cultivated in the streets of Surry Hills and, with the help of his father, in his backyard and the nearby Moore Park. Although described by M. A. Noble [q.v.11], his schoolmate, as a 'short, spare, narrow-shouldered boy', Trumper excelled at batting, bowling and fielding. At 15 he played with the Carlton club and at 16 with the South Sydney club where he had the awe-inspiring advice and example of Syd Gregory [q.v.4]. Playing for the New South Wales Juniors eighteen against Andrew Stoddart's England eleven on 22 December 1894, he disregarded a severe cold to score 67 runs, a final schoolboy triumph that led to selection for New South Wales against South Australia in January 1895. He scored 11 and 0, beginning inauspiciously a career with his home colony and State of 73 matches which produced 5823 runs at an average of 51.08, with 15 centuries and 29 half-centuries; a fast bowler, he took 33 wickets at 34.97: some highlights were 292 in a day against Tasmania, including a century before lunch, in 1898; 100 in 58 minutes against Victoria in 1906; and 201 against South Australia in 1913. He missed the 1908-09 season through illness. When Noble retired in December 1909, the New South Wales Cricket Association appointed Austin Diamond captain. Trumper favoured the previous practice of the captain being selected by the players and withdrew from the team for 1909-10. Appointed captain next season, he led the State 24 times for 15 wins, 4 draws and 5 losses.

Although he had won the Pattison Trophy with 674 runs in intercolonial games in 1898-99, Trumper was included late, as fourteenth man on reduced financial terms, in the 1899 team to tour England. Batting at number 6 in the second Test in June at Lord's, he made 135 not out. After becoming the first Australian to score 300 in England—against Sussex in July—he was admitted as a full member of the team. This tour began a Test career of 48 matches—including 8 against South Africa with 2 centuries—in which he totalled 3163 runs at 39.05: his figures against England were 2263 at 32.80, highest score 185 not out, with 6 centuries and 9 half-centuries. Scoring 11 centuries, he excelled in

the 1902 tour when, described by *Wisden* as 'the best batsman in the world', he made 2570 at 48.49 in a season marked by such 'bad weather and wet wickets' that fires were needed in the dressing-rooms in the early months; opening in all matches, he became the first batsman to record a century before lunch in a Test—at Old Trafford on 24 July—and the first batsman to make two centuries in one match (of three days)—against Essex in July. On the way home in October he hit 218 against Transvaal in South Africa.

In the first Test against (Sir) Pelham Warner's England team in Sydney in December 1903 Trumper scored 185 not out in 230 minutes; next month in the second Test in Melbourne he opened on a sticky wicket and, with 74 out of a total of 122 in the first innings, was the last man out. In the 1903-04 Tests Trumper scored 574 runs at 63.78. During the 1905 tour of England he was handicapped by a torn back-muscle and was fifth in the averages. In the fourth Test against England in Melbourne in February 1908 he failed to score, his only 'pair' in any match. In his last tour in 1909 again he did not dominate the team, but contributed much to its success.

South Africa sent its first team to Australia for the 1910-11 season. Trumper conjured up his pristine form in the second Test in Melbourne, reaching 159 in 171 minutes; coming in at number 5 with the total at 111, he compiled 214 (not out) of a total of 465 in the Adelaide Test, won by the tourists: he headed the series averages with 661 at 94.43. Vice-captain, under Clem Hill [q.v.9], against the English tourists in 1911-12, Trumper became the first to score six centuries in Anglo-Australian Tests—in Sydney in December 1911; opening in what proved his final Test, he scored 50 in the second innings of the last Test in Sydney, 1912.

Together with W. W. Armstrong, A. Cotter, V. S. Ransford [qq.v.7,8,11], Hanson Carter and Hill, Trumper resented the appointment of a manager by the new Australian Board of Control for International Cricket Matches and declined to join the 1912 Australian team to visit England. At the invitation of (Sir) Arthur Sims, a strong Australian side toured New Zealand in February-March 1914: batting at number 9 at Christchurch on 28 February, Trumper dazzled a large crowd with 293 runs in 178 minutes, and moved Viscount Cobham to write that his 'glory shone for one last moment with an unearthly brilliance'. Trumper's final game was for his club, Gordon, against Petersham at Chatswood Oval on 24 October 1914; tired and sick, he scored 4 runs.

Trumper's first-class batting figures are: 255 matches, 16 939 runs, highest score 300 not out, average 44.58; he made 42 centuries and 87 half-centuries; he took 172 catches, and 64 wickets at 31.73. Neville Cardus has tried to portray him: 'We can no more get an idea of Trumper's [winged] batmanship by looking at the averages and statistics than we can find the essential quality of a composition by Mozart by adding up the notes'. It is a sign of his unique place in a game which spawns statistics, assiduously audited, that he is above and beyond them.

Cricket was rooted in the cultural consciousness of the Australian nation as it was formed in the 1890s and established in 1901. Trumper starred at the Federation carnival in Sydney on 4 January that year in winning the ball-throwing contest with 120 yards 1 ft. 6 ins. (110.19 m): his fast, flat throw reflected his baseball skill and was a feature of his sweeping fielding. By then he was just under six feet (182.9 cm) tall, fair-complexioned, with grey-blue eyes, 'not too muscular and above all graceful and courtly'. His 335 in 180 minutes for Paddington at Redfern Oval on 31 January 1903 became part of the folk-lore of Sydney. Trumper was Australians' romantic figure in their *belle époque*, 1890-1914. He is cricket's supreme batting stylist, timeless and unassailable in his symmetry of artistry and elegance.

He played every stroke in the game with that peerless grace and timing that disguises power. Trumper perfected shots, such as leg drives off his pads and toes, that became part of the repertoire of all great batsmen after him. Some of his strokes have proved impossible for others, notably his leg glances with his left or right foot raised, and his 'yorker shot' which he forced square on either side, or, by rapid footwork, lofted over the bowler. C. B. Fry has tried to define his batting: 'He . . . played his strokes with a swing from the wrists which was not a flick, but rather, as it were a stroking effect'. Trumper's drives were similar to a master golfer's: high back lift, fluent arc and immaculate follow through. His square, back and late cuts, and leg deflections, were executed with precision and beauty of movement. A. A. Lilley, England's wicket-keeper, observed him closely many times and saw that 'his foot-work was perfection'. This gift was part of his computer-like ability to sight the direction, flight, length and pace of the ball quicker than any other batsman, and helps to explain his unrivalled skill on uneven, bumping, sticky and wet wickets. He played at a time when uncovered wickets restricted batsmen, as the contemporary statistics for both fast and slow bowlers show. Moreover, in England all first-class matches were of three days only. Thus, Trumper's triumph in the 1902 tour was *sui generis*; but, as *Wisden* observed in its obituary on him, he played that year as only a young man could. He never repeated that success, though he

flashed golden glimpses of his prowess almost to the end.

Victor looked on life as one shining summer in which a man should score a quick century, then get out and give his mates a turn. A tee-totaller, non-smoker, and an Anglican, on 7 June 1904 at St Patrick's Catholic Cathedral, Melbourne, he married Sarah Ann Briggs who was a sister-in-law of J. J. Kelly, Australia's wicket-keeper; she loved cricket, Victor was her beau idéal and she shared his happy-go-lucky disposition. Each enhanced the other's life. They lived with Victor's parents at Paddington, moving with them to Chatswood in 1909. Annie accompanied him on the 1905 tour of England. She did improve somewhat his chaotic way with clothes; but not with cricket bats which he treated cavalierly, discarding them often, disdaining rubber grips (and batting gloves), and scoring the binding of the handles with broken glass, the better to hold them high for his flowing strokemaking.

Business fitted into his dream of summer. In August 1904 he opened a sports store in Market Street with Carter; in 1909, with J. J. Giltinan and others, he formed a sports and mercery store in George Street (near Wynyard Station) and by 1912 turned it into Victor Trumper and Dodge Ltd. The restructuring matched Victor's precarious incompatibility with commerce. His repute, association with Giltinan and friendship with 'Dally' Messenger [q.v.10] were important in the foundation of Rugby League in 1908; he was a fallible, and brief, treasurer of the league. Annie dabbled in business, too; her 1912-13 venture with Dudley King resulted in a debt of £1040 to E. C. Clifton being added to Victor's liabilities. His testimonial match, 7-11 February 1913, raised £2950 13s. 3d. which was wisely placed in a trust fund by the New South Wales Cricket Association. T. J. Houghton [q.v.9], an organizer of the event, sued for commission, alleging that Victor had told him, 'Don't worry; you'll get paid all right'; but he got no money and lost the case.

Trumper was generous and handsome, and, on the cricket field, often resplendent. But a delicate tinge always shadowed his grace. From at least 1908 the darkness gradually deepened. By late 1914 an insidious kidney disease began to take its final toll. By the first Anzac Day he was confined to bed. On 21 June he entered St Vincent's Hospital, to die there on 28 June 1915. Buried in the Anglican section of Waverley cemetery, he was survived by his wife (d. 1963), a 9-year-old daughter and a 1-year-old son.

W. G. Grace, the 'Great Cricketer', died four months later. If, as K. S. Ranjitsinhji wrote, Grace turned cricket from 'an accomplishment into a science', then Trumper lifted it to a level of art beyond the reach of all but himself. And, in achieving this, he reworked the charter of cricket from a Victorian artefact into an Edwardian palimpsest, with spacious Australian flourishes all but replacing the English script.

In February 1917 administration of Trumper's intestate estate, valued at £5, was granted to E. C. Clifton. In January 1919, when interstate games recommenced after World War I, the Victorian team laid a wreath on Trumper's grave.

Ranjitsinhji, *The jubilee book of cricket* (Edinburgh, 1897); C. B. Fry, *Great batsmen* (Lond, 1905); A. E. Knight, *The complete cricketer* (Lond, 1906); A. A. Lilley, *Twenty-four years of cricket* (Lond, 1912); M. A. Noble, *The game's the thing* (Lond, 1926); N. Cardus, *The summer game* (Lond, 1929); A. Mitchell, *84 not out* (Lond, 1962); J. Arlott (ed), *Cricket* (Lond, 1967); J. H. Fingleton, *The immortal Victor Trumper* (Syd, 1978); *Great knock* (Christchurch, NZ, 1978); A. Mallett, *Trumper* (Melb, 1985); P. Sharpham, *Trumper* (Syd, 1985); *Wisden Cricketers' Almanack*, 1903, 1916; *Sydney Mail*, 12 Oct 1932. BEDE NAIRN

TRUSCOTT, WILLIAM JOHN (1886-1966),

footballer, was born on 9 October 1886 at Lithgow, New South Wales, third son of William John Truscott, a miner from Cornwall, and his native-born wife Susanna(h), née Strickland. In 1899 Mrs Truscott took the children to join their father at Kalgoorlie, Western Australia. Young William left school at 14. Nicknamed 'Nipper' as a boy for his quickness in Rugby Union, at Kalgoorlie he played top-grade Australian Rules football with Mines Rovers (one hundred games from 1906) and worked as a postman.

On 22 May 1912 at the Wesleyan Church, Kalgoorlie, Truscott married Alice Stenlake Huxham; they moved to Perth that year where he became a postmaster. He was with East Fremantle Football Club from 1913 until 1927, enjoying success as player, captain and captain-coach, and making five carnival appearances (1908, 1911, 1914, 1921 and 1924). He was only 5 ft. 9 ins. (175.3 cm) tall and weighed 10 st. 5 lb. (65.8 kg), but made up for his slight physique by pace and cleverness. Truscott's anticipation ensured Western Australia's first carnival victory against Victoria in 1921: as the Victorian forward Dick Lee [q.v.10] prepared a place-kick at goal that would have put his side ahead, Truscott sensed his change of tactics, intercepted his attempted handpass and effected a clearance as the siren sounded. In 404 games for Mines Rovers, East Fremantle and Western Australia, 'Nipper' was renowned for his ability to read the play, for the accuracy of his passing, for his astute leadership and for his fairness; a top centreman who could play in most other positions, he won numerous medals and best-player awards. Vice-captain (1913-15) and captain (1916-22) of East Fremantle, he played in three premiership teams and in seven that were runners-up. Truscott was the first Australian Rules footballer to play in five Australian championships. He later acted as coach, club and State selector, club secretary and delegate.

He practised twice a week and played sport every Saturday, cricket in summer, football in winter. As a wicket-keeper and batsman, he was in the State side that met W. M. Woodfull's [q.v.] Australian XI on its way to England in 1930. Truscott was also a superb leg spinner, but preferred to be behind the stumps. In retirement he became a first-division lawn bowls player, a winner of several club championships and a member of premiership sides. Partnered by Harry Snook, he won an Australian pairs bowls title in 1955.

Truscott was, as well, captain of the East Fremantle Volunteer Fire Brigade and a member of the East Fremantle Town Council. He was a Freemason. Survived by five daughters and two sons, he died at Bayswater, Perth, on 20 June 1966 and was cremated. One of the first sportsmen nominated for the Western Australian Institute's Hall of Fame in August 1985, in the following December he was listed in the Sport Australia Hall of Fame.

D. Heinrichs, *The jubilee book of the East Fremantle Football Club* (Perth, nd, 1948?); J. Lee, *Old Easts* (Perth, 1976); J. Lee and F. Harrison, *The South Fremantle story*, 2 vols (Fremantle, 1976); J. Lee et al, *The footballers* (Perth, 1985).   JACK LEE

TRYON, HENRY (1856-1943),

scientist, was born on 20 December 1856 at Buckfastleigh, Devon, England, son of Henry Curling Tryon, gentleman, and his wife Elizabeth Anne, née Obree. Educated locally at Sherwood College, Henry later abandoned medical studies at University College, London, to pursue his interest in natural science. In Sweden, New Zealand (while managing a grazing property for his father) and from 1882 in the North Queensland sugar-lands, he collected plant and insect specimens, many of which he donated to the Queensland Museum in 1882-83.

Appointed honorary clerical and scientific assistant at the museum in 1882, Tryon was officially employed there from 4 September 1883 and promoted to assistant curator in 1885. On 22 December he married English-born Henrietta Powys Foy with Anglican rites at St John's Church, Brisbane. From 1887 he also undertook scientific work for the

Department of Agriculture, improving the quality of pleuro-pneumonia vaccines and investigating the fruit-fly problem on the Darling Downs. His work for a government board of inquiry into mange-affected stock in 1887-88, and for a New South Wales royal commission into the destruction of rabbits in 1888-89, was widely acclaimed. These secondments created friction between the museum and department which was exacerbated by Tryon's 'disrespectful and antagonistic' attitude to the museum curator; the dissension ended in 1893 when Tryon was retrenched.

He became government entomologist in August 1894 and vegetable pathologist in 1901. His expedition to New Guinea in 1895-96 acquired sixty-six new varieties of sugarcane, of which Badila was to prosper. The author of several papers on prickly pear after 1899, Tryon was appointed in 1911 to a government board of advice headed by Professor B. D. Steele [q.v.]. In 1912-14 Tryon and Professor T. H. Johnston [q.v.9], who were dubbed 'the prickly pair', travelled abroad to investigate remedies and imported cochineal insects which succeeded against tree pear, but Tryon's efforts to rear cactoblastis failed. He described bacterial wilt of the potato, introduced lantana-fly (*Agromyza* [now *Ophiomyia*] *lantanai*) and identified and named buffalo-fly (*Lyperosia* [now *Haematobia irritans*] *exigua*) in 1912.

A naturalist of the old school, Tryon had wide-ranging scientific interests. Linnaeus, rather than Darwin [q.v.1], was his model: he loved precise, practical work in taxonomy, anatomy and the biological control of pests, but showed little interest in natural philosophy. He combined keen eyesight and physical vigour with meticulousness and intellect; he was equally at home in the field where he adopted an easy loping gait, in the laboratory, and in meetings of scientific associations where he was 'the terror of inexperienced or ill-prepared speakers'. Tall, pale and of medium build, he could be irascible and over-critical in both personal and public relationships. Conflict often resulted.

Founding secretary of the Royal Society of Queensland (1883-88) and its representative at meetings to form the Australasian Association for the Advancement of Science in 1886, Tryon resigned from the society in 1891 after clashing with its council; with the exception of two stormy years, he remained outside the society until 1920; he was given life membership in 1929 in recognition of his scientific contribution. In his career he wrote at least 150 reports and papers. His association with various field naturalists' clubs included the Gould [q.v.4] League of Bird Lovers of which he was a president.

Retiring from the public service in 1925, he

continued as a 'temporary' to 1929. Tryon then lived in some poverty as a quasi-pensioner of the State. Survived by a daughter, he died in Brisbane Hospital on 15 November 1943 and was cremated. The Queensland fruit-fly *Dacus tryoni* was named after him.

A. Musgrave, *Bibliography of Australian entomology 1775-1930* (Syd, 1932); P. Mather et al, *A time for a museum* (Brisb, 1986); *Qld Naturalist*, May 1945; *Procs of Roy Soc of Qld*, 56, 1945, 71, no 2, 1960; Public Service Bd (Qld), Personnel file (QA).
                                              G. N. LOGAN

TUBB, FREDERICK HAROLD (1881-1917), soldier and grazier, was born on 28 November 1881 at Longwood, Victoria, fifth child of Harry Tubb, teacher, and his wife Emma Eliza, née Abbott, both English born. His father, head teacher at the local school, subsequently took up a selection in the area. Fred obtained his merit certificate and left school to manage the farm; he later worked his own land. He was 5 ft. 5¾ ins. (167 cm) tall, an extrovert and a born leader. After volunteer service with the Victorian Mounted Rifles (1900-02) and the Australian Light Horse (1902-11), he joined the 60th Battalion, Australian Military Forces, and was commissioned second lieutenant in 1912. He transferred to the 58th Battalion in 1913.

Appointed to the Australian Imperial Force on 24 August 1914 as a second lieutenant in the 7th Battalion, Tubb was promoted lieutenant on 1 February 1915. He reached Gallipoli on 6 July and was gazetted captain on 8 August. On the same day he took over a vital sector of captured trench at Lone Pine, with orders to 'hold it at any cost'. Early on the 9th the Turks launched a furious attack, advancing along a sap which had been barricaded with sandbags. From the parapet, with eight men, Tubb fired at the enemy; two corporals in the trench caught enemy bombs and threw them back or smothered them with greatcoats. Although Tubb was blown from the parapet and the barricade repeatedly wrecked, each time it was rebuilt. He inspired his men, joking and shouting encouragement. A huge explosion blew in the barricade and killed or wounded most of the defenders. Wounded in the arm and scalp, Tubb was left with Corporals A. S. Burton and W. Dunstan [qq.v.7,8]; he led them into action, shooting three Turks with his revolver and providing covering fire while the barricade was rebuilt. A bomb burst, killing Burton and temporarily blinding Dunstan. Tubb then obtained additional help, but the Turks did not renew the attack.

Evacuated that evening, Tubb was taken to England to convalesce. For his gallantry at Lone Pine he was awarded the Victoria Cross.

An emergency appendicectomy left him with an incision hernia and he was invalided to Australia; he arrived home in April 1916 to a hero's welcome. Having persuaded an A.I.F. medical board that he was fit, he rejoined his battalion in France in December and was promoted major on 17 February 1917. His company had an important role in the Menin Road attack, 3rd battle of Ypres, on 20 September. Before the battle he was troubled by his hernia, yet refused to be evacuated. With dash and courage he led his company to its objective, but was hit by a sniper; while being taken out on a stretcher, he was mortally wounded by shell-fire. Tubb was buried in the Lijessenthoek military cemetery, Belgium, and is commemorated by Tubb Hill, Longwood, and a memorial tree in the Avenue of Honour, Euroa, Victoria. His V.C. is on display in the Hall of Valour, Australian War Memorial, Canberra. Three of his brothers, Arthur Oswald (lieutenant, 60th Battalion), Frank Reid, M.C. (captain, 7th Battalion) and Alfred Charles, a signaller, also served in the A.I.F.

C. E. W. Bean, *The story of Anzac*, 2 (Syd, 1924) and *The A.I.F. in France*, 1917 (Syd, 1933); A. Dean and E. W. Gutteridge, *The Seventh Battalion, A.I.F.* (Melb, 1933); L. Wigmore (ed), *They dared mightily*, second ed revised and condensed by J. Williams and A. Staunton (Canb, 1986); *London Gazette*, 15 Oct 1915; *Euroa Advertiser*, 4 Sept 1914; *Euroa Gazette*, 1 Sept 1915; Tubb personal diaries (held by author, Brighton, Melb); personal information.   H. MURRAY HAMILTON

TUCK, MARIE ANNE (1866-1947), artist, was born on 5 September 1866 at Mount Torrens, in the Adelaide hills, daughter of Edward Starkey Tuck, teacher, and his wife Amy Harriet, née Taylor, both English born. With her three sisters and three brothers, she received a liberal education at her father's school. From 1886 Marie attended James Ashton's [q.v.7] Norwood Art School in the evenings and worked for a florist by day. Wishing to study in Paris, she began teaching at nights. In 1896 she moved to Perth where she again taught painting and worked for a florist; she saved carefully and in 1906 left for France. She altered her age, subtracting six years.

She idolized her mentor, Rupert Bunny [q.v.7], whose lessons she paid for by cleaning his studio, fuelling the stoves and sweeping snow from the door. Marie spent summers in Étables, Brittany, painting village life. In 1908 she sent a huge painting 'The Fish Market' to Adelaide for the 11th Federal Exhibition of the (Royal) South Australian Society of Arts; the National Gallery of South Australia bought it for 100 guineas. That year she exhibited 'Les Commères' and 'Fishwife' at the salon de la Société des Artistes Français, Paris. Her work was hung in the next four salon showings and in 1911 she received honorable mention for her 'Toilette de la Mariée', now in the Queen Adelaide Club.

After the outbreak of World War I Tuck returned home where she taught life-drawing and painting at the South Australian School of Arts and Crafts. She insisted on nude models; her natural dignity and authority ensured that her request was accepted. Still frugal, she built a small live-in studio and garden at Frewville where students gathered on Saturdays to eat nasturtium-leaf sandwiches, drink mulberry wine and talk about Paris. Her 1920 exhibition was criticized by the *Bulletin* for including slapdash pictures, but her *plein air* work was praised by the *Advertiser* at her 1924 and 1933 exhibitions. Marie continued to teach (until 1939), to paint portraits and to execute large religious works, including those for Reims Cathedral, France.

She loved music and owned a silver-stringed spinet. At work she wore a shift, buttoned in front, with loose sleeves; on festive occasions, she chose lavish trimmings. She was barely 5 ft. (152 cm) tall. Her spiky, grey hair was arranged like a Japanese doll, her face and hands were pale and freckled, her lips thin. What mattered were the eyes, faded with age to a luminous green-grey, the irises rimmed with light. A dedicated and inspiring teacher, with a sweet voice, she had many devoted students, among them Ivor Hele and John Dowie.

Although unmarried, Marie Tuck regarded brides as 'those fortunate ones'. When France fell in 1940 she had a stroke, but continued to paint, with difficulty, until her death on 3 September 1947 at Glen Osmond. Born a Methodist, she had adopted Anglicanism. Her paintings are in the art galleries of South Australia, New South Wales and the Northern Territory. At her 1971 retrospective, Dowie commented that she 'had the dancing, broken touch of a painter interested in light and atmosphere. Her palette was high-keyed and pure ...she ...taught us what an artist should be'.

Catalogue of the National Gallery of South Australia (Adel, 1946); R. Biven, *Some forgotten, some remembered* (Adel, 1976); N. Benko, *Art and artists of South Australia* (Adel, 1969); C. Ambrus, *The ladies' picture show* (Syd, 1984); *Critic* (Adel), 27 Sept 1905; Sth Aust Soc of Arts, *Kalori*, Mar 1964; J. Robertson, 'Marie Tuck', in Personalities remembered (Radio talk, 11 Dec 1971, ms, Mortlock Lib); family papers and letters (held by Mrs J. Stephenson and author, Adel); personal information.   RUTH TUCK

TUCKER, CHARLES (1857-1928), customs agent, politician and pastoralist, was born on 20 February 1857 at Walkerville, Adelaide, son of William Henry Tucker, storekeeper, and his wife Eliza, née Samler. Educated at F. F. Unwin's school, Walkerville, and at J. L. Young's [q.v.6] Adelaide Educational Institution, Charles worked on his father's farm near Goolwa. About 1880 he entered a shipping office at Port Adelaide and then joined E. Malpas & Co., shipping and customs agents; their partnership was dissolved six months later, leaving Tucker as sole owner. On 19 October 1885 at St Bartholomew's Anglican Church, Norwood, he married Mary Elizabeth Patterson. He was mayor of Port Adelaide in 1890-93 and of Adelaide in 1894-98. By instituting unpopular spending cuts, he improved the corporation's financial position; he remained on the council until 1907.

An Independent, who generally supported Charles Kingston [q.v.9] and was helped by him, Tucker advocated free trade and Federation. Sidney Webb saw him as 'a tall, spare, heavy-moustached and swarthy man, with a slow and ungraceful manner, extremely anxious to be deferential and polite, but exceedingly awkward'. A controversial opportunist, Tucker drew considerable newspaper comment during election campaigns: when he stood for the House of Assembly seat of North Adelaide in 1896 he was attacked by Cornelius Proud who alluded to Tucker's marital separation and philandering, and claimed that he was morally unfit for parliament. Tucker did not sue. In 1899 he was returned for Encounter Bay, but, because of a violation of the Electoral Code Act, had to contest the seat again at a by-election in July. In a highly publicized contest with King O'Malley [q.v.11], Tucker allegedly declared that, if elected, he would give his salary to charity; O'Malley retorted that he could do the same 'if he were an agent in the Customs'. Voters supported Tucker's opposition to household suffrage and his wish to develop Victor Harbor as a port: as a conservative, he held the seat until 1902 and Alexandra in 1902-06.

While detested by many people, Tucker rose as a public figure. He was first president of the Port Adelaide branch of the Australian Natives' Association, a governor of the Botanic Garden board, a commissioner of the National Park board and of the destitute and lunatic asylums, chairman of the Adelaide Hospital board, a member of the Adelaide Licensing Bench, and a patron of sporting clubs, charities and the Prisoners' Aid Association. He was a Freemason.

From the 1880s Tucker had speculated in mining at Silverton and Broken Hill, New South Wales, and in Western Australia. In South Australia he concentrated on the northeast, pioneering the Mannahill goldfields and the Trinity Mutooroo Copper Mine; when his syndicate took it over, he became chairman of directors of the Balhannah Goldmining Co. and he was also a director of West Callington Copper & Silver Mining Co. His Western Australian interests included membership of the Collie coalfield syndicate and directorship of several Coolgardie mining companies, among them the Londonderry Console. His underhand dealings caused the Stock Exchange of Adelaide to take steps in 1896 to remove companies with which he was associated from its lists. In 1902 he sued James Hutchison [q.v.9] for libel.

On 12 February 1907, as customs agent for John Martin & Co. Ltd, Tucker was found guilty of having defrauded the Customs Department during the 1890s of duties payable on goods imported by the firm. His brother and nephew were also implicated. The amount involved approached £33 000 of which Tucker's share had been about £2000 a year for more than a decade. Tucker was sentenced to two years imprisonment with hard labour; the *Observer* cautioned against 'the pretensions of smooth-tongued and clever individuals of gentlemanly address and suitably captivating manners'. It had been South Australia's longest criminal trial: there were 97 witnesses and some 8000 exhibits, and the case ran for 31 days. Because of his rash mining ventures, Tucker was virtually bankrupt. After his release from prison, he rented the Metropolitan Hotel in Grote Street. He managed Nullarbor station from 1913 and later owned a share of the Nullarbor Pastoral Co. He died intestate on 5 December 1928 at North Adelaide Private Hospital, survived by his wife and their two daughters, and was buried in North Road cemetery.

R. Cockburn, *Pastoral pioneers of South Australia*, 2 (Adel, 1927); A. J. Hannan, *The life of Chief Justice Way* (Syd, 1960); B. Webb, *The Webbs' Australian diary, 1898*, A. G. Austin ed (Melb, 1965); R. M. Gibbs, *Bulls, bears and wildcats* (Adel, 1988); *City of Adel Mayor's Report*, 1897-98; *Critic* (Adel), 27 Feb 1907; *Observer* (Adel), 8 Dec 1894, 16 Feb 1907; *Register* (Adel), 25, 27 Apr 1896; *Chronicle* (Adel), 8 Dec 1928.   VIVIEN STEWART

TUCKER, HORACE FINN (1849-1911) and GERARD KENNEDY (1885-1974), Anglican clergymen, were father and son. Horace was born on 13 October 1849 at Cambridge, England, third child of Joseph Kidger Tucker, clergyman, and his wife Elizabeth, née Finn. Joseph was appointed Australian agent of the British and Foreign Bible Society, and the family arrived in Sydney in 1861.

Educated at Moore Theological College, New South Wales, Horace was made deacon in 1873 and ordained priest in 1874. On 10 September 1873 he had married Caroline Lavinia, daughter of William Adams Brodribb [q.v.3] at St Andrew's Anglican Church, Brighton, Melbourne. His first parishes were in central Victoria where his sermons and pioneering spirit attracted the attention of Bishop Moorhouse [q.v.5]. Promoted in 1880 to the prosperous Melbourne parish of Christ Church, South Yarra, Tucker set up three mission churches and established a grammar school.

During the depression of the 1890s Horace and Rev. Charles Strong [q.v.6] promoted a scheme for resettling the unemployed in country areas. In 1892-94 Tucker Village Settlements, of about 200 families, were established in Gippsland and central Victoria, but were unable to continue due to lack of capital, worsening economic conditions and mismanagement. Recognizing their efforts, the government passed a Settlement of Lands Act (1893) to provide for future village community settlements. Horace published The new Arcadia (1894), a novel based on the ideals of the Tucker settlements, as well as a book of verse, After many days (1905), a study of the Christian saints, Lights for lesser days (1909), and articles on social issues.

Elected in 1894 a canon of St Paul's Cathedral, Melbourne, he retired from Christ Church in 1908, but continued parish work in outer suburbs until he died of a cerebral haemorrhage at Glen Iris on 22 December 1911. He was buried in St Kilda cemetery. His wife, three daughters and three sons survived him. A tall man of striking appearance —bald in later life—with a high forehead and luxuriant dark beard, Tucker was remembered by his parishioners for his good-humour, compassion and public service.

His son, Gerard Kennedy, was born on 18 February 1885 at South Yarra, Melbourne. From childhood he wanted to follow his father and grandfather into the Church. His years at Melbourne Church of England Grammar School were undistinguished; small and slight, he had a severe stammer which seemed likely to prevent him from entering the ministry. On leaving school, he worked briefly in a sugar factory and on a relation's farm, but neither experience proved successful and his father finally agreed that he should study for the priesthood. In 1908 Gerard entered St John's Theological College, Melbourne; with four other students, he approached Archbishop Henry Lowther Clarke [q.v.8], offering to work as celibate priests among the poor in the inner city. The idea was rejected as impractical, but it foreshadowed Tucker's later achievement.

Having failed his final examinations through extreme nervousness, in 1910 he offered his services as deacon to a parish in north-west Australia; he was totally unsuited to outback conditions and after a few months returned to Melbourne. There he was ordained priest in 1914, becoming curate of St George's, Malvern. On the outbreak of war he asked to be posted overseas as a chaplain. When this request was refused, he enlisted as a private soldier and sailed for the Middle East in December 1915. Three months later he was appointed chaplain to the Australian Imperial Force and served in Egypt and France until late 1917 when he was invalided back to Australia. In 1919 he published As private and padre with the A.I.F.

In 1920 Tucker was appointed to a parish near Newcastle, New South Wales, where he met Guy Colman Cox who shared his dream of a community of serving priests and in 1930 they founded the Brotherhood of St Laurence. Its four original members pledged to remain unmarried while part of the brotherhood, to live frugally and to practise an active community life. The first B.S.L. Quarterly Notes were published in 1932 for their supporters; over the next forty years they aired many important social issues.

At the invitation of Archbishop Head [q.v.9], in 1933 the Brotherhood of St Laurence moved to Melbourne where Tucker became curate at St Peter's Church, Eastern Hill, and missioner of St Mary's Mission, Fitzroy. In 1937-42 he was vicar of St Cuthbert's, East Brunswick. His first project was a hostel for homeless, unemployed men. In 1935 he devised a plan to move them and their families to a nearby farming community. Like his father's earlier schemes, this project was not altogether successful, but Gerard's settlement at Carrum Downs remained and by 1944 had become an effective community retirement village. It provided housing and activities for the elderly and later expanded to include self-contained flats for the infirm, as well as a cottage hospital.

Other major welfare schemes initiated by Fr Tucker included a hostel for homeless boys, a club for elderly pensioners, a seaside holiday home for poor families and an opportunity shop. His slight frame, clear blue eyes, horn-rimmed spectacles and hesitant voice became familiar to the people of Melbourne as he campaigned for the abolition of slums. He was appointed O.B.E. in 1956.

Gerard had moved in 1949 to Carrum Downs where he soon embarked on his new project, 'Food for Peace'. He encouraged residents at the settlement to contribute from their pensions to send a shipment of rice to India. Supporting groups formed throughout Australia and in 1961, as Community Aid Abroad, they became a national organization. Tucker published pamphlets in support of the project and, in 1954, an autobiography.

Another settlement for the elderly,

St Laurence Park, opened at Lara, Victoria, in 1959. Tucker moved into its first cottage where he remained until his death at Geelong on 24 May 1974. He was buried in Melbourne general cemetery.

I. R. Carter, *God and three shillings* (Melb, 1967); C. R. Badger, *The Reverend Charles Strong and the Australian church* (Melb, 1971); J. Handfield, *Friends and brothers* (Melb, 1980); *People* (Syd), 20 Dec 1950, 27 Mar 1963; *Australasian*, 4 July 1896; *Argus*, 23 Dec 1911; *Herald* (Melb), 6 Sept 1947, 5 Jan 1957.   RUTH CARTER

TUCKER, THOMAS GEORGE (1859-1946), classical scholar, was born on 29 March 1859 at Burnham, Buckinghamshire, England, son of Charles Tucker, agent, and his wife Elizabeth, née Rolfe. He was educated at Northampton Grammar School, the Royal Grammar School at Lancaster and at St John's College, Cambridge (B.A., 1882; M.A., 1885; Litt.D., 1890), where he was Brown's medallist (1879, 1880), Craven scholar (1881), senior classic and chancellor's medallist and fellow (1882). Plagued by bronchitis, he travelled abroad and in 1883 became founding professor of classics and English at the new Auckland University College, New Zealand. During his first week there, he narrowly survived a boating accident in which his only professorial colleague drowned.

In 1885 Tucker was appointed professor of classical philology at the University of Melbourne after the resignation of H. A. Strong [q.v.6]. His inaugural lecture on 'The place of the classics in a liberal education' prompted much discussion. In 1892 Tucker represented Melbourne at the tercentenary of the University of Dublin and received an honorary D.Litt. He served as president of the professorial board (1902) and dean of the faculty of arts (1904-13). His reputation as a lecturer of great ability extended into the public domain where he was much in demand, whether by the Beefsteak Club, the Socialist Hall, the Pleasant Sunday Afternoon or the Medical Students' Society. He was a trustee of the Public Library, museums and National Gallery of Victoria. Accounted the 'literary oracle of Melbourne' in the 1890s, he exercised considerable influence through his Saturday leaders in the *Argus*. In 1890-91, with (Sir) Walter Baldwin Spencer [q.v.], he edited the *Australasian Critic* which, although it fell victim to declining sales in the depression, was a monument to the idealism and community of thought among the younger professors.

Appearing before the royal commission on the University of Melbourne in 1902, Tucker gave evidence which provided a valuable record of his views on education. The university faced a financial crisis through embezzlement by its accountant and, when the chair of modern languages became frozen on E. E. Morris's [q.v.5] death, Tucker undertook an honorary lectureship in English for almost two years.

Tucker's literary output was prodigious. In classical scholarship his reputation rested securely on his editions and commentaries on Aeschylus: *Supplices* (1889), *Choephori* (1901), *Seven against Thebes* (1908). In his day his Aeschylean editions were ranked for dramatic insight and lucidity with Sir Richard Jebb's famous editions of Sophocles. Tucker's translations of *Agamemnon*, *Prometheus bound* and *Persians* were published in 1935. He also produced works on Thucydides's Book VIII (1892), Aristotle's *Poetics* (1899), Plato's *Republic* (1900) and Aristophanes's *Frogs* (1906), while his elegant lecture on Sappho (1914) enjoyed an extraordinary vogue. Among Tucker's general works were *Life in ancient Athens* (1907) and *Life in the Roman world of Nero and St Paul* (1910); his lively and imaginative Latin grammar (1907) was often reprinted.

A lifelong interest in linguistic evolution was apparent in Tucker's *Introduction to the natural history of language* (1908) and in *A concise etymological dictionary of Latin* (1931) on which he had worked for many years. Some scholars, however, regretted that he did not devote his time to completing his Aeschylus. His literary interests and knowledge were reflected in *The foreign debt of English literature* (1907) and in books on Shakespeare and on literary appreciation. Tucker also published textbooks on English literature and grammar, one with (Sir) Walter Murdoch [q.v.10], another with (Sir) Robert Wallace [q.v.]. His numerous papers and lectures were also published, some of the latter in *Things worth thinking about* (1890) and *Platform monologues* (1914).

Of Tucker's role as an arbiter of public taste, E. Morris Miller [q.v.10] wrote appreciatively, yet Geoffrey Dutton dismissed him as an enemy of modernity. (Sir) Walter Murdoch wrote to Alfred Deakin [q.v.8]: 'Classical scholars—who have a way of claiming a monopoly of literary taste—have certain well-defined limitations and Tucker, as you say, is probably cut off from enjoyment of all literature in which the individual note is sounded'. D. H. Rankin balanced earlier eulogies of Tucker as 'a living library' and 'a temple of the Muses' against perceptible austerities in his style and thought.

In 1919 Tucker retired, as emeritus professor. Next year he was appointed C.M.G.; family tradition maintains that he declined a knighthood. For reasons of health, he lived in Sydney, but retained contact with university life, filling in for Professors Woodhouse [q.v.]

and Michie [q.v.10] at the universities of Sydney and Queensland. George Robertson [q.v.11], of Angus & Robertson, employed him, among other literary advisers, to read manuscripts and 'lick them into shape' for publication. Although many authors resented this 'tuckering', Robertson valued it highly and C. E. W. Bean [q.v.7], for one, ultimately applauded his conscientiousness and sense of style. While Tucker failed to detect the significance of the early work of Christopher Brennan [q.v.7], he was enthusiastic about Frank Dalby Davison's *Man-shy*.

On 9 November 1882 Tucker had married Annie Mary Muckalt (d. 1933) in St Paul's parish church, Shireshead, Lancashire. On 9 January 1934 in Melbourne he married Anne Sophie Henrietta, née Hamilton (d. 1941), widow of Theyre à Beckett Weigall [q.v.]. His stepdaughter, Joan Lindsay, has left an affectionate portrait of him: 'Tall slim surprisingly upright even in old age and always something of a dandy, gloves and a light cane, a broad brimmed fedora hat, patent leather shoes, large pearl tiepin and an unusually high white collar . . . were typical accessories of his wardrobe. The lean craggy face with its gingery grey moustache and bright blue eyes was . . . vivacious and . . . full of personal charm'. Tucker died at Stope Cove, Devon, England, on 24 January 1946, survived by the two daughters and son of his first marriage.

Joan Lindsay, *Time without clocks* (Melb, 1962); *Walter Murdoch and Alfred Deakin on 'Books and men'*, ed J. A. La Nauze and E. Nurser (Melb, 1974); A. W. Barker (ed), *Dear Robertson* (Syd, 1982); D. McCarthy, *Gallipoli to the Somme* (Syd, 1983); G. Dutton, *Snow on the saltbush* (Melb, 1984); Roy com on the University of Melbourne, Minutes of evidence, *PP* (Vic), 1903, 2 (20), p 15, Final report, 1904, 2 (13), pp 97, 138; *Alma Mater* (Univ Melb), 1, no 9 (1896), p 14, 7, no 4 (1902), p 161; *Melb Univ Mag*, 24, no 2 (1930), p 27; Classical Assn of Vic, *Iris*, 1987, no 1, p 3; *Table Talk*, 1 Sept 1893, 29 May 1896; *Age*, 3 Jan 1953; Univ Melb Archives.
K. J. McKay

TUCKER, TUDOR ST GEORGE (1862-1906), artist, was born on 28 April 1862 at Finchley, Middlesex, England, second of five children of Charlton Nassau Tucker, retired Bengal Cavalry officer, and his wife Harriet, née Mason. The family had traditional ties with India: Henry St George Tucker, chairman of the East India Co., was his grandfather. Tudor chose the independent path of an artist, later describing it as 'a very painful & up-hill struggle'. He came to Melbourne in 1881 for his health. High-spirited, with a broad knowledge of art, music and philosophy, he was an early member of the Buonarotti Club. Between 1883 and 1887 he trained

at the National Gallery schools under George Folingsby [q.v.4] and was awarded prizes for drawing in 1884, 1886 and 1887. Tucker joined in landscape-sketching excursions and taught drawing to support himself. During 1882 and 1883 he exhibited with the Victorian Academy of Arts.

In May 1887 Tucker left for Europe. With E. Phillips Fox [q.v.8], he studied in Paris at the Académie Julian and under Gérôme at the Ecole des Beaux-Arts where he won a gold medal. He also painted in *plein air* artists' colonies. At Etaples he produced his first major picture, 'A Picardy Shrimp Fisher', with which he made his début at the Salon de la Société des Artistes Français in 1891. Returning to Melbourne in July 1892, Tucker occupied a studio at Flinders Lane, later moving to the Cromwell Buildings in Bourke Street. A councillor of, and exhibitor with, the Victorian Artists' Society between 1892 and 1898, he held studio shows in 1892 and 1895. He contributed to major Sydney exhibitions and the Australian Exhibition at the Grafton Galleries, London, in 1898. Although his art was well regarded and purchased by two Victorian public galleries, patronage was limited. In 1893, together with Fox, Tucker established the Melbourne School of Art, based on French academic practices; from 1894 they conducted a lively, outdoor summer school at Charterisville.

Tall and slender, with a sauntering walk, Tucker had dark-blue eyes, refined features and soft, golden-brown hair. In failing health, he returned to London where he displayed his Australian works. By 1899 he had settled at Chelsea, but continued to exhibit widely—at the Royal Academy, at Birmingham and at Liverpool. He held his final 'Sea and Sunlight' show in 1906. On 21 December that year he died of phthisis at Hearne House, Hayes, Middlesex, and was buried with Anglican rites in the local churchyard.

Tucker's contribution has been underestimated. He was esteemed by fellow artists and Melbourne reviewers noted his advanced understanding of French art; his ability to theorize and communicate ideas enlarged local knowledge of Impressionist colour theories. His own work shows a refined colour sense and a delicate feeling for light effects; academic training is evident in his figure painting. Apart from portraits, landscapes and nudes, he painted figure compositions, sometimes quasi-narrative in character. Tucker is represented in the Australian National Gallery, Canberra, the National Gallery of Victoria, Warrnambool Art Gallery, in major private collections and at Derby, England.

J. Clark and B. Whitelaw, *Golden summers* (Syd, 1985); *Table Talk*, 26 Aug 1892, 5 July 1895, 2 Oct 1896; *Middlesex and Buckinghamshire Advertiser*,

29 Dec 1906, 5 Jan 1907; *Argus*, 10 Aug 1929; *Financial Review*, 6 Apr 1978; R. Zubans, Emanuel Phillips Fox (1865-1915): the development of his art, 1884-1913 (Ph.D. thesis, Univ Melb, 1980); Buonarotti Club Minutes *and* Vic Artists' Soc, Minute-books (LaTL); Tucker to E. Lance, letter, 5 Jan 1894 (Warrnambool Art Gallery, Vic).

RUTH ZUBANS

TUCKETT, FRANCIS JOHN (1875-1917) and LEWIS (1879-1960), soldiers, were brothers. Francis was born on 1 March 1875 at Beaufort, Victoria, fifth child of Alfred Curtis Tuckett, a brickmaker from Bristol, England, and his Irish wife Maria, née Bryans. About 1878 Alfred took up farming at Marraweeney, near Violet Town, where Lewis, his seventh child, was born on 1 April 1879. The children were educated locally.

A smallish, stocky man, Francis (or Jack as he was known) served in the militia with the Victorian Mounted Rifles for two years before going to Western Australia and becoming a telegraphist at Eucla in 1895. Moving to Kalgoorlie, he married Elspeth Maria Morrison on 9 June 1898 with Presbyterian forms; they were to have six children. In Perth in 1904 he joined the (Royal) Australian Engineers, serving first with the 8th Half Company and from 1909 with the 30th Signal Company. He was commissioned second lieutenant on 16 March 1913.

Jack Tuckett was appointed to the 3rd Divisional Signal Company, Australian Imperial Force, on 3 March 1916; his eldest son FRANCIS CURTIS (1899-1953) was allotted to the company six days later as a sapper. Born at Coolgardie on 28 July 1899 and educated at Victoria Park, young Francis was a bank clerk when he managed to enlist in the A.I.F. on 28 December 1915. Father and son embarked in May 1916 for training in England; Jack was promoted lieutenant in September. They proceeded to France in November where their company was responsible for providing and maintaining communications with forward units in the war zone. Lieutenant Tuckett was recommended for the Military Cross for his work in the Ypres sector in September and early October 1917; he was killed in the 2nd battle of Passchendaele on 14 October before his award was promulgated. His mates wrote to his wife that he had died while 'seeking to alleviate the distress of others'. A keen cricketer, he had been presented with the bat used when a side from his company was successful against a 10th Australian Infantry Brigade team: his family later gave it to the Western Australian Cricket Association.

Sapper Tuckett attended his father's funeral at Ypres Reservoir North cemetery. For his gallantry in operations prior to and on 12 October, Francis Curtis Tuckett was awarded the Military Medal. He was transferred to Headquarters in April 1917 and his appointment was terminated in November, after his return to Australia on compassionate grounds. Later, as a 'gun' shearer, he roamed the country. On 8 November 1953 he died of lung cancer in Royal Prince Alfred Hospital, Sydney, and was buried in the Field of Mars cemetery with Methodist forms. He was survived by his wife Eileen Theresa, née Sheridan, whom he had married at the Sacred Heart Catholic Church, Hughenden, Queensland, on 14 November 1931, and by their daughter.

Lewis Tuckett, like his elder brother, joined the Western Australian Postmaster-General's Department as a letter carrier in 1900 and became a telegraphist. He served in the citizen forces from 1909. Two weeks after marrying Edith Emma Keedwell at St George's Anglican Cathedral, Perth, on 11 August 1914, he enlisted in the A.I.F. Promoted sergeant, he embarked for Egypt with the 1st Divisional Signal Company in October.

Tuckett's company was attached to the 2nd Australian Infantry Brigade and landed on Gallipoli on 25 April 1915. He was awarded the Military Medal for his work in maintaining communications during the consolidation of the front line and at Cape Helles when the brigade attacked Krithia. Transferred to the 8th Battalion, he was commissioned second lieutenant on 1 December.

In Egypt in February 1916 Tuckett was promoted lieutenant. He was transferred to the 4th Divisional Signal Company next month and went in June to France where, as signals officer for the 13th Australian Infantry Brigade, he was responsible for communications with the forward battalions. He was mentioned in dispatches three times during operations at Mouquet Farm, Fleurbaix, Somme, Ypres and Flers. Disregarding his own safety at the attack and seizure of Noreuil in April 1917, he kept communications in working order with every unit. For this action he was awarded the Military Cross.

Later that month Lewis Tuckett was transferred to the 3rd Divisional Signal Company; promoted captain, he was second-in-command. Following the death of his brothers, Jack and Philip, he was granted two months compassionate leave early in 1918 to visit his family in Australia. Back in France in August, he served with the 4th Divisional Signal Company; he returned to Australia in July 1919 and his A.I.F. appointment terminated in September. He continued in the Australian Military Forces until December 1931 when he was placed on the retired list.

After the war Tuckett had resumed his job as a postal employee and later became a supervisor at the General Post Office, Perth. With blue eyes, dark brown hair and a fair complexion, he became a father figure to Jack's children and was an active member of Legacy, the Returned Sailors' and Soldiers' Imperial League of Australia and the Anglican Church. Survived by his wife and a son, he died at the Repatriation General Hospital, Hollywood, Perth, on 12 February 1960 and was cremated.

The Tucketts' youngest brother, PHILIP SAMUEL (1884-1916), was the fourth member of the family involved in providing communications at the battle front. Born on 1 November 1884 at Violet Town, he was a survey hand on the construction of the transcontinental railway before enlisting in the A.I.F. in Perth on 3 January 1916. Promoted sergeant, he embarked with the 3rd Pioneer Battalion in June for training in England. Arriving in France, he was allotted to the 49th Battalion; two days after being commissioned second lieutenant, he was killed by shell-fire while inspecting telephone lines at Flers on 24 November 1916. His brother Lewis witnessed his burial at Bull's Road Military cemetery.

Another brother, Frederick William (1873-1922), was postmaster at Halls Creek in the Kimberleys, Western Australia; in August 1917 he operated on a seriously injured stockman by following instructions telegraphed to him from a surgeon in Perth. The incident reinforced public recognition of the need for a flying doctor service.

E. Hill, *Flying doctor calling* (Syd, 1948); R. D. Williams (comp), *World War I military medals to Australia* and *World War I military crosses to Australia* (Melb, 1982); *London Gazette*, 27 Oct 1916, 2 Jan, 1, 15 June, 25, 28 Dec 1917, 25 Jan 1918; *West Australian*, 7, 11 Aug 1917, 19 Apr 1986; Unit embarkation nominal rolls, 1914-18 war *and* troopship records *and* war diaries, 1st, 3rd *and* 4th Divisional Signal Company, AIF (AWM); information from Mrs W. M. De Landgrafft, Boyup Brook, WA and Mr R. Tuckett, Altona, Melb.

R. E. COWLEY

TUCKETT, JOSEPH HELTON (1890-1922), soldier and auctioneer, was born on 19 March 1890 at South Yarra, Melbourne, son of Arthur Helton Tuckett, auctioneer, and his wife Margaret, née Gibson, both Melbourne born. Joseph attended Melbourne Church of England Preparatory Grammar School (1898-1900), Malvern Grammar School and Hamilton Academy before starting work as an auctioneer. About 1913 he became a partner in his father's firm, Arthur Tuckett & Son.

Two days after enlisting in the 5th Battalion, Australian Imperial Force, Tuckett married Edith Eliza Eva ('Queenie') Fenton on 24 August 1914 at St Peter's Anglican Church, Melbourne. On 16 September he was promoted sergeant and transferred to the Australian Army Ordnance Corps. He em-

barked for the Middle East on 21 October with the 1st Division headquarters; promoted staff sergeant next January, he sailed for Gallipoli via Lemnos on 5 April 1915. Brought to notice for his gallantry and valuable services from 25 April to 5 May, he was awarded the Military Medal and promoted warrant officer, class one.

In Egypt on 21 February 1916 Tuckett was commissioned lieutenant and appointed deputy assistant director of ordnance services, 4th Division, with the temporary rank of captain. Proceeding with the division to France, he was confirmed in rank on 20 August. For over two years he played a pivotal role in the often hazardous task of providing stores to forward units. He was awarded the Military Cross on 1 June 1917 for his work, promoted major in November and thrice mentioned in dispatches. Appointed temporary assistant director of ordnance services to the Australian Corps in October 1918, he became the A.I.F.'s senior ordnance officer in France on 4 December. He was A.D.O.S., Australian Corps headquarters, with the temporary rank of lieutcolonel from March 1919; in September, with the honorary rank of lieut-colonel, he embarked for home. His A.I.F. appointment terminated in January 1920.

A small man with blue eyes, brown hair and a fair complexion, Tuckett left Australia about 1921 to work as a gazetted official in the Chief Engineer's Department, Iraq. On the night of 25-26 March 1922 he was shot dead by Arab intruders in his bungalow in Engineer Field Park, Baghdad. Survived by his wife, he was buried in the local war cemetery.

Joseph's cousin, Lieutenant Richard Joseph Tuckett (1890-1954), was awarded the Military Cross for his services at the battle of Dernancourt in April 1918.

J. B. Kiddle (comp and ed), *War services of Old Melburnians 1914-1918* (Melb, 1923); Melb C of E Grammar School, *Liber Melburniensis* (Melb, 1937, 1965) and *Melburnian*, 8 Dec 1954; C. E. W. Bean, *The A.I.F. in France*, 3, 5 (Syd, 1929, 1937); *Argus*, 31 Mar, 1 Apr 1922; information from Mr R. Tuckett, Altona, Melb, and Mr I. H. Tuckett, Cranbrook, WA.

R. E. COWLEY

TUCKFIELD, WILLIAM JOHN (1881-1969), dentist and academic, was born on 15 December 1881 at Belfast (Port Fairy), Victoria, seventh child of Rev. James William Tuckfield, Wesleyan minister, and his wife Mary Ann, née Patterson, both Australian born. His grandfather Rev. Francis Tuckfield [q.v.2] had established the Buntingdale Mission for Aborigines near Geelong in 1838.

'Tucky', as William was known, received the diploma of the Australian College of Dentistry and was registered as a dentist in 1902 by the Dental Board of Victoria. On 12 April 1911 at St Matthew's Anglican Church, Prahran, he married Marcella Mabel Monckton. He served in the Australian Army Medical Corps (Dental Services) in 1915-18, becoming honorary captain in July 1917.

Elected a member of the faculty of dental science, University of Melbourne, in 1908, he was dean in 1922-23; he retired in 1959, having been acting professor of dental prosthetics since 1949. He edited the *Australian Journal of Dentistry* from 1914 to 1956 when he became editor emeritus of the new *Australian Dental Journal*. His editorials, articles and letters, devoted to the support of the profession, revealed an uncompromising approach that bore testimony to his missionary forebears. With boundless mental and physical energy, he worked seven days a week in private and hospital practice, teaching, editing and engaging in dental politics. He was president of the Odontological Society of Victoria (1910), the Alumni Society of the Australian College of Dentistry (1921) and the Australian Dental Association (1939-41).

Chairman and president of the Australian College of Dentistry and the Dental Hospital in 1915-16, he still worked there at the age of 72 as building officer. His lifelong interest in visual aids had developed from the magic lantern through the deep focus camera to colour cinematography in which he made a significant contribution to clinical teaching. He retired in 1963 and resigned from the council in 1967.

An outstanding clinician, Tuckfield had a high level of technical skill which was communicated in his only book, *Full denture technique* (Melbourne, 1944). Although he showed no interest in working for higher qualifications either through study or research, he never failed to help others to succeed. His achievements were recognized by the award of honorary degrees from the Northwestern University, United States of America (D.Sc., 1925) and the University of Melbourne (D.D.Sc., 1944; LL.D., 1963), and by an honorary fellowship in dental surgery from the Royal College of Surgeons, London (1948).

'Tucky' had an immense zest for life. In his earlier years he was a keen pioneer motorist and an amateur golfer. In spite of his strict upbringing, he was a free-thinker. In 1967 he went to live with a son in Brisbane where he died on 19 December 1969 and was cremated. Both his sons had served as flying officers in World War II; the younger was killed in action. Tuckfield's portrait by William Dargie is at the Royal Dental Hospital, Melbourne.

Aust Dental J, Feb 1970; *Univ Melb Gazette,* 26, no 1, Mar 1970; Aust College of Dentistry, Minutes 1897-1967, *and* Melb Dental Hospital, Minutes 1890-1967, *and* Faculty of Dental Science, Univ Melb, Minutes 1908-1959 (held at Dental Faculty Lib, Roy Dental Hospital, Melb).

H. F. ATKINSON

TUDOR, FRANCIS GWYNNE (1866-1922), hatter and politician, was born on 29 January 1866 at Williamstown, Melbourne, second surviving son of John Llewellyn Tudor, ballastman, and his wife Ellen Charlotte, née Burt, both Welsh born. The family moved to Richmond and Tudor was to be a Richmond man for the rest of his life. On leaving the Richmond Central State School, he worked in a sawmill and a boot factory before being drawn to the felt hat trade. It soon became both a passion and a passport to the wider world. After an apprenticeship at the Denton Hat Mills in Abbotsford, he went 'on tramp' around Victoria and then to England where he worked in London, Birmingham, Liverpool and at the famous Tress works at Manchester. On 2 January 1894 he married Alice Smale (d. 1894) at the Congregational Chapel, Denton, Lancashire. Tudor dreamed of becoming the manager of the finest hat factory in the world; he succeeded in becoming vice-president of the London branch of the Felt Hatters' Union and assistant to the general secretary of the national organization. As district representative of the Felt Hatters' Union of Connecticut, United States of America, he witnessed the effectiveness of the 'union label'. After persuading the English union to adopt the same principle, he returned to Australia and to a job in the Denton Mills. Full of ideas for improving conditions in the trade, he quickly rose to the presidency of the Felt Hatters' Union and took a seat on the Victorian Trades Hall Council. By 1900 he was president.

'Everyone in Richmond knew Tudor', so the young president of the Trades Hall Council was the obvious choice as the Political Labor Council's candidate for the new Federal seat of Yarra. He won it in March 1901. Before long it was the safest Labor seat in the country. His high principles tempered by genuine liberalism, Tudor was very much in the mould of respectable artisan radicalism. A deeply kind man and a deacon of the Congregational Church, he deplored sectarianism and appalled extreme Protestants by supporting Home Rule for Ireland. He was a lifelong teetotaller and non-smoker, but would cheerfully attend the Liquor Trades' picnics. On 6 January 1897 he had married Fanny Jane Mead at Richmond. Despite the demands of a large family, his home was open to his constituents and their manifold vexations. A keen patron of local sport, whenever he was invited, he went. His street meetings (held by lamplight) to which people were summoned by an auctioneer's bell, remained part of Richmond's oral lore for over sixty years.

In parliament, he did well: immediately elected Labor whip and assistant party secretary, in 1904 he became secretary. In 1908 he was made minister for trade and customs and retained the portfolio (1908-09, 1910-13, 1914-16) into Hughes's [q.v.9] first government. An efficient administrator, with an eye for detail, he made friends and earned respect on both sides of the House, and was considered to be the most moderate of the Victorian Labor members. Yet, he remained at heart a unionist, preferring to discuss conditions in the hat trade rather than parliamentary politics. R. A. Crouch [q.v.8] assessed him as 'not a good or deep speaker, but a good friend and an indefatigable member for his constituents'. Tudor was not destined for greatness.

During World War I, as Hughes's government wrestled over the principle of conscription, Tudor prevaricated, waiting, he claimed, for cabinet's decision. His Richmond supporters, shocked by the tragedy of Pozières, had already made up their minds. By the second week of September 1916, the Richmond P.L.C. lost patience and announced a series of street meetings at which Mr Tudor would speak against conscription. Left without an alternative, Tudor resigned from cabinet. After Hughes broke away, Tudor was elected leader of the parliamentary Labor party in November 1916. Under him, the party lost the 1917 election, but had a slim victory in the conscription referendum. As leader of the Opposition he offended few and refused to be drawn into acrimony. Nonetheless, Labor was again defeated in 1919. Tudor's health began to fail in 1921 and he was increasingly incapacitated, but the party refused to allow him to resign.

Tudor died of heart disease on 10 January 1922 at his Richmond home and was buried in Melbourne cemetery after a state funeral at which Prime Minister Hughes was a pallbearer. Tudor's wife, three sons and three daughters survived him.

J. McCalman, *Struggletown* (Melb, 1984); G. Souter, *Acts of parliament* (Melb, 1988); *Punch* (Melb), 15 Mar 1917; *Age* and *SMH*, 11 Jan 1922.   JANET McCALMAN

TULLOCH, ERIC WILLIAM (1883-1926), brewer, soldier and rower, was born on 16 April 1883 at Ballarat, Victoria, eldest son of William George Tulloch, brewer, and

his wife Agnes Ann, née Wheeldon, both Ballarat born. Educated at Melbourne Church of England Grammar School (1897-99), he represented the school in football and rowed in the first eight and four. In 1901-02 he won the Victorian Champion VIII's title for the Albert Park Rowing Club and in 1902-04 represented the State in the victorious interstate eight-oared crew.

After studying brewing under Auguste de Bavay [q.v.8], bacteriologist of the Foster Brewery, Melbourne, Tulloch was brewer at R. Marks & Co., Maldon, Victoria, in 1904-06. For the next two years he was head brewer at the Swallow Brewery, Perth. In that city on 15 April 1908 at St John's Anglican Church he married Lillian Jane Temby.

A commissioned officer in the Citizen Military Forces, Tulloch joined the Australian Imperial Force in January 1915. As captain in the 11th Battalion, he landed at Gallipoli on 25 April. He was wounded that day while achieving his objective, the southern slopes of Battleship Hill, and was probably the closest officer to enemy lines until repelled.

Recovering in Australia, he was posted in October 1917 to France where he was gassed in the second battle of Passchendaele and fought on the Somme at Cappy. On 23 August 1918 near Chuignolles he commanded two companies and captured Froissy Wood; on 18 September at Hargicourt, near Villeret, with two others Tulloch overpowered and captured the crews of two enemy machine-guns. He was given command of the 12th Battalion and awarded the Military Cross and Bar. Appointed officer-in-charge of the rowing section, sports branch, in February 1919, Tulloch coached the A.I.F. crew which won the King's Cup at Royal Henley.

On his return Tulloch took up a senior position at the Victoria Brewery where he worked until his death. He was an original member of Legacy and was gazetted in 1921 lieut-colonel, 22nd Battalion, Commonwealth Military Forces. He coached the Melbourne Grammar first eight which won the Head of the River in 1923 and finished second in 1924. That year he was appointed to the Old Melburnians council.

Early on the morning of 8 May 1926 he disturbed an intruder in his room at the boarding house, Lauriston Hall, East Melbourne. During a struggle Tulloch was fatally shot. No motive for the killing could be established and the identity of the murderer has never been discovered. Tulloch's funeral was conducted with full military honours. After a service at Melbourne Grammar chapel, the procession, more than a mile long, proceeded to Brighton cemetery by way of St Kilda Road which was lined by thousands of people. His wife, who had been in Sydney receiving medical treatment, survived him; they had no children.

C. E. W. Bean, *The story of Anzac* (Syd, 1921), and *The A.I.F. in France, 1918* (Syd, 1942); J. B. Kiddle (comp and ed), *War services of Old Melburnians 1914-1918* (Melb, 1923), and *Liber Melburniensis 1848-1936* (Melb, 1937); *Aust Brewing and Wine J*, 20 June 1906, 20 May 1926; *Argus*, 9, 11 May 1926; *Truth* (Melb), 15, 22 May, 12, 19 June, 3 July 1926; Inquisition, inquest no 723/1926 (PRO Vic).   P. C. DANE

TUNBRIDGE, WALTER HOWARD (1856-1943), architect and soldier, was born on 2 November 1856 at Dover, Kent, England, son of John Nicholas Tunbridge, bricklayer, and his wife Ann, née Denne. Educated at Eythorne, Walter arrived in Australia as an assisted immigrant in 1884 and established an architectural practice at Townsville, Queensland, later that decade. By 1902 the firm Tunbridge & Tunbridge, civil engineers, architects and surveyors, was prominent in North Queensland.

Commissioned in the Mounted Infantry, Queensland Land Forces, in February 1889, Tunbridge was promoted lieutenant in December. His unit was called out to protect non-union labourers during the 1891 shearers' strike and in June 1892 he was promoted captain. Transferring to the Queensland Artillery (Townsville) Garrison Battery with the rank of major in November 1898, he left for South Africa on 1 March 1900 in command of the 3rd (Queensland) Mounted Infantry Contingent. After operations in Rhodesia in April and May, his unit moved to the Transvaal in July and saw action at Elands River and Rhenoster Kop. Early in 1901 it served in the Cape and Orange River colonies. For his services, Tunbridge was appointed C.B., mentioned in dispatches, awarded the Queen's South Africa Medal with five clasps and made brevet lieut-colonel. Returning home, he rejoined his artillery unit and was aide-de-camp to the governor-general (1902-09).

Following his marriage on 7 April 1904 to Leila Emily Brown at All Saints Anglican Church, Brisbane, Tunbridge established a branch of his firm in Melbourne; he practised there until 3 August 1914 when he became censor for the 3rd Military District. Next week he was deputy chief censor and on 17 August was appointed lieut-colonel in the Australian Imperial Force. Certain line of communications units were required and Tunbridge was given command of the 1st Australian Division Ammunition Park (Mechanical Transport) and commissioned to raise its six officers and 468 men. A supply column was also formed under Lieut-Colonel A. Moon. With limited understanding of the use of mechanical transport in the supply services of the Armed Forces, Tunbridge was

guided by an article in the *New Zealand Military Journal*: he inspected and purchased about 200 vehicles, and provided the required workshops and accessories.

He arrived in England with the two units on 15 February 1915. Due to a lack of spare parts, his varied collection of lorries (some of them German) was replaced by standard British models, but his mobile workshops were admired for their ingenuity and retained. Renumbered as part of the British Army (300th and 301st Mechanical Transport Companies, A.S.C., A.A.S.C.), the units were sent to France in July. On 1 August Tunbridge assumed command of a reorganized British V Corps Ammunition Park; the 8th (301st) Company became the 17th Divisional Ammunition Sub-park and the 9th (300th) the division's supply column. With the support of Lieut-General Allenby, V Corps commander, Tunbridge used his spare men and vehicles to form a second sub-park which was attached to the 23rd Division.

Remaining with V Corps mainly in the Ypres Salient until the Australian divisions arrived in France, Tunbridge became commanding officer of 1 Anzac Corps Ammunition Park on 25 April 1916. After the battle of the Somme he arranged for the publication of the *Rising Sun* to help cheer the men facing winter on the front. On the reorganization of supply columns and ammunition parks in January 1917, he was appointed senior mechanical transport officer of 1 Anzac Corps; at the height of the 3rd battle of Ypres in September, his responsibilities were extended to incorporate the whole of the A.I.F. in France.

Promoted colonel on 1 June 1918, Tunbridge transferred to the retired list in January 1920 and returned home; his A.I.F. appointment ended in June. He had worked outstandingly under intense pressure from bad weather, mechanical breakdowns and desperate calls for supplies from the front line. Mentioned in dispatches five times, he was appointed C.M.G. (1917) and C.B.E. (1919), and made a brevet colonel in the Australian Military Forces. He resumed his career as an architect in Melbourne and retired in the mid-1930s. Survived by his wife, son and two daughters, he died at his Hawthorn home on 11 October 1943 and was buried in Box Hill cemetery.

Aust Defence Dept, *Official records of the Australian military contingents to the war in South Africa*, P. L. Murray ed (Melb, 1911); C. E. W. Bean, *The A.I.F. in France, 1916-18* (Syd, 1929, 1933, 1937, 1942); *London Gazette*, 16, 19 Apr 1901, 31 Dec 1915, 13 June 1916, 1 June, 25, 28 Dec 1917, 3 June, 11 July 1919; *Argus*, 14 Oct 1943; card index: personnel, AIF, 1914-18 (AWM).   CHARLES GLYN-DANIEL

TUNN, JOHN PATRICK (1892-1955), soldier and insurance agent, was born on 8 July 1892 at Glasgow, Scotland, son of John Tunn, pawnbroker, and his wife Catherine, née Shearer. Educated at St Mungo's Academy, Glasgow, Tunn migrated with his parents to Brisbane about 1910. He worked as a cabinetmaker, began accountancy studies and in 1916 became a clerk in the State Government Insurance Office.

Enlisting in the Australian Imperial Force on 19 May 1916, he was posted to the 23rd Reinforcements, 9th Battalion, and taken on strength at Ribemont, France, on 28 May 1917. From August he was attached to headquarters, 1st Australian Division, on military police duty; promoted corporal in October, he returned to the 9th on 28 December. For 'splendid' work during an abortive attack on the German garrison at Meteren on 23-24 April 1918, Tunn was recommended for an award: although it was not approved, he was commissioned second lieutenant in the field on 20 May.

A 'seven seconds Mills bomb', without its pin, was accidentally dropped on 19 July in operations leading to the recapture of Meteren. Running to the bomb and holding it to the ground, Tunn saved his platoon from the effects of the explosion, but lost his right forearm and sustained other injuries. Recommended for the Victoria Cross, he was awarded the Albert Medal for 'gallantry displayed in saving life' as the enemy was not being actively engaged at the time. Only two other members of the A.I.F.—Sergeant David Coyne and Captain William Geake [qq.v.8]—received this award.

Returning to the S.G.I.O., Tunn qualified as an associate of the Federal Institute of Accountants. On 16 September 1919 at St Brigid's Catholic Church, Red Hill, Brisbane, he married Mary Louisa Sherman. He moved to the Queensland Probate Insurance Co. Ltd (later the Equitable Life Assurance Company of Australasia Ltd) where from 1935 he was a manager. In 1946 he joined the National Mutual Life Association of Australasia Ltd, but deteriorating health (the result of gas attacks during the war) prompted him to move to the drier climate of Dalby where he operated a newsagency in 1947-51. Frequent hospitalization necessitated his return to Brisbane. There he again worked in the S.G.I.O. until 1955 when he was classified as totally and permanently disabled.

Of middle height and sturdy build, 'Jock' was a teetotaller with a modest and unassuming manner. He was president of the Indooroopilly and Dalby bowling clubs, choirmaster of the Indooroopilly choral society and, despite his physical disability, an occasional organist at his local Catholic church. A foundation member of the Limbless Soldiers' Association of Queensland, he drafted the constitution of its provident society and was insurance adviser of the Hibernian Association of Queensland. Survived by his wife, two sons and two daughters, Tunn died of asthma in the Repatriation Hospital, Greenslopes, Brisbane, on 12 October 1955 and was buried in Toowong cemetery.

C. E. W. Bean, *The A.I.F. in France*, 1918 (Syd, 1937); N. K. Harvey, *From Anzac to the Hindenburg Line* (Brisb, 1941); C. M. Wrench, *Campaigning with the fighting 9th* (Brisb, 1985); *London Gazette*, 15 Oct 1918; *Reveille* (Syd), 1 Jan 1939; information from and family papers held by Mr V. P. Tunn, Scarborough, Brisb.   BETTY CROUCHLEY

TUNNECLIFFE, THOMAS (1869-1948), bootmaker, trade unionist and politician, was born on 13 July 1869 at Coghills Creek, Victoria, son of John Tunnecliffe, a bootmaker from England, and his Irish wife Sarah, née Thompson. Thomas's early years were unsettled by the death of siblings and by an interrupted state school education due to his family successively shifting to Newlyn, Dean, Clunes, Newbridge and Ballarat.

Following in his father's trade, Tunnecliffe moved in 1886 to North Melbourne where he opened a bootmaker's shop which also became a centre for earnest discussion of contemporary social issues. Active in the Victorian Operative Bootmakers' Union, of which he was to become president and treasurer, he became involved in the radical political sects which flourished during the 1890s. He was president of the Knights of Labor; a delegate to the International Socialist Congress at Sydney in 1888; a member of the Victorian Socialists' League, the Australian Natives' Association and the Land Nationalisation Society; an original member of the *Tocsin* and other co-operatives; and treasurer and co-founder—with Frank Anstey [q.v.7]—of the Victorian Labour Federation in 1898. He was later president of the Trades Hall Council and the Eight Hours' Committee.

An earnest believer in self-improvement, Tunnecliffe took first prize for deductive logic at the Working Men's College in 1892. Throughout his career he maintained a steady literary output, mostly on political subjects: among his better-known pamphlets were *The problem of poverty* (1904) and *Successful socialism* (1906). At various stages he contributed to *Tocsin* and its successor *Labor Call*, to *Ross's* [q.v.11 R. S. Ross] *Monthly* and *Stead's Review* which he edited in 1925-27.

He entered parliament in 1903, winning the Legislative Assembly seat of West Melbourne for the Labor Party at a by-election, but the seat was abolished; despite vigorous campaigns for Melbourne in 1904 (and the Senate in 1906), he did not return to State parliament until 1907 when he won the provincial seat of Eaglehawk. In the meantime he supported Tom Mann's [q.v.10] Victorian Socialist Party. On 12 February 1908 at West Melbourne Tunnecliffe married with Presbyterian forms Florence Bertha Bishop (d. 1911), a music teacher.

During his thirteen years as member for Eaglehawk he won respect as a well-read and forceful debater whose unusually rapid delivery was spiced with benign but pointed wit. He served on the public accounts committee in 1912-21 and was a member of the 1909 royal commission which investigated Sir Thomas Bent's [q.v.3] dubious land dealings. With the decline in Eaglehawk's mining population, Tunnecliffe's electoral support diminished and he was defeated by (Sir) Albert Dunstan [q.v.8] in 1920. *Punch* saw Tunnecliffe as round faced and fresh complexioned, only his greying moustache suggesting his 50 years.

Returning to Melbourne, Tunnecliffe served as secretary of the Public Service Association in 1920-24. In August 1921 he re-entered the Legislative Assembly as the member for Collingwood, at the centre of John Wren's [q.v.] patronage network. In 1924 he was appointed chief secretary in the short-lived Prendergast [q.v.11] government. Two years later the State Labor caucus elected him deputy leader and, when the first Hogan [q.v.9] ministry took office in May 1927, he became minister for railways and electrical undertakings. The high point in his career coincided with the most difficult years of the Depression. In the second Hogan ministry (1929-32) he was again appointed chief secretary, which put the old socialist in the uncomfortable position of having to defend the police against allegations of brutality at unemployment demonstrations. As acting premier in early 1932, he presided over a minority government under pressure from its Country Party colleagues to implement the Premiers' Plan in the face of opposition from his party machine. When he refused, the government was defeated and lost the subsequent election in a landslide victory to the United Australia Party-Country Party coalition.

With the defection of Hogan, Tunnecliffe was elected leader of the Opposition, a position he held until 1935 when Labor moved to the cross-benches. In 1937-40 he was Speaker. In 1940 a royal commission investigated allegations that he had accepted bribes from monopoly interests to prevent the passage of the Milk Board Act of 1939. Owing to the 'evasive and unsatisfactory' key witness, Commissioner C. Gavan Duffy [q.v.8] made no charges. Tunnecliffe served as a backbench 'elder statesman' until ill health

obliged him to resign in August 1947. He died at his Clifton Hill home on 2 February 1948 and was given a state funeral at Fawkner crematorium. Warmly remembered as one of Victorian Labor's pioneers, he was survived by his second wife Bertha Louise, née Gross, to whom he had been married by Rev. Charles Strong [q.v.6] at Armadale on 31 July 1913, and by their son and daughter.

LA Vic, *One hundred years of responsible government in Victoria, 1856-1956* (Melb, 1957); L. T. Louis, *Trade unions and the Depression* (Canb, 1968); V. Burgmann, *'In our time'* (Syd, 1985); *PD* (Vic), 27 Apr 1948, p 669; *Stead's Review*, 1 May 1926; *Tocsin*, 29 Mar 1906; *Punch* (Melb), 9 Dec 1920; *Labor Call*, 28 Aug 1924, 6 Feb 1948; *Age*, 3 Feb 1948; Tunnecliffe papers *and* S. Merrifield collection (LaTL).　　　　　　　PETER LOVE

TURLEY, JOSEPH HENRY LEWIS (1859-1929), politician, was born on 24 April 1859 at Burton St Michael, Gloucester, England, son of Charles Turley, master shoemaker, and his wife Agnes, née Oliver. Educated at Brixham, Devonshire, Harry went to sea as a youth. After arriving in Brisbane in 1879, he became a wharf labourer and union activist. On 15 May 1886 in Brisbane he married Mary Smith with Presbyterian forms.

Secretary and later president of the Wharf Labourer's Union, Turley was a member of an intercolonial defence committee organized by W. G. Spence [q.v.6] that took over the conduct of the 1890 maritime strike. During the 1891 shearers' strike Turley was a union delegate to negotiating conferences in Sydney. In May 1893 he won the Queensland Legislative Assembly seat of Brisbane South for Labor. Next year he assisted E. H. Lane [q.v.9] to reform the Socialist League in Brisbane. In September he was one of the Labor parliamentarians who were sensationally suspended during the acrimonious debate on the peace preservation ('coercion') bill which was designed to counter the pastoral workers' strike.

Turley lost Brisbane South in March 1899. Recognized as one of Labor's 'strongest and most hard-headed men', he regained the seat at a by-election in July and served as home secretary from 1 to 7 December in the short-lived Dawson [q.v.8] Labor ministry. Defeated for Carnarvon in March 1902, and unsuccessful in contesting Maryborough later that year, he 'got out his old dungarees, searched out his dog-hook, and marched stolidly down to the wharves to look for work'. Committed to 'the abolition of coloured aliens', he had unsuccessfully contested the Federal seat of Oxley in 1901, but was returned to the Federal parliament as a senator in 1903.

President of the Senate in 1910-13, he caused a minor but symbolic furore in 1910 when he rejected the accoutrements of his office for ordinary dress in what was seen as 'a disdainful gesture against the trappings and traditions of the Old World'. Turley was a humble man who had once fought and chastised his supporters for trying to carry him in triumph after an election victory. His inner strength was mirrored in his physique: 'massy shoulders, bossed with muscle', a great neck, powerful hands and a 'strong, heavily jawed face, with still, quiet, steady eyes'. A Congregationalist, a Freemason and a man of few words, he confined himself in debate mainly to industrial affairs of which he had personal knowledge.

Turley remained with the Labor Party through the 1916 split over conscription, a stand that cost him his Senate seat in 1917. He failed to regain it in 1919 and 1925. In 1919 he had been appointed shipping master in the Queensland Harbours and Rivers department; when the post was abolished in 1921 he became a storeman in the Commonwealth Mercantile Marine office. He died suddenly in a Brisbane street on 5 June 1929 and was buried in South Brisbane cemetery. His wife, a son and three daughters survived him.

E. H. Lane, *Dawn to dusk* (Brisb, 1939); D. J. Murphy et al (eds), *Prelude to power* (Brisb, 1970); *Punch* (Melb), 4 Aug 1910; *Daily Standard* (Brisb), 6 June 1929; *Worker* (Brisb), 15 Jan 1910, 12 June 1929.   BRIAN F. STEVENSON

TURNBULL, ARCHIBALD (1843-1901), Christian Socialist clergyman, was born on 16 February 1843 in Sydney, son of Henry Turnbull, shoemaker, and his wife Mary, née Drummond. Repelled by convict transportation, Henry moved his family in 1849 to Collingwood, Melbourne, where he was later a councillor (1860-64, 1866-69) of the East Collingwood Borough. On leaving school, Archibald worked in his father's shop which had become a meeting-place for radicals and protectionists. On 13 October 1862 he married with Presbyterian forms his cousin Harriet Turnbull in Sydney; for the next decade they moved frequently between there and Melbourne.

In 1866 Turnbull abandoned the bootmaking trade to become a city missioner in Melbourne and to prepare for the Anglican ministry. He was made deacon at Blackwood, Victoria, in 1877. Next January Harriet, a mother of five, eloped with a local bank clerk who was a member of the church council.

Turnbull was granted a divorce in September 1878; on 17 June 1879 at Christ Church, Geelong, he married with Anglican rites an 18-year-old governess, Ada Louisa Taylor.

After four years as deacon in rural Victorian parishes, Turnbull left the Church to join the United Evangelists ministering in the slums of Melbourne. In 1884 he moved to Adelaide where he worked with the Salvation Army until, after quarrelling with its leaders, he formed the Christian Crusaders. Returning to the Anglican Church in 1886, he served as curate at Balmain, Sydney, and at Cobargo in the Goulburn diocese where he was ordained priest in 1889.

Next year Turnbull became assistant curate at New Town, Hobart. Provoked by his militant Christian Socialism, Bishop Montgomery [q.v.10] removed him in 1892 to Perth in northern Tasmania. Turnbull returned to New Town in 1893 and, with permission but without financial support, established a Church of England People's Mission. His shortened Anglican service with its political sermon and light musical items proved popular.

Concerned at the plight of Hobart's unemployed, in 1894 Turnbull led a forceful employment campaign, establishing a labour bureau and lobbying politicians. On 29 June he was escorted by 750 of the unemployed to the House of Assembly where they petitioned, without success, that he be allowed to speak of their grievances. With the help of the Trades and Labor Council, Turnbull formed a Labor and Liberal Political League through which, as president, he pursued his political objectives: freer education, better housing, prohibition of 'sweating', adult suffrage, adequate payment of members and reform or abolition of the Upper House. He criticized Bishop Montgomery who in May 1895 withdrew his licence as an Anglican priest. Turnbull's church became known as 'Our Father's Church'.

Moving in 1896 with his family to Carlton, Melbourne, he founded a Labour Church in Bourke Street. The church developed close links with the Victorian Socialists' League and co-operated with it in May Day activities. In July 1898 Ada founded the Women's Social and Political Crusade, an organization of labour women which became a focus for feminist opposition to the suffrage provisions of the 1898 Federal bill. Predeceased on 19 June 1899 by his wife whom he had described as his 'indispensable' colleague and 'greatest chum', Turnbull died of septicaemia on 10 March 1901 following a long illness and was buried in Melbourne general cemetery after a service performed by Rev. Charles Strong [q.v.6]. Four daughters and a son of his first marriage, and the daughter and son of his second, survived him.

B. Barrett, *The inner suburbs* (Melb, 1971); V. Burgmann, *'In our time'* (Syd, 1985); *PTHRA*, 12, no 2, Nov 1964; *Observer* (Adel), 8 Mar 1884; *Mercury*, 23, 24, 31 May, 5 June, 12, 14 July 1894, 27 Apr, 31 May 1895; *Tocsin*, 26 Jan, 9 Mar 1897, 26 May, 9 June, 7, 28 July 1898, 21 Mar 1901; *Age*, 11, 13 Mar 1901; F. Kelly, The 'Woman Question' in Melbourne 1880-1914 (Ph.D. thesis, Monash Univ, 1982); Merrifield collection (LaTL); Divorce procs, Turnbull v. Turnbull and Horne, VPRS 283, 1878/370, box 33 (PRO Vic).   DIANE LANGMORE

TURNBULL, ERNEST (1892-1974), film exhibitor and distributor, was born on 7 February 1892 at Port Melbourne, son of David Walter Turnbull, furniture-dealer, and his wife Mary Ann, née McGrath, both Melbourne born. He attended the local state school.

In World War I Turnbull served with the 5th Battalion, Australian Imperial Force, from 1914. After his return in 1917, he worked for the Department of Repatriation. Actively involved in the newly formed Returned Sailors' and Soldiers' Imperial League of Australia, he was Victorian president (1921-24, 1926-28) during a period in which numerous district branches were established, pensions were secured for veterans, Anzac Day was declared a holiday in Victoria and the soldier-settlement scheme was stabilized. While acting as federal president of the league, Turnbull largely negotiated acceptance of the principle of giving preference in employment to returned servicemen. In 1929 he represented Australia at the British Empire Service League Convention in London where he spoke at the Albert Hall before 70 000 returned servicemen. He later became a patron and life member (1937) of the R.S. & S.I.L.A. and showed a continuing interest in the work of Legacy.

In 1930 Turnbull was one of the founders of the Australian Citizens' League, formed to raise money for the Conversion Loan. Its object achieved, the group re-formed as the Victorian branch of the All for Australia League under Turnbull's presidency. Once J. A. Lyons's [q.v.10] United Australia Party government was secured, the league disbanded. Turnbull resisted repeated invitations to enter politics.

His career in the film industry had begun in 1923 with his appointment as assistant publicity officer to the government's cinema and photographic branch where he was responsible for the *Know your own country* series. On 26 November 1925 at Christ Church, South Yarra, he married with Anglican rites Joyce Illma, daughter of Charles Herschell, a leading film producer in Melbourne who specialized in documentaries. As managing director from 1928 of British Dominion Film Ltd,

Turnbull established Australian distribution outlets for British films and in 1932 introduced an 'all-British' policy at selected cinemas throughout Australasia, commencing with the Athenaeum Theatre, Melbourne. By this time British films had captured 25 per cent of a market where, four years previously, they had barely a toe-hold. In the late 1930s the company was named Gaumont British Dominions Film Distributors Pty Ltd. It supplied British films to the Hoyts circuit through Fox Film Corporation (A'sia) Pty Ltd, of which Turnbull was appointed general manager in 1936.

With his wife, Turnbull was involved in many charities. During World War II he initiated the collection at Hoyts cinemas of contributions to the 'Bundles for Britain' campaign, and was president of the Merchant Navy Club committee. Throughout the war Fox Movietone News (together with its only major competitor, Australasian News) contributed to the dissemination of information about the conflict and to the building of morale on the home front. When the Federal government set up a National Films Council (1940) to co-ordinate film activities for the war effort, Turnbull was appointed to the committee.

In December 1941 he succeeded C. E. Munro as managing director of Hoyts Theatres Ltd in which the Fox Film Corporation (A'sia) Pty Ltd held a controlling interest; Turnbull was also chairman (1953-63) of Fox. A period of expansion saw the introduction of wide-screen processes, such as Cinemascope and Cinerama, in which he took a personal interest, and the opening in 1954 of Australia's first drive-in theatre at Burwood, Melbourne; the period of decline began with the challenge of television. After a brief retirement, Turnbull returned in 1966 as chairman of Hoyts Theatres Ltd and Twentieth Century Fox Film Corporation (Aust) Ltd.

A chevalier of the Légion d'honneur for his fund-raising efforts for French widows and orphans of Indo-China (Vietnam), Turnbull was appointed C.B.E. in 1960. He died on 24 July 1974 at Rose Bay, Sydney, and was cremated. His wife, son and daughter survived him.

Everyone's, 7 Sept 1932; *Showman*, 15, no 1, 15 May 1963; *A'sian Exhibitor*, 1 Aug 1963; *Table Talk*, 9 Apr 1931; Turnbull papers (NL); family papers held by and information from Mrs J. Turnbull, Hawthorn, Melb.   INA BERTRAND

TURNBULL, GILBERT MUNRO (1890-1938), writer, architect and civil servant, was born on 11 September 1890 at Llandudno, Carnarvonshire, Wales, son of James Turnbull, hotelkeeper, and his wife Elizabeth, née

Munro. Educated privately at Fleetwood, Lancashire, England, Gilbert worked briefly for the *Fleetwood Chronicle* and qualified as an architect before adventuring professionally to the United States of America, Canada, Mexico, Tahiti and, in 1913, Papua.

After trading copra and planting coconuts, in February 1915 he took employment at Samarai as a clerk in the treasury and postal department. Promoted draughtsman with the department of public works in Port Moresby in December 1916, he frequently acted as superintendent; from about 1920 to 1934 he was government architect with the right of private practice. In a financially depressed capital built almost entirely of wood and galvanized iron, Turnbull used the new technology of reinforced concrete for spartan, functional buildings such as the European hospital, the treasury and post office; he also designed the Samarai war memorial hall and plantation compounds. Intrepid, lively in conversation, gregarious, but sharp with fools, Turnbull accompanied villagers on fishing expeditions. He travelled to remote areas, observing how Australians seldom extended mateship to Papuans and how fragile so-called civilization was 'at the jungle's edge'. His 1936 obituary of the bombastic *kiap*, C. A. W. Monckton [q.v.10], ironically defined 'pacification' as making Papua 'safe for company promoters'.

Frequently using the pseudonym 'Tauwarra' (Motu for 'fighting-man'), Turnbull published in Australian journals over 150 anecdotal paragraphs, numerous articles and at least 90 short stories. Three of his novels were serialized: *Disenchantment* (1932), *Paradise plumes* (1934) and *Mountains of the moon* (1935). A fourth novel, *Portrait of a savage* (Sydney, 1943), created arguably 'the most complex character in colonial fiction before World War II'. Rejected by eight English and three Australian publishers as 'unclean', *Portrait* was probably too topically related to the notorious case of an alleged child molester, Sergeant Stephen Gorumbaru, who had been executed in 1934 under Sir Hubert Murray's [q.v.10] White Woman's Protection Ordinance. Though Turnbull had defended the Americans' use of lynch law in 1922, the novel compassionately depicted a mission-reared Papuan, caught in the conflict of imported and tribal values, who is hanged after being falsely accused of rape by a White 'seductress'. Despite Beatrice Grimshaw's [q.v.9] stylistic advice, *Portrait* was richly textured with passages of Gothic horror. It was reviewed as 'new literature' about 'New Guinea's unequal race relations', a perception possibly influenced by wartime appreciation of the 'fuzzy wuzzy angels'.

Turnbull retired to Urunga, New South Wales, in 1934. He died at Bellingen of respiratory disease on 7 September 1938 and was buried in the Anglican section of the local cemetery. His wife—Jean Doris, née Winn, whom he had married on 31 August 1921 in the Presbyterian manse at Armidale, New South Wales—and daughter survived him. His unfinished novel 'Maraguna' was completed by his biographer, Lewis Lett, but never published.

A. Inglis, *Not a white woman safe* (Canb, 1974); N. Krauth (ed), *New Guinea images in Australian literature* (Brisb, 1982); Territory of Papua, *Annual Report*, 1914-1934; *J of Cwlth Literature*, 17, no 1, 1982, p 51; information from Mrs J. Turnbull, Ebor, NSW, Mrs B. Dowling, Glen Fernaigh, via Dorrigo, NSW, Mr I. and Mrs E. Champion, Weston Creek, Canb.   HELGA M. GRIFFIN

TURNER, ALFRED JEFFERIS (1861-1947), paediatrician and entomologist, was born on 3 October 1861 in Canton, China, eldest of six children of Frederick Storrs Turner, missionary, and his wife Sophia Mary, née Harmer. Educated in England at Amersham Hall and the City of London School, in 1878 he began medical studies at University College, London, graduating with first-class honours (M.B., M.R.C.S., 1884; M.D., 1886).

He arrived in Australia in 1888. Next year Turner became first resident surgeon at the Hospital for Sick Children, Brisbane, and continued as its honorary visiting physician after he entered private practice in 1893. He qualified for the Cambridge Diploma in Public Health in 1901 and from 1904 was visiting medical officer to the Diamantina Hospital for Chronic Diseases.

Despite his natural reserve, Turner was active in the Medical Society of Queensland and in 1904 was president of its successor, the State branch of the British Medical Association. His clinical research and influence helped to reduce the number of children's deaths in Queensland: he introduced the diphtheria anti-toxin (1895) and, with J. L. Gibson [q.v.8], diagnosed hookworm-induced anaemia (1892) and lead poisoning (1897). Moreover, he advocated breast-feeding of infants, health education for expectant and nursing mothers, and the establishment of antenatal clinics. He played a pivotal role in combating the bubonic plague epidemic of 1900 and in making the notification of tuberculosis compulsory in 1904. Following his participation in the campaign for the Infant Life Protection Act (1905), Turner established the first infant welfare clinic in Queensland in 1909. Two years later he took a leading place in pressing for the repeal of the 1868 Act for the Prevention of Contagious

Diseases which he thought discriminated against women.

Considering himself obliged to assist the war effort, Turner went to England in 1916 and joined the Royal Army Medical Corps. He returned to Brisbane after the Armistice and became director of the Central Tuberculosis Clinic in 1927 and first (part-time) director of infant welfare from 1926 until he retired from clinical practice in 1937. Under his directorship the service expanded from 14 to 104 infant welfare clinics, while infant mortality in Queensland dropped from 50.7 to 35.6 per thousand births registered, the second lowest rate of all the Australian States.

In his spare time Turner was a keen amateur entomologist who specialized in Lepidoptera and named 450 new genera and four new families. President of the Entomological Society of Queensland (1930) and a member of other learned societies, he bequeathed his collection of over 50 000 moths to the Council for Scientific and Industrial Research, Canberra. He published 240 articles in entomological and medical journals.

Because of his mild manner and love of children, Turner acquired the sobriquet 'Gentle Annie'. An obituarist noted his effacing qualities, his 'slight, almost translucent figure, quiet, small voice', and inability to sound his Rs; yet, through the quaintness, he showed a subtle humour and 'some unusual quality of strength'. Turner died in Brisbane without issue on 29 December 1947 and was cremated. He was survived by his wife, Hilda Constance, née Roehricht, whom he had married on 2 February 1898 in St Nicholas's Anglican Church, Sandgate, Brisbane.

A. Musgrave, *Bibliography of Australian entomology, 1775-1930* (Syd, 1932); M. J. Thearle, 'Dr Alfred Jefferis Turner—a man before his time', in H. Attwood and R. W. Home (eds), *Patients, practitioners, techniques* (Melb, 1985); R. Patrick, *A history of health and medicine in Queensland, 1824-1960* (Brisb, 1987); Annual report of the acting director of infant welfare to 30 June 1938, *PP*(Qld), 1938, 2, p 105; *MJA*, 17 Apr 1948, p 517; Roy Soc Qld, *Procs*, 60 (1949), p 69, and for Turner's publications; *Courier Mail*, 30 Dec 1927; M. J. Thearle, Dr Alfred Jefferis Turner, 1861-1947. His contribution to medicine in Queensland (M.D. thesis, Univ Qld, 1988).   JOHN THEARLE

TURNER, DORA JEANNETTE (1888-1953), educationist, was born on 8 January 1888 at Portland, Tasmania, daughter of George Arthur Turner, bank clerk, and his wife Mary Louisa, née Ikin. She was educated at Devonport Primary and Launceston High schools. Beginning her professional career in 1906 as an assisted teacher at Westwood, Chudleigh and Beaconsfield, she completed a one-year certificated course in 1909 at the Hobart Teachers' Training College and taught in four primary schools. In 1924, as first teacher-in-charge, she opened the Girls' Welfare School at Newtown. Consisting of one classroom and a kitchen, it had an enrolment of eight pupils aged between 12 and 14. Its establishment marked the Tasmanian Department of Education's recognition of the need for a 'special' education for some children.

Her first priority was to create an environment in which her students would gain confidence in their abilities and advance in self-esteem. The curriculum aimed at personal development. Emphasis was placed on skills for independent living, with a minimum of academic work to support the practical curriculum. Her approach succeeded. Dora was a born teacher whose discipline was never apparent. Although she had no specific training in educating children with intellectual disabilities, she combined an innate understanding of their needs with her solicitude and dedication to ensure that her pupils enjoyed their years at school and gained the means to enable them to become self-respecting citizens.

The school moved in 1930 to Mather House, a two-storey building in Murray Street, Hobart. The schoolrooms were on the ground floor, with living quarters for Dora and her sister Mary, also a teacher, on the upper. These premises proved more suitable because they were larger, nearer the city, and adjacent to the Elizabeth Street Practising School with which there was limited interaction. An additional twenty-two girls were soon enrolled.

A serious, somewhat austere woman, upright and well groomed, Dora worked untiringly for the underprivileged. She was highly respected and belonged to the New Town Methodist Church. Her hobbies included embroidery, cake decorating, gardening, sketching and bridge. Throughout her twenty-seven years as principal Miss Turner made self-reliance the watchword of her school. Firm yet kind, she encouraged students to take pride in their appearance and fostered positive attitudes toward learning. She managed the school with efficiency and economy. Her programmes were clearly enunciated, her expectations high but realistic. After resigning on 1 May 1951, she worked as a relief teacher until she suffered a stroke and died in Calvary Hospital, Hobart, on 12 October 1953. She was cremated at Cornelian Bay. In 1955 the Tasmanian Department of Education honoured her by changing the name of the Girls' Welfare School to the Dora Turner School.

Mercury, 15 Oct 1953; P. E. M. Griffiths, A history of Dora Turner School, formerly Girls'

Welfare School 1924-1974 (M.Special Ed, Univ Tas, 1981); Education Dept (Tas), records.

GLEEWYN SPROD

TURNER, ETHEL MARY (1870-1958), author, was born on 24 January 1870 at Balby, Yorkshire, England, second child of Bennett George Burwell, commercial traveller, and his wife Sarah Jane, née Shaw (d. 1923). Burwell died in Paris in Ethel's infancy; on 21 August 1872 in the register office, Yarmouth, Sarah Jane Shaw married Henry Turner, a widower with six sons; they were to have a daughter Jeannie Rose (b. 1873). Ethel and her elder sister LILIAN WATTNALL BURWELL (1867-1956) took their stepfather's name and were known by it throughout their professional careers. Turner, a factory manager, fell into financial difficulties and left only £200 when he died at Coventry in August 1878.

Next year Mrs Turner migrated with her daughters to Sydney. On 31 December 1880 she married Charles Cope, a clerk in the Department of Lands and brother of William Cope [q.v.8]; their son Charles Rex completed the three-level family. Ethel Turner's autobiographical novel, *Three little maids* (1900), describes her mother's struggle to maintain her family in genteel poverty and presents the third marriage as a means of rescue.

Ethel and Lilian were educated at Sydney Girls' High School where they ran their own magazine, the *Iris*, in opposition to the *Gazette*, edited by Louise Mack [q.v.10]. In January 1889, after Ethel left school, the sisters founded and co-edited a sixpenny monthly, the *Parthenon*, which lasted for three years until its printers, Gordon & Gotch, were sued for libel; the magazine sold about 1500 copies a month and made about £50 annually for its editors. Ethel contributed the 'Children's Page' and serial romances for adults: both she and Lilian planned to become novelists. In 1893 Ethel published a story in the *Bulletin* and was earning £100 a year as editor of the 'Children's Page' of the *Illustrated Sydney News*. The paper folded next year, but as 'Dame Durden' she edited the 'Children's Page' in the *Australian Town and Country Journal* until it ceased publication in 1919.

For diversion from a more ambitious work, she wrote her first children's book, *Seven little Australians*. On the recommendation of William Steele, Melbourne representative of the English firm of Ward, Lock & Bowden, it was published in London in 1894. The first edition sold out in weeks and 'Ethel Sibyl Turner' (as she styled herself) was launched as a children's writer.

The Sydney suburban setting, the quiet comedy, the refusal to idealize family life and the insistence on the distinctive nature of Australian childhood experience set *Seven little Australians* apart from its contemporaries. Although the novel shows the influence of Charlotte Yonge's *The daisy chain* (1856) and Louisa May Alcott's *Little women* (1868), it reverses the literary conventions of these works. When its heroine, the rebellious Judy Woolcot, dies after a ring-barked tree falls on her, there is none of the customary religious consolation for a young life cut short. The irascible Captain Woolcot (a version of Turner's stepfather Charles Cope) never becomes a model father; the other Woolcots remain imperfect; and, while the family fortunes vary, they do not essentially change. The domestic realism is sustained in the second Woolcot novel, *The family at Misrule* (1895).

Deploring the 'free and easy, somewhat rowdy associations due to [the Australian] atmosphere, climate, environment and the influence of The Bulletin', in 1895 Steele urged Ethel Turner to consolidate her reputation by spending some time in English literary circles. She refused to leave Sydney and delay her wedding to the young barrister HERBERT RAINE CURLEWIS (1869-1942), to whom she had been unofficially engaged for four years. They were married at St John's Anglican Church, Gordon, on 22 April 1896.

Herbert was born on 22 August 1869 at Bondi, eldest son of native-born parents Frederick Charles Curlewis, brickmaster, and his wife Georgina Sophia, née O'Brien. Educated at Newington College and the University of Sydney (B.A., 1890; LL.B., 1892), he was admitted to the Bar on 17 March 1893; practising mainly in common law, after an early struggle he prospered. Curlewis had some literary talent and, as a student, wrote Latin and Greek verses and some love poems dedicated to Ethel Turner. In *The mirror of justice* (1906), a layman's introduction to legal process, he emphasized the human interest of the courtroom as well as the intricacies of the law. He edited the *Australasian annual digest* of leading decisions in 1905-15 and lectured on the law of procedure, evidence and pleading at the university in 1911-17. Fluent in Italian and a member of the (Royal) Australian Historical Society, he was also attracted by anything mechanical. Appointed a judge of the Industrial Arbitration Court in 1917, he became District Court judge on 1 July 1928. He earned a reputation for severity, especially for his insistence that correct English should be spoken in the cases over which he presided. Curlewis retired in 1939.

The marriage was happy: each fostered the other's career. They rented a cottage at Mosman until their own house, Avenel, overlooking Middle Harbour, was completed in 1903. Their daughter was born in 1898 and their son in 1901. Ethel was prominent in Sydney's literary and social life, and enjoyed skating, tennis, golf and surfing. In 1910-11 the family travelled abroad. On their return, Ethel published *Ports and happy havens* (1911). Creating a garden absorbed a good deal of her time and her love of growing things is evident in her novel, *The ungardeners* (1925).

Her writing showed a continuing tension between her enjoyment of popular and commercial success and her wish to break free from the restrictions of juvenile fiction. Ethel's publishers always insisted that her work should remain within the range of the sheltered young reader. Her use of Australian slang in *The little larrikin* (1896) brought a rebuke from Steele. When she published with Hodder & Stoughton in 1913, she found similar prohibitions.

During World War I Ethel Turner organized ambulance and first aid courses, campaigned for conscription and worked for patriotic causes. With Bertram Stevens [q.v.], she edited *The Australian soldiers' gift book* (1917). She also embarked on a temperance crusade in *St. Tom and the dragon* (1918). A wartime trilogy—*The cub* (1915), *Captain Cub* (1917) and *Brigid and the cub* (1919)—is notable for its freedom from anti-German hysteria and for its sympathetic portrayal of a reluctant Anzac; the ideal of loyalty to Empire is combined with a strong sense of Australian nationalism.

A recurring theme in the Turner novels is that of the conflicting demands of the creative and the domestic life. Whatever restrictions Ethel may have felt as author, wife and mother, they did not diminish her productivity. Thirty-four volumes of fiction, three of verse, a travel book, plays, some miscellaneous verse and prose testify to her talent, and her discipline. Before World War I she had planned to start a children's newspaper; in 1920 she suggested the idea to the editor of the *Sydney Sun*; when it fell through, she edited (1921-31) 'Sunbeams', the children's page in the *Sunday Sun*. A member of the Sydney P.E.N. Club, in 1936 she joined C. H. Bertie, (Sir) Walter Murdoch, G. V. Portus [qq.v.7,10,11] and a dozen others who each contributed a chapter to *Murder pie*. Ethel was an excellent manager of her financial and literary affairs; she gave time and money to various charities, and was a generous friend to less affluent writers, among them Henry Lawson [q.v.10] with whom she shared the affliction of deafness.

Her daughter ETHEL JEAN SOPHIA (1898-1930) was born on 7 February 1898 at Mosman and educated at Sydney Church of England Girls' Grammar School. Jean published poems and stories as well as four novels: *The ship that never set sail* (1921), *Drowning maze* (1922), *Beach beyond* (1923)

and *The dawn man* (1924). These appeared under the Ward Lock imprint, in identical format to the novels of Ethel and Lilian Turner. Her talent, however, was quite unlike that of her mother and aunt. Instead of domestic comedy and stories of love and marriage, Jean Curlewis wrote adventure stories with a strong sense of place. Yet, while they evoke the Sydney of sun and surf beaches, they are essentially novels of ideas. She was not at ease with the happy ending of most children's fiction: her characters accept compromise or defeat as the price of adulthood. When she married Percie Leonard Charlton, medical practitioner, on 23 October 1923 at St Luke's Anglican Church, Mosman, her health was already causing concern. After two years in Europe where Charlton did postgraduate work, she returned to Sydney looking 'fragile and sad'. Soon afterwards she was found to have tuberculosis. She died in Sydney on 28 March 1930, her promise as poet and novelist unfulfilled.

Her mother's last novel, *Judy and Punch*, was published in 1928. Although this book was prompted by Ward Lock's belief that another Woolcot novel was the best way to challenge the pre-eminence of Mary Grant Bruce's [q.v.7] Billabong books, there may have been personal significance in the re-emergence of Judy at a time when Ethel faced her own daughter's death.

Survived by their son Adrian, Curlewis died at Avenel on 11 October 1942 and Ethel Turner died at Mosman on 8 April 1958; she was buried in the Anglican section of Northern Suburbs cemetery. Extracts from her diaries, kept since she had left school, were published in 1979 and 1982. Her portrait by Jerrold Nathan is held by the family.

Her elder sister Lilian was born on 21 August 1867 at Lincoln, England. Her childhood, like that of Ethel, was disrupted by the deaths of her father and first stepfather, by financial insecurity, migration to Australia and by her mother's remarriage. Charles Cope, who was possessive—even obsessive —but generally indulgent towards Ethel, was strict and disagreeable with Lilian. Ethel, fairhaired and blue-eyed, was the prettier of the sisters, the more talented and, in spite of her fragile appearance, the more vital. Lilian's career, too, was eclipsed by her sister's early success. Though Lilian's first novel, *The lights of Sydney* (1896), won first prize in an open competition organized by the London publisher Cassell & Co., it led nowhere. Accepting what she saw as a lesser aim, she turned to the 'flapper' novel: stories of love and ambition written for schoolgirls and young women. In a format identical to that of her sister's work ('as alike as tins of jam', Ethel remarked), Lilian Turner published twenty novels with Ward, Lock & Co.

between 1902 and 1931. Most were competent, none was outstanding. *Betty the scribe* (1906) deals with the clash between literary ambition and domestic responsibility; *Paradise and the Perrys* (1908) and *Three new chum girls* (1910) express her mildly feminist impulses, but suggest no future for the independent woman. While family life is shown to be drudgery, marriage seems the only realistic goal.

Lilian Turner's own life was marked by financial hardship and ill health. At the time of her marriage to Frederick Lindsay Thompson (d. 1924), dentist, on 22 February 1898 at St John's Anglican Church, Gordon, she was over 30, although (as Ethel had also done) she understated her age. Thompson was unemployed for long periods; Lilian had to keep writing to support her family, and had to accept financial help from her sister. Something of the Turner literary ability shone in her son Lindsay who published boys' adventure and school stories. There was a strong bond of loyalty and affection between Ethel and Lilian, but to the best-selling author, the judge's wife, the woman of means, it was inevitable that Lilian should become 'Poor Lil'. When she died on 25 August 1956 at Turramurra, survived by her two sons, all her books were out of print, while her sister's *Seven little Australians* had been translated into many languages, staged and filmed (1939). Its frequent reprintings and an Australian Broadcasting Commission television version in 1973 have confirmed its status as one of Australia's few unquestioned children's classics.

H. T. E. Holt, *A court rises* (Syd, 1976); B. Niall, *Seven little Billabongs* (Melb, 1979); P. Poole (comp), *The diaries of Ethel Turner* (Syd, 1979) and *Of love and war* (Syd, 1982); *Cassell's Mag*, Jan 1909, p 191; *Lone Hand*, 1 Nov 1915, p 355; *People* (Syd), 28 Feb 1951, p 13; *Hist Studies*, no 71, Oct 1978, p 297; *SMH*, 7 June 1916, 20 June 1917, 11 Aug 1928, 12 Oct 1942; Ethel Turner papers (ML *and* NL) *and* diaries (ML); Curlewis family papers (ML).   BRENDA NIALL

TURNER, FRED (1852-1939), horticulturist and botanist, was born on 17 April 1852 at Burton Salmon, near Pontefract, Yorkshire, England, son of Charles Turner, gardener, and his wife Anne, née Terry. Educated privately, then at Thirsk and York, he became interested in applied aspects of botany and horticulture at the royal nurseries at Handsworth, Yorkshire, and Hammersmith, London. He collected plants in Britain, Europe, the Canary Islands and South Africa.

In 1874 he left the Royal Vineyard Nursery, London, to work at the Brisbane Botanic Gardens. Encouraged by the director Walter

Hill, he improved the gardens and was praised in parliament. Turner married Welsh-born Jane Isabella George, daughter of a gardener, at All Saints Church, Brisbane, on 5 September 1877. During extensive botanical excursions on which he spent six weeks with the Aborigines, he collected 'upwards of 10 000 specimens', among them the Fraser Island creeper (*Tecomanthe hillii*) which he boldly declared was 'the rarest Australian plant'. In 1879 he became curator of the Queensland Acclimatisation Society's gardens and plantations at Bowen Park, Brisbane, winning awards for his 'comprehensive and unique collection of plants of commercial importance'.

Joining the grounds staff of the Botanic Gardens, Sydney, at seven shillings a day in April 1880, he worked amicably under the director Charles Moore [q.v.5] in the Garden Palace Grounds. Next year Turner was invited 'to re-design and beautify Hyde Park, Sydney'; he 'removed about 60' Moreton Bay figs 'in one year' and planted groups of the palm, *Phoenix canariensis*, as well as various deciduous and evergreen species.

In May 1890 Turner was appointed economic botanist in the new Department of Agriculture. He received 'over 2000 letters' in 1892 and in 1890-93 contributed some 140 articles to the department's *Agricultural Gazette of New South Wales*. He mainly wrote about crops, weeds and toxic plants, grasses, pasture plants and agricultural procedures. His retrenchment in 1893 was criticized as 'a public calamity'.

Contributing from 1885 to the *Australian Town and Country Journal*, Turner also wrote regularly for the *Sydney Morning Herald* for over twenty years. A member of the Linnean Society of New South Wales from 1891 and a councillor (1897-1912), he had contributed over 100 papers to its *Proceedings* by 1922. In addition, he published a *Census of the grasses of New South Wales* (1890), *Forage plants of Australia* (1891), *Australian grasses* (1895) and *Australian grasses and pasture plants* (1921) which was illustrated by his daughter Mary.

In 1907 Turner completed three manuals for Anderson & Co., seedsmen, the copy for which was declared to be 'the acme of perfection and neatness, characteristic no doubt of the man'. That year he gave evidence before the royal commission on forestry. His work became widely acclaimed. The forthright Yorkshireman attacked J. H. Maiden [q.v.10] and E. Breakwell, implying that both of them had drawn excessively from his own writings and illustrations without due acknowledgement.

Known to F. M. Bailey, W. R. Guilfoyle, Sir Ferdinand von Mueller, William Woolls, William Farrer, J. J. Fletcher and A. H. S. Lucas [qq.v.3,4,5,6,8,10], Turner succeeded

Mueller as consulting botanist to the Western Australian government. Nominated by Mueller as a fellow of the Royal Horticultural Society, London, in 1888, he also became a fellow of the Linnean Society of London in 1892. H. C. L. Anderson [q.v.7] had 'never known' Turner 'to be puzzled' by any of the thousands of plants sent to him, and Bailey named the rosaceous plant from Barron River, *Pygmeum turnerianum*, in his honour (1893).

Turner recorded that he had travelled over 50 000 miles (80 465 km) 'on the Australian continent from Cleveland Bay and Kuranda in Northern Queensland to the vicinity of Perth in Western Australia', collecting material and popularizing indigenous fodder plants. Although awarded 'seven medals and four diplomas', he remained somewhat disillusioned after his retrenchment. His unpublished autobiography, written and presented to the Mitchell [q.v.5] Library when he was 73, virtually omitted all personal details. He was a sturdy, earnest man with closely cropped hair, a trimmed moustache and goatee, who spent his leisure growing such commercial plants as cotton in his garden at Chatswood. Fred Turner died in hospital at Chatswood on 17 October 1939 and was buried in the Anglican section of Northern Suburbs cemetery. Predeceased by his wife and a son, he was survived by two daughters and a son.

Chamber of Manufactures of Aust, Federal Council, *Aust Industry*, 1906; F. Turner, Autobiography (ms, 1925, ML); Turner papers (NL); Roy Botanic Gardens, Syd, Archives.

L. A. GILBERT

TURNER, SIR GEORGE (1851-1916), premier and Commonwealth treasurer, was born on 8 August 1851 in Melbourne, son of English migrants Alfred Turner, cabinet-maker, and his wife Ruth, née Dick. Following education at the National Model School until 14, he entered the solicitor's office of John Edwards, member of the Legislative Assembly. On 10 August 1872, two days after his twenty-first birthday, on 25 shillings a week, Turner married English-born Rosa Morgan at St James's Cathedral, Melbourne. That year he joined the Australian Natives' Association and became treasurer of a city branch. He matriculated in 1874, 'passing well' in English, history and Euclid. Articled in 1875 to Samuel Lyons, an A.N.A. founder, he completed the articled clerks' course at the University of Melbourne, was admitted as an attorney in 1881 and became Lyons's partner in Collins Street. Holding office in several friendly societies, Turner joined the

Freemasons in 1882 (and from 1896 was senior grand warden). He was elected to St Kilda City Council (1885-1900), was mayor in 1887-88, and was said to have been 'never more at home, never more himself, "plain George", than after a council meeting in the mayoral supper room'.

Elected to the Legislative Assembly in March 1889 as a Liberal Protectionist for St Kilda, Turner was one of a dozen new parliamentary members from the A.N.A. Quiet at the start, he had his chance in April 1891 as commissioner for trade and customs in Munro's [q.v.5] ministry. He continued in this portfolio and also became solicitor-general from February 1892 when Shiels [q.v.11] replaced Munro. James Service [q.v.6] soon remarked that he had never known a better minister for customs.

Struggling in the depths of the depression, the Shiels ministry fell on 18 January 1893 and was succeeded by (Sir) James Patterson's [q.v.5] government during the period of the bank crashes and further grave revelations of financial chicanery. Eventually, on 28 August 1894, Turner carried a no confidence motion by four votes. He had just been elected Liberal leader, despite his earnest plea of unsuitability: Sir Graham Berry [q.v.3] was discredited by failure as Shiels's treasurer, Shiels was in bad health and Deakin [q.v.8] stood aloof. Benjamin Hoare [q.v.9] suggested Turner to David Syme [q.v.6] who was persuaded that he was the best of a bad lot; Deakin and (Sir) Isaac Isaacs [q.v.9]—the *Age*'s henchmen—proposed him in caucus, but Turner was widely regarded as a mere stopgap. His policy for the election on 20 September featured direct taxation and company reform. The *Age* was in fine campaigning form; the traditional Liberal forces, public servants and trade unionists rallied; to its surprise, the government was routed by some 65 (including 14 Labor) to 30 seats.

Thus, aged 43, the quiet 'little man in the shabby brown suit and the cheap spectacles' became Victoria's first Australian-born premier. He was also treasurer. The ministry's inner driving-force was three other radical native-born, Isaacs, (Sir) Alexander Peacock [q.v.11] and (Sir) Robert Best [q.v.7], but the rest were comparatively conservative. Coincidentally, radical governments led by (Sir) George Reid [q.v.11] and Charles Kingston [q.v.9] also held office in 1894-99 and achieved much. Inheriting a huge accumulated deficit, very high unemployment and large-scale emigration to Western Australia, Turner necessarily had comparatively modest objectives.

Determined to redeem Victoria's disgrace, he grimly cut costs, slashing public works, education and defence; in 1895-97 public works expenditure was one-sixth that of New

South Wales. Amid conservative frenzy, he immediately carried a graduated income tax (which began at £200), although he dropped other proposals for taxes on 'surplus wealth' and land. Isaacs's comprehensive reform of company law was largely mangled by the Legislative Council, but his insolvency legislation passed almost intact. Following a royal commission, in 1896 local savings banks were amalgamated in the State Savings Bank of Victoria with useful provision for loans to farmers, yet the bank's proposed monopoly of note issue had to be abandoned. In 1896 the Factories Act, with its provision for wages boards, was carried by Peacock; compromises had to be reached with the council, but the strength of the anti-sweating movement backed by the *Age* was such that for once the council was not prepared to provoke a constitutional crisis against a near-unanimous assembly. Although Turner's consensus approach lessened party tension, it also involved avoidance of contentious issues. The government all too often followed the will of the House, referring many matters to royal commissions and boards of inquiry; in 1896 it even treated tariff reform as an open question: some duties were consequently slightly reduced.

In mid-1897, with the other premiers, Turner attended Queen Victoria's diamond jubilee celebrations, was appointed K.C.M.G. and a privy counsellor, and awarded honorary degrees by the universities of Oxford and Cambridge. On his return he spoke at a civic reception, in 'new serio-comic vein', about his honours and the 'duchessing' (he was agreeably surprised by the dukes whom he had assumed would be 'stuck up'), and confessed to having been 'altogether out of my element' at Buckingham Palace. According to Lady Turner, 'All the other Premiers' wives were awfully afraid. But I wasn't. I went up to the Princess of Wales and talked to her . . . These royalties are very glad to be talked to as if they were human beings. She was very nice and said when I left, "Tell the Australian people I like you very much my dear"'.

Turner had returned to an election in October. In his policy speech he promised a period of 'rest and quiet', and won with a barely reduced majority; perhaps unwisely he made no ministerial changes. In 1897-98, and the following financial year, revenue at last exceeded expenditure. Edward Shann [q.v.11] later commented: 'the faithful solicitor cut expenditure to the minimum, refused every suggestion of fresh borrowing abroad, and forced Victoria to reduce her budget to health and order'. In 1898, however, Syme had to demand some renewal of public works. The only major legislation of Turner's second term was Best's revision of land legislation in 1898 and next year, at last, abolition of plural

voting for the assembly. The government complied with party and popular feeling in offering a contingent for the South African War.

When country Liberals and disaffected radicals crossed the floor, Turner was defeated on 30 November 1899 by Allan McLean [q.v.10] who had resigned from the ministry in opposition to the Federation bill. Deakin refused Turner's offer of the Liberal leadership. In November 1900 the Turner Liberals, still supported by Labor, had a sweeping electoral victory; Turner's close ally William Trenwith [q.v.] and John Burton (another Labor man) became ministers. The premier's main achievement before he resigned in February 1901 to enter Federal politics was to legislate on a temporary basis for old-age pensions, but the details were botched.

In January 1895 Turner had attended the premiers' conference which arranged for the Australasian Federal Convention; he and Kingston prepared the draft enabling bill which Victoria passed in March 1896. In March 1897 Turner topped the poll for the Victorian representatives and—such was his popularity—was cheered at many stations on the way to Adelaide for the first session. A determined Federationist, he was anxious about the future of Victorian manufacturers: they had the advantage of early protection, but lacked the huge black coal resources of New South Wales. At a preliminary sitting his suggestion that (Sir) Edmund Barton [q.v.7] be asked to frame resolutions led to Barton's election as convention leader. Next day Turner gave the first formal speech. Eschewing fine sentiments, he clearly stated the issues and his opinions thereon. The delegates appreciated his practical, businesslike approach and freely cheered him. On the constitutional committee Turner opposed a strong Senate and resisted the claims of the less-populated colonies. On the finance committee, however, he had a rebuff which shook his confidence when Reid wrecked his financial plan. Though he was disregarded, Turner drew attention to the words 'absolutely free' in the eventual Section 92: 'We ought to be careful about using words which may have a wider interpretation than was originally intended'.

At the Sydney session Turner won further respect, even from the local press, for his moderation and co-operativeness. Early in 1898 in Melbourne he reached a dignified compromise with Reid over railway rates. At the convention's conclusion Turner and his colleagues had doubts about the draft Constitution, especially over possible effects on Victorian rural producers—and the *Age* was initially hostile. After Deakin and the A.N.A. had converted Syme, Turner announced full government support in April; by May he asserted that rejection of the bill would be a disaster and disgrace. After the failure to gain a sufficient majority vote in New South Wales, Turner chaired the premiers' meeting of January 1899 when Reid's proposed amendments were broadly adopted. Turner's motion for Federal territory within New South Wales was carried, and he may have suggested the minimum distance from Sydney. Later in the year he presided at the final meeting of the Federal Council of Australasia.

He took a leading part in December 1900 in correcting the 'Hopetoun [q.v.9] blunder'. At first he wavered. Some of his colleagues and Syme favoured accepting Sir William Lyne [q.v.10] as prime minister, seeing him as a stauncher Protectionist than Barton. Turner, however, joined (Sir) Frederick Holder [q.v.9] in Sydney; his intimation that they, as well as Barton and Deakin, would not join Lyne settled the matter. Turner may have been in touch with Hopetoun; ten years later Deakin recorded: 'Hopetoun implored T. help him out of hole. Nerve entirely gone—T. told him sit tight'. So, resigning the premiership to Peacock and elected the member for Balaclava, Turner joined Barton's ministry as treasurer, a post for which he had an unrivalled claim.

Turner presented the first four Commonwealth budgets. Governments were committed to no taxation other than customs and excise. Turner aimed to pass to the States more than the constitutionally guaranteed three-quarters of the revenue—and did so every year. His estimates were remarkably accurate and he kept the promise that the cost of Federation would be small. He bore with Kingston the burden of the 1902 tariff legislation. Barton eventually praised Turner's work in cabinet, but considered him to have been a little over-cautious as treasurer.

By 1904 Turner was generally regarded as a non-party man. J. C. Watson [q.v.], forming the first Labor ministry, wanted him to stay on as treasurer. When Watson was defeated in August, Reid offered Turner joint leadership; he refused because of illness, but accepted the treasurership again. He was greatly upset when Deakin did not consult him in 1905 before his 'notice to quit' speech, but there was no lasting breach. Content to retire at the 1906 election, Turner maintained his 'air of bourgeois good humor' in parliament to the last.

Continually plagued by illness, Turner was often exhausted. Early in 1898 and in February-March 1901 he was out of action for several weeks; in June 1904, after two operations, he was unconscious and delirious for several days: it was 'touch and go'.

About 1904 the Turners moved from their St Kilda cottage to Summerlea, a mansion in Riversdale Road, Hawthorn. He resumed his practice in Collins Street with his son George John (who was to die in a railway accident in 1908), but incorporated it with Corr & Corr in 1907. From 1906 Turner was chairman of commissioners of the State Savings Bank of Victoria. He enjoyed bowls and gardening. Survived by his wife and daughter, he died suddenly at his home on 13 August 1916 of heart disease and was buried in St Kilda cemetery with Anglican rites. A bust by Mackennal [q.v.10] is in Parliament House, Canberra, and a portrait by H. F. Allkins is in St Kilda City Hall. Turner's estate was sworn for probate at £3789.

Turner has been grossly underestimated as a politician. He dominated his cabinet, was master of the assembly and highly respected in the House of Representatives. He was a capable speaker, lucid in exposition and able in debate—dull, no doubt, but Victorian voters had had enough of the high-flown oratory of Deakin and Shiels. Turner's capacity for work, mastery of detail, patent integrity, frankness, unpretentiousness and geniality won general trust. He also had a very keen sense of public opinion. (Sir) Frederic Eggleston [q.v.8] described him as a 'super-efficient pedestrian' whose 'all-round skill was astonishing'. According to Deakin, he was the 'ideal bourgeois . . . in dress, manner and habits exactly on the same level as the shopkeepers and prosperous artisans [also] in his uprightness, straightforwardness, domestic happiness and regularity of habits'. Turner took professional advice well. Yet, he was opportunistic, lacked theoretic basis ('had to find his principles as he went') and tackled each question as if a new brief. Deputations on the whole appreciated his informality in receiving them in his shirtsleeves. Mistrusted by the business classes, he was in general sympathetic to the 'have-nots'. He lacked imagination and it cannot be claimed that he had, or tried to implement, any coherent radical programme.

Reid came greatly to admire Turner, as did J. R. Collins [q.v.8] of the Commonwealth Treasury for his 'quick insight', 'searching analysis' and kindness in working relationships. Turner was also popular with the press. Despite his good education, he was extremely narrow, intellectually and culturally; one known exception to the charge that he never read a book was James Bryce's *American Commonwealth* (London, 1888). Turner's basic shyness and diffidence, and his trick of screwing his head to one side, were aspects of an appealing personality which he developed into a persuasive and convincing style.

G. H. Reid, *My reminiscences* (Lond, 1917); B. Hoare, *Looking back gaily* (Melb, 1927); J. B.

Cooper, *The history of St. Kilda* (Melb, 1931); H. L. Hall, *Victoria's part in the Australian Federation movement* (Lond, 1931); E. H. Sugden and F. W. Eggleston, *George Swinburne* (Syd, 1931); *The Cambridge history of the British Empire*, vol 7, pt 1 (Cambridge, 1933); A. Deakin, *The Federal story*, J. A. La Nauze ed (Melb, 1963); C. E. Sayers, *David Syme* (Melb, 1965); R. R. Garran, *Prosper the Commonwealth* (Syd, 1958); J. A. La Nauze, *Alfred Deakin* (Melb, 1965) and *The making of the Australian Constitution* (Melb, 1972); A. W. Martin (ed), *Essays in Australian Federation* (Melb, 1969); J. D. Rickard, *Class and politics* (Canb, 1975) and *H. B. Higgins, the rebel as judge* (Melb, 1984); *PD* (Vic), 1891, p 3103, 1894, p 1384; *Argus*, 14, 19 Aug 1897, 14 Aug 1916; *Punch* (Melb), 16 June 1904; *Bulletin*, 25 Aug 1904; *Age*, 14 Aug 1916; Deakin *and* Turner papers (NL); Crouch memoirs (LaTL).

GEOFFREY SERLE

TURNER, JAMES ALFRED (1850-1908), artist, was born on 11 February 1850 at Bradford, Yorkshire, England, son of John Turner, bank accountant, and his wife Rhoda, née Oddy. He arrived in Victoria some time before 1874, the year of his earliest-known Australian painting, 'View down Collins Street from Spring Street'. In 1884 James Oddie [q.v.5] commissioned him to execute fourteen paintings of bush life which Oddie donated to the newly founded Ballarat Fine Art Gallery. Turner had several Melbourne addresses: at William Street in the 1870s and at least two in Collins Street in the 1880s. In 1888 he bought a twenty-acre (8.09 ha) bushland property with a small dwelling ('The Gables') at Kilsyth, near Croydon, at the foot of the Dandenong Ranges.

That year his paintings 'Saved' and 'Fighting for Home' received 3rd awards of merit in the Melbourne Centennial (International) Exhibition which also included the work of Tom Roberts, John Mather, Girolamo Nerli and Frederick McCubbin [qq.v.11,10]. On 29 October 1890 at St Peter's Church, East Melbourne, Turner married Annie Margaret Williams; they lived at Hawthorn; she died in the following year after the birth of a stillborn child. Turner returned to Kilsyth in 1893 and remained there until 1907. Local rural and bush life supplied subjects for his paintings which *Table Talk* described as being of 'peculiar exactness'. He was recognized in 1894 as 'our best known painter of incident'. On 1 May 1900 he married Mary Ann Thomas (d. 1950), daughter of the founder of Thomastown, at the Government Statist's Office, Melbourne.

A prolific painter, Turner was a master of oil and water-colour. He also worked in gouache. He painted chiefly to please himself, 'without any suspicion of pot boiling', never allowing work to leave his hands until he was thoroughly satisfied. Generally content with 'homely incidents and quiet aspects of nature', he sometimes painted large works such as 'The Homestead Saved' (90 cm by 151 cm) which sold for $82 000 in 1980. Bushfires were a subject he handled well, probably because he had seen them at first hand: the *Argus* asserted in 1908 that 'No man has ever painted the realism of a forest fire and its fighting better'. Turner was an exhibiting member of the Victorian Artists' Society, the Australian Art Association, the Victorian Academy of Arts, the Yarra Sculptors' Society and the Melbourne and New Melbourne art clubs. The first of his paintings to be reproduced on postcards was published in Melbourne about 1904. It proved popular and forty-six of his rural and bush-life works were issued in colour. No other colonial painter's work was published in such volume and Turner postcards are still sought by collectors.

Turner died suddenly of heart disease on 13 April 1908 at Canterbury and was buried with Anglican rites in Box Hill cemetery. He had no children.

Table Talk, 21 Nov 1901; *Argus*, 8 May 1890, 16 Apr 1908; *Aust Financial Review*, 15 Nov 1973.

SHIRLEY C. JONES

TURNER, JOHN WILLIAM (1849-1913), educationist, was born on 14 May 1849 at Parramatta, New South Wales, son of Henry Turner, shoemaker, and his wife Ellen, née Armstrong. He attended St John's School, Camden, before becoming a pupil-teacher at St Peter's School, Cook's River, in 1864. Two years later he was appointed assistant teacher at the metropolitan St Barnabas's School and in 1869 took charge of Mount Tarana Public School. He married Martha Lees with Anglican forms at St Andrew's Cathedral, Sydney, on 28 June 1870; they were to have eight children.

Promoted that year to Wellington where he impressed Frederick Bridges [q.v.3], Turner returned to Sydney as head of a George Street school which was soon resited and renamed Blackfriars Public School. Here his career blossomed. In 1889 he became head of Fort Street Model School and master of method at the Fort Street Training School. His role was extended in 1893 when the two institutions were amalgamated under the one head. He supervised the introduction of secondary education to the school, was commanding officer of the cadet corps and found time to produce an operetta or cantata each year. A strict disciplinarian, he was affectionately known by his pupils as 'The Boss'.

In 1902 Turner and (Sir) George Knibbs [q.v.9] were appointed by the See [q.v.11] government to investigate overseas developments in primary, secondary, technical and other branches of education. Visiting seventeen countries, they published a three-volume report on their return in 1903; of the 231 recommendations it contained, Turner's were the more financially practicable. Although their work contributed to subsequent reforms, Peter Board's [q.v.7] more succinct analysis had greater impact.

Appointed assistant under-secretary to Board in the Department of Public Instruction on 8 February 1905, Turner succeeded Knibbs as superintendent of technical education in June 1906. An efficient administrator, he did his best in the post, but realized that Board gave priority to improving primary and secondary education. Turner fought to obtain appropriate facilities, encouraged staff involvement in decision-making and fostered technical education in country regions. While aware of his branch's shortcomings, he was prevented by ill health from helping in its reconstruction; begun in 1912, the task was completed by his successor James Nangle [q.v.10]. Taking extended sick-leave, Turner planned to retire.

Although dedicated and hard-working, Turner may not have been entirely fitted for the roles he was called upon to perform from 1902. He was remembered by a former pupil as 'stockily built' and 'square headed', with 'a clear, steady, direct gaze'. A keen sportsman, he was a trustee of the Athletic Sports Ground at Moore Park and encouraged the teaching of swimming. He was a Freemason, a foundation member (president 1900-02) of the Public Service Association of New South Wales, and sometime vice-president of the Boys' Brigade and the short-lived Child Study Association. Survived by his wife, two daughters and a son, Turner died of diabetes at his Summer Hill home on 24 July 1913 and was buried in Rookwood cemetery.

Cyclopedia of N.S.W. (Syd, 1907); L. E. Gent, *The Fort Street centenary book* (Syd, 1949); A. R. Crane and W. G. Walker, *Peter Board* (Melb, 1957); *Technical Gazette of NSW*, 3, pt 3, 1913; *SMH*, 10 Mar 1902, 25 July 1913; *T&CJ*, 22 Mar 1902, 7 May, 30 July 1913; *Syd Mail*, 12 Apr 1902; J. Cobb, History of technical education in New South Wales to 1949 (ts, Syd, 1988, held by Mr N. Neill, Dept of Technical and Further Education, Syd). R. PHILPS

TURNER, WALTER JAMES REDFERN (1884-1946), poet and critic, was born on 13 October 1884 in South Melbourne, eldest son of WALTER JAMES TURNER (1857-1900), warehouseman, and his wife Alice May, née Watson. Born on 3 July 1857 at Geelong, Victoria, the father became prominent in Melbourne's musical activities. Organist at St James's Cathedral and later at St Paul's Church, he was appointed to teach music at the Working Men's College in 1888; he also composed ballads and directed the People's Promenade Concerts at the Melbourne Cricket Ground. He died at Kew on 5 April 1900 and was buried in Box Hill cemetery.

Educated at Carlton State School, Scotch College and the School of Mines before working as a clerk, Walter junior recalled his Melbourne boyhood in his fictional autobiography, *Blow for balloons* (1935). In 1907 he went to London to become a writer. Spending ten months in Germany and Austria in 1913-14, he wrote satirical sketches for the *New Age* and concert reviews for the *Musical Standard*. He returned to England before the outbreak of World War I and, although he served in the Royal Garrison Artillery in 1916-18, his literary career flourished. In 1916 he published the first of sixteen volumes of poetry. His work gained prominence when it appeared in *Georgian poetry* in 1917 and 1919. On 5 April 1918, at St Luke's parish church, Chelsea, he had married Delphine Marguerite Dubuis (d. 1951); they remained childless.

Following the war, Turner's activities introduced him to leading literary and intellectual figures in Bloomsbury and at Garsington, the home of Lady Ottoline Morrell. He was music critic for the *New Statesman* (1915-40), *Truth* (c.1920-37) and the *Modern Mystic* (1937); drama critic for the *London Mercury* (1919-23) and the *New Statesman* (1928-29); literary editor of the *Owl* (1919) and the *Daily Herald* (1920-23); and had plays produced. Although he still admired and was influenced by Georgian poets such as Walter de la Mare, in 1922 he withdrew in disillusionment from the last *Georgian poetry* anthology and experimented with a more modern verse in *The seven days of the sun* (1925). While committed to rhythm, music, sensibility and imagination, Turner's poetry also pursues his metaphysical interests and reveals a philosophic idealism that relates closely to Platonism and the thought of Kierkegaard. Yeats valued Turner's modernity and philosophic energy, and in the late 1930s they collaborated in British Broadcasting Commission poetry programmes.

As music critic, Turner distinguished himself by the independence, originality and outspokenness of his views. He published studies of Beethoven (1927), Wagner (1933), Berlioz (1934) and Mozart (1938), but also revered modern composers such as Stravinsky, and was one of London's most receptive commentators on the new music of Schönberg, Berg, Webern and Hindemith. He regarded Artur Schnabel as the greatest pianist of the age and became his close friend. In his late years Turner continued a prolific and varied literary output, writing poetry, short stories, criticism and drama. He was literary editor of the *Spectator* (1941-46) and general editor of the *Britain in pictures* series. He died of cerebro-vascular disease at his Hammersmith home on 18 November 1946.

A. D. Hope, *Native companions* (Syd, 1974); C. W. F. McKenna, *W. J. Turner, poet and music critic* (Gerrards Cross, Eng, 1989); *The Times*, 20, 23 Nov 1946.

C. W. F. McKenna

TWEDDLE, ISABEL MAY (1875-1945), artist, was born on 26 November 1875 at Deniliquin, New South Wales, third daughter of Henry William Hunter, builder, and his wife Emma Louisa, née Peers, both English born. Isabel studied at the National Gallery schools, Melbourne, in 1894-97; there she acquired the nickname 'Diana' and met Ada May Plante [q.v.11] with whom she was to work closely. On leaving the gallery schools, Isabel worked as a photographic tinter, rented a city studio and exhibited occasionally with the Victorian Artists' Society. Having married Joseph Thornton Tweddle [q.v.] on 30 March 1904 at the Methodist Church, St Kilda, she accompanied him to Europe about 1907. She attended Max Meldrum's [q.v.10] classes (*c.*1915-20), and executed decorative and refined pastel portraits which had an affinity with the work of Jessie Traill [q.v.]. Meldrum's influence persisted in Isabel's ability to build her subject through patterns of light and shade, working thinly and directly across the canvas. She was a foundation member (1917) of the Twenty Melbourne Painters. During 1921 the Tweddles lived in England.

Her awareness of Post-Impressionism developed in Melbourne in the wake of Arnold Shore and William Frater [qq.v.11,8]. She joined the Women's Art Club in 1926 and quickly became a leading exhibitor. Her studies overseas strengthened her position in modernist circles. In London in 1927 and 1933 she exhibited work painted in Scandinavia, the Mediterranean region, Australia and the Pacific, and in the 1930s she visited the Solomon Islands, New Guinea, Japan and Germany.

While she used her husband's prominence to advance Post-Impressionist art and attempted to influence National Gallery purchases through his trusteeship, her own strong personality brought added prominence to modernism in Melbourne. A foundation member (1932) of the Contemporary Art Group and committee-member (1938) of the Contemporary Art Society, she was president (1930-31 and 1941-45) of the Melbourne Society of Women Painters and Sculptors, and publicly opposed the Australian Academy of Art. Although some envied her affluence, her art was accepted by critics such as Basil

Burdett [q.v.7] who described her as a 'forceful, vigorous painter and a fine colourist'. Her gestural expressionism, as well as her prominence, may have encouraged younger artists —such as Sybil Craig, Peggie Crombie and Jessie Mackintosh—to adopt a spontaneous style in the 1930s in preference to the formal design taught by George Bell [q.v.7].

Survived by her son and two daughters, Isabel died of cancer on 9 July 1945 at her Toorak home and was cremated. Direct and intuitive in her work, she left few statements about her art and destroyed a number of her paintings shortly before her death. For Tweddle, the 'moderns' were Matisse, Cézanne and Van Gogh; she believed that 'modern art . . . brought back to painting the vitality and sincerity which had been suppressed by academic treatment'.

C. Reddin, *Rupert Bunny himself* (Melb, 1987); *Art and Aust*, Nov 1938; *Argus*, 19 Apr 1933; *Herald* (Melb), 12 Sept 1930; *Bulletin*, 30 July 1925; J. Peers, History of the Melbourne Society of Women Painters and Sculptors (forthcoming); family information.

JULIET PEERS

TWEDDLE, JOSEPH THORNTON (1865-1943), businessman and philanthropist, was born on 14 April 1865 at Winlaton, Durham, England, eighth child of Thomas Tweddle, butcher, and his wife Mary, née Reay. Educated at the local council school, he had some commercial experience with an ironmongery firm at Newcastle upon Tyne; when Joseph's health collapsed, his father helped him to emigrate to Victoria in 1887. Tweddle worked at Mincha West on the farm of Henry Angus, to whose brother he had probably brought a letter of introduction; he later partnered the brothers in constructing irrigation works at Kow Swamp and at Benjeroop. When the latter scheme failed due to drought, Tweddle took a clerkship with the Colonial Gas Association Ltd, Melbourne, and then with a firm of solicitors. On 5 April 1893 he married Lilian Billis (d. 1895) at Auburn with Presbyterian forms.

As an accountant, in 1896 he joined Andrews Bros Pty Ltd, a woollen and manchester warehouse in Flinders Lane. By 1899 he was a director. In 1904 Joseph married Isabel May Hunter [q.v. Tweddle]. He was a member in 1915-16 of a royal commission, chaired by Alexander Cooch [q.v.8], to inquire into the Victorian Public Service: its report was scathingly critical of management and operations. Tweddle had been appointed managing director of Andrews Bros in 1915. The firm, whose business expanded greatly during World War I, had branches in every State. A London office made regular trips to

England obligatory for Tweddle; in 1933 he became chairman of directors.

Councillor (1915-39) and president (1935-39) of Queen's College at the University of Melbourne, and a councillor of Wesley College (1921-43), he funded extensions to both institutions which were completed in 1923. Influenced by Maude Primrose (promoter of the Visiting Trained Nurses' Association of Victoria and of the Truby King or Plunket system of baby health care) and by Dr J. W. Springthorpe [q.v.], Tweddle financed the Tweddle Hospital for Babies and School of Mothercraft as the training centre for Plunket and Primrose nurses: it opened at Footscray in 1924. From 1918 he had farmed at various locations in Victoria, initially in partnership with E. H. Flack [q.v.8], and was a prize-winning breeder of Friesian cattle, Suffolk sheep and Percheron horses. In a notable taxation case in 1942 he appealed successfully against the disallowance of deductions for pastoral losses when the High Court of Australia concluded that it was not the function of tax legislation 'to dictate to taxpayers in what business they shall engage or how to run their business profitably or economically'.

An effective public speaker, if inclined to floridity, Tweddle was tall and prepossessing. He attributed his philanthropy to the influence of a devoutly Methodist upbringing. A connoisseur of art and an enthusiastic collector, he was a trustee from 1921 of the Public Library, museums and National Gallery of Victoria. Described as 'one of the best-known figures in business, pastoral and art circles in Melbourne', he died on 16 July 1943 at Richmond and was cremated. His wife, son and two daughters survived him; his estate was sworn for probate at £118 878; Queen's College holds his portrait.

G. A. L. Gunn (ed), *The Australian income tax reports* (Syd, 1944); *Methodist Spectator*, 15 Dec 1920, 16 Aug 1922, 4 Apr 1923; *Age* and *Argus*, 9 Feb 1916, 19 July 1943; *Kerang New Times*, 15 Feb 1916, 22 Dec 1922; *Herald* (Melb), 23 Mar 1923, 19 July 1943; information from Mrs A. Tweddle and Mrs M. F. Elmore, Melb.   JOHN LACK

TYE, CYRUS WILLMOT OBERON (1879-1946), public servant, was born on 14 January 1879 at Macdonaldtown, Sydney, son of Thomas Tye, butcher, and his wife Eugenie, née Cozens, both native-born. Educated at Newington College, in 1897 he joined the Department of Public Instruction. Transferring to the Department of Lands as a clerk in 1900, he was involved with closer settlement. On 20 March 1907 Tye married Constance Isabel Elizabeth Cauthra Hall with Presbyterian forms at Rockdale; they were to have a son and two daughters. A keen cricketer, after World War I he took up baseball and later played golf.

Appointed in 1912 as special clerk to Joseph Davis [q.v.8], director-general of public works, Tye enrolled that year as a part-time student at the University of Sydney and qualified in 1915 with a diploma in economics and commerce. He assisted John Spence [q.v.] with the Norton Griffith & Co. contract in 1916 and in June 1917 became secretary to the minister for public works. In 1920 he was promoted to assistant accountant in the department and was under secretary in 1925-29. As an associate of the Commonwealth Institute of Accountants, Tye was one of the first permanent heads to have accounting qualifications and experience.

In 1925 Britain undertook to provide loan funds at a low interest rate for development schemes in Australia that would increase the migration of British workers. When the Commonwealth government failed to recommend sufficient projects and immigration to New South Wales fell in 1929, the Bavin [q.v.7] government set up the Migration Agreement Executive Committee to make arrangements for construction schemes within the State. In May Tye was appointed director of development within the Premier's Department, in charge of the committee and concurrently secretary and executive officer of the Council for the Prevention and Relief of Unemployment. The Wyangala Dam scheme was the first of the projects aimed at developing the resources of the State and attracting British migrants. The committee was maintained by premiers J. T. Lang [q.v.9] and (Sir) Bertram Stevens [q.v.]; Tye also served on other government boards and was an executive member of the committee organizing the sesquicentenary celebrations in 1938.

During World War II Tye took on numerous responsibilities in the public service. Manager of the Government Stores Department, he was a member of the State Liquid Fuel Control Board and in 1942 had charge of the State Charcoal Undertaking for the Department of Road Transport and Tramways. A diabetic, he died of a coronary occlusion at his home at Mosman on 31 March 1946 and was cremated with Anglican rites; his wife and a daughter survived him. Tye's success in administration under changing governments, his training and experience in financial management, and his ability to take on substantial and varied responsibilities made him a notable professional administrator.

Report respecting the Imperial migration agreement, *PP* (NSW), 1923 (1); *SMH*, 14, 16 June 1924, 17 Apr 1929, 4 Oct 1939, 2 Apr 1946.

LENORE COLTHEART

TYRRELL, JAMES ROBERT (1875-1961), bookseller and publisher, was born on 3 July 1875 at Darlington, Sydney, son of George Tyrrell, dealer, and his wife Mary, née Colgan. His father, born on the Isle of Wight, had served in the Crimean War before trying his fortune on the New South Wales goldfields; his mother had come to Queensland from Ireland. Jim attended the Pigeon Ground (Public) School at Balmain and Petersham Superior Public School; the Tyrrells moved to Newtown during his boyhood. At the age of 13 he began work with Angus and Robertson [qq.v.7,11], running errands, delivering books in a billycart and 'keeping an eye on the front' (the books displayed outside the shop). Relations within 'the family' were close: Tyrrell's early reading was guided by Angus and his first exercise as an independent bookseller (at night in a shop near the university) was encouraged by Robertson's generosity in allowing him to choose freely from discards.

Already enmeshed in the world of books, Tyrrell spent ten months in London and Edinburgh as a buyer for the firm in 1897-98. His tour was part business, part pleasure, both an expansion of his knowledge and contacts in the book trade, and a pilgrimage to the 'literary shrines' of England and in particular Scotland. On his return, he married Matilda Bourne, daughter of a museum curator, on 17 August 1898 at St Stephen's Anglican Church, Newtown. Tyrrell stayed with Angus and Robertson for seventeen years, acquiring an invaluable training in the craft of bookselling and an enviable knowledge of Australiana and its major collectors.

Again with the friendly support of Robertson, Tyrrell set up in business in 1905, with a partner, on the corner of Castlereagh and Market streets. Like many of Sydney's booksellers, he was to move premises several times. After five years of indifferent success, he made a fresh start in Adelaide, finding ideal premises at 128 Gawler Place. Dealing in art as well as books, he began the diversification of activities which was to characterize his return to Sydney; he also rekindled that entrepreneurial pleasure he had experienced at Angus and Robertson's of playing a constructive part in building public and private collections, and of running an establishment which was seen as a focal point by writers and bibliophiles.

Returning in 1914 to Castlereagh Street, Sydney, Tyrrell not only expanded the twin strands of bookselling and art-dealing, but formed a publishing company, Tyrrell's Ltd, in which J. F. Archibald [q.v.3] among others held shares. Prominent on its list, which also reflected Tyrrell's abiding interest in early Sydney, were Henry Lawson's [q.v.10] volume of verse, *My army, o my army!* (1915),

Zora Cross's [q.v.8] *Songs of love and life* (1917) and a volume of caricatures by the cartoonist David Low [q.v.10]. Tyrrell himself compiled and published a collection of Aboriginal place-names (1933) and wrote a short reminiscence of David Scott Mitchell [q.v.5] in 1936.

Testimony to Tyrrell's fascination with collectable items, and the breadth of his knowledge and interests, was his acquisition of the established Hunter Street business, Antiques Ltd, and in August 1923 of Tost & Rohu, 'Taxidermists, Tanners, Furriers and Island Curio Dealers', 'the queerest shop in Sydney'. In financial straits in the late 1920s, Tyrrell added a museum to this shop in Martin Place. From 1935, when he moved to 281 George Street, he concentrated on books; his son Eric later took over the burden of management.

In *Old books, old friends, old Sydney* (1952) Tyrrell records something of his boyhood and progress as an independent bookseller and art dealer; it is less an autobiography than a collection of often anecdotal reminiscences of the years (1888-1905) he spent with Angus and Robertson. Its sequel, *Postscript: further bookselling reminiscences* (1957), has notes on Henry Kendall, W. H. Traill and J. B. Stephens [qq.v.5,6] and includes the uncollected poems of James Lionel Michael [q.v.5] as transcribed by Kendall.

Tyrrell writes modestly, but with a strong sense of having been privileged to witness and take part in a formative period in Australian cultural history. His style is matter-of-fact, his memory keen and his observation sharp. Skills honed in the pursuit of Australiana reveal themselves in the vivid clarity with which he records the 'picturesque cavalcade' of 'bookfellows' that passed before him. Among his acquaintances were booksellers Angus, Robertson, George Robertson of Melbourne, William Dymock [qq.v.6,8] and Fred Wymark [q.v.]; writers such as Lawson, Archibald, A. B. Paterson, C. J. Dennis, [qq.v.11,8], 'Steele Rudd' [q.v.8 A. H. Davis], A. G. Stephens [q.v.], 'the alliterative quintet of Brennan, Brady, Brereton, Bedford, and Becke' [qq.v.7]; visitors to Sydney like Mark Twain and Robert Louis Stevenson; artists and illustrators including Norman and Lionel Lindsay [qq.v.10] and Low; collectors, among them Mitchell, (Sir) William Dixson [q.v.8], A. B. Triggs, H. L. White [qq.v.] and A. H. Turnbull from New Zealand; and other bibliophiles prominent in public life, such as Sir Henry Parkes and W. M. Hughes [qq.v.5,9]. The book provides invaluable glimpses of these and other figures, and casts light on their engagement at a critical time in the collection and preservation of Australiana.

Best remembered as the doyen of sellers of

second-hand books, Tyrrell died at Cammeray, Sydney, on 30 July 1961 and was cremated. His wife, son and daughter survived him. Perhaps the most poignant tributes to Tyrrell's role in their common pursuit are those of poets who knew and frequented one or other of his shops—Lawson's 'Song of Tyrrell's bell', Roderic Quinn's [q.v.11] 'Tyrrell's bookshop', and Kenneth Slessor's 'In Tyrrell's bookshop':

> Broadsheets there are, of horrid hangman's tales;
> Yellow-stained maps from some forgotten book;
> Journals of convict years in New South Wales,
> And Captain Cook.
>
> Mottled monastic tomes of Cicero;
> Ballads of murder, testaments of thieves;
> Shakespeares in brindled duodecimo,
> With rusty leaves.
>
> Long forgot relics of a dead decade:
> All that is old, and nothing that is new—
> Here, in the shadows, half an earth has made
> Last rendezvous.

Aust Booksellers Assn, *The early Australian booksellers* (Adel, 1980); *People* (Syd), 20 Mar 1957, p 48; *SMH*, 15 Dec 1945, 27 Mar 1954, 22 Feb 1958; *Sun-Herald*, 6 Aug 1961; Tyrrell papers (ML).   W. S. RAMSON

TYRRELL, THOMAS JAMES (1880-1942), trade unionist and politician, was born on 14 April 1880 at Coonamble, New South Wales, son of Patrick Tyrrell, a labourer from Ireland, and his native-born wife Isabella, née Dunn. The family moved to Sydney where Thomas was educated at Patrician Brothers' School, Redfern. Employed by the Sydney Municipal Council, from his early twenties he took an interest in trade union affairs; he became president of the Municipal Employees' Union of New South Wales and campaigned to obtain an award for council workers.

Federal president of the expanded Federated Municipal and Shire Council Employees' Union of Australia in 1916, Tyrrell was its State secretary in 1917-42. Having achieved registration of the union with the Commonwealth Court of Conciliation and Arbitration in 1919, he saw his union's membership double to 12 000 by 1925. He was also a member of the Local Government Superannuation Board (1927-34). Aware of the moderate aspirations of most of his unionists, he sought meliorative reforms from Federal or State Labor governments and encouraged

support through the union's journal, the *Counsellor*. He was associated with the J. T. Lang [q.v.9] faction, and worked with Albert Willis [q.v.] and Edward Magrath [q.v.10] in the 1920s.

A member of the Labor executive in 1916-17 and 1919-23, Tyrrell was able to adapt to the changing political climate and was a senior vice-president of the party in 1923-26. With Magrath, he was nominated in July 1925 to the Legislative Council; in 1933 Tyrrell was elected to the reconstituted council for nine years. In November 1925 the right-wing Australian Workers' Union had publicly castigated him as an 'example of the stupid fury and reckless unscrupulousness of those who mismanage' the Labor Party in New South Wales for having moved a resolution debarring unions connected with the Labor Council from affiliating with the party.

Jim (or Jimmie) Tyrrell remained popular among his supporters. Broad-shouldered, with a handlebar moustache when younger, in later years he gave shrewd and practical advice in a terse, staccato manner. A director of the *Labor Daily* in 1926-37, Tyrrell was appointed general manager in April 1929 and —despite suffering concussion when he fell from a tram in March 1930—acting managing director on 1 April 1931. He supported Lang's moves to increase his control over the newspaper, but was deposed by a meeting of the paper's 'rebel' directors in February 1938.

Wage reductions, retrenchments and the undercutting of awards for his union members gradually exhausted Tyrrell's energies on the industrial front. In 1934 he had been involved in setting up Labor Motor Funerals Ltd to extend services and general assistance to unionists and the public; the company prospered and in 1937 paid a 10 per cent dividend. As an active chairman of the *Century* company, he was to combat stiff competition from other labour newspapers.

Dispirited at his ousting from the *Labor Daily*, Tyrrell rallied to assist the early mobilization of labour to wartime needs. Survived by a son, he died of a cerebral tumour on 31 October 1942 at Earlwood and was buried in the Catholic section of Botany cemetery. His estate was sworn for probate at £689.

J. T. Lang, *I remember* (Syd, 1956); B. Nairn, *The 'Big Fella'* (Melb, 1986); *Counsellor*, 1 Jan 1916, p 6, Oct 1942, p 5; *Aust Worker*, 13 June 1923; *SMH*, 6 May 1924, 30 July, 7 Oct, 26 Nov 1925, 24 Mar 1930, 10 Feb 1938, 3 Nov 1942; *Labor Daily*, 30 July, 10 Nov 1925, 1 Apr 1931, 23 July 1935, 24 Sept 1937; *Daily Guardian*, 24 Aug 1925; *Daily Telegraph* (Syd), 3 Sept 1925; *Century* (Syd), 3 Jan 1941; *Truth* (Syd), 1 Nov 1942.

FRANK FARRELL

U

ULM, CHARLES THOMAS PHILIPPE (1898-1934), aviator, was born on 18 October 1898 at Middle Park, Melbourne, third son of Emile Gustave Ulm, a Parisian-born artist, and his Victorian wife Ada Emma, née Greenland. Charles was educated at state schools in Melbourne and Sydney (after his family moved to Mosman) and began work as a clerk in a stockbroking office. Emulating his grandfather and uncle who had fought in the Franco-Prussian War, as 'Charles Jackson' he enlisted in the 1st Battalion, Australian Imperial Force, on 16 September 1914: his height of almost six feet (182.9 cm) gave credence to his stated age of 20. He embarked for Egypt in December and was among the first troops to land at Gallipoli on 25 April 1915. Wounded in action that month, he was returned to Australia and, as a minor, discharged from the A.I.F. at his parents' request. In January 1917 he re-enlisted under his own name; while serving with the 45th Infantry Battalion on the Western Front, in July 1918 he was badly wounded and evacuated to Britain before being demobilized in March 1919.

Imbued with an entrepreneurial spirit and a vision of successful commercial airlines, Ulm had returned to Sydney with £3000 (from a £50 English investment) and backed several short-lived aircraft companies. On 20 November 1919 at St John's Anglican Church, Darlinghurst, he married Isabel Amy Winter. Reckless and restless, Ulm probably went to Western Australia. Having divorced his wife in 1927 and been granted custody of their son, he married Mary Josephine Callaghan on 29 June at North Sydney Congregational Church.

Backed by Sun Newspapers Ltd, in 1927 Ulm and (Sir) Charles Kingsford Smith [q.v.9] circumnavigated Australia in a Bristol Tourer in 10 days and 5 hours, more than halving the record. They acquired sufficient funds to plan the first trans-Pacific flight from the United States of America to Australia. In a borrowed, three-engined Fokker (later named the Southern Cross) they left Oakland, California, with two American crewmen on 31 May 1928; Ulm acted as co-commander and co-pilot. Facing unknown hazards after Hawaii, they encountered severe tropical storms: they tried to fly above the clouds, but were forced to descend to only two hundred feet (61 m) to avoid running out of fuel before landing at Suva on 5 June. They reached Brisbane on 9 June, after 83 hours and 19 minutes flying time. The journey made Ulm and Kingsford Smith popular heroes: both were awarded the Air Force Cross and given honorary commissions in the Royal Australian Air Force; Southern Cross became their property.

In extreme weather conditions on 10 September they made the first trans-Tasman flight, from Sydney to Christchurch, New Zealand, in fourteen hours. Ulm at last received his pilot's licence. He also enjoyed sailing and belonged to the Royal Air Force Club, London, the (Royal) Aero Club of New South Wales and the Legacy Club of Sydney; he was, as well, a captain in the Ligue Internationale des Aviateurs.

Kingsford Smith and Ulm formed Australian National Airways Ltd in December 1928 to operate unsubsidized passenger, mail and freight services. Deciding in March 1929 to fly to London to buy aircraft, they were lost for thirteen days after Southern Cross was forced to land near the desolate north-west Australian coast. During the massive search, Keith Anderson, a former colleague, died. Although Ulm had previously made suggestive remarks, the rumour that he had arranged the incident to obtain publicity was not substantiated by the Air Inquiry Committee. He flew with Kingsford Smith to London when the flight was resumed on 25 June. Henceforth Ulm devoted himself to managing A.N.A. Hit by the Depression and aircraft losses, the company went into liquidation in February 1933; Ulm bought one of the remaining aeroplanes and renamed it Faith in Australia.

In 1933 he flew this aircraft to England with (Sir) Gordon Taylor [q.v.] as navigator, but, after damaging the aeroplane in Ireland, had to cancel the projected around-the-world flight. Returning to Australia, they established a new record of 6 days, 17 hours and 56 minutes. In April 1934 Ulm flew the first official mail from Australia to New Zealand; in Faith in Australia he completed the return trans-Tasman flight in 28 hours and 44 minutes flying time; he flew the Tasman eight times in all. In August he carried the first official airmail from Australia to New Guinea and back. Hoping to establish a trans-Pacific service between Australia, Canada and the United States, in September he formed Great Pacific Airways Ltd and bought an Airspeed Envoy, Stella Australis, with long-range (3800 miles, 6115 km) fuel tanks. On 3 December 1934, with a crew of two, Ulm flew from Oakland for Hawaii. Stella Australis failed to arrive. Despite an extensive sea search, no trace of it was ever found. Ulm's wife and the son of his first marriage survived him; his estate was sworn for probate at £742.

With dark brown, curly hair and an olive complexion that indicated his French ancestry, Ulm was regarded with considerable affection by those who worked with him. A practical visionary with a keen sense of humour, he displayed drive, energy, extraordinary precision in thought and courage in adversity. It was his responsibility to arrange the financial and administrative aspects of his flights with Kingsford Smith and his organization was impeccable.

P. G. Taylor, *VH-UXX: the story of an aeroplane* (Syd, 1937); *Notable citizens of Sydney* (Syd, 1940); I. R. Carter, *Southern Cloud* (Melb, 1963); J. Pickering, *The routes of the Valkyries* (Lond, 1977); E. Rogers, *Faith in Australia* (Syd, 1987); *Reveille* (Syd), 1 Jan 1935; *SMH*, 25 June 1929, 13 Dec 1934; Ulm papers (ML).   JOHN MCCARTHY

ULRICH, THEODORE FRIEDERICK (1888-1963), soldier and clerk, was born on 10 December 1888 at Ararat, Victoria, son of German-born Augustus Charles Theodore Ulrich, stock agent, and his Irish wife Catherine, née Darling. He was the youngest of nine children, only five of whom survived to adulthood.

The family moved to Melbourne where Ulrich was educated at Carlton and Wesley colleges. He then worked for Connibere [q.v.8], Grieve & Connibere as a clerk, played cricket for a Carlton team and, aged 22, became a second lieutenant in the 1st Battalion, 6th Australian Infantry Regiment. In 1912 he joined the 63rd Infantry (East Melbourne) Regiment, as militia adjutant. On 14 August 1914 he was appointed lieutenant in the 6th Battalion, Australian Imperial Force, and embarked for Egypt on 19 October.

The battalion landed at Gallipoli on 25 April 1915; two days later Ulrich was promoted captain. For the next seven months he experienced the horrors and hardships of the peninsula before being evacuated sick on 22 November. He returned to his unit in February 1916 and sailed to France a month later, having been promoted major. In July he was appointed brigade major of the 2nd Brigade. He carried out his duties ably during the terrible Somme operations and was awarded the Distinguished Service Order late in 1916. From February to July 1917 he again gave 'conspicuous good service' to his brigade and was mentioned in dispatches.

On 6 July Ulrich became second-in-command of the 8th Battalion. On 20 October, during the 3rd battle of Ypres, he was wounded, but remained on duty. He returned to the 6th Battalion a few days later. His commanding officer, Lieut-Colonel C. W. D. Daly,

was killed on 13 April 1918 near La Motte; next day Ulrich was appointed lieut-colonel with temporary command of the battalion. The allies' last great offensive was launched on 8 August; in the following two days Ulrich's battalion fought at Lihons, a battle which was, Ulrich confided to C. E. W. Bean [q.v.7], 'a very heavy time' for the 6th. On the 23rd the unit fought near Herleville Wood. Despite heavy artillery and machine-gun fire, Ulrich continually advanced with his troops, keeping closely in touch with his men and controlling their movements. Although the course of the battle at times became obscure, he was able to grasp situations and exploit opportunities. He was awarded a Bar to his D.S.O. By the time the war ended he had been thrice mentioned in dispatches.

After returning to Melbourne in May 1919, Ulrich commanded militia units and worked at various jobs. In the mid-1920s he owned a butcher's shop and for a long time was an office-holder in the Victorian Automobile Chamber of Commerce. On 30 June 1926 he married Ida Violet Ferris at All Saints Anglican Church, St Kilda. With the outbreak of World War II Ulrich was given command of the 12th Australian Garrison Battalion at Broadmeadows. He led the unit until early 1945 when he retired from the army.

Thereafter Ulrich worked at several clerical, accounting and managerial positions. He joined the Brunswick sub-branch of the Returned Sailors', Soldiers' and Airmen's Imperial League of Australia in 1949 and occupied his spare time with golf, reading and carpentry. Survived by his wife and son, he died on 12 December 1963 at his Brunswick home and was cremated. In the words of a member of his family, Ulrich was 'at his best in the army and perhaps a little "out of place" in civilian life'.

C. E. W. Bean, *The A.I.F. in France*, 1918 (Syd, 1942) and *Anzac to Amiens* (Canb, 1946); *Age*, 14 Dec 1963; Bean diaries and official historian's biog cards and AIF nominal roll and honours and awards (AWM); information from Mr P. Ulrich, Brisb.

MATTHEW HIGGINS

UNAIPON, DAVID (1872-1967), preacher, author and inventor, was born on 28 September 1872 at the Point McLeay Mission, South Australia, fourth of nine children of James Ngunaitponi, evangelist, and his wife Nymbulda, both Yaraldi speakers from the lower Murray River region. James was the Congregational mission's first Aboriginal convert. David attended the mission school from the age of 7. In 1885 he left to become a servant to C. B. Young who encouraged his interest in philosophy, science and music. Back at Point McLeay from 1890, Unaipon read widely, played the organ and learned boot-making at the mission. A non-smoker and tee-totaller, he grew frustrated at the lack of work for educated Aborigines at mission settlements and in the late 1890s took a job as storeman for an Adelaide bootmaker before returning to assist as book-keeper in the Point McLeay store. On 4 January 1902 at Point McLeay he married a Tangani woman from the Coorong, Katherine Carter, née Sumner, a servant.

By 1909 Unaipon had developed and patented a modified handpiece for shearing. He was obsessed with discovering the secret of perpetual motion. In 1914 his repetition of predictions by others about the development of polarized light and helicopter flight were publicized, building his reputation as a 'black genius' and 'Australia's Leonardo'. Between 1909 and 1944 Unaipon made patent applications for nine other inventions, including a centrifugal motor, a multi-radial wheel and a mechanical propulsion device, but the patents lapsed.

His fame, urbanity, fastidious manner of speech and Aboriginal identity confounded current stereotypes: Unaipon embodied the potential—in White terms—for Aboriginal advancement. His lectures for the Anglican Church stressed improvement: 'Look at me and you will see what the Bible can do', and his rhetorical skills were shared by other Point McLeay Aborigines.

In 1912 Unaipon led a deputation urging government control of Point McLeay Mission; next year he gave evidence to the royal commission into Aboriginal issues and became a subscription collector for the Aborigines' Friends' Association. For fifty years he travelled south-eastern Australia, combining this work with lectures and sermons in churches and cathedrals of different denominations. In addresses to schools and learned societies he spoke on Aboriginal legends and customs, and about his people's future. He also demonstrated his inventions, but his public requests for financial support provoked the disapproval of the mission authorities. His wife (d. 1928) stayed at home; their marriage was not happy.

From the early 1920s Unaipon studied Aboriginal mythology and compiled his versions of legends; he was influenced by the classics and by his researches into Egyptology at the South Australian Museum. The A.F.A. funded publication of *Hungarrda* (1927), *Kinie Ger—the native cat* (1928) and *Native legends* (1929). Unaipon sold these and other booklets while employed by the A.F.A. His articles, beginning on 2 August 1924 in the Sydney *Daily Telegraph*, were written in a prose that showed the influence of Milton and Bunyan; they pre-dated the work of other Aboriginal writers by over thirty years.

Unaipon published poetry in the 1930s and more legends in the 1950s and 1960s. Gathered before 1930, the legends are in his surviving manuscript in the Mitchell [q.v.5] Library: they were commissioned and published by W. Ramsay Smith [q.v.11], without acknowledgment, as *Myths and legends of the Australian Aboriginals* (London, 1930). Unaipon also wrote 'My life story' and 'Leaves of memory' (A.F.A. *Annual Reports*, 1951 and 1953).

In the 1920s and 1930s he influenced government Aboriginal policy. Assisted by friends like Rev. J. H. Sexton [q.v.11], Dr Herbert Basedow [q.v.7], Sir George Murray [q.v.10] and Dr Charles Duguid, Unaipon remained relatively free from the official restraints usually placed on Aborigines. In 1926 he appeared before another royal commission into the treatment of Aborigines. That year he also advocated a model Aboriginal state in an attempt to provide a separate territory for Aborigines in central and northern Australia; his involvement in the movement may have contributed to his arrest in November on vagrancy charges.

In 1928-29 he assisted the Bleakley [q.v.7] inquiry into Aboriginal welfare. By then the best-known Aborigine in Australia, Unaipon was accepted as his people's spokesman. His skill in manipulating members of the press—who invariably described him as a full-blood Aborigine—lent authenticity to his statements at a time when governments were concerned with the so-called 'half-caste problem'. In 1934 he urged the Commonwealth to take over Aboriginal affairs and proposed that South Australia's chief protector of Aborigines be replaced by an independent board. Educated Aboriginal men from Point McLeay and Point Pearce supported him, among them Mark Wilson [q.v.]; their view that the Aborigines' transition to European society should be facilitated through education was supported by the A.F.A. and was later expressed in the Commonwealth's assimilation policy. Unaipon's preference for gradual change was highlighted by his disagreement with the New South Wales branch of the Australian Aborigines' League over its National Day of Mourning on Australia Day, 1938.

In 1953 Unaipon received a Coronation medal. He continued to travel on foot in Adelaide and country centres, where he was often refused accommodation because of his race, and was still preaching at 87. In his nineties he worked on his inventions at Point McLeay, convinced that he was close to discovering the secret of perpetual motion. Survived by a son, he died at Tailem Bend Hospital on 7 February 1967 and was buried in Point McLeay cemetery.

Portraits of Unaipon by S. Wickes and L. Wilkie [q.v.] are in the South Australian

Museum. In 1988 the national David Unaipon award for Aboriginal writers was instituted and an annual Unaipon lecture was established in Adelaide.

G. Rowe, *Sketches of outstanding Aborigines* (Adel, 1955); J. Horner, *Vote Ferguson for Aboriginal freedom* (Syd, 1974); G. Jenkin, *Conquest of the Ngarrindjeri* (Adel, 1979); L. A. Murray (comp), *The new Oxford book of Australian verse* (Melb, 1986); A. Markus, *Blood from a stone* (Syd, 1988); A. Shoemaker, *Black words, white page* (Brisb, 1989); *Bible in the World*, 1 Aug 1911; *Southerly*, 39, Sept 1979, p 334; *Advertiser* (Adel), 12 Apr 1907, 27 Apr 1914, 9 Nov 1936, 9 Feb 1967; *Observer* (Adel), 10 Oct 1925; *Register* (Adel), 14 July 1926; *News* (Adel), 22 July 1959; Aborigines' Friends' Assn *Annual Report*, 1964, *and* records (Mortlock Lib).   PHILIP JONES

UNWIN, ERNEST EWART (1881-1944), Quaker educationist, was born on 13 July 1881 at Folkestone, Kent, England, son of Uriah John Unwin, bricklayer, and his wife Sophia Jane, née Martin. He was educated at the Quaker schools of Saffron Walden and Ackworth, and graduated (B.Sc., 1901) at the University of Leeds. He taught at Ackworth in 1901-04, became a lecturer in science at the University of Leeds, gained his M.Sc. in 1908 and from 1908 to 1912 taught at Bootham School, York. On 7 April 1910 he married Ursula Dymond Thorp at The Friends' Meeting House, Carlton Hill, Leeds. In 1912 Unwin became senior science master at the Quaker school, Leighton Park, Reading; his first book, *Pond problems* (Cambridge, 1914), was a science textbook for schools. As a conscientious objector during World War I, he was given leave to teach and published two more books, *As a man thinketh* (London, 1919) and *Religion and biology* (London, 1922).

In 1923 Unwin answered what he felt was a 'call to service' in Australia by accepting the headmastership of the co-educational Friends' School in Hobart, a position which he was to hold until his death. The years 1923-44 witnessed major growth in the school. Unwin embarked on an ambitious rebuilding plan in which he enlisted substantial financial support from English Quakers. He brought a new dynamic of educational leadership to his school and to education in Tasmania, introducing new subjects of art, physiology and botany to the senior school curriculum, and giving priority to science in his building plans. A gifted water-colour artist and teacher of art, he was also a pioneer in the field of educational broadcasting.

His influence and leadership spread beyond his school. In 1925 Unwin was largely responsible for setting up the Association of Headmasters and Headmistresses of the Indepen-

dent Schools of Tasmania, and was secretary of that association until 1944. Invited by the Tasmanian government in 1935 to be a member of the board of inquiry into education, he was secretary of the State's committee on educational extension in 1942-43. Unwin had a wide-ranging involvement in community activities: becoming a member of the Royal Society of Tasmania in 1923, he sat on its council (1926-42 and 1944) and served two terms as vice-president (1933-34 and 1940-41). He was a member of the council of the University of Tasmania in 1927 and president of the Tasmanian Council of Churches in 1928 and 1933.

Ernest Unwin believed that a school should inspire a love of truth, an appreciation of beauty and a willingness to serve the community. To his students, he was often the subject of intense curiosity. One of them described him as 'short and stockily built', with slightly bowed legs, fresh complexion, fair hair and penetrating blue eyes. Customarily he wore a bowler hat and carried pigskin gloves, while in winter he donned spats. Survived by his wife, son and daughter, he died of a coronary occlusion on 20 September 1944 in Hobart and was cremated.

W. N. Oats, *The Friends' School, 1887-1961* (Hob, 1961), and *The rose and the waratah* (Hob, 1979); Roy Soc Tas, *Procs*, 1944.
        WILLIAM N. OATS

UPFIELD, ARTHUR WILLIAM (1890-1964), writer and bushman, was born on 1 September 1890 at Gosport, Hampshire, England, eldest of five sons of James Oliver Upfield, draper, and his wife Annie, née Barmore. Named William Arthur, he was known to his relations as 'Arker-Willum' and grew up to be Arthur. Educated at Blenheim House, Fareham, he was mostly reared by his grandparents and apprenticed to Puttock & Blake, surveyors of Gosport. At the age of 19 he was sent at his father's wish to Australia.

Arriving in Adelaide late in 1910, Upfield immediately responded to the call of the outback, roaming through New South Wales and Queensland until war was declared. He enlisted in the Australian Imperial Force on 22 August 1914. Allotted to the Light Horse Brigade Train, he went to the Middle East; he was a driver with the Australian Army Service Corps and took part in the Gallipoli campaign. At the British Consulate General, Alexandria, Egypt, he married Anne Douglass, a nurse, on 3 November 1915. Acting sergeant on several occasions, Upfield was sent to England in 1916 and to France next year.

Discharged in London in October 1919, after returning to Australia in 1920 he separated from his wife. Upfield resumed bush work and spent some time in Western Australia. Encouraged by the wife of a station-owner of a Darling run in New South Wales, he began to write and soon turned to the popular genre of crime fiction. Although *The house of Cain* appeared in 1928, his first novel was *The Barrakee mystery* (London, 1929) which originally had a White sleuth: during rewriting, it gained the character of the detective Napoleon Bonaparte, a part-Aborigine who had graduated from the University of Queensland. Upfield claimed that 'Bony' was based upon the part-Aborigine Leon Wood, a wise man, a skilled tracker and a good friend.

Many novels steadily followed. Upfield gained some notoriety when the plot of *The sands of Windee* (London, 1931) was apparently used by a murderer in Western Australia. Leaving the bush in 1931, but unable to live from royalties, Upfield became a feature writer with the Melbourne *Herald*; he lived at Airey's Inlet, Victoria, where he later set *The new shoe* (New York, 1951). When Doubleday & Co. of New York republished *The mystery of Swordfish Reef* (Sydney, 1939) in 1943, it sold 22 000 copies. Upfield became a major figure in international crime fiction, the first foreigner to be a full member of the Mystery Writers of America. He wrote full time, moving about Australia with Jessica Hawke, his long-time companion and the author (or perhaps co-author) of his biography. In 1948 he led a 5000-mile (8046.5 km) expedition through the Kimberleys, Western Australia, for the Australian Geographical Society.

Irritation at the failure of literary circles to acknowledge him as a creative artist inspired Upfield to write one of his most sharply effective novels, *An author bites the dust* (Sydney, 1948), in which a pillar of the literary establishment is brought down in more ways than one. Presenting himself as 'a story teller first and last', Upfield claimed 'I'm not a literary figure and don't want to be'. He was 'a crusty man', who appeared 'slight, wiry, buttoned up and outwardly irascible', with hazel eyes, 'weatherbeaten face, grizzled hair, ears like jug handles, a glass of whisky in his hand and the ubiquitous grey homburg on the chair beside him'.

Unassuming but spiky, at once simple and complex, Upfield had done most of the jobs that he wrote about, from stockmen's cook to camel-driving fence-patroller. He acquired considerable learning about aspects of Aboriginal lore, which he respected, even revered; he was also familiar with the elemental forces that gave him a numinous sense and that so dominate his plots, such as in *Death of a lake* (Melbourne, 1954) and *Bony and the white savage* (London, 1961).

Survived by his son, Upfield died on 12 February 1964 at Bowral, New South Wales, and was cremated. The last of his twenty-nine 'Bony' titles, *The Lake Frome monster* (London, 1966), was completed by J. L. Price and Dorothy Strange. In the mystique of the bush, Upfield saw elements of epic power in Australian life. In contrast, his rather dry style and meticulous plotting seem distinctly smaller in scale. But that is part of Upfield's impact, creating a worm's eye view of awesome natural grandeur, a sense of human inadequacy in a dominating continent.

J. Hawke with A. Upfield, *Follow my dust* (Lond, 1957); J. Reilly (ed), *Twentieth-century crime and mystery writers* (NY, 1985); J. Symons, *Bloody murder* (Lond, 1984); *Aust J*, 1 Dec 1935, p 1701, 1 Jan 1936, p 100, 1 Feb 1936, p 238, 4 Mar 1937, p 852; *People*, 27 Aug 1954, p 12; *Walkabout*, May 1964, p 37; *Armchair Detective*, Nov 1974; *This Australia*, 5, no 3, Winter 1986, p 53; *Age*, 21 Jan 1961.

STEPHEN KNIGHT

URQUHART, FREDERIC CHARLES (1858-1935), police commissioner and administrator, was born on 27 October 1858 at St Leonards-on-Sea, Sussex, England, son of Frederic Day Urquhart, army officer, and his wife Charlotte, née Goldie. Having attended All Saints School, Bloxham, Oxfordshire, and Felstead (military) School, Essex, he served as a midshipman before migrating to Queensland in 1875. He worked in the sugar and cattle industries, and became a telegraph linesman at Normanton in 1878.

Reputedly an accomplished horseman who had some acquaintance with Aborigines, he joined the Queensland Native Mounted Police Force on 27 April 1882 as a cadet and was installed as sub-inspector in charge of the Gulf, Cape York and Torres Strait districts. Urquhart was summoned to Cloncurry in 1884 to lead a detachment of armed settlers and police against the Kalkatunga (Kalkadoon) Aborigines; in a campaign that culminated in pitched combat at Battle Mountain the Kalkatungu were slaughtered and their armed resistance ended. He transferred in 1889 to the general police. In the far north he searched for survivors from the ill-fated *Quetta* in Torres Strait in 1890. He charted Albatross Bay, and the Embley and Hay Rivers, publishing his findings in the *Proceedings of the Royal Society of Queensland* (1897). 'Well read', with a 'cultivated intelligence', Urquhart wrote bush verse which included *Camp canzonettes* (1891) and *Blood stains* (1919).

Suffering from repeated sickness, he transferred to Brisbane in 1896. Next year he was promoted inspector, second class, and in 1898 took charge of the criminal investigation branch. His administration was severely criticized in 1899 by a royal commission which drew attention to his 'impulsive and exacting temperament' and his 'vindictive and tyrannical nature', but, with the support of the police commissioner and political friends, Urquhart survived. Appointed chief inspector on 1 July 1905, he was prominent in police action during the 1912 general strike. Despite some objections, he was appointed Queensland's fourth commissioner of police on 1 January 1917; he held the position until 16 January 1921, introducing little in the way of reform. He figured in the police action against the 'red flag' rioters in Brisbane in 1919 and was involved with loyalist groups during and after World War I.

Appointed administrator of the Northern Territory on 17 January 1921, Urquhart was sent to Darwin 'to clean up the place'. His mission brought him into confrontation with the 'socialistic extremists' of the North Australian Industrial Union; to counter their industrial and political power, he supported the formation of the Northern Territory Workers' Union. Urquhart welcomed restraining measures introduced by the Commonwealth government's Observance of Law Ordinance (1921) which legitimized police control of public meetings, abolished trial by jury except for capital cases, and enforced payment of taxes. Next year citizens without certain property qualifications were prevented from voting at municipal elections.

Mounting local public opposition over taxation without representation and the imprisonment of tax defaulters led in 1922 to the appointment of one member for the Northern Territory with limited voting rights in the House of Representatives. Faced with unemployment and a depressed economy, Urquhart had to carry out retrenchments, repatriate Chinese and find relief work for one hundred Europeans.

After he retired as administrator on 16 January 1926, Urquhart settled at Clayfield, Brisbane. Predeceased by his wife, Annette, née Atkinson, whom he had married at St Peter's Church, Melbourne, on 7 November 1891, he died at St Helen's Private Hospital on 2 December 1935 and was buried in Toowong cemetery with Anglican rites. A daughter and two sons survived him.

Police Dept (Qld), *A centenary history of the Queensland Police Force, 1864-1963*, C. Lack comp (Brisb, 1964); A. Powell, *Far country* (Melb, 1982); P. F. Donovan, *At the other end of Australia* (Brisb, 1984); D. J. Mulvaney, *Encounters in place* (Brisb, 1989); Roy Com to inquire into the constitution, administration and working of the criminal investigation branch of the police force of Queensland, Report, *V&P* (Qld), 1899, 4, pp 167-8, 174; *Qld Police Union J*, July 1986, p 16; NT, *Annual Report*, 1921-27; personnel file, Qld Police Dept, A/47932 (QA).   W. Ross Johnston

V

VACCARI, GUALTIERO (1894-1978), merchant and philanthropist, was born on 12 April 1894 at Sant' Agostino, Ferrara, Italy, second child of Carlo Vaccari, merchant, and his wife Olinda, née Pavesi. Educated at the local elementary school, the Royal Technical School of Finale Emilia, Modena, and the Royal Institute of Commerce, Bologna, Gualtiero was employed by a bank at Bologna before learning of opportunities in Victoria from an uncle at Bendigo. In 1912 Vaccari migrated to Melbourne where, while working as an assistant in the Italian consulate for six years, he studied accountancy. In 1921 he founded G. Vaccari & Co.: as an agent for well-known Italian companies, he imported such products as synthetic fibres, ball- and roller-bearings, and cotton goods. In 1936 he was appointed cavaliere of the Order of the Crown of Italy.

In the hothouse Italo-Australian politics of the period he was a leading figure, under fire from both sides: the Fascists accused him of lacking *cameratismo* (comradeship), while the anarchists vilified his class position. Although Vaccari was a good politician, he preferred a day at his Queen Street office to a stormy evening at the Club Cavour. Naturalized in July 1939, he became an advocate for Italians, especially for conscripted aliens, civilian internees and prisoners of war; his support of non-political Italians who were interned in Victoria secured the release of many. On the recommendation of Archbishop Mannix [q.v.10], in November 1943 the Federal government appointed Vaccari an honorary liaison officer for the Italian community in Australia. At A. A. Calwell's request, Vaccari made an analysis of Australia's post-war immigration needs; his business office provided assistance to the war effort, mounting drives among the Italian community to raise war loans. On 14 October 1946 at the registrar's office, Launceston, Tasmania, he married Elda Nicoletti, an Italian-born teacher. Vaccari was appointed a commander (1955) and grand officer (1977) of the Order of Merit of the Italian Republic.

In 1962 his increasingly diversified business, by then in La Trobe Street, became a proprietary company. He was instrumental in the establishment of a Melbourne branch of the Italian Welfare Association (Comitato Assistenza Italiano) in 1966 to which he gave financial support. In 1972 he created the Gualtiero Vaccari Foundation which endowed a chair of Italian studies at La Trobe University, granted money to the Art Foundation of Victoria to purchase Italian works for the State's national gallery, and established the Elda Vaccari Hostel at North Fitzroy and the Vaccari Italian Historical Trust. He also contributed to the Italian Community Service Fund. His outstanding achievement was as instigator of the Vaccari Homes for the Aged at South Morang.

Handsome, with keen eyes and a ready smile, he was 5 ft. 7 ins. (170.2 cm) tall and solidly built. A modest man who valued courtesy and precision, he kept his own counsel and rarely raised his voice. Vaccari died at his Toorak home on 9 September 1978 and was buried in Boroondara cemetery, Kew. His wife and two sons survived him; his estate was sworn for probate at $153 435. Two portraits are held by the family.

G. Cresciani, *Fascism, anti-fascism and Italians in Australia, 1922-1945* (Canb, 1980); R. Pascoe, *Buongiorno Australia* (Melb, 1987); N. Randazzo and M. Cigler, *The Italians in Australia* (Melb, 1987); M. Montagna, *I rifugiati ebrei italiani in Australia e il movimento antifascista (1942-1946)* [Italia Libera] (Cuneo, Italy, 1987); *Labour Hist*, May 1976, no 30, p 26; C. Finkelstein, untitled ms biog (held by author, Toorak, Melb); Vaccari papers (held by Footscray Inst of Technology, Melb).

ROBERT PASCOE

VALE, MAY (1862-1945), artist, was born on 18 November 1862 at Ballarat, Victoria, second of twelve children of William Mountford Kinsey Vale [q.v.6], stationer, and his wife Rachel, née Lennox, both London born. In 1872 the family moved to Melbourne where May attended Honiton College, St Kilda. During her father's appointment to London in 1874-78, she went to school there and also attended the Royal School of Art at South Kensington. Back in Melbourne, she studied at the National Gallery schools (1879-86, 1888-89) under G. F. Folingsby and Frederick McCubbin [qq.v.4,10]. At Mayfield, built for Georgiana McCrae [q.v.2] and purchased by William Vale in 1886, May gave her first art lessons.

In 1890 she returned to London and studied under Sir James Linton for two years, then attended the Académie Julian in Paris for six months. On her journey home she painted David Syme's [q.v.6] portrait; in 1892 she took a studio in Swanston Street and undertook commissions; in 1895 she moved to Flinders Buildings and set up an art school. A member (1883) of the Buonarotti Society, Vale was a councillor (1900, 1903-04) of the Victorian Artists' Society and foundation member (1888) and councillor (1901-02) of the Yarra Sculptors' Society. Some of her major works were illustrated in that society's 1902 exhibition catalogue. That year she moved to Elizabeth Street. In 1906 Vale again went to London where she studied enamelling at the Chelsea Polytechnic and attended the Burbeck Institute; she also revisited Paris and the Académie Julian. Her pictures were shown in the Australian Exhibition of Women's Work (1907) and at the V.A.S. in 1908. On 20 August at the register office, Chelsea, she married Alexander Gilfillan, a mining engineer and a friend of her youth when they had both been members of the Congregational Church.

Arriving once more in Melbourne, she exhibited in 1909 and 1910, and showed her first enamels with the Yarra Sculptors. In an interview published in *Southern Sphere* (1910) she rightly claimed to be a pioneer of landscape and portraits in enamel, a difficult medium in which she excelled. During World War I she held exhibitions at the V.A.S. (1915) and Besant Hall (1916) before spending time in New South Wales. She returned in 1917 and exhibited work painted there, mostly small panels of the Illawarra Ranges and the south coast.

In 1918 she exhibited for the first time with the Women's Art Club. With the exception of 1922, she exhibited annually throughout the 1920s at the Athenaeum, or in her Oxford Chambers studio where she also held classes. Working in the Australian 'impressionist' tradition, over the next decade she enjoyed painting excursions from her cabin at Diamond Creek. After her husband's death in Singapore in July 1940, May went to live at her brother's house at Black Rock and twice exhibited there during World War II. Although not obtrusive, her personality was vibrant and animated. Pleasant in appearance, with brown hair and eyes, she was robust and independent in attitude. She died on 6 August 1945 at Black Rock and was buried in Cheltenham cemetery. She is represented in the National Gallery of Victoria, the Art Gallery of New South Wales, and regional galleries at Castlemaine and Warrnambool.

L. B. Cox, *The National Gallery of Victoria, 1861 to 1968* (Melb, 1970?); J. Burke (ed), *Australian women artists* (Melb, 1980); Public Lib, Museum and National Gallery of Vic, *Annual Reports*, 1870-1889; *Southern Sphere*, 1 Dec 1910, p 37; Buonarotti Club Minutes (LaTL); Artists files, indexes and press-clippings (Art, Music and Performing Arts Lib, SLV); packet 7 and miscellaneous correspondence, 1872-75, and of National Gallery of Vic, 1871-72 (PRO Vic); family information.

JOYCE MCGRATH

VAN DER SLUICE; *see* RENE

VAN RAALTE, HENRI BENEDICTUS SALAMAN (1881-1929), etcher, was born on 11 February 1881 at Lambeth, London, son of Dutch-born Joel Van Raalte, merchant, and his English wife Frances Elizabeth, née Cable. Educated at the City of London School, St John's Wood Art Schools and the Royal Academy of Arts schools, he became an associate of the Royal Society of Painter-Etchers and Engravers, and exhibited at the Royal Academy of Arts, London. Henri migrated with his brother to Western Australia in 1910 and on 6 July 1912 at the Claremont registrar's office married Katherine Lyell Symers.

As a timber-getter he enjoyed 'bush art-wandering': in his eyes the tuart trees symbolized the grandeur of his adopted landscape and few of his Australian etchings treated the human figure as central. His first major gum tree etching, 'The Monarch' (1918), shown at the Royal Academy in 1920, realized a record price in Australia (£45) and his work was praised by (Sir) Lionel Lindsay [q.v.10] in *Art in Australia* (1918); much of it had an imaginative, disturbed quality.

In 1914 Van Raalte had settled in Perth where, he claimed, 'Art was dead'. He worked in a department store before teaching at several schools; his private classes grew into the Perth School of Art by 1920. In 1916, when Perth's citizens had given him a printing press, his art appeared in the *Westralia gift book.* He held a successful, one-man exhibition in 1919.

Sending work to the Melbourne dealer W. H. Gill, he remarked: 'Some of the stuff is good, some isn't. I like it all because I did it. I regret I didn't do it all better!' It sold well. In 1920 and 1924 there were exhibitions of his work at Preece's [q.v.11] Gallery, Adelaide. Van Raalte was a founder (1920) of the Australian Painter-Etchers' and Graphic Art Society. Considered a pioneer of Australian etching, he also specialized in aquatint and drypoint: his distinctive transmission of mood was more expressionistic than that of his peers, although his prolific output sometimes degenerated to mere scene-recording.

Following Gustave Barnes's [q.v.7] death, in 1922 Van Raalte went to Adelaide to become the curator at the Art Gallery of South Australia. His manner was volatile and outspoken, but the *Advertiser* also found him 'unaffected, courteous and a capital raconteur'. The gallery's crypt was 'a hopeless confusion', with valuable canvases in the cleaners' lavatory. Additional space, conservatorial and curatorial facilities, and extra staff were needed. The collection of works, Van Raalte said drily, made the gallery 'a pleasant backwater'. He developed and catalogued the large print collection. A council-member of the South Australian Society of Arts, he was president of its offshoot, the Sketch Club, which he helped to found. He soon resigned from both the Society of Arts and the Painter-Etchers in protest against mediocrity and 'the shackles imposed . . . by amateurs'. In 1924 the United Arts Club was formed in Adelaide, with Van Raalte as president; it ran a highly successful Artists' Week which exhibited the work of interstate and local artists.

He had strong support among the art fraternity, but next year Van Raalte's problems with some members of the gallery's board intensified. During his absence, the chairman Sir William Sowden [q.v.] overrode his decision not to hang certain inferior works. In January 1926 Van Raalte resigned and issued a press statement calling the board 'a company of ignoramuses'. In March ¡Sowden also resigned.

The etcher retired with his wife, three sons and his press to a rented cottage at Second Valley, on the coast, where he produced some of his finest work. Alcohol became his demon. Despite his acceptance by the local community, to whom the dapper artist was a familiar figure in his old T-model Ford, Van Raalte's melancholy was exacerbated by financial stress. On 4 November 1929, in his wife's absence, he sent two of his sons for the doctor, then shot himself in the head. He died an hour later and was buried in the nearby Bullaparinga cemetery.

In December a memorial exhibition of his work was held in Adelaide. Van Raalte had influenced the development of print-making in Australia during the inter-war years in what was a world-wide revival and he had been one of the first to produce colour etchings. His work is in most State galleries, the Australian National Gallery, the British Museum and in many private collections.

J. Gooding, *Western Australian art and artists 1900-1950* (Perth, 1987); Art Gallery of WA, *Bulletin*, 1979; Art Gallery of SA, *Bulletin*, 1980; *Australasian*, 13 Mar 1926; *Advertiser* (Adel), 6 Nov 1929.   CHRISTABEL CHAPPELL (SPROTT)

VANZETTI, EUGENIO (1844?-1908?), financier and entrepreneur, was born near Verona, Italy. Having studied chemistry and metallurgy, and gained mining experience in France and Spain, he migrated about 1879 with his wife and daughter to New South Wales. As a chemist and medical practitioner in Forbes, Parkes, Mount Hope, Broken Hill and Cobar, he incidentally broadened his knowledge of mining. He was granted approval to mine for gold in New South Wales in 1892 and, as the representative of commercial interests, took his family to the Western Australian goldfields in 1894. To his business drive, Eugenio added the grooming and courtesy 'of a widely travelled and well-read Italian gentleman'. 'I am', he said, 'a staunch believer in the mineral resources and future prosperity of Western Australia'. By 1896 Vanzetti had perhaps more capital than any individual in the colony; he had held Great Boulder shares until they reached £8.

Having travelled to London in 1895, he floated the Water Trust, Mining & Quartz Crushing Co. of Western Australia Ltd with a capital of £250 000 to develop his Golden Pig mine at Southern Cross. For his Colonisation Co., he also visited the area near Lucca, Italy; there, backed by the Italian consul in Sydney, he recruited twenty-five peasants to settle on his Seabrook Estate near Northam, Western Australia. They were to be followed by 300 families to form an Italian colony which would include farmers, winemakers and sericulturists who worked for his companies. He was negotiating to reopen a silver mine at Kendinup and claimed to have floated companies worth £515 000 in London. On this trip he also brought his orphaned nephew Francesco back to Perth.

In June 1896 Vanzetti announced that his Water Trust Co. at Seabrook, on the Yilgarn railway, was ready to begin operations. Its plant included an 80-head stamp battery, assay office, storehouses, blacksmith's shop and rolling-stock from South Australia. The company was to crush ore from the Golden Pig and backload water for sale in Coolgardie. Later that year Vanzetti publicized his Western Australian Industrial & Mining Tramway Co. which proposed to build railways to carry ore to a terminus near Newcastle. Vanzetti again took his wife and daughter to London in 1897 where he planned to capitalize the tramway company to the extent of £2 million. In 1898 he opened the magnificent Alhambra Café in Hay Street, Perth. Next year Vanzetti & Co.'s grandiose schemes were crumbling: changing cost factors rendered his mining ventures unprofitable and the machinery was dismantled.

Turning his attention to the Australian wine industry, in 1900 Vanzetti sailed to Italy; cancer delayed his next foray to London. By 1902, when his wife and daughter arrived in Milan, he had joined an Italian mining company. In 1904 the flow of Italian migrants to Western Australia provoked an outcry and a royal commission on non-British immigrants was established to investigate whether they were arriving under illegal contracts. Alfredo Gaddini, one of Vanzetti's first recruits, was a key witness. Eugenio Vanzetti died probably in Italy in 1908.

W. B. Kimberley, *History of West Australia* (Melb, 1897); J. Gentilli, *Italian roots in Australian soil* (Perth, 1983); *British A'sian*, 2 May, 24 Oct, 28 Nov 1895, 29 Sept 1898, 6 Sept, 13 Dec 1900; *Australasian*, 6 Apr 1895, 4 Jan 1902; *Morning*

Herald, 21 Jan, 8 Feb, 17 June, 29 Oct 1896, 11 Jan 1897.   ROBERT PASCOE

VARDON, JOSEPH (1843-1913), printer and politician, was born on 27 July 1843 at Hindmarsh, Adelaide, eldest son of Ambrose Edward Vardon, shoemaker, and his wife Elizabeth, née Painter. Educated at Moody's School, Hindmarsh, and James Bath's School, North Adelaide, at 13 Joseph found work on a farm before being apprenticed to Henry Denyer Hilton, a printer in the city. On 26 December 1864 Vardon married Mary Ann Pickering (d. 1905) at Brompton. In 1870-74 he published the Strathalbyn *Southern Argus* and in 1871 established Webb, Vardon & Pritchard (later Vardon & Sons Ltd) which grew to be one of Adelaide's biggest printing and publishing companies; it was eventually absorbed by the *Advertiser*. Vardon was president and secretary (for twenty-three years) of the South Australian Typographical Society and belonged to the Master Printers' Association. He became a director of the Adelaide Fruit and Produce Exchange Co. Ltd and State president of the Australian Natives' Association. A Freemason, he was a deacon and in 1892 lay chairman of the South Australian Congregational Union; he studied elocution and in 1904-08 served as president of the Young Men's Christian Association. Mayor of Hindmarsh in 1888-91, he later sat on both the Adelaide and Unley city councils.

Having thrice attempted to win a seat in the House of Assembly, Vardon represented Central in the Legislative Council in 1900-06. He was commissioner of public works and minister of industry (1904-05) in J. G. Jenkins's [q.v.9] government, and chief secretary and minister of industry in (Sir) Richard Butler's [q.v.7] cabinet (March-July 1905). Vardon led the government in the Upper House and advocated the temperance cause. Robust, genial and optimistic, self-made without being ostentatious, he proved a 'plodding' politician, though he was liked and regarded as 'broad-minded', even 'cosmopolitan': he went abroad several times. He was president of the State and national branches of the Liberal Union of Australia in 1910-13, and of the Effective Voting League of South Australia. In 1906 he had been a senator for South Australia, but next year, owing to technical irregularities, his election was declared void. At the fresh election, in 1908, Vardon won easily and held his seat until 1913; unpleasant incidents during that campaign affected his health. Survived by four sons and a daughter, he died of a cerebral haemorrhage on 20 July 1913 in Adelaide and was buried in Hindmarsh cemetery; his estate was sworn for probate at £19 139. The Vardon Memorial Congregational Church at King's Park no longer exists, but Hindmarsh Historical Society holds his portrait.

His eldest son EDWARD CHARLES (1866-1937) was born on 10 November 1866 at Hindmarsh and educated at North Adelaide Grammar School. After joining his father's firm, he became chairman of directors of Mile End Cold Stores Ltd, of the Adelaide Fruit and Produce Exchange Co. Ltd, and of the East End Market. On 28 August 1888 at the Congregational Church, Port Adelaide, he married Ellen Peel. He was president of the South Australian Chamber of Manufacturers (1910-12) and of its federal body, and sat on the Apprentices Advisory Board of South Australia. Like his father, he was a Freemason. Edward was a National (1918-21) and Liberal (1924-30) member for Sturt in the House of Assembly; in 1921-22 he was a senator for South Australia. Although sincere and charming, he never won the respect accorded his father. Survived by his daughter, Edward died of coronary thrombosis on 23 February 1937 at Unley Park and was cremated.

H. T. Burgess (ed), *Cyclopedia of South Australia*, 1 (Adel, 1907); *PP* (SA), 1887 (27), 1907 (51) (52) (61), 1921 (24); *Quiz* (Adel), 3 Mar 1905; *Mail* (Adel), 18 May 1912; *Advertiser* (Adel), 21 July 1913, 17 Feb 1921, 24 Feb 1937; *Register* (Adel), 21 July 1913; *Chronicle* (Adel) and *Observer* (Adel), 26 July 1913.   MALCOLM SAUNDERS

VARLEY, GEORGE HENRY GISBORNE (1852-1936), journalist and politician, was born on 7 April 1852 in London, son of William Waterloo Gisborne Varley, picture-dealer, and his wife Ann, née Daston. With his parents, he reached Sydney on 4 September 1856 in the *Lloyds*; having attended school at Maitland, he joined the *Maitland Ensign* in 1866 as an apprentice. He later moved to the Wallsend *Miner's Advocate*, a small weekly started by James Fletcher [q.v.4], transferring with it on the paper's incorporation into the *Newcastle Morning Herald* in 1876. Catering to public interest, Varley introduced reports on handball, athletics and coursing as special features; he also acted as handicapper for the Wallsend Jockey Club and was secretary of the Wallsend and Plattsburg Athletic Club. In covering the first race meeting at Tamworth (1878), he wrote a comprehensive review of the district.

At West Maitland registry office Varley had married 16-year-old Jane Louise Brackenreg, daughter of an innkeeper, on 26 January 1871. Moving his family to Grafton when he became manager and part-owner of the bi-weekly *Clarence and Richmond Examiner* in

1881, he involved himself in community organizations, such as the Grafton Water Brigade, and continued his interest in athletics. By 1887 he was sole proprietor of the *Examiner* and turned his tri-weekly into a leading provincial newspaper. He remained sole proprietor, manager and editor until 1905 when he moved to Sydney and undertook the duties of the metropolitan office, exercising control through local staff heads. In 1915 a Grafton company, including (Sir) Earle Page [q.v.11], was formed and the paper became the *Daily Examiner*; Varley retained a controlling interest.

His championing of dairy farmers aided the establishment of the Grafton Dairy Co. Ltd, of which he was chairman. Varley persuaded the New South Wales Fresh Food & Ice Co. Ltd to operate on the Clarence, with strategically located creameries. A leading member of the Clarence River Railway Construction and Harbour Improvement League, he lobbied hard but unsuccessfully for the Clarence-New England connexion, then turned his attention to the construction of the coastal line. He was a generous supporter, lay canon and synodsman of the Church of England, and displayed a liberal and catholic spirit in the publication of religious news.

In 1904 Varley became a director (later managing director) of the New South Wales Country Press Co-operative Co. Ltd (Country Press Ltd from 1921). As a committee-member of the Sydney Chamber of Commerce, he served on its country sectional committee. He was also a committee-member of the Australian Provincial Press Association (1909-27), a member of the Empire Press Union, a councillor of the Metalliferous Mining Association and belonged to the Aborigines Protection Board (1910-16).

Nominated to the Legislative Council in 1917, Varley proved a sturdy champion of country interests, but did not seek election to the reconstituted House in 1933. Later years saw him increasingly active as a vice-president of the Royal Agricultural Society of New South Wales. Survived by his wife, two daughters and four sons, Varley died on 28 April 1936 at his Bellevue Hill home and was buried in South Head cemetery.

SMH, 7 May 1917, 9 Apr 1924, 16 Nov 1932, 29 Mar 1934, 30 Apr 1936; *Sun* (Syd), 7 Apr 1924; *Daily Examiner* (Grafton), 30 Apr, 1 May 1936; information from Mrs N. Mackey, Grafton, Mrs M. Timbrell and Mrs R. Howell, Lismore, NSW.

JOHN ATCHISON

VAUDE, CHARLIE (1882?-1942), comedian and radio personality, was born probably on 9 June 1882 in London, son of Charles John Ridgway, printer, and his wife Mary, née McCarthy. Named Charles Joseph, he was reared and educated 'within the sound of Bow-bells'. In his youth he frequented music-halls and learned to imitate the patter and songs of such comedians as George Robey and Wilkie Bard. Because his family opposed a stage career, Charles became an errand-boy and later a carpenter's apprentice. Keen to be free of his indentures, he lied about his age and enlisted at Guildford, eventually joining the Royal West Surrey Regimental Band and playing at Edward VII's coronation.

About 1902 Ridgway migrated with his family to Australia. During two years as a casual labourer in Western Australia he pursued his interest in the stage, but found Perth a theatrical 'graveyard'. Seeking backing for his pierrot show, he went to Adelaide and obtained an engagement at Broken Hill where he met Bill Bartington. Ridgway adopted the name 'Charlie Vaude' and, with Bartington, formed the team of 'Vaude and Verne' in a double act which they took to Melbourne and to New Zealand for (Sir) Benjamin Fuller [q.v.8].

Before long 'Vaude and Verne' appeared at Harry Rickards's [q.v.11] Opera House in Melbourne. On the Tivoli circuit their act consisted of quick-fire patter, topical gags and songs, with Vaude ad-libbing on prominent personalities. From 1911 they worked for Hugh D. McIntosh [q.v.10]. While on tour in North Queensland after World War I under Birch, Carroll [q.v.7] & Coyle Ltd, Vaude leased a Rockhampton theatre and formed his own company. When his lease expired he traversed Queensland as far west as Longreach. By then, his type of live theatre was in decline.

In 1930 Vaude was hired by 3DB as an experiment to 'pep-up' its radio advertising. He soon proved his worth during the station's night broadcasts of the 1930 Test cricket matches in England. With a new straight man, the portly Renn Millar, Charlie provided gags and songs to keep the audience amused while the experts deciphered the vital information from cables. The programme resumed in 1934 and in 1938. Other triumphs followed, among them the 'Smile Away Club' which in 1937 boasted 37 000 members, including Prime Minister Lyons [q.v.10] and his wife. Charlie joked and sang on 3DB's C. & G. Minstrel Show, hosted community singing and tours of country towns, and acted as the ratbag professor of Bonehead College. He was a mainstay of 3DB's charity effort. His name was a household word and his humour was always clean.

Ridgway was married twice: on 25 September 1911 at St Jude's Anglican Church, Carlton, to 17-year-old Lilias May Roots (d. 1931), an actress, and on 5 October 1935 at Northcote with Presbyterian forms to Leila

Halliday Sach, a dancer. He died of cancer on 29 October 1942 at his Northcote home and was buried in Melbourne general cemetery. His wife and the son of his first marriage survived him. Gregarious, talkative and funny, Vaude was much loved; in returning that attachment, he showed an understanding of his public's need for mirth and camaraderie in the hard years of the Depression.

B. McLaughlin, *From wireless to radio* (Melb, nd); C. A. Grant, *500 Victorians* (Melb, 1934); *Table Talk*, 21 Aug 1930; *Sporting Globe*, 10, 17, 24 June 1939; *Sun News-Pictorial*, 30 Oct 1942; information and memorabilia held by Mrs L. H. Vaude, Elwood, Melb.   DAVID DUNSTAN

VAUGHAN, CRAWFORD (1874-1947), premier and journalist, and JOHN HOWARD (1879-1955), lawyer and politician, were brothers. Crawford was born on 14 July 1874 in Adelaide, eldest son of Alfred Vaughan, civil servant, and his wife Louisa, née Williams; Crawford's grandfathers had been Chartists. From Norwood and Marryatville public schools, he attended Prince Alfred College in 1888-89. Beginning his working life as a clerk, he ventured briefly to the Western Australian goldfields, returned to Adelaide where he was employed by the Crown Lands Department and in the late 1890s practised freelance journalism.

Secretary (1899-1904) of the Single Tax League of South Australia, Vaughan was also a committee-member of the Effective Voting League. In 1898 he campaigned unsuccessfully for the Anti-Commonwealth Bill League. A clever writer, in 1899-1904 Vaughan edited *Quiz*, a radical newspaper, and opposed the British cause in the South African War. Running as an Independent, he was defeated for the House of Representatives (1901), the House of Assembly seat of Torrens (1902) and the Senate (1903). A Unitarian, on 8 June 1906 at Norwood he married Evelyn Maria Goode (d. 1927), a novelist and member of the Women's Non-Party Political Association.

Joining the United Labor Party in 1904, Vaughan won Torrens at the State election next year. Earnest and quietly-spoken, he rose within Labor's hierarchy: honorary secretary (1905-06), vice-president (1907-08) and president (1908-09) of the party, he was parliamentary whip in April-June 1909. His sister Dorothy [q.v.] was simultaneously making her way in the U.L.P. On 3 June 1910 Vaughan became treasurer and commissioner of crown lands and immigration in John Verran's [q.v.] ministry. A polished parliamentarian, Vaughan developed into an effective administrator: the conservative *Register* considered him 'one of the intellectual forces

of the House of Assembly'. In 1910 he secured legislation which gave the government power to purchase compulsorily large estates for closer settlement. Verran's government was defeated in 1912; when he resigned in July 1913, caucus elected Vaughan to the parliamentary leadership unopposed.

He built support for Labor, particularly in rural areas; his moderation and white-collar background endeared him to many among Adelaide's middle classes. Vaughan helped Labor to overcome the Liberal Union's electoral redistribution of 1913 and to win a majority of six in the 1915 election at which he was returned for the seat of Sturt.

Unusually young, at 40, for a premier, he held as well the portfolios of treasurer and minister of education, and dominated the government. Most of his ministers had little experience of trade unions who scathingly called the cabinet the 'black-coated brigade'. The inclusion of the premier's brother Howard and his brother-in-law Clarence Goode made the ministry appear clannish. For all that, it substantially improved the education system by restructuring the department's senior bureaucracy, by extending the years of compulsory school attendance and by providing better facilities for the intellectually and physically disabled. Moreover, the government enabled women to serve in the police force and as justices of the peace, while it also improved workers' access to the arbitration system and diminished the court's punitive powers against trade unions. Legislation introduced in 1915-16 established war service land and housing schemes, in addition to a wheat pool. Although often frustrated by a hostile Upper House, the government's legislative achievements were generally impressive. In 1915, however, it passed a law designed to close Lutheran primary schools, thus discriminating against South Australians of German origin. Lack of fiscal restraint was the administration's major weakness: the budget deficit almost trebled.

Beyond parliament, Crawford Vaughan's moderate reformism proved unacceptable to impatient radicals in the U.L.P. With the Australian Workers' Union, they demanded more far-reaching legislation throughout 1915-16. For reasons of temperament and with an eye to electoral reality, the premier refused. Strained relations between Vaughan and the A.W.U.'s secretary F. W. Lundie [q.v.10] were exacerbated in 1916: the premier announced his approval of the introduction of conscription for compulsory military service overseas; in September he convened the National Referendum Council to promote the 'Yes' campaign in the plebiscite. To Lundie and the U.L.P.'s anti-conscription industrial wing, Vaughan's stand was confirmation that he should not represent working-class Labor voters. In February 1917, after prolonged inter-factional abuse and Lundie's uncompromising lobbying, Vaughan and other Labor parliamentarians who had favoured conscription (most of caucus) were declared by a U.L.P. conference to be disloyal to the party. Regarding the decision as 'intolerable and vindictive', Vaughan and his allies formed the National Labor Party, later styling themselves the National Party. Apart from losing some of its best parliamentary talent, Labor's expulsion of Vaughan and his followers virtually signalled the end of middle-class influence within the party for decades.

Vaughan's government lost its majority as a result of the split. Convinced that public opinion backed him, he clung to the premiership: he argued that, if the National Party held its ground, the Liberal Union would eventually be compelled to participate in a National-dominated coalition. Even when the Liberals defeated the government on an adjournment motion in July 1917, Vaughan remained optimistic. Despite his private attempts to persuade their financial backers to force Liberal politicians into line and his spurious public claims that they may have been influenced by 'German' interests, the Liberals held firm. After much dispute, they offered Vaughan and the Nationalists a minority role in a coalition cabinet: concerned that the public had tired of inter-party squabbling, in August the Nationalists accepted.

Incensed by his colleagues' betrayal, Vaughan declared that they 'were like a lot of panic-stricken sheep, quite willing to be driven either to the shearing shed or the slaughter-house'. He refused a post in A. H. Peake's [q.v.11] coalition cabinet. Feeling 'a bit nervy', in November Vaughan accepted an invitation from the government of the United States of America to lecture to industrialists in that country on their duty to support the war effort. While abroad, he unsuccessfully tried to retain Sturt at the 1918 election by standing as an Independent Nationalist and allowing his wife to campaign on his behalf. His approaches to interstate Nationalist Party contacts to pre-select him for a seat in the House of Representatives also failed. Vaughan remained in America throughout 1918, at first attached to Lord Reading's British War Mission to the United States and later as an honorary representative of the Australian government. He spoke in twenty-one States and met President Wilson. Next year Vaughan was a delegate of the English-Speaking Union at the Paris peace conference; he then lectured in Britain. In 1920 he delivered the Lowell lectures at Boston, on Australian industrial legislation.

From 1920 Vaughan lived mainly in Sydney where he dabbled in business as managing director (1921-24) of the British-Australian Cotton-Growing Association; in the early 1930s he became involved in several unremunerative gold-mining ventures. He had unsuccessfully contested the New South Wales Legislative Assembly seat of Ryde as a member of the Progressive Party in 1925 and Hartley as a Nationalist in 1927. Involved in several conservative lobby groups, in 1929 he was campaign director of the New South Wales Prohibition Alliance; in 1936-38 he was honorary secretary of the British-American Co-operation Movement for world peace; and he was briefly secretary of the Professional Business Men's Association of New South Wales. On 29 May 1934 Vaughan married Millicent Fanny Preston Stanley [q.v.11] at St John's Church, Toorak, Melbourne. In 1933-35 he was chief leader-writer for the Adelaide *News*. He also wrote radio plays and books, publishing *Golden wattle time* (Sydney, 1942), a fictional account of Adam Lindsay Gordon's [q.v.4] life, and *The last of Captain Bligh* [q.v.1] (London, 1950). Survived by his wife and by a daughter of his first marriage, Vaughan died at Elizabeth Bay, Sydney, on 15 December 1947. After a state funeral in Adelaide, he was buried with Anglican rites in Centennial Park cemetery. His estate was sworn for probate at £860.

His brother Howard was born on 14 November 1879 at Norwood. He attended the local public school and Prince Alfred College (1894-96), won the 1898 Roby Fletcher [q.v.4] scholarship for logic and psychology, and graduated at the University of Adelaide (LL.B., 1900). Admitted to the Bar in 1901, Howard formed a partnership with R. P. A. von Bertouch. He also joined the Effective Voting League. Having drafted South Australia's first bill for proportional electoral representation in 1902, he saw it annually rejected by parliament on eight occasions. Between 1906 and 1910 he thrice unsuccessfully contested the House of Representatives seat of Wakefield for Labor before winning the South Australian Legislative Council seat of Central in 1912. He was vice-president (1911-13) of the South Australian Tramway Employees' Association and president (1913-14) of the State branch of the U.L.P. A Unitarian, on 11 August 1909 Howard married Heléna Maud Fry (d. 1954) at St Matthew's Church, Adelaide: they were to remain childless.

On 3 April 1915 he became attorney-general in his brother's ministry. Although able and gifted with 'an engaging personality', he produced little progressive legislation. His support for conscription brought about his banishment from the U.L.P. in 1917. In July Howard Vaughan enlisted in the 10th Battalion, Australian Imperial Force; on active service in France, he was commissioned in

314

November 1918 and returned to Australia next year. He unsuccessfully contested the House of Assembly seat of Sturt as a Progressive Country Party candidate in 1921.

In Adelaide he resumed his legal practice with K. H. Kirkman as a partner in the 1920s and K. L. Litchfield in 1936-41. Vaughan sat on the Burnside District Council (1921-29) and was chairman (1921-42) of the local branch of the Australian League of Nations Union. Appointed C.B.E. in 1932, he was State consul for Czechoslovakia in 1929-37 and was awarded that country's Order of the White Lion in 1937. Howard Vaughan died in Adelaide on 21 August 1955 and was buried in Centennial Park cemetery.

F. S. Wallis, *Labour's thirty years record in South Australia* (Adel, 1923); *Lone Hand*, 1 July 1915; *Univ Studies in History*, vol 4, no 2, 1963-64; *Advertiser* (Adel), 24 July 1913, 17 Apr 1945, 16 Dec 1947, 24 Aug 1955; *Register* (Adel), 29 Mar, 2 Apr 1915; S. Weeks, The relationship between the Australian Workers' Union and the South Australian Labor Party, 1908-1918 (B.A. Hons thesis, Flinders Univ, 1981); G. Grainger, The Liberal Union-National Party coalition government in South Australia 1917-1920 (M.A. thesis, Flinders Univ, 1983); Aust League of Nations Union, SA branch, Official Reports (Mortlock Lib); CP 360/11 (AA, Canb).   G. GRAINGER

VAUGHAN, DOROTHY (1881-1974), social reformer, was born on 22 October 1881 at Norwood, Adelaide, daughter of Alfred Vaughan, civil servant, and his wife Louisa, née Williams. Proud of her Chartist forbears, she took part in her family's wideranging political and social discussions; like her brothers Crawford and John Howard [qq.v.], she advocated social justice and equality of the sexes. Her calm expression, sturdy build and serious nature did not inhibit her 'sparkle of fun'.

Despite never earning her living, Dorothy joined the United Labor Party and in 1910 organized a women's branch at Norwood; she became secretary of an 'All Nations' fair which raised funds for Labor's *Daily Herald* and 'gave the impetus' for country Labor women's committees. In 1913, under Howard Vaughan's presidency, she was among three women elected to the U.L.P. executive and initiated improved women's organization. As Unitarian representative on the British Girls' Welfare League in 1912-14, she assisted immigrant 'domestic helpers'; she had participated in the Unitarian Women's League from its foundation (1912). Appointed a justice of the peace in 1917, she later presided over the Women Justices' Association. In 1927-29 she was one of three female directors of the Adelaide Co-operative

Society Ltd and demonstrated her concern for poor families.

Dorothy helped to redraft the Women's Non-Party Political Association's platform in 1912. President in 1932-35, she envisaged a new social order: she guided campaigns for equal parental guardianship, improved children's courts, the appointment of women to public boards, and—with Jeanne Young [q.v.] —for proportional representation. In the Woman's Christian Temperance Union from 1936 to 1954 she was at different times State superintendent of 'equal citizenship', 'petitions and legislative', and 'prison work'. President of the Henley Beach Union in 1949-54, she also supported single-tax leagues.

In 1916 the Crawford Vaughan government had appointed her to the State Children's Council. It was responsible for wards of the state: their detention or placement in private homes, their release, and the supervision of foster-mothers and illegitimate children. Miss Vaughan was the visitor for Rose Park and an active council-member. Lacking the expertise and resources to meet the children's needs, the councillors were derided by A. A. Edwards [q.v.8] for their ineffectual gentility. In 1927 Miss Vaughan was an assiduous foundation member of the Children's Welfare and Public Relief Board which replaced the council. Her concern for 'wayward' girls contributed to the closure of Barton Vale Reformatory which was reopened as Vaughan House Training School for Girls in 1947. Its inmates often stayed overnight with her and visited her after their release. Appointed M.B.E. in 1954, she retired from the board in 1962, a bespectacled, benign old lady.

She was devoted to her brother Howard and her decades of unpaid public work epitomized the social idealism of their time. Dorothy Vaughan died on 14 July 1974 at the Methodist Aldersgate Village, Felixstow, Adelaide, and was cremated.

M. Harry, *A century of service* (Adel, 1986); *PP* (SA), 1928 (23), 1948 (23), 1963 (23); *Weekly Herald* (Adel), 3 May 1913; *Register* (Adel), 2 Jan 1915; *Advertiser* (Adel), 1 Jan 1954, 22 Dec 1962; Children's Welfare and Public Relief Bd, Minutes, 1927-28, *and* State Children's Council, Minutes, 1916-27 (PRO SA); League of Women Voters, Minutes (misc), 1909-15, 1927-36, *and* Minutes of Executive and Cttee Meetings, 28 Feb 1912, July 1932-35, *and* League of Unitarian and other Christian Women, Minutes, 1914-26 *and* Woman's Christian Temperance Union, Annual Reports, 1936-54 (Mortlock Lib); information from Mrs P. Duguid, Kent Town, Adel.   HELEN JONES

VAUGHAN, MILLICENT; *see* PRESTON STANLEY

315

VENN, HENRY WHITTALL (1844-1908), pastoralist and politician, was born on 27 October 1844 in Adelaide, second son of Robert Venn, a prosperous butcher of Port Adelaide, and his wife Elizabeth, née Evans. Locally schooled, Harry worked for the merchandisers Ormond & Co. at Robe, then joined the Melbourne-based Denison Plains Pastoral Co. which was planning to start a sheep-station in the remote north of Western Australia. The company's representatives arrived at Fremantle in 1865 but never reached their goal. In 1866 Venn took part in two exploring parties in the Pilbara before taking up Karratha station on the Maitland River. Starting with one hundred of the company's sheep and some Hereford cattle, he increased his stock to 8000 before selling out in 1878. He settled at Dardanup and Prinsep Park, two properties in the fertile south-west, near Bunbury. Here he spent the rest of his life with his wife Charlotte, sister of (Sir) George Shenton [q.v.6], whom he had married on 10 December 1874; they were to adopt three sons.

In February 1880 he won the Legislative Council seat of Wellington by one vote from the long-serving (Sir) James Steere [q.v.] and kept it until 1901, transferring in 1890 to the Legislative Assembly when parliament became bicameral. An advocate of bold developmental policies and responsible government, Venn came to the fore in 1882 as spokesman for a land-grant railway to the Kimberley district. In 1887 he chaired an important royal commission on agriculture which, in over three years of activity, made 'many long and tedious journeys, at seasons not always the most pleasant or convenient'. The Venn commission's findings foreshadowed the great agricultural push of the early twentieth century: the commission confirmed Western Australia's suitability for wheat-growing and dairying, advocated the planting of softwoods, and recommended an agricultural bank, agricultural education and government repurchase of large estates for subdivision. In 1889 Venn also chaired an inquiry into disease among cattle.

When self-government came in 1890, Venn was commissioner of railways and director of public works in (Sir) John Forrest's [q.v.8] ministry. In five years Venn trebled the mileage of government railways, doubled their earnings and kept down costs. He backed the development of Western Australia's first coalfield at Collie. The unprecedented pressures of a gold rush, however, placed great strain on the transport system and public complaints grew. In 1894 Forrest considered transferring Venn to the Lands Department, but did not. In September 1895 Venn was widely attacked in parliament, one member complaining that his 'pompous manner seemed to say "stand on one side"'. A bald, portly man, with a red face and heavy moustache, conventional and prolix, Venn was more competent than his manner suggested, but found himself inadequately supported and was no master of public relations. In February 1896 a Perth public meeting passed resolutions against the railway administration. Forrest asserted that funds for additional rolling-stock had never been refused. Sensing implied censure, Venn accused Forrest in the press of disloyalty. When asked to resign from the ministry, he refused three times; on 8 March Forrest requested Governor Sir Gerard Smith [q.v.11] to withdraw Venn's commission. As Venn put it, he was 'dismissed in his nightshirt'.

The rest was anticlimax. A convinced Federationist, Venn was a substitute delegate to the Australasian Federal Convention from August 1897 but made no mark. In 1900 he was Western Australian commissioner to the international exhibitions at Paris and Glasgow. Out of parliament after April 1901, he failed to win the Federal seat of Perth in 1903; next year he applied unsuccessfully to become agent-general in London. Considered an austere recluse, Venn passed his final years at Dardanup where he died of heart disease on 8 March 1908; he was buried in the Anglican section of Bunbury cemetery. His estate was sworn for probate with a deficit of £7844.

Roy Com on agriculture, Report, *V&P* (WA), 1891-92 (1); *PD* (WA), 1895, p 905; *West Australian*, 28 Feb-11 Mar 1896; *Bunbury Herald*, 10, 12 Mar 1908; B. Gleeson, The life of H. W. Venn (ms, Battye Lib).

G. C. BOLTON

VENNARD, ALEXANDER VINDEX (1884-1947), journalist, was born on 11 July 1884 at Vindex station, near Winton, Queensland, son of Irish-born Joseph Vennard, labourer, and his Scottish wife Jane, née Sutherland. In 1890 the family moved to the Normanton district whence, at 13, Alexander stowed away and worked for two years on pearling luggers in Torres Strait. After rejoining his family and attending school in Brisbane, he resumed his adventures in the Pacific until he contracted malaria.

Establishing himself as a journalist in Brisbane, he worked at Bowen and Proserpine before becoming editor of the *Port Denison Times*. On 13 October 1910 he married Isabel Emily Nicol with Presbyterian forms at Proserpine. The couple settled in Sydney where Vennard wrote for the *Sydney Morning Herald, Sun, Bulletin* and London *Daily Mail.* Again smitten by wanderlust, he took his swag and left home in 1913. At Coonamble, as 'Frank Reid', he enlisted in the 18th Battalion, Australian Imperial Force, on 5 April 1915; by October he was fighting on Gallipoli with the 5th Brigade.

Evacuated to Egypt, Reid contributed articles to local and English newspapers. He transferred to the Imperial Camel Corps and served in the Libyan desert, Sinai and Palestine. Described as a 'hard case' who 'never shirked his duty or his punishments', he was wounded and hospitalized at Gaza in 1917. At Moascar camp, near Ismailia, he met David Barker with whom in 1918 he produced *Kia Ora Coo-ee*, a monthly magazine for Australian and New Zealand troops. When Charles Barrett [q.v.7] joined them, circulation rose from 3000 to 15 000. After being discharged in Sydney in May 1919, Reid wrote short stories for *Smith's Weekly* for nearly two years.

Lured to the north, he contributed articles to *Cummins* [q.v.8] & *Campbell's Monthly Magazine*, and a regular column 'On the Track' for the *North Queensland Register*, Townsville, for about twenty-five years. He adopted the pseudonym 'Bill Bowyang' after the straps buckled over trousers below the knees. Collecting yarns, ballads and anecdotes about bush life, and gathering contributions from readers, Vennard published—in addition to his column—at least nine booklets of 'bush recitations'. As 'Frank Reid' he also wrote *Toilers of the reef* (1925), a book for children, and *The fighting cameliers* (1934), a breezy, historical narrative permeated with digger insouciance. His *Romance of the Great Barrier Reef* was published posthumously (1954). He wrote other occasional pieces under the pen-names 'Island Exile', 'Island Trader', 'Wirraroo', 'Fossicker', 'Maurice Dean' and 'Frank Neil'. Having risen from printer's devil to author, he knew every line of the Inky Way.

A constant friend to bushmen and 'diggers', Vennard in later life had a bedraggled appearance: 'His black creased shoes were untied; his unpressed serge pants were held by a leather belt and he wore an open necked khaki shirt. He was stout, and his rugged features proclaimed him as a lover of the open spaces'. He had huge hands and kindly grey eyes. Survived by his wife, two sons and two daughters, Vennard died of heart disease in Bowen hospital on 16 February 1947 and was buried in the local cemetery.

E. M. Barker, *The story of 'Bill Bowyang'* (Bowen, Qld, 1978); *Kia Ora Coo-ee*, 15 July 1918; *Topic*, 19 June 1947; *Cummins & Campbell's Monthly Mag*, Mar 1947; *Islands Review*, 1, no 4, Jan-Mar 1969, p 14; *Bowen Independent*, Oct 1924, 28 May 1927; *Nth Qld Register*, 1 Dec 1973.

HUGH ANDERSON

VERBRUGGHEN, HENRI ADRIEN MARIE (1873-1934), musician, was born on 1 August 1873 in Brussels, only son of Henri Joseph Verbrugghen, textile manufacturer, and his wife Elisa, née Derode. He made his début at the age of 9. With the support of Eugène Ysaÿe and Joseph Wieniawski, Henri overcame parental determination that he study medicine and in 1886 entered the Royal Conservatoire of Music of Brussels, graduating with first prize in 1889. Having visited London with Ysaÿe in 1888, Verbrugghen gave violin recitals in England, but declined to make a world tour with Amy Sherwin [q.v.6] in 1890 and worked mainly in Belgium as an orchestral violinist.

From 1893 he played intermittently with the new Scottish Orchestra Company at Glasgow, becoming concertmaster and assistant conductor under (Sir) Frederic Cowen in 1903. Verbrugghen played with summer orchestras in Wales at Llandudno (1895-97) —where he married the singer Alice Emma Beatrice Beaumont on 21 September 1898 in the parish church—and Colwyn Bay (1898-1902). Appointed professor of violin, chamber music, orchestra and opera at the Glasgow Athenæum in 1904, he was also professor of violin at the Royal Irish Academy of Music, Dublin, and appeared as soloist with the Berlin Philharmonic Orchestra. For four seasons from 1903 he was concertmaster for the Queen's Hall Orchestra summer promenade concerts in London under (Sir) Henry Wood.

His interest in conducting stimulated by Ysaÿe, Verbrugghen studied closely the techniques of the conductors under whom he played, among them Saint-Saëns, Lamoureux and Kes. He appeared often as a soloist and in 1907 gave the English première of the Sibelius concerto; he also played in string quartets, forming his own in 1903. In 1911 he was appointed conductor of the Glasgow Choral Union. Although he conducted in Paris, Brussels, Berlin, Munich and St Petersburg, his greatest success was a five-day Beethoven Festival with the London Symphony Orchestra and the Leeds choir in 1914.

Chosen directly from 173 applicants by A. C. Carmichael [q.v.7], in 1915 Verbrugghen was selected as foundation director of the New South Wales State Conservatorium of Music for a term of five years. He reached Sydney in August, followed by his wife and family next February. His early staff appointments included Roland Foster, Alfred Hill, Frank Hutchens, Cyril Monk and Arundel Orchard [qq.v.8,9,10,11]. An inspiring teacher, Verbrugghen himself took classes in advanced chamber music, the diploma, the select choir and the students' orchestra. He was determined to establish an institution of international standing and one in the

European rather than the English musical tradition.

His energy and charm persuaded the government to bring out the other members of the Verbrugghen String Quartet and to provide musical scholarships. The quartet gave twenty-four concerts each year (the entire corpus by Beethoven being always included) and Verbrugghen made introductory talks a popular feature of these performances. He also established a symphony orchestra of 45 members (96 after three years) which rapidly acquired an outstanding reputation and became the New South Wales State Orchestra. It toured New Zealand, Melbourne and Adelaide, as well as giving numerous concerts in Sydney and at the conservatorium. In 1921 the orchestra gave 180 concerts, most of which Verbrugghen conducted. An instance of his drive and his passion for Beethoven (a London critic had called him 'the Beethoven conductor *par excellence*') was the thirteen performances of the *Missa solemnis* that he directed over three years.

Verbrugghen acquired a few enemies (he insisted, for instance, on proper decorum at concerts) and by 1921 his orchestra was in financial difficulties when John Storey's [q.v.] government decided to withdraw support unless substantial funds were guaranteed by public subscription. A Melbourne fund was established under Sir James Barrett [q.v.7] and the New South Wales fund was directed by Ernest Wunderlich [q.v.]. That year T. D. Mutch [q.v.10], the minister of public instruction, offered a three-year extension of Verbrugghen's directorship at £1500 a year and a maximum fee of £1500 annually as conductor (£20 per concert). The proposed fees proved unacceptable to Verbrugghen: he had received 'not one penny piece' for conducting and felt that the government did not want the director to earn more than a senior bureaucrat.

He took extended leave in 1922, visiting Britain and the United States of America. After conducting the Detroit Symphony Orchestra, he was invited by the chairman of the Minneapolis Symphony Orchestra to be one of five guest conductors for the 1922-23 season. Within two months he was offered a three-year contract as permanent conductor at a salary of $25 000. Negotiations with the New South Wales government continued, but agreement could not be reached. Verbrugghen formally resigned his Sydney position late in 1922 and began a successful nine-year term with the Minneapolis Symphony Orchestra; the other members of his quartet joined him.

As in Sydney, he broadened the repertoire with works by Stravinsky, Honegger and Bloch, sometimes to the outrage of his subscribers; he often reduced the strings when conducting Beethoven in the interests of authentic balance. His performances were said to be of the 'cerebro-dramatic school of conductors' and he was described as a 'flaming little volcano' on the podium. Verbrugghen's interest in novelty and experiment led him to include jazz-influenced works in his concerts and to employ a pillowslip full of peanut shells to achieve a particular sound in his orchestration of Hill's song, 'Waiata Poi'. He made few solo appearances for he found the concomitant nervousness debilitating.

With an elegant, waxed moustache and 'dark eyes so bright and keen that they convey a sense of inextinguishable youth', Verbrugghen was 'one of those short men who produce a tall effect on the beholder'. A colleague described him as genial in temperament, but capable of being domineering when the occasion demanded it. He had a fund of stories, 'some decidedly Rabelaisian in character', and a surprising fondness for horses and their breeding. A man of wide knowledge with highly cultivated tastes, he was especially well-informed on painting and sculpture. 'Most performers', he once observed, 'practise too much and think too little. Knowing history, philosophy and other things helps make a good musician'.

On 26 October 1931 Verbrugghen suffered a cerebral haemorrhage and collapsed during a rehearsal. He recovered sufficiently to head the music department of Carleton College, Northfield, Minnesota, but never directed his orchestra again. Survived by his wife, daughter and three sons, he died of hypertensive renal disease on 12 November 1934 at Northfield and was cremated.

NSW Conservatorium of Music, *Programme, Beethoven Festival,* 18-22 October 1920 at Adelaide Town Hall (Syd, 1920); W. A. Orchard, *The distant view* (Syd, 1943) and *Music in Australia* (Melb, 1952); R. Foster, *Come listen to my song* (Syd, 1949); *Musical Times* (Lond), 1 June 1914, p 369, 1 June 1930, p 497; *Theatre Mag,* 1 July 1915, p 17; *Lone Hand,* 1 Oct 1915, p 324; *SMH,* 22 June 1922, 3 Jan 1923, 14, 15 Nov 1934; *New York Times,* 13 Nov 1934; Carleton College Archives, Northfield, Minnesota, USA; K. Hince collection (NL); Verbrugghen family collection (held by Mrs W. D. McFarland, Fort Benton, Montana, USA).

JOHN CARMODY

VERCO, SIR JOSEPH COOKE (1851-1933), physician and conchologist, was born on 1 August 1851 at Fullarton, Adelaide, sixth child of James Crabb Verco, builder, and his wife Ann, née Cooke, both from Cornwall, England. A serious boy, Joseph made a museum of shells in his backyard. He attended J. L. Young's [q.v.6] Adelaide Educational Institution (1863-67) and worked briefly for the South Australian railways before entering the Collegiate School of St Peter. Enrolling at the University of London (M.B., 1875; M.D., 1876; B.S., 1877), he won four gold medals. He was admitted as licentiate of the Royal College of Physicians (1875) and fellow of the Royal College of Surgeons (1877), and became a midwifery assistant at St Bartholomew's Hospital (1877).

Returning to South Australia, Verco registered as a general practitioner in 1878, but gradually specialized as a physician and proved a skilled diagnostician. He was one of the earliest doctors in Adelaide to use a case-records system: when this became onerous, he learned shorthand. Honorary physician at the Adelaide Hospital and honorary medical officer at the Adelaide Children's Hospital, he attempted in 1888 to remove a hydatid of the brain in one of the first of such operations in Australia. With (Sir) Edward Stirling [q.v.6], Verco had founded the University of Adelaide's medical school in 1885; he was a precise, if unexciting, lecturer in medicine (1887-1915) and also a clinical teacher at the Adelaide Hospital; his students found him reserved, punctilious and severe, and nicknamed him 'holy Joe'.

Despite an attack of enteric fever, in 1887 Verco presided over the first Intercolonial Medical Congress of Australasia which was held in Adelaide. He was a foundation member and president (1886 and 1914-19) of the South Australian branch of the British Medical Association and a council-member of the University of Adelaide (1895-1902 and 1919-33). His most important publications were his entries in T. C. Allbutt's A system of medicine (London, 1897, 1907) and his review (1879) of South Australian statistics on consumption.

A devout member of the Churches of Christ, Dr Verco was a Sunday School superintendent and a temperance advocate; he gave generously to the Kermode Street Church in North Adelaide where he worshipped. He also wrote hymns and religious poetry. The flowing black beard of his youth was later trimmed to a point; his grave dignity was matched by his formal dress. On 13 April 1911 at North Adelaide he married Mary Isabella Mills. Recognized as the city's leading physician, he was knighted on his retirement next year.

Verco revived his boyhood love of the sea. Using his brother William's ketch, he learned the techniques of dredging and—often with his nephews—collected shells, corals, crabs, sponges and other marine life. W. G. Torr [q.v.] and Stirling sometimes accompanied Verco whose gifts of shells, specimens, books, apparatus and money to the South Australian Museum eventually helped to form one of the world's outstanding collections. He

hired tugs for longer trips along the Great Australian Bight and off the coast of Western Australia. From these journeys, he published papers in the transactions of the Royal Society of South Australia (1895-1918), in the records of the museum (1922-28) and in the proceedings of the Malacological Society of London (1931). Verco kept extensive diaries and was moved to write at least one love poem; the manuscript of his sea travels was later edited by Bernard Cotton as Combing the southern seas (1935). The South Australian Naturalist (August 1933) included a bibliography of Verco's work in malacology. Honorary conchologist at the museum from 1914, he methodically and succinctly described 169 new species and subspecies. A fish, a crustacean and a number of molluscs were named after him.

President of the Royal Society of South Australia in 1903-21, Verco presented £1000 to found its research and endowment fund. He donated £5000 in 1926 to the Medical Sciences Club of South Australia to establish the Australian Journal of Experimental Biology and Medical Science and supported many other institutions, financially and administratively, among them the Adelaide Children's Hospital and the Queen Victoria Convalescent Home. Survived by his wife, Sir Joseph died childless at his North Terrace home on 29 July 1933 and was buried in West Terrace cemetery. He is commemorated in the Verco Theatre at the Institute of Medical and Veterinary Science, Adelaide (with a bronze portrait plaque), and in the Verco Ward, Royal Adelaide Hospital. In 1928 the Royal Society of South Australia struck the Sir Joseph Verco medal for distinguished scientific investigations carried out by its members.

H. R. Taylor, The history of Churches of Christ in South Australia, 1846-1959 (Adel, 1959); P. W. Verco, Masons, millers and medicine (Adel, 1976); Lancet, 12 Aug 1933; British Medical J, 12 Aug, 16 Sept 1933; MJA, 16 Sept 1933; Malacological Soc (Lond), Procs, 15 Nov 1933; Sth Australiana, 2, no 2, Sept 1963; A. A. Lendon, The Medical School of S.A. (1885-1935), ts and Personalities remembered, ABC radio scripts: J. Ashton on Dr J. C. Verco, and Sir J. C. Verco's diaries and medical notes (Mortlock Lib); Univ Adel Archives; SA Museum Archives; information from Dr P. W. Verco, Adel.   R. V. SOUTHCOTT

VERNON, HOWARD (1848-1921), singer and comedian, was born on 20 May 1848 at Batman's Swamp, Melbourne, and baptized John, son of Richard Lett, brickmaker, and his wife Jane Catherine, née Williamson. At the age of 15 John worked as a clerk, at 16 as a tea-taster and blender. His first Melbourne stage appearance was as a tenor in a concert at which Johann Kruse [q.v.5] played a violin obbligato. When Vernon appeared to share the applause, amusing everyone but Kruse, George Coppin [q.v.3] remarked to Vernon: 'My boy, you are a comedian'. He also sang and acted with Walter Montgomery, W. S. Lyster [qq.v.5] and Coppin; in 1873 he performed as primo comico in a season of *opéra bouffe* conducted by G. B. Allen, husband of leading soprano Alice May, and subsequently joined them in the company they took to the East. In Sydney on 2 February 1870 as Norman Letville he had married an actress, Mary Jane Walker (d. 1905); they were to have nine children.

By 1874 Vernon had formed a small group of singers which he named the Royal English Opera Company. They toured Australia, New Zealand, India, China and other Eastern countries, and in 1877 went to Japan. Vernon visited England, playing Ange Pitou in *La fille de Madame Angot* and Fritz in *La grande duchesse* with the Alice May company. He then performed at San Francisco, United States of America, as a member of Emilie Melville's company.

In Singapore in 1876 Vernon and Alfred Plumpton produced *Trial by jury*, aided by the band of the 74th Highlanders who were stationed there; they also staged *Trial by jury* and *The sorcerer* at Bombay, India. On his return to Australia, Vernon joined J. C. Williamson [q.v.6] and began the long series of Gilbert and Sullivan opera performances on which his fame largely rests. In May 1881 he appeared in *The pirates of Penzance* in Melbourne; in November he played Bunthorne in *Patience* in Sydney. Other roles in which he gave the first Australian performances were Ko-Ko *(The Mikado)* 1885, King Hildebrand *(Princess Ida)* 1887, Wilfred Shadbolt *(The yeomen of the guard)* 1889, Don Alhambra *(The gondoliers)* 1890 and King Paramount *(Utopia Ltd)* 1906. Esteemed by Australasian theatre-goers for his mastery of such roles, Vernon had—in each opera—one character which was regarded as his by right and merit. Alfred Cellier, the conductor at the Savoy Theatre, London, who had worked with both Gilbert and Sullivan, declared that Vernon's interpretations compared with anything seen in London.

On 8 March 1906 at Sorell, Tasmania, as Howard Vernon he married an actress and singer, LAVINIA FLORENCE DE LOITTE (1881-1962), daughter of William Henry de Loitte, accountant, and his wife Florence Lavinia, née Herbert (known as Adams), comtesse de Vilme-Hautmont. Born on 15 March 1881 at Balmain, Sydney, Vinia de Loitte, as she was known on stage, became the toast of Sydney in 1904 as Fifi in *The belle of New York*. That year she met Vernon when they both performed in *Patience*. They frequently appeared

together, both in Australia and abroad, and in 1909 gave musical entertainments at the Brussels exhibition. She published a booklet, *Gilbert and Sullivan opera in Australia* (*c.*1933).

After several years in Britain, Vernon came home to Melbourne in 1914, retired from the stage and ran a book shop at Richmond. In 1920 J. C. Williamson Ltd gave a benefit for him, but failing health prevented his appearance. Vernon died at Prahran on 26 July 1921 and was buried in Brighton cemetery with Anglican rites; his estate was sworn for probate at £47. He was survived by his wife who died on 22 August 1962, and by two daughters and two sons of his first marriage, one of whom used the stage name 'Victor Prince'.

P. Downes, *Shadows on the stage* (Dunedin, NZ, 1975); H. Love, *The golden age of Australian opera* (Syd, 1981); E. Irvin, *Dictionary of Australian theatre 1788-1914* (Syd, 1985); *Age* and *SMH*, 27 July 1921; *Argus*, 27, 29 July 1921; *Table Talk*, 4 Aug 1921; *Sun* (Syd), 24 Aug 1962.

JOAN MASLEN

VERNON, WALTER LIBERTY (1846-1914), architect and soldier, was born on 11 August 1846 at High Wycombe, Buckinghamshire, England, eldest son of Robert Vernon, banker's clerk, and his wife Margaret, née Liberty. Educated at the Royal Grammar School, High Wycombe, and at Windsor, Walter was articled in 1862 to the London architect W. G. Habershon; he attended Sir Robert Smirke's lectures at the Royal Academy of Arts and went at night to the South Kensington School of Art.

On completing his articles, Vernon worked for Habershon & Pite and from 1869 took charge of their branch office in Wales. On 11 August 1870 in the Dock Street Chapel at Newport, Monmouthshire, he married Margaret Anne Jones (d. 1919). He then ran an office for the London architect Charles Moreing at Hastings where he set up his own practice in 1872. Vernon went on sketching trips through Holland, Belgium and Germany, and carried provisions across the Prussian lines during the siege of Paris. Suffering from bronchial asthma, he spent a year recuperating at Malta. A member (fellow, 1883) of the Surveyors' Institution from March 1880, he opened an office in Great George Street, London, while retaining his practice at Hastings. When his asthma recurred in 1883, he was advised to leave England: the family sailed in the *Ballaarat*, reaching Sydney on 3 November.

Commissioned to build a department store for David Jones [q.v.2] Ltd (George and Barrack streets, 1885), Vernon designed his own home, Penshurst, at Neutral Bay in 1884. He bought adjoining land where he designed and built several villas. From 1 October that year until February 1889 he was in partnership with W. W. Wardell [q.v.6]. Vernon assisted with works already in progress, designed buildings and supervised Wardell's Melbourne projects in 1884-85. Vernon was an alderman on East St Leonards Municipal Council in 1885-90. Elected a fellow of the Royal Institute of British Architects in 1885, he joined the (Royal) Art Society of New South Wales in 1884, (Sir) John Sulman's [q.v.] Palladian Club and the Institute of Architects of New South Wales in 1887, and the Sydney Architectural Association in 1891.

On 1 August 1890 Vernon had been appointed government architect in the new branch of the Department of Public Works which had been created to allow private architects to compete for the design of all public buildings estimated to cost over £5000. The government architect was to supervise the construction, with a commission paid to the selected architect. For new work below £5000 and for all alterations and maintenance, Vernon was required to make do with the remnants of James Barnet's [q.v.3] staff (73 in 1890, reduced to 44 by 1893). Of three competitions held, only one resulted in a completed building (Grafton gaol, 1891). By the end of 1894 Vernon showed that the new system cost twice as much as designs from his own office: competitions were never reinstated during his tenure.

When building revived in the mid-1890s, he was permitted more staff. Unlike his predecessor, Vernon saw major city public buildings as 'monuments to Art', large in scale and finely wrought in stone (the main facade of the National Art Gallery of New South Wales, 1904-06); suburban buildings took on the scale and character of their surroundings (Darlinghurst fire station, Federation Free Style, 1910); and country buildings were designed with cross-ventilation, shady verandahs and sheltered courtyards (Bourke Court House, Federation Free Style, 1900).

In running the branch, Vernon insisted on the highest quality of design, the use of improved materials and construction methods, and the application of business-like procedures. Reserving the right to approve designs, he delegated project responsibility to capable officers. This sound basis allowed flexibility for such tasks as providing illuminations and decorations for the Commonwealth celebrations and supervising statutory by-laws like the Theatres and Public Halls Act, 1908.

From 1901 Vernon had executed many site studies for the future Federal capital and later maintained that his most important duty had been his part in contributing to the eventual choice of Canberra. He was appointed in 1909 to the Federal Capital Advisory Board which negotiated with the New South Wales government for the transfer of land and formulated the conditions for a competition to design the city. Believing that Australians possessed insufficient knowledge of town planning to be able to do justice to the great possibilities, he advocated a world-wide competition. He supported Walter Burley Griffin [q.v.9] in *Building* on 12 June 1913 when a departmental scheme, largely drawn up by C. R. Scrivener [q.v.11], was substituted for Griffin's winning plan.

As well as serving on many government boards and inquiries, including the royal commission on the Sydney water supply (1902), Vernon belonged to the Australian Club (from 1884), United Service Institution of New South Wales (1889) and Aerial League of Australia (1909); he was president of the Broughton Club (1910-12) and of the architecture and engineering section of the Australasian Association for the Advancement of Science (1913); he was also a commissioner for the Franco-British Exhibition, London (1908), a trustee of the Australian Museum, Sydney (1909), vice-president of the Millions Club (1913) and a councillor of the Town Planning Association of New South Wales (1913).

A man of military stamp, Vernon was consumed by his interests in architecture and soldiering. In England he had served in the 4th Battalion of the Oxfordshire Light Infantry. He joined the New South Wales Lancers in January 1885 and was commissioned in March next year. Promoted captain (1893), he commanded the New South Wales Lancers contingent at Queen Victoria's diamond jubilee (1897) and was promoted major (1899). As lieut-colonel, Vernon commanded the 1st Australian Light Horse Regiment (New South Wales Lancers) in 1903-07 and, as colonel, the 2nd Light Horse Brigade in 1907-10; he was awarded the Volunteer Officers' Decoration in 1905.

By August 1911, when he retired, his staff numbered 152 and the government architectural office for New South Wales was an efficient public service machine. Vernon resumed private practice and found time for gardening, as well as for collecting furniture, pictures, armour and weapons. Since 1895 he had lived at Wendover, Normanhurst. Survived by his wife, two sons and two daughters, he died at Darlinghurst on 17 January 1914 of septicaemia and gangrene after the amputation of his leg, and was buried in the Anglican section of Gore Hill cemetery. The Vernon lectures in town planning, instituted at the University of Sydney in 1916, were endowed in his honour.

His elder son HUGH VENABLES (1877-1935) was born on 20 February 1877 at St Mary-in-the-Castle, Hastings, Sussex, England. Known as Venables (often Ven), he was educated at the Grammar School, Scone. On 1 November 1897 he joined the New South Wales Lancers as a trooper. He went to South Africa in November 1899 and took part in operations in Cape Colony, in the relief of Kimberley and in the Orange Free State. Awarded the Queen's South Africa Medal with three clasps, he contracted enteric fever in March 1900; he was commissioned in 1903. Vernon trained as an architect, probably under Howard Joseland [q.v.9] with whom he was in partnership in 1903-14. On 31 January 1907 at St Mark's Anglican Church, Darling Point, Vernon married Mary Stephens (d. 1966).

A major in the 1st Light Horse Regiment, Australian Imperial Force, he embarked in October 1914, commanded the regiment when it was dispatched to Gallipoli on 8 May 1915 and was mentioned in dispatches. Transferred to the 4th Division Ammunition Column in April 1916 at the invitation of (Major General Sir) Charles Rosenthal [q.v.11], he was promoted lieut-colonel and took the unit to France in June 1916. After the battle of Fromelles he was awarded the Distinguished Service Order and was again mentioned in dispatches. He came home in December 1918.

Returning to civilian life and to architectural practice, Vernon resumed militia service (1921-26) and was awarded the Volunteer Officers' Decoration in 1924. Active in several South African War veterans' associations, he was State president and a trustee of the Returned Sailors' and Soldiers' Imperial League of Australia, a member of the Soldiers' Children Education Board, a director of the United Service Insurance Co. Ltd, a foundation member of the Legacy Club of Sydney, and a councillor and fellow of the Institute of Architects of New South Wales. Vernon's practice was mainly in domestic architecture in Sydney and Canberra. Survived by his wife, daughter and two sons, he died of chronic nephritis on 3 July 1935 at Warrawee and was buried beside his father.

Walter's younger son GEOFFREY HAMPDEN (1882-1946) was born on 16 December 1882 at Hastings, Sussex. Educated at Sydney Church of England Grammar School (Shore), he studied medicine at the University of Sydney (M.B., Ch.M., 1905). He was appointed captain in the 4th Light Horse Field Ambulance, Australian Imperial Force, on 4 March 1915, and served in the Middle East as regimental medical officer of the 11th Light Horse; he was awarded the Military Cross for 'gallantry and devotion to duty' under heavy fire on 8 August 1916 near the Hod el Beheir

oasis, Sinai; promoted major in January 1917, he was wounded in action in November at Tel el Sheria and returned to Australia in August 1918. He lowered his age by eight years and enlisted in the Australian Army Medical Corps in 1942. As a captain, he served in Papua-New Guinea as medical officer with the 39th Australian Infantry Battalion on the Kokoda Track, becoming a legend among Australian troops and a hero to the Papuans. 'Doc' Vernon died on 16 May 1946 and was buried on Logea Island, Papua.

P. V. Vernon (ed), *The Royal New South Wales Lancers, 1885-1985* (Parramatta, NSW, 1986); *PP* (Cwlth), 1906, 2 (29), p 389, 1909, 2 (47), p 16; *A'sian Builder and Contractor's News*, 19 Nov 1887, 8 June 1889; *Building* (Syd), 11 Sept 1909, p 38, 12 June 1913, p 46, 12 Feb 1914, p 101, 12 May 1914, p 99; *SMH*, 5 Nov 1883, 17 Jan, 2 Sept, 2 Oct 1884, 26 Feb 1889, 20 Feb 1890, 17 Mar 1914, 5 July 1935; *Daily Telegraph* (Syd), 12 Feb 1914; P. L. Reynolds, The evolution of the government architect's branch of the NSW Department of Public Works: 1788-1911 (Ph.D. thesis, Univ NSW, 1972); D. Jones, Walter Liberty Vernon (architect): 1846-1914 (B.Arch thesis, Univ NSW, 1977); Executive Council (NSW), Minute-book, 12, 1890, *and* Dept of Public Works (NSW), Annual Report, 1909, *and* Federal Capital Site Comm, 1889-1902 (NSWA); Neutral Bay Land Co records *and* W. W. Wardell letter-books, 2 (ML); Dept of Home Affairs papers (AA, Canb); Vernon family papers (held by Mr P. V. Vernon, Lindfield, Syd).

PETER REYNOLDS

VERRAN, JOHN (1856-1932), miner and premier, was born on 9 August 1856, and baptized in the pit at Gwennap, Cornwall, England, twin son of John Spargoe Verran, copperminer, and his wife Elizabeth Jane, née Harvey. The family migrated to South Australia in 1857, living for eight years in Kapunda before moving to the Cornish settlement at Moonta. Having received only a few months elementary education, at the age of 10 John started work as a 'pickey-table boy' in the copper-mines. The ministers of the Primitive Methodist Church encouraged him to read and influenced him by their support of trade unionism. Through teaching in the Sunday School and through preaching, he learned to argue a case in public and was later to say, 'I am an M.P. because I am a P.M.' After a short spell gold-mining in Queensland, Verran returned to Moonta where he was a miner for over thirty years and a popular president of the Amalgamated Miners' Association (1895-1913). As a gradual reformist, he was suspicious of direct action. On 21 February 1880 at Moonta he had married Catherine Trembath (d. 1914); they were to have eight children.

Defeated in the elections of 1896 and 1899,

Verran was returned as Labor member for Wallaroo in the South Australian House of Assembly by-election of 1901. In 1909, on the death of Tom Price [q.v.11], premier of a Labor-Liberal coalition, Verran took over the Labor leadership and the coalition was dissolved. Labor won the subsequent election and on 3 June 1910 he became premier of the first all-Labor government in South Australia; he was also commissioner of public works.

His administration lasted less than twenty-one months. Shortly after taking office, it faced a drivers' strike which led to riots in the streets of Adelaide and to criticism of Verran's handling of the problem. The ministry spent considerable sums on railways and harbours, and its Advances for Homes Act (1911) allowed the State Bank of South Australia to grant loans to poorer people, but the Legislative Council thwarted the government's attempt to establish state brickyards and timber mills. Relations between the assembly and the council bedevilled the government; Verran petitioned the British parliament to legislate to override the council; in January 1912 he called an election over the Upper House's power to veto legislation passed by the Lower. Labor lost. One factor in his defeat had been the transport strike on the eve of the elections which divided the labour movement and frightened voters. Having lost support within his party, Verran resigned the leadership. He was excluded from Crawford Vaughan's [q.v.] Labor cabinet in 1915-17.

During World War I Verran became a vituperative critic of South Australians of German birth or descent. He made no allowances for those from pioneer families or for those who had been naturalized: 'They have German names and a German is a German. I have no bowels of compassion on this matter'. Wishing such persons to be removed from government departments, he also supported the closure of Lutheran schools and introduced a bill to prevent 'Germans' from voting in State elections, unless their sons had enlisted.

The bluff, flamboyant Verran was short and stout, with a goatee that had been full and black in his youth. While he often used Cornish idiom, his grammatical lapses gave a comical dimension to his repartee: 'Ef yore brains wuz dynamite and they wuz to iggs-plode, 'twouldn't blaw yer 'at off'. His parliamentary speeches were replete with Biblical allusions and stories were repeated for years about his idiosyncratic sermons: 'There are no flies on God' was one of his comments on the divinity. 'Honest John' was an 'unconventional champion of the conventions' who was respected even when he espoused unpopular causes.

In the national debates over conscription in 1916-17 Verran supported W. M. Hughes

[q.v.9] and became a Nationalist. Campaigning for conscription, he alienated his Moonta constituency and lost his seat in 1918 to R. S. Richards [q.v.11], a fellow Methodist and future Labor premier. Verran lost when he again contested Wallaroo as an Independent in 1921 and a Liberal in 1924. President of the National Party in South Australia in 1922, he unsuccessfully stood for the Senate that year and for the House of Representatives in 1925. The South Australian parliament appointed him to a casual vacancy in the Senate in 1927; he was defeated at the elections next year. He found it hard to get work, but was employed briefly as a timekeeper for a construction company and as a supervisor on the wheat stacks at Wallaroo.

Apart from the Methodist Church and Freemasonry, Verran's main interest was the temperance movement. He had signed the pledge as a young man and joined the Rechabites. 'Your signboard has fallen down', he once said to a publican, pointing to a drunkard in the gutter. Verran often appeared on temperance platforms, especially during the State referendum on early-closing in 1915. Survived by three sons and four daughters, he died at Unley on 7 June 1932; after a State funeral he was buried in Moonta cemetery.

His son JOHN STANLEY (1883-1952) was born on 24 December 1883 at Moonta. With his brothers and sisters, he experienced a strict Methodist upbringing which was relieved by his mother's wit and flexibility. Having worked in the mines as a youth, he took a job as a clerk at Port Adelaide and became president of the State branch of the Federated Clerks' Union and of the Australian Government Workers' Association. On 21 April 1913 in the Methodist manse, South Terrace, Adelaide, he married Ethel Clara Watson; they were to have two children before they divorced. He was a Labor member of the House of Assembly for Port Adelaide in 1918-27, but failed in his bid to enter the Senate in 1931. Survived by his son and daughter, John Stanley Verran died of a coronary occlusion on 30 August 1952 and was buried in Moonta cemetery.

H. T. Burgess (ed), *Cyclopedia of South Australia*, 1 (Adel, 1907); O. Pryor, *Australia's little Cornwall*, (Adel, 1962); D. J. Murphy (ed), *Labor in politics* (Brisb, 1975); D. Dunstan, *Felicia, the political memoirs of Don Dunstan* (Melb, 1981); D. Jaensch (ed), *The Flinders history of South Australia* (Adel, 1986); *PD* (SA), 24 Nov 1915, 31 Oct 1917; *Mail* (Adel), 20 July 1912; *Australasian*, 8 July 1922; *News* (Adel), 7 July 1931; *Chronicle* (Adel), 16 July 1931; *Advertiser* (Adel), 8 June 1932, 2 Sept 1952, 16 June 1984; *Aust Christian Cwlth*, 17 June 1932; R. J. Miller, The fall of the Verran government, 1911-12 (B.A. Hons thesis, Univ Adel, 1965).
                                    ARNOLD D. HUNT

'VESTA'; see ALLAN, STELLA MAY

VICARS, SIR JOHN (1857-1936) and SIR WILLIAM (1859-1940), manufacturers and businessmen, were born on 29 September 1857 and 24 May 1859, at Tillicoultry, Clackmannanshire, Scotland, eldest sons of John Vicars [q.v.6] and his wife Anne, née Moor. Settling at Rockhampton, Queensland, in 1863, the family moved to Sydney in 1871. John and William completed their education at Sydney Grammar School and entered their father's woollen mill in Sussex Street. After the retirement of John senior in 1887, John and his brothers William and Robert (1867-1921) moved the factory to a larger site at Marrickville in 1893; they later acquired the Sydney Woollen Mills Ltd at Parramatta. On 8 November 1893 John married Sophia Aspinall Harvie at St Andrew's Presbyterian Church, Sydney. After twenty years with John Vicars & Co., he formed a partnership with James P. Johnson as Messrs Johnson & Vicars, woolbrokers, wool-scourers and fellmongers, with offices at Circular Quay and works at Botany.

During World War I Vicars was active in patriotic causes and an executive-member of the French-Australian League of Help. He did outstanding voluntary work as chairman of the State Wool Committee from 1917 and as chairman of the British Australian Wool Realization Association Ltd (1920-24). For many years he was on the executive and sometime chairman of the Wool Buyers' Association, treasurer of its soldiers' convalescent hospital and a member of the Tariff Board in 1923. Next year he was knighted.

In 1928 Sir John joined the board of the Australian Gas Light Co., and later the boards of Australian Steam Pty Ltd, Caledonian Collieries Ltd, Howard Smith [q.v.6] Ltd, the Equitable Permanent Benefit, Building, Land and Savings Institution, and the National Mutual Life Association of Australia Ltd.

He had an abiding faith in Australia and its workers; the *Bulletin* wrote that 'physically, mentally and in character—he was "a big Australian"'. A golfing enthusiast, he was a president and captain of the Australian Golf Club and a member of the New South Wales Club. Survived by his wife, he died in Sydney on 28 February 1936 and was cremated.

William Vicars was co-proprietor, with his brother Robert, of John Vicars & Co. and a director of the Sydney Woollen Mills Ltd. At the Presbyterian Church, Rockhampton, on 23 July 1884 he married Mary Emily Hutton. He also became prominent in the business life of Sydney and was noted for his philanthropy. In 1900-01 and 1914 he was president of the

Chamber of Manufactures of New South Wales.

After World War I he championed the cause of returned servicemen; he was chairman of the State Repatriation Board in 1919-20 and of its purchase and contract and orphan education boards until 1922. In 1921 he and Robert gave Pitt Town Farm to the Church Social Campaign to train needy ex-servicemen for the land. Long associated with the work of the Australian Red Cross Society, in 1920 he became chairman of its convalescent homes committee and in 1921 chairman of the New South Wales division of the society. He was appointed C.B.E. in 1920 and knighted in 1922. In tribute, his employees paid for his portrait to be painted by Norman Carter [q.v.7].

Sir William fought to overcome prejudice against locally-manufactured woollen fabrics; as a result of his efforts, 'Vicars, Marrickville' became the hallmark throughout Australia for quality tweeds, serges, woollens, blankets and rugs. Returning from an overseas visit in December 1926, he averred that American fabrics were neither better nor cheaper than Australian.

He was also a director of Amalgamated Wireless (Australasia) Ltd (chairman, 1922), the Commercial Banking Co. of Sydney (1924-28, 1933-39), Home Recreations (Australia) Ltd and the Australian board of Royal Exchange Assurance of London. In 1932-33 Vicars was one of the trustees appointed to reopen the Government Savings Bank as the Rural Bank of New South Wales. A founder of the National Club and member of the Union Club, he played golf regularly.

Distinguished-looking, with strong features and a King George V beard, he had an easy nature, entirely devoid of anything stilted or pompous: quoting the epistle of Saint James, a friend saw in Vicars 'no variableness, neither shadow of turning'. Survived by his wife and daughter, Sir William died at his Rose Bay home on 20 October 1940 and was buried in South Head cemetery. His estate was sworn for probate at £114 818.

Marrickville Council (comp), *A history of the Municipality of Marrickville 1861-1936* (Syd, 1936); *Aust Manufacturers' J*, 15 July 1910; *Lone Hand*, 1 Jan 1912; *P.F.A. Q Mag*, Dec 1920, p 14; *Sydney Tatler*, 7 Dec 1922; *Bulletin*, 4 Mar 1936; *Pastoral Review*, 16 Nov 1940; *SMH*, 22 July, 22 Oct 1921, 2 Jan, 2, 10 June 1922, 1 Jan 1924, 13 Dec 1926, 26 Aug 1931, 29 Feb 1936, 21, 30 Oct 1940; *Syd Mail*, 18 Jan 1922; *Daily Telegraph* (Syd), 13 Feb 1922.   G. P. WALSH

VICKERS, ALLAN ROBERT STANLEY (1901-1967), flying doctor, was born on 3

June 1901 at Caniambo, Euroa, Victoria, son of Robert Vickers, farmer, and his wife Jessie Scott, née Louden. His Victorian-born parents later ran a store near Albury, New South Wales. Allan was educated at Albury High School and the University of Sydney (M.B., 1926), but his studies were broken by the chronic asthma that persisted for the rest of his life. Following a period as resident medical officer at Albury Hospital and as general practitioner at Queanbeyan, he worked briefly in a tuberculosis sanatorium at Waterfall.

With the prompting of Rev. John Flynn [q.v.8], Vickers joined the Aerial Medical Service of the Presbyterian Australian Inland Mission and in 1931-34 was medical superintendent at Cloncurry, North Queensland. In hazardous flights to outback locations which lacked proper landing facilities, Vickers averaged 25 000 miles (40 233 km) a year in his de Havilland 50 cabin biplane (DH50) which was equipped with a battery-operated portable transmitter. After financial support for the mission had been eroded by the Depression, in 1933 he began a publicity and fund-raising drive that led to the formation of an independent body, the National Aerial Medical Service of Australia. On 1 February 1934 he married Lilias Hinah Ella Whitman at St Andrew's Anglican Church, Cloncurry. That month he resigned from the A.I.M.

Resident medical officer (1934-35) at Broome, Western Australia, Vickers next established that State's first flying doctor base at Port Hedland. He saw its role as providing preventive and routine medicine, rather than merely emergency services. In charge of the two hospitals at Port Hedland and another at Marble Bar, he was also quarantine officer, resident magistrate, protector of Aborigines, mining warden and inspector of fisheries. During World War II Lieut-Colonel Vickers was commanding officer (1939-43) of the 110th Australian General Hospital, Perth, and a councillor and vice-president of the Western Australian section of the National Aerial Medical Service. He was recalled by the Queensland section of what was, after 1942, the Flying Doctor Service, and established its second base at Charleville in 1943: he was chief medical officer there in 1951-54. As a Nuffield fellow in 1954, he canvassed in England for the development of the flying doctor service on a British Commonwealth basis. Back in Australia he was appointed medical superintendent and supervisor of bases in Queensland.

A Freemason and a commander of the Order of St John of Jerusalem (1946), Vickers was appointed O.B.E. in 1951 and C.M.G. in 1955. He became medical consultant to the federal council of the Royal Flying Doctor Service of Australia in 1964. Elder statesman of the movement at his retirement in 1966,

Vickers had employed all his tenacity, resilience and force of character in its service. His quiet and self-effacing manner was belied by deep-set 'eager and vivacious' eyes. Returning as ship's doctor from a voyage to England, Vickers died of heart disease aboard the *Imperial Star* off Cape Town on 30 October 1967. His ashes were scattered from a R.F.D.S. plane over Cloncurry; his wife and two sons survived him.

J. Bilton et al, *The Royal Flying Doctor Service of Australia* (Syd, 1961); W. S. McPheat, *John Flynn* (Lond, 1963); *MJA*, 6 Jan 1951, p 51, 4 May 1968, p 5; M. J. Richards, Allan Vickers, flying doctor (M.A. thesis, JCU, 1979); Vickers papers *and* C. Duguid papers *and* J. Flynn papers *and* G. Simpson papers *and* Aust Inland Mission papers (NL).

MICHAEL J. RICHARDS

VICKERS, WILLIAM (1893-1969), soldier and newsagent, was born on 17 September 1893 at Wellington, Shropshire, England, son of Samuel Vickers, agricultural labourer, and his wife Sarah Ann, née Picken.

Enlisting in the Australian Imperial Force in Perth on 7 January 1915, Vickers stated that he was a winch driver of North Dandalup. He was posted to the 12th Battalion and reached Gallipoli on 7 May; evacuated to England with dysentery on 26 August, he rejoined his unit in March 1916, two weeks before it moved from Egypt to France. He was wounded at Pozières on 24 July and was away from the battalion until 22 September. Promoted lance corporal in January 1917 and corporal in March, he was transferred to the 3rd Training Battalion in England on 10 May. After completing a Lewis-gun course, he returned to the 12th in October.

On 3 November, near Broodseinde Ridge, Vickers helped to force a German patrol back to its post; with Vickers leading, the post was then rushed and he killed three men. He was awarded the Military Medal and on 15 November promoted lance sergeant. Having attended the 3rd Brigade non-commissioned officers' course from 17 February 1918, he was promoted sergeant on 13 March. He commanded a section of his platoon in an attack at Meteren on 23 April with such dash that the enemy fled from the first objective after suffering numerous casualties. Vickers took a bombing team to the second objective, capturing a machine-gun, inflicting further loss and taking several prisoners. Next day he inspired his men to repel repeated counter-attacks. He was awarded the Distinguished Conduct Medal.

On the night of 2 June at Mont de Merris, Vickers led his section against a machine-gun, killed the crew and captured their weapon.

During the consolidation he went out alone and brought in fifteen prisoners who were in shell-holes in front of the Australian lines. The battalion historian recorded that Vickers' 'strength and bravery were miraculous and his language fiery'. For this operation he won his third gallantry decoration, a bar to his D.C.M. Again wounded on 24 July at Rouge Croix Switch, he was evacuated to England; he left for Australia still medically unfit on 10 December and was discharged from the A.I.F. on 21 June 1919.

Having returned to England where he worked as a railway servant, on 12 October 1920 at St Agatha's parish church, Sparkbrook, Warwickshire, Bill Vickers married Alice Hilda Rowland whom he had met in 1916 while recuperating in Wales. They remained in Britain and he retired as a newsagent to Paignton, Devon, where he died on 25 December 1969, survived by his wife (d. 1981) and their only son.

L. M. Newton, *The story of the twelfth* (Hob, 1925); C. E. W. Bean, *The A.I.F. in France*, 1918 (Syd, 1942); *London Gazette*, 23 Feb 1916, 3 Sept, 30 Oct 1918; Honours and awards, 1914-18 war, 1st Division, Aust Army (AWM).

ANTHONY STAUNTON

VIDLER, EDWARD ALEXANDER (1863-1942), publisher, journalist and author, was born on 13 August 1863 in London, son of Thomas Collins Vidler, surgeon dentist, and his wife Amelia Gould, daughter of George Bennett and god-daughter of John Gould [qq.v.1]. Educated at a private school at Gravesend, at 17 Edward was employed by Cassell & Co., publishers, where he was largely responsible for the publication of R. L. Stevenson's *Treasure Island* in volume form. Migrating to Melbourne in 1888, Vidler worked as a freelance journalist and critic. On 28 December 1889 he married Florence Jessie Byrchall at St Barnabas's Anglican Church, Balwyn. Moving to Geelong as part-proprietor and editor of the *Evening News*, he was founder and secretary of the Geelong Progress League, a founder and life member of the Geelong Art Gallery and a life member of the Geelong Public Library. His involvement in regional affairs extended to Warrnambool where he was secretary of the chamber of commerce and the progress league. He published commemorative volumes on Geelong (1897) and Warrnambool (1907).

Returning to Melbourne by 1897, he edited the *Tatler*, a weekly magazine of art, literature, music and drama. His poetic play, *The rose of Ravenna*, was published by George Robertson [q.v.6] & Co., booksellers, who in 1908 appointed him head of their publishing

department. When this department closed in 1918, Vidler began publishing on his own account, while continuing to work as a journalist, lecturer and literary agent. He concentrated on work by local artists and authors in an attempt to popularize Australian art and literature, but few of his publications made money and the business folded in 1930. Vidler also suffered financial losses with the demise of the *Spinner*, the magazine through which he promoted Australian verse.

The active interest that Vidler displayed in all branches of the arts was the stimulus for the foundation of the Australian Institute of Arts and Literature in 1921. Artists, writers and musicians were drawn together with the primary objectives of promoting artistic and literary appreciation and furthering the development of the arts in Australia. While Vidler's initial enthusiasm had helped the institute to become established as a focal meeting place, declining membership forced it to disband in 1931.

A keen naturalist, Vidler wrote and published books on Australian flora and fauna. In 1932, when appointed an honorary joint curator of the Maranoa Gardens at Balwyn, he helped to design the structure of native plantings. He was essentially a man of ideas, rather than practicalities, whose lack of organizational ability appears to have prevented him from achieving financial success, but his consistent support of Australian art and letters was recognized by the award in 1939 of a pension from the Commonwealth Literary Fund. Vidler died on 28 October 1942 at Surrey Hills. Survived by his wife, son and daughter, he was buried in Box Hill cemetery.

F. T. Macartney, *Furnley Maurice* (Syd, 1955); *Aust Musical News*, 1 Aug 1922, p 47; *Vic Naturalist*, 59 (1942-43), p 180; *Table Talk*, 1 Mar 1900, p 6; *Age* and *Herald* (Melb), 3 Nov 1942; B. Morris, Edward Vidler: man of contradictions (lecture delivered at Warrnambool Public Lib, 10 Mar 1983); information from Mr J. P. Holroyd, Windsor, Melb.
LURLINE STUART

VIGANO, MARIO ANTONIO FRANCESCO BATTISTA VIRGINIO (1888-1966), restaurateur, was born on 27 August 1888 at Olgiate Comasco, Lombardia, Italy, son of Ferdinando Vigano, architect, and his wife Antonia, née Azzali. Educated at Milan, Mario studied law at the University of Pavia, but did not graduate. As a young man he served in the 1911-12 war against Turkey. In 1912 he travelled to Canada where he met Italian-born MARIA TERESA Ferrari (1884-1969) and about October 1914 married her in Winnipeg. Vigano found work in a Vancouver hotel and with the Canadian Pacific Railways.

Enlisting in the Canadian Expeditionary Forces in 1917, he served until 1919 as a private in the 29th Vancouver Battalion and was awarded the D.C.M. during operations in France.

Resident again in Italy from 1919, Vigano was unsympathetic to the Mussolini régime and migrated with his family, arriving in Melbourne in January 1928. Working first as a waiter at Scott's Hotel in Collins Street, then as a partner in a catering business, he obtained a lease and later purchased the Melbourne Club Hotel, 198 Exhibition Street, which he opened as Mario's in 1932. From modest beginnings its restaurant was expanded to some 200 covers and offered an extensive menu, basically Italian in style. Vigano brought several chefs from Italy to his kitchens. Moderately priced and well-serviced, the restaurant was popular for family celebrations; situated in the theatre district, it also attracted a clientele from all social strata: Mario's became the most widely patronized of Melbourne's Italian restaurants.

Of middle height (5 ft. 8 ins., 172.7 cm), with a powerful physique and erect stance, Vigano was clean-shaven and broad faced, with a wide mouth and sunny expression. In his restaurant he dressed formally in striped trousers and dark jacket. Something of a 'showman', at times flamboyant in manner, he was always a prominent figure among the diners. He was naturalized in 1933. Following the success of his restaurant, he bought a property at South Morang where he entertained in generous fashion and indulged his liking for riding. In 1955 he took over 'the Latin' freehold from Camillo Triaca [q.v.].

Maria Teresa Vigano often assisted in the restaurant. A painter of distinction who had studied at the Brera Academy of Art, Milan, in 1909-10, she exhibited in Rome (1963) and Adelaide (1965). Mario Vigano died at his hotel on 16 February 1966 and was buried with Catholic rites in Preston cemetery. He was survived by his wife, a daughter, and a son who carried his father's name to the restaurant of the Brighton Beach Hotel which he owned in 1968-89. Mario's was purchased in 1966 by Triaca's son David who ran it until 1968. Maria Teresa died in Melbourne on 26 February 1969. A commemorative exhibition of her work was held at the Victorian College of the Arts Gallery in 1981. She is represented in the National Gallery of Victoria, and eight of her paintings hang in her granddaughter's restaurant, Mietta's, Melbourne.

M. G. Henderson, *500 Victorians* (Melb, 1934); *Pix*, 22 Jan 1966; *Age*, 17 Feb 1966; naturalization papers (AA); information from Mrs D. J. O'Donnell, Parkville, Melb, and Mr F. G. Vigano, Mount Eliza, Vic.　　　　　　　　　　W. S. BENWELL

VILLIERS, VICTOR ALBERT GEORGE CHILD-; *see* JERSEY

VINCENT, ALFRED JAMES (1874-1915), cartoonist, was born on 9 February 1874 at Launceston, Tasmania, son of William Thomas Vincent, groom, and his wife Frances, née Wilks. Alf came to notice at the age of 17 with the publication of his drawings and caricatures, *Skits: a memento from the Tasmanian Exhibition, Launceston, 1891-92*, and to prominence in 1896 when he was offered a staff position on the *Bulletin* with the privilege of later acquiring shares worth £3000 in that company.

From his top-floor studio in Collins Street which once belonged to Arthur Streeton [q.v.], Vincent drew full-page comments on Melbourne affairs, caricatures of public personalities and jocular sketches of life in the slums, on the racecourses, at the theatres and around the streets. His themes—like those of Phil May [q.v.5]—were of city life, the high and the low. From an early age, Alf studied the 'leaving-out' technique pioneered by May and acknowledged the influence of his idol. Although derivative, Vincent's pen-drawing style did have individuality, noticeably in his quality of line, composition and figure grouping, together with the evocative suggestion of locale in his backgrounds.

As with all *Bulletin* staff artists, Vincent was called upon to illustrate short stories and features for its sister magazine, the *Lone Hand*, and for its book publishing division. With five other *Bulletin* artists, he illustrated the first edition (1899) of Steele Rudd's [q.v.8 A. H. Davis] *On our selection*, creating the images of Dad and Dave for all succeeding cartoonists. One of Melbourne's best-dressed men, Vincent was a leading light in the affairs of the Savage Club for whose celebrated smoke-nights he illustrated programme covers. He donated a selection of his works for the permanent cartoon display at the club's Bank Place rooms.

Because of his sensitive disposition, Alf Vincent was occasionally something of a trial to his friends who nevertheless accepted him as they found him: at times charming, with his delightful, quiet humour; at others irritating in his melancholy fits of despondency. Speculation about his nervous collapse and tragic suicide on 6 December 1915 at Manly, Sydney, has centred on his work being too imitative of Phil May to have rewarded him with contemporary renown. Survived by his wife Phyllis May, née Potter (d. 1916), whom he had married with Anglican rites at St James's Old Cathedral, Melbourne, on 5 April 1913, and by their daughter, Vincent was buried in Manly general cemetery. There are collections of his drawings in the State art galleries in Melbourne and Sydney.

D. M. Dow, *Melbourne Savages* (Melb, 1947); V. Lindesay, *The inked-in image* (Melb, 1970); *Aust Worker*, 9 Dec 1915.   VANE LINDESAY

VINCENT, JAMES (1895-1950), soldier and farmer, was born on 20 October 1895 at Willoughby, Sydney, son of Thomas Vincent, labourer, and his wife Virginia, née Brooks. He left school at 14, worked for five years as an oil company storeman, was a member of the militia for two years and joined the Australian Imperial Force in December 1914.

With a 'very bad feeling inside', Private Vincent sailed for Egypt in February 1915 with reinforcements for the 13th Battalion. He landed at Anzac Cove on 6 May. Three days before that, he had sharpened his bayonet. 'God help the Turks for everyone aboard means business', he recorded in his diary. Wounded once and twice evacuated because of illness, he volunteered to return to Gallipoli and was in one of the last groups to leave on 19 December. He had learned 'the horrors of war'. Promoted corporal in March 1916, he joined the 45th Battalion which reached France in June. On the Western Front Vincent repeatedly proved his skill and daring. He was twice mentioned in dispatches and, despite differences with his officers, was promoted company sergeant major in February 1917.

An unprecedented bombardment began the allied advance east of Messines, Belgium, on 7 June. For his work during the assault on Owl Trench, Vincent won the Distinguished Conduct Medal. With his battalion shattered and most of its officers dead, he encouraged the survivors to further efforts, scouted for intelligence and rescued wounded men during the next seventy-two hours. Commissioned in the field as second lieutenant on 21 June, Jimmy returned to his battalion as a scout officer in March 1918, following training in England.

Lieutenant Vincent won the Military Cross for service on 5 April at Dernancourt, France, scouting continuously under heavy machine-gun fire. A Bar was added when he again displayed continuous gallantry and ability east of Hamel on 8-11 August. He laid jumping-off tapes in near-impenetrable fog, guided tanks and troops into position, led a patrol that pinned down the enemy with three Lewis-guns, and saved many casualties. On patrol he captured more than one hundred of the enemy.

Wounded on 17 July, he was seconded to the 5th Army for courts martial in October. His brigadier, S. C. Herring [q.v.9], recorded that he was 'a really remarkable soldier'.

Vincent's elder brother Edward (19th Battalion) was killed in action on 5 June 1918. James was demobilized in Australia in April 1919.

City life was unbearable for him after the war. From 1924 he was a wheat farmer at Wongonbra, near Lockhart, New South Wales. At Lockhart, on 10 February 1926, he married a schoolteacher, Mabel Clare Steenholdt (d. 1985), her wedding ring being made from the lucky sovereign James had carried throughout the war. In 1938 the family purchased a grazing property, Pine Tree, near Armidale. James was a bush craftsman, an avid reader and a respected local figure; quietly spoken, with brown eyes and hair, he was 5 ft. 6 ins. (168 cm) tall.

He loved the sea and in 1949 built a house overlooking Port Macquarie where he died of heart disease on 25 October 1950. Survived by his wife, two daughters and a son, he was buried in the local cemetery with Anglican rites. His diaries, faithfully kept for most of the war, provide a lively record of his service.

C. E. W. Bean, *The A.I.F. in France*, 1918 (Syd, 1942); recommendation files for honours and awards, AIF, 1914-18, entries under Vincent (AWM); J. Vincent, transcript of diaries 1914-17 (held by author, Canb) information from Mrs M. White, Guyra, NSW.   GRAHAM MCLENNAN

VINCENT, ROY STANLEY (1892-1965), newspaper proprietor and politician, was born on 6 February 1892 at Uralla, New South Wales, eleventh child of New Zealand-born Frank Walter Vincent, journalist, and his wife Sarah, née Rampling, from Armidale. The Vincents had long been involved with northern newspapers. Educated locally, Roy and his brother Reginald began publishing the *Don Dorrigo Gazette and Guy Fawkes Advocate* in 1910.

Enlisting in the Australian Imperial Force on 17 September 1915, Roy Vincent embarked with the 20th Battalion for Egypt. He arrived in France with his battalion in March 1916 and two months later was seriously wounded and gassed; he never fully recovered. He embarked for Sydney in September and was discharged in November. Becoming president (1918) of the Dorrigo branch of the Returned Sailors' and Soldiers' Imperial League of Australia, he was a member (1918-20) of the local repatriation committee. On 19 December 1919 he married Ethel Gertrude Hardwicke at St Stephen's Anglican Church, Dorrigo. A foundation member of the North Coast Development League, Vincent advocated improved port facilities at Coffs Harbour and a north-coast rail service; he was also a leader of the Northern New State

Movement and an active publicist of its campaign.

Standing as a Progressive for the seat of Oxley in 1922, he was returned to the Legislative Assembly and joined (Sir) Michael Bruxner's [q.v.7] 'True Blues'. Vincent held Oxley in 1925 and represented Raleigh from 1927 to 1953; he was sometime whip and secretary of the Country Party and an executive-member of the New England division of the United Country Movement. He brought to parliament 'a clear and vigorous mind'. A fine speaker, with the ability to get 'to the core of things', he won the respect of his colleagues. He was secretary for mines and minister for forests from 18 June 1932 to 16 May 1941 in the Stevens [q.v.]-Bruxner and Mair [q.v.10]-Bruxner coalitions; briefly in 1938 he was, as well, minister for agriculture. Vincent launched a progressive policy of re-afforestation and conservation. His Forestry (Amendment) Act of 1935 reconstituted the Forestry Commission under E. H. F. Swain [q.v.] and provided for the creation of national forests. In *Declaration of the Nightcap National Forest* (1937) Vincent expressed his view that such areas should be managed with 'the same care and attention as . . . any large business'.

In 1938 Vincent was responsible for the Soil Conservation Act under which a conservation service was created and a soil research station opened at Cowra. He established the fuel research committee in the Department of Mines (1935) and helped to draft uniform regulations for civil aviation in Australia. Appointed chairman of the State Coal Control Committee in 1940 to ensure the availability of coal for defence and industry, he succeeded D. H. Drummond [q.v.8] as deputy leader in July 1950.

Quiet and unassuming, Vincent was well-read and practical. For relaxation, he fished and played billiards and snooker. He belonged to the Aborigines Protection Board (1923-37). Forced by ill health to retire from public life in 1953, he devoted himself to his garden at Pymble. Survived by his wife, two sons and two daughters, he died in Concord Repatriation General Hospital on 5 June 1965 and was cremated.

U. Ellis, *The Country Party* (Melb, 1958); D. Aitkin, *The colonel* (Canb, 1969) and *The Country Party in New South Wales* (Canb, 1972); *PD* (NSW), 1965, 57, p 33; *Bulletin*, 6 July 1932; *SMH*, 7 Nov 1933, 29 Mar 1935, 16 Sept 1937, 22 May 1940, 13 Jan 1961, 7 June 1965.   MICHAEL STURMA

VINER, WILLIAM SAMUEL (1881-1933), chess-master, was born on 5 December 1881 at East Maitland, New South Wales, only son of William Samuel Viner, an English tinsmith, and his native-born wife Elizabeth,

née Blackwell (d. 1884). After schooling, at the age of 14 he learned chess from his father and by 1897 had joined the Sydney School of Arts Chess Club. Having visited Broken Hill, in 1898 father and son went to Boulder City on the Western Australian goldfields. They helped to form a chess club and young William succeeded in local matches. Back east two years later, he played brilliantly in Sydney Suburban Chess Association matches and was runner-up in the School of Arts club championship.

Returning to Boulder City in January 1900, Viner worked as a plumber; he won the local chess handicap tournament and the West Australian championship. Early next year he became a clerk with the Perth Gas Co. Ltd. He was again State champion in 1901, 1903 and 1905, and won the Perth Chess Club's handicap tournament three times. In response to a challenge issued by the club to re-establish the dormant Australian championship, in 1906 he beat the Victorian champion C. G. M. Watson. Submitting that the title should be based on an official tournament, the New South Wales Chess Association alone refused to recognize Viner's claim to the title. Next year he won the New Zealand championship.

Shifting to Bellingen, New South Wales, in 1911 to help on his father's dairy farm, Viner successfully defended his Australian title against Dr L. B. Lancaster in 1912 and against the New South Wales champion Spencer Crackanthorp in 1913. Next year Viner competed in the British championship tournament at Chester and came seventh. Back home, he enlisted in the Australian Imperial Force on 12 January 1915 and embarked with the 11th Battalion on 19 April for Egypt. Evacuated sick, he spent two terms in hospital and served in A.I.F. depots in England from August 1916 before being demobilized in Perth in June 1918. On 10 July at the Anglican Church of St Mary the Virgin, West Perth, he married Alice Lily May Hutt. He later took over the Bellingen farm, but sold out in December 1923; he worked as an attendant at the Goulburn Mechanics' Institute until 1927, then as a clerk in Sydney.

Viner lost the Australian title to Watson at the new Australian Chess Federation's 1922 championship congress. Next year Viner challenged the new champion; unable to play, Watson resigned the title to him. Viner retained it at the second official tournament in 1924, but lost in 1926. He was inactive until 1931 when he played in interclub matches; in 1932 he became an adjudicator for the State chess association. At the 1932-33 congress, despite failing health, he shared second place. Survived by his wife, a two-month-old daughter and four young sons, he died of cancer in Royal Prince Alfred Hospital,

Sydney, on 27 March 1933 and was buried in Botany cemetery.

Quiet and modest, Viner was remembered for his cheerfulness and convictions. A strong positional player, a 'fighter' rather than a 'stylist', he had an indomitable will to win.

Aust Chess Review, 20 Dec 1930, 20 Apr 1933; *Aust Chess Lore*, 1981, 1982, 1984, 1985, 1986; *Daily Telegraph* (Syd), 22 Apr 1899, 2 May 1900; *Maitland Mercury*, 15 July 1899; *Australasian*, 15 Apr 1933.   JOHN VAN MANEN

VINEY, HORACE GEORGE (1885-1972), soldier and journalist, was born on 8 June 1885 at Parkside, Adelaide, son of George Viney, chaff merchant, and his wife Grace Stodden, née Burnard. He attended the Grote Street Pupil Teachers' School and in 1903 studied arts at the University of Adelaide. A lieutenant in the Commonwealth Military Cadet Corps (1908-11), he was commissioned in the 1st Battalion, 10th (Adelaide Rifles) Australian Infantry Regiment, in January 1911. Qualifying for appointment to the Administrative and Instructional Staff, Australian Military Forces, in February 1912, he was promoted provisional lieutenant in March. Next November he served at the Special School of Instruction, Albury, New South Wales, and in July 1913 was appointed adjutant in the 23rd Light Horse Regiment.

On 20 August 1914 Viney joined the 3rd Light Horse Regiment, Australian Imperial Force, as an adjutant. Promoted captain, he embarked for Egypt in October and landed on Gallipoli on 12 May 1915. During a spell in hospital he was promoted major and rejoined his regiment as commanding officer of 'B' Squadron on 11 October. Shortly before leaving Gallipoli in December, he was appointed deputy assistant adjutant and quartermaster general, 2nd Australian Division. In Egypt Viney was transferred to the 18th Battalion as brigade major, 5th Infantry Brigade, on 1 February 1916 and sailed for France next month. For his actions at the battle of the Somme in September, when his brigade helped to hold a portion of the line at Pozières, he was awarded the Distinguished Service Order. Appointed D.A.A. and Q.M.G., 1st Australian Division, on 13 October, he undertook staff training from December until February 1917. Returning to 1st Division headquarters in Belgium, he was appointed deputy assistant adjutant general on 7 April and assistant adjutant and Q.M.G., with promotion to lieut-colonel, on 23 July. For his valuable services at Ypres in September-October he was appointed C.M.G.

Viney married Darragh O'Neill at the Harrow parish church, Middlesex, England, on 6 June 1918. He became assistant Q.M.G., Australian Corps, on 16 November, embarked for home on 18 July 1919 and his A.I.F. appointment ended on 17 November. He had been mentioned in dispatches five times, appointed C.B.E. and awarded the French Croix de Guerre. Posted to the Staff Corps, A.M.F., Viney left for England in November 1920 to undertake the senior course at the Staff College, Camberley. Back in Australia in February 1922, he served as a staff officer until August when he transferred to the unattached list; he was placed on the reserve of officers in 1927 with the rank of lieut-colonel.

In civilian life Viney took up journalism and joined the literary staff of the Adelaide *Advertiser*; in 1936 he was commissioned by the Adelaide Chamber of Commerce to write *A century of commerce in South Australia*. He moved to Victoria in 1939. Called up for full-time duty with the militia staff, he was appointed deputy assistant director of ordnance services in December that year. He transferred to the reserve in 1941 and was placed on the retired list in June 1945.

While working as a clerk in Sydney, Viney was an active member of the Returned Sailors', Soldiers' and Airmen's Imperial League of Australia and helped to form the Kings Cross sub-branch. After his wife's death, on 25 June 1955 at the registry office, Sydney, he married Margaret Jane Lillian Browne; when he retired in 1958, they moved to Springwood. Survived by his wife and by a son of his first marriage, Viney died there on 7 March 1972. He was cremated with Presbyterian forms.

C. E. W. Bean, *The story of Anzac*, 1, 2 (Syd, 1921, 1924) and *The A.I.F. in France*, 1916-18 (Syd, 1929, 1933, 1937, 1942); *Mountain Gazette*, 15 Mar 1972; card index: personnel, AIF, 1914-18 *and* nominal roll, 3rd Light Horse Regiment, AIF, at embarkation 22 Oct 1914 *and* war diary, 3rd Light Horse Regiment *and* 5th Aust Infantry Brigade, AIF *and* recommendation files for honours and awards, AIF (AWM).   MICHAEL SHEPHERD

VIRGO, JOHN JAMES (1865-1956), administrator and evangelist, was born on 22 April 1865 at Glenelg, Adelaide, eldest of eight children of Caleb Virgo, carpenter, and his wife Mary, née Swan. Leaving Glenelg Grammar School, Jack worked as a clerk and joined the South Australian Literary Societies' Union. On 7 November 1886 in Adelaide he married Lucy Stapleton Crabb (d. 1915); they were to have a daughter and three sons. He became acting secretary of the Adelaide Young Men's Christian Association; following the secretary's conviction for embezzling association funds, Virgo was confirmed in the position in 1887. Membership and activities increased. He established the Our Boys' Institute as a separate branch and developed educational and sporting programmes with Christian emphases. He also began the famous Sunday-night Theatre Royal evangelical services which attracted between one and two thousand people. Virgo conducted the choir and led the singing in a fine baritone voice; a practised elocutionist, he delivered a spiritual message as the evening's climax.

His muscular Christianity suited the Y.M.C.A. Lacking the 'sissified complexes of the goody-goody', he had a gregarious nature and a gentle tolerance; he seemed incapable of indignation. In 1894 he attended the jubilee international Y.M.C.A. conference in London and in 1900 became secretary of the Australasian Union of Y.M.C.A.s. In 1903 he was appointed secretary of the Y.M.C.A., Sydney. Its new premises were extensive, with a large gymnasium ('build the man' was one of his mottoes), concert hall, accommodation, library and clubrooms. Virgo soon raised £15 000 to repay the association's debt. He promoted a fourfold programme involving physical, social, educational and spiritual activities, instituted Sunday-night evangelical meetings and took part in Christian crusades.

Virgo became general secretary of the London Central Y.M.C.A. in 1911. As national field secretary during World War I, he raised massive funds for the war effort and addressed a total of some two million soldiers on the Western Front. Two of his sons had enlisted. In 1918 he was appointed C.B.E. and next year became the English representative on the World's Alliance of Y.M.C.A.s. He retired in 1925.

On 12 October 1920 in the parish church of St Michael, Handsworth, Virgo had married Emmeline Dorothy Aston, a clergyman's daughter. They lived in the country where she bred champion bulldogs and he wrote his memoirs, *50 years of fishing for men* (1930). He was a corporator of the International Young Men's Christian Association College at Springfield, Massachusetts, United States of America. Wearing a homburg, Jack travelled widely, often revisiting Australia; at 70, on his tenth world tour, he delivered 101 speeches in 80 days. In Melbourne he had declared: 'There is not enough of real Christianity . . . there is too much of the mushy type. Too much flowery beds of ease and singing oneself away to everlasting bliss, and too little laying hold on life'. Survived by his wife, Virgo died on 2 August 1956 at Parkstone, Dorset. His estate was sworn for probate at £9016.

Young Men's Christian Assn, *Y.M.C.A. who's*
who and annual (UK), 1934; J. T. Massey, *The Y.M.C.A. in Australia* (Melb, 1950); *Observer* (Adel), 26 Mar 1921; *The Times*, 18 Apr 1925, 4 Aug 1956; *Herald* (Melb), 17 Aug 1929; *Table Talk*, 29 Aug 1929; J. W. Daly, The Adelaide Y.M.C.A. (B.A. Hons thesis, Univ Adel, 1972).

JIM DALY

VOGT, GEORGE LEONARD (1848-1937), journalist and editor, was born on 1 November 1848 at Frankfurt am Main (Germany), son of Johann Hermann Vogt, printer, and his wife Maria Elisabeth, née Kellner, a former operatic singer. The family arrived in Melbourne on the *Marco Polo* on 6 December 1856, lived at Kew and later settled in the Scarsdale district where Johann established the *Grenville Advocate*. On his father's death in 1864, George was apprenticed to a Ballarat printer and became caught up in political reform movements.

In June 1870 Vogt joined his brother John in Gippsland; they founded a newspaper, the *Bairnsdale Courier*, in which they recorded many of the activities of reform groups. Vogt left the paper in 1871 and returned to Melbourne to partner the printer Charles Jones in the publication of the *Internationalist*; it ran for twelve issues between February and May 1872, and continued as the *Australian International Monthly* for another two issues. Both of these papers supported the formation of the Democratic Association of Victoria which espoused the cause of the First International (formed in London in 1864).

Moving to Ballarat, Vogt worked for a local paper and married Scottish-born Margaret Young with Presbyterian forms on 10 January 1877. Next year he took over the management of the *Bairnsdale Courier* from his brother. When it ceased publication in March 1879, George founded the *Bairnsdale Liberal News* which was to become in 1881 the *Bairnsdale and Bruthen News*. In 1890 he and John launched Gippsland's first and only daily paper, the *Gippsland Daily News*; the venture failed and they were both bankrupted. While John revived the *Courier*, George went to Melbourne about 1894 where he worked as a printer at Malvern. Shifting to Ballarat, he began a pioneering cork-cutting business.

Back in Melbourne in 1899, Vogt was employed from 1901 on the Federal Hansard printing staff. He again became associated with the radical press: with Thomas J. Windlow, he set up a workers' co-operative newspaper, the *People's Daily*, to provide a 'liberal democratic' penny daily in opposition to the *Argus* and *Age*. Against great odds, their paper was published from November 1903 to June 1904. A short, wiry man, Vogt saw himself as a 'fighting journalist' and a champion of the workers.

When the paper folded, George retired with his family to run a cork factory, Vogt Bros Pty Ltd, later the Cork & Crown Seal Co. Pty Ltd. At his Brunswick home he entertained many of his friends in the labour movement, including several politicians. In retirement he wrote for journals such as *Labor Call*, produced papers on contemporary and historical subjects, and lobbied successfully for a tariff on imported corks (1908). Vogt died at Brunswick on 12 April 1937 and was cremated. His wife, three daughters and six sons survived him.

Labor Call, 25 June, 9 July 1931, 19 Dec 1935; *Labour Hist*, Nov 1964, no 7, p 14, May 1965, no 8, p 22; W. Trevena, Country newspaper people: a select biographical dictionary of country newspaper men and women working in Victoria between 1840 and 1980 (M.A. thesis, Univ Melb, 1985); Vogt papers (LaTL).

J. D. ADAMS

VOIGT, EMIL ROBERT (1883-1973), athlete, political organizer, engineer and radio-manager, was born on 21 January 1883 at Ardwick, Lancashire, England, son of Emil Robert Voigt, a German-born mantle salesman, and his wife Elizabeth, née Robb. Educated locally at Ross Place school, he joined the Slade Harriers and later Manchester Athletic Club. In 1905-06 he studied in Austria. Very short, fair, wiry (8 st. 3 lb., 52.2 kg) and a vegetarian, Voigt won the five-mile race at the 1908 London Olympic Games. He was British four-mile (1908-09) and one-mile (1910) champion, and competed in Europe, including Russia, in 1909.

A master engineer, familiar with German, French, Italian and Spanish, Voigt arrived in Melbourne in June 1911. He became Victorian mile champion in 1912 and started Voigt & King, mechanical engineers, at Armadale. On 5 September 1913 at East Melbourne registry office he married Minnie Boardman, from Salford, England; in October they moved to Sydney, but left for England next April. In World War I he ran a welding and brazing works at Manchester.

In February 1921 Voigt returned to Sydney and controlled the research bureau of the Labor Council of New South Wales. He became one of the 'Trades Hall Reds', favourite bogeymen for conservatives and a target of the Federal secret service. At a March 1922 economic conference he clashed with W. M. Hughes [q.v.9], and at Sydney University Union in April he supported revolution in a debate with W. A. Holman and D. R. Hall [qq.v.9]. In April 1923 he urged communists and Labor to unite. Although he was denounced by his Dee Why neighbours, and linked with Jock Garden [q.v.8] and A. C. Willis [q.v.] as 'extremists of the extremist

kind', he apparently never joined the Communist Party of Australia, but regarded it as part of the nemesis of capitalism. In July 1923 he left for Los Angeles, United States of America.

Returning to Australia in February 1925, with enthusiasm for radio and its nationalization, he chaired the Labor Council's wireless committee and founded 2KY radio in October. From July he was Willis's private secretary. Voigt sat on the 1926 Labor conference's committee which revised party rules, was minutes secretary of the conferences and briefly belonged to the inner group controlling the State executive in 1927-30. From May 1927 he managed United Distributors Ltd. Founding chairman (1927-30) of the Australian Federation of Commercial Broadcasting Stations and president (1927-30) of the Radio Manufacturers' Association of New South Wales, in January 1929 he became manager of 2KY (and its boxing commentator) and in April assistant secretary of the Labor Council.

With J. T. Lang [q.v.9] in the ascendant, from 1930 Voigt's influence waned; in 1934 R. A. King defeated him for the secretaryship of the Labor Council. While Voigt was visiting Europe, Soviet Russia and U.S.A. in 1935, his position at 2KY was challenged. In January 1936 he resigned and in March left for London where he set up Broadcast Enterprises Ltd and recorded radio programmes for the Dominions. In 1940-45 he co-founded H.V.H. Engineering Ltd, Hereford, which made aircraft parts. Moving to New Zealand, he was a partner in Monro Foundries Ltd (1947-52) and James Motors (1956-60). Survived by his wife and three sons, Voigt died at Auckland on 15 October 1973. A restless, contradictory idealist, he had served Australia's early wireless industry and fought in the cockpit of 1920s Sydney Labor politics.

M. Goot, 'Radio Lang', in H. Radi & P. Spearritt (eds), *Jack Lang* (Syd, 1977); B. Nairn, *The 'Big Fella'* (Melb, 1986); *Athletic News* (Manchester), 1 June, 20 July 1908; *Referee*, 2 Sept 1908, 14 June 1911, 1 Oct 1913, 15 Apr 1914; *SMH*, 4, 6 Mar, 1 Apr 1922, 16 Jan 1929; *Daily Telegraph* (Syd), 1 Feb 1927, 6 Aug 1935; *Aust Worker*, 8 Mar 1922, 11 Apr, 18 July 1923, 4 Feb 1925; NSW Labor Council minutes (ANUABL); information from Miss R. Voigt, Springwood, NSW, and Mr E. Voigt, Auckland, NZ.

CHRIS CUNNEEN

VON DOUSSA, HEINRICH ALBERT ALFRED (1848-1926), horse-racing promoter and politician, and CHARLES LOUIS (1850-1932), politician and lawyer, were born on 27 April 1848 at Adelaide and 17 May 1850 at Hahndorf, South Australia, sons of Emil Louis Alfred von Doussa, farmer, and his wife Anna Dorothea, née Schach; Emil later entered the Hahndorf firm of Gunther & von Doussa, chemists. Both his sons were educated at T. W. Boehm's [q.v.7] Hahndorf Academy; Alfred proceeded to the Collegiate School of St Peter in Adelaide, whereas Louis was privately tutored. After leaving school, Alfred accompanied his father to the New Zealand goldfields. He was later involved in several Western Australian gold-mines and became chairman of directors of Mount Benson Goldmining Co. When Emil retired to Germany, Alfred maintained the pharmacy while continuing as clerk to the Echunga Council (1871-1926). On 15 October 1885 at Gawler he married Helena Theresa Doudy.

A handsome, genial and impulsive man, Alfred numbered his friends in hundreds. He was a political force among local Germans and in 1901-21 represented Southern District in the Legislative Council where he became known for his liberal views. A member of seven royal commissions, five of which concerned railways, he sat on the railways standing committee and urged the construction of the Pinnaroo line to develop the Mallee region. As a vigorous sportsman into his fifties, he especially enjoyed rifle-shooting. But this 'prince of organisers' is best remembered as secretary of the Onkaparinga Racing Club from its foundation in 1875 to 1924; he instituted its Oakbank Easter races which grew to be one of Australia's premier picnic meetings. Survived by his wife, two daughters and a son, Alfred died at Hahndorf on 1 August 1926 and was buried in the local cemetery. His estate was sworn for probate at £193. The von Doussa Steeplechase at his old club commemorates him.

Louis was articled in 1866 to J. J. Bonnar and admitted to the Bar in 1871. On 16 April 1874 at Strathalbyn he married Agnes Bowman; they were to have seven children. He was a man of 'cultured and resilient brain' whose social gifts made his company sought. He practised in every jurisdiction of the State's Supreme and lower courts, and in the High Court of Australia. An ardent Federationist, from 1899 he represented Mount Barker in the House of Assembly, but lost his seat in 1902 when the electorate was restructured; adverse publicity surrounding his introduction of the judges' retiring allowances bill (1901) possibly contributed to his defeat.

In 1903 he, too, entered the Legislative Council as a representative for Southern; he was attorney-general and minister for education in J. G. Jenkins's [q.v.9] government. A nervous breakdown forced him to leave the ministry next year and the council in 1905. Four of his children had died young, and Agnes died after the birth of a daughter in 1886. At Elsternwick, Melbourne, on 17 March 1900 Louis married with Presbyterian forms an Irish widow, Robena Frances Farrar, née Smyth; they were to have no children. In retirement Louis represented the State in lawn bowls; an Anglican and a Freemason, as was his brother, he fostered the arts and agriculture at Mount Barker, 'the town I love'. He died there on 27 May 1932 and was buried in the local cemetery. His estate was sworn for probate at £19 883, much of which was bequeathed to Mount Barker where an obelisk was erected in his memory.

H. T. Burgess (ed), *Cyclopedia of South Australia*, 1 (Adel, 1907); S. Bessant, *Oakbank* (Adel, 1984); *Critic* (Adel), 4 Mar 1899; *Quiz* (Adel), 2 June 1932, 13 July 1933; *Observer* (Adel), 4 Apr 1896, 6 Mar 1899, 3 Dec 1921, 7 Aug 1926; *Register* (Adel), 25 Nov 1921, 2 Aug 1926, 25 Nov 1931; *Advertiser* (Adel), 2 Aug 1926, 28 May 1932; *Mount Barker Courier*, 3 June 1932; information from Mr R. McOmish, Mount Barker, SA.

WRAY VAMPLEW

VON SKERST; *see* SKERST

VONWILLER, OSCAR ULRICH (1882-1972), professor of physics, was born on 18 February 1882 at Paddington, Sydney, second child of John Ulrich Vonwiller, a Swiss-born merchant, and his native-born wife Josephine, née Hug. Oscar was educated at Paddington Superior Public School and Sydney Boys' High School where he was dux (1898) and won a Barker [q.v.3] scholarship and Horner exhibition. At the University of Sydney (B.Sc., 1902) he enrolled in engineering, but changed to science, graduating with the University medal and first-class honours in physics and mathematics. Appointed junior demonstrator in physics (1902) and assistant lecturer (1910), he published—with Professor J. A. Pollock [q.v.11]—his first scientific paper on electric waves in the *Philosophical Magazine*. They also produced a textbook, *Practical physics* (1907, 1918).

At Woollahra on 30 December 1907 Vonwiller married with Presbyterian forms a cousin Annie Vera Bennett, niece of Samuel Bennett [q.v.3] of the *Evening News*. Assistant professor from 1913, Vonwiller published several articles on the electrical properties of solids: selenium, molybdenite and silicon. During World War I he shouldered Pollock's duties, but was incapacitated by pneumonic influenza for months in 1919-20. His wife Vera died suddenly in 1920. On 1 January 1925 at St Stephen's Presbyterian Church, Sydney, he married a divorcee Elsie Isobel Bridges, née Whiteman.

He was promoted associate professor in 1921 and again took charge when Pollock died in office next year. Appointed to the chair in 1923, Vonwiller completed the plans for the new physics building which opened in 1925. He had only three members of staff until 1938 and had to carry an increasing load as his subject rapidly advanced, particularly under the sway of quantum mechanics.

Despite the difficulties, Vonwiller switched his chief interest in physics to the neglected but important area of optics, particularly spectroscopy. He produced several competent papers: following his leave in 1929 at Utrecht, Netherlands, one of them was published in the American *Physical Review*. In 1939-41 he was dean of the faculty of science and member of the senate. At the onset of World War II, as a member of the Commonwealth panel he organized the Sydney contribution to optical munitions, producing anti-aircraft gun-sights and pioneering the work of reconditioning thousands of requisitioned binoculars.

A scholar in a community of scholars, Vonwiller used his knowledge of the classics with telling effect; his writings on historical figures, such as Newton and Galileo, showed freshness and independence; he understood, lectured on and debated the great themes of science, philosophy and religion; he was in the vanguard of those concerned with the social applications of science. Vonwiller gave of his services freely and headed the university union (1914-15), science society and rifle club. He was foundation president of the Science Teachers' Association of New South Wales, president of the Royal Society of New South Wales (1930) and of section A, Australian and New Zealand Association for the Advancement of Science (1935), a member of the Physical Society, London, the British Astronomical Association and of the boards of visitors of Sydney Observatory (1930-61) and the Mount Stromlo Observatory, Canberra (1944-55), fellow of the Institute of Physics, London (1927) and the Australian Institute of Physics (1963), and treasurer of the Australian National Research Council (1934-40).

In the 1930s his wife ran their farm at Castle Hill. Retiring in 1946, Vonwiller lived at Kangaroo Valley, but continued to make contributions to science, to university life and to the *Union Recorder*. In his prime he was of medium build, with grey hair and a serene, open face, conveying the same impression as his measured writing style. He died in Lewisham Hospital, Sydney, on 30 July 1972 and was buried in the Catholic section of Northern Suburbs cemetery. He was survived by a son of each of his marriages. Vonwiller's portrait by Erwin Reiner (1954) is held by the University of Sydney.

Philosophical Mag, 3 (1902), p 586; *Physical Review*, 35 (1930), p 802; Roy Soc NSW, *J*, 3 (1931), p 333, 76 (1942), p 316; ANZAAS, *Report of Meeting*, 22 (1935), p 38; *Syd Univ Science J*, 1936, p 24; Univ Syd Union, *Union Recorder*, 7 Oct 1937, p 215; *Aust J of Science*, 1 (1938), p 30; *Syd Mail*, 26 Apr 1902; *SMH*, 25 Apr 1923, 15 Sept 1925, 20 Aug 1927, 8 May 1930, 15 Sept 1936; *Daily Telegraph* (Syd), 15 Sept 1925; Vonwiller papers *and* Professorial Bd minutes (Univ Syd Archives).

J. B. T. McCAUGHAN

VOSPER, FREDERICK CHARLES BURLEIGH (1869-1901), journalist and politician, was born on 23 March 1869 at St Dominick, Cornwall, England, son of Charles Walter Vosper, prison warder, and his wife Emma, née Lane. Educated at Truro, he served briefly in the Royal Navy before migrating to Maryborough, Queensland, in 1886. After working for the *Eidsvold Reporter* and the *Maryborough Chronicle*, he was sub-editor of the Charters Towers *Northern Miner* until 1890 when he became editor of the *Australian Republican*. He adopted the name Burleigh and later added two years to his age.

A professed atheist, he fought for causes such as republicanism, political separation for the goldfields and miners' safety; he also opposed Asian immigration. Vosper defended working men's rights in the press and on public platforms, and was the author of two pamphlets, *A social armistice* and *Legalised robbery* (1891). As editor of the *Republican*, he wrote the inflammatory 'BREAD or BLOOD' editorial which condoned 'revolution throughout Australasia' in the course of the 1891 shearers' strike. After two trials he was acquitted of seditious libel, but was convicted in 1892 of inciting a riot during a miners' dispute and sentenced to three months hard labour. On his release Vosper considered entering the Queensland parliament, then moved to Sydney and Melbourne where he worked on *Truth* and *Workman*.

Next year he reached the Western Australian goldfields town of Cue and joined the *Murchison Miner*. In 1893-94 he was employed by several newspapers at Cue, Geraldton and Perth (where he began the short-lived *Miner's Right*), before editing the influential *Coolgardie Miner*. He was, as well, a correspondent for the *Mining Journal* and the *West Australian Review*, and wrote a guidebook, *The prospector's companion* (1894). Vosper joined several political movements in 1894-97, proving himself a bold platform speaker with a gift for repartee. He was prominent in the National League, the Gold Diggers' Union, the Goldfields Protection and Advancement League, and the Electoral Registration League. In mid-1895, while touring the colony as delegate of the Anti-Asiatic

League, he edited the *Geraldton Express* and used it to attack Sir John Forrest's [q.v.8] policies.

Because of his popularity in the eastern goldfields, in 1897 Vosper turned to parliamentary politics. Rebuffed by the Political Labor Party, as he had been in Queensland, he ran as an Independent for the Legislative Assembly seat of North-East Coolgardie and won easily. He supported votes for women, compulsory arbitration, a minimum wage, payment of members, liberalization of the electoral laws and triennial parliaments. Although he lived in Perth, he regularly visited the goldfields. On 11 November in St John's Anglican Church, Perth, Vosper married a widow, Venetia Ann Nicholson, née Finn; they were to remain childless. Using their combined capital, he joined Edward Ellis in establishing the *Sunday Times*. After Ellis's death in 1898, Vosper became editor and consolidated his reputation for scathing attacks on Forrest and his party. An Adelaide journalist regarded Vosper in 1901 as unstable and vain, seeing him as an editor who overloaded his newspaper with references to himself. Vosper was tall and thin, with a sallow complexion, prominent jaw, and black, shoulder-length hair. A dramatic figure, he was far more than a political showman: contemporaries agreed that he was courageous, intelligent, well-read and that he had a magnetic personality; but he also made many enemies.

From 1897, in parliament and outside it, he devoted time to goldfields' disputes, to the government's mental health policies and to Federation. In each area he revealed his attachment to principle, albeit in opposition to popular opinion. With regard to Federation, he thought that Western Australia should join, though only on the best possible terms, and eventually campaigned for a 'No' vote. His oppositionist stand estranged him from the goldfields-based 'Separation for Federation' movement. Vosper achieved more success in promoting penal reforms, including changes to the Lunacy Act. He sat on six select committees: one in 1899 reported favourably on the bill to establish the Commonwealth of Australia. An admirer of Cecil Rhodes, Vosper supported the South African War. He was a member of the Australian Institute of Mining Engineers, founded the State branch of the Geological Society of Australasia and presented his collection of a thousand mineral specimens to the Western Australian Museum.

Vosper never spared himself. Although his hard drinking had ended when he married, he suffered illnesses caused by overwork. He and his wife, of necessity, lived frugally; by November 1900 he was in financial difficulty and, with the abolition of his electorate, Vos-per stood for the Senate as a liberal free trader. Soon after announcing his platform, he suffered an attack of appendicitic erysipelas; having received Catholic rites, he died on 6 January 1901 and was buried in Karrakatta cemetery; his gravestone reads: 'Nevertheless I Live'. He left an estate of less than £5.

J. Kirwan, *My life's adventure* (Lond, 1936); V. Courtney, *All I may tell* Critic (Adel), 12, 19 Jan 1901; *Univ Studies in History*, 5 (1967); *Westerly*, 4, Dec 1977; *Geraldton Express*, 7, 21 June, 19 July 1895; *Coolgardie Miner*, 10, 17, 30 Apr 1897; *Kalgoorlie Miner*, 31 July 1900; *Sunday Times* (Perth), 13 Jan 1901; J. Kirwan papers *and* Vosper papers (Battye Lib). E. JAGGARD

VOSS, FRANCIS HENRY VIVIAN (1860-1940), medical practitioner, was born on 9 August 1860 at Hackney, London, son of Robert Voss, solicitor, and his wife Charlotte, née Smith. Educated at the Church of England Grammar School, Hackney, he gained some experience as an assistant to the family's doctor before passing the University of Cambridge entrance examination and entering London Hospital. There he studied under Dr Hughlings Jackson, Sir Jonathan Hutchinson and other leading medical men. On 11 August 1881 Voss received permission to practise as a licentiate of the Society of Apothecaries (M.R.C.S., 1882; F.R.C.S., 1885). He served his internship at London Hospital and worked for a year at Whitechapel Infirmary.

Reaching Bowen, Queensland, in November 1885 as locum tenens for Dr Thurston, Voss was additionally employed as government health officer. Next year he moved to Rockhampton where he was assistant immigration agent (in the quarantine area) in 1887, government medical officer (1888-1927) and visiting government surgeon from 1891. Soon after arriving, he established a flourishing practice and attracted two doctors from overseas. The 'Rockhampton triumvirate' ran two private hospitals; Voss improved the only maternity ward, separated it administratively from the Benevolent Asylum and established a training school for nurses. A disciple of Joseph Lister, he was an outstanding medical practitioner, especially in obstetrics and gynaecology. He was considerate to mothers, whether they were married or not; in return, they revered him.

In 1897 Voss bought a large block in Talford Street on which to build a modern private hospital. In the following year he visited the United States of America and England—the first of his three visits—to gather new ideas and purchase equipment. He returned with an X-ray machine, improved sterilizers and detailed plans. The hospital was built in 1900. A pioneer among private practitioners in establishing his own pathology laboratory, Voss became a foundation fellow of the Royal Australasian College of Surgeons in 1927.

A colleague remembered him as wise, honest and trustworthy, as a veritable godsend in a district stretching five hundred miles (805 km) inland. On call twenty-four hours a day, Voss still found time for private study: he indulged his love of literature in his fine private library, knew the Bible and belonged to the Home Reading Union and the Natural Science Circle. He contributed to local sanitation and educational developments, and was a member and chairman of the Girls' Grammar School Trust, vice-president of the Rockhampton Jockey Club, patron of the cricket association and a Freemason. For many years he was surgeon-captain of local naval volunteers in the Queensland Defence Force and commanded the Rockhampton branch of the Ambulance Corps.

Predeceased in 1926 by his wife Lottie Kerrod, née White, whom he had married at St Paul's Church, Rockhampton, on 11 January 1888, Voss retired to Sydney in 1929. He died at his Bellevue Hill home on 15 February 1940 and was cremated with Anglican rites. Of his two sons and three daughters who survived him, all but one daughter became medical practitioners.

Alcazar Press, *Queensland, 1900* (Brisb, nd); W. Watson & Sons Ltd, *Salute to the X-ray pioneers of Australia* (Syd, 1946); L. McDonald, *Rockhampton* (Brisb, 1981); *MJA*, 13 Apr 1940; *Morning Bulletin*, 2 Feb 1929, 16 Feb 1940; *SMH*, 19 Feb 1940; information from Miss V. Voss *and* Dr D. M. Sear, Rose Bay, Syd.   LORNA MCDONALD

W

WADDELL, THOMAS (1854?-1940), pastoralist and premier, was born in Monaghan, Ireland, son of John Waddell and his wife Ann, née Mossman. The family migrated in 1855 and settled at Lake George, New South Wales, where John became a grazier. Educated at Goulburn High School, at 15 Thomas worked as a shop assistant and was clerk of petty sessions at Collector in 1876-80. An awakening interest in business took him into horse- and cattle-dealing; in partnership with his brother George, he soon took up Mileela, Wyuna Downs and Wangamana stations in the far west and spent five rough years managing them. The brothers sold out in the boom of the 1880s.

In 1887 Waddell topped the poll for the Legislative Assembly seat of Bourke; next day parliament was dissolved and he had to contest the seat again (successfully). In February he moved to Sydney and on 27 May at Christ Church St Laurence married Elizabeth James, a 19-year-old from Orange. Waddell combined an active political career with numerous business activities. He acquired new pastoral interests in the outback, including Fort Bourke station with (Sir) Samuel McCaughey [q.v.5] whom he later bought out.

Having held Bourke in 1889, Waddell lost the seat in June 1891, but regained it four months later, defeating Donald Macdonell [q.v.10] at a by-election; thereafter he represented Cobar (1894-98), Cowra (1898-1904), Belubula (1904-13) and Lyndhurst (1913-17). A Protectionist and an advocate of Federation, he served as colonial treasurer under (Sir) John See [q.v.11] in 1901-04, but wished that his old friend (Sir) Joseph Carruthers [q.v.7] 'were a member of our cabinet'.

Tall and grave, Waddell had to cope with the State's finances at a time of severe drought and won respect in the House. His tight financial policies enabled him to reduce the deficit in the 1903 budget which gained reluctant praise from the Opposition. He was generally regarded as a 'useful lieutenant' who lacked the strength of character to be a leader. When See resigned as premier in June 1904, he favoured W. P. Crick [q.v.8] as his successor. The governor, Sir Harry Rawson [q.v.11], indicated that he was not prepared to send either for Crick who had been 'drinking to excess' at Executive Council meetings, or for B. R. Wise [q.v.] whom Rawson regarded as able but unreliable. After canvassing his colleagues, See reported that Waddell was marginally favoured over John Perry [q.v.11]. Waddell formed a Protectionist ministry on

17 June, but inherited a divided party; Crick and Wise declined to serve under him and the government was soundly defeated by the Liberals who formed a ministry under Carruthers on 30 August.

Retaining only twelve seats, Waddell fashioned the Progressive Party from the remnant of the Protectionists; in 1907 he led the Progressives to defeat. The party disintegrated after May when Waddell accepted the post of colonial secretary under Carruthers. (Sir) Charles Wade [q.v.] became premier in October and Waddell again became colonial treasurer. He reduced income tax and repealed stamp duty, but the government was embroiled in contentious industrial relations and land legislation; Labor won the election in 1910. A member of the Farmers and Settlers' Association, Waddell was one of eleven Liberals who formed a country faction at the 1913 elections. In April next year he was involved in early moves to found a State country party which he saw as the first step towards a 'united front in opposition to the overbearing tyranny of unionism and Socialism gone mad'. In 1917 he was nominated to the Legislative Council.

As a founder in 1918 and first chairman, Waddell was closely associated with the McGarvie Smith [q.v.11] Institute which controlled the production of anthrax vaccine. He was a director of the City Bank of Sydney, Queensland Insurance Co. Ltd and Modern Lighting Ltd, and chairman of the Austral Malay Rubber Co. Ltd and the Commonwealth Wool & Produce Co. Ltd. A long-standing opponent of government intervention in the economy, Waddell frequently wrote to the newspapers, criticizing government spending and taxation, and advocating selling off the railways; appearing before the basic wage inquiry in 1921, he opposed higher wages. He belonged to the Australian Club, enjoyed shooting, played chess and handled a billiard cue 'with some skill'. In 1933 he did not stand for election to the reconstituted Legislative Council.

He died at his Ashfield home on 25 October 1940 and was cremated with Presbyterian forms. His wife, three sons and four daughters survived him. Waddell had identified with the individualism of bush life; though his strong views were not always accepted, it was said that 'his word is taken when another politician's oath would not be believed'.

PD (LC NSW), Oct 1928; *Catholic Press*, 20 Sept 1902, 29 Jan, 1 Oct 1903, 16 June, 18 Aug 1904; *T&CJ*, 3 July 1907; *Fighting Line* and *Daily*

Telegraph (Syd), 19 Aug 1913; Land (Syd), 1 May 1914; SMH, 22 Oct 1915, 29 June, 17 Sept 1921, 1 Jan 1931, 26 Oct 1940; See and Carruthers papers (ML); CO 418/32, f218 (PRO microfilm, NL).

A. R. Buck

WADDY, PERCIVAL STACY (1875-1937), Anglican clergyman, was born on 8 January 1875 at Carcoar, New South Wales, second son of Richard Waddy, a bank clerk from India, and his native-born wife Elizabeth Ann, daughter of John Stacy [q.v.6]. After the family moved to Morpeth, Stacy attended East Maitland Grammar and The King's School, Parramatta. He captained King's, played cricket for the Cumberland district against Lord Sheffield's English team in December 1891, and won the Broughton and Forrest [qq.v.1] exhibition. At Balliol College, Oxford (B.A., 1897; M.A., 1901), he read law and excelled at cricket. Capped for the university after scoring 107 not out against Surrey, Waddy played against Cambridge (1896 and 1897) but declined to assist the 1896 Australian touring team, preferring to travel home to visit his family.

Abandoning his intended career as a barrister for welfare and religious service at Oxford House in London's East End, he was made deacon on 18 December 1898 and ordained priest on 21 December 1899 by Bishop Mandell Creighton of London. Waddy had great gifts as a teacher, organizer, writer and sportsman. His physique was superb and he had an attractive personality, though tinged with acerbity. He almost did too many things too well to give his full attention to one activity and sometimes resented the consequent lack of recognition, but his faith was constant and his vocation as a clergyman unwavering.

Returning to New South Wales in 1900, Waddy married Etheldred Spittal at St James's Church, Morpeth, on 28 October 1901. Working in the Newcastle diocese, he served at the cathedral, Stockton and Singleton, combining parochial work with pamphleteering and raising money for a lectureship in memory of his mentor Bishop Stanton [q.v.6]. He also played cricket for Northern district and in December 1903 made 93 and 102 against (Sir) Pelham Warner's visiting Englishmen.

In October 1906 Waddy accepted an invitation to become headmaster of The King's School. At a time of expansion and change, he founded a junior school (1908), set up a house system and began 'land classes' for boys without academic pretensions. All boys over 12 now had to belong to the school cadet corps and wear its distinctive uniform. Popular and vigorous, Waddy attended the Delhi Durbar (1911) with a party of cadets and wrote about it.

A part-time chaplain from 1908, during World War I Waddy was twice refused leave by the school council to enlist in the Australian Imperial Force; in May 1916 he resigned and, despite Archbishop Wright's [q.v.] disapproval, became an army chaplain. Waddy was always to regret this action, but believed he had no alternative. He served in France with the 3rd and 1st Battalions, and in August 1917 sailed for Egypt. In October he was transferred to headquarters, Desert Mounted Corps, where he became senior chaplain and an honorary major with the Light Horse.

The Middle East was to claim him. Following a spell in Australia in 1918, Waddy returned to become a canon of St George's Cathedral, Jerusalem, archdeacon of Palestine with responsibility for education, and chaplain of the Order of St John of Jerusalem (1922); he published two local guides and gathered material for his popular Homes of the Psalms (London, 1928). Appointed secretary in 1924 of the Society for the Propagation of the Gospel in Foreign Parts, he moved to London.

Faced with the society's decreasing finances and the fading attractiveness of mission work, Waddy embarked on tours to North America, the Far East and Pacific, India and Africa. He preferred travel to administration and proved an effective inspector of missions. A prolific author of devotional works, he also wrote detective stories with a biblical setting. He was a canon of Peterborough, preached at Oxford, maintained his interest in Freemasonry, substituted golf for cricket, and developed into a competent pen-and-ink artist. His constitution was weakened by hard travelling in difficult regions: Waddy contracted cerebral malaria on the Gold Coast, Africa, and died in the Hospital for Tropical Diseases, London, on 8 February 1937, survived by his wife, three sons and two daughters.

S. M. Johnstone, The history of The King's School, Parramatta (Syd, 1932); E. Waddy, Stacy Waddy (Lond, 1938); Wisden Cricketers' Almanack, 1893, 1905, 1938; Aust Bd of Missions, ABM Review, 1 Mar 1937; The King's School Mag, May 1937, p 2; Church Times, 12 Feb 1937; The Times, 13, 18 Feb 1937; Aust Church Record, 25 Feb 1937; Church Standard, 2 Apr 1937; P. J. Yeend, Aspects of the history of The King's School, Parramatta (M.A. thesis, Macquarie Univ, 1980); P. S. Waddy files (The King's School Archives).   K. J. Cable

WADE, ARTHUR (1878-1951), geologist, was born on 12 November 1878 at Halifax, Yorkshire, England, son of Samuel Wade, master butcher, and his wife Sarah, née

Gathercole. From school at Isleworth, London, he went to the Royal College of Science (University of London) and won its Murchison medal and prize (1903). He taught geology at the Liverpool Municipal Technical School and in 1906 was elected a fellow of the Geological Society of London. In 1909 he was appointed a senior demonstrator at the Royal School of Mines, London. Having worked in Egypt on the geology of petroleum, he graduated D.Sc. (1911) from the University of London and pioneered the teaching of that subject at the Imperial College of Science and Technology.

In 1913 Wade was recommended to the Australian government to further the search for oil in Papua where inspections by J. E. Carne [q.v.7] and the government geologist E. R. Stanley had encouraged the decision to sponsor a survey. Wade produced his *Report on petroleum in Papua* in 1914 and visited the Territory intermittently until 1919. As director of oilfields, he reported on petroleum prospects for the Commonwealth government between 1915 and 1919 when he resigned to become an industrial consultant. In 1920-24 he worked in Africa, North America and Australia; later, based in London, he shifted his attention to southern Europe and Poland. On 29 January 1924 at Pace Baptist Church, Mississippi, United States of America, he had married Mayme Lou Souter.

Resuming his antipodean career with the Freney Kimberley Oil Co. in 1933, Wade made his most significant contributions to Australian geology. Over the next two years, with rarely more than a surveyor and a couple of assistants, he used innovative aerial reconnaissance combined with ground traverses to cover much of the Canning Basin in Western Australia. He systematically recorded its stratigraphy and found evidence in the basin of ancient barrier reefs of Devonian age. With the petrologist R. T. Prider, he also studied leucite-bearing volcanic rocks in the West Kimberley area. A member (1936) of the Commonwealth Oil Advisory Committee and successor to W. G. Woolnough [q.v.] as chairman (1938), in 1940 Wade became geological adviser to the Shell (Queensland) Development Co. of Australia. During World War II he served on the staff of the United States Army, South-West Pacific Area (1943-44), and with Allied Intelligence (1944-46). He was a freeman of the city of London, and a councillor and fellow of the Institute of Petroleum.

An erudite and fluent writer, Wade contributed many papers to scientific journals. He also wrote poetry: his *Vagabond verse* (Melbourne, 1917, 1918, Brisbane, 1947) was said to have been first published without his knowledge. In addition he claimed authorship of the *Borneo book for servicemen* (c.1944).

A man 'notably equable in temperament', kind, considerate and a good companion, Wade yet had 'all the tenacity of purpose and bluntness of a true Yorkshireman'. He died on 8 April 1951 after a heart attack while surfing at Mermaid Beach, Queensland, and was cremated. His wife survived him, as did their son and daughter after whom the volcanic Mounts Cedric and Gytha in the West Kimberleys are named. The mineral wadeite is named after their father.

Qld Government Mining J, 20 Mar 1951; American Assn of Petroleum Geologists, *Bulletin*, 35, 1951, p 2643; Geological Soc of Lond, *Q J*, 107, 1952, p lxi; *Earth Sciences Hist*, 6, no 2, 1987, p 159; personal information.   T. G. VALLANCE

WADE, BENJAMIN MARTIN (1883-1958), building contractor, businessman and politician, was born on 12 July 1883 at Tenterden, New South Wales, eighth child of William Martin Wade, a blacksmith from England, and his native-born wife Anne, née Hogan. Educated at Stannifer and Inverell Superior public schools, Ben worked briefly for the Department of Lands at Narrabri, then tried teaching, before going to Sydney to learn the building trade.

Establishing a successful business at Inverell about 1907, Wade won building contracts there and in neighbouring towns. By 1909 he had bought a brickworks and later owned five timber-mills. After marrying Bertha Mathilde Oberle (d. 1923) on 18 April 1917 at St Patrick's Catholic Church, Laidley, Queensland, he bought into F. & E. Thomas, cordial manufacturers, and began making ice-cream; by 1923 he held the controlling interest. He was a director of Kautz Pty Ltd, bakers and pastry-cooks, ran the Inverell picture theatre and an undertaking business, and held four grazing properties; in 1931 he began to grow tobacco as a share-farmer. On 10 January 1927 at the Sacred Heart Church, Randwick, Sydney, he had married a widow Claire Vaughan Reece, née Williams (d. 1952).

Having unsuccessfully contested the New South Wales Legislative Assembly seat of Barwon for the Country Party in 1930, Wade won it in 1932 and held it until he resigned in 1940. With the confidence of a 'self-made' man, in parliament he spoke often and on a wide range of issues, expressing the rural populism of the time. He frequently criticized the Stevens [q.v.]-Bruxner [q.v.7] coalition, and opposed D. H. Drummond [q.v.8] on technical education and on a new public library for Sydney. Engaging in heated exchanges with Labor members, he wanted all industrial awards cancelled, a 48-hour week, lower taxes, lower bank interest and lower solicitors' fees. Although attempts were made in the House to discredit him in 1934, he was appointed chairman of the 1936-37 select committee inquiry into the tobacco industry and in 1941 became a member of the Australian Tobacco Board.

Defeated for the Federal seat of Gwydir in 1940 and 1946, Wade also failed in 1944 to regain his State seat. By 1950, when he unsuccessfully sought endorsement for Bruxner's seat of Tenterfield, his outspokenness had left him with few friends in the party hierarchy. Standing as an Independent, he lost to Bruxner.

Wade had been chairman of the local railway league in 1923 and was a member of the North-West County Council (1940-51, 1954-58), the Better Communications League and the New England Regional Committee. An alderman on Inverell Municipal Council (1921-23, 1948-52, 1953-58) and mayor in 1956-58, he was a member of the local Chamber of Commerce and the Pastoral and Agricultural Association, as well as of the Graziers' Association of New South Wales.

Ben Wade was a big man with an 'open countenance'. He belonged to the New South Wales Rifle Association and regularly contested the King's prize; he also enjoyed bowling, fishing and gardening. A diabetic, on 21 May 1953 he married a nurse Lillian May Sanderson in the sacristy of the Sacred Heart Church, Inverell. Survived by his wife, and by a son and two daughters from each of his previous marriages, he died on 20 December 1958 at Inverell and was buried in the local cemetery.

D. Aitkin, *The Country Party in New South Wales* (Canb, 1972); E. Wiedemann, *World of its own* (Inverell, NSW, 1981); *PD* (NSW), 27 June 1934, p 1350; *PP* (NSW), 1937-38, 1, p 933; *Aust Country Party*, 1 Jan 1935; *Inverell Times*, 3, 22, 24 Dec 1958.
                                    BRUCE MITCHELL

WADE, SIR CHARLES GREGORY (1863-1922), premier and judge, was born on 26 January 1863 at Singleton, New South Wales, eldest of six sons of William Burton Wade, a civil engineer from Shropshire, and his native-born wife Anne McBean, née Duguid. His brothers included Leslie and (Sir) Robert [qq.v.]. Greg was educated at All Saints College, Bathurst (1874-76), and The King's School, Parramatta (school captain, 1879-80, and colour sergeant of cadets, 1880). Winning the Broughton and Forrest [qq.v.1] exhibition in 1880, he read classics at Merton College, Oxford (B.A., 1884). Described as 'a Hercules of a man' and regarded as one of the finest wing three-quarters of his day, he played Rugby football for Oxford and represented England eight times. He also excelled at tennis, rowing and shooting. Called to the Bar at the Inner Temple, London, on 19 May 1886, he returned to Sydney and was admitted to the colonial Bar on 1 September. At All Saints Church, Petersham, he married Ella Louise Bell, daughter of a civil engineer, on 9 April 1890.

As a crown prosecutor in 1891-1902, mainly on the western circuit and in the Central Criminal Court, Wade fought his cases tenaciously; his convictions in 1895 included those of W. P. Crick, George Dean and T. E. Rofe [qq.v.8,11]. He published several legal treatises, acted as a District Court judge and conducted four inquiries between 1898 and 1902 into colliery explosions and disasters. A foundation member of the Council of the Bar of New South Wales in 1902, he practised in the new Industrial Arbitration Court where he was increasingly briefed by coal-owners. He took silk in 1906. A. B. Piddington [q.v.11] thought that Wade was 'never brilliant or dextrous, but had a kind of massive personal strength which made his careful and thorough work tell'.

Supported by the Liberal and Reform Association (president from 1908), People's Reform League, New South Wales Alliance for the Supression of Intemperance, Loyal Orange Institution and Australian Protestant Defence Association, Wade was elected to the Legislative Assembly for Willoughby in September 1903. He represented Gordon, an upper-middle-class seat, in 1904-17. In February 1904 he committed himself to local option without compensation.

Although a political novice, in August 1904 Wade was appointed attorney-general and minister of justice in (Sir) Joseph Carruthers' [q.v.7] ministry. He introduced many legal reforms, among them protection of neglected children, and defended the independence of the judiciary. In June 1905 Labor members accused Wade of having administered the Industrial Arbitration Act unfairly. His social reforms appealed mainly to respectable Protestants of some means. His Liquor (Amendment) Act of 1905 was a victory for the temperance movement, and legislation on betting and lotteries in 1905-06 struck principally at gambling among young people and the working classes. Wade's rectitude drove his enemies to revile him as a hypocrite.

The ministry was bedevilled by scandals uncovered by the royal commissioner, (Sir) William Owen [q.v.11], who inquired into the administration of the Lands Department (1905-06). Charges were levelled that Wade (and Carruthers) wanted no action against Crick that might disturb their political arrangements or their pastoral friends. In August 1905 W. A. Holman [q.v.9], Labor deputy leader, exempted Wade from charges of obstructing the royal commission, but when Wade accepted official advice against further prosecution of Crick and W. N. Willis [q.v.] he endured malicious attacks.

Carruthers resigned after winning the election of September 1907. Wade succeeded him and took the portfolios of premier, attorney-general and minister of justice. He confided to Carruthers: 'I almost shudder at the responsibility of the position. I feel my want of experience is my great stumbling block—I must trust to luck & a strong constitution to pull us through'. To Melbourne *Punch*, Wade had the characteristics of the British bulldog —courage, tenacity, obstinacy, pugnacity and loyalty. His speeches were prosy, dreary and humourless; his voice especially when excited was 'harsh, even rasping', in contrast to Holman's mellifluous tone. Wade was a governor (1901-22) of The King's School, a member of the Australian Club and a trustee (1908-18) of the National Art Gallery of New South Wales. An imposing figure with 'a strong and powerful face', he was a shy and aloof man whose few friends included Archbishop Wright [q.v.].

Attempting to conciliate critics who thought the government indifferent to common people, Wade supported legislation to fix minimum wages for all employees, admitted that legalism had helped to frustrate the arbitration system, favoured extended old-age pensions, promised encouragement to the 'industrious and thrifty', and introduced a bill to provide court defence for the poor (an idea which he had earlier ridiculed). The government continued to pass reforming measures of a mildly progressive kind. Wade re-established the ministry of agriculture, authorized work to begin on Burrinjuck Dam and won general praise in December 1907 when he persuaded C. H. Hoskins [q.v.9] to take over William Sandford's [q.v.11] ironworks at Lithgow, to fulfil the government contracts and to pay compensation to Sandford.

From November 1907 political life had been largely dominated by looming industrial strife in the collieries over mechanization and redundancy. Wade negotiated with both sides and proposed an independent tribunal to settle the dispute, on condition that the miners went back to the pits. By 21 November the immediate threat had waned. In March 1908 he introduced a new industrial disputes bill, substituting wages boards for the existing cumbersome arbitration, and banning strikes and lockouts. Labor accused him of planning to destroy trade unionism.

Governor Sir Harry Rawson [q.v.11] reported to the Colonial Office in January 1909 that Wade had 'proved himself a high-minded, capable and strong Minister, and in the handling of some delicate and complicated matters has exhibited great tact, judgment and discretion'. Stubborn in defending State rights, Wade told Alfred Deakin [q.v.8] in

October 1907 that 'the general sentiment . . . is almost one of hostility': relations with the Commonwealth, already strained by the wire-netting case and by squabbles over the Federal capital site, were exacerbated by Deakin's New Protection and proposed financial arrangements.

In introducing amendments in December 1909 to the Industrial Disputes Act (including retrospective imprisonment for inducing unionists to strike), Wade provoked a Labor motion of no confidence which he imprudently ignored. Labor members withdrew from the Assembly for two days. The incident demonstrated Wade's parliamentary ineptitude. Following further coal strikes, in December the government arrested some union leaders, including Peter Bowling [q.v.7], under the 'Coercion' Act.

Throughout the coal strike of 1909-10 Wade's actions favoured the mine-owners. His argument that the government should protect the community from 'socialistic agitators' could not save him from public reaction to his severity. The Crown Lands (Amendment) Act (1908), giving leaseholders the right to convert to limited freehold, had been carried against strong Labor protest. Rumours persisted that Wade wanted the chief justiceship. His many reforms seemed unimportant.

Aware that his government was losing ground to Labor and alarmed by the swing against Deakin's Fusion ministry, Wade argued that Federal and State issues were separate and unavailingly tried to consolidate the Liberal position. His controversial plan to limit the size of parliament was dropped. He courted popularity by making Saturday a half-holiday in Sydney and Newcastle and by introducing a limited Workmen's Compensation Act. Wade's was very much a 'one-man government': nothing that he and his claqueurs did could save the Liberals; the election in October 1910 gave Labor a majority of two.

As leader of the Opposition, Wade made seemingly partisan objections to the Murrumbidgee Irrigation Area legislation. He engaged with Holman in passionate exchanges over Bowling's conviction and release, and missed his chance to force Holman to the polls in July 1911. In August Wade was outmanoeuvred again when Holman persuaded the Liberal Henry Willis [q.v.] to accept Labor nomination as Speaker. In 1913 a royal commission cleared Arthur Griffith [q.v.9] of Wade's charges of maladministration. The Liberals were overwhelmingly defeated that year.

Accused by Holman in 1915 of breaking their political truce, Wade laid the foundations of an alliance with the emerging Country Party and assisted the estrangement of Holman from the Labor Party. After the defeat of the conscription referendum in 1916, he and Holman helped to establish a national government. With his family, Wade departed on a trip to the United States of America and England; he allayed his anxiety at crossing the Atlantic by buying gutta-percha life-saving suits which he tested in the Hudson River. In 1917 he was appointed agent-general in London. He gave seven lectures at University College, London, published as *Australia: problems and prospects* (1919). Knighted in 1918, he was known as Sir Charles and was appointed K.C.M.G. in 1920.

In December 1919 Wade accepted a puisne judgeship in the Supreme Court of New South Wales. He served on royal commissions into gas and electricity prices in 1920-21 and had established himself as a fair, courteous and dignified judge when he died suddenly of heart disease on 26 September 1922 at his Potts Point home. He was buried in the Anglican section of South Head cemetery after a state funeral. His wife, two sons and twin daughters survived him. By then much of the bitterness of earlier years had subsided and Wade's integrity and dedication to public service were praised generously by men who had formerly opposed him.

Cyclopedia of N.S.W. (Syd, 1907); A. B. Pidding-ton, *Worshipful masters* (Syd, 1929); H. V. Evatt, *William Holman* (Syd, 1945); W. A. Steel and J. M. Antill, *The history of All Saints' College, Bathurst, 1873-1934* (Syd, 1936); *British A'sian*, 12 Apr 1917; *Punch* (Melb), 28 Nov 1907, 19 Aug 1909, 1 Jan 1914; *Fighting Line*, 19 Aug 1913; *T&CJ*, 20 Nov 1917; *SMH*, 27 June 1911, 3 June 1920, 27, 28 Sept 1922, 13 Sept 1923, 10 Sept 1926; Deakin papers (NL); Carruthers papers (ML); CO 418/62, f324, /72, f35 (PRO microfilm, NL).

JOHN M. WARD*

WADE, JOHN (1842?-1931), cornflour manufacturer, was born in Yorkshire, England, son of David Wade, manufacturer, and his wife Mary, née Stockwell. Reaching Sydney with his father and two brothers in December 1858 in the *Duncan Dunbar*, John became a storekeeper at Forbes where he married Margaret Crawford, a servant, on 28 June 1863 with Presbyterian forms; they were to have thirteen children. About 1866 he established a general store at Dungog, the centre of a maize-growing district.

Since most cornflour was imported from Britain, Wade saw an opportunity to establish a local cornflour-milling industry: by 1878 he had engaged Mr McDonald from the English cornflour manufacturers, Brown & Polson Ltd, to construct a four-storey, brick-and-wood mill with imported machinery on his partner's (R. L. Alison) land at Cooreei Bridge

on the Williams River. Labour proved a problem: the men were new to the work and, because there were insufficient women to do the packing, the cornflour had to be sent in large sacks to Sydney. Nonetheless, local farmers profited from higher prices for their maize.

An active member of the Methodist Church, Wade was conference representative and circuit steward at Dungog, and later at Ashfield and Mosman. He helped to found the Dungog School of Arts with an abiding friend Rev. Dr J. E. Carruthers who served at that town in 1871-73. Wade was also a founder (1881) and chairman of the Williams River Steam Navigation Co. Ltd. As a Protectionist, he twice unsuccessfully contested the Legislative Assembly seat of Durham.

When maize production declined with the introduction of dairying, John Wade & Co. moved its cornflour and starch manufacturing activities to Sydney in 1888. 'Wade's cornflour' was widely advertised and became a popular Australian household commodity. He retained control until selling out in 1908 to Brown & Polson. Although later bought by Clifford Love [q.v.10] & Co. Ltd, 'Wade's cornflour' continues to be marketed.

Margaret Wade was involved in welfare work for the Wesleyan Church and was a member of the Ashfield branch of the Woman's Christian Temperance Union; she died in 1900. On 19 August 1903 at Brighton, Melbourne, Wade married Sarah Jane Clark, née Kernaghan, widow of Robert Clark [q.v.3]. Survived by two sons and four daughters of his first marriage, Wade died at Mosman on 16 September 1931 and was buried in Rookwood cemetery; the service was conducted by Carruthers.

J. E. Carruthers, *Memories of an Australian ministry 1868 to 1921* (Lond, 1922); *T&CJ*, 14 Sept 1878; *Methodist* (Syd), 6 Oct 1900, 26 Sept 1931; *SMH*, 17, 19 Sept 1931; *Dungog Chronicle*, 22, 25 Sept 1931.

GAIL REEKIE

WADE, LESLIE AUGUSTUS BURTON (1864-1915), civil engineer, was born on 20 June 1864 at Singleton, New South Wales, son of English-born William Burton Wade, civil engineer, and his native-born wife Anne McBean, née Duguid. (Sir) Charles Gregory and (Sir) Robert Blakeway [qq.v.] were his brothers. Leslie was educated at All Saints College, Bathurst, and at The King's School, Parramatta. Joining the Department of Public Works on 1 July 1880 as a cadet, he was articled to W. C. Bennett [q.v.3] and trained as a surveyor in the field with John Cardew, working on Sydney's ocean outfall sewerage scheme.

An outstanding athlete, Wade played

Rugby Union football for New South Wales against Queensland (1883, 1888) and Britain (1888). In February 1890 he joined the recently formed water conservation branch of the Department of Mines and Agriculture as assistant engineer under Hugh McKinney, remaining with the branch when it was transferred to the works department in May 1892. He was directly involved in the planning and construction of major public works, including the Lachlan River storage, and the Cataract Dam for Sydney's water supply. On 29 December 1896 at St John's Anglican Church, Parramatta, Wade married Ethel Constance, daughter of Charles Lloyd [q.v.5].

Promoted principal engineer of the water supply and sewerage branch in March 1901, Wade visited the United States of America in December 1903 to investigate the most suitable and economical type of dam for a proposed reservoir on the Murrumbidgee River. As principal engineer for rivers, water supply and drainage from July 1904 (chief engineer, 1906), he urged the State government to build the Burrinjuck Dam. He was closely associated with its construction and supervised the planning of the diversion canals which channelled water to the Murrumbidgee Irrigation Area, carved out of the arid plains north-west of Narrandera.

In 1908 Wade's health collapsed from the cumulative strain of overwork; taking leave, he investigated engineering practices in Europe. Soon after returning to duty in April 1909, he was made chief engineer for irrigation and drainage; when the branch was divided in August 1911 he became chief engineer for irrigation. He was also executive officer and secretary of the Murrumbidgee Irrigation Trust from January 1911. On 1 January 1913 he was appointed commissioner for water conservation and irrigation with a staff of 250 and responsibility for all irrigation programmes in the State. Wade directed the settlement and development of the M.I.A., exercising the powers of a virtual pro-consul from his headquarters at Leeton. His administrative style blended authoritarianism with paternalism, though he claimed that he tried to see things from the perspective of the battling settler. He was loath to delegate responsibility and his administration was marred by friction with his subordinates, while his skills in land settlement and social planning were also criticized. Because duties took him to Sydney, he was often absent from the M.I.A. Despite his shortcomings, he brought dedication and energy to the task of establishing a sound basis for a venture into irrigated land settlement.

Survived by his wife and four daughters, Wade died at his Double Bay home on 12 January 1915 of coronary heart disease and was buried in Waverley cemetery. News of his sudden death was received in the M.I.A. with the dismay and reverence that usually attend the passing of the great. Wade Shire was designated in his honour.

Cyclopedia of N.S.W. (Syd, 1907); C. J. Lloyd, *Either drought or plenty* (Syd, 1988); *Irrigation Record*, 1 Feb 1915; *British A'sian*, 11 Mar 1915; *SMH*, 13, 14 Jan 1915; *T&CJ*, 20 Jan 1915.

C. J. LLOYD

WADE, SIR ROBERT BLAKEWAY (1874-1954), orthopaedic surgeon, was born on 27 January 1874 at Bathurst, New South Wales, son of English-born William Burton Wade, civil engineer, and his native-born wife Anne McBean, née Duguid. (Sir) Charles and Leslie [qq.v.] were his brothers. Robert attended Sydney Grammar School and studied medicine at the University of Sydney (M.B., 1896; M.D., 1904; Ch.M., 1907). He was resident medical officer at Royal Prince Alfred Hospital and in 1897 joined the staff of the Hospital for Sick Children (Royal Alexandra Hospital for Children) where he became honorary registrar and anaesthetist in 1901; he was awarded his doctorate for a thesis on ether anaesthesia. Honorary assistant surgeon (1901-13), honorary surgeon (1913-33) and consultant (from 1934), he had been associated with (Sir) Charles Clubbe [q.v.8]; Wade developed an interest in orthopaedic surgery and became director of the gymnasium and massage department in 1912. At St John's Anglican Church, Darlinghurst, on 13 June 1903 he had married Maude May, a nurse and daughter of T. F. Furber [q.v.8]; they were to have three daughters.

A major in the Australian Army Medical Corps, during World War I Wade was surgeon at the Military Hospital, Randwick; promoted lieut-colonel, he became consultant orthopaedic surgeon. Following his involvement with children during the poliomyelitis epidemic in 1915-16 and with the orthopaedic problems of wounded soldiers, he became particularly interested in the treatment of cripples, and in preventive medicine and rehabilitation.

Active and vocal as a councillor (1917-33) and president (1925-26) of the State branch of the British Medical Association, Wade was inaugural president (1937) of the orthopaedic section of the Australasian Medical Congress. He published in the *Medical Journal of Australia*. An able administrator, he was vice-president (1920-33) and president (1933-43) of the board of management of the R.A.H.C. He was a foundation fellow (1927) of the (Royal) Australasian College of Surgeons (president 1935-37); chairman of his State's medical board, the Australian Advisory Council for the Physically Handicapped and the

New South Wales Institute of Hospital Almoners; a director, vice-chairman and honorary surgeon at the Prince Henry Hospital, and an honorary at Marrickville and Royal South Sydney hospitals.

In improving health care in the community, Wade played an outstanding role. At the R.A.H.C. he was largely responsible for establishing the Physically Handicapped Children's School (1930), the department of social work (1930), speech therapy unit (1931) and orthopaedic clinic (1932). As lecturer in paediatric surgery at the hospital from 1924 and at the university in 1926-32, he took a large part in making the R.A.H.C. clinical school a major undergraduate teaching facility of the university: he publicly declared the need for a chair in child health and paediatrics four years before it was established in 1949. In his Clubbe oration (1945) Wade also expressed his beliefs in the 'need to improve both the social welfare and the general health of our people', in the importance of 'ample supplies of suitable food at prices possible for everyone' and in 'slum clearance and building of sanitary houses for all'. He saw and sought broad ends and considered that good health began pre-natally and in childhood.

Solid, self-contained and seemingly unhurried, Wade had presence, without any aura of self-importance, and was as readily approached by adults as by children. Rather than irony or humour, his smile revealed the pleasure and interest he showed in his patients, colleagues and friends. For relaxation, he belonged to Royal Sydney Golf Club and went trout-fishing. Elected honorary fellow of the Royal College of Surgeons, England, in 1937, he was knighted next year. Survived by a daughter, he died on 13 May 1954 at Bathurst, where he had spent his last years in retirement, and was cremated. A portrait by Joshua Smith is held by the R.A.H.C.; another by W. B. McInnes [q.v.10] is held by the R.A.C.S., Melbourne.

D. G. Hamilton, *Hand in hand* (Syd, 1979); *MJA*, 4 Aug 1945, 7 Aug 1954; *Bulletin of the Post-Graduate Committee in Medicine of the University of Sydney*, Oct 1965, p 111; information from Dr R. S. Cameron, Woollahra, Syd; personal recollections.

C. R. B. BLACKBURN

WADE, ROBERT THOMPSON (1884-1967), palaeichthyologist, clergyman and schoolmaster, was born on 8 October 1884 in Dublin, eldest son of Robert Wade, prison governor, and his wife Sarah Anne, née Thompson. In 1890 the family arrived in Australia and settled at Bathurst. Educated at All Saints College, which he represented at cricket and Rugby football, young Robert was head boy and won the J. B. Watt [q.v.6] exhibition in 1901. At the University of Sydney (B.A., 1905; M.A., 1924), he came under the influence of (Sir) Edgeworth David [q.v.8] and graduated with honours in geology and mathematics. That year he began teaching science at Barker [q.v.3] College, Hornsby.

Made deacon by Bishop Camidge [q.v.7] on 15 March 1908, Wade married Mary Adderley Kearney on 18 December at St Philip's Church, Sydney. On 6 June 1909 he was priested by Bishop Stone-Wigg [q.v.] and became curate at St Paul's, Wahroonga with Hornsby. Having left Barker briefly in 1910 for a senior curacy at St John's, Darlinghurst, he returned as senior master and in 1917 acted as headmaster. Wade taught physics, chemistry and geology, and organized field excursions.

In 1918 he founded Headfort College, Killara; among his pupils was (Sir) John Gorton, a future prime minister. The strain on Mary's health from running the domestic side of the school obliged Wade to sell his foundation in 1928 to the Congregational Union. In May he was appointed senior science master at The King's School, Parramatta.

Between 1925 and 1929 Wade collected hundreds of fossil fish from the Brookvale brick pits: he sent some to the noted palaeichthyologist Sir Arthur Smith Woodward in England, but worked on others and described them. With a grant from the Australian National Research Council, he entered Clare College, Cambridge (Ph.D., 1931), to continue his studies on vertebrate palaeontology.

Scholarly, energetic and talented, in 1932-35 Wade taught at Challows School, Devon, and Sutton Vallance School, Kent. He visited Australia to collect more specimens and sold his collection of Australian Mesozoic fishes to the British Museum (Natural History) which published his memoir, *The Triassic fishes of Brookvale, New South Wales* (1935). After a short term as dean of Christ Church Cathedral in the Falkland Islands, he returned with his wife to Sydney in 1936. Wade was a locum tenens at St John's Church, Milsons Point, then headmaster of Broughton [q.v.1] School for Boys, Newcastle (1938-40). He came back to King's in January 1941 and retired in May 1949.

Wade published six papers on Triassic and Jurassic fishes in the *Journal and proceedings* of the local Royal Society between 1930 and 1953. His valuable descriptive work enlarged on that of Woodward and others, and brought Australian Mesozoic fishes 'into relationship with one another and with the general subject of Palaeicthyology'. In retirement he lived at Manly near his favourite collecting ground. After 1953 Mary's and his own ill health forced him to give up scientific work. Predeceased by his wife, he died without issue on 23 September 1967 at Eastwood and was cremated.

W. A. Steel, *History of All Saints' College, Bathurst, 1873-1934* (Syd, 1936); S. Braga, *Barker College, a history* (Syd, 1978); Roy Soc NSW, *J*, 64 (1930); *Nature* (Lond), 20 July 1968, p 311; *C of E Hist Soc J*, 20, no 1, Mar 1975.   G. P. WALSH

WADSWORTH, ARTHUR (1864-1931), librarian, was born on 19 December 1864 at Windsor, Melbourne, eighth child of Robert Wadsworth, clerk, and his wife Julia Lucy, née Guillaume, both English born. His father was clerk of the Victorian Executive Council in 1875-89. Arthur was educated at All Saints Grammar School, East St Kilda, and studied at the University of Melbourne in 1880 before joining the Victorian parliamentary library next year. On 6 May 1891 he married Lilian Johnston Pengelley at All Saints Church, St Kilda. When Wadsworth succeeded the parliamentary librarian Richard Church in 1901, the newly elected Commonwealth representatives enjoyed the use of the Victorian Parliament House, with its library and staff, until the establishment of a Federal capital. Wadsworth was thus to have charge of the Commonwealth library for over twenty-six years while also being titular head of the State parliamentary library. His formal transfer to the Commonwealth service, not gazetted until 1927, was backdated to 1925.

As Commonwealth parliamentary librarian Wadsworth was responsible to a parliamentary committee more than usually jealous of its powers, particularly as its members had rejected a suggestion by Prime Minister (Sir) Edmund Barton [q.v.7] that an additional board of experts might advise them on the formation of the new library. Since their chairman controlled most financial and administrative matters, Wadsworth had little independent authority. Nevertheless, he built up a strong collection of official publications, laid the foundation for a general reference collection, acquired some important basic Australiana and compiled two catalogues (published in 1906 and 1911). He was also responsible for the first five issues of the *Commonwealth parliamentary handbook* in 1915-26 and was executive officer for the library's multi-volume publication, *Historical records of Australia*, in 1914-25. Possessing an 'encyclopaedic knowledge and a card-index memory', he was much in demand by politicians in search of information or quotations with which to embellish their speeches. Between 1909 and 1917 Wadsworth defended himself, with commendable restraint, against the unsubstantiated criticisms of E. A. Petherick [q.v.5]: embittered by his lack of

responsibility within the library, Petherick had accused Wadsworth of incompetence, ignorance and a lack of probity in dealing with booksellers. Wadsworth retired in 1927.

Tall, with a distinguished appearance and bearing, 'Waddy' was deeply interested in art and the theatre. An *habitué* of Fasoli's dinners, he was regarded by his friend Allan Wilkie [q.v.] as one of Australia's leading Shakespearian students. Wadsworth was an active Anglican and extended his interests to astronomy, physics and music. A sociable man, he included among his companions Sydney booksellers George Robertson [q.v.11] and Fred Wymark [q.v.], and Melburnians W. R. Maloney [q.v.10], E. A. Parr, Margareta Webber, and A. H. Spencer [q.v.] who described him as a 'whole man'. Wadsworth died on 21 April 1931 at Kew and was buried in Box Hill cemetery. His wife, daughter and two sons survived him.

Sun News-Pictorial, 22 Apr 1931; Parliamentary Lib Archives (Canb); NL Archives (NL) and Petherick papers *and* C. McDonald papers (NL); information from Mrs D. Lamb, Melb, and Sir H. White, Canb.   PAULINE FANNING

WAGER, RHODA (1875-1953), jewellery designer, was born on 10 March 1875 at Mile End Old Town, London, one of five children of George Wager, warehouseman, and his wife Jane Annabella, née James. Brought up at Bristol, she attended the local art school, then studied drawing and painting at the School of Art, Glasgow (1897-1903). She exhibited metalwork and jewellery at the Glasgow Art Club in 1901 and at Cork, Ireland, next year. From 1903 she was a member of the Glasgow Society of Lady Artists and showed regularly with them. Returning to Bristol, Miss Wager taught art at St Mary's girls' school. She spent her holidays making jewellery under Bernard Cuzner, a talented silversmith who had designed Liberty & Co. Ltd's 'Cymric' jewellery in 1899.

Late in 1913 Rhoda went to live on her brother's sugar plantation in Fiji. Settling in Sydney in 1918, she resumed jewellery-making. On 24 January 1920 at the registrar general's office she married a 41-year-old widower Percival George, a marine surveyor and son of Julian Rossi Ashton [q.v.7].

A member of the Society of Arts and Crafts of New South Wales, Rhoda Wager later joined the Melbourne and Brisbane societies, showing annually at their exhibitions. Her jewellery was displayed and sold on commission at Farmer [q.v.4] & Co. Ltd's city store. At 42 Martin Place, her studio had a display section which attracted clients from the Australia, Carlton and Metropole hotels. She was soon able to employ an assistant Walter

Clarence Clapham and in 1928 was joined by her niece Dorothy Wager. About 1930 Rhoda moved premises to the State Office Block, Market Street, and later to Rowe Street and Victoria Arcade Chambers. She retired in 1946.

A review of her hand-wrought jewellery at the Dunster Galleries, Adelaide, in 1925, stated that her 'work is wrought from beginning to end. Each flower, stem and leaf or berry is made separately and soldered on bit by bit'. The 170 pieces exhibited included 'brooches with pearls, corals, black onyx and calchedony; earrings of lapis lazuli and amethysts; chains and pendants of opals and turquoise'.

Occasionally, she advertised in women's magazines and in December 1929 her work was illustrated in *Art in Australia*. Rhoda's favourite stones were opals and yellow sapphires, for they caught the sun; she used Australian motifs such as gum leaves in her foliage decoration. A tiny, silver plate bearing the name 'Wager' was soldered on her work when practicable. World War II restricted her to making wedding and engagement rings. Over twenty-five years she produced some twelve thousand pieces of jewellery, all meticulously recorded in her sketch-books (1921-46).

Generous, lively and witty, she was passionate about her art; strong-willed and determined, she was a clear-headed, industrious businesswoman. Moving to Queensland in 1951, Rhoda Wager died childless in Brisbane on 2 December 1953 and was cremated with Anglican rites. Her work provides a link with the English Arts and Crafts Movement, and with jewellery designers like Cuzner and Sybil Dunlop.

I. Anscombe and C. Gere, *Arts and crafts in Britain and America* (NY, 1978); C. Gere, *Victorian jewellery design* (Lond, 1972) and *European and American jewellery 1830-1914* (Lond, 1975); *Art in Aust*, Dec 1929; *Observer* (Adel), 29 Aug 1925; D. M. Wager, The biography of Rhoda Wager (ms, 1980) *and* Autobiography (ms, 1981) held by author, Woollahra, Syd.   ANNE SCHOFIELD

WAGG, HENRY CHRISTOPHER; *see* WEBB, CHRIS

WAINWRIGHT, JOHN WILLIAM (1880-1948), public servant, was born on 27 November 1880 at Naracoorte, South Australia, son of Charles Wainwright, head teacher, and his wife Anne, née Brooke. William attended his father's schools at Naracoorte and at Eudunda where he remained for two more years as an unpaid pupil-teacher. Having attended Adelaide High School and done further pupil-teaching, he entered the Training College whence he studied at the University of Adelaide in 1903-04. After a years teaching at North Adelaide Model School, he resigned and is said to have worked as a tailor's assistant. In 1908 Wainwright joined the public service and in 1910 became a clerk in the audit section of the Chief Secretary's Department. Three times during World War I he tried to enlist, though told on each occasion that he could never be accepted; a childhood accident had left him with a glass eye. In the State service he rose to be inspector (1923), assistant auditor-general (1928), then auditor-general from 1934 until his retirement in 1945. When few State public servants had much education, he was one of several ex-schoolteachers who led the South Australian service. During and after World War II he also served the Commonwealth as its South Australian deputy director of war organization of industry and in the secondary industries division of the ministry of post-war reconstruction.

His private life had some coldness. William's mother had died in his infancy. When the boy was 7, his father married an Englishwoman, Emma Brooke, but she was widowed when William was 23 and they shared a house for the rest of her life. Her health began to fail in 1920. On 26 March 1921 in the Church of the Immaculate Conception, Ivanhoe, Victoria, Wainwright married with Catholic rites Agnes Matilda Samuels, a clerk. They were described as a tough pair who shared a housekeeping rather than a passionate partnership; with no children of their own, they adopted a daughter who found little warmth in their household, left it as soon as she could, and was bequeathed nothing.

In 1910-17, as an evening student, Wainwright had qualified as an accountant (A.I.C.A., 1922) and completed an undistinguished degree (B.A., 1917). His economics texts included one by the orthodox Alfred Marshall and one by J. A. Hobson, an 'under-consumptionist' forerunner of J. M. Keynes. When the university later employed Wainwright as a part-time lecturer in public finance, he set texts by Henry George [q.v.4], Arthur Pigou and Hugh Dalton. He was citing Keynes's work, and predicting multiplier effects of industrial changes in South Australia, before Keynes published *The general theory of employment, interest and money* (London, 1936). With (Sir) Leslie Melville, Wainwright wrote a pamphlet, *The economic effects of Federation* (1929). It had two main themes: the balance between Commonwealth and State power had shifted, divorcing financial resources from investment responsibilities and handicapping the States' developmental efforts; and that shift combined with the Commonwealth's tariff policies to disadvantage those States which produced the least protected goods and relied most on exporting primary products.

Both Labor and non-Labor governments appointed Wainwright to commissions and committees of inquiry, and used him as a general economic adviser. He sat on royal commissions on the railways (1930), dairy produce industries (1933), transport (1937) and electricity supply (1931, 1945), and on boards and committees concerned with public service efficiency, secondary industries, public transport, regional development, forestry, dairying, abattoirs, building materials, taxation, and financial relations with the Commonwealth. Their reports express a consistent approach to economic development and management which many of his associates attributed to Wainwright and which is also clear in his auditor-general's reports and his other writing.

His principles were those of a Keynesian theorist with a practical gift for effective business regulation. They included the following: when approaching any industry's problems, government should survey the relevant experience and policies of other States and the world outside. It should try to see the industry 'whole' and in its economic context; for example, a rail or road policy should minimize the social cost of transport (the total costs of public and private transport by rail, truck, bus and car). Where natural monopoly allows price fixing, the fixing may best be done by government; Wainwright designed ingenious patterns of price control which preserved cost-cutting and competitive incentives. Whether public control might best be achieved by regulating, or by owning the industries concerned, should be decided by considerations of public interest alone.

To Wainwright, public enterprises could be as efficient as private ones, provided that they were not directed by their managers (who may be self-indulgent), or by politicians (who may be pork-barrellers), or by representatives of the industries with which they deal (who may put private before public interests). Like private companies, they should have boards of directors. Their directors should be disinterested, non-executive, and should include both experts and laymen. The model has prevailed in South Australia since.

Wainwright was not the initiator of South Australian industrialization. The State already made motor bodies, agricultural machinery and metal products. His originality lay in reasoning that technical progress meant that—merely to maintain employment—any given population must continually *increase* its manufacturing activity because primary production, limited by its natural resources, had no such capacity to expand

output in step with increasing productivity per head. The more productive the primary industries, the fewer people they could employ; the more competitive the secondary industries, the more they should be able to employ. Wainwright and others devised an industrial strategy to keep costs of production in Adelaide lower than those in the eastern States by more than the cost of transporting manufactured goods to their main markets in those States. Government agencies supplied cheap land, rail connexions, power, water, sewerage, planning and advisory services and (during and after the war) factories and credit. Cheap public housing was built in the industrial suburbs. Price control was applied to many necessaries, especially the components of the cost-of-living index to which local wage rates were linked. Compared with their eastern competitors, low money wages benefited employers, while equal real wages made for industrial peace.

Besides monetary incentives, Wainwright believed that economic development also needed a productive culture and collective purpose. In 1942 he and Tom Garland, a communist union secretary, founded a movement called Common Cause. Its priority was to intensify the war effort. In the longer run it hoped to 'generate a new and vital attitude to society and ourselves': business and labour leaders, churchmen and academics managed to agree on statements of social purpose, and on the need for social research as an aid to political consensus. Wainwright wrote: 'We need to know more about our State and its affairs and the needs of the people, needs for housing, defence, education, unemployment, public finance, families and the decline in birth rates, social evils and their cure . . . and when we know more, a strong public opinion will grow up'. His driving purpose seems to have been to use his and others' brains to remodel the economy so as to generate less poverty and unemployment.

As Australia recovered from the Depression, South Australian industry revived and grew impressively. Much credit for that was claimed by (Sir) Thomas Playford's Liberal and Country League government (1938-65). As to how much of the recovery was simply cyclical, and how much it owed to Wainwright's influence and the government's measures, experts disagree; but in Wainwright's lifetime South Australia's industrial growth was proportionately the nation's fastest.

In person Wainwright was a short, ordinary-looking man. Contemporaries described him as efficient, logical, self-effacing, humourless; some thought his glass eye the kinder of the two. He worked long hours and was a hard-driving taskmaster. In most things he cared for the substance and despised the show. He never appeared in *Who's who*. He belonged to no church. He liked tennis and music, and belonged to the Adelaide Dual Club. Wainwright offended his wife and adopted daughter in his last years by preferring the company of young women he met at tennis. To one of them he bequeathed his house and savings, after providing for his widow during her lifetime. He died of a coronary occlusion on 12 November 1948 at Fullarton, Adelaide. His will directed that there be no advertisement of his death or burial, and that his body be taken to the Glen Osmond cemetery in a plain coffin in his own car. His efficiency had died with him: the car broke down and had to be towed.

K. Sheridan (ed), *The state as developer* (Adel, 1986); *Aust J of Politics and Hist*, May 1962; *Aust Economic Review*, Mar 1984; T. J. Mitchell, The industrialisation of South Australia 1935-1940 (B.A. Hons thesis, Univ Adel, 1957); R. F. I. Smith, The Butler government in South Australia, 1933-1938 (M.A. thesis, Univ Adel, 1964).

HUGH STRETTON
PAT STRETTON

WAINWRIGHT, WILLIAM EDWARD (1873-1959), mining and metallurgical engineer, was born on 3 January 1873 at Upper Holloway, London, son of Edward Harley Wainwright, schoolmaster, and his wife Maria, née Brooks. Edward brought his family to Adelaide in 1879 when he was offered a teaching post at the Collegiate School of St Peter.

Educated at Prince Alfred College, William proceeded to the South Australian School of Mines and Industries where he gained diplomas in metallurgy (1892) and mining (1894). His first appointment, in 1895, was as battery manager at Ivanhoe Gold Mines, Kalgoorlie, Western Australia. Next year he was made mill-manager at Queen Margaret Gold Mine, Bulong, near Kalgoorlie. In 1898 he joined the staff of the South Mine of Broken Hill South Ltd, Broken Hill, New South Wales; in 1903 he became manager, in 1918 general manager, then consulting engineer in 1937, before retiring in 1941.

Under Wainwright's leadership the South Mine achieved and maintained a leading position world-wide in mining and metallurgical practice and research. He developed efficient mine-management systems and built a staff of outstanding competence, while exercising a moderating influence in Broken Hill's difficult industrial scene and promoting the welfare of employees. He was among the earliest to apply modern technology to problems of health and ventilation in Broken Hill's mines.

In 1926 the Commonwealth government appointed him chairman of the technical committee to report on the gold-mining industry at Kalgoorlie and at the Sons of Gwalia mine, Leonora, Western Australia. He was also a member of the executive committee of the Imperial geophysical experimental survey. In 1930 Wainwright led the Australian delegation to the third Empire Mining and Metallurgical Congress, held in South Africa. Vice-chairman of the council of the Standards Association of Australia and chairman of its Victorian committee, he was a member of the executive of the Australian National Research Council, the Victorian committee of the mining advisory panel of the Council for Scientific and Industrial Research, as well as of the engineering faculty and the appointments board, University of Melbourne. He served as director of several companies including N.K.S. (Holdings) Ltd and Noyes Bros (Melbourne) Ltd.

A member of the Australasian Institute of Mining and Metallurgy from 1902, Wainwright was a councillor in 1908-59, president in 1919 and 1930, and honorary treasurer in 1943-59. Awarded the Institute medal in 1936, he was made an honorary member in 1950. He initiated an endowment fund and founded a student prize. Wainwright was also a member of the Institution of Mining and Metallurgy, London. After fifty years membership of the American Institute of Mining and Metallurgical Engineers he was admitted in 1953 to its 'Legion of Honour'.

Of middle height and medium build, Wainwright had a thick moustache and receding hair. He dressed conservatively. A good companion, with a pleasant sense of humour, he belonged to the Broken Hill Club, and to the Australia and Rotary clubs in Melbourne. He was a warden at St Paul's Anglican Church, Caulfield. Predeceased by his wife Emily Constance, née Goode, whom he had married on 27 October 1900 in the chapel of St Peter's College, Adelaide, Wainwright died at his Caulfield home on 3 May 1959 and was cremated. Two daughters and three sons survived him.

W. S. Robinson, *If I remember rightly*, G. Blainey ed (Melb, 1967); G. Blainey, *The rise of Broken Hill* (Melb, 1968); B. Carroll, *Built on silver* (Melb, 1986); *Univ Melb Gazette*, Oct 1959; A'sian Inst of Mining and Metallurgy records (Parkville, Melb); Univ Melb Archives; information from Mrs H. M. Bean, Claremont, Perth, and Mrs H. Beith, Ivanhoe East, Melb.   D. F. FAIRWEATHER

WAITE, EDGAR RAVENSWOOD (1866-1928), zoologist and museum director, was born on 5 May 1866 at Leeds, Yorkshire, England, second son of John Waite, bankers clerk, and his wife Jane, née Vause. Edgar left the Leeds Parish Church Middle Class School for the borough accountant's office; his enthusiasm for natural science led him to read biology at Owens College, Manchester. In 1888 he was appointed assistant curator, and in 1891 curator, of the museum of the Leeds Philosophical and Literary Society (later Leeds City Museum) where he distinguished himself by cataloguing the collections, staging live exhibits, encouraging research and providing informative services. On 7 April 1892 he married Rose Edith Green at St Matthew's parish church, Leeds.

In 1893-1905 Waite was assistant curator in charge of vertebrates at the Australian Museum, Sydney. He accompanied the trawling expedition of H.M.C.S. *Thetis* and in 1899 published its scientific results. In 1906 he was appointed curator of the Canterbury Museum, Christchurch, New Zealand. His many improvements included the introduction of exhibits and new display techniques, and the establishment (1907) and editing of the *Records of the Canterbury Museum*. Apart from his faunal work, the extensive studies he undertook of New Zealand and Antarctic fishes established him as a leading ichthyologist. Waite frequently participated in major land and sea expeditions, among them (Sir) Douglas Mawson's [q.v.10] first subantarctic cruise in 1912, and edited *Scientific results of the New Zealand government trawling expedition, 1907* (Canterbury, 1909, 1911), as well as writing 'Fishes of the Australasian Antarctic Expedition'. Early in 1914 he was appointed director of the South Australian Museum, a position he held until 1928. He established (1918) and edited the museum's *Records*. After leading the museum's expedition to Strzelecki and Cooper creeks (1916), he published the results in 1917 in the *Transactions of the Royal Society, South Australia*. In 1918 he made collecting trips to New Guinea, New Britain and New Ireland, and in 1926 inspected museums in the United States of America and Europe.

Waite published diversely and prolifically, mostly on vertebrate taxonomy, particularly fishes, reptiles and mammals: his important and well-known work on *The fishes of South Australia* was published by the British Science Guild (Adelaide, 1923), as was *The reptiles and amphibians of South Australia* (Adelaide, 1929, edited by H. M. Hale). He was active in the Yorkshire Naturalists' Union, the Conchological Society of Great Britain and Ireland, the Leeds Naturalists' Club and the Leeds Geological Association. A fellow (1890) of the Linnean Society and a corresponding member of the Zoological Society, London, he was senior vice-president of the Royal Society of South Australia and councillor of the South Australian Zoological and Acclimatization Society. He was also an editor of the South Australian handbooks committee of the British Science Guild, a member of the Flora and Fauna Board of South Australia and of the Linnean Society of New South Wales, and a founding member and president of the South Australian Aquarium Society.

His early research on Australian vertebrate fauna had been highly regarded. Before Waite moved to New Zealand, he was already a leading ichthyologist and herpetologist; he later rose to be a world authority on the fishes of the Australasian-Antarctic region. An exceptionally capable and innovative museum administrator, by the mid-1920s he was at the zenith of his professional standing. Versatile, thorough, meticulous and highly productive, he had formidable accomplishments and had greatly influenced the development of natural science in South Australia.

Almost 5 ft. 11 ins. (180.3 cm) tall, Waite was bespectacled, with a domed forehead, symmetrical face, aquiline nose and an Edwardian beard. Imposing but gentle, with a dry sense of humour, he was held in affection and esteem by all who knew him well. Though reserved and of a retiring disposition, he possessed extraordinary enthusiasm and energy which extended to hobbies as varied as motor cycling, drawing, painting, photography, aquarium-keeping, philately and playing the flute.

Plagued with recurring ill health after having contracted malaria in New Guinea in 1918, Waite became gravely ill early in 1928 before leaving Adelaide to attend a meeting of the Australasian Association for the Advancement of Science in Tasmania. He died of enteric fever on 19 January 1928 in Highbury Hospital, Hobart, and was cremated. His wife and son survived him.

Sth Aust Museum, *Records*, May 1928, p 344, June 1956, pp i, 1; Roy Soc SA, *Trans*, 52, Dec 1928, p 1; *Mercury* and *Register* (Adel), 20 Jan 1928; family papers (held by Mr D. R. Waite, Croydon, and Mrs I. Sloman, Melb); personal notes from Prof N. B. Tindale, Palo Alto, California, USA; Waite papers (Sth Aust Museum *and* PRO SA); information from Mr P. C. D. Brears, director of museums, Leeds, Eng.   C. J. M. GLOVER

WAITE, WILLIAM CHARLES NIGHTINGALE (1880-1973), soldier and auctioneer, was born on 8 September 1880 in Adelaide, son of English-born parents, William Nicholas Waite, licensed victualler, and his wife Anna, née Weston. Educated at St Bartholomew's Church of England School, Norwood, and Prince Alfred College, Adelaide, he joined the South Australian Garrison Artillery (militia) in 1897.

With the outbreak of the South African War, Waite embarked for active service in November 1899 as a corporal with the 1st South Australian Contingent. After twelve months of campaigning he returned home and re-enlisted with the 6th (Imperial Bushmen) South Australian Contingent in 1901 as a lieutenant. The unit operated in Transvaal, Cape Colony and the Orange River Colony, and Waite was mentioned in dispatches. When the contingent completed its service Waite remained in South Africa as an intelligence officer; at the war's end he settled at The Springs, a mining centre near Johannesburg. He later worked for a large mining corporation in the Rand. On 13 March 1907, at Germiston, Transvaal, he married a Queenslander, Florence Alberta Thomas. They were to have three children. That year they returned to Adelaide and in 1908-09 Waite was city manager for Reynella Wine Vaults. In 1910 he became a livestock-dealer. He kept up his military associations as a second lieutenant and then a lieutenant in the field artillery.

Having worked as a stock auctioneer at Willunga, Waite joined the Australian Imperial Force as a lieutenant on 20 August 1914 and was posted to the 3rd Field Artillery Brigade; shortly before embarkation he was promoted captain and transferred to the 3rd Field Artillery Brigade Ammunition Column. His unit landed at Gallipoli on 25 April 1915 and Waite served there until the evacuation in December, first commanding the 7th Field Artillery Battery and then the 8th. For his Gallipoli service he was awarded the Military Cross and was mentioned in dispatches. One of his proudest possessions was an 18-pounder cartridge case from No. 4 gun of the 8th F.A.B.: he averred that he had disobeyed orders by waiting another five minutes in order to fire the last artillery round of the campaign.

After a brief time in staff appointments in Egypt, Waite was transferred in March 1916 to the newly formed 4th Division, A.I.F., as lieut-colonel commanding the 24th Field Artillery Brigade. In June he embarked for France and the brigade went into action at Bois Grenier and Fromelles, and at Ypres, Belgium. Waite took command of the 11th Field Artillery Brigade from January 1917. He served as an artillery brigade and group commander in operations on the Somme, at Bullecourt, Ypres, Messines, Dernancourt and Villers-Bretonneux, received the Distinguished Service Order, particularly for his work at Fromelles, Ypres and the Somme, and was again mentioned in dispatches. In August 1918 he was invalided home.

After demobilization Waite became an auctioneer, valuer and agent in Adelaide. He retained his commission in the militia and in

1926-30 commanded the 10th Battalion (Adelaide Rifles). In World War II he resumed full-time military duties, initially as camp commandant at Wayville and Woodside, and later as deputy director of recruiting at Keswick Barracks, Adelaide.

Waite's service to the nation in three wars was outstanding; he also served the community well, being an active participant in ex-servicemen's organizations, a visiting justice of the peace to the South Australian Department of Prisons for twenty-seven years and a member of the Burnside Town Council for seventeen. The Colonel Waite Memorial Oval at Kensington Gardens, Adelaide, honours his service to the council. He was a Freemason and a keen tennis player. Healthy and active until late in life, Waite cut a dapper, cheery and sprightly figure; his erect bearing and precise habits reflected years of disciplined military life. At 90 he presided over the last memorial meeting of Boer War veterans. He was especially well known as chief marshal on Anzac Days in Adelaide; proudly mounted on a dapple-grey charger, he led the parade on twenty-nine occasions.

Predeceased by his wife, Waite died at Norwood on 25 December 1973 and was cremated. He was survived by a son and two daughters. His brother, Arthur Cyril Roy, also served as an artilleryman in the A.I.F. and won the Military Cross.

Aust Defence Dept, *Official records of the Australian military contingents to the war in South Africa*, P. L. Murray ed (Melb, 1911); C. E. W. Bean, *The story of Anzac*, 1, 2 (Syd, 1921, 1924) and *The A.I.F. in France*, 1916-18 (Syd, 1929, 1933, 1937, 1942); *Reveille* (Syd), June 1932, p 20; nominal roll, 3rd Field Brigade Ammunition Column at embarkation 20 Oct 1914, *and* war diaries, 3rd, 11th and 24th Field Artillery Brigades, AIF *and* recommendation files for honours and awards, AIF (AWM); Prince Alfred College, Kent Town, Adel, archives; information from Mr A. D. Garrett, Kensington Gardens, Adel.   S. N. GOWER

WAKELIN, ROLAND SHAKESPEARE (1887-1971), artist, was born on 17 April 1887 at Greytown, New Zealand, youngest of seven children of Richard Alfred Wakelin, an English-born timber merchant, and his wife Emily, née Noakes, from Auckland. Roland began sketching and painting as a boy. Educated at Wellington Technical School on a scholarship in 1902-03, while employed with the Land and Income Tax Department he continued night and Saturday art classes at the school under Henri Bastings and H. Linley Richardson and exhibited at the New Zealand Academy of Fine Arts.

Having visited his brother in Sydney in 1908, Wakelin settled there in 1912. He enrolled in classes at the Royal Art Society of New South Wales in 1913, studied life-drawing at night under Antonio Dattilo-Rubbo and Norman Carter [qq.v.11,7], and on Saturdays painted with Dattilo-Rubbo. On 15 October 1913 Wakelin married Rachel Estelle Robinson at the William Street Methodist parsonage. He joined the State land tax branch of the Commonwealth Treasury in November. The same year one of Dattilo-Rubbo's pupils, Norah Simpson, returned from abroad with reproductions of works by Cézanne, Gauguin, Matisse and Picasso; her revelation of modern painting, combined with an exhibition of the expatriate Phillips Fox [q.v.8], inspired Wakelin. In 1916 he gained long-term employment as a commercial artist with (S. Ure) Smith [q.v.11] & Julius.

During the next few years Wakelin, with fellow pupils Roy de Maistre and Grace Cossington Smith [qq.v.8,11], painted experimental works (breaking the picture space into touches of bold colour) which culminated in Wakelin's and de Maistre's colour-music paintings, or 'synchromies', shown in 1919. That year they executed completely abstract paintings, though did not exhibit them. At the same time Wakelin and his friends did not abandon their interest in realism: his 1916 masterpiece, 'Down the hills to Berry's Bay', has a vibrancy in its broken colour and an arabesque movement that anticipates the abstract paintings of 1919; equally communicated is the artist's sense of place, his love of the light, colour and atmosphere of his harbour city.

Under the pervasive and persuasive influence of Max Meldrum [q.v.10], Wakelin briefly abandoned his pursuit of colour until he visited London in 1922. Working as a freelance commercial artist for three years, he at last saw original paintings by the French artists. He was impressed by exhibitions of van Gogh and Gauguin at the Leicester Galleries, London, but when he returned to Sydney in 1924 Cézanne's paintings dominated his ideas about art for several years. Wakelin exhibited his paintings of London and Paris to open John Young's Macquarie Galleries in 1925 and enjoyed artistic if not commercial success. In the late 1920s he was championed by Ethel Anderson, the writer, who displayed his paintings at her home in 1930. The National Art Gallery of New South Wales in 1935 bought his 'Mount Wellington, Tasmania'. A member of the Society of Artists, Sydney, and of the Contemporary Group, he was later a foundation member of the Australian Academy of Art, Canberra.

From 1934 Wakelin's paintings entered a romantic phase of sonorous colour, depicting his beloved harbour and the intimate subjects of domestic life: backyards, still lifes, and portrait and figure studies of his family and friends. Never able to rely on a secure income from his painting, in World War II Wakelin did mechanical drawing in the Postmaster-General's Department and taught for a year at the National Gallery schools in Melbourne.

Back in Sydney he taught part time at the University of Sydney and for Dora Sweetapple at the Woollahra Arts Centre. With his quiet charm and unselfish nature, he was greatly respected by fellow artists, particularly his colleagues of the Northwood group, Lloyd Rees, George Lawrence and Marie and John Santry. A 'happy man with simple tastes', Wakelin had a bass voice and a repertoire of popular songs; he and his wife held Gilbert and Sullivan, Bach or Mozart evenings, depending on the company. Between bursts of painting, he read Shakespeare, Flaubert, Dickens and detective stories.

Wakelin exhibited for some forty years, often at the Macquarie Galleries, and was given a major retrospective by the Art Gallery of New South Wales in 1967. Survived by his wife, son and daughter, he died at Rose Bay on 28 May 1971 and was cremated without clergy. He is represented in all major Australian public collections.

J. Hetherington, *Australian painters* (Melb, 1963); Art Gallery of NSW, *Roland Wakelin retrospective*, cat (Syd, 1967); L. Walton, *The art of Roland Wakelin* (Syd, 1987); *Art in Aust*, 1, no 1, Feb 1922, p 70, Mar 1925, p 15, 15 Aug 1934, p 22; *Art and Aust*, 4, no 4, Mar 1967; *B.P. Magazine*, 1 Dec 1930, p 51; *Hemisphere*, 17, no 4, Apr 1973, p 13; *SMH*, 1 Feb 1922, 8 Sept 1928, 24 Sept 1930, 5 Oct 1932, 4 July 1934, 27 June, 3 July 1935, 23 July 1936, 18 Aug 1937, 15 May 1942, 5 Apr 1967, 29 May, 6 June 1971; *Sydney Mail*, 8 Feb 1922; Aust artists, biog files (Art Gallery of NSW, Syd); H. de Berg tapes (NL).   BARRY PEARCE

WALDER, SIR SAMUEL ROBERT (1879-1946), businessman and politician, was born on 8 October 1879 in Sydney, son of Samuel Walder, sailmaker, and his wife Mary Ann, née Hatton, both native-born. Educated at Cleveland Street Public and Christ Church St Laurence schools, at 13 Samuel entered his father's sail, tent and tarpaulin manufacturing business as an apprentice. When his father died, Walder took over as manager, aged 18. Under his guidance the firm expanded and was floated as a limited company in 1911. It made its name by supplying tents to the Australian Army in World War I.

On 22 March 1911 Walder had married Elsie Helena Blunt, a milliner, at St Martin's Anglican Church, Kensington. In 1924 he retired as managing director of S. Walder Ltd, which remained a family company, to devote himself to 'the interests of the city'. Standing for the Citizens' Reform Association, he was elected to Sydney Municipal

Council at a by-election for Flinders Ward; he served as an alderman until 1927 (when the council was abolished) and for Macquarie Ward from 1930 until he retired in 1941 due to ill health. In evidence before the 1926 parliamentary select committee he denied allegations of involvement in bribery. Having been the C.R.A.'s party secretary since 1925, he became lord mayor in 1932, the worst year of the Depression: he chaired the Citizens' Employment Committee which placed over 3000 people in a 'Back to Work' programme within two months. He advocated civic improvements, notably the extension of Martin Place to Macquarie Street, and effective civil administration; he also devised a scheme in 1932 for civic employees to receive retiring allowances. Knighted in January 1933, he was elected vice-chairman of the city council finance committee in 1935.

As an Imperial patriot, Walder regarded Labor supporters as disloyal. He was a vice-president of the National Association of New South Wales in 1930-32 and a member of the committee that negotiated its merger with the All for Australia League to form the United Australia Party, of which he was a vice-president in 1933-39. Nominated to the Legislative Council in September 1932 and elected to the reconstituted council in November 1933 for nine years, he served until his defeat in April 1943. He criticized the 'frenzied' efforts of the Lang [q.v.9] government to alleviate unemployment and to introduce a basic wage tax in the early 1930s. Although the *Sydney Morning Herald* in 1933 described Walder as 'an influential although unobtrusive figure in State politics', he never gained ministerial rank.

Restricting his business interests, he was a director of the Eagle, Star and British Dominions Insurance Co. Ltd, Lowe Bros Ltd, Monsoon Waterproof Co. and National Studios Ltd, and chairman of Sargents [q.v.11] Ltd. Having been prominent in the harbour bridge celebrations in 1932, Walder chaired the finance committee for Australia's 150th Anniversary Celebrations Council in 1938 and supported the establishment of a festival to attract tourists to Sydney.

An active philanthropist, he was president of the Allies' and the China days funds, and of Hammond's [q.v.9] Pioneer Homes Ltd, Liverpool, a director of Royal Prince Alfred Hospital (1933-35) and a member of the Rotary Club of Sydney. Lady Walder was also active in welfare work, especially in finding employment for women and the young. Sir Samuel took a keen interest in the Church of England and introduced an annual 'Civic Service' at St Andrew's Cathedral. During World War II he chaired the council's National Emergency Services committee, advocating the construction of underground air-raid shelters and the hosing down of hoodlums who persisted in smoking through blackout tests.

Walder lived with his family at Deauville, Point Piper. Handsome, with clear-cut features and dark hair, he enjoyed golf, yachting and motoring, and belonged to Tattersall's, the New South Wales, Millions, Australian and Elanora Country clubs. Survived by his wife, son and daughter, he died of cancer on 24 November 1946 at Woollahra and was buried in Waverley cemetery. His estate was sworn for probate at £88 261.

V&P (LA NSW), 1926, 4, 2nd S, p 677; *United Aust Review*, Jan 1933; *SMH*, 11 Aug, 11 Oct 1924, 4 Feb 1925, 8, 9, 21 Oct 1926, 10 Dec 1931, 1 Apr, 1 Sept, 13 Oct, 11 Nov 1932, 2 Jan 1933, 19 Feb, 25 Sept, 25 Oct 1941, 25 Nov 1946; *Daily Telegraph*(Syd), 25 Nov 1946; T. D. Mutch, An account of the family of William Walder (ML).

PETER SPEARRITT

WALDOCK, ARTHUR JOHN (1872-1961), Baptist minister, was born on 6 June 1872 at Kew, Melbourne, son of John Waldock, an English-born schoolteacher and Congregational lay preacher, and his wife Mary Hannah, née Day, from Jersey. Arthur was educated in New South Wales and trained for the ministry under the Baptist education committee. Assistant pastor at Bathurst from 1892, he completed his training in 1896 and was sent to Hinton. On 28 October he married Charlotte Godfrey (d. 1946) at Raglan. He was ordained next year at the Bathurst Street Church, Sydney. While pastor at Auburn for nine years from 1899, he published a volume of sermons; he was president of the Baptist Union of New South Wales (1906 and 1918) and from 1915 of the New South Wales Baptist Theological College where he lectured on Church polity; he also served on federal Baptist committees.

When Waldock was superintendent (1908-24) of the Baptist Home Mission Society, the number of churches more than doubled, staff increased from five to forty and the annual income grew from £230 to £10 000. In 1922 he represented Australia at the Baptist World Alliance meetings in England and travelled for eight months in North America and Europe, coming home with an honorary doctorate of divinity from Georgetown College, Kentucky. Due to 'internal dissensions', he resigned his superintendency in 1924, claiming that no man could work for the denomination 'while certain elements were in it'. As pastor of the Mosman Church (1924-29) he sought to mobilize Protestant opinion against what he regarded as the unnatural religious malaise of the Australian people. He was appointed president of the New South Wales

Council of Churches in 1928, but was not prepared to support wireless dramatization of Bible stories on the grounds that it would 'cheapen the Bible in the estimation of the coming generation'.

In 1924 Waldock secured a church site in Canberra and was to chair the interdenominational church council. The first Baptist minister in Canberra, he made frequent pronouncements on moral issues and denounced the government's proposal in 1930 for a local lottery to relieve unemployment. He was an ardent advocate of the Empire Day movement and commended the White Australia policy: while he thought that multiculturalism would create problems of identity and weaken Australia's 'British' moral character, he regarded Dutch and Swiss migrants as capable of becoming 'safe' citizens. A militant Christian, he held fast to nineteenth-century values.

Waldock maintained a vigorous ministry until his retirement in 1948; his sermons appeared weekly in the *Canberra Times*. Having attended conferences abroad in 1936, he returned to initiate the 'forward movement' which raised money for extension work, including a homes trust and a business college for girls. During World War II he was president-general (1941-44) of the Baptist Union of Australia. With receding hair and a dark moustache, he had a subtle sense of humour and had been the lead tenor in the (Royal) Sydney Philharmonic Society. A well-known and respected figure in Canberra, he served on numerous committees ranging from the Australian National University council to a hockey club. Predeceased by his son and daughter, Waldock died in Canberra on 1 May 1961 and was buried in Northern Suburbs cemetery, Sydney.

A. C. Prior, *Some fell on good ground* (Syd, 1966); R. K. Robb, *Fifty capital years* (Canb, 1979); R. D. Holly, *Further capital years* (Canb, 1989); *Aust Baptist*, 10 May 1961; *SMH*, 24 Sept 1918, 19 July, 26 Sept 1924, 2 May 1928, 2 Dec 1930, 9 Sept 1941; Waldock papers (Baptist Church Archives, Canb and Syd).   NIEL GUNSON

WALES, SIR ALEXANDER GEORGE (1885-1962), businessman and politician, was born on 11 October 1885 at Richmond, Melbourne, eldest of seven children of Alexander Wright Wales, contractor and quarry-owner, and his wife Rosanna, née Poynton, both Victorian born. After his father was blinded in an industrial accident, George left Brunswick State School at 14 and became a railway labourer before working at a quarry. In 1903 he joined the Commonwealth public service as a clerk and began studying at night. The fruits of his determination to improve himself were seen in his appointment in 1907 as secretary of the Albion Quarrying Co., in which his family had interests. Subsequently its managing director and chairman, Wales was the recognized force behind the company's expansion. As a building industry contractor, he travelled throughout Australia, constantly extending his commercial interests and becoming a director of the Hardware Co. of Australia Pty Ltd, the Twentieth Century Building and Investment Society, the Albion Sand Co. and the Geelong Brick Co. On 5 September 1911 he married Ethel May Bromet at Christ Church, Brunswick, with Anglican rites.

Beginning his public career in 1914, Wales was elected to the Brunswick council; having been mayor (1917-18) like his father before him, he resigned in 1924. Next year he progressed to the Melbourne City Council as representative of Lonsdale Ward. During the ensuing twenty-nine years he was a member of most council committees and chairman (1937-39) of the public works committee. In 1936 he was president of the Metropolitan Fire Brigades Board. Chairman of the council's decorations committee for Melbourne's centenary, he served three successive terms as lord mayor (1934-37). Wales received the customary reward—a knighthood—with which he was invested at Buckingham Palace by King George VI whose coronation he attended in 1937.

In 1919 Wales had unsuccessfully contested the Victorian Legislative Assembly seat of Melbourne North; in 1936, with United Australia Party support, he was nominated to the Legislative Council. He resigned two years later following the disclosure that he was a principal shareholder in a firm successfully tendering for State government contracts. Although Wales disclaimed knowledge of the firm's business arrangements, he did not recontest the seat, although eligible so to do. In 1942 he made a bid to re-enter the Legislative Council, but failed.

An early director of the Alba Petroleum Co. of Australia (later Ampol), Wales helped the development of the industry and visited the United States of America in 1943 and 1946. Impressed by that country's wartime shipbuilding efforts and an admirer of its people's enterprise, he actively supported closer ties with the United States. While president (1947-48) of the Melbourne Chamber of Commerce, Wales was a vocal critic of the Federal Labor government: as a staunch antisocialist, he was a focus for conservative opposition to the Curtin and Chifley governments; he attacked Chifley's plans to nationalize the banks, and accused the government of doctrinaire economic policies, laxity in regard to trade unions and failure to stimulate production.

Energetic, with a strong sense of civic

responsibility, Wales was a patrician at heart. He was burly in appearance, with a bullet head, short hair and an implacable moustache; goodnatured, but phlegmatic, he admired poise and detested argument. While unsuccessful in parliament, he was a natural leader in business and civic politics. A powerful force in the Melbourne City Council, he opposed democratic reforms such as the creation of a Greater Melbourne Council and the abolition of plural voting, but advocated the redevelopment of city-owned property like the Eastern and Western markets which took place after his shock defeat in the council election of 1954.

Survived by his wife and daughter, Wales died on 31 May 1962 at Elsternwick and was buried in Coburg cemetery. His estate was sworn for probate at £27 391. The family holds his portrait by William Dargie.

Graphic, 29 Nov 1934; *Herald* (Melb), 29 Nov 1932, 10 Oct 1934, 30 June, 27 July 1938, 10 Feb, 9 Mar 1948, 27 Aug 1954; *Age*, 10 Oct 1934, 9 July 1947, 9 Jan 1948, 1 June 1962; *Sun News-Pictorial*, 9 Mar 1937, 11 Aug 1938, 4, 17 July 1942, 18 June 1943, 21 May 1947, 28 Apr 1949, 26 Aug 1954; *Argus*, 5, 31 Mar, 22 May 1948.

DAVID DUNSTAN

WALEY, SIR FREDERICK GEORGE (1860-1933), colliery manager and businessman, was born on 27 May 1860 near Cavendish Square, London, son of Simon Waley Waley, stockbroker, and his wife Anna Hendelah, née Salomons. Educated at University College School, Frederick served with the 20th Middlesex (Artists) Rifle Volunteers in 1877-79. He married 17-year-old Evelyne Jane Crossan (d. 1886) on 20 September 1881 at Marylebone parish church; they were to have one daughter.

Arriving in Queensland with his wife in 1883, Waley worked for Burns, Philp [qq.v.7,11] & Co. Ltd before moving to Sydney in 1885 as its first secretary. He established the coal business Mitchell & (Woolcott) Waley in 1886 which was absorbed in 1893 by his Sydney-based Bellambi Coal Co. Ltd (founded 1888); thereafter he was general manager and chairman. On 22 February 1887 he married with Anglican rites Edith Maude Woolcott, daughter of a solicitor, at Yarra Flats, Lilydale, Victoria.

A justice of the peace from 1887, Woolcott-Waley was an alderman on North Sydney Municipal Council (1894-96) and campaigned for a deepwater harbour at Port Kembla in 1897. He served with the Volunteer Naval Artillery from 1890, retiring with the rank of lieutenant in 1900. He had divorced his wife in 1898 and on 15 September 1900 married Ethel Kate O'Connor at Christ Church, North Sydney. In 1905 the Waleys moved to Mowbray Park, an 800-acre (323.8 ha) property at Picton where Frederick proved an efficient manager and established a school for the children of his workers and for those of neighbouring farmers.

During World War I Waley was appointed captain in the Royal Australian Naval Brigade and acted as Commonwealth representative on the Naval Coal Board, officer-in-charge of the Naval Transport Coaling Battalion and president of the Northern and Southern Coal Purchase Board. During the 1917 general strike he enrolled non-union labourers to coal hospital ships and troop transports.

Chairman of the Southern Colliery Proprietors' Association (1920-31), Bundi Tin Dredging Co. in the Federated Malay States, Voxophone Co. (from 1923) and Red Funnel Fisheries Ltd (1927-31), Waley was also a director of W. E. Smith Ltd and Anderson's Industries Ltd (hatters and furriers). He was an executive-member of the New South Wales division of the Australian Red Cross Society, the Big Brother Movement and the Navy League, and a life governor and trustee of the Women's Hospital. His wife gave Mowbray Park with 180 acres (72.8 ha) of the surrounding land to the Commonwealth government in 1919 as a home for shell-shocked soldiers. Waley was appointed C.B.E. in 1920 and knighted in 1923; having served as honorary vice-consul for Norway since 1908, he was invested knight of the Order of Saint Olaf in 1921.

At times of industrial dispute Waley was a formidable combatant who consistently opposed the demands of the Miner's Federation. At an economic conference in February 1922, he extolled the merits of capitalism while denouncing 'nonsensical talk of revolution and violence'. In October he objected to the extended use of electric lighting in mines, even though traditional oil lighting had resulted in a high incidence of nystagmus among miners. Articulate and deeply conservative, he told the Commonwealth royal commissions on national insurance (August 1925) and on child endowment (November 1927) that any 'recompense for unemployed miners' should not remove 'the incentive to work', and that workers should 'maintain their own children'.

A member of Royal Sydney Yacht Squadron who affected a jaunty nautical appearance and habitually used his naval title, in 1923 he donated the Waley Cup for an annual race. He was interested in polar exploration and helped to equip Captain Scott's *Discovery*. Clean-shaven, with classically moulded features, he belonged to the Junior Carlton and Bath clubs in London, and at home to the Warrigal, Imperial Service and Royal Sydney Golf clubs; he was also patron of the Woonoona

Bowling Club. Sir Frederick died on 29 November 1933 at his Elizabeth Bay home and was cremated. He was survived by his wife, their twin daughters, and by two sons and a daughter of his second marriage. His estate was sworn for probate at £47 285. Waley's portrait by John Longstaff [q.v.10] hangs in Mowbray Park, now again in private hands.

Aust National Review, 18 Jan 1923, p 18; *Triad* (Syd), 1 Jan 1925, p 28; *SMH*, 20, 23 Jan 1917, 7 May 1921, 28 Feb, 7 Oct 1922, 1 Jan 1923, 3 Feb, 25 Aug 1925, 18 Nov 1927, 10 Jan, 30 June 1930, 30 Nov 1933; *Illawarra Mercury*, 1 Dec 1933; B. Burgmann, The industrialization of Wollongong with special reference to Australian Iron and Steel Pty Ltd (Ph.D. thesis, Macquarie Univ, 1986); information from Mr J. Ruffels, Randwick, Syd.

ANDREW MOORE

WALKER, ALAN CAMERON (1864-1931), architect and craftsman, was born on 27 August 1864 in Hobart Town, fourth son of Robert Walker, merchant, and his wife Emma Jane, née Cameron; he was a grandson of John Walker [q.v.2]. Educated at The Hutchins School, Hobart, Alan was articled in 1882 to the architect Henry Hunter [q.v.4], studied under Professor Roger Smith in 1887-88 at University College, London, and recorded buildings for (Sir) Banister Fletcher. In 1888 he was admitted as an associate of the Royal Institute of British Architects. Arriving in Melbourne in November, Walker practised with Ellerker & Kilburn, and subsequently on his own. He served on the Council of the Royal Victorian Institute of Architects and led a breakaway group of progressives. His published papers on architectural subjects included an address to the Australasian Association for the Advancement of Science in 1892.

Having married Mabel Marianne Robertson (d. 1918) on 5 June 1889 at St Andrew's Anglican Church, Brighton, in 1895 Walker brought his family to Hobart where he had built a fashionable home, Huonden. He went into practice with Douglas Salier in 1901 and formed a partnership with Archibald Johnston in 1911. President of the Tasmanian Association of Architects (1906-07, 1915-16 and 1923-25), Walker was first chairman of the Board of Architects of Tasmania in 1930. He also helped to prepare the architectural syllabus for the Hobart Technical College where he lectured.

Thoroughly grounded in Classical and Gothic Revival architecture, as well as being acquainted with the work of Richard Norman Shaw and C. F. A. Voysey, Walker reflected English and American trends in his Hobart buildings. The influence of Henry Hobson Richardson's Romanesque Revival style is evident in Walker's execution of the National Mutual Life Building (1906). The General Post Office (1901) and Public Library (1904-06) are free interpretations of the Classical Revival, while the cloisters (1929) and tower (1931) of St David's Cathedral display his understanding of the Gothic. Walker's exploration of materials is expressed in these buildings, as well as in St Raphael's Church, Fern Tree (timber, 1892), and Werndee, for Sir Elliott Lewis [q.v.10], (polychrome brick, 1902-03). In 1926 several of Walker's designs were included in an exhibition in London of Dominion architecture.

Walker had also served on the Council of the Art Society of Tasmania in 1897-1900. A keen metalworker who had studied enamelling in England, he exhibited in various media and brought the ideas of the English Arts and Crafts Movement to Tasmania. He provided the impetus for the establishment of the Arts and Crafts Society of Tasmania, becoming its first president in 1903.

On 11 March 1922 he married Daisy May Hook at St Columba's Anglican Church, Hawthorn, Adelaide. Tall, well-built and invariably well-dressed, he was 'the image of a country gentleman'. By nature he was unassuming, approachable and energetic, and had a genuine concern for the underprivileged. Survived by his wife, and by the son and daughter of his first marriage, he died suddenly of valvular heart disease on 12 December 1931 at his Fern Tree home and was buried in Cornelian Bay cemetery.

Art, antique and historical exhibition, cat (Hob, 1931); J. M. Freeland, *The making of a profession* (Syd, 1971); Roy Aust Inst of Architects (Tas chapter), *An architectural guide to the city*, Hobart (Hob, 1984); C. Miley, *Beautiful and useful* (Launc, 1987); *Building and Engineering J*, 22 Dec 1888; *Tribune* (Hob), 6 Sept 1876; *Mercury* (Hob), 18 June 1929, 14, 15 Dec 1931; Tas Assn of Architects *and* Tas Chapter of Architects, Minute-books (Hob); The Hutchins School archives (Hob); information from the firm Crawford, Cripps and Wegman, architects (Hob). BRENDAN LENNARD
CAROLINE MILEY

WALKER, ALLAN SEYMOUR (1887-1958), physician and medical historian, was born on 19 June 1887 at Richmond, New South Wales, son of Thomas Walker and his wife Kate, née McCredie, both native-born schoolteachers. Allan had an outstanding scholastic record, winning a scholarship to Sydney Boys' High School and silver medals for English at the junior and senior public examinations. In 1906 he entered the medical school of the University of Sydney (M.B., 1910; Ch.M., 1911; M.D., 1922), graduating with first-class honours. After two years as a resident medical officer at Royal Prince

Alfred Hospital, he engaged in general practice at Parkes in 1913-20 and served at home from 1915 in the Australian Army Medical Corps (honorary captain 1916). At St John's Anglican Church, Parramatta, he had married Beatrice Mary Phillips on 24 March 1914.

Returning to the university in 1921 for postgraduate work in pathology, next year Walker graduated M.D. with the university medal. He practised at Summer Hill, Sydney, in 1922-27; after further postgraduate experience in England in 1926, he became a consultant physician. At R.P.A.H. he was honorary morbid anatomist (1920-25), assistant physician (1922-33), physician (1933-45) and consulting physician (1945-58). A demonstrator in pathology at the university (1928-38), he lectured in clinical medicine from 1937. He was also consultant physician to St George, Canterbury, Western Suburbs and Parramatta district hospitals, and physician and director of the Queen Victoria Homes for Consumptives. His students found him a sound and sympathetic teacher, with wide and up-to-date knowledge. He also published several papers that reflected his interest in pathology and neurology.

A councillor of the New South Wales branch of the British Medical Association (1934-39), Walker was invited to join the Association of Physicians of Australasia and was honorary secretary when it became the Royal Australasian College of Physicians in 1938. As its first honorary secretary, he helped to set up an administrative system which formed a model for other professional associations. After his resignation in 1944, he was a council-member until 1956 and vice-president in 1948-50.

Having enlisted in the Australian Imperial Force in October 1939, Walker was promoted lieut-colonel and appointed senior medical specialist in the 2nd/1st Australian General Hospital. By February 1940 he had established a hospital on the Gaza Ridge in Palestine: he wrote a perceptive account of its activities and vicissitudes in the *Medical Journal of Australia* (1942). Twice mentioned in dispatches, he returned to Australia in December 1941 and, as consultant physician to land headquarters, Sydney, twice went to New Guinea. He was discharged in June 1944.

Despite his interest in medical journalism, Walker declined appointment as a war historian in 1944 largely because he felt obliged to return to teaching, given the absence of experienced clinicians on war service. Following the death of R. M. Downes [q.v.8] in March 1945, Gavin Long persuaded Walker to take over the 'great and important task' of producing the medical series of Australia's involvement in World War II. Formally appointed editor with the pay of colonel

(which brought significant financial loss over the years), Walker reversed the pattern of his predecessor A. G. Butler [q.v.7] by first producing the volume on *Clinical problems of war* (1952). Appreciating the impracticality of involving a range of specialized authors (as Downes had envisaged), Walker wrote this book himself, as well as the succeeding volumes, *Middle East and Far East* (1953) and *The Island campaigns* (1957). He had completed much of the final volume on the medical services of the Royal Australian Navy and the Royal Australian Air Force when ill health compelled him to resign in 1956. Walker brought to his work a scholarly and literary background, as well as professional and administrative experience. He had travelled extensively to attend all but the first meeting (1946) of the Official Medical Historians' liaison committee and chaired the second in Canberra in 1949.

Sensitive and somewhat self-effacing, Walker loved music, the arts and literature. His volumes are lucidly written, with many an apt turn of phrase; in Long's words he was a 'philosophical scientist-historian, with something very definite to say and a gift of saying it'. An excellent physician, Walker had a strong sense of duty and was motivated by altruism rather than by a wish for self-aggrandizement. On his return from the war, his closest colleagues noticed that he had lost something of his earlier spirit, but his enthusiasm returned with his appointment as medical war-historian. Survived by his wife, son and two daughters, Walker died of cerebrovascular disease on 8 January 1958 in R.P.A.H. and was cremated with Presbyterian forms.

MJA, 25 July 1942, 17 May 1958; *J of the AWM*, 12 Apr 1988; Walker file (Roy A'sian College of Physicians Archives, Syd); records, including diaries of G. Long (AWM).

BRYAN GANDEVIA
G. L. McDONALD

WALKER, DAME EADITH CAMPBELL (1861-1937), philanthropist, was born on 18 September 1861 at The Rocks, Sydney, only child of Scottish parents Thomas Walker [q.v.2], merchant, and his wife Jane, née Hart. The family moved to Yaralla on the Parramatta River at Concord in 1870. After his wife died in December, Walker brought his sister Joanna (d. 1890) from Scotland to look after Eadith, whose childhood was shared by Annie Masefield; the girls were educated at home, but attended dancing classes in the city. Strictly raised, Eadith was taught that wealth brought responsibilities and obligations.

In 1886 she inherited her father's estate, sworn for probate at £937 984. She commissioned (Sir) John Sulman [q.v.] (who married Annie Masefield in 1893) to design additions to Yaralla in the 1890s. To the traditional English grounds she added exotic plants, and employed European stonemasons to build a sunken garden, an Italianate terrace and a grotto; her home had, as well, a swimming pool, croquet lawn, and tennis and squash courts. A keen oarswoman, Eadith was vice-president (1895) of the Sydney Rowing Club; she was also a patron of the Yaralla cricket club and leased land to (Royal) Sydney and Concord golf clubs. She loved animals, especially her dogs, and was an executive-member of the Animals' Protection Society of New South Wales (Royal Society for the Prevention of Cruelty to Animals).

Before World War I Miss Walker showed flair in organizing lavish balls, children's parties on a grand scale, fêtes and charitable functions at her home; her guests included visiting royalty and other dignitaries. Widely travelled and interested in music and art, she brought back memorabilia: after visiting New Delhi for the 1903 Coronation Durbar, she built an Indian room to house some of her treasures; on another occasion she brought home a Norwegian house that was re-assembled at Yaralla. She enjoyed reading, accumulated an extensive library (which she bequeathed to Women's College, University of Sydney) and collected valuable glass, porcelain, paintings and antique furniture. She was a founder of the Queen's Club (1912) and a life-member of the Royal Art Society of New South Wales.

Far from frivolous, Miss Walker was to perpetuate her father's philanthropies and generously supported the Thomas Walker Convalescent Hospital that he had founded. She was an executive-member of, and a sub-scriber to, many charitable organizations, among them the Women's Industrial Guild, Queen's Jubilee Fund, Royal Alexandra Hospital for Children and the Royal Hospital for Women, Paddington. Eadith also supported religious and educational institutions, including local churches and the University of Sydney. She maintained her staff in their old age and built cottages for needy men.

World War I sharpened the focus of her endeavours. An executive-member of the State division of the Australian Red Cross Society, she was a member of its finance committee and a delegate to the central council in Melbourne. Working through the Red Cross and later the Returned Sailors' and Soldiers' Imperial League of Australia, she personally did much for ill and disabled servicemen, and set up 'The Camp' at Yaralla for those with advanced tuberculosis. Miss Walker established and maintained a library at the Prince of Wales Hospital and donated her house at Leura for use by consumptive servicemen.

She formed friendships with returned soldiers and occasionally established them in small businesses. Appointed C.B.E. in 1918 and D.B.E. in 1928, she was described as fiercely patriotic, loyal to the Empire and 'a Britisher to the Backbone'.

Eadith never married; her aunt Joanna reputedly had instilled in her a fear of fortune-hunters. In maturity, she looked imposing, and was rather full-faced with gently waved, grey hair. A shy, but strong and capable woman who disliked publicity, she spent most of her later years at the Astor, Macquarie Street. Dame Eadith died at Yaralla on 8 October 1937, her dog Cobber beside her. Returned servicemen and boy scouts lined the approach to the chapel at Rookwood where she was cremated; her ashes were buried at St John's Anglican Church, Ashfield. Her estate, sworn for probate at £265 345, was disposed of in accordance with the terms of her father's will after the Walker Trusts Act was passed in 1939.

H. Tanner & Associates Pty Ltd, *Yaralla estate Concord* (priv print, Syd, nd); J. R. Lawson and F. E. de Groot, *Estate of the late Dame Eadith Campbell Walker to be sold. Yaralla*, auctioneers' cat (Syd, 1938); G. N. Griffiths, *Some houses and people of New South Wales* (Syd, 1949); A. L. May, *Sydney rows* (Syd, 1970); S. Coupe, *Concord, a centenary history* (Syd, 1983); Women's Industrial Guild, *Annual Report*, 1891; *Home*, 1 Nov 1924; *Reveille* (Syd), 1 Nov 1937; *Annual Report* of Roy Alexandra Hospital for Children, 1891-1922, *and* Roy Soc for the Prevention of Cruelty to Animals, 1894-1937, *and* Aust Red Cross Soc, NSW division, 1914-37, *and* Junior Red Cross, NSW branch, 1917-37; *SMH*, 19 June 1914, 23 June 1924, 22 Sept, 26 Nov 1927, 4 June 1928, 15 Oct 1937; *Daily Mail* (Syd), 13 Oct 1937; *Syd Mail*, 13 Oct 1937.

J. MacCulloch

WALKER, FRED (1884-1935), merchant and industrialist, was born on 5 January 1884 at Hawthorn, Melbourne, second of three sons of native-born parents Harry Walker, merchant, and his wife Emily Mary, née Haussen, and was only 6 when his father was killed in an industrial accident. Educated at Caulfield Grammar School, in 1899 Fred joined J. Bartram & Sons, produce and export merchants, where he became familiar with canning and refrigeration. In January 1903, aged 19, he set up his own import and export business, Fred Walker & Co., in Hong Kong. He returned to Melbourne in 1908 to establish himself in the export and import of a variety of commodities, mainly food; in 1910 Walker began to can meats, butter, dripping and Red Feather brand cheese (preserved with sulphite) for export to Asia, South Africa and—during World War I—England.

In 1908 Walker had been commissioned in the Australian Garrison Artillery, Australian Military Forces; transferring to the 13th Infantry Brigade in 1913, he was promoted captain in 1916, but, because of the importance of the production of foodstuffs, did not join the Australian Imperial Force. In 1918 he began to manufacture Bonox and in 1920 secured the former South Melbourne College, Albert Park, to consolidate his manufacturing. In 1918 the business had been extended to Sydney and in 1919 to Adelaide and New Zealand. Due largely to post-war readjustments in world trade, he suffered severe financial reverses. Faced with a deficiency of over £80 000, he persuaded his bank and his creditors to back him in the formation of a new company, Fred Walker & Co. A Melbourne accountant, E. V. Nixon, was appointed chairman, Walker was managing director, and two other directors represented his creditors who accepted debentures to the value of Walker's indebtedness. A period of consolidation and rationalization followed.

In 1923, when the company was struggling, Walker courageously appointed a chemist, C. P. Callister [q.v.7], to develop a yeast extract. Under the tradename Vegemite, it was marketed in 1924. That year Walker undertook the canning of meat and fish pastes at Launceston, Tasmania, then at Dandenong, Victoria; in 1925, following experimental work by Callister, Walker arranged with James L. Kraft of Chicago to manufacture processed cheese in Melbourne. The Kraft Walker Cheese Co. was registered in May 1926 and manufacturing began in September. This company was separate from, but managed by, the staff of Fred Walker & Co. and in May 1930 Walker became chairman. By late 1930 manufacturing for both companies was consolidated and, thanks to processed cheese, Walker had traded his way out of debt.

Walker had drive and presence, but was uneasy in addressing groups of people—even his employees, in whose welfare he was genuinely interested. A workers' social club was established in 1927; morning tea breaks commenced in 1928; a modest staff canteen and first-aid facilities soon followed. Walker's introduction in 1932 of the Bedaux system of time-and-motion study was based on his wish to make factory-work less arduous. As scientifically-designed work systems increased productivity, bonuses paid to employees rose and jobs in the companies were keenly sought.

President (1933-34) of Melbourne Rotary Club, Walker was a supporter of the Boy Scouts' Port Melbourne Settlement for underprivileged children. He was a director of the Young Men's Christian Association and a staff member of the Lord Somers' [q.v.]

Camp. After some years of ill health, Walker died of hypertensive heart disease on 21 July 1935 at his Auburn home and was buried in Boroondara cemetery. On 15 May 1913 at St Columb's Anglican Church, Hawthorn, he had married Mabel Ashton Perrin who, with their daughter, survived him.

Although Walker's financial skills did not match his foresight, when freed from financial oversight he was able to plan and organize effectively. With his instinct for technology and with Callister's support, he established a sound manufacturing base in the 1920s. His will provided for the Fred Walker prize for postgraduate chemistry at the University of Melbourne. After his death his business was absorbed by the Kraft Walker Cheese Co. in which the American Kraft Co. had the major shareholding.

J. S. Legge, *The Naval and Military Club, Melbourne, 1881-1962* (Melb, 1962); *Smith's Weekly* (Syd), 23 May 1931; *Argus*, 22 July 1935; Kraft Walker Cheese Co. Pty Ltd records *and* Fred Walker & Co. Pty Ltd records (held by Kraft Foods Ltd, Port Melbourne); information from Mrs S. Alsop, Mount Eliza, Vic.   K. T. H. FARRER

WALKER, SIR HAROLD BRIDGWOOD (1862-1934), army officer, was born on 26 April 1862 at Dilhorne, Staffordshire, England, son of James Harold Walker, Church of England clergyman, and his wife Mary, née Bridgwood. Educated at Shrewsbury School, and for a year at Jesus College, Cambridge, he was commissioned as a lieutenant in the Duke of Cornwall's Light Infantry in May 1884 and served in the Sudan until 1886. While on leave, Walker married Harriett Edith Coulthard at Plymstock parish church, Devon, on 15 December 1887. After a career in which he saw service in India, the South African War and Ireland, in November 1914 he was appointed brigadier general on the General Staff in India. On 12 December he became chief of staff to Lieut-General Sir William Birdwood [q.v.7] in the Anzac Corps. According to C. E. W. Bean [q.v.7], in his looks and likings 'Walker was an English country gentleman'. From the first, his wish was 'to throw himself into the fighting'.

A man of strong opinions, Walker opposed the landing on Gallipoli, maintaining that the operation had no chance of success. His distaste for staff work also led him to delegate the task of drawing up detailed plans for the operation to Lieut-Colonel Andrew Skeen, an outstanding staff officer. While Walker concentrated on supervising the tactical training of the troops, Skeen 'dominated the conferences of various staffs in the *Minnewaska's* saloon'. The first officer of Birdwood's staff to land on Gallipoli, shortly before 8 a.m. on 25 April 1915, Walker went ashore to keep personal touch with the fighting; by 11 a.m. he took over the New Zealand Infantry Brigade whose commander had fallen ill during the sea voyage.

On the left flank of the Anzac position, Walker's Ridge was of vital tactical importance. With the Turks making a determined effort to gain the ridge, Walker completed a personal reconnaissance on the morning of the 28th. E. E. Herrod [q.v.9], who overheard Walker's appreciation of the situation, later wrote that 'had he been reading from a carefully-prepared text book, I doubt whether it could have been stated better. The wealth of information conveyed in proper sequence, the positive and negative made clear, the topography of the front, the enemy and our own troops, their numbers, disposition and condition etc—all this was rounded off by a few, but decisive words of appeal for water and food for our men. My heart warmed to him'.

A few days later the New Zealand brigade commander returned to duty and Walker was placed in command of the 1st Infantry Brigade, Australian Imperial Force. On 15 May General (Sir) William Bridges [q.v.7] was mortally wounded and Walker replaced him as commander of the 1st Division until General J. G. Legge [q.v.10] took charge. On 24 June Walker returned to the 1st Brigade. Although some Australian brigadier generals objected to Legge's appointment because he was junior to them, Walker raised no objection: he considered it 'natural and proper for the Commonwealth to desire its command to be in the hands of an Australian'. On 26 July Legge left Anzac and Walker resumed command with the temporary rank of major general. Thereafter, the jaunty figure of 'Hooky' (with his cap tilted over one eye) and other divisional staff officers were 'too often seen nipping around insecure trenches or making their way over the top . . . for any man to have any doubts about their willingness to share the dangers'. Walker commanded the division at Lone Pine, although he had strongly objected to the plan of attack. In September he was half-buried by a shell which burst in his dugout; a fortnight later, while inspecting a post on Silt Spur, he was severely wounded by machine-gun fire: characteristically, he refused attention until another wounded soldier had received treatment.

Walker saw no more of the fighting on Gallipoli and did not return to the division until March 1916. His rank of major general had been confirmed on 1 January. He led his Australians against Pozières and in the spring of 1917 through the outpost zone of the Hindenburg line. That summer he organized three attacks in the battle of Passchendaele. His last major engagement was at Hazebrouk from April to July 1918. In the three years that he commanded the division Walker welded it into a fighting force probably unsurpassed in the British armies. He was an astute and trusted leader as well as a humane operational commander who made no secret of his affection for his troops; the affection was reciprocated to an uncommon degree. At all times scrupulous in his care of the division, he was reluctant to commit it to an attack unless convinced that the results would more than warrant the losses; he even threatened to resign his command rather than sacrifice his men unjustifiably.

In accordance with Birdwood's wishes, Walker was among the last British officers to leave the A.I.F. On 3 July 1918—'to the deep regret of his officers and men'—he relinquished command of the 1st Division. General (Sir) Thomas Glasgow [q.v.9] replaced him. The influence of a small quota of British officers, of whom Birdwood and Walker were outstanding, 'was beyond computation', according to Bean, 'especially in the standards set by them for personal conduct'. Awarded the Distinguished Service Order in 1902, and appointed C.B. in 1915, K.C.B. in 1918 and K.C.M.G. in 1919, Walker won several foreign decorations and was nine times mentioned in dispatches in World War I.

From July 1918 Sir Harold commanded the 48th British Division in Italy and from March to July 1919 all British forces in that country. Returning to a territorial command in England, he was promoted lieut-general in 1923 and was commander-in-chief, Southern Command, India, from 1924 until 1928 when he retired from the army. He died at Crediton, Devon, on 5 November 1934, survived by his wife and two sons, one of whom became an admiral in the Royal Navy.

C. E. W. Bean, *The story of Anzac* (Syd, 1921, 1924) and *The A.I.F. in France*, 1916-18 (Syd, 1929, 1933, 1936, 1942); *Reveille* (Syd), July 1933, Apr, Dec 1934, Jan 1935; records (AWM).

A. J. SWEETING

WALKER, HURTLE FRANK (1890-1975), champagnemaker and artilleryman, was born on 5 October 1890 at Magill, near Adelaide, one of five children of John Walker, labourer, and his New Zealand-born wife Henrietta, née Ward. His lifetime association with the South Australian wine industry began at the age of 10 when he obtained exemption from Magill Public School to pick grapes. Setting off at dawn on the long walk to the vineyards, with his lunch and a bottle of cold tea in a sugar bag slung over his shoulder, the schoolboy worked a back-breaking, eleven-hour day for 7s. 6d. a week.

At 14 Walker left school to take a job as an errand-boy with Auldana Winery. His duties ranged from escorting the manager's son to school and loading casks of claret on to bullock-waggons to picking olives and working in the wine cellars 'at anything that was going'. As he grew into a tall, sinewy, curly-haired young man, he mastered the fundamentals of the industry so thoroughly that at 21 he was placed in charge of the sparkling-wine cellars. A good athlete (at school he was the only boy able to scale the flagpole), Walker played representative football and tennis and won trophies for long-distance cycling. On 7 September 1915 he enlisted as a private in the Australian Imperial Force; he embarked from Melbourne on 5 January 1916 with the 2nd Reinforcements for the 6th Field Artillery Brigade.

In France Walker served with several artillery formations before joining the 6th Brigade at Belley-sur-Somme on 19 July. He remained with the unit until the war ended, by which time he had been gassed and twice wounded; he had also risen to the rank of sergeant major and become, in the words of the unit war diary, 'the most decorated non-commissioned officer of the Brigade'. His courage and stamina in handling horses, limbers and heavy ordnance amid carnage earned him the Distinguished Conduct Medal and the Military Medal and Bar.

The D.C.M. had been won in June 1917 at Messines, Belgium, where—under shell-fire and with ammunition exploding—Walker displayed 'the greatest gallantry and initiative' in assisting his battery commander to save the guns and ammunition from a fire. At Hooge, Belgium, in October he gained the M.M. to which a Bar was added for his actions on 18 September 1918 near Le Verguier, France, when shells hit a field artillery team, wounding or killing four horses and pinning the driver beneath the wagon. While a bombardment of high explosive and gas shells continued, Walker extricated the driver and released the surviving horses.

Invalided back to Australia in 1919, he spent six months in a military hospital before returning to the wine industry and helping to establish the Romalo cellars of Australian Wines Pty Ltd. In 1926 he was appointed manager of the company, a position he held until his retirement. On 25 July 1923 at St Paul's Church, Adelaide, he had married Ellen Eliza Grattan of Elliston, South Australia. They were to have two children. A brave and energetic man, with a record of achievement in both the technical and business sides of winemaking, Walker died at Norwood on 23 August 1975, survived by his daughter and son.

London Gazette, 14 Aug 1917, 1 Feb 1918, 17 June 1919; *Advertiser* (Adel), 25 Aug 1975; War diary, 6th Field Artillery Brigade, AIF (AWM); Jack Ludbrook & Associates, Hurtle Walker of Romalo (ts, c.1965) held by Mr N. Walker, Magill, Adel, who also supplied information.   ERIC SPARKE

WALKER, JAMES (1863-1942), builder, soldier and public official, was born on 16 August 1863 at Banbridge, County Down, Ireland, son of Isaac Walker, builder, and his wife Rose Ann, née McCann. Little is known of his family and early life. After migrating to Australia about 1881, Walker settled as a builder at Charters Towers, Queensland, where he married New Zealand-born Emily Jane Meredith with Anglican rites on 4 August 1897. He served as a lieutenant in 1900-01 with the Imperial forces in the South African War and was awarded the Queen's medal with three clasps. In 1905 he was promoted captain in the Queensland Volunteer Defence Force and acted as paymaster on Thursday Island in 1914 while completing a building contract there. In August Walker was appointed captain in the Australian Imperial Force. Promoted major in 1915, he commanded the 25th Battalion from October to December at Gallipoli, and later in France and Belgium. He was mentioned in dispatches and awarded the Distinguished Service Order (1916), the Serbian Order of the White Eagle and the Czechoslovakian War Cross. Discharged medically unfit in April 1917, he was subsequently in charge of the call up of reservists in Australia.

In March 1919 he was appointed commissioner for war service homes. Influenced by Walker's distinguished military career and by a laudatory reference that he was very competent and 'good with men', Senator E. D. Millen [q.v.10] had recommended the appointment when Walker was technically an undischarged bankrupt. In 1910 as director and joint guarantor of the Golden Copper Mine, Charters Towers, Walker had resigned after discovering that the managing director held two-thirds of the shares. When the Bank of Australasia eventually called up the overdraft, Walker declined any responsibility. Only days before he embarked with the A.I.F., the bank had issued a writ and in his absence Walker had been declared bankrupt in October 1915, although actually in a sound financial position. As commissioner, Walker quickly made enemies by reducing the inflated price of materials and by dealing fearlessly with unscrupulous contractors, land agents and 'rings' formed to exploit the Department of Repatriation. He also confronted the Commonwealth Bank, in its capacity as constructing and marketing authority, over its demand that the commission pay architects' fees which Walker argued should be included in the purchase price of a house. Millen and the solicitor-general supported Walker, and the bank was later reduced to a financial agency. The resignation of the New South Wales deputy commissioner for war service homes, Major J. W. D. Evans, whose quarrel with Walker's administration was widely publicized, undermined confidence in the commission's operations.

Contrary to explicit ministerial direction, Walker had stockpiled land and acquired bulk supplies of building materials by purchasing timber areas and sawmills in an attempt to control costs in a time of shortages. His strict policy of employing returned servicemen, even when they were not the most suitable, was exacerbated by his unrealistic support of day-labour in a buoyant building market. Surprised that the minister should direct him in matters for which he believed himself legally responsible, Walker was insensitive to political realities. Neither he nor the government fully understood the relationship between a minister and a statutory authority. These problems were ventilated in the proceedings and reports of the Parliamentary Joint Committee of Public Accounts which censured Walker as an incompetent administrator. In March 1921, even before its final report (July 1922) was tabled, his appointment was cancelled on the pretext that he was an undischarged bankrupt. The acting minister for repatriation, A. S. Rodgers [q.v.11], declared that Millen had not known of the bankruptcy, but Colonel J. M. Semmens, chairman of the Repatriation Commission that replaced Walker, publicly disagreed. In upholding the decision, the treasurer Sir Joseph Cook [q.v.8] insisted that the dismissal did not reflect on Walker's ability, but the former commissioner's lawyers saw him as a scapegoat for adverse publicity and internal unrest in the government.

Walker returned to contract building in Sydney, Brisbane and Canberra. He was a distinguished rifle and revolver shot. He was, as well, chairman (1935) of the St John Ambulance Association of New South Wales. Walker died on 24 January 1942 in Sydney and was cremated. His wife, a son and a daughter survived him.

PD (Cwlth), 1920-21, pp 7287, 10395; R. L. Wettenhall, 'Administration debacle 1919-23', *Public Administration* (Syd), 27, no 4, 1964, and for bibliog; *Brisbane Courier*, 1 Jan 1917; *SMH*, 1, 19, 21 July 1919, 26-27 Jan 1942; *Age*, 27 Feb 1919; *Argus*, 21-23 Mar, 11 Apr, 7-9, 18, 22-23 July, 5, 6, 8, 23, 26, 31 Aug 1921; *Bulletin*, 28 July 1921; Repatriation, War Service Homes, Dismissal of Lt Col Walker, A457, item G403/2 (AA).

D. I. McDONALD

WALKER, JAMES THOMAS (1841-1923), financier and politician, was born on 20 March 1841 in Edinburgh, fifth son of John William Walker, wine merchant, and his wife Elizabeth, née Waterston. John ran Castlesteads station, Boorowa, New South Wales, in 1845-49; having sold it to Hamilton Hume [q.v.1], he returned with his family to Scotland. Educated at the Edinburgh Institution, then at King's College, London, James went back to Scotland for two and a half years to learn office management. In March 1860 he joined the London staff of the Bank of New South Wales, of which his cousin Thomas Walker [q.v.2] was a director. James sailed for Queensland in 1866 to manage the bank's Townsville, and later its Toowoomba, branch and was appointed assistant inspector of Queensland branches in 1879. On 16 April 1868 he had married Janette Isabella Palmer at Range View, Toowoomba. Foundation general manager (1885-87) of the Royal Bank of Queensland, he resigned to become manager and trustee in New South Wales for Thomas Walker's wealthy daughter (Dame) Eadith Campbell Walker [q.v.].

Deeply interested in the constitutional aspects of Federation, Walker was a member of the People's Federal Convention at Bathurst in 1896. There he propounded a detailed scheme for Federal finance. A delegate to the Australasian Federal Convention (1897-98), he was dismissed by Alfred Deakin [q.v.8] as 'a mere commercial man' and ignored by the Adelaide finance committee. His Sydney admirers feared that he was 'one crying in the wilderness', but he published the speeches he delivered to the convention in Sydney as *Draft Commonwealth bill* (1897). To the great satisfaction of *Liberty*, Walker's proposals were adopted at the Melbourne sittings 'in preference to the ideas set forward by the politicians which were found to be quite impractical'. He was returned at the head of the New South Wales Senate poll in 1901, and sat as a Liberal and a Free Trader in four Federal parliaments before retiring in June 1913.

Walker had resigned his presidency (1897) of the Bank of New South Wales before entering parliament, but retained a directorship (1895-1921). He owned Mount Ubi estate at Wide Bay, Queensland, and was a veteran director of such leading companies as Burns, Philp [qq.v.7,11] & Co. Ltd and the Australian Mutual Provident Society. Keen but composed and exuding rectitude, with classic features enhanced by elegant whiskers, Walker was, nonetheless, warm-hearted and capable of fiery response. An 'old and valued' member of the Highland Society and president (1903-19) of the Australian Golf Club, Sydney, he was chairman of the Thomas Walker Convalescent Hospital, and a director of the Royal

Prince Alfred Hospital and the Burnside [q.v.7] Presbyterian Orphan Homes. He sat on the finance committee of the Presbyterian Church of Australia and was a councillor of Women's and St Andrew's colleges, University of Sydney. Vice-president of the Australian Economic Association and a fellow (1886) of the Institute of Bankers, London, he was 'prominently identified' with the Bankers Institute of New South Wales. Survived by his wife, three sons and two daughters, he died on 18 January 1923 at Woollahra, Sydney, and was buried in South Head cemetery. His estate was sworn for probate in New South Wales at £27 697.

A. Deakin, *The Federal story*, J. A. La Nauze ed (Melb, 1963); R. Norris, *The emergent Commonwealth* (Melb, 1975); *Liberty* (Syd), 23 Dec 1896, 25 Feb, 26 Nov 1897, 29 Mar, 27 Apr 1898; *Scottish A'sian*, 21 Feb 1923; *Punch* (Melb), 3 Jan 1907; *SMH*, 19, 20 Jan 1923; Deakin papers (NL); Walker papers (ML).   MARGARET STEVEN

WALKER, JEAN NELLIE MILES (1878-1918), nursing sister and army matron, was born on 16 November 1878 at Port Sorell, Tasmania, daughter of Alfred Miles Walker, farmer, and his wife Louisa Mary Glover, née Wilkinson. Privately educated until 1893, she enrolled at the Collegiate School, Hobart, then trained at Hobart General Hospital in 1903-06. Having stayed on as staff nurse and later sister, in 1908 she entered private nursing. In early 1913 she completed six months training in obstetrical nursing at the Women's Hospital, Melbourne, following which she served as matron of private hospitals at Tallangatta, Victoria, and Darlinghurst, Sydney.

Joining the Australian Army Nursing Service Reserve in 1906 and becoming principal matron in 1909 of the 6th Military District (Tasmania), Miles-Walker (as she sometimes styled herself) was one of twenty-five nurses who sailed for Egypt with the Australian Imperial Force in November 1914. After several weeks with the British in Alexandria, she joined her own unit, the 2nd Australian General Hospital, at Mena House, Cairo. During the first rush of wounded from Gallipoli she took charge at Mena House while the matron was at the Ghezireh Palace Hotel, also run by the 2nd A.G.H. 'Never Matron had better assistance', Ellen Gould [q.v.9] later wrote of Jean and her counterpart at Ghezireh. From September 1915 to January 1916 Sister Walker worked in the British hospital ship *Gascon* which carried patients from Anzac Cove, Cape Helles, Mudros and Salonika to Malta, Gibraltar, England and Egypt. She was

next attached as temporary matron to the 1st Australian Stationary Hospital at Ismailia, Egypt, where wounded from the battle of Romani were treated.

When the 3rd Australian Auxiliary Hospital opened at Dartford, England, in October 1916, she had been promoted matron. In the following July she became matron with the A.A.N.S. staff of the 5th British Stationary Hospital at Dieppe, France; from September 1917 to April 1918 she acted as matron of the 3rd A.G.H. at Abbeville, replacing Grace Wilson [q.v.]. While the allies retreated from Amiens in April, the hospital was used as a casualty clearing station: its remaining twenty-four nurses cared for some 1800 patients—many of whom were badly wounded—as bombs fell in the area. After a further term at Dieppe, Matron Walker went to London and on 19 October was attached to the 2nd A.A.H. at Southall. When working in the 1st Group Clearing Hospital at Sutton Veny, Wiltshire, she fell ill during the Spanish influenza epidemic.

Jean, who had never married, died of influenza on 30 October 1918 in the British military hospital, Sutton Veny, and was buried in the graveyard of nearby St John's Church. She had been mentioned in dispatches and awarded the Royal Red Cross (1st class) in 1916.

M. Tilton, *The grey battalion* (Syd, 1934); A. G. Butler (ed), *Official history of the Australian Army Medical Services in the war of 1914-1918*, 1-3 (Melb, 1938, Canb, 1940, 1943); *A'sian Trained Nurses Assn Register of Members*, 1916; *London Gazette*, 1, 29 Dec 1916; *Collegiate School Mag*, Dec 1916, p 10, Dec 1918, p 2; *A'sian Nurses J*, 15 Jan 1917, p 7, 15 Mar 1918, p 88, 15 Mar 1919, p 75; *SMH*, 25 Dec 1918; Butler papers *and* honours and awards, 1914-18 war, Aust Army (AWM); information from Mrs R. Charlston, Royal Hobart Hospital and Mrs R. Whitehouse, St Michael's Collegiate School, Hob.   JAN BASSETT

WALKER, JOHN (1855-1941), Presbyterian minister, was born on 17 April 1855 at Oxton, Cheshire, England, son of Scottish parents David Walker, builder, and his wife Jemima Elizabeth, née Blackie. After schooling at Birkenhead, Walker spent five years as a Liverpool merchant's clerk. A committed Presbyterian from 1871, he worked for the American revivalists, D. Moody and I. Sankey, in their 1875 Liverpool mission, and with Professor Henry Drummond.

Migrating to Sydney for health reasons in 1876, Walker was befriended by J. H. Goodlet [q.v.4]. Walker's evangelistic interests led him to enter St Andrew's College in 1879 to train for the Presbyterian ministry. Licensed to minister at Burwood in 1881, he was ordained in 1882 and sent as first Presbyterian minister to Germanton (Holbrook) where he pioneered the nearby parishes of Tumbarumba, Culcairn, Corryong and Upper Murray. On 13 June 1883 he married Jessie Dight (d. 1932) at Richmond. Next year he became evangelist at Bathurst.

After visiting England, Walker was called in 1888 to the new Sydney parish of Woollahra. His parish paper, as the *Messenger*, became the official organ of the Presbyterian Church of New South Wales. With James Cameron, he edited its two-volume *Centenary history* (1905). For the General Assembly, he convened committees on religion and morals, and on foreign missions; in 1899 he was appointed commissioner of the Centenary Thanksgiving Fund and in five years raised over £50 000; he was founding secretary (1899-1905) of the evangelical New South Wales Council of Churches. His pastoral abilities and zeal were recognized: he was inducted as moderator of the General Assembly on 6 May 1902 and issued his address, *Some urgent Church problems*. The Stccl [q.v.6] lecturer in pastoral theology at St Andrew's College in 1906, he published his lectures as *The King's business* (1908).

At St Andrew's Kirk, Ballarat, Victoria, from 1908 to 1926, Walker was president of the Ballarat College council and wrote sundry poems. As Presbyterian chaplain with the Australian Imperial Force, he sailed to England in a troop-ship in 1917 and visited Australian soldiers in French and British hospitals. His five sons were serving with the A.I.F. (three were killed in action) and his daughter Janet nursed with a British unit at Salonica, Greece.

Moderator-general of the Presbyterian Church of Australia in 1918-20, he published his address, *The Protestant Catholic Church: and Church union for greater Christian service* (Melbourne, 1918). Spruce, with a full moustache, Walker belonged to the Naval and Military Club, Melbourne, and was a philatelist.

To raise funds to build and endow a Presbyterian church and manse in Canberra, Walker was appointed commissioner of the national General Assembly (1926) and inducted as the first minister of St Andrew's in February 1927. Despite the Depression, he raised more than £50 000. In 1930 the University of Edinburgh conferred an honorary D.D. upon him. Walker retired to Sydney on 31 December 1933. Survived by his wife, two sons and two daughters, he died at Woollahra on 14 September 1941 and was buried in Waverley cemetery.

C. A. White, *One hundred years of the Presbyterian Church in N.S.W.* (Syd, 1937); Presbyterian Church of NSW, *Minutes of Proceedings of General Assembly*, 1942; *T&CJ*, 17 May 1902; *SMH*, 8 Mar 1932, 15 Sept 1941; *Canb Times*, 16 Sept 1941; Walker papers (Ferguson Lib, Syd).

ROBERT WITHYCOMBE

WALKER, LUCY ARABELLA STOCKS WHEATLEY; see GARVIN, LUCY

WALL, DOROTHY (1894-1942), author and illustrator, was born on 12 January 1894 at Kilburnie, Wellington, New Zealand, daughter of Charles James William Wall, soldier, and his wife Lillian, née Palethorpe, both English born. From the age of 10 Dorothy won scholarships and studied at the Christchurch School of Art and Wellington Technical School. Migrating to Sydney in 1914, she joined the *Sun* newspaper; in October she had an illustration in the *Lone Hand*; in 1920 her children's story, *Tommy Bear and the Zookies*, was published. On 4 November 1921 at St Alban's Anglican Church, Five Dock, she married Andrew Delfosse Badgery, a clerk.

She won recognition as an illustrator of children's books with her work for J. J. Hall's *The crystal bowl* (1921). Her rather florid cherubs and pixies, Art Nouveau fairies and naturalistic animals shared similarities with the work of Ida Sherbourne Outhwaite [q.v.11]. Wall continued to illustrate books for other writers, including *Jacko—the broadcasting kookaburra* (1933) and *The amazing adventures of Billy Penguin* (1934) for Brooke Nicholls, and *Australians all* (1934) for Nellie Grant Cooper. An ardent defender of Australian flora and fauna, Wall drew to educate as well as to entertain.

In 1933 she published her most famous book, *Blinky Bill: the quaint little Australian*, based on stories told to her only child, Peter. *Blinky Bill grows up* (1934) and *Blinky Bill and Nutsy* (1937) followed. While later critics have objected to the anthropomorphizing of her characters—animals dressed in trousers, dresses, aprons and bonnets act out suburban domestic situations in a stylized bushland setting—successive generations of children have delighted in the mischievous koala with his 'boyish' characteristics of adventurousness, impudence and curiosity.

Despite the success of Blinky Bill, Dorothy Wall still struggled to establish herself professionally and financially. Divorced in 1934, after she had removed herself and her son to a cottage at Warrimoo in the Blue Mountains, she wrote to her publishers, Angus & Robertson [qq.v.7,11] Ltd: 'I've never cared for the honour and glory of seeing my name in print. £.S.D. is what matters to me now'. They gave her supplementary work, illustrating book jackets, for each of which she was paid about three guineas. Touched by the determination of this 'little battler', W. G. Cousins encouraged her, sending her advances, buying at her request lottery tickets (in which she had unflagging faith) and helping her pursue her schemes to sell her cartoons to American movie companies or her Blinky Bill motif to English china firms.

Depressed and ill, in 1937 Wall went back to the country of her birth and became an illustrator for the *New Zealand Herald* and *Auckland Weekly News*. Although financially secure and comfortable for the first time, she increasingly missed the sunshine, the 'beautiful gum trees and the hard old stones and shrubs of the bush'. Her health improved, she resigned her job and in July 1941 returned to Sydney. She told Cousins: 'I'll have to start the battle over again but I feel much better and more able to combat disappointment'. Six months later, she died of pneumonia on 21 January 1942 at Cremorne. Survived by her son, she was buried in Northern Suburbs cemetery. *The complete adventures of Blinky Bill*, first published in 1939, was reprinted fifteen times between 1940 and 1965.

H. M. Saxby, *A history of Australian children's literature, 1841-1941* (Syd, 1969, 1971); M. Muir, *A history of Australian children's book illustration* (Melb, 1982); *Truth* (Syd), 30 Sept 1934; *SMH*, 4 Oct 1934, 27 Jan 1942; Angus & Robertson correspondence (ML).   DIANE LANGMORE

WALLACE, ARTHUR COOPER ('JOHNNY') (1900-1975), footballer and barrister, was born on 5 September 1900 at Macksville, New South Wales, second child of native-born parents Matthew Wallace, storekeeper, and his wife Isabel, née Gellatley. He attended Sydney Grammar School where he played Rugby, rowed in three successive winning eights in the Athletic Association of the Great Public Schools 'Head of the River' regattas and was senior prefect in 1919. Resident in St Andrew's College, he studied arts at the University of Sydney in 1920-22, won a rowing blue and excelled at Rugby Union. A slim, dark and elegant three-quarter, he donned the waratah-crested jersey for the 1921 New South Wales Rugby tour of New Zealand.

Awarded a Rhodes scholarship in 1922, Wallace read jurisprudence at New College, Oxford (B.A., 1925) and was called to the Bar at Lincoln's Inn on 17 September 1925. He gained Rugby blues in 1922-25. Of Caledonian stock, he was chosen with Ian Smith from Melbourne and two other Oxonian pals to play for Scotland. The Oxford three-quarter line proved a major strength in the 1925 Scottish 'Grand Slam'. 'Johnny' Wallace played nine times for Scotland and was in seven winning sides.

Returning to Sydney, Wallace was admitted to the New South Wales Bar on 12 March 1926. He played with Glebe-Balmain and captained the 1927-28 Waratahs' tour of Britain, France and Canada (since 1986 regarded as a fully Australian representative side). His captaincy was a success: Wallace's team played exciting, open football with forwards and backs linking efficiently; they won against Ireland, Wales and France, but lost to Scotland and England.

Back in Australia, Wallace gave up Rugby and became vice-principal of St Andrew's College in 1928. On 5 January 1929 he married Betty Jean Simson with Presbyterian forms at Gunnedah; they were to have two daughters. In 1930 Wallace settled down at his native Macksville as a grazier where he remained for a decade. His interest in Rugby remained active and he coached the State and Australian sides against the 1937 Springboks *en route* for New Zealand and glory. In spite of the rain, on a very damp Sydney Cricket Ground the New South Wales team played a magnificent running and passing game, thrashing South Africa 17-6, with four tries to one.

Divorced in June 1941, Wallace married Floris Ada Jago, a nursing sister, at Paddington, Sydney, on 14 July. He had been provisionally commissioned in the Australian Imperial Force in 1939, but was discharged next year after being injured in an accident. From October 1941 he served as a captain in the Australian Army Legal Department until 1944, then as hirings officer until 1946. Practising at the Bar in Sydney until 1955, he was admitted as a solicitor on 29 July and worked in the Crown Solicitor's Office until 1966.

A life member and vice-president of the New South Wales Rugby Union, Wallace coached the Wallabies on their 1953 tour of South Africa where he again advocated a 'running with the ball' game. A smoker and a drinker, he died of myocardial infarction on 3 November 1975 at The Entrance and was cremated. He was survived by the two sons of his second marriage.

'Johnny' Wallace may be remembered as the player, captain and coach who helped, in difficult times, to put Australia back on the Rugby Union world map.

R. McWhirter and A. Noble, *Centenary history of Oxford University Rugby Football Club* (Oxford, 1969); J. Pollard, *Australian Rugby Union* (Syd, 1984); *SMH*, 11 Nov 1921.   J. P. BODIS

WALLACE, ARTHUR KNIGHT; *see* AHERN, ELIZABETH

WALLACE, ELIZABETH; see AHERN, ELIZABETH

WALLACE, GEORGE STEVENSON (1895-1960), comedian, was born on 4 June 1895 at Aberdeen, New South Wales, son of George Stephenson Wallace, painter, and his wife Catherine Mary Ann, née Scott, both native-born. Known as 'Broncho', George senior began touring in minstrel shows. George junior appeared on stage at the age of 3 as a pirate in a Sydney pantomime and was the infant member of a family song-and-dance act until his parents divorced. A juvenile busker on the Pyrmont waterfront, he was later apprenticed in his stepfather's ink factory. He spent his youth knocking about North Queensland as a farm-hand and canc-cutter before he joined a road show at 16.

On 3 January 1917 at the People's Evangelic Mission House, Brisbane, Wallace married Margarita Edith Emma Nicholas, a barmaid, and brought her to Sydney next year. Early in 1919, after an unpaid trial performance of acrobatic clog-dancing at the Newtown Bridge Theatre (one of Harry Clay's city and suburban vaudeville houses), he was engaged at £4 a week. The bill changed weekly and the audience knew what it wanted. Wallace soon introduced his wife to feed him patter and their 2-year-old son to join in acrobatic poses. The family act did not last, but 'Wee Georgie Wallace' partnered his father occasionally before Wallace and his wife separated in 1924.

Late in 1919 Jack Paterson and Wallace had teamed up at the Newtown Bridge Theatre as 'Dinks' and 'Onkus' ('The Two Drunks'), a knockabout comedy act inspired by the success of 'Stiffy' and 'Mo' [q.v.11 Rene]. A year later they were Clay's most popular performers, regularly playing to full houses. The partnership survived for five years, while Paterson's role steadily diminished. By mid-1922 Clay was advertising new programmes of vaudeville and revue by 'Onkus and His Merry Company'.

In 1925 Wallace joined the Fuller [qq.v.8] circuit for £20 a week. His talents both as a performer and as a witty song and revue sketch writer soon prompted the Theatre Magazine to predict, 'in the face of theatrical providence', that one day he would be 'Australia's greatest comedian'. Wallace was small and tubby, with goggle eyes, mobile expression and a croaking voice. Baggy trousers precariously hitched at half-mast beneath his protruding stomach, a checked shirt and a battered felt hat were his trade marks. He had the audience rolling in the aisles. Astonishingly agile, he perfected the art of falling

on his left ear and built a repertoire of absurd tales about such characters as Stanley the Bull, the Drongo from the Congo and the so-refined bus conductress, Sophie the Sort. Unusually in his profession, he did not try to steal scenes. The Theatre Magazine described him as 'irresistibly funny without ever descending to the vulgar': his humour was larded with a robust yet innocent country flavour that contrasted strikingly with the pungent comic styles of his great contemporaries Roy Rene and Jim Gerald. Going to see every new George Wallace revue was said to have become 'a pleasant habit' with his admirers.

The Depression and competition from films created difficulties for vaudeville, but Wallace found new successes on the stage, in film and in pantomime—though never as a Dame. As Dandy Dick he appeared with Gladys Moncrieff [q.v.10] in the Australian musical, Collits' Inn (1933), by 'Varney Desmond' [q.v.10 Monk], and took the role of Asticot in The beloved vagabond (1934). Wallace made seven films, re-working his earlier revue scripts as the screenplays for His Royal Highness (1932) and Harmony Row (1933), and collaborating in writing the scenarios for A ticket in Tatts (1934), Let George do it (1938) and Gone to the dogs (1939). Songs he composed included the popular World War II tune, A brown slouch hat. He taught himself to play the piano, saxophone and guitar, and was a good caricaturist and amateur landscape painter; as another hobby, he made dolls from felt. Passionately fond of animals, particularly horses, he had a chicken farm at Rooty Hill.

Joining the Tivoli circuit in the early 1940s, Wallace earned £120 a week. He also appeared in two more films, as the barber in The rats of Tobruk (1944) and the stage-manager in Wherever she goes (1951). From 1949 he had a weekly radio show on the Macquarie network; he later played opposite Gerald in such nostalgic variety shows as Thanks for the memory (1953) and The good old days (1957), staged by Harry Wren. Heart disease forced Wallace into semi-retirement in 1957. Survived by his son, he died of chronic bronchitis and emphysema on 19 October 1960 at his Kensington home, Sydney, and was cremated with Anglican rites.

J. West, Theatre in Australia (Syd, 1978); A. Pike and R. Cooper, Australian film 1900-1977 (Melb, 1980); H. Love (ed), The Australian stage (Syd, 1984); J. Stewart, An encyclopaedia of Australian film (Syd, 1984); Theatre Mag (Syd), 1 Apr, 2 June, 1 Nov 1919, 1 Jan, 1 Mar, 1 Oct 1920, 1 June 1922, 2 Mar, 1 Apr, 1 May, 1 June 1925; People (Syd), 28 Feb 1951, p 25; A'sian Post, 3 June 1954; Herald (Melb), 9 Dec 1944, 21 Aug 1957; SMH and Sun (Syd), 20 Oct 1960; Sun-Herald, 23 Oct 1960.   STUART SAYERS

WALLACE, SIR ROBERT STRACHAN (1882-1961), university vice-chancellor, was born on 1 August 1882 at Old Deer, Aberdeenshire, Scotland, son of John Wallace, master blacksmith, and his wife Christina, née Hay. Robert was educated locally at Gordon's College and on a scholarship at the University of Aberdeen (M.A., 1904), gaining first-class honours in English language and literature. Having taught at his old school, he proceeded to Christ Church, Oxford (B.A., 1907); there he was awarded the Holford exhibition in English and took first-class honours in English literature. Wallace returned as assistant-professor to Aberdeen where he married Mary Murray McAdam on 28 July 1909 with Congregational forms.

Appointed to the chair of English language and literature at the University of Melbourne in 1912, Wallace was a dedicated teacher and scholar. He also proved an able administrator as dean of the faculty of arts (1914-17), vice-president (1917, 1922-24) and president (1925-27) of the professorial board, and chairman of the extension board. While in Melbourne he was general editor of the *Australasian Shakespeare* series, and edited *Twelfth night* (1916) and *Holinshed's chronicles* (1917, 1923). He also published *An historical English grammar* (1921) and, with (Sir) Archibald Strong [q.v.], *English prose and verse* (1923).

On 23 February 1917 Wallace had enlisted as a gunner in the Field Artillery, Australian Imperial Force. Commissioned in November, he was posted next year to the A.I.F. Education Service, Cambridge, England, and appointed director of the Australian Corps Central School at Rue, France. He was responsible to Bishop Long [q.v.10] for organizing the corps school as a training centre for matriculation, accountancy and civil service examinations. His A.I.F. appointment terminated on 3 November 1919.

In 1927, on the unanimous decision of the senate of the University of Sydney, Wallace was appointed vice-chancellor. On his arrival with his family in January 1928, he was unimpressed with the dilapidated buildings, and with the unkempt grounds whose beauty he set about restoring, assisted later by Professor E. G. Waterhouse [q.v.] and relief workers during the Depression.

Confronted with the severe problems brought about by a decrease in the government grant, Wallace had to cope with salary reductions, lack of essential equipment and financial stringency in all aspects of university life. That the university weathered the storm while developing some new courses and maintaining academic standards was largely due to his careful administration and ability to obtain co-operation and loyalty from a staff under considerable pressure. New chairs were established, including the Bosch [q.v.7] chairs in medicine, surgery and bacteriology. A degree course in divinity and several new diploma courses were also introduced.

Wallace benefited from his contacts within the government through his involvement as the Commonwealth's chief censor for cinematographic films (1922-27) and as a member (1932-35) of the Australian Broadcasting Commission. A major achievement was the decision of the State government in 1937 to increase the university's statutory endowment to a permanent £100 000. Wallace, however, feared that too much government assistance might endanger the university's autonomy and aimed to find further income from independent sources.

Among the major building projects undertaken in his term of office were a new medical school, biology laboratories, the departments of biochemistry and geography, and a lecture theatre which bears his name. Sancta Sophia College was incorporated into the university, the veterinary farm at Badgerys Creek was purchased with the assistance of a grant from the (John) McGarvie Smith [q.v.11] Institute (1936) and the plant breeding station at Curlewis was established (1944). Wallace was also a founder of the New England University College at Armidale.

The careful and wise handling of students was a strong point of his vice-chancellorship. Students respected Wallace's fairness and understanding which he demonstrated especially in regard to the Commemoration Day celebrations and in the creation of the students' representative council. He tried to satisfy the graduates (who had long sought representation on the senate) by establishing the standing committee of convocation.

Generally on good terms with his staff and almost always available, Wallace was thought by some critics to be unable to take a stand on certain issues because of influences brought to bear on him. His close friends included professors Archibald Charteris [q.v.7] (his legal adviser) and Leslie Wilkinson [q.v.] (whose work he admired), and Eric (Lord) Ashby. A keen supporter of freedom of speech for academics, Wallace gave prudent support to the controversial Professor John Anderson [q.v.7].

In World War II Wallace faced the task of guiding the university through the attendant problems of manpower restrictions, the urgency of wartime research and the lack of essential equipment. He had known grief at the death of his eldest child and grieved anew when the university's casualty list lengthened. Responsible for successfully implementing the Commonwealth Reconstruction Training Scheme for ex-service men and women, he saw a dramatic expansion in the number of students and staff. Nevertheless, his last years were ones of increasing frustration. Unable and unwilling to adjust to large-scale administration, he increasingly passed to younger men the committee-work which he hated. Knighted in 1941, Wallace was glad to retire in 1947 from what had been a challenging but arduous and, at times, soul-destroying decade.

Tall and spare, with an Aberdonian accent, a soft and hearty chuckle and a dry sense of humour, Wallace had a vigorous, energetic temperament much influenced by his religious upbringing. He was a firm man, of great integrity, but his moralistic sense of justice was at times marred by hastiness of judgement. He was devoted to his family and kept his private sphere separate from his university life. Mary presided over a happy home. Among his sporting interests were cricket and golf. Wallace retired to Canberra where he died on 5 September 1961. Survived by his wife and two sons, he was buried with Presbyterian forms in Canberra cemetery.

E. Scott, *A history of the University of Melbourne* (Melb, 1936); G. Blainey, *A centenary history of the University of Melbourne* (Melb, 1957); H. Dow (ed), *Memories of Melbourne University* (Melb, 1983); *Reveille* (Syd), Dec 1932; Univ Syd, *Gazette*, June 1952, Oct 1961; *SMH*, 16 June, 8 July 1927, 5 Apr, 30 Nov 1928, 24 May 1932, 1 Jan 1941, 7 Sept 1961; *The Times*, 8 Sept 1961; Univ Syd Archives.   URSULA BYGOTT

WALLER, MERVYN NAPIER (1893-1972), artist, was born on 19 June 1893 at Penshurst, Victoria, son of William Waller, contractor, and his wife Sarah, née Napier, both Victorian born. Educated locally until aged 14, he then worked on his father's farm. In 1913 he began studies at the National Gallery schools, Melbourne, and first exhibited water-colours and drawings at the Victorian Artists' Society in 1915. On 31 August of that year he enlisted in the Australian Imperial Force, and on 21 October at Carlton married with Presbyterian forms Christian Marjory Emily Carlyle Yandell (d. 1954), a fellow student and artist from Castlemaine. Serving in France from the end of 1916, Waller was seriously wounded in action at Bullecourt in May 1917; his right arm had to be amputated at the shoulder. While convalescing in France and England he learned to write and draw with his left hand. After coming home to Australia and being discharged in February 1918, he exhibited a series of war sketches in Melbourne, Sydney, Adelaide and Hobart in 1918-19 which helped to establish his reputation.

He continued to paint in water-colour, taking his subjects from mythology and classical legend, but exhibited a group of linocuts in 1923. Waller had prepared his first, though unsuccessful, mural design for a competition in 1921 and in 1927 completed his first major mural for the Menzies Hotel, Melbourne. Next year his mural 'Peace after Victory' was installed in the State Library of Victoria.

Visiting England and Europe in 1929 to study stained glass, the Wallers travelled in Italy where Napier was deeply impressed by the mosaics in Ravenna and studied mosaic in Venice. He returned to Melbourne in March 1930 and began to work almost exclusively in stained glass and mosaic. In 1931 he completed a great monumental mosaic for the University of Western Australia; two important commissions in Melbourne followed: the mosaic façade for Newspaper House (completed 1933) and murals for the dining hall in the Myer [q.v.10] Emporium (completed 1935). During this time he also worked on a number of stained-glass commissions, some in collaboration with his wife. Waller was, as well, senior art teacher in the applied art school of the Working Men's College, Melbourne.

Between 1939 and 1945 he worked as an illustrator and undertook no major commissions. In 1946 he finished a three-lancet window commemorating the New Guinea martyrs for St Peter's Church, Eastern Hill. In 1952-58 he designed and completed the mosaics and stained glass for the Hall of Memory at the Australian War Memorial, Canberra. He was appointed O.B.E. in 1953 and C.M.G. in 1959. On 25 January 1958 in a civil ceremony in Melbourne Waller had married Lorna Marion Reyburn, a New Zealand-born artist who had long been his assistant in stained glass. A heart attack in 1966 did not prevent him from continuing his work. He died on 30 March 1972 at Ivanhoe, Melbourne, and was cremated. His wife survived him; his estate was sworn for probate at $104 238.

Waller's early work was strongly influenced by Pre-Raphaelite and late-nineteenth century British painters; his monumental works show an increasingly classical and calmly formal style, using timeless and heroic figure compositions to express ideas and ideals, sometimes with theosophical or gnostic overtones.

J. Hetherington, *Australian painters* (Melb, 1963); N. Draffin (comp), *The art of Napier Waller, 1893-1972* (Melb, 1978).   NICHOLAS DRAFFIN

WALLIS, ALFRED RUSSELL (1888-1963), trade union official and conciliation commissioner, was born on 16 April 1888 at North Carlton, Melbourne, son of William Wallis, a carpenter from London, and his Tasmanian-born wife Mary Ann, née

Gorman. After attending Horsham and Moreland state schools, he served an apprenticeship as a cutter in the men's tailoring trade and worked as a journeyman in several Melbourne factories. Aged 18, he was converted to Tom Mann's [q.v.10] socialism and joined the Victorian Socialist Party; in 1906 he was imprisoned for thirty days for taking part in its free-speech campaign.

On his release from prison, Wallis became active in the Victorian Clothing Operatives' Union which covered pressers, cutters and trimmers. He represented it on the Trades Hall Council and on the Wages Board; he was also elected a member of the executive of the V.S.P. The stress of these activities, in addition to his paid factory work, induced a breakdown and he went to the country to recuperate.

In 1908 Wallis resumed his trade union career, this time with the newly amalgamated Federated Clothing Trades Union of Australia (Victorian branch) which embraced the tailors and tailoresses as well as the V.C.O.U. Next year he was elected president of the Victorian branch and represented the union on the Trades Hall Council, the Wages Board and the Eight Hours' Committee. In 1912 he was elected full-time paid organizer and thereafter represented the union at the State Australian Labor Party conferences and at union conventions. From 1920 Wallis acted as secretary to the rapidly expanding Victorian branch of the Clothing Trades Union and edited its short-lived journal, the *Clothing Trades Gazette*. On 5 March 1921 he married fellow unionist Josephine Wood at St Joseph's Catholic Church, Collingwood.

A leader of union opposition to the Premiers' Plan, Wallis stood unsuccessfully as a Labor candidate for the Senate in 1931. Next year he was elected president of the Victorian Trades Hall Council. In 1933 the Federal government appointed him Australian workers' delegate to the International Labour Conference in Geneva, Switzerland. On his return, he was general secretary-treasurer of the Amalgamated Clothing and Allied Trades Union (1934-44), while remaining secretary of the Victorian branch.

In 1942 Wallis became one of the workers' representatives on the wartime Women's Employment Board. He resigned his union positions in 1947 when appointed a Commonwealth conciliation commissioner. Wallis retired in 1953 after union protest at his accepting a directorship of North Deborah Mining Co. N.L. He died on 3 August 1963 at Fitzroy and was cremated. His wife survived him; there were no children.

Described as a 'grim visaged man, always careful with his dress', Alf Wallis was a controversial figure who evoked strong personal and political antipathies among employers and unionists. His prejudicial attitudes towards women and Jews were especially resented by many in the clothing trades. Wallis's career was marked by a steady shift from left to right, or, as he said, from 'rebel' to 'diplomatist'.

L. J. Louis, *Trade unions and the Depression* (Canb, 1968); B. Walker, *Solidarity forever* (Melb, 1972); *Aust Clothing Trades J*, Apr 1940, p 2, Nov 1941, p 13; *Labor Call*, 26 July 1923; *Sun News-Pictorial*, 29 Mar 1933; *Labor Daily*, 3 Oct 1933; *Herald* (Melb), 13 June 1932, 28 Mar, 3 Oct 1933, 12 Apr 1935, 6 Oct 1936, 13 May 1938, 10 Oct 1947, 2, 3, 4 Dec 1952, 6 Apr 1953, 7 Aug 1963; B. Ellem, A history of the Clothing and Allied Trades Union (Ph.D. thesis, Univ Wollongong, 1986); R. Frances, The politics of work: case studies of three Victorian industries, 1880-1939 (Ph.D. thesis, Monash Univ, 1988); M. Brodney papers (LaTL).

RAELENE FRANCES

WALLIS, FREDERICK SAMUEL (1857-1939), printer and politician, was born on 22 November 1857 at Macclesfield, South Australia, eldest son of Richard Wallis, shoemaker, and his wife Anne, née Gamble. While attending Norwood Grammar School, Sam worked as a newspaper-boy. Apprenticed in 1872 to J. H. Lewis, printer of the *Protestant Advocate*, he joined the *South Australian Register* as a compositor in 1877 and rose to proofreader six years later.

A lay preacher of the Unitarian Christian Church and secretary of its mutual improvement association, Wallis published a booklet about truth and the Trinity, *Three ones* (1879), under the pseudonym 'Arith Metic'. He was president (1884-87) of the South Australian Typographical Society and represented it in 1886 at meetings of the Fourth Intercolonial Trades Union Congress in Adelaide and of the Australasian Typographical Union in Melbourne. Sincere, straightforward and conscientious, he was a councilmember of the South Australian Temperance Alliance. His neatness, clipped moustache and serious expression indicated restraint. He did not marry and lived with his mother at Goodwood Park.

Sacked in 1888 for joining a strike at the *Register*, he remained rueful: 'that was my first and last'. As unpaid secretary (1887-1909) of the typographical society, Wallis was a delegate to the United Trades and Labour Council, sat on the committee responsible for building the Trades Hall, and attended the Selborne Hotel meeting on 7 January 1891 which formed the Legislative Council Elections Committee, precursor of the United Labor Party. Next year he gave evidence to the shops and factories commission. President (1896) of the U.T.L.C. and its secretary (1897-1909), he compiled the *Trades Hall*

Review for twelve years from 1897. During the 1890s he worked night shifts at the *Advertiser*. In 1901-04 he was vice-president of the U.L.P. and in 1905 secretary of the Women Employees' Mutual Association.

Having unsuccessfully contested three elections, in 1907-21 he represented Central in the Legislative Council where he was chief secretary and minister of industry (March-June 1909) in Tom Price's [q.v.11] cabinet, chief secretary (1910-12) under John Verran [q.v.], Opposition leader in 1912-13, and a member of eight government inquiries. Expelled from the Labor Party in 1916 for supporting conscription in World War I, Wallis regained membership in March 1917, but two years later was again forced out and eventually joined the National Party. In 1925 he was debarred from his trusteeship of the Trades Hall after publicly admonishing striking seamen.

Active in the Boy Scouts' Association, Wallis was a board-member of the Royal Institution for the Blind, a South Australian vice-president of the League of the Empire, and a Freemason. One of the founders of the local branch of the Royal Geographical Society of Australasia, he helped to produce its *Centenary history of South Australia* (1936). He had published *Thirty years' record of the Labor Party in South Australia* (1923) and in 1937-38 wrote a column about labour history in the *Weekly Herald*. He died on 13 November 1939 in Adelaide; following a state funeral, he was buried in West Terrace cemetery.

H. T. Burgess (ed), *Cyclopedia of South Australia*, 1 (Adel, 1907); Roy Geog Soc of A'sia, SA branch, *Procs*, 40, 1938-39; *A'sian Typographical J*, June 1897; *Quiz and the Lantern*, 1 Sept 1898; *Univ Studies in Hist*, 4, no 2, 1963-64; *Worker* (Brisb), 5 Jan 1901; *Mail* (Adel), 21 Mar 1914; *Observer* (Adel), 3 Mar, 7 Apr 1917, 11, 18 Feb 1928; *Advertiser* (Adel), 13 Oct 1937, 14 Nov 1939; newspaper-cuttings (Mortlock Lib).   SUZANNE EDGAR

WALLIS, WILLIAM DANE (1882-1955), soldier and rural worker, was born on 14 February 1882 in Perth, son of William Alfred Wallis, builder, and his wife Harriett Henrietta Maria, née Jones. Enlisting for service in the South African War, young William left Fremantle in March 1900 as a bugler with the 3rd Western Australian (Mounted Infantry) Contingent which merged with a contingent from Victoria to be known as the '3rd Bushmen'; it served under Lieut-General Carrington in Rhodesia and, after the relief of Eland's River, under Lord Methuen and General Plumer.

Returning to Western Australia in May 1901, Wallis took up farming at Wagin. On 19 March 1908 he married Beatrice Annie Clark

in the local Methodist Church. Giving his occupation as commercial traveller and his marital status as single, he enlisted in the Australian Imperial Force on 17 August 1914 and, with the rank of sergeant, left for Egypt in October with the 8th Battery, 3rd Field Artillery Brigade. Commanded by Major A. J. Bessell-Browne [q.v.7], the battery landed at Gallipoli on 25 April 1915 but its guns were not immediately brought ashore. On 4 May two field-guns were hauled up the precipitous slopes of Plateau 400. Under orders from Major General (Sir) William Bridges [q.v.7], Wallis led one of the crews which, three times on 5-6 May, used dragropes to bring its gun onto the crest whence it bombarded the enemy trenches at a range of 450 yards (411 m) while fully exposed to cross-fire. Awarded the Military Medal, he was mentioned in dispatches and commissioned on 16 August in the 1st Divisional Artillery; he was promoted lieutenant in December.

In March 1916 he embarked from Egypt for the Western Front with the 23rd Battery which became part of the 21st F.A. Brigade in May and saw action at Pozières. Evacuated ill in December, Wallis returned to the front in April 1917 and was appointed divisional trench mortar officer, 5th Divisional Artillery. He was promoted temporary captain next month, mentioned in dispatches for his 'initiative and determination' in the Ypres sector from July, and confirmed in rank on 5 September.

Commended for his work in the line from February to September 1918, Wallis won the Military Cross for his action on 17 October: while his unit supported the advance from the Selle River, he fearlessly rode forward on a motor cycle and obtained valuable information about the attacking troops. Promoted major that month, he was appointed commander of the 5th Divisional Ammunition Column and attended training at the School of Artillery, Shoeburyness, England. In January 1919 he was awarded a Bar to his Military Cross.

In December Wallis arrived in Australia; his A.I.F. appointment ended in March 1920. Although his wife and two children remained in Western Australia, he was demobilized in New South Wales. He worked as an agricultural labourer before becoming a clerk at Casino where he was a foundation member (1925) and later president of the sub-branch of the Returned Sailors' and Soldiers' Imperial League of Australia. In World War II he served as an enlistment officer; he was a board member (chairman 1944-50) of Casino Memorial Hospital and was prominent in the town's sporting activities. Wallis died in Concord Repatriation General Hospital on 28 March 1955 and was cremated with Anglican rites.

Aust Defence Dept, *Official records of the Australian military contingents to the war in South Africa*, P. L. Murray ed (Melb, 1911); C. E. W. Bean, *The story of Anzac*, 2 (Syd, 1924), and *Two men I knew* (Syd, 1957); *Reveille* (Syd), 1 May 1955; *Richmond River Express*, 30 Mar 1955; records (AWM).
GEORGE DICKER

WALPOLE, HERBERT REGINALD ROBERT SEYMOUR (1853-1928), professional organizer, was born on 6 December 1853 at Balderton, Nottinghamshire, England, son of Robert Seymour Walpole, Church of England clergyman, and his wife Elizabeth, née Apthorpe. He claimed connexion with the illustrious Walpole family. Educated, by his own account, at 'the Temple, in Brighton, Sussex', at 17 Walpole travelled in the United States of America where his father had bought a ranch. He returned to England in 1874 and soon afterwards migrated to Australia. Employed by the Bank of Australasia, he was sent to New Zealand; following ill health, he came back to work on stations in the backblocks of New South Wales. On 23 August 1882 he married Jane Sophia Kent in the Church of the Holy Trinity, Launceston, Tasmania. His appointment as secretary to the Calcutta Exhibition (1883-84) in India marked the start of his career as an organizer. Walpole was a commissioner for Victoria at the Centennial International Exhibition in Melbourne (1888) and at the Paris Exhibition (1889). He claimed to have qualified in England as a metallurgical and mining engineer.

During the Constitutional referenda campaigns of 1898 and 1899, Walpole was organizing secretary of the Australasian Federation League of Victoria. Hailing the telephone as 'that instrument of absolute necessity', he relished aggressive campaigning and used his Voluntary Fighting Brigade of 'sharpshooters' to harass 'the enemy' at political meetings. Concerned about a reluctant turn-out for the second referendum, he persuaded Sir George Turner [q.v.] to issue a certificate to those who voted in 1899.

In 1902 Walpole became organizer and secretary of the Victorian Employers' Federation, the prototype for similar organizations in other States. He also helped to found the Employers' Federation of New South Wales in 1903. Later, as secretary of the Central Council of Employers of Australia which produced the journal, *Liberty and progress*, he was in touch with similar bodies in North America; he was instrumental, as well, in setting up the Australian Women's National League and the Anti-Socialist Alliance which were part of the employers' developing political strategy. On six months leave in 1908, he raised money in London for the forthcoming Federal election which, Walpole averred, would decide 'who was to be top dog in this country'. An expert on new industrial legislation of concern to employers, he was credited with instigating Constitutional challenges in the High Court of Australia which succeeded in restricting the Commonwealth's role. Conceding that he was worth even more, the V.E.F. in 1906 increased Walpole's annual salary from £350 to £500.

Tall and lean, nicknamed 'Tallpole', he had become something of a Melbourne identity, but his abrasive and confrontationist style denied him popularity: Walpole admitted in 1908, though not without satisfaction, that many looked upon him as 'the most unpopular man in Australia'. For this reason the federation sought to minimize his visibility as an organizer in bodies such as the A.W.N.L. In 1909 the *Argus* criticized his lack of discretion; next year Walpole resigned for reasons of health. Rewarded with a testimonial purse of sovereigns, he was acknowledged as 'largely responsible for the proud position which the Federation occupies'.

Survived by his five daughters and a son, Walpole died on 2 July 1928 at his home at Heidelberg, Melbourne, and was buried in Phillip Island cemetery, Victoria.

J. Smith (ed), *Cyclopedia of Victoria*, 3 (Melb, 1905); J. Rickard, *Class and politics* (Canb, 1975) and *H. B. Higgins* (Syd, 1984); *Review of Reviews* (A'sian ed), 15 June 1898; *Liberty and progress*, 25 May 1908, 25 Jan 1911; *Punch* (Melb), 7 Nov 1907; *Argus*, 21 Oct 1909; Council and executive minute-books (Vic Employers' Federation, Melb).
JOHN RICKARD

WALSH, HENRY DEANE (1853-1921), engineer, was born on 16 September 1853 in Dublin, son of John Edward Walsh, barrister, and his wife Blair Belinda, née MacNeill. John was conservative member of the House of Commons for the University of Dublin, attorney general for Ireland in 1866 and master of the rolls for Ireland. Henry was educated at Portora Royal School, Enniskillen, and at Trinity College, Dublin (B.A., B.A.I. [Engineering], 1874). Captain of the university football club, he was foundation secretary of the Irish Football Union in 1874 and played twice for Ireland against England in 1875. He was engaged on engineering works in England in 1875-76, then joined the Great Southern and Western Railway Co. in Ireland.

Migrating to New South Wales in 1877, Walsh joined the Department of Public Works in January 1878 as a surveyor for the Sydney water supply scheme. Appointed resident engineer at Newcastle in 1879, he took charge of constructing the Walka pumping station and reservoir, and supervised flood protection works on the Hunter River at

Maitland. He married Lucy Gwendoline Steele at St Thomas's Anglican Church, Enfield, Sydney, on 23 April 1879.

Promoted supervising engineer in January 1891, Walsh was confirmed as district engineer in 1895. He was responsible for all public works programmes from Lake Macquarie to the Queensland border. At Newcastle, Walsh developed a new harbour basin and Walsh Island (site of the State dockyards), built midstream in the Hunter River from dredged silt. He was appointed an official member of the Hunter District Water Supply and Sewerage Board in 1892, succeeding Alexander Brown [q.v.7 John Brown] as president in 1896.

On the establishment of the Sydney Harbour Trust in 1901, Walsh moved to the capital as engineer-in-chief. His engineering and administrative abilities were evident in the remodelling of Dawes and Millers points, including the design and construction of the Walsh Bay and Jones Bay wharves and cargo-handling systems. Almost £5 million was spent on the Sydney harbour front under his direct supervision. Appointed commissioner of the trust in 1913, he retired in 1919.

In 1891 Walsh had joined the Royal Society of New South Wales (president, 1909) and contributed papers to its proceedings. He was a member of the Institution of Civil Engineers, London, from 1889 and of its local advisory committee (1902-21). Closely involved with the Church of England, he was a Freemason, a member of the Boy Scouts' Association's council, and honorary district treasurer for the New South Wales centre of the St John Ambulance Association (1909-21). Genial, witty and tactful, he was adept at handling difficult situations; he endeared himself alike to the 'humblest workmen on the wharves' and to his superiors. For relaxation, he played golf and tennis.

The death of his only son in 1916 bereft Walsh of his usual cheer and energy. Survived by his wife and five daughters, he died of arteriosclerosis on 29 August 1921 at his Roseville home and was buried in the of Field of Mars cemetery. His achievements were commemorated in the eponymous designation of Walsh Island in Newcastle Harbour and Walsh Bay on Sydney's waterfront.

S. Diffley, *The men in green* (Lond, 1973); *Cyclopedia of N.S.W.* (Syd, 1907); *DNB*, vol 20, 1964-65; J. W. Armstrong, *Pipelines and people* (Newcastle, 1967) and (ed), *Shaping the Hunter* (Newcastle, 1983); Roy Soc NSW, *J*, July 1922, p 7; *Syd Harbour Trust Officers J*, 1, no 4, Sept 1925, p 14; *The Times*, 14 Dec 1875; *Newcastle Morning Herald*, 1, 22 Apr, 9, 13 May 1901; *SMH*, 30 Aug 1921; S. Schreiner, Research notes on H. D. Walsh (Research School of Social Sciences, ANU).

P. N. TROY
C. J. LLOYD

WALSH, JAMES MORGAN (1897-1952), author, was born on 23 February 1897 at Geelong, Victoria, son of Thomas Patrick Walsh, accountant, and his wife Kate, née Morgan, both Australian born. James went to local Catholic schools and then to Xavier College, Melbourne, leaving in 1912 to work in his father's stock and station business. He later said that it was from a clerk's stool at Geelong that he launched himself as a writer. His first short story was published in 1913, his first novel, *Tap Tap Island*, illustrated by Percy Lindsay [q.v.10], in 1921.

The Walsh family moved to Melbourne in 1922. Encouraged by the success of *The lost valley* (1921), James became a full-time writer in 1923. On 1 January 1925 at St Joseph's Catholic Church, Port Melbourne, he married Louisa Mary Murphy. That year they settled in London where they were friendly with Roy Bridges [q.v.7] and his circle. James and Louisa revisited Australia in 1927-29.

One of Australia's most prolific authors, Walsh produced fifty-eight novels under his own name. As 'H. Haverstock Hill' he produced five crime adventures of the Pacific islands, in the genre of Louis Becke and Beatrice Grimshaw [qq.v.7,9]. Three others were written under the pseudonym 'Jack Carew'. References to him as 'the Australian Oppenheim' and 'the Australian Edgar Wallace' indicate both his popular status and the range he covered. He produced international spy sagas like E. Phillips Oppenheim and tales of urban crime like Wallace, as well as straight adventure yarns and a huge number of short stories: he reported that in 1929 he had thirty accepted by magazines. His work was translated into many languages.

Much of Walsh's output was produced for the London thriller mills and has little Australian interest: he rewrote *The white mask* (1925) from an Australian to an English setting to achieve publication in London. *The lost valley* is set in Victoria's Western District, and two of his later titles, *The man behind the curtain* and *The league of missing men* (both published 1927), are formal mysteries set in Australia. The latter in particular is a novel of some impact, mixing as it does the familiarities of detection and romance with some more searching speculations about identity, business practices and, ultimately, the limits to policing in the modern state. Here at least Walsh fulfilled his aspiration to be 'the author of one good psychological novel'.

A prodigious reader from childhood, Walsh was a dedicated and by no means undignified writer of good-quality, popular material. Dark haired, strong featured and distinctly Celtic in appearance, he was seen by 'Little Malop' of the Melbourne *Age* as being 'as mild a man as ever cut a throat on paper'. From 1938 Walsh lived at Weston-super-Mare, Somerset. Survived by his wife, son and daughter, he died there on 29 August 1952.

R. Bridges, *That yesterday was home* (Syd, 1948); *All About Books*, 21 Jan, 18 July 1929, 20 Jan 1930; Education Dept (Vic), *Educational Mag*, Sept 1948; *Herald* (Melb), 22 Jan 1927; *Age*, 17 Jan 1931.

STEPHEN KNIGHT

WALSH, JOHN JOSEPH (1862-1926), detective, was born on 14 February 1862 at Kilfinnane, County Limerick, Ireland, son of James Walsh, farmer, and his wife Ellen, née Bourke. John attended school in Ardpatrick and in 1879-81 studied medicine at Queen's College, Royal University of Ireland, Cork. He migrated to Sydney and joined the police force on 24 November 1881. Three years later he arrived in Queensland where he served as a constable at Townsville and Bowen, then transferred to the north-western district of New South Wales in 1887. At Perth in 1891 he joined the Western Australian police force and spent six years at country stations, including the goldfields. Assigned to the detective branch in 1897, he worked at Fremantle and Kalgoorlie before becoming detective-sergeant in charge of the Fremantle office in 1905. On 18 April 1900 at St Mary's Catholic Cathedral, Perth, he had married Mary Jane Newell, a niece of Bishop Gibney [q.v.8].

Theft was endemic on the eastern goldfields where stolen ore was treated in illicit furnaces hidden in thick bush. Although such practices were widely accepted, the losses suffered by mine-owners led to a royal commission in 1906 and to the establishment next year of a gold-stealing detection staff, based at Kalgoorlie but operating independently of local police. Transferred there in 1908, Walsh took charge of both the detective branch and the gold-stealing staff. He was 5 ft. 9 ins. (175.3 cm) tall, dark and trim, with hazel eyes and a bushy moustache; he had a reputation for absolute integrity, excelled in boxing, running and weight-lifting, and was an experienced bushman. Among his staff was Detective-Sergeant Alexander Pitman.

From 1912 Walsh was a sub-inspector at Perth, heading the criminal investigation branch; promoted inspector in 1916, he returned to Kalgoorlie in 1920 in charge of the gold-stealing detection staff. Four years later the squad was reduced by four, leaving only Walsh and Pitman to police the entire area. Threats were made against them; their wives returned to Perth. On 28 April 1926 the two men set out for an unknown destination. Because of the need for secrecy, they did not inform the Kalgoorlie station of their proposed movements.

On 12 May their charred and dismembered bodies were found in a disused shaft, some six miles (9.7 km) south-west of Kalgoorlie. A week later their bicycles were found in the bush 17 miles (27.4 km) to the south-east. A gold-treatment plant was nearby and evidence indicated that the murders had occurred there. Perth detectives joined the search for the killers. On 6 June three local men—Evan Clarke, Phillip Treffene and William Coulter—were arrested. Clarke turned King's evidence, swearing that he had only assisted in disposing of the corpses. Treffene and Coulter were found guilty of murder and hanged.

Survived by his wife, daughter and three sons, Walsh was buried in Karrakatta cemetery; his estate was sworn for probate at £52. A monument commemorating Walsh and Pitman was erected outside Perth's police headquarters in 1929 and rededicated at Adelaide Terrace in 1988.

J. S. Battye (ed), *Cyclopedia of Western Australia*, 1 (Adel, 1912); H. E. Graves, *Who rides* (Lond, 1937); J. Coulter, *With malice aforethought* (Perth, 1982); *V&P* (LA WA), 1906, 2 (14), p 5; *Western Argus*, 2 May 1905; *West Australian*, 13 May 1926; *SMH*, 13, 14 May, 26 Oct 1926; WA Police Dept, Community Affairs branch files *and* police occurrence books, gold stealing detection staff, 1907-10 (BL); NSW police register (ML); Qld Police Dept, Community Relations branch (QA).

MOLLIE BENTLEY

WALSH, THOMAS (1871-1943), seaman and trade unionist, and ADELA CONSTANTIA MARY PANKHURST (1885-1961), feminist, were husband and wife. Tom was born on 15 January 1871 at Youghal, County Cork, Ireland, son of Patrick Walsh, cobbler, and his wife Mary, née Murphy, who died soon after their son's birth. Raised by his aunts, Tom had little schooling, but read widely. He went to sea and in 1893 arrived in Brisbane, hoping to join William Lane's [q.v.9] New Australia venture in Paraguay, but lacked the necessary £60. He joined the Social Democratic Vanguard and worked as a seaman in coastal ships. On 18 November 1899 he married native-born Margaret O'Heir with Catholic rites at Cairns.

Moving to New South Wales, Tom was agent at Newcastle in 1908 for the Federated Seamen's Union of Australasia. By 1909, when he backed the militant Peter Bowling and clashed with W. M. Hughes [qq.v.7,9] during the coal strike, Walsh was a polished platform speaker. He belonged to the union's federal executive in 1909 and was New South Wales branch secretary in 1912. Suffering from tuberculosis, Margaret died on 6 April 1914; their three daughters were cared for by

Ethel and Robert Ross [q.v.11] in Melbourne where Tom was based throughout the war.

Adela was born on 19 June 1885 at Chorlton upon Medlock, Manchester, Lancashire, England, third daughter of Richard Marsden Pankhurst, barrister-at-law, and his wife Emmeline, née Goulden. A liberal intellectual, Richard supported working-class self-improvement movements. Although he died when Adela was aged 9, his widow and daughters pursued varying goals in the belief that they were carrying out his wishes. Adela attended Manchester School for Girls, and the Disley Road school as a trainee teacher. Although she did not complete her training, she was moved by observing the effects of poverty on the children at the school.

Her mother and sisters, Christabel and Sylvia, were members of the Independent Labour Party (for which Adela distributed literature) and founders of the Women's Social and Political Union which demanded the franchise for women. Adela became a paid organizer for the W.S.P.U., operating mainly in Yorkshire where contact with working-class women developed her interest in improving conditions for them. She believed that, once women had the vote, children would not be allowed to suffer. Though less than five feet (152.4 cm) tall, Adela was a compelling speaker. She suffered from bronchitis and, after being several times imprisoned as a militant suffragette, withdrew from the campaign exhausted. After some training in agriculture at Studley College, Warwickshire, she accompanied Mrs Helen Archdale to Italy. Estranged from her mother and Christabel, Adela sailed for Australia with only £20.

Arriving in Melbourne in April 1914, she found work in the one area in which she was experienced and expert: she became an organizer for Vida Goldstein [q.v.9] and remained with the anti-war and anti-conscriptionist Women's Political Association and Women's Peace Army. Adela Pankhurst was their best speaker. She also joined the Victorian Socialist Party and used the suffragette tactic of repeated questioning to disrupt her opponents' meetings. While living with her close friends the Rosses, she met Tom Walsh. Both Tom and Adela campaigned actively against conscription: they hated the wicked loss of life and feared that the cost of the war would prove a barrier to future improvement in the workers' standard of living. For repeatedly defying the ban on public gatherings, Adela was treated with increasing severity. Sentenced to gaol after leading a demonstration in Melbourne against the high price of food, she was on remand when she and Tom were married in Melbourne by Rev. Frederick Sinclaire of the Free Religious Fellowship on 30 September 1917. Although it was later said that she married Tom to avoid deportation (which Hughes was considering), they were devoted to one another.

Having refused Hughes's offer of release on the condition that she not speak in public, Adela returned to gaol in October to serve four months. Despite a petition signed by thousands, she was not released until January 1918. With Tom, she moved to Sydney where their five children were born. Adela did some organizing for the Social Democratic League and wrote for the *Seamen's Journal*. General secretary of the Seamen's Union, Tom organized its 1919 strike and was imprisoned for three months in Melbourne.

The Walshes were foundation members of the Communist Party of Australia: Adela envisaged a new order (involving communal kitchens, architect-designed worker housing and free books) in which none would want. She ran a speakers' class and wrote and spoke at its meetings, but both she and Tom soon withdrew from Communist Party activities.

As federal president of the union from 1922, Walsh used the tactic of delaying a ship's sailing until the seamen's demands were met; as a result, his union gained improved conditions in Australian vessels. Its success led to moves by shipowners to have the union deregistered; the Commonwealth Government Line of Steamers chartered British ships and sailed under British articles to avoid paying Australian union rates and thus provoked strike action by waterside unions and the seamen. In an attempt to break the union, in 1925 the Commonwealth government had it deregistered, charged Walsh with inciting the Waterside Workers' Federation of Australia and passed special legislation aimed at deporting Walsh and Jacob Johnson. When British seamen went on strike later that year, the Australian union supported them and helped to arrange temporary accommodation for them. The government then moved to deport Walsh and Johnson: after the Deportation Board found against them, the two were arrested and held at Garden Island, pending an appeal which was upheld.

The events of 1925 had made it clear that depressed wages in international shipping endangered local standards. The Commonwealth government had threatened during the shipping strike to suspend the Navigation Act to permit low-wage shipping on coastal runs. Realizing that continued militancy would cost the union its recent gains, Walsh repeatedly clashed with Johnson over strategy and control of the union until Tom was finally defeated late in 1928. He then attempted, unsuccessfully, to form a new union committed to industrial peace and was not readmitted to the Seamen's Union until 1936.

Increasingly known as an anti-communist, in 1928 Adela founded the Australian Women's Guild of Empire which raised money to relieve suffering among women and children in working-class suburbs. She toured industrial areas, speaking at factories and workplaces on the need for industrial co-operation. In her view, the correct response to the Depression was to increase efficiency and raise productivity. The family increasingly depended on what Tom could earn from journalism (William Andrade [q.v.7], the bookseller, had named him as one of the two best-read men in Melbourne) and on Adela's income as speaker and organizer for the guild. Her administrative skill, eloquence and anti-communism attracted large numbers of middle-class supporters. The guild provided a motor car to enable her to extend her message to a wider audience. Braving picket lines to speak against strikes, she often met a hostile reception.

Tom's and Adela's internationalism led them to sympathize with Japan's efforts to industrialize and to secure a share of the China market; they also thought that Japan would make a better trading partner for Australia than the United States of America. As the likelihood of war in Europe grew, they increasingly urged that Australia negotiate a trade agreement with Japan. In December 1939-January 1940 they visited that country as guests of the Japanese government; it was the only holiday they had ever taken. On their return, they assured Australians that Japanese intentions were pacific.

Adela's following among the British Guild of Empire fell away. She was briefly drawn to an ill-omened association with the Australia First Movement, founded by W. J. Miles [q.v.10] and another disillusioned ex-communist P. R. Stephensen [q.v.]. In the panic that followed the bombing of Pearl Harbour, Adela was interned in March 1942. She was prepared to sacrifice principle: Tom was dying and she wanted to be with him at home. Her appeal failed, but she was released on 13 October, two days after beginning a hunger strike. Tom's death in North Sydney on 5 April 1943 marked the end of her public life. Survived by three daughters of his first marriage, and by a son and three daughters of his second, he was buried in the Unitarian section of Northern Suburbs cemetery.

Adela maintained her optimistic outlook on human nature and her faith that human institutions could operate for equal benefit to all. Her naive generosity and trusting spirit brought affection and loyalty from her friends, and baffled distrust from her opponents. Survived by a son and two daughters, she died on 23 May 1961 in a Wahroonga hospital and was buried with Catholic rites beside her husband.

D. Mitchell, *The fighting Pankhursts* (Lond, 1967); B. Muirden, *The puzzled patriots* (Melb, 1968); B. Fitzgerald and R. Cahill, *The Seamen's Union of Australia, 1872-1972* (Syd, 1981); *People* (Syd), 9 May 1951; *Daily Standard*, 4 Apr 1914; *SMH*, 16 Jan, 11 Feb, 4 Apr, 13, 15 May, 2, 3, 4, 7, 12, 15 Sept, 18 Oct, 7, 21, 27 Nov, 12, 19 Dec 1925, 1, 2 Apr 1926, 16 Feb 1940, 19 May, 26 June 1942, 8 Apr 1943; Seamen's Union of Australia papers (ANUABL); Imprisonment and release of Adela Walsh 1917-18, A456 item W26/148/239 pt 1 (AA); Walsh and Pankhurst papers (NL); S. Hogan, *Stirring times* (ms held by author).

SUSAN HOGAN

WALTER, WILLIAM ARDAGH GARDNER (1860-1940), magistrate, was born on 13 August 1860 at Wilton, Somerset, England, son of Octavius Gardner Walter, solicitor, and his wife Prudence, née Ardagh. Educated at Taunton College School, William migrated to Western Australia in 1885 and bought a cattle property at Tanjanerup, near Nannup. On 20 September 1887 at St Paul's Anglican Church, Bunbury, he married Lucille Jane Thomson (d. 1947); they were to have a daughter and a son who was killed in World War I.

In 1891 Walter sold his station and entered government service. After helping to compile the census, he became warden of the new Murchison goldfield. From 1893 he was resident magistrate for the Blackwood area and registrar of Greenbushes tin-mining district; he quarrelled with the under secretary of crown lands over advice allegedly tendered by the latter on the issuing of mining leases. Walter was acting police magistrate at Perth in 1902 and then resident magistrate for three years at Geraldton; he was appointed second stipendiary magistrate at Kalgoorlie in 1909, acting warden of its mining district in 1911 and, after two years on the Murchison fields, first magistrate at Kalgoorlie.

In March 1918 he fined the leader of the parliamentary Opposition Phillip Collier [q.v.8] £25 plus costs for utterances 'likely to cause disaffection' during the conscription plebiscite. The fine was subsequently remitted and costs refunded in an undefended action before the High Court of Australia. A big, swarthy man with an iron-grey moustache, in 1919 Walter aroused hostility in trade union and labour circles when, after clashes between rival unions at Kalgoorlie, he refused bail for a number of Australian Workers' Union strikers and sent them to Perth for trial; it was later revealed that he had travelled to Perth for fire-arms to quell the disturbances. Workers disliked what they saw as his favouritism towards the Chamber of Mines and the Returned Sailors' and Soldiers' Imperial League of Australia; but one court reporter, while suspecting that Walter knew more about men than about the law, admired his judgements for their tolerance and compassion.

Walter left the goldfields in 1920 to become third stipendiary magistrate in Perth and was promoted second magistrate next year. Returning from a holiday in Burma in May 1924, he refused to resign and was compulsorily retired by the newly elected Collier Labor government. Victimization was alleged, but Collier remained adamant. Walter had shone at Rugby football and rowing in England, and at tennis and cricket in Western Australia; he coached women scullers on the River Swan and belonged to the Western Australian Turf Club. He was a member of Hannans Club and of the senate of the University of Western Australia; a vice-president of the Weld Club, he became its secretary in 1925, but resigned next year and went home to England where he died at Pembury, Kent, on 10 March 1940.

Truthful Thomas, *Through the spy-glass* (Perth, 1905); J. S. Battye (ed), *Cyclopedia of Western Australia*, 2 (Adel, 1913); T. S. Louch, *The history of the Weld Club* (Perth, 1980); *PD* (WA), 1924, p 535; *V&P* (WA), 1893, 2 (A 11); *Kalgoorlie Miner*, 22 Dec 1917, 9, 13 Mar 1918, 7, 13 Nov 1919; *West Australian*, 26, 29, 31 May, 29 Aug 1924; *Blackwood Times*, 26 Oct, 2 Nov 1966.

DAVID BLACK

WALTERS, GEORGE THOMAS (1853-1926), Unitarian minister, was born on 23 October 1853 at Liverpool, Lancashire, England, son of William Miles Walters, carver and gilder, and his wife Katherine, née Yelverton. Educated at the local elementary school and a private academy at Everton, he considered commerce before deciding that he wished to be a Baptist minister. While preparing himself for the ministry, he worked for Nettlefold & Chamberlain, screw manufacturers, of Birmingham.

Since childhood, when his Baptist upbringing had encouraged his taste for preaching and engendered nightmares about hell, Walters had sought religious truth; at 15 he rejected the Baptist chapel and restlessly visited the churches of Liverpool. Having rejected the Trinity and the doctrine of eternal torment, he entered Rawdon College, Yorkshire, believing that he was 'already tainted with heresy'. During his training, exposure to the Biblical criticism of D. F. Strauss and J. E. Renan further challenged his acceptance of orthodox Baptist doctrine. Reading a pamphlet which propounded Unitarian beliefs, he found what he had been seeking. After studying at the Unitarian College, Manchester, he was appointed to Burnley, Lancashire (1876-78), and Aberdeen,

Scotland (1878-84). On 8 August 1876 at Upperthorpe Chapel, Yorkshire, he married Marian Radcliffe (d. 1886).

In 1884 Walters was appointed by the British and Foreign Unitarian Association of London to the Melbourne Unitarian Christian Church at Eastern Hill. For four years he presided over its burgeoning and wealthy middle-class congregation, supervising the building of a handsome church and establishing a Social Union to broaden cultural activity among his adherents. He contributed to Melbourne's intellectual life through the Shakespeare and Shelley societies, and through his journal, *Modern Thought*, begun in 1885.

An intense, dark, bearded man, balding later in life, Walters preached with eloquence and 'incisive force', but his congregation became increasingly uneasy about his secular interests and his radical political and theological views. The church committee challenged his policy of inviting prominent laymen into the pulpit and almost succeeded in prohibiting a debate on the Irish question, chaired by Walters who held republican sympathies. When in 1888 they reinstated the Lord's Prayer in the service, he resigned in protest.

Accompanied by his wife Myra Aimée, née Tuckett, whom he had married with Presbyterian forms at Queenscliff on 4 October 1886, Walters transferred to the Hyde Park Unitarian Church, Sydney. Active in the Dickens [q.v.4] Fellowship, he wrote a Biblical drama, *Joseph of Canaan*, which was produced to great acclaim in 1895 by George Rignold [q.v.6 Rignall] at Her Majesty's Theatre, Sydney, and then in Melbourne. Walters' other plays, *Thou fool* and *Under the Southern Cross*, were later performed. He was a member of the board of the Pitt Town Co-operative Settlement, the council of the Womanhood Suffrage League and the Sydney Mechanics' School of Arts committee. As in Melbourne, he established a lively literary and social union within the church.

In 1898, after conflict with the church committee, Walters led almost all his congregation out of the Unitarian Church and set up a branch of the Australian Church which met at the Independent Order of Oddfellows' Temple. In 1903 the two congregations amalgamated as the Australian Unitarian Church. From pulpit and through pamphlets he preached essentially the faith that he had discovered as a student, although his understanding evolved in response to the challenge of scientific thought. His early lyrical expositions of nature as the revelation of the deity were by the 1890s tempered by an acceptance of the Darwinian doctrine of natural selection which, in turn, led him by 1916 to espouse eugenic theory. He continued his ministry until 16 November 1926 when he was knocked down by a car and killed at Mosman. Survived by the son and daughter of his first marriage, he was cremated.

E. Wilson, *The story of the Sydney Unitarian Church 1850-1974* (Syd, 1974); D. Scott, *The halfway house to infidelity* (Melb, 1980); J. Roe, *Beyond belief* (Syd, 1986); T. W. H. Leavitt, *Australian representative men*, 2 (Melb, 1887); *Age*, 29 May 1888; *Table Talk*, 3 Feb 1893, 25 Nov 1926; *SMH*, 5 June 1918, 2 July 1920, 25 Dec 1923, 10 Nov 1924, 27 May, 3 June 1925, 17, 18 Nov 1926; *Bulletin*, 25 Nov 1926; Unitarian Church (Syd), Minutes (ML); H. G. Turner papers (LaTL).

DIANE LANGMORE

WALTERS, HENRY LATIMER (1868-1929), public servant, was born on 24 January 1868 at Newcastle, New South Wales, fourth surviving child of Joseph Walters, engine driver, and his wife Mary, née Evans, both Welsh born. Joining the New South Wales Department of Public Works as a clerk in 1883, Henry transferred to the Government Printing Office; he next worked in the Department of Lands. On 12 June 1895 he married Edith Rebecca Cole at Marrickville with Congregational forms. In 1899 Walters was promoted accountant in the Treasury. After Federation, he joined the Commonwealth Department of Home Affairs as its accountant, and moved to Melbourne. Within this department he developed a close association with the foundation of Canberra.

The 1916-17 Blacket [q.v.7] royal commission on the Federal capital administration criticized Walters for his accounts system and for the limited direction he had given to the accounts clerk in the Federal capital. Independent advice received by W. A. Watt [q.v.], the minister for works and railways, supported Walters, and was used to discredit Blacket's conclusions generally. Walters' reputation was in no way harmed and later in 1917 he was appointed chief clerk in the Commonwealth Department of Works and Railways. In 1926 he succeeded W. D. Bingle [q.v.7] as departmental secretary and was also appointed commissioner for war service homes. Mindful of the legacy of Colonel James Walker's [q.v.] controversial term as commissioner, Walters pursued 'efficiency, sympathy and economy'. He visited operations in all the States, revised procedures and staffing, and achieved a substantial reduction in administrative expenses.

A tall, robust man, Walters had 'simple tastes' and was 'kindly in disposition, exceedingly devout, and overflowing with good humor'. Prominently identified with the Baptist Church, he was a gifted lay preacher. He was esteemed in the Commonwealth Public Service and in 1928 was awarded the Imper-

ial Service Order. Walters died of stomach cancer on 17 March 1929 at St Kilda, Melbourne, and was buried in Cheltenham cemetery. He was survived by his wife, son and two daughters.

J. Gibbney, *Canberra 1913-1953* (Canb, 1988); *PP* (Cwlth), 1917, 2, p 1, 1926-28, 2, p 347; *Age* and *Argus*, 19 Mar 1929; *Canb Times*, 5 Dec 1964.

IAN CARNELL

WALTON, THOMAS UTRICK (1852-1917), industrial chemist, was born on 17 June 1852 at Greenock, Renfrewshire, Scotland, third child of Utrick Walton, a customs officer from Cumberland, and his wife Elisabeth, née Dickinson. Educated at the academy, Greenock, at the University of Glasgow (B.Sc., 1873) where he won prizes and awards, and at Anderson's University (1876-78), he was admitted to the Institution of Civil Engineers (1873) and worked in sugar refineries at Greenock until 1880. Recruited by (Sir) Edward Knox [q.v.5] to develop scientific procedures for the Colonial Sugar Refining Co., Walton migrated in the *Cotopaxi*, reaching Sydney on 11 March 1881. On 20 March 1889 he married Mary Hamilton at St George's Presbyterian Church, Sydney.

With Gustav Kottmann (a beet-sugar chemist from Berlin), Walton developed a system of chemical control which monitored the movement of cane-sugar from the farms through the mills and refineries to the final market products. He trained large numbers of school-leavers in routine polarimetric analysis before they were sent into the field. A high degree of efficiency resulted, allowing the company to survive in difficult economic times. The control system became a model for the Australian sugar industry and also internationally. Walton and his central laboratory staff, including Thomas Steel [q.v.], also undertook advanced investigation of a wide range of other technical problems.

A member of the Institution of Civil Engineers, London, from 1873, Walton was elected a fellow of the (Royal) Institute of Chemistry of Great Britain and Ireland in 1880 and of the Chemical Society, London, in 1884. From its foundation in 1903 until his death, he was honorary secretary of the Sydney section of the Society of Chemical Industry.

A practising Congregationalist, Walton served in 1888-92 as secretary of the Pitt Street Church, Sydney; from 1894 he attended the Trinity Church, Strathfield. His only recreation seemed to be his garden at Burwood. Survived by three daughters and a son, he died of acute colitis on 1 February

1917 at Darlinghurst and was buried in Rookwood cemetery. Tributes were paid to his personal and civic qualities.

A. G. Lowndes (ed), *South Pacific enterprise* (Syd, 1956); R. W. Home (ed), *Australian science in the making* (Cambridge, Eng, 1988); *Scottish A'sian*, Oct 1913, p 2123; *International Sugar J*, July 1917, p 320; Inst of Chemistry, *Procs*, 1917, p 17; *SMH*, 2 Feb 1917; *Aust Worker*, 8 Feb 1917; *Aust Christian World* (Syd), 9 Feb 1917; *T&CJ*, 28 Feb 1917; Colonial Sugar Refining Co. staff records and correspondence (ANUABL); family information.

H. G. HOLLAND

WAND, JOHN WILLIAM CHARLES (1885-1977), Anglican archbishop, was born on 25 January 1885 at Grantham, Lincolnshire, England, son of Arthur James Henry Wand, butcher, and his wife Elizabeth Ann Ovelin, née Turner. Although his father was a staunch Calvinist, his mother fostered John in the Church of England. Educated at the King's School, Grantham, and at St Edmund Hall, Oxford, where he took first-class honours in theology (B.A., 1907; M.A., 1911), he prepared for ordination at Bishop Jacob Hostel, Newcastle upon Tyne, and was made deacon in 1908 and ordained priest in 1909. He served curacies at Benwell and Lancaster, and on 11 October 1911 married Amy Agnes Wiggins (d. 1966) at St Leonard's parish church, Watlington, Oxfordshire.

Appointed vicar-choral of Sarum in 1914, on the outbreak of war Wand enlisted as chaplain and reached Gallipoli in July 1915. He was padre to the 2nd Australian Hospital and, after being invalided home with paratyphoid fever, served in France.

Demobilized in March 1919, he was made perpetual curate of St Mark's, Salisbury, where St Clair Donaldson [q.v.8] was bishop. In 1925 Wand became fellow and dean of Oriel College, Oxford, and university lecturer in church history. Eight years later Bishop Francis Batty [q.v.7] procured his nomination to the see of Brisbane. Wand was consecrated in St Paul's Cathedral, London, on 1 May 1934 and enthroned in St John's, Brisbane, on 5 September.

His arrival in Queensland was almost immediately clouded by the accidental death in Switzerland of his only son Paul. Furthermore, those who had wanted a local dignitary as their new bishop united to oppose Wand. His attempts to eradicate slackness made him appear authoritarian to his clergy. Sturdy in appearance, shy and gracious, Wand was often seen as being aloof and something of an intellectual snob. The decision to move St Francis's Theological College from Nundah to the Bishopsbourne property proved un-

popular, although Wand's relations with its students won him their respect and affection. His establishment of a property and finance board to handle the economic problems of the diocese did not meet with general favour.

As a member of the University of Queensland senate, Wand worked to promote biblical studies. During his episcopate he wrote a weekly article for the *Courier Mail*, translated the New Testament epistles and gave the Moorhouse [q.v.5] lectures in Melbourne in 1936; he consecrated the cathedral of St Peter and St Paul, Dogura, New Guinea, in 1939 and made a lecture tour of the United States of America in 1940. He argued in support of a new constitution for the Church, but thought that the proposed appellate tribunal should have a majority of bishops, rather than legal laymen, to determine points of doctrine. With his friend Bishop Batty, he supported the early ecumenical movement.

During World War II, when Brisbane resembled a garrison town, Wand and his wife worked for the Soldiers, Sailors and Airmen's Help Society. His 1942 address to the Royal Society of St George defended the British war effort and was published as a pamphlet, *Has Britain let us down?* It prompted questions in the Federal parliament and attracted the attention of such British politicians as Brendan (Viscount) Bracken and (Sir) Winston Churchill. Early in 1943 Wand was surprised to be offered the see of Bath and Wells. He left Brisbane in July.

Two years later he was translated to the see of London where post-war difficulties, including the rebuilding of shattered city churches, challenged and revealed his administrative gifts. As bishop, Wand was a privy counsellor; in 1955 he was appointed K.C.V.O.; in 1946-57 he was prelate of the Order of the British Empire. After resigning his see in 1956, he officiated as canon and treasurer of St Paul's Cathedral, London, until 1969 and edited the *Church Quarterly Review*. A wide-ranging and facile historian, he wrote forty books, among them a *History of the modern church* (1930), *History of the early church* (1937), *White* [q.v.] *of Carpentaria* (1949), *Anglicanism in history and today* (1961) and an autobiography, *The changeful page* (1965). Survived by a daughter, Wand died on 16 August 1977 at the College of St Barnabas, Lingfield, Surrey, and was cremated. An obituary in the *Church Times* paid tribute to his scholarship, administrative genius and unsentimental piety.

DNB, 1971-80; *Brisb Diocesan Newsletter*, no 25, Nov 1977; K. Rayner, The history of the Church of England in Queensland (Ph.D. thesis, Univ Qld, 1962); Diocesan Archives, Brisb; London Diocesan Archives, St Paul's Cathedral; personal information.

F. R. ARNOTT*

WANLISS, DAVID SYDNEY (1864-1943), army officer and judge, was born on 20 February 1864 at Perth, Scotland, second son of Thomas Drummond Wanliss, a newspaper proprietor at Ballarat, Victoria, and his wife Eliza, née Henderson, both Scottish born. David attended Ballarat College and Trinity College, Cambridge (B.A., LL.B., 1887). Called to the Bar at the Inner Temple, London, on 19 November 1888, he returned to Victoria in 1890 and practised at Ballarat and in Melbourne. On 25 April 1895 at Scots Church, Melbourne, he married with Presbyterian forms Jessie Guthrie (d. 1922). He helped to write a second edition of his brother-in-law (Sir) William Irvine's [q.v.9] *Justices of the peace* (1899).

On 12 January 1901 Wanliss joined the militia as a lieutenant in the Victorian Scottish Regiment; he became its commanding officer in February 1911 and was promoted lieut-colonel in February 1913. By then the regiment had been reorganized as the 52nd Battalion, yet Wanliss continued to call it the Victorian Scottish. Like his father he was proud of having been born in Scotland, and when on 18 August 1914 he was appointed commanding officer of the 5th Battalion, Australian Imperial Force, he tried to fill it with men of Scottish ancestry. He succeeded in recruiting about a quarter of the battalion from Victorian Scottish veterans and men with Scottish surnames. In addition, he filled one of the battalion's eight companies with former pupils from private schools. Battle was to obliterate these distinctions, but in 1921 Wanliss's photograph, as the frontispiece of the 5th Battalion's history, showed him in the tartan of the Victorian Scottish.

Wanliss led his battalion at the landing on Anzac and through the hectic days that followed, and in the terrible battle of Krithia, on Helles, on 8 May 1915. From that month he acted intermittently as commanding officer of the 2nd Brigade, but in late July was evacuated with typhoid, and after time in a hospital on Malta was repatriated in January 1916. He had proved a competent but not outstanding leader: aged 51 in 1915, he was a little old for the trials of Gallipoli, yet the 5th Battalion remembered him as 'the father of the regiment', and he was appointed C.M.G. and mentioned in dispatches in November 1916. Wanliss Gully on Anzac was named after him.

In mid-1916 Wanliss returned to A.I.F. service as officer commanding the 1st Australian Divisional Base Depot at Étaples, France, and then various A.I.F. depots in England. In March 1917 he was appointed officer commanding the 65th Battalion of the proposed 6th Division; when the division was disbanded, he returned to depot service. His A.I.F. appointment was terminated in July 1918. From November he served for thirteen months as commandant of the 6th Military District (Tasmania).

In April 1921 Wanliss was appointed chief judge of the Mandated Territory of New Guinea where he served with several old comrades from the 5th Battalion until August 1937. He was considered a humane judge who showed concern for the welfare of New Guineans. Retiring to Brighton, Melbourne, Wanliss died there on 25 September 1943 and was buried in Eltham cemetery. He was remembered as a warm-hearted and generous man. On 22 May 1923 at Christ Church, South Yarra, he had married with Anglican rites Evelyn Muriel Bryant. She survived him, as did the only son of his first marriage, John Guthrie, who had served with him in the A.I.F.

Wanliss's brothers also earned distinction. The eldest was John Newton Wellesley [q.v. H. B. Wanliss]. Another, CECIL (1866-1933), was born at Ballarat on 19 October 1866, graduated from the Royal Military College, Sandhurst, England, in 1886, and joined the South Lancashire Regiment as a lieutenant. By August 1914 he was lieut-colonel commanding the regiment's 2nd Battalion at the battle of Mons. There he became the first Australian officer in World War I to lead a battalion into battle, the first to be wounded and the commander of the first battalion to mount a bayonet charge against the Germans. Following the retreat from Mons, he was one of several commanders who were suspended. Later exonerated, he served out the war commanding training battalions in England and was appointed O.B.E. in 1919. After post-war service in Germany, he retired in September 1920. From 1925 he lived in Switzerland; he died suddenly at Kensington of coronary vascular disease on 3 October 1933 while visiting London.

A third brother, Ewen (1873-1966), was a good district cricketer and served as a private and lieutenant with the 4th Imperial Bushmen in the South African War. In 1903-10 and 1922-58 he was an associate to judges in the Supreme Court of Victoria, in 1910-20 a grazier, and in 1920-22 private secretary to Irvine, then lieut-governor of Victoria. A fourth brother Neville (1876-1962) was in turn a Queensland jackeroo and a clerk in New Zealand. In January 1915, aged 38, he enlisted as a private in the 21st Battalion, A.I.F. He served at Gallipoli, but was discharged in August 1917. He became a clerk in Melbourne.

A. W. Keown, *Forward with the Fifth* (Melb, 1921); C. E. W. Bean, *The story of Anzac*, 1, 2 (Syd, 1921, 1924); Hist Cttee of the Women's Centenary Council (comp), *Records of the pioneer women of Victoria 1835-1860* (Melb, 1937); W. G. Mein, *History of Ballarat College, 1864-1964* (Ballarat, Vic, nd, 1964?); *Reveille* (Syd), Oct 1933; information from Mrs B. Morrison and Mr T. Wanliss, Melb.

BILL GAMMAGE

WANLISS, HAROLD BOYD (1891-1917), soldier and orchardist, was born on 11 December 1891 at Ballarat, Victoria, elder child of JOHN NEWTON WELLESLEY WANLISS (1861-1950), solicitor, and his wife Margaret, née Boyd. Newton, brother of David Sydney Wanliss [q.v.], was educated at Ballarat College and Trinity College, Cambridge (B.A., LL.B., 1884; M.A., 1887). He became a solicitor at Ballarat and was active in the Federation campaign. Harold was also educated at Ballarat College (dux 1908) and travelled with his father in Europe before attending Hawkesbury Agricultural College, New South Wales, for one year (dux 1912). In 1913 he took up 295 acres (119.4 ha) near Lorne, Victoria, to plant an orchard, and nearby found the falls on the Erskine River which were later named after him.

Serious, popular, dark haired and well built, a non-drinker and non-smoker, Harold Wanliss lived plainly, rose early and worked hard. He had 'special powers of application' and fine instincts for the future of Australia and the civilizing mission of Empire. In August 1914 he broke his leg in a riding accident which prevented him from joining the Australian Imperial Force, but typically he spent his convalescence studying the history and theory of war. After enlisting on 28 April 1915, he was selected for officer training at Broadmeadows. Promoted second lieutenant in July 1915, he embarked with the second reinforcements of the 29th Battalion on 29 December.

In March 1916 Wanliss was posted to the 14th Battalion. He was chosen to lead its first raid in France against the German trenches in the Bois Grenier sector on the night of 2-3 July. Although the raid was personally planned by Brigadier General (Sir) John Monash [q.v.10], it was a disaster. The raiders found the German wire uncut, and were caught by German machine-gun and artillery fire. Almost all the eighty-nine raiders—picked men, 'the flower of the A.I.F.'—were hit, and they failed to take a prisoner. Wanliss showed exceptional courage and leadership. He led his party through the uncut wire and, although wounded three times, cleared a section of the German front trench; he then covered the withdrawal of his men and, under heavy fire, continued to direct them until he collapsed from loss of blood. He won the Distinguished Service Order, the first A.I.F. subaltern so decorated in World War I.

Recovering from his wounds, Wanliss rejoined his battalion on 27 September. He became battalion adjutant in January 1917 and a captain on 6 March, and in these months helped to make an already famous battalion one of the most efficient in the A.I.F. His work was marked by attention to detail and untiring concern for his men, notably during the 1st battle of Bullecourt in April. He began a range of recreational activities for troops out of the line, including a series of lectures and debates on post-war Australia and the Empire. In mid-1917 Wanliss requested transfer to a fighting company and was made commanding officer of 'A' Company on 13 August. On 26 September he led it into the battle of Polygon Wood. Just as he reached his battalion's objective a German machine-gunner shot him through the heart, throat and side. He died instantly, and was buried where he fell.

In addition to his D.S.O., Wanliss had been mentioned in dispatches and twice recommended for a decoration, and his comrades mourned his death. 'Many brave men—many good men have I met . . . but he was the king', his colonel wrote. A brother officer thought him 'the best man and the best soldier and the truest gentleman in our Brigade', while one of his men called him 'the finest Officer ever I met'. Australia's loss was at least as grievous. C. E. W. Bean [q.v.7] reported the opinion of Monash and others that Wanliss was 'possibly destined, if he lived, to lead Australia'. Wanliss had spent his A.I.F. leaves studying new industries which might benefit post-war Australia, and searching for various kinds of work for disabled ex-servicemen. His death demonstrates that Australia's World War I losses cannot be measured simply by numbers.

Harold's sister MARION BOYD WANLISS (1896-1984), born on 28 December 1896, attended the University of Melbourne (M.B., B.S., 1920; M.D., 1929); after research into cancer as a postgraduate in Vienna, she practised as a physician at Camberwell, Melbourne, and later in Collins Street. She became an honorary physician at the Queen Victoria Memorial Hospital. A member (1928) of the Royal College of Physicians, London, and a fellow (1954) of the Royal Australian College of Physicians, she was also a prominent conservationist. She died on 28 June 1984; in accordance with her will, her body was delivered to the university's medical school.

After World War I Newton Wanliss wrote the story of his son's battalion, *The history of the Fourteenth Battalion, A.I.F.* (1929). One of the best 1st A.I.F. unit histories, it reveals a competent researcher, a good writer, and a proud and grieving father. On 12 November 1943 he concluded his will: 'I desire to place on record the pride that I have always felt in the achievements and characters of my two children . . . and . . . my gratitude for the companionship and devotion they have both invariably extended towards me'. His son had been dead for 26 years.

N. Wanliss, *The history of the Fourteenth Battalion, A.I.F.* (Melb, 1929); C. E. W. Bean, *The A.I.F. in France, 1916-17* (Syd, 1929, 1933); Hist Cttee of the Women's Centenary Council (comp), *Records of the pioneer women of Victoria, 1835-1860* (Melb, 1937); W. G. Mein, *History of Ballarat College, 1864-1964* (Ballarat, nd, 1964?); *Reveille* (Syd), May 1932; *MJA*, 29 Sept 1984; Red Cross files (AWM); information from Mrs B. Morrison and Mr T. Wanliss, Melb.   BILL GAMMAGE

WANT, JOHN HENRY (1846-1905), barrister and politician, was born on 4 May 1846 at Glebe, Sydney, fourth son of nine children of Randolph John Want [q.v.6], solicitor, and his wife Hariette, née Lister. Educated at Rev. W. H. Savigny's Collegiate School, Cooks River, and Sydney Grammar School, Jack reputedly spent some time at Caen, France. Entering Randolph's office, he became dissatisfied with the monotony of legal practice and worked on the land in Queensland and at a mine in which his father had an interest at Lithgow, New South Wales. Attracted back to the law, Want read in the chambers of (Sir) Frederick Darley [q.v.4] and was admitted to the Bar on 13 November 1869. At St John's Anglican Church, Darlinghurst, on 20 December 1870 he married Mary Selina Augusta Prince; they were divorced in 1884.

Without professing any profound interest in legal doctrine, Want was suited by temperament to the theatre of the courtroom and established a pre-eminent reputation as an advocate who was to command an extensive practice, particularly in criminal and *nisi prius* cases. His skill with a jury was widely acknowledged. Over six feet (182.9 cm) tall, with a rugged jaw, flashing eyes and 'fierce moustachios', he addressed the jury in 'a voice full and sonorous', with a homely and familiar style marked by the use of proverbs and colloquialisms. 'Bluff and unconventional', he was never more dangerous than when 'toying with his watch-chain'. He emerged as an authority on shipping matters: 'nobody knew more about the rules of navigation, or the harbour regulations'. Frequently appearing as a junior with W. B. Dalley [q.v.4] in 'heavy cases', Want was appointed a Queen's Counsel in 1887, but declined elevation to judicial office. He was, in his own words, much attracted by 'the active life and excitement of my profession'.

Elected to the Legislative Assembly in 1885 for Gundagai, Want served as attorney-general from October to December 1885 and from February 1886 to January 1887 in the ministries of (Sir) George Dibbs and Sir Patrick Jennings [qq.v.4]. While in office he prosecuted F. A. Wright [q.v.6] and others in 1886 for conspiring to defraud the commissioner of railways; he also persuaded Darley to accept the chief justiceship. A staunch free trader, Want was unable to continue supporting the protectionists, Dibbs and Jennings, but was unwilling to join Sir Henry Parkes [q.v.5]. When the latter ignored his criticism of the appointment of W. M. Fehon [q.v.8] as chief commissioner of railways, Want carried a motion for adjournment against the ministry on 9 January 1889 and precipitated Parkes's surprise resignation. Being about to visit Japan, Want declined the governor's commission to form his own ministry. He represented Paddington in 1889-91 before temporarily retiring from politics. As in his legal career, Want was not driven to pursue high office and never enjoyed certain backing in parliament. In 1894 he was nominated to the Legislative Council and, save for ten weeks in 1898, was (Sir) George Reid's [q.v.11] attorney-general from 18 December 1894 until resigning in April 1899.

Of a singularly independent character, Want was deeply committed to the colony he served. Aspiring to be 'the arch destroying angel of Federation', that 'hydra-headed monster', he was an intransigent—if not an extravagant—opponent of any system of federal union for the Australian colonies. 'Faderation', as he dubbed it, could only result for his own colony in 'the surrender of our independence and liberty', beneficial though union might be for the others. His purpose was 'to protect New South Wales, not to sell it into bondage'. Following Reid's famous 'Yes-No' speech on the Federation enabling bill in March 1898, Want resigned from office on 4 April the better to oppose Federation, only to rejoin the ministry on 18 June after the first referendum. Reid's failure in the interim to fill the vacancy excited the Federationists' suspicion.

On 25 November 1898 at St Stephen's Anglican Church, Kurrajong, Want had married Nina Ventry, née Everest, a 42-year-old widow with two daughters. He defended Dean O'Haran in Arthur Coningham's [qq.v.11,8] divorce case in 1900-01 and later defended the solicitor T. M. Slattery [q.v.11]. In 1904-05 Want opposed Sir Josiah Symon's [q.v.] attempt to move the High Court of Australia's principal seat to Melbourne.

Vigorous and robust, Want threw 'the same energy into his amusements as into his serious avocations'. Like his father, he was a member of Royal Sydney Yacht Squadron and enjoyed sailing down to Hobart or fishing on Port Hacking, dressed like 'a pirate bold'. He was a trustee of (Royal) National Park and a member of the Board of Fisheries, in which capacity he did much to develop and to protect the fisheries of the colonies, as well as advocating the introduction of trout to inland waters. A generous foe and a loyal friend, he was a member of the Union Club, a patron of the turf, a motorist and an inveterate traveller.

Survived by his wife, Jack Want died from complications of aortic valve disease on 22 November 1905 at Darlinghurst; he was buried in Waverley cemetery, his coffin being borne by six K.C.s—(Sir) Alexander Gordon [q.v.9 Margaret Gordon], (Sir) William Cullen, C. E. Pilcher, R. M. Sly, A. B. Smith, [qq.v.8,11] and Reid.

B. R. Wise, *The making of the Australian Commonwealth, 1889-1900* (Lond, 1913); W. Blacket, *May it please Your Honour* (Syd, 1927); A. B. Piddington, *Worshipful masters* (Syd, 1929); P. Loveday and A. W. Martin, *Parliament factions and parties* (Melb, 1966); J. M. Bennett (ed), *A history of the Bar of New South Wales* (Syd, 1969); *PD* (LC NSW), 1897, pp 2100, 2111, 2117; *British A'sian*, 16 Feb 1899; *Express* (Syd), 17 Dec 1885; *Arrow* (Syd), 21 Nov 1905; *SMH*, 23 Nov 1905; *Truth* (Syd), 26 Nov 1905; *T&CJ*, 29 Nov 1905; Parkes correspondence (ML).   PAUL FINN

WARD, ELIZABETH JANE (1842-1908), milliner and philanthropist, was born on 27 March 1842 in Sydney, daughter of William Garland, farrier, and his wife Sarah, née Jenks, both Parramatta born. Baptized with Anglican rites, she was educated at Mrs Chandler's ladies' seminary in Liverpool Street. Having worked as a milliner from the age of 15, she claimed to have become head milliner at Farmer [q.v.4] & Co.'s store. On 18 July 1863 she married with Wesleyan forms Charles Ward, a house-painter from Shrewsbury, England; they were to have seven sons. She managed millinery businesses in King Street and later Oxford Street.

An active, voluntary parishworker for the Church of England, Mrs Ward was a leading member of a women's network of evangelical activists after she moved to Surry Hills in 1883. As a founder and secretary of the Sydney Women's Prayer Union, she advocated sabbatarianism and public prayers. She was an executive-member of the Surry Hills branches of the Exhibition of Women's Industries and Centenary Fair (1888) and of the Girls' Friendly Society. With members of the Young Women's Christian Association of Sydney, she conducted gospel services at the Church Rescue Home for the Intemperate and Fallen [Women].

She worked for the Sydney Ladies' United Evangelistic Association and for the committees of G. E. Ardill's [q.v.7] Jubilee Home and Registry Office for Young Women, the Queen's Jubilee Fund and the third Australasian Conference on Charity (1891-92); she also joined the National Council of Women of New South Wales. A member of the Women's Federal League, she wrote letters to the newspapers advocating Federation.

Gentle but resolute, Elizabeth was a 'most indefatigable worker'. Having helped to found the ladies' committee of the Sydney City Mission, she organized midnight suppers for prostitutes and distributed cards inviting them to call on her when 'in need of advice or sympathy'. As superintendent of the mission's biblewoman for the Rocks district, she publicized the 'terrible reality' of sweating and the poor's need for material as well as spiritual succour. After 1901 she assisted the elderly to apply for old-age pensions.

Ward was a member of the Woman's Christian Temperance Union of New South Wales from 1884; she was later a vice-president and life member. From 1889 she campaigned for, and wrote pamphlets on, female suffrage as a Christian duty and a means to temperance. Joining the short-lived Women's Suffrage League of New South Wales in 1890, she became colonial superintendent of the W.C.T.U.'s franchise department in 1892; in addition, she took charge of the evangelistic and press departments.

Her autobiography, *Out of weakness made strong* (1903), revealed her conviction of divine direction. She believed that women had 'a distinct and separate point of view', with 'their own homes to protect, and special wrongs to right'. Her work was motivated by a belief in the spiritual sisterhood of all women.

Survived by four sons, Elizabeth Ward died of heart disease on 29 May 1908 at Watsons Bay and was buried in the Anglican section of Waverley cemetery.

Mrs J. Williams and Mrs A. Holliday (eds), *Golden records* (Syd, 1926); Syd City Mission, *Annual Reports*, 1886-95; *Syd City Mission Herald*, 15 Jan 1903, 1 July 1908; J. Godden, Philanthropy and the woman's sphere, Sydney, 1870-c1900 (Ph.D. thesis, Macquarie Univ, 1983); Syd City Mission, Minutes, 1894-96 (ML).

JUDITH GODDEN

WARD, FREDERICK FURNER (1872-1954), Labor Party secretary, was born on 11 May 1872 at Bowden, Adelaide, son of English-born Frederick Rousseau Ward, miller, and his wife Eliza, née Shiels. Educated at Port Adelaide Public School, at 14 he started work as a clerk with Malcolm Reid & Co., timber and iron merchants; he became an accountant, a traveller and eventually manager of the firm; later he was chief metropolitan traveller for Lion Timber Mills.

On 16 June 1897 at the Port Adelaide Presbyterian Church he married Jessie McInnes Fraser (d. 1954).

For over twenty years Ward chaired the 'Labor Ring' in the Botanic Park on Sunday afternoons. Having joined the Port Adelaide Democratic Club, he became a foundation member of the United Labor Party; he was its full-time secretary in 1922-44 and a board member of the *Workers' Weekly Herald*. He was president of the Saw Mill and Timber Workers' Union, a member of the Australian Workers' and of the Federated Clerks' unions, president and secretary of the Agricultural Implement and Machinery and Ironworkers' Association, and a delegate to the Port Adelaide and the United trades and labour councils in South Australia. He was also president of the State branches of the Movement Against War and Fascism, the Workers' Educational Association and the Dickens [q.v.4] Fellowship. Being prominent in the Socialist League of South Australia did not preclude him from acting as superintendent of Lefèvre's Peninsula Presbyterian Sunday School. Ward was a tall, laconic, but quite obstinate and dogmatic man. At his desk he sat bolt upright; on walks he strode. Possessing impeccable manners, he dressed rather eccentrically, with wing collars, tussore shirts, and in summer a pith helmet; he cultivated a drooping moustache and smoked cigars. He played Australian Rules football when young and still played cricket at 73; he was a delegate to the South Australian Cricket Association and the South Australian Football League.

Ward was never adequately rewarded by the Labor Party. Deriving rent from Adelaide properties, he enjoyed financial security; for years, especially during the 1930s, he paid his own and sometimes his assistant secretary's salaries. He thrice failed to enter State parliament (1912, 1918, 1921) and twice unsuccessfully contested the Senate (1931 and 1937). Elected in 1946, he became the oldest person to enter that House (1 July 1947). There he stayed, quietly, until defeated in 1951 when he became a partner in the City Land Agency, Adelaide. The safe Senate seat had been compensation for having, to his dismay, lost the party secretaryship in 1944; as a meticulous organizer, he had taken no leave in seventeen years. Ward was an anti-conscriptionist in World War I and a vehement anti-communist in the 1920s; he then became more radical and alienated some right-wingers; by 1947 the local Communist Party extolled 'old Fred', the 'battler' and 'Labor stalwart'; in 1948 he was chairman of the South Australian branch of the Australian-Russian Society.

Survived by his son and daughter, Ward died on 31 December 1954 at Largs Bay and was buried in Cheltenham cemetery. Port Adelaide's streets were lined with mourners.

Communist Party of Aust, *Catholic Action at work* (Syd, 1946); R. Cooksey (ed), 'The great Depression in Australia', *Labour Hist*, 1970, no 17; J. Moss, *Sound of trumpets* (Adel, 1985); *Politics* (Syd), 6, no 1, May 1971, p 77; *Labour Hist*, Nov 1976, no 31; *Daily Herald*, 9 Feb 1923; *Advertiser* (Adel), 14 Sept 1944, 30 Sept 1946, 1, 5 Jan 1955, 10 June 1983; *Chronicle* (Adel), 14 Sept 1944; *Workers' Weekly Herald*, 26 Nov 1937, 15, 22, 29 Sept, 20 Oct 1944; *Tribune* (Adel), 2 Sept 1944, 11 July 1947; *Sunday Mail* (Adel), 1 Jan 1955; *News* (Adel), 3 Jan 1955; J. Playford, History of the left-wing of the South Australian labour movement, 1908-36 (B.A. Hons thesis, Univ Adel, 1958); R. Pettman, Factionalism in the Australian Labor Party: a South Australian case-study, 1930-1933 (B.A. Hons thesis, Univ Adel, 1967); D. J. Hopgood, A psephological examination of the South Australian Labor Party from World War One to the Depression (Ph.D. thesis, Flinders Univ, 1974); personal information. MALCOLM SAUNDERS

WARD, FREDERICK WILLIAM (1847-1934), journalist, was born on 5 April 1847 at Taranaki, New Zealand, fourth son of Rev. Robert Ward, Primitive Methodist missionary, and his wife Emily, née Brundle. Frederick attended Wesley College and Seminary, Auckland, and saw active service as a scout when the Maori Wars engulfed Taranaki in 1863-64.

Accepted for the Primitive Methodist ministry in 1866, Ward was first sent to Brisbane and then to Newcastle in New South Wales. As an early advocate of Methodist union, he resigned in 1869 to join the Wesleyan Church, serving at Mudgee (1869), St Leonards, Sydney (1870-71), Bathurst (1872-74) and Ashfield (1875). Having been ordained in 1873, on 22 March he married 19-year-old Amy Ada Cooke at St Leonards.

Leaving the ministry in 1876 to devote himself to journalism, Ward next year became editor of the Wesleyan *Weekly Advocate*. The position provided an entrée into the Fairfax [qq.v.4,8] family's organization: in 1879-84 Ward edited their weekly, the *Sydney Mail*, and also the evening paper, the *Echo* (1883-84). Seriously committed to country interests and distribution, the *Mail* competed with J. F. Archibald's [q.v.3] *Bulletin* in the 1880s. As editor, Ward encouraged new literature, serializing 'Rolf Boldrewood's' [q.v.3 T. A. Browne] *Robbery under arms* in 1882-83 in spite of opposition on moral grounds from (Sir) James R. Fairfax.

Persuaded by Watkin Wynne [q.v.], Ward left the Fairfax newspapers in 1884, taking with him L. J. Brient [q.v.7], and headed a powerful editorial team which was recruited that year to revitalize the ailing *Daily Telegraph*. Under his leadership, by 1888 that newspaper had doubled the circulation of the Fairfax-owned *Sydney Morning Herald.* In May 1890 Ward resigned after a dramatic confrontation with the board over his editorial independence. He went to London and immersed himself in the newspaper world, working as cable correspondent for the *Age,* but the continuous night-work and a severe winter affected his health and he came home after twelve months.

On behalf of the New South Wales secretary for public works, (Sir) William Lyne [q.v.10], Ward undertook a water-management survey of the Darling River. He later accompanied the eccentric shipping entrepreneur James Huddart [q.v.4] to Canada to negotiate that country's participation in the 'All-Red' cable route linking the Empire; accompanied by several Canadians, he returned to Brisbane in March 1893 to campaign for a Pacific cable.

Described by his lifelong friend C. B. Fletcher [q.v.8] as a big man with striking red hair and a voluminous beard, as outspoken, progressive and of unflagging energy, Ward attracted attention and was quickly appointed editor of the *Brisbane Courier.* He resigned in 1898 to become principal leader-writer for the Melbourne *Argus.* In 1903 he was reinstated as editor of the Sydney *Daily Telegraph* at the invitation ('it was almost an apology') of the directors. He was awarded an honorary doctorate by the University of Glasgow in 1909 when he attended the first Imperial Press Conference in London.

Although Ward retired from the *Daily Telegraph* in 1914, after spending two years in England he edited the Brisbane *Telegraph* until December 1920. His last years were spent at his home at Kirribilli, Sydney. Predeceased by his wife, and survived by two sons and two daughters, he died there on 1 July 1934 and was buried with Presbyterian forms in South Head cemetery.

Dictionary of NZ biog, 2 (Wellington, 1940); C. B. Fletcher, *The great wheel* (Syd, 1940); R. B. Walker, *The newspaper press in New South Wales, 1803-1920* (Syd, 1976); *Church Heritage,* 4, no 2, Sept 1985, p 122; *ISN,* 15 Feb 1887; *SMH,* 16 Dec 1916, 3 July 1934; Deakin papers (NL); information from Rev E. G. Clancy, Uniting Church in Aust Church Records and Hist Soc, Nth Parramatta, Syd.

KATHY MOIGNARD

WARD, HUGH JOSEPH (1871-1941), actor and theatrical entrepreneur, was born on 24 June 1871 at Preston Retreat, Philadelphia, Pennsylvania, United States of America, son of Hugh Ward, an American-born labourer, and his English wife Mary, née O'Connor. Educated in Philadelphia, at 16 Hugh joined a minstrel troupe and learned his trade with stock companies at Salt Lake City, Denver, San Francisco, Philadelphia and Pittsburgh. It was a hard school: after twelve years he had a repertoire of over 300 parts and had endlessly 'talked the philosophy of acting' with fellow thespians. On 30 June 1897 he married Mary Grace Miller in St Paul's Cathedral, Pittsburgh.

Accompanied by his wife, Ward visited Australia with Charles H. Hoyt's comedy company, arriving in Sydney on 10 June 1899. He first appeared as the decrepit dude in *A stranger in New York*; on tour he also played Ben Guy in *A trip to Chinatown.* Engaged as a comedian by J. C. Williamson [q.v.6] for the Christmas pantomime, *Little Red Riding Hood,* Ward then joined Williamson's Royal Comic Opera Company, playing in most of the Gilbert and Sullivan operas and performing his favourite role, Cyrus Gilfillan, in *Florodora* (1900-01). He was 'one of the greatest masters of make-up known to the Australian stage'.

In July 1903 Ward returned to the United States. At Christmas he was a sensation with his scarecrow dance in the pantomime, *Humpty Dumpty,* at Drury Lane, London. Described by one critic as 'all on hinges', Ward was a 'slim and dazzling dancer', 'a master of eccentric attitudes'. After a dancing turn at the Empire with Adeline Genée, in December 1904 he again appeared at Drury Lane, this time as a baboon, illustrating the Darwinian theory with grotesque humour. Following a five month season in Paris, he played for a year in New York under Marc Klaw and Claude Erlanger.

Having organized an English company with George Willoughby, Ward opened in Sydney in May 1906 in *The man from Mexico* and toured Australasia for eighteen months. Returning to London in 1908, he formed his own comedy company and played in India, Burma, China and the Straits Settlements. He brought the company to Australia and settled his wife and children in Sydney. Grace Miller Ward became well known on the concert platform and as a teacher of singing; she 'discovered' Gladys Moncrieff [q.v.10]. In 1909-10 *A bachelor's honeymoon* and *The fencing master* proved popular throughout Australasia; in New Zealand, Ward raised £27 000 for hospitals in Wellington and at Dunedin. He appeared for the last time on the stage in *The girl from Rector's* in Brisbane in April 1911 and joined J. C. Williamson Ltd as managing director in Sydney in May.

Described by Claude Mackay as 'well-groomed, middle-sized, with sparkling blue eyes and boyish manner', Ward visited Europe and North America on behalf of the government and from 1913 sat on the advisory committee that chose Henri Verbrugghen [q.v.] as foundation director of the

New South Wales State Conservatorium of Music. After Williamson's death in 1913, Ward became managing director of 'the Firm', but sometimes differed with (Sir) George Tallis [q.v.]. Ward frequently went abroad in search of plays and talent, competing with the Taits [qq.v.].

Already known for his success in raising money for hospitals in Sydney, to Governor Sir Gerald Strickland [q.v.] Ward was 'the man who starts all the big things'. During World War I he and his wife worked for innumerable patriotic causes; Grace sang at concerts and entertained the troops. Asked by the government to organize Belgian Day, Hugh raised £142 000. He was the moving spirit in promoting 'Australia Day', collected for the Australian Red Cross Society and personally induced subscriptions of over £5 million to the Commonwealth war loans. With the peace, Ward helped to organize victory celebrations and the visits of Viscount Jellicoe, General Sir William Birdwood [q.v.7] and the prince of Wales. Appointed chevalier of the Belgian Order of Leopold II in 1919, Ward was twice unsuccessfully recommended for a knighthood. He was naturalized in 1922.

Resigning as managing director of J.C.W. in 1922, he set up Hugh J. Ward Theatres Pty Ltd in partnership with the Fullers [qq.v.8]. He was a member of the Green Room Club, London, the White Rats Actors' Union of America and the famous New York club, The Lambs. A founder of the Millions Club (1913), Ward was a director of Sydney Hospital (1918-41). Retiring in 1926, he became a devotee of the cinema; a member of the executive committee for the sesquicentenary celebrations, he tried to arrange the visit of an Empire cricket team in 1938. A 'white-haired, merry-faced veteran', Hughie was a great raconteur who kept friends amused for hours.

Survived by his wife and two sons, Ward died of a coronary occlusion on 21 April 1941 at his Potts Point home and was cremated with Presbyterian forms. His estate was sworn for probate at £33 805.

British A'sian, 20 Apr 1911, 23 Apr 1914; *Theatre Mag* (Melb, Syd), 1 Aug 1914, p 12, 1 Jan 1918, p 17, 1 Oct 1919, p 17, 2 Aug 1920, p 3; *SMH*, 12 June 1899, 22 Feb 1917, 26 Mar, 5 Apr 1918, 6 Sept, 27 Nov 1919, 9 Mar 1922, 30 Aug 1923, 1 Oct 1926, 7 Feb 1931, 22 May, 23 Nov 1936, 22, 26 Apr 1941, 28 Dec 1952; *Argus*, 26 Feb, 16 Dec 1900; *Australasian*, 4 July, 19 Dec 1903, 13 Feb 1904, 9, 23 June, 28 July 1906, 18 Sept 1915; *Bulletin*, 5 July 1906, 22 July, 12 Aug 1909, 24 Feb 1910, 18 May 1911; *Daily Telegraph* (Syd), 27 May 1911, 25 Aug 1915; *Punch* (Melb), 4 July 1912, 3 June 1915, 16 Mar 1922; *Table Talk*, 22 Apr 1926; CO 440/15 f477, 447/118 f18 (PRO microfilm, NL); Naturalization file, A1/28/8913 (AA).   MARTHA RUTLEDGE

WARD, JOHN FREDERICK (1883-1954), schoolmaster, was born on 20 July 1883 at Newton, Lancashire, England, son of John Ward, master butcher, and his wife Mary Ann, née Russel. The family migrated to Adelaide in 1886 and lived at Norwood. Educated at the local primary school, young John won a scholarship to Prince Alfred College; its Methodism accorded with family adherence. He topped the colony's senior public examinations in 1889, with credits in his eight subjects and first place in four. Further scholarships helped him to graduate from the University of Adelaide (B.A., 1903) with first-class honours in classics, at a higher level than any previous student. His M.A. (1908) in classics received similar honours.

He taught at Prince Alfred College in 1904-05 and 1910-19; in the interval he was second master at Rockhampton Grammar School, Queensland. On 21 December 1912 at the Congregational Church, Subiaco, Perth, Ward married Florence Winifred Braddock who later became president of the Adelaide Young Women's Christian Association. Poor eyesight frustrated his attempts to enlist in the Australian Imperial Force. In 1920 he was appointed headmaster of Thornburgh College, Charters Towers, Queensland, and in 1923 foundation headmaster of Wesley College, Perth. Respected for his learning, he believed in a classical base for education and aimed to produce fine Christian gentlemen. In 1930 he achieved his ambition of becoming headmaster of Prince Alfred College, and followed his predecessors John Hartley and Frederic Chapple [qq.v.4,7] in emphasizing mathematics and science; like them, he enjoyed almost unlimited authority and dominated the school. Ward also shared a belief in the value of hard work, demonstrating it especially through detailed supervision of school affairs in the Depression and in World War II when the school's resources were strained. Prince Alfred College lacked the endowment and prestige of its Adelaide rival, the Anglican Collegiate School of St Peter, a lack which he felt keenly.

Although he introduced drawing and reintroduced German in 1939, Ward hardly changed the courses. Physically, the school scarcely altered. Few left it without firm impressions of their headmaster: a tall, bespectacled, white-haired figure whose thunderous temper too often obscured his sensitive nature; a fine scholar, of religious but not bigoted conviction; a leader respected by many students and by his staff. One teacher, Hal Porter, described him as a 'straight-backed Methodist Olympian'. A member of the South Australian government's education inquiry committee in 1942, Ward also belonged to the councils of the University of Adelaide and of Lincoln College. He was a founder and chairman (1943-46) of the Australian Headmasters' Conference, and a long and staunch member of the Australian Student Christian Movement. Appointed O.B.E. in 1948, he retired that year and wrote *Prince Alfred College* (1951). On the last day of his life he quoted the precept by which he had always been guided: 'Faith is putting into your life the substance of what you believe'. He died on 18 August 1954 in North Adelaide and was buried in Centennial Park cemetery; he was survived by his wife, two daughters and a son, the historian Russel Ward.

H. Porter, *The paper chase* (Syd, 1966); R. M. Gibbs, *A history of Prince Alfred College* (Adel, 1984); R. Ward, *A radical life* (Melb, 1988); *Aust Intercollegian*, Oct 1954; *Prince Alfred College Chronicle*, Oct 1954; *Advertiser* (Adel), 1 Aug 1929, 19 Aug 1954; *Aust Christian Cwlth*, 16 Aug 1929; family and private information.   R. M. GIBBS

WARDLAW, ALAN LINDSAY (1887-1938), pastoralist, soldier and parliamentarian, was born on 23 July 1887 at Rock House, Avoca, Tasmania, son of James Bennett Wardlaw, farmer, and his wife Dora Dove, née Miller. After attending state schools, he helped his mother to run a butchery at Scottsdale and later purchased an interest in a small sheep-station. At 24 he assumed management of Mineral Banks, a mixed farming property near Ringarooma, and was later regarded as one of the State's best judges of stock and a very able horseman. He served with the militia from 1907.

On 20 May 1916 Wardlaw transferred to the Australian Imperial Force as a second lieutenant and joined the 12th Battalion in France in March 1917. He was promoted lieutenant in April. Wounded during the battle of Bullecourt in May, he earned a special mention in Sir William Birdwood's [q.v.7] corps orders. In August 1918, while Wardlaw was fighting in the front line near Amiens, one of his legs was shattered by shell-fire. It was a crushing blow to the young soldier and he considered himself lucky to live through it. When he returned to Australia in May 1919 his disability made farm life impossible; even though he had purchased Mineral Banks in partnership with H. G. Salier, he decided to enter public life.

He brought to politics commitment and zest. After serving on the local council, in May 1920 Wardlaw was elected to the Legislative Council as Nationalist member for South Esk, and represented that electorate until December 1938. He was chairman of committees in 1926-28 and held the honorary portfolio of minister for agriculture in 1932-34. He was always active in matters affecting the man on the land; probably no other Tasmanian in these years accepted more honorary offices in working for his industry or carried them out more effectively.

Wardlaw's services in government and wide knowledge of agriculture were recognized by successive Tasmanian premiers: both (Sir) John McPhee and Sir Walter Lee [qq.v.10] appointed him minister without portfolio and leader of the House—in McPhee's cabinet from June 1928 to March 1934 and in Lee's ministry in 1934. His genial manner endeared him to them as it did to most other contemporary Tasmanian politicians. Wardlaw was a man of the highest principles and an able speaker. Outside parliament his interest in public affairs was intense. He was appointed C.M.G. in 1935.

On 3 November 1925, at Launceston, he had married Olive Hart with Methodist forms. Survived by his wife and two daughters, Wardlaw died of hypertensive cerebrovascular disease on 24 December 1938 in St Margaret's Hospital, Launceston, and was buried in Carr Villa cemetery.

Examiner (Launc) and *Mercury*, 27 Dec 1938; personal information.   R. A. FERRALL

WARK, BLAIR ANDERSON (1894-1941), army officer and quantity surveyor, was born on 27 July 1894 at Bathurst, New South Wales, fourth child of Alexander Wark, a gas engineer from Scotland, and his native-born wife Blanche Adelaide Maria, née Forde. Educated at Fairleigh Grammar, Bathurst, St Leonards Superior Public School (North Sydney High) and Sydney Technical College, Blair worked as a quantity surveyor while pursuing his military interests. A senior cadet in 1911-12, he enlisted in the 18th (North Sydney) Infantry, Australian Military Forces, and was provisionally commissioned in 1913.

On 5 August 1915 Wark was appointed to the Australian Imperial Force and embarked for Egypt with the 30th Battalion in November. A captain from 20 February 1916 and a company commander, he reached the Western Front in June. He was wounded in the battle of Fromelles. On his return to duty in November, he joined the 32nd Battalion. His conduct at Fromelles and in action at Sunray Trench in March 1917 led to his recommendation for the Distinguished Service Order. Though no award was made, he was promoted major on 27 April. In late September and early October, while in command of the front line east of Ypres, his vigorous patrolling and personal reconnaissance kept his sector secure and enabled him to repulse one counter-attack and to thwart another. He won the D.S.O. for this achievement and for his previous courage and devotion to duty. In May 1918 he was mentioned in dispatches.

Experienced and self-reliant, careless of his own safety, yet solicitous for his men, at the age of 24 Wark was given temporary command of the 32nd Battalion in operations against the Hindenburg line that began on 29 September. Often moving ahead of his troops in the face of heavy fire, he secured the help of a passing tank near Bellicourt and attached two hundred leaderless Americans to his command before rushing a battery of 77mm guns which were firing at his rear companies: he captured four guns and ten of their crews. With two non-commissioned officers, he surprised and captured fifty Germans near Magny-la-Fosse. On 1 October he 'dashed forward and silenced machine-guns which were causing heavy casualties'. For his bravery he was awarded the Victoria Cross. His brothers Alexander and Keith also served in the A.I.F.; Keith won the Distinguished Conduct Medal.

On 31 May 1919 at the parish church, Worthing, Sussex, Wark married Phyllis Marquiss Munro and returned to Australia where his A.I.F. appointment was terminated in September. He became a principal of Thompson & Wark, quantity surveyors, a director of several companies, a councillor of the National Roads and Motorists' Association, a committee-member of the Hawkesbury Race Club and a life governor of the Benevolent Society of New South Wales. Divorced in 1922, Wark married Catherine Mary Davis on 10 December 1927 at St Stephen's Presbyterian Church, Sydney.

In April 1940 he was appointed to the 1st Battalion, A.M.F., and assumed command on 26 July with the rank of temporary lieutcolonel. While bivouacked at Puckapunyal, Victoria, he died suddenly of coronary heart disease on 13 June 1941. Wark was cremated after a military funeral at which it was said that he 'liked the wind in his face and lived the life of three men'. His wife, their son and two daughters survived him.

L. Wigmore (ed), *They dared mightily* (Canb, 1963); B. Greaves (ed), *The story of Bathurst* (Syd, 1976); C. E. W. Bean, *The A.I.F in France*, 1918 (Syd, 1942); *Reveille* (Syd), 1 Dec 1933, 1 July 1941; War diary, 30th and 32nd Battalion, AIF (AWM); letters and family papers (held by Mr B. Wark, Wahroonga, Syd).   RICHARD GORRELL

WARNER, WILLIAM LLOYD (1898-1970), anthropologist and sociologist, was born on 25 October 1898 at Colton, California, United States of America, son of William Taylor Warner and his wife Belle, née Carter. After serving in the infantry as a private in World War I, he graduated in anthropology (A.B., 1925) from the University of California, Berkeley. Warner was fortunate in his close association with luminary anthropologists and proved eclectic in adapting their diverse methodologies. Taught by R. H. Lowie and A. L. Kroeber, he was also stimulated by B. K. Malinowski who visited Berkeley and recommended a Rockefeller Foundation fellowship for Warner at the University of Sydney's new anthropology department under A. R. Radcliffe-Brown [q.v.11]; on the latter's advice, the Australian National Research Council extended the fellowship for two years.

In 1927-29 Warner worked in north-east Arnhem Land, based at Milingimbi Methodist Mission. His major research included investigations into Aboriginal social structure, group and individual inter-relations, including economics, physical conflict and ceremonial life. In addition, he documented material culture, excavated middens and made the first serious assessment of the influence of Macassan trepangers on Aboriginal society. His anthropometric measurements of 307 Aborigines were later analysed by W. W. Howells. Warner became celebrated for his exposition of the system of kinship and marriage among the various clans of his so-called Murngin people. His findings stimulated the 'Murngin controversy', a voluminous dialogue to which distinguished anthropologists still contribute. He analysed his data in Sydney during 1929 and several original articles followed. Considering Warner to be 'exceptionally able' and his work 'as good as any piece of research' conducted in Australia, Radcliffe-Brown predicted that he 'will do brilliant scientific work'.

After leaving Australia in 1929, Warner taught anthropology, sociology and social ethics at Harvard University until 1935. *A black civilization: a social study of an Australian tribe* (New York, 1937, 1948, 1964) elaborated his field-work, often incorporating earlier publications verbatim. Outstanding for its scope and detail, its status is that of an anthropological classic. Associate professor (1935-41) and professor (1941-59) of sociology at the University of Chicago, and thereafter professor of social research at Michigan State University, Warner applied the anthropological techniques he had used for studying small-scale Aboriginal societies to contemporary industrial cities. Influenced by G. E. Mayo [q.v.10], he pioneered the study of American social classes. His extensive publications included the collaborative Yankee City series (five volumes) and *Democracy in Jonesville* (New York, 1949). Warner founded Social Research Inc., a motivational research firm, in 1946, editing with N. H. Norman *Industrial man: business men and business organizations* (New York,

1959); his professional image was possibly enhanced by his industry and neatly clipped moustache.

With Mildred Hall, whom he had married on 12 January 1932, he wrote *What you should know about social class* (Chicago, 1953). Warner died in Chicago on 23 May 1970 and was cremated; his wife, a son and two daughters survived him. He was esteemed by a colleague as 'the greatest of the empiricists'.

Papers of the Peabody Museum of American Archaeology and Ethnology, 16, 1937; *Oceania*, 41, 1970, p 77; *American J of Sociology*, 76, 1970-71; *New York Times*, 24 May 1970; *Washington Post*, 25 May 1970; Warner's collection of 102 Arnhem Land photographs (Aust Inst of Aboriginal Studies, Canb); Aust National Research Council papers (NL).   D. J. MULVANEY

WARNES, MARY JANE (1877-1959), Country Women's Association founder, was born on 18 July 1877 at Fullarton, Adelaide, youngest daughter of Thomas Fairbrother, a gardener from England, and his wife Jane Mears, née Clarke. Mary was educated at the Misses Newman's private school, Parkside. On 12 February 1900 at St Augustine's Church, Unley, she married Isaac James Warnes (1871-1944). They lived at Koomooloo, an isolated property in the arid north-east of the State. Only infrequently did they make the eighty-mile (129 km) round trip by horse and buggy to Burra, the nearest town. Mary later recalled going into shops to buy unnecessary trifles as an excuse to speak with other women. After her sister Deborah married Isaac's brother, and came to live only seven miles distant, the sisters bicycled along bush tracks once a week to meet half-way for the pleasure of company; but, within two years, Deborah's death in childbirth left Mary again 'marooned on an island of men'.

By the 1920s country women's associations were being formed in the eastern States and in 1926 the National Council of Women called an informal meeting in Adelaide which Mrs Warnes attended. She was by then living at Wahroonga, some twelve miles from Burra. On her return from Adelaide, she immediately invited women from the eleven local districts to form the Burra Women's Service Association. Founded in November 1926, it was the first of three hundred State branches of the Country Women's Association. President of the Burra branch, Mary was prominent in the establishment of the C.W.A.'s metropolitan branch in Adelaide and was State president (1929-41).

In 1929 she was a delegate to the Rural Women's Conference, London, held under the auspices of the International Council of Women, which moved towards creating the Associated Country Women of the World; by 1986 sixty-two nations belonged to the A.C.W.W. As the wife of 'one of the best-known pastoralists in the State', Mrs Warnes travelled extensively at home and abroad, and took an active interest in the family's sheep-holdings, of which she was a director. Cultured, tall and dignified, but gentle and kind, she gave and received great affection. In addition to making a special study of the conditions of country women and children, she was a councillor and president of the women's branch of the State Liberal Federation and of its Burra branch, president of the Leighton Women's Guild, a member of the National Council of Women of South Australia and of the League of Nations Union, and State country representative of the Victoria League. In 1936 she was appointed M.B.E.

Survived by three sons, Mary Warnes died on 19 June 1959 at Eastwood, Adelaide, and was buried in Burra cemetery. A memorial window is in the Burra Anglican church of St Mary the Virgin, and rooms in the Burra and the Adelaide C.W.A. are named in her honour. In 1986 she was allocated a plaque on the North Terrace pavement, Adelaide, which commemorates leading figures in South Australia.

National Council of Women of SA Inc, *Greater than their knowing* (Adel, 1986); SA Country Women's Assn, *So we grow* (Adel, 1954); *Queenslander*, 11 Oct 1928; *Observer* (Adel), 2 Feb 1929; Country Women's Assn Archives, Adel; St Mary's Church, Burra, SA, Archives; information from Mr R. Warnes, Nth Adel, and Mrs R. Jennison, Burra, SA.   NANCY ROBINSON WHITTLE

WARREN, HUBERT ERNEST DE MEY (1885-1934), missionary, was born on 2 March 1885 at Prahran, Victoria, son of William Robert de Mey Warren, agent, and his wife Selina Jane Cornish, née Horrell; both parents were of Cornish descent. After being educated at All Saints Grammar School, St Kilda, Warren served his apprenticeship to Robison Bros & Co., Melbourne, marine engineers, before becoming a ship's engineer. Converted at a George Grubb Mission, Warren trained for the Anglican ministry at Moore College, Sydney, being made deacon in 1910 and ordained priest in 1911. In 1913 he joined the Church Missionary Society's Aboriginal mission at Roper River in the Northern Territory and was appointed superintendent in October. On leave in Sydney, he married Ellie May Potter on 6 April 1915 at St Andrew's Cathedral.

Physically strong and over six feet (182.9 cm) tall, Bert Warren had a tough physique, an open nature and an infectious laugh. In 1916-21 he explored the east Arnhem Land coast and islands in a small launch called the *Evangel* to find sites for 'a chain of missions' on the west of the Gulf of Carpentaria. In recognition of this work he was made a fellow (1918) of the Royal Geographical Society of Victoria. Returning from furlough in 1919, he completed an historic 3000-mile (4828 km) journey from Sydney to the Roper River in a T-model Ford. In 1921 Warren started the C.M.S. mission at the Emerald River on Groote Eylandt to house and train children of mixed descent from camps and towns in eastern areas of the Northern Territory. Contact was also established with the local Aborigines. Despite appalling isolation and hardship, the mission developed: in 1925 Captain (Sir) Hubert Wilkins [q.v.] praised its work and in 1928 Commissioner J. W. Bleakley [q.v.7] commended it in his survey of Northern Territory missions. In 1929 the C.M.S. adopted a policy aimed at evangelizing the Aborigines. Relieved of his position and given a years leave, Warren served at the understaffed Roper River mission. To the Aborigines, he was 'long fella cobberlile'—a gecko.

Appointed rector of Cullenswood in Tasmania in 1932, Warren led a 'peace expedition' to Arnhem Land in 1933-34. In response to the killing of five Japanese trepangers, two white beachcombers and a policeman by Aborigines on the east Arnhem Land coast, police had planned a punitive expedition. The C.M.S. intervened and—with the approval of the Commonwealth government—Warren, Rev. A. J. Dyer and D. H. Fowler made contact with the Aborigines implicated in the incident and persuaded them to go to Darwin. The nature of their trials emphasized the incongruity of the court system for Aborigines in remote areas.

Warren then accepted nomination to the parish of St Thomas, Enfield, Sydney. On 19 October 1934 the aircraft *Miss Hobart*, on which he flew from Launceston bound for Melbourne, disappeared over Bass Strait. His wife, two sons and two daughters survived him. Warren's colleagues saluted him as 'one of Christ's gallant men' and the Groot Eylandters wrote: 'He was like our father and he treated us as his children, so a person who does that to us shall never be forgotten'.

C. C. Macknight (ed), *The farthest coast* (Melb, 1969); K. Cole, *Groote Eylandt pioneer* (Melb, 1971) and *The Aborigines of Arnhem Land* (Adel, 1979); *Oceania*, 17, 1947; *Mercury*, 20, 22 Oct 1934.

KEITH COLE

WATERHOUSE, BERTRAND JAMES (1876-1965), architect, was born on 8 February 1876 at Leeds, Yorkshire, England, son of James Waterhouse, grocer, and his wife Sarah, née Turner. Bertrand reached Sydney in the *Gulf of Mexico* with his mother and two sisters in March 1885 and was educated at Burwood. Known as 'B.J.', he studied architecture at Sydney Technical College while articled to John Spencer. On 6 July 1898 Waterhouse married 19-year-old Lilian Woodcock (d. 1955) at Christ Church St Laurence. Joining the professional relieving staff of the Department of Public Works in March 1900, he worked in the harbours and rivers branch and became a relieving architectural draftsman.

In partnership with J. W. H. Lake from 1908, Waterhouse built up a substantial practice, particularly in the Cremorne-Neutral Bay area. In 1917-18 he served as assistant commissioner in the Australian Comforts Fund with the 1st Division, Australian Imperial Force, in France and Belgium. Until the mid-1920s his domestic architecture drew on the Arts and Crafts Movement, with steeply gabled roofs, extensive use of sandstone in the basements, shingle tiles and roughcast exterior wall surfaces. Thereafter his style showed a strong Mediterranean influence, a notable example being May Gibbs's [q.v.8] house, Nutcote, with textured stucco walls and symmetrical, twelve-paned, shuttered windows. His non-residential designs included warehouses, churches, picture theatres and university buildings, some with Leslie Wilkinson [q.v.]; in the 1920s he produced the winning design for the Young Women's Christian Association's new premises in Liverpool Street. Most of his better-known work was completed before the Depression.

Active in the Institute of Architects of New South Wales, Waterhouse was vice-president seven times between 1913 and 1948. He was secretary and treasurer of the Federal Council of the Australian Institutes of Architects (1922-24), and councillor of the Royal Australian Institute of Architects (1932-34) and of its New South Wales chapter (1934-48). President of the Board of Architects of New South Wales (1929-49), Waterhouse promoted architectural education, acting as examiner at Sydney Technical College and sitting on its advisory committee. Having taken a keen interest in town planning in Sydney, he was increasingly invited to advise the Federal Capital Commission on major projects in Canberra; in 1938 he was appointed to the National Capital Planning and Development Committee and later served as its chairman until 1958.

An excellent pencil draughtsman, Waterhouse had exhibited drawings at annual exhibitions of the (Royal) Art Society of New South Wales from 1902. He travelled through Europe in 1926 with Lionel Lindsay and Will Ashton [qq.v.10,7], and in 1932 exhibited his drawings at the Macquarie Galleries, Sydney. A trustee of the National Art Gallery of New South Wales from 1922, Waterhouse was president in 1939-58; he was also State president of the Society of Arts and Crafts. He spoke extensively, advocating more orderly planning of Sydney and the preservation of parks and old buildings such as Hyde Park Barracks; in addition, he wrote articles on contemporary art and historical papers on European art and architecture. For relaxation, he sketched and played tennis.

A fellow of the Royal Institute of British Architects (1928) and of the R.A.I.A. (1931), Waterhouse was appointed O.B.E. in 1939 and received the King George V jubilee (1935), King George VI coronation (1937) and Queen Elizabeth II coronation (1953) medals. Survived by two sons and a daughter, he died on 21 December 1965 at his Neutral Bay home and was cremated with Anglican rites. His portrait by Mary Edwards (1940) is held by the R.A.I.A., Sydney, and another by William Dargie (1958) by the Art Gallery of New South Wales.

I. and M. Stapleton, *Twentieth century buildings of significance* (Syd, 1979); R. Irving et al, *Fine houses of Sydney* (Syd, 1982); *Architecture in Aust*, Feb 1921, July 1926, Feb 1927, July 1932, Oct 1943, July 1949, Jan 1966; *Building* (Syd), Oct 1927; *SMH*, 3, 15 Aug 1929, 18 Jan 1966; *Bulletin*, 17 Apr 1940; *Daily Telegraph* (Syd), 15 Oct 1943; *Canb Times*, 23 Dec 1965; R. E. Apperly, Sydney houses: 1914-1939 (M.Arch thesis, Univ NSW, 1972); A. Ashton, B. J. Waterhouse: a tribute (ms, 1965, copy held by author); Trustees of the National Art Gallery of NSW, Annual Reports *and* Minutes of mthly meetings; Lionel Lindsay papers (ML); National Trust of Australia (NSW), listings; family papers, printed cats and other articles held by author. MICHAEL WATERHOUSE

WATERHOUSE, EBEN GOWRIE (1881-1977), linguist and camellia expert, was born on 29 April 1881 at Waverley, Sydney, second son of native-born parents Gustavus John Waterhouse, mercantile clerk, and his wife Mary Jane, daughter of Ebenezer Vickery [q.v.6]. Like his brother Gustavus Athol [q.v.], Gowrie was known by his second name. He was educated at Waverley Public School, Sydney Grammar School and the University of Sydney (B.A., 1903; M.A., 1919), gaining first-class honours in English, French and German in his bachelor's degree.

After teaching in private schools, Waterhouse sailed for Europe in 1906. He took specialized courses and improved his skills in French and German. In 1907 he lived with a family in Paris where he met Janet Frew Kellie (d. 1973), a student from Scotland; he later visited her family at their home, Eryldene, Kilmarnock. Having attended the

Institut Tilly [q.v.] in Berlin, he came home in 1909.

At Sydney Grammar School Waterhouse's language teaching was so innovative and effective that it led in 1912 to his appointment as senior lecturer in modern languages at Teachers' College, Sydney. Before taking up the post, he returned to Scotland to marry Janet with Church of Scotland forms on 1 October at Kilmarnock. Back in Sydney, they bought land at Gordon and commissioned Hardy Wilson [q.v.] to design a house that they named Eryldene; over many years Waterhouse enhanced the buildings with a beautiful and complex garden, making extensive use of camellias and azaleas, with other trees and shrubs of pleasing form. In 1939 he was to establish Camellia Grove Nursery and generate a momentum of renewed, worldwide interest in these plants.

To help schoolteachers of French, Waterhouse published booklets on the direct method of instruction: he submitted *The teaching of the French verb* (1918) for his master's degree which was awarded first-class honours. His *Liederbuch* (1932)—a collection of folk songs, student songs and popular lyrics —had a similar aim for teachers of German. In the field of literary criticism, he published his Goethe centenary lecture (1932) which conveyed his sensitivity to literary values and his capacity to arouse a like quality in his students.

On the enforced resignation of C. J. Brennan [q.v.7], in 1926 Waterhouse was appointed McCaughey [q.v.5] associate professor of German and comparative literature at the University of Sydney. He recognized the desirability of adding Italian to his languages and later promoted its teaching at the university. While overseas in 1934, he was granted audiences by Hitler and Mussolini. Waterhouse was head of department for almost twenty years and professor of German in 1938-45: he encouraged mastery of the spoken and written language, a knowledge of its structure, and the appreciation of its literature and culture. He produced many outstanding Germanists, among them his successor R. B. Farrell.

From the 1920s Waterhouse took a leading role in the Alliance Française, the Dante Aligheri Art and Literary Society, and the Modern Languages Association, and was president of the Australian Limited Editions Society from 1939. He was a connoisseur of art and culture, and made many friends in the consular and artistic communities with whom he enjoyed intelligent conversation over a good meal. A trustee of the National Art Gallery of New South Wales (1938-62), he was its president in 1960-62.

His success with the garden of Eryldene led him to influence landscape gardening within the university: he converted the Quadrangle from an unsightly mess into a dignified area, turfed and paved; he produced the vice-chancellor's luxuriant courtyard; and he planted well-grown camellias around the main building, and in the grounds of Teachers' College and Royal Prince Alfred Hospital.

In retirement Waterhouse learned Japanese and studied the origins and nomenclature of Australian camellias. He examined records of the plants imported by Sir William Macarthur [q.v.5] of Camden Park, checked surviving specimens and collected catalogues from camellia nurseries in North America, Europe and Australasia. Waterhouse demonstrated that the camellia known as *Aspasia* in Australia was a Macarthur seedling quite different from the European *Aspasia* and that it had prior claim to the name. Other discoveries were revealed in his books, *Camellia quest* (1947) and *Camellia trail* (1952), which were written in clear, attractive prose and handsomely printed on selected paper, with illustrations by Adrian Feint and Paul Jones.

With a sure touch in recognizing the hybrids that grew under his camellias from unintended cross-fertilization or from seeds he obtained from others, Waterhouse propagated many old and new specimens. He helped to found the State branch of the Australian Camellia Research Society (1954) and the International Camellia Society (1962). Among the honours he received were the gold medals of the Goethe-Institut, Munich, West Germany (1957), and of the Royal Horticultural Society, London (1966); he was appointed officier d'Académie (*les Palmes Academiques*) by the French government (1923), *cavalieri* of the Order of Crown of Italy (1933), O.B.E. (1962) and C.M.G. (1976). Survived by three sons, Waterhouse died on 17 August 1977 at Killara and was cremated with Anglican rites. His house and garden were acquired in 1980 by the Eryldene Trust which was established with the support of the Ku-ring-gai Municipal Council.

M. Armati, *E. G. Waterhouse of Eryldene* (Syd, 1977); *People* (Syd), 7 Sept 1955; *Univ Syd News*, 1977, 9, 168; *SMH*, 14 Sept 1923, 25 June 1932, 24 Apr 1934, 9 Apr 1935, 2 May 1939, 30 Aug 1957, 18 Aug 1977.
W. M. O'NEIL

WATERHOUSE, GUSTAVUS ATHOL (1877-1950), entomologist, was born on 21 May 1877 at Waverley, Sydney, eldest of five children of Gustavus John Waterhouse, a Tasmanian-born mercantile clerk and later a Sydney Municipal Council alderman, and his native-born wife Mary Jane, daughter of Ebenezer Vickery [q.v.6]. He grew up in a family interested in scientific pursuits: his father collected Pacific Island artefacts and his mother was a notable shell-collector. Athol was educated at Waverley Public School and went with his brothers, Eben Gowrie [q.v] and Leslie Vickery, to Sydney Grammar School where he spent lunch hours browsing in the Australian Museum next door.

In 1896 Waterhouse enrolled at the University of Sydney (B.Sc., 1899; B.E. [mining], 1900; D.Sc., 1924). Graduating with first-class honours in geology and palaeontology in 1899, he was influenced by Professor (Sir) Edgeworth David [q.v.8] and studied volcanic dykes in the Triassic rocks around Sydney. From 1900 to 1926 Waterhouse was assistant assayer at the Sydney branch of the Royal Mint. At Waverley on 12 September 1902 he married Beatrice Talbot Stretton with Methodist forms. They lived at Killara where Athol cultivated native plants, bred butterflies and carried out hybridization experiments. Later he took his family for holidays in a cottage at (Royal) National Park where he collected insects. On the outbreak of war in 1914 he volunteered, but was rejected for active service with the Australian Imperial Force; he then organized and drilled the Roseville Rifle Club.

Having joined the Field Naturalists' Society, Waterhouse won a prize for a collection of local sea shells in 1893; he had helped to revive the society in 1900 and was president (1906-07 and 1914-15). A member of the local Linnean Society from 1897, he was a councillor (1912-43) and president (1921-23); as treasurer (1926-28 and 1930-43), he placed the society's finances on a secure footing. He was president of the Royal Zoological Society of New South Wales (1924-25), a member of the Australian National Research Council (1926-51), honorary secretary of the local Royal Society (1923-25) and general treasurer of the Australian and New Zealand Association for the Advancement of Science (1934-46), presiding over section D (zoology) at the Auckland meeting in 1937. It was due to his suggestion that Science House was built as a permanent home for Sydney's scientific societies.

Meanwhile Waterhouse added to the butterfly collection he had begun in 1893, while continuing his observations and taxonomic studies. In 1903 he had prepared a catalogue of Australian butterflies; in 1914, with George Lyell, he published *Butterflies of Australia*; in 1932 he produced *What butterfly is that?*, illustrated by Neville Cayley [q.v.7]. In addition, Waterhouse wrote over fifty scientific papers. He was honorary entomologist for the Australian Museum from 1919 and a trustee (1926-47); when president in 1930, he presented his collection and library to the museum.

Waterhouse was a meticulous and dedicated worker whose taxonomic studies were detailed and thorough. In 1924 his work on the hybridization of sub-species belonging to the genus *Tisiphone* earned him his doctorate and the university medal. In 1928-29, during its formative years, he served as curator and executive officer of the division of economic entomology of the Commonwealth Council for Scientific and Industrial Research. According to (Sir) George Julius [q.v.9], Waterhouse resigned because of 'his Chief and Canberra'.

Accompanied by his wife, Waterhouse visited England in 1936. He worked in the British Museum (Natural History) and studied Lord Rothschild's collection at Tring and the Meyrick collection at Marlborough. A fellow of the Royal Entomological Society, London, he was elected a special life member in 1943.

A kindly man, learned in many fields, Waterhouse took a deep interest in ancient history and philately, and encouraged amateur collectors. Dapper, with deep-set eyes and a bushy moustache, he was a director of E. Vickery and Sons Ltd and Coal Cliff Collieries Ltd (chairman 1938-43). Among his later activities, he spent months identifying butterflies which had been stolen from the Australian and other museums to enable them to be restored to their rightful owners. Survived by his wife, two daughters and two sons, he died at Pymble on 29 July 1950 and was cremated with Anglican rites. A third son had been killed on active service in New Guinea in World War II.

Aust Museum Mag, 5, 1935, p 372, 10, no 3, 1950, p 78; Linnaean Soc NSW, *Procs*, 78, no 14, 1953; *SMH*, 13 July 1968; G. A. Waterhouse staff file *and* executive correspondence (CSIRO Archives, Canb).   J. W. EVANS

WATERHOUSE, WALTER LAWRY (1887-1969), agricultural scientist, was born on 31 August 1887 at West Maitland, New South Wales, third son of John Waterhouse, a Tasmanian-born schoolteacher, and his wife Hephzibah, née Lawry, a New Zealander. Walter was educated at Sydney Boys' High School where his father was headmaster (1896-1915). After two years commercial experience, he entered Hawkesbury Agricultural College, gaining its diploma in 1907. He was headmaster of a Methodist high school in Fiji before enrolling in 1911 in the new agricultural science course at the University of Sydney (B.Sc.Agr., 1914); he graduated with first-class honours and the University medal.

In 1915 Waterhouse declined the 1851 Exhibition science scholarship, opting instead to enlist in the 2nd Battalion, Australian Imperial Force, on 21 June. Commissioned in December, he sailed for Egypt in January 1916. Crossing to France with his battalion, he attended a bombing school and was awarded the Military Cross for 'conspicuous gallantry in the capture of an enemy's strong post' at Pozières in July. He was severely wounded in the shoulder in November and invalided home in January 1917.

Awarded the Walter and Eliza Hall [qq.v.9] agriculture research fellowship in 1918, Waterhouse attended the Imperial College of Science and Technology, London, and obtained its diploma (1921). He returned to Sydney via the United States of America, spending some time at the University of Minnesota where he developed a lifelong association with Elvin Charles Stakman, a notable rust researcher. In 1921 Waterhouse was appointed lecturer in agricultural botany (as well as plant pathology, genetics and plant breeding in 1923) at the university under (Sir) Robert Watt [q.v.]. On 6 September 1924 Waterhouse married with Presbyterian forms Dorothy Blair Hazlewood in her father's house at Epping; they were to have three daughters.

Centring his research interests on the cereal rusts, Waterhouse pioneered the assessment of annual changes in their pathogenic variability and demonstrated that new races of rust could arise on the alternative hosts of both stem and leaf rust of wheat, namely *Berberis vulgaris* and *Thalictrum sp.* respectively. His investigations indicated the importance of Australian grasses as hosts in the persistence over the summer of economically important rusts. In 1929 the University of Sydney's first doctorate in agriculture was conferred upon him for a thesis on Australian rusts.

Waterhouse is chiefly remembered by Australian farmers for producing successful wheat varieties which he bred for rust resistance, baking quality and yield. In 1937 he released the varieties Hofed and Febweb which rapidly gained acceptance among wheat-farmers especially on the north-west slopes of New South Wales. The variety Gabo, released in 1945, had the greatest impact: it became for a time the leading wheat variety grown in Australia and also gave high yields in other countries, such as Mexico.

Influencing three decades of students, Waterhouse was a severe taskmaster who refused to tolerate shoddy work. The essence of his approach to teaching was captured by his colleague Professor Eric (Lord) Ashby:

He brought to lecture room and laboratory an austere integrity, a quiet dedication to the training of agricultural scientists which touched even the less sensitive of his students and made a life-long impression on those who fully appreciated his talents. There was a *gravitas* about his whole approach to teaching which influenced colleagues and students alike. The secret of his success was that for him the scientific career and the upright life were indivisible.

Appointed reader in agriculture in 1937, Waterhouse became research professor in 1946. Although a prodigiously hard and methodical worker, he did not involve his undergraduate students directly in his evolving research interests. The laboratory tasks he set them could never be completed within the scheduled hours which caused conflict with other members of staff when students were absent from their classes.

Active in scientific circles, Waterhouse was an executive-member of the Australian National Research Council and of the State committee of the Council for Scientific and Industrial Research; he was also president of the Linnean (1935) and Royal (1937) societies of New South Wales, and of section K (agriculture) of the Australian and New Zealand Association for the Advancement of Science (1939). He was awarded the Farrer (1938 and 1949) and (W. B.) Clarke [qq.v.8,3] (1943) memorial medals, the local Royal Society (1948) and Australian Institute of Agricultural Science (1949) medals, and the James Cook [q.v.1] medal (1952); in addition, he received the first E. C. Stakman award of the University of Minnesota in 1956. Appointed C.M.G. in 1955, Waterhouse was a fellow of the Australian Academy of Science (1954) and the Australian Institute of Agricultural Science (1960).

Dignified and self-effacing, kind and dedicated, Waterhouse showed a devotion to his family which carried over to his relationships with his students, by whom he was affectionately (though confidentially) known as 'Wally'; he took a personal interest in their careers and was willing to give them advice whenever they sought it. Quietly spoken, he embodied courtesy and good manners: no man, so far as is known, ever succeeded in following Waterhouse through a doorway, no matter how hard he tried. Despite his modesty and gentle ways, he was a man of action and determination when occasion demanded it.

Upon his retirement in December 1952, the university's research committee acknowledged his 'outstanding' contribution. Waterhouse then spent time in writing up his research which had been set back by his heart attack in 1942. Survived by his wife and daughters, he died at Concord on 9 December 1969 and was cremated.

Linnean Soc of NSW, *Procs*, 45, pt 3, 1971, p 260; *Records of the Aust Academy of Science*, 2, no 3, Nov 1972, p 76; *SMH*, 17 Dec 1952; *The Times*, 15 Jan 1970; K. O. Campbell, 'Emeritus Professor W. L. Waterhouse—an obituary', Professorial Bd minutes, 15 Dec 1969 (Univ Syd Archives).

KEITH O. CAMPBELL

WATERWORTH, EDITH ALICE (1873-1957), welfare worker, was born on 18 October 1873 at Castleton, Lancashire, England, daughter of Henry Hawker, joiner, and his Irish-born wife Emma, née Hamilton. The family migrated to Queensland where Edith was educated at Brisbane Girls' Grammar School. She taught for fourteen years at state schools before marrying with Methodist forms JOHN NEWHAM WATERWORTH (1867-1949) on 5 October 1903 in Brisbane. John was born on 2 June 1867 at Scarborough, Yorkshire, England, son of John Gwin Waterworth, joiner and undertaker, and his wife Margaret Ruth, née Newham. In 1887 he had followed his family to Tasmania and taken work as a tailor in Queenstown; his travels took him to Brisbane in 1895 where he became a Baptist lay preacher, acquired some competence with hypnosis and described himself as a 'magnetic healer'.

After their marriage John and Edith lived in Sydney while he studied optometry under Harry Cole; they then settled at Launceston where John established himself as an optician. Moving his family and business to Hobart about 1909, he unsuccessfully contested seats in the House of Assembly: first Wilmot as a Liberal Democrat in 1909, next Denison as a Labor candidate in the 1912 and 1913 elections; he remained a staunch Labor supporter. Waterworth was instrumental in obtaining Tasmania's Opticians Act (1913) and in 1916 formed a partnership with R. M. Ross, a fellow optician. Withdrawing from public life to support his wife's welfare work, John indulged his love of reading and passion for organ music at their home in West Hobart.

Edith also stood unsuccessfully for the Tasmanian parliament, contesting Denison in 1922 and 1925 as an Independent endorsed by the Women's Non-Party League, of which she was president from 1929. In the former election (in which she received 6.5 per cent of the vote) Mrs Waterworth campaigned on rights for deserted wives, for widows and for their children; a member of the Women's Criminal Law Reform Association, she called for the admission of women to juries, the appointment of women justices, and new procedures to ensure that women had the support of a female companion when they were cross-examined. In the latter election (in which she polled fewer votes) she stressed health issues, such as maternity hospitals and bush nursing services, as well as the need for a domestic science training centre. Likening the state to a large home which needed both sexes to manage it, she argued that women had a special place in public affairs as guardians of the human race.

Mrs Waterworth attended the congress in Washington, D.C., of the Women's International League for Peace and Freedom in 1924 and the International Alliance of Women for Suffrage and Equal Citizenship which met in Berlin in 1929. She toured Tasmania in 1935, fund-raising for the King George V and Queen Mary maternal and infant welfare appeal on the slogan 'Make Motherhood Worthwhile'. Concerned with the falling birth-rate, she appreciated that, to raise the status of motherhood, the position of women in the home had to be improved. In 1937 she convened a State-wide conference aimed at co-ordinating welfare work for women and children; it led to the formation of the Tasmanian Council for Mother and Child which she chaired for eighteen years. She was also founder and secretary of the Child Welfare Association.

Active on the National Council of Women, the National Fitness Club, the Free Kindergarten Association and the Board of Censors of Moving Pictures, Edith went on numerous deputations to ministers and gave copious testimony to parliamentary inquiries. A former columnist (as 'Hypatia') in the Hobart *Mercury*, she established good relations with the paper's proprietors, but her frequent and outspoken letters to the editor earned her the sobriquet 'Mrs Hot Waterworth'. Appointed O.B.E. in 1935, she was unsuccessful when she stood for the Legislative Council seat of Hobart in 1943. Her husband died in Hobart on 3 August 1949 and was cremated; his estate was sworn for probate at £33 026. Survived by three sons, Edith Waterworth died at her Sandy Bay home on 6 November 1957; she, too, was cremated.

Mercury, 9 June 1922, 7, 22 May, 2 June 1925, 10, 17 July 1935, 4 Aug 1949, 7 Nov 1957; J. Waters, To help the mothers and save the babies: an episode in Tasmania's population debate (B.A. Hons thesis, Univ Tas, 1983); Chief Secretary's Dept *and* Health Services Dept, correspondence (TA); C. Wright, Biog sketch of J. N. Waterworth (copy held by ADB, Canb).   JILL WATERS

WATKINS, DAVID (1865-1935), miner and politician, was born on 5 May 1865 at Wallsend, New South Wales, third son of John Watkins, miner, and his wife Mary Ann, née Hopkins, both of whom had migrated from Wales. On leaving Wallsend Public School at the age of 13, David began work in the local office of the *Newcastle Morning Herald*. In

1881 he was employed as a timber-getter and next year entered the Wallsend colliery as a water-baler and wheeler; two years later he started at the coalface.

In his father's house Watkins married Marion Alice Arthur (d. 1933) with Wesleyan forms on 30 July 1890. In the aftermath of the defeats of the maritime strike, he became secretary of the Wallsend lodge of the Australasian Coal and Shale Employees' (Miners') Federation and sought to rebuild the union and to pursue its claim for working refuse and pillars. Active in local affairs, he was a member of the committee of management of the district hospital, a founder of the Wallsend and Plattsburg Musical and Literary Society, and a supporter of the Wallsend Choral Society and minstrels; in addition, he conducted at the eisteddfod.

Embarking on a parliamentary career in 1894, Watkins won the new Legislative Assembly seat of Wallsend for the Labor Electoral League, standing as a Protectionist: despite causing disquiet among some members of the league, he gained the favour of the Licensed Victuallers' Association by advocating local option with compensation; he saw the election as a fight between capital and labour, and feared that payment of members might be abolished. Watkins gave evidence to the 1895 royal commission on the coal-mining regulation bill which resulted in improved mine safety and ventilation. He was 'not a fluent speaker', but his reputation grew and Wallsend became a safe Labor seat.

In June 1901 Watkins moved to the House of Representatives and held the Newcastle seat until 1935. He focused on local issues and remained an unequivocal Protectionist. A member of the 1903 royal commission on the bonuses for manufacturers bill, he enthusiastically supported such assistance to develop a local iron and steel industry which would benefit his electorate. He served under Andrew Fisher [q.v.8] as government whip (1910-13) and Opposition whip (1909-10 and 1913-14), and was secretary of the parliamentary party (1908-17). Watkins chaired the parliamentary delegation which visited Papua in 1911 and was an Australian member of the Empire Parliamentary Association in England in 1916. In 1920-28 he was temporary chairman of committees.

A 'short, clean shaven' man with merry eyes and the debating style of a 'healthy middleweight', Dave Watkins enjoyed racing and had 'as sharp an eye for form and possibilities' as any tipster. Following his continued support for the banking and arbitration policies of the Scullin [q.v.11] government, he faced his greatest test in 1931: at the urging of the Northern Miners, the Lang [q.v.9]-dominated central executive of the New South Wales Labor Party expelled Watkins and preselected another candidate for Newcastle. The contest between Watkins (representing the Federal interest) and James Kidd (the Lang Labor candidate) was bitterly fought and split the electorate; Watkins managed to hold the seat with a greatly reduced majority. The 1934 election saw a return of his electoral support.

An active Freemason, Watkins was involved in Mark Master Masonry and belonged to the Newcastle and District Cambrian Society and the Australasian Society of Patriots. Survived by four sons and three daughters, he died of cancer on 8 April 1935 at Newcastle and, after a Methodist service, was buried with Masonic rites in the Anglican section of Sandgate cemetery. His second son, David Oliver Watkins, easily won the ensuing by-election.

Although Watkins never attained ministerial rank and did not always please Labor's left-wing members, he was, at the time of his death, one of only three members of the first Commonwealth parliament who retained an unbroken record of parliamentary service. Unlike W. M. Hughes and Sir George Pearce [qq.v.9,11], Watkins did not change his party allegiance; nor did he change his electorate, as Hughes had done.

R. Gollan, *The coalminers of New South Wales* (Melb, 1963); B. Nairn, *Civilising capitalism* (Canb, 1973); *Newcastle Morning Herald*, 7, 10, 24 July 1894, 18 July 1934, 9 Apr 1935; *Punch* (Melb), 27 Sept 1906; *SMH*, 9 Mar, 28 Apr, 24 July 1931, 26 July 1934, 9 Apr 1935; *Daily Telegraph* (Syd), 28 Apr 1931; *Worker* (Syd), 10 Apr 1935; *Labor Daily*, 31 July, 28 Sept 1931; Crouch memoirs (LaTL).

HILARY KENT

WATRIAMA, WILLIAM JACOB (1880?-1925), soldier and patriot, was born probably on 30 August 1880 at Tuo village, Maré, one of the Loyalty Islands of New Caledonia, son of Waupo, a servant of the chiefly Naisiline clan, and his wife Sera Wakanude. Adhering to the London Missionary Society, the family was Protestant.

From an early age Watriama showed remarkable independence. About 1887 he left Maré to work as a household servant in Nouméa. Subsequently he joined a Société le Nickel vessel which he deserted in Sydney in 1891. In his first years in Australia he was possibly helped by Rev. John Jones of the L.M.S. who had been expelled from Maré by the French in 1887. Watriama later made a living as a gardener and house-painter. In 1907 he lived at the Methodist mission headquarters in Castlereagh Street, Sydney.

Watriama first came to public notice in 1911 through a campaign he launched urging the end of French rule over New Caledonia and its dependencies. He saw an influx of Japanese labourers there as the start of a Japanese invasion of the South Pacific and as a threat to the security of Australia. Accordingly, he declared himself to be the exiled 'King of the Loyalty Islands' and in that assumed role sought to persuade the British and Australian governments to annex New Caledonia and so abort the Japanese menace. He twice attempted to visit New Caledonia, but was deported each time. Although unsuccessful, his cause did enjoy considerable public following, while his pretensions to royalty were generally treated sympathetically.

As the recipient of this attention Watriama is a figure of some historical interest, for he was one of the few Black men to attain such a degree of acceptance in White Australian society. Much of his support was due to his war record. In 1901-02 he had served in the South African War as a trooper with the 2nd New South Wales Mounted Rifles. In 1914 he joined the Australian Naval and Military Expeditionary Force which occupied German New Guinea and, *en route* to Rabaul, helped to train troops aboard the *Berrima*. Enlisting as a private in the Australian Imperial Force in December 1915, he served with the 5th Australian Training Battalion in England and with the 18th Battalion, A.I.F., in France. He was discharged on 5 December 1917. His most dramatic demonstration of patriotism occurred during an Anzac Day service in 1921: with a party of ex-servicemen, he hoisted a Union Jack above Sydney Town Hall in protest at the alleged disloyalty of the lord mayor W. H. Lambert [q.v.9].

On 21 March 1916, before departing on active service, Watriama had married Ethel May Tipping at Wesley Church, Melbourne. They lived at Northbridge, Sydney. Survived by his wife, daughter and son, he died of cancer on 5 January 1925 at Mater Misericordiae Hospital, Sydney, and was buried in the Methodist section of Northern Suburbs cemetery. Prime Minister Hughes [q.v.9] delivered a eulogy at the graveside.

Evening News (Syd) and *Sun* (Syd), 6 Jan 1925; *Daily Telegraph* (Syd) and *SMH*, 7 Jan 1925; *Aust National Review*, 23 Jan 1925; H. Laracy, 'W. J. Watriama: pretender and patriot (or a black man's defence of White Australia)', (seminar paper presented at ANU, 3 June 1987).   HUGH LARACY

WATSON, ARCHIBALD (1849-1940), professor of anatomy, was born on 27 July 1849 at Tarcutta, New South Wales, eldest son of Sydney Grandison Watson, pastoralist, and his wife Isabella (d. 1861), née Robinson.

Educated at a national school in Sydney and in 1861-67 at Scotch College, Melbourne, Archibald excelled in scripture and was a champion light-weight boxer. Acting as his father's agent, he arrived at Levuka, Fiji, on 10 March 1871. He was aboard the *Carl* on her 1871-72 blackbirding venture in the Solomon Islands and kept a diary. The captain Joseph Armstrong was later sentenced to death for murder and atrocities committed during her previous voyage. On returning to Levuka, Watson was arrested and charged with piracy; J. S. Butters [q.v.3] stood bail. On 16 July 1872 Watson was discharged from his bail on entering into his own recognizance of one thousand dollars and left for Melbourne.

In 1873 he travelled to England and Germany where he studied medicine at the Georg-August Universität of Göttingen (M.D., 1878) and the Université de Paris (M.D., 1880). In England he obtained the licentiate (1880) of the Society of Apothecaries, London, and became a member (1882) and fellow (1884) of the Royal College of Surgeons. While assistant demonstrator of anatomy at Charing Cross Hospital Medical School, he studied surgery under Joseph Lister.

Appointed Elder [q.v.4] professor of anatomy at the University of Adelaide in 1885, Watson also became lecturer in pathological anatomy (1887-1903) and in operative surgery (1887-1919). Using vivid language and rapid blackboard sketches, he taught with dramatic intensity. Following a dispute in 1895 over a nursing appointment involving Margaret Graham [q.v.9], the government did not reappoint the board of the (Royal) Adelaide Hospital and the honorary doctors resigned in protest. Watson became consultant surgeon, hoping to continue the teaching of medical students there. After the arrival of Dr William Ramsay Smith [q.v.11] and Dr Leith Napier, the new board dismissed Watson for criticizing Napier, but later reinstated him.

Watson initially contributed to medical meetings and based his publications on practical experience. He had developed the habit of recording daily the details of patients seen and operations witnessed; his style was terse, his descriptions precise; his diagrams were finely drawn in pencil, black ink, crayons and water-colours. He also kept daily accounts of expenses. Most of his accounts and surgical notebooks have been preserved. Probably Australia's most precious surgical literary artefact, the notebooks cover the period 1883-1937 and record operations and postmortems performed in Australia, England, the United States of America, South Africa (while consultant surgeon, Natal Field Force, during the South African War) and in Egypt

and Greece (while consultant pathologist with the rank of major, 1st Australian Stationary Hospital in 1915-16). He visited China, South America, Japan, Russia and New Zealand where he usually watched leading surgeons operate, but regarded Sydney's Sir Alexander MacCormick [q.v.10] as pre-eminent. Watson was himself to influence Australian surgery through his mastery of anatomy, his association with practising surgeons and by his passion for the preservation of tissues.

An erratic, histrionic genius, he flouted convention and dressed in an old canvas coat. Short, bearded and bespectacled, he spoke six languages and had a firm voice, acid wit and racy vocabulary. He was loved by his family and close friends who called him Archie, by most of his students and colleagues who called him 'Proffie', and by children to whom in later life he had an instant appeal. 'Wattie' was kind to nurses and considerate to the less fortunate. He built elaborate stratagems against those who offended him and then let the matter rest. For transport, he rode a succession of motor cycles in Adelaide and through the country. Having sold the properties he inherited, he lived in boarding houses, at clubs—he belonged to the Athenaeum, Melbourne—or with friends.

Having crossed the equator at the age of 10, he became an inveterate seafarer. In 1923 he was engaged on several coastal vessels; in retirement he travelled to such places as Iceland and the Falkland Islands. He recorded details of his paramours in his personal diaries: he entered the names in Greek, his sexual experiences in Fijian and his actions often in variations of a coloured Maltese cross. Watson spent much of his last four years on Thursday Island, studying the Aborigines and collecting marine specimens. He died on 30 July 1940 on the island and was buried there with Anglican rites. A memorial lecture at the University of Adelaide commemorates him; his portrait by W. B. McInnes [q.v.10] hangs in the university's anatomy department. His estate was sworn for probate at £58 601; in accordance with his will, his personal letters, stored in the South Australian Museum's crypt, were burnt.

Roy Soc SA, *Trans*, 16, pt 2, 1893; *Lone Hand*, 1 Jan 1914; *Adel Univ Mag*, 2, no 1, Sept 1919; *MJA*, 12 Oct 1940, p 361, 27 Sept 1947, p 381, 29 Apr 1950, p 549; Adel Medical Students Soc, *AMSS Review*, Aug 1961, p 19; R. G. Elmslie, 'The colonial career of James Patrick Murray', *Aust and NZ J of Surgery*, 49, no 1, 1979; *SMH*, 20-23 Nov 1872, 1 Mar 1873, 30 Sept 1930, 30 July 1936; *Observer* (Adel), 15 Feb 1896, 20 Jan 1900, 26 May 1928; *News* (Adel), 31 July 1940; *Chronicle* (Adel), 15 Aug 1940; GRG 2/5/23, 43 *and* D5390 [Misc] *and* PRG 128/12/7 and 30/5/7-9 (Mortlock Lib); Roy A'sian College of Surgeons Archives (Melb); Marston collection, folders 33-71, especially MS 1682/65 no 3847-49 (NL); Attorney-general and Justice Dept, Special bundles, 1836-76, 4/2698B (NSWA); Land Claims Commission 1875-82, claim no 606, 782 998 (National Archives of Fiji, Suva).

RONALD ELMSLIE
SUSAN NANCE

WATSON, CHARLES HENRY (1877-1962), administrator and pastor of the Seventh Day Adventist Church, was born on 8 October 1877 near Yambuk, Victoria, one of twelve children of Henry Greaves Watson, a native-born labourer, and his English wife Sarah Jane, née Pettingill. Henry later became a woolclasser and ran a small store; Charles followed his father into the wool-buying business. On 23 March 1898 at St Peter's Church, Yambuk, he married with Anglican rites Elizabeth Mary Shanks, a neighbour and childhood friend. Although brought up in the Church of England, in 1902 Charles and Elizabeth became Seventh Day Adventists. In order to study for the ministry he moved with his family in 1907 to Avondale School for Christian Workers, Newcastle, New South Wales.

Following his ordination on 14 September 1912, Brother Watson was called to Queensland and immediately elected president of the Queensland conference. Moving to Sydney, he became vice-president (1914) and president (1915) of the Australasian Union Conference of Seventh Day Adventists. Deeply interested in missionary work, he furthered programmes designed to promote his faith among Australian Aborigines and South Pacific islanders. He visited the United States of America in 1918 to attend the S.D.A. General Conference at San Francisco. In 1920, when the Australasian Conference Association Ltd was established as a legal holding body for the Church, he became its general manager. During this time he helped to reorganize the Adventist health food operations and developed the successful Sanitarium Health Food Co: its profits were used to advance the work of the Church, especially the Adventist school system in Australia.

A talented administrator, Watson was elected vice-president and associate treasurer of the S.D.A. General Conference in 1922. For the next four years he was attached to headquarters near Washington, D.C., and travelled throughout the world on Church business. In 1926 he returned to Australia and resumed the presidency of the Australasian Union Conference. Recalled to the United States in 1930 to serve as president of the S.D.A. General Conference, he was the only non-American to hold that position. The Depression had dramatically reduced Church income and Watson was obliged to prune expenditure ruthlessly. By 1936 he was able to report that the Church was operating on a balanced budget and that there had also been considerable growth in Seventh Day Adventism both at home and in the mission fields.

Pastor Watson came back to Sydney in 1936 and resumed his work in the Church as president of the Australasian Conference (1936-38) and of the Australasian Division (from 1938). He retired to Turramurra in 1944. Survived by his wife, two daughters and two sons, he died at Wahroonga on 24 December 1962 and was buried in Northern Suburbs cemetery.

D. F. Neufeld et al (eds), *Seventh Day Adventist Encyclopedia*, 10 (Washington, DC, 1966); D. A. Ochs, *The past and the presidents* (Nashville, Tennessee, USA, 1974); R. W. Schwarz, *Light bearers to the remnant* (Mountain View, California, USA, 1979); G. Land (ed), *Adventism in America* (Grand Rapids, Michigan, USA, 1986); *SMH*, 13 Oct 1922, 2 Aug 1934, 26 Dec 1962; *Review and Herald* (Washington, DC), 31 Jan 1963.   W. J. BREEN

WATSON, CHARLES VINCENT (1882-1930), public servant and soldier, was born on 2 June 1882 at Horsham, Victoria, son of New Zealand-born George Rollaston Watson, civil engineer, and his English-born wife Catherine Elizabeth, née Donnelly. Educated at Xavier College, Kew, he was a pupil-architect and, after qualifying in 1905, assistant engineer and architect with the Victorian Public Works Department. Transferring to the Commonwealth Public Service, he became assistant examiner of architectural and engineering patents in the Attorney-General's Department.

Having served in the volunteer junior cadet corps from 1896 and as a reservist from 1901 in the Victorian Rifle Corps, in 1907 Watson was commissioned second lieutenant in the 1st Battalion, 5th Infantry Regiment. Promoted lieutenant in 1909, he joined the headquarters of the Australian Intelligence Corps in 1910 as staff officer to Colonel (Sir) James McCay [q.v.10]. A captain from 1911, Watson transferred to the Victorian district section of the Intelligence Corps in 1912. On 8 October he married Eileen Catherine Ryan at St Mary's Catholic Church, Hawthorn.

On the outbreak of World War I Watson volunteered for service with the Australian Imperial Force, but was retained in Australia for duty with the intelligence section of the general staff at district headquarters, Melbourne, and as chief instructor of the A.I.F. Officer Training School at Broadmeadows, Victoria, and officer commanding the A.I.F. training camp at Liverpool, New South Wales.

Promoted major in April 1915, he was granted the honorary rank of lieut-colonel in October 1916 for meritorious service.

In July 1917 Watson obtained his release to serve overseas. As a major he transferred to the 58th Battalion, A.I.F., attended a three-month senior officers' course at Aldershot, England, and joined his unit at Courset, France, in January 1918 as a company commander. In April he was involved in operations at Vaire and Villers-Bretonneux, in the latter action as a 'special intelligence officer' employed on forward reconnaissance for which he was congratulated in corps orders.

Watson was appointed commanding officer of the 58th Battalion in May and led it at Hamel in July (when it was engaged east of Ville-sur-Ancre) and at Amiens in August. For this work he was awarded the Distinguished Service Order. He took part in the capture of Péronne in September, and his gallantry and leadership during the Australian attack on the Hindenburg line near Bellicourt (29 September–3 October) was recognized with a Bar to his D.S.O. The citation to this award referred to his prompt action 'under very heavy shell-fire in personally reconnoitring and ascertaining the exact situation at a critical time [which] enabled him to make dispositions restoring the situation'. He was twice mentioned in dispatches for service during 1918 and awarded the Légion d'honneur.

Transferred to London in December as assistant provost marshal at A.I.F. Headquarters, in 1919 Watson represented the A.I.F. on the board which conducted the inter-allied games organized by the American general, J. J. Pershing. In September Watson assumed the additional duties of officer commanding the Australian Provost Corps. He returned to Australia in January 1920 and his A.I.F. appointment ended in May.

Watson resumed his public service career, rising to controller-general of patents and registrar of trade marks and designs in 1923. He represented the Australian government at an industrial property convention at The Hague in 1925 and was chairman of the Central War Gratuity Board. Prominent in Melbourne's sporting and club life, he was a committeeman of the Naval and Military Club and a member of the Athenaeum.

Continuing his links with peacetime soldiering through the 2nd Battalion, 24th Infantry Regiment, in 1920 Watson had been given command of the 2nd Battalion, 58th Infantry; placed on the unattached list in 1924, he became temporary colonel commanding the 15th Infantry Brigade in 1927 and was promoted colonel in 1929.

On 10 February 1930, following an operation for appendicitis, Watson died in a South Yarra private hospital and was buried in Box Hill cemetery with military honours. His wife and two sons survived him.

H. E. Renfree, *History of the Crown Solicitor's Office* (Canb, 1970); C. D. Coulthard-Clark, *The Citizen General Staff* (Canb, 1976); C. E. W. Bean, *The A.I.F. in France, 1918* (Syd, 1937, 1942); *London Gazette*, 31 Dec 1918, 1 Jan, 2 Apr, 11 July, 10 Dec 1919; *Reveille*, 31 Mar 1930; *SMH*, 11 Feb 1930; *Queenslander*, 13 Feb 1930; records (AWM).

C. D. COULTHARD-CLARK

WATSON, ELLIOT LOVEGOOD GRANT (1885-1970), biologist, writer and mystic, was born on 14 June 1885 at Staines, Middlesex, England, elder son of Reginald Grant Watson, gentleman, and his wife Lucy, née Fuller. The younger son died in 1899, the father soon after. The mother—a fanatical Darwinist—dedicated her life to her firstborn. He was educated at Bedales School, Petersfield, and Trinity College, Cambridge (B.A., 1909), graduating with first-class honours in natural sciences.

In 1910 Watson set out ahead of Alfred Brown [q.v.11 Radcliffe-Brown] who had invited him to join an expedition to Western Australia to investigate Aboriginal marriage customs. Watson's mother and stepfather followed him to Perth. Taken by the entrepreneur Dorham Doolette [q.v.8] to see his mine at Bullfinch, near Southern Cross, Watson lived with the miners, collected insects for European entomologists and fell in love with the Australian bush, which, he said, changed his life. By October Brown's small party, joined by Daisy Bates [q.v.7], was encamped near Sandstone. Brown established contact with the Aborigines, but his relations with Bates grew increasingly distant, as Watson's *But to what purpose: the autobiography of a contemporary* (London, 1946) makes clear. After a police raid on the Aboriginal camp, Brown and Watson retreated to Bernier and Dorré islands, off Carnarvon. In March 1911 the party disbanded. Brown and Watson travelled up the Gascoyne River, then Watson made a leisurely return to England by way of Fiji and Canada. He revisited Australia in 1912. His travels in the Pacific and, later, the Middle East and Northern Europe, left him permanently at odds with Western civilization. The autobiography and *Journey under the southern stars* (London, 1968) give vivid accounts of his journeys.

Despite a nervous breakdown shortly before World War I, Watson enlisted in the British Army and was seconded to do biological research. After 1918 his mother's legacy supported his Bohemian life in London. On 17 July 1919 at Hampstead register office he married Katharine Hannay.

Watson wrote more than forty books, including fiction, travel accounts and studies of philosophy. His finest works, about the English countryside, are classics of their kind. His first novel, *Where bonds are loosed* (London, 1914), was based on hospital politics observed on Bernier Island; it was made into a film, unfortunately lost. *The desert horizon* (1923), *Daimon* (1925), *The partners* (1933) and *The nun and the bandit* (1935) are better novels. Much of this fiction reflects the violence of his hidden feelings. Always restless, Watson moved his family from one country house to another. His main source of income was writing, lecturing and broadcasting. He kept in touch with Owen Barfield, Havelock Ellis and Carl Jung; one of his greatest admirers was the naturalist Frank Fraser Darling, in whose company Watson gathered material for his novel, *Priest island* (1935).

Distinguished by a precise as well as a poetic evocation of the landscape and by an empathy with the Aborigines, Watson's Australian novels are also important for their use of the desert as a metaphor of the Unconscious and, metaphysically, as an image of the Void as the womb of all possible manifestations. In this respect he is a pioneer in Australian literature. Watson faced the desert with awe, not fear, and had a real affinity with the bush.

Survived by his wife and two daughters, Watson died at Petersfield, Hampshire, on 21 May 1970 and was buried in nearby Steep churchyard. A conspectus of his writings, edited by Dorothy Green, was published in 1990.

D. Green, *The music of love* (Melb, 1984); Watson family papers (NL); information from Mrs K. Watson, Lynton, Devon, and Mrs J. Spence, Duddleswell, Sussex, England.

DOROTHY GREEN

WATSON, JAMES FREDERICK WILLIAM (1878-1945), editor, historian and medical practitioner, was born on 27 June 1878 in Sydney, fourth child of James Watson [q.v.6], a merchant from Ireland, and his Scottish wife Margaret Salmon, sister of James Ewan [q.v.4]. Educated at Sydney Grammar School, Fred attended the University of Sydney (M.B., Ch.M., 1903). He was resident surgeon at Toowoomba Hospital, Queensland, for five months and assistant medical superintendent at the nearby Hospital for the Insane in 1903-05.

In 1906 he joined the surgeon (Sir) Neville Howse [q.v.9] at Orange, New South Wales. On 12 September Watson married Muriel Palmerston Marks at St Mark's Anglican Church, Darling Point, Sydney. When the partnership with Howse was dissolved in 1908, Watson took his family to Europe where he studied X-rays in 1909. Returning to Sydney, he maintained medical rooms in Macquarie Street for about two years, but made no serious attempt to establish a career in radiology.

Recognized as a knowledgeable collector of Australiana, Watson was appointed a trustee of the Public Library of New South Wales in October 1910. He served on the 1911 sub-committee investigating the library's internal administration and was honorary acting principal librarian in January-June 1912. Watson was recommended by the trustees as librarian, but F. M. Bladen's forced retirement had offended the Public Service Board and, after bitter wrangling, W. H. Ifould [q.v.9] was appointed.

Meanwhile, Watson developed his flair for documentary research. His first major publication, *The history of Sydney Hospital* (1911), was commissioned and published within six months. It could not have been attempted without familiarity with *Historical records of New South Wales*, edited by Bladen between 1892 and 1901, and James Bonwick's [q.v.3] transcripts of official papers in London. While acting librarian, Watson had inherited the responsibility for supervising continuing work on the transcripts. In August 1912 he was formally appointed editor for the *H.R.N.S.W.* series that was expected to resume publication.

The Library Committee of the Commonwealth Parliament managed the project on behalf of the government (which had agreed to finance it in 1907). On Watson's recommendation the project was renamed *Historical records of Australia*; its scope was enlarged to include all Australian colonies and the *H.R.N.S.W.* chronology was abandoned in favour of seven subject-based series. Watson surveyed government offices in Sydney and Hobart, discovering hundreds of early colonial records. He produced some of these in facsimile as *The beginnings of government in Australia* (1913). In 1914 the first volume of *H.R.A.* appeared.

His untutored prose attracted such criticism that George Arnold Wood [q.v.], professor of history at the University of Sydney, was appointed literary consultant. Watson's style gradually improved, though Wood was never able to convince him of the need to provide evidence of his documents' location. Watson took advice in good part, but could not always afford to act upon it: scholarship took time and the library committee was in a hurry.

Despite several financial setbacks, Watson had a private income and would not commit himself to *H.R.A.* on a professional, salaried basis. He was not always sensible about money matters or tactful in dealing with colleagues. The need to re-negotiate short-term contracts with the library committee and the adherence to payment by volume tried everyone's patience. Watson's wish to serve abroad with the Australian Imperial Force was thwarted, but work on *H.R.A.* was suspended from mid-1917 until January 1919. The last contract was signed on 13 July 1922.

By the time Watson realized that the task was beyond one person, his relationship with the library committee was ruptured beyond repair, leading to well-publicized legal proceedings in 1925-26 (which he won) and to the collapse of *H.R.A.* Series I (governors' dispatches) had been virtually completed and two other series begun. Almost single-handed between 1914 and 1925 Watson had collated, edited and supervised through the press thirty-three volumes of documents covering the period from 1786 to 1848; despite their flaws, they effectively laid the foundations for the study of much of Australia's colonial history.

Like Bonwick and Bladen, Watson promoted the idea of government archive offices at State and national levels. By 1924 problems with the location and control of records in all States had become so severe that he contemplated suspending the publication programme and creating a Commonwealth archives. A similar idea was developed in a report on the future of *H.R.A.*, compiled by Professor (Sir) Ernest Scott [q.v.11] with some assistance from Wood. Watson refused to co-operate with the preparation of the report which was unkind to him.

Reputedly expecting to be appointed government archivist, in 1927 Watson moved to the Canberra district. There he bought Gungahleen where he lived until 1940. He was an elected member of the Federal Capital Commission in 1929; within six weeks he resigned, alleging maladministration and raising doubts about the commission's legality.

Watson shielded his family from the tumult that surrounded his professional and financial worries. He took special delight in the last of his children, James, whose death in 1940 at the age of 19 came as a severe blow. A sociable man, Watson enjoyed dinner parties and, in a short career as owner, had won the Victoria Racing Club's Cup Steeplechase with Pilot on 3 November 1908. A member of the Australian Club and the Royal Australian Historical Society, he was responsible for the first Canberra imprint when he published *A brief history of Canberra* in 1927. Other works included a contentious monograph about James Cook's [q.v.1] voyages (1933) and a stream of communications to the press on sundry topics. His unpublished manuscripts include an autobiography.

Survived by his wife and three daughters, Watson died of cancer on 22 January 1945 at Vaucluse, Sydney, and was buried in Rookwood cemetery; his estate was sworn for probate at £2574. His reputation had suffered from controversy not always of his own making.

J. F. Watson (comp), *Papers relating to the editing of the Historical Records of Australia* (Syd, 1926); *Hist Studies*, 20, no 79, Oct 1982; *Australasian*, 7 Nov 1908; *SMH*, 12 Aug 1926, 16 Apr 1927, 12 Mar, 6 May 1929, 24 Jan 1945; A. M. Mitchell, Dr Frederick Watson and Historical Records of Australia (Paper delivered at ANU, 1 May 1980, copy held by ADB); Watson family papers (NL); G. A. Wood papers (Univ Syd Archives); Hist Records of Australia correspondence (NL and SLNSW); Cwlth Parliamentary Lib correspondence (AA); information from Miss P. Watson, Syd.

ANN M. MITCHELL

WATSON, JAMES HENRY (1841-1934), businessman and historian, was born on 2 December 1841 at East Stonehouse, Devonshire, England, third son of Robert Watson, a clerk in the Royal William Victualling Yard, and his wife Agnes, née Thomson. Educated at the New Grammar School, Plymouth, James planned to follow his eldest brother into the navy, but, on the latter's death at sea, acquiesced in his mother's wishes and took a position in his uncle's furnishing warehouse at Newcastle upon Tyne. In 1861 Watson found employment with a London firm.

Offered a position with Buckley [q.v.3] & Nunn, drapers in Melbourne, he arrived in the *Yorkshire* on 21 February 1864. When he had served out his contract, he partnered a shipmate on a small station on Quail Island, Western Port, before joining Farmer [q.v.4] & Co. Ltd in Sydney. Watson returned to Victoria in 1868 and worked for several months at Ballarat and Clunes, then signed on a ship bound for Bombay where he entered the service of the Great Indian Peninsula Railway Co. Discharged with a serious foot injury (eventually cured by a Parsee doctor), he sailed for Liverpool.

After three months in England, Watson returned to Melbourne on Cup Day 1872 and became a draper at Geelong. On 24 March 1875 at South Yarra he married Emma Grundy with Congregational forms. In 1880 he moved to Sydney to become a department manager for David Jones [q.v.2] Ltd. A founder (1889) of Beard, Watson & Co., carpet warehousemen, he retired from business in 1901 on the eve of its expansion into Beard, Watson Ltd, carpet warehousemen, upholsterers, cabinet-makers and general house furnishers. Having previously served with the British militia, the Royal Victorian Volunteer Artillery (Melbourne) and the Duke of Edinburgh's Highlanders (Sydney), in 1885 Watson had helped to form the Hunters Hill Corps, Reserve Corps of Infantry. In 1889 he was promoted captain, 1st Infantry Regiment, New South Wales; he resigned his command in 1892 and remained in the reserve of officers until 1902.

In retirement Watson indulged a passion for historical research. A pioneer in the study of Australian history, he was a member of the (Royal) Australian Historical Society from 1904 and president in 1909, 1926 and 1927. As honorary research secretary (1915-32), he answered a myriad of questions about local and family histories (including the vexed subject of convict ancestry), and indefatigably explored graveyards and cemeteries in search of genealogical information. He was made a fellow of the R.A.H.S. in 1916 and a life member in 1925. An authority on church and maritime history, and on early Sydney, he frequently contributed to periodicals such as the *Scottish Australasian*. He was a staunch Anglican and a member of synod for fifteen years.

Straight-backed, trim-bearded, keen-eyed and sprightly, Watson was a familiar figure in the city streets. Predeceased by his wife, he died at North Sydney on 11 February 1934 and was buried in Gore Hill cemetery. Two daughters and a son survived him. His estate was sworn for probate at £2709.

Scottish A'sian, Aug 1917; *Oddfellow*, 15 Dec 1924, 15 Feb 1934; *JRAHS*, 20, pt 7, 1934, 73, pt 4, 1988; *SMH*, 24 Feb 1926, 3 Dec 1929, 12, 13 Feb 1934; Watson papers (ML); information from Mr R. Swift, Collaroy, Syd.   DIANE LANGMORE

WATSON, JOHN CHRISTIAN (1867-1941), trade unionist, prime minister and company director, was born on 9 April 1867 at Valparaiso, Chile, son of Johan Christian Tanck and his wife Martha, née Minchin (or Skinner). Tanck was chief officer of the brig *Julia* which had arrived at Port Chalmers, New Zealand, from Talcahuano, Chile, on 24 December 1865; he married Martha at Port Chalmers on 19 January 1866; they departed in the *Julia* for Guam on 2 February. On 15 February 1869 at Waipori, New Zealand, Martha Tank [*sic*] married George Thomas Watson; her son Chris became part of her new family.

Chris Watson went to school at Cave Valley, leaving at 10 to become a nipper on railway construction works. After helping on his father's farm, at 13 he was apprenticed as a compositor to the *North Otago Times*. In 1882, described as a 'lanky, alert-looking, youth', he was with the *Oamaru Mail* and in 1886 was a member of the local typographers' union and of the New Zealand Land League. Losing his job in 1886, he migrated

to Sydney where he took work as a stablehand at Government House. Briefly a compositor on the *Daily Telegraph* and *Sydney Morning Herald*, he was influenced by W. H. Traill [q.v.6] to move in 1888 to the new protectionist paper, the *Australian Star*.

By then Watson was about 5 ft. 10 ins. (177.8 cm) tall, with sapphire-blue eyes, dark brown hair, moustache and budding beard: his athletic appearance and strength complemented his good looks. A rower and Rugby footballer, he was a great card-player, good at billiards and enjoyed a glass of beer. On 27 November 1889 in the Unitarian Church, Liverpool Street, Sydney, he married English-born Ada Jane Low, a 30-year-old dressmaker. Watson had developed his debating and speaking skills by renewing his industrial work in the Typographical Association of New South Wales. His proficiency, dedication and gregariousness facilitated his rise in the union, and he became the father of the *Star*'s chapel. In January 1890 he was elected a delegate to the New South Wales Trades and Labor Council at the time when P. J. Brennan [q.v.3] was intensifying his campaign for trade union support for the council's direct intervention in politics: Watson backed Brennan, and in May became leader of a subcommittee that sought to establish a newspaper to advance their political objectives.

He was a sympathetic observer of the preliminaries of the maritime strike, which began on 16 August, and of its defeat by November. Watson increased his involvement with the T.L.C.'s renewed drive for political action, taking part in the debates in March 1891 that produced a platform and organizational structure for the Labor Electoral League (Labor Party). On 14 April he became foundation secretary of its West Sydney branch, and was the chief organizer of the local campaign which captured the electorate's four seats in the Legislative Assembly for Labor at the general election on 17 June. He was defeated for the post of secretary of the T.L.C. on 16 July.

As well as trade unionists and other manual workers, the Labor Party attracted individuals and groups motivated variously by self-aggrandizement, shades of nebulous socialism, single-taxism and fiscalism. Watson's ideal worker was a protectionist trade unionist—though he tolerated free traders—and he wanted as many as possible of them in the branches to maintain the laborism which he saw as the main source of the new party and the basis of its survival and growth. To him, trade unionism exemplified mateship, and was pragmatic, powerful and versatile enough to sustain Labor by adaptation to democratic pressures and changing circumstances. He noticed contemporary advanced social and economic doctrines, but was too practical minded to be unduly swayed by them, though he toyed with 'State socialism'.

Radiating friendliness and respect for others, Watson moved to the centre of Labor action, his authority assured by his rapport with individuals no less than by his exceptional courage and common sense. Elected vice-president of the T.L.C. in January 1892, he inspired the settlement in June of a dispute between the council and the executive of the Labor Party; in terms of that agreement, he became, at 25, both president of the council and chairman of the party. On 24 October 1893 he chaired a large public meeting, seeking relief for the 'thousands of unemployed'; in 1894 he was joint treasurer of a co-operative village settlement that aimed to reduce unemployment.

During the Broken Hill miners' strike, on 15 September 1892 Watson (on horseback) had led a procession, headed by a T.L.C. deputation, to Parliament House to encourage the thirty-five disunited Labor parliamentarians to support a censure motion against Sir George Dibbs's [q.v.4] government. He backed James Toomey's [q.v.] plans to reunite the members of the Legislative Assembly and to reform the role of country Labor branches, and he oversaw the organizing of a special unity conference that met on 9-11 November 1893 at Millers Point. Looking and sounding like a born leader, Watson chaired the turbulent gathering with confidence: the parliamentarians' solidarity pledge was reworded, firm direction given that the divisive fiscal question had to be 'sunk', and four backsliding M.L.A.s were expelled. At the annual party conference in March 1894, which confirmed the decisions of November 1893, Watson vacated the chair to ensure that the T.L.C. retained its representation on the Labor Party executive.

In the ensuing acrimonious debate with the parliamentarians about solidarity and the wording of the pledge, Watson took a decisive lead: he stressed the primacy of conference rulings as he balanced the conflicting demands exerted by the party branches and executive, and the T.L.C. whose power was being undermined by an economic depression. More than any other individual, including W. A. Holman and W. M. Hughes [qq.v.9], Watson influenced events to reconstruct the Labor Party. By the July 1894 general election, it had set the seal on its basic institutional forms of the sovereignty of conference, caucus solidarity with accepted pledge, and the potent role of the executive. With Toomey's help, Watson won the south-western seat of Young at the 1894 election. The fifteen 'solidarity' M.L.A.s elected James McGowen [q.v.10] as their leader: they held a virtual balance of power and backed the

government of (Sir) George Reid [q.v.11], a free trader with whom Watson found some common ground.

Having resigned his T.L.C. and party positions, Watson joined the Australian Workers' Union and led moves to readjust country branches to the new circumstances of the Labor Party, following the temporary demise of the T.L.C. Opposing the separatist tendencies of W. G. Spence [q.v.6], general secretary of the A.W.U., Watson became president of the provincial council of the Australian Labor Federation, which was dominated by the A.W.U.; at the 1895 Labor Party conference he argued for a compromise that would recognize the importance of the country branches. At meetings of the L.E.L. and the A.L.F. on 23-24 May a new constitution was adopted, reflecting Watson's vision of a harmonious amalgamation of city and country interests. The party's official name became the Political Labor League; Watson was a member of its executive.

With McGowen and Hughes, Watson completed the formidable trio who led the Labor parliamentarians. Reid was not dominated by them, but his new liberalism was responsive to their pressure for increased social and economic action by the state, especially after the 1895 election when his majority was reduced and eighteen Labor members were returned. Watson mastered the forms and procedures of the Legislative Assembly. He polished his speaking skills, reaching a high standard of direct and cogent argument, the more effective because of his unfailing courtesy, tact and good temper; but he was no orator. He was loyal to McGowen, frequently negotiating on his behalf with the premier and ministers. He also nursed his electorate and at the 1898 election, with Federation the main issue, withstood a strong challenge from R. E. O'Connor [q.v.11]. By then Watson was an accomplished and diligent parliamentarian, accepted as a distinguished Labor man, with some intercolonial repute. He regarded the party as the best for employees, but counselled them that 'you can't revolutionize society in four or five years'.

Federation increasingly overrode politics in 1895-99, and Labor had to adapt to it. Watson was active in shaping party policy on the great national movement. He was one of ten Labor candidates nominated for the Australasian Federal Convention on 4 March 1897: none was elected. The party, perforce, endorsed Federation, but regarded the draft Commonwealth constitution as undemocratic; when it was submitted to a referendum on 3 June 1898, they opposed it, with Watson prominent in the campaign. The referendum failed, and a general election was held on 27 July, essentially to determine the fine details of a constitution acceptable to New South

Wales. Nineteen Labor M.L.A.s were returned, including Holman. Of necessity, Federation remained Reid's first priority, but his hold on government was now precarious; he was opposed by a motley group of protectionists, individualists and disaffected free traders who, while mostly ostensible Federationists, would not have been able to transpose their discordant provincialism into firm constitutional proposals for another referendum. Labor, with Watson backing McGowen, kept Reid in office against the objections of Holman and Hughes whose first priority was not Federation.

Watson was devoted to the idea of a referendum as an ideal feature of democracy. To ensure that Reid might finally bring New South Wales into national union on an amended draft constitution, Watson helped to negotiate a deal, involving the party executive, that included the nomination of four Labor men to the Legislative Council. At the March 1899 annual party conference, Hughes and Holman moved to have those arrangements nullified and party policy on Federation changed, thus thwarting Reid's plans. Watson, for once, got angry; he 'jumped to his feet in a most excited manner and in heated tones . . . contended . . . that they should not interfere with the referendum'. The motion was lost. The four party men were nominated to the council on 4 April and the bill approving the second referendum, to be held on 20 June, was passed on 20 April.

These events revealed that Watson's will matched his clear political thinking. Like all the Laborites, he opposed the final terms of the Commonwealth Constitution, but knew that the party could do nothing about it, and, unlike Holman and Hughes, he believed that it should be submitted to the people. Nevertheless, with all but two of the Labor parliamentarians, he campaigned against the 'Yes' vote at the referendum. When the Constitution was accepted, he agreed that 'the mandate of the majority will have to be obeyed'. He had made an essential contribution to that democratic decision.

With Federation adopted by New South Wales, Reid's control of parliament deteriorated. His related loss of reforming zeal caused Labor to lean to Hughes's and Holman's view that the party should seek further concessions from (Sir) William Lyne [q.v.10] who replaced (Sir) Edmund Barton [q.v.7] as leader of the Opposition on 23 August 1899. Eventually, Watson and a majority of caucus, excluding McGowen, were persuaded that they should transfer their support to Lyne. On 7 September Labor's nineteen votes were decisive in removing Reid.

By 1900 Watson's beard had flowered into an elegant Vandyck. Looking 'like a Viking', he was conspicuous at the intercolonial conference of Labor delegates that met in Sydney on 24 January 1900 under the auspices of the New South Wales executive; a Federal party and a short platform were approved. On 26 January the New South Wales conference recommended a draft pledge, based on the local form, to the 'Interstate Labor Parties'. These events were the formal beginnings of the Federal branch of the Australian Labor Party: many had assisted its birth, but none more than Watson.

He decided to enter Federal politics and in March 1901 won the House of Representatives seat of Bland which included his State electorate. The twenty-two Labor members who had been returned met in Melbourne on 7 and 8 May, and Watson became chairman of the party; soon after parliament assembled on 9 May, he was accepted as Federal Labor's first leader.

Watson headed a new party infected with residual colonial loyalties, free trade and protectionist doctrines, and diffused collectivism. And it operated in a national parliament divided by tenacious fiscalism and governed by a minority Protectionist ministry. Watson had little regard for Barton, the first prime minister, but respected Alfred Deakin [q.v.8], the attorney-general and a liberal Protectionist. Fiscalism masked the conservatism and liberalism that was mixed uneasily in both non-Labor parties: Reid led the Free Trade Opposition which harboured a majority conservative wing. Watson mastered this complex situation, reaffirming the pragmatism which anchored the Labor Party and which was inherent in the political forms of laborism derived from time-honoured trade unionism. He and the party concluded that the chance of any potential reform legislation approaching Labor's platform lay with the Protectionists, especially Deakin; holding the balance of power, Labor backed the government.

So Watson had to display the utmost political finesse throughout his pioneering leadership. Without precedents, and with only fitful help from fragmented and sometimes embryonic State branches, he was caught in the mercurial initial stages of the consolidation of Labor and the realignment of minority parties in the new parliament. His immediate task was to flesh out the unity of Labor and to show that, though novel and apparently sectional, it was as relevant to Australian politics as the old, eclectic, fiscal parties which were stacked with established colonial politicians. He began this strategy in 1901 in the debate on the immigration restriction bill which had unanimous parliamentary and electoral support for its principle of the exclusion of non-White peoples. His speeches projected contemporary rhetoric, but their basic and enduring theme emphasized that the Labor

Party was a distinct and original entity in the mainstream of national life.

The attainment of a truly protectionist tariff was a complementary major objective for Watson who linked it with the 'New Protection' which had its beginnings in Victoria in the late 1890s. This important part of policy reinforced Watson's personal relations with Deakin who became prime minister in September with Labor support. But Watson had to proceed with caution, for there were several Labor free traders, not least Hughes and (Sir) George Pearce [q.v.11]. The 1902 tariff was a compromise, and at the 1903 election Watson stressed that the Labor Party had no ties with either fiscal party. Labor took 23 House of Representatives seats, the Protectionists 26 and the Free Traders 25: Labor also gained 10 of the 19 Senate seats it contested. Watson's style and methods had received popular approval. He was the confirmed captain of one of the 'three elevens' now in the field.

Deakin said that only a coalition could govern and, in general terms, he was right. Yet, the degree and form of the partnership posed a particular problem for Watson who wanted Labor's platform enacted, but could not afford to allow the party to lose its identity. The new Federal parliamentary situation resembled that of 1895-99 in New South Wales. Remaining independent, the Federal Laborites again supported Deakin; when he refused to bring State public servants under the conciliation and arbitration bill, they voted against him. Watson became prime minister on 27 April 1904, with fickle Protectionist support.

Caucus agreed that Watson should select the first Labor ministry and allocate portfolios. His judicious balancing act had been justified, but he had committed his party to a complex system, with virtually no immediate chance of effecting a legislative programme based on the Labor platform: the party's aspirations were distorted and its developing Federal structure strained. This quandary, which in various forms would continue to harass doctrinaire Laborites, held other problems for Watson. As prime minister he felt keenly the inherent personal conflicts of a reformist government which was responsible to the nation through parliament, and at the same time answerable to non-parliamentary segments that he had done so much to create. His predicament was illustrated by his need to appoint H. B. Higgins [q.v.9], from the radical wing of the Protectionist Party, as attorney-general.

Administratively, Watson's minority government performed with credit; its short term in office was essentially part of the process of the formation of a two-party parliamentary system. With caucus approval, on 26 May Watson sounded out Deakin on a temporary accord. It was in vain: many Protectionists opposed Labor, and Deakin objected to the party's institutional checks. The government fell on 12 August over the conciliation and arbitration bill, defeated by a combination of Reid's Free Traders and conservative Protectionists. Reid became prime minister.

Now leader of the Opposition, Watson pursued his plans for a protectionist tariff; in September Labor formed a joint platform with the radical Protectionists, headed by Lyne and (Sir) Isaac Isaacs [q.v.9], hoping to remove Reid who in 1905 began an 'anti-socialist' campaign. On 26 June Watson wrote to Deakin, assuring him of Labor's support if he moved against Reid. Deakin again became prime minister on 5 July. But that month the Inter-State (Federal) Labor Conference ruled that no coalition should be formed with any other party, that the existing alliance with the Protectionists should be restricted to the current parliament, that caucus should elect ministries and that no immunity should be given to any Protectionists at the next election.

Watson had mixed feelings about those binding decisions. Immersed in the minutiae of making parliament work, he had attempted to integrate the Labor Party into its proceedings while seeking as much reformist legislation as possible. His period as prime minister had confirmed his position as a major politican, adept at requisite compromise and attached (as nearly all members were) to the clubbable atmosphere of parliament. His immediate reaction was that he had been let down and that conference had no sympathy with his vexatious parliamentary mission. Again he got angry.

Nevertheless, his resentment was more than balanced by his loyalty to the Labor Party. Watson had continued to take a prominent part in State and interstate (Federal) conferences; in 1902 he had had placed on the Federal platform a plank, for a competitive national (Commonwealth) bank; he maintained his close, friendly links with innumerable country and city Laborites—these were increased in 1905 when Cardinal Moran [q.v.10] declared that Labor's 'socialism' was not incompatible with Catholicism. On 27 July 1905 Watson eased his dilemma by composing a letter of resignation as party leader in which he explained his side of the contretemps; but, having second thoughts and responding to the entreaties of his colleagues who knew his worth, he withdrew the letter on 2 August.

Watson's country seat was abolished at a redistribution for the December 1906 election at which he won South Sydney. The new parliament had a majority of Protectionists. Labor had twenty-six seats. Deakin remained prime minister. Watson informed him that

Labor did not want office unless its policy, including land taxation, could be implemented, but argued that protection could now be effected. To ensure that the Labor free traders would agree on that, Watson stressed the danger of Reid's 'anti-socialism' and the advantages of 'New Protection'. Firm protectionist tariffs, with Imperial preferences, were in sight by October 1907, and were formally enacted next year.

Recognizing that his arduous foundational work for the parliamentary Federal Labor Party had been completed, Watson resigned as leader on 24 October 1907 and was replaced by Andrew Fisher [q.v.8]. Additional reasons for Watson's decision were his physical and mental fatigue, together with his wife's ill health and her objections to his frequent absences from home. Moreover, he possessed little money and had concluded that his managerial skills might be put to some lucrative use. He did not contest South Sydney at the 13 April 1910 election which Labor won outright. By then the fiscal parties had fused as the conservative Liberal Party under Deakin. The two-party contest had begun. Watson's wisdom and tolerance had facilitated that historic political rationalization. Labor could now build on his sure-footed pioneering.

With the prestige of an ex-prime minister added to his popularity, Watson continued to work for the Labor Party. He also had to make a living. On behalf of a syndicate hoping to find gold, he had visited South Africa in December 1908, but that enterprise failed, as did his speculation in land at Sutherland, Sydney. Association with A. R. Tewksbury [q.v.] and F. W. Hughes [q.v.9], in which he used his wide range of contacts and organizing ability, netted him some income. By 1920 Watson was a director of F. W. Hughes Pty Ltd, a leading wool and textile business, and his protectionism and friendship with Prime Minister Hughes had helped the company during World War I. But in 1910-16 Watson's main work was with the A.W.U. He assisted in the publication of the *Worker*; through his directorship of Labor Papers Ltd, he promoted the union's plans to produce a daily newspaper to be called the *World*: the war ended that project, but in 1914 Macdonell [q.v.10] House in Pitt Street was acquired by the A.W.U. and Watson had an office there until 1916. In February 1915, with Ada, he had left on a trip to England; having returned through the United States of America in August, he reported to Prime Minister Fisher on the war situation.

Continuing to attend Labor Party conferences, both State and Federal, Watson was not always a delegate, but was persistently influential: his prudently modified 'socialist' objective had been adopted as early as the 1905 Federal conference. He campaigned prominently at elections and belonged to the New South Wales executive in 1910-11 and 1913-15. In 1913, with Kate Dwyer [q.v.8] and others, he revised the fighting platform. Claims were made in Labor circles and the press that he 'bossed' the party: they were not correct, but the complaints pointed to his authority as he complemented the power of the A.W.U. His objective of strengthening the Federal branch against the State organizations led him to consider seriously national unification in place of Federation. In 1911, when backing the referendum to increase Commonwealth powers, he clashed with Holman and broke with (Sir) George Beeby [q.v.7] who said that Watson was 'disgruntled'. Watson replied, 'The Labor movement has always treated me generously, I have nothing to be disgruntled about'. After Labor's win in the 1913 State election, he remarked: 'The Labor Party has continued to grow because of the intrinsic justice of its cause'.

Like Hughes and many other Laborites, Watson had interpreted Labor's traditional anti-militarism as being compatible with a national policy that accepted compulsory military training for home defence. With Hughes, who was prime minister, in 1916 Watson perceived Britain as so endangered as to justify the extension of that policy to the conscription of Australians for overseas service in World War I. Although explicable in terms of the devotion many Australians felt towards the mother country as the corner-stone of the Empire, this judgement led inexorably to the expulsion from the Labor Party of Watson, Hughes, Holman and many more in September-November 1916. Watson's vast capacity for compromise failed this agonizing test.

In 1915 he had joined the Universal Service League to help recruit volunteers; in December 1916 he played a leading part in the formation of the Australian Democratic Labor League to provide a political organization for 'National' governments formed by Hughes and, in New South Wales, Holman. By January 1917 the new party, with majority non-Labor elements, was discreetly called the National Federation and Watson was promoting it in Melbourne: it soon became known as the National Party. Watson had campaigned for Hughes at the conscription referendum in October 1916; he worked for the National Party at the March 1917 election in New South Wales, won by Holman, and at the May 1917 Federal election, won by Hughes; he also spoke for conscription at the second referendum in November. Watson's interest in the new party waned when Holman lost in 1920, but he had links with it until the 1922 Federal election when he helped Hughes and his old A.W.U. friend, Hector Lamond [q.v.9], and denounced 'extremists in the Labor Party and the Country Party'.

From August 1915, as honorary organizer of the scheme to provide employment for returned soldiers, Watson had pioneered the placing of ex-servicemen on the land. In 1915 he published the pamphlet, *Returned soldiers. Employment and settlement*; his article, *The Labour movement*, had appeared the year before.

By 1920 Watson had shaved off his moustache and beard as his hair greyed. The depilation sapped his striking appearance: he looked kinder and more amiable; but his iron will surfaced on the rare occasions when gentle persuasion seemed likely to fail. He joined the council of the newly established National Roads Association on 22 March 1920 and on 16 August became its president, a position he held until his death. His leadership and administrative capacity turned the N.R.A. into the National Roads and Motorists' Association in December 1923. Appreciating that motoring would become a mass activity, for twenty years he publicized the association's policies and discussed them with governments, helping to make the N.R.M.A. Australia's leading motoring organization. On 2 April 1928, as chairman of the Traffic Advisory Committee, he submitted a valuable report on Sydney's traffic problems.

Ada died, childless, on 19 April 1921. On 30 October 1925 Watson married a 23-year-old Western Australian, Antonia Mary Gladys Dowlan, in the same church as his first wedding. Having visited the United States of America on business in 1922, he expanded his commercial interests in the 1920s: associated with G. R. W. McDonald [q.v.10] in Brisbane Metal Quarries Ltd, he became a director of another of F. W. Hughes's companies, Alexandria Spinning Mills Ltd, and in 1927 of Yellow Cabs of Australia Ltd, with Tewksbury.

Remaining an ardent protectionist, Watson congratulated James Scullin [q.v.11] on Labor's win at the 1929 Federal election and welcomed his government's increased tariffs; in 1931, as president of the New South Wales branch of the Australian Industries Protection League, he gave evidence to a select committee of the Legislative Council and criticized J. T. Lang's [q.v.9] arbitration bill. Watson disliked Lang and supported the 1931 Premiers' Plan to alleviate the Depression. He remained fond of a bet on the horses, and in the 1930s was a trustee of the Sydney Cricket Ground. His support was decisive in (Sir) William Walkley's plans to establish the Australian Motorists Petrol Co. Ltd (Ampol) and Watson became its first chairman of directors in 1936. He revisited New Zealand several times.

Watson remained friends with his fellow Labor Party pioneers of 1890-1910 and formed associations with later ones, among them John Curtin and (Sir) William McKell. He was a pallbearer at Holman's funeral in 1934. Survived by his wife and daughter, Watson died at his Double Bay home on 18 November 1941. His estate was sworn for probate at £3573. He was cremated after a state funeral from St Andrew's Anglican Cathedral: among the pallbearers were Sir Joseph Cook, Albert Gardiner [qq.v.8], Curtin and McKell. Making an exception for a party expellee, the Federal Labor caucus passed a motion of condolence and regret. W. M. Hughes said, 'I am overwhelmed by the blow his death has given me'.

Watson's portrait (1913) by Julian Ashton [q.v.7] is in the Prime Minister's Lodge, Canberra.

L. F. Crisp, *The Australian Federal Labour Party, 1900-1951* (Lond, 1955); L. F. Fitzhardinge, *William Morris Hughes*, 1 (Syd, 1964); J. A. La Nauze, *Alfred Deakin* (Melb, 1965); P. Ford, *Cardinal Moran and the A.L.P.* (Melb, 1966); M. Lake, *The limits of hope* (Melb, 1987); G. Souter, *Acts of parliament* (Melb, 1988); W. G. McMinn, *George Reid* (Melb, 1989); B. Nairn, *Civilising capitalism* (Melb, 1989); *V&P* (LA NSW) 1892-93, 8; *PP* (LA NSW) 1928, 1; *PP* (LC NSW) 1930-32, 5; B. Nairn, 'J. C. Watson in New South Wales politics, 1890-1894', *JRAHS*, 48, no 2, 1962; *Aust J of Politics and Hist*, May 1962; B. Nairn, 'J. C. Watson: A genealogical note', *Labour Hist*, no 34, May 1978; *Catholic Press*, 2 July 1903; *Bulletin*, 28 Apr 1904; *British A'sian*, 14 July 1910; *Punch* (Melb), 4 May 1911, 7 May 1914; *Daily Telegraph* (Syd), 20 Nov 1913; *SMH*, 23 Dec 1916, 28 Nov 1917, 16 Nov, 13 Dec 1922; *Canb Times*, 18 Jan 1966; A. Wilkinson, The NRMA story (ts, Syd, 1964, held by NRMA Archives, Syd); Trades and Labor Council records, 1890-94 (ML) *and* Deakin papers *and* Watson papers (NL); Crouch memoirs (LaTL); Series A, 16/3361 (AA).   BEDE NAIRN

WATSON, PHEBE NAOMI (1876-1964), educationist and women's leader, was born on 23 May 1876 in Adelaide, daughter of Edward Watson, clerk, and his wife Sarah Ann, née Goldsmith. Educated privately, from 1892 Phebe was a pupil-teacher at Goodwood Public School. Entering the Training College for a one-year course in 1896, she taught briefly at Quorn, transferred to Mitcham, then went to Woodville. In 1902, as assistant at Grote Street Public School, she began her connexion with the training of pupil-teachers and in 1908 became assistant at the Observation School, Currie Street. Appointed head teacher of its model country school in 1916, she became mistress of method in 1921 and assumed full charge of training country teachers.

In 1923-36 Miss Watson rose from lecturer (mistress of method) to senior lecturer at Adelaide Teachers' College. As women's warden from 1926 she was concerned with moral issues facing young people, a concern she voiced emphatically as a witness before the 1927 royal commission on the cinema. Somewhat severe in appearance, strong-browed, firm-mouthed, with keen eyes behind heavily-rimmed spectacles, she extended her interest in the students' welfare to their subsequent teaching appointments. She used the knowledge that she gained from them in the evidence she gave before the 1937 Industrial Court hearing on proposed salary cuts and attested to the depressed living conditions of young women teachers in outback schools.

Phebe Watson and her lifelong friend Adelaide Miethke [q.v.10] were respectively secretary and president of the Women Teachers' League, an affiliate of the South Australian Public School Teachers' Union. Resentful at the failure of the organization to achieve adequate restoration of salaries for women teachers, six hundred of the thousand women members of the union withdrew to form the South Australian Women Teachers' Guild in 1937. Watson was its first president. Active in the National Council of Women of South Australia (treasurer 1925-35, secretary 1935-37), she was honorary secretary of the Women's Centenary Council of South Australia and one of five compilers of *A book of South Australia: women in the first hundred years* (1936). Appointed M.B.E. in 1937, she was vice-president of the National Council of Women of Australia in 1936-41. During World War II she organized the Women's Voluntary Services in the State.

Her commitment to education led Watson into other public activities. During World War I she had been secretary of the South Australian Children's Patriotic Fund. She was editor (1930-37) of the *Children's Hour* for the Department of Education, and a lecturer in art and literature for the Young Women's Christian Association of which she was a board-member. A commissioner (1933-36) of the Girl Guides' Association, she had launched a guide company at the teachers' college in 1925 and in 1945 was involved with training guides for refugee work in Europe. She was also a founder and president of the Adelaide Women's Club. In 1946 she moved to Melbourne where she lived at Brighton Beach and pursued her interest in book-collecting. Almost blind, she returned to Adelaide about 1960. She died on 19 September 1964 at Glengowrie and was cremated.

B. K. Hyams, *Learning and other things* (Adel, 1988); Adel Teachers' College, *Torch*, Dec 1936; *SA Teachers' J*, Nov 1964; *Advertiser* (Adel), 22 Sept 1964; B. K. Hyams, State School Teachers in South Australia 1847-1950 (Ph.D. thesis, Flinders Univ, 1973).   B. K. HYAMS

WATSON, STANLEY HOLM (1887-1985), railway engineer and soldier, was born on 24 October 1887 at Parkside, Adelaide, eldest of eight children of Harry Watson, a clerk with the Hydraulic Engineers' Department, and his wife Adelaide Elizabeth, née Menz. Educated at Plympton Primary and Sturt Street Advanced schools, Stan studied engineering at the School of Mines and the University of Adelaide. In 1904 he was apprenticed in the South Australian Railways for five years as a draftsman. On 12 June 1911 he married with Catholic rites Leila Vera McBride at Clarence Park.

Having joined the 6th Field Troop of Engineers (militia) as a second lieutenant in 1910, by August 1914 he was lieutenant and commanding officer of the 28th Signalling Company, Engineers. He was appointed to the Australian Imperial Force as lieutenant commanding headquarters section, 1st Australian Divisional Signal Company, on 19 August, left for Egypt in October and reached Gallipoli on 25 April 1915. With lines established, Watson and several 2nd Australian Field Company sappers constructed the first pier at Anzac Cove: using a defused Turkish shell as a pile-driver, they completed the jetty on 18 June; it was named 'Watson's Pier'. Appointed second-in-command, and officer commanding No.1 Section, of the 2nd Divisional Signal Company on 26 July, Watson was promoted captain in November. On 11 December Brigadier General (Sir) Brudenell White [q.v.] gave him responsibility for the lines covering the Anzac withdrawal on the nights of 18 and 19 December. On the 20th Watson sent the final signal: 'Evacuation complete 3.45 a.m. —casualties unknown'; he then left by the last lighter. He was mentioned in dispatches for 'distinguished and gallant services' in the evacuation of Gallipoli.

Reaching France in late March 1916 with the 2nd Divisional Signal Company, Watson was attached to artillery headquarters on 18 April and took part in every 2nd Division engagement in France and Belgium. Following the Somme battle for Pozières Ridge in July and August, he was recommended for the Military Cross for his services in the Albert Area, Gallipoli and Pozières. At Flers and Fricourt during November and December he 'showed great gallantry and devotion to duty in maintaining lines and controlling linesmen' and was awarded the Military Cross. Watson commanded the 2nd Divisional Signal Company from December 1916 and was awarded the Order of the White Eagle of

Serbia. Promoted major in January 1917, he followed the German retirement from Butte de Warlencourt through Bapaume to the Hindenburg line in March and April, and served in the battle of Bullecourt in May. He was mentioned in dispatches in September for his work at Bapaume and Bullecourt.

Continuously in the Somme area from March 1918, after the battle of Hamel in July Watson laid a system of cables almost to the front lines. General Sir John Monash [q.v.10] made him responsible for communications for the battle of Amiens which commenced on 8 August. Watson received a special mention in dispatches in November and in January 1919 was awarded the Distinguished Service Order for his work on the Somme from August to 3 September 1918, especially prior to 8 August 1918. A natural leader, he 'was one of the most efficient and successful commanding officers of Signals in the First World War'.

Discharged in January 1919, Watson rejoined the South Australian Railways. He was acting resident engineer at Bordertown and Quorn, then superintendent at Peterborough in 1922 and in Adelaide in 1924. The State commissioner of railways sent him abroad in 1928 to study train control systems before their introduction in South Australia. General traffic manager from 1935, Watson became deputy commissioner of railways in 1948 and held the post until his retirement in 1952. For his services to transport he was appointed C.B.E. in 1958. During World War II, as a lieut-colonel, he had been Commanding Royal Engineer in South Australia.

Predeceased by his wife and son, and survived by his two daughters, Watson died in Adelaide on 5 May 1985. After a service at St Michael's Anglican Church, Mitcham, he was buried in Centennial Park cemetery. In delivering the eulogy, Brigadier Phillip Greville concluded: 'Colonel Watson combined the steadiness of the battle-wise soldier with the intellectual discipline of the civil engineer. He was, in one sense, a simple man—simple and direct as the railway lines he built—and just as purposeful'.

C. E. W. Bean, *The story of Anzac*, 2 (Syd, 1924); *London Gazette*, 11 July, 13, 29 Dec 1916, 15 Feb, 25, 28 Dec 1917, 31 Dec 1918, 1 Jan 1919, 21 Jan 1937, 30 Dec 1958, 6 Jan 1959; J. H. Thyer, *Royal Australian Corps of Signals: Corps history 1906-1918* (ms, Adel, 1974, AWM); Watson biog file (Aust war records section, AWM); correspondence with Mrs R. Funder, held by author, Paynesville, Vic.

JEAN P. FIELDING

WATSON, WILLIAM (1864-1938), businessman and politician, was born on 13 May 1864 at Peg Leg, near Sandhurst (Bendigo),

Victoria, fifth child of William Watson, quartz-miner, and his wife Hannah, née Horren, both English born. After leaving Guildford Public School at 13, Watson worked as a farm-labourer, axeman, miner, navvy, bricklayer, dairyman and commercial traveller; while employed in a rural general store, he learned the basics of the pork industry. On 2 April 1888 at Campbells Creek, near Castlemaine, he married Eliza Annie Showell.

In 1889 Watson started his own grocery store in Melbourne, but in 1895 moved to Western Australia with his family, £375 and a horse and cart. At Fremantle he opened a grocery store and a tea-room, then a store in Perth, and leased land at Hamilton Hill to establish a pork abattoir and bacon and sausage factory. Having acquired several more grocery stores, he was one of the first local businessmen to use motor vehicles for deliveries. After 1918 he changed the emphasis of his business from retailing to manufacturing and wholesaling smallgoods. Two of his sons died in action in World War I. Watson was a liberal contributor to the Fremantle War Memorial fund and his generosity towards ex-servicemen earned him honorary life membership of the Returned Sailors' and Soldiers' Imperial League of Australia.

His aversion to 'machine' politics and his support for prohibition during the war led him to contest the Federal seat of Swan as an Independent in 1918. Though unsuccessful, Watson was returned for Fremantle in 1922, and in 1925 when his opponent was Labor's John Curtin. Watson did not stand for election in 1928 or 1929. Prompted by the economic crisis, he came out of retirement in 1931, stood again as an Independent and took the seat from Curtin. In tribute to Watson's oratory, the *Age* described him as 'Australia's Abraham Lincoln'. While he invariably blamed party politics for class divisions in society and occasionally criticized non-Labor governments during his years in the House of Representatives, on vital issues Watson remained one of the conservatives' staunchest supporters. He retired in August 1934 due to ill health. In 1937 he relinquished the directorship of the family business to his sons.

Known affectionately as 'Old Bill', he was a successful businessman, community leader, inventor and student of ancient history who owned a large personal library. He was also a charitable man who helped those in need, regardless of their political or religious beliefs: during a 1920s waterside workers' strike at Fremantle, he had distributed food parcels to destitute lumpers. Survived by his wife, three of his sons and three daughters, Watson died at Peppermint Grove, Perth, on 21 December 1938 and was buried in the Methodist section of Fremantle cemetery; his estate was sworn for probate at £29 412. His political success had sprung from the general esteem in which he was held: John Curtin, a pallbearer at Watson's funeral, called him a 'generous and friendly opponent'.

West Australian, 22 Dec 1938; interview with Mr H. A. Watson, May 1984, oral history records *and* biog of W. Watson, ms (Fremantle City Lib, Perth).   NOELENE DOOHAN

WATSON, WILLIAM THORNTON (1887-1961), army officer, was born on 10 November 1887 at Nelson, New Zealand, son of Tasmanian-born Robert Watson, blacksmith, and his Victorian wife Annie, née Harford. Educated at Nelson, William came to Australia and by 1912 had been selected as a front-row forward in the New South Wales Rugby Union football team.

Giving his occupation as salesman, Watson enlisted in the Australian Naval and Military Expeditionary Force on 8 August 1914 and took part in operations in New Britain and New Ireland. Discharged in January 1915, he enlisted in the Australian Imperial Force on 19 March and, as a gunner, was posted as a reinforcement for the 1st Divisional Artillery. He embarked from Sydney on 26 June, landed at Gallipoli on 14 August and two days later joined the 1st Field Artillery Brigade.

After service on Gallipoli and in Egypt, in March 1916 he proceeded with his unit to France where his temporary promotion to sergeant was confirmed on 22 April. During operations on the Somme from 26 October 1916 to 15 January 1917 Watson showed 'conspicuous gallantry and devotion to duty' by going to the aid of wounded men under heavy fire. He was awarded the Distinguished Conduct Medal and posted to England for officer training. Commissioned on 7 September, he joined the 2nd Field Artillery Brigade that month and was wounded in action in Belgium on 17 November.

Promoted lieutenant on 7 December, he returned to duty in April 1918 and was at Foucaucourt on 27 August, acting as forward observation officer with the infantry. When the advance was impeded by enemy machine-gun fire, Watson worked his way forward and directed three batteries barraging the German machine-gun posts. For his conduct he was awarded the Military Cross. At Nauroy on the night of 2-3 October Watson's battery was bombarded with gas shells; although gassed himself, he stayed with the unit and attempted to save the life of a wounded officer. His 'energy and devotion to duty' won him a Bar to his M.C.

In 1919 Watson captained the A.I.F. Rugby XV in the King's Cup competition. After his A.I.F. appointment was terminated and his name transferred to the reserve of officers, in 1920 he captained New South Wales against New Zealand. Back in New Guinea, in 1920-25 and 1932-39 he engaged in copra production and gold-mining. Having married American-born Cora May Callear on 14 September 1929 at St Stephen's Presbyterian Church, Sydney, in 1935 he established their home at Columbiana, Ohio, United States of America.

With the outbreak of World War II Watson returned to Australia and served in the 2nd Australian Garrison Battalion from March 1940. In June he was promoted temporary captain and posted to the Papuan Infantry Battalion, a unit comprising Papuan soldiers and Australian officers and non-commissioned officers. Soon after Japan entered the war, Watson became commanding officer of the P.I.B. The battalion, an element of Maroubra Force, was dispersed between Awala and the north coast when the Japanese landed at Buna and Gona on 22 July 1942. Outnumbered, the P.I.B. fell back before the advancing Japanese; its remnants linked up with leading troops of the 39th Battalion, fought rearguard actions at Gorari and Oivi, and rejoined Lieut-Colonel W. T. Owen, the Maroubra Force commander at Deniki.

Having abandoned the position prematurely, Owen reoccupied Kokoda on 28 July, his force reduced to about eighty men. The Japanese attacked that evening. With Owen mortally wounded, Watson—'a bluff outspoken man, quick in thought and speech'— took command. The defenders withdrew to Deniki where Watson remained in command until 4 August when he was relieved by the arrival of A.I.F. reinforcements and a more senior commander. For his bravery and example during the withdrawal, Watson was awarded the Distinguished Service Order and promoted major on 1 September 1942. The P.I.B. subsequently carried out useful work, patrolling the flanks of the Australian-American forces as they pushed northward. Watson relinquished his command on 30 March 1944 and on 7 July was transferred to the reserve of officers.

After the war Watson returned to the United States and was Australian vice-consul in New York (1945-52). Survived by his wife, daughter and son, he died on 9 September 1961 in the Veterans Administration Hospital, Brooklyn, New York.

C. E. W. Bean, *The A.I.F. in France*, 1918 (Syd, 1942); D. McCarthy, *South-West Pacific area—first year* (Canb, 1959); *SMH*, 26 Jan 1921, 18 Dec 1942, 21 Sept 1961; AWM holdings, including G. Long, Official history 1939-45 war, ms records.   A. J. SWEETING

WATSON, WILLIAM WALKER RUSSELL (1875-1924), soldier, dentist and company director, was born on 19 May 1875 at Balmain, Sydney, son of native-born parents William George Watson, surgeon, and his wife Emily Jane, née Walker. Educated at Sydney Boys' High School (where he was a cadet bugler) and the University of Sydney, Watson entered the dental profession. He joined the New South Wales Scottish Rifles and in 1896 was commissioned second lieutenant in the 4th Infantry Regiment.

He served as a lieutenant, New South Wales Mounted Rifles, in the South African War. As a staff officer in the 2nd Imperial Mounted Infantry Corps, he was dispatched to demand the surrender of Pretoria; under heavy fire at Dainsfontein, he risked his life to rescue a wounded man. For his service in the Orange Free State, Cape Colony and the Transvaal, he was mentioned in dispatches and promoted captain. In 1902 he commanded the New South Wales detachment of the Australian Coronation Corps at the crowning of King Edward VII. Watson was promoted major in 1905 and lieut-colonel in 1912. On 9 November 1904, at St Mark's Church, Darling Point, Sydney, he had married Minnie Sarah, daughter of Samuel Hordern [q.v.4] and sister of (Sir) Samuel Hordern [q.v.9]; they were to remain childless.

Watson was appointed commanding officer of the infantry battalion of the Australian Naval and Military Expeditionary Force raised in August 1914 to seize German Pacific territories. Virtually unopposed, by December his troops had secured New Britain, New Guinea, New Ireland, Nauru, and the Admiralty and Solomon Islands. In January 1915 he returned to Australia with Colonel William Holmes [q.v.9]; both gave evidence before a court of inquiry into looting by the A.N. & M.E.F.

On 16 March Watson took command of the 24th Battalion, Australian Imperial Force, and reached Gallipoli on 5 September. As his brigade commander Colonel Richard Linton had died at sea after a troopship had been torpedoed, Watson temporarily commanded the 6th Brigade for its landing. On the night of 10-11 September the 24th took over positions at Lone Pine. In addition to hardship caused by the onset of cold weather, they suffered casualties from suffocation in the shallow tunnels and dug-outs when the Turks bombarded them in November. During the evacuation of Gallipoli, Watson successfully commanded the 6th Brigade rear parties; for his service on the peninsula he was appointed C.B. and again mentioned in dispatches.

In March 1916 the 24th Battalion sailed for France and in April moved into the line at Fleurbaix. Near Albert, on the night of 7-8 August a shell burst in an old gun-pit occupied by battalion headquarters. Watson was the sole survivor. Admitted to hospital with shell-shock, he resumed command on 12 October. He took charge of the 2nd Division Training School in November. In May 1917 he resumed command of the 24th Battalion, but in July returned to England where he had charge of the 17th Brigade; in September he was appointed commandant of the Overseas Training Depot near Warminster. He immediately convened a court martial to deal with outstanding cases, re-wrote standing orders and introduced more effective training programmes. He was promoted colonel on 1 June 1918. Desertion by Australian troops on leave in England had increased. On one occasion, when a draft paraded before returning to France, a soldier protested that he would not go unless he were carried. Watson had him tied to an ambulance and dragged with the draft until he begged to be released. In December Watson was appointed C.M.G.; in January 1919 he became commander of the A.I.F. depot at Sutton Veny.

From April until July Watson took special leave to participate in the A.I.F. non-military employment scheme and was involved in the manufacture of cardboard at Anthony Hordern [q.v.4] & Sons in London. He embarked for Australia in September and was awarded the Légion d'honneur in December. After demobilization he became chairman of directors of Cumberland Paper Board Mills Ltd, a member of the New South Wales Club and the National Club, and an adherent of the National Party.

Allegedly as the result of a chill caught at the funeral of Brigadier General Henry Finn [q.v.8], Watson died in Sydney of septicaemia on 30 June 1924 and was buried with Anglican rites in South Head cemetery. He was survived by his wife. Typical of the better A.I.F. commanders, he was respected by his troops; he was intensely loyal to them, but would not tolerate those who sought to evade their responsibilities.

Aust Defence Dept, *Official records of the Australian military contingents to the war in South Africa*, P. L. Murray ed (Melb, 1911); W. J. Harvey, *The red and white diamond* (Melb, 1920); C. E. W. Bean, *The story of Anzac*, 2 (Syd, 1924) and *The A.I.F. in France*, 1916-1918 (Syd, 1929, 1933, 1937, 1942); S. S. Mackenzie, *The Australians at Rabaul* (Syd, 1927); *London Gazette*, 18 Apr 1901, 3 June, 11 July 1916, 2 Jan 1917, 31 Dec 1918; *Despatch*, Sept 1978; *SMH*, 10 Jan, 2, 24 Apr, 7 Aug 1900, 26 Feb, 2 May 1901, 1, 2 July 1924; AWM records *and* War diary, 24th Battalion *and* Overseas Training Brigade (AWM); W. W. R. Watson, Personal scrap-book, 1900-1922 (ML); information from Univ Syd, Syd High School, Major J. Cotter, Syd, and Mr K. W. Watson, Balgowlah, NSW.
                                        R. SUTTON

WATT, ERNEST ALEXANDER STUART (1874-1954), shipowner, pastoralist and patron of the arts, was born on 8 December 1874 in Sydney, third son of Scottish-born John Brown Watt [q.v.6], merchant, and his native-born wife Mary Jane, daughter of G. K. Holden [q.v.4]. Educated in England at Clifton College, Bristol, Ernest took the history tripos at King's College, Cambridge (B.A., 1896; M.A., 1901).

Coming home on his father's death in 1897, Watt inherited a share in Llanlillo station, Walgett. He married Annie Elizabeth Caroline Weston on 3 April 1900 at St Mark's Anglican Church, Darling Point, and took her to London; they had two daughters before being divorced. Called to the Bar at the Inner Temple on 26 January 1905, Watt read for a year with the eminent counsel Frank Newbolt, then joined David L. Thompson & Co., stockbrokers. He published *Love letters of a genius* (1905) which he had translated from the French of Prosper Mérimée, *Pauline's book of poetry* (1911) and an anthology, *A diary and other indiscretions* (1914).

On 22 February 1912 at the register office, Hanover Square, Watt married Marie Margeurite Beerbohm, a 22-year-old niece of Max Beerbohm. Rejected for active service, Watt taught at Boxgrove School, Guildford, Surrey. His marriage soon ended in divorce. On 23 June 1917 at the Guildford register office he married Bertha Marion Ada Campbell, daughter of Dr A. J. Brady of Sydney and widow of Captain Prowse, R.N.; they were to have a daughter. *To Bertha and other verses* appeared in 1919.

Back in Sydney by 1920, Watt was a director of the family shipping firm, Gilchrist, Watt & Sanderson Ltd, the Liverpool and London and Globe Insurance Co. Ltd, Wallarah Coal Co. Ltd, Sayers, Allport Pty Ltd and Koitaki Para Rubber Estates Ltd (New Guinea); he was also founding chairman of the New South Wales Cremation Co. Ltd. He extended his pastoral interests to Kurrabooma, Moree, and cattle stations in Queensland (Strathmore, Bowen, and Glen Prairie, Rockhampton). While supporting the Empire and the Church of England, he was not politically-minded, though he described himself as a 'Democrat'.

His tribute to his brother, *Oswald Watt* [q.v.] (1921), brought Ernest into close contact with his co-editors Sydney Ure Smith [q.v.11] and Bertram Stevens [q.v.]. In 1922 Watt became a director of Ure Smith's Art in Australia Ltd and took a great interest in the *Home*, swamping the office with glamorous and giggling misses, eager to be photographed. In 1927 he bought, and with Hugh McCrae [q.v.10] edited, the short-lived magazine, *New Triad*. Watt was a generous supporter of Australian artists and writers,

especially the Lindsay brothers [qq.v.10], and collected good paintings. (Sir) Charles Lloyd Jones [q.v.9] became his close friend.

A popular man about town, Watt belonged to the Union and Australian clubs in Sydney and to the Melbourne Club. He loved the theatre and acted in amateur productions, once playing the title role in *The importance of being earnest*. He had played cricket at Cambridge; later he took up bridge and was a member of Royal Sydney Golf Club; a racehorse owner, he belonged to the Australian Jockey and Rosehill Racing clubs and had a seat in the private stand at Newmarket, England.

Again divorced, on 2 September 1929 Watt married 23-year-old Ruth Edmunds Massey in the registry office, Sydney. They lived with their daughter at Darling Point and later at Point Piper. About 5 ft. 10 ins. (177.8 cm) tall, with light brown hair and blue eyes, Watt 'spoke with a quiet, pleasant drawl and moved with a leisurely gait as though time were no object. He was immensely vague, pre-occupied and unpredictable ... capable of flashes of anger'. His personality baffled Leon Gellert, who was 'very, very fond of him'. Survived by his wife and by his four daughters, Watt died at Paddington on 18 February 1954 and was cremated with Anglican rites. His estate was sworn for probate at £117 265.

Daily Telegraph (Syd) and *SMH*, 19 Feb 1954; *Sunday Telegraph* (Syd), 15 Jan 1967; family information from Lady Street, Syd.

MARTHA RUTLEDGE

WATT, SIR ROBERT DICKIE (1881-1965), agricultural scientist, was born on 23 April 1881 at Knocklandside, near Kilmaurs, Ayrshire, Scotland, second son of John Watt, farmer, and his wife Agnes Taylor, née Dickie. Watt's elder brother Hugh became professor of church history at the University of Edinburgh and moderator of the General Assembly of the Church of Scotland. After early education at Kilmaurs, Robert entered Kilmarnock Academy. From the age of 16 he worked on his father's home farm, a tenancy within Lord Rowallan's estate, for three years before enrolling in arts and later science at the University of Glasgow (M.A., 1903; B.Sc., 1905). Some of the agricultural subjects were taught at the affiliated West of Scotland Agricultural College. Watt also obtained national diplomas in dairying, and in agriculture (with first-class honours and first place in Britain).

Awarded a Carnegie research scholarship, he undertook research at Rothamsted Experiment Station outside London in 1905-07. He was appointed agricultural chemist in the Transvaal Department of Agriculture at

Pretoria. In 1908 he became chief chemist, but next year accepted the foundation chair of agriculture in the faculty of science at the University of Sydney.

Reaching Sydney from Britain in February 1910, Watt single-handedly began to devise an agricultural curriculum of university standard; the first four students were admitted in 1911. Watt relied to some extent on members of the science faculty and part-time lecturers from the New South Wales Department of Agriculture, but inevitably taught much of the course himself. Moreover, he had to persuade the State government to fund the construction of an agriculture building, a goal which was achieved early in 1916. On 3 June that year at Randwick he married Marjorie Dymock (Madge) Forsyth, by whom he was to have a daughter; they lived at Vaucluse (1929-46).

In 1920 agriculture became a faculty in its own right with Watt as dean until 1946. He was a fellow of the senate of the university in 1934-35 and 1946. In 1921 he had succeeded in having W. L. Waterhouse [q.v.] appointed to the staff. Thereafter they had a fruitful association and together established the reputation of the Sydney faculty. Watt concentrated on teaching and administration, leaving to Waterhouse the task of instilling in undergraduates the essentials of scientific discipline and a knowledge of agricultural research procedures.

His role in the emerging science of agriculture led to Watt's appointment to the State and executive committees of the Commonwealth Advisory Council of Science and Industry (1916-19) and its successor, the Institute of Science and Industry (1919-26). He investigated prickly pear and helped to eradicate 'bunchy top', a serious virus disease of bananas. With the formal establishment in 1926 of the Commonwealth Council for Scientific and Industrial Research, Watt chaired the State committee until 1941 (and was *ex officio* on its council); he remained a member until 1965.

In 1922 Watt chaired the Murray Lands Advisory Committee, appointed by the New South Wales, Victorian and Commonwealth governments to report on the suitability of Murray River lands as irrigation settlements. He was a trustee of the Public Library of New South Wales (1915-46), member of the Australian National Research Council (1919-54), president of section K (agriculture) of the Australasian Association for the Advancement of Science (1924) and president of the Royal Society of New South Wales (1926). State (1935) and federal (1939-40) president of the Australian Institute of Agricultural Science, he was elected a fellow in 1960. A life member of the Royal Agricultural Society of New South Wales (1935), he received the

Farrer [q.v.8] memorial medal in 1950 and was knighted in 1960.

After he retired in 1946, Watt maintained his professional interests and did research on Australian agricultural history which he published as *The romance of the Australian land industries* (1955). For a time he acted as executive officer of the Men of the Land Society. He was a keen golfer and a member of the Royal Sydney Golf Club from 1941.

A tall, upright, distinguished figure, Watt was reserved but well spoken with his Scottish brogue. He observed and expected the proprieties of the time (he did not meet his students in private unless gowned) and he tolerated no nonsense. He took a keen interest in his students' extracurricular activities and actively encouraged them in their sporting endeavours. He was well liked, even loved, by the many students who passed through his hands, being affectionately known by them privately as 'Robert Dickie'. In committee he spoke only after due consideration and was generally respected, but he could be determined in his own bailiwick and authoritarian in university administrative matters.

Survived by his wife and daughter, Sir Robert died in St Vincent's Hospital of a brain tumour on 10 April 1965. He was cremated after a service at St Stephen's Presbyterian Church, Macquarie Street, of which he had been an elder since 1928. A portrait of him by Arthur Murch is held by the university and the original agriculture building has been named after him.

N. Yeates, *Robert Dickie Watt Kt.* (priv pub, Coffs Harbour, NSW, 1987); *T&CJ*, 5 Jan, 2 Mar 1910; *SMH*, 16 Apr 1965.   KEITH O. CAMPBELL

WATT, WALTER OSWALD (1878-1921), airman, grazier and merchant, was born on 11 February 1878 at Bournemouth, Hampshire, England, youngest son of Scottish-born John Brown Watt [q.v.6], merchant, and his native-born wife Mary Jane, daughter of G. K. Holden [q.v.4]; his elder brother was Ernest Alexander Stuart Watt [q.v.]. After his mother's death when he was aged 1, Oswald spent ten years in Sydney before being educated in England at Clifton College, Bristol, and Trinity College, Cambridge (B.A., 1899; M.A., 1904). Returning to Sydney in 1900, he was commissioned second lieutenant in the New South Wales Scottish Rifles and in 1902 was appointed an aide-de-camp to the State governor. He bought Howlong station at Carrathool and had interests in Llanillo, Goonal and Gunningrah, New South Wales, as well as in Queensland cattle-stations, Strathmore at Bowen and Glen Prairie at Rockhampton. On 27 September 1902 at St John's Anglican Church, Toorak, Melbourne, he married

Muriel Maud, daughter of Sir Hartley Williams [q.v.6]. Having learned to fly at Salisbury Plain, Wiltshire, England, Watt set up as a civilian pilot in 1911.

Following his divorce in 1913, he spent several months flying his Bleriot XI in Egypt and travelled to France in 1914. Thinking that Britain would not be involved in a European war, he offered his services and his plane to the French and became an ordinary soldier in the Aviation Militaire section of the French Foreign Legion. He was awarded the Légion d'honneur and the Croix de Guerre, and given the brevet rank of captain. As he was not a French citizen, he could not be placed in a position of command. In 1916 he transferred to the newly formed Australian Flying Corps, with the rank of captain and command of B Flight, No.1 Squadron, then stationed in Egypt.

In September he was promoted major and took command of No.2 Squadron which was being formed in Egypt. The new squadron was sent to England for training in early 1917 and arrived on the Western Front in September. C. E. W. Bean [q.v.7] visited No.2 Squadron after the battle of Cambrai and recorded his impressions of its work: 'They are winning themselves a magnificent name, this first Australian fighting squadron ... It is Watt who has worked them up to this remarkably high level of conduct and general tone'. As squadron commander Watt worked long hours, rising at 5 a.m. to give moral support to his dawn patrols; according to Bean, the heavy fighting at Cambrai had left Watt 'very wan ... he fell asleep after dinner'. In February 1918 Watt—by then a lieut-colonel —was promoted to command the four squadrons (Nos. 5, 6, 7 and 8) of the Australian training wing at Tetbury, Gloucestershire, England. He excelled as a leader who inspired his crews with his ideals of service. The novelist W. J. Locke visited him after the Armistice and noted 'there was not one who ... did not confide to me his pride in serving under a leader so distinguished'.

Watt came back to Australia in 1919. He had been appointed O.B.E. that January and was elected president of the New South Wales section of the Australian Aero Club. After the war he lobbied politicians for improved safety measures in civil aviation; he was known for his generosity to former A.F.C. comrades and for his efforts to find them employment. In 1920 he was offered the position of controller of civil aviation, but declined because of business commitments: he was a partner in Gilchrist, Watt & Sanderson Ltd, the family shipping firm, and a director of the Australian Alum Co., the Great Britain Tin Mining Co., the Sogeri Para Rubber Co. and Art in Australia Ltd. 'Toby' Watt drowned at Bilgola Beach, Newport, New South Wales, on 21 May 1921. He was buried with full military honours and his ashes were interred in St Jude's churchyard, Randwick; his estate was sworn for probate at £176 846; he was survived by his only son.

Oswald Watt (Syd, 1921); F. M. Cutlack, *The Australian Flying Corps* (Syd, 1923); K. Isaacs, *Military aircraft of Australia, 1909-1918* (Canb, 1971); *Reveille* (Syd), 1 June 1939; *Daily Telegraph* (Syd), 23 May 1921; *SMH*, 2 June 1921; information from Mr A. Fraser, Canb, and Mr C. Schaedel, Adel.

SUSAN JOHNSTON

WATT, WILLIAM ALEXANDER (1871-1946), premier and acting prime minister, was born on 23 November 1871 at Barfold, near Kyneton, Victoria, eleventh and youngest child of James Michie Watt, a farmer who had migrated from Scotland about 1843, and his Methodist wife Jane, née Douglas, from Ireland. After James's death in 1872, the family moved to Phillip Island and some six years later settled in North Melbourne. Billy attended the Errol Street State School and was a newsboy. He joined an ironmongery, then a tannery, as a clerk, and, after ten years supporting his mother and a sister, became accountant and eventually a partner in a hay and corn store, Barwise & Co. On 21 December 1894 he married Florence Carrighan at the Presbyterian Church, Parkville; she was to die after childbirth in 1896.

'A precocious boy, a smart lad, and a clever young man', Watt had ambitions of becoming 'the complete orator', but learned to fight in Royal Park and a lasting rumour associated him with a local 'push'. He read voraciously, frequenting the Public Library, and from 1888 undertook night studies at the Working Men's College in accountancy, grammar, logic, mental philosophy and elocution. By 1893 he was secretary of the North Melbourne Debating Club. W. S. Robinson recalled his brother (Sir) Arthur [qq.v.11] and Watt at the Parkville Literary and Debating Society addressing 'the assembled multitude, chiefly in the form of my solitary self, on political issues'. Watt also gathered friends for weekly discussions of topical questions.

He joined the Australian Natives' Association, probably before 1890. The North Melbourne team, with Watt winding up, won the metropolitan debating competition three times in the mid-1890s. A delegate (1895-1901) to annual conferences and a president of the metropolitan committee, he was famous for his recitation of 'The Man from Snowy River' at smoke-nights. From 1894 he was an executive member of the A.N.A.-inspired Australasian Federation League of Victoria and campaigned vigorously for the 'holy cause' in 1898, especially at the crucial A.N.A. conference in March at Bendigo.

In October 1897 Watt had been elected to the Legislative Assembly for Melbourne North over the fiery Labor member George Prendergast [q.v.11]. The *Age* and conservative voters backed Watt in a turbulent campaign; always combative, he enjoyed the cut and thrust. Although anti-socialist, he stood for radical liberal reform of 'a social order, where the *few* sit on the shoulders of the *many*'. He was soon identified with other A.N.A. members known as the 'Young Australia' group who, indignant first with Premier Turner's [q.v.] equivocation over the Federal bill, later criticized the government's cautious land, taxation and factories legislation. In October 1899 Watt was boldly sceptical about the wisdom of sending a contingent to the South African War, but later became conventionally bellicose.

The 'Young Australia' group helped to dismiss Turner in November and Allan McLean [q.v.10] invited Watt to become postmaster-general: he was the only city member in cabinet and, at 28, reportedly the youngest cabinet minister in the Empire; he survived a desperately hard-fought ministerial election. A capable minister who tried hard to bring about the penny post and the Pacific cable connexion, he was sometimes accused of autocracy and egotism. The realities of office tempered his radicalism but, having isolated himself from the Turner-Labor alliance, he lost his seat at the November 1900 election.

Watt stood unsuccessfully for the first Commonwealth Senate as a Protectionist, and was twice more defeated for the assembly, but helped his idol Alfred Deakin [q.v.8] to build a national Liberal organization. Having opened an estate agency and moved to Moonee Ponds, he was returned to the assembly for Melbourne East in October 1902 and for Essendon in June 1904. He was a supporter in principle of his friend (Sir) William Irvine [q.v.9], but concentrated on establishing an independent position; seeing Labor as the chief enemy, he determined to bring about a two-party alignment. He still staunchly supported reform of the Legislative Council, the female franchise, further factory legislation and protection of the weak. With his friend J. A. Boyd [q.v.7], he sniped at Premier Bent [q.v.3]. According to (Sir) Frederic Eggleston [q.v.8], 'The history of the Bent Ministry is a duel between Bent and Watt; for a long time Bent was invulnerable, but ... he gradually succumbed'. John Murray [q.v.10] resigned from the ministry in August 1906 and allied himself with Watt. They eventually brought down Bent on 3 December 1908 and won the following election.

After Murray became premier on 8 January 1909 in a composite ministry, largely of countrymen, Watt was treasurer almost uninterruptedly until June 1914. He was the government's driving force, even before acting as premier for six months in 1911 and before the tiring Murray passed the premiership to him in May 1912. W. L. Baillieu, J. D. Brown and George Graham [qq.v.7,9] were leading colleagues. An expanding economy supported rural development policies, decentralization, lavish government spending and further instalments of 'state socialism'. The government swept to victory at the November 1911 election.

As always the Legislative Council obstructed. In 1909-10 it rejected compulsory land acquisition, radical land taxation and optional preferential voting; but it tolerated the establishment of state secondary education (Watt had vigorously supported Frank Tate [q.v.]) and in 1911 gave way on land taxation and preferential voting. Guided by Elwood Mead [q.v.10] in the purchase of irrigable lands, the government furthered closer settlement which it linked with railway construction and assisted immigration. In 1911-12 it undertook a massive legislative programme, involving wholesale reorganization of public services. The Country Roads Board was established, the Melbourne Harbor Trust reorganized and electrification of suburban railways was accepted. Hospitals and charities, workers' compensation and Greater Melbourne legislation had to be delayed. Watt significantly developed 'state socialism' in Victoria—'anything the State can do for the State better than others, let the State do'— and especially the use of the statutory corporation.

Absent from February to July 1913, Watt impressively negotiated a large conversion loan in England. In 1912 many of his nominal supporters had begun to caucus as a 'country party'. Hoping to force reconstruction of the ministry, in July 1913 Donald McLeod [q.v.10] moved a want of confidence motion and attacked in particular the transfer of government functions to 'irresponsible boards'. Watt replied with harsh invective and the countrymen withdrew. In December, however, he introduced redistribution legislation, re-valuing a metropolitan vote merely from 50 to 60 per cent of a non-metropolitan vote. Enough countrymen voted with Labor to defeat the government, whereupon Watt resigned and the Labor leader George Elmslie [q.v.8] was commissioned. Master of the situation, Watt brought his followers to heel: Labor was defeated after one week in office and he reconstructed his ministry with additional radical Liberals. He then enacted workers' compensation legislation, but postponed redistribution, Greater Melbourne, and hospitals and charities regulation.

Watt developed his unrivalled reputation as a financier during the long negotiations between Commonwealth and States for adjustments after the initial ten-year financial agreement. His proposals at the 1914 premiers' conference concerning State debts and a national borrowing policy were far-sighted, if premature: Watt looked to unification in the distant future. Meanwhile, he fervently opposed the Fisher [q.v.8] Labor government's attempts in 1911 and 1913 to transfer major powers by referendum, in the belief that the States must continue to control developmental policies. At the 1912 premiers' conference he took the lead in formulating proposals by the States to transfer powers voluntarily. He resisted the new Commonwealth Bank's encroachment on the State banks' activities. In 1913-14 he contributed crucially to the final difficult settlement of the Murray Waters Agreement.

Eggleston studs his account of Watt with superlatives—the dominant force in Victorian politics, a man who tackled the hard problems, a great parliamentarian, orator and debater—but Watt could be rash and sometimes lapsed into intolerance and scorching sarcasm. Roy Bridges [q.v.7], the *Age* journalist, became Watt's close friend and regarded him as 'a great Australian, generous, sympathetic, democratic, unpretentious'.

It was widely believed that Deakin regarded Watt as his successor. His oration at Deakin's funeral was to be generally regarded as superb. Just before the outbreak of World War I, 'after 48 hours self-searching', Watt yielded to party blandishments and, as an obvious potential prime minister, resigned the premiership in order to contest Balaclava and campaign for (Sir) Joseph Cook's [q.v.8] government; he comfortably defeated John Curtin and thanked Herbert Brookes [q.v.7] for the 'part you played in dragging me across'.

Labor's victory in September 1914 was a setback to Watt who must have expected a ministry. He threw himself into support for the war effort and, apprehensive of divisiveness, muted his criticisms of the government's war measures. His negotiations late in 1915 with (Sir) Alexander Peacock [q.v.11] avoided a referendum by securing an offer from the premiers to transfer limited powers for the duration of the war. From July 1915 Watt was a member of the parliamentary war committee. He was already convinced that the government should introduce conscription and his fiery patriotic speeches made him the darling of the powerful Australian Women's National League. Yet his attack on Frank Brennan [q.v.7] for 'pigeon-livered' pacifist tendencies led to Brennan challenging him to meet at a recruiting office; Watt avoided the issue.

The failure of the conscription plebiscite and the Labor split in November 1916 led Watt, Irvine and J. N. H. Hume Cook [q.v.8] to work for a national government. The non-party National Referendum Council (of which Watt had been joint secretary) was a useful basis for a 'Win-the-War' party. The process took ten weeks. Sir John Forrest [q.v.8], Irvine and Cook all claimed leadership: Watt knew it had to be Hughes, and threatened Cook with the secession of Victorians from the Liberal Party. The National Federation was launched in Melbourne on 9 January 1917; the Liberal Party was finally coerced on 8 February and the National ministry was formed on 17 February. Watt had been chief architect and drafter of policy.

Hughes preferred Watt as treasurer, but was obliged to give Forrest the post: Watt had to be content with works and railways, and saw the transcontinental railway through its final stages. He supported Hughes in holding the second conscription plebiscite and in the fiasco of charging T. J. Ryan [q.v.11] with conspiracy. When Hughes kept his pledge to resign, Watt advised Governor-General Munro Ferguson [q.v.10] not to commission Forrest with whom he had repeatedly clashed in cabinet. After Hughes resumed office, he and Watt conspired to make Forrest a lord; once Forrest resigned, Watt at last became treasurer on 27 March 1918, having acted for a month. In April Hughes and Cook sailed for London. Watt was acting prime minister, eventually for sixteen months.

Almost his first action was to introduce a formal agenda for and minutes of cabinet meetings. In order to ensure (Viscount) S. M. Bruce's [q.v.7] success at the Flinders by-election in May, in return for the withdrawal of the Farmers' candidate he promised and later carried out introduction of preferential voting. Cabinet accepted General Sir William Birdwood's [q.v.7] recommendation of (Sir) John Monash [q.v.10] as commander of the Australian Corps. Late in the year Watt abruptly gazetted Jens Jensen [q.v.9] out of the ministry after an adverse royal commission report on defence expenditure. He quickly pulled the Nationalist politicians together and conciliated Labor by modifying coercion to stimulate voluntary recruitment. Leading a weak and weary ministry while in precarious health, he brought comparative calm to government, but told Hughes several times that he hoped he would soon return to relieve him.

Watt had found both the Treasury and the Prime Minister's Office in confusion. War finance was in a parlous state and a huge debt was mounting for Britain's maintenance of Australian troops. In July he insisted that the premiers stop borrowing and reduce public works. His austere budget heavily increased taxation; he introduced a bill, abandoned with the peace, that required subscription to war loans according to means. Fearful for the future, he continued austerity during 1919. His concern for State rights was now subordinated to the needs of the nation.

Hughes, in England, had often taken initiatives without consultation. Watt, however, was also tactless and inconsiderate, and their acerbic exchanges in hundreds of often delayed ciphered cables inevitably led to friction, especially over extension of the wool agreement with the British government and wheat sales. After the Armistice innumerable issues of external policy arose which the government had not discussed before Hughes's departure. Watt and the cabinet became increasingly concerned about the prime minister keeping them uninformed and about his public confrontations with the Imperial government. They backed him when Lloyd George accepted President Wilson's Fourteen Points without consulting the Dominions, but, sensitive to Imperial ties, resisted his assertion of particular Australian interests and his campaign for separate Dominion representation at the peace conference: Hughes took no notice. Watt established a Pacific branch of the Prime Minister's Department under E. L. Piesse [q.v.11], without consulting the prime minister. Hughes began selling Commonwealth ships, without notifying Watt. Cabinet joined Hughes in opposition to Wilson's insistence on League of Nations control of German colonies, but preferred Imperial annexation and Australian administration to Hughes's demand for Australian annexation. In response to Hughes's offensive attitude to Japan, Watt issued a statement of admiration for Japan's conduct as a British ally. Hughes and Watt had developed a deep antagonism. After Hughes returned in August 1919, Watt had to be persuaded to continue in the government beyond the December election.

A supercilious Munro Ferguson at first was restive about Watt's casual methods, his limited appreciation of the governor-general's constitutional role and his disinclination to take the award of honours entirely seriously. He eventually came to admire Watt's broadmindedness and his 'grasp of the financial and commercial situation . . . he is extremely reasonable and a very pleasant man to discuss business with. He can see both sides of a case and his judgement can be relied on'. It was doubtful if even Hughes had rendered better war service.

In April 1920 Watt sailed for England for vital financial negotiations. Meanwhile Hughes pursued negotiations on wool, without informing him. In June Watt resigned as treasurer, in a distraught state: 'I was credentialled to London as a Minister Plenipo-

tentiary, but upon my arrival had no greater powers than a messenger boy'. On his tardy return in October, he delivered a detailed self-defence in parliament, charging Hughes with deliberately setting out to destroy a rival, but was generally disregarded. Watt had married Emily Helena Seismann at Essendon on 24 April 1907 and had five young children for whom he was anxious to provide. He had refused a knighthood, partly because he considered he had inadequate means to live up to it, but had delighted in his appointment as privy counsellor in 1920; he was also made commander of the Légion d'honneur.

Though seeming to be, almost inevitably, the next prime minister, Watt had muffed the chance. Over the next two years he veered between deciding to leave politics for a business career and making a last throw for high office. In 1918-19 he had been incapacitated for weeks with heart trouble and nervous tension. His health now improved. A lone wolf, he attacked Hughes's wool policy, and Cook's and Bruce's budgets, and rarely attended party meetings. He lost all credibility with Nationalist politicians who looked to (Sir) Walter Massy-Greene [q.v.10] as Hughes's likely replacement. Watt was behind much Victorian criticism within the party in 1922, but publicly remained aloof from the anti-Hughes Liberal Union. He often conferred, however, with (Sir) Earle Page [q.v.11], an admirer who saw him as a possible leading colleague in the future.

When Hughes was deposed early in 1923 in favour of Bruce and Page, Watt was feared as too much of a danger to leave free on the back-benches: he was offered and accepted the speakership for one term. By this stage Watt was essentially a conservative Imperialist who opposed equal status of the Dominions with Britain. The radical Victorian Deakinite strain disappeared as an influence in Commonwealth politics. He was a very successful Speaker, quick, decisive and popular; his weekly afternoon teas helped to promote 'fruitful social intercourse between the parties'. In 1926 he resumed sniping against the government, yet his stature was such that his party endorsement was renewed. He was active in debate in 1927 over the Financial Agreement with the States which he eventually accepted; in 1944, in his preface to Deakin's The Federal story, he finally declared himself a unificationist. After parliament moved to Canberra, he attended less than half the sitting-days and spoke rarely. On medical advice, he resigned his seat in July 1929.

From 1922 Watt had been chairman of Australian Farms Ltd which aimed to attract migrants with capital; it was liquidated in 1925. As chairman, he saw Dunlop-Perdriau [q.v.11] Rubber Co. successfully through the Depression, but declined a governing directorship. From his base in Collins House, he was also chairman of the Aeolian Co. (Aust) Ltd, British Dominion Film Ltd, Jalan Kebun Rubber Co., Taranaki Oil Fields Ltd, Rolfe & Co. Ltd and of the local boards of Silverton Tramway Co. Ltd and Zinc Corporation Ltd, and a director of QANTAS Empire Airways Ltd and other companies. During the Depression he was notably sympathetic to the unemployed and workers suffering wagecuts. A member of the Imperial Federation League, he was first Victorian president of the English-Speaking Union and revered King George V and Queen Mary. He was never happier than when watching Test cricket as chairman of the Melbourne ground trustees.

With deep-set eyes, Watt had a broad, pugnacious face and was clean-shaven. Known in middle age as William, Will or Willy (never as Bill), he began to compensate for his early teetotalism and remained a pipe-smoker. His manner was breezy, his humour witty though mordant, his aplomb marred by fits of temper; his intimates included W. S. Robinson (to whom he was 'always a wonderful friend and helper'), W. L. Baillieu and W. A. Holman [q.v.9], and he had many Jewish friends. A fine player of bridge, he was a convivial member of the Yorick, Athenaeum, West Brighton and Victoria Golf clubs; he disliked pomp, formality and attending Government House. He was a masterful parent. A stroke in 1937 partly disabled him. An agnostic, he died at his Toorak home on 13 September 1946 and was cremated; his wife, two sons and three daughters survived him. His estate was sworn for probate at £37 256. Portraits by Phillips Fox and Longstaff [qq.v.8,10] are held in the Savage Club, Melbourne, and in Parliament House, Canberra.

E. H. Sugden and F. W. Eggleston, *George Swinburne* (Syd, 1931); R. Bridges, *That yesterday was home* (Syd, 1948); E. C. G. Page, *Truant surgeon*, A. Mozley ed (Syd, 1963); W. S. Robinson, *If I remember rightly*, G. Blainey ed (Melb, 1967); F. C. Green, *Servant of the House* (Melb, 1969); L. F. Fitzhardinge, *The little digger* (Syd, 1979); P. G. Edwards, *Prime ministers and diplomats* (Melb, 1983); *Punch* (Melb), 26 July 1906, 29 July 1909, 23 May 1912; *Table Talk*, 1 Nov 1928; *Argus*, 25 May 1912; *Age*, 9 Apr 1938; J. S. Anderson, W. A. Watt: a political biography (M.A. thesis, Univ NSW, 1972); J. Hume Cook, Recollections and reflections. The story of my life, ts, 1935 *and* Brookes *and* Deakin *and* Groom *and* Makin *and* Novar papers (NL); family information.   JOHN ANDERSON
GEOFFREY SERLE

WATT, WILLIAM SHAND (1876-1958), mining engineer and meteorologist, was born on 2 January 1876 at Green Island, Dunedin, New Zealand, sixth of eleven children of Dr Michael Watt, Presbyterian minister, and his wife Isabella, née Shand, both Scottish born. He attended the Otago Boys' High School, Dunedin, and the Otago School of Mines, gaining an associateship in mining and a certificate of metallurgical chemistry and assaying (1900). In 1902 he obtained an associateship in metallurgy.

He spent time at Kalgoorlie, Western Australia, before lecturing in mining engineering at the Zeehan School of Mines, Tasmania. On 2 January 1907 at St Paul's Church, Ascot Vale, Melbourne, Watt married Hilda Muriel Maude with Anglican rites; they were to remain childless. At Zeehan Watt acted as meteorological observer in addition to teaching. In 1911 he came first in a competitive examination for the post of Tasmanian divisional officer in the newly established Commonwealth Bureau of Meteorology. In 1921 he transferred to Melbourne as head of the bureau's climatological section. He was appointed assistant director in 1927 and in June 1931 succeeded H. A. Hunt [q.v.9] as Commonwealth meteorologist.

The promotion was not straightforward: there was concern in meteorological circles that the position had been inadequately advertised abroad and reservations were held about the calibre of the local applicants. Within the public service itself the post was eagerly contested. As acting Commonwealth meteorologist Watt successfully appealed against the initial appointment of H. Barkley, the bureau's assistant research director.

Watt's term as Commonwealth meteorologist coincided with the expansion of aircraft services that led to a demand for more accurate weather forecasting. To assist in the 1934 London to Melbourne air race, the bureau established an office in Darwin which later became an integral part of the war effort. During the 1930s meteorological offices were opened at Australian airports. The bureau's staff grew dramatically and Watt introduced a special education section which offered formal training courses for meteorologists and observers. In August 1935 he represented Australia at a British Empire meteorology conference in London and went in September to a larger international gathering in Warsaw. In 1937 he attended a conference in New Zealand which considered meteorological aspects of the proposed trans-Tasman air services. He retired in 1941. Survived by his wife, Watt died on 15 April 1958 in Brighton Private Hospital, Melbourne, and was cremated.

Sharing with his father the advantages of a liberal education, Watt was versed in the classics as well as in engineering and science. The bureau remembered him as a man of wit, with 'a reminiscence or story to suit every occasion'. His brother Dr Michael H. Watt

(1887-1967) was director-general of health in New Zealand in 1931-48.

Argus, 7 Jan, 24 Feb, 21 Apr, 19 June 1931, 28 Nov 1934, 21 June, 23 Aug, 19 Sept, 30 Oct 1935; information from Bureau of Meteorology, Melb, *and* Hist Records Cttee, Presbyterian Church, Dunedin, *and* Otago Boys' High School, *and* Otago School of Mines.   HEATHER NASH

WATTERSTON, DAVID (1845-1931), journalist, was born on 2 January 1845 at Balgone Barns, Haddingtonshire, Scotland, youngest son of James Watterston and his wife Catherine, née Broadwood. He came to Victoria with his parents in 1853 and was educated privately and at denominational schools in Melbourne. In 1860, after being employed for two years as a lawyer's clerk, he moved with his widowed mother and two sisters to Queensland where he worked as a junior reporter with the *Ipswich Herald (Queensland Times)*. Joining the *Brisbane Courier* in 1865, he became a member of its parliamentary reporting staff, while also contributing articles to the *Queensland Express* and *Queensland Guardian*.

In 1869 Watterston returned to Melbourne as a reporter for the *Argus*; he remained in that post until 1873 when he went to London to receive specialist treatment for eye trouble. Back in Victoria in 1875, he worked briefly for the Department of Education where one of his colleagues was J. F. Archibald [q.v.3]. Watterston rejoined the *Argus* in 1876 and was sent to the United States of America to cover the Philadelphia Centennial Exhibition. In 1879 he accompanied the Victorian premier (Sir) Graham Berry [q.v.3] to London and covered Berry's unsuccessful mission to persuade the secretary of state for the colonies to introduce a bill into the Imperial parliament to amend the Constitution of Victoria. Watterston represented the *Argus* at the Sydney International Exhibition at the Garden Palace and in 1880 took charge of newspaper work connected with the exhibition in Melbourne. He was special correspondent for the *Argus* during the Australian tour of the princes, Edward (duke of Clarence) and George (King George V), in 1881. Later that year he became chief of the *Argus* reporting staff.

Appointed editor of the *Australasian* in 1885, Watterston held that position with distinction for eighteen years. From 1903 to 1906 he was editor of the *Argus*, after which he became representative of the trustees of the Edward Wilson [q.v.6] estate on the council of management of the *Argus* and *Australasian*. He retired in 1928. Respected for his wit, insight and knowledge of public affairs, he showed as an editor 'rare literary discrimi-

nation, a just sense of values and a mastery of detail'. He believed that he served the proprietors best when he served the public best.

Seen by Melbourne *Punch* in 1914 as 'a tall, gaunt, stern, grey-haired, grey-bearded man', Watterston was regarded as one of the ablest newspapermen of his generation. He had been part of a brilliant coterie of writers for the *Argus* in the 1880s and 1890s, among them Marcus Clarke and 'The Vagabond', J. S. James [qq.v.3,4]. An enthusiastic amateur botanist, Watterston numbered among his many friends (Sir) Baldwin Spencer [q.v.], whom he had recruited as science writer for the *Australasian*. Watterston was a member of the Melbourne Club and a life member of the Yorick Club where his portrait by John Longstaff [q.v.10] was hung. He died, unmarried, at his Armadale home on 23 July 1931 and was buried in Boroondara cemetery.

H. Gordon, *An eyewitness history of Australia* (Adel, 1976); D. J. Mulvaney and J. H. Calaby, '*So much that is new*' (Melb, 1985); *Newspaper News* (Perth), 1 Aug 1931; *Punch* (Melb), 6 Aug 1914; *Argus*, 24 July 1931; *Bulletin*, 29 July 1931.
                                                    JOHN HURST

WATT DE BEUZEVILLE, WILFRED ALEXANDER; *see* DE BEUZEVILLE

WAY, SIR SAMUEL JAMES (1836-1916), chief justice and lieutenant-governor, was born on 11 April 1836 at Portsmouth, Hampshire, England, eldest son of James Way, a Bible Christian minister, and his wife Jane, née Willis. Samuel attended Shebbear College, Devon, and a private school run by a Unitarian minister at Chatham, Kent. In 1850 James Way migrated with his wife and younger children to Adelaide to become superintendent of his Church in South Australia, leaving Samuel behind to complete his education. On 6 March 1853 he joined his family in Adelaide, in time for the Sunday evening service. Articled to Alfred Atkinson, he was admitted to the Bar on 23 March 1861. He proved to be an industrious and competent practitioner whose career was forwarded by fortuitous events: Atkinson became insane shortly before Way's admission, leaving his junior to run the practice; after Atkinson's death in July, Way bought the practice for £1000, payable by instalments. In 1863 he appeared before a select committee of the House of Assembly for a claimant in the dispute over leases to the Moonta copper mines. This controversy occupied the attention of the Supreme Court for two years and ultimately went to the Privy Council.

In 1867 Way was retained by the government in an action before the governor and Executive Council for the amotion of Justice Boothby [q.v.3] from the Supreme Court; Way conducted proceedings and delivered the final address. That year he took a partner, enabling him to concentrate on the barrister's side of the practice. In 1869 he holidayed in England where he was concerned in two appeals to the Privy Council. Two years later he took silk.

Elected in February 1875 to the House of Assembly for Sturt, in June Way became attorney-general in (Sir) James Boucaut's [q.v.3] ministry; when Chief Justice Sir Richard Hanson [q.v.4] died suddenly next year, Way replaced him. Although there were precedents for his elevation from attorney-general to chief justice, Way's appointment was disapproved by the bench and by his partner (Sir) Josiah Symon [q.v]. The puisne judges E. C. Gwynne and R. I. Stow [qq.v.4,6] were so affronted that they ostracized Way in private, permanently in the first case, temporarily in the second. His acceptance involved exchanging an income of almost £6000 a year for a salary of £2000, but he had saved some £40 000 in fifteen years practice and could afford it. That he attained the chief justiceship while still under 40, and without either financial backing or university qualifications, was testimony to his skill and energy.

On 27 March 1876 he took his seat on the bench of the Supreme Court which he was to occupy for nearly forty years. His life entered a period of autumnal splendour during which, while assiduously attending to his judicial duties, Way was also prominent on most of South Australia's educational, cultural and philanthropic bodies. Out of his wig he was a softly spoken man; but he drew attention by the challenging poise of his head which was always slightly held back.

Way sat in the court's various jurisdictions. He promoted a reorganization of the circuit court system, and the fusion of law and equity along the lines of the English Judicature Acts. He invented the summons for immediate relief. He formalized judicial dress on the English model, not only the black gown and wig in vogue before him, but the scarlet and ermine of the Criminal Court. He presided over royal commissions, notably that of 1883 into the administration of the Destitute Act: its recommendations partially alleviated the plight of boys on a rotting hulk used as a reformatory training ship, and the servitude of unmarried mothers to washtub and mangle, and urged the establishment of a state children's relief board. Sitting with his colleagues Boucaut and (Sir) William Bundey [q.v.3] in

almost unbroken harmony from 1884 to 1903, Way dominated the court; on the only instance in which he was in the minority, he was upheld in the Privy Council.

A council-member of the new University of Adelaide before his elevation, Way was vice-chancellor (1876) and chancellor (1883-1916). There was criticism of these appointments because of his lack of tertiary qualifications and experience; on ceremonial occasions he wore his judge's wig and gown in lieu of the academic dress to which he was not entitled. Prominent among those who promoted the establishment of the Adelaide Children's Hospital, he was president of the board from its foundation in 1876 until 1915. In addition, he was president (1893-1908) of the Public Library, Museum and Art Gallery of South Australia and was active in Freemasonry and in Bible Christian affairs. He helped to effect the union in 1900 of the three Methodist sects into the United Methodist Church of Australia and New Zealand, and remained a staunch member of the Methodist Conference. In 1872 he had bought Montefiore, a North Adelaide mansion where he spent the rest of his life; while at the Bar he also bought Sea View, a farm near Noarlunga; on his property at Kadlunga he grazed the improved Shropshire sheep which he had introduced into Australia. He was delighted when a great pastoralist greeted him in Sydney not as the chief justice, but as 'the breeder of Shropshires'.

From 1876 Way sometimes acted as governor during an interregnum or in the incumbent's absence. Late in 1890 he was appointed lieut-governor of South Australia for life. Governor Kintore [q.v.5] made this arrangement with the Imperial authorities without cabinet's knowledge; the announcement came after Way had departed on a world tour. Fêted in England and awarded an honorary doctorate of civil law at the University of Oxford in 1891, he visited Shebbear College and presented it with a neighbouring farm.

Greater honours awaited him. An Imperial Act of 1895 allowed up to five colonial judges to enter the judicial committee of the Privy Council. Way was chosen as the Australasian representative. The appointment—which involved negotiations to gain support from the other Australasian colonies—was forwarded by (Sir) Langdon Bonython [q.v.7], proprietor and editor of the Adelaide *Advertiser*, and, more grudgingly, by Premier Kingston [q.v.9]. In 1897 Way left to take his seat. He heard appeals from India, China, South Africa, Jamaica and New South Wales. He was awarded an honorary LL.D. by the University of Cambridge. According to his letters, he was received with deference and showered with attention by official and legal dignitaries and by society hostesses. In some quarters, however, he experienced iciness and condescension. Way went home in October and never sat on the Privy Council again, ostensibly because of the failure of either the Imperial or the various Australian colonial governments to pay his salary and expenses.

On 11 April 1898, his 62nd birthday, Way married Katharine Gollan, late Blue, née Gordon, a 44-year-old widow with a grown family. Though he had several times refused a knighthood (perhaps because his senior puisne Boucaut was a K.C.M.G.), Way accepted a baronetcy with alacrity in 1899. It would have been a little presumptuous, he wrote, to have 'declined a dignity which was accepted by Sir Walter Scott', and he was proud to have become, as he saw it, the first Methodist baronet in the British Empire.

From this point, Way's official life began a slow decline in status and supremacy. While taking no official part in the Federation movement, he strove unsuccessfully behind the scenes to prevent any restriction on the power of the Privy Council to grant leave to appeal from the High Court of Australia. His attitude to the High Court was one of suspicion and distrust: 'That Court was no more needed than the fifth wheel to a coach'. In 1906 he refused the offer of a seat on that court; he could hardly be expected to 'tramp about the Continent as a subordinate member of the itinerant tribunal'. The High Court soon demonstrated a propensity to reverse the decisions of the State courts in a disproportionate number of cases. Its actions made a great difference to Way's method of working. Formerly he had delivered most of his judgements extempore. He now made a practice of reserving them, and then delivered them at some length. The resulting delays were eventually discussed in parliament. While he long escaped the correction of the High Court, in 1909 he was inevitably reversed, for the first time in thirty-four years (*Dashwood* [q.v.8] v. *Maslin*).

The retirements of Bundey (1904) and Boucaut (1905) had left Way somewhat lonely on the bench. He received what might well have been a salutary shock when (Sir) John Gordon [q.v.9] dissented in the first case that he heard in the Full Court, but later found Gordon an excellent judge and an agreeable colleague; and he was pleased when his former associate and subsequent successor (Sir) George Murray [q.v.10] was appointed to the Supreme Court in 1912. As the twentieth century's second decade took its course, Way began to fail. Lady Way's death in May 1914 came as a heavy blow. Diagnosed as suffering from cancer, Way went to Sydney where, in July, Sir Alexander MacCormick [q.v.10] amputated his left arm. Characteristically, Way wrote an eleven-page description of his journeys there and back, the operation and his convalescence.

He returned to the bench in October 1914 and struggled on with his many duties. The cancer recurred. He presided over the university commemoration in December 1915 and sat twice in the Full Court in the week that followed. On 8 January 1916 he died at his North Adelaide home and was buried in his parents' grave in West Terrace cemetery. His estate was valued for probate at £55 000 (gross). There were thirty-five beneficiaries, the most considerable legacy going to his widowed sister; his library of 15 000 volumes was willed to the university. Way's voluminous, shrewd and candid letter-books are in the Mortlock Library of South Australiana. It is said that his sister burnt his personal diaries.

Sir Samuel Way was not a great jurist. His pragmatic cast of mind inhibited intensive historical research or jurisprudential analysis. At times he strained the law to produce the result which he thought justice and common sense demanded (see *De Pledge* v. *Australian United Steam Navigation Co.*, 1904). But he was conscientious, intelligent and industrious, and his verdicts gave general satisfaction. His judgement in the celebrated corset case (*Weingarten* v. *Wills & Co.*, 1906), which took nearly four hours to read, demonstrated his ability to marshal and assess a complex array of facts.

There was a touch of vanity about him, and an element of the complacency and self-satisfaction of his era. For all that, Way was by nineteenth-century standards a great man who left an enduring mark on South Australian life. Beatrice Webb had found him a 'grizzled, bearded little man, insignificant in features, voluble and diffusive in speech, with more authority than dignity in his manner; he neither pleases nor impresses . . . At first he seems a fussy little methodist . . . presently you discover that he is both good and wise. With intimacy one learns to appreciate his wide experience of men and things, his large-minded cultivation and above all his continuous application in advancing what he believes to be right'. Way's portrait by G. A. J. Webb is in the Supreme Court, Adelaide; his statue stands in North Terrace near the university.

A. J. McLachlan, *McLachlan* (Melb, 1948); A. J. Hannan, *The life of Chief Justice Way* (Syd, 1960); B. Webb, *The Webbs' Australian diary, 1898*, A. G. Austin ed (Melb, 1965); A. D. Hunt, *This side of heaven* (Adel, 1985); C. Bridge, *A trunkful of books* (Adel, 1986); A. C. Castles and M. C. Harris, *Lawmakers and wayward Whigs* (Adel, 1987); *PP* (SA), 1883-84, 4 (228), 1885, 4 (228); *Quiz and the Lantern*, 26 Apr 1890; *Honorary Magistrate*, 26 Feb 1924; *Critic* (Adel), 2 May 1904; *Advertiser*

(Adel), 15 May 1914, 17, 18 Jan 1916, 17 Mar
1960.   J. J. BRAY

WAY LEE, YET SOO WAR (c.1853-
1909), merchant, was born at Tungkun, near
Canton, China, the only child of a rice-miller.
By his first wife, Way Lee had a son Yett King
Sum. Arriving in Sydney alone in 1874, Way
Lee stayed briefly with his uncle, the merchant Way Kee of George Street, and
attended schools in Sydney and Brisbane for
two years.

Working for his uncle, by 1878 he had
established Way, Lee & Co., an importing
firm in Adelaide. Its branches spread to the
colony's far northern settlements, western
New South Wales and the Northern Territory; its contracts included providing supplies
to the South Australian government for
the Port Augusta-Hergott Springs (Marree)
railway.

Planning to visit China in 1887 after the
death of his father, Way Lee offered to bring
Chinese labour for the Daly River Plantation
Co. in the Northern Territory. He also
thought that Chinese families should be
allowed to migrate—perhaps to a district
solely for Chinese settlement—and to cultivate unused Australian land. Chinese commissioners who visited Adelaide for the
Jubilee Exhibition that year arranged for Way
Lee, Mei Quong Tart [q.v.5] and two others to
present a memorial from Australian Chinese
to the Peking government. During their visit
Way Lee was appointed a mandarin of the
fourth degree.

Concerned for the welfare of Australia's
Chinese inhabitants, Way Lee promoted
education and endeavoured to improve their
living and working conditions; he advocated
restricting the import and use of opium and
recommended that the practice of smuggling
Chinese by sea into Western Australia be
abolished. Furthermore, he tried to facilitate
intercolonial travel for the Chinese. Although
he had been naturalized in 1882, Way Lee
experienced an embarrassing poll-tax incident when travelling to New South Wales in
1888; Sir Henry Parkes [q.v.5], who was on
the same train, took his part.

In 1889 Way Lee married Margaret Ann
McDonald. He became a Freemason and was
recognized as a leader of Adelaide's Chinese
community, many of whom lived near his tea
merchant's premises in the West End of the
city. More prosperous than they were, he was
accepted by other Adelaide businessmen and
dignitaries whom he hosted at Chinese New
Year dinners. For the larger community, he
provided fireworks on Guy Fawkes night. On
platforms and in the press he deplored anti-
Chinese feeling and legislation: 'The Aus-

tralian people are always very kind to me, but
the law worse than the people'. He collected
money for the victims of flood and famine in
China. A genial man, he spoke English fluently
and followed political and municipal affairs.

He anticipated appointment as Chinese
vice-consul for South Australia, but died of
chronic nephritis and amyloid disease at his
Rundle Street home on 21 August 1909, survived by his wife, two of their daughters (Vera
Pretoria and Lily) and their son (Jack Ernest),
as well as by the son of his first marriage.
Next day thousands surged through West
Terrace cemetery expecting to witness peculiar Chinese rites. They were disappointed.
The burial was conducted with Presbyterian
forms. Way Lee's estate was sworn for probate at £1000 and included his musical instruments, jewellery and property in China and
South Australia. On 12 December 1911 in the
Supreme Court of South Australia his widow
successfully contested his will against its
executor, her daughter Lily.

Quiz (Adel), 1 Nov 1889; *Advertiser* (Adel), 9
Sept 1887, 29 Mar 1888, 23 Aug 1909; *Observer*
(Adel), 4 Feb, 7 Apr, 30 June 1888, 2 Feb 1889;
Register (Adel), 24 Feb, 11 May, 1, 2 Oct 1888, 23
Aug 1909.   R. M. GIBBS

WAYN, AMELIA LUCY (1862?-1951),
historical researcher, was born probably in
1862 in Germany, daughter of Rev. Arthur
Wayn, Anglican clergyman, and his wife
Amelia, née Ibbotson. Her father, who had
been ordained priest in New South Wales in
1854 and had later been a curate in England,
became curate at St Andrew's Church,
Evandale, Tasmania, in November 1864. For
the next thirty years Amelia accompanied her
father (widowed in 1877) around the various
parishes in which he was the incumbent;
following his retirement, in 1896 she trained
as a nurse at Launceston Public Hospital.
Moving to Hobart, she ran the Fairfield
Private Hospital, initially in partnership with
Miss McDowall, in 1900-15. Amelia then
went to Launceston as matron-in-charge of
the military base hospital until she was
demobilized in 1921.

For the compilation of *The historical records
of Australia*, funding was negotiated between
the Tasmanian and Commonwealth governments to employ a person to arrange and
index Tasmanian archival records, dating
from the 1820s, which were held by the Tasmanian Chief Secretary's Department. In
March 1921 Miss Wayn was appointed in a
temporary capacity as a 'lady indexer'. She
quickly became the one who answered
requests received by the Tasmanian government for all manner of historical information
and was recognized as the 'authority on the

historical records of the State'. Over the next twenty-five years she undertook work and provided replies for a wide range of researchers. By the early 1930s the funding for her indexing had been reduced to a minimal honorarium in token recognition of her voluntary labours.

In January 1941 she was appointed M.B.E.: although the citation referred primarily to her contribution to historical research, it also mentioned her various charitable works. In 1942 the Tasmanian government finally allocated increased funds to pay its annalist. Amelia continued her indexing and research until 1949 when a full-time archivist was formally appointed under the Public Records Act (1943). Miss Wayn died in Hobart on 11 August 1951 and was cremated at Cornelian Bay.

Although she did not publish any books herself, Amelia Wayn contributed greatly to the work of others through the provision of information, research and assistance without which many publications would have been the poorer, or may not have been possible at all. Her major legacy to researchers, however, were the indexes and compilations that she created for records prior to 1856 in Tasmania. These are now held in the Archives Office of Tasmania and include substantial compilations dealing with governors' dispatches, shipping, the military and the civil service. The massive index which now bears her name is, despite its idiosyncracies and errors, an invaluable starting point for any researcher engaged on the early period of European settlement in Tasmania and provides a lasting memorial to her work.

Mercury, 24 Sept 1901, 14 Aug 1951; Premier's Dept, Recommendations and associated correspondence related to the granting of honours *and* Premier's *and* Chief Secretary's Dept, General correspondence *and* Wayn compilations (TA).

IAN PEARCE

WEARNE, WALTER ERNEST (1867-1931), grazier and politician, was born on 2 September 1867 in Sydney, son of James Teare Wearne, flour-miller, and his wife Emily, née Dengate, both English born. While attending Cleveland Street Public School, Walter made a lifelong commitment to teetotalism. His education continued in public schools at Inverell and at Bingara where James opened his own flour-mill and sawmill in 1881.

Walter spent eight years acquiring a thorough knowledge of these industries. On 16 November 1887 at Bingara he married with Wesleyan forms Clara Louisa Bridger (d. 1892); they were to have two children. Secretary of most Bingara organizations, Wearne was first clerk of Bingara Municipal Council (1889-1910). He branched out as an auctioneer and commission agent, established the stockyards in 1890, and was licensed as a government and municipal valuer. On 25 September 1894 at Piedmont he married with Anglican rites Alice May Capel, a squatter's daughter. Wearne acquired 250 acres (101.2 ha) in 1903 on the Gwydir River and by 1920 had consolidated Beaufort into a 5000-acre (2024 ha) mixed farm.

A public spirited man who 'knew the land and believed in the land', Wearne was a gifted raconteur, skilled musician and elocutionist. He was an executive-member of the Farmers and Settlers' Association (1909-22) and defeated George Black [q.v.7] for the seat of Namoi in the Legislative Assembly in 1917 when both stood as Independent Nationalists. Wearne represented Namoi until 1927 when he won Barwon as a Nationalist. While a F.A.S.A. representative on the National Association of New South Wales, he had believed that country interests were endangered and formed the country parliamentary committee. With two sons at the front, Wearne and his wife were active in war work and in promoting the welfare of soldiers. To boost morale, he wrote *The voluntary camp song* during the 1917 general strike in which his brother Reginald shot dead a striker, Mervyn Flanagan.

When (Sir) George Beeby [q.v.7] resigned from cabinet in July 1919, Wearne and E. A. Buttenshaw [q.v.7] joined him; next year Wearne was elected leader of the Progressives. Short, squat, bluff and big-hearted, he was a trustworthy politician and keen debater, but faced a dilemma in defending country interests. Premier James Dooley [q.v.8] resigned in December 1921. After consulting his party and insisting on the priority of decentralization as a condition, Wearne joined Sir George Fuller's [q.v.8] seven-hour cabinet on 20 December as secretary for lands and minister for forests. Wearne enjoyed the overwhelming support of his electorate, but the party split when (Sir) Michael Bruxner [q.v.7] and his 'True Blues' refused to countenance any coalition. Genuinely upset by the 1921 split and by the lack of endorsement of his actions, Wearne bore with honour the 'jihad' waged against him by W. W. Killen.

As deputy leader in the coalition 'Coffinship Cabinet' (1922-25), Wearne held his previous portfolios. Aided by Under-Secretary C. P. Fleming, he paid meticulous attention to soldier settlement, promoted voluntary subdivision of larger estates and secured the border railways agreement (Barnes to Balranald). His spectacular achievement was 'Ziff Wearne's Circus and Menagerie' train which carried sceptical politicians to the

Pallamallawa-Warialda prickly pear infestations, a tactic successful in securing the passage of his Prickly Pear Act of 1924, despite lampooning by metropolitan newspapers. His pioneering leadership with *Cactoblastis cactorum* achieved wide recognition. Wearne strained his health by a punishing schedule of office hours. He renewed the coalition pact prior to the 1925 election, but resigned as deputy.

Exhausted by ministerial office, Wearne did not contest the 1930 election. He died on 17 January 1931 at Molong Private Hospital, Sydney, and was cremated after a service at Bondi Junction Methodist Church. His wife, daughter and four sons survived him, as did the son and daughter of his first marriage; his estate was sworn for probate at £8138.

U. Ellis, *The Country Party* (Melb, 1958) and *A history of the Australian Country Party* (Melb, 1963); B. D. Graham, *The formation of the Australian Country Parties* (Canb, 1966); B. Batterham (comp), *Bingara—a collection of historical stories* (Bingara, NSW, 1977); D. Aitkin, *The colonel* (Canb, 1969); R. Milliss, *City on the Peel* (Syd, 1980); Aust Soc for Labor Hist (Syd branch), *Hummer*, special issue no 21, Labor Day, 1988; *SMH*, 16, 28 Apr 1920, 19 Jan 1931; *Scone Advocate*, 17 Apr 1925; Wearne family papers held by, and information from Mr and Mrs J. T. Wearne, Beaufort, Bingara, NSW.
JOHN ATCHISON

WEATHERBURN, CHARLES ERNEST (1884-1974), mathematician, was born on 18 June 1884 at Chippendale, Sydney, fifth child of Henry Weatherburn, engineer, and his wife Amelia, née Cummins, both English born. Educated at Blackfriars School and Sydney Boys' High School (captain in 1900), Charles attended the University of Sydney (B.A., 1904; B.Sc., 1905; M.A., 1906; D.Sc., 1916) and was awarded the university medal in mathematics. H. S. Carslaw [q.v.7] wrote: 'He is without doubt the most distinguished of the Mathematical graduates of Sydney in the thirty-one years during which I have been head of our Department'. On a travelling scholarship in 1906, Weatherburn entered Trinity College, Cambridge (B.A., 1908; M.A., 1915), where he was exhibitioner (1907) and major scholar (1908). At St Andrew's Anglican Church, Summer Hill, Sydney, on 6 March 1909 he married his childhood sweetheart Lucy May Dartnell (d. 1972); they were to have three sons.

From 1909 he taught mathematics and physics at Sydney Boys' High School and tutored in these subjects at St Paul's College at the university until 1911. That year he was appointed lecturer in mathematics and theoretical physics at Ormond [q.v.5] College, University of Melbourne, where J. H. Michell [q.v.10] encouraged Weatherburn to write

Elementary vector analysis (London, 1921) which was reprinted fourteen times before its revision in 1955. Like Michell, he was a man of refinement, reserved and highly principled. In 1923 Weatherburn was appointed to the chair of mathematics and natural philosophy at Canterbury University College, University of New Zealand. Michell and E. J. Nanson [q.v.10] had earlier recommended his original work on integral equations and relativity; Weatherburn added *Advanced vector analysis* (London, 1924) and the two-volume *Differential geometry* (Cambridge, 1927, 1930) to his publications. In March 1929 he took up the foundation chair of mathematics at the University of Western Australia.

A grant (1935-36) from the Carnegie Corporation of New York led to his meeting the American mathematicians L. P. Eisenhart and O. Veblen, and to his *Riemannian geometry and the tensor calculus* (Cambridge, 1938); in 1946 Weatherburn presented a copy of his *First course in mathematical statistics* (Cambridge, 1946) to fellow mathematician Eamon de Valera, long-time president of Ireland. Despite Weatherburn's prolific output of books and papers, his other responsibilities were not neglected. Running his department single-handed, and with the help of a lecturer after 1938, drew from him 'businesslike qualities of a very high order'. He was unstinting in his assistance to students. His peers acknowledged his gift of lucid exposition, his love of teaching and his power of easy control in his classes. Weatherburn retired in 1950.

The Royal Society of New Zealand had awarded him the Hector medal in 1934 and in 1951 the University of Glasgow conferred upon him an honorary doctorate of laws. Survived by two sons, Weatherburn died on 18 October 1974 at Claremont, Perth, and was cremated with Presbyterian forms. A mathematics lecture theatre at the University of Western Australia had been named (1971) in his honour.

J of the Aust Mathematical Soc, 21, 1976, p 1; *British A'sian*, 16 Mar 1911; *Australasian*, 18 Feb 1911; *Western Mail* (Perth), 31 Jan 1929; *West Australian*, 19 Oct 1974; H. Weatherburn diary (held by Mr D. C. Weatherburn, Lindfield, Syd); Weatherburn papers held by author; personal information.
A. K. WEATHERBURN

WEATHERLY, LIONEL JAMES (1881-1962), pastoralist, was born on 12 May 1881 at Billilla, Wilcannia, New South Wales, only son of WILLIAM WEATHERLY (1839-1914), sheep-farmer, and his wife Jeanie Thompson, née Wilson, both Scottish born. In 1859 William had come to family friends Robert Hood and the Chirnsides [qq.v.9,3] in Victoria to gain rural experience. He intended to settle in Queensland, but an outbreak of scab in New South Wales closed the border, forcing him to sell his sheep at a disastrous loss. In 1863 he returned with Willie Hood from Hungerford, Queensland, in three weeks, riding only one horse each over the 1100 miles (1770 km). William repaid his debts by working for the Chirnsides and subsequently became managing partner in T. Chirnside & Co., holding a one-sixth share in their 450 000 acres (182 111 ha) at Billilla. On 19 December 1878 he married Jeanie with Presbyterian forms at Earlston, Berwickshire, Scotland, and returned to Billilla. With George and A. E. Bowes Kelly [q.v.9], in 1884 he bought a one-fourteenth share (for £150) in the new Broken Hill mine from (Sir) Sidney Kidman [q.v.9]; William's half equity made his fortune. A fellow (1890) of the Royal Geographical Society, London, he had moved in 1888 to Brighton, Melbourne, and invested systematically in land, buying a string of properties after 1895.

Lionel was educated at Cumloden School, St Kilda, and Trinity Hall, Cambridge (B.A., 1904; M.A., 1908). His right side was partially paralysed in his youth, though his affliction did not prevent him from fox-hunting in England in 1908. On his return in 1909, his father gave him ownership of the major part of Woolongoon at Mortlake, Victoria, and the lease of the balance, and in 1910 he took over the management of two other properties. At Longwood on 27 April 1911 Lionel married Faerlie Alice Ffloyd Chomley: the bishop of Wangaratta officiated. William Weatherly died on 1 September 1914 at Brighton, survived by his son and two daughters. Lionel tried to enlist during World War I, but was rejected because of his paralysis. As well as running his own flock (6000 strong in 1915), he worked for the Red Cross, supervised properties for enlisted owners and was president of the local repatriation committee. After the war he donated two farms (888 acres, 359 ha) for soldier settlement and voluntarily sold nearly 16 000 acres (6475 ha) to the Closer Settlement Board to provide another forty-six farms. Involved in numerous local activities, he was a member (1919-26) and president (1922-23) of the Mortlake Shire Council, but was forced to retire due to ill health. A committee-member of Mortlake hospital, he was also involved in the formation of the rural fire brigade.

From 1909 Weatherly was a member of the Pastoralists' Association (later Graziers' Association of Victoria); elected to its council in 1910, he was State president in 1921-25. He represented the association on the federal council in 1921, 1922 and 1924, and was federal president at the Melbourne convention in 1924; he remained on the State executive until 1947. Appointed to the Australian Meat Council in 1922, he represented it next year in South Africa, England and the Netherlands. In 1925 he resigned from the Wool Growers' Council, being reluctant to represent it while he opposed Sir John Higgins's [q.v.9] plan for the post-war marketing of wool. Weatherly was a committee-member and president (1951-52) of the Australian Sheepbreeders' Association and a councillor of the Polwarth Sheepbreeders' Association. Keenly interested in thoroughbred horses, he was a member of the Victoria Racing and the Camperdown Turf clubs.

A devout Presbyterian and church elder, Weatherly was generous and intelligent, with a fine sense of humour. Although he was seldom critical of others, he set, and achieved, such high standards for himself that contemporaries regarded him with awe. Sir Chester Manifold was prepared to place him 'right up at the top of all the managers of properties'. Weatherly handed over Woolongoon to a son in 1944 and retired to Camperdown. In 1962 he donated £25 000 towards a Haileybury College branch school at Keysborough. Survived by his wife, daughter and two sons, he died on 19 December 1962 at his Camperdown home and was buried in Ellerslie cemetery.

J. Smith (ed), *Cyclopedia of Victoria*, 1 (Melb, 1903); C. E. Sayers, *Shepherd's gold* (Melb, 1966); H. B. Ronald, *Wool past the winning post* (Melb, 1978); J. O. Randell, *Teamwork* (Syd, 1983); J. Bowen, *Kidman the forgotten king* (Syd, 1987); *Pastoral Review*, 16 Sept 1914, 18 Jan 1963; L. G. Lomas, The western district farmer 1914-27 (Ph.D. thesis, Monash Univ, 1979); Aust Sheepbreeders' Assn records; Polwarth Sheepbreeders' Assn records; Mortlake Shire records; Weatherly family papers (LaTL); information from and family papers held by Mr W. Weatherly, Mortlake, Vic.

ROBERT HOOD

WEATHERLY, MAY ISABELLA (1868-1950), headmistress, was born on 22 May 1868 at Ballarat, Victoria, eldest of three children of Bolton Stafford Bird [q.v.3], clergyman, and his Scottish-born wife Helen, née Chisholm. Educated in Hobart and at Methodist Ladies College, Kew, Melbourne, she matriculated in 1893 and taught at M.L.C. until 1895 when she went to Rockhampton Girls' Grammar School, Queensland, for a year. Enrolling at the University of Tasmania (B.A., 1904), she taught part-time at Hobart schools while studying for her degree.

Senior mistress from 1904 at Queen's College, Ballarat, in 1907 May Bird became headmistress of New England Girls' School at Armidale, New South Wales. Her stay was short: she left after one quarter and, on 16 July, at St Paul's Anglican Cathedral,

Melbourne, married James Weatherly, a Scottish-born grazier of Wallaloo Park, Stawell, Victoria. He was a 63-year-old widower with five daughters, one of whom she had taught and comforted on the death of the previous Mrs Weatherly. When James died in 1914, May returned to Tasmania to stay with her parents on Bruny Island. There she found peace and happiness, and continued to live on the island after her mother and father died.

Having long advocated formal education in 'home management', in 1928 Mrs Weatherly left Bruny Island to become the founding principal of a new homecraft hostel which eventually found a permanent location at Invergowrie, Hawthorn, Melbourne. This large bluestone house and extensive garden was presented to the Association of Headmistresses of Girls' Registered Secondary Schools of Victoria by the family and trustees of the Sir William McPherson [q.v.10] estate. May Weatherly had a great rapport with the young and a talent for bringing out the best in them. She 'guided the hostel through the first difficult years, as perhaps no one else could have done' and gave professional training to future housewives. In 1932 Miss Margaret Kirkhope joined her as co-principal and in 1938 Mrs Weatherly retired.

During World War II she took on the voluntary task of organizing a day nursery in South Yarra (sponsored by the Women of the University Patriotic Fund) which provided care for the children of mothers engaged in essential war work. At the request of the Melbourne Technical College, she also prepared and corrected papers for a correspondence course in home-making offered to women in the armed services.

In retirement she lived at Malvern with her sister Ann, widow of Rev. A. H. Garnsey [q.v.8]; Mrs Weatherly died there on 2 November 1950 and was cremated. In 1957 the May I. Weatherly Memorial Hall was added to Invergowrie; her portrait hangs in the main house, occupied in the 1980s by the Victorian Post-Secondary Education Commission.

New England Girls' School, *Milestones and memories* (Armidale, 1945); *Truth* (Melb), 15 June 1929; Univ Tas Lib Archives; information from Mrs M. Lawton, Berwick, Vic, and Mrs S. White, Deepdene, Melb.   HEATHER B. RONALD

WEATHERS, LAWRENCE CARTHAGE (1890-1918), undertaker and soldier, was born on 14 May 1890 at Te Kopuru, near Dargaville, New Zealand, son of John Joseph Weathers, labourer, and his wife Ellen Frances, née McCormack, both Adelaide born. Aged 7, he sailed with his parents to Adelaide; the family settled in rural South Australia and Lawrence was sent to Snowtown Public School. By 1913 he had become an undertaker and may have sensed —if he did not understand—where paths of glory lead. On 10 September he married a 23-year-old, Melbourne-born domestic servant, Annie Elizabeth Watson, at her father's home in the Adelaide suburb of Unley; the young couple lived nearby at Parkside and were to have one child.

Enlisting in the Australian Imperial Force on 3 February 1916, Weathers embarked with the 43rd Battalion in June. After further training on Salisbury Plain, England, in November he was taken with units of the 3rd Division to the Western Front. Sickness confined him to hospital from January to April 1917. On the night of 10 June, during an operation at Messines, Belgium, he was wounded and was away from his battalion until 3 December. Promoted lance-corporal on 21 March 1918, he was gassed on 26 May at Bois L'Abbé in the Villers-Bretonneux sector, France, but rejoined his unit within a month.

After the capture of Mont St Quentin, the duty of clearing a small area criss-crossed with barbed wire entanglements north of Péronne fell to the 43rd Battalion on 2 September. The major objective was Scutari trench. The unit went forward at 5.35 that morning, but was halted by scything fire. From the vanguard Weathers attacked the enemy garrison and killed its leader. Replenishing his stock of bombs, with three others he went back into the fray. Given cover by a comrade's Lewis-gun, Weathers seemed oblivious to danger as he scaled the German parapet and hurled his bombs into the trench below. By 7 a.m. resistance ceased. He took three machine-guns and 180 prisoners back to his lines. His uniform caked in mud, with blood streaming down his face and five days stubble, Weathers looked quite a 'card' to his mates when he returned with souvenired German binoculars and pistols festooning him like a Christmas tree. The strain and the release of nerves showed in his chatter of how he had 'put the wind up' the enemy. He was recommended for the Victoria Cross.

Promoted temporary corporal on 10 September 1918 (his fifth wedding anniversary), Weathers received a short respite from action before moving with his battalion to attack the Hindenburg line between Rosnoy and Bony. At dawn on the 29th the engagement commenced; wounded by shell-fire, Weathers died before dusk. He never knew of his V.C. which was gazetted on Christmas eve. Buried in Unicorn cemetery, Vendhuille, France, he was survived by his wife and son. His elder brother Private Thomas Francis Weathers, 9th Light Horse Regiment, had died from wounds on 15 June 1915 at Gallipoli.

K. R. Cramp, *Australian winners of the Victoria Cross in the Great War 1914-19* (Syd, 1919); E. J. Colliver and B. H. Richardson, *The Forty-third Battalion* (Adel, 1920); C. E. W. Bean, *The A.I.F. in France*, 1918 (Syd, 1942); L. Wigmore (ed), *They dared mightily*, revised and condensed by J. Williams and A. Staunton (Canb, 1986); *SMH*, 30 Dec 1918; *Argus*, 5 July 1941; card index: personnel, AIF, 1914-18 (AWM).   JOHN RITCHIE

WEAVER, REGINALD WALTER DARCY (1876-1945), real estate agent and politician, was born on 18 July 1876 at Kickerbill station, Murrurundi, New South Wales, twelfth child of English-born parents Richard Weaver, grazier, and his wife Fanny Seymour, née Weaver. Educated at Newington College, Sydney, Reg joined two of his brothers in a stock and station agency at Forbes before setting up on his own at Condobolin and Narrandera in the mid-1890s. On 19 April 1899 he married Gertrude Susan Bond Walker at St Andrew's Anglican Cathedral, Sydney. During the South African War rumours about his horse-trading deals in that country earned him the nickname 'Red Reggie', one much favoured by his opponents.

An alderman on Condobolin (1898-1900) and Narrandera (1902) Municipal councils, Weaver was active in the Farmers and Settlers' Association. By 1910 he was living at Dubbo. Defeated as a Liberal for the State seat of Ashburnham in 1910 and for Macquarie in 1913 (after a temporary bankruptcy), he attributed Labor's victory in the latter election to manipulation of the rolls. An inquiry exonerated Labor, but found Weaver's own organizers guilty of fraudulent roll-stuffing. Moving to North Sydney in 1916, he established his real estate business and in 1917 entered the Legislative Assembly for Willoughby. Re-elected (for North Shore) in 1920, he briefly retired from politics in 1925, citing business reasons.

Engaging passionately and resolutely in the causes he espoused, Weaver was a fervent Imperialist and pro-conscriptionist. He was rejected as medically unfit for the Australian Imperial Force in 1916, but eventually enlisted in August 1918. Demonstrating his talent for rhetoric, he recruited sixty men to his own platoon and even campaigned on the waterfront for members of the 'one big union on the Western front'. He raised over £25 000 for the War Loan and was discharged from the A.I.F. in December.

An implacable foe of socialism, Weaver earned the unremitting hostility of the trade unions for reporting militant strike leaders to the railway commissioners in 1917; for the next decade he opposed their re-employment, while defending the reinstatement of the 'Loyalists'. At the trial of Donald Grant [q.v.9]

and other members of the Industrial Workers of the World, Weaver was accused of helping to procure the evidence of a key police witness. In 1923 he denied that he had tried to bribe W. J. Thomas with £500 to inflame violence on the coalfields and implicate the Communist Party of Australia in a conspiracy that he hoped to use for his own political ends. As suspicious of Catholicism as he was of Communism, Weaver was a leading spokesman of the Australian Protestant Defence Association; he railed against Sinn Feiners and Irish prelates like Daniel Mannix and Michael Kelly [qq.v.10,9], and feared an invasion of Catholic immigrants.

In politics Weaver was admired for his independence of mind. More than once he crossed the floor and was often in severe conflict with his own premier. His debating flair was legendary: he could demolish members of J. T. Lang's [q.v.9] Opposition with satirical verse, delighting both parliament and press. Weaver was vice-president of the National Party (1919-32) and a councillor of the United Australia Party (1932-38). Representing Neutral Bay in 1927-45, he served as secretary for mines and minister for forests in the Bavin [q.v.7] government from April 1929. Taking over the worsening dispute on the northern coalfields, he believed the struggle to be communist-inspired and made possible by unemployment relief and child endowment. By December, when the miners refused to accept reduced wages, Weaver opened the mines with volunteer labour and police protection. Violent clashes occurred at Rothbury, resulting in death and injury; unemployment relief was stopped, confirming Weaver as Labor's arch-enemy.

In Opposition from 1930, Weaver was elected deputy leader of the United Australia Party in New South Wales in 1932. A member of the Sane Democracy League, he was believed by Naval Intelligence to be a covert leader of the New Guard (with which he explicitly sympathized). In 1932 Weaver became minister for health and public works in (Sir) Bertram Stevens' [q.v.] cabinet. Abandoning larger political themes, he travelled extensively and concentrated on the expansion of hospitals. His determination to exert more control over hospital administration and his banning of honorary doctors from local hospital boards brought him into conflict with State branch of the British Medical Association. He decreed that new doctors would henceforward be required to have a years hospital residency, but an unfortunate reference to the few who lacked this qualification as 'duds' was interpreted by outraged doctors as a slur on the medical profession. In the ensuing fuss in 1935 Stevens found him 'too extreme in personal independence' and possessing a 'needlessly sharp tongue'. Weaver refused to back down. Stevens and his cabinet resigned on 21 August. A new government was reconstructed without Weaver who again resigned from parliament.

In 1937 he was returned for Neutral Bay and was elected Speaker; he held firm sway over the House until the McKell government swept to power in 1941. Weaver was cleared in 1938 by (Sir) Percival Halse Rogers' [q.v.11] inquiry into Lang's allegations of fraud and corruption in the sale of state enterprises in 1933 when Weaver was responsible minister. As controller of salvage in 1940-41, he was diligent but controversial.

Elected leader of the new Democratic Party in 1944, he was now leader of the Opposition. Efforts to merge with the Liberal Democratic Party of Australia were deadlocked over questions of party organization and by acrimony between the leaders, Weaver and E. K. White. Discord existed within the Democratic Party and, although Weaver resigned as its president, he remained leader of the parliamentary Opposition. In December both parties agreed to enter the new Liberal Party formed by (Sir) Robert Menzies.

Survived by his wife, son and three daughters, Weaver died in Hornsby Hospital of a coronary occlusion on 12 November 1945 and was cremated with Christian Science forms. His estate was sworn for probate at £1114. A man of powerful convictions, he had lived, as he said, 'in an atmosphere of contention, criticism and condemnation', but had served the State with energy and dedication.

W. J. Thomas, *A Red revolution for £500! an account of the Weaver-Thomas conspiracy case* (Syd, 1923); *PD* (NSW), 30 Aug 1923, p 565; *V&P* (LA NSW), 1938-39-40, 6, p 747; *Fighting Line* (Syd), 19 July 1913; *SMH*, 17 Dec 1913, 9 Oct, 13 Sept 1918, 17, 21 June 1921, 22 May, 14 July 1922, 19 Nov 1923, 21 Sept 1928, 28 May, 21, 22 Nov, 11, 13, 17 Dec 1929, 11 Mar 1930, 12, 14, 25 May 1932, 6 Aug, 5 Dec 1934, 1, 12, 14 Feb 1935, 11 Jan, 12 Feb, 3 Mar 1938, 10 Feb, 5 Aug, 6 Sept, 18 Dec 1944, 13 Nov 1945; *Daily Telegraph* (Syd), 3 Aug 1923; Intelligence reports, SP 1141/1/13, MP 1049/9 file 1887/2/35 (AA); information from Dr A. W. Martin, Research School of Social Sciences, ANU.   HELEN BOURKE

WEBB, CHRIS (1866-1948), boatman, was born on 17 October 1866 at Blues Point, North Sydney, and named Henry Christopher, seventh child of William Webb Wagg, a boatman from Farnmouth, England, and his Sydney-born wife Sarah, née Turner. He began working for his father (a yachtsman who was known as 'Old Billy Webb') on lighters carrying stone for St Patrick's College, Manly. Starting his racing as for'ard hand for his brother Charlie, Chris first won as helms-

man with the 14-foot canvas dinghy, *Latona*, in 1884 when he took the J. W. Durning trophy. In later seasons he skippered the 'fourteen', *Violet*, to twelve wins, and in 1891-93 the 24-footer, *Mantura*, to eleven. On 3 September 1892 at Redfern he married Nellie Eliza Rogers with Wesleyan forms.

By 1903 Webb had won 100 races and been placed 118 times in 23 yachts of various classes, but his reputation as 'the best-known, the most successful, and perhaps the most popular skipper of open sailing boats on the waters of Port Jackson' was gained in 18-footer races. Pioneered by Mark Foy [q.v.8], these handicap events over a triangular course on Sydney Harbour, featuring craft with coloured sail identifiers, became a popular sport from 1891. Crews included working watermen, and owners were often boat-builders. Spectators watched from Clark Island and from ferries; illegal betting enhanced the excitement. Webb came to dominate local events, probably receiving some of the owners' prize-money. He also contested intercolonial and Australian 'eighteen' championships, winning with Sam Williams's *Australian* in Brisbane in 1897, with W. M. 'Watty' Ford's *Australian* (formerly *Arline*) in Perth Flying Squadron Challenge Cup races in 1908 (in Perth), 1909 (Sydney) and 1910 (Perth), with *Golding* in the 1912 Interstate Championship (Sydney) and with *Australian* in the 1914 Mark Foy Challenge Cup (Perth).

Employed until the 1930s by Sydney Ferries Ltd as a night-watchman who also dampened engine fires and hosed decks, Webb lived at North Sydney; about 1924 he moved to a boatshed and refreshment kiosk which he ran at The Spit, Middle Harbour. Returning to competition in 1922, with George Press's *H. C. Press II* he won the Mark Foy Challenge Cup in 1924 (Sydney), 1925 (Perth) and 1927 (Sydney). He last contested an Australian championship in 1937.

This incomparable record and his longevity as a helmsman were due to his knowledge of rigging and trimming, and to aquaintance with 'every swirl of a Harbour eddy': one journalist quipped that Webb could get 'the most for his boat out of a fishtail swish'. Short, quiet (nicknamed 'Rowdy'), moustached and pipe-smoking, he was 'cool, skilful and reliable'; his face 'tanned by many an exposure to strong winds and hot suns, wears a rather thoughtful expression. His dark brown eyes, deep set, show an undaunted nature'. Predeceased by his wife and survived by their three daughters, he died on 9 June 1948 at Beauty Point, Mosman, and was buried with Anglican rites in Northern Suburbs cemetery. In March 1942, aged 75, Webb had won his last 'eighteen' race in Sydney; it was for the title, 'Cock o' the Harbour'.

SMH, 11 Feb 1884, 2 Mar 1942, 10 June 1948; *Referee*, 5 Jan 1898; *Sydney Mail*, 13 May 1903; *Western Mail* (Perth), 30 Jan 1909; *Arrow* (Syd), 27 Feb 1909; *Sun* (Syd), 21 Aug 1916; *Daily Mirror* (Syd), 17 Nov 1962, 15 Feb 1964; information from and scrap-books held by Mr K. Ravell, Mosman, Syd.   CHRIS CUNNEEN

G. N. Hawker, *The parliament of New South Wales, 1856-1965* (Syd, 1971); J. A. La Nauze, *The making of the Australian Constitution* (Melb, 1972); *PD* (LA NSW), 1903, pp 40, 56, 1904, 2nd S, p 33; Roy Soc NSW, *J*, 54 (1920), p 35; *SMH*, 18 July 1919; Carruthers correspondence *and* Parkes correspondence (ML).   WILLIAM E. FOX

WEBB, FREDERICK WILLIAM (1837-1919), public servant, was born on 20 February 1837 in Sydney, son of John Webb, an Irish-born civil servant in the commissariat, and his wife Mary, née Bell. Educated at private schools, Frederick joined the public service as a sessional extra in the Legislative Council on 20 October 1851.

His first permanent appointment was in the Post Office where he worked in 1853-60; he was to draw upon this experience as a witness before the 1862 board of inquiry into the management of that department. On 19 April 1860 Webb obtained a position in the printing branch in the Legislative Assembly. He progressed steadily, promotion of staff being strictly by seniority. At St Thomas's Anglican Church, Willoughby, on 2 June 1866 Webb married Irish-born Charlotte Elizabeth Hickson; she died in childbirth next year. On 25 May 1872 he married Emily, youngest daughter of John Piper MacKenzie and granddaughter of Alexander McKenzie [q.v.2], at St James's Anglican Church, Sydney; they were to have four children.

Clerk assistant from 1 February 1873, Webb acted briefly as clerk of the Legislative Assembly in 1877 and in 1885, before being appointed to that position on 21 February 1888. He was responsible for the accuracy of records, the custody of all documents and control of the staff; he also had to be at hand to advise the Speaker and chairman of committees at any hour of the day or night. As clerk of the Legislative Assembly, Webb was appointed secretary to the National Australasian Convention held in Sydney in 1891; he acted as an adviser at the Australasian Federal Convention and was clerk to its finance committee in Adelaide in 1897.

Distinguished-looking, kindly, 'modest and efficient', Webb was praised for his 'valuable assistance' and 'unswerving loyalty', and came to be seen as 'inseparably associated' with the Legislative Assembly. He was held in 'affectionate esteem' by his staff. Appointed C.M.G. in 1894, he was elected a member of the Royal Society of New South Wales in 1897. After twelve months sick-leave, he retired on a pension in January 1904 and had more time to go shooting and fishing. Survived by his wife, daughter and a son, he died at Manly on 17 July 1919 and was buried in the local cemetery. His estate was sworn for probate at £9749.

WEBB, JESSIE STOBO WATSON (1880-1944), historian, was born on 31 July 1880 at Ellerslie station, near Tumut, New South Wales, only child of New Zealand-born Charles Henry Webb, grazier, and his Scottish wife Jessie, née Watson. Her mother died in giving birth to her and her father was killed in an accident when she was 9 years old. Sent to Melbourne to her mother's family, she was educated at Balaclava College and the University of Melbourne, graduating (B.A., 1902; M.A., 1904) with first-class honours in history and political economy, and in logic and philosophy; she shared the J. D. Wyselaskie [q.v.6] scholarship in English constitutional history and won the Cobden Club medal. In 1908 she joined the history department at the university and remained there for the rest of her life, becoming a senior lecturer (1923) and acting professor (1925, 1933-34 and 1942-44).

Her main interest was in ancient history, particularly that of Greece, and she spent her leave at the British School of Archaeology in Athens and in visiting classical sites, on one occasion travelling through Crete on a mule. In 1922-23 she accompanied Dr Georgina Sweet [q.v.] on a journey from Cape Town to Cairo. Ancient history, as Miss Webb taught it, was exciting: she kept abreast of the archaeological work which was revolutionizing the subject and communicated to her students her sense of being at the frontier of knowledge. Sir Keith Hancock recorded that it was the living interest of history as taught by Jessie Webb and (Sir) Ernest Scott [q.v.11] which caused him to become a historian rather than a classical scholar. Gladly as Miss Webb learned and taught, the most earnest efforts of her colleagues could not persuade her to write or publish. She underestimated her ability and scholarship, and probably felt handicapped by distance from ancient sites, great libraries and professional colleagues which could not be bridged by rare periods of overseas leave.

Jessie was a splendid example of the 'new woman' of the generation which came to maturity in the 1890s. Almost alone from childhood, she developed a character both independent and responsible, and confronted life with courage and indomitable gaiety. She was highly intelligent, wise, witty and very kind. Emancipated herself, she did all in her power to help other women to lead fuller and more interesting lives, but as she was rational and good-humoured her feminism aroused no hostility and she was as much liked by men as by women. She was a founder of University Women's College, the Victorian Woman Graduates' Association (president 1924-25), the Catalyst Society of professional women and the Melbourne Lyceum Club (president 1920-22). In 1923 she was alternate delegate to the League of Nations assembly.

Having continued, as acting professor, to administer the history department from her hospital bed, Miss Webb died of cancer on 17 February 1944 at St Kilda and was cremated. She is commemorated in the Jessie Webb Library of the history department at her university.

W. K. Hancock, *Country and calling* (Lond, 1954); *Hist Studies*, no 9, Oct 1944; information from Mrs J. Paisley and the late Prof N. D. Harper, Melb.   KATHLEEN FITZPATRICK

WEBB, WILLIAM ALFRED (1878-1936), railway administrator, was born on 16 May 1878 at Eaton, Ohio, United States of America, son of William Porter Webb, medical practitioner, and his wife Nancy Lavinia, née Campbell. Educated locally, at the age of 12 he left home and began work as a messenger-boy on the Colorado Midland Railway. He rose from traffic clerk to telegraphist, studied shorthand at night-school and became stenographer to the general manager. Appointed secretary to the president of the Colorado and Southern Railway in 1900, by 1911 Webb was assistant to its vice-president. He became general manager of the Texas Central Railroad and in 1914 general manager, operations, of the Missouri, Kansas and Texas Railroad Co. His rapid promotion in the private enterprise American railroads had given him a practical grounding in every aspect of rail management.

When the United States entered World War I the government assumed control of all railroads and in 1918 Webb was made general manager, under Federal control, of a large regrouped system of south-west lines. Tensions between North and South railway managements, personal and parochial conflict, and Federal obstinacy placed Webb in an untenable position and he resigned in 1919. He was appointed a member of Railroad Board of Adjustment No. 1, Washington, D.C., which was principally concerned with the settlement of industrial disputes. Eleven months later, amid post-war national railroad discord and uncertainty, he again resigned to become vice-president and general manager of the St Louis south-west system. In 1922 he was elected president of the prosperous Cambria

and Indiana Railroad. Once more he resigned, having accepted the position of chief commissioner of the South Australian Railways. His salary of £5000 per annum was to be a source of much future criticism.

With his wife Alice, née Van Stone (whom he had married on 4 December 1907 at Denver, Colorado), and their two sons, Webb arrived in Adelaide on 16 November 1923. A tall, well-built, clean-shaven man, he had a striking personality and force of character. Inheriting an outdated and uneconomic system, characterized by fragmented authority, ponderous decision-making and a complex, pyramidal administrative structure, he revolutionized railway management by rationalizing the basis of operations. He recognized the need to reduce gross and to augment net ton miles by increasing full carload lots, and introduced large trucks and locomotives, heavy track, stronger bridges and efficient practices. His most important changes to working methods occurred in 1924-26: the train control organization was introduced in 1924, high capacity bogie freight cars in 1925 and large power locomotives in 1926. Webb's dramatic railway rehabilitation left few aspects untouched by forced technological change and innovation, and even included the complete reconstruction of the Islington workshops.

Remembering the catastrophic attempts of the United States government to institute central control of railroads in World War I, Webb decentralized the S.A.R. administration, giving his carefully chosen divisional superintendents almost complete autonomy over the lines within their jurisdiction, while he concentrated on high managerial policy. He created a public management system which was less interventionist and tried to deliver services efficiently. Despite his advanced ideas, he had no time for trade unions, or for those who did not embrace the virtues of hard work for a fair wage. He was merciless, though not vindictive, to subordinates who did not measure up to his exacting standards.

His programme was costly and sometimes extravagant. It occasioned continuous political and public controversy, interspersed with vitriolic personal attacks from numerous and influential enemies. Webb pushed ahead with his plans, regardless of the source of criticism, and did not disguise his contempt for the parliamentary process or its representatives. His expenditure became an issue in South Australian elections. The effects of significant railway deficits on the State's shaky financial situation partly accounted for the defeat of both the Hill [q.v.9] Labor government in 1927 and the Butler [q.v.7] Liberal administration in 1930.

Having declined the offer of a further term,

Webb returned to America in May 1930, unhappy but wealthy. The strain of the previous seven years had not been helped by his refusal to take any holidays, and the former teetotaller had been driven to whisky by the pressure of endless criticism. His public image was not enhanced by a final argument over his allowances and by the revelation that he did not have to pay any income tax.

Following his departure the re-elected Hill government sought to tackle the financial problems of the Depression. Webb's administrative reforms were dismantled and the old hierarchy was reinstated to preside over forty years of technological stagnation and traditionalism. For all that, his rehabilitation of the S.A.R. did enable it to undertake an enormous transport task in World War II and laid the footing for the reforms of Australian National Railways when it later took over the country lines of the S.A.R.

In 1935 Webb was appointed general manager of the Texas Centennial Exposition; credited with its success, he was approached to become manager of the projected World's Fair, New York (1939). Since 1933 he had been troubled by hypertensive cardiac disease. The long hours and the strain of organizing the centennial worsened his condition. Webb died of an intercranial haemorrhage on 9 August 1936 at Dallas, Texas. After a state funeral, he was buried in the Hillcrest memorial cemetery with Presbyterian forms. His wife and sons survived him.

R. I. Jennings, *W. A. Webb, South Australian Railways commissioner, 1922-1930* (Adel, 1973), *and* The introduction and evolution of safe working systems on the South Australian Railways 1854-1986 (Ph.D. thesis, Flinders Univ, 1988), and for bibliog.   REECE JENNINGS

WEBBER, WILLIAM THOMAS THORNHILL (1837-1903), Anglican bishop, was born on 30 January 1837 in Upper Grosvenor Street, London, son of William Webber, surgeon, and his wife Eliza, née Preston. Educated at Tonbridge School, Kent, Norwich Grammar School and Pembroke College, Oxford (B.A., 1859; M.A., 1862), he was made deacon in 1860 and ordained priest in 1861. Webber was curate at Chiswick in 1860-64 and vicar of St John the Evangelist, Holborn, from 1864. The archbishop of Canterbury E. W. Benson nominated him to succeed Mathew Hale [q.v.4] as bishop of Brisbane. Webber was consecrated on 11 June 1885 in St Paul's Cathedral, London, and enthroned on 17 November in St John's Pro-Cathedral, Brisbane.

Skilled in fund-raising, administration and the style of team organization identified with inner-London clergy houses, Webber was a mildly ritualistic Tractarian who held strongly anti-Erastian views of the exclusive rights of bishops and synods to determine Church matters. His insistence that the Church of England had a 'duty to care for the Nation's life' reflected the influence upon him of J. B. Lightfoot and Thomas Arnold, and indicated his eclectic approach to theology.

In 1886 Webber addressed synod on the threefold strategy which shaped his episcopate: the sub-division of his diocese, the recruitment of a talented clergy and the eradication of 'mere congregationalism' which limited parochial commitment to local concerns. He appointed coadjutor bishops to look after the distant regions, raised £10 000 to endow a new diocese of Rockhampton, removed Church property from local trustees to a Church of England corporation and subsidized clerical stipends. He also commissioned John Loughburgh Pearson to design a cathedral, like Truro's, as a symbol that 'the Diocese—not the Parish—is the unit of the Church'.

Webber brought clergymen from Oxford and Cambridge for five-year tours of duty in Queensland. In 1887 he had synod petition for the establishment of a university and in 1897 he established a theological college in All Saints Rectory, Wickham Terrace; his hope that the college would be attached to the tertiary institution was dashed by an Act of 1899 which excluded theological studies from the proposed university. Webber led the Bible in State Schools League in Queensland, urged the diocese to establish secondary schools, appointed missioners to minister to railway navvies and to the Chinese, attracted to the diocese a sisterhood which cared for orphans, and endowed a brotherhood for priests in western Queensland.

Despite economic difficulties, Webber raised £65 000 for diocesan projects in 1885-95 and another £32 000 towards the cathedral whose foundation stone was laid in 1901. He toured England four times, pursuing for the colonial churches a portion of the profits expropriated from Queensland by English and other investors. Falling ill in 1902, he returned to Brisbane where he directed the building of the cathedral and persuaded synod to elect a bishop coadjutor. Webber died on 3 August 1903 of heart disease and was buried in Toowong cemetery. His Queensland estate was sworn for probate at £9041, a substantial proportion of which was bequeathed to his diocese.

C of E Diocese of Brisb, *Procs of Synod*, 1884-1904 and *Year Book*, 1890-1904; K. Rayner, The history of the Church of England in Queensland (Ph.D. thesis, Univ Qld, 1962); Webber papers (C of E Diocesan Archives, Brisb).   GEORGE P. SHAW

WEBER, CLARENCE ALFRED (1882-1930), athlete and physical culturist, was born on 27 March 1882 at Brighton, Melbourne, seventh surviving child of Robert Gustaf Frederick Weber, a German-born market-gardener and Methodist lay preacher, and his Victorian-born wife Eliza, née Head. Clarence was successful as a young athlete, winning three sprint and hurdles titles at the Victorian championships in 1900; turning to cycling, he won two Victorian amateur titles in 1902.

Attracted to the nascent physical culture movement, exemplified by Eugene Sandow (who visited Australia in 1902) and George Hackenschmidt (who came regularly between 1904 and 1907), Weber opened a health and strength college in Flinders Street. As 'Professor' Weber, he taught—in addition to wrestling—body-building, correct breathing and *poses plastiques* to both men and women. Run in partnership with John Rice, who was his wrestling second, the college became a well-known feature of the Melbourne sporting scene.

Hackenschmidt, the world's champion wrestler, encouraged Weber to take up the sport in 1904. His first major bout in November resulted in his opponent, 'the turbanned alien' Buttan Singh, being chased down St Kilda Road by a crowd enraged at the Indian's foul tactics. Weber lost again to him in July 1905, but defeated Buttan for the Australian heavyweight championship in November 1906.

On 19 December 1906 Weber married Louisa Peck (d. 1918) at the Methodist Church, Waverley. A bout of sunstroke contracted on his honeymoon caused him virtually to withdraw from wrestling to concentrate on business, but he made a successful comeback in 1908, winning the Australian title with a victory over the New Zealand-based Scot, Alexander Bain, in September 1911. In 1913 Weber retired undefeated, but was persuaded to return in 1923 when he again won the heavyweight title from Billy Meeske, a former pupil who was fourteen years his junior. No longer the dominant force of yore, Weber lost bouts to visiting Americans and a 'giant Finn', only retained his title on a foul against Meeske in July 1926 and finally lost to him in September in his last appearance in the ring. Thereafter he devoted himself to his college and to charitable work, under the influence of his wife Ivy Lavinia [q.v.], late Mitchell, née Filshie, whom he had married at Brighton with Methodist forms on 7 March 1919.

Six feet (182.9 cm) tall, weighing up to fourteen stone (88.9 kg), beautifully proportioned, handsome as well as strong (he registered a number of weight-lifting records in the early 1900s), he was termed 'Adonis' as well as 'Hercules': 'girls, all enthusiastic Weberites', leavened the normally masculine gallery itself given to voicing 'a hum of admiration' at his appearance.

After a day spent lecturing during a Victorian health week, while washing his hands before dinner Weber collapsed and died of a coronary occlusion on 20 November 1930 at his Mont Albert home. Survived by his wife, seven children of his first marriage and three of his second, he was buried in Brighton cemetery; his estate was sworn for probate at £10 292.

Argus, 31 Oct 1904, 27 Nov 1905, 6 Sept, 21 Nov 1911, 10 May, 28 Aug, 3 Sept 1923, 26 May, 25 June, 1, 23 July, 11 Aug 1924, 12 July, 20 Sept 1928, 22 Nov 1930; *Referee*, 9, 16 Nov, 7 Dec 1904, 25 Jan, 21 June, 5 July 1905, 21 Nov 1906, 15 May 1907, 10, 24 May, 27 Sept 1911, 27 Mar 1912; *Age* and *Sun News-Pictorial*, 22 Nov 1930; information from Mr W. Crocker, Ainslie, Canb.

W. F. MANDLE

WEBER, HORACE GEORGE MARTIN (1887?-1968), organist, was born probably on 9 May 1887 at Parkside, Adelaide, fourth of eight children of Albert George Conrad Weber, music teacher and piano mechanic, and his wife Sophie Lydia, née Peryman, singer. Horace was educated at St Cyprian's Day School and Pulteney Street School. Encouraged by his parents and taught by his father, he learned the piano and organ. He was a chorister at St Peter's Cathedral (1898-1903) and assistant organist (1899). In 1905-06 he studied piano at the Elder [q.v.4] Conservatorium.

Appointed in 1909 organist and choirmaster at St John's Cathedral, Napier, New Zealand, on 3 April 1911 Weber married Adelaide-born Annie May Shakeshaft at St Thomas's Anglican Church, Wellington. Returning to Australia, he was organist at the North Adelaide Baptist Church in 1913-17. Now recognized as a leading concert organist, he gave many recitals in churches and at the Adelaide Town Hall. In 1919 he was given a three-year contract at the Grand Theatre, Adelaide, playing the newly installed Wurlitzer Duplex for silent films.

Weber played the organ in many theatres in New South Wales, Western Australia and Victoria—his last engagement was at Melbourne's Regent and Plaza theatres in 1948-49—but his years (1924-29, 1933-34 and 1938-44) at Australia's first full-scale 3m/15r Wurlitzer at the new Capitol Theatre, Melbourne, were the highlight of his career. The opening night (8 November 1924) featured the film, *The Ten Commandments*, a large orchestra and Weber as 'master organist'. In 1963 when the Capitol closed its organ, he was principal recitalist, his performance still brilliant and whimsical. The Dendy Theatre, Brighton, bought the organ and in 1967 Weber re-opened it. His repertoire was always varied, from classical (Bach, Reger, Widor) to hymns, hit parade songs and his signature tune, *Look for the silver lining*. As a teacher of classical and theatre organ, he excelled.

In the late 1920s 'talkies' had reduced the importance of theatre organists who subsequently only provided entertainment before and between films. Intermittent and enforced idleness was probably a contributing factor to Weber becoming alcohol-dependent and unemployed. In private life he experienced tragedies. His wife had died in childbirth in 1921, leaving him with three small children, one of whom died in 1923. On 17 October 1927 at St Mark's Anglican Church, Fitzroy, he married Welsh-born Gladys May Sylvester; they had three children, of whom one died in 1928. Weber and his wife separated in 1946. 'Down and out', he lived at Gordon House (a refuge for homeless men) in Bourke Street, Melbourne. In 1949 Rev. Wesley Bligh of the Armadale Baptist Church befriended Weber and encouraged him to become his organist and choirmaster. Respected by the congregation and choristers, and applauded for his recitals and broadcasts, he at last enjoyed years of peace.

A tall, erect, courteous and private man, with twinkling blue eyes and 'elf-like humour', Weber 'brought the skill of the classical organist into the world of popular entertainment'. Predeceased by his wife, and survived by the two sons of his first marriage and by a son and daughter of his second, he died on 4 October 1968 at Fitzroy and was cremated. In 1987 the Theatre Organ Society of Australia (Victorian Division) held the Horace Weber Centenary Celebration Concerts to honour its former patron.

Theatre Organ, Spring 1964; *Age*, 5 Oct 1968; R. Brown, Funeral oration (held by Mr J. Ferguson, Mt Waverley, Melb); information from Mr E. Wicks, Ivanhoe, Mr H. Hodge, Glen Iris, and Mr J. Ferguson, Mt Waverley, Melb, and Mr W. and Mrs M. Weber, Mornington, Vic.　　Joyce Gibberd

WEBER, IVY LAVINIA (1892-1976), physical culturist and politician, was born on 7 June 1892 at Captains Flat, New South Wales, third child of John Filshie, schoolteacher, and his wife Elizabeth, née Seaman, both native-born. Educated at Dungog and raised as a Presbyterian, she worked in Sydney, possibly at Reuters newsagency, and on 11 December 1915 at the Sacred Heart presbytery, Mosman, married with Catholic rites Thomas Mitchell, a stock and station agent. He was killed in action in France in May 1917, leaving her with a baby son. Living with her parents in Melbourne, Ivy enrolled in the Weber and Rice Health and Strength College and on 7 March 1919 married its principal, Clarence Weber [q.v.], a widower with seven young children—they were to have three of their own. Domestic help with the children allowed Ivy to run the women's classes at the college.

In 1930 Clarence Weber died suddenly. Ivy took a job with the Berlei Corset Co., lecturing on figure control. Subsequently she worked as an organizer for the United Country Party and for the Hospital Benefits Association. A woman of 'immense vitality', she gave radio talks on physical culture, served on the management committee of the Queen Victoria Hospital (1930-34) and by 1937 was an office-bearer of the Playgrounds Association and the Red Cross Society. She was president of the Local Option Alliance (1939-43) and of the Australian Temperance Council (1941-43). As an executive-member of the National Council of Women (1934-39), she played a leading part in the establishment of a physical education course at the University of Melbourne; she was also a member of the National Fitness Council in 1939-53.

In June 1937 the League of Women Electors had been formed to endorse women parliamentary candidates under the banner of 'Mother, Child, Family, Home and Health'. Ivy Weber was the league's president and its candidate for the Legislative Assembly seat of Nunawading at the 1937 State election. Standing as an Independent, she advocated free education and a national health scheme. Tall, 'very good-looking, with a pleasing voice and poise', she defeated the sitting member, becoming the second woman to be elected to the Victorian parliament and the first at a general election. In parliament she successfully argued for the appointment of a woman to the Housing Commission (1938). Re-elected twice, she resigned in 1943 to contest the Federal seat of Henty for the 'Women to Canberra' movement of which she was president. She polled fifth in a field of six; two years later she was decisively beaten when she stood for the State seat of Box Hill.

After leaving parliament, Mrs Weber held organizing jobs with the Department of Supply, the Country Party, the Australian Women's Movement Against Socialism and worked for the blind. Survived by her two sons and two daughters, she died at Camberwell on 6 March 1976 and was cremated. Ivy Weber believed that girls should put 'marriage and motherhood before any other career'; yet she also maintained that women should be active in public life. She managed to do both by 'working a tremendous lot of over-time'.

A. Lemon, *Box Hill* (Melb, 1978); M. Bevege et al (eds), *Worth her salt* (Syd, 1982); M. Sawer and M. Simms, *A woman's place* (Syd, 1984); F. Kelly and M. Lake (eds), *Double time, women in Victoria, 150 years* (Melb, 1985); V. Davies, Ivy Lavinia Weber (unpublished biog study, LaTL); Weber cutting-book (held by Ms V. Davies, Fitzroy, Melb).

GEOFF BROWNE

WEBSTER, CHARLES ERNEST (1861-1936), merchant and businessman, and EDWIN HERBERT (1864-1947), business-man and yachtsman, were born on 21 October 1861 and 20 June 1864 in Hobart Town, second and fourth sons of Alexander George Webster [q.v.6], merchant, and his wife Louisa Harriett, née Turnley. Educated at The Hutchins School, in 1879 Charles joined the family's wool and grain store on Hobart's Old Wharf. The firm became known as A. G. Webster & Son Ltd. He enthusiastically pro-moted the import of agricultural implements and machinery, including fan winnowing mills, the Reid and Grey double-furrow plough, the Hornsby steam plough and the Wolseley [q.v.6] sheep-shearing machine. By 1889 the business had opened machinery branches at Launceston, Devonport and Burnie, and had published *Webster's Tasmanian Agricultural-ist and Machinery Gazette* which provided in-formation on scientific farming. In its capacity as a general agent, the firm also imported the first motor car to Tasmania—a Reo—which it assembled locally. In 1916 it organized the introduction of the Boving turbines for the hydro-electric station at Waddamana.

The collapse of the Van Diemen's Land Bank on 3 August 1891 had threatened Web-ster & Son, a major shareholder, with finan-cial catastrophe. Charles replaced his father as general manager that year and presided over a period of steady growth. In 1910, when the firm was registered as an incorporated company, Charles was managing director; on his father's death in 1914, Charles became chairman of directors and retained that post until 1936, save for an interval in 1924-30 when (Sir) Alfred Ashbolt [q.v.7] filled it.

A fine gymnast in his youth, Charles also hunted, played polo and was an amateur com-edian. He took a keen interest in yachting and, with H. W. Knight, had founded the Derwent Sailing Boat Club in 1880. On 9 August 1899 at the Church of the Epiphany, Mandeville, New Zealand, he married Louisa Margaret Bell, a grazier's daughter; they were to remain childless. President of the Hobart Amateur Horticultural Society, Charles was an expert in the hybridization of daffodils. He rented and managed Glen Lynden, an orchard at Glenorchy, and was also president of the local Royal Agricultural Society and the King-ston Beach Golf Club. He was esteemed for his charity. Survived by his wife, Charles Webster died at Potts Point, Sydney, on 23 September 1936 and was cremated with Anglican rites. His estate was sworn for pro-bate at £71 204.

Edwin was also educated at The Hutchins School and entered the family firm where he distinguished himself in its mercantile and financial affairs. On 10 February 1904 in Hobart he married Edith Maud Hudspeth, an Anglican clergyman's daughter. Edwin became a director of the family company in 1910. Responsible for the marketing of wool, he has been credited with organizing the first international wool auctions in the State. He also played a significant role in exporting Tas-manian apples which led to his appointment as director of the Tasmanian Stevedoring Co. Edwin contributed to the growth of the family firm into a State-wide pastoral and merchant company with offices in the major towns of Tasmania, as well as in Melbourne, Sydney and Hong Kong. In 1920-21 he served as an alderman on Hobart City Council. He was, as well, a prominent exhibitor at the Hobart Amateur Horticultural Society's functions.

An enthusiastic yachtsman and first-class helmsman, he promoted the design and build-ing of a Tasmanian yacht class and in 1911 collaborated with the shipbuilder Alfred Blore. In 1925-29 Edwin helped to develop the Derwent class yacht. With Leslie Nor-man, he compiled *A hundred years of yachting* (1936), a valuable guide to boating and recreation on the Derwent River. Survived by his wife and three sons, Edwin Webster died on 31 July 1947 at Greystanes, his home at Sandy Bay, Hobart, and was cremated. His estate was sworn for probate at £20 568.

George Alexander (1860-1911), A. G. Webster's eldest son, became a qualified doc-tor and practised in England and Victoria; injured *en route* to the South African War, he specialized in treating consumptives in Hobart.

Webster Limited, *Tasmania's pioneering com-pany* (Hob, 1981); *Tas Mail*, 13 Feb 1904, 21 Jan 1931; *Mercury*, 13 Dec 1911, 11 Feb 1922, 25 Sept, 2 Oct 1936, 1 Aug 1947; Webster papers (Univ Tas Archives).   PETER CHAPMAN

WEBSTER, ELLEN (1877-1965), grazier and politician, was born on 14 October 1877 at Reedy Creek, near Inverell, New South Wales, sixth child of Phillip Callachor, hawker, and his wife Mary, née Fitzgerald, both from Ireland. Phillip prospered on the land and Ellen was educated at home, Emer-ald Vale, Yetman. Residing in Sydney with

432

her aunt, Margaret Ann Fletcher, she retained her country connexions and claimed to have begun medicine at the University of Sydney. Politically aware, through her family's links with the Progressive (Country) Party, she joined the Labor Party after she met WILLIAM MAULE (McDOWELL) WEBSTER (1885-1958). They married on 26 July 1921 in the vestry of St Patrick's Catholic Church, Sydney, and went to live at Forbes.

William was born on 3 January 1885 at Forbes, son of Edward Webster, grazier, and his wife Ellen, née Crooks. A stock and station agent, in 1928 he took over the Arcot estate near Forbes. By then he was president (1927-28) of the New South Wales branch of the Australian Labor Party. Ellen matched his enthusiasm; she was a delegate to country conferences and a member of the party executive in 1927-29. Both were keen followers of the leader J. T. Lang [q.v.9] who in 1931 appointed William a member of the Closer Settlement Advisory Board on which he served until 1939. In November 1930 Ellen had been among eighty Laborites whom Lang nominated to Governor Sir Philip Game [q.v.8] for appointment to the Legislative Council; though legal proceedings forestalled any action, Ellen was one of the first two women appointed to the council in November 1931.

Tall, firmly built, with glasses and bountiful hair, Ellen Webster had an expressive and amiable face. She was cheerful, a great raconteur and name-dropper; her friendliness could easily turn into benevolence, and she contributed much to Church and charities. She became a conscientious and energetic parliamentarian, adhering to Lang's party during the intense internecine strife that succeeded the expulsion of Lang and his followers from the A.L.P. in March 1931. After Lang's dismissal in May 1932, and his electoral defeat next month, she remained loyal to him. Yet, despite her protests, she was placed in an unwinnable position on Lang's party ticket for election to the reconstituted Legislative Council in December 1933: 'Well, I've been dumped', she said, 'but I can still raise a smile'. She remained active in the Labor Party and did not follow Lang when he defected in 1943. Expelled in the great party split over the industrial groups in the mid-1950s, she joined the Democratic Labor Party in 1957.

The Websters had a home at Randwick, Sydney, as well as at Forbes. William was the Australian member of the British Phosphate Commission in 1946-52. When he died on 20 April 1958, Ellen took over the management of Arcot. In ill health in the 1960s, she lived at Randwick with her nephew John Callachor Fletcher. He was her main beneficiary when she died, childless, on 20 October 1965 at Darlinghurst and was buried in Randwick cemetery.

B. Nairn, *The 'Big Fella'* (Melb, 1986); *SMH*, 7 Apr 1928, 28 July 1933, 8 Aug 1934; *Labor Daily*, 18 May 1932; *Daily Telegraph* (Syd), 16 Dec 1933; *Sun* (Syd), 17 Jan 1957; information from Rev F. Fletcher, Erskineville, Syd.   BEDE NAIRN

WEBSTER, WILLIAM (1860-1936), quarryman and politician, was born on 7 June 1860 at Everton, Lancashire, England, son of John Webster, labourer, and his wife Elizabeth, née Poynton. One of a large family, William left school at 13 to work in the Welsh quarries. Migrating to New South Wales in 1879, he quarried stone at Pyrmont and, by diligent saving, was able to bring the rest of his family to Sydney. By 1880 he was prominent in the Quarrymen's Union of New South Wales and financial secretary of the Trades and Labor Council. On 7 June 1883 at St Clement's Anglican Church, Marrickville, he married Jane Buckney. Webster Bros, the quarrying firm he founded at Marrickville, was among the first in New South Wales to observe an eight-hour day and standard wage.

Having been a member of the Marrickville Municipal Council from 1887, Webster surmounted the legal technicalities of the case arising from a disputed election to the Petersham Council in 1890 to act successfully as his own counsel: when a new election was ordered, he was returned with an overwhelming majority. Defeated in the 1890s when he stood for the New South Wales Legislative Assembly seats of Canterbury, Petersham and Wickham, he withdrew his candidature for Marrickville during the 1893 depression when his building business collapsed. Webster returned to his trade at Narrabri, quarrying stone for the Moree courthouse. Despite his previous opposition to the Federation bill, in 1901 he contested the Federal seat of Gwydir. From 1901 to 1903 he was the first Labor member to represent Moree in the assembly where he invoked reform of land administration. A hardworking local politician, he made it his business to know 'the pet name and birthday of every child' in his electorate. In 1903 he resigned and won Gwydir for Labor. He never forgot his constituency and, though swamped with considerable correspondence, took care to attend personally to letters and requests.

He was an instigator, member and chairman of the royal commission on postal services (1908-10) whose critical findings on the service under the Deakin [q.v.8] administration became a catalyst for the government's defeat. In pursuit of these criticisms, Webster —'the man with the iron jaw'—delivered a famous stonewalling speech on 9 July 1909 which lasted 10 hours and 57 minutes; a time limit, adopted three years later, preserved his record. In the first Hughes [q.v.9] government Webster was appointed postmaster-general on 27 October 1915. In 1916 he left the Australian Labor Party over conscription: as one of the twenty-four ex-members who joined Hughes in the National Labor government, he retained his portfolio until 3 February 1920. Webster successfully impeached the Department of Works for waste and extravagance in developing the Federal capital. He was defeated in the December 1919 election.

Retiring to Wentworthville, to his books, his garden and an occasional game of bowls, Webster died on 8 October 1936 at Parramatta and was cremated. His wife, daughter and two sons survived him.

L. F. Fitzhardinge, *The little digger* (Syd, 1979); P. M. Weller (ed), *Caucus minutes, 1901-1949* (Melb, 1975); *V&P* (LA NSW), 1902, 5, p 750; *Lone Hand*, 16 June 1919; *Punch* (Melb), 4 Oct 1910, 25 June 1914, 11 Nov 1915; *SMH*, 28 Oct 1915, 14 Feb, 9 May, 10, 23 Oct, 2 Nov 1916, 21 Aug 1919, 9 June 1933, 12 Oct 1936.   CHRISTINE WISE

WEEDON, SIR HENRY (1859-1921), businessman and lord mayor, was born on 26 March 1859 in Melbourne, son of Henry Weedon, grocer, and his wife Emily, née Emery, both London born. At the age of 21 he was employed as a decorating contractor and undertook work on Parliament House and its library, the Melbourne Town Hall, Government House and the Victorian court at the Hobart exhibition. An able businessman with a talent for financial organization, Weedon was a managing partner of the successful Talma Photographic Studios of Sydney and Melbourne. He was also involved in gold-dredging in the Bright, Castlemaine and Gippsland districts of Victoria, chairman of investment companies in Melbourne and Sydney, and managing director of the Globe Motor Co. in South Melbourne.

Elected in 1899 to the Melbourne City Council for Albert Ward which he continued to represent until his death, Weedon was lord mayor in 1905-08 and an alderman in 1913. He was chairman of the council's parks and gardens committee and of the Alexandra Gardens committee. In 1906 he had represented Victoria at the Christchurch exhibition in New Zealand. While acting as commissioner for Victoria at the Franco-British Exhibition, London, he was knighted in 1908.

An Oddfellow and a Freemason, Weedon assisted a wide variety of community organizations and charities. He was a chairman of the Tramways Trust, a trustee and treasurer

of the Public Library, museums and National Gallery, a member of the Fire Brigades' Board, a trustee of the Exhibition Building, a manager of the Fawkner cemetery and founding chairman of the Macedon Water Trust. A governor of the Melbourne, Alfred, Homeopathic, Women's and Children's hospitals, the Sutherland Home, the Carlton Refuge, and the Deaf and Dumb Asylum, he was also a member of the faculty of veterinary science at the University of Melbourne.

Following the resignation of Sir Samuel Gillott [q.v.9], in 1907 Weedon was returned to the Legislative Assembly for the seat of East Melbourne; as a Ministerialist, he supported Sir Thomas Bent [q.v.3] and served on the royal commission into tramway fares in 1910-11. Defeated in the 1911 election, he unsuccessfully contested his former seat in 1912 and 1914 before representing Melbourne Province in the Legislative Council in 1919-21.

Noted for his courtesy and genial nature, Weedon was a philanthropic urban liberal of the old school who was remembered for his frock-coat and bell-topper, and for his somewhat erratic grammar. He was thrice married with Anglican rites: to Emily Ellard (d. 1896) on 26 December 1880 at St Jude's Church, Carlton; to Fanny Dudley Cohen (d. 1913) on 5 August 1896 at All Saints Church, St Kilda; and to Florence Maud Mary McCarron on 17 April 1915 at St Mary's Cathedral, Auckland, New Zealand. Survived by his wife, and by a son of his first marriage, Weedon died of cerebro-vascular disease on 26 March 1921 at Darlinghurst while holidaying in Sydney and was buried in Melbourne general cemetery. His estate was sworn for probate at £9349.

J. Smith (ed), *Cyclopedia of Victoria*, 1 (Melb, 1903); *PD* (Vic), 6 July 1921; *Table Talk*, 17 Nov 1899, Annual 1905; *Argus*, 10 Oct 1905, 28, 31 Mar 1921; *Leader* (Melb), 14 Oct 1905; *Age*, 28, 31 Mar 1921; *Bulletin*, 7 Apr 1921.

DAVID DUNSTAN

WEIGALL, CECIL EDWARD (1870-1955), barrister, was born on 28 March 1870 in Sydney, son of Albert Bythesea Weigall [q.v.6], headmaster, and his wife Ada Frances, née Raymond, granddaughter of James Raymond [q.v.2]. With his eight brothers and sisters, Cecil lived at Sydney Grammar School where he was educated and captained the school in 1888. At Corpus Christi College, Oxford (B.A., 1893), he was captain of cricket, rowed stroke for the eight and graduated with fourth-class honours in *literae humaniores*.

On returning to Sydney in 1893 he studied law and, after passing the Barristers Admission Board examinations in 1895, was admitted to the Bar on 19 May 1896. He recorded industrial arbitration cases in 1905-11. On 20 April 1912 he married Maude Lyman Sise at All Saints Anglican Church, Dunedin, New Zealand. Entering the New South Wales Public Service as assistant parliamentary draftsman in July 1920, Weigall became parliamentary draftsman (1921), crown prosecutor and assistant law officer (1922) in rapid succession. He was appointed solicitor-general on 27 December 1922 and took silk on 22 April 1925.

As solicitor-general Weigall was the principal non-political legal adviser to the State government: he deputized for the attorney-general and assisted with administrative functions within the Department of the Attorney-General and Justice; he also helped to prepare legislation, represented the Crown as counsel in civil and criminal matters, and became an authority on criminal law and procedure. He published, sometimes as co-author, standard legal works on the Acts covering industrial arbitration (1906), infants' custody, maintenance and protection (1908), child welfare (1924), deserted wives and children (1932) and, most notably, four editions of the standard New South Wales text on criminal law and procedure (1930, 1940, 1947 and 1957).

A keen sportsman, Weigall played social cricket for I Zingari (Australia) and golf until he was in his seventies. He belonged to the Australian Jockey, Royal Sydney Golf and the Union clubs, and was a member of the Sydney Cricket Ground. He was, as well, a voracious reader of detective stories.

A bout of typhoid fever early in the century left him with increasing deafness. Weigall continued to appear regularly in the Court of Criminal Appeal, but, in his later career, required the assistance in court of a law officer to relay indistinct statements from the bench. He admired succinctness in a judge and his asides to the officer about one verbose justice became legendary among the Sydney Bar. Weigall's shy, quiet and gentle manner, compounded by his affliction, meant that communication with him was often difficult in his last years, yet he was held in great affection by members of the crown law office.

Awarded the King George V silver jubilee (1935) and King George VI coronation (1937) medals, Weigall did not retire until 1953. Survived by his wife and two daughters, he died on 11 June 1955 at Darling Point, Sydney, and was cremated. His estate was sworn for probate at £7178.

Aust Law J, 21 May 1953, p 24; K. Mason, 'The office of solicitor general for New South Wales', *Bar News* (NSW), 1988; *SMH*, 1 June 1922, 13 June 1955; information from Mrs A. Bury and Mrs M. Maxwell, Bellevue Hill, Syd.   KEITH MASON

WEIGALL, THEYRE à BECKETT (1860-1926), barrister and judge, was born on 10 February 1860 at Elsternwick, Melbourne, son of Theyre Weigall, clerk, and his wife Marion, née à Beckett, both London born. Educated at Melbourne Church of England Grammar School where he won the matriculation classics exhibition, he studied law at the University of Melbourne (LL.B., 1880), gaining first-class honours and several exhibitions. He was called to the Bar in 1881. When his uncle (Sir) Thomas à Beckett [q.v.3] was elevated to the bench of the Victorian Supreme Court in 1886, Theyre succeeded to much of his large practice. On 7 April 1890 at St David's Anglican Cathedral, Hobart, Weigall married Anne Sophie Henrietta, daughter of Sir Robert Hamilton [q.v.4], governor of Tasmania.

Specializing in equity work, procedure and company law, Weigall became renowned as an expert on the administration of trusts. Appointed a K.C. in 1906, he practised widely in the High Court of Australia and the Supreme Court of Victoria. When he was offered a place on the Supreme Court bench about 1920, he refused it: he regarded himself as an equity specialist, and was averse to criminal cases because of his opposition to capital punishment. In 1923, however, he did accept an appointment as acting judge: he was excused criminal matters and actually sat in chambers. Learned, capable and cautious, he was well regarded by his colleagues.

A kindly, humorous and witty man, charming and courteous, Weigall 'never lost a friend or made an enemy', according to (Sir) Isaac Isaacs [q.v.9]. These two men had been close since they were law students and academic rivals; another friend from school years was (Sir) Edward Mitchell [q.v.10]. Weigall was a vigorous man of simple tastes and boyish enthusiasms, with a spare frame and bright, blue eyes. He loved monthly bushwalks with members of the Wallaby Club; he played tennis all his life and in 1909-26 was president of the Lawn Tennis Association of Victoria; cycling was another abiding pleasure. A sociable man, he was a member of the Bohemian, Melbourne, Royal Yacht and Royal Melbourne Golf clubs. He was also active in the affairs of his old school.

His daughter Joan Lindsay commented that although her father was 'a firm believer in stabilised marriage, the Church of England, Debentures and the Melbourne Club', he was in small matters somewhat heedless of conventions. Thus, he rode an out-of-date push-bike and apparently liked shabby, old clothes. She attributed this fondness for the unconventional and old-fashioned to his à Beckett heritage. Weigall died suddenly of pneumonia at his St Kilda home on 8 June 1926 and was buried in Brighton cemetery; his estate was sworn for probate at £63 699. He was survived by his wife, who later married Professor T. G. Tucker [q.v.], three daughters and a son.

J. L. Forde, *The story of the Bar of Victoria* (Melb, 1913); P. A. Jacobs, *A lawyer tells* (Melb, 1949); Joan Lindsay, *Time without clocks* (Melb, 1962); D. Lindsay, *The leafy tree, my family* (Melb, 1965); A. Dean, *A multitude of counsellors* (Melb, 1968); *Australasian*, 9 Dec 1882, 14 Dec 1891, 25 Dec 1897, 25 Nov 1911, 12 June 1926; *Argus* and *SMH*, 9 June 1926.   RUTH CAMPBELL

WEIGALL, SIR WILLIAM ERNEST GEORGE ARCHIBALD (1874-1952), governor, was born on 8 December 1874 in London, fifth son of Henry Weigall, artist, and his wife Lady Rose Sophia Mary Fane, author and niece of the 1st duke of Wellington. Educated at Wellington College, Berkshire, and the Royal Agricultural College, Cirencester, Archie became an estate manager. Joining the Northampton and Rutland Militia, he was awarded the Queen's medal in the South African War and was promoted major. On 16 August 1910 in the Metheringham parish church, Lincolnshire, he married a divorcee Grace Emily, Baroness von Echardstein, only child of the deceased furniture magnate Sir John Blundell Maple who had left a fortune of £2 153 000; the couple settled at Petwood, Woodhall Spa; Weigall farmed and also represented Horncastle in the House of Commons as a Conservative-Unionist (1911-20).

In 1919 he agreed to succeed Sir Henry Galway [q.v.8] as governor of South Australia. Appointed K.C.M.G. in 1920, Weigall arrived in Adelaide in June. Four months later he told the prince of Wales that his hardest job was 'holding my tongue'. The Colonial Office had wrongly advised him that the State government would pay his staff's salaries, which, with his servants' wages, absorbed all but £300 of his own salary. In the official sphere Weigall was shocked that 'sums voted . . . for one specific purpose are transferred to another without reference to Parliament'. Like Governor Sir Day Bosanquet [q.v.7], he failed to prevent his ministers spending much of the State's revenue before parliament had granted supply. Weigall concluded in 1921 that 'State Governors and State Legislatures are now anachronisms': he advised the Colonial Office that the division of power between Commonwealth and States had produced 'farcical' and 'chaotic' results, and that a unitary system of government was desirable.

A tall, balding, cigar-smoking gentleman, with a moustache and a stammer, Weigall disliked making long speeches, but his wit and interest in farming made him popular: he con-

vened a conference which led to the establishment of an agricultural high school and to legislation compelling the registration and licensing of bulls. In public his wife, who was a good speaker, promoted social and philanthropic work; behind the official scene, she suffered a number of miscarriages. In December 1921 Weigall sought leave to resign for 'private and financial' reasons: he claimed that he had not realized 'what the results of British taxation were going to be'. They left Adelaide on 24 April 1922. Their departure prompted the premier, Sir Henry Barwell [q.v.7], to raise the governor's salary.

Becoming chairman of directors of Australian Chilled Meat & Food Supplies Ltd, Weigall accepted directorships in the Clarence Hatry companies: he lost his capital when they crashed in 1929; though his fellow directors were gaoled for forgery or conspiracy, he was not prosecuted. Thereafter he was dependent upon his wife's money. As chairman of the Royal Empire Society (1932-38), Weigall revisited South Australia in 1935 and 1937. A chairman of the Royal Veterinary College, in 1938 he was created baronet and King of Arms of the Order of St Michael and St George. Predeceased by his wife in 1950 and survived by their only daughter, he died at Ascot, Berkshire, on 3 June 1952; his English estate was sworn for probate at £17 479.

Critic (Adel), 28 Jan 1920; P. A. Howell, 'Pursuing further varieties of vice-regal life', *J Hist Soc of SA*, no 17, 1989; *Evening Standard*, 23 Jan 1920; *Punch* (Melb), 5 Feb 1920; *Argus*, 18 Feb 1920; *Observer* (Adel), 16 Oct 1920; *The Times*, 27 Mar 1929, 17 Mar 1930, 4, 5 June 1952; *Chronicle* (Adel), 20 June 1929; *Herald* (Melb), 16 Mar, 10 Dec 1934, 5 Apr 1951; Weigall papers (Kent Archives Office, UK); CO 418/194, /210, /222 (NL); information from Mr E. Veniard, Seacliff, Adel.

P. A. HOWELL

WEINDORFER, GUSTAV (1874-1932), naturalist and conservationist, was born on 23 February 1874 at Spittal an der Drau, Kärnten, Austria, son of Johann Weindorfer, district governor, and his wife Pauline, née Tscheligi. Gustav was educated at Villach and at an agricultural school at Mödling, near Vienna. After compulsory military service, he worked in the wine industry and migrated to Australia in 1900.

Obtaining a clerical position in Melbourne with Pfaff, Pinschof [q.v.11] & Co., Weindorfer became honorary chancellor at the Austro-Hungarian consulate in 1901. A mountaineer and an amateur botanist, he joined the Field Naturalists' Club of Victoria that year and the local branch of the Royal Geographical Society of Australasia in 1903; he gave public lectures and published in the

Victorian Naturalist, the *Leader* and the *Australasian.* Weindorfer sent Australian plants and seeds to the Museum of Natural History, Vienna, and to other collectors, and organized holiday camps in the Victorian Alps for botanists.

Naturalized in 1905, he married fellow club member Kate Julia Cowle with Methodist forms at Stowport, Tasmania, on 1 February 1906. They bought 100 acres (40.5 ha) in 1910 at Kindred, near Devonport, where Kate's family held land; Weindorfer proved an excellent farmer. Impressed by Cradle Mountain during his first climb in January 1909, he determined to make it a national park: with Kate, Gustav shared his dream of establishing a chalet for bushwalkers and mountaineers in the valley below. He named local features, wrote articles on the project in the Launceston *Weekly Courier* and in the *Victorian Naturalist,* and urged the government to build a road to the area.

In 1912 Weindorfer began building Waldheim ('home in the forest'), using King Billy pine from the site. As a horse and cart could approach no closer than 8.7 miles (14 km), 'Dorfer' carried baths and stoves on his back. First opened at Christmas 1912, Waldheim became a popular resort. Its courtly and jovial host often sang to his guests and had a mischievous sense of humour. Carved on the wall of the chalet was the motto: 'This is Waldheim, where there is no time and nothing matters'.

After his wife died in April 1916, Weindorfer experienced isolation. Although he was a justice of the peace and had tried to join the Australian Imperial Force, he became a target for anti-German prejudice; selling his farm at Kindred in 1917, he ran Waldheim single-handed, while acting as ranger. He also travelled, lectured and kept official weather records. Weindorfer died of coronary vascular disease on 5 May 1932 in Cradle Valley and was buried there. His property was eventually added to the adjoining 158 000 acres (63 941 ha) stretching from Cradle Mountain to Lake St Clair which, as a result of his efforts, had been proclaimed a reserve in 1922. A granite cairn over his grave was unveiled in 1938.

G. F. J. Bergman, *The hermit of Cradle Mountain* (np, 1955?) and *Gustav Weindorfer of Cradle Mountain* (Launc, 1959); M. Lake, *A divided society* (Melb, 1975); *Walkabout,* Apr 1966; *Examiner* (Launc), 17 Aug 1929, 11 May 1932; Weindorfer papers (ML); biog card index (Basser Lib, Canb).

RAYMOND F. TILLEY

WEINGARTH, JOHN LEOPOLD (1862-1925), surveyor, was born on 8 June 1862 in Sydney, second son of Henry Weingarth, a baker from Sobernheim, Prussia, and his Irish wife Bridget, née Kenny. Educated at St Stanislaus's College, Bathurst, John was an enthusiastic sportsman, good footballer and all-round athlete. He entered the Department of Lands as a cadet draughtsman, worked as an assistant to Edward McFarlane in the Western Land District and was licensed as a surveyor on 6 July 1883. Weingarth practised as a departmental surveyor in the Western Division, then joined J. T. Cahill in partnership in Sydney in 1886 before setting up on his own. On 30 June 1891 at St James's Catholic Church, Glebe, Weingarth married Gertrude Lawn; they were to have four children. In 1903 he corresponded with Sir Edmund Barton [q.v.7] about the choice of a site for the Federal capital.

Active and successful, Weingarth soon became one of the State's most experienced private surveyors, known for his identification surveys, road formation and street alignments. His advice as an expert witness was eagerly sought in lawsuits. He published *Identification surveys: freehold title and Torrens title* (1913), a standard reference still esteemed by surveyors for its clarity and accuracy; it is used, *inter alia,* by lawyers in assessing the culpability of negligence of surveyors and in deciding whether to sue for damages.

Expert in the design and formation of racecourses, Weingarth supervised their construction at Randwick, Rosehill, old Warwick Farm, Kensington, Rosebery Park and Epping. As official surveyor to the Australian Jockey Club, he also designed new Warwick Farm and the 1921 improvements at Randwick. His scientific approach weighed carefully the relationships of curves, centrifugal forces, safety and equal opportunities, while his observations on galloping horses, stride and landing expanded significantly the standard textbooks.

After his sons Jack and Delman qualified as surveyors, in January 1919 he established J. Weingarth & Sons, licensed surveyors; the firm suffered an initial setback when Jack, who had served with the Royal Australian Flying Corps and was interested in the potential of aerial survey, died in an accident in England. A visit to the United States of America in 1922 enabled Weingarth to study the latest methods of road construction; he later convassed the comparative costs and advantages of new technologies for laying asphalt roads.

A council-member for many years and president (1915-16) of the Institution of Surveyors, New South Wales, he was a member of its board of examiners and later edited the *Surveyor.* His series on pioneer surveyors (1916-20) provided a detailed account of the progress of the profession; his interests spread into local history and he became an active member of the Royal Australian Historical Society. Weingarth's articles on the Macleay, Nambucca and Bellinger districts provide the first trained and critical linking of map and land records with these areas.

Survived by his wife, a daughter and a son, Weingarth died of an aneurysm of the aorta on 7 March 1925 at his home in Etham Avenue, Darling Point, and was buried in Waverley cemetery after a service in St Mary's Cathedral. His Castlereagh Street firm continued until Delman's death in 1962.

Surveyor (Syd), Mar 1925; *JRAHS*, 11, no 3, 1926; *SMH*, 1 Oct 1921, 27 Sept 1922, 9, 10 Mar 1925; *Catholic Press*, 12 Mar 1925; letters of Sir E. Barton to J. L. Weingarth (ML); information from Messrs J. C. and G. F. Weingarth, Syd, J. M. Naughton, Cheltenham, Syd, J. Weingarth, Lismore, T. J. Stewart, Armidale, P. Pardy, Glen Innes, and Mrs D. Bowden, Kempsey, NSW.   JOHN ATCHISON

WEIR, STANLEY PRICE (1866-1944), army officer and public servant, was born on 23 April 1866 at Norwood, Adelaide, son of Alfred Weir, carpenter, and his wife Susannah Mary, née Price. Educated at Norwood Public School, Stanley joined the South Australian Lands and Survey Department in 1879 and at 19 enlisted in the Volunteer Military Force. On 14 May 1890 at the Christian Chapel, Norwood, he married Rosa Wadham (d. 1923). Weir was an active member of the Churches of Christ and president (1924) of their conference. Commissioned in the South Australian Militia in 1890, he continued to serve with the Australian Military Forces, commanding the 19th Infantry Brigade from 1912 and gaining promotion to colonel next year. Meanwhile, he had steadily advanced in his civil employment.

On 17 August 1914 Weir was appointed to the Australian Imperial Force as a lieut-colonel and given command of the 10th Battalion. Embarking in October, the battalion trained in Egypt and on Lemnos, and was one of the first two A.I.F. units to land at Gallipoli on 25 April 1915. Five days later, half its officers and soldiers had become casualties. Despite his age, Weir impressed C. E. W. Bean [q.v.7] with his powers of endurance, but fell ill in September and had to be evacuated. He rejoined his command in Egypt in March 1916. Transferred to the Western Front, the 10th Battalion was involved in the fierce fighting at Pozières and Mouquet Farm in July and August. Exhausted, Weir asked to be relieved and returned to Australia where his A.I.F. appointment was terminated on 14 December. For his gallantry and his consistent skill, tact and judgement in command, he

won the Distinguished Service Order. He was also mentioned in dispatches and awarded the Russian Order of St Anne (with swords). Aide-de-camp (1917-20) to the governor-general, he retired from the A.M.F. in March 1921 as an honorary brigadier general.

His repatriation ahead of the bulk of returning servicemen combined with the South Australian government's policy of preference for veterans in its employment to propel Weir to the top of the public service. He had become the State's first public service commissioner in 1916. Given the task of classifying and regularizing the service, he proved ineffectual: he was unable to cope with political and personal conflicts within the service and the government, and was soon disregarded by individual ministers and by the cabinet. Amendments to the Public Service Act in 1925 cleared the way for his replacement in 1930. In the eighteen months before his retirement in 1931, he was simultaneously chairman of the Central Board of Health and the Children's Welfare and Public Relief Board. Succeeding Ramsay Smith [q.v.11], he avoided controversy in the first of these roles, while performing the second with energy, compassion and insight.

Prominent in religious, charitable and welfare activities, Weir continued this work after his retirement. To the end of his life, he remained a public servant in the best sense of the term. He was general secretary of the Adelaide Benevolent and Strangers' Friend Society and contributed to the formal training of social workers; he was also an honorary matrimonial conciliation commissioner, president of Our Boys' Institute and a member of such bodies as the Masonic Lodge and the Cheer Up Society which had a strong service orientation. On 27 April 1926 at Kensington Park, Adelaide, he had married Lydia Maria Schrapel. Survived by his wife, and by the son and daughter of his first marriage, he died on 14 November 1944 at his home in St Peters, Adelaide, and was buried in West Terrace cemetery.

C. E. W. Bean, *The story of Anzac*, 1 (Syd, 1921) and *The A.I.F. in France*, 1916 (Syd, 1929); H. R. Taylor, *The history of Churches of Christ in South Australia, 1846-1959* (Adel, 1959); *Report of the committee of inquiry into the public service of South Australia* (Adel, 1975); B. Dickey, *Rations, residence and resources* (Adel, 1986); D. Jaensch (ed), *The Flinders history of South Australia. Political history* (Adel, 1986); *Chronicle* (Adel), 16 Nov 1944; Public Service Bd (SA), Personnel cards, *and* Minutes of Public Service Commissioner's Office (SA), *and* Central Bd of Health (SA), *and* Children's Welfare Dept and Public Relief Bd (SA), *and* Adel Benevolent and Strangers' Friend Soc (PRO SA); Bd of Management of Our Boys' Inst (Mortlock Lib).

NEVILLE HICKS
JUDITH RAFTERY

WELCH, ERIC WILFRED (1900-1983), sporting commentator, was born on 28 October 1900 at Clifton Hill, Melbourne, son of Lionel John Samuel Welch, an accountant from England, and his native-born wife Margaret Jane, née Gordon. Educated at Gold Street State School, Clifton Hill, and Melbourne High School, he enlisted in the 14th Battalion, Australian Imperial Force, in May 1918 and served as a private. After World War I Welch studied science for two years at the University of Melbourne, but abandoned his course when 'race meetings and poker schools clashed with the lecture times'. In 1922 he went to Rabaul, New Guinea, as a bacteriologist for the Commonwealth Department of Health and worked there until joining the Melbourne *Argus* as a junior reporter in 1924.

Live radio broadcasts of horse-racing began in Melbourne in 1925; in that year Welch called the first of eighteen thousand races in his career. He left the *Argus* to join 3LO radio as a full-time broadcaster in 1927; in that year he called the first of twenty-seven Melbourne Cups. On 14 February 1928 at the Randwick registry office, Sydney, he married Zalda Gouldston. For reasons never publicly disclosed—but probably related to a Supreme Court writ served on Welch for allegedly 'enticing' a woman away from her husband—he was dismissed by the Australian Broadcasting Commission on 30 December 1933. In February 1934 he was employed by 3DB, for which he worked until 1954.

Banned from on-course calling until 1945, Welch and his competitors found improbable and difficult vantages from which to continue their work. Half a mile (805 m) from the winning post at Flemington, from the loft of the Pioneer Hotel he accurately picked the dead heat in the 1934 St Leger. Complementing his race-calling with broadcasts of cricket, tennis and boxing, he took his turn to be thrown from the ring at West Melbourne Stadium while purportedly describing the wrestling. For more than a quarter of a century he was an organizer, with Charlie Vaude [q.v.], of the Children's Hospital appeal. Each year he described Anzac Day marches with an intimacy born of his acquaintance with many of the participants.

Welch loved to drink (not on race-days) and to gamble, but advised punters: 'Never bet on anything that can talk'. His was a cavalier life. He narrowly escaped death (a passenger drowned) when he drove a Rolls Royce off South Wharf in January 1939. He paid off his Thornbury house when Rimfire (80/1) won the Melbourne Cup in 1948. In World War II Welch was a censorship liaison officer. He later diversified his radio work by hosting a classical music programme and serving as a panellist on the quiz show, 'Information Please'.

In 1954 Welch resigned from full-time radio work and became licensee of Kirkpatrick's Hotel, Mornington. When television broadcasting began in 1956, he joined Channel Nine as a racing commentator, then worked as promotions executive until his retirement in 1965. Weathering various licensing offences, he managed his hotel into the 1970s. He died at Mt Martha, Victoria, on 25 July 1983 and was cremated. Accurate and colourful, Welch's descriptions set the standard for such subsequent race-callers as Bill Collins who said that Welch had 'the best voice ever heard on radio'.

Listener In, 6 Nov 1929, 10 Sept 1932; *Truth* (Melb), 4 Feb 1933; *Herald* (Melb), 11 Dec 1933, 10, 24 Feb 1934, 21 Jan 1939, 13 Dec 1947, 2 June 1954, 26, 28 July 1983; *Sun News-Pictorial*, 4, 6 Jan 1934, 6 Nov 1945, 3, 26 June 1954, 7 Nov 1980, 26, 27 July 1983; *Sporting Globe*, 12 June 1954; *Age*, 1 Jan 1934, 30 Apr 1955, 25 Mar 1965, 26 July 1983; information from ABC Archives (Syd).

PETER PIERCE

WELLISH, EDWARD MONTAGUE (1882-1948), mathematician, was born on 14 April 1882 at Darlinghurst, Sydney, second son of Albert Wellisch, a Hungarian-born architect, and his English wife Kate Sophia, née Moody. Educated at Fort Street Model School, Edward studied arts at the University of Sydney (B.A., 1903; M.A., 1906) as an evening student, graduating with first-class honours and the University medal for mathematics. In 1907 he went to England and read at Emmanuel College, Cambridge (B.A. [Research], 1909). In the Cavendish Laboratory he tested (Sir) Joseph Thompson's view that, during the passage of electrons through a gas, some of the electrons become attached to molecules, giving rise to negative ions. In 1909 his work was communicated by Thompson to the Royal Society, London. Wellish was awarded the Clerk Maxwell scholarship for research and in 1911 appointed assistant professor of physics at Yale University, United States of America. Returning to Sydney in 1915, he took up a lectureship in applied mathematics at the university. He had anglicized his surname by 1920.

Heavily built, Wellish spoke slowly and was rather taciturn. To undergraduates, he seemed somewhat forbidding, but they appreciated that his lectures were models of clarity and his work at the blackboard magnificent; they respected him for the 'simplicity and uprightness of his character'. Those who later joined the department found him to be conscientious, kind and modest, with a quiet sense of humour and totally without malice.

On 18 March 1925 at St Peter's Anglican Church, Newcastle, Wellish married Margaret Ann Buxton, a schoolteacher.

Skilled in both experimental and theoretical research, he developed the equipment required for his research on the passage of electricity through gases, and also worked on the necessary electromagnetic theory. In 1927 the London Mathematical Society published his paper on electric and magnetic displacements. Next year Wellish received a grant to continue the research work he had begun at the Cavendish Laboratory. The results of his experiments were published in the *Proceedings* of the Royal Society, London, in 1931. He took sabbatical leave in 1924 and 1934.

Appointed associate professor of applied mathematics in 1926, Wellish was a member of the Royal Society of New South Wales and for many years chaired the syllabus committee in mathematics; he was a member of the Board of Secondary School Studies and chief examiner in mathematics for the public examinations. From September 1941 he was acting professor in charge of the department. In poor health, he had hoped to retire in 1942, but did not do so until the end of 1945.

Wellish died of a coronary occlusion on 22 July 1948 at his Roseville home and was cremated. He was survived by his wife; their only son had died as a baby. Wellish had sacrificed his own research interests for the needs of the students and the department. 'His character and sense of duty were such that he judged the sacrifice worth the while in the interest of mathematical education'.

Aust Mathematics Teacher, 9, 1953, p 26; Depts of Pure and Applied Mathematics, Univ Syd, *Aust Mathematical Soc Gazette*, 13, 1986, p 29; *SMH*, 24 July 1948; Univ Syd Archives; information from Assoc Prof H. Mulhall, Wollstonecraft, Syd.

DENIS E. WINCH

WELLS, LAWRENCE ALLEN (1860-1938), explorer, was born on 30 April 1860 at Yallum Park, Penola, South Australia, second son of Thomas Allen Wells, squatter, and his wife Isabella Elizabeth, née Kelsh. Educated at Donovan's National School, Mount Gambier, and later by private tutors, Larry entered the South Australian Survey Department in 1878, becoming a cadet the following year. At 23 he joined the Northern Territory and Queensland Border Survey; pegging of the 651-mile (1047.7 km) line to the Gulf of Carpentaria was completed in 1886.

He was surveyor in 1891 for the Elder [q.v.4] Scientific Exploring Expedition, led by David Lindsay [q.v.10] and administered by the South Australian branch of the Royal Geographical Society of Australasia. It set out to investigate the country between Warrina, South Australia, and the Western Australian coast. Drought caused the expedition to be diverted and exacerbated dissension among the personnel. The loyal Wells became leader. His zeal enabled the team to complete part of the exploration and to discover the East Murchison goldfields. Later, his evidence was crucial in exonerating Lindsay. On 22 September 1892 in St John's Anglican Church, Adelaide, Wells married Alice Marion Woods.

Appointed in 1896 to head the Calvert [q.v.7] Scientific Exploring Expedition, Wells engaged the camel driver Bejah Dervish [q.v.7] with whom he formed a lifelong friendship. Like the 1891 expedition, this trip was well planned, directed by the R.G.S.A., and foiled by the arid interior: the 850-mile (1368 km) projected route from Lake Way to the Fitzroy River crossed heavy, high sandridges, the continent's last major uncharted area. After leaving Separation Well one of the two parties—comprising Charles Wells, Larry's cousin, and George Jones, Lindsay's nephew—perished from thirst in the Great Sandy Desert. The tragedy terminated the expedition, at the first of its proposed three stages. Although he had spent months backtracking to find his comrades' bodies, as the leader Wells was vilified by press and public in Adelaide; two years were to pass before a parliamentary select committee praised his conduct.

Having promised his family that he would give up exploring, Wells worked from 1897 for the South Australian Pastoral Board, but in 1903 led the government's North-West Prospecting Expedition, accompanied by Herbert Basedow [q.v.7]. Wells customarily befriended the Aborigines and they named him 'Eagle-eyed Man'. Known as 'the last of the great inland explorers', he was modest and reticent, but was willing to reminisce among his intimates over lunch in a city café. In 1908 he completed a trigonometrical survey of the Victoria River district, Northern Territory, and later held administrative positions in the State and Federal public services where he was involved with land taxes. Chairman of South Australia's Land Board from 1918, he retired in 1930 and was appointed O.B.E. in 1937.

At 72 Wells led the Endeavour Expedition through the Great Victoria Desert in search of minerals; next year he and his prospecting party almost succumbed to thirst near McDouall Peak. After being struck by a rail car at Blackwood, Adelaide, he died on 11 May 1938. Survived by his wife and two daughters, he was buried in Mitcham cemetery. His estate was sworn for probate at £925.

W. and C. Steele, *To the great gulf* (Adel, 1978); *Quiz and the Lantern*, 17 June, 22, 29 July, 4 Nov 1897, 22 Dec 1898; *PRGSSA*, 39 (1937-38), 85 (1985); *Advertiser* (Adel), 28 June 1892, 13 Mar 1933, 12, 13 May 1938; *Chronicle* (Adel), 1 May 1930, 9 Nov 1933; Personalities remembered, ABC radio script, D5390 (misc) no 3 *and* PRG 315 (Mortlock Lib).   CHRISTOPHER STEELE

WELSBY, THOMAS (1858-1941), company director, politician and sportsman, was born on 29 November 1858 at Ipswich (Queensland), fourth child of William Welsby, carpenter and later contractor, and his wife Hannah, née Bilsborough, both English born. Educated locally at John Scott's and Ipswich Boy's Grammar schools, Thomas joined the Bank of New South Wales in Brisbane in October 1874. Resigning as ledgerkeeper in May 1879, he joined the Australian Joint Stock Bank in Brisbane. In July 1884 he left to practise as a public accountant, trustee and auditor; he became a member of the Brisbane Stock Exchange, operated a shipping partnership and audited the Brisbane Municipal Council accounts until 1893.

A member of Booroodabin Divisional Board in 1893-1902 (chairman 1897-1900), Welsby was chairman of the New Farm State School committee in 1899-1905 and honorary treasurer of the Brisbane Chamber of Commerce in 1899-1908. Instrumental in the formation of the Engineering Supply Co. of Australia in 1903, he was a director of the Royal Bank of Queensland and had interests with (Sir) Robert Philp [q.v.11] in mining and with G. C. Willcocks, a railway contractor. Welsby was also a trustee for the Mount Garnet railway debentureholders (1901-15).

The chairmanship of directors of Queensland Brewery Ltd (1907-19) stamped Welsby's commercial importance and made him one of Brisbane's elite. He had stood unsuccessfully for the Legislative Assembly as a candidate for Fortitude Valley in 1899, 1902 and 1909; as a Ministerialist he won North Brisbane in 1911 and held Merthyr from 1912 to 1915. Nicknamed 'Bung Bung', he generally disliked parliamentary life. His maiden speech was principally about the Ipswich railway workshops near his childhood home. He deplored the passage of the Liquor Act of 1912, believed that St Helena prison should be moved to Woogaroo and the island be converted to a recreational park, and considered that State or local authorities should take over the Brisbane Tramways Co. He wanted government to assist industry by building railways, dredging the Brisbane River, and financing exploration on the Cloncurry and Palmer mining fields.

A 'club man', tall, well-built and amiable, Welsby loved history and sport. Foundation honorary treasurer (1913), president (1936-37) and vice-president (1917-36, 1937-41) of the Historical Society of Queensland, he advocated that the government subsidize the society to collect Queensland's early records. He bequeathed his large library to the society and his portrait hangs over the entrance. Welsby wrote seven books about the history of the Moreton Bay region: *Schnappering* (1905), *Early Moreton Bay* (1907), *The discoverers of the Brisbane River* (1913), *The history of the Royal Queensland Yacht Club* (1918), *Memoirs of Amity* (1922), *Sport and pastime in Moreton Bay* (1931) and *Bribie the basketmaker* (1937). He also wrote a pamphlet, *The story of Newstead House* (1939), as well as four papers for the society's journal, all demonstrating his enthusiasm for recording Queenslanders' reminiscences and for using original documents in research.

In August 1882 Welsby had been manager and half-back for Queensland's first intercolonial Rugby Union team which played in Sydney. He helped to revive the code in 1928, was a life member of the Queensland Rugby Union (president 1929-39) and donated the Welsby Cup. Foundation secretary of the Brisbane Gymnasium in 1882, he sponsored boxing matches and formed the Queensland Amateur Boxing and Wrestling Union in 1909. With a house at Amity on Stradbroke Island, Welsby was patron of the Amateur Fishing Society from 1916; a founding member of the Royal Queensland Yacht Club in 1885, he was commodore in 1903-19.

There was much sadness in his life: his father and two brothers had died by 1879; his wife Margaret Gilchrist, née Kingston, whom he had married with Presbyterian forms on 21 February 1893 at East Brisbane, died ten years later, and their only son died in childhood. Survived by two daughters, Welsby died on 3 February 1941 at New Farm, Brisbane, and was cremated. His estate was sworn for probate at £14 354.

PD (Qld), 1911-12, pp 1173, 2481, 1912, pp 390, 1271, 1935, 2810, 1913, pp 247, 2623, 1914, p 412; *Pugh's Almanac*, 1891-1903; *JRHSQ*, 4, no 5, 1952, p 619, 6, no 1, 1959, p 268, 11, no 4, 1983, p 126; *Courier Mail*, 4 Feb 1941; Aust Joint Stock Bank, Qld staff book *and* Bank of NSW, Register of officers (Westpac Bank Archives); Brisb Chamber of Commerce, Minutes, 1895-1909 (OL); Carlton and United Breweries (Qld) Ltd, Minutes 1888-1919 (CUB Ltd, Brisb); New Farm State School file (QA).   RUTH S. KERR

WELSH, DAVID ARTHUR (1865-1948), pathologist, was born on 19 November 1865 at Montrose, Forfarshire, Scotland, son of David Welsh, sheep-farmer, and his wife Emma, née Hall. Receiving his early education at Arbroath, in 1883 he entered the

University of Edinburgh (B.A., 1887; M.B., Ch.M., 1893; M.D., 1897). He took first-class honours three times—in mathematics with the Drummond scholarship (1887), in clinical medicine and pathology with the Murchison scholarship (1893), and, with a gold medal, for his doctoral thesis on the structure and function of a parathyroid (1897).

Moved by what he had seen of patients' physical suffering and social problems, on first graduating Welsh had become a resident physician to Sir Thomas Fraser at the Royal Infirmary which he found the 'most interesting time in my life and the most precious part of my training'. He then spent about a year at the Morningside Asylum where he came into contact with Ford Robertson. As junior assistant in pathology at the university, Welsh worked directly under Robert Muir, a lifelong colleague and friend, whose sister Elizabeth he married in Edinburgh on 11 April 1899 with United Presbyterian forms. He also tutored in medicine. The importance of pathology to the practising clinician was to remain one of his obsessions.

Appointed foundation professor of pathology in 1901 at the University of Sydney, in March 1902 Welsh joined (Sir) Thomas Anderson Stuart and J. T. Wilson [qq.v.] in a triumvirate ('Taffy', 'Andy' and 'Jummy' to their students) who transplanted the traditions of the Edinburgh school to a new environment.

His department consisted of three rooms: the professor's 'retiring room', a single laboratory and a practical classroom; the lecture theatre and museum were shared. Welsh's responsibility was to teach pathology (all branches of laboratory medicine) to veterinary and dental as well as medical students, and also to provide (unaided) the pathology services to Royal Prince Alfred Hospital. At first, his enthusiasm and experience compensated for the lack of facilities and inadequate support staff. He established an innovative teaching programme with excellent practical classes, particularly in haematology, and continued to emphasize the contribution of pathology to day-to-day clinical problems. Welsh maintained his own clinical expertise and was elected a fellow of the Royal College of Physicians, Edinburgh, in 1911.

In collaboration with several colleagues in Sydney, Welsh published clinical descriptive papers, and a number of reports on Australian marsupial species. His most important scientific work concerned immunological reactions. In a long series of papers with Henry Chapman [q.v.7] he described the quantitative aspects of immune precipitation. Their most significant finding was that antibody (not antigen as previously believed) contributes the bulk of the mass of immune precipitates. Welsh's family and academic ties with Edin-burgh remained strong and most of this work was published both in Australian and Scottish journals.

The rapid development of laboratory medicine in the early twentieth century entailed a heavier work-load for Welsh. By 1925 it was clear that a single pathologist could not hope to provide diagnostic services for a large modern hospital while maintaining the research and teaching obligations of a university department. Dean of the faculty of medicine in 1927-29, Welsh wrote little over the next decade. He increasingly relied on didactic lecturing and depended on Muir's famous textbook for teaching. The separation of the hospital and the university department of pathology in 1925 brought some relief, but necessitated the abandonment of Welsh's plan to integrate laboratory and clinical training in the advanced years of the medical course. He retired in 1935.

Welsh next turned his interest to the problems of malignant disease and to the effects of ionizing radiation on cell biology. He collaborated with his son Arthur and Drs Amphlett and Kenny at the new radium institute at R.P.A.H. in studies of squamous cancer and radiation. Treatment of his own skin condition led to the formation of epithelioma and to the amputation of his foot. The consequent pain and disability clouded his final years and diminished the pleasure he took in his beloved golf. Survived by his wife and son, he died at his Wahroonga home on 13 May 1948 and was cremated. His estate was sworn for probate at £2292.

J. A. Young et al (eds), *Centenary book of the University of Sydney faculty of medicine* (Syd, 1984); Univ Syd, *Medical J*, 1933, p 97; *MJA*, July 1948, p 24.
                                    YVONNE COSSART

WENDT, JOACHIM MATTHIAS (1830-1917), silversmith, was born on 26 June 1830 at Dägeling, near Itzehoe, Holstein, son of Joachim Matthias Wendt, smith, and his wife Christina, née Schlichting, who died when he was aged 9. Raised by his father and two sisters, he was apprenticed to a watchmaker and learned the silversmith's craft. He migrated to Adelaide in 1854 where he set up as J. M. Wendt, watchmaker and jeweller. His business flourished, enabling him to move to premises in Rundle Street.

The quality of his workmanship and design was recognized at the New Zealand Exhibition of 1865, held in Dunedin, where his silverware and jewellery won first prize. For the duke of Edinburgh's visit to Adelaide in 1867, Wendt's firm produced four presentation caskets; the duke commissioned further work and appointed him 'Jeweller to His Royal Highness' in the colony of South

Australia. Wendt's staff had expanded to include twelve silversmiths and in 1869 he opened another shop at Mount Gambier. That year on Christmas Day at his North Terrace home he married with Unitarian forms Johanna Maria Caroline, late Koeppen, née Ohlmeyer, a widow with four children.

Wendt's silverwork included extravagant naturalistic creations, stylish Edwardian domestic designs and pieces which showed restrained Regency taste. At its best, it ranks with the finest produced in Australia in the second half of the nineteenth century. Among his important commissions was the salver presented to E. M. Young [q.v.6] in 1870 (now held by the Australian National Gallery, Canberra); Wendt also submitted a pair of prize-winning epergnes to the Paris Universal Exhibition of 1878. Commercial success encouraged him in 1888 to open a further branch at Broken Hill, New South Wales; his model of the Block 10 mine was executed five years later. In 1901 he supervised the production of the silver casket which was presented by the citizens of Adelaide to the duke of York. Seeking profitable investments, Wendt became a member of the syndicates that built the Adelaide Arcade (which he subsequently owned) and the Theatre Royal in Hindley Street. His interests were diverse: by the turn of the century he was developing 60 000 acres (24 281.4 ha) of scrub land in the Tintinara district.

In 1903 his son Julius and stepson Hermann Koeppen-Wendt became partners in the firm and took over its management. Upright and honest, with heavy-lidded eyes, a trim beard and a sense of serenity, in his retirement Wendt received expressions of affection from his employees and tenants. Although he had been naturalized in 1864, he deflected anti-German sentiment during World War I by stressing his Danish origins and by lauding the British Empire. Survived by his wife, and their son and two daughters, he died on 7 September 1917 at his home in Wakefield Street, Adelaide, and was buried in North Road cemetery. His estate was sworn for probate at £33 883. Wendts Pty Ltd has continued to operate to the present.

W. F. Morrison, *The Aldine history of South Australia* (Adel, 1890); Wendts Ltd, *Wendts 100 years 1854-1954* (Adel, 1954); K. Albrecht, *19th century Australian gold and silver smiths* (Melb, 1969); J. B. Hawkins (ed), *Australian silver, 1800-1900* (Syd, 1973); *Observer* (Adel), 30 June 1906, 15 Sept 1917.   RICHARD PHILLIPS

WENTWORTH-SHIELDS, WENTWORTH FRANCIS (1867-1944), Anglican bishop, was born on 2 April 1867 at Lewisham, London, son of Francis Webb Shields, a civil engineer with Australian experience, and his wife Adelaide, née Baker. Educated at St Paul's School and the University of London (B.A., 1890; M.A., 1893), he was made deacon on 18 December 1898 and ordained priest on 24 December 1899 by Bishop Talbot of Rochester. Curate at Plumstead (1898-1900) and St George's Church, Bloomsbury (1900-1903), he married Annie, fourth daughter of Bishop William Boyd Carpenter, on 3 April 1902 in the palace chapel, Ripon, Yorkshire. They sailed for North Queensland in 1903 to join his cousin Bishop Barlow [q.v.7].

Designated to St James's Cathedral, Townsville, Wentworth-Shields found that Barlow had been translated to Goulburn, New South Wales; to the chagrin of the hard-pressed tropical clergy, he followed him south; he helped Barlow to put his disordered diocese on an effective basis. After brief tenures at Cooma, St Saviour's Cathedral and Wagga Wagga, Wentworth-Shields returned to Goulburn and assumed a variety of roles: cathedral precentor, archdeacon of Wagga Wagga, joint-commissary, examining chaplain and warden of the new Bishop's College which trained ordinands. A fine teacher and scholar, he was a good cathedral man, but less happy when dealing with the affairs of a rural archdeaconry. His family connexion with the bishop did not always help matters. In March 1910 he resigned his Goulburn offices and took temporary charge of the fashionable All Saints Church, St Kilda, Melbourne. Late that year he became rector of St James's Church, Sydney.

At St James's, Archbishop Wright [q.v.] had been involved in conflict over liturgical matters. Wentworth-Shields's appointment represented a grudging compromise by the parish. He soon introduced a more moderate ritual, allayed parochial resentment and conciliated the diocesan authorities. A superb preacher, he attracted crowds by the sheer force of his pulpit oratory and the spiritual intensity of his message. He was ideally suited to a city church which could encourage his strengths and cope with his administrative shortcomings. Even his quite monumental absent-mindedness became an idiosyncrasy rather than a disadvantage. Steering his church successfully through the tensions of World War I, he was elected bishop of Armidale in October 1916 and consecrated by Archbishop Wright on 21 December.

Reduced by the separation of the Grafton diocese in 1914, Armidale gained from the spread of closer (and, later, soldier) settlement; the city itself had schools and a theological college. Wentworth-Shields was effective as an intellectual mentor of the diocese and able to play a part in national Church affairs, but failed to give local leadership.

Although he grew impatient with the grind of country work, he never lost the charm and sympathy that ensured his personal popularity.

The death of his wife in 1927 made Wentworth-Shields anxious to return home; he had never thought of himself as truly Australian. Having resigned in 1929, next year he took up the wardenship of St Deiniol's Residential Library, Chester; he held this agreeable, scholarly office until 1939, while acting as assistant bishop to the archbishop of Wales. Survived by two sons, Wentworth-Shields died at Chester on 13 September 1944.

R. T. Wyatt, *The history of the diocese of Goulburn* (Syd, 1937); K. J. Cable, *St. James' Church, Sydney* (Syd, 1982); *Southern Churchman* (Goulburn), 1 Mar 1945; *SMH*, 22 Sept 1916, 20 Apr 1927, 18 May 1929; *Aust Church Record*, 5 Oct 1944.

K. J. CABLE

WENZ, PAUL (1869-1939), grazier and writer, was born on 18 August 1869 at Reims, France, third of five children of Emile Wenz, wool-merchant, and his wife Marie, née Dertinger, natives of Wurtemberg who had settled at Reims in 1858. Emile owned spinning-mills and later opened wool-buying agencies in Melbourne, Sydney and Perth. Paul was educated in Paris in 1879-88 at the Ecole Alsacienne, an exclusive Protestant college; he became and remained a friend of fellow pupil André Gide. After military service in the artillery with another friend Joseph Krug of the champagne-producing family, Wenz was trained in the family firm and spent eight months in London. He disliked the European business world, however, and left in 1892 for a long tour of the family wool interests.

Over 6 ft. 4 ins. (193 cm) tall, energetic and loving the outdoors, Wenz felt immediately at home in Australia and spent two years jackarooing in Victoria, New South Wales and the Queensland Gulf country. He went briefly to New Zealand in 1896, visited the Pacific islands and worked in South America before arriving back in France in 1897. Wenz returned to New South Wales as a settler and in April 1898 purchased Nanima, a property on the Lachlan River between Forbes and Cowra. On 15 September he married Harriet Adela Annette (Hettie) Dunne (d. 1959), daughter of a pastoralist. They were happily married, but childless. Wenz was a successful grazier who took a keen interest in innovative agricultural methods, particularly lucerne growing and irrigation; he invented a charcoal-burning tractor and believed in water-divining. He also oversaw his family's wool-buying agencies and travelled regularly to Sydney and Melbourne as a director of Wenz & Co.

In 1900 *L'Illustration* began publishing his short stories, written in French but set in Australia or the Pacific islands. Two volumes of such stories were later published: *A l'autre bout du monde* (Paris, 1905) and *Sous la croix du sud* (Paris, 1910). These stories all bear traces of the *Bulletin*'s influence. In 1908 Wenz published in Melbourne his only book written in English, a novella, *Diary of a new chum*. Until 1910 he used the pseudonym 'Paul Warrego'. He also published several translations from English into French, notably of his friend Jack London's *Love of life* (1914), and wrote other stories that were not set in Australia. His first novel, *L'homme du soleil couchant* ('The sundowner', Paris, 1923) appeared in serial form in the *Revue de Paris* in 1915.

Stranded in Europe with his wife on the outbreak of war in 1914, Wenz was mobilized at once and served as a liaison officer with British and Australian troops in French military hospitals, while Hettie worked for the Red Cross. Posted to London in 1916, he accompanied an Australian mission to Morocco as liaison officer and interpreter in April 1919 before returning to Australia in November. Inspired by his war experiences, he published two small collections of stories and a novel, *Le pays de leurs pères* (Paris, 1919). He published two more novels with Australian settings, *Le jardin des coraux* (Paris, 1929) and *L'écharde* (Paris, 1931), a book on his experiences as a grazier and a fanciful memoir of his childhood.

Wenz's concise style, vivid description and dry irony are shown to advantage in his short stories which achieved some success; his novels are less sure and attracted little attention. His early writings show him as an amused apologist for Australia to the French, but his post-war novels and stories express a more matter-of-fact Australian identity. He regularly visited Europe, but in the 1920s and 1930s became more actively involved in the Australian literary scene and made friends with Miles Franklin, Dorothea Mackellar, Nettie Palmer [qq.v.8,10,11], G. B. Lancaster and Frank Clune. In 1931 Nettie described Wenz's overpowering presence: 'In he came with his Norman blue eyes from Rheims, his fresh colouring under white hair, his broad shoulders that made you wonder how the man had ever found a horse strong enough to carry him'. He endeavoured to get his novels and stories translated and published in Australia, and to have his works included in school and university curricula.

Survived by his wife, Wenz died of pneumonia on 23 August 1939 in a hospital at Forbes and was buried with Anglican rites in the local cemetery. His estate was valued at

£40 664; the Forbes library was left his portrait by Paul Laurens.

N. Palmer, *Fourteen years* (Melb, 1948); A. P. L. Stuer, *The French in Australia* (Canb, 1982); J.-P. Delamotte, biog sketch in P. Wenz, *L'écharde* (Paris, 1986); M. J. Blackman, biog sketch in P. Wenz, *Diary of a new chum and other lost stories* (Syd, 1990); *Tas J of Education*, 4, no 3, June 1970, p 93; *Bulletin*, 4 Apr 1934; *Monde*, 14 June 1985; E. Wolff, *A French-Australian writer: Paul Wenz* (Ph.D. thesis, Univ Melb, 1948); Wenz & Co. archives (Univ Melb Archives); Wenz papers *and* S. M. Franklin papers (ML); A. Gide papers (Bibliothèque Jacques Doucet, Paris).

MAURICE BLACKMAN

WESCHÉ, AWDRY GORDON (1865-1938), shipping manager, and PHOEBE ELLEN (1871-1950), charity worker, were husband and wife. Gordon was born on 7 July 1865 at Bombay, India, son of William Francis Wesché, stockbroker, and his wife Helen, née Venn. Reared and educated in England, in 1881 he entered the London office of the Peninsular and Oriental Steam Navigation Co. Ltd. After working for the company in Bombay from 1886, he joined the Sydney office as passenger clerk in 1889 and was promoted chief clerk (1900) and assistant superintendent (1906). He belonged to the Union Club from 1903.

At St Nicholas's Anglican Church, Goulburn, on 14 February 1901 Wesché married Phoebe Ellen Twynam. She was born on 10 June 1871 at Goulburn, second of eight children of Edward Twynam, a district surveyor from England, and his native-born wife Emily Rose, née Bolton, who was a sister of Mary Windeyer [q.v.]. Brought up at Riversdale, Goulburn, Phoebe was widely read and extremely practical, with 'the brownest, black-fringed eyes'; she loved horses and racing, and trout fishing in the mountains with her husband.

In Sydney Mrs Wesché was a councilmember of the Australian Bush Nursing Association, a vice-president of the Bush Book Club, a committee-member of the Rawson [q.v.11] Institute for Seamen, the Twilight League and the immigrant home at Dawes Point, and a founder (1912) and a vice-president of the Queen's Club. She became a close friend of Lady Poore who in 1909 published verses in the *Spectator* about her:

There's nothing Phoebe cannot do.
She'll break a horse, or patch a shoe,
A page of Browning she'll construe . . .

The Weschés visited England in 1912. Appointed superintendent of the P. & O. Co. in Australia that year, Gordon was founding chairman (1912-15) of the Oversea Shipping Representatives Association, vice-president (1912-13) of the Sydney Chamber of Commerce and a member (1914-19) of the Commonwealth Shipping Board. When the management of the P. & O. in Australia was taken over by Macdonald Hamilton & Co. in 1917, he became resident managing partner in Sydney. In 1925 he took temporary charge of the Brisbane branch.

On the outbreak of World War I, Mrs Wesché had been a founding member of the executive of the New South Wales division of the British Red Cross Society; as honorary secretary of the Voluntary Aid Detachment, she worked long hours at the George Street depot. In October 1915 her remarks about the execution of Edith Cavell were misrepresented in the *Sunday Times* and led to questions in the Legislative Asembly. In November she visited England where she remained for several years. Returning in 1918, she became State director of the Voluntary Aid Detachment.

In December 1926 Wesché sailed for England on retirement leave, accompanied by his wife. With little money, Phoebe soon became the companion of Louisa, wife of Sir Kenneth Anderson, at The Yair, Galashiels, Selkirkshire, Scotland. Troubled by a drink problem, Wesché died on 29 December 1938 at South Kensington, London. By 1943 Phoebe had returned to New South Wales to live with two of her sisters. Survived by her son, she died at Riversdale on 21 August 1950 and was cremated.

Lady Poore, *Recollections of an admiral's wife 1903-1916* (Lond, 1916); *Australasian*, 9 Jan 1915; *Daily Telegraph* (Syd), 1 Sept 1915; *SMH*, 28, 29 Oct 1915, 8 Mar 1917, 27 July 1920, 2 Dec 1926.

MARTHA RUTLEDGE

WEST, JOHN (1856-1926), journalist, horticulturist and irrigation pioneer, was born on 23 August 1856 at Armstrongs Diggings, Mount Ararat, Victoria, eldest son of English-born Isaac West, goldminer, and his Scottish wife Ann, née McMann. A garden help and stablehand at 13, 'with a very imperfect education', West joined Brunnings Nursery, St Kilda, and attended night-school to qualify as a state schoolteacher. He taught at Tatura, and at Murungi in the Goulburn Valley where his family selected land after his father died (1876) in a mine accident. When rust ruined the local wheat crop in 1878, West advocated vine and fruit culture as alternatives: his campaign in the *Shepparton News* gained much attention and for some years before resigning his teaching post he was that newspaper's farming editor. On 7 April 1882 he married with Presbyterian forms Mil(l)vina Gardiner at Pentland Hills, near Bacchus Marsh.

Active in shire and local interests, he was

secretary (1885-89) of the Mooroopna hospital. With his brother, West printed the *Goulburn Valley Yeoman*. In 1885 he founded the *Euroa Advertiser*, and occasionally freelanced for the *Argus* and *Australasian*. In 1886 he was one of a syndicate of five who purchased two farms (730 acres, 296.6 ha) for £5 per acre which were to provide the basis for Ardmona—the first irrigation settlement in Victoria. (Chaffey brothers [q.v.7] secured their grant the same year.) Most of the land was subdivided into holdings of less than 15 acres (6.1 ha) and sold at £12 to £15 per acre.

With his 'heart and soul in the industry', West took up Milvina, his own 22 acres (8.9 ha), and began planting for intense cultivation in 1887. Using irrigation, he worked 20 000 trees, raised currants and grapes, and culled a legendary 300 cases of tomatoes from three-quarters of an acre (0.3 ha). West Bros Nursery supplied thousands of vine cuttings for Chaffey Bros, and propagated peach, pear and apricot stock for the orchardmen of Ardmona. A paper which West presented at an irrigation conference in 1890 advocated methods used today. In that year Alfred Deakin [q.v.8], commissioner of water supply in the Gillies [q.v.9] administration, sent West to California, United States of America, to study irrigation. On his return, West toured Victoria, lecturing on what he had seen. He undertook the training of future horticulturists and in 1894 had nine men working at Milvina, each of whom paid him a £25 fee for the experience. A government bonus (£2 per acre for vines and £3 for fruit trees) encouraged planting at Ardmona after 1898.

Deeply interested in public life, especially from the viewpoint of the 'man on the land' (a phrase he was reputed to have coined), West was prominent in Victoria's pre-Federation politics. In 1894, when he founded the Triple Reform League under the uncompromising banner 'Victoria must part with her high duties or with her farmers', he was seen by *Table Talk* as a 'coming man of politics'. An advocate of Federation at the People's Federal Convention at Bathurst in 1896, next year he was one of five non-parliamentary Victorian nominees for election to the Australasian Federal Convention (1897-98). He held meetings throughout the State, making his appeal particularly to country electors as the only candidate resident outside Melbourne. Though one of the '*Argus* ten', he finished fifteenth in a field of twenty-nine. Having unsuccessfully contested the Legislative Assembly seat of Warrnambool in 1897, he was defeated for the Federal seat of Moira by T. J. Kennedy [q.v.9] in 1901. West was a founding member of the Kyabram reform movement whose protests against extravagance and call for public economy helped to bring down Sir Alexander Peacock's [q.v.11] government in 1902.

In 1903 West joined the staff of the *Argus* (after a public farewell from Ardmona) and represented the paper at the 1907 Imperial and Navigation conferences in London. In 1909-19 he was secretary of the National Union, an organization interested in constitutional matters. He retired to farm at Toolern Vale where he was president of the local bushfire brigade, a member of the Melton exhibition committee and a 'keen' proponent of a district water scheme. In 1923-26 he was secretary of the Bacchus Marsh Agricultural and Pastoral Society. Survived by two sons and a daughter, West died of a cerebral haemorrhage on 22 February 1926 at Toolern Vale and was buried in Melton cemetery.

H. L. Hall, *Victoria's part in the Australian Federation movement, 1849-1900* (Lond, 1931); D. M. McLennan (comp), *History of Mooroopna, Ardmona and district* (Mooroopna, Vic, c1936); W. S. James, *A history of Shepparton* (Shepparton, Vic, 1938); C. S. Martin, *Irrigation and closer settlement in the Shepparton district*, J. L. F. Woodburn ed (Melb, 1955); R. West, *Those were the days* (Shepparton, Vic, 1962); N. H. Bossence, *Todwan and the shire of Rodney* (Melb, 1969); G. Nice, *Hospitals are people* (Melb, 1976); *Australasian* and *Table Talk*, 15 Sept 1894; *Kyabram Free Press*, 26 Feb 1925; *Bacchus Marsh Express*, 27 Feb 1926.

MARGARET STEVEN

WEST, JOHN EDWARD (1852-1931), plumber, trade unionist and politician, was born on 27 January 1852 at Lambeth, London, son of John Edward West, brass finisher, and his wife Elizabeth Ann, née Hearne. Jack was apprenticed to a plumber and from the age of 17 was associated with the Ancient Order of Foresters. On 18 March 1874 at St Andrew's parish church, Holborn, he married Susannah Sarah Metcalfe (d. 1925). After visiting New Zealand, they arrived in Sydney in 1875 and settled at Paddington. In time they 'reared a family of seven daughters and two sons—all native of East Sydney'.

Able to balance a belief in the worth of diligent improvement with a clear appreciation of the British class system and his place within it, West set up business as a plumber and by 1879 had brought together the operative plumbers, gasfitters and galvanized-iron workers into a single union, the Operative Plumbers' Society. Next year he was a delegate to the Trades and Labor Council and secretary of a committee of union organizations pressing for the introduction of technical education. Secretary of the Trades and Labor Council from 1880, West was president in 1887-1907. As chairman of its parliamentary committee, he supported the political

Labor movement and saw the successful establishment of the Labor Party which owed much to the firm but meliorative approach championed by West and other T.L.C. leaders.

As a delegate to the Intercolonial Trade Union congresses held after 1879, West supported the proposed Commonwealth Constitution. He declined to stand for the first Federal parliament, preferring to concentrate his energies on maintaining progress with the Trades Hall building project which had occupied his attention for years. Although he belonged to the Master Plumbers' & Sanitary Engineers' Association and was an employer, he was active in the movement for an eight-hour day. He stood unsuccessfully against (Sir) George Reid [q.v.11] for the Federal seat of East Sydney in 1906 and next year contested the State seat of King; West was eventually returned to the House of Representatives for East Sydney in 1910.

A natural back-bencher, he combined conscientious attention to his constituency with union commitments and his business as a master plumber. West was an 'unconscious humourist': he retained a Cockney-like speech and in 'his pebbly voice' hurled 'the most deadly insult in the most incomprehensible English at an opponent with all the rollicking amiability of a man who has just made a good joke'. He almost lost pre-selection in 1917, but throughout the 1920s steered a middle course in his electorate: he criticized the Bruce-Page [qq.v.7,11] government for the slow progress of the temporary parliament house in Canberra, campaigned for the priority of the Australian flag on all Commonwealth office buildings, opposed the deportation of Tom Walsh [q.v.] and Jacob Johnson, and argued that all talk of Labor's association with 'Bolshevism and Communism was moonshine'. West's public boast about family life and local achievement, which he made after Labor's Federal victory in 1929, typified his approach to society and underlined his commitment to establishing an 'improving community'.

As the rift between the Scullin and Lang [qq.v.11,9] governments widened in late 1930, speculation was rife that West would at last have to vacate his seat at the next election, leaving it open to the angry young men at Trades Hall. Survived by nine children, West died at midnight on 5 February 1931 at his Darlinghurst home and was buried in Waverley cemetery. His successor as member for East Sydney was the fiery E. J. Ward. Tributes to West's parliamentary service ranged from that of his close friend Scullin to those of Lang supporters and conservatives; in 1932 a bronze memorial to West was unveiled at the Sydney Trades Hall building, itself a testimony to his practical drive.

Historical Studies; selected articles, M. Beever and F. B. Smith eds, 2nd s (Melb, 1967); M. Easson (comp), *110th anniversary of the Labor Council of New South Wales* (Syd, 1981); B. Nairn, *Civilising capitalism* (Canb, 1973); *Punch* (Melb), 19 Oct 1911; *SMH*, 20 Jan 1917, 18 Nov 1919, 10 May 1922, 3 May 1924, 14, 22 Sept, 21 Oct 1925, 30 Mar, 15 May 1926, 24 Nov 1930, 6, 7, 9, 19 Feb, 3 Apr 1931, 29 Feb 1932; *Aust Worker*, 13 Feb 1919, 11 Dec 1929; *Bulletin*, 11 Feb 1931; *Queenslander*, 12 Feb 1931.   FRANK FARRELL

WEST, WINIFRED MARY (1881-1971), educationist, was born on 21 December 1881 at Frensham, Surrey, England, second of six children of Charles William West (d. 1891), schoolmaster, and his wife Fanny, née Sturt. In 1891 the family moved to Farnham. On a scholarship, Winifred boarded at Queen Anne's School, Caversham, Berkshire, in 1894-1900. She read mediaeval and modern languages at Newnham College, Cambridge (1900-03), where she qualified for an arts degree and played hockey.

While teaching at Guernsey Ladies' College (1903-06), she became engaged to an Australian and followed him to New South Wales in 1907: on the voyage she fell in love with an explorer in the British Antarctic Expedition and broke her engagement. Staying in Sydney, she taught private pupils, among them Helen Simpson [q.v.11], and drew shells for Charles Hedley [q.v.9] at the Australian Museum. She studied painting with Julian Ashton [q.v.7] and played hockey at Rushcutters Bay where she met Phyllis (d. 1973), daughter of (Sir) Charles Clubbe [q.v.8]. In 1908 they founded the New South Wales Women's Hockey Association; they also played for the State.

A critic of contemporary education, Miss West was persuaded to implement her own ideas. After two years in England, where she taught at Harrogate Ladies' College and Miss Clubbe studied physical education, they returned to Sydney in 1912. Believing that children should be taught in rural surroundings, in July 1913 at Mittagong they opened Frensham, a girls' boarding-school, with a borrowed £1000 and the help of Winifred's mother, sister Frances and friend Margaret Hartfield who had all arrived in New South Wales. In 1920 Winifred's other sister Margaret and her husband Arthur Topp, who became school secretary, settled at Mittagong.

With a rich speaking voice, 'glossy brown hair' and a wonderful smile, Winifred had personal magnetism and an infectious enthusiasm. Frensham had a family atmosphere and soon became known as an unusual school: with non-denominational religion, few rules, and no competitions, marks or prizes, it emphasized music, art and drama, as well as academic subjects and sport. There was always provision for examination and non-examination courses. Fees were £30 a quarter in 1913. Stressing self-discipline and flexibility, Miss West aimed to develop the whole nature—aesthetic and spiritual, intellectual and physical. Intense, impatient, talented yet practical, she was also a gardener, a spinner, a cellist and a bridge player.

Laying foundations for the future, Miss West insisted on the involvement of staff, past and present girls, parents and friends. She lived simply and could be shrewd with money. When a suitable house or piece of land came on the market, she bought, confident that funds would be forthcoming. From 1918 she held informal council meetings. In 1930 two companies—Frensham School Ltd and Holt Property Ltd as owner of the buildings and extensive grounds (including uncleared bush) —were formed to safeguard the school's existence and to prevent its exploitation for financial gain.

Retiring as head of Frensham in 1938, Miss West continued to live nearby with Miss Clubbe. In 1941 Winifred opened Sturt in Frensham's grounds to provide spinning, weaving and carpentry for 14-year-olds from Mittagong Public School. Professional production began in 1951 with the arrival of a German master weaver and in 1954 a pottery was established. Eventually Sturt flourished with pupils of all ages and both sexes, mainly from the Berrima district, and became known internationally for its crafts.

A member of the British Music Society, Miss West was a vice-president of the New Education Fellowship in the 1930s. With Phil Clubbe she travelled abroad in 1921, 1927 and 1931, and visited the Soviet Union in 1935. Winifred made friends outside the school with educationists, artists and musicians, including J. D. M. Moore [q.v.10], (Dame) Sybil Thorndyke, Ernest Llewellyn and (Sir) Keith Hancock. Convinced that Frensham and more particularly Sturt should be involved with the community, she founded the Berrima District Education Club and worked for the Young Women's Christian Association, as well as for the Children's Library and Crafts Movement.

As a governing director of the Frensham and Holt companies until 1971, Miss West had encouraged the foundation (1953) of Gib Gate, near Mittagong, a primary boarding-school for girls; in 1968 her dream of alternative progressive education for seniors was realized at Hartfield, one of the school's houses. Frensham School Ltd changed its name to Winifred West Schools Ltd in 1955. Miss West was appointed M.B.E. in 1953 and C.B.E. in 1971.

Christianity was the foundation stone of each school and of Winifred West's life: she chose as Frensham's motto 'In Love Serve One Another'. Late in life she disagreed with many people, principally on educational matters. Still impatient and unsatisfied, she died on 26 September 1971 at Bowral and was cremated with Anglican rites.

P. Kennedy, *Portrait of Winifred West* (Syd, 1976); *SMH*, 1 June 1953, 1 Jan 1971; *Age*, 27 Nov 1976; *Canb Times*, 18 Dec 1976; West papers (ML); miscellaneous publications, papers and personal documents, including copies of *Frensham Chronicle* and minutes of governors' and council's meetings, Frensham School Ltd (held by author, Mittagong, NSW).
PRISCILLA KENNEDY

WESTMACOTT, CHARLES BABINGTON (1864-1934), actor-manager, was born on 5 February 1864 at Mayfair, London, son of Augustus Frederick Westmacott, gentleman and elocutionist, and his wife Hannah, née Lyons. Educated at Westminster School, Charles learned of the theatre from his father's friends. He arrived in Australia in 1884 and worked as a jackaroo near the Lachlan and Bogan rivers, New South Wales; on losing his job, he turned to the stage. Impressing George Rignold [q.v.6 Rignall] with his 'resonant public school voice', Westmacott made his stage debut in *Held by the enemy* at Her Majesty's Theatre, Sydney, on 29 October 1887. He continued to play bit parts for the company until engaged in May 1889 by Williamson [q.v.6], Garner & Musgrove [q.v.5]. In 1890 he appeared in Melbourne with Kyrle Bellew [q.v.7] and Mrs Brown-Potter in *Romeo and Juliet* and *Camille*.

Visiting London, on 3 August 1893 Westmacott married Rosa Butler (d. 1927) at the register office, Kensington. Back in Sydney next year, he played in a series of Rignold's melodramas and in 1895 joined L. J. Lohr's company at the Criterion; his portrait of Freddy in *The Guv'nor* was considered his best role. Organizing his own company in December, he opened at Sydney's Theatre Royal with a musical comedy, *Pat, or the bells of Rathbeal*, which Ellen Todd [q.v.] regarded as one of his 'happiest inspirations'. The company played to packed houses in Melbourne from March until June 1896. In September he was joint manager with John Barnett when Marius Sestier opened Lumière Cinématographe in Sydney. Forming another company, Westmacott leased Her Majesty's Theatre and opened with a pantomime in December. He moved to the Theatre Royal in February 1897 and, when his season ended abruptly early in April, was given a farewell benefit.

Unable to pursue his career because of his wife's ill health, Westmacott eventually visited New Zealand with C. R. Standford's company in 1901, arranging the advance bookings and winning audiences with his infectious laugh. Hired by Musgrove in 1903 to manage Nellie Stewart's [q.v.] New Zealand appearances and her farewell season in Sydney, Westmacott performed with her in *A country mouse*. In 1909 he managed Cosens Spencer's [q.v.] Theatrescope Co. in Adelaide before conducting (Sir Rupert) Clarke [q.v.8], Meynell & Gunn's tour there and in Western Australia. He also managed tours for Oscar Asche [q.v.7] and Lily Brayton (1910, 1912), H. B. Irving (1911) and Beaumont Smith (1915).

Succeeding E. J. Tait [q.v.], Westmacott was general manager for J. C. Williamson Ltd in Sydney from 1916 to 1934, with a stint (1917-19) in the Melbourne position. He was commissioned temporary lieutenant in the 2nd Battalion, 22nd Infantry Regiment, Australian Military Forces, in 1918 and served as transport officer at Richmond, Melbourne. An energetic worker for the Red Cross and Australian Comforts Fund, he was appointed O.B.E. in October and, in 1919, was secretary of the Theatrical Managers and Proprietors' Association.

Known for his tact, 'Westie' (or 'Sir Charles') was portly, affable and charming, with 'amazingly expressive eyes'. He coached newcomers to 'the Firm' in rum-and-milk sessions at the Australia Hotel and related his reminiscences in radio programmes and newspaper articles. A regular churchgoer, he belonged to the English Public Schools Association, the Royal Sydney Yacht Squadron, the Millions Club, Sydney, and the Athenaeum Club, Melbourne. Having retired in January 1934, he died on 21 October at Darlinghurst and was cremated after a service in St Andrew's Anglican Cathedral.

Mrs R. H. Todd, *Looking back* (Syd, 1938); E. Reade, *Australian silent films* (Melb, 1970); C. Kingston, *It don't seem a day too much* (Adel, 1971); *NZ Illustrated Mag*, May 1901; *Bulletin*, 3, 10 Apr 1897, 24 Oct 1934; *SMH*, 27 May 1899, 24 June, 18 July 1919, 25 Nov 1933, 20 Jan, 22 Oct 1934; *Australasian*, 12 Oct 1918; *Sydney Mail*, 31 Jan 1934; *Daily Telegraph* (Syd), 22 Oct 1934.

GILLIAN FULLOON

WESTON, THOMAS CHARLES GEORGE (1866-1935), horticulturist, was born on 14 October 1866 at Poyle, Middlesex, England, son of Thomas Weston, journeyman tailor, and his wife Elizabeth, née Newell. Leaving school at 13, he learned horticulture at a number of places, serving a term as gardener at Drumlanrig Castle, Dumfriesshire, Scotland. In 1896 he migrated to New South Wales; two years later he was appointed gardener-in-charge at Admiralty House, North Sydney. On 20 April 1898 he married English-born Minimia Cockshott at St Andrew's Anglican Church, Summer Hill. In 1908 he went to Federal Government House, Sydney, as head gardener; four years later he became superintendent of the State Nursery, Campbelltown. In May 1913 he was made officer-in-charge of afforestation, Canberra.

At a remote rural location, infertile, windy and rabbit infested, Weston's task was to create an urban landscape consonant with the capital city to be built at Canberra. He was also expected to establish a local forestry industry. Weston set down on paper his four objectives: to establish a first-class nursery, to raise stocks of plants likely to prove suitable, to reserve all local hilltops and improve their tree cover, and to seek out and procure useful seeds. Fully aware of contemporary interest in the soil, he appreciated the opportunity—'which amounts almost to a duty'—of 'wresting a little more from nature's inexhaustible storehouse' to 'add materially to human comfort and enjoyment'.

He speedily established a small experimental nursery and then a large plant propagation nursery, and travelled widely in search of seed. There was little scientific knowledge about horticulture suitable to the area, although a few local established gardens featured exotic conifers and deciduous trees. From this very restricted base, Weston sought to expand the number of species that might grow in Canberra and carried out extensive, scientifically-planned trials. His correspondence with the botanist J. H. Maiden [q.v.10], director of the Botanic Gardens, Sydney, indicated how advanced Weston was in the experimental breeding of eucalypts. Responsible to W. B. Griffin [q.v.9], Weston had differences of opinion with his superior over what tree species should be grown; in at least one instance, at Griffin's insistence, Weston carried out an onerous planting which proved to be a failure: Weston's sensitivity to the native environment stood out in sharp contrast to Griffin's intransigence.

In November 1926 Weston retired to Sydney, but was retained in a consultative capacity until May 1927. In that month he was appointed M.B.E. He died of cancer on 1 December 1935 at Turramurra and his ashes were scattered in the park he had designed at Parliament House, Canberra. His wife and three daughters survived him. The *Sydney Morning Herald* paid tribute to Weston as 'a poet, an artist and a tree-planter in one'; his influence extends throughout the nation's capital and marks a significant development in Australian landscape architecture. A street and a park in Canberra are named after him.

The Weston Memorial Trust Fund is administered by the Royal Australian Institute of Parks and Recreation (Australian Capital Territory Region).

Canb Hist J, Sept 1979; *Aust Parks and Recreation*, Aug 1982, p 47; *Canb Times*, 2 Dec 1935; *SMH*, 5 Dec 1935; R88/2131 (NSWA); CP/209/1 (AA).
                                            GREG MURPHY

WETHERSPOON, JOHN (1844-1928), farmer and politician, was born on 13 July 1844 at Newburgh, Fifeshire, Scotland, son of Andrew Wetherspoon, labourer, and his wife Helen, née Marr. The family came to Sydney in 1853. John was soon employed in the New England district as a shepherd; by the age of 19 he was an overseer; at 24 he became manager of Trinkey station on the Liverpool Plains. On 20 December 1871 Wetherspoon married Catherine Crothers (d. 1926) with Presbyterian forms at Gowrie, Patricks Plains. Gaining title (probably after selection) to 100 acres (40.5 ha) south of Glen Innes, he made it the nucleus of his eventual 1600-acre (648 ha) property, Glencoe, which he acquired without 'dummying'. He built a fine, brick residence surrounded by hedges, avenues and many 'home-country' trees.

President of Glen Innes Pastoral and Agricultural Society (1888), Wetherspoon had charge of the northern exhibit at the Sydney Royal Show for many years. He helped to secure the Glen Innes Experiment Farm in 1902. An early member of the Farmers and Settlers' Association, he served on its executive (1901-14) and was vice-president (1904-09 and 1911-14). He was also a member of the Severn Shire temporary council in 1906 and a director of the Glen Innes Pastures Protection Board (1907-28) and the Land Newspaper Co Ltd (1911-14).

A free trader and Federationist, Wetherspoon was defeated for the Glen Innes seat in the Legislative Assembly in 1895 and 1898 (as an Independent). He was nominated to the Legislative Council in 1908. At first he advocated matters close to his interests: the importance of land to the welfare of the nation, the value of closer settlement and the need to break up large estates. He advocated the planting of trees, and supported railway extension and immigration (when land was available). After 1910 he seldom spoke in the House and attended only about one-tenth of the sittings.

In 1890 Wetherspoon had published *Warblings from the bush*. Written between 1862 and the 1880s, his verse revealed a strong patriotism for a united and democratic Australia springing from Anglo-Saxon strains, the blood of Scotland and 'Erin's better sons'. Some of his poems cast the Abor-

igines as foes. Self-educated, he was proud of his writing and sent a copy of the book to Sir Henry Parkes [q.v.5], adding: 'you were the friend of poor Henry Kendall [q.v.5] and . . . are inclined to woo the muse at times'.

A devout Presbyterian, Wetherspoon supported his Church and praised Rev. Alexander Cameron, the local minister. Wetherspoon became more Scottish as he aged. He was a founder and vice-president of the local Caledonian Society (1892), chief in 1894-96 and actively involved thereafter. A man of grit, determination and faith, he died at Glencoe on 12 June 1928. In the rain and bitter cold, preceded by pipers playing *Loch Aber no more* and *Lord Lovat's lament*, he was buried beside his wife in the local cemetery. Their only daughter survived them.

PD (NSW), 11 Sept 1928, p 3; *Scottish A'sian*, Dec 1914, p 3250; *Glen Innes Examiner*, 23 Feb 1926, 14 June 1928; *Land* (Syd), 15 June 1928; Parkes correspondence (ML).   BRUCE MITCHELL

WETTENHALL, MARCUS EDWY (1876-1951), fruit-grower, farmer and politician, was born on 26 January 1876 at Carrs Plains, near Stawell, Victoria, sixth child of Holford Highlord Wettenhall [q.v.6], pastoralist, and his wife Mary Burgess, née Dennis. Roland Ravenscroft [q.v.] was his brother. Educated at the local state school, and at Toorak and Geelong colleges, Marcus matriculated in 1893. He was an outstanding athlete who won 29 of his 35 starts, including the Victorian Amateur Athletic quarter-mile championship (1896) and the open half-mile (1896, 1897). On 27 January 1903 he married Leila Ashton Warner at St David's Anglican Cathedral, Hobart.

While managing his father's orchard, Glen Holford, near Pomonal, Wettenhall patented a grading machine for apples and was president (1902) of the Central Fruitgrowers' Association of Victoria. In 1909 at Mernong he took up a 3000-acre (1214 ha) subdivision of Carrs Plains which, though he moved to Melbourne in 1917, he continued to farm until 1923. He was a member (1926-35) of the Federal Council of Woolgrowers and Victorian delegate to the Wool Research Conference in London in 1930.

Having joined the anti-socialist People's Party in 1912 to fight 'tooth and nail' against the establishment of the Commonwealth Bank, by 1920 he had become the bank's supporter and regarded the 'Socialist bogy' as a 'flabby golliwog'. In October 1920 Wettenhall won the Legislative Assembly seat of Lowan for the Victorian Farmers' Union. Although he did not live in his electorate, he won six elections and from September 1923 to March 1924 was honorary minister assisting the minister of agriculture in the Lawson-Allan [qq.v.10,7] government. Of middle height and medium build, with brown hair, pale complexion and sharp features, Wettenhall was a 'straight shooter' who was described in 1924 as 'a man of punch who does not ask for leave to use it'. His speeches in the assembly were frequent, vigorous and well argued: they focused on agriculture, the development of Portland harbour, transport and education.

A pioneer of the bulk handling of wheat in Victoria, he had designed and built his own silos at Mernong in 1919. He was convinced that Portland could become 'the Odessa of Australia', and his persistent arguments helped to bring about a royal commission on Victorian outer ports in 1923. Anticipating the event by ten years, in 1924 Wettenhall advocated the creation of a ministry of transport. He insisted that closure of the local state school had changed 'the whole trend' of his life by compelling him to move to Melbourne for the sake of his children's education. Thereafter, he worked tirelessly to improve educational opportunities in rural areas. A member (1924-40) and chairman (1938-39) of the Council of Agricultural Education, he was also a councillor (1925-40) of the University of Melbourne.

Wettenhall served on the statute law revision committee and was parliamentary representative on the sports committee of the Victorian Centenary Council (1934-35). In 1935 he lost his seat when the Country Party allowed two candidates to contest it. Finding defeat incomprehensible, he again stood for Lowan as an Independent in 1940, but forfeited his deposit. Survived by his wife, three sons and a daughter, Wettenhall died on 25 January 1951 in East Melbourne and was buried in Brighton cemetery.

A. Henderson (ed), *Early pioneer families of Victoria and Riverina* (Melb, 1936); C. E. Sayers, *Shepherd's gold* (Melb, 1966); *Farmer's Advocate*, 6 June 1924; *Countryman* (Melb), 15 Feb 1935; Wettenhall papers (Vic Parliamentary Lib); information from Mr H. R. Wettenhall, Mount Martha, Vic.
GEOFF BROWNE

WETTENHALL, ROLAND RAVENSCROFT (1882-1965), dermatologist, was born on 13 March 1882 on the family property at Carrs Plains, near Stawell, Victoria, seventh son of Holford Highlord Wettenhall [q.v.6] and his wife Mary Burgess, née Dennis. Marcus Edwy [q.v.] was his brother. From Geelong College, Roland went to the University of Melbourne (M.B., B.S., 1906) where his career was more distinguished for ability in athletics and lacrosse than for academic achievement.

On graduating, Wettenhall spent a resident period at the Hobart Hospital. Thereafter, except for war service, his medical practice was exclusively in dermatology to which he was introduced and in which he was trained by his cousin Herman Lawrence. Having married Jane Vera Creswick on 6 April 1910 at St George's Anglican Church, Malvern, Wettenhall went to London for further medical experience. With the outbreak of World War I, he joined the Royal Army Medical Corps, serving as regimental medical officer to the Royal Munster Fusiliers in France and on a hospital ship in the Mediterranean. He returned to Australia in 1916 and transferred to the Australian Army Medical Corps, attaining the rank of major.

Discharged in 1919, Wettenhall obtained honorary dermatological appointments at the Hospital for Sick Children and the Alfred Hospital, although his major work was to be as honorary dermatologist to the Melbourne Hospital in 1922-42. He was also dermatologist to the Repatriation Department and a consultant to the War Pensions Assessment Appeals Tribunal after World War II. A foundation fellow of the Royal Australasian College of Physicians (1938), Wettenhall was president of the dermatology section of the Australasian Medical Congress (British Medical Association) in Sydney in 1929. In 1937 he became president of the Victorian branch of the British Association of Dermatology and Syphilology. He was a foundation member of the Dermatological Association of Australia (Australian College of Dermatology) in 1948.

Until his retirement in 1959, Wettenhall's private practice continued to be extensive. His major interests, derived from Lawrence, were related to radium and superficial X-ray therapy which he used for a wide range of conditions; he was also a master of the ancient art of prescription writing. In later years he had some pastoral interests and a property at Mount Martha. Although 'averse to writing', Wettenhall possessed wide historical knowledge and genealogical expertise which was reflected in his presidency (1952-55) of the Royal Historical Society of Victoria and election to fellow in 1962, and in his foundation presidency (1941-49) of the Genealogical Society of Victoria. He belonged, as well, to the Royal Australian Historical Society and the Australasian Pioneers' Club, Sydney.

A lover of his garden and of native wildflowers, Roly had a strong sense of family and wide cultural interests. Friendly, philanthropic and generous with his knowledge, he yet could appear autocratic. His wife's death in 1928 intensified his religious practice; he was an elder of the Toorak Presbyterian Church for almost forty years. Survived by two sons, he died at Parkville on 21 July 1965 and was buried in Brighton general cemetery.

One-third of his estate, sworn for probate at £149 509, was shared between Geelong College, St Andrew's Hospital and his local church.

VHM, 36, no 3, Aug 1965; *Aust J of Dermatology*, 1968, no 9, p 274; *Age*, 23 July 1965; Wettenhall papers (Roy A'sian College of Physicians, Syd); information from and family papers (held by Dr H. N. Wettenhall, Toorak, Melb).   BRYAN GANDEVIA

WHATMORE, HUGH EDWARD (1860-1939), Salvation Army officer, was born on 6 April 1860 in London, son of John Whatmore, shoemaker, and his wife Elizabeth, née Westgate. After schooling, Hugh was apprenticed to a leading firm of optical, surveying and instrument makers. In 1877 at Whitechapel he was converted by the Christian Mission which next year became known as the Salvation Army. Joining as a soldier, he was commissioned in 1882 and rose rapidly to staff captain. Posted overseas by General William Booth, Whatmore served in Sweden and in the United States of America where he married fellow English Salvationist Mary Woodward on 8 August 1886.

Promoted major in 1892, Whatmore pioneered the army's work in Italy before returning to England in 1896 to become successively junior field secretary, provincial secretary, commander of the North London and Western provinces and in 1904 field secretary for Great Britain. Appointed international secretary in 1911, he visited South Africa and in 1914 attended the Swedish annual congress; he was *en route* to Finland when war was declared. Evacuated from Berlin, in 1915 he toured Korea, Japan, southern India, Ceylon and the Dutch East Indies before taking command of work in Holland. He was appointed commissioner of international training at Clapton, England, in 1919.

Following James Hay's [q.v.9] separation of the Australian administration into two territorial commands, Whatmore was appointed commissioner of the 'eastern territory' (New South Wales and Queensland). Hoping to create a revival of 'red-hot' religion, he arrived in Sydney with his wife on 7 January 1922 to find that a more practical Christianity was required. He expanded the League of Mercy, extended slum work, opened the William Booth Memorial Institute for Men, Albion Street, and homes for the aged at Burwood and Collaroy, and organized free seaside holiday camps for poor city children. He purchased a large new building in Elizabeth Street for territorial headquarters, was closely involved with training subordinates, and opened several new corps and the Sword and Shield brigade to promote Bible reading.

Travelling extensively throughout his territory, he regularly visited Brisbane.

Whatmore addressed the annual congresses of the 'southern territory' (Victoria, Tasmania, South Australia and Western Australia) early in 1926 and learned of his transfer there as territorial leader. He arrived in Melbourne in July and began touring his vast area of responsibility, campaigning vigorously against gambling, intemperance and smoking. Although he gave priority to 'relief work' over 'developmental work', he continued to hold officer-training sessions and established successful annual congresses for young people.

Exhausted and in ill health, Whatmore was recalled to London in June 1928 to attend a meeting of the Salvation Army High Council. He then went to Canada for the Toronto congress and visited San Francisco and Los Angeles before returning to London for further meetings. Back in Australia, in April-May 1929 he conducted the centenary congresses celebrating William Booth's birth and in September opened the Gill Memorial Home for Men, Melbourne. A regular contributor to *War Cry* and other periodicals, he began wireless broadcasting of army meetings. By his retirement in April 1930 he had extended the Bethesda Hospital, Melbourne, and opened more than thirty new halls and homes in his territory. He was farewelled affectionately when he sailed for England.

Described as 'a great spiritual leader', Whatmore was a gentle yet determined man in whom a shrewd administrative ability was combined with kindness, sympathy and tact. He died at Hackney, London, on 29 March 1939, survived by his wife, who had ably assisted him throughout his long years of service, and by four daughters, two of whom were Salvation Army officers.

R. Sandall, *The history of the Salvation Army*, 1-6 (Lond, 1947); H. P. Dale, *Salvation chariot* (Melb, 1952); L. Tarling, *Thank God for the Salvoes* (Syd, 1980); *Salvation Army Yearbook*, 1933, 1935; *War Cry* (Adel), 1 Sept 1921, 10 Apr 1926, 10 May 1930, 15 Apr 1939; *SMH*, 9 Jan 1922, 2 May 1930, 10 Aug 1936, 31 Mar 1939; *Argus*, 1 Feb 1930.

L. M. HEATH

WHEATLEY, FREDERICK WILLIAM (1871-1955), headmaster and cryptographer, was born on 7 June 1871 at Kapunda, South Australia, son of James Edward Wheatley, music teacher, and his wife Wilhelmina Magdalena, née Basedow. Educated at Prince Alfred College, Adelaide, in 1890 Frederick joined the teaching staff of Way College. On 28 June 1898 at St Peter's Anglican Church, Glenelg, he married Alice Ruth Kimber; they were to have three children. He taught at

Prince Alfred College from 1901, studied at the University of Adelaide (B.A., 1904), then transferred to King's College, Goulburn, New South Wales, in 1905. Appointed headmaster of Rockhampton Grammar School next year, he resigned in 1911 after clashing with the school board. Meanwhile he had become a captain (1908) in the Senior Cadets and had begun an association with the proposed Royal Australian Naval College, helping to draft the academic syllabus and college regulations.

Enrolling at Lincoln College, Oxford, Wheatley studied the ionization of gases and graduated B.Sc. in 1913; in that year the University of Adelaide awarded him a D.Sc. Before returning to Australia, he visited Germany where he improved his knowledge of the language and, by his own account, had conversations with Admiral von Tirpitz and General von Hindenburg. Appointed senior naval instructor on 6 February 1914, he joined the R.A.N.C. at Osborne House, Geelong, Victoria, to teach mathematics and physics. On the outbreak of World War I he was seconded to Navy Office, Melbourne, to work with Captain W. H. C. Thring [q.v.] and was placed in charge of intercepted enemy radio messages. With the aid of a captured code-book, he discovered the cypher key used to encrypt messages sent by Vice Admiral Graf von Spee's Pacific Squadron. Wheatley's brilliant work earned him the thanks of the Admiralty: the intelligence he supplied may have validated the decision to position the Royal Navy's superior forces which destroyed von Spee's ships in the battle of the Falkland Islands in December. He was later to exaggerate the impact of his code-breaking on the battle's outcome.

In 1915 Wheatley returned to the R.A.N.C. which, during his absence, had been relocated at Jervis Bay, New South Wales (later Australian Capital Territory). He became headmaster in 1920, the year when the academic staff were reclassified as civil officers. Throughout his tenure the college suffered from its geographical isolation and faced threat of closure. These problems may have cramped Wheatley's intellectual capacity and contributed to his sensitivity to real or imagined slights. While a difficult colleague, he was a proficient educationist and gained the affection of the cadets among whom he was known as 'Pa'. Bespectacled, with blue eyes and curly hair, he was an imposing figure, despite being only 5 ft. 8 ins. (172.7 cm) tall. He left the R.A.N.C. in 1930 when it was transferred to Flinders Naval Depot, Victoria, taking with him the appreciation of the Naval Board for his 'conspicuous success' in educating cadets to standards which enabled them as officers to take high places in examinations during subsequent training with the R.N.

From January 1931 to February 1932 Wheatley was director of studies at the Cranbrook School, Sydney. Appointed C.B.E. in 1932, in his retirement he was an office-bearer in the Royal Empire Society. Survived by a son and daughter, he died on 14 November 1955 at Cremorne and was cremated. His son Ross served in the Royal Australian Navy in 1914-53 and held the rank of acting captain.

F. B. Eldridge, *A history of the Royal Australian Naval College* (Melb, 1949); P. Beesly, *Room 40* (Lond, 1982); T. A. Clinch, *The history of the Rockhampton Grammar School, centenary 1881-1980* (Rockhampton, 1982); I. Cunningham, *Work hard, play hard* (Canb, 1988); *Cranbrookian*, 11, no 1, Aug 1930, no 3, May 1931; *Reveille* (Syd), July 1932, June 1934; *SMH*, 17 May, 20 Sept 1930, 31 Jan 1931, 3 June 1932, 6 Sept 1934, 4 Feb, 24 May 1938, 15 May 1940, 13 June 1947, 12 Aug 1949, 7 Feb 1952; Cranbrook School Council, Minutes; Roy Aust Naval College records; Navy Office records (AA, Melb); records (AWM); information from Admiral Sir Victor Smith, Red Hill, Canb, and Commander I. Cunningham, Ballarat, Vic.

ROBERT HYSLOP

WHEELER, ANNIE MARGARET (1867-1950), soldiers' welfare worker, was born on 10 December 1867 at Saunders Station, Dingo, Queensland, eldest surviving child of Alexander Stuart Somerville Laurie, grazier, and his wife Margaret, née Stevenson, both Scottish born. Educated at the Rockhampton convent school, she received some training at Sydney Hospital and engaged in private nursing on her return. At the Cathedral Church of St Paul, Rockhampton, on 24 February 1896 she married Henry Gaudiano Wheeler of Cooroorah Station, near Blackwater. After his death in 1903, Annie again made Rockhampton her home. In March 1913 she took her only daughter Portia to England to visit relations and to complete her education.

On the outbreak of hostilities in August 1914, Mrs Wheeler felt compelled to contribute to the war effort. She worked as a probationer nurse in a hospital near Eastbourne, Sussex, and joined the Australian Natives' Association and the Australian War Contingent Association. Frustrated by the organizational problems of the latter body, she resigned in order to serve Australian troops who came from central Queensland, together with their relations: distance, the uncertainty of mail, censorship of the press and a shortage of reliable information had caused them anguish.

Moving to London where she took up residence near the Australian Army Headquarters and the Anzac Buffet, Mrs Wheeler endeavoured to contact all soldiers from central Queensland, whether they were wounded, imprisoned, or in the trenches. She kept a detailed card index on them, corresponded with servicemen on the battlefield, forwarded packages and mail, provided for their needs and supervised the care and comfort of those in hospital. For soldiers on furlough, she supplemented restricted allowances and advanced funds when they experienced bureaucratic delays. To them, she became known as the 'Mother of the Queenslanders'. Families in Queensland sent letters and parcels through her: this was the only mail many diggers received. By 1918 over 2300 men were on her books.

Each fortnight Mrs Wheeler sent home detailed letters which were published in the *Capricornian* and the *Morning Bulletin*. A special fund to support her work was set up at Rockhampton; early in 1918, when she experienced poor health, Nurse May MacDonald was sent to assist her. The Commonwealth government provided a free passage for Annie Wheeler's return in November 1919.

Rockhampton accorded her a hero's welcome: over 5000 people met her train; cheering soldiers towed her car through the streets to a public reception; further functions followed in other towns. The Returned Sailors' and Soldiers' Imperial League of Australia made her an associate member and she was appointed O.B.E. in 1920. Presented with a house at Emu Park, near Rockhampton, she lived there from 1921 to 1947, then moved to Surfers Paradise. Survived by her daughter, Annie Wheeler died there on 23 October 1950 and was cremated. A plaque at Mt Thompson Memorial Gardens, Brisbane, bears the words 'She lived not unto herself'.

Just the link between (Rockhampton, 1917); *Aust Pastoralist, Grazing, Farmers' and Selectors' Gazette*, Dec 1917; *Capricornian*, 29 Nov 1919; Wheeler papers (OL); information from Mrs P. Fox and Mrs B. Williams, Brisb.   M. D. O'HAGAN

WHEELER, CHARLES ARTHUR (1880-1977), artist, was born on 4 January 1880 at Dunedin, New Zealand, son of John Edward Wheeler, labourer, and his wife Victoria Julia, née Francis, both English born. After John's death, Julia moved with her family to Williamstown, Melbourne, about 1891. Apprenticed in 1895 to C. Troedel [q.v.6] & Co. as a lithographic artist, Charles began part-time study next year at the Working Men's College; in 1898 he took drawing classes at night in the National Gallery schools under Frederick McCubbin [q.v.10] and in 1905 joined the painting class under L. Bernard Hall [q.v.9]. Some five years later Wheeler

held his first one-man show. In 1910 the National Art Gallery of New South Wales purchased his painting, 'The Portfolio', and the National Gallery of Victoria acquired 'The Poem'. Wheeler exhibited with the Victorian Artists' Society in 1908-10 and with the Australian Art Association in the 1920s and 1930s.

In April 1912 he had travelled to London, visiting Paris and the Prado in Madrid to see the work of Velazquez. In the following year he exhibited 'Le Printemps' at the Salon de la Société des Artistes Français, Paris, and in 1914 went to the Netherlands. Returning to England before the outbreak of World War I, he enlisted in the 22nd Battalion, Royal Fusiliers. He was awarded the Distinguished Conduct Medal (1916) for his actions at Vimy Ridge, but refused a commission and remained a sergeant. Demobilized in February 1919, Wheeler took a studio at Chelsea and exhibited 'Autumn Afternoon' and 'Golden Hours' at the Royal Academy of Arts, London. Back in Melbourne, he held an exhibition at the Athenaeum Gallery in March 1920. For some years a private teacher of drawing and painting, he became assistant drawing instructor at the National Gallery in 1927 and drawing-master in 1935. During these years Wheeler's work was at the height of its popularity, especially his nudes; he was, as well, a fine portraitist and a competent landscapist who won the New South Wales Art Quest prize (1929), the George Crouch prize (1932 and 1934) and the Archibald [q.v.3] prize (1933). In 1939-45 he was painting-master and head of the gallery schools. He was appointed O.B.E. in 1951.

About 5 ft. 8 ins. (172.7 cm) tall and handsome, Wheeler was softly spoken, gentle and sincere. Considered a thorough gentleman, he was much respected, particularly at the Savage Club of which he was sometime president. His restraint—and a certain fastidiousness—were reflected in his approach to painting: he assiduously applied traditional academic principles and distrusted modernist innovation. He held his final show at the Athenaeum Gallery in November 1970. Wheeler died in Melbourne on 26 October 1977 and was cremated. He never married. His estate was sworn for probate at $137 276. A self-portrait (1922) is held by the National Gallery of Victoria. He is represented in State galleries, the Australian National War Memorial, Canberra, the University of Melbourne and the Castlemaine Art Gallery.

J. S. MacDonald, *The art of Charles Wheeler*, *O.B.E., D.C.M.* (Melb, 1952); J. Hetherington, *Australian painters* (Melb, 1963); *Art in Aust*, no 7, 1919; *Argus*, 20 Jan 1927; *Manuscripts*, 6, 1933.   M. W. H. PENNINGS

WHEELER, JOHN (1853-1915), accountant, Orangeman and politician, was born on 18 December 1853 in Sydney, son of Aaron Wheeler, sawyer, and his wife Elizabeth, née Hawkins, both English born. Upon leaving school, John worked with his father for two years before joining in 1870 the Newcastle-Wallsend Coal Co.'s head office in Sydney. On 7 August 1878 he married Hannah Clarke at Petersham Congregational Church; they were to have five children. He became a qualified accountant and in the early 1900s the company's general manager.

The prevailing climate of sectarianism had prompted Wheeler, an active Congregationalist, to join the Loyal Orange Institution of New South Wales in 1870. Entering its New South Wales Grand Lodge in 1872, he was grand master in 1886, 1894-1909 and 1912 (by which time Orangeism was less influential) and sometime grand president of the Loyal Orange Institution of Australasia. A dedicated Freemason, from 1883 he was a member of the Protestant Alliance Friendly Society of Australasia's New South Wales grand council, its grand master in 1885-94 and for a time vice-president of its federal council.

Having lived in the suburb since 1867, Wheeler was an alderman on Petersham Municipal Council in 1884-92, 1896-1901 and 1904-13; he was mayor in 1886-91 and 1912-14. A council-member of the Municipal Association of New South Wales for twenty years from 1886, when not a Petersham alderman he represented Wallsend. For much of that time he was the association's senior vice-president. He strongly supported the movement for a Greater Sydney and for a city railway.

Defeated in 1887, Wheeler was elected to the Legislative Assembly for Canterbury behind (Sir) Joseph Carruthers [q.v.7] in 1889. At his public meetings and in parliament Wheeler eschewed sectarianism and espoused free trade, municipal reform and local option. Standing again in 1891, he was the object of rowdy attention from supporters of the new Labor Party, probably because of his opposition to aspects of the coal mines regulation bill which he believed unnecessarily restricted the rights of the proprietors. As in 1889, he appealed to working men, claiming to support an eight-hour day and quoting Henry George [q.v.4]. Wheeler was narrowly returned, but unseated after a recount.

An energetic joiner of organizations, he was a good chairman and an able administrator. He served on royal commissions on the improvement of the city of Sydney and its suburbs (1908) and on food supplies and fish (1911-13). Anti-Catholicism was an integral part of his outlook, but he gave it no prominence in seeking parliamentary or municipal office. Like others from the second rank of business, such as Thomas Jessep [q.v.9], Wheeler linked Protestant sectarianism, temperance and evangelical Christianity with free trade and liberalism, laying the foundation for much of the electoral support gathered in the 1904 election by the Liberal Party under the leadership of his old friend Carruthers.

Forced by ill health to resign from business, Wheeler died of a cerebral haemorrhage on 18 April 1915 at his Strathfield home and was buried in the Independent section of Rookwood cemetery. He was survived by his wife, three daughters and a son.

Cyclopedia of N.S.W. (Syd, 1907); W. A. Stewart (comp), *Early history of the Loyal Orange Institution, N.S.W.* (Syd, 1926); A. M. Shepherd (comp), *The story of Petersham 1793-1948* (Syd, 1948); *SMH*, 16 June 1891, 19 Apr 1915; M. Lyons, Aspects of sectarianism in New South Wales circa 1865 to 1880 (Ph.D. thesis, ANU, 1972).   MARK LYONS

WHEEN, ARTHUR WESLEY (1897-1971), soldier and librarian, was born on 9 February 1897 at Sunny Corner, New South Wales, second son of Harold Wheen [q.v. J. G. Wheen], Wesleyan minister, and his native-born wife Clara Isabel Morze, née Black. Arthur grew up in the country towns of his father's calling and attended Nowra and South Bathurst Public schools. When his father was posted to Sydney in 1910, Arthur continued his education at Gordon Public and Sydney Boys' High (1911-14) schools. He won an exhibition to Teachers' College and in 1915 studied arts at the University of Sydney.

On 15 October Wheen enlisted in the Australian Imperial Force and embarked for Egypt in December. He was posted as a signaller to the new 54th Battalion at Tel-el-Kebir on 16 February 1916 and crossed to France in June. For repairing cut telephone lines and maintaining communications in the midst of enemy artillery barrages 'at great personal risk and self sacrifice', he was awarded the Military Medal and two Bars: at Petillon in July 1916, at Beaulencourt in March 1917 and at Villers-Bretonneux on 25 April 1918. Meanwhile, he was promoted lance corporal on 17 January 1918 and corporal a week later. Having attended an officers' training course at Oxford, England, he was commissioned on 7 May and promoted lieutenant on 7 August. Wounded in action in September 1917 and again in September 1918, he was invalided home, reaching Sydney in March 1919.

Chosen that year as Rhodes scholar for New South Wales, Wheen left for England in July 1920 to read modern history at New

College, Oxford (B.A., 1923). His health broke down and he took third-class honours. In January 1924 he was appointed assistant librarian at the Victoria and Albert Museum, London. He detested ambition and personal advancement, and refused early promotion to chief librarian, but became acting keeper in 1939 and keeper of the library in 1945.

Returning to Australia briefly in September 1926 after the death of his father, on the voyage out Wheen met Aldwyth Lewers, sister of Gerald Lewers, the sculptor, and married her on 20 October 1928 at the register office, Kensington, London. They made their home at Jordans, among a Quaker community in the Chiltern Hills, Buckinghamshire. Aldwyth ran the property as a smallholding. Their younger daughter died of meningitis on 13 January 1939, aged 5; their elder, Gretchen, was evacuated to Australia during World War II and never again lived in England.

Wheen mixed in literary circles that included (Sir) Herbert Read and T. S. Eliot. His only listed original work is a short story, 'Two masters', first published in the *London Mercury* in November 1924. A highly gifted linguist, he was better known for his translations from the German, most notably that of Erich Maria Remarque's *All quiet on the Western Front* which has remained a classic in Wheen's version since its appearance in March 1929. Between then and 1937 Wheen translated four more German war novels (two of them Remarque's), a scholarly treatise on Virgil and a book on Bushman art.

To his friends Wheen revealed his singular verbal talents in conversation and in correspondence: surviving letters disclose a delightful range of wit, oblique fancy, irreverent humour and erudition. Tall, with striking blue eyes and an expressive face, he was a 'spellbinder', both as speaker and listener. His friend J. F. Head described his 'extraordinarily penetrating and logical intellect'. Wheen had a wide knowledge of English and foreign literature, both classical and modern, but was naturally in sympathy with the *avant-garde* of the 1920s and 1930s, taking particular interest in Pablo Picasso and Georg Grosz; he also encouraged young British artists. He bought extensively for the museum's art library, tracking down important publications in Eastern European and Oriental languages, and adding to the section on aesthetics and the philosophy of art. Another contribution to the library was the subject index which he began in 1936.

On retirement in 1962 Wheen took up pottery at Jordans and continued to advise former colleagues. Survived by his wife and daughter, he died in Amersham hospital, Buckinghamshire, on 15 March 1971 and was cremated without religious rites.

Reveille (Syd), 1 Mar 1935; *SMH*, 28 Sept 1918, 1 Mar, 12 Nov 1919, 1 Dec 1920, 29 Jan 1924, 22 Sept 1926, 5 Apr 1971; *The Times*, 19 Mar 1971; Wheen *and* M. Aurousseau papers (NL); J. F. Head papers (held by Soc of Antiquaries of Lond); information from Messrs R. Lightbown and J. P. Harthan, Lond.

SALLY O'NEILL

WHEEN, JOHN GLADWELL (1858-1929), Methodist minister, was born on 27 April 1858 at Ecclesall Bierlow, Yorkshire, England, son of Edwin Wheen, a master grocer of Sheffield, and his wife Agnes, née Gladwell. The Wheen children were raised as Methodists and attended Carver Street chapel and private schools with their friend Joseph Woodhouse (1860-1924). Trained for a commercial career, John joined the town clerk's staff and became secretary of Sheffield public hospital. He was also a superintendent at Red Hill School. His sister Margaret Agnes, who was to marry Woodhouse in 1888, arrived in Melbourne in August 1882, followed by her brothers John and Herbert later that year; Woodhouse reached Sydney in 1884.

In 1883 John Wheen became a Wesleyan Methodist home missionary. Next year he was ordained and served in various parts of Melbourne. In 1888 he moved to Charlton and on 25 April married Sheffield-born Eliza Ellen Lief at the Wesleyan Methodist Church, Hawthorn. Stationed in Tasmania from 1890, he returned to Melbourne in 1899. As president (1907-08) of the Victorian and Tasmanian conference, he proved an able administrator and he was called to the foreign missions office in Sydney in 1908 to assist Benjamin Danks.

Although Wheen did not become general secretary of missions until 1910, he is remembered with George Brown and John Burton [qq.v.3,7] as a great missionary promoter. He presided over the reconciliation of the Tongan Church, largely engineered by Rodger Page [q.v.11], went to Samoa, New Britain, the Solomon Islands and India, and also visited Fiji three times (once with G. J. Waterhouse and Jacob Garrard [q.v.4]). Wheen's promotion of education as the principal means of evangelizing was reflected in his enthusiasm for the Thomas Baker Memorial College, Davuilevu, Fiji, the co-racial Suva boys' school, and the Wesleyan high school at Azamgarh, India. His support of government grants and his legalistic approach to mission problems brought him into conflict with progressives like Burton.

Elected president of the New South Wales conference in 1919, Wheen next year attended the Wesleyan Methodist conference in London and the World Conference on Faith and Order in Geneva. In 1926-29 he was president general of the Methodist Church of Australasia. Shortly after retiring, he died at Ashfield on 13 November 1929 and was cremated. His wife, son and two daughters survived him; his daughter Agnes was foundation headmistress of Annesley Methodist Girls' School at Bowral. To J. E. Carruthers, Wheen was 'an able preacher, an effective platform speaker, a man of affairs, with a special aptitude for big things'.

His brother HAROLD (1867-1926) was born on 28 June 1867 at Oldland, Gloucestershire; he trained as a pharmacist, came to Sydney in 1889 and opened a business at Waverley. Entering the Wesleyan ministry in 1891, he served at Bourke, Wilcannia, Sunny Corner, Jamberoo, Bathurst and Paddington, Sydney. He was general secretary of the young people's department, and president of the State Council of Religious Education and in 1923-24 of the Christian Endeavour Union. He died at Roseville, Sydney, on 18 June 1926, survived by his wife Clara Isabel Morze, née Black, whom he had married at Mudgee on 26 March 1895, and by their eleven children, including Arthur [q.v.].

The Wheen brothers and their brother-in-law Woodhouse had formed an influential triumvirate in Sydney in charge of Methodist outreach: foreign missions, young people and home missions respectively. All three promoted church union and total abstinence, reinforcing the conservative image of Methodism in the first quarter of the twentieth century.

J. E. Carruthers, *Memories of an Australian ministry 1868 to 1921* (Lond, 1922); A. H. Wood, *Overseas missions of the Australian Methodist church* (Melb, 1975-87); *SMH*, 12 Mar 1925, 19, 21 June 1926, 14 Nov 1929; *Adel Chronicle*, 21 Nov 1929. NIEL GUNSON

WHELAN, JAMES PAUL (1864-1938), wrecker, was born on 30 June 1864 at Stawell, Victoria, second son of eight children of James Whelan, miner, and his wife Mary, née Brett, both Irish born. His father died from phthisis in 1885, leaving the family destitute. Big and strong as a youngster, Jim went to Melbourne at the age of 19; by carting timber during the 1880s building boom, he saved enough money to buy his own horse and dray, and became a well-known figure around the wharves. On 17 March 1896 at St Joseph's Catholic Church, Collingwood, he married Elizabeth White, a barmaid and daughter of a coachman. In 1892 Whelan was given a start as a wrecking contractor by the builder David Mitchell [q.v.5] who wanted to demolish some shops in Swanston Street and who offered the wrecked materials as sole payment. The experience enabled Whelan to survive the 1890s depression by buying and wrecking empty cottages in East Brunswick. Establishing premises there as a timber merchant, he was to become Melbourne's leading wrecker.

The London and American Supply Stores, the Leviathan Clothing Co. and Monahan's [q.v.5] buildings in Swanston Street, the Yarra Bend asylum, McCracken's [q.v.5] brewery, the old Melbourne Hospital, and all manner of mansions, cottages and skyscrapers fell to Whelan's hammers. His methods were crude but effective. Buildings were gutted with pick and hammer until only the walls remained: rather than being knocked down, these were pushed inward. Whittled away, brick by brick, by 'cats' on top, the rubble was removed by 'bulls' below, leaving a vacant site displaying a hoarding that read: 'Whelan the Wrecker Is Here'. This famous advertisement had prosaic origins as a site directive to delivery men; a change to the past tense supplied a familiar Melburnian dictum for Australian servicemen in both World Wars who posted it on areas of enemy devastation.

Eventually, Whelan was to wreck buildings for whose construction he had carted timber, and in one reversal of activity he painstakingly moved St James's Cathedral from William and Collins streets to its present site in King Street, Melbourne. Although he boasted that he had never received a claim from a member of the public, Whelan experienced many accidents himself. His arm and leg were broken in the collapse of a brick kiln; his head was struck by a brick dropped from six storeys; his last accident, a fall from four storeys, left him with a permanent limp and kept him off the top of buildings thereafter. It did not keep him from demolition sites where his lanky frame, complete with black bow-tie and billycock, could be seen sitting on a box as he directed activity.

Big, jovial, and tough, Whelan was a benevolent patriarch who provided members of his extended family with jobs and houses, and retained his workers throughout the 1930s Depression when there were few contracts. Barely able to read or write, he paid cash for everything and managed both men and finances in his major concerns. As a proprietary company with a capital of £20 000, the business passed wholly to his sons shortly before he died at Fitzroy on 2 March 1938. Survived by his wife, three sons and three daughters, he was buried in Melbourne general cemetery; his estate was sworn for probate at £19 759.

Herald (Melb), 21 June 1930, 16 Jan 1932, 2 Mar 1938, 31 Dec 1955; *Sun News-Pictorial*, 9 Jan 1932; *Smith's Weekly* (Syd), 19 Feb 1927; *SMH*, 31

May 1963; *Argus*, 23 Jan 1937, 12 Feb 1938; information from Mr M. Whelan, Brunswick, Melb.

DAVID DUNSTAN

WHIDDON, SAMUEL THOMAS (1848-1905), importer, boot manufacturer and politician, FRANK (1877-1947) and HORACE WILLIAM (1879-1955), wool merchants, scourers and combers, were father and sons. Samuel was born on 26 June 1848 at Hoxton New Town, London, son of Samuel Cephus Whiddon, plasterer, and his wife Sarah, née Fossey. Aged 5, he arrived in Sydney with his parents and, after schooling, became a messenger-boy with Thomas Williams, boot importer and manufacturer. Having spent fourteen years learning the trade, he took over the firm, T. Williams & Co., which he moved to larger premises in Pitt Street by 1895. At the Congregational Church, Surry Hills, he had married Sydney-born Kate Gertrude Fogarty on 25 August 1869.

Appointed a justice of the peace in 1885, Whiddon was electoral returning officer and member of the School Board for South Sydney. He was a director of the Sydney Permanent Freehold Land and Building Society, a founder and president of the Pitt Street Congregational Literary and Social Union, and a member of the Free Trade, Land and Reform League. In 1894-1904 he represented Sydney-Cook in the Legislative Assembly as a free trader and liberal supporter of (Sir) George Reid [q.v.11]. Politically active in social matters until failing sight intervened, he favoured the eight-hour day, early closing, old-age and invalid pensions, and women's franchise and parliamentary candidature. Survived by four sons and three daughters, he died of a cerebral haemorrhage on 20 September 1905 at his Glebe home and was buried in Randwick cemetery.

His second and third sons, Frank and Horace, were born on 25 March 1877 and on 21 February 1879 in Sydney. Educated at Fort Street Model School, in 1895 they were apprenticed to wool-scourers. In January 1900 they formed Whiddon Bros, a wool-scouring business at Botany and in 1906 acquired Messrs Johnson's and Vicars's [q.v.] works on the water reserve there. On 5 June 1906, at the Pitt Street Congregational Church, Frank married Alice Maude Curnow (d. 1919), granddaughter of William Curnow [q.v.8]. Horace married her sister Lillian Weiss Curnow at the Congregational Church, Newtown, on 25 July 1907.

Whiddon Bros Ltd became a public company in January 1910 with authorized capital of £50 000 in £1000 shares; Frank was chairman and managing director; Arthur, the eldest brother, was secretary. In 1911 wool combing was added to scouring and fell-mongering activities. By 1938 the firm had acquired the adjacent Bridgewater Wool Scouring Co.; it had also entered into an arrangement with Buzacott & Co. Ltd for establishing on their site the Lan-O-Leen Co. to produce sheep dip, agricultural sprays and the sheep food, Vita-Pro-Teen. By this time Frank and Horace had gained control of the assets of the firm which was reconstituted as Whiddon Pty Ltd.

Frank was a prominent and dedicated Free-mason. Initiated into Lodge Neutral Bay No. 267, he became worshipful master in 1916; past junior grand warden in 1938 and deputy grand master in 1943, he was installed as grand master of United Grand Lodge of New South Wales on 13 August 1945 in Sydney Town Hall. Whiddon was a member of the council of advice of the Liverpool and London and Globe Insurance Co. and a director of Rogers Meat Co. Ltd. He belonged to Royal Sydney Yacht Squadron and was a founding member of (Royal) Prince Edward Yacht Club. A member of the Australian Jockey Club, he also enjoyed motoring and golf. In June 1944 he succeeded Sir Henry Braddon [q.v.7] as president of the English-Speaking Union.

Of medium build, white-haired, brisk and punctilious, Frank Whiddon died on 1 September 1947 at his home in Wolseley Road, Point Piper, and was cremated with Masonic rites. He was survived by his wife Blodwen, née Jones, whom he had married on 4 September 1923 at the Presbyterian Church, Epping, by their daughter, and by the son and two daughters of his first marriage. Probate of his estate was sworn at £48 990. He is commemorated by Lodge Frank Whiddon No. 739 and by the Frank Whiddon Masonic Homes.

On Frank's death, Horace became chairman of directors of the family firm. Secretary of the Wool Employers' Federation, he was a member (1941) of the State Wool Committee and in January 1943 was appointed chairman of the advisory committee of the wool and basil industry under the director-general of manpower. He was a councillor of the Royal Agricultural Society of New South Wales and a keen horticulturist; he chaired the society's horticulture and building and works committees, sat on the horse committee and was honorary assistant ringmaster; he became a vice-president in 1946. President of trustees of (Royal) National Park (1934-49) and a director of Royal Prince Alfred Hospital, he was a life member of the New South Wales Rugby Union and a member of the New South Wales and National clubs.

Portly, florid, pipe-smoking and good-natured, Horace was prominent in the United Australia Party and chairman of its electoral conference in Croydon, the seat (1927-40) of his friend (Sir) Bertram Stevens [q.v.]. In September 1934 Whiddon was elected to the Legislative Council of New South Wales where he was inactive (never making a speech) until his second term expired in April 1955. Survived by his wife and son, he died at his Enfield home on 11 May 1955 and was cremated.

J. Jervis and L. R. Flack, *A jubilee history, 1888-1938, of the Municipality of Botany* (Syd, 1938); *N.S.W. Freemason*, 9, no 3, Oct 1976; *Pastoral Review*, 16 June 1955; *Daily Telegraph* (Syd), 14 June 1894; *T&CJ*, 27 Sept 1905; *SMH*, 11, 18 July 1894, 21 Sept 1905, 26 May 1932, 9 Sept 1933, 29 Mar, 3 Aug, 28 Sept 1934, 17 July 1936, 4 Dec 1937, 2 June, 23 Sept 1938, 19 Apr 1941, 27 Jan 1943, 30 June 1944, 14 Aug 1945, 20 May 1946, 9 Jan, 2 Sept 1947, 12 May 1955; information from Mr M. Cowan, Canb.　　G. P. WALSH

WHIDDON, WILLIAM HENRY (1858-1949), taxation commissioner and lotteries director, was born on 17 October 1858 at Woolloomooloo, Sydney, sixth child of Samuel Whiddon, builder, and his wife Sarah Maria, née Fossey, both from London. William became a clerk and lived at Surry Hills. On 24 April 1878 he married with Independent forms Elizabeth Ann Timms at Emerald Hill, Melbourne; they were to have ten children. He acquired an office in Fitzroy Street, Sydney, and about 1890 with James Summons set up as a cordial manufacturer. Whiddon entered the New South Wales Treasury as a temporary clerk in March 1895 and remained closely connected with income tax legislation and collection.

Appointed senior assessor in the State taxation branch in July 1905, he became commissioner of taxation on 1 January 1914. At a conference in Melbourne in July 1923 he cogently advocated uniform taxation forms for State and Federal purposes: he and the Federal taxation commissioner Robert Ewing [q.v.8] designed the form for subsequent collections. Whiddon and the other State commissioners were concurrently appointed deputy Federal commissioners late that year.

At the 1928 royal commission on the Commonwealth Constitution, Whiddon alleged that the atmosphere of the newly amalgamated department was 'very clouded'. In addition to a long backlog of claims awaiting settlement by 'ignorant' Federal staff, there was evidence of 'criminal' dealings between taxation officials and hoteliers. In March Prime Minister S. M. (Viscount) Bruce [q.v.7] arranged with the State premier for an inquiry to be held, but further action was frustrated by Ewing, who took exception to Whiddon's 'regrettable reflections' on members of his staff, and by Whiddon's impending retirement at the age of 70. From December he was retained as assessor and member of the local Income Tax (Management) Board.

On 22 June 1931 he was appointed first director of the State lottery, established by the Lang [q.v.9] government in December 1930 as part of its 'feverish search for new sources of revenue'. Whiddon revelled in his new public role; in Lang's view he was the 'ideal man to launch the scheme' because of his theatrical presence. Although the United Australia Party criticized his appointment, it proved popular with the lottery-buying public.

A reversal in Whiddon's career occurred in 1933. The Public Service Association of New South Wales chafed at his exercising sole power to appoint lottery staff. He was not reappointed lottery director in June; two months later his membership of the Income Tax Board was terminated. Having become the subject of allegations of criminal offences, Whiddon appeared in Central Police Court on 24 October and 19 December; he was fined £2 and £10 for selling shares in a lottery ticket in contravention of the Gaming and Betting (Amendment) Act. The controversial sale of two tickets bearing the same number had also brought him to court on 28 November. In a taxation appeal in 1935 Whiddon was named for having allowed, while commissioner, that betting proceeds from racing should not be regarded as income.

A genteel-looking, bespectacled man, Whiddon was one-time conductor of the Metropolitan Liedertafel and Petersham Choral Society. His other keen interest was horse-racing and he was chairman (1930-32) of Tattersall's Club. A widower, on 16 October 1939 at the Congregational Church, Newtown, he married Agnes Martha Cole. Survived by her, and by a son and five daughters of his first marriage, he died on 29 May 1949 at his Hurlstone Park home and was buried in the Anglican section of Manly cemetery. His estate was sworn for probate at £15 626.

J. T. Lang, *I remember* (Syd, 1956); B. Nairn, *The 'Big Fella'* (Melb, 1986); Roy Com on the Constitution, Procs, *PP* (Cwlth), 1928, 5, p 1292; *T&CJ*, 31 Dec 1913; *SMH*, 12 Sept 1923, 9, 20 Mar, 14 June, 18 Dec 1928, 15 May 1930, 14 Nov 1931, 20 May 1932, 3, 22 June, 26 Aug, 10, 29 Nov, 20 Dec 1933, 11 Dec 1935, 30 May 1949.

PETER SPEARRITT

WHITE, ALEXANDER HENRY (1882-1915), army officer and maltster, was born on 9 May 1882 at Ballarat, Victoria, fifth child of

Alexander White, a maltster from Scotland, and his English wife Eliza, née Collison. Educated by a private tutor and at Grenville College, Ballarat, Alexander followed his father and brother into the malting business, joining Wendouree Malt House. He became a citizen-soldier in 1899: his 'whole heart and soul was in his military work from the time he joined the old (Victorian) Mounted Rifles in Ballarat after leaving school'. Commissioned in March 1904, he gained steady promotion and by 1914 was brigade major in the 5th Light Horse Brigade. On 22 October 1913 he had married Myrtle Louise Glasson at St Peter's Anglican Church, Ballarat.

Transferring to the Australian Imperial Force on 21 September 1914, White was given command of the 8th Light Horse Regiment. He was promoted lieut-colonel on 1 January 1915, eight weeks before the regiment embarked for Egypt as part of the 3rd Light Horse Brigade. The unit landed at Gallipoli on 21 May to be employed as infantry. White was wounded in action on 27 June, but resumed command on 4 July.

At 4.30 a.m. on 7 August 1915 the 3rd Light Horse Brigade mounted a bayonet assault on the Turkish trenches at The Nek. Seven minutes earlier, due to an error, the preliminary bombardment had ceased, allowing the enemy to prepare for the attack. White led the first of his regiment's two waves, but was shot down a short distance from his trench. Of the 300 officers and soldiers under his command, 153 died with him and 80 were wounded within minutes. The charge has endured as one of the best-known episodes of the Gallipoli Peninsula campaign: it was the subject of a painting by George Lambert [q.v.9] and the setting for the finale in the 1981 Australian film, *Gallipoli*.

C. E. W. Bean [q.v.7] criticized White for leading the charge instead of remaining to supervise the operation; had he stayed behind he might have lent support to Lieut-Colonel N. M. Brazier, the commanding officer of the accompanying 10th Light Horse Regiment, in his appeals to Lieut-Colonel J. M. Antill [q.v.7], brigade major of the 3rd Light Horse Brigade, to halt the third and fourth waves of the assault. A sensitive man and a conscientious, brave and respected officer, White was mentioned in dispatches for his bold action. His wife survived him, as did their only son, Alexander John Middleton, who joined the Australian Army Medical Corps during World War II and was made a prisoner of war by the Japanese in 1942.

C. E. W. Bean, *The story of Anzac*, 2 (Syd, 1924) and *The A.I.F. in France, 1918* (Syd, 1942); *Argus*, 8 Oct 1915; records (AWM); information from and personal papers held by Mrs M. McPherson, Bulleen, Melb.

PETER BURNESS

WHITE, Sir CYRIL BRUDENELL BINGHAM (1876-1940), soldier, was born on 23 September 1876 at St Arnaud, Victoria, seventh child of John Warren White, stock agent and retired army officer, and his wife Maria, née Gibton, both Dublin born. The family moved to Queensland in 1881 and lived on pastoral stations in the Gympie, Charters Towers and Gladstone areas before settling at Clayfield, Brisbane. Although he was unsuccessful as a pastoralist, in 1885 John became president of the Brisbane Stock Exchange. Brudenell was educated at Brisbane Central Boys' School and for one year at Eton Preparatory School, Nundah. He had wanted to be a barrister, like his grandfather, but at the age of 16 took a job as a bank clerk and studied in his spare time.

While based at Gympie, he became friends with (Sir) Thomas Glasgow [q.v.9]; through this connexion, and with the assistance of Captain C. B. Steele, White was provisionally commissioned on 7 October 1896 in the 2nd Queensland (Wide Bay and Burnett) Regiment. Transferring to the permanent forces, he was commissioned on 7 June 1899 in the Queensland Regiment of the Royal Australian Artillery, was stationed at Thursday Island in 1900-01 and continued to serve in the Australian Military Forces. On 18 February 1902 he embarked for service in South Africa with the 1st Battalion, Australian Commonwealth Horse. The unit engaged in minor operations in the western Transvaal and Bechuanaland; hostilities ended in June and White wrote: 'I would have liked to see a little fighting'. Sailing for Australia next month in the poorly equipped *Drayton Grange*, he went among a group of mutinous soldiers who threatened to 'toss him in a blanket' and placated them.

In January 1904 he was detached from his duties with the artillery in Victoria and appointed aide-de-camp to Major General Sir Edward Hutton [q.v.9], general officer commanding the A.M.F. His one year association with Hutton, during which the two formed a lasting friendship, marked the beginning of White's formative years as a staff officer. Promoted temporary captain, he travelled extensively with the G.O.C. and learned much about the state and organization of the infant Australian Army. On 15 November 1905 at Christ Church, South Yarra, White married Ethel Davidson with Anglican rites. Next year, nominated by Hutton, he became the first A.M.F. officer to attend the British Army Staff College, Camberley, England. He began the course with relatively little regimental experience and limited active service. That he graduated well up in his class-list was testimony to his ability and capacity for hard work, traits which increasingly brought him to the notice of his superiors. Returning to Australia, he was promoted captain and in

March 1908 joined the staff of the chief of intelligence, Colonel (Sir) William Bridges [q.v.7], who shared many of his views. By the end of the year White was again in Britain, serving on exchange as a general staff officer, 3rd grade, at the War Office.

His attachment to the War Office gave him experience in handling large forces and developed his skills in planning and administration; it also introduced him to officers with whom he would later work and deepened his 'commitment to the British Empire'. Writing regularly to Bridges, he elaborated an Imperial view of Australian defence which contrasted to the more independent stance of officers such as Lieut-Colonel J. G. Legge [q.v.10]. In January 1909 White wrote: 'I have always held that an Imperial General Staff must of necessity be able to accomplish more than any local one'. He favoured bringing Australian forces under the British Army Act in time of war, and opposed the creation of an Australian navy. The need for trained officers in Australia led to his recall and to his appointment on 1 January 1912 as director of military operations at Army Headquarters, Melbourne. He had been promoted major the previous year.

In his new post he was responsible for developing strategic policy and administering the military system recently formulated by Legge and Lord Kitchener. White maintained and updated Bridges's mobilization plans for home defence and supported the concept of a citizen force. Although pleased by the depth of Imperial sentiment among politicians, especially in the Labor Party, he was frustrated by the refusal of successive defence ministers to allow contingency planning for war between Britain and Germany. In 1912, however, (Sir) George Pearce [q.v.11] approved talks with New Zealand representatives on common action to be taken were either country attacked. It was agreed that a jointly-manned division would be fielded. Instructed by Pearce to work in secrecy, White compiled specifications for raising, equipping, training and dispatching the Australian portion of such a force. In July 1914 he was made acting chief of the General Staff, pending Legge's return from Britain. Next month, as a result of his earlier planning, White was able to endorse the government's offer to the United Kingdom of a force of 20 000 men to proceed overseas at short notice in the event of war.

When Bridges was appointed in August 1914 to command the Australian Imperial Force he chose Lieut-Colonel White as his chief of staff. Drawing on White's plans, the two worked closely to create the force and to establish administrative arrangements to preserve its separate identity within the British Army. By December the first contingent

of the A.I.F. was training in Egypt. With Bridges, White planned the landing of the 1st Australian Division at Gaba Tepe, while expressing the view that the total force to be used in the assault on Gallipoli was inadequate. In the confusion of the landing on 25 April 1915, he accompanied Bridges on his rapid tour of A.I.F. positions and helped to pull together the disorganized threads of command and communications. He was 'the perfect complement to Bridges' until the latter's death in May. Next month White was awarded the Distinguished Service Order for his exceptional efforts as a staff officer. On 1 October he became brigadier general, General Staff, Australian and New Zealand Army Corps, and began his long partnership with Lieut-General Sir William Birdwood [q.v.7] who took permanent command of the A.I.F. that month. White was the logical choice for a position which involved operational duties, the administrative control of the A.I.F., and issues of policy between the Australian government and the British commander of its overseas forces.

With Birdwood's departure to act as commander-in-chief at Imbros in October 1915, White remained at corps headquarters. There he planned and supervised the evacuation of Anzac, the most successful operation of the campaign. Put into effect in three stages, his plan lulled the Turks into thinking that a lessening of activity was part of preparations for winter; on the night of 19-20 December the last 10 000 men were evacuated, transported to Imbros and thence to Egypt; the withdrawal was accomplished without incident or casualties. White was twice mentioned in dispatches for his work at Gallipoli. In Egypt he had the principal role in implementing the expansion of the A.I.F. to four divisions. One of the new divisional commands might have gone to him, but Birdwood chose to maintain continuity in the force's administration. Appointed C.B., White embarked for France on 29 March 1916 as B.G.G.S., I Anzac Corps.

His authority over the A.I.F. on the Western Front was pervasive. It was generally recognized that he was responsible for running the corps, while Birdwood exercised command through regular and direct contact with the men. Notwithstanding his close relationship with 'his' Australians, Birdwood's administration and organization were weak, and his tactical acumen suspect. White more than compensated for these shortcomings. When General Sir Douglas Haig rebuked the Anzac Corps staff after a failure at Pozières Heights in July 1916, it was White who showed him 'in detail, item by item' that the criticism was unfounded. Haig was sufficiently impressed to reply: 'I daresay you are right, young man'. Moreover, White understood the need to provide for the comfort and well-being of the troops, notably in the dreadful winter of 1916-17 when there was an urgent requirement to build camps, roads and railways. Because it became known that he could get things done, problems were referred to him: 'During this, the most difficult period of the A.I.F.'s existence', he wielded unprecedented influence.

Although concern had already been expressed that he was 'being kept back on account of his usefulness as a staff officer', as Birdwood had admitted in a letter to Hutton in September, White was promoted temporary major general on 1 January 1917 and continued as Birdwood's chief of staff. Throughout the advance to the Hindenburg line in March, he constantly advised the divisional commanders and maintained control in the unfamiliar conditions of fighting on the move. Finding that Haig had not been informed of the need for the Australian divisions to rest, White told a senior British staff officer in May that he would never again recommend sending an Australian force overseas unless its representative had direct access to the commander-in-chief. At times his responsibilities bore hard upon him. Writing to his old friend Brigadier General (Sir) John Gellibrand [q.v.8] next month, after the two costly battles of Bullecourt, he vented his dissatisfaction with Birdwood and the remainder of the staff. Yet, he attributed his irritability to tiredness: 'I know in my innermost heart that all I need is a certain amount of rest and freedom from responsibility and I will see the world in correct perspective again for a while'.

In July 1917 White rejected Haig's suggestion that he take command of the corps, arguing that Birdwood's position with the Australians was too valuable to lose. C. E. W. Bean and (Sir) Keith Murdoch [qq.v.7,10] agitated behind the scenes later in the year to have White placed in command, though to no avail. He was appointed C.M.G. in December. Following the collapse of the British Fifth Army in the German offensive of March 1918, General Birdwood was selected as its commander, opening the question of who should lead the newly formed Australian Corps. On learning in May that Major General Sir John Monash [q.v.10] would be appointed and that White would go to the Fifth Army with Birdwood, Bean and Murdoch revived their campaign: their aim was to have Monash promoted general and made general officer commanding the A.I.F. in England, thus leaving White to take the corps. White gave them no encouragement and dissociated himself from their manoeuvres. Monash's appointment had been proper and deserved. As arrangements stood, administrative command of the A.I.F. would remain nominally with Birdwood, but in effect with White, thereby enabling him to retain control of the cherished force he had done so much to create and advance. For these reasons, White suppressed personal ambition for what he held to be a greater good. On 1 June he took up duties as major general, General Staff, Fifth Army, and had little further involvement in operations.

Sent to London to preside briefly over the Demobilization and Repatriation Branch, he was promoted temporary lieut-general and made chief of staff, A.I.F., on 28 November 1918. He was appointed K.C.M.G. on 1 January 1919. For his services after Gallipoli, he received five foreign decorations, was appointed aide-de-camp to King George V and mentioned in dispatches five times. His brilliant war record had been due to his loyalty, professionalism, intelligence and the capacity to work harmoniously with successive leaders. 'A tallish, wiry man with elegant carriage, direct and compelling blue eyes and a dominant nose', he had personal charm which cloaked a strong will.

His brother DUDLEY PERSSE WHITE (1867-1947) had also served in the war. He was born on 31 July 1867 at Minnieboro station, near Glenorchy, Victoria. Commissioned in the Queensland Land Forces in 1889, he transferred to the permanent forces and by 1913 was a lieut-colonel, Administrative and Instructional Branch, A.M.F. On 25 March 1904 he married Lynette Charlotte Yaldwyn with Anglican rites at St John's Pro-Cathedral, Brisbane. Appointed to the A.I.F. in November 1916, he commanded the 13th Light Horse Regiment on the Western Front from May 1917 to the end of hostilities. He was promoted brevet colonel, A.M.F., for specially meritorious service, mentioned in dispatches and awarded the Belgian Croix de Guerre. Having retired in 1922, Dudley White went to live in England and died on 15 April 1947 at Much Marcle, Herefordshire.

Returning to Australia in June 1919, Sir Brudenell found that his first peacetime task was to join Legge, Sir James McCay [q.v.10] and George Swinburne [q.v.] on a committee which considered the future organization of the A.M.F. Their report recommended a modified system of compulsory military training and a citizen force structure of six infantry and two mounted divisions—some 180 000 men. In February 1920 the committee, enlarged to comprise six generals of the former A.I.F., produced a second report. Minor changes to the earlier proposals were suggested. Becoming chief of the General Staff on 1 June, White was prepared to implement the proposals, but faced savage cuts in defence spending. Rather than building a citizen army, as he had hoped, he found himself preserving as much of it as he could in a nucleus organization which would be capable of expansion in an emergency.

Retiring as C.G.S. in June 1923, White was appointed chairman of the newly constituted Commonwealth Public Service Board. Although his primary task was to reclassify the service, he also supervised the progressive transfer of departments from Melbourne to Canberra. In 1927 he made the Federal arrangements for the visit of the duke and duchess of York and was appointed K.C.B. He had been appointed K.C.V.O. in 1920 for organizing the tour of the prince of Wales. Wishing to remain within weekly commuting distance of his grazing property, Woodnaggerak, near Buangor, Victoria, where he had established his home, he chose not to move to Canberra and in 1928 declined a further term on the Public Service Board. That year he became chairman and superintendent for Australia of the New Zealand Loan & Mercantile Agency Co. Ltd. His withdrawal from public office enabled him to build up his pastoral interests and to enjoy the simple pleasures he preferred. He read widely, with a special interest in history. Ever ready to give his time to charitable and service organizations, he was a trustee of the A.I.F. Canteen Funds Trust and the Baillieu [q.v.7] Education Trust, and a member of the Australian War Memorial Board and the Board of Management of the Alfred Hospital. President (1934), he was prominent in the affairs of the Melbourne Club.

Claims have been made that White was involved in right-wing 'secret armies' in the 1920s and 1930s. The evidence for such assertions is circumstantial at best, consisting mainly of hearsay in police intelligence files which alleges that he was prominent in the 'White Army'; this organization, however, took its title from the political associations of the colour and not from White's surname. A man of sensitivity and intellect, he believed in the rule of law. His training and experience had finally persuaded him that democracy was 'right in principle'. He later argued that there was 'no need for national guards, legions, or such like organizations': citizens should be encouraged to support their elected political leaders. Though patrician in manner and very conservative in his views, he was an improbable political vigilante.

Placed on the retired list in the rank of honorary lieut-general in August 1939, White was recalled to be C.G.S. on 15 March 1940, following the death in office of Lieut-General E. K. Squires [q.v.]. His sense of duty compelled him to accept the post—which brought promotion to general—even though at 63 years of age he believed himself to be out of date: 'I feel like Cincinnatus called from his farm. And may I say that I much prefer being Cincinnatus at the plough although I do appre-

ciate the honour paid to me'. One of White's first acts as C.G.S. was to recommend Lieut-General Sir Thomas Blamey for command of the new A.I.F. In April he urged that Blamey and the 7th Division should sail as soon as possible to join the 6th Division; in May and June he recommended that the A.I.F. should be brought into the fighting without delay, preferably assisting the beleaguered French. Meanwhile, he grappled with the problems of training and munitions supply.

His second term as C.G.S. was too short to affect the course of Australia's effort in World War II. White's greatest achievement had been in the previous conflict: one of the founders of the A.I.F., he had become its 'tactical and administrative commander in all but name'. A consummate chief of staff, his distinction in the role had denied him senior command and the public recognition that went with it. Nevertheless, Bean described him as the greatest man he ever knew, and his judgement was shared by many. On 13 August 1940 White flew from Melbourne in the company of three Federal ministers, J. V. Fairbairn, Sir Henry Gullett [qq.v.8,9] and G. A. Street [q.v.]; their aircraft crashed near Canberra aerodrome, killing all on board. After a service at St Paul's Cathedral, Melbourne, with state and military honours, White was buried in Buangor cemetery. His wife, two daughters and two sons survived him; his estate was sworn for probate at £20 699. A portrait of White by John Longstaff [q.v.10] is in the Australian War Memorial and he is commemorated by a bronze plaque in the Church of St John the Baptist, Canberra.

C. E. W. Bean, *The story of Anzac* (Syd, 1921, 1924) and *The A.I.F. in France, 1916-18* (Syd, 1929, 1933, 1937, 1942) and *Two men I knew* (Syd, 1957); G. Serle, *John Monash* (Melb, 1982); D. M. Horner (ed), *The commanders* (Syd, 1984); M. Cathcart, *Defending the national tuckshop* (Melb, 1988); *RHSQ Hist Papers*, 10, no 1, 1975-76; *Herald* (Melb), 6 June 1931, 16 Mar 1940; *SMH*, 13 Jan 1973; White papers (NL, AWM and Lady Derham, Melb).

JEFFREY GREY

WHITE, CYRIL TENISON (1890-1950), botanist, was born on 17 August 1890 in Brisbane, son of Henry White, mercantile broker, and his wife Louisa, née Bailey, both Queensland born. Cyril was educated at South Brisbane State School before his appointment in 1905 as pupil-assistant to the colonial botanist of Queensland, a position which had been held by F. M. Bailey [q.v.3], his maternal grandfather. Combining simplicity and accurate detail, White's early work included the 976 line-drawings in Bailey's book, *A comprehensive catalogue of Queensland plants* (1913), which was a new edition of his *Catalogue of the indigenous plants of Queensland* (1890). The 1913 publication also incorporated several colour plates of paintings by M. E. Rowan [q.v.11].

In 1917 White succeeded his uncle J. F. Bailey [q.v.7] as Queensland's government botanist, a position he was to hold until his death. He collected species throughout Queensland, from other Australian States, and from New Guinea (1918) and New Caledonia (1923). Aided by international exchanges, he built up an important reference collection in the Queensland Herbarium. His insistence on full provenance data on all mounted specimens was a major step in modernizing the herbarium. On 21 October 1921 at South Brisbane he married with Baptist forms Henrietta Duncan Clark, an enthusiastic field naturalist and hiker.

As government botanist White helped pastoralists by identifying noxious weeds and by evaluating native pastures and fodder plants; he also assisted the timber industry. His books, *An elementary textbook of Australian forest botany* (1922) and *Principles of botany for Queensland farmers* (1938), became texts at the University of Queensland where he lectured in forest botany. His numerous publications included a 42-part series on weeds (1915-26) and a series on 41 Queensland trees (1921-27), both in the *Queensland Agricultural Journal*; with W. D. Francis he wrote for the *Queensland Naturalist* (1924-34) a 12-part illustrated series on eucalypts of the Brisbane district. An authority on tropical botany, White was chiefly interested in the taxonomy of woody plants. He maintained a close association with the Arnold Arboretum at Harvard University, United States of America, publishing a monograph on North Queensland rainforest species in its *Contributions* (1933). In 1939-40 he was Australian liaison officer at the Royal Botanic Gardens, Kew, London. He instructed forestry companies of the Australian Army in New Guinea in 1944 and conducted forestry surveys in the British Solomon Islands in 1945.

White relished bushwalking and camping, and led excursions of the Queensland Naturalists' Club. He served on its council and on that of the Royal Society of Queensland, and was active in several other horticultural and geographical societies. An energetic and convivial man who had a fund of anecdotes, he encouraged younger scientists and was affectionately known as 'C.T.'

Awarded the Mueller [q.v.5] medal in 1946, he received an honorary M.Sc. in 1948 from the University of Queensland. Survived by his wife and two daughters, White died of heart disease at his home at Kangaroo Point, Brisbane, on 16 August 1950 and was cremated. In 1951 the Queensland Naturalists'

Club instituted the annual C. T. White memorial lecture.

Procs of Roy Soc Qld, 62, no 3, 1950, p 35, and for list of publications; *Qld Naturalist*, 14, no 3, Jan 1951, p 42.   R. SUMNER

WHITE, DANIEL (1834?-1923), carriage-builder, was born probably on 19 September 1834 at Roscrea, County Tipperary, Ireland, eldest son of Edward White, mechanic, and his wife Margaret, née Guilfoyle. While Daniel was still an apprentice in his father's blacksmith shop, Edward's death left him responsible at 17 for his mother and her seven children. The family migrated to Victoria in 1861 and Daniel easily found employment in Melbourne workshops. On 2 June 1868 at St Mary's Catholic Church, Geelong, he married his countrywoman Sarah Delaney, a milliner. Possessed of £180 by March 1869, White began his own carriage-building business 'in a small way' in Swanston Street, Melbourne.

In the following decade White's carriages, in which 'lightness, sound workmanship and artistic ornament were happily blended', were showered with medals and prizes at exhibitions in Melbourne, Sydney and London. The business quickly became one of the best known of its kind in Melbourne. White's versatile employees (some of whom were with him for decades) produced a range of vehicles including buggies, waggonettes, landaus and Victorias. A celebrated four-in-hand drag was made to order for the 2nd marquess of Normanby [q.v.5] and an exact copy in crimson and gold, trimmed with maroon velvet and yellow silk lace, was built for the King of Siam in 1882. In the early 1880s White moved his plant and showrooms to a site in Grant Street, off St Kilda Road. With its modern, steam-powered machinery, and about one hundred employees, it was considered one of the most complete carriage-making workshops in Australia; when White converted to a limited liability company (with a capital of £60 000) in March 1888, the shares were quickly oversubscribed. Refusing to use other than the best imported materials, he opposed protection, telling one official inquiry: 'I would like to see everything free as the air that blows on the mountain top'.

For three years Daniel White & Co. Ltd was able to pay a remarkable dividend of 10 per cent, but the depression drew White in 1892 to attend to the branch he had opened in Western Australia some five years earlier. On his return in 1896, he found his Melbourne company facing daunting claims. Perhaps it was his lovable disposition and Irish eyes twinkling in a smooth and placid face rather than his blacksmith's robustness that persuaded timber merchant James Moore to build him a new shop in Sturt Street, South Melbourne. After 1904 White entered the automobile trade, building bodies for imported chassis, and holding the agency for Simms Welbeck and Duryea Power Carriages. His original company in Grant Street went into voluntary liquidation in 1908.

A life member of the Coach and Waggon Builder's Association, White was an office-bearer in the Melbourne Chamber of Commerce. In 1877 he had moved the motion that created a local chamber of manufactures, of which he was president (1883-84) and honorary treasurer for thirty-eight years. He represented the chamber on the Working Men's College council: at the smoke-night to honour his retirement from its presidency in September 1923, his 'vigour, shrewdness and humour, and kindliness incomparable' were recognized affectionately. He died on the 24th of that month in St Vincent's Hospital, Fitzroy, and was buried in Melbourne general cemetery. Two sons survived him; his estate was sworn for probate at £5304.

A. Sutherland, *Victoria and its metropolis*, 2 (Melb, 1888); *V&P* (LA Vic), 1894, 2 (37), p 563, 1895-96, 3 (71), p 219; *A'sian Trade Review*, 5 June 1882, p 296; *A'sian Coachbuilder and Saddler*, 15 Nov 1894, p 115; *VHM*, 43, May 1972, p 802; *Melb Bulletin*, 6 Oct 1882; *Argus*, 26 Sept 1923.

MARGARET STEVEN

WHITE, ELLEN GOULD (1827-1915), Seventh-day Adventist prophet and author, was born on 26 November 1827 near Gorham, Maine, United States of America. She and her twin sister Elizabeth were the youngest of eight children of Robert Harmon, hatmaker, and his wife Eunice, née Gould. An accident at the age of 9 ended Ellen's formal education. In 1843 the Harmons were deprived of fellowship in the Methodist Church because of their sympathies with the Millerite movement and its adventist views. Next year Ellen began experiencing what she claimed were visions. On 30 August 1846 at Portland, Maine, she married Pastor James Springer White (d. 1881), a minister of the Christian Connection and an Adventist adherent. Ellen played a key role in forming the Seventh-day Adventist Church in the 1860s and in developing its evangelistic outreach, working for the movement in the U.S.A. and in Europe in 1885-88.

Invited to visit Australia by the Church's foreign mission board, she arrived in Sydney on 8 December 1891 with one of her four sons and a staff of four women. By this time Mrs White was generally regarded by Seventh-day Adventists as possessing the prophetic gift and was firmly established as one of the Church's most influential members. Only 5 ft. 2 ins. (157.5 cm) tall, she had strong features, compelling eyes and dark hair, severely parted in the middle. Her son WILLIAM CLARENCE (1854-1937), a Seventh-day Adventist minister, acted as her editorial assistant and publishing manager. He travelled extensively throughout the eastern states of Australia and in New Zealand, speaking at Church meetings. William played a major role in establishing health-food manufacture in Australia. In 1894 he was appointed head of the Australasian Union Conference which he had helped to develop, but three years later was released to assist with his mother's literary work.

Moving to Melbourne, Ellen was based there until August 1894, in Sydney until December 1895, and at Cooranbong, New South Wales, until her return to America in 1900. Despite severe attacks of rheumatism, she travelled throughout Tasmania, Victoria, South Australia, New South Wales, Queensland and New Zealand, attending Church meetings and giving public lectures to audiences sometimes numbering thousands. Her topics ranged from health reform and temperance to biblical interpretation and prophecy. Adventist Church leaders in Australia and abroad often sought her counsel.

A prolific writer, she sent hundreds of letters and regular contributions to Adventist Church papers in the U.S.A. and Australia. While in Australia White completed *Thoughts from the mount of blessing* (Battle Creek, U.S.A., 1896), *The desire of ages* (Mountain View, U.S.A., 1898), *Christ's object lessons* (Battle Creek, U.S.A., 1900), a devotional work and the sixth of a nine-volume series, *Testimonies for the church*, in which she outlined her theory of education. She regarded Avondale College, Cooranbong, as a model which exemplified her ideas on the need for educating the whole person—mentally, socially, physically and spiritually. Fascinated by the conflict between good and evil, and its reflection in history, White was inspired to write a series of books that are referred to as 'The Conflict of the Ages' series. More than ninety of her books are now in print and some 60 000 pages of her unpublished typescript are held at the research centre named after her at Avondale College.

Through her emphasis on the combination of religion, health and education, White played a formative role in the Church's identity, although her authority as a prophet within the Church was to become the subject of controversy in the 1970s. Her influence had led directly to the organization of Adventist day schools in Australia, and to the establishment of Avondale College and the Sydney Sanitarium (later the Sydney Adventist Hospital) at Wahroonga. She had also guided the development of the Church's administrative structure in Australia and encouraged the manufacture of health foods by the Adventist-owned Sanitarium Health Food Co.

Back in the U.S.A., she worked in the southern States and influenced the establishment of her Church's centre in Washington, D.C.; in 1909 she helped to found the College of Medical Evangelists at Loma Linda, California. Survived by two sons, Ellen White died on 16 July 1915 at St Helena, California, and was buried beside her husband in Oak Hill cemetery, Battle Creek, Michigan.

Seventh-day Adventist Encyclopedia, 10 (Washington DC, US, 1976); A. L. White, *Ellen G. White*, 4 (Washington DC, US, 1983); A. J. Ferch (ed), *Symposium on Adventist history in the South Pacific 1885-1918* (Syd, 1986); M. F. Krause, The Seventh-day Adventist church in Australia 1885-1900 (M.A. thesis, Univ Syd, 1968); A. N. Patrick, Ellen Gould White and the Australian women, 1891-1900 (M.Litt. thesis, Univ New Eng, 1984); E. G. White letters, 1847-1914 and manuscripts, 1845-1914 and W. C. White letters, 1891-1907 (Ellen G. White SDA Research Centre, Avondale College, Cooranbong, NSW).

GARY KRAUSE

WHITE, GILBERT (1859-1933), poet, author and bishop, was born on 9 June 1859 at Rondebosch, Cape Colony, South Africa, son of Francis Gilbert White, clergyman, and his wife Lucy, née Gilderdale; Gilbert was named after his great-grand-uncle, the naturalist. The family returned to England in 1861 and Gilbert was educated at Fettes College, Edinburgh, and Oriel College, Oxford (B.A., 1881; M.A., 1885; honorary D.D., 1908). Made deacon in 1883, he was priested in 1884 by the bishop of Truro. A lung condition necessitated emigration and he arrived at Townsville, North Queensland, in September 1885. White became successively rector of Charters Towers (1886), Herberton (1888) and Ravenswood (1891), and archdeacon of Townsville (1892). On 24 August 1900, in Sydney, he was consecrated first bishop of Carpentaria and was enthroned in November on Thursday Island.

Though an indifferent sailor, in order to visit his 'amorphous lump' of a diocese White bought and often navigated a ketch crewed by South Sea islanders. His apostolic 'orgy of travelling' included a journey in 1901 from Port Darwin to Alice Springs, Oodnadatta and Adelaide; *en route* he held services at cattle- and telegraph-stations and made geological, botanical and anthropological observations. In June 1905 he personally founded an Aboriginal mission on the Mitchell River and in 1907 explored the Roper River for another mission site. Next year he negotiated the resettlement on Moa Island of Melanesians deported from Queensland.

From July 1915 to September 1925 White was first bishop of Willochra, another sparsely settled diocese, in South Australia. He spent ten years travelling, and founded and edited *The Willochran*.

An 'austere Tractarian' despising popularity and ecclesiastical politics, he attended every general synod from 1891 where his forthrightness enlightened debates on social issues. In 1916 he helped to revive the Australian Board of Missions. Seeing World War I as a crusade for 'the liberties of mankind', White supported conscription and the League of Nations, and opposed a rigid White Australia policy as impeding northern development. In 1920 he attended conferences at Lambeth, England, and Geneva, Switzerland, and in 1925 was Australian representative at the Stockholm ecumenical conference.

'Tall, gangly, with spindly legs and straggling beard', ill at ease in society, he wrote fluently and read Greek and Latin, French, German, Italian and Spanish. His *Melchior and other verses* (Gateshead, 1893), including poems composed on the lonely ride from Irvinebank to Herberton, *Night and other verses* (Townsville, 1897) and *The world's tragedy and other poems* (Thursday Island, 1910) were privately printed; 'Australia: a poem' (1913) and 'Australia: 1917', both critical of society and politics, first appeared anonymously in the *Sydney Morning Herald*. Two collected volumes, *Poems* (London, 1919) and *The later poems of Gilbert White* (Morpeth, 1930), reveal a religious mysticism, a love of nature and a habit of preaching, within the confines of traditional poetic techniques. In 1922 and 1926 volumes of his sermons were published in London. His best-known works were travelogues, *Across Australia* (Brisbane, n.d.; London, 1909), *Round about the Torres Straits* (London, 1917; 1925) and *Thirty years in tropical Australia* (London, 1918; 1925).

In 1926 White retired to Epping, Sydney, and joined the boards of the *Church Standard* and the Australian Board of Missions whose *Review* he edited until November 1932. He died at his home on 1 April 1933 and was buried in Northern Suburbs cemetery. He never married; from 1886 successive maiden sisters had kept his house.

J. W. C. Wand, *White of Carpentaria* (Lond, nd); J. O. Feetham and W. V. Rymer (eds), *North Queensland jubilee book 1878-1928* (Townsville, 1929); *Aust Bd of Missions Review*, 1 Nov 1932, 1 May 1933; *J of Religious History*, 2, no 3, 1963; *SMH*, 3 Apr 1933; *The Times*, 3, 6 Apr 1933; *Church Standard*, 7 Apr 1933.   RUTH TEALE

WHITE, HAROLD FLETCHER (1883-1971), grazier and soldier, was born on 13

June 1883 at Saumarez, near Armidale, New South Wales, son of Francis John White, grazier, and his wife Margaret, née Fletcher, both native-born. Francis John (1855-1935) was a son of Francis White, and a nephew of James White [q.v.6] and of Frederick Robert White (1835-1903) of Booloominbah.

In 1894 Harold belonged to the first group of pupils at the New England Proprietary School (later The Armidale School); he proceeded to the University of Sydney where he studied arts and engineering for two years, and worked with Pitt, Son & Badgery [qq.v.5,3] Ltd. In 1906 he returned to manage some of his family's New England properties at Guyra and lived on his selection at Ward's Mistake. On 19 October 1911 at St Peter's Anglican Cathedral, Armidale, he married Evelyn Augusta Bigg Curtis; they made their home on Bald Blair station, near Guyra.

Known by his friends as 'Bill', in 1906 he had joined the 6th Light Horse, Australian Military Forces, and in April 1914 was promoted captain in the 5th Light Horse. In March 1916 he was appointed to the Australian Imperial Force as a captain in the 33rd Battalion; he was promoted major on 1 May and embarked three days later as officer commanding 'D' Company. The 33rd Battalion reached France in November and went into the line at Armentières. White was wounded on 8 February 1917 and was out of the unit until 11 April. Within days of learning of the death of his infant son whom he had never seen, White was engaged in action at Messines, Belgium, on 6-10 June and was awarded the Distinguished Service Order. The citation spoke of 'his utter disregard of personal danger, his indomitable will and his tireless energy' during his ninety-six hours in the front line.

Having attended the officers' school at Aldershot, England, from January to March 1918, White was promoted lieut-colonel in April; he commanded the 36th Battalion until June and then the 35th for the rest of the war. He led the 35th in action south of the Somme in August at Mont St Quentin and in September in operations against the Hindenburg line. Between 1917 and 1919 he was thrice mentioned in dispatches, received the French Croix de Guerre and was appointed C.M.G. White's reputation with his men was that of a hard but fair man. He was intense, serious and lacked a sense of humour. After embarking in April 1919 to return to Australia, he received further promotions in the A.M.F. in 1920 and 1921, and in 1926 was placed on the reserve of officers as a lieut-colonel.

White returned to Bald Blair and continued the pasture and stock improvements which he had commenced before the war; he also concentrated on improving his family's Aberdeen Angus stock and from 1924 began to exhibit

and win prizes at the Royal Easter Show, Sydney. In 1926 34 000 acres (13 759 ha) of the F. J. White Bald Blair estate was sold to promote closer settlement and White concentrated on improving his property of 5200 acres (2104 ha). By the 1950s he had changed a swampy and useless place into a prosperous farm.

Throughout the 1920s and 1930s White had been prominent in local and regional affairs. He was a councillor for the Guyra shire in 1911-29, vice-president of the Northern New State Movement in 1922 and a supporter of the Country Party. Like many ex-officers, he showed alarm at post-war political trends and took part in the Old Guard movement. He had no time for the New Guard. In September 1932 he was nominated to the Legislative Council: he did not like politicians, did not speak in the House and retired in April 1934 when the council was reconstituted.

White backed the regional economic and educational innovations of the 1930s and 1940s: he was a director of the New England and North-West Producers Co. Ltd and was active in the movement to obtain wool-selling facilities at Newcastle; he was also a director of Armidale Newspapers Ltd. He sat on the council of The Armidale School and supported the campaign for a university college at Armidale; a member of the Advisory Council of New England University College in 1938-53, he was a council-member of the university in 1954. Survived by his wife, two sons and two daughters, he died on 20 February 1971 at Armidale and was buried at Guyra with Anglican rites.

C. E. W. Bean, *The A.I.F. in France*, 1916-18 (Syd, 1929, 1933, 1937, 1942); *Armidale Express*, 18 Oct 1961; *Northern Daily Leader*, 23 Feb 1971; *SMH*, 25 Feb 1971; AWM records; information from Dr A. Moore, Campbelltown, and Mr R. H. F. White, Bald Blair, NSW.   BRUCE MITCHELL

WHITE, HENRY ELI (1876-1952), theatre architect, was born on 21 August 1876 at Dunedin, New Zealand, son of English parents Joseph Eli White, bricklayer, and his wife Susanna, née Scholfield. On leaving school, Henry joined Joseph's contracting business and learned bricklaying, painting, plumbing and carpentry while studying engineering and architecture. Finding it difficult to work with his father, he established his own business as a builder in 1896. 'Big Henry' was over six feet (182.9 cm) tall and weighed more than 16 stone (101.6 kg). He married Margaret Hallinan at Dunedin on 24 December 1900; they were to have four children.

Although his first major project was a tunnel on the Waipori River hydro-electric scheme, White gravitated towards theatre design: he was interested in using steel frames and reinforced concrete, and in the problems of ventilation, acoustics and visibility posed by auditorium design. By 1905 he had established himself at Christchurch. With the contract to build His Majesty's Theatre, Wellington, for (Sir) Benjamin Fuller [q.v.8] in 1912, White moved his thriving practice to that city where he also built the Midland Hotel.

By 1915 White was building theatres in Australia for Hugh McIntosh [q.v.10] and was well placed to take advantage of the boom in theatre investment in the 1920s. He adapted from the American architect John Eberson the 'atmospheric' style, one which was supposed to evoke an exotic garden or courtyard and used Spanish, Moorish, Venetian and Indian motifs. White's theatres in Sydney (where he made his headquarters) included the Capitol, the St James (for the Fullers) and the Majestic (Elizabethan) at Newtown. His only significant industrial project in Sydney was the Bunnerong power station, begun in 1925. He designed over 130 theatres, among them the Tivoli, Brisbane, and the St James Theatre, Wellington, New Zealand.

Sydney's baroque State Theatre (opened in June 1929) is White's best-known work. The building, which includes shops and an office block in Market Street, cost Union Theatres Ltd £1 million in an attempt to entice middle-class film-goers. The auditorium was divided into three levels of comfort and expense. Much loved by audiences for its excessive Art Deco ornamentation, its interior made lavish use of marble, gold and ivory decoration, and featured paintings, sculpture and exotic objects (such as the 'Fujiyama cameo', removed during World War II). The cinema's lavatories were named the 'Empire Builder's', 'Pompadour' 'Futurist' and 'Pioneer' rooms.

The Depression marked the end of White's architectural career. He won a competition to design a college at Auckland, but plans were shelved; he closed his office and lost money through farming in New Zealand. By 1937 he was back in Sydney. His plans for a block of flats at Point Piper were disallowed by Woollahra Municipal Council. Although his cement manufacturing project near Bathurst fell through, dolomite was discovered on the site and during World War II his company supplied it for windows and light bulbs made in Australia. White spent much time sailing and big-game fishing.

Survived by his wife and two sons, he died on 3 March 1952 at Kings Cross, Sydney, and was cremated with Anglican rites. He had reputedly earned over £1 million in architectural fees, but was not an astute businessman; his estate was sworn for probate at £1147.

R. Thorne, *Cinemas of Australia via USA* (Syd, 1981); J. Tulloch, *Australian cinema* (Syd, 1982); *Theatre* (Syd), Aug 1914, p 20; *Parade*, Mar 1960, p 30; *SMH*, 10 June 1925, 2 May 1928, 23 Dec 1930, 1 Oct, 5 Nov 1937, 23 Feb 1938, 7 Sept 1955; *Daily Mirror* (Syd), 7 Sept 1955; correspondence to the author from Mr G. Thornton, Wellington, NZ.

JULIAN THOMAS

WHITE, HENRY LUKE (1860-1927), pastoralist and philanthropist, was born on 9 May 1860 at Anambah, near Maitland, New South Wales, third son of Francis White [q.v.6 James White], pastoralist, and his wife Mary Hannah, née Cobb, both native-born. From Calder House, Redfern, Sydney, Henry went in 1875 to The Goulburn School, Garroorigang, where he learned his lessons, and how to play cricket and to blow birds' eggs. Qualifying as a surveyor in 1884, 'H.L.' (as he was known in the family) next year became manager of Belltrees, near Scone.

He and his brothers bought and divided the family estates in 1889. The eldest Francis John went to Saumarez, New England; the second JAMES COBB (1855-1927) stayed on at the family headquarters, Edinglassie, near Muswellbrook; from the estate, Henry and his three younger brothers (William, Arthur and Victor) purchased Belltrees where Henry remained as managing partner.

In dynastic unions, James had married Emmeline Eliza (d. 1926), daughter of Edward Stanley Ebsworth of Bronte House, Waverley, on 13 April 1882 at St John's Anglican Church, Darlinghurst, Sydney; at St Mary's Anglican Church, Waverley, Henry married her sister Louisa Maude on 14 April 1887 and Arthur married another sister Millicent on 19 January 1893. Maude and Millicent at Belltrees, and Emmeline at Edinglassie, gave a close-knit stability to domestic life.

Influenced by his uncles' standards, Henry endeavoured to improve his stock and was receptive to new ideas. He took charge of the merino stud (based on Havilah blood) and of wool production. It took five months each year to shear 96 000 merinos and 10 000 crossbreds; Wolseley [q.v.6] shearing machines were installed in 1902. In addition, he bred horses and red poll Shorthorn, Durham and Aberdeen Angus cattle. Belltrees also had two pony stallions and a small thoroughbred stud: Charge won the 1896 Australian Jockey Club Derby and Parapet the 1900 Doncaster. The brothers acquired additional land by selection, lease and private purchase; by 1901 Belltrees spread over more than 145 000 acres (58 680 ha).

In 1905 White instructed his architect J. W. Pender to design a large, good, plain, brick

468

homestead at Belltrees. Completed in 1907, the house had fifty-two rooms and fifty-seven squares of verandah. The station's population of some 250 was provided with a store and post office, community hall, chapel, cricket pitch, and with the means for lavish celebrations on Queen Victoria's birthday; from 1912 White photographed station life. He released trout fingerlings in the creeks, established a plantation of a thousand eucalypts, and peppered the government botanist J. H. Maiden [q.v.10] and departmental heads with dozens of inquiries.

A member of the provisional council in 1906, White was foundation president of Woolooma (Upper Hunter) Shire Council until 1927. Threatened by a Federal land tax in 1911 and 'tired of the worry of management', he offered to sell 140 000 acres (56 657 ha) for closer settlement; because the area was mountainous and too far from a railhead, the government refused the proposal. By 1915 the sale of 40 000 acres (16 188 ha) on the open market brought some relief. The family firm subscribed generously to war loans and presented two aeroplanes to Britain.

Reckoning that a man 'must have a hobby in the bush' as 'a relief from the sheep, cattle and dog talk', White resumed his boyhood interest in stamp-collecting. He began to specialize, from 1897 buying and amalgamating the collections of other philatelists. In 1917 he presented the H. L. White Collection of the stamps of New South Wales to the Mitchell [q.v.5] Library and later donated the stamps of Western Australia, Queensland and Tasmania. He became a fellow of the Royal Philatelic Society, London. Encouraged by Albert Spencer [q.v.], White also collected Australian books. The Belltrees library housed more than 2000 rare items, with specialized sub-collections such as philately, ornithology and F. M. Harpur's cricket books, as well as some works which, to his nephew Patrick White, had a 'faintly pornographic' tone. He recalled Henry—the only White uncle he liked—as 'a short man of fiery complexion, his eyes as cold as blue glass until they blazed with enthusiasm or anger'.

In the hobbies he pursued, as in all else, 'H.L.' sought perfection. His wealth allowed him to buy the finest books and stamps, just as he bought the best breeding-stock, but their acquisition presented no real challenge. In 1907, however, he decided to add to his small collection of birds' eggs and began by purchasing S. W. Jackson's [q.v.9] collection. White employed him, among others, to search for rare birds and rarer eggs, and appointed him curator of the Belltrees collection. Between 1908 and 1924 White published short articles in the *Emu*. A member of the Royal Australasian and British Ornithologists' unions and of the (Royal) Zoological Society of New South Wales, he was also a corresponding fellow of the American Ornithologists' Union. In 1917 he gave some 8500 Australian birdskins to the National Museum of Victoria, with a complete register and index. Eggs were White's most loved possession: over 4200 clutches of eggs of Australian birds, meticulously documented, remained at Belltrees until his death when they were transferred to the museum.

After World War I White spent more time entertaining family and friends, and following polo and cricket (he sat in the same seat in the members' stand at the Sydney Cricket Ground to watch every Test played there for twenty-five years). He made substantial gifts to the Church of England, the Scone hospitals, the Liberal and Reform Association, and other causes. He quietly helped local people and the unfortunate, and gave sweets to children who opened gates for him. Survived by his wife, son and two daughters, White died of cancer on 30 May 1927 at Belltrees and was buried in Muswellbrook cemetery. His estate was sworn for probate at £185 360.

Born on 29 November 1855 at Belltrees, James Cobb White was educated at Newcastle Grammar School and in Sydney, before becoming manager of Edinglassie. After 1889 he turned the station into one of the showplaces of New South Wales and acquired properties in Queensland and the Northern Territory. A strong believer in the value of stud stock, in the early 1920s he was a founder and president of the Aberdeen-Angus Herd Book Society of Australia. He periodically imported bulls from England and built up the country's largest pedigreed Angus herd. Among his neighbours he was renowned as a water-diviner.

Nominated to the Legislative Council in July 1908, though 'never very active' in the work of parliament, James was 'attentive to his public duties': he was president of the Denman Shire Council, the Upper Hunter Pastoral and Agricultural Association and the local hospital, and a member of the Licensing Court and of the local Pastures Protection Board. He died on 18 January 1927 at Muswellbrook and was buried in the local cemetery. His three sons and two daughters inherited his estate which was sworn for probate at £236 691.

E. J. Brady, *Australia unlimited* (Melb, 1918); J. White, *The White family of Belltrees* (Syd, 1981) and *Land settlement and selection in the Belltrees region* (Newcastle, 1988); P. White, *Flaws in the glass* (Lond, 1981); *PD* (LA NSW), 19 Jan 1927, p 471; *Pastoral Review*, 16 May 1925, 16 Feb, 16 June 1927; *Aust Museum Mag*, 3, no 3, July-Sept 1927, p 102; *Aust Zoologist*, 5, 1927-29, p 120; *Syd Mail*, 16 Nov, 30 Nov 1901, 24 June 1927; *Scone Advocate*, 21 Jan, 31 May, 3 June 1927; *SMH*, 31 May 1927, 7

May 1960; H. L. White letter-books, 1885-1927, station diaries, photograph albums and family papers (Belltrees, Scone, NSW).   NANCY GRAY

WHITE, JAMES (1861-1918), sculptor, was born 2 December 1861 at Liverpool, Lancashire, England, son of Robert White, journeyman shipwright, and his wife Janet, née Dunn. Apprenticed to a plasterer, James studied modelling at South Kensington. He made anatomical models for London hospitals and, while an assistant to the Scottish sculptor John Rhind, executed a bas-relief of John Hunter, surgeon, for the University of Edinburgh.

Having arrived in Sydney about 1884, White worked for Achille Simonetti [q.v.6] in 1888-90 on Governor Phillip's [q.v.2] monument, Botanic Gardens. In 1892 White won the competition for an allegorical group on the pediment of the Metropolitan Board of Water Supply and Sewerage building; he was paid £252 for the completed stone figures. In the 1890s he also produced some of the stone life-size sculptures for the Department of Public Instruction building's Bridge Street facade. At Hamilton, Victoria, on 28 June 1893 he married with Presbyterian forms Jamesina Dunn, a hotelkeeper's daughter.

White had begun showing with the Art Society of New South Wales in 1891 and with the Society of Artists, Sydney, in 1896. His exhibits included his modified neo-classical plaster bust of Professor (Sir) Thomas Anderson Stuart [q.v.] (1894), a realist statuette of a bushranger, and busts of R. B. Smith [q.v.6] (1896) and 'Conamdatta—Northern Queensland Aboriginal' (1897). White advertised his willingness to sell any of his works cast in plaster or bronze, or carved in marble. In 1897 at his small foundry at Petersham he used the lost wax process to cast a statue of William Bede Dalley [q.v.4] (Hyde Park). He campaigned vigorously for commissions for public statuary to be given to Australian sculptors. Failing to obtain the commission for a statue of Sir Thomas Elder [q.v.4] in Adelaide in 1899 (after opposition from Eccleston Du Faur [q.v.4]), White cast at his Annandale foundry a bronze bust of Sir Edwin Smith [q.v.6].

Technically versatile and ingenious, in the early 1900s White became the busiest sculptor in Australia. In 1902, with the group 'In Defence of the Flag', he was the first sculptor to be awarded the Wynne prize. The enlarged cast-bronze version was sent to Perth as a war memorial next year. His numerous commissions included a carved marble statue (1904) of John McDouall Stuart [q.v.6] for Adelaide and his monumental cast-bronze statue of Sir John Robertson [q.v.6] in the Botanic Gardens, Sydney. White used the electrolytic copper deposit method to produce large statues of Queen Victoria and Prince Albert for Royal Prince Alfred Hospital. He worked repoussé copper for the figure of 'Commerce' (1902-03) for the Royal Exchange building, Sydney. A founding member of the National Guild of Applied Arts and Crafts, he had moved to Melbourne by 1906.

White's reputation as an artist was shattered by the costly (£6218) marble Queen Victoria monument (1907), Melbourne. He had intended the Queen to be in bronze, but accepted the committee's demands for allegorical figures and marble. While publicly acceptable, the work was anathema to such arbiters of taste as Bernard Hall [q.v.9]. Although White received a few more commissions, by 1909 his large-scale operations ceased. His last work of any size was the marble funerary monument (1912) in Waverley cemetery, Sydney, for Harry Rickards [q.v.11].

Survived by his wife, son and two daughters, White died of cancer on 14 July 1918 while visiting Brisbane and was buried in Toowong cemetery with Baptist forms. His estate was sworn for probate at £70. There are hints that White's career owed much to his ability to compromise, to his persuasive tongue, to his bombast and to his great reserves of physical energy.

K. Scarlett, *Australian sculptors* (Melb, 1980); *A'sian Builder and Contractor's News*, 12 Nov 1892, p 238; *AAA*, 2 Mar 1903; *A'sian Art Review*, 1 Apr 1899, p 20, 1 July 1899, pp 18, 21, 1 Sept 1899, p 12; *Lone Hand*, Aug 1907, p 380; *Observer* (Adel), 21 Nov 1903; *SMH*, 11 May 1904; *Advertiser* (Adel), 6 June 1904; *Age*, 25 May 1907; *Argus*, 27 Sept, 29 Nov 1910, 20 July 1918, and camera supp, 1 Dec 1928; Annual exhibition cats, Art Soc of NSW, 1892, 1894, *and* Soc of Artists, 1896, 1897.   NOEL S. HUTCHISON

WHITE, JESSIE McHARDY (1870-1957), army principal matron, was born on 24 July 1870 at Yarra Flats, near Healesville, Victoria, fifth surviving child of John Williamson, farmer, and his wife Mary, née McHardy, both Scottish born. On 21 December 1893 at Scots Church, Melbourne, Jessie married with Presbyterian forms Thomas James White, a book-keeper of Fitzroy; they were to remain childless. Following her husband's death in 1896, Mrs White took up nursing. She completed her general training at the Alfred Hospital (December 1896 to February 1900) and her midwifery training at the Women's Hospital (February 1900 to March 1901). By 1906 she was running a private hospital in Melbourne and had joined the Australian Army Nursing Service Reserve.

In October 1914 Sister White embarked

with the first contingent of the Australian Imperial Force, arriving in Egypt on 4 December. Attached to a British military hospital, she also served in a hospital ship and was briefly matron of the 1st Australian General Hospital. A reorganization of the Australian Army Medical Corps led to her appointment early in 1916 as principal matron of the A.I.F. in England. Following the arrival in London of Matron-in-Chief Evelyn Conyers [q.v.8], White embarked for Australia in August, having been awarded the Royal Red Cross (1st Class) for her services.

In response to a request from London in April 1917, it was decided to send Australian nurses to staff four British general hospitals at Salonica (Thessaloniki). Matron White resumed active service on 5 June as principal matron in charge of a contingent of 364 nurses, organized into units comprising one matron and ninety nurses for each hospital. She was also matron of No.1 Unit which arrived at Salonica on 30 July to take over a tent hospital with over 800 beds, located during summer at nearby Hortiach. The second and third units were soon in position, but all members of the fourth were not present until June 1918. While ministering to sick and wounded soldiers, she and her staff contended with poor living conditions, extremes of temperature, threats to their safety from marauders, and with flies, lice, malaria, dysentery and typhus.

Efficient and self-reliant, but isolated from administrative support, White was given additional powers to promote and repatriate nurses; meanwhile she steadfastly preserved her contingent's separate identity. Her severe treatment of one subordinate matron did not negate Matron White's essential humanity. Moved by the burial of a British nurse, she wrote: 'I was glad to have been there and felt that we had left the little one—she was only twenty-three—in safe keeping'. The principal matron spent her leisure hours enjoying the beauty of her natural surroundings.

Jessie White was appointed M.B.E., mentioned in dispatches, and awarded the Greek Medal for Military Merit and the Serbian Order of St Sava in recognition of her work at Salonica. She returned to Australia on 28 June 1919 and her A.I.F. appointment terminated on 7 August. Continuing her nursing career until late in life, she was active in the affairs of returned nurses and served for twenty-five years as president of the Salonica Sisters' Group. She died on 26 October 1957 at East Hawthorn, Melbourne, and was cremated. Her estate was sworn for probate at £31 773.

A. G. Butler (ed), *Official history of the Australian Army Medical Services in the war of 1914-1918*, 1-3 (Melb, 1938, Canb, 1940, 1943); *Mufti*,

Dec 1957; *Herald* (Melb), 10 Oct 1916, 29 July 1919, 28 Oct 1957; records (AWM).

PERDITTA M. McCARTHY

WHITE, JOHN (1853-1922), company director and politician, was born on 9 November 1853 at Dumbarton, Scotland, son of Alexander White and his wife Ellen, née Anderson. Marrying Maggie Frame with Church of Scotland forms on 10 April 1877 at Glasgow, John migrated with his family to Queensland in 1883. At Bundaberg he formed a partnership with George John Young, a stationer, and became sole proprietor in 1897. Having bought shares in the Bundaberg Foundry Co. in 1888, he was prominent in the syndicate which floated it as a limited company in 1898 and was its chairman in 1900-22. Soon rivalling Walkers Ltd at Maryborough in heavy engineering for the sugar and mining industries, the company was reconstructed under White's direction after a disastrous fire in 1919 revealed that it was severely underinsured.

In 1906 White became chairman of the newly formed Bundaberg Co-operative Insurance Association; he established Carricks Ltd, a substantial sawmilling and furniture company; and he invested in Waterloo Ltd in 1908 which relocated the Waterloo Sugar Mill closer to its growers. His achievements led him to declare that he was a director of 'Queensland Unlimited'.

Thrice chairman of the Bundaberg Chamber of Commerce, and a founder and long-serving chairman of the Bundaberg Harbour Board, White campaigned enthusiastically for irrigation and held the Legislative Assembly seat of Musgrave in 1903-04 and 1907-15, as a Ministerialist and a Liberal respectively. He became chairman of the Farmers' Parliamentary Union in 1911 and first chairman in 1913 of the (Queensland) Country Liberal Party. In December 1912 he was appointed secretary for agriculture and stock in the Denham [q.v.8] ministry. Losing his seat in the 1915 election, White moved to Brisbane.

A businessman rather than a professional politician, he had voted for a reduction in parliamentary salaries, and opposed the land tax and the repurchase of landed estates. He wanted governments to use railway construction to enhance land revenue and favoured state enterprise to help farmers and miners remain independent. He offered to manage Gin Gin Central Sugar Mill until it was viable and criticized Premier (Sir) Arthur Morgan and Walter Maxwell [qq.v.10] for foreclosing on it in 1904. Thriving on interjections and bringing humour to many debates, in 1912 White was proposed by Edward Theodore [q.v.] as Speaker, but declined. As minister, in

1914 White piloted through parliament the co-operative agricultural production bill to provide funds for building factories in a range of primary production areas. He promoted business principles in his department, directed State research farms to aim at self-sufficiency and gave autonomy to Gatton Agricultural College. His support for the American Meat Trust in 1914 was repudiated by the home secretary John Appel [q.v.7].

John White died of a cerebral haemorrhage on 13 June 1922 at the Royal Hotel Bundaberg and was buried in the local cemetery with Presbyterian forms. He was survived by three daughters, his son having died in 1915. White's estate was sworn for probate at £43 921.

Newspaper Cartoonists' Assn of Qld, *Queenslanders as we see 'em* (Brisb, 1915); U. Ellis, *A history of the Australian Country Party* (Melb, 1963); *PP* (Qld), 1911-12, 2, p 1048; *PD* (Qld), 1904, p 172, 1912, p 3; *Aust Sugar J*, 14, no 4, 7 July 1922, p 233; *Daily Standard*, 11 Dec 1912; *Brisbane Courier*, 13 June 1922; Bundaberg Foundry Co. *and* Bundaberg Co-operative Insurance Assn *and* Waterloo Ltd, records (QA).   JOHN D. KERR

WHITE, MYRTLE ROSE (1888-1961), author, was born on 30 August 1888 at Acacia Dam, near Broken Hill, New South Wales, third of ten children of native-born parents Mark Albert Kennewell, miner, and his wife Dinah Ann, née Adams. The birth was dramatic. Travelling with bullock teams and looking for land to settle, Dinah gave birth alone in a tent, during a dust storm in which her husband became lost while fetching a lidwife. The family moved to the Barossa Valley, South Australia, and Myrtle's schooling, 'picked up here and there', was completed at a small private school in Williamstown. She often visited her aunt who had a hotel near Packsaddle, north-west of the Darling River. Myrtle was a domestic servant when she married Cornelius White, a cab proprietor, in St Peter's Anglican Church, Broken Hill, on 19 October 1910.

From 1915 when their daughter Doris was 4, Cornelius managed Lake Elder station, near Lake Frome, South Australia. Life was lonely and anxious: the Whites were the only Europeans in the area; Myrtle's two sons were sickly and doctors unobtainable; they collected their mail fortnightly, but stores came twice yearly and fresh vegetables were rare. Yet the family remained cheerful. In 1922 they moved to the west Darling district where Con managed seven stations for Sir Sidney Kidman [q.v.9], including Morden and Wonnaminta, comprising over a million acres (404 690 ha).

When her three children were older and she had some leisure, White began writing. At Wonnaminta, despite endless interruptions, she worked meticulously on her drafts which she typed with one finger. The result was *No roads go by* (Sydney, 1932), an account of life at Lake Elder, rather in the tradition of Mrs Gunn's [q.v.9] *We of the Never-Never*. With humour and resilience, White described the remote station surrounded by sand 'insidiously creeping up the six-foot iron fence, which was our frail barrier against all that moving country'. Drought, flood and near death were presented in intense but restrained prose. Two sequels followed: *Beyond the western rivers* (Sydney, 1955) and *From that day to this* (Adelaide, 1961).

In 1937 Con was forced to retire and the Whites opened Cricklewood, a guest house at Aldgate in the Adelaide hills. Con died three years later. Their two sons enlisted in the Royal Australian Air Force. Alan survived World War II, but Garry was missing in action; his mother, a Methodist and spiritualist, always believed that he would return. Encouraged by Dame Mary Gilmore [q.v.9], Myrtle White also formed friendships with Jean Devanny, Miles Franklin [qq.v.8] and Gwen Meredith. When leases on the big stations were re-allocated, Wonnaminta fell to her daughter Doris and son-in-law Jim Chambers. Myrtle visited them and travelled with them overseas where she assisted several orphanages in India.

Although Myrtle White also wrote three novels, only *For those that love it* (Sydney, 1933) was published. While visiting her son Alan at Lalla Rookh, near Port Hedland, Western Australia, she died on 11 July 1961. Her ashes were interred in Con's grave at Centennial Park cemetery, Adelaide, and at Wonnaminta.

G. Dutton, *The Australian collection* (Syd, 1985); W. H. Wilde, *Courage a grace* (Melb, 1988); *SMH*, 14 Jan 1956; *Advertiser* (Adel), 13, 19 July 1961; White correspondence (Mortlock Lib); Miles Franklin correspondence (ML); Hazel de Berg tapes *and* White papers (NL).   ROBIN EADEN

WHITE, SAMUEL ALBERT (1870-1954), ornithologist and conservationist, was born on 20 December 1870 at Reedbeds (Fulham), Adelaide, son of Samuel White, ornithologist [q.v.6], and his wife Martha Elsea, née Taylor. Educated at several private schools, he claimed to have received his best schooling at Christian Brothers' College and retained allegiance to Catholicism. From the age of 16 Samuel made his first extensive birdwatching expeditions, along the Murray River and to Western Australia. He also became a noted racehorse owner. He inherited money and received income from land rents and agistment fees. During the South African War he had two tours of duty and was temporarily promoted captain, a title he used thereafter. In 1903 he made a big-game expedition in Africa and collected scientific specimens along the east coast. On 19 April 1906 in Adelaide he married Ethel Rosina Toms (d. 1926) in two ceremonies with Anglican and Catholic rites; they were to remain childless.

His most arduous and important work as a naturalist occurred when he collaborated with G. M. Mathews [q.v.10] on *The birds of Australia* (London, 1910-27). To this end, White mounted major collecting expeditions, often accompanied by his wife. He travelled with camels to Alice Springs and beyond (1913), with a government team to the Musgrave and Everard ranges (1914), and with the South Australian Museum expedition to Cooper Creek (1916); he also went to the Nullarbor Plains (1917-18), with Sir Edgeworth David and Professor Walter Howchin [qq.v.8,9] to the Finke River (1921), and in 1922 led the great adventure from Adelaide to Darwin and back, using three Dort motor cars supplied and serviced by Adelaide mechanics Cyril and Murray Aunger.

White's outstanding achievement lay in completing an ornithological survey of the whole of South Australia and much of the Northern Territory. He was the first European to see several species and regarded the Princess Alexandra parrot as the world's most beautiful bird. A keen conservationist, he was a central figure in the declaration of national parks in the State and was a noted spokesman on insects, birds and botany. He had cultivated the friendship of the Aborigines of Central Australia and defended them publicly.

A short, wiry man, with a handlebar moustache, White addressed public meetings, schools and government seminars, attracting large attendances and becoming known throughout Australia. He also contributed to the press, wrote booklets about his journeys, and saw his work published in scientific journals at home and abroad: a list appears in H. M. Whittell's [q.v.] *The literature of Australian birds* (Perth, 1954). White's most notable publications included *The Gawler Ranges* (1913), *Into the dead heart* (1914) and *The life of Samuel White* (1920).

President of the South Australian Ornithological Association (1904 and 1911) and of the Royal Australasian Ornithologists' Union (1914-16), White was a corresponding member of the British Ornithologists' and the American Ornithologists' unions. He chaired the Advisory Board of Agriculture and was State chief commissioner (1923-31) of the Boy Scouts' Association. In St Mary's Catholic Cathedral, Sydney, on 12 July 1927 he married 22-year-old Muriel Mary Fisher; they toured Asia and the Pacific. White died on 19 January 1954 at his home, Weetunga, Fulham, and was buried in Morphett Vale cemetery; his wife, son and daughter survived him.

G. M. Mathews (ed), *Austral avian record*, 3 (Lond, 1919); H. M. Whittell, *The literature of Australian birds* (Perth, 1954); R. Linn, *Nature's pilgrim* (Adel, 1989), and for bibliog; *SA Ornithologist*, 21, pts 2-3, 25 June 1954; *Syd Mail*, 22 Feb 1922; *Observer* (Adel), 23 Apr 1904, 1 May 1926, 9 July 1927; *Advertiser* (Adel), 20 Jan 1954.

R. W. LINN

WHITEHOUSE, JOSEPH HOWELL (1874-1954), organbuilder, was born on 26 May 1874 at West Derby, Lancashire, England, son of Benjamin Burton Whitehouse, organbuilder, and his wife Lucy, née Howell. Joseph learned his craft with the Norwich firm of Norman Bros (later known as Norman & Beard before amalgamating with Hill & Son). On 24 December 1896 he married Amelia Jones at St Mark's parish church, Birmingham. The couple migrated to Brisbane, arriving on 12 July 1897; there Joseph joined his elder brother Benjamin who had come in 1883 and begun installing organs the following year.

The brothers were at first associated with J. S. Marlor and were listed as importers of pianos, organs and musical instruments. Joseph also tuned pianos and harps, and repaired player-pianos. From 1903 the brothers traded as B. B. Whitehouse & Co., the name which appeared on the organs they built until 1921 when Whitehouse Bros was established exclusively as organbuilders.

Gaining a virtual monopoly within Queensland of organ building, as well as of organ maintenance, repair, tuning and rebuilding, the firm won contracts in that State for at least ninety instruments during Joseph's lifetime; it extended its business, constructing or rebuilding organs in every State except South Australia where J. E. Dodd [q.v.8] held the market. Such success testified to the solid and reliable workmanship in their instruments. The sensitive voicing of their sound might have been questioned: the company never made metal pipes, but installed ranks which were made and pre-voiced overseas. Nevertheless, it did manufacture all wooden pipes, chests and consoles: the first organ made by Whitehouse in 1899 functioned without major repair until its restoration in 1985. The presence of so many organs in Queensland with a design later considered inadequate was due less to requests from largely untrained players than to the forceful personality and stubborn convictions of Whitehouse himself.

To the public, clients and senior members of the organ fraternity, he was at all times a courteous English gentleman; with employees, he tended to dismiss as inferior any opinion other than his own. He never left Australia, nor did any member of his staff. If his attitude to organ design was parochial and insular, his tonal aesthetic both created and reflected contemporary tastes. His early instruments, in particular, sound robust, especially when sited in an auditorium of generous resonance. Survived by his wife, son and a daughter, Whitehouse died at his Toombul home on 28 February 1954 and was cremated. His estate was sworn for probate at £8950. His son Joseph and grandson Kevin continued the business until 1982.

G. Cox, *Gazeteer of pipe organs in Australia* (Melb, 1976); G. D. Rushworth, *Historic organs of New South Wales* (Syd, 1988); information from Mrs R. O. Reinhold and Mr H. L. Whitehouse, Brisb, and Mr K. M. Whitehouse, Palmwoods, Qld.

ROBERT K. BOUGHEN

WHITELEGGE, THOMAS (1850-1927), naturalist, was born on 7 August 1850 at Stockport, Cheshire, England, son of Moses Whitelegg, an illiterate bricklayer, and his wife Elizabeth, née Grant. Born into poverty, Thomas left school at the age of 8 and worked in factories around Cheshire. Apprenticed to a hatter, he broke his indentures. He lived as a fugitive for two years on a farm at Hurstbrook, Lancashire, where he developed an interest in natural history and obtained work as a journeyman with a hat manufacturer who was sympathetic to his plight.

When his life became less troubled, Whitelegge read and attended lectures in natural history. Interested in geology, he began a fossil collection which brought him into contact with the local societies of artisan naturalists. In 1874 he joined the Ashton-under-Lyne Linnean Botanical Society and began to study botany. He quickly gained a reputation for his knowledge of local natural history, particularly microscopic pond life. In his early twenties he founded the Ashton Biological Society, began publishing authoritative natural history articles in local newspapers and taught botany at the Albion Schools. On 26 July 1880 he married Ellen Steele in the United Methodist Free Church, Ashton-under-Lyne. His research into plant reproductive strategies led him into a correspondence with Charles Darwin [q.v.1].

After his mother died, Whitelegge migrated with his family in 1882; they reached Sydney in the *Euterpe* on 12 February 1883. Finding work as a plasterer and in a brewery, he soon met Rev. Julian Tenison-Woods [q.v.6], president of the Linnean Society of New South Wales. Proposed for membership by (Sir) William Macleay [q.v.5], Whitelegge attended the society's weekend gatherings at Macleay's Elizabeth Bay House. He also joined the Royal Society of New South Wales that year. Through this circle of naturalists and professional scientists, he met E. P. Ramsay [q.v.6], curator of the Australian Museum, where he was given a temporary position. Whitelegge investigated oyster pests of New South Wales for the museum's trustees in 1884 and in 1887 was appointed senior scientific assistant in charge of lower invertebrates. That year his wife died after childbirth, leaving five children, the youngest two hours old.

Whitelegge was a biologist in the broadest sense. As a botanist, he was an authority on mosses and produced a catalogue of the frondose mosses of Australia. As a zoologist, he wrote on many invertebrate phyla: Protozoa, Porifera, Cnidaria, Annelida, Crustacea and Echinodermata. Between 1897 and 1907 he published important papers on the invertebrates of Funafuti, on those of Port Jackson, and on the crustaceans and sponges collected by the *Thetis* expedition. His most important work was the 'List of the marine and freshwater Invertebrates of Port Jackson and neighborhood': the Royal Society of New South Wales published it in its *Journal and Proceedings* in 1889 and awarded him a special medal. His descriptions of the benthic environment of the inner port are still used as a base line for measuring environmental change.

A councillor (1890-96) of the local Linnean Society, Whitelegge was elected a fellow (1889) of the Royal Microscopical Society, London. He taught botany for many years at the Sydney Mechanics' School of Arts and at Sydney Technical College. Thin-faced, with a bony nose, dark hair and handlebar moustache, he was 'unassuming and modest of bearing'. In 1908 he resigned from the Australian Museum, but retained a small post at the National Herbarium, Botanic Gardens. He remained an active associate of the museum and the gardens, though he stopped publishing in 1908. Survived by two daughters and a son, Whitelegge died on 4 August 1927 in Royal Prince Alfred Hospital, Sydney, and was buried in Rookwood cemetery.

Aust Museum Mag, 3, no 4, 1927, p 133; Linnean Soc NSW, *Procs*, 53, 1928, p 3; *Records of the Aust Museum*, 17, no 6, 1929, p 264, and for publications; *SMH*, 9 Aug 1927; Hunt Inst biogs (Basser Lib, Canb); Whitelegge papers (ML).

JIM LOWRY
GWEN BAKER

WHITFELD, HUBERT EDWIN (1875-1939), university vice-chancellor, was born on 14 March 1875 in Sydney, seventh child of Edwin Whitfeld, schoolmaster, and his wife Eleanor, née Cooke, both English born. Educated at Sydney Grammar School and the University of Sydney (B.A., 1897), he graduated with first-class honours in classics and philosophy, and was university medallist in classics. After teaching for two years, he studied engineering (B.E., 1902) at the university. Whitfeld then went to Western Australia where he spent the next ten years as a metallurgist and mine-manager in the Murchison district. On 17 June 1912 he married Frances Matilda Zahel at St Paul's Retreat, Glen Osmond, Adelaide. When the University of Western Australia was established in 1913 he was appointed foundation professor of mining and engineering. In 1916-19 he worked for the British Ministry of Munitions, as an inspector of munitions in the United States of America and as a technical adviser in the Explosives Supply Department, London.

By the University of Western Australia's process of rotation, Whitfeld was vice-chancellor in 1913-15 and 1925-27. Retaining his philosophic interests, he deliberately sought to maintain a close correlation between scientific and humanitarian studies. His policy ensured a measure of unity and inter-faculty co-operation, but was not always appreciated by such colleagues as the chemist N. T. M. Wilsmore [q.v.], though it was strongly supported by other foundation professors like (Sir) Walter Murdoch [q.v.10]. In 1927 Whitfeld was appointed first permanent vice-chancellor and was to hold that office until his death. Under his direction, in the early 1930s the university moved to its attractive site by the Swan River at Crawley. Aided by the munificent bequests of Sir John Hackett [q.v.9] and in collaboration with the architect Rodney Alsop [q.v.7] and the gardeners Oliver Dowell and George Munns, Whitfeld contributed much to the layout and landscaping of the campus.

Academic administration was severely restricted by World War I and by the Depression. Whitfeld's expansion of the university's art collection and his establishment of residential facilities for both male and female students aroused some opposition. Such criticisms were more than offset by his imaginative leadership and personally persuasive influence: 'He charmed as Socrates charmed. His infectious gaiety of spirit and of mind dissolved any barrier of years'. A former president of the University of Sydney undergraduates' association, the vice-chancellor attracted the active support of young people, even if some of them were later to complain that Whitfeld did not always live up to the

expectations he had encouraged in them. In retrospect, his contemporaries subscribed to the view that his greatness lay in the fact that his mind was never closed to an idea, nor his door to a colleague.

Though not a 'conference man', he played his part—despite the disabilities imposed by distance—in the interstate co-operation of the handful of Australian universities. More significant for the university was the close relationship which developed between Whitfeld and the president of the Carnegie Corporation of New York, Dr F. Keppel. The frequent award of Carnegie travelling fellowships to the teaching staff enabled them to take advantage of the sabbatical leave which Whitfeld recommended to offset the isolation of Crawley. Another beneficiary was the university's adult education board and, particularly, its library: successive grants to the latter were consistent with Whitfeld's view of the young university's service to the community at large and in accord with emphasis he gave to the range and quality of undergraduate teaching rather than to costly and specialized research.

Despite his charm, Whitfeld was not prominent in social functions outside the university. He preferred to devote his leisure to Evoe, a small vineyard he cultivated at Upper Swan, the homestead of which had been designed for him by Alsop. Whitfeld was appointed C.B.E. in 1933. Survived by his wife, he died on 31 July 1939 in Perth and was cremated with Anglican rites. A memorial bust (1965) by John Dowie stands in the court which bears Whitfeld's name at the university.

F. Alexander, *Campus at Crawley* (Melb, 1963); *Aust Q*, 4, no 4, Dec 1940; *West Australian*, 1 Aug 1939, 12 Apr 1965; W. Somerville, A blacksmith looks at a university (BL and Reid Lib, Univ WA).

FRED ALEXANDER

WHITFORD, STANLEY R. (1878-1959), politician, was born on 5 June 1878 at Moonta, South Australia, youngest child of Richard Whitford, a miner from Devonshire, and his Cornish wife Emma, late Prior, née Matthews. Stanley attended local primary schools, then was employed for seven years by a blacksmith. In 1898 he attended night-classes at the Moonta School of Mines and learned mine surveying on Saturdays. He worked on the Western Australian goldfields in 1899-1908 and next at Wallaroo, near Moonta. Having been a navvy, in 1909 he joined the South Australian Railways as a porter. On 1 October 1910 in the Methodist Church, North Adelaide, he married Edith Thyra Dixon, a schoolteacher.

Stan, as he preferred to be called, kept his

Cornish accent. He became an organizer and secretary of the Australian Railways Union and, later, the Australian Workers' Union. His reading included the work of Henry George [q.v.4], Tom Paine and Karl Marx. After opposing conscription in World War I, as a Labor candidate he unsuccessfully contested the Federal seats of Barker (1917) and Boothby (1919); he was president of the State branch of the Australian Labor Party in 1919-20. Whitford was defeated for the House of Assembly seat of Victoria in 1918, but won North Adelaide in 1921. A Freemason, he was a member of the Adelaide City Council (1922-24), a delegate to the South Australian Football League and president (1923-24) of the Workers' Educational Association. Losing his parliamentary seat in 1927, he became a clerk on the wharfs before Sir Wallace Bruce [q.v.7], a businessman and a leading conservative, gave him a job in the Adelaide Cement Co., a house and gifts of money.

In 1929-41 Whitford was a Labor member for Central in the Legislative Council where he was briefly minister of immigration, repatriation and irrigation in 1930, minister of agriculture and commissioner of forest lands in 1930-33, and chief secretary from October 1930 to April 1933. He was almost surprised to find 'that zig-zagging through the State by bike, coach and train, I became Chief Secretary and Acting Treasurer'. Balding and bespectacled, he dressed the part: wing collars, polka-dot ties and a pipe. His most humane legislation was the Destitute Persons Relief Act (1931).

Modest and self-effacing, he owned prize-winning coursing dogs. Trotting enthusiasts applauded his bill to allow totalizators at meetings, though it was not passed. He also had support from the right-wing Citizens' League of South Australia. In 1931 Whitford was expelled from the A.W.U. and the A.L.P. for supporting the Premiers' Plan. Backed by the Liberal Federation, he and like-minded colleagues held office as the Parliamentary Labor Party under L. L. Hill and R. S. Richards [qq.v.9,11] until 18 April 1933. Thereafter Whitford was an Independent Labor member, as well as a commercial traveller.

A self-trained elocutionist, he entertained at lodge meetings and concerts. In 1939 he described workers as maggots and praised Hitler: 'can't we take our hats off to such an organiser? I do'. During World War II he lost his seat and his advertising agency for Scotch whisky; he then worked in a munitions factory until 1943. Crippled by arthritis, he spent his last eleven years bed-ridden in hospital where he wrote his unpublished autobiography. Survived by two sons, Whitford died on 13 December 1959 in Royal Adelaide Hospital and was buried in West Terrace cemetery.

Daily Herald (Adel), *Labor's thirty years record in South Australia* (Adel, 1923); Universal Publicity Co, *The official civic record of South Australia* (Adel, 1936); *Labour Hist*, no 31, Nov 1976; *Advertiser* (Adel), 14 Dec 1959; S. Whitford, ms autobiography (Mortlock Lib).   A. R. G. GRIFFITHS

WHITHAM, JOHN LAWRENCE (1881-1952), soldier, was born on 7 October 1881 at Jamalpur, Bengal, India, son of Lawrence Yates Whitham, a major in the Indian Army who brought his wife Ellen and family to Hobart in 1886 and joined the local police force. John worked as a clerk and in his spare time served in the volunteers from 1898.

In 1902 he went to the South African War as quartermaster sergeant of the Tasmanian company of the 3rd Battalion, Australian Commonwealth Horse. At the war's end he transferred to the South African Constabulary with whom he remained until 1904. He then served with the Tasmanian Senior Cadets and was commissioned lieutenant in 1908. In 1910 he embarked upon his full-time military career: commissioned lieutenant in the Administrative and Instructional Staff in July, he was posted to South Australia; in 1912 he was selected for duty on the staff of the inspector general; he was a captain when World War I began.

With the formation of the Australian Imperial Force, Whitham was given command of a company of the 12th Battalion. He embarked on 20 October 1914 and, after training in Egypt, landed with the battalion at Anzac on 25 April 1915. He led his company throughout the first day until he was wounded and evacuated. He rejoined the battalion in May, as a major and its second-in-command. In August he briefly commanded the battalion, but next month was invalided ill and did not return to Anzac.

In Egypt in February 1916 he was appointed deputy assistant adjutant and quartermaster general for the 2nd Australian Division. After crossing to France and following the Pozières operations, he was transferred to A.I.F. Headquarters staff as a lieut-colonel. In May 1917 he was given command of the 52nd Battalion, a unit formed partly from his old 12th Battalion. Several weeks later he led his battalion throughout the bloody fighting beyond Ypres, Belgium. Whitham's battalion was billeted near Locre, France, when the German 1918 offensive commenced. He assisted in having the brigade rushed south and on 3 April placed his men in a defensive position near Dernancourt. During the month the 52nd Battalion played a vital role in two of the most critical actions in which the Australians were engaged on the Western Front. He commanded the battalion when the Germans attacked at Dernancourt on 5 April and, twenty days later, led it in the counter-attack which recaptured Villers-Bretonneux. The repulse at these two points blunted the enemy's offensive and saved the city of Amiens.

In May the depleted 52nd Battalion was disbanded and Whitham was transferred to command the 49th. Next month he was sent as an instructor to the Senior Officers' School at Aldershot, England, and rejoined his command too late to lead it in battle before the war ended. He remained in France and England throughout 1919 as a liaison officer with British Army Headquarters. In 1920 he attended staff college at Camberley. On 12 April he married Olive Young, née Le Pays, a widow, at St John's parish church, Littlewick, Berkshire. They came to Australia in 1921. Between the wars Whitham was director of organization and personal services, and base commandant in Tasmania (1933-35), Queensland (1935-37) and Victoria (1937-39). Too old for active service in World War II, he commanded the Volunteer Defence Corps in Victoria. In 1944 he transferred to part-time duty and retired in 1946 as an honorary lieutgeneral.

A thoroughly professional soldier, both as a staff and a regimental officer, Whitham had been appointed C.M.G. in January 1916; following his work at Villers-Bretonneux in 1918 he was awarded the Distinguished Service Order. He was mentioned in dispatches three times. 'Tall and distinguished in appearance; courteous to the point of gentleness; dignified but lacking any trace of pomposity; stern . . . but . . . courteous', he was also described by C. E. W. Bean [q.v.7] as 'one of the nearest among Australian battalion commanders to Chaucer's "parfit gentil knight"'. General Whitham retired to Wahroonga, Sydney. Survived by his wife, he died of cancer on 12 May 1952 in Concord Repatriation Hospital and was cremated.

L. M. Newton, *The story of the Twelfth* (Hob, 1925); C. E. W. Bean, *The A.I.F. in France*, 1918 (Syd, 1937); *Reveille* (Syd), Feb 1939.

PETER BURNESS

WHITINGTON, FREDERICK TAYLOR (1853-1938), Anglican priest, was born on 13 July 1853 in Adelaide, son of William Smallpiece Whitington, merchant, and his wife Mary Emily, née Martin. With his parents opposing his wish to be a clergyman, he worked in his father's firm and later became an articled clerk. At 21 he was employed as a court reporter by the Adelaide *Register* and eventually rose to be sub-editor. At St Paul's Church on 1 October 1878 he married Katie

Lisette (d. 1929), daughter of (Sir) Richard Butler [q.v.7].

Made deacon in 1877 and ordained priest in Adelaide in 1879, Whitington was mission chaplain at Port Pirie in 1877-80. When his wife's health deteriorated they moved to Adelaide in March 1880 to the parish of St Mary on Sturt. Bishops' supply chaplain and bursar at St Barnabas's Theological College in 1882-83, he served as organizing chaplain of the Bishops' Home Mission Society in 1883-89. Having enrolled at the University of Adelaide, he graduated LL.B. in 1886. He was an honorary canon of St Peter's Cathedral from 1887 and was incumbent of the rural parish of Kapunda in 1887-91.

Attracted to Brisbane by the challenge of missionary work, Whitington was appointed missionary chaplain attached to St John's Pro-Cathedral and first general secretary of the Australian Board of Missions (1892). While visiting New Guinea, he contracted recurring malaria and doctors advised him to move to a colder climate. In 1893 he was made assistant incumbent and canon of St David's Cathedral, Hobart. In 1895 he became rector of St John's Church, Newtown, and archdeacon of Hobart, a position he retained until his retirement in 1923. He was also vicar general from 1895 and administered the diocese during the absences of Bishops Montgomery and Mercer [qq.v.10]. Whitington became senior chaplain to the Armed Forces in Tasmania in World War I and held the rank of colonel. He served for eighteen years on the council of the University of Tasmania. His scholarly work included biographies of Bishop Short [q.v.6], Bishop Broughton [q.v.1] and A. R. Russell, dean of Adelaide.

The archdeacon was a popular cleric. An advanced churchman with a deep love of Anglo-Catholic liturgy, he was scholarly, genial and eloquent; his delightful wit and humour endeared him to people of all classes, within the Church and beyond it. Editor of the Tasmanian diocesan monthly newspaper, *Church News*, Whitington was also a long-standing member of general synod, and widely known and respected throughout the Australian Anglican Church.

Predeceased by his son and survived by his daughter Mary Agnes who had always lived with her father, Whitington died in Hobart on 29 November 1938 and was buried in St John's cemetery, Newtown, after a service in All Saints Church, South Hobart.

W. R. Barrett, *History of the Church of England in Tasmania* (Hob, 1942); D. Hilliard, *Godliness and good order* (Adel, 1986); *Church News* (Hob), July 1893, May 1895, May 1923, Dec 1938, Sept 1939; *All Saints Parish Paper*, Aug 1929; *Year Book of the C of E in Tas*, 1930; *Examiner* (Launc) and *Mercury*, 30 Nov, 2 Dec 1938.

LOUIS V. DANIELS

WHITTELL, HUBERT MASSEY (1883-1954), ornithologist, soldier and farmer, was born on 24 March 1883 at Stratford, Essex, England, son of Alfred Leighton Whittell, engineer, and his wife Amire Campbell, née Henderson. Educated in India, Germany and England, in 1899 Hubert began studying medicine at the University of Edinburgh where he joined the University Company of the Royal Scots Regiment. His hobby was birdwatching. He abandoned medicine, chose an army career and was commissioned in 1904. Next year he sailed for Bombay. Appointed in 1907 to the 56th Punjabi Rifles, Indian Army, he played hockey for All India, rode well and went big-game hunting. Whittell studied Urdu, Pushtu and Persian, collected early north-west Indian coins and published papers on the history of the area. On home leave in 1909, he was engaged to Sydney Margaret O'Hara Hodgkins, a clergyman's daughter, whom he married on 26 October 1911 in St Thomas's Cathedral, Bombay.

During World War I Lieutenant Whittell served in France, Belgium and Egypt; he was twice mentioned in dispatches, promoted major in 1919 and appointed O.B.E. next year. Migrating with his family to Western Australia in 1926, he developed an orchard and dairy farm at Bridgetown. He joined the Royal Australasian Ornithologists' Union in 1929 and was convenor of its checklist committee and president (1941-43); he was also vice-president of the Gould [q.v.1] League of Bird Lovers of Western Australia.

Whittell began an egg and skin collection. In the field he was always willing to undertake camp chores. A skilled and patient taxidermist, he often prepared skins in the field and provided specimens for G. M. Mathews [q.v.10] who named *Pachyptila salvini whittelli* in his honour. Determined to preserve a stable nomenclature, Whittell ranged throughout the State and made many trips in search of three rare birds of the southwest: he succeeded in collecting the Western whip-bird.

A restless, spare man, with blue-grey eyes and a clipped English accent, 'the Major' retained his military outlook and relished command. Hard but fair, he was impatient with trivialities. When acquaintances became friends, his good nature made him a congenial companion. He published in natural history journals, including *Emu*. In collaboration with D. L. Serventy, he produced *A handbook of the birds of Western Australia* (1948, 1951)—a standard work of reference—and *A systematic list of the birds of Western Australia* (1948). For twenty years, with references overflowing into every room of his home, Whittell worked on his monumental *The literature of Australian birds* (1954).

A member of the St John Ambulance Association, the Returned Sailors' and Soldiers' Imperial League of Australia, and the Western Australian Naturalists' Club, Whittell was a keen conservationist who served on the State Fauna Protection Advisory Committee from 1946. He was also active in agricultural societies, at local shows and as a chronicler of Bridgetown history. Survived by his wife, daughter and two sons, he died on 7 February 1954 at Nannup District Hospital and was buried in the Anglican section of Bridgetown cemetery. Whittel [*sic*] Island, north-west of Perth, is named after him.

Emu, 4, 1937, p 280, 54, 1954, p 61; Dept of Fisheries and Fauna (WA), *Mthly Service Bulletin*, 3, no 3, 1954, p 69; *West Australian*, 8 Feb 1954; information from Mrs J. Brockman, Busselton, WA.
TESS KLOOT

WHITTINGHAM, ARTHUR HERBERT (1869-1927), grazier and politician, was born on 20 September 1869 at Dunedin, New Zealand, son of George Whittingham, merchant, and his wife Selina, née Davidson. The family moved to Victoria about 1871 where George became a principal of Whittingham Bros, a large pastoral firm with holdings in Queensland, New South Wales and South Australia. Educated at Kew High School and Geelong Church of England Grammar School, in 1888 Arthur entered Trinity Hall, Cambridge, to study arts. He then enrolled in medicine at the University of London, training for more than three years at St Mary's Hospital, but his studies were interrupted by the deaths of his father and eldest brother. Whittingham returned to Australia to look after the family interests.

Having gained experience on Canally station at Balranald, New South Wales, Whittingham was sent in 1901 to manage Alice Downs, a property near Blackall in central Queensland which his father and brother John had taken up in 1878. With his brother Harold, Arthur bought the run in 1903; six years later he bought out Harold's interest. The Alice Downs merinos were sedulously and scientifically increased to some 80 000; Whittingham and his manager avoided overstocking in order to produce a high quality fleece. Periodic land resumptions—to meet the demands of closer settlement—reduced the size of the property, but Whittingham added to his holdings by buying Anthony, Anthony North, Lancevale and Westhill stations in central Queensland.

Keenly interested in the pastoral industry, Whittingham was elected president of the United Graziers' Association in 1913 and held the post for twelve years. His term of office coincided with the membership's shift from large property owners to predominantly smallholders and farmer-graziers: he used 'firm and tactful handling' to facilitate the transition. An active participant in local government, Whittingham had unsuccessfully contested the Legislative Assembly seat of Barcoo in 1907. Appointed to the Legislative Council in July 1912, he bitterly opposed Labor amendments to the land Acts and the move to abolish the council which eventually terminated his parliamentary career in 1922.

On 4 June 1913 at St John's Anglican Cathedral, Brisbane, Whittingham had married Cecile Viva Condamine Taylor. The childless couple lived at Mayfield in the Brisbane suburb of Hamilton and made their home a focus of social activity in the 1920s. Cecile was described as 'Queensland's best dressed woman'. A horse-racing enthusiast, Whittingham owned Lordacre which won the Queensland Turf Club Derby Stakes (1916) and Clairvaux which won the Brisbane Thousand (1924). He was a prominent Freemason who belonged to several clubs and associations which promoted sporting, cultural and humane interests. He was also a director of the Blackall Wool Scouring, the Union Trustee and the Australian Mutual Life and Finance companies, and for some years was consular agent for Italy.

Survived by his wife, Whittingham died of heart disease on 20 June 1927 at Mater Misericordiae Private Hospital, Brisbane. He left an estate sworn for probate in Queensland at £234 608. His widow contested the will, but his bequest to Geelong Grammar of some £100 000 remained. The school received a further $221 875 in 1972 after the death of his widow.

M. Fox, *The history of Queensland, its people and industries*, 1 (Brisb, 1919); *Pastoral Review*, 15 Sept 1910, 16 July 1927; Geelong C of E Grammar School, *Corian*, Dec 1975; *Courier Mail*, 5 June 1913, 21 June 1927, 21, 22 June 1934; *Queenslander*, 23 June 1927; *Truth* (Brisb), 12 Feb 1933, 24 June 1934.
                              DIANNE BYRNE
                         BRIAN F. STEVENSON

WHITTLE, JOHN WOODS (1882-1946), soldier, was born on 3 August 1882 at Huon Island, near Gordon, Tasmania, son of Henry Whittle, labourer, and his wife Catherine, née Sullivan. John enlisted as a private in Tasmania's 4th (2nd Imperial Bushmen) Contingent which reached South Africa on 24 April 1901, saw action in the Cape Colony and returned to Tasmania in June 1902. Soon after, he enlisted in the Royal Navy and served for five years as a stoker before joining the Permanent Military Forces. On 23 July 1909 at the archbishop's house, Hobart, he married with Catholic rites Emily Margaret Roland; they were to have six children.

Transferring to the Australian Imperial Force on 6 August 1915, Whittle was given the rank of acting corporal and in October sailed as a reinforcement for the 26th Battalion. By April 1916 he was in France with the 12th Battalion. Wounded in action on 18 June, he was promoted sergeant in October. Early in 1917 he was involved in the fighting during the German withdrawal to the Hindenburg line. At dawn on 27 February his battalion attacked the outpost villages of Le Barque and Ligny-Thilloy. On the left flank with Captain J. E. Newland's [q.v.11] 'A' Company, Whittle bombed an enemy machine-gun post, forced the Germans to flee and won the Distinguished Conduct Medal.

The 12th Battalion carried out a diversionary attack on the village of Boursies on 9 April 1917; Whittle led his platoon in the initial assault. The Germans resisted fiercely and counter-attacked at 10 p.m. Whittle checked and steadied the forward posts until Newland came forward to organize the defence and regain lost ground. After a four-day spell out of the line, the battalion advanced close to Lagnicourt. At 4 a.m. on 15 April the enemy mounted a surprise counter-attack. 'A' Company was forced from its trenches to a sunken road where Newland and his men made a stand. Whittle saw the Germans bringing up a machine-gun. He 'rushed alone across the fire-swept ground', attacked the enemy with bombs before the weapon could be brought into action, killed the crew and captured the gun. For his heroism at Boursies and Lagnicourt he was awarded the Victoria Cross.

Wounded again during the German offensive of March 1918, and once more in late July, Whittle returned to Australia with other V.C. winners in October 1918 to take part in a planned recruiting drive. Following the Armistice, he was discharged on 15 December and lived in Sydney. He made a desperate plea in 1932: 'I have been trying to struggle on for some time, but the children are badly in need of boots and clothing for the winter, and I cannot get any work'. Within a month he was employed by the Western Assurance Co. On 7 February 1934 he saved a small boy from drowning in an ornamental pool in University Park; though Whittle departed without giving his name, the deed became widely known.

Survived by his wife, three daughters and a son, he died of a cerebral haemorrhage on 2 March 1946 at Glebe and was buried in Rookwood cemetery. Whittle and Newland were the only Australian V.C. winners of World War I to have been permanent servicemen before the war. One of Whittle's sons, Ivan Ernest, had joined the A.I.F. and was killed in September 1943 when a bomber crashed into the 2/33rd Battalion marshalling area near Port Moresby, Papua New Guinea.

Aust Defence Dept, *Official records of the Australian military contingents to the war in South Africa*, P. L. Murray ed (Melb, 1911); L. M. Newton, *The story of the twelfth* (Hob, 1925); C. E. W. Bean, *The A.I.F. in France*, 1917 (Syd, 1933); L. Wigmore (ed), *They dared mightily* (Canb, 1963); *Reveille* (Syd), 1 Apr 1946, 1 Jan 1969; *SMH*, 28 Aug 1918; *Argus*, 12 Oct 1918.

STEPHEN ALLEN

WHITTON, IVO HARRINGTON (1893-1967), golfer, was born on 9 December 1893 at Moonee Ponds, Melbourne, son of Percy Whitton, accountant, and his wife Eliza Lord, née Harrington, both Tasmanian born. Educated at Melbourne Church of England Grammar School where he captained the preparatory school cricket team, he is said to have taken up golf seriously at the age of 14 when passed over for the first eleven. He practised in the paddocks surrounding his home in Munro Street, Armadale, and in 1908 joined the Caulfield Golf Club in which his father was an active member. When it moved to Oakleigh that year, becoming the Metropolitan Golf Club, Ivo won the last medal on the old course and the first on the new. He was club champion three times before the war; on 11 November 1911 he set two course records (71 in the morning and 69 in the afternoon), taking the monthly medal despite a handicap of plus four. He won his first Australian Open championship in 1912 and is the only Australian golfer to have won it five times (1912, 1913, 1926, 1929 and 1931), and that as an amateur.

On leaving school in 1911, Whitton had joined the woolbroking firm of A. R. Lempriere (the Australian amateur golf champion in 1913) who allowed him time for golf in off-seasons. Late that year Whitton went to England and in 1914 competed in the British amateur championship. When World War I broke out he returned home; on being rejected by the Australian Imperial Force, he went back to England and served in the Royal Garrison Artillery. He gained his commission and served at Salonica. Contracting malaria, he was invalided home.

After the war Whitton worked as a wool-appraiser for the Commonwealth government in 1919-20 before returning to wool-buying. In 1926 he joined the sports-goods firm of A. G. Spalding & Bros, becoming a director in 1931 and later general manager. In addition to his 'opens', he won numerous amateur championships including the Australian (1922, 1923), the Victorian (1919-20, 1922-24) and the New South Wales (1929). In 1920 he won the Helms award for the outstanding athlete of the year. He published an instructional book, *Golf*, in 1929.

Having joined the Royal Melbourne Golf Club in 1913, Whitton was club champion nine times in 1920-36, its captain in 1947-50, and was made an honorary life member in 1953. He represented the club on the Victorian Golf Association and the Australian Golf Union. From 1948 to 1953 he was a member of the rules of golf committee of the Royal and Ancient Golf Club of St Andrews, Scotland, and in 1951 was the Australian delegate to a conference in Britain to unify the rules. In 1960 the V.G.A. established the Ivo Whitton Trophy to be awarded annually to the best amateur.

A modest but tenacious player, Whitton also enjoyed the 'club' and social side of golf; his other interests included tennis, fishing and photography. He had married Evelyn Jessie Jennings, herself a good golfer, at All Souls Anglican Church, Sandringham, on 9 June 1920. Survived by his wife, son and two daughters, Whitton died at Sandringham on 2 July 1967 and was buried in Cheltenham cemetery. The R.M.G.C. established the Ivo Whitton Cup in his memory.

Age, 4 July 1967; *Table Talk*, 24 Feb 1927; *Daily Mirror*, 4 Feb 1985; information from Mr W. I. Whitton, South Yarra, Melb, and Royal Melb Golf Club.

A. G. L. SHAW

WHYTE, WILLIAM FARMER (1877-1958), journalist and author, was born on 13 December 1877 at Bombala, New South Wales, and named William James Rodney, fourth of eight children of Henry Peter Whyte, an Irish-born storekeeper, and his English wife Constance Sophia Rodney, née Ricketts. After attending Bombala and Orange Superior Public schools, William joined the *Bombala Times* and, from the age of 19, worked in Sydney as a journalist on the *Daily Telegraph*.

Then he travelled—to Auckland, New Zealand, as a sub-editor on the *New Zealand Herald* (1907-10), and to Samoa and Tonga. He contributed to the *Cyclopedia of Samoa* (Sydney, 1907) and collaborated with H. J. Moors on *With Stevenson in Samoa* (London, 1910). On 30 June 1909 he married his first cousin Hilda Gorman Cusack Whyte in St Paul's Anglican Church, Auckland. Whyte toured the United States of America in 1910 as manager of a Maori troupe which performed in New York, Chicago and San Francisco; he interviewed President Taft, Andrew Carnegie and Thomas Edison for articles commissioned by the *Sydney Morning Herald* and other Australian newspapers.

In September Whyte joined the *Sydney Morning Herald* and became that paper's most versatile descriptive writer, 'touching nothing'—as his editor Thomas Heney [q.v.9] observed in Dr Johnson's words—'which he did not adorn'. Due to the Commonwealth Electoral Act's requirement that editorials on Federal elections and referenda should be signed, W. Farmer Whyte's name became well known for his vigorous wartime editorials in an era of predominantly anonymous journalism.

Tall and prematurely greying, Whyte had sensitive features dominated by an aquiline nose. His engaging personality, professional ability and varied interests won him a wide range of friends. In 1918 he chaired the Australian Journalists' Association's inquiry into the general subject of education for journalists. He was an active member of the (Royal) Australian Historical Society and the Sydney branch of the Dickens [q.v.4] Fellowship, honorary secretary of the Shakespeare Society of New South Wales (1911-16) and joint honorary secretary of the State's Shakespeare Tercentenary Memorial Fund in 1916. An omnivorous reader and a writer of verse, he particularly admired Shakespeare, the French classics and the romantic school established by Victor Hugo.

Although he was twice appointed to newspaper editorships, Whyte's tenure at the Brisbane *Daily Mail* (1918-21) and the Sydney *Daily Telegraph* (1921-23) was relatively brief. Preferring self-employment, or perhaps simply uncomfortable in editorial chairs, he joined the Federal parliamentary press gallery in Canberra in 1927. There, for the rest of his life, he conducted the Federal News Service, supplying political articles and his *Canberra Times* column ('Over the Speaker's Chair') to country newspapers throughout Australia. In 1937-39 he edited a monthly magazine, *Australian National Review*, about which he corresponded with Miles Franklin [q.v.8]. He enjoyed chess, was involved in local social and community life, and remained a member of the Johnsonian Club, Brisbane, and the Bread and Cheese Club, Melbourne.

In 1952 Whyte edited the *Australian parliamentary handbook* and in 1955 published an extensive, though not definitive, biography of the prime minister whom he had known for much of his own career, W. M. Hughes [q.v.9]. Farmer Whyte worked to within a few days of his death in Canberra on 16 November 1958. Survived by his wife, two sons and two daughters, he was buried in Canberra cemetery.

Lone Hand, 1 July 1918; *Sydney Mail,* 28 Aug 1912, 1 June 1922; *Canb Times* and *SMH,* 17 Nov 1958; John Fairfax Ltd (Syd) archives; M. Franklin *and* M. Gilmore papers (ML); information from I. Hamilton and R. Chalmers, Canb.

GAVIN SOUTER

WICKENS, CHARLES HENRY (1872-1939), statistician and actuary, was born on 16 October 1872 at Kangaroo Flat, Sandhurst (Bendigo), Victoria, fourth child of English-born Charles Wickens, farmer, and his Irish wife Margaret, née Quinn. Educated at the local state school, Charles worked in the family orchard and through private study qualified as an associate of the Institute of Actuaries by 1896. He moved to Western Australia in search of employment and joined the State Public Service as a temporary assistant clerk in April 1897. Promoted to the Statistical Bureau in 1899, he was appointed assistant compiler and departmental actuary in July 1901, responsible for conducting the State census of that year. In 1905 Wickens constructed the first life tables for Western Australia based on census data. Next year he represented the State at the first conference of Commonwealth and State statisticians, and was awarded the Messenger prize by the Institute of Actuaries, London, for an essay on the collection and analysis of mortality and population data.

His growing reputation as a vital statistician led in November 1906 to his recruitment as a compiler by the Commonwealth statistician, (Sir) George Knibbs [q.v.9], to the newly created Commonwealth Bureau of Census and Statistics. In 1913 he was appointed supervisor of census; under Knibbs, he conducted the census in 1911, 1915 and 1921. During this period Wickens constructed Australian life tables for the decennia 1881-90, 1891-1900 and 1901-10 which were published in the census reports of 1911 and 1921. These pioneering works, which enabled comparisons between the States, found that life expectancy had increased since 1890 and that female rates of mortality were generally lower than those of males. For the 1921 census Wickens introduced mechanical tabulating equipment which incorporated the 'Hollerith' punched-card system for sorting and counting data. In August 1922 Wickens succeeded Knibbs as Commonwealth statistician; two years later his title was expanded to Commonwealth statistician and actuary.

Initiating an era of greater co-operation between State and Commonwealth bureaus, Wickens convened annual conferences to ensure uniformity in the collection and tabulation of statistical data. Successfully negotiating the transfer to the Commonwealth of the Tasmanian bureau in 1924, Wickens brought a rare infusion of university-educated officers—including L. F. Giblin [q.v.8]—into the public service. In the later 1920s the bureau's activities grew significantly to meet demands for the analysis of data concerning wealth measurement, domestic finance and international trade. Wickens' role as government adviser began with the formulation of

481

the Commonwealth superannuation scheme in 1923. In 1927 he was Commonwealth representative in London at the 8th International Actuarial Congress and at an Imperial conference which aimed to set uniform standards for trade, agricultural and other statistics. He also investigated social insurance schemes in preparation for the development of national insurance proposals by (Sir) Earle Page [q.v.11].

Called to advise the royal commission on national insurance (1923-27) and the parliamentary accounts committee, he represented the government before the Commonwealth Court of Conciliation and Arbitration on the 1930 basic wage case. Wickens, Giblin and the bureau played a major part in providing economic advice to the Bruce-Page and Scullin [qq.v.7,11] governments, assembling information on Australia's financial and trade position during the 1930 crisis and assisting Sir Otto Niemeyer's investigations. In collaboration with Giblin, J. B. Brigden, E. C. Dyason [qq.v.7,8] and (Sir) Douglas Copland, Wickens produced *The Australian tariff: an economic inquiry* (Melbourne, 1929). He also wrote extensively for professional journals. A fellow (1918) of the Royal Statistical Society and of the Institute of Actuaries (1920), he was a foundation member and chairman (1928) of the Economic Society of Australia and New Zealand, and president (1924) of the Actuarial Society of Australasia. Finding recreation in walking, golf and bowls, he was also sometime president of the Prahran Rifle Club.

In February 1931 he suffered a stroke and was invalided from the service in April 1932. Wickens died of a cerebral haemorrhage on 30 July 1939 at Balwyn, Melbourne, and was buried in Brighton cemetery. He was survived by his wife Gertrude Emma, née Howard, whom he had married at St James's Anglican Church, Melbourne, on 3 May 1909, and by their son. Widely recognized as one of the ablest government statisticians of his generation, Wickens was respected as an economist, an indefatigable worker and a congenial colleague.

C. Forster and C. Hazlehurst, 'Australian statisticians and the development of official statistics', *Year book Australia* (Canb, 1988); *Aust J of Statistics*, 16, no 2, 1974, p 71.

CAMERON HAZLEHURST
MARGOT KERLEY

WIECK, GEORGE FREDERICK GARDELLS (1881-1973), soldier, was born on 18 August 1881 in Brisbane, son of George Johann Heinrich Wieck, printer, and his wife Caroline Maria Friederika Gerhardina, née Riebstein; both parents had arrived from Schleswig-Holstein in 1864. One of nine children, George grew up on the family farm and was educated at Toowoomba. On 23 September 1898 he enlisted in the Queensland Permanent Artillery. He served in the South African War, sailing with the machine-gun section of the 1st Queensland Mounted Infantry in November 1899 and taking part in the relief of Kimberley and engagements at Driefontein, Sanna's Post, Pretoria, Belfast and Komati Poort. At Sanna's Post on 31 March 1900 he was a member of a nine-man rearguard when a company of the Q.M.I. was outflanked by Boers; their horses caught in quicksand, seven men were captured. Wieck was recovered from the enemy on 4 June. One of three Australians selected for Lord Roberts's Colonial Mounted Bodyguard in July, he rejoined his unit in November.

Reaching Brisbane in January 1901, Wieck joined the Queensland contingent sent to Melbourne for the opening of Federal parliament. Posted to Thursday Island for two years, he returned to Brisbane in March 1904 as a sergeant instructor with the 9th Australian Infantry Regiment; in May 1907 he was classified as staff company sergeant major. He married Nellie Gannon with Anglican rites on 20 March 1907 at Christ Church, Milton, Brisbane. In November 1908 he went to England for courses of instruction; returning in January 1910, he was sent to the army school at Albury, New South Wales, to train non-commissioned officers. He next became assistant instructor at the School of Musketry. In March 1912 he was commissioned lieutenant and posted to Adelaide.

On the outbreak of World War I Wieck was appointed captain in the Australian Imperial Force in November 1914 and adjutant of the 9th Light Horse, with which unit he served in Egypt, Gallipoli and Sinai. In March 1916 he was promoted major and became brigade major of the 15th Infantry Brigade under Brigadier General H. E. Elliott [q.v.8], serving in the Canal Zone and later on the Western Front. He showed considerable moral courage in standing up to Elliott who—during the German withdrawal to the Hindenburg line in March 1917—ordered a risky daylight advance in secret contravention of a direct order by the divisional commander, Major General (Sir) Talbot Hobbs [q.v.9]. As the two battalions were moving into position, Wieck told Elliott that unless he advised Hobbs of his intention, Wieck would do so himself. Elliott gave way, and a message from divisional headquarters immediately cancelled the attack.

Transferred in July 1917 as general staff officer, grade 2, to the 3rd Division under Major General (Sir) John Monash [q.v.10], Wieck took part in the battle of Passchendaele and played a particularly active staff officer's role during the division's deployment at the Somme to stem the German offensive of March 1918. In May he became G.S.O. 1 of the 1st Division and was temporarily promoted lieut-colonel. Awarded the Distinguished Service Order and mentioned four times in dispatches, he embarked for Australia in April 1919. In Adelaide he became chief instructor at an army school before being transferred in 1920 to the Royal Military College, Duntroon, as instructor in tactics. In January 1924 he was posted as senior administrative officer at Perth headquarters. He was appointed O.B.E. in 1937 and retired in April 1940.

Recalled to duty that year, Wieck established A.I.F. training camps before retiring as honorary colonel in 1941. A keen student of geography and history, in retirement he researched and published histories of the volunteer movement in Western Australia, the Northam Army Camp and the United Service Institution. He founded and managed an army museum, using as its basis his own large collection which was later donated to the State museum. A champion rifle-shot, cricketer and hockey player in his youth, he later became a keen gardener and collector of geological specimens. Survived by two sons and two daughters, he died in Perth on 28 August 1973 and was cremated with Methodist forms. His portrait, painted by Margaret Johnson about 1938, remains in the family's possession.

C. E. W. Bean, *The story of Anzac*, 2 (Syd, 1924), and *The A.I.F. in France*, 1916-18 (Syd, 1933, 1937, 1942); J. E. Lee, *Duntroon* (Canb, 1952); P. Pedersen, *Monash as military commander* (Melb, 1985); *London Gazette*, 2 Jan, 1 June, 25 Dec 1917, 28 May 1918, 7 May 1937; *Sabretache*, Jan 1974, Feb 1975; *West Australian*, 30 Aug 1973; information from Miss M. Wieck, Floreat Park, Perth.

C. D. COULTHARD-CLARK

WIEDERMANN, ELISE; see PINSCHOF, CARL LUDWIG

WIENHOLT, ARNOLD (1877-1940), army officer, adventurer, pastoralist, politician and author, was born on 25 November 1877 at Goomburra station, near Allora, Queensland, eldest son of Edward Wienholt [q.v.6], pastoralist, and his Victorian-born wife Ellen, née Williams. Educated in England at Eton, Arnold returned to Australia and gained experience in the pastoral industry. Enlisting in the 4th (Queensland Imperial Bushmen) Contingent, on 18 May 1900 he embarked for South Africa; he was promoted sergeant in June and established a reputation for firmness and fairness. The contingent saw

twelve months active service before being disbanded in Brisbane on 10 August 1901.

In 1908 Wienholt became manager of Wienholt Estates Co. of Australasia Ltd and was responsible for the firm's Queensland properties. He was a good cattleman and devised his own method of dealing with the ravages of tick. Entering politics in 1909, he was the member for Fassifern in the Legislative Assembly until 1913. That year, having failed to win the Federal seat of Wide Bay, he decided to go on safari to German South-West Africa (Namibia). While hunting, he was mauled by a wounded lion; his wrist was mangled and he lost full use of his right hand.

Learning of the outbreak of World War I, Wienholt made his way to Rhodesia. His offer to scout for the British was refused and he returned to Brisbane. In March 1915 he sailed for Africa accompanied by Ivan Lewis, a friend and one of his station managers. They served briefly on border patrol as special service troopers in the British South African Police, then enlisted in the East Africa Mounted Rifles. Early in 1916 they were seconded to the Intelligence Branch and Wienholt was promoted warrant officer. Leading a patrol into German East Africa (Tanzania), he collected valuable information before being wounded and captured on 1 July. He escaped six months later and spent fifteen days crossing unfamiliar country to regain his own lines. For his gallantry he was awarded the Military Cross. Wienholt performed further successful reconnaissance missions, among them an arduous six-month expedition during which his party was frequently attacked by superior enemy forces. His courage and endurance won him the Distinguished Service Order in October 1918. A bar to his M.C. had been gazetted in September; he had also been promoted captain.

Two months after arriving home, on 29 April 1919 Wienholt married Enid Frances Sydney Jones at St Philip's Anglican Church, Sydney. They made their home at his property, Washpool Farm, near Kalbar, Queensland. That year he was elected to the House of Representatives as National Party member for Moreton and immediately urged the government to repeal restrictions on German settlers disfranchised during the war. A prudent businessman, he spoke against public indebtedness and state enterprise. He voted in accordance with his conscience on all matters except 'motions of censure or want of confidence'. He did not contest the 1922 election. In 1930 the Fassifern electorate returned him to the assembly. Retaining the seat in 1932, he did not contest the 1935 election. He had published *The story of a lion hunt* (London, 1922), an account of his adventures on safari and in World War I, and gone lion-hunting on four occasions between 1923 and 1929.

Following the Italian invasion of Ethiopia, Wienholt arrived in Addis Ababa in December 1935 as war correspondent for the Brisbane *Courier Mail*. Two months later he joined the Ethiopian Red Cross as a transport officer and left for the front. Impeded by Italian air attacks and hostile tribesmen, he skilfully assisted various philanthropic groups to retreat to the capital. He recorded his experiences in *The Africans' last stronghold: in Naboth's vineyard* (London, 1938) and continued to promote the Ethiopian cause in Australia and England, but failed to gain official or public support for his stand. On the outbreak of World War II he sailed to Aden; while awaiting Italy's entry into the war, he learned Arabic and Amharic. In anticipation of a commission in the British Army, he was ordered on 31 August 1940 to proceed overland from the Sudan to Ethiopia in charge of a small party of natives. Wienholt's group was a component of Military Mission 101, a force tasked with fostering rebellion against Italy. Ambushed and wounded, probably on the morning of 10 September, he was last seen scrambling into the bush and was presumed to have died.

Of military bearing, with a moustache and short beard, Wienholt had been alert and restless. At Eton 'he was conspicuous as a straight running, fearless boy of great energy'. The boy was father to the man: he never smoked or drank alcohol, and his physical fitness more than once saved his life. Although taciturn, he liked to tell a good yarn, and to listen to one. As a soldier and scout, he was brave and resourceful, in the style of the heroes in his book, *The work of a scout* (London, 1923). A man of 'ruthless integrity and exacting truthfulness', he abhorred sentimentality and exaggeration. Consequently, his books understated his deeds. An 'uncompromising individualist', he had affection for the peoples of Africa. Wienholt lived much of his life alone, and died alone for a cause which he embraced eagerly and with passion. His wife survived him, as did their only daughter Anne who became a prominent artist. His Queensland estate was sworn for probate at £174 978.

P. E. von Lettow-Vorbeck, *My reminiscences of East Africa* (Lond, 1920); M. J. Fox (comp), *The history of Queensland* (Brisb, 1921); A. D. Mickle, *Many a mickle* (Melb, 1953); C. G. Grabs, *Australian, and a hero* (Toowoomba, Qld, 1987); W. Thesiger, *The life of my choice* (Lond, 1987); *Canb Times*, 11 May 1968; R. C. Foot, Arnold Wienholt: a biography of an independent Australian (ms, held by Mrs R. C. Foot, Clareville Beach, Syd); Wienholt collection (Fryer Lib, Univ Qld).

P. J. GREVILLE

WILCOX, DORA; *see* MOORE, WILLIAM

WILDER-NELIGAN, MAURICE (1882-1923), soldier and district officer, was born on 4 October 1882 at Tavistock, Devon, England, son of Canon John West Neligan and his wife Charlotte, née Putland. Maurice Neligan was educated at Queen Elizabeth's Grammar School, Ipswich, and Bedford Grammar School. On 18 February 1905 he married a divorcee Frances Jane Wyatt at the register office, Paddington, London. They were to have one daughter.

Enlisting in the Royal Horse Artillery in September 1910 as Maurice Wilder, he lowered his age and gave Auckland, New Zealand, as his birthplace. He served in the ranks for about a year before leaving his family in London and going to Sydney. He next appeared as a weighbridge clerk in a sugar mill at Proserpine, Queensland, and lived at Kelly's Club Hotel, Brandon, where he established a close friendship with the publican's family. In August 1914 he enlisted as a private soldier in the 9th Battalion, Australian Imperial Force, again as Maurice Wilder, and was promoted sergeant on 1 January 1915. From the landing on Gallipoli on 25 April he was in his element. On the 26th he carried in a wounded man under heavy fire, collected stragglers and led them back to the firing-line. For this action he was awarded the Distinguished Conduct Medal. Officer casualties were heavy: although he was only the battalion's orderly-room sergeant, he was soon acting as adjutant of the 9th and was commissioned as second lieutenant on 28 April. On the night of 27 May he led a raid on a Turkish post near Gaba Tepe, inflicting casualties and bringing back a prisoner without firing a shot and without losing a man; his careful planning of the operation ensured its swift success. Wounded in June and evacuated to Egypt, he discharged himself from hospital and made his way back to the 9th.

He was appointed adjutant and temporary captain in September, and obtained official promulgation of a change of name to Wilder-Neligan. The transfer of the A.I.F. to France in 1916 brought him wider opportunities. He planned and carefully trained the troops for a major raid near Fleurbaix, launched on the night of 1-2 July. Its success was recognized by the award of the Distinguished Service Order to Wilder-Neligan who, despite serious wounds, had continued to command until all his men had returned. After recovering, he took part in desperate fighting at Bullecourt in May 1917 and in the 3rd battle of Ypres. For brief periods that year he was acting commanding officer of the 9th Battalion and of the

10th. Promoted lieut-colonel, he returned to the 10th on 30 June as its commander; 'within a few months [he] infused into that battalion a special eagerness'. His determined and imaginative training prepared it for the battle of Polygon Wood in September—with brilliant results.

Perhaps his greatest achievement was the capture of Merris in July 1918, described by the inspector general of training in the British Expeditionary Force as the 'best show ever done by a battalion in France'. Wilder-Neligan was awarded a Bar to his D.S.O. for this innovative and daring operation. He was prominent in the great series of battles beginning on 8 August. In the fighting for Lihons he moved 250 yards (228 m) ahead of his battalion, taking a signalling lamp which he flashed red for halt and take cover, and yellow for advance. In this way he brought the 10th into position in support of the 9th with only one man wounded. His tactical skill was buttressed by his tireless care for the well-being of his men, their clothing and fitness as well as their rations. Above all he was an organizer, some said the best in the A.I.F. To C. E. W. Bean [q.v.7] he was 'a restless and adventurous spirit', 'an impetuous, daredevil officer but free of the carelessness with which those qualities are often associated'. His eccentricities were famous and were often shown in the embarrassing way he treated his officers, but much was forgiven so masterly a commander. If the rank and file cursed him, they also trusted him. He was mentioned in dispatches four times; in 1918 he was appointed C.M.G. and awarded the French Croix de Guerre.

Wilder-Neligan's A.I.F. appointment terminated in Queensland in October 1919. He had been thinking of obtaining an administrative post in the Australian 'military or civil dependencies', but it was not until March 1920 that he joined the military administration of New Guinea as a lieutenant. He began as temporary deputy district officer attached to the Rabaul garrison. On 9 May 1921, when military government ended, he transferred to the civil administration, becoming district officer at Talasea, New Britain. Early in January 1923 he was called to Rabaul by the administrator to answer allegations of financial malpractice made by a former German planter. Although Wilder-Neligan appears to have resigned, he set out for Rabaul by sea. He went ashore to stay at the village of Ekerapi and to rest for a few days. On coming to wake him on 10 January, his servant found that Wilder-Neligan was dead. A coronial inquest by the acting district officer at Talasea found that the cause of death was unknown and that there were no suspicious circumstances. Survived by his wife and daughter, Wilder-Neligan had died intestate and in debt. His remains were buried on Garua Island, near Talasea, in accordance with his wishes; his wife placed a memorial stone on the grave.

Big in stature, 'solidly built and of upright and soldierly bearing', Wilder-Neligan was outstanding among those for whom the war meant a liberation of their faculties and for whom it provided stimulation and purpose. With only modest training and experience, he learned quickly, coming to understand war in France in the same terms as Sir John Monash [q.v.10], but with an even clearer appreciation of the possibilities of the battlefield owing to his intimate experience of it. He was lucky in that he survived, but it was his courage, his sheer tactical brilliance and his unceasing care for his soldiers that made 'Mad Neligan' a legend in his day. He was and remains a mysterious figure, save for the brief years of his military achievement.

C. E. W. Bean, *The story of Anzac* (Syd, 1921, 1924), and *The A.I.F. in France*, 1916-18 (Syd, 1929, 1933, 1937,-1942); C. B. L. Lock, *The fighting 10th* (Adel, 1936); N. K. Harvey, *From Anzac to the Hindenburg Line* (Brisb, 1941); C. M. Wrench, *Campaigning with the fighting 9th* (Brisb, 1985); *Reveille* (Syd), Sept 1930, Mar 1931, Mar 1941; Wilder-Neligan personal file A518, 852/1/886 (AA, Canb).   A. J. HILL

WILDMAN, ALEXINA MAUDE (1867-1896), journalist, was born on 28 February 1867 at Paddington, Sydney, eighth daughter and eleventh child of English parents Edwin Wildman, clerk, and his wife Elizabeth, née Stevens. Ina began writing as a schoolgirl. In 1885 she complained in person when her verses were rejected by the *Bulletin*. Despite the editor J. F. Archibald's [q.v.3] view that women could not write poetry, 'the bright, audacious schoolgirl with original ideas' soon became a regular contributor of prose and verse. Wildman joined the *Bulletin* staff where she spent the whole of her brief career; her column, written as 'Sappho Smith', appeared weekly from 28 April 1888 to 22 August 1896; it was an instant success, and probably the most widely read part of the *Bulletin* by the early 1890s.

Headed by a Phil May [q.v.5] cartoon of a disdainful dowager with fan and pince-nez, the column usually appeared on its own page and took the form of a letter to 'my dear Moorabinda'; it contained 'a medley of all sorts of things that are running through my head', as well as 'interesting items of fashionable intelligence' observed by Wildman and her readers whose contributions would 'at all times be thankfully received and acknowledged'.

The weekly letter cast a sharp, sarcastic eye over vice-regal events, balls ('the usual bareback show'), garden parties, weddings, at-homes and sporting fixtures, together with behaviour at plays and concerts, and even confirmations at St Andrew's Cathedral. Then, as now, Sydney society provided rich pickings for the satirist. Amid snippets of gossip, she also provided thoughtful remarks and insights, such as her comment on the compelling style of famed ex-Fabian socialist and theosophical lecturer Annie Besant who was in Australia in 1894: 'quite a little East Lynne on wheels'.

Wildman's scepticism extended to 'she-Suffragists' and the 'New Woman', an irony given her early independence and professionalism, yet in accord with *Bulletin* misogyny. Gaucheries, especially those of women, were often noted by 'Sappho Smith'. She constantly derided pretension, whether British or Australian in origin, but her racist references to 'the Chosen People' and Brisbane as a 'city of yellow-faced men' may have merely reflected the magazine's editorial predilections.

A *Bulletin* sub-editor described Wildman as slender, attractive rather than pretty, charming of manner and childlike in some respects. Another journalist Ellen Todd [q.v.] found her 'a sympathetic soul', unexpectedly vulnerable, an impression strengthened by her wistful, romantic poems. Wildman fell ill early in 1894; a holiday in Queensland failed to restore her health. She died of nephritis on 15 November 1896 at Waverley and was buried in the Anglican section of the local cemetery. Often referred to as 'the incomparable Ina Wildman', she was celebrated by her colleagues as a brilliant writer and a good comrade; her brief, bright career was an encouragement to many women journalists. Eight of her poems (1884-92) are preserved in a volume of press-cuttings in the Mitchell [q.v.5] Library, Sydney.

S. Lawson, *The Archibald paradox* (Melb, 1983); J. Roe, *Beyond belief* (Syd, 1986); P. Clarke, *Pen portraits* (Syd, 1988); *Cosmos*, 1 Sept 1984; *Bulletin*, 21 Nov 1896; D. O'Reilly newspaper cuttings (ML).   J. I. ROE

WILKIE, ALLAN (1878-1970), actor-manager, was born on 9 February 1878 at Toxteth Park, Lancashire, England, son of James John McKinlay Wilkie, engineer, and his wife Mary Kate, née Bowyer. Educated at Liverpool High School, as a young man Allan worked in a merchant's office, but he was so inspired by the performances of Osmond Tearle that he decided to embrace 'the free, spacious, romantic life of the Shakespearean actor'. Moving to London, he became an understudy and soon graduated to roles in touring companies, including that of Beerbohm Tree. On 4 February 1904 at All Saints parish church, Kensington, London, Wilkie married Iné de la Garde Cameron, a 21-year-old actress. Disdainful of the genteel theatre of the West End, at 27 he launched his own touring company. His first Shakespearian venture was *The merchant of Venice*, a play that was to be associated with his name. A divorcee, on 22 July 1909 at the register office, Chapel-en-le-Frith, Derbyshire, he married Frediswyde Hunter-Watts (d. 1951), a 22-year-old actress in his company who soon became his leading lady.

In 1911 Wilkie seized an opportunity to take his company to India; over the next two years he also played in Ceylon, Singapore, Malaya, China, Japan and the Philippines. Returning to England, he accepted an invitation to join a company in South Africa: he and his wife were there at the outbreak of World War I and decided to travel to Australia where Frediswyde had relations.

Having toured New Zealand with Nellie Stewart [q.v.] in 1915, Wilkie and Hunter-Watts were invited by entrepreneur George Marlow to head a Shakespearian company which launched a season at the Princess Theatre in Melbourne in January 1916. As very little Shakespeare had been professionally performed in Australia for a generation, local actors were inexperienced in it; nevertheless, boosted by vice-regal patronage, the season was a success and led to a national tour. Wilkie ambitiously launched his own 'permanent' Shakespearian company in September 1920 and challenged theatrical superstition by opening with *Macbeth*. This production, with its stylish, simplified staging which enabled the play to be given with only one brief interval, had considerable impact. By 1924 the company had totted up one thousand consecutive performances and he earned a commendation from Prime Minister S. M. (Viscount) Bruce [q.v.7] for 'performing a duty of a national character'. Next year Wilkie was appointed C.B.E. In 1926, after a fire at Geelong destroyed the company's sets and costumes, a public appeal was launched to save 'a national institution' and raised almost £3000.

Faced with the difficulty of finding a theatre in Sydney, in 1928 Wilkie enterprisingly rented the Majestic at Newtown and played a highly successful season, following which he toured suburban theatres and halls. In early 1930, as the Depression and 'talkies' were beginning to exact their toll, he astonished the pundits by attracting full houses in Melbourne for a season of eighteenth-century comedy. In Sydney, however, the company faltered. Wilkie attempted to retrieve the situation by staging Doris Egerton Jones's [q.v.9] *Governor Bligh* [q.v.1], a play written at his suggestion, which aroused some controversy but enjoyed only modest success. The company's next season in Melbourne proved so disastrous that Wilkie disbanded his players in October 1930. For a decade he had struggled to make his company part of the cultural establishment, engaging support from governors, politicians and education departments for his remarkable marathon which saw the production of twenty-seven Shakespearian plays in capital cities and country towns throughout Australasia, as well as a relentless effort to win government subsidy for classical theatre.

Wilkie was not, as Colin Bingham put it, an Irving. An impressive figure, nonetheless, with a moon-shaped face, he could command the stage, and his portrayals were usually thoughtful and effective. As a director, he combined skill and vision. A romantic and anti-modernist, he saw the practical advantages of a simpler staging of Shakespeare which allowed for more pace and textual authenticity. (Dame) Ngaio Marsh saw his productions as having 'a thrust and drive and an absence of tarting-up'. Wilkie founded the *Shakespearean Quarterly*, published in Sydney in 1922-24. Hunter-Watts, described by Hal Porter as 'an actress in the chilly classic mode', was accomplished and versatile, though never a robust performer.

After the company's demise, the Wilkies survived by reciting Shakespeare in country towns; in February 1931 they played in the first Australian professional production of Noël Coward's *Hay fever*. They left Australia in September and spent most of the remainder of their lives in Canada, the United States of America and Britain. In 1955 Wilkie visited his son Douglas, a journalist in Melbourne. On 19 October 1962 Allan Wilkie married Bertha Winifred Martin at the Church of St Columba-by-the-Castle, Edinburgh. Survived by her, and by the son of his second wife, he died on 6 January 1970 at Rothesay, Isle of Bute, Scotland.

H. Porter, *Stars of Australian stage and screen* (Adel, 1965); M. Skill, *Sweet Nell of old Sydney* (Syd, 1974); C. Bingham, *The beckoning horizon* (Melb, 1983); *SMH*, 13 June 1924, 3 June 1925, 8 Jan 1970; *Table Talk*, 10 Mar 1927; Shakespearean productions, 1928-30 *and* A. Wilkie, All the world my stage (mss, LaTL).   JOHN RICKARD

WILKIE, LESLIE ANDREW ALEXANDER (1878-1935), artist, was born on 27 June 1878 at Royal Park, Melbourne, eldest son of David Wilkie, a gardener from England, and his native-born wife Mary Frances, née Rutherford. Educated at Brunswick College, in 1895 Leslie returned there as a junior teacher. In 1896-1901 he attended the National Gallery schools under Bernard Hall [q.v.9] and was a prizewinner in 1900. Having completed his first important commission for a full-length portrait in 1903, Wilkie set off next year on a tour of galleries in Europe and Britain to study the works of the masters and those of his distinguished relations (he was a grand-nephew of Sir David Wilkie, R.A.). Returning to Melbourne in 1905, he worked briefly as art critic for the *Age*, was elected (1906) a council-member of the Victorian Artists' Society and deputized in 1907-08 for Frederick McCubbin [q.v.10] at the National Gallery.

At Kew on 6 November 1913 Wilkie married with Presbyterian forms Alma Rubina ('Nani') Tunnock (d. 1930). He held a successful exhibition in 1914 at his city studio in the Austral Buildings; there, and at a college in Mornington, he also taught art. His portrait of Senator Sir Albert Gould [q.v.9] was accepted by the Historic Memorials Committee of the Federal government. During World War I Wilkie sold pictures and painted banners to assist the Australian Red Cross Society. An exhibitor for over twenty years with the Victorian Artists' Society, between 1916 and 1933 he also exhibited regularly with the Australian Art Association and was its secretary in 1923-25. His entry in the Sydney Society of Artists' exhibition of Australian art, shown locally and in London in 1923, had won praise in both cities. Having joined the art staff of both the *Argus* and the *Australasian*, and having sat on judging panels for exhibitions at the National Gallery of Victoria, in September 1926 he exhibited in Sydney with A. E. Macdonald. Wilkie was a conscientious and careful portraitist who painted in the tradition of the Royal Scottish Academy; his work showed considerable 'vitality, in spite of its restraint'.

Slight in build, with a domed head and sensitive features, he was modest and retiring, and never seemed in robust health. In 1926 he was appointed curator (later director) of the Art Gallery of South Australia where he proved efficient, painstaking and popular. He was a council-member of and taught at the South Australian School of Arts and Crafts, and exhibited with the (Royal) South Australian Society of Artists (1927 and 1928) and with the United Arts Club of Adelaide. Elected (1930) to the Royal Drawing Society, London, he became president (1932) of the R.S.A.S.A. In 1934 he joined a University of Adelaide anthropological expedition to Central Australia and painted portraits of Aborigines near Cooper Creek; these works were later exhibited at the A.G.S.A.

After an operation for appendicitis, Wilkie died in an Adelaide private hospital on 4 September 1935, survived by his only daughter. He was buried in St Saviour's Anglican Church cemetery, Glen Osmond. His work as a teacher and administrator, and perhaps his isolation in Adelaide from the stimulus of old friends, had limited his artistic opportunities during the Depression. Wilkie's paintings are in the National Library of Australia and the Australian War Memorial, Canberra, in State and regional galleries, the State Library of Victoria and the Athenaeum Club, Melbourne.

Gadfly (Adel), June 1908; *Art in Aust*, 7, 1919; *Herald* (Melb), 2 Aug 1907; *SMH*, 7 Sept 1926; *News* (Adel), 4 Sept 1935; *Advertiser* (Adel), 5 Sept 1935; J. McGrath, The Australian Art Association, 1912-1933, against the social background of the period (B.Soc.Sci. special study, RMIT, 1974); information from Mr D. A. Wilkie, Beaconsfield, Vic.   JOYCE MCGRATH

WILKIN, FREDERICK JOHN (1855-1940), Baptist clergyman, was born on 3 May 1855 at Cambridge, England, eldest of ten children of William Wilkin, master shoemaker, and his wife Emma, née Allen. In 1861 the family migrated to Victoria and settled at Castlemaine where William set up business as a boot repairer. They became active members of the newly constituted (1862) Baptist Church. By the age of 19 Frederick had decided to enter the Christian ministry. Accepted as a ministerial candidate by the Victorian Baptist Association home mission committee, he began his training in 1875 at the Congregational College at Carlton, Melbourne. Three years later he was appointed minister of Eaglehawk Baptist Church. On 10 September 1878 at Carlton he married with Congregational forms Louisa Jane Thwaites, a teacher at Fitzroy Model School.

In 1880 Wilkin moved to a pastorate at Kerang from where, for nineteen years, he undertook pioneering home mission work, travelling widely to establish preaching stations in northern Victoria. During this period he wrote tracts, published articles in the *Kerang Home Missionary* (which he edited) and took part in public debates on social issues. He was an irrigation enthusiast and a crusader for the temperance movement. In 1899-1906 Wilkin served at Brighton, Melbourne. He was also home mission superintendent for Victoria in 1892-1911 (full time from 1906).

A keen scholar, Wilkin continued extramural studies at the University of Melbourne (B.A., 1892; M.A., 1896) and the Melbourne College of Divinity (B.D., 1914; D.D., 1921). From 1912 until his retirement in 1937, he exercised a significant influence over the training of denominational leaders through his work as tutor and (from 1920) professor of theology at the Victorian Baptist Theological College.

President of the Victorian Baptist Association (later Union) in 1894-95 and secretary in 1912, 1914-20 and 1923, Wilkin was also secretary of the advisory board and the home mission committee, as well as editor of the denominational paper, the *Southern Baptist*. He published *A romance of home missions* (1927) and *Baptists in Victoria* (1939). A strong advocate of a Baptist Union of Australia, he served from 1926 as foundation secretary of its educational board. From 1914 he led an annual ministers' retreat at his Anglesea holiday home which was later given to the Baptist Union of Victoria for the same purpose.

Amiable and bearded, with twinkling eyes beneath rather fierce brows, Wilkin was known as the 'grand old man' of the Victorian Baptists; he was respected for his leadership and loved for his warmth and humility. Predeceased by his wife, he died on 10 January 1940 at his Canterbury home and was buried in Box Hill cemetery; two daughters and three sons survived him.

B. S. Brown, *Members one of another* (Melb, 1962); *Vic Baptist Witness*, 6 June 1938, 5 Feb 1940; J. G. Manning, Frederick John Wilkin, ms, 1984 and I. D. Chalmers, The life of Dr F.J. Wilkin and his contribution to Baptists in Victoria, unpublished paper, 1988 (Baptist Union of Vic Archives).   JILL MANTON

WILKINS, SIR GEORGE HUBERT (1888-1958), war correspondent and photographer, polar explorer, naturalist, geographer, climatologist and aviator, was born on 31 October 1888 at Mount Bryan East, South Australia, thirteenth child of Henry Wilkins, farmer, and his wife Louisa, née Smith. As a child, George experienced the devastation caused by drought and developed an interest in climatic phenomena. Reared as a Methodist, he studied engineering part time at the South Australian School of Mines and Industries, then pursued interests in photography and cinematography in Adelaide and Sydney. In 1908 he sailed for England to work for the Gaumont Film Co.

As a newspaper reporter and cameraman, Wilkins visited different countries; he also learned to fly and experimented with aerial photography. As a war correspondent and photographer, in 1912 he covered the fighting between the Turks and Bulgarians. From 1913 to 1916 he was second-in-command on Vilhjalmur Stefansson's Canadian Arctic expedition: Wilkins became adept in the art of survival in polar regions, added to his scientific knowledge and conceived a plan to improve weather forecasting by establishing permanent stations at the poles.

Returning to Australia, on 1 May 1917 he was commissioned as second lieutenant in the Australian Imperial Force (Australian

Flying Corps). By August he had been transferred to the general list and was at I Anzac Corps headquarters on the Western Front. Appointed official photographer in April 1918, he was tasked with providing 'an accurate and complete record of the fighting and other activities of the A.I.F.' as a counterpart to Captain J. F. Hurley's [q.v.9] propaganda work. In June Wilkins was awarded the Military Cross 'for bringing in some wounded men'. With Hurley's departure, he was promoted captain on 11 July and took charge of No.3 (Photographic) Sub-section of the Australian War Records unit. His routine was to visit the front line for part of each day that troops were engaged in combat and periodically to accompany infantry assaults. During the battle of the Hindenburg line, on 29 September he organized a group of American soldiers who had lost their officers in an enemy attack and directed operations until support arrived. Awarded a Bar to his M.C., he was also mentioned in dispatches. The A.I.F. published his edited *Australian war photographs: A pictorial record from November 1917 to the end of the war* (London, 1918).

In January 1919, as photographer, Wilkins joined C. E. W. Bean's [q.v.7] mission to reconstruct Australia's part in the Gallipoli Peninsula campaign. He entered the England to Australia air race that year, but his aircraft, a Blackburn Kangaroo, experienced engine failure and crash-landed in Crete; he arrived in Australia by sea in July 1920 and his A.I.F. appointment terminated on 7 September. Engaging in further polar exploration, in 1920-21 he made his first visit to the Antarctic, accompanying J. L. Cope on his unsuccessful voyage to Graham Land. Wilkins next took part in Sir Ernest Shackleton's *Quest* expedition of 1921-22 on which he made ornithological observations.

While in the Soviet Union in 1922-23 surveying and filming the effects of famine, he was asked by the trustees of the British Museum to proceed to tropical Australia and collect specimens of the rarer native fauna, principally mammals. Wilkins's book, *Undiscovered Australia* (New York, 1929), showed the extent and quality of his work over two and a half years from 1923; in addition to mammals, the collections included plants, birds, insects, fish, minerals, fossils and Aboriginal artefacts. When a projected Antarctic expedition failed through lack of funds in 1926, he began a programme of Arctic exploration by air. The enterprise culminated in his great feat of air navigation: in April 1928, with Carl Ben Eielson as pilot, he flew from Point Barrow, Alaska, United States of America, eastward over the Arctic Sea to Spitsbergen (Svalbard), Norway. He was knighted in June, and awarded the Patron's medal of the Royal Geographical Society of London

and the Samuel Finley Breese Morse medal of the American Geographical Society. His book, *Flying the Arctic* (New York, 1928), publicized the achievement. On 30 August 1929 in the registry office, Cleveland, Ohio, Wilkins married Suzanne Evans, an Australian-born actress known by her stage name 'Suzanne Bennett'. Though they were to remain childless, the marriage was a happy one and both parties pursued their own careers.

Sir Hubert had carried out the first aerial explorations of the Antarctic in November 1928 and January 1929. While most of his discoveries were later shown to have been erroneous, his 'reconnaissance greatly influenced the course of all subsequent exploration in the area'. He visited Antarctica again in 1930 and attempted next year to reach the North Pole by taking a surplus United States Navy submarine, renamed *Nautilus*, under the pack-ice. Mishaps and mechanical failures caused the venture to be abandoned, amid ridicule of his ideas. Wilkins's account of the operation appeared in *Under the North Pole* (New York, 1931). In collaboration with Lincoln Ellsworth, he made four further expeditions (1933-34, 1934-35, 1935-36 and 1938-39) to the Antarctic continent. During 1937 and 1938 he played a major role in the search for the Russian aviator Sigismund Levanevsky who disappeared on a flight from Moscow to Fairbanks, Alaska. In these years Wilkins also advanced techniques of flying by moonlight, made scientific observations and experimented with telepathy.

At the outbreak of World War II he offered his services to the British and Australian governments, but was rejected on account of his age. Wilkins nonetheless became involved in a number of missions for United States government agencies, visiting the Middle East, South-East Asia and the Aleutian Islands. From 1942 he was a consultant and geographer with the U.S. Army Quartermaster Corps which sought his advice on rations and equipment suitable for use in conditions of extreme cold. He held other defence-related scientific posts, and served in the U.S. Weather Bureau and the Arctic Institute of North America.

A fellow of the Royal Geographical Society and the Royal Meteorological Society (1923), Wilkins could be dismissive of conventional scientific method. He was primarily a field explorer and pioneer who worked to a clear, long-range plan, based on his conviction of the necessity for a world-wide meteorological organization. Yet, his curiosity drew him irresistibly to new ideas and projects. In 1955 he was granted an honorary D.Sc. by the University of Alaska. Despite his solitary nature, he was a good mixer and companion. Tall and athletic, he had physical drive and courage to match his mental endurance, and he held deep religious convictions.

Wilkins lived to learn in August 1958 of the under-ice transits of the Arctic Sea by the submarines U.S.S. *Skate* and U.S.S. *Nautilus*. He died suddenly in his hotel room at Framingham, Massachusetts, on 30 November 1958 and was cremated; four months later his ashes were scattered from the *Skate* at the North Pole. Lady Wilkins survived him and wrote affectionately of a husband whose only contact with her for extended periods had been through his letters. Her portraits of Wilkins, and those by Vuk Vuchinich, Roland Hinton Perry and James Peter Quinn, were in her possession at the time of his death. Another by Reynolds Mason hangs at the entrance of the Wilkins arctic test-chamber in the Army Quartermaster Research and Engineering Center, Natick, Massachusetts.

C. E. W. Bean, *The A.I.F. in France*, 1917-18 (Syd, 1933, 1937, 1942), and *Gallipoli mission* (Canb, 1948); US Dept of the Navy, *Antarctic bibliography* (Washington, DC, 1951); *DNB*, 1951-60; J. Grierson, *Sir Hubert Wilkins* (Lond, 1960); R. A. Swan, *Australia in the Antarctic* (Melb, 1961); L. Thomas (comp), *Sir Hubert Wilkins . . . autobiography* (Lond, 1962); M. L. Olsen, *Saga of the white horizon* (Lymington, UK, 1972); *Polar Record*, 9, no 62, May 1959.   R. A. SWAN

WILKINSON, ARTHUR GEORGE (1911-1940), speedway motor cyclist, was born on 27 August 1911 at Millthorpe, New South Wales, third son of native-born parents John Wilkinson, butcher, and his wife Jessie May, née Toshack. While at South Bathurst Public School, Arthur saved the money to buy his first bicycle by working after school as a paper-boy. On leaving school he was employed as a butcher-boy and purchased his first motor cycle, a Douglas, for £3 10s. Within twelve months he was setting speed records on the dirt track at Bathurst sportsground. After he won the unofficial New South Wales championship, competing against Lionel van Praag, a public fund was established to send him to Britain.

From 1929 'Bluey' Wilkinson raced with the West Ham club in East London. A favourite with spectators because of his daring riding, he was dubbed 'the red-headed miracle'. Following a racing collision in which he found his handlebar bent inward, he introduced curved handlebars to motor cycle speedways. He also ceased the practice of thrusting out or trailing the leg while cornering. Selected to ride for Australia against England in 1930, he failed to score, but in later Tests amassed a total of 359 points, more than any other rider.

On 12 October 1936 Wilkinson married Muriel Vick in the register office, Westminster, London; they were to remain childless. Through the 1930s he attracted huge crowds. Regarded as the favourite for the 1937 world championship, he was injured in a fall a week before the event and forced to withdraw. He visited New South Wales that year, won the Australian championship and achieved an unbroken sequence of thirty-seven wins in Sydney.

Back in Britain, in 1938 Wilkinson won the Scottish championship and set new records at many tracks. In September he won the world championship at Wembley stadium. The result was popular: he had suffered an injury the previous night and rode with his shoulder in plaster. He came out of retirement in 1939 to give a Royal command performance, then turned to management and promotion of speedway racing, but the sport was virtually suspended during World War II.

The Wilkinsons were keen travellers and thrice went to the United States of America. In March 1940 they returned to Sydney and lived at Bellevue Hill. Riding his motor cycle at Rose Bay on 27 July, Wilkinson was involved in a collision with a lorry, fractured his skull and died almost instantly; Muriel, who was riding pillion, was severely injured, but survived. He was buried in Bathurst cemetery with Anglican rites.

Quiet, modest, reserved, and seemingly incapable of fear, Wilkinson had enjoyed the support and affection of speedway spectators for his breathtaking performances. He tutored and guided many riders who later achieved prominence. At Bathurst, Wilkinson Place commemorates his name, while the lights at the sportsground were erected in his memory.

Speedway World (Great Britain), 7 Sept 1938; *Parade*, Oct 1964; *SMH*, 11 May, 3 Sept, 2, 26 Dec 1938, 20 Jan 1939, 4 Mar, 29 July, 1 Aug, 24 Sept 1940; *Daily Mirror* (Syd), 28 Sept 1963, 12 Oct 1987; information from Mrs M. Baxter, Benowa, Qld, Mrs J. Green, Bathurst, NSW, and Mrs N. Bennett, Guildford, Syd.   JAMES PRIOR

WILKINSON, AUDREY HAROLD (1877-1962), vigneron, was born on 29 July 1877 at Five Dock, Sydney, son of Frederick Albert Wilkinson (d. 1883), a 'gentleman vigneron' from England, and his Adelaide-born wife Florence Mary Hindmarsh, daughter of George Milner Stephen [q.v.2] and granddaughter of Rear Admiral Sir John Hindmarsh [q.v.1]. Frederick had come to Pokolbin, New South Wales, about 1865 and planted the first wine grapes at Oakdale in 1866; he also selected a property (Côte d'Or) for his father and others (Mangerton, Coolalta and Maluna) for his brothers Charles, John and William respectively. The family became dominant in establishing viticulture in the Pokolbin area.

Having briefly attended West Maitland Public School and been tutored at home, at the age of 15 Audrey took charge of Oakdale and managed the property for the remainder of his life, mostly working the vineyard with his brother Garth. His activities were bound up with the affairs of his property (which combined wine production and dairying) and focused on the district rather than beyond it. In 1901 he became secretary of the Pokolbin and District Vinegrowers' Association (1901-14) which has been credited with influencing the passage of the first effective Wine Adulteration Act (1902) in New South Wales. He was also active in its successor, the Pokolbin and District Agricultural Bureau, and kept the rainfall figures for Pokolbin for over half a century.

Tall and slight, with keen blue eyes and an ascetic face, Wilkinson was a lifelong teetotaller. Commissioned in the 4th Australian Light Horse Regiment in 1913, he was promoted captain of the 6th L.H.R. but did not see service overseas during World War I. He enjoyed playing tennis at home and occasionally visited Sydney. At Christ Church Cathedral, Newcastle, Wilkinson married Beatrice Blomfield on 12 April 1921 with Anglican rites; they were to remain childless. For much of their married life she helped to run the vineyard and did office work, but by 1949 was almost entirely bedridden.

Courteous and cultured, Wilkinson did business 'in the old reliable, trustworthy way'; his 'outlook on men and affairs also dated from other times'. Oakdale slowly declined during the lean years of the Hunter wine industry from the 1930s. Wilkinson's wine-making reputedly involved squeezing grapes into clean kerosene tins and fortifying the juice with spirits. He continued to drive his 1920 Buick. Faced with changing times, he did not adapt, preferring to spend his days writing, and attending to Beatrice. Survived by his wife, he died at Cessnock on 30 July 1962 and was cremated.

Cyclopedia of N.S.W. (Syd, 1907); M. Lake, *Hunter winemakers* (Brisb, 1970); *Cessnock Eagle*, 28 Oct 1949, 3 Aug 1962; W. P. Driscoll, A history of the Hunter valley wine industry in the nineteenth century (M.A. thesis, Univ Newcastle, 1970); Wilkinson family papers (including A. Wilkinson, Reminiscences of the early days, paper read to Cessnock Hist Soc, 9 Aug 1954) *and* Wilkinson diaries, 1872-1961 (ML); Pokolbin and District Vinegrowers' Assn, Minute-book, 1901-14 (held by author).   W. P. DRISCOLL

WILKINSON, DOROTHY IRENE (1883-1947), headmistress, was born on 22 May 1883 at Upholland, Lancashire, England, eldest daughter of Rev. Christopher George Wilkinson (1855-1929), Anglican clergyman, and his wife Florence, née Shann. Recruited by Bishop Montgomery [q.v.10], in 1889 Wilkinson brought his family to Tasmania and served in the diocese. In 1896 Dorothy went home to complete her schooling at the Clergy Daughters' School, Casterton, Westmorland.

Returning to Tasmania, she discovered a love of teaching while assisting her father, headmaster of Launceston Church Grammar School. In 1909 she entered the University of Melbourne (Dip.Ed., 1912; B.A., 1913; M.A., 1921) where she played hockey for the university and graduated with honours in history. After teaching briefly at the Church of England Girls' Grammar School, Melbourne, Dorothy returned to Launceston and in 1915 established the Girls' Grammar School which in six years built up an enrolment of two hundred pupils.

In 1920 Miss Wilkinson was appointed headmistress of Sydney Church of England Girls' Grammar School, Darlinghurst, in succession to Edith Badham [q.v.7]. After failing to persuade the Church to move the school, or to buy the adjoining property (Rosebank), she initiated an extension and renovation programme, converting the school hall into a chapel in 1926. That year she introduced a house system. She took a years leave in England and Palestine in 1929. On her return, her own ill health and the stresses of the Depression occasioned difficulties, but by 1935 the school had a record 365 students. In 1941 she established a wartime branch of the school at Leura in the Blue Mountains.

Originally known as 'Stickybeak', she cleverly altered the nickname to 'Stick' by which she became affectionately known to the girls who admired her readiness to stick by them. She moved quickly about the school, wearing an academic gown and her golden hair in a bun. Miss Wilkinson was a dedicated High Church Anglican, devoid of extremism; she wrote prayers and hymns, notably the chapel hymn, *Luceat lux vestra*. She provided her students with an education grounded in the Christian faith, while encouraging them to enter and excel at public examinations.

Committed to wider issues of education, Miss Wilkinson served as honorary secretary (1923-47) of the Association of Headmistresses; a councillor of the Teachers' Guild of New South Wales (vice-president, 1934-35) and of the Teachers' Central Registry, she was also a member of the New Education Fellowship and the Gurney Soubeiran [q.v.] Trust. She endeavoured to raise the salaries of teachers in non-government schools and battled, with minimal success, against clerics who regarded teaching as a 'calling'.

Wilkinson

Retiring in May 1947, she handed on to her successor Barbara Chisholm a flourishing and profitable school with an enrolment of 450 pupils. Dorothy Wilkinson moved to Wahroonga. On 18 September, alighting from a bus at Neutral Bay, she fell beneath the vehicle and was crushed to death. Following a funeral service at St Andrew's Cathedral, she was cremated. Her estate was sworn for probate at £8222. In 1970 the Dorothy Wilkinson Library was opened at S.C.E.G.G.S.; the school holds her portrait (1933) by Adelaide Perry.

SCEGGS Council, *Sydney Church of England Girls' Grammar School 1895-1955*, W. Sharland ed (Syd, 1958) and G. Appleton ed (Syd, 1972); SCEGGS, *Lux*, June 1945, jubilee no; *SMH*, 12 Oct 1920, 9 May, 19, 20 Sept 1947; information from Mrs M. Maltby and Mrs D. Straesser, SCEGGS Archives, and Mrs I. Vandervord, Bellevue Hill, Syd.   CAROLINE SIMPSON

WILKINSON, JOHN FRANCIS (1864-1935), physician, was born on 13 April 1864 at Collingwood, Melbourne, son of William Wilkinson, tailor, and his wife Harriet Emily, née Ezard, both Yorkshire born. John was educated at Boston's Grammar School, Preston, and at Alexander Sutherland's [q.v.6] Carlton College, of which he was dux. Graduating from the University of Melbourne (M.B., 1885; B.S., 1886) with first-class honours in medicine, he married Celia Harmer with Wesleyan forms on 20 September 1887 at Bundoora.

After a year as resident medical officer at the Melbourne Hospital, Wilkinson moved to Bright in north-eastern Victoria where he practised for ten years. Returning to Melbourne in 1897, he commenced practice in Collins Street, and was appointed honorary demonstrator and lecturer in clinical biochemistry at the university, a post which he held for twenty-five years. Under Professor (Sir) Charles Martin [q.v.10] he trained himself in physiological chemistry and graduated M.D. in 1899. According to W. A. Osborne [q.v.11], Wilkinson became the foremost clinical biochemist in Melbourne, and one of the first to establish a private laboratory. His particular interests were the fractional test meal and the opaque bismuth meal X-ray examination which he introduced with H. M. Hewlett [q.v.9]. He was an early advocate of massive doses of iron for anaemia, and popularized the dietary treatment of peptic ulcer and diabetes. His *Synopsis of lectures delivered . . . at the Walter and Eliza Hall* [qq.v.9] *Institute, Melbourne Hospital* (1923) was an important contribution to Australian gastroenterology. After seeing insulin used clinically in Canada in September 1922, Wilkinson persuaded the

Insulin Committee of the University of Toronto that it should be manufactured under licence by the Commonwealth Serum Laboratories in Melbourne. He demonstrated his initial results to a meeting of the Victorian branch of the British Medical Association in June 1923 and to the Australasian Medical Congress in Melbourne in November.

Endowed with energy, Wilkinson gave undergraduate and postgraduate lectures, and was a regular contributor at clinical meetings. Honorary physician from 1903 to the Melbourne Hospital, he was editor (1901-07) of the *Intercolonial Medical Journal of Australasia*, president (1912) of the Victorian branch of the British Medical Association and a member (1929-34) of council of the University of Melbourne. A layman of the Methodist Church, he was a councillor of Wesley and Queen's colleges.

During his years at Bright, Wilkinson enjoyed exploring the Victorian Alps and helped to establish Mount Buffalo as a tourist resort. A founder and first secretary of the Alpine Club, he took part in the first winter ascent of Mount Feathertop (1889) and The Horn (1890). His reminiscences were published as a booklet, *The romance of Buffalo* (1942). Wilkinson's Lookout is named after him.

Sturdy of body, Wilkinson was a handsome man with a naval beard. He was a progressive physician and a competent anaesthetist. Meticulous in his examinations and investigations, and clear and precise in his writings, he was esteemed by his colleagues. He died of complications from acute appendicitis on 29 March 1935 in St Ives Hospital, East Melbourne, and was buried in Melbourne general cemetery. His wife, a daughter and three sons survived him.

MJA, 11 May 1935, 23 July 1938; Aust Medical Assn, Vic branch, Archives, Melb; Cwlth Serum Laboratories Archives, Melb.
                              RICHARD TRAVERS

WILKINSON, LESLIE (1882-1973), professor of architecture, was born on 12 October 1882 at New Southgate, Middlesex, England, younger son of Edward Henry Wilkinson, commercial clerk, and his wife Ellen, née Barker. A delicate boy, Leslie was educated at St Edward's School, Oxford, and at the Royal Academy of Arts' school of architecture in London where he won the silver (1903) and gold (1905) medals; travelling studentships (1904, 1905) allowed him to tour France, Italy and Spain, as well as Britain. Wilkinson was a first-class draftsman, quick and accurate: his student drawings illustrated his immediate enchantment with Mediterranean architecture.

Articled in 1900 to the London architect James S. Gibson, Wilkinson became his assistant in 1903 and worked on commercial and municipal projects. In 1907 he was made an associate of the Royal Institute of British Architects; next year he became assistant to Professor F. M. Simpson at University College, London, and was assistant professor in 1910-18. He married Alice Dorothy Ruston (d. 1947) at St Stephen's parish church, Ealing, on 11 April 1912.

With the outbreak of World War I, Wilkinson enlisted in the Territorial Force, was commissioned in the University of London Officers' Training Corps in October 1914 and promoted lieutenant in June 1915. He dressed in tailcoat and top hat for his interview in 1918 for the new chair of architecture at the University of Sydney; his application was in the form of an illuminated address; his eminent referees ensured that he easily obtained the post.

Travelling through North America, Wilkinson arrived in Sydney on 19 August to be met by the premier, lord mayor and other dignitaries. Appointed to a chair within the faculty of science, he threw his considerable energy into gaining approval for a faculty of architecture which was created, with himself as dean, in 1920. In the four-year course he emphasized philosophy, theory and practice of design, aesthetics and attractive rendering; subjects included free-hand and water-colour drawing, and the history of architecture.

To Wilkinson, architecture was an art and those who practised it were discriminating gentlemen to whom good manners were all important. His emphasis on the intellectual and artistic over the more mundane aspects of construction and practice sometimes brought him into conflict with other members of the profession. In 1926 the Institute of Architects of New South Wales protested at the weakness of the students' practical knowledge; as a result, Alfred Hook was appointed associate-professor in charge of construction and related scientific fields, while Wilkinson was restricted to architectural design and history. Throughout his thirty years teaching his 'forceful personality' had a profound influence on the school and its graduates.

Appointed university architect in 1919, he did some of his best work as part of his master plan for the university, such as completing Edmund Blacket's [q.v.3] Gothic Revival quadrangle. In 1923 Wilkinson incorporated the Italian palazzo façades, removed from the George Street premises of the Commercial Banking Co. of Sydney, into a new chemistry building at the university. He designed the Mediterranean-style physics building (1926), but his finest work often relied on making the best of an established building by opening up vistas and using existing elevations and spaces.

Exceptionally tall (6 ft. 5 ins., 195.6 cm), fair-complexioned and pink-cheeked, with a clipped moustache (and in later life a goatee), the patrician Wilkinson made such pronouncements as 'it is not so important to be in style as to have style'. One of his staff, the cartoonist George Molnar, observed that an 'Olympian peace' surrounded him. Wilkinson had soon come to appreciate the quality of Australia's colonial heritage which, with Mediterranean architecture, became the main influence on his work, both as teacher and practising architect. He disliked modern buildings. His kindred spirits were William Hardy Wilson [q.v.] in Sydney, Walter Bagot in Adelaide and Robin Dods [qq.v.7,8] in Brisbane whose work raised the popularity of colonial revival architecture in the 1920s and 1930s.

Retaining the right to private practice, Wilkinson carried out domestic and ecclesiastical commissions. He designed some thirty houses and flats, and altered many more. Greenway, the first home he built (in 1923 for himself), was at once a Mediterranean villa and a colonial Georgian house; in the 1960s he was still designing houses of the same character. His work was always fashionable. Among his important houses are Samuel Hordern's home at Bellevue Hill (1936), Maiala at Warrawee (1937), Greyleaves, Burradoo (1934), and Hazeldean, Cooma (1937). Of his flats, his best is Silchester, Bellevue Hill (1930), a four-storey block in the Mediterranean style. As diocesan architect, he was responsible for a number of Anglican church buildings, among them his skilful completion of Blacket's St Michael's, Vaucluse.

Wilkinson was an artist, more than a conservator: he saw nothing to condemn in his proposal to convert Elizabeth Bay House into flats, or in basing the colours for repainting (1958) Blacket's ceiling in St Matthew's Church, Windsor, on a Capstan cigarette-box which he happened to have in his pocket. He was involved, however, with campaigns to save Burdekin House in the 1930s and Subiaco in the 1960s, and he resigned from the Union Club in 1956 in protest at the members' decision to demolish their Wardell [q.v.6]-designed clubhouse.

A fellow of the I.A.N.S.W. from 1918, Wilkinson was a councillor (from 1921) and president (1933). On the formation of the State chapter of the Royal Australian Institute of Architects in 1934, he became its first president; he was awarded its Sulman [q.v.] medal in 1934 and 1942, and its first gold medal in 1961; that year its housing award was named in his honour. Appointed O.B.E. in 1969, he received an honorary D.Litt. from the University of Sydney in 1970.

Survived by his son and two daughters, Wilkinson died on 20 September 1973 at Vaucluse and was cremated. Judy Cassab's and Norman Carter's [q.v.7] portraits of him are held by the University of Sydney; another is held by the family.

G. Beiers, *Houses of Australia* (Syd, 1948); S. Falkiner (ed), *Leslie Wilkinson a practical idealist* (Syd, 1982); *Art in Aust*, 1919; *Art and Aust*, Sept 1974; *Architecture in Aust*, Dec 1973; *SMH*, 6 Feb, 22 Aug 1918, 16 May 1961, 20, 21 Sept 1973; information from Miss B. Wilkinson, Syd.

CLIVE LUCAS

WILKS, WILLIAM HENRY (1863?-1940), fuel merchant, politician and public servant, was born in Sydney, son of Joseph Henry Wilks, a sea-captain from Bristol, England, and his native-born wife Susannah (d. 1863), née Harris. After attending Balmain Public School, he was associated with W. M. Hughes [q.v.9] in various odd-job enterprises before setting up a wood and coal yard at Balmain. President of the New South Wales Literary and Debating Societies' Union for two years, Wilks joined the Free Trade Association of New South Wales and in 1887 was elected to its council.

A Freemason from an early age, in 1888 he was grand master of the Grand Lodge of Scotland. Having entered politics, he became associated with the Loyal Orange Institution of New South Wales. His 'strong democratic views' led him to support Labor's entry into parliament in 1891, but the split in the party next year disillusioned him. He became active in the Free Trade, Land and Reform League, the more radical wing of the Free Trade Party then being consolidated by (Sir) George Reid [q.v.11]. On 19 July 1894 Wilks married Florence Matilda Vincent (d. 1926) at St Barnabas's Anglican Church, Sydney, and in August was elected to the Legislative Assembly for North Balmain as a free trader at the general election which brought Reid to office.

In the House, Bill Wilks became something of a licensed joker, but held off Labor challenges in his working-class constituency. His speeches, although infrequent, were long and rambling, yet occasionally effective. Believing that the ostensible cause of the censure motion against Reid in 1899 hid a conspiracy to prevent the premier from obtaining the first Federal prime ministership, Wilks strongly defended his leader: he attempted to defuse the motion with an amendment to separate the issue of the payment to J. C. Neild [q.v.10] (which was most likely to win Labor Party support) from the main Opposition case —a shrewd but unsuccessful move.

A 'rollicking looking man', Wilks had a 'strong moustache, continually bitten at the ends'. He was member for Dalley in the House of Representatives from 1901 to 1910 and whip in the Reid-McLean [q.v.10] government in 1904-05. His Orange connexions made him useful to Reid when the latter found himself embroiled with Cardinal Moran [q.v.10] in the sectarian controversies which muddied early Federal politics, but the journalist who described Wilks in 1906 as 'one of the great political directors who, working behind the scenes, determine who shall strut the public stage' greatly exaggerated both his influence and that of the L.O.I. Chairman of committees in 1905-07, Wilks chaired the royal commission on postal services in 1908.

Losing his seat to Labor in 1910, he was appointed to the public service as a land valuer in Melbourne and remained in that post until he retired in 1928. He married Edna Eunice Hinchcliffe in St Paul's Cathedral, Melbourne, on 6 August 1927. Survived by his wife, and by two sons and three daughters of his first marriage, he died at his Camberwell home on 5 February 1940 and was buried in Box Hill cemetery.

Daily Telegraph (Syd), 27 June 1894; *Punch* (Melb), 25 Jan 1906; *Age*, 7 Feb 1940; *SMH*, 7, 9 Feb 1940; Crouch memoirs (LaTL).

W. G. MCMINN

WILLCOCK, JOHN COLLINGS (1879-1956), engine driver and premier, was born on 9 August 1879 at Frogmore, Boorowa district, New South Wales, sixth child of Joseph Willcock, miner, and his wife Ellen, née Webb, both English born. Educated at Sydney Boys' High School, John worked in a bakery before moving to Western Australia in 1897 where he was employed on the Fremantle harbour works for two years. Beginning as a railway engine cleaner, by 1902 Willcock had become a railway fireman at Geraldton; after 1912 he was an engine driver, and an active member and official of the Engine Drivers', Firemen's and Cleaners' Union. On 24 September 1907 he had married Sicily Ann Stone at St Francis Xavier's Church, Geraldton; they were to have six children.

During World War I Willcock belonged to several patriotic groups, including Geraldton's confidential recruiting committee. He was a co-founder of the local labour women's organization, president (1914-17) of the district council of the Australian Labour Federation and a member (1917-23) of the branch executive of the Amalgamated Workers' Union.

Narrowly defeated as Labor candidate in the Legislative Assembly by-election for

Geraldton in April 1917, he captured the seat in the September general election and moved to Perth. Shortly afterwards he became secretary of the parliamentary Labor Party, then in opposition. Led by Phillip Collier [q.v.8], Labor won power in April 1924 and Willcock was minister for railways and justice until the government's defeat in April 1930; between April 1924 and June 1928 he was also minister for police. In 1927 he succeeded W. C. Angwin [q.v.7] as deputy premier and deputy leader of the party, but lost the latter position to Alexander McCallum [q.v.10] in 1930. After Labor's landslide victory in 1933, Willcock again became minister for railways and justice, and held the education portfolio until March 1935 when he regained the deputy leadership. Following Collier's retirement as party leader, on 19 August 1936 Willcock was commissioned as premier, treasurer and minister for forests.

In its early years in office his government —like its predecessor—concentrated on agricultural development and the construction of public works. Though his administration refused to provide full-time employment for men on relief, or to implement a 40-hour week for the State's workforce, Willcock was able to maintain a co-operative relationship with the entire labour movement. He was a conscientious and competent administrator with a penchant for carefully balanced budgets. Disliking extravagance, he rarely made use of government vehicles, preferring instead to drive his own car or to travel by public transport. In the late 1930s he introduced direct government involvement to encourage diversification of Western Australia's economy: development of a range of small secondary industries was fostered, many of which were in production by the mid-1940s. In 1939-41 Willcock and his cabinet extended carefully considered support for a Jewish proposal for a migrant settlement in the East Kimberley region.

A keen Imperialist, Willcock represented the State branch of the Empire Parliamentary Association at the coronation of King George VI in 1937 and strongly supported Australian involvement in World War II. His opposition, however, to John Curtin's attempts to expand the Commonwealth's wartime powers caused some disquiet in the Western Australian labour movement; although Willcock eventually relented, the tension remained. Throughout his eighteen years as minister and nine as premier, he was beset by bouts of serious illness which hospitalized him on occasions and eventually forced him to give up his forestry portfolio in December 1943 and to retire to the back-bench on 31 July 1945. He left parliament in March 1947. That year he was converted from Methodism to Catholicism.

With his full moustache, spectacles and fob watch-chain, Willcock presented a picture of respectability. Described as 'quiet, solid and likeable', and as 'disarmingly modest', he was popular with his party colleagues and respected for his honesty and sincerity. Yet, as premier, he had been prepared to act without consulting caucus. His amiable demeanour masked a shrewd and alert mind, and stories abounded of his powers of observation. He held personal prejudices against university education, but was a keen reader and an astute student of public affairs. More of a conversationalist than an orator, he could still make lengthy speeches in parliament without recourse to written notes. Survived by his wife, three daughters and a son, Willcock died on 7 June 1956 in St John of God Hospital, Perth; after a state funeral, he was buried in Karrakatta cemetery. His estate was sworn for probate at £16 707.

I. N. Steinberg, *Australia—the unpromised land* (Lond, 1948); V. Courtney, *Perth and all this* (Syd, 1962); G. C. Bolton, *A fine country to starve in* (Perth, 1972); C. T. Stannage (ed), *A new history of Western Australia* (Perth, 1981); G. S. Reid and M. R. Oliver, *The premiers of Western Australia 1890-1982* (Perth, 1982); *Geraldton Express*, 1 Oct 1917; *West Australian*, 26 July 1945, 8 June 1956; R. F. Pervan, The Western Australian Labor movement, 1933-47 (M.A. thesis, Univ WA, 1966).

NOELENE DOOHAN

WILLIAMS, ALFRED (1863-1913), educationist, was born on 16 October 1863 at St Ives, South Australia, eldest son of John Henry Williams, miner, and his wife Emma Mary, née Davey, both Cornish migrants. The family moved to Moonta where Alfred became a pupil-teacher in 1876 at the local public school. Following an outstanding year at the Training College and the University of Adelaide in 1881, he received good appointments at five primary schools and by 1900 was headmaster of Norwood Public School. He made it the top State school in South Australia and attracted the interest of educational and political leaders: inspectors noted how 'intensely interested' the children were in work which was 'a pleasure and not a task'. In Adelaide on 11 July 1885 Williams had married Matilda Coombs. A protégé of the former inspector-general of schools J. A. Hartley [q.v.4], he was committed to the ideas of the new education which aimed to foster intelligence rather than learning by rote. He also retained a 'belief in social equality' from his Methodist working-class background: he thought that, with the aid of scholarships, schools should be ladders for bright children of all classes to climb to university.

Guided by these ideals, Williams set out to reform South Australia's Education Department. A committee-member from 1892 of the Adelaide Teachers' Association, he was its delegate to the South Australian Public School Teachers' Union of which he was president (1903-05). Supported by prominent Adelaide intellectuals, he launched a public campaign to replace the stolid inspector-general L. S. Stanton with G. C. Henderson [q.v.9], professor of history and English at the university. Frank Tate [q.v.], the director of education in Victoria, inspired Williams through his visits to South Australia and through his summer schools in Victoria.

Tom Price's [q.v.11] coalition government moved quickly in 1905 to reform education and appointed Williams as director. Becoming —in his own words—'a missionary' in the cause of new education, he held several congresses which introduced teachers to new methods of child-centred learning and aroused public interest and support. He selected promising teachers to study interstate and then to act as leaven in South Australia: Lydia Longmore [q.v.10] and Elsie Claxton (infant teaching), A. G. Edquist (nature study) and W. J. Adey [q.v.7] (secondary teaching). Williams also appointed Bertie Roach [q.v.11] as editor of *The Children's Hour*: used as a textbook in reading, history, nature study and geography, his schoolpaper cheaply and effectively introduced Australian content to curricula.

Conscious of the teachers' burden in having to cover a range of subjects, Williams encouraged integration: Australian history for all classes beyond the infant grades was made possible from 1906 by its association with geography and reading. He supported teachers by providing higher salaries, better designed houses and schools, smaller classes and medical inspection of children. Williams also moved to end the distinction between provisional and permanent teachers by introducing in 1911 a minimum six months training for all. The establishment of the Observation and Practising School in Adelaide in 1908 and the separation of the Training College from the university in 1913 further strengthened professional training.

Although Williams's most significant achievement was to change attitudes towards primary education among students, teachers and the community, his work in secondary education is better known. With Tate, in 1907 he had visited Europe and the United States of America and learned how backward Australia was. Williams created Adelaide High School in 1908 by combining the Adelaide Continuation School with the Advanced School for Girls; next year the continuation classes in several large country towns were constituted as district high schools: by 1911 they numbered eighteen. A threefold increase in the number of scholarships that

year greatly extended secondary schooling. Despite Williams's concern for the working boy, in the field of technical education little could be done until the passing of the Education Act in 1915 and the appointment next year of Dr Charles Fenner [q.v.8] as superintendent.

A dynamic man of medium build, bespectacled, with deep eyes and a determined mouth, Williams was fired by the potential of education to develop children and, through them, South Australia. He was an avid reader and a fine speaker. A council-member of the University of Adelaide, he was also a fellow of the Royal Society of St George. Although gifted with organizational ability, he overestimated how much one person could achieve. Refusing to relax in the evenings or on weekends, he was forced by ill health to take periods of extended leave in 1910-12. He did not live to see many of the changes he had recommended. The advances he had made under Price slackened with the premier's death and the coalition's collapse in 1909. Survived by his wife, daughter and five sons, Williams died in a coma from diabetes mellitus on 18 February 1913 at his Torrensville home and was buried in North Road cemetery.

C. M. Thiele and R. Gibbs, *Grains of mustard seed* (Adel, 1975); P. Miller, *Long division* (Adel, 1986); Reports of minister of education, *PP* (SA), 1907-14; *PP* (SA), 1908, 3 (65); *Education Gazette* (SA), 1906-13; *Advertiser* (Adel) and *Register* (Adel), 19 Feb 1913; H. Beare, The influence of Alfred Williams and the Price ministry on public education in South Australia (M.Ed. thesis, Univ Melb, 1964); E. H. Kwan, Making 'good Australians': the work of three South Australian educators (M.A. thesis, Univ Adel, 1981).   ELIZABETH KWAN

WILLIAMS, EDWARD DAVID (1842-1909), businessman and politician, was born on 24 September 1842 at Talerddig, Montgomeryshire, Wales, son of Edward Williams, miller, and his wife Ann, née Howells. Educated at a private school, he worked in the woollen industry until, aged 17, he went to Shrewsbury where he learned English before moving to London in 1860. After four years in an uncle's grocery store, he decided to try his luck in Victoria. He arrived in 1864. Having briefly visited the central goldfields, he returned to Melbourne and to the grocery trade for three years. Moving to Lancefield and then Ballarat for another three years, eventually as the proprietor of his own business, he went to Castlemaine in 1871. On 26 December 1872 at Winchelsea he married Jane Jones with Anglican rites. Prospering as a general storekeeper, Williams gradually extended his interests to real estate and wholesale dealing. He acquired extensive gold-mining investments at Castlemaine, Campbells Creek, Chewton and Fryerstown, had interests in dredging companies and was chairman of the Castlemaine mining board.

A borough councillor for twenty-three years from 1886, Williams was three times mayor (1892, 1898 and 1907). In September 1894, after outpolling the premier, (Sir) James Patterson [q.v.5], he was elected to the Legislative Assembly for the seat of Castlemaine as a 'local and liberal' candidate on a platform of financial restraint, moderate protection, Federation, progressive income taxes and imposts on unimproved land. In an unremarkable career he was to be returned at three further elections before retiring in June 1904. Insisting that he entered parliament 'not to follow men but to support measures', he was vocal on issues (like mining) that touched his constituency, but also favoured liberal causes such as factory legislation, pensions, fair parliamentary representation and reform of the Legislative Council. In 1899 he sponsored a private member's bill to regulate the trusteeship of the Congregational ministerial training college. He was also a persistent champion of female suffrage on the grounds that 'our wives, our mothers, and our sisters possess as much common sense and as sound a judgement as the men'.

A leading promoter of the Castlemaine Woollen Co. Ltd from the formation of a provisional committee in September 1874, Williams had become its first secretary, principal shareholder, major mortgagor, and chairman from August 1885. The company was notable for its marketing initiative and concentration on the mixed cotton and wool fabrics shunned by its rivals. As managing director from January 1891, he was largely responsible for the mill's particular success with flannels and blankets. Sympathetic to wage-earners at large, but patriarchal towards his own employees, Williams was known for his geniality, self-reliance, business acumen and zest for work. He was a leading Congregationalist, deacon and Sunday School superintendent. He died suddenly on 17 October 1909 at his Castlemaine home and was buried in the local cemetery. His wife, two sons and four daughters survived him. His estate was sworn for probate at £11 978.

A. Sutherland, *Victoria and its metropolis*, 2 (Melb, 1888); Roy Com on the tariff, *V&P* (Vic), 1883, 4 (50), 1884, 2 (9); Bd appointed . . . to enquire into the effect of the fiscal system of Victoria upon industry and production, *PP* (Vic), 1894, 2 (37), 1895-96, 2 (3); *PD* (Vic), 1895-96, p 3567, 1902-03, p 50; *Table Talk*, 21 Dec 1894; *Mount Alexander Mail*, 6 Sept 1894, 18 Oct 1909; *Argus*, 18 Oct 1909; Castlemaine Woollen Co. Ltd papers (Univ Melb Archives).   GRAEME COPE

WILLIAMS, FRANCIS EDGAR (1893-1943), anthropologist and public servant, was born on 9 February 1893 at Malvern, Adelaide, son of David Williams, architect, and his wife Annie, née Good. Educated at Kyre College, a Baptist school, and the University of Adelaide (B.A., 1914), he graduated with first-class honours and several awards. Although selected as a Rhodes Scholar in 1915, Williams enlisted in the Australian Imperial Force, serving for two years as a lieutenant in France and subsequently as a captain with Dunsterforce in Persia.

After the war Williams took up his scholarship at Balliol College, Oxford, where in 1921 he studied under R. R. Marett and gained a diploma in anthropology with distinction. In 1922 he was appointed assistant government anthropologist in the Territory of Papua, then firmly governed by (Sir) Hubert Murray [q.v.10]. Williams was promoted to government anthropologist in 1928, a post he held for the rest of his life. In December 1926 he had married Constance Laura Denness, a kindergarten teacher from Vancouver, Canada.

During his distinguished anthropological career Williams undertook a remarkable amount of field-work. Of his nineteen years in the Territory, he spent more than five living in Papuan villages. Murray suspected that he was 'quite indifferent to discomforts', though Williams admitted to a 'sheer dislike of long isolation'. He completed major studies of seven distinct and widely separated cultures: Vailala (Purari Delta, 1922-23), Orokaiva (Northern Division, 1923-25); Keraki (Morehead River, 1926-32); Koiari (Central Division, 1929-31); Elema (Gulf Division, 1923-37), Foi (Southern Highlands, 1938-39), and Keveri (Eastern Division, 1940). He also made shorter studies of at least a dozen other societies.

Of the many reports he wrote for the Papuan government, four were published as monographs by Oxford University Press: *Orokaiva magic* (1928); *Orokaiva society* (1930) for which in 1928 he had been awarded an M.A. honours degree by the University of Adelaide; *Papuans of the Trans-Fly* (1936) which gained him a B.Sc. from Oxford (1934); and *Drama of Orokolo* (1940) for which he received an Oxford D.Sc. (1941). Among his other honours were the Wellcome gold medal for anthropological research (1933), the Cilento medal (1935) and a Rockefeller fellowship (1933-34). In 1939 he was elected president of the anthropology section of the Australian and New Zealand Association for the Advancement of Science.

A careful and thorough ethnographer, Williams nevertheless admitted to being an indifferent linguist who rarely made the effort to learn vernaculars. His writing style was clear, candid, unpretentious, and at times wryly self-deprecating. While not a major theorist, he was a searching and rigorous one, who made some strikingly original theoretical observations. His analyses of certain systems of kinship and marriage, for example, foreshadowed exchange theory and the structuralism of Claude Lévi-Strauss.

While accepting in part the reigning doctrine of British functionalism, he had the practical experience to judge its limitations. For him, a culture was not an 'integrated system', but 'always . . . to some extent a hotch-potch and a sorry tangle'. In his isolation from the academy Williams developed his own approach and addressed those issues he saw to be salient in the cultures he studied, rather than those which his academic colleagues (notably Bronislaw Malinowski and A. R. Radcliffe-Brown [q.v.11]) deemed to be important. The result was a body of published work unusual in its ethnographic range, integrity and pragmatic focus, albeit one unjustly neglected by his peers.

Although his published work has lasting scientific value, it was as an applied anthropologist concerned with 'native welfare' that Williams was employed; his salary was provided from a native benefits fund raised by taxing Papuans. An essential qualification for the job was the ability to get on with Murray whose large ego brooked no opposition. Williams was companionable, modest, yet forthright, and Murray respected him. Both were benevolently paternalistic in their attitude to Papuan welfare, but Murray did not take kindly to unsolicited advice, and Williams's innumerable recommendations were usually ignored. With Murray's warm approval, Williams founded and edited a monthly newspaper in simple English, the *Papuan Villager* (1929-42): designed to promote 'native education', its sententious content and patronizing tone made it more a vehicle for colonial propaganda.

Williams advocated the 'blending of cultures': the best of traditional arts and ceremonies with the most progressive elements of European culture, such that the Papuan remained recognizably himself. An impossibly fine line had to be drawn, for Williams abhorred crude 'Europeanization'. Christianity, he allowed, had to be part of the blending process. A rationalist himself, he was, nonetheless, largely sympathetic toward the work of the missions, while deploring the destructive effects of over-zealous missionaries. He attempted to interpret Papuan cultures so that they might be appreciated and even admired by Europeans for their rich artistic and ceremonial achievements. The *hevehe* ceremonies of Orokolo in particular impressed him deeply and he argued powerfully (but to little avail) for their preservation. His

greatest coup, perhaps, was to prevent the suppression of the 'bull-roarer cult' in the Gulf of Papua.

He supported land reform, but—surprisingly for an anthropologist—was against communalism, believing that the sooner Papuans became individualistic peasant proprietors the better. He promoted the idea of village self-government, yet held no hopes of more general political developments in Papua: 'There is always the need for sober Toryism in our guardianship of the native'.

In May 1941, when the Pacific War was imminent, Williams was made responsible for air-raid precautions in Port Moresby. Soon afterwards he enlisted in Brisbane where he served with military intelligence, compiling manuals for the Allied Geographical Section. In early 1943 he returned to Papua to serve as a liaison officer with the rank of captain in the Australian New Guinea Administrative Unit. On 12 May 1943 he was killed in a plane crash in the Owen Stanley Range. Survived by his wife and son, he was buried in a military cemetery at Bomana.

F. West, *Hubert Murray* (Melb, 1968) and (ed), *Selected letters of Hubert Murray* (Melb, 1970); E. Schwimmer (ed), *Francis Edgar Williams* (Brisb, 1976); T. Austin, *Technical training and development in Papua 1894-1941* (Canb, 1977); *Oceania*, 14, no 2, Dec 1943, p 91; D. J. F. Griffiths, The career of F. E. Williams, government anthropologist of Papua, 1922-43 (M.A. thesis, ANU, 1977); Williams papers, 1921-43 (National Archives of Papua New Guinea).   MICHAEL W. YOUNG

WILLIAMS, GEORGE DAVIES (1879-1947), naval officer and public servant, was born on 17 September 1879 at St Dogmaels, Pembrokeshire, Wales, son of John Williams, master mariner, and his wife Margretta, née Davies. Educated at St Dogmaels and Cardigan, in 1896 George followed his father into the British mercantile marine and by 1908 had become chief officer of the White Star Line training ship *Mersey*. He joined the Royal Naval Reserve in 1909 and came to Australia in 1911 to take up a post as captain superintendent of the Victorian training ship, *John Murray*. In that year he was awarded a testimonial on vellum by the Royal Humane Society, London, for having saved a youth from drowning.

Promoted lieutenant on 16 January 1913, Williams had been mobilized and was serving on loan with the Royal Australian Navy within three weeks of the outbreak of World War I. His initial appointment was to the flagship H.M.A.S. *Australia*, engaged in operations against the German territories in New

Guinea. From January to October 1916 he served in H.M.A.S. *Sydney* before reverting to the Royal Navy. Made acting lieut-commander in 1917 for meritorious service in the fleet, in 1918 he was given command of H.M.S. *Marguerite*. During 1919 he commanded the Paddle Mine Sweeping Flotilla which operated in the Aegean and Black seas. For his mine-clearance work, he was awarded the Distinguished Service Order in March 1920.

Williams returned to Australia in 1920 to be chairman of the Subordinate War Gratuity Board (Naval); later that year he assumed the position of deputy director of navigation, Navigation Branch, Sydney. His responsibilities included the conduct of courts of inquiry, the provision of pilots and the maintenance of lighthouses. On 5 May 1921 he married Helen Isabel Sheppard at St Stephen's Presbyterian Church, Sydney; they were to remain childless. From 1932 Federal and State navigational services were progressively rationalized. When the Maritime Services Board of New South Wales was formed in 1936, Williams was initially vice-president, then president from November 1937. The M.S.B. played a central role in the sesquicentenary celebrations of 1938 and Williams was appointed C.M.G. next year.

The commencement of hostilities in 1939 saw Williams seconded to Melbourne as controller of shipping and deputy chairman of the Shipping Control Board, but the organization remained dormant until 1941, by which time he had returned to his M.S.B. duties. Increased attacks on shipping in Australian waters after Japan entered the war led to the expansion of the system of convoys and escorts. A commander (R.N.R. retired list) from 1923, Williams was again posted to loan service with the R.A.N.; on 13 March 1942 he took charge of the Naval Control Service in Sydney which was responsible for the assembly of ships into convoys and for their briefings before sailing. Tall, with drawn features, cheerful, forthright and kindly, he served in this appointment until March 1946.

Survived by his wife, Williams died of osteomyelitis of the cervical vertebrae on 29 August 1947 in St Luke's Hospital, Sydney, and was buried in South Head cemetery.

S. J. Butlin, *War economy, 1939-42* (Canb, 1955); S. J. Butlin and C. B. Schedvin, *War economy, 1942-45*, 2 (Canb, 1977); *SMH*, 23 Dec 1920, 5 Oct 1932, 1 Feb 1936, 13 Nov 1937, 8 June, 12 Sept 1939, 2 Apr 1942, 30 Aug 1947; *Smith's Weekly* (Syd), 18 Nov 1939; information from Naval Hist Section, Dept of Defence (Navy Office), Canb, and from the librarian, Maritime Services Bd Reference Lib, Syd.   BOB NICHOLLS

WILLIAMS, HAROLD JOHN (1893-1976), baritone, was born on 3 September 1893 at Woollahra, Sydney, third child of Owen Williams, a Victorian-born plumber, and his Scottish wife Isabella, née Wylie. Leaving Woollahra Superior Public School at 14, Harold worked as a messenger-boy, then as a railway stores clerk. He sang with the Waverley Methodist Church choir as a boy soprano and later a baritone, but found 'football and cricket were the most absorbing affairs of my life': he played for Waverley Cricket Club (1906-15) and Rugby Union as wing three-quarter for Eastern Suburbs, representing New South Wales against New Zealand in August 1914. Of middle height, he had a sallow complexion, grey eyes and brown hair.

Enlisting in the Australian Imperial Force on 24 July 1915, Williams sailed in the *Argyllshire* in May 1916 as a corporal in the 9th Field Ambulance; his vigorous ballads were popular at shipboard entertainments. After military training in England, he was promoted sergeant in August, went to France in November 1916 and saw action at Armentières. In January 1917 he was transferred at General Sir William Birdwood's [q.v.7] request to the entertainment unit, 'Anzac Coves'. By contrivance, he rejoined the 9th Field Ambulance in March, saw action at Passchendaele and Messines, and was regimental quartermaster sergeant from December.

On leave in England in 1918, Williams sang at a private party at Sheffield; several musical luminaries insisted that he should begin lessons as soon as possible. In August he transferred to the 1st Australian Auxiliary Hospital, Harefield, where he met Dorothy Mason, a staff nurse in the Australian Army Nursing Service. He began to study in London with Charles Phillips and strove to overcome his own lack of basic musical knowledge. Attached to A.I.F. Headquarters in London from April 1919, he married Dorothy in the St Marylebone parish church on 5 May and was demobilized in July.

Reassured that he had 'a fine natural voice', Williams entered numerous competitions. Although his début recital in December at the Wigmore Hall, London, was kindly received by the critics, he remained as secretary to the Stearn Electric Lamp Co. until 1920. After ridding himself of his Australian accent, he received a great deal of musicale, concert and oratorio work throughout England. That year he began a long association with the Columbia Gramophone Co. (also recording under such names as 'Geoffrey Spencer'). He sang in the 1924 stage première of Coleridge-Taylor's *Song of Hiawatha* in London under (Sir) Eugene Goossens and, with the exception of 1929, in all later performances until 1939.

A famous Elijah in Mendelssohn's oratorio, Williams appeared with most of the greatest conductors of his time, including Toscanini, Walter, Klemperer, Barbirolli, Boult and Beecham. When in England he sang in every season of Sir Henry Wood's Promenade Concerts in 1921-51. An acclaimed performer in *The dream of Gerontius*, Williams often worked with Elgar. He sang at his memorial service in 1934, at the coronation of King George VI in 1937, and was one of sixteen soloists for whom Vaughan Williams wrote the *Serenade to music* in 1938.

Apart from his vocal beauty and musicianship, Harold Williams was renowned for his breath control and for the clarity of his diction in English music. Although the concert hall was his natural *milieu*, he also performed such roles as Iago (*Otello*), Wolfram (*Tannhäuser*) and Tonio (*Pagliacci*) with the British National Opera Company until its demise in 1929, and for sixteen seasons sang such parts as Mephistopheles (*Faust*) and Boris (*Boris Godunov*) at Covent Garden. He belonged to the Savage Club, London, took a house at Selsey, Sussex, played village and club cricket, and reputedly never missed a Test match; his friends included Alan Kippax, Stan McCabe [qq.v.9,10] and Bill O'Reilly.

Having toured Australia in 1929 for J. & N. Tait [qq.v.], Williams was urged by the Australian Broadcasting Commission to return for the Beecham tour of 1940; he was an important touring soloist throughout World War II and also taught at the New South Wales State Conservatorium of Music. When the Argonauts session was established on A.B.C. radio in 1941, Williams was 'Orpheus' and sang requests as well as the programme's theme song. He left the session temporarily in 1946 to return to Britain for the inaugural Edinburgh Festival in 1947.

In 1952 he rejoined the conservatorium staff at the request of Goossens, its director. Williams sang in opera and concerts until his voice failed him in a Melbourne performance of *Elijah* in December 1953. He once said that he had 'never overcome the onslaught of nervousness'. Although he had some notable pupils, he was not a strikingly successful teacher of voice production; further, he knew almost nothing of the Lieder repertoire and had little strength in languages. He was appointed M.B.E. in 1966 and retired in 1972. Survived by twin daughters, he died on 5 June 1976 at Gordon, Sydney, and was cremated.

W. A. Orchard, *The distant view* (Syd, 1943); I. Moresby, *Australia makes music* (Melb, 1948); L. Evans, *'Hello Mr Melody Man'* (Syd, 1983); K. S. Inglis, *This is the ABC* (Melb, 1983); *People* (Syd), 14 Dec 1955, p 35; *Referee*, 12 Aug 1914; *Table Talk*, 6 June 1929; *SMH*, 1 Oct 1934, 8 Feb 1941, 8 Apr 1944, 28 July 1949, 13 Sept 1952, 21 Dec 1953, 11 June 1966; Williams papers (NL); personal information.

JOHN CARMODY

WILLIAMS, HAROLD PARKYN (1881-1933), journalist and broadcasting pioneer, was born on 24 June 1881 at Ipswich, Queensland, son of Rev. William Henry Williams, Wesleyan clergyman, and his wife Emma, née Carroll, both English born. After leaving school, he briefly joined a firm of warehousemen, then trained as a journalist on country newspapers in New South Wales. He was editor of the Bathurst *National Advocate* and later the *Bathurst Times*. On 25 February 1911 he married Ethel Elizabeth Waite with Methodist forms at Neutral Bay, Sydney. He loved singing and conducted choral societies.

In 1911 he became foundation editor and manager of the *Land*, the weekly newspaper of the Farmers and Settlers' Association of New South Wales, which he ran for a decade. The paper's 'vigorous cartoons and spirited political articles gave new direction to the association's activities' and reflected Williams's commitment to the formation of an effective country party. During the 1922 elections he was appointed foundation general secretary of the Australian Country Party and he was to play an important part in subsequent election campaigns. Williams travelled extensively. In North and South America and South Africa on behalf of the Associated Farmers' Federation of Australia, he had investigated the formation of a world wheat pool in 1919 and he explored markets for the Australian Meat Council in 1923.

In 1924 Williams joined the Sydney 'A class' radio station 2FC and became assistant manager of New South Wales Broadcasting Ltd. When the Australian Broadcasting Co. took over in 1928 he was appointed director of news, sporting and utility services, and gave radio commentary on the news. In August 1932 he was appointed general manager of the newly established Australian Broadcasting Commission, at a salary of £2000 per annum. In a statement made at this time he declared that 'Australians should realize that they had pioneered many aspects of broadcasting, especially in the provision of utility services and in the description of sporting and other events'. He was one of the first to initiate eyewitness descriptions of horse-races by radio and in 1930 proposed cable coverage of Test cricket matches in England. As manager he prepared and presented the A.B.C.'s case before the royal commission on performing rights (1932-33).

Active in Australian Country Party and Nationalist negotiations which arranged the formation of the Bruce-Page [qq.v.7,11] ministry, Williams found that his political affiliations led to charges that he was merely a United Australia Party appointee. On 15 September 1932 J. A. Beasley gave notice in the House of Representatives that, if Labor won government, Williams should prepare to 'pack up his traps and get out rather than be pushed out'. Survived by his wife and daughter, Williams died of coronary vascular disease on 4 March 1933 at his Double Bay home, Sydney, and was cremated. He was remembered for his immense simplicity and lack of affectation, and for his ability, courtesy and sense of fairness.

U. Ellis, *A history of the Australian Country Party* (Melb, 1963); D. Aitkin, *The Country Party in New South Wales* (Canb, 1972); A. W. Thomas, *Broadcast and be damned* (Melb, 1980); K. S. Inglis, *This is the ABC* (Melb, 1983); *Land* (Syd), 27 Jan 1911; *Argus*, 6, 12 Aug 1932; *SMH*, 6, 7 Mar 1933.

MARGOT KERLEY

WILLIAMS, HARRY LLEWELLYN CARLINGTON (1915-1961), golfer, was born on 12 July 1915 at Elsternwick, Melbourne, son of Eric Llewellyn Williams, manufacturer and importer, and his wife Emma Madge Dagmar, née Halfey, both Victorian born. Educated at Brighton Grammar School, Harry began playing golf at Elsternwick at the age of 10 and was elected a junior member of Commonwealth Golf Club in 1927. He won his first monthly medal next year with a gross score equal to standard scratch and also played in the club's senior pennant team. In 1931 he resigned from Commonwealth and joined Victoria Golf Club and that year won both the Australian and Victorian amateur championships. His great rival was the New South Wales junior, Jim Ferrier: during the 1930s Williams showed his superiority by winning six of their seven individual encounters, though Ferrier beat him in the Australian Open and amateur championship in 1939.

His inheritance from his father who died in 1933, together with his mother's income from the estate of her father, enabled Williams to practise and to play continuously. He won the Victorian amateur championship again in 1934, 1935, 1936 and 1939, and the Australian amateur for the second time in 1937. He never won the Australian Open, but was runner-up to Gene Sarazen from the United States of America in 1936. Urged by Sarazen to go to the U.S.A. as a professional, Williams refused. Apparently his mother, a possessive woman, dissuaded him from taking up an offer which would probably have made him a millionaire, as she did his touring Great Britain with an Australian team in 1938. Perhaps his heart was not in the game. In one competition against 'bogey', he is said to have

been 8 up after nine holes, when he left for the races, marking a loss against the remaining nine—though in the event his score of 'one down' left him the winner. Tall and lean, Williams hit a very long ball and was in 1937 —in Sarazen's judgement—the greatest left-hander in the world and the greatest Australia had produced.

Chronic asthma cut short Williams's army service with the Citizen Military Forces (1940-42) and he did not play golf seriously after World War II. He and his mother seem to have been poor financial managers, and the family fortune dwindled as rising prices, the turf, alcohol and unemployment took their toll. He died with his mother by carbon monoxide poisoning in their flat at East Kew on 13 December 1961. Harry Williams was cremated at Springvale.

D. Lawrence, *Victoria Golf Club 1903-1988* (Syd, 1988); *Age*, 15 Dec 1961; *Sun* (Syd), 8 Jan 1980; *Herald* (Melb), 4 Jan 1986.

A. G. L. SHAW

WILLIAMS, HENRY ROBERTS (1848-1935), mining director and politician, was born in 1848 at St Just, Cornwall, England, son of William Lanyon Williams, miner, and his wife Elizabeth, née Roberts. With his mother he arrived in Victoria in 1860 and settled at Sandhurst (Bendigo), where his father had pioneered quartz mining and opened up the Williams United mine. As a young man, Henry gained practical experience both underground and as an engine driver in his father's mine; he studied at night at Bendigo High School and received private tuition. In 1874 he became manager of the mine and invested widely in mining companies in the boom of the early 1880s.

Elected to the Eaglehawk borough council in 1874, Williams was also president of the Bendigo National Reform League. In May 1877 he was returned to the Legislative Assembly as member for Mandurang. A staunch supporter of (Sir) Graham Berry [q.v.3], he was minister for mines in Berry's government from August 1880 to July 1881. In 1878 Williams had been a member of the Victorian crown lands commission of inquiry which examined the workings of the 1869 Land Act. Defeated in 1883, he failed to win Sandhurst in a by-election that year and Mandurang in 1885. After the Mandurang electorate was divided, Williams represented the new mining constituency of Eaglehawk in 1889-1902. He was minister of railways and vice-president of the Board of Land and Works (1894-99), and minister of health (1895-99) in the Turner [q.v.] government. During his parliamentary career he sat on ten different royal commissions, select committees and boards of inquiry. Defeated by the Kyabram Reform Movement's candidate Hay Kirkwood in 1902, he again stood unsuccessfully in 1908.

Committed to miners' welfare, in 1879 Williams had opposed the attempt of the major Bendigo mine-owner, George Lansell [q.v.5], to reduce wages. Following his election to parliament Williams sought to reform the practice of tributing in mines: in 1897 he helped to have the Mines Act amended in order to introduce a subsistence wage for tributers. When moves were made to repeal this section in 1902, he called upon miners to insist on their rights, claiming that, as a mine-owner and director, he had always paid tributers full wages. Williams supported other liberal initiatives: he argued for an old-age pension that was more than 'a mere starvation allowance', supported the extension of the franchise to women in 1902 and condemned the sacking of married women teachers.

Like many of his fellow Cornish migrants at Bendigo, Williams was a practising Methodist and a vigorous temperance campaigner. A leading Freemason, he was a justice of the peace and a councillor of the Bendigo School of Mines. He was twice married at Eaglehawk: to Kate Gruby (d. 1891) with Presbyterian forms on 11 June 1878, and to Louisa Cyrena Davidson with Methodist forms on 5 December 1892. Williams died at Murrumbeena, Melbourne, on 12 November 1935 and was buried in Eaglehawk cemetery. His wife survived him, as did four daughters and a son of his first marriage.

G. Mackay, *The history of Bendigo* (Melb, 1891); W. B. Kimberly, *Bendigo and its vicinity* (Ballarat, 1895); J. Smith (ed), *Cyclopedia of Victoria*, 1 (Melb, 1903); *Argus* and *Bendigo Advertiser*, 14 Nov 1935.
                                        CHARLES FAHEY

WILLIAMS, MARY BOYD BURFITT (1882-1956), physician and pathologist, was born on 9 November 1882 at Redfern, Sydney, fifth child of native-born Charles Trimby Burfitt, auctioneer, and his Irish wife Annie, née Fitzmaurice. After a parish primary education, Mary was awarded a scholarship to St Mary's College, Rosebank. She followed her two elder brothers Walter [q.v.7] and James to the University of Sydney (B.A., 1905; B.Sc., 1908; M.B., 1909; Ch.M., 1910), gaining Professor Haswell's [q.v.9] prize for zoology and sharing the Renwick [q.v.6] scholarship for general proficiency.

Graduating in 1909 with first-class honours, Burfitt was appointed resident medical officer at Royal Prince Alfred Hospital where, with Elsie Dalyell, she succeeded Jessie Aspinall [qq.v.8,7]. When an attempt was made to

curtail their treatment of males, the women called on Professor (Sir) Thomas Anderson Stuart [q.v.] who promised them his support. They found that those who opposed their professional advancement were not the male doctors, but members of the nursing staff and laywomen. Mary was the first woman to become senior resident at the hospital. Interested in pathology, in 1911 she presented to the Australasian Medical Congress one of the earliest accounts of blood culture from living patients.

That year Dr Burfitt applied for residency at the Women's Hospital, Crown Street, Surry Hills, to gain obstetric experience. Opposition to her application by the hospital secretary and some women on the hospital board led to the publication of several articles on the controversy in the *Evening News*. The other candidate withdrew because of Burfitt's superior academic record. Mary rented a room in an Albion Street terrace house adjacent to the hospital and arranged at her own expense for a telephone connexion between her bedroom and the hospital.

On completing her residency at Crown Street, Burfitt built up a large general practice at Glebe (1912-24), and served as honorary physician (1912-38) at Lewisham Hospital where she established the pathology department and served as honorary pathologist. On 19 January 1921 at St James's Catholic Church, Forest Lodge, she married Grosvenor John Williams who had graduated in medicine in 1916. She was a consulting physician in Macquarie Street in 1924-52.

A founder and councillor (1929-53) of Sancta Sophia College, University of Sydney, she was also president of the University Catholic Women's Association. Survived by her husband and by three sons who followed her into medical practice, she died on 30 November 1956 at Bellevue Hill and was buried in Waverley cemetery.

MJA, 11 May 1957; information from Dr G. Burfitt-Williams, Syd, and Dr W. Burfitt-Williams, Mudgee, NSW.
                                        ROSSLYN FINN

WILLIAMS, SIR RICHARD (1890-1980), air force officer and aviation administrator, was born on 3 August 1890 at Moonta Mines, South Australia, eldest child of Richard Williams, miner, and his wife Emily, née Hodge. Educated to junior secondary level at Moonta Public School, Richard was employed as a telegraph messenger, then as a bank clerk. Aged 19, he enlisted in the South Australian Infantry Regiment, Australian Military Forces, and was commissioned in 1911. To achieve his objective of a commission in the permanent forces, he went in September 1912 as a sergeant to a special school of instruction at Albury, New South Wales. Three months later he was promoted lieutenant, Administrative and Instructional Staff. On 17 August 1914 he attended the first war-flying course held at the Central Flying School, Point Cook, Victoria. Instruction lasted three months; on its completion, he and the three other graduates rejoined their units. Williams performed administrative duties until July 1915 when he returned to Point Cook for two months advanced aviation training. Expecting to depart for India at short notice, on 21 August he married 38-year-old Constance Esther Griffiths (d. 1948) with Methodist forms at the Collins Street Congregational Church, Melbourne. They were to remain childless.

Late in 1915 the decision was made to raise a complete Australian unit for service with the Royal Flying Corps. Appointed captain in the Australian Imperial Force on 5 January 1916, Williams was posted as a flight commander to No.1 Squadron, Australian Flying Corps. The squadron's members arrived in Egypt in April. Initially dispersed among R.F.C. units, they began operations as a separate entity in December, supporting the Egyptian Expeditionary Force in the advance towards Palestine. Early in 1917 Williams exhibited conspicuous gallantry, when, under anti-aircraft fire, he attacked and scattered Turkish troops; on another occasion he rescued a pilot shot down behind enemy lines. He was awarded the Distinguished Service Order. Given command of No.1 Squadron in May, 'Dicky' supported his officers in a vigorous mess life, though he was abstemious in his own habits. His dealings with his subordinates were formal, correct and fair, and earned him respect. Twice mentioned in dispatches in January 1918, he was promoted temporary lieut-colonel on 28 June and seconded to command the 40th (Army) Wing, Palestine Brigade, R.F.C. Comprising his own and three British squadrons, the wing had been formed five months earlier.

After a brief period as temporary brigade commander, Williams was appointed O.B.E. in January 1919. His war service was to be further recognized with his appointment (1920) to the Order of the Nahda by the King of the Hejaz. From March to October 1919 he was staff officer, aviation, at A.I.F. Headquarters, London. His duties entailed liaising with British authorities on the organization and equipment required for a proposed Australian air force. Returning home, he was made brevet lieut-colonel, A.M.F., on 5 January 1920 and sat on a board of navy and army officers tasked with developing a policy for the new force: he was the army's aviation specialist; the navy was represented by Major S. J. Goble [q.v.9]. Because the army continued the project, Williams had free rein and

a strong influence on its outcome. In November an Air Board, similar to the existing Naval and Military boards, was established; Williams was senior member and Goble next in authority; both had the rank of wing commander.

At the Air Board's first meeting, Williams tabled proposals for the establishment of the (Royal) Australian Air Force and had the satisfaction of seeing his new service come into being on 31 March 1921. His position as first air member was circumscribed. To compensate for his comparative youthfulness and assumed lack of administrative experience, and in an attempt to achieve a 'compromise between exclusive control of Australian air power by either the army or the navy', an Air Council had been formed in 1920 to oversee the board. Positioned administratively between the board and the minister for defence, the council ensured that the air force was kept to an auxiliary role. Tension between the services, financial stringency, an emphasis on navy in Imperial defence planning and the perception of a low risk of war—all hindered Williams's efforts to formulate air power doctrine and to create a separate identity for the R.A.A.F., as well as contributing to his personal conflict with Goble. His title was changed to chief of the Air Staff in 1922. Next year he attended the British Army Staff College, Camberley, and spent six months at the Royal Air Force Staff College, Andover, graduating from both.

Promoted group captain on 1 July 1925, Williams was immediately embroiled in controversy over the navy's plan, which Goble had sanctioned in his absence, to establish a fleet air arm. Considering that the proposal would have weakened the air force, he manoeuvred skilfully and succeeded in having it shelved. Between September and December 1926, with a co-pilot and mechanic, he flew a seaplane on a round trip from Point Cook, along the Australian east coast to Papua, New Guinea, New Britain and the Solomon Islands. The object of the flight was to study the area from a defence point of view and to gain experience in operating away from base. For accomplishing the feat without serious incident or delay, he was appointed C.B.E. in 1927. Having acted in the rank since April, he was promoted air commodore on 1 July. Three weeks later he took off on a flight around Australia; after covering an additional leg from Adelaide to Tennant Creek, he again returned safely. During the Depression, amid urgings by senior navy and army officers, in 1929 and 1932 successive governments considered the abolition of the air force as a separate service. Having weathered the crises, in 1933 Williams attended the Imperial Defence College, London.

On 1 January 1935 he was promoted air

vice marshal, finally gaining equivalent rank with the other service chiefs. In May he was appointed C.B. That year the minister for defence (Sir) Archdale Parkhill [q.v.11] contemplated manning three new squadrons (approved as part of general rearmament) with members of the Citizen Air Force. Williams resisted stoutly and won the day. He and Parkhill worked together more harmoniously to foster the development of the Australian aircraft industry: the Commonwealth Aircraft Corporation was formed in 1936.

Meanwhile, the entry into service of new aircraft and technology stretched the resources of existing personnel. This problem, together with an increase in flying hours, resulted in a higher number of accidents. Responding to pressure in parliament and from the press, the government invited Marshal of the R.A.F. Sir Edward Ellington to report on the organization and efficiency of the Australian air force. Williams clashed with Ellington whose report of July 1938 was released to the newspapers before senior R.A.A.F. officers had seen it. Although he found that organization and development had been sound, Ellington criticized the administration of operational training. The Air Board challenged his conclusions and cast doubt on his figures which showed that the R.A.A.F. accident rate in relation to flying hours had been higher than that of the R.A.F. Armed with information from Goble that the chief of the Air Staff had been responsible for operational training, the Lyons [q.v.10] government announced that Williams would be sent abroad for two years duty with the R.A.F. to broaden his experience. He learned of the decision in the press.

After a short attachment to the Air Ministry, early in 1939 he became air officer in charge of administration at Coastal Command headquarters, R.A.F. War with Germany began on 3 September and in February 1940 Williams came back to Australia to be air member for organization and equipment. J. V. Fairbairn [q.v.8], minister for air, had wanted him to be chief of the Air Staff, but Prime Minister (Sir) Robert Menzies decided that a senior R.A.F. officer—Air Marshal Sir Charles Burnett—should command the R.A.A.F. On taking up their appointments in March, Burnett was promoted air chief marshal and Williams temporary air marshal. To Williams's chagrin, the government acquiesced in Burnett's policy of using the Australian air force as a reservoir for the R.A.F., thereby denying it the corporate identity enjoyed by the A.I.F. In October 1941 Williams arrived in London to set up and command R.A.A.F. Overseas Headquarters, an administrative centre for the increasing number of personnel serving in Europe and the Middle East. When the Japanese attacked

Pearl Harbour, Hawaii, on 7 December, he was swiftly recalled. His expectation that he would succeed Burnett was not realized and from 1942 he served for the remainder of the war as R.A.A.F. representative, Washington, D.C.

Williams had been given 'the principal hand in establishing Australia's Air Force' and had justly earned the title of 'father' of the R.A.A.F. Yet his 'seventeen years of resisting attacks by the army and the navy, of coping with inert, economy-minded governments, and generally handling the unspectactular job of building an air force in peacetime' had been taxing. He had fought strenuously for his service and had not been above the use of subterfuge to advance its interests. His acrimonious relationship with Goble and the occasional, unavoidable friction with politicians, senior public servants and fellow uniformed officers had left their legacies. Although noted for his courtesy, ready smile and sparkling eyes, Williams was 'not a too-forgiving man'. It would have befitted the end of his career had he led the air force in World War II, but Prime Minister Curtin had refused to consider him. Williams later claimed in his autobiography, *These are facts* (Canberra, 1977), that the secretary for defence (Sir) Frederick Shedden had informed Curtin of his rift with Goble to discredit him.

Ceasing duty in June 1946 to become director-general of civil aviation, Williams retired from the R.A.A.F. on 14 September. In this new role he supervised the expansion of domestic and international commercial aviation during the post-war years. His department created the network of airfields, communications and related support services required by the industry, while maintaining an enviable safety record. He was appointed K.B.E. in 1954. On his retirement next year, he joined the board of Tasman Empire Airways Ltd. Federal president (from 1940) of the Air Force Association, he used that institution to stimulate public debate on the future of air power in Australia's defence. He was a member of the Naval and Military, and Athenaeum clubs, Melbourne.

On 7 February 1950 at Wesley Church, Melbourne, Williams had married 49-year-old Lois Victoria Cross. Predeceased by her, he died on 7 February 1980 in St George's Hospital, Kew, and was cremated. Some seven hundred mourners had attended his air force funeral and seventeen aircraft flew past. Septimus Power's [q.v.11] portrait (1924) of Williams is in the Australian War Memorial, Canberra.

F. M. Cutlack, *The Australian Flying Corps* (Syd, 1923); L. W. Sutherland, *Aces and kings* (Syd, 1935); J. Herington, *Air war against Germany and Italy 1939-1943* (Canb, 1954); D. N. Gillison, *Royal*

Australian Air Force 1939-1942 (Canb, 1962); L. J. Wackett, *Aircraft pioneers* (Syd, 1972); J. M. McCarthy, *Australia and Imperial defence 1918-39* (Brisb, 1976), and *A last call of Empire* (Canb, 1988); J. E. Hewitt, *Adversity in success* (Melb, 1980), and *The black one* (Melb, 1984); D. M. Horner, *High command* (Canb, 1982), and (ed), *The commanders* (Syd, 1984); H. Rayner, *Scherger* (Canb, 1984); *Aircraft* (Melb), Mar 1980; *Canb Times*, 8 Feb 1980.   A. D. GARRISSON

WILLIAMS, ROBERT ERNEST (1855-1943), teacher, journalist, town clerk and soldier, was born on 13 August 1855 at Ballarat, Victoria, son of English-born Robert Williams and his Welsh wife Catherine, née Newman, both schoolteachers. In 1852 they had migrated to Ballarat where Robert failed as a miner and a farmer. An adventurous boy, the second of ten children, Ernest left school at 11 to run errands. He became a clerk, then trained and worked as a teacher for about ten years. On 4 June 1884 he married Annie Clara de Hylton at St Paul's Anglican Church, Ballarat.

In 1881 Williams had switched to journalism on the *Ballarat Courier*, of which he became editor in 1889. A humane radical-liberal, he gave trenchant support to labour during the 1890s strikes. He prompted Alfred Deakin and (Sir) Alexander Peacock [qq.v.8,11] on such issues as the basic wage and old-age pensions, and promoted Ballarat as 'Golden City'. Like locally-born contemporaries in the South Street Debating Society, he read omnivorously and enjoyed discussion. He championed his friend G. E. Morrison when Bishop Thornton [qq.v.10,6] belittled his criticism of missionaries in China. Williams held racist and imperialist views, but supported colonial independence.

Of average height, tough and wiry, with a strong forehead and nose, piercing eyes and a flashing smile, Williams was genial company. Despite his intellect, he was essentially a man of action. He loved cricket, golf, hiking and riding. In 1881 he had enrolled in the Ballarat militia, which thereafter shaped the way he thought and organized. He topped a Victorian officers' course, was commissioned in 1884 and rose quickly to become lieut-colonel (1895) commanding the 3rd Battalion (Ballarat Rifles). From 1907 to 1911 he was colonel in charge of the 2nd Infantry Brigade. Scornful of humbug and pretence, and distrustful of staff officers, Williams prized local autonomy and efficiency. He challenged officers to bring out 'the natural and acquired qualities, powers and resources of soldiers'. Although approachable, he expected high standards and delighted in rivalling crack British regiments at rifle-shooting, marching and drill. Frustration galled him in 1900 when the *Ballarat Courier* would not release him to lead Victoria's South African contingent.

Appointed town clerk of Ballarat West in 1902, Williams promoted the city, advocated decentralization, organized visits by celebrities and masterminded the erection at Ballarat of Victoria's major memorial to the South African War. He was made a justice of the peace in 1911.

On 26 July 1915, during the peak of Australian Imperial Force enlistments, Senator (Sir) George Pearce [q.v.11] recalled Williams from the reserve and, with a day's notice, made him commandant of military forces in Victoria. Against opposition from permanent staff, Williams reformed the Broadmeadows camp, routed its prostitutes, and decentralized the accommodation and administration of 100 000 troops under training. He transformed attitudes to venereal disease by treating it as a medical issue, cleaned up the camp at Langwarrin and encouraged its demoralized inmates; outstanding results were achieved at that military base when he put a young Gallipoli veteran, Lieutenant W. T. Conder [q.v.8], in charge. By far the best State commandant, Williams was mentioned in dispatches, appointed C.M.G. (1917) and promoted from brigadier to major general. At the end of hostilities he was appointed to boards and commissions that dealt with price-fixing, the property of aliens and the influenza scourge.

Returning to Ballarat in 1919, Williams resigned from the position of town clerk and accepted an invitation from Theodore Fink [q.v.8] to write leaders for the Melbourne *Herald*, of which Williams became a director (1923-35). Sent on the Commonwealth government's relief mission in 1923, he cabled reports on the Yokohama earthquake. Japan excited him, as later did Mussolini's civic reforms. In the *Herald* Williams ventilated long-standing concerns about slum clearance, the subservience of the Australian Army to the British, and the importance of physical training for youths.

In the 1930s Williams wrote many charming reminiscences for the *Ballarat Courier* and a lively history, *The old Third and the new Seventh* (1935). Much affected by his wife's death in 1918, he became withdrawn and egotistical, a Dickensian figure in a charcoal-grey raincoat and bowler hat. Survived by a son and a daughter, he died on 7 July 1943 at St Kilda, Melbourne, and was cremated.

M. M. McCallum, *Ballarat and district citizens and sports at home and abroad* (Ballarat, 1916); E. Scott, *Australia during the war* (Syd, 1936); W. Bate, *Lucky city* (Melb, 1978); *Newspaper News* (Syd), 1 May 1935; *Punch* (Melb), 29 June 1916; *Herald* (Melb), 3 Apr 1935, 8 July 1943;

Ballarat Courier, 8 July 1943; family papers (held by Mrs K. Nailer, Fitzroy, Melb).

WESTON BATE

WILLIAMS, SUSANNAH JANE (1875-1942), classical scholar and educationist, was born on 15 September 1875 at Castlemaine, Victoria, second daughter of Edward David Williams, a grocer from Wales who later entered the Legislative Assembly, and his native-born wife Jane, née Jones. Having attended (Sir) James McCay's [q.v.10] Castlemaine Grammar School, Susie was a resident at Trinity College Hostel, University of Melbourne (B.A., 1897); she was Annie Grice scholar (1894-95) and gained first-class honours in classics and comparative philology. In England, at Newnham College, Cambridge (1897-1900), she produced brilliant work, but completed the classical tripos with an upper second; during one vacation she had toured Greece and Asia Minor and in 1897-98 read archaeology at the University of London.

Back home, Miss Williams tutored in classics at Trinity College, University of Melbourne, and from 1902 taught English and classics at Melbourne Church of England Girls' Grammar School, becoming chief of staff in 1908. From 1914 she again tutored at Trinity; her teaching was enhanced by her beautiful voice. In 1919, as acting principal at Trinity College Hostel, she directed expansion and refurbishing.

In June that year Miss Williams succeeded Louisa Macdonald [q.v.10] as principal of the non-denominational Women's College, University of Sydney; with forty students it was the largest and oldest university women's college in Australia. Some councillors had feared that an Australian would limit its 'cultural outlook', but all had been impressed by her credentials.

As principal, Miss Williams acted on her belief that able women should attend university, in accommodation equal to men's, with good food and exercise, and with civilized surroundings. Although funds were short, the college expanded to house seventy students. Its somewhat Edwardian atmosphere dissipated as regulations were relaxed; students took over administrative duties and were encouraged in extra-scholastic activities and community work.

Vice-president of the Sydney University Social Service Society, president of the Sydney University Women Graduates' Association and a committee-member of many university associations, Miss Williams was a practising Congregationalist who arranged through the Sydney University Christian Union for students to study and discuss public questions. She was founding president of the Women Justices' Association of New South Wales and also served on the national board of the Young Women's Christian Association, the executive committee of the National Council of Women of New South Wales and the board of the Rachel Forster Hospital for Women and Children.

'Of distinguished appearance', Miss Williams seemed reserved and intellectually intimidating to some students, but her kindness was unreserved. Her conversation was wide-ranging, cultured and stimulating. On her retirement in 1935, she left her successor a buoyant institution; its new wing (1937) was named after her. She cut short a visit to England in 1936 when pressed to become temporary principal of University Women's College, Melbourne; she remained there until 1938. Suffering from progressive muscular atrophy from 1940, she shared a Melbourne cottage with her old friend Emma Christina ('Dolly') Tonks. Susie Williams died on 27 May 1942 at Castlemaine and was cremated; her portrait by W. B. McInnes [q.v.10] is held by University Women's College.

W. V. Hole and A. H. Treweeke, *The history of the Women's College within the University of Sydney* (Syd, 1953); E. I. Lothian, *University Women's College, University of Melbourne* (Melb, 1955); L. Gardiner, *Janet Clarke Hall 1886-1986* (Melb, 1986); Univ Syd Union, *Union Recorder*, May-June 1942; *SMH*, 10 Apr 1920, 7 Oct 1922, 6 June 1925, 24 Feb 1926, 21 Mar 1930, 8 Nov 1933, 15 Dec 1938; *Sydney Mail*, 13 Nov 1929; *Herald* (Melb), 21 Oct 1936; Trinity College Hostel 1919: an unofficial record (ms, held by Janet Clarke Hall, Univ Melb); S. J. Williams diaries (held by Mrs H. Vellacott, Castlemaine, Vic).

PATRICIA HORNER

WILLIAMS, SIR WILLIAM DANIEL CAMPBELL (1856-1919), surgeon and soldier, was born on 30 July 1856 in Sydney, eldest child of William James Williams, medical practitioner, and his wife Ellen Ann, née Titterton, both English born. Educated at the New School, Sydney, and Sydney Grammar School, Williams went to London to study medicine at University College (M.R.C.S., 1879; L.R.C.P., 1880). After a years internship at its hospital, he returned to Sydney and practised at Darlinghurst. Williams was appointed honorary surgeon at St Vincent's Hospital in 1885. He had married Florence Severn on 21 June 1881 at the parish church, Lee, Kent; they were to have two sons and a daughter.

In 1883 Williams became staff surgeon of the New South Wales Artillery with the rank of captain. He enjoyed soldiering and was dedicated to developing army medical services. The embarkation of the New South Wales contingent to join the British force in the Sudan in 1885 enabled him, as its principal medical officer, to test his ideas and observe the medical arrangements of an army in the field. That year Williams was promoted major, mentioned in a special dispatch and awarded the Khedive's Star. He also trained at Aldershot, England, and qualified as an instructor in army medical services.

Back in Australia he was made P.M.O. of the army in New South Wales. Based on his advice, the reorganized medical service in 1888-91 included a well-trained Permanent Medical Staff Corps. They were equipped with light ambulance wagons, built to Williams's innovative design, which had attracted attention in the Sudan and which were more advanced than those in the British Army. He also proposed mounted stretcher-bearers for mounted units, lighter stretchers and intensive training for those using them, and he insisted that medical units in the field must be 'under one command . . . possess adequate and trained reserves and an ample reserve of equipment'. Major General (Sir) Edward Hutton [q.v.9], commandant in New South Wales in 1893-96, extolled the excellent organization, high standard of efficiency and enthusiasm of all ranks in the New South Wales army medical service.

On the outbreak of war in South Africa in 1899 Williams mobilized two medical contingents of the New South Wales Army Medical Corps, trained, equipped and ready for active service. When they went into the field they created a sensation due to their mobility and to the excellence of their ambulances and transport. In fast-moving mounted operations Williams's mounted stretcher-bearers kept up with the units they were supporting; unlike the British medical commanders, he kept his field hospitals and bearer companies working together. He thus anticipated the field ambulance system which was introduced into the British and Australian armies in 1906. Made temporary colonel in South Africa, in January 1900 Williams was appointed P.M.O. of the Australian and New Zealand forces serving there. He was present at the relief of Kimberley and Sunnyside, and was variously P.M.O. to Hutton's Mounted Division and to major forces under Colonel (General Sir) Ian Hamilton and Lieut-General Sir Archibald Hunter. A British war correspondent described Williams as 'the first man I have met who seems to be a master of Army medical work in the field'. For his service in South Africa, Williams was promoted surgeon general in January 1901, mentioned in dispatches and appointed C.B. He was also appointed a Knight of Grace of the Order of St John of Jerusalem.

Coming home in January 1901, he resumed his practice and his work at St Vincent's Hospital. In January 1902 Hutton arrived as general officer commanding in Australia with a brief to organize an Australian Army. He appointed Williams director general of medical services from 1 April 1902, with the task of creating the Australian Army Medical Corps from the disparate and small colonial services. Although he was appointed consultant surgeon to St Vincent's Hospital in Melbourne when he moved to that city to begin work at Army Headquarters, Williams virtually ceased private practice. His organization of the A.A.M.C. was achieved within the narrow limits imposed by defence policy and funding. As surgeon general, Williams was the only regular officer of the A.A.M.C. He established the units which would operate with a field force, but was unable to set up clearing hospitals and base hospitals. He did establish the Australian Army Nursing Service and a reserve of officers, but his proposal of 1906 for a dental service was rejected. Despite inadequate resources, from the beginning he aimed at a high standard of training. The advent of 'universal' military service in 1911 increased the number of units in the A.A.M.C., yet it did not remedy the shortages of ambulances and equipment.

In August 1914 Williams asked for the post of director of medical services with the Australian Imperial Force. 'Without egotism', he wrote, 'I can safely say that my services would be of great value'. Major General (Sir) William Bridges [q.v.7] agreed and 'Mo' Williams made ready for his third war. He was 58, overweight and in poor health. The degree to which 'his outlook had become self-contained and restricted by immersion in the past' is arguable, but there is no doubt that 'he made a bad impression on Bridges' during the voyage to Egypt. C. E. W. Bean [q.v.7], who was with A.I.F. Headquarters, thought that Williams treated the voyage 'rather as he might a month at his club'. Bridges increasingly turned to the dynamic Lieut-Colonel (Sir) Neville Howse [q.v.9] who was Williams's staff officer.

By going on to London in November 1914, Williams weakened his position. While he did valuable work there—buying motor ambulances, medical equipment and drugs for the A.I.F.—the fact that Bridges allowed him to go was significant. Williams returned to Egypt in February 1915 and encountered an embarrassing situation. No one wanted him. The British D.M.S. in Egypt, Major General Sir Richard Ford, expected to have direct control of all A.A.M.C. units. Bridges neither supported Williams against Ford, nor ensured that a medical section was established in the Australian Intermediate Base under Colonel V. C. M. Sellheim [q.v.11]. With one staff sergeant and one clerk, Williams was isolated, without status or responsibility. Bridges had him attached to the office of the D.M.S., Egypt, for Anzac affairs and Williams suffered the humiliation of being graded by the War Office as a deputy director of medical services. He was even excluded from discussions on the provision of hospital ships for the A.I.F.

On 25 April he again embarked for London. There he made arrangements for A.I.F. convalescents and introduced a system for invaliding to Australia. On his return voyage he received a cable in Malta stating 'that his services were not required in Egypt'. Frustrated and embittered, Williams was ordered back to London where he was attached to the Australian High Commission and had little to do. In September his former staff officer Howse was appointed deputy director of medical services, Anzac Corps, and became D.M.S. of the A.I.F. in November. Williams was totally eclipsed. After Howse arrived in London in April 1916, Williams was soon able to return to Australia. His appointment as K.C.M.G. in June and a mention in dispatches may have mitigated a little the harshness of his fate. In declining health he decided to return to his wife in London in December and was placed on the army retired list on 1 January 1917.

Williams was a great pioneer. He was also the victim of extraordinary circumstances. The nebulous status of the A.I.F. and the attitude of British senior officers to 'colonial' forces were aggravated by the failure of his own commander to support him. Bridges was so obsessed with the training of his 1st Division that he deliberately tried to avoid the administrative problems of the A.I.F. With Williams set adrift, 'the medical problems of the A.I.F. were not the recognized business of anyone in particular' until late in 1915.

After returning alone to Melbourne, Williams died of cardiac disease on 10 May 1919 in Caulfield Military Hospital. Survived by his wife and children, he was buried in Brighton cemetery with full military honours. His estate was sworn for probate at only £540.

Aust Defence Dept, *Official records of the Australian military contingents to the war in South Africa*, P. L. Murray ed (Melb, 1911); C. E. W. Bean, *The story of Anzac*, 1, 2 (Syd, 1921, 1924) and *The A.I.F. in France*, 1916 (Syd, 1929) and *Two men I knew* (Syd, 1957); A. G. Butler (ed), *Official history of the Australian Army Medical Services in the war of 1914-1918* (Melb, 1938); J. Gurner, *The origins of the Royal Australian Army Medical Corps* (Melb, 1970); R. L. Wallace, *The Australians at the Boer War* (Canb, 1976); *MJA*, 31 May 1919, 17 Apr 1948; *Aust Army J*, Oct 1958.   A. J. HILL

WILLIAMS, WILLIAM HENRY (1852-1941), scholar and critic, was born on 7 November 1852 at Kings Norton, Worcestershire, England, son of William Williams, merchant's clerk, and his wife Amelia Burley, née Arden. He attended Newark Grammar School and entered Trinity College, Cambridge, in 1872. The award of a sizarship helped him through an academically distinguished career in which he gained a foundation scholarship, an English declamation prize, the New Testament Greek prize and the Jeston exhibition. He graduated with first-class honours in the classical tripos (B.A., 1876; M.A., 1879) and became assistant master and senior classics master at Leys School, Cambridge, until 1883.

In 1884 Williams took up the headmastership of Newington College, Sydney. The school's authorities described him as 'essentially a scholar of liberal outlook' who broadened the curriculum in arts and science. In 1885 he established Newington's first science laboratory. He believed that college education should include 'some of the graces and amenities of life without neglecting the realities'. In 1892 the college council decided that the combined position of governor and headmaster should be held by a clergyman. Williams resigned his post.

In 1894 he became a lecturer and in 1896 the foundation professor of classics and English literature at the newly established University of Tasmania. He occupied the chair until his retirement in 1925. During part of that time he was dean of the faculty of arts and chairman of the professorial board. In March 1926 he was made professor emeritus. He was also a trustee of the State Library of Tasmania from 1921 to 1936.

Although Williams wrote no books, he edited or wrote introductions to twenty-five publications. These included editions of Thackeray and Dryden, and notes on *Twelfth night*, *Macbeth*, *King Lear* and *The tempest*. The majority, however, concentrated on pre-Shakespearian works and support E. Morris Miller's [q.v.10] claim that Williams was an authority on Elizabethan and pre-Elizabethan English. Giving emphasis to dramatists, Williams paid special attention to Udall's *Ralph Roister Doister* which he edited with P. A. Robin in 1901. He published three other articles on this comedy and also made a case for Udall's authorship of *Jacke Jugeler* which Williams edited in Hobart from photographs of the original owned by the duke of Devonshire. In 1905 Williams contributed the introduction and notes to the Clarendon Press publication, *Specimens of English drama*. In addition to writing on Chaucer, Langland and Marlowe, he also edited classical texts.

On 7 April 1883 Williams had married Ethel Swindells (d. 1926) at St Luke's parish church, Chesterton, Cambridgeshire. They had two sons and a daughter. On 19 June 1931 Williams married Ruth Mary Newbery in the Davey Street Congregational Church,

Hobart. Survived by her, and by the sons of his first marriage, he died at St Anne's Rest Home, Hobart, on 12 September 1941. He was buried with his first wife in the Primitive Methodist section of Cornelian Bay cemetery.

Univ Tas, *Calendar*, 1927, 1932; *T&CJ*, 7 July 1888; *Mercury*, 13 Sept 1941; S. G. Claughton, Biog sketch of W. H. Williams (ts, held by *ADB*, Canb); Univ Tas Archives.   J. C. HORNER

WILLIAMSON, FRANCIS SAMUEL (1865-1936), poet and schoolteacher, was born on 18 January 1865 at Fitzroy, Melbourne, son of English-born William Williamson, coachmaker, and his Scottish wife Mary Ann, née McCoy. After completing his schooling at Scotch College, Melbourne, he was appointed in 1882 a pupil-teacher with the Education Department at Flemington State School. He resigned in 1884 when at North Melbourne State School.

In 1888-94 Williamson taught at Wesley College, Melbourne. A popular junior master, he was inclined to give his classes a singsong instead of formal work 'whenever the cheerful whim or the occasional hangover made him rebel at orthodox behaviour'. 'Long Bill' was regarded as 'the epitome of the easy-going school' which A. S. Way [q.v.6], the headmaster, saw 'dimly and kindly through his thick spectacles'. Sir Frederic Eggleston [q.v.8] was more severe: while a good poet who inspired many boys with a love of poetry, Williamson 'was irregular and though he was kept on for many years . . . became almost an outcast'. In 1894 he joined A. H. S. Lucas's [q.v.10] staff at Newington College, Sydney, but returned to Wesley in 1902. Apart from his usual classroom duties, Williamson participated in rowing, cricket and the cadets until the end of 1904 when he was dismissed, apparently for drunkenness.

Over six feet (182.9 cm) tall and well proportioned, Williamson 'carried himself like the proverbial lord'. A 'golden talker', he belonged—with Bernard O'Dowd, Marie Pitt, Frederick Sinclaire [qq.v.11] and others—to a discussion group called 'The Heretics'. In 1912 a collection of Williamson's poetry, *Purple and gold*, named after Wesley's colours, was published by T. C. Lothian [q.v.10]. It contained twenty-eight poems: two relating to the school, 'Before the Boat Race' and 'Flag Song', were set to music by the headmaster L. A. Adamson [q.v.7] and printed in the *Wesley College song book*. Williamson's most famous poem, 'The Magpie's Song', which appeared in several anthologies in the 1920s and 1930s, had been published in *Purple and gold*. A 1940 edition of this book, enlarged to fifty-five poems by

R. H. Croll, was introduced by Sir John Latham [qq.v.8,10] who saw in Williamson's poems 'a lyrical quality of delicate beauty'.

After 1905 Williamson spent the remainder of his career as a temporary head teacher in the Education Department, usually staying a few months only, never in the same school twice, and at places as far apart as Lavers Hill and Bonang, though the majority of his appointments were in Gippsland. Between 1905 and 1930 he was head teacher in fifty-four rural schools. Following his retirement, Williamson was given a Commonwealth literary pension. His last years were spent in Melbourne where he died on 6 February 1936 and was cremated. He never married. Percival Serle [q.v.11] considered him a strange case of an educated man writing a fair amount of verse of small merit until in middle life 'something blossomed in him and he wrote half a dozen quite beautiful poems'.

R. H. Croll, *I recall* (Melb, 1939); G. Blainey et al, *Wesley College* (Melb, 1967); *Landfall*, 113 (Mar 1975); Brady papers (ML); Eggleston papers (NL); Serle papers (LaTL).   HUGH ANDERSON

WILLIS, ALBERT CHARLES (1876-1954), miner, trade unionist and politician, was born on 24 May 1876 at Tonyrefail, Glamorganshire, Wales, son of James Willis, sinker, and his wife Louisa, née Morse. From the age of 10 Albert worked in a Monmouthshire mine, but also attended Brynmaur Board School and later, on a bursary, the London Labour College and classes at Ruskin College, Oxford, and King's College, University of London. In 1899 he became a lay preacher of the Church of God and on 1 October 1901 married Alice Maud Parker at St Mary's parish church, Haggerston, London. A labour intellectual steeped in the industry of coal, Willis was a founding secretary of the Cardiff Workers' Educational Association. He became president of the western district branch of the South Wales Miners' Federation and Labour representative on the Monmouthshire County Council before deciding to migrate to Australia.

Arriving in Sydney in 1911, he presented himself to the secretary of the Trades Hall, E. J. Kavanagh [q.v.9]. Willis began work at Balmain in the State-owned coalmine, but soon changed to the Illawarra district where there was a higher percentage of Welsh miners. At a time of heightened interest in industrial issues among the southern miners of New South Wales and of strike activity in 1912, Willis was a clear-minded and far-sighted advocate of reorganization; acting secretary in 1913, he became president of the Illawarra Miners' Association. For his wider basis of support in the Illawarra, Willis depended on Nonconformist Protestants, a section of society beguilingly similar to that in Wales. He moved easily between miners' lodges and Protestant churches, perceiving them to be closely linked.

The experience of war hastened the trend towards reorganization and unity between the northern and southern coalfields and culminated with the formation in 1915 of the Australasian Coal and Shale Employees' Federation (Miners' Federation); J. M. Baddeley [q.v.7] was its president and Willis secretary (1916-25). During World War I disaffection among the miners increased, direct action was pursued and anti-conscription sentiments grew. Assuming a leading role in shaping and channelling the developing radical outlook, Willis favoured the tactic of confining disputes to a single mine or district while other pits worked. A member of the Industrial Section (from 1918 Industrial Vigilance Council), he was elected vice-president of the New South Wales branch of the Australian Labor Party in 1916. Drawn into the disastrous general strike of 1917, Willis and Kavanagh were gaoled, charged with conspiring to strike and neglecting their duty as public officers; the charges were later withdrawn.

Willis used the débâcle of the strike's defeat to take the Miners' Federation to leadership of the One Big Union movement, drawing on concepts associated with the De Leonite version of the American Industrial Workers of the World. This revitalization drive generated enthusiasm in the wider labour movement and culminated in the decision of the miners' central council in 1921 to reconstitute their union as the Workers' Industrial Union of Australia (Mining Department). The struggle with the dominant Australian Workers' Union for leadership of the One Big Union movement led in 1919 to Willis's expulsion from the State branch of the Labor Party. With others who were expelled, he moved towards the far left and to leadership of the Industrial Socialist Labour Party. His own enthusiasm did not long survive the new party's first electoral rebuff; he then sought to stem the drift of radical unionists to Marxist-Leninism and helped to popularize the guild socialist ideas of G. D. H. Cole.

As secretary of the council of action established by the All-Australian Trade Union Congress of 1921, Willis tried to implement its programme in an atmosphere of declining militancy and a period of considerable turmoil. The council failed as a co-ordinating instrument in a strike action late in 1922, but next year the anger of the rank and file led to the victory of a coalition of unionists and parliamentarians against the A.W.U. faction led by John Bailey [q.v.7] in the State A.L.P. Willis re-entered the party in 1922 and was State branch president in 1923-35. With the new

parliamentary leader J. T. Lang [q.v.9], he soon excluded the Communists, though he later offered a renewed alliance to the 'Trades Hall Reds' associated with J. S. Garden [q.v.8].

In 1924-31 Willis was chairman and managing director of the Labor Daily, then financed by the Miners' Federation. Contemporaries believed that, through his newspaper, Willis exerted great influence over Lang: Vernon Goodin observed to Voltaire Molesworth [q.v.10] that the 'bland, subtle, apparently unassuming' Willis was 'the most powerful political potentate Australia had ever known'; H. V. Evatt similarly noted that, while allowing Lang to wear the imperial purple, Willis—with Garden—retained 'the real direction and control'. Nominated to the Legislative Council in 1925, Willis was vice-president of the Executive Council under Lang in 1925-27 and 1930-31.

A weakening of Protestant identification with the Labor Party during the war and renewed sectarianism in its aftermath undermined Willis's appeal even within the close-knit mining community. His own emphasis on Methodist rather than Marxist inspiration for labour ideals further narrowed his bases of support on the left. Willis's attempt with Rev. A. E. Talbot [q.v.] in 1923-25 to establish the Industrial Christian Fellowship failed, though it contributed to his reputation as an anti-Catholic employer while editor of the Labor Daily.

Short, stolid, with hair receding to baldness by his late forties and a face in perpetual repose, the 'King Coal of Australia', as he had been portrayed by his critics in the press, was now at the limit of his political achievement. Lang brought Willis's political career to an end. He appointed him agent-general for New South Wales in 1931 and, on the eve of his departure for London, presented him with 'a sterling gold albert [watch chain] for an Albert of sterling gold'. In Willis's absence Lang gained effective control of the Labor Daily. Recalled from London when the Lang government fell, Willis faced an openly hostile Labor machine. He resigned from the Legislative Council in 1933 to contest the by-election for the assembly seat of Bulli, but failed against the official Labor candidate, despite strong support from some radical unions and the Socialisation Units within the party. Again expelled from the State branch of the A.L.P., Willis sued Lang for libel over statements made during and after the by-election; following an appeal to the High Court, Lang won. In 1934-36 Willis was a member of the Federal Labor executive and in 1934 unsuccessfully contested the Federal seat of Barton.

Willis increasingly withdrew to his home at Burraneer, Sydney. His immense experience in arbitration and industrial relations was drawn upon during World War II when he was a conciliation commissioner and chairman of the Commonwealth Central Coal Authority (1943-47). Predeceased by his wife, he died on 22 April 1954 at Cronulla and was cremated. His son and two daughters survived him.

R. Gollan, *The coalminers of New South Wales* (Melb, 1963); I. Turner, *Industrial labour and politics* (Canb, 1965); R. Cooksey, *Lang and socialism* (Canb, 1971); M. Dixson, *Greater than Lenin?* (Melb, 1977); H. Radi and P. Spearritt (eds), *Jack Lang* (Syd, 1977); R. B. Walker, *Yesterday's news* (Syd, 1980); F. Farrell, *International socialism and Australian labour* (Syd, 1981); B. Nairn, *The 'Big Fella'* (Melb, 1986); *J of Religious Hist*, no 4, Dec 1963, p 303; *SMH*, 14, 28 Nov, 5, 18 Dec 1916, 13, 14, 24 Nov 1917, 18 Aug 1921, 19, 23 May, 26 Sept, 29 Nov 1933, 24 Apr 1954; *Punch* (Melb), 1 May 1919; *Aust Worker*, 13 June 1923; *Daily Standard*, 4 Feb 1925.　　　FRANK FARRELL

WILLIS, ERNEST HORATIO (1867-1947), architect and political organizer, was born on 30 November 1867 at South Yarra, Melbourne, son of Samuel Willis, contractor and later mayor of Prahran, and his wife Cassandra Alice, née Wragge, both English born. Educated at Wesley College in 1882-85, Ernest joined the architectural firm of William Salway, completing his articles in 1887. He entered into partnership with Rupert Nicholson, mainly designing flats and public buildings in the Prahran area, and in 1922 was made a fellow of the Royal Victorian Institute of Architects.

A member of the Prahran City Council (1908-20), Willis was mayor in 1913-14 and 1918-19. On the outbreak of war, he organized a local patriotic fund, a Red Cross society, a recruiting depot and the construction of war widows' homes. In 1920 he was appointed O.B.E. He had a long municipal career: a vice-president of the board of the Alfred Hospital (1925-41), he also served on the Tramways Board and the Melbourne and Metropolitan Board of Works.

In December 1916 Willis was elected secretary of the Prahran branch of the National Party. Two years later he became secretary to the National Union: it organized financial support for the National Party and later the United Australia Party, while retaining independence from them. The business of the union was carried out almost solely by Willis and its successive presidents, particularly (Sir) Robert Knox [q.v.9]. Their influence extended to party branches in South and Western Australia. Although the National Union was often seen as a front for a coterie of Melbourne businessmen seeking to control the party, Willis was widely respected: his

advice was sought by every conservative prime minister from W. M. Hughes [q.v.9] to (Sir) Robert Menzies. Not ambitious himself, Willis preferred to work behind the scenes, playing a vital role in resolving many crises, most notably the replacement of (Sir) John Latham by Joseph Lyons [qq.v.10] as U.A.P. leader in 1931. Willis retired as secretary in June 1944.

Of middle height and lightly framed, Willis had married Richmond-born Isabella Moffat with Presbyterian forms on 20 April 1900 at Brighton Beach, Melbourne; they had three children. His chief relaxation was horse-racing and he belonged to the Victoria Racing Club and the Victoria Amateur Turf Club. Predeceased by his wife and survived by their two sons, Willis died at his Malvern home on 10 March 1947 and was buried in St Kilda cemetery.

J. B. Cooper, *The history of Prahran 1836-1924* (Melb, 1924); R. Cooksey (ed), 'The great Depression in Australia', *Labour Hist*, 1970, no 17; C. Hazlehurst (ed), *Australian conservatism* (Canb, 1979); *Age*, 27, 28, 31 Oct 1922, 19, 21, 22 Nov 1941; *Herald* (Melb), 9 June 1944; *Argus*, 11 Mar 1947.　　　ANDREW SLOAN

WILLIS, HENRY (1860-1950), politician, was born on 6 April 1860 at Port Adelaide, South Australia, son of John Willis, a mariner from England, and his wife Jane, née Emmerson. Educated at the local grammar school where he won distinction as a debater, Henry later worked in his father's tannery at Hindmarsh. A committee-member of the South Australian Literary Societies' Union, from 1884 he was a member of its first, second and fourth parliaments. By 1885 Willis had established his own tannery at Hindmarsh and 'got in early into Broken Hill silver mines'. He served on Hindmarsh Municipal Council (1884-86) and the local board of health.

Arriving in Sydney in 1888 intending to study for the Church of England ministry, Willis married Annie Louisa Moore on 20 September 1889 at St Peter's Church, Campbelltown; they were to have five children. He launched into municipal politics: he was first mayor of Cabramatta and Canley Vale (1893), served on the Camden (from 1897) and Randwick (1899-1902) councils, and strongly advocated unification at the 1900 Metropolitan Municipal Reform Conference. Meanwhile, he read the lives of famous statesmen and joined the Sydney School of Arts Debating Club.

Elected to the House of Representatives for Robertson in 1901, Willis supported (Sir) George Reid's [q.v.11] Free-Trade government. Re-elected in 1903 and 1906, he was defeated in 1910, but was returned in

October to the New South Wales Legislative Assembly as a Liberal for the Upper Hunter.

In July 1911 Labor lost its majority of one in the assembly and sought an Opposition member as Speaker. Believing the position to be non-partisan, Willis was persuaded to offer himself to avert an unnecessary dissolution. He became Speaker on 24 August 1911 amid a twenty-four-hour opening sitting marked by unprecedented scenes of disorder and violence. Convinced that he had betrayed the party, his fellow Liberals vilified him as a 'Judas' and 'political leper'.

Having observed parliaments in Europe and embraced the ideals of Robert Lowe [q.v.2], Willis acted to protect the privileges and dignity of parliament and its members by enlarging the Speaker's powers. He claimed authority to remove members, censor their speeches and questions, and to exclude journalists from the press gallery; he also reconstructed the reporting department, established a separate department for the sergeant-at-arms, appointed a full-time secretary to the Speaker and reorganized the duties of clerical officers. His reforms, however, were ephemeral.

Such measures inflamed both Liberal and Labor members. In one incident in September 1911, when the sergeant-at-arms had failed, Willis called in the police to eject seven Liberals for continued disorder in the House. Unduly censorious on occasions, he incurred several civil actions for assault and illegal ejection (including a successful one by John Perry [q.v.11] in 1911). Dubbed 'a putty Napoleon', Willis was repeatedly caricatured and ridiculed as a figure of folly throughout his 'reign of terror'. His overbearing presence and insensitive manner alienated support. Possessing 'audacious vanity' and supreme self-confidence, he faced increasing press and parliamentary indignation. He resigned on 22 July 1913, dispirited that the terms on which he had accepted the Speakership had still not been honoured, and was defeated at the next election.

A sturdily-built man of middle height, clean-shaven, with a dark, sunburnt face, close-cropped grey hair, a game leg and a 'child-like' smile, Willis personified one Victorian ideal of the cultivated gentleman. He was well read, and noted for his literary and satirical eloquence in parliament. An enthusiastic yachtsman, he lived in a house built in 1903-05 at Middle Harbour and named Innisfallen Castle, after a ruined abbey at Killarney, Ireland. Before retiring, he devoted time to his Queensland cattle property, Kooringa Downs, Roma, one of the four estates he owned. Survived by his wife, a son and two daughters, Willis died at his Middle Harbour home on 23 February 1950 and was buried in Northern Suburbs cemetery. His estate was sworn for probate at £621.

G. N. Hawker, *The parliament of New South Wales, 1856-1965* (Syd, 1971); *NSW State Reports*, 11 (1911), p 479; *Lone Hand*, 1 Nov 1912; *Daily Telegraph* (Syd), 26 June 1894; *Punch* (Melb), 5 Oct 1911; *Worker* (Syd), 24 July 1913; *SMH*, 24 June 1932, 24 Feb, 15 July 1950; R. A. Crouch memoirs, 1900-46 (LaTL); family information, including letter from Mrs U. R. Douglas, Castle Cove, Syd, 28 July 1977.

PETER SPEARRITT
ELIZABETH STEWART

WILLIS, WILLIAM NICHOLAS (1858-1922), politician, newspaper proprietor, land agent and publisher, was born on 3 August 1858 at Mudgee, New South Wales, third child of native-born parents John Willis, a blacksmith who later went to California, and his wife Margaret, née Lehane. Nicholas was educated at the local denominational school and, after the family moved to Sydney, at St Mary's School. Starting work as an office-boy at the age of 9 to help to support his mother, he took sundry jobs and attended night-school. A 'singularly handsome boy with engaging manners', he was employed at the Victoria Theatre and appeared as 'W. N. Kingston' with William Creswick's Shakespearian company in 1877-78. Willis then became a shop assistant at Dubbo and soon succeeded as a hawker along the Macquarie, Darling and Bogan rivers.

In partnership (1879-88) with T. L. Richardson, Willis opened and managed stores at Girilambone, Nyngan, Mulga and Brewarrina. On 25 January 1888 he married Mary Hayes at St Mary's Catholic Cathedral, Sydney. 'Restless and dynamic', Willis was a plucky—and lucky—investor: he owned the *Central Australian and Bourke Telegraph* and that year took up a homestead lease, Tarrion, at Brewarrina. Having unsuccessfully stood for the Legislative Assembly in 1887, he won Bourke as a Protectionist in February 1889.

Moving to Sydney, Willis established himself as a land and financial agent with George McNair and advertised that he required no 'black-tracker to show him through the land laws'. He made and lost several fortunes through his pastoral interests. Holding his seat in 1891, he represented the Barwon in 1894-1904, after surviving a petition from Donald Macdonell [q.v.10] to unseat him in 1894. Willis was defeated for the Darling in 1904.

A rowdy, hard-drinking gad-fly and a racing crony of W. P. Crick [q.v.8], he repeatedly introduced bills to restrict cruelty to camels, to amend the Masters and Servants Act and to repeal the Agreement Validating Act; less determinedly, he tried to regulate hawkers, reduce the cost of litigation, amend the Sunday laws, introduce the totalizator and enfranchise women. None of his bills was enacted. A 'ready, fluent, forcible speaker', he used parliament for his own ends and 'brought off many remunerative coups', but achieved no eminence, although he did serve on the royal commission into crown tenants in 1900.

In August 1890 Willis and McNair had founded *Truth*, with A. G. Taylor [q.v.6] as editor; the scurrilous newspaper rapidly achieved circulation figures of over 30 000. Struck off the roll of magistrates later that year for publishing an allegedly treasonable letter, Willis denied responsiblity and cognizance. He promptly protected himself by selling *Truth* to partners, among them Crick and John Norton [q.v.11] with whom he had a full-blooded fight in King Street in 1893. Although ownership was deliberately obscured, Willis remained a major shareholder; after protracted litigation, he sold out to Norton in 1896, probably as the result of blackmail.

Having pioneered the South African market with fodder and horses for the British Army, Willis recruited Australian bushmen as scouts and sharpshooters for the South African War. He visited that country in 1902 and reputedly acquired property in Madagascar. While Crick was secretary for lands in 1901-04, Willis was profitably involved in land transactions of a shady nature involving leases that required ministerial assent; he also took up two large leases in his wife's name by 'dummying'. John Haynes [q.v.4] in the *Newsletter* constantly alleged that Willis and Crick were corrupt. Soon after (Sir) William Owen's [q.v.11] appointment in 1905 as royal commissioner into the administration of the Lands Department, Willis thought it politic to leave the country.

When Haynes failed to have him extradited from Perth, Willis fled to Natal, South Africa. Although he temporarily foiled extradition, he returned to Sydney under police escort in July 1906 to face criminal charges of obtaining money by false pretences, fraud and conspiracy (with Crick). Twice the jury disagreed and he was discharged. A picaresque character, Willis was described in Melbourne *Punch* as 'a stout, florid man, whose vigour seems unabated by trouble, who challenges attention by his strong individualism, who talks in the racy vernacular of the street, and who may be relied upon to put up a good fight'. In 1909 he published *The life of W. P. Crick*.

Prudently removing himself to London about 1910, Willis wrote *What Germany wants* (1912) and a racing romance, *Bluey Grey* (1912). He established the Anglo-Eastern Publishing Co. and wrote books with salacious titles, such as *White slaves in a*

Piccadilly flat (1913). His son, who had served with the 6th Light Horse Regiment, Australian Imperial Force, joined him in partnership after the war and probably wrote for the company as 'Bree Narran'. Marie Stopes was horrified at Willis's implication in *Wedded love or married misery* (1920) that she was encouraging immorality. Survived by his wife and six daughters in Australia, and by his son, Willis died suddenly of coronary vascular disease on 3 April 1922 at Lambeth, intestate and penniless.

C. Pearl, *Wild men of Sydney* (Syd, 1959); R. B. Walker, *The newspaper press in New South Wales, 1803-1920* (Syd, 1976); R. Hall, *Marie Stopes* (Lond, 1978); *V&P* (LA NSW), 1890, 1, p 516, 3, p 869, 1894-95, 1, p 901; *PP* (NSW), 1906, 2, p 1; *PD* (NSW), 22 Dec 1899, p 3750; *AAA, All About Australians*, 1 Sept 1905, p 446; *T&CJ*, 9 Mar 1889; *SMH*, 27 Oct 1877, 9 Mar 1878, 28 Feb 1900, 24, 26 Apr 1918, 7 Apr 1922; *Catholic Press*, 20 Apr 1905; *West Australian*, 19 July 1905; *Australasian*, 17 Feb 1906; *Daily Telegraph* (Syd), 28 July 1906; *Punch* (Melb), 2 Aug 1906; Case of W. N. Willis, A2 05/3530 (AA, Canb).　　　MARTHA RUTLEDGE

WILLMORE, HENRIETTA (1842-1938), musician, was born on 27 March 1842 in London, daughter of Raymond Percival, literary editor, and his wife Henrietta, née Street. Lacking formal musical training, she overcame this handicap and emerged as a proficient pianist, much in demand in musical circles. At Chester on 25 September 1862 she married Alfred Mallalieu, a property-owner; with their infant daughter, they arrived in Brisbane in the *Prince Consort* on 12 May 1864.

From 1866 Brisbane audiences responded enthusiastically to Mrs Mallalieu. As an accompanist or soloist in numerous concerts, she introduced a widening repertoire of classical music, frequently in collaboration with her friend R. T. Jefferies [q.v.9]. Her long teaching career began in 1867 through economic necessity when her husband's attempt to establish a printery ended in insolvency. Henrietta became music mistress at Mrs Thomas's Academy for Young Ladies. She later taught at other schools and, after her husband's death, increased her private classes. Dedicated and determined, she often took promising pupils without charge and gave freely of her skills and organizing ability to further the cause of music.

Undeterred by popular prejudice, she decided to become an organist. Her teacher was Walter Graham Willmore whom she married in All Saints Church, Brisbane, on 28 December 1885: they were unhappy and eventually parted. Henrietta was organist at St John's Pro-Cathedral from 1882 to 1885, at Wickham Terrace Presbyterian Church and at other churches, and pioneered organ recitals and organ-based concerts in Brisbane. The vogue for such entertainments did not last and her fund-raising concerts to retain the Exhibition Building's Willis organ were considered overly classical and met with a cool reception. In contrast, her recitals in Sydney in 1890 proved successful, her pedalling being judged remarkably fine. On a visit to South Africa in 1896 she won praise for 'preserving a calm dignity and firm seat at the instrument while attacking all difficulties'. Her final appearances were chamber music recitals in Brisbane in 1911 with members of the Jefferies family and her protégé Percy Brier [q.v.7].

Willmore believed in women's political rights and responsibilities. She served on the executives of the Queensland Women's Suffrage League and the Woman's Franchise Association of Queensland; a founding member of the Brisbane Women's Club, she was president of the Queensland Women's Electoral League's Toowong branch and, during World War I, of the Belgian Relief Fund for which she was awarded the medal de la Reine Elisabeth. The Willmore Discussion Club was formed in 1931 in her honour.

Survived by two daughters and one son of the five children of her first marriage, she died at Wynnum, Brisbane, on 22 August 1938 and was buried in Bulimba cemetery with Anglican rites. There is a Henrietta Willmore memorial chair, carved by L. J. Harvey [q.v.9], in Women's College, University of Queensland; Mallalieu Home (her former house at Toowong) is a hostel for female music students.

R. K. Boughen, An account of the music of St John's Cathedral Brisbane from 1843-1887 (M.A. Qual thesis, Univ Qld, 1974); B. J. Hebden, Life and influence of Mr Richard Thomas Jefferies (M.A. Qual thesis, Univ Qld, 1980); F. J. Ericksen, The bands and orchestras of colonial Brisbane (Ph.D. thesis, Univ Qld, 1987); E. Mallalieu, Short sketch of the life of Henrietta Willmore, one of the early pioneers of music in Brisbane, from the year 1865 (nd, ts, OL); M. A. Ogg, Memories of early Brisbane, as sketched and told to Ernest Briggs (nd, ts, OL); Willmore cutting-book (OL). BETTY CROUCHLEY

WILLMOTT, FRANCIS EDWARD SYKES (1870-1941), orchardist and politician, was baptized on 21 August 1870 at Kirkley, Suffolk, England, son of Rev. Henry Willmott and his wife Anne Maria, née Sykes. Francis was educated at Hurstpierpoint, Sussex. After being rejected for the army, in 1886 he came with his brother to Western Australia for farming experience. Having spent two years on E. R. Brockman's property in the south-west, Willmott was variously a tutor, drover, prospector and stockman in the Gascoyne and the eastern goldfields. On 8 April 1896 at St Mary's Church, Busselton, he married Brockman's daughter Frances Edith. Willmott farmed briefly before becoming a supervisor on the construction of the Coolgardie-Esperance road, and on the water-supply works at the goldfields and Mundaring weir. He was government forest ranger (1897-1914) in the south-west where he acquired his orchard, Applewood, at Bridgetown.

In 1914 Willmott won the Legislative Assembly seat of Nelson, the newly formed Country Party's only seat outside the wheatbelt. When he replaced the pro-Laborite James Gardiner [q.v.8] in March 1915 as parliamentary leader of the party, the change was deemed to give Alexander Monger [q.v.10], the assertive president of the Farmers and Settlers' Association, greater influence in promoting a more conservative alliance. Though more amenable than Gardiner, Willmott stood firm on certain issues, often supporting Labor and countering undue F.A.S.A. pressure. With Gardiner and C. F. Baxter, he was censured for accepting—without party approval—a ministerial position in June 1917 in (Sir) Henry Lefroy's [q.v.10] National coalition government; in 1918 he was publicly admonished by Monger for inadequate involvement in Country Party affairs. Willmott remained a minister without portfolio under (Sir) Hal Colebatch and (Sir) James Mitchell [qq.v.8,10] until 13 April 1921. In that year Willmott lost the parliamentary leadership of his party which opted for a leader unencumbered by government responsibilities.

In May 1921, shortly after losing Nelson to an Independent, he won the Legislative Council seat of South-West Province from the endorsed Country Party candidate. As a 'Mitchell government supporter', Willmott admitted having 'many enemies' within his party and blamed the party's refusal to pre-select him on his long-standing refusal to promote the interests of Westralian Farmers Ltd in parliament. In 1923 he condoned the Country Party's executive decision not to re-endorse four sitting members for the 1924 election, a move which contributed to a major split in the party. He lost his seat in May 1926.

Noted for his 'jovial and happy nature', Willmott became involved in property development at Bridgetown. A sometime president of the West Australian Fruit Growers' Association, he was a director of South-West Co-operative Dairy Farmers Ltd. In failing health, he retired to Busselton in 1938. Survived by his wife, daughter and three sons, Willmott died on 29 January 1941 at Subiaco,

Perth, and was buried with Anglican rites in Bridgetown cemetery.

B. D. Graham, *The formation of the Australian Country Parties* (Canb, 1966); *Periscope*, 11 July 1919; *Blackwood Times*, 27 May 1921, 7 Feb 1941; *West Australian*, 15, 16, 19 Aug 1918, 5, 31 July 1919, 25 May 1921, 30 Jan 1941; D. W. Black, The National Party in Western Australia, 1917-1930: its origins and development with an introductory survey of 'Liberal' Party organisation, 1901-1916 (M.A. thesis, Univ WA, 1974). BETTY CARTER

WILLSHIRE, WILLIAM HENRY (1852-1925), police officer, was born on 10 March 1852 in Adelaide, son of James Doughty Willshire, schoolmaster, and his wife Emily Elizabeth, née Schlenkrich. He joined the South Australian Police Force in 1878 and was posted to Alice Springs in 1882, gaining rapid promotion to first-class mounted constable in 1883.

Following the wounding of two Europeans by Aborigines in 1884, Willshire used his bushcraft and physical endurance to set a pattern of relentless 'dispersal'. Late in 1884 he took command of a native-police detachment of six armed men. Ostensibly appointed to protect settlers, they made reprisals for cattle spearing their standard duty. Willshire was transferred temporarily to the Daly River where his troop 'pacified' that region. Returning to Alice Springs, in 1886 he established the police station at Heavitree Gap, building an outpost at Boggy Hole on the Finke River downstream from Hermannsburg. Complaints by missionaries led to its abandonment after three chained 'escaping' prisoners were shot in the back by police. Disliking paperwork, Willshire often failed to report his activities; by 1890 Aboriginal deaths associated with his actions certainly exceeded the official number of thirteen.

In 1891 Willshire's men attacked sleeping Aborigines camped at Tempe Downs station. Two men died and their bodies were cremated. F. J. Gillen [q.v.9], Alice Springs subprotector of Aborigines, investigated the reported episode and committed Willshire to Port Augusta for trial for murder. As he was the first policeman to be so charged, and colonists felt their rights challenged, emotions ran high: public subscriptions provided Willshire's £2000 bail and retained Sir John Downer [q.v.8] for his defence. Aboriginal witnesses attended, but problems over accepting their evidence resulted in Willshire's popular acquittal. Having prudently stationed him at southern centres, his superiors transferred him in 1893 to the Victoria River district where he was able 'to commit mayhem at will'. Sensing further notoriety, in 1895 the government posted him perma-

nently in the south. Willshire resigned in 1908, after audaciously applying for appointment as State protector of Aborigines. Although that post was inappropriate, his credentials were unquestionable for his subsequent twelve years as nightwatchman at the Gawler Road abattoir, Adelaide.

Contemporaries praised Willshire as an authority on Aboriginal society because he published four short accounts between 1888 and 1896. Sometimes vivid, they reflected the settlers' ethos: containing some reasonable anecdotal ethnology and word lists, they are distinguished more for their sexual overtones, boastful sadism and racial triumphalism. 'It's no use mincing matters', he rhapsodized in *The land of the dawning* (Adelaide, 1896), 'the Martini-Henry carbines at the critical moment were talking English in the silent majesty of these eternal rocks'.

Willshire portrayed himself as a heroic frontiersman, rendering the land safe for civilization. Settlers praised his 'daring and efficient devotion to duty', but his terrorism survives in Aboriginal oral tradition. He was contemptuous of Aboriginal lives and culture, and condoned female exploitation—'perhaps the Almighty meant them for use as He has placed them wherever the pioneers go'. J. J. Healy aptly described Willshire's *A thrilling tale of real life in the wilds of Australia* (Adelaide, 1895) as 'grotesque, almost schizophrenic, fictions'; it was largely autobiographical.

Willshire died in Adelaide on 22 August 1925. He had married Ellen Sarah Howell on 13 September 1896 at Port Lincoln. His wife, a son and a daughter survived him.

R. Clyne, *Colonial blue* (Adel, 1987); D. J. Mulvaney, *Encounters in place* (Brisb, 1989); *Aust Literary Studies*, 8, no 3, May 1978; *Observer* (Adel), 16 Oct 1897, 19 July 1924, 5 Sept 1925; *Quiz*, 30 Apr 1896.   D. J. MULVANEY

WILMOT, FRANK LESLIE THOMPSON ('FURNLEY MAURICE') (1881-1942), poet, bookseller and publisher, was born on 6 April 1881 at Collingwood, Melbourne, second of five children of Henry William Wilmot (1855-1907), ironmonger, and his wife Elizabeth Mary, née Hind, both Australian born. Henry was a socialist, a follower of William Morris and well versed in various handcrafts. Frank was educated at Clifton Hill and North Fitzroy State schools, leaving at 13 to join E. W. Cole's [q.v.3] Book Arcade.

He began writing verse as a child: when he was 11 he sent a poem to the *Bulletin*—J. F. Archibald [q.v.3] replied encouragingly—and he was first published in the *Tocsin*; the poem was captioned 'A 16-year old Democrat sends the following'. Thus began his association with Bernard O'Dowd [q.v.11], a mentor and in some respects a model. Wilmot began to dream of some day publishing and editing 'a first-class literary periodical'. In 1901-02, on his own primitive press, he produced eight lively issues of the monthly, *Microbe*, which he largely wrote; Joseph Conrad was then his chief literary enthusiasm. He continued to print and publish occasional books, notably through his Galleon Press. After steady rejection of his poems by the *Bulletin*, possibly because of A. G. Stephens' [q.v.] prejudice against him, he was accepted in 1905-06 as 'Furnley Maurice', the pseudonym he continued to use. His verse and prose began to be published widely at home and occasionally abroad. On 24 August 1910 at Christ Church, St Kilda, he married with Anglican rites Ida Lizzie Meeking; they settled at Surrey Hills and were to have two sons. His *Bay and Padie book: kiddie songs* (1917) was commercially successful over four editions.

A down-to-earth democrat, always a man of the people attracted to popular pastimes, Wilmot had been involved on the fringes of the Victorian Socialist Party. Although he could see most sides of the question, he saw World War I primarily in terms of its folly and wickedness; his pacifist leanings were expressed in his 'To God from The Warring [Weary] Nations' (1916) and he worked against conscription. He joined Vance Palmer and Frederick Sinclaire [qq.v.11] in their movement to define and encourage national sentiment and contributed to the latter's *Fellowship*. With his friends Frederick Macartney, Henry Tate [q.v.] and others, in 1916 Wilmot founded the Melbourne Literary Club and printed its journal, *Birth*. In the early 1920s he joined the Y Club, associated with the Pioneer Players and was a leading member of the literary club established by Percival Serle [q.v.11] whom he assisted in compiling *An Australasian anthology* (1927). Later prominent in the Fellowship of Australian Writers, he campaigned against book censorship and lectured for the Commonwealth Literary Fund of whose advisory body he was a member.

Wilmot remained with the Book Arcade, eventually as manager, until its demise in 1929; his occupation aided his developing command of world literature in breadth and depth, and he became a natural focus for Melbourne writers and littérateurs. He bought Cole's lending library and also launched out as a bookseller in Little Collins Street, but was saved in the Depression by appointment early in 1932 as the first full-time manager of the Melbourne University Press and Bookroom. His initial salary of £300 was raised to £450 from 1934; he did his share of counter work and had no separate room until 1940. The

business mildly flourished, with profits from publishing (less than £1000 a year) outstripping bookselling. The half-dozen books published annually included S. H. Roberts's *The squatting age in Australia*, Morris Miller's [q.v.10] *Australian literature*, Brian Fitzpatrick's *The British Empire in Australia*, and —an especial pleasure—R. D. FitzGerald's *Moonlight acre*. 'Is it so good that it is our duty to lose money by publishing it?', he asked his reader A. A. Phillips. Wilmot also published, once editing, once co-editing, three profitable anthologies for schools. While he fitted in congenially at the university, he considered it 'remote from life and unaware of its own inherent snobbery'.

Always totally up-to-date in awareness of contemporary poets, he read W. B. Yeats, Rupert Brooke and the Georgians, and especially Ezra Pound and other Americans; E. E. Cummings and Carl Sandburg were lasting influences. Although attracted early to the colloquial, Wilmot wrote predominantly in conventional styles in his earlier substantial volumes—*Unconditioned songs* (1913), *Eyes of vigilance* (1920), *Arrows of longing* (1921), and the lyrical *The gully and other verses* (1929) which reflected his love for the Dandenongs. But in an essay in his volume, *Romance* (1922), he condemned current Australian poetry as 'the last word in conventional English verse production'. He continued doggedly to experiment, striving to reflect 'everyday life and language' and to extend poetry's frontiers. His belief in spontaneity involved an unwillingness to revise.

He found his full voice eventually in *Melbourne odes* (1934), his major volume:

The juggernauting trams and the prolonged
Crash of the Cafeterias at noon
Are silenced . . .

In such titles as 'The Victoria Markets Recollected in Tranquillity' and 'Upon a Row of Old Boots and Shoes in a Pawnbroker's Window' he mused—with flashes of humour—on the state of the nation, the demoralization and stagnation of the Depression, and the theme of city versus country.

Wilmot was prolific: many of his stories, essays and plays were unpublished, though four of his plays were produced. His critical work in *All About Books* and elsewhere was outstanding in a sorry period—he reviewed Xavier Herbert's *Capricornia* and Patrick White's *Happy Valley* enthusiastically and in 1938 noticed signs of 'an independent culture in Australia . . . growing and revealing itself secretly, unconsciously, unexpectedly'. A collection of his criticism is needed. His literary reputation has survived only precariously, but a major article in *Meanjin* (1982) by David Headon claimed him as 'the first Australian modernist' and demanded his reconsideration, especially as 'the most important forerunner of Australia's modernist movement in poetry'.

Apart from his deep knowledge of literature, Wilmot was many-sided, well informed on world and national affairs, knowledgeable about classical and popular music (he played the piano), a skilled carpenter as well as printer. He was sceptical and agnostic—not quite a rationalist: 'human affairs were seventy-five per cent humbug'. He had natural, good, though unpolished, manners, with a distaste for attitudinizing. His conversation was unassertive, marked by sardonic, chuckling wit. He was widely respected for 'generous devotion to unpopular causes and impersonal ends'. He was a quintessentially Melbourne man.

Survived by his wife and sons, Wilmot died suddenly of heart disease on 22 February 1942 at his home. His estate was sworn for probate at £2563. Serle selected an edition of his *Poems* (1944). The revealing, highly individual preface to *Melbourne odes* had concluded: 'I have had my share of attention and appreciation, and, from a deep love of the craft I practise, have carefully avoided that frightful publicity which . . . debases everything it touches'.

V. Palmer, *Frank Wilmot (Furnley Maurice)* (Melb, 1942); H. Anderson, *Frank Wilmot (Furnley Maurice): a bibliography and a criticism* (Melb, 1955); F. T. Macartney, *Furnley Maurice* (Syd, 1955); D. R. Walker, *Dream and disillusion* (Canb, 1976); *Aust Q*, 15, June 1943, p 108; *Meanjin Q*, 33, no 1 (1974), 41, no 4 (1982); Wilmot papers (ML).   GEOFFREY SERLE

WILSMORE, NORMAN THOMAS MORTIMER (1868-1940), professor of chemistry, was born on 23 January 1868 at Williamstown, Melbourne, only child of English parents Thomas Wilsmore, solicitor, and his wife Marianne Maria, née Norman. After being dux at Caulfield Grammar School, in 1887 Norman entered the University of Melbourne (B.Sc., 1890; M.Sc., 1893). On 28 June 1894 at St John's Anglican Church, Camberwell, he married Leonora Jessie Little, the first woman science graduate of the university.

For three years he did research in London under Professor Sir William Ramsay and Norman Collie; in 1897-1901 he worked with Professor Walther Nernst at the Georg-August University of Göttingen, Germany, and in 1901-02 assisted Professor Richard Lorenz at the Federal Polytechnic, Zurich, Switzerland. Wilsmore published an important paper on electrode potentials and in 1903 returned to University College, London, as Ramsay's assistant in inorganic chemistry

and, later, his assistant-professor. In 1907 Wilsmore was a co-discoverer of keten, a new organic compound, and received his D.Sc. from the University of Melbourne; in the fields of electrode potentials and keten chemistry he demonstrated a brilliant mind.

In 1913 Wilsmore took up the foundation chair of chemistry at the new University of Western Australia; his department was housed in a wood and iron structure that had been transferred from the goldfields and re-erected in Irwin Street, Perth. During the early years he had little equipment and no assistants.

Becoming an honorary director of the War Munitions Supply Co. Ltd of Western Australia in September 1915, he undertook war work in the British Department of Explosives Supply in 1917-18. He returned to Perth in 1919 and concentrated on teaching and administration. While 'Willie' never awarded a first-class honours degree, his second-class graduates were welcomed by other chemistry schools. He served six terms as dean of science, was a member of the university senate (1916-22) and vice-chancellor in 1924-25. Twice president of the State committee of the (Royal) Australian Chemical Institute, Wilsmore was president of its council (1937); a member of the State committee of the Council for Scientific and Industrial Research, he was an original fellow and vice-president (1933-34) of the Australian National Research Council; he was also a fellow of the (Royal) Institute of Chemistry of Great Britain and Ireland.

His last years in the university were unhappy. Despite his shyness, Wilsmore had a caustic tongue and quarrelled bitterly with Vice-Chancellor Whitfeld [q.v.] and others over the design of a new science building on the Crawley campus. When a plan showed a lavatory beside his main lecture theatre, the professor exploded: 'I have no intention of lecturing to an obligato of flushing cisterns'. He demanded that lower priority be given to aesthetic features in order to save money for equipping the laboratories. On losing the argument, he refused to help in planning the building and did not attend its opening. Slight and spare, of less than middle height, Wilsmore was severely myopic, with pale blue eyes, white hair and beard. When he finally retired in 1937 he declined the title emeritus because its dictionary definition included 'having become unfit for service; worn out'. He became a consultant to the local chemical firm Plaimar Ltd. Survived by his wife and son, he died on 12 June 1940 at Claremont, Perth, and was cremated. He is commemorated by the Wilsmore prize for chemistry.

F. Alexander, *Campus at Crawley* (Melb, 1963); *Aust J of Science*, 3, 1940, p 31; *J of the Chemical Soc*

(Lond), 1940-41, p 59; Roy Aust Chemical Inst, *Procs*, Jan 1958; N. S. Bayliss, The Chemistry School, University of Western Australia (ms, 1988, School of Chemistry, Univ WA) *and* Reminiscences. The School of Chemistry, University of Western Australia, 1913-1970 (ms, Univ WA Archives); Registrar's office file 986 *and* UWAA files 0287, 0433, 0434 (Univ WA Archives).

B. K. DE GARIS

WILSON, ALEXANDER WILLIAM (1870-1949), dairy industry manager, was born on 20 March 1870 at Goldie, Lancefield, Victoria, son of Joseph Wilson, farmer, and his wife Prudence, née Robinson, both Irish born. Educated at Scotch College, Melbourne, Alexander spent a year at the city headquarters of the Bank of Victoria. In 1889 he joined the Colonial Bank and the following year was appointed accountant at its Camperdown branch. He resigned in 1899 to begin dairy-farming on Glenora, his newly acquired 314-acre (127 ha) property at Mirboo North. In 1901 he became secretary of the Mirboo North Dairy Co. Ltd, a small co-operative butter factory which, like others at the time, was struggling to survive: Wilson's banking experience helped to put the company on a sound financial basis. In 1902-05 he was a member of the Mirboo Shire Council.

Having represented the Mirboo North co-operative before a royal commission on the butter industry (1904-05) which exposed unscrupulous practices by marketing agents, Wilson became an advocate of a co-operative selling company. When the Gippsland Butter Factories Co-operative Produce Co. Ltd (later Gippsland and Northern Co-operative Co. Ltd) was formed in 1905, he was appointed its secretary. On 10 June 1908 he married Marion Ferres Ogilvy at Christ Church, St Kilda. That year he became general manager of the Gippsland co-operative.

Under Wilson the company expanded to encompass the sale of grain, seed, livestock and land; it established its own butter-box factory, its own insurance company and, after 1920, its own weekly newspaper, *The G & N Co-Operator*. Arguing that, by co-operation, farmers and graziers could retain control of their industry and maximize their returns, Wilson wrote in 1912: 'Co-operation in its many forms is one of the greatest social movements in active operation in the civilized world today'. He was active in the formation of the Australian Producers Wholesale Co-operative Federation Pty Ltd, a federation of distributing co-operatives formed in 1918, of which he remained chairman until his death. A director of Empire Dairies Ltd, London, he had instigated the formation and was a director of The Overseas Farmers' Co-operative Federation Ltd, a London-based distributor

for Australian co-operatives. Wilson was also a member of the Australian Dairy Produce Board from its inception in 1924 until its restructuring in 1948, having the distinction of moving its first and last motion.

A dynamic personality, he was widely respected for his knowledge of the dairy industry and of agricultural marketing; *Smith's Weekly* commented in 1939 that Wilson attracted directorships and chairmanships 'as naturally as a magnet picks up steel'. He was very tall and walked with a slight stoop; though appearing aloof, he was fond of congenial company and made himself accessible to those seeking advice. He enjoyed tennis and motoring. Deeply religious, he was an elder of the Hawthorn Presbyterian Church. Wilson died on 10 December 1949 at his Woodend home and was buried in Box Hill cemetery. His wife and two sons survived him; his estate was sworn for probate at £17 473.

J. Smith (ed), *Cyclopedia of Victoria*, 3 (Melb, 1905); *G & N Co-Operator*, 5 Feb, 29 Apr 1948, 15 Dec 1949; Gippsland and Northern Co-operative Co Ltd, *Annual Reports*, 1905-55.

GREG S. J. BRINSMEAD

WILSON, ARTHUR MITCHELL (1888-1947), obstetrician, was born on 24 August 1888 in South Melbourne, only son of Victorian-born parents David Wilson (d. 1891), chemist, and his wife Helen, née Mitchell. Arthur won scholarships in 1902 to Scotch College and in 1907 to Ormond [q.v.5] College, University of Melbourne. He gained blues in athletics and football, graduated (M.B., B.Ch., 1911; M.D., 1913) and took a post as a resident medical officer at the Melbourne Hospital. Having made a trip to China as a ship's surgeon, he joined the resident staff at the Women's Hospital under R. H. J. Fetherston [q.v.8] who helped to influence his love for obstetrics.

At Scots Church, Melbourne, on 6 May 1915 Wilson married with Presbyterian forms Sarah Marguerita, a 24-year-old typist and daughter of the cricketer R. W. McLeod. As a captain in the Australian Imperial Force, Wilson had been allotted to the 3rd Australian General Hospital and embarked on 18 May. He served at Gallipoli, in Egypt and in France. Promoted major (25 February 1916) and lieut-colonel (2 May 1918), he commanded the 7th Field Ambulance; he thought that surgeons should be as close to the front line as possible and wrote a report on ways of transporting casualties. Twice mentioned in dispatches, he was awarded the Distinguished Service Order for his work near Amiens in August 1918. He embarked for Melbourne on

24 January 1919 and his A.I.F. appointment terminated on 31 May.

Commencing private practice at Prahran with R. N. Wawn, in 1920 Wilson became honorary obstetric surgeon at the Women's Hospital. In 1926 he was appointed lecturer in obstetrics and gynaecology at the university; he proved a popular teacher and had charge until R. M. Allan [q.v.7] accepted the new chair in 1929. Wilson was a foundation fellow (1929) of the Australian branch of the Royal College of Obstetricians and Gynaecologists.

From 1931 he concentrated on his private and consulting practices. The most eminent Victorian obstetrician of his day, he delivered on average one thousand babies a year. The wives of more than six hundred doctors had him attend their labour. Wilson's judgement, experience, gentleness and manipulative technique achieved excellent results: in his care, only one mother died from caesarean section during his ten-year term at the Women's Hospital. He worked at all hours. When he relaxed by going to the Melbourne Cricket Ground, he carried a pocketful of pennies with which to telephone to inquire about his patients' progress. In 1943 he broke professional custom by writing a signed letter to the *Herald* expressing his concern at the shortage of beds for maternity cases in inner-suburban hospitals.

Spare and drawn, Wilson was unassuming, equable and kind, with a manner that dispelled fear. He devoted his life to helping people and retained sympathy for the poor: he kept his fees low and is said to have never refused a request for help. Ingenuous by nature, he paid little attention to his appearance, and liked a cup of tea, a cigarette and a chat. Survived by his wife, two daughters and two sons, he died of cancer on 19 December 1947 at Epworth Private Hospital, Richmond, and was cremated. His estate was sworn for probate at £25 615.

C. Macdonald (ed), *A book of remembrance*, 1 (Melb, 1956); J. Peel (ed), *The lives of the fellows of the Royal College of Obstetricians and Gynaecologists 1929-1969*(Lond, 1976); *MJA*, 24 Apr 1948, p 545, 2 July 1955, p 1; *VHM*, Feb 1961, p 141; *Herald* (Melb), 12 May 1943.　　　　JOHN RITCHIE

WILSON, DAVID (1830?-1899), dairy expert, was born at Glasgow, Scotland, son of John Wilson, cotton spinner, and his wife, Mary, née Donald. David arrived in Victoria in the *Marco Polo* in 1854 with his wife Grace, née Elliott, whom he had married at Kelso, Roxburghshire, in 1853. After running sheep, he became a dairy-farmer at Inverleigh and then at Springbank, Mount Egerton. Keenly interested in improving practices and the quality of the product, he made a systematic study of dairying and was an early importer of the de Laval mechanical cream separators for farm use: he demonstrated and publicized the value of separators in saving the time involved in setting milk and skimming cream, and in reducing microbial contamination and improving quality. Wilson's butter was so good that Melbourne grocers paid a premium for it. He won major prizes at the Ballarat and Geelong shows; his achievement set an example for others to follow. In 1881 he successfully exported butter to Britain.

Appointed State dairy expert in 1888, Wilson superintended the government's model dairy at the Centennial International Exhibition. In 1889 he organized a travelling dairy under the management of Alexander Crawford who, during the next two years, covered northern and western Victoria, demonstrating the cream separator and instructing farmers in its operation. With regard to churning, butter working and packing, Wilson's and Crawford's initiatives facilitated the transition from making butter by hand to its production in centralized factories. Convinced of the importance of co-operation in the industry, Wilson drew up plans and articles of association for co-operative factory companies. He was a founding member of the Dairymen's Association of Victoria.

From 1889 Wilson supervised the beginnings of Victoria's butter export industry. Having visited Europe in the early 1890s to study 'pasteurized and fermentized' butter, in 1893-94 he recommended the adoption of pasteurization and predicted that it would eliminate the need for boric acid as a preservative. He also stressed the importance of fodder conservation, culling and breeding, testing cows individually and hygienic methods. At his instigation, a pasteurization plant designed by A. N. Pearson [q.v.11] was installed at Tungarmah in 1899. Wilson was also responsible for the appointment of Henry Potts [q.v.11] to lecture to factory managers and buttermakers, and of Robert Crowe [q.v.8] as an instructor in the use of the pasteurizer.

Widowed in 1895, Wilson married with Presbyterian forms Mary Stewart, a teacher, on 17 November 1897 at Geelong. He died of abdominal cancer on 26 August 1899 at his South Yarra home. Survived by his wife, and by six daughters and three sons of his first marriage, he was buried in Boroondara cemetery.

Cwlth Dept of Primary Industry, Agr Production Branch, *Dairy farming in Australia*, G. T. Laffan ed (Melb, 1964); K. Sillcock, *Three lifetimes of dairying in Victoria*(Melb, 1972); *PP*(Vic), 1895-96, 4 (92), p 743; *J of Agr* (Vic), July 1951; *Weekly Times* (Melb) and *Leader* (Melb), 2 Sept 1899.

K. T. H. FARRER

WILSON, DORA LYNNELL (1883-1946), artist, was born on 31 August 1883 at Newcastle upon Tyne, England, daughter of James Wilson, agent, and his wife Annie Maria, née Green. The family migrated to Victoria next year. Dora was educated at Somerset School and Methodist Ladies' College, Melbourne. Known as 'Wiltz' to her colleagues, she studied at the National Gallery schools in 1901-06 under Bernard Hall and Frederick McCubbin [qq.v.9,10]. She was impressed by the Anders Zorn etchings in the gallery collection and, together with Jessie Traill [q.v.] and Janie Wilkinson Whyte, took lessons from John Mather [q.v.10]. Their etchings were reproduced in the *Lone Hand* (1907) and constituted some of the earliest efforts in the medium by women. In 1907 she contributed to the Australian Exhibition of Women's Work in Melbourne. Like her colleague Janet Cumbrae Stewart [q.v.8] with whom she was compared, Wilson excelled in pastels. From 1910 her studio, 'a picturesque and ancient rookery' at Temple Court, Collins Street West, was the meeting place of the 'Waddy', a group of ex-students who in 1913-14 exhibited as 'The Twelve Melbourne Painters'.

Wilson's reputation grew steadily. Her etchings, pastels and oils of still life, nudes and portraits (especially of children) were noted for their fine draughtsmanship. Although they were sometimes criticized for using tired themes or for being overly 'sweet' and 'coy', they sold well. In 1923 she contributed to the Exhibition of Australian Art at Burlington House, London. *Woman's World* reproduced on its cover her painting, 'Reve d'Or', which had been accepted at the Salon des la Société des Artistes Français, Paris, and the magazine described Dora's sense of humour, 'quaint personality' and 'shy, self-deprecating manner'.

In the mid-1920s she began to concentrate on the street scenes for which she is best remembered. She invested them with particular atmospheric effects, such as dappled light filtered through trees. Opening her exhibition 'The Lure of Melbourne' at the Fine Art Society Gallery in May 1931, Sir William Branton commented on the novel sight of 'a woman in a motor car with an easel in front of her . . . painting the life of the busy city'.

Following a commission from Sir Baldwin Spencer [q.v.] to paint European landmarks, in 1927 Wilson had gone abroad for two and a half years; she toured the Continent and Britain with photographer Peg Clarke, sometimes travelling on foot and often sleeping in barns. In 1928 Wilson exhibited at the Beaux Arts Gallery, London, and next year at Australia House. Her style, dependent on a bright palette and on simple, broad impasto brushwork, was praised by Arthur Streeton [q.v.] in 1931 for its freshness and freedom from 'the depressing appearance of black paint'. Her art, while not embracing modernism, did show the influence of its basic tenets, as the critic Basil Burdett [q.v.7] and the artist Blamire Young [q.v.] appreciated. In the 1930s Dora painted a series of Australian historical pictures, concentrating on the Victorian era, which were shown in Melbourne in 1935.

During World War II Wilson worked with the Women Painters' Service Group. She died of cancer on 21 November 1946 in East Melbourne and was cremated with Presbyterian forms. Her estate was sworn for probate at £7400. She is represented in most State galleries and the Castlemaine and Bendigo galleries, Victoria.

Home, 1 June 1921, p 14; *Woman's World*, 1 Sept 1923, p 501; *Argus*, 20 Mar 1930, 7 May 1931; *Age*, 8 May, 20 June 1931.

MARY ALICE LEE

WILSON, FRANK (1859-1918), businessman and premier, was born on 12 May 1859 at Monkwearmouth, Durham, England, son of John Wilson, timber merchant, and his wife Sarah Martha, née Walker, who died soon after Frank's birth. Educated at Sunderland, at a Moravian college in Germany and at Wesley College, Sheffield, he was apprenticed to a Sunderland timber merchant and shipbroker. At 19, Frank joined his elder brother in establishing an engineering works at Sunderland. On 25 May 1880, at the local Whitburn Street Chapel, Wilson married Annie Phillips with Wesleyan Methodist forms. Following a strike by engineers, in 1886 he migrated to Queensland where he operated his own business before being appointed manager of A. Overend & Co. Ltd, railway contractors, flour-millers and machinery merchants in Brisbane.

Moving to Western Australia as managing director (1891-99) of the Canning Jarrah Timber Co., Wilson also became a mining agent and a director of Fremantle Gas & Coke Co. Ltd, Eureka Milling Co. and the Perth Brick Co. After a spell with the Jarrah Wood & Sawmills Co., he turned his interest to coal-mining and was to remain associated with Collie Coalfields Pty Co. Ltd as a substantial shareholder and, by the time of his death, managing director. President (1899-1902) of the Perth Chamber of Commerce, he was sometime president of the Timber Merchants' and Sawmillers' Association, as well as of the Coalowners' Association of Western Australia which he established.

A Perth City councillor (1896-99), Wilson was elected to the Legislative Assembly for the seat of Canning in 1897; he had campaigned against Sir John Forrest's [q.v.8] government on such issues as the proposed Coolgardie water scheme, Federation and high customs duties on food. After an electoral redistribution, Wilson was returned for Perth in 1901. Having voted consistently with George Leake's [q.v.10] administration, he accepted appointment as minister for mines and commissioner of railways under A. E. Morgans [q.v.10] who supplanted Leake on 21 November: this about-face contributed to Wilson's defeat with two other ministers in the ensuing ministerial by-elections. He unsuccessfully contested Claremont in a 1902 by-election, but in June 1904, while serving as employers' representative in the Arbitration Court, won Sussex as an Independent. In August 1905 he became minister for works in (Sir) Cornthwaite Rason's [q.v.11] newly formed Liberal government. Before stepping down in May 1906, Rason had recommended Wilson as his successor, but the latter could not obtain sufficient support and became deputy premier, holding the treasury, education and agriculture portfolios under (Sir) Newton Moore [q.v.10]. Wilson was responsible for legislation introducing income and land taxation, and for the establishment of Perth Modern School (on the initiative of Cecil Andrews [q.v.7]); he temporarily lost favour during a financial recession and was demoted to the works portfolio in June 1909. When Moore resigned for health reasons in September 1910, Wilson became premier and colonial treasurer.

Wilson's first term as premier produced legislation to establish the University of Western Australia and preferential voting, but a controversial electoral redistribution failed to prevent a landslide loss in October 1911 to the Labor Party led by John Scaddan [q.v.11]. While visiting England to attend the coronation of King George V, Wilson had been granted the freedom of the city of Sunderland. Appointed C.M.G. in 1911, he was a member (1911-16) of the senate of the University of Western Australia, and vice-president and president of the Liberal League in 1912-14. The formation of the Country Party in 1914 hampered his efforts to defeat Scaddan and, although the government lost its majority in late 1915, it was not until July 1916 that Wilson formed his second ministry. Still plagued by the Country Party, at one stage he offered his resignation. In June 1917 he and his close colleague (Sir) James Mitchell [q.v.10] were ousted from office as a result of manoeuvres associated with the formation of the wartime National coalition ministry.

Wilson, who had strongly backed the war effort as president of the National Referendum Council, was by then gravely ill. He lost his seat by four votes to a Country Party candidate in October 1917. Survived by his wife, three sons and six daughters, he died of cancer on 7 December 1918 at his Claremont home and was buried in Karrakatta cemetery. His estate was sworn for probate at £16 523.

Strong and stubborn, Wilson had a quick mind and did not suffer fools gladly; he attracted opposition from Labor and some in his own party for his conservatism and for the potential conflict of interest between his political and business dealings. A measure of opportunism and lack of political acumen hindered his parliamentary career, but he was a very successful businessman and a prominent figure in the community. Notable for his publicly avowed moral values, he was a loyal friend and a much-loved father.

W. B. Kimberly (ed), *History of West Australia* (Melb, 1897); C. P. Bryan, *Frank Wilson esq* (Perth, 1912); J. S. Battye (ed), *Cyclopedia of Western Australia*, 1-2 (Adel, 1912, 1913); A. R. Grant, *Memories of parliament* (Perth, 1937); B. D. Graham, *The formation of the Australian Country parties* (Canb, 1966); Roy Com on the Collie coalfields, Report, *PP* (WA), 1905, 2 (9), p 271; *West Australian*, 19 Nov 1895, 2, 19 Apr 1897, 9, 10 Dec 1918; L. B. McIntyre, The development of trade unionism in Western Australia and the operation of industrial conciliation and arbitration, 1900-1914 (M.A. thesis, Univ WA, 1972); F. D. Adams, A biography of Sir Newton James Moore with special reference to his role in Western Australian politics (M.A. thesis, Univ WA, 1973); D. W. Black, The National Party in Western Australia, 1917-1930: its origins and development with an introductory survey of 'Liberal' Party organisation, 1901-1916 (M.A. thesis, Univ WA, 1974); scrap-book of press cuttings relating to F. Wilson's time in office, 1911 (BL); information from Ms L. Wilson, Subiaco, Perth.

DAVID BLACK

WILSON, GORDON CAMPBELL (1895-1929), soldier and airman, was born on 6 October 1895 at Minmi, New South Wales, fifth surviving child of William Wilson, a miner from Scotland, and his Tasmanian-born wife Agnes Cecilia, née Jackson. Educated at public schools and Newcastle Technical College, he became an apprentice patternmaker with the engineering firm A. Goninon & Co. Ltd.

At the outbreak of World War I Wilson was a member of the 39th Fortress Company, Engineers, Australian Military Forces, and soon after transferred to the Australian Imperial Force. He embarked from Sydney as a lance corporal with the 1st Field Company, Engineers, in October. After training in Egypt, his unit was among the first to land at Gallipoli on 25 April 1915 and Wilson's work in trench consolidation during that day's desperate fighting came under special notice. Although wounded during the first month, he remained on duty, distinguishing himself in mining and trench construction, until relieved in November. He was mentioned in dispatches and later awarded the Distinguished Conduct Medal for his Gallipoli service and for his work as a section sergeant of the 5th Division, Engineers, particularly during the battle of Fromelles, France, in July 1916.

Transferring to the Australian Flying Corps in December, Wilson was commissioned as a second lieutenant, A.F.C., in April 1917 and graduated as a pilot. In June he joined No.68 Squadron (later designated the 2nd Squadron) A.F.C., and flew De Havilland 5 aircraft. With other pilots of the three new A.F.C. squadrons soon to mobilize for overseas service, he was detached to a Royal Flying Corps squadron in France to gain practical experience in war flying. Wilson joined No.32 Squadron, R.F.C., in late July, but was wounded while carrying out low-level strafing during the 3rd battle of Ypres, Belgium. Rejoining his squadron in England, he was appointed flight commander, promoted captain and accompanied the squadron to France in September. Equipped with aeroplanes inferior in performance and armament to enemy fighters, the squadron received special training in ground attack and played an important part—though with heavy casualties—in the battle of Cambrai in November: no fewer than six squadron pilots, among them Wilson, were awarded the Military Cross on the same day for their difficult and dangerous low-level bombing and strafing in support of ground operations. Clashes with the Germans were frequent and Wilson was credited with the destruction of one enemy aircraft which he shot down and then blew to pieces with a bomb.

Recalled to England in February 1918 to strengthen the expanding A.F.C. training organization, Wilson served as a flight commander, flying instructor and commanding officer in No.8 (Training) Squadron. He was awarded the Air Force Cross in June 1919 for distinguished war service and returned to Australia that month. His A.I.F. appointment ended in July. His brothers, Ronald and Alexander, had also served at Gallipoli.

Among the first war pilots to engage in civil aviation in Australia, 'Skipper' Wilson worked as a licensed pilot and ground engineer in a number of aviation enterprises and was associated with Charles Ulm [q.v.]. Without government support, however, virtually all these post-war aviation ventures failed; from time to time Wilson took other jobs, such as opal-mining. On 11 March 1929, while employed by New South Wales Airways Ltd, he travelled by car to retrieve an aeroplane; the driver lost control of the vehicle near Bogan Gate and Wilson was killed in the accident. At his funeral service held in St Philip's Church, Newcastle, representatives of municipal, aviation and ex-service organizations, together with friends like Ulm and (Sir) Charles Kingsford Smith [q.v.9], paid tribute to Wilson's character, war service and contribution to civil aviation. He was buried in the Presbyterian section of Sandgate cemetery. Wilson was engaged to be married at the time of his death.

C. E. W. Bean, *The A.I.F. in France*, 1916 (Syd, 1929); F. M. Cutlack, *The Australian Flying Corps* (Syd, 1923); R. McNicoll, *The Royal Australian Engineers 1902 to 1919*, 2, *Making and breaking* (Canb, 1979); *London Gazette*, 28 Jan, 29 Dec 1916, 1 Feb 1918, 3 June 1919; *Aircraft* (Melb), 20 June, 20 July 1921, 1 Jan 1926, 30 June 1928; *Sabretache*, Jan 1977; *Parkes Post*, 12 Mar 1929; *Newcastle Morning Herald*, 13, 15 Mar 1929; War diaries, 2nd *and* No 8 (Training) Squadron, Aust Flying Corps, *and* Nominal roll (embarkation), 1st Field Company, Engineers, AIF (AWM); information from A. Goninon & Co Ltd, Newcastle, NSW, *and* Mr C. Schaedel, Park Holme, SA.   ALAN FRASER

WILSON, GRACE MARGARET (1879-1957), nursing sister and army matron-in-chief, was born on 25 June 1879 in South Brisbane, eldest child of John Pearson Wilson, clerk, and his wife Fanny Campbell, née Lang, both Scottish born. Educated at Brisbane Girls' Grammar School, Grace entered Brisbane Hospital as a probationer in 1905 and gained her certificate in 1908. In London she trained in midwifery at Queen Charlotte's Lying-in Hospital before joining the staff of the National Hospital for the Paralysed and Epileptic (Albany Memorial).

Back in Queensland, she became matron of Brisbane Hospital in July 1914. Joining the Australian Army Nursing Service in October, she was appointed principal matron of the 1st Military District. On 15 April 1915 Wilson transferred to the Australian Imperial Force; as principal matron of the 3rd Australian General Hospital, she embarked for England in May. The hospital was transferred to Lemnos to treat Anzac casualties; with her staff, she arrived there in early August to find conditions 'too awful for words'. Their equipment had been delayed: there were few tents and mattresses, no beds, and only spirit lamps for cooking and sterilizing. Encouraging the nurses to contend with such primitive conditions, she soon created order out of chaos; by 13 August the hospital was treating 900 patients. Dysentery became a later problem and winter brought men suffering from frost-bite and gangrene. Despite all difficulties, the hospital's mortality rate was only 2 per cent.

Early in 1916 the 3rd A.G.H. was transferred to Abbassia, Egypt. Mentioned in dispatches three times that year, Matron Wilson was awarded the Royal Red Cross, 1st class, in May. She moved with the hospital to Brighton, England, in October, and to Abbeville, France, in April 1917. The unit initially had 1500 beds and expanded to 2000.

In September she was appointed temporary matron-in-chief at A.I.F. Headquarters, London, to relieve Matron Conyers [q.v.8]. Although Wilson enjoyed the administrative experience, she longed to be back with 'her family' at Abbeville. Returning there in April 1918, by judgement, tact and ability she ensured a high standard of conduct. Again mentioned in dispatches in December, she was appointed C.B.E. on 1 January 1919. After the 3rd A.G.H. was dismantled in May, she was posted to the 3rd Australian Auxiliary Hospital at Dartford, Kent, before coming home to Queensland in January 1920. Her A.I.F. appointment ended in April.

As matron from November 1920 of the Children's Hospital, Melbourne, Wilson improved conditions for her nurses and succeeded in winning trainees a nominal wage. Openly critical of the hospital committee, she resigned two years later and bought a private hospital, Somerset House, in East Melbourne. In January 1933 she became matron of the Alfred Hospital. Determined to improve the standard of nursing, she formed a training school committee, appointed two tutor sisters and introduced an orientation course for probationers.

Wilson had become matron-in-chief of the army nursing reserve in August 1925. Awarded the Florence Nightingale medal in 1929, she led the A.A.N.S.'s coronation contingent in London in 1937. She resigned from the Alfred when she was called up for full-time duty in World War II. Appointed to the A.I.F. in September 1940, she served in the Middle East until ill health forced her return to Australia in August 1941; her A.I.F. appointment ended next month. On 15 September 1943 she became executive officer, nursing control section, Department of Manpower Directorate (Victoria).

A life member of the Australasian Trained Nurses' Association, Wilson was a councilmember of the Royal Victorian Trained Nurses' Association and sometime president of its successor, the Royal Victorian College of Nursing; she helped to establish postgraduate training courses. Three times president of the Returned Nurses' Club, she was a trustee of the Edith Cavell Trust Fund and of the Shrine of Remembrance, and in 1953 was made a life member of the Returned Sailors', Soldiers' and Airmen's Imperial League of Australia. She was also active in the Australian Red Cross Society and the Girl Guides'

Association, and belonged to the Lyceum Club.

Tall, slim and attractive in her youth, Wilson had that 'rare quality which inspired deep and lasting loyalty'. A self-disciplined leader, she had a sympathetic ear for her staff; believing it a privilege to help soldiers, she was proud of the A.A.N.S. She had a great gift for living.

During a visit to London, on 12 January 1954 Grace Wilson married Robert Wallace Bruce Campbell at Holy Trinity parish church, Roehampton. Survived by her husband, she died on 12 January 1957 in the Repatriation General Hospital, Heidelberg, Melbourne, and was cremated after a service with full military honours at Christ Church, South Yarra.

Who's who in the world of women, 1 (Melb, 1930); A. S. Walker, *Medical services of the R.A.N. and R.A.A.F.* (Canb, 1961); L. Gardiner, *Royal Children's Hospital Melbourne 1870-1970* (Melb, 1970); A. M. Mitchell, *The hospital south of the Yarra* (Melb, 1977); R. Goodman (ed), *Queensland nurses* (Brisb, 1985) and *Our war nurses* (Brisb, 1988); H. Gregory, *A tradition of care* (Brisb, 1988); *UNA*, Jan 1957; Roy Brisb Hospital nursing records; Roy Vic College of Nursing records; Aust Army Nursing Service, Seniority lists (AWM) *and* records (Dept of Defence, Canb); G. Wilson personal diary, WWI (copy held by author); information from Mrs M. Weedon, c/- Mrs J. Campbell, Aspley, Brisb.

JANICE McCARTHY

WILSON, HERBERT WARD (1877-1955), lecturer in science, was born on 29 September 1877 at Bradford, Yorkshire, England, fifth child of William Wilson, joiner, and his wife Fanny, née Ward. The family migrated to Australia in 1883, settling at Dimboola, Victoria, where William became a farmer and builder. Herbert attended a local school and in 1894 joined the Education Department. While teaching in remote areas of the colony, he matriculated in 1896. Fascinated by natural history, he made it his lifelong study; though reference books were few, he was encouraged by naturalists and was well prepared when it became a school subject in the early 1900s. At exhibitions held in various inspectorates, Wilson's talents were quickly recognized. Chosen to undergo special instruction at the Melbourne Training College, he completed the course brilliantly and was appointed lecturer in nature study; as deputy to J. A. Leach [q.v.10], he assisted him with publications.

In 1908 Wilson commenced a diploma of agriculture with honours in agricultural botany at the University of Melbourne, but college duties and World War I interrupted his course. Enlisting in the Australian Imperial Force on 11 March 1915, he served at

Gallipoli, in Egypt and in France where he gave instruction in gas warfare and liaised between armies in France and the Chemical Warfare Committee, London. Promoted lieutenant (1917) and captain (1918), he was demobilized in July 1919 with the rank of major; awarded the Military Cross (1918) and the Belgian Croix de Guerre avec palme (1921), he was twice mentioned in dispatches and was appointed O.B.E. (1919).

Returning to civilian life, 'the major' resumed work at the teachers' college and his studies at the university (B.Sc., 1920; M.Sc., 1925). He shared the 1922 MacBain [q.v.5] research scholarship for botany and later lectured on the subject at the university. In 1924-42 he was lecturer in method for geography and biological science at the university's school of education; in 1927-52 he lectured in botany at the Victorian College of Pharmacy and was examiner to the Pharmacy Board of Victoria. Retiring from the Melbourne Teachers' College in 1942, Wilson requested and was granted permission to continue at the pharmacy college until the last of his ex-servicemen students had completed the course.

A member of the Royal Australasian Ornithologists' Union, the Bird Observers' Club, the Field Naturalists' Club of Victoria and the Microscopical Society, Wilson had been responsible for founding the Gould [q.v.1] League of Bird Lovers of Victoria (1910) and for its subsequent spread to other States: in 1963 a perpetual trophy was named in his honour. He had also been awarded the Natural History medallion in 1943. Stout and 5 ft. 10 ins. (177.8 cm) tall, he covered his bald head with a black skull-cap. His forthright manner and dominant personality hid a dedicated and highly disciplined nature; his descriptive language, humour and unconventional manner of teaching transmitted enthusiasm to his students. Survived by his son, Wilson died at his Caulfield home on 1 October 1955 and was cremated; he left an estate sworn for probate at £11 122. His wife, Myra Hester, née Smith, whom he had married at St John's Anglican Church, Camberwell, on 22 May 1920, had predeceased him.

Univ Melb Gazette, 11, no 6, Nov 1955, p 84; *Vic Naturalist*, 72, pt 10, Feb 1956, p 148; *Education Mag*, 13, no 3, Apr 1956, p 97; *A'sian J of Pharmacy*, 49, no 585, Sept 1968, p 669.

TESS KLOOT

WILSON, JAMES ALEXANDER CAMPBELL (1879-1963), dentist, was born on 14 October 1879, at Carlton, Melbourne, twelfth child of Thomas Wilson, stone merchant, and his wife Martha, née Moffatt, both Scottish born. Educated at New College, Box Hill, in 1896 James enrolled in the Australian College of Dentistry, Melbourne (M.A.C.D., 1901); he also passed the Dental Board of Victoria's examinations. He graduated (D.D.S., 1903) from the University of Pennsylvania, United States of America, and went to England for further experience and study. On 16 August 1905 he married Agnes Rose (d. 1931) at the Congregational Church, Stockport, Cheshire. Returning to Australia in 1905, he took a locum-tenency in Perth where he began his own practice in 1909.

Commissioned in the 11th Australian Infantry Regiment in 1908, Wilson held the rank of captain in the 88th Perth Infantry by August 1914. He was appointed major in the Australian Imperial Force in May 1915 and served briefly at Gallipoli with the 28th Battalion. Invalided to England with amoebic dysentery, he was discharged as medically unfit in April 1916 on his return to Fremantle.

Foundation secretary (1909) of the Western Australia Dental Society, Wilson was a member from 1910 (chairman, 1922-53) of the Dental Board of Western Australia and used that body as a base for his energy and talents. Following changes in 1920 to the Dentists Act (1899) which greatly reduced professional morale, he confided to Wynn Needham, the registrar of the board, his determination to see a dental hospital and dental school established in the State. With the co-operation of the board, dental classes were introduced in 1922 at Perth Technical School and the Perth Dental Hospital opened in 1927. Wilson's particular skill was in leading, inspiring and reconciling conflicting factions: he chose his colleagues carefully, even recruiting some of his strongest opponents to serve on the board of management of Perth Dental Hospital where they became staunch supporters of the scheme they had originally fought.

On 3 December 1932 he married Laura McCrae at St Patrick's Anglican Church, Inglewood. Innately modest and kind, Jim Wilson was 5 ft. 6½ ins. (168.9 cm) tall; alert and lively, he had a keen wit, a ready sense of fun and a love of sport, particularly motoring. At the investiture of his C.B.E. (1953) in Perth in 1954, Queen Elizabeth II inquired what branch of medicine he represented; when Wilson replied, 'the gentle art of painless dentistry', the Queen responded: 'Had I the time, I would debate that remark with you!'

After his retirement in 1953, Wilson practised part time at Rockingham when no district dentist was available. On a return trip, his car collided with a bus and he was fatally injured; he died in Royal Perth Hospital on 20

April 1963 and was cremated. He was survived by his wife, their son and daughter, and by two sons of his first marriage.

J. S. Battye (ed), *Cyclopedia of Western Australia* (Adel, 1912, 1913); R. F. Stockwell, The history of Perth Dental Hospital *and* The origins of the dental profession in Western Australia (tss, held by Dental School Lib, Perth, Lib of RWAHS and BL); information from Mrs L. Wilson, Sth Perth, Miss E. H. Wilson, Innalloo, Perth, and Mrs M. Norman, Mundaring, WA.   R. F. STOCKWELL

WILSON, JAMES LOCKIE (1880-1956), pastoralist and studmaster, was born on 29 August 1880 at St Leonards, Sydney, fifth surviving son of David Wilson, merchant, and his wife Annie, née Struth, both Sydney born. Educated at Sydney Grammar School and Hawkesbury Agricultural College, Richmond, he served in the South African War in 1899-1901. He purchased Calliope station, near Gladstone, Queensland, in 1905 in partnership with P. J. C. McDouall whose daughter, Jessie, he married with Anglican rites on 18 April 1906 in the Church of the Good Shepherd, Belford, New South Wales.

On 8 February 1916 Wilson enlisted in the 11th Battalion, Australian Imperial Force, and was promoted sergeant in May. Attached to the 1st Australian Tunnelling Company in 1917, he helped to drive a 110-foot (33.53 m) tunnel beneath Hill 60 near Ypres and to plant 40 tons (40 640 kg) of high explosives under the enemy. Embarking in January 1919, he was discharged in April.

With McDouall, he bought Calliungal, Rannes and Balcomba stations, all in central Queensland. Balcomba, on the Mackenzie River, was 209 square miles (541.3 km²). By the 1930s Calliope and its associated stations ran 45 000 head of cattle. The partners founded a Hereford stud in 1919 and a Poll Hereford stud in 1936. Wilson was a councillor of both breed societies; Calliope Herefords became champions at Brisbane and Sydney shows from the 1920s.

An executive member of the United Graziers' Association for twenty-seven years, Wilson chaired its cattle committee. He and Edward Archer [q.v.7] were responsible for the formation in 1936 of the Central Coastal Graziers' Association (affiliated with the U.G.A.) which catered for the specialist needs of beef producers. Wilson's commitment to the British Hereford (*Bos taurus*) led him to oppose the introduction into Queensland of tropical Zebu cattle (*Bos indicus*) by the Council of Scientific and Industrial Research in 1933. The powerful influence of the U.G.A. cattle committee restricted experimental breeding by the C.S.I.R. to privately-owned stations. Despite criticism of the mongrel-

izing of British breeds, the development of tropically adapted Brahman stock eventually revolutionized the beef cattle industry in northern Australia.

As director (from 1912) and chairman (1923-34) of the Port Curtis Co-operative Dairy Association Ltd, Wilson was largely responsible for its expansion to seven butter factories in central Queensland in the interwar period. In 1925 he led a band of primary producers who broke a waterside workers' strike at Gladstone. Wilson was a member of the Gladstone Harbour Board from its inception in 1914 until 1942, a Calliope Shire councillor for over twenty years and president of the Gladstone Show Society. As a member of the Royal National Association (president 1948-51), he initiated many reforms in the showing of beef cattle. He was appointed C.B.E. in 1955. Survived by three daughters and a son, Wilson died on 13 November 1956 at Toowoomba and was cremated.

Calliope tropicalised Herefords (Brisb, nd, 1969?); L. McDonald, *Gladstone* and *Cattle country* (Brisb, 1988); *Pastoral Review*, 17 Dec 1956, p 1547; family information supplied by Mr R. W. L. Wilson, Banana, Qld.   LORNA McDONALD

WILSON, JAMES THOMAS (1861-1945), anatomist, was born on 14 April 1861 at Moniaive, Dumfriesshire, Scotland, son of Thomas Wilson, a Free Church schoolmaster, and his wife Helen, née Brown, also a teacher. James was educated by his parents and by an eccentric medical naturalist, Dr T. B. Grierson; at the University of Edinburgh (M.B., C.M., 1883), he also pursued an interest in philosophy with two friends, J. S. Haldane and James Lorrain Smith, subscribing to the Idealist school of T. H. Green and Edward Caird. There followed six months as resident house surgeon under John Duncan at the Royal Infirmary, Edinburgh, two winter sessions demonstrating anatomy under Professor Sir William Turner at the university and three voyages to China as ship's surgeon.

For reasons of health, finances and career prospects, in 1887 Wilson accepted (Sir) Thomas Anderson Stuart's [q.v.] offer of appointment as demonstrator in anatomy at the University of Sydney's new medical school and arrived in Sydney on 22 February 1887 in the *Orient* with Professor (Sir) Mungo MacCallum [q.v.10] who became an intimate friend. In 1890 Wilson became the first occupant of the Challis [q.v.3] chair of anatomy. That year on 4 September at Chalmers Presbyterian Church, Adelaide, he married Jane Elizabeth Smith, sister of his Edinburgh friend. Jane died on 14 July 1891, leaving a 3-day-old daughter. On 14 September 1898 at

Woollahra Presbyterian Church, Sydney, he married Mabel Mildred Millicent (d. 1944), daughter of Sir Julian Salomons [q.v.6].

A keen naturalist from boyhood, Wilson readily espoused Edinburgh's traditional emphasis on comparative anatomy. His great achievements were to found in Sydney an anatomy school in the Edinburgh mould and to build a tradition of research which drew international respect. He taught anatomy as a biological science, emphasizing dissection and museum and laboratory techniques in which he was highly accomplished. For thirty years he ran a rapidly expanding department with heavy teaching commitments, assisted only by a small technical staff and teams of student demonstrators.

Tall, spare and severe, but really the kindest of men, a dull lecturer who yet inspired his students by his fierce dedication to his subject, 'Jummy'—as he was called by staff and students (except in his presence)—was at his best in the laboratory 'advising, criticizing and, above all, encouraging, all with great vehemence'. With the physiologist (Sir) Charles Martin [q.v.10], Wilson led a distinguished group of researchers, including (Sir) Grafton Elliot Smith and J. P. Hill [qq.v.11,9], in the first sustained and authoritative studies by locally-based scientists of Australia's native fauna. A self-supporting, interdisciplinary, informal postgraduate team, they kept abreast of British, European and American developments. Wilson's contribution to the first international congress of anatomists in Geneva (1905)—on his work with Hill on the embryology of the platypus—was accorded first place by *Nature*'s reviewer. In 1909 Wilson was elected a fellow of the Royal Society, London. Anderson Stuart built the Sydney medical school; Wilson furnished it with a reputation.

His research effort declined as his teaching and administrative loads increased, and as colleagues dispersed, but his enduring interest in neurology led him to build an excellent undergraduate course in neuro-anatomy and generated a growing enthusiasm for postgraduate neurological research. As president of the anatomy, physiology and pharmacology section of the Australasian Medical Congress (1908), he reviewed current work, controversies and clinical implications in neurology which had, he claimed, 'almost won rank as a distinct branch of biological science'.

Well versed in literature, theology and especially philosophy, Wilson tried to reconcile deep religious sensibilities with materialist science. In two fine addresses as president (1898-99) of the Linnean Society of New South Wales he challenged the vitalist views of his friend Haldane. A mechanist who regularly attended church and took communion as 'a toast to the Almighty', and a devout Christian who yet denied the divinity of Christ, Wilson pursued scientific truth with religious dedication. With fellow Idealists (Sir) Francis Anderson [q.v.7] and MacCallum, he promoted adult education through University Extension Board lectures, the Workers' Educational Association, the Toynbee Guild and the Student Christian Movement. He joined colleagues like Archibald Liversidge and (Sir) Edgeworth David [qq.v.5,8] to stimulate and gain recognition for science through the Australasian Association for the Advancement of Science, the Royal Society of New South Wales, the Linnean Society and the Australian Museum, Sydney. Wilson addressed medical congresses and student medical societies, and in 1916 helped to inaugurate at the university a society for combating venereal diseases. As an Imperialist, he supported the Victoria League, the Round Table and the Australian National Defence League.

Having been commissioned in 1898 in the New South Wales Scottish Rifles, 5th Infantry Regiment, Wilson was promoted captain in 1899; a major, he succeeded Lieut-Colonel Gerald Campbell [q.v.7] as commandant in 1907. In 1908-13 he was appointed State commandant of the new Australian Intelligence Corps. With David, in 1900 he had sponsored the Sydney University Volunteer Rifle Corps. On the outbreak of war, Wilson was immediately called up with the rank of lieut-colonel to organize and command the censor's office, 2nd Military District (New South Wales). Ill health forced his retirement in December 1915; he was mentioned in military orders for 'meritorious services'. On 1 December 1917 he was recruited as an honorary adviser to the intelligence section, General Staff; he retired from the army in August 1920.

An able but unwilling administrator, Wilson was chairman (1908-13, 1916-20) of the professorial board and *ex officio* fellow of the senate from 1916. He emerged as a university leader of energy, wisdom and integrity as the board became more assertive on staff and curriculum questions and on broad education issues. In 1919 his administrative burden increased due to post-war student numbers and the McCaughey [q.v.5] bequest. He devised an improved faculty system with provision for research, planned a new anatomical institute and pushed for the establishment of a second chair in physiology. A long rift between the two leaders of the medical faculty ended with the death of Anderson Stuart in 1920. Dean of medicine for the first time, Wilson promptly reclaimed histology (microscopical anatomy) from the physiology department. Before he left New South Wales in August 1920 to take the chair of anatomy at the University of Cambridge he arranged for his young protégé John Hunter [q.v.9] to succeed him. In 1924 Wilson declined to return to Sydney as the university's first executive vice-chancellor.

At Cambridge he expanded the routine clinical fare of anatomy and introduced new courses. Elected a fellow of St John's College (1920), the Zoological Society of London and the Cambridge Philosophical Society (president 1924-26), Wilson began to mellow long before he retired in 1934. In England he served Australian universities on selection committees for academic appointments and as an executive councillor (1921-38) of the Universities' Bureau of the British Empire. He was a councillor of the Anatomical Society of Great Britain and Ireland (president 1922-24) which, on his eightieth birthday, dedicated volume 76 to the 'Nestor' of British anatomists. Wilson died on 2 September 1945 at Cambridge and was cremated. The daughter of his first marriage survived him, as did the three daughters and three sons of his second. At the University of Sydney he is commemorated by an anatomical museum and a portrait by William Nicholson.

C. D. Coulthard-Clark, *The Citizen General Staff* (Canb, 1976); J. A. Young et al (eds), *Centenary book of the University of Sydney faculty of medicine* (Syd, 1984); *Cambridge Review*, 10 Nov 1945; *Nature* (Lond), and *MJA*, 29 Dec 1945; *Obituary Notices of Fellows of the Roy Soc*, 6, no 18, Nov 1949; *Bulletin of the Post-Graduate Cttee in Medicine, Univ Syd*, Apr 1950; Wilson family papers (temporarily held by author); Wilson papers *and* Univ Syd Senate and Professorial Bd minutes (Univ Syd Archives).

PATRICIA MORISON

WILSON, JOHN PURVES (1852-1932), headmaster, was born on 1 April 1852 at Dalkeith, Edinburgh, son of James Wilson, railway platelayer, and his wife Isabella, née Pringle. Migrating with his parents to Victoria, John was educated at the Flinders National School, Geelong, and the University of Melbourne (B.A., 1875; M.A., 1877; LL.B., 1882; LL.D., 1885) where he gained third- and fourth-year exhibitions in law. On 6 January 1874 he married English-born Harriet Vile with Methodist forms at Geelong.

After teaching for the Education Department, Wilson was appointed mathematics master at Presbyterian Ladies' College, East Melbourne. His infectious enthusiasm for his subject and his distinctive blend of bullying and coaxing earned the school regular matriculation honours and the exhibition in 1890. On George Tait's [q.v.] resignation, Wilson became vice-principal in 1879 under Andrew Harper [q.v.9] and, on the latter's resignation in 1889, headmaster. Dr Wilson was then a strong, stocky man, with Dundreary whiskers and 'a face full of character'.

Henry Handel Richardson [q.v.11] in *The getting of wisdom* portrayed him unsympathetically: 'A tiny little nose was as if squashed flat on his face, above a grotesquely expressive mouth ... He had small short-sighted, red-rimmed eyes, and curly hair', but even the prickly Laura soon found herself 'bewitched' by his exuberance. He was a vital force in the school, teaching cricket, editing the school magazine, *Patchwork*, and, above all, encouraging intellectual aspirations in his female students. After retirement in 1906, he remained involved with the school council and Old Collegians' Association.

In 1907 he was acting master and tutor at Ormond [q.v.5] College during the absence of (Sir) John MacFarland [q.v.10]. From 1910 until his death Wilson was a member of the university council and in 1911-28 chairman of its finance committee. He served on the committee which proposed a radical reorganization of the administration of the university in 1913 and on that which initiated a student loan fund in 1919. A foundation member (1884) and president (1901-03) of the Melbourne Shakespeare Society, Wilson was president of the Incorporated Association of Secondary Teachers of Victoria in 1904 and 1910, and published two mathematical textbooks. He was active in the Presbyterian Church, a councillor of Scotch College, president of the Melbourne Orphanage, and a director of Langridge Mutual Permanent Building Society and the Victorian Malay Rubber Plantation.

Tributes from colleagues and pupils portray Wilson as an endearing man with a simplicity of character, a bubbling sense of humour and unfailing good nature. It is difficult to reconcile these impressions with the anti-papist, pro-conscriptionist Wilson who wrote in 1918 of that 'archdevil of hypocrisy, lying and treachery—Herr Mannix' [q.v.10] and his cohorts of 'Irish, whose highest ideal is to shoot a man from behind a hedge, and cold-footers and shirkers . . . [and] sentimental old women'.

Predeceased by his wife and two sons, Wilson died at his Kew home on 28 May 1932 and was buried in Melbourne general cemetery. Two daughters survived him. His estate was sworn for probate at £27 578. A portrait by Josephine Muntz-Adams, commissioned by the General Assembly of the Presbyterian Church of Victoria in 1906, is in Presbyterian Ladies' College.

J. Smith (ed), *Cyclopedia of Victoria*, 2 (Melb, 1904); E. Scott, *A history of the University of Melbourne* (Melb, 1936); M. O. Reid, *The ladies came to stay* (Melb, 1960); K. Fitzpatrick, *PLC Melbourne* (Melb, 1975); *Vic Presbyterian Messenger*, 3, 10 June 1932; *Age, Argus, Herald* (Melb), 28 May 1932.

DIANE LANGMORE

WILSON, LACHLAN CHISHOLM (1871-1947), lawyer and soldier, was born on 11 July 1871 at Logan River, Queensland, third child of Charles Wilson, farmer, and his wife Ann Mary, née Chisholm, both Scottish born. Educated at Brisbane Grammar School, Wilson was admitted to the Queensland Bar in 1895; he then practised at Townsville where he married Sydney-born Nellie Grant Hartley at St James's Anglican Pro-Cathedral on 27 June 1903.

He had fought in the South African War as a corporal in the 2nd Queensland Mounted Infantry Contingent, serving in the advance to Johannesburg and Pretoria, the battle of Diamond Hill and other actions. Commissioned in the 15th Light Horse Regiment in 1904, he trained with other future leaders of the Light Horse under Lieut-Colonel (Sir) Harry Chauvel [q.v.7]. Promoted major in 1911, Wilson was second-in-command of the Moreton Regiment after his return to Brisbane. There he entered into a partnership with E. K. Tully to form one of Queensland's leading law firms.

Joining the Australian Imperial Force as a major on 30 September 1914, in November Wilson transferred from the 7th Light Horse Regiment to the 5th (Queensland) Regiment of which he became second-in-command. He landed at Gallipoli in May 1915 and took charge of the 5th on 1 August after its commanding officer was killed. A lieut-colonel from that date, Wilson mounted a successful raid against Bird Trenches near Gaba Tepe on 23 August; in November, after repulsing a Turkish attack, he seized positions known thereafter as Wilson's Lookout.

In April 1916 he led the advance of the Anzac Mounted Division across the Suez Canal when the Turks attacked near Romani. Wilson took part in almost all the major engagements between the battle of Romani (4-5 August 1916) and the capture of Damascus (October 1918). He introduced the Queensland spear-point pump to obtain water in the desert: it was a portable device which could raise water quickly; with canvas troughs, it simplified the watering of the horses.

When Brigadier General J. R. Royston [q.v.11] returned to South Africa on the eve of the 3rd battle of Gaza (30 October 1917), Wilson was given command of the 3rd Light Horse Brigade as colonel and temporary brigadier general. Short and stocky, quiet and shy, Wilson was the antithesis of his predecessor. In the 2nd battle of the Jordan (30 April to 4 May 1918) he seized Es Salt with astonishing speed and, when the Turks counter-attacked, succeeded in withdrawing his brigade from a perilous situation. Forty miles (64.4 km) behind the Turkish lines after the breakthrough at Megiddo (20 September-

ber), Wilson's brigade advanced southwards on Jenin, capturing three or four times their own number. On 1 October Wilson changed the course of the battle for Damascus by boldly directing his brigade through the city at dawn, leaving thousands of Turks cut off while his regiments pressed up the road to Homs. He called off the pursuit on 2 October after taking another 2000 Turks; in a fortnight the 3rd Brigade had captured over 11 000 prisoners.

While Wilson was at Moascar early in 1919 waiting to embark for Australia, a rebellion broke out against British rule in Egypt. He was ordered to Zagazig where he soon had seven regiments under his command. Clashes with rioters cost his troops about twenty casualties, but by April the violence had subsided and repatriation was resumed. Wilson was appointed C.B. and C.M.G., awarded the Distinguished Service Order and the French Croix de Guerre, and mentioned in dispatches six times.

After a brief period on the unattached list, Australian Military Forces, Wilson was aide-de-camp to the governor-general in 1923-27 and commanded the 11th Infantry Brigade in 1925-29. He was commander, 1st Cavalry Brigade, in 1929-31 and State commandant for Queensland of the Volunteer Defence Corps in 1941-42.

Wilson's law partnership prospered and he extended his business interests as a director of the Australian Mutual Provident Society. He was chairman of directors of Cribb & Foote and of Alexanders Pty Ltd. The welfare of ex-servicemen and women became one of his chief activities and he collaborated with Captain H. Wetherell in writing *The Fifth Light Horse Regiment 1914-1919* (Sydney, 1926). Survived by his wife, son and a daughter, Wilson died at his New Farm home on 7 April 1947 and was buried in Toowong cemetery.

H. S. Gullett, *The A.I.F. in Sinai and Palestine* (Syd, 1923); C. E. W. Bean, *The story of Anzac*, 2 (Syd, 1924); S. Brugger, *Australians and Egypt* (Melb, 1980); *Reveille* (Syd), May 1936; *Qld Digger*, May 1947.   A. J. HILL

WILSON, SIR LESLIE ORME (1876-1955), soldier, politician and governor, was born on 1 August 1876 in London, son of Henry Wilson, stockbroker, and his wife Ada Alexandrina, née Orme. Educated at St Michael's School, Westgate, and St Paul's School, London, he was appointed second lieutenant in the Royal Marine Light Infantry in 1895, lieutenant in 1896 and captain in 1901.

After serving (1899-1901) in the South African War in which he was wounded, mentioned in dispatches, and awarded the

Queen's Medal with five clasps and the Distinguished Service Order, he was aide-de-camp (1903-09) to Sir Harry Rawson [q.v.11], governor of New South Wales. On 10 June 1909 at Christ Church, Mayfair, London, Wilson married Winifred May, eldest daughter of Charles Smith [q.v.6], a Sydney merchant.

While a captain of the Berkshire Royal Artillery (Territorials), Wilson won Reading in the 1913 elections and took his seat in the House of Commons in early 1914. With the outbreak of war he was made a temporary lieut-colonel in the Royal Marines and given command of the Hawke Battalion of the Royal Naval Division. Following service at Gallipoli, during which he was again mentioned in dispatches, Wilson was sent to France in 1915 where, in the following November, he was severely wounded. He was appointed C.M.G. in 1916.

In late 1918 he became parliamentary assistant secretary in the war cabinet, in 1919 chairman of the National Maritime Board, and in 1921 parliamentary secretary to the treasury and chief Unionist whip. At the historic Carlton Club meeting in October 1922 he sided with the Conservative breakaway. Having won South Portsmouth at a by-election, he was sworn to the Privy Council in 1922 and served as chief government whip. In 1923 he was appointed G.C.I.E. and governor of Bombay.

The uneasy system of diarchy by which India was governed, together with the serious depression of the cotton textile industry on which Bombay so largely depended, made the position of governor no sinecure. Sir Leslie dealt with the most serious and prolonged strike in the history of the Indian manufacturing industry with firmness and goodwill. He preferred persuasion to intervention. As chief scout of Bombay he improved facilities for education, while his Governor's Hospital Fund (keenly supported by Lady Wilson) increased the efficiency of voluntary institutions. In 1928 he completed his office and in 1929 was appointed G.C.S.I.

On 13 June 1932 Wilson was sworn in as governor of Queensland. Although he had accepted a less exacting and responsible charge than Bombay, he carried out his constitutional, social and philanthropic duties with zest. A regular traveller to remote areas of the State, he was particularly interested in the welfare and progress of North Queensland. Closely associated with organizations as diverse as the Australian Institute of International Affairs and the Kennel Association of Queensland, he was the driving force behind the Bush Children's Health Scheme. In 1935 the University of Queensland awarded him an honorary LL.D. and in 1937 he was appointed G.C.M.G..

The Queensland government obtained a second quinquennial appointment for Wilson, followed by three annual extensions necessitated by the war: in all, he served fourteen years as governor, a British gubernatorial tenure unequalled since Jonathan Duncan's term at Bombay. Handsome and courteous, Wilson had natural presence. His affable nature, keen interest in sport and the unflagging support he and Lady Wilson gave to organizations and service functions during the war years were warmly regarded by Queenslanders.

Wilson left office on 11 April 1946 and retired to England, but revisited Australia several times to see his son who had a property in Queensland. Survived by his wife, son and daughter, Sir Leslie died in hospital at Chertsey, Surrey, England, on 29 September 1955 after a road accident. His portrait by William Longstaff [q.v.10] hangs in Parliament House, Brisbane.

Queensland and Queenslanders (Brisb, 1936); F. Brockway, *Inside the Left* (Lond, 1942); *PD* (Qld), 6 Aug 1946, p 1; *Brisbane Courier*, 17, 25 Feb, 1 June 1932; *Queenslander*, 16 June 1932; *The Times*, 1 Oct 1955; Wilson collection (Fryer Lib, Univ Qld).   PETER CAHILL

WILSON, MARK (THRALRUM) (1870?-1940), Aboriginal leader, was born in the Lewurindjerar clan of the Jaralde people in the vicinity of Murray Bridge, South Australia, son of Long Billy and Emily Liwuni, later the wife of Bob Wilson. Thralrum grew up in the Aboriginal mission at Point McLeay where he became a teacher both of Christian ethics and general curriculum at the Raukkan school in 1886. Speaking English and Ngarrindjeri (Jeraldkeld), as a young man he was a prominent spokesman for his people at the mission in their negotiations with the management of the Aborigines' Friends' Association. His status and willingness to express his opinions were reflected in 1889 when he was deputed to write a letter of protest over the association's choice of a superintendent after the death of Frederick Taplin. Under some pressure from the mission authorities, Wilson left Raukkan for Adelaide about 1891.

He worked subsequently in various jobs, including shearing, and as a driver for an Adelaide doctor. In 1895 he issued an address of welcome on behalf of South Australian Aborigines to the new governor, Sir Thomas Buxton [q.v.7], and was described by the South Australian *Register* as a 'very intelligent native'. G. K. Jenkin, a historian of Ngarrindjeri culture and society, characterized Wilson as one of the 'most dynamic and influential'

Aboriginal leaders in the colony by the turn of the century.

Like his friend and contemporary David Unaipon [q.v.], Wilson was raised in a strongly Evangelical environment, but it is possible that the extent to which such leaders of that generation retained and transmitted respect for, and details of, traditional knowledge, has been underestimated. Wilson was able to follow Christianity, achieve fluency in the English language, mix with non-Aborigines, remain in employment, yet still keep firmly fixed within Aboriginal society and beliefs. He is gaining recognition in modern Nunga society for his role in passing on memory of the older ways. Little is known of the middle period of his life, but by the 1930s he was well known in the State as an authoritative spokesman for his people on traditional Aboriginal matters. He was acquainted with the anthropologist R. M. Berndt and demonstrated to him the construction of tree-canoes. Another anthropologist, H. K. Fry, recorded aspects of traditional culture told to him by Wilson. In 1937 the Aborigines' Friends' Association recognized Wilson as a distinguished 'old boy' who had been raised and trained by their teachers. For his part, Wilson acknowledged the help of the association in saving the lives of the Ngarrindjeri in the nineteenth century.

Described as an 'Aboriginal labourer', Wilson died of heart disease on 25 November 1940 at Royal Adelaide Hospital. He was unmarried. His burial is unrecorded. On his death the association described him as 'one of the outstanding leaders of the native race, well versed in native traditions, lore and legends. He possessed musical ability, was a capable teacher and speaker and a good chairman' who would be missed by those for whose rights he had been an ardent advocate.

G. Jenkin, *Conquest of the Ngarrindjeri* (Adel, 1979); Aborigines' Friends' Assn, *Annual report*, 1937, 1940.
PETER READ

WILSON, SIR REGINALD VICTOR (1877-1957), businessman and politician, was born on 30 June 1877 in Adelaide, son of James Wilson, commercial traveller, and his wife Elizabeth Ann, née Tonkin. Educated at Riverton and Whinham College, North Adelaide, he worked briefly in a store at Happy Valley, then for six years with H. A. and W. Goode at Port Pirie. In 1898 he bought a store at Broken Hill, New South Wales. On 12 February 1901 he married Lily May Suckling at Holy Trinity Church, Riverton. Poor health brought him to Adelaide in 1903, but he returned in 1906 to Broken Hill where he purchased a grocery business. Becoming a Freemason, Wilson joined the Chamber of Com-

merce and was treasurer of the Silver City Show Committee. In 1908 he was elected an alderman, but in November 1909 transferred his business to Adelaide where he was mayor of St Peters in 1916-17. He unsuccessfully contested the Legislative Assembly seats of Torrens (1912) and East Torrens (1918).

Chosen by the Farmers and Settlers' Association as a candidate in a composite National Party team, Wilson was elected to the Senate in 1919. In parliament he soon came to the attention of S. M. (Viscount) Bruce [q.v.7]. As a member of the royal commission inquiring into Cockatoo Island dockyard (1921), Wilson was conspicuous for his tough questioning and his thoroughness was confirmed by his work on the wireless agreement committee (1921-22). An honorary minister (1923-25) in the Bruce-Page [q.v.11] government with some responsibility for health and immigration, in March 1923 Wilson was nominated by Bruce as chairman of the commission responsible for organizing an Australian pavilion for the British Empire Exhibition at Wembley, London: an integral part of the 'men, money and markets' programme, the pavilion aimed to stimulate immigration, promote foreign investment and extend and open up markets. Wilson's handling of his task drew lavish praise and marked the turning-point of his career. He accompanied Bruce to London in September where he added his voice to the pressure for preference for Australian produce, and was described as 'one of the most capable and business-like ministers who had ever visited England'. In Britain he also discussed a proposed migration agreement and reorganized Australia House 'from top to bottom'. Those who met him warmed to his bluff and breezy personality, valued his candour and forcefulness, and—according to Bruce—regarded him very much as 'a typical Australian'. Wilson subsequently negotiated a reciprocal trade agreement in Canada, visited New York and attended the opening of the Wembley exhibition. He returned to Australia in June 1924.

His meteoric political career continued when Bruce appointed him minister for markets and migration on 16 January 1925. The new portfolio made him *ex officio* deputy president of the Commonwealth Board of Trade. Although he had joined the Country Party, Wilson did not identify with either the Country or Nationalist groupings; nor did he attend meetings of either parliamentary party. As a ministerialist, he believed that he should not have to seek party pre-selection. Angered by his attitude, the South Australian Country Party omitted him from its Senate team: not even Page's intervention induced it to relent. Wilson had fourth place on the non-Labor ticket for the Senate at the general election in December 1925 and was defeated.

Bruce asked him to remain until his term expired (June 1926). Wilson was widely tipped to succeed Sir Joseph Cook [q.v.8] as high commissioner in London. Instead, in January 1926, he was appointed K.B.E.

Sir Victor remained very much a public figure. In the late 1920s he moved to Sydney. As president (1927-39) of the Motion Picture Distributors' Association, he was periodically accused of preferring American to Australian and British film interests—an allegation he flatly rejected. A director of the Australian General Insurance Co. from 1938, he was senior vice-chairman (1938-57) of the Royal North Shore Hospital board, a member (1938-46) of the National Health Research Council and chairman (1939-57) of National Press Pty Ltd. He owned a pastoral property at Mudgee and was part-owner of another near Kingoonya, South Australia.

Wilson was a tireless and cool-headed fighter. Popular and unpretentious, he remained 'just his natural self'—a knight who liked to be called 'Vic'. Predeceased by his wife and son, he died at his Neutral Bay home on 13 July 1957 and was cremated with Anglican rites. Two daughters survived him.

Advertiser (Adel), 6 Jan 1920, 17 Jan 1925, 21 Jan 1926, 15 July 1957; *SMH*, 10 Feb 1923, 17 Jan 1925, 21 Jan 1926, 30 June 1939; *Observer* (Adel), 24 Jan 1925, 23 Jan 1926; *Register* (Adel), 21 Jan 1926; *Chronicle* (Adel), 6 July 1933; *Sun-Herald*, 14 July 1957; Wilson papers (held by Mr T. W. Ilbery, Greenwich, Syd, and Mr L. Wilson, Moonamby, near Mudgee, NSW.   MALCOLM SAUNDERS

WILSON, WALTER HORATIO (1839-1902), solicitor and politician, was born on 15 July 1839 at Rhos-y-Medre, Denbighshire, Wales, son of Benjamin Frederick Wilson, clerk, and his wife Anne, née Sands. Educated at Ellesmere School, Shropshire, England, in 1853 Walter migrated with his family to Melbourne where he served his articles of clerkship. On 18 April 1862 he married with Anglican rites Elizabeth Hannah Field (d. 1886) at Christ Church, St Kilda. Admitted as a solicitor in 1863, he moved with his wife to Brisbane in 1865 where he was allowed to practise unconditionally in the Supreme Court from 1866.

Suffering ill health from overwork, he took N. J. R. Wilson, the son of an Ipswich merchant, into partnership in 1879 and left next year for the United States of America and England. At Trinity College, London, he pursued his love of music by studying harmony and composition. Returning to Australia in 1881, he founded the Brisbane Musical Union, became president of the Liedertafel, and was organist and choirmaster at St Thomas's Anglican Church, Toowong, for

twelve years: his repertoire included his own anthems, 'O how amiable are Thy dwellings' and 'Teach me Thy way'.

Involved in numerous community activities, Wilson held broad liberal views and attracted the notice of (Sir) Samuel Griffith [q.v.9] with whom he also had business dealings. Although he had declined the premier's invitation in the early 1880s to stand for the assembly seat of Enoggera, Wilson accepted nomination to the Legislative Council in July 1885; he remained on the council for the rest of his life. He was postmaster-general and government representative in the council (1887-88), leader of the council (1890-94, 1898), minister without portfolio (1890-93, 1894-98), postmaster-general (1893-94, 1898), secretary for public instruction (1893-94, 1899) and minister of justice (1898-99). He supported Federation and was responsible for the standard of time bill in 1894.

On 22 November 1893 Wilson had married Rose Mary Harding at St John's Pro-Cathedral, Brisbane. He had also taken H. B. Hemming as a partner in his firm. Contemporaries regarded Wilson as a temperate and just man with deep sympathies for those in need. His firmness, courtesy and tact often secured him his way in the House and beyond it. In 1900 he was appointed C.M.G. Wilson died suddenly at his Toowong home on 28 February 1902 of acute intestinal obstruction and was buried in Toowong cemetery. He was survived by his wife, a son and daughter of his first marriage, and two sons and a daughter of his second. His estate was sworn for probate at £22 294.

Alcazar Press, *Queensland, 1900* (Brisb, nd); R. S. Browne, *A journalist's memories* (Brisb, 1927); R. J. N. Bannenberg, *Queensland parliamentary handbook* (Brisb, 1983); *Brisbane Courier*, 30 Mar 1878, 5 Dec 1888, 1 Mar 1902; *Queenslander*, 8 Mar 1902; St Thomas's Church, Toowong, Easter meetings, minute-book (C of E Diocesan Archives, Brisb); Queensland Law Soc Archives, Brisb.
                                           J. C. H. GILL

WILSON, WILLIAM HARDY (1881-1955), architect, was born on 14 February 1881 at Campbelltown, New South Wales, second of four surviving sons of William Joshua Wilson, agent, and his wife Jessie Elizabeth, née Shepherd, both native-born. Living with his parents at Burwood, Billy attended (1893-98) Newington College; he passed the junior public examination, played cricket in the first XI and captained the first Rugby XV. In 1899-1904 he was articled to Harry Kent of Kent & Budden, architects, and attended Sydney Technical College at night; he qualified in 1904 and was president of the Architectural Students' Society. Meanwhile, he had taken lessons from the artist Sydney Long [q.v.10] and exhibited water-colours with the Royal Art Society of New South Wales in 1903-04.

Having sailed for England in 1905, Wilson was employed in the office of William Flockhart, architect, of New Bond Street, London, and passed the intermediate and final examinations of the Royal Institute of British Architects (1906, 1908). He joined the Chelsea Arts Club, served as its secretary and made friends with George Lambert [q.v.9] and Arthur Streeton [q.v.]. With Stacey Neave, Wilson travelled in Europe and the United States of America where he was attracted by the early architecture of the eastern States and impressed by the colonial revival style.

Back in London, Wilson lived at Chelsea and collected antique furniture and *objets d'art*. Returning home in 1910, on 22 November he married Margaret Rachel Reid McKenzie (d. 1939) at St Stephen's Presbyterian Church, Sydney. By then he was calling himself Hardy. In 1913 he entered practice with Neave in George Street. Determined to make Australians as aware of their early colonial heritage as Americans had become of theirs, Wilson had begun to make drawings of colonial buildings in New South Wales and Tasmania: he 'looked at buildings with a painter's eye as much as an architect's', even noting the plants in their gardens. Finding Julian Ashton [q.v.7] 'a beacon of hope in a city of indifference', Wilson exhibited regularly with the Society of Artists; with Ashton, Elioth Gruner [q.v.9] and others, he founded the Fine Arts Society, a small commercial gallery. His work was to be included in the 1923 Exhibition of Australian Art at Burlington House, London.

Wilson's architectural commissions consisted almost entirely of houses and small commercial buildings: work at this scale best suited his talents. His admiration of early Australian architecture influenced the design of his houses: two of his best-known were built in Sydney's northern suburbs. The colonial house, Horsley, provided the source of his design for Eryldene, Gordon, completed in 1914 for E. G. Waterhouse [q.v.]. Similarly, Clarendon at Windsor was the model for his home, Purulia, Wahroonga, completed in 1916.

That year Neave joined the army and their office closed. Wilson continued to work at Purulia on his drawings and in 1920 *The Cow Pasture Road* was published by Art in Australia Ltd. The firm re-opened that year in Spring Street with a new partner John Berry. At a time when Australian domestic architecture was characterized by complexity of shape and detail, Wilson's revival of a simple Australian colonial idiom constituted a signif-

icant development. Wilson, Neave & Berry's design (1922) for Peapes & Co. Ltd's menswear store in George Street was a scholarly adaptation of the eighteenth-century English Georgian style to a medium-rise city commercial building.

Wilson contributed to *Art in Australia*, the *Home, Sydney Morning Herald* and other journals. His architectural works and writings, with the houses and teaching of Professor Leslie Wilkinson [q.v.], encouraged many Australian architects in the 1920s and 1930s to adopt a composite idiom of Australian colonial, British Georgian and Mediterranean vernacular influences. Visiting China in 1921, Wilson was greatly impressed by the architecture of Peking and avowed his intention to evolve an architectural style for Australia which would combine the best of the Oriental and Occidental worlds: he designed Celestion, a Chinese-style house that was never built.

In 1922 he finished his drawings of old colonial architecture, sold Purulia and went to England and Europe where he sought the best printmakers and printers. In Athens he wrote the introduction to *Old Colonial architecture in New South Wales and Tasmania* (Sydney, 1924); it contained fifty collotype reproductions of his drawings which were executed by Max Jaffe in Vienna. Returning to Sydney in 1925, Wilson became increasingly dissatisfied with the local profession and with the standard of workmanship in the building industry. In 1926 the Commonwealth government purchased his drawings of old colonial architecture for £3000. His 'last effort in the art of architecture' was a small Chinese teahouse erected at Eryldene in 1927; he left the partnership, and travelled through Europe to London where he lived at St John's Wood. In 1929 *The dawn of a new civilization* was published in London: in this autobiographical work Wilson referred to himself in the third person as 'Richard Le Measurer'.

Again returning to Sydney, Wilson moved in 1930 to Melbourne and next year to Flowerdale Farm in north-western Tasmania where he farmed very badly, wrote for the Burnie *Advocate* and published a fantasy, *Yin Yang* (1934). In Melbourne again from 1935, he was recommended by the trustees of the National Gallery of Victoria in September 1936 to be director, but the government appointed J. S. MacDonald [q.v.10]. In 1938 Wilson acquired a property at Wandin, near Mount Dandenong, and on 27 February 1940 at St John's Anglican Church, Toorak, married a widow Elsie Rose Hughes MacLean, née McMurtrie; they lived in her home at Kew, Melbourne, when not at Wandin. He was an inveterate walker and sustained his love of birds by keeping poultry.

In his later years Wilson published *Collapse of civilization* (1936); *Grecian and Chinese architecture* (1937), profusely illustrated with his own drawings and printed on goatskin vellum by Percy Green [q.v.9]; the autobiographical *Eucalyptus* (Wandin, 1941); *Instinct* (Wandin, 1945); and *Atomic civilization* (1949): all were limited editions. Convinced of the supreme importance of the creative artist, Wilson believed that Western society was decadent and materialistic, needing to be revitalized by a fusion of East and West. A mystic, with down-to-earth moments, he reiterated his belief in a unified world civilization. He had presented fifty of his drawings of Grecian and Chinese architecture to the Commonwealth National Library in 1935. In 1954 he gave that library forty-six drawings and plans for a visionary city, redolent of China, to be built at Kurrajong in the Blue Mountains of New South Wales; fourteen of the drawings were published in *Kurrajong: sit-look-see* (Kew, 1954).

Sydney Ure Smith [q.v.11] described Wilson as 'exceptionally tall, with a studious head, always with a rather quizzical expression—at times a kindly smile hovered around his mouth. He was an impressive character—dominant, dogmatic at times, appreciative and enthusiastic about the particular idea he was propounding ... Extremely impatient ... he was quick to make up his mind about a person's character!'. Survived by his wife, and by the son of his first marriage, Wilson died on 16 December 1955 at Richmond, Melbourne, and was cremated with Presbyterian forms. His portrait by George Henry is held by the Art Gallery of New South Wales.

S. Ure Smith and B. Stevens (eds), *Domestic architecture in Australia* (Syd, 1919); National Trust of Australia (NSW), *William Hardy Wilson, a 20th Century colonial, 1881-1955*, exhibition cat (Syd, 1980), and for bibliog; *Home*, June 1920, p 11, 1 Mar 1922, p 12; *South West Pacific*, no 21, 1949, p 7; *SMH*, 2 May, 14 June 1922, 23, 24 Sept 1936, 6 Oct 1944, 17 Jan 1981; R. E. Apperly, Sydney houses 1914-1939 (M.Arch thesis, Univ NSW, 1972); information from Mrs C. Simpson, Bellevue Hill, Syd.   RICHARD E. APPERLY

WILTON, JOHN RAYMOND (1884-1944), mathematician, was born on 2 May 1884 at Belfast (Port Fairy), Victoria, son of Charles Richard Wilton, architect, and his wife Annie Isabel, née Gladstones, both native-born. His early years were spent at Mount Barker, South Australia, where his father (later chief of the Adelaide *Advertiser*'s literary staff) was editor of the *Mount Barker Courier*. Educated at Prince Alfred College in 1891-1901, Raymond won the old collegians' scholarship and an Angas [q.v.3] engineering

exhibition. At the University of Adelaide (B.Sc., 1903) he graduated with first-class honours in mathematics and in physics. Professor (Sir) William Bragg [q.v.7] described Wilton as having had the greatest natural genius for mathematics among any of his students; on his advice, in 1904 Wilton proceeded to Trinity College, Cambridge (B.A., 1907; M.A., 1911). Awarded a sizarship in 1905, he also won the Jeston scholarship; in the mathematical tripos examination of 1907 he was fifth wrangler; next year he took the second part of the natural science tripos and gained first-class honours in physics.

After a period of research in the Cavendish Laboratory, Cambridge, in 1909 Wilton was appointed assistant lecturer in mathematics at the University of Sheffield. On 5 September 1910 at St John's Church, St Teath, Cornwall, he married Annie Martha Gladstone (d. 1932). The University of Adelaide awarded him its first D.Sc. in mathematics in 1914; by 1916 he had published a prodigious twenty-five research papers on partial differential equations, hydrodynamics and elliptic functions.

During World War I he suffered as a pacifist. Before the introduction of conscription, Wilton had undertaken X-ray work in a Sheffield hospital, but in 1916 was directed to London where repetitive tasks and financial privation contributed to his breakdown in June 1918. After the war he joined the Society of Friends and taught briefly at one of their schools. Having accepted an assistant lectureship in mathematics at Owens College, Victoria University of Manchester, under (Sir) Horace Lamb [q.v.5], in 1919 Wilton was appointed (Sir Thomas) Elder [q.v.4] professor of mathematics at the University of Adelaide.

Back in Adelaide in 1920, he found the mathematical courses much the same as those he had attended as an undergraduate. Although he revised the curricula, as well as those at the senior school level, he was not successful in encouraging honours students, only eight of whom graduated between 1920 and 1940. In 1926-34 Wilton published twenty-six research papers on analysis and number theory: his sustained research gained him a doctorate in science from the University of Cambridge in 1930 and the Lyle [q.v.10] medal in 1935 from the Australian National Research Council.

In his 1954 address on Australian contributions to mathematics (Sir) Thomas Cherry rated Wilton's research as second only to that of J. H. Michell [q.v.10]. H. S. Carslaw [q.v.7] and C. H. Hardy regarded Wilton's work as that 'of a fine mathematician, with admirable taste and a natural inclination towards deep and difficult problems ... He might perhaps have made a bigger name if his taste had been less fine, and he had been content to work in fields which offer cheaper rewards'.

Beyond mathematics, Wilton's prime interests were music and literature. He read Dante's *Divine comedy* in Italian several times a year for twenty years. The Faculty of Arts at the University of Adelaide acknowledged him as 'a scholar of powerful and sensitive intellect who united highly specialised learning with a broad and deep culture, and a gentleman of unassuming demeanour, warm sympathy, just judgment and steadfast devotion to principle'. Active in the Society of Friends, he was clerk (1934-37) of the General Meeting for Australia, twice president of the South Australian Council of Churches, Australian treasurer of the Save the Children Fund and was associated with the Student Christian Movement.

A stroke in 1941 so impaired Wilton's speech and memory that 'he had to learn mathematics afresh, even his multiplication tables'. In 1944 he returned to lecturing, but died of a cerebral haemorrhage on 12 April at the Wakefield Street private hospital, Adelaide, and was buried in West Terrace cemetery. His wife Winifred Aimée, née Welbourn, whom he had married on 25 May 1936 at the Friends Meeting House, North Adelaide, survived him, as did their daughter.

R. M. Gibbs, *A history of Prince Alfred College* (Adel, 1984); C. Stevenson, *The millionth snowflake* (Adel, 1987); J. R. Wilton, *These three: love, faith, hope* (Adel, 1945); Lond Mathematical Soc, *J*, 20, 1945, p 58; R. B. Potts, 'Mathematics at the University of Adelaide', *Aust Mathematical Soc Gazette* (Depts of Pure and of Applied Mathematics, Univ Syd), 4, 1977, p 37.   R. B. POTTS

WILTON, OLIVE DOROTHEA GRAEME (1883-1971), actress and producer, was born on 17 April 1883 at Bath, Somerset, England, eldest daughter of John Gauler Wilton, solicitor, and his wife Agnes Emily, née Kitching, an amateur actress. Olive was educated at home by governesses and later attended the Bathwick Ladies' School. Her parents then enrolled her at the Ben Greet school of acting, London.

She made her debut as a parlourmaid in (Sir) Arthur Pinero's *The second Mrs. Tanqueray*; conspicuous for her 'red-gold hair', at 17 she played opposite Courtenay Thorpe in F. Marion Crawford's *A cigarette-maker's romance* which toured England. Engagements followed as Princess Flavia in Anthony Hope's *The prisoner of Zenda*, as Viera in *A cigarette-maker's romance* and as Glory in (Sir Thomas) Hall Caine's *The Christian*. Edward Terry chose her for the name part in Pinero's *Sweet Lavender* in the New York production of the play. From that time her success was assured and she took leading roles in many popular contemporary plays in London and the provinces.

Against her family's wishes, on 5 March 1906 at St Luke's parish church, Chelsea, Olive married an actor, Benjamin Arthur Cornell. They came to Australia that year with Grace Palotta and the Willoughby and Ward [q.v.] London Company, and made return visits under different managements. In 1909 she was engaged in London by William Anderson [q.v.7], an enthusiastic producer of Australian plays, who saw her perform a dangerous ride on stage because the stand-in jockey was too drunk. 'Tall, commandingly beautiful, and polished in manner and speech', she had spirit and verve, and was dedicated in every detail of her work. In 1910 Wilton starred in *The squatter's daughter*, a full-length Australian film which enjoyed box office success.

A divorcee by the outbreak of World War I, she decided to remain in Australia: she toured interstate with J. C. Williamson [q.v.6] Ltd and other companies, travelling for long periods by train and ship. During these years Olive Wilton played opposite such actors as Julius Knight, Frank Harvey and Emélie Polini [q.v.11]; two of her greatest successes were as the Empress Josephine in *A royal divorce* and as Mrs Dubedat in G. B. Shaw's *The doctor's dilemma*.

In 1920 Wilton settled in Tasmania. Using her own money, she produced and presented four plays each year at Hobart's Theatre Royal, beginning with Pinero's *His house in order*. She also began drama classes and formed the Olive Wilton Company which staged a series of performances at the Hobart Town Hall. Able to attract patronage and to interest prominent citizens in her work, she was instrumental in the formation of the Hobart Repertory Theatre Society on 21 July 1926. Its first performance, *Mice and men*, was produced by Wilton at the Theatre Royal next year. She remained the society's major producer until 1933 when commitments to education, radio and the arts forced her to relinquish her position, but she returned occasionally as a guest producer.

Olive Wilton was superintendent of speech at the Teachers' College in 1927-46; she qualified as a licentiate in the art of speech at the university in 1938. A member of the Australian Music Examinations Board in Hobart (1936-48) and of the Australian Broadcasting Commission's State advisory committee (1946-49), she represented Tasmania on the federal executive of the British Drama League, Sydney, and on the Arts Council of Australia in 1948-52. Her passionate regard for the traditions of the theatre and for the welfare of fellow actors had led her to attend a meeting in Melbourne in 1910 for the protection of Australian actors against exploitation by certain theatre companies; she was later a member of the first federal executive committee of the Actors' Association. In 1959 Wilton was appointed O.B.E. She died on 8 June 1971 in Hobart and was cremated; her only child Junee Cornell (b. 1911), a radio and stage actress, survived her.

H. Porter, *Stars of Australian stage and screen* (Adel, 1965); *Hobart Repertory Theatre Society golden jubilee 1926-1976* (Hob, 1976); *Illustrated Tas Mail*, 9 June 1921; *Mercury*, 30 June 1938, 17 June 1944, 9 June 1971; information from Mrs J. C. Williams, Hob.   JOHN MOORE

WILTSHIRE, AUBREY ROY LIDDON (1891-1969), banker and soldier, was born on 28 May 1891 at Longwood, Victoria, son of Rev. Albert Arthur Wiltshire and his wife Sara, née Hodgson, both Victorian born. Educated at Euroa High School, he matriculated and became a clerk with the local branch of the Bank of Australasia in March 1907; he was transferred to Sale in 1911 and to the bank's principal office in Collins Street, Melbourne, in 1912.

He served three years in the senior cadets, joined the militia and in 1913 was commissioned in the 56th Infantry (Yarra Borderers). Promoted lieutenant in February 1915, Wiltshire transferred next month to the 22nd Battalion, Australian Imperial Force: his family had agreed that he could enlist and that his brother John was to take care of their mother. According to family accounts, Aubrey soon afterwards met John in an army camp and found that he had joined the 23rd Battalion; he never spoke to him again. John was commissioned on active service and won the Military Cross and Bar.

Aubrey was promoted captain in May and, on reaching Gallipoli in August, was appointed unit adjutant. In the evacuation of the peninsula in December he had charge of the battalion's last party. He remained adjutant until April 1916 when he was given command of a company in France. Placed in charge of training a 200-strong brigade raiding-party, he had overall command of an attack on German lines at Armentières on the night of 29-30 June for which he was complimented in Army Corps orders. While in charge of 'C' Company at Pozières, he was wounded on 27 July. During his convalescence recommendations went forward citing his good work in commanding his company and his personal gallantry in reconnaissance; he was awarded the Military Cross. Returning to his unit, he was promoted major in October and made second-in-command;

between October 1916 and February 1917 he temporarily commanded the battalion.

At the 2nd battle of Bullecourt in May 1917 Major General (Sir) John Gellibrand [q.v.8] who regarded Wiltshire as 'a specially trusted assistant' employed him on crucial liaison duties with a British division on the left of the 6th Australian Brigade. On 10 June Wiltshire was promoted lieut-colonel and appointed to command the 22nd Battalion; aged 26, he was one of the youngest Australian battalion commanders. He was 'cool and resolute in a crisis; a careful planner who was prepared to push his men, ruthlessly if necessary, to reach his objectives'. For his work at Broodseinde, Belgium, in October he was awarded the Distinguished Service Order. He took temporary command of the 6th Brigade for several short periods in 1918; he was thrice mentioned in dispatches and appointed C.M.G. His A.I.F. appointment ended in November 1919.

Wiltshire resumed work with the Bank of Australasia. He transferred as an accountant to Ballarat where, on 29 August 1922, he married Jean Alice Margaret Craig Morrison with Presbyterian forms. He was appointed manager of a Melbourne branch in 1923; returning to head office as acting accountant in 1925, he became sub-manager in 1931. Meanwhile, he also continued his militia career: in 1920-21 he was temporary commanding officer of the 2nd Battalion, 22nd Infantry Regiment; in 1921-24 he commanded the 8th Battalion and in 1924-28 the 24th.

In 1932 Wiltshire went to Perth as inspector and manager of the bank's operations; from there he was appointed manager of the Sydney office in December 1933. His name was put forward as the next superintendent in 1935, but the bank's directors considered him too young for the post. Sent to London in 1938, he returned and became manager of the Collins Street branch. In July 1940 he was seconded to the Department of Defence Co-ordination for six months as inspector-general of administration. He was eventually appointed superintendent of the bank in April 1944 when his qualities of energy and experience were recognized as essential to revitalizing its operations. In 1949 his position was renamed general manager in preparation for a merger with the Union Bank which produced the Australia-New Zealand Bank in 1951. One of two joint general managers, he was the first sole general manager from December 1953 until his retirement in July 1954. Survived by his wife and a daughter, Wiltshire died in East Melbourne on 1 June 1969 and was cremated. His estate was sworn for probate at $339 066.

C. E. W. Bean, *The A.I.F. in France*, 1916-18, 3, 4, 6 (Syd, 1929, 1933, 1942); E. Gorman, *With the Twenty-Second* (Melb, 1919); S. J. Butlin, *Australia and New Zealand Bank* (Melb, 1961); D. T. Merrett, *ANZ Bank* (Syd, 1985); *London Gazette*, 29 Dec 1916, 28 May, 3 June, 31 Dec 1918, 3 June, 11 July, 1 Aug 1919; *Listening Post*, June 1932; *Reveille* (Syd), June 1932, May 1933, Feb 1934; RAHS, *J*, 25, 1939; *Age*, 3 June 1969; Wiltshire papers (ML); personal file (AWM); information from Mr R. A. D. Hood, Hexham, Vic.

C. D. COULTHARD-CLARK

WINCHCOMBE, FREDERICK EARLE (1855-1917), woolbroker and politician, was born on 26 April 1855 at Brunswick, Melbourne, second son of John Phillimore Winchcombe, a quarryman from Wales, and his English wife Julia Sophia, née Earle. In the 1860s the family moved to the Young and Yass districts of New South Wales. Educated at Christ Church St Laurence School, Sydney, Frederick joined the woolbroking firm of Mort [q.v.5] & Co. and gradually became a wool expert and auctioneer. In his youth he played cricket for South Sydney club. At Christ Church St Laurence he married Annie Amelia Henson (d. 1952) on 25 September 1878.

After Mort's firm amalgamated with R. Goldsbrough [q.v.4] & Co. Ltd, Winchcombe resigned in 1888 and next year joined Duncan Carson [q.v.7], C. L. Wallis and E. J. Turton to form Winchcombe, Carson & Co., woolbrokers, stock and station agents; he was its chairman. In September 1899 the firm was incorporated with a nominal capital of £150 000. Winchcombe, Carson & Co. Ltd became Winchcombe, Carson Ltd in 1910. Its large woolstores in Wattle Street, Pyrmont, begun in 1893-94, made effective use of the local terrain for easy handling; Winchcombe, Carson's turnaround of 86 000 bales in 1905 was claimed as an Australasian record; it soon became one of the best-known pastoral firms in eastern Australia with over thirty branches in New South Wales and twenty-five in Queensland.

A lean man of middle height whose close-cut hair emphasized the triangular shape of his face, Winchcombe was prominent in the public and business world of Sydney. He was a commissioner for the 1893 Chicago exhibition, an executive member of the Patriotic Fund for the South African War and an active vice-president of the Royal Agricultural Society of New South Wales. Three times president of the Sydney Chamber of Commerce (1907-08, 1909-10, 1914-15), he was a director of the Australian Mutual Provident Society, Atlas Assurance Co. Ltd and James Martin & Co. Ltd, and chairman of Ruthven Ltd, a Queensland pastoral company.

Winchcombe represented Ashfield in the Legislative Assembly from November 1900, but resigned in August 1905 due to business pressures. On his return from Europe, he was nominated to the Legislative Council on 24 September 1907 and was a member of the Board of Health (1907-10). In parliament he generally adopted a conservative stance on industrial and rural issues, but he agreed in principle with women's franchise, closer settlement and the eight-hour day, and supported the wages board system for dealing with industrial disputes. He strongly opposed the fair rents bill (1913) and the Workmen's Compensation Act (1916), arguing instead for a 'national insurance scheme' to which employees would contribute.

A councillor of the Liberal and Reform (later National) Association, Winchcombe outlined his political views in a series of articles in the Brisbane *Monthly Record* which were republished under the title *As it strikes me* (1916). Maintaining that there were no 'classes' in Australia, he attacked labour's 'go slow policy' and the tactics of the Industrial Workers of the World; he praised the qualities of the Australian bushman and advocated better worker and technical education, 'bonus-giving' and easier access to the land; he urged employers to study workers' literature and to look at industrial questions from the workers' point of view.

A sincere Christian, Winchcombe was a parishioner of St Mark's, Darling Point, and a member of the Christ Church Improvement Association. Although neither 'a temperance reformer nor a total abstainer', he favoured early closing in 1915 as a necessary act of self-denial during 'the stress of a great and serious war'. He organized the Chamber of Commerce War Food fund, helped to establish the State Wool Committee, and was a foundation member of the Universal Service League, trustee of the Regimental Comforts Fund and vice-president of the Soldiers' Club.

In 1917 he went to England to visit his two sons on active service with the Australian Imperial Force. On his way back to Australia, the *Mongolia* struck a mine and sank in the Indian Ocean: Winchcombe was among those rescued, but died of pneumonia on 29 June 1917 in the military hospital at Bombay and was buried in Sewri cemetery. He left an estate valued at £56 109. His wife, two sons and two daughters survived him. His elder son Kenneth joined the firm in 1907, becoming a director in 1926; his daughter Edyth married (Sir) Thomas Bavin [q.v.7].

Pastoral Review, 15 Nov 1906, 16 Feb 1911, 15 Feb 1913, 16 Sept 1914, 16 July 1917; *A'sian Insurance and Banking Record*, 21 July 1917; *T&CJ*, 13 Oct 1900, 4 July 1917; *SMH*, 2, 9 July 1917; *Fighting Line*, 21 July 1917; *Aust Worker*, 5 July 1917; Carruthers papers *and* Winchcombe family, Letter-books, 1913-17 and news-cuttings, 1906-57 (ML).

G. P. WALSH

WINDEYER, JOHN CADELL (1875-1951), obstetrician, was born on 27 November 1875 at Raymond Terrace, New South Wales, second son of John Windeyer, an English-born farmer, and his native-born wife Isabella Mowbray, née Cadell, and grandson of Archibald Windeyer [q.v.2]. Jack was educated at The King's School, Parramatta, and the University of Sydney (M.B., Ch.M., 1899; M.D., 1926).

After working at Sydney Hospital as resident medical officer, he went overseas with his friend (Sir) George Wilson. They trained together in obstetrics and gynaecology at University College Hospital, London, the Rotunda Hospital, Dublin, and in Vienna. In 1901 Windeyer qualified as licentiate of the Royal College of Physicians, London, and member of the Royal College of Surgeons, England. Returning to Australia that year, he worked in the pathology department of Sydney Hospital, specializing in the pathology of the female genital tract. At St James's Church, Turramurra, he married Aileen Spencer Evans on 17 October 1911 with Anglican rites.

Appointed honorary assistant surgeon in 1904 to the Royal Hospital for Women, Paddington, and senior surgeon in 1919, Windeyer maintained an association with this institution throughout his career. In 1909 he persuaded Professor (Sir) Thomas Anderson Stuart [q.v.] that clinical (bedside) teaching in obstetrics was an essential extension of didactic lectures. At Paddington in 1912 he began an ante-natal clinic, the longest surviving continuous clinic in Australia. He recognized the special needs of new-born infants and in 1926 established the position of honorary neo-natal paediatrician (filled by Margaret Harper [q.v.9]) at the Royal Hospital when such a post was a singular exception rather than the rule.

Teaching was an integral part of Windeyer's life: he was examiner in gynaecology for the university (1915-20), and an acting lecturer (1918), lecturer (1920-25) and foundation professor of obstetrics from 1925. His slogan was always 'to try and make childbirth safer for the mother'. As dean of the faculty of medicine (1930-31 and 1939), he was ex officio a fellow of the university senate and a director of Royal Prince Alfred Hospital; he was also a member of the university cancer research committee.

Windeyer wrote widely on clinical subjects related to obstetrics and gynaecology. His best known publication was the pamphlet, *Methods of ante-natal abdominal palpation* (1926), which had formed the basis of his doctoral thesis: under the title *Diagnostic methods*, it ran to six editions.

A foundation fellow of the (Royal) Australasian College of Surgeons (1927), he was elected a foundation fellow of the Royal College of Obstetricians and Gynaecologists, London, in 1929 and chaired its dominion reference committee which was established in Australia in 1932. Windeyer presided over the obstetrics and gynaecology section at several national meetings of the British Medical Association. He was a committee-member (1918-29) and honorary consulting physician (from 1923) of the Royal Society for the Welfare of Mothers and Babies; he served on the Nurses' Registration Board (1925-41), the editorial committee of the *Australian and New Zealand Journal of Surgery* (1928-48), the obstetric research committee of the National Health and Medical Research Council (1937-41), the Medical Board and the New South Wales Post-Graduate Committee in Medicine; he was chairman of the medical appointments advisory committee of the Hospitals Commission of New South Wales, a trustee of the King George V Memorial Fund (for maternal and infant welfare) and a member of the special medical committee investigating maternal mortality in 1939.

An impressive and likeable man, 5 ft. 10 ins. (178 cm) tall, with dark (later grey) hair, Windeyer was known as the 'Grand old man of the Royal'. His manner was firm rather than aggressive. He shook his large head during lectures just as he did in conversation. To Bruce Mayes, his successor, as to others, it was 'inconceivable' that Windeyer could be known by any other sobriquet than 'Daddy'.

After retiring from his chair in 1941, Windeyer gave more time to his hobbies of gardening and fishing. A keen tennis player well into his sixties, he belonged to the Union and University clubs. Survived by his wife, two sons and a daughter, he died of a coronary occlusion on 15 August 1951 at Wahroonga and was cremated. Of his children, Ella and John graduated in medicine from the University of Sydney.

P. N. Walker-Taylor (ed), *Senior year book, University of Sydney Medical School* (Syd, 1926); J. Peel, *The lives of the Fellows of the Royal College of Obstetricians and Gynaecologists 1929-1969* (Lond, 1976); I. A. McDonald et al, *Super Ardua* (Melb, 1981); J. A. Young et al (eds), *Centenary book of the University of Sydney faculty of medicine* (Syd, 1984); *MJA*, 19 Jan, 16, 23 Feb 1952, pp 24, 239, 272; family papers held by Dr J. S. Windeyer, Longueville, Syd.   RODNEY P. SHEARMAN

WINDEYER, MARY ELIZABETH (1837?-1912), suffrage campaigner, and MARGARET (1866-1939), librarian, were mother and daughter. Mary was baptized on 2 April 1837 at Buxted, Sussex, England, second daughter of nine children of Rev. Robert Thorley Bolton, a clergyman of the

Church of England, and his wife Jane Martha, née Ball. The Boltons arrived in Sydney in the *Strathfieldsaye* on 25 July 1839. Mary spent her childhood at Hexham where she married (Sir) William Charles Windeyer [q.v.6] on 31 December 1857. Between 1859 and 1876 nine children were born of the marriage, the third daughter dying in infancy. During bouts of ill health, Mary took her children to stay with her mother-in-law at Tomago. Both women were devout; both offered William political advice.

Initially directing her philanthropy towards saving infant life, in 1874 Mary supported a foundling hospital—to 'remove temptation to infanticide'—and its reorganization in 1875 as a home (later Infants' Home, Ashfield) for destitute and homeless new mothers, provided they remained in residence to breast-feed their babies. For older children in need of care, she favoured 'boarding out' from orphanages, a system which her friend Caroline Emily Clark [q.v.3] had begun in South Australia. William Windeyer's report on public charities reflected Mary's views. Their friendship with (Sir) Henry Parkes [q.v.5] helped Mary's lobbying and facilitated a grant for an experimental 'cottage home'. The campaign concluded with the passage of the State Children Relief Act (1881) and the establishment of a board to oversee the fostering of children from the colony's orphanages; Mary Windeyer was a board-member (1881-86 and 1889-97). In 1886 she and William visited England.

Back in Sydney she organized the Exhibition of Women's Industries and Centenary Fair 1888, and, with proceeds from a sale of work, financed the Temporary Aid Society which lent money to women who had encountered financial difficulties. Mary's philanthropy broadened into a programme of moderate feminist reforms, encompassing higher education, expanded employment opportunities especially in the professions, improved hospital facilities and political rights. Lady Windeyer was foundation president of the Womanhood Suffrage League of New South Wales. When the rules which she had modelled on Mary Lee's [q.v.10] advice were changed in 1893, she resigned as president, but remained active in the campaign as convenor of the franchise department of the Woman's Christian Temperance Union.

She was an honorary secretary for the second Australasian Conference on Charity in 1891 and a committee-member of the Thirlmere Home for Consumptives. In her endeavours to promote economic independence for women, Lady Windeyer sponsored a silk-growing co-operative, a shorthand writers and typists' society, and hospital training for nurses. As organizer of the women's industries section of the colony's exhibit at the 1893 World's Columbian Exposition, Chicago, United States of America, she asserted that women's work went 'beyond the product of the needle'. Her proposal in 1893 for a women's hospital had dual aims: to help poor women and to train nurses. Beginning as a district service, the hospital opened its own premises in 1896 and, at a new location, became the Women's Hospital, Crown Street, Sydney.

Margaret, her fifth daughter, was born on 24 November 1866 in Sydney. Sharing her mother's endeavours to advance women's opportunities and political rights, she belonged to Louisa Lawson's [q.v.10] Dawn Club and issued invitations for the meeting at her parents' home at which the Women's Literary Society was formed, the nucleus of the later Womanhood Suffrage League. Margaret joined the league's executive and became a member of the committee formed to establish Women's College within the University of Sydney.

Appointed a commissioner to the Chicago exhibition in 1893, she contacted other women's organizations in the United States and attended the World's Congress of Representative Women. On her return, she convened the meeting that established the National Council of Women of New South Wales and served as corresponding secretary (1896-97). It was to Margaret that Maybanke Wolstenholme [q.v.7 Anderson] turned in 1895 on feeling the strain of producing *Women's Voice*, though nothing came of her offer to hand over the paper to Margaret. Mother and daughter were in England in 1897, Mary preparing to travel to Canada for the world convention of the W.C.T.U. and Margaret to attend the International Council of Women, when William died unexpectedly. Mary returned to live at Tomago, taking an interest in farm management, her local church and the Newcastle Kindergarten Society. Survived by five daughters and three sons (including Richard and William [qq.v.]), she died at Tomago on 3 December 1912 and was buried in the Anglican section of Raymond Terrace cemetery. Her estate was sworn for probate at £11 408.

Margaret went to New York where in August 1899 she satisfactorily completed the two-year course at New York State Library. After further experience, including an appointment at the library of Wells College, Aurora, New York, she came back to Sydney. Her earlier applications for employment in Australia had been rejected on the grounds of her sex and age, but H. C. L. Anderson [q.v.7] had encouraged her to become thoroughly acquainted with Dewey's classification. On 22 July 1901 her appointment to the Public Library of New South Wales as a cataloguer was secured with the introduction of special library entrance examinations. Several able women joined the staff about this time. In January 1910 Margaret was appointed assistant to the Mitchell [q.v.5] Library collection, but was twice passed over for the position of senior cataloguer. Anderson praised her as 'an expert in the Dewey system and a cataloguer of more than usual intelligence'; F. M. Bladen minuted that she was very diligent and very efficient, but later librarians found her difficult. She retired in 1926.

In these years Margaret was extensively engaged in feminist activities and was reputedly one of the best speakers in Sydney. She served on the council of Women's College in 1907-39, and worked for the Kindergarten Union of New South Wales, the Parks and Playgrounds Movement, the Professional Women Workers' Association and the National Council of Women (although never on its executive, she was made honorary life president in 1918).

Book clubs and children's libraries became Margaret's special interest. In 1909 she helped to start the Bush Book Club with which she remained associated until 1939. She urged the Playgrounds Movement to introduce books to its establishments and the City of Sydney Public Library to open a children's book room. She lived with her sister Jane at Elizabeth Bay. Margaret Windeyer died on 11 August 1939 in St Luke's Hospital, Darlinghurst, and was cremated with Anglican rites.

H. Radi (ed), *200 Australian women* (Syd, 1988); *SMH*, 5 Mar 1896, 15, 21 Aug 1939; *Bulletin*, 23 May 1903; *Daily Telegraph* (Syd), 22 Apr 1907; M. R. Talbot, The Library Association of Australasia, 1896-1902 (Ph.D. thesis, Monash Univ, 1985); J. Cleary, Women librarians at the Public Library of New South Wales: the first generation (ts, 1989, copy held by J. Cleary, Univ Newcastle Lib); Parkes papers *and* Scott family papers *and* Windeyer papers (ML).   HEATHER RADI

WINDEYER, RICHARD (1868-1959), barrister, and WILLIAM ARCHIBALD (1871-1943), solicitor, were born on 9 September 1868 and on 9 April 1871 at Darlinghurst, Sydney, eldest and second sons of (Sir) William Charles Windeyer [q.v.6], barrister, and his wife Mary Elizabeth [q.v. Windeyer], née Bolton. The brothers were educated at Sydney Grammar School and the University of Sydney: Richard was a resident of St Paul's College, edited *Hermes* and graduated B.A. in 1891; William (B.A., 1893) was a member of the Australian Rifle team in 1891. They later belonged to the Australian and University clubs.

A committee-member (1893) of the Articled Clerks' Association, from 1892

Richard was judge's associate to his father before being admitted to the Bar on 10 August 1894. He built up a solid practice, beginning on the Hunter River and Northern circuits; in Sydney he practised at Denman Chambers. On 23 December 1891 at All Saints Church, Petersham, he married Mabel Fuller Robinson (d. 1957).

His skill as an advocate brought him a leading practice, particularly in common law, criminal law and divorce. Windeyer took silk in 1917 and was an acting Supreme Court judge from November 1936 to February 1937. He was counsel in the much-publicized Norton [q.v.11] and Field divorces; he appeared for P. S. Brookfield, T. D. Mutch [qq.v.7,10] and E. E. Judd who claimed before a royal commission in 1918 that police had procured false evidence in the 1916 conspiracy trials of D. M. Grant [q.v.9] and other members of the Industrial Workers of the World; and he acted for the Australian Newspaper Proprietors' Association in their successful press censorship contest with Arthur Calwell in World War II (1944). Windeyer retired in 1946. Sir Garfield Barwick later testified to his courage and resource as counsel, and described him as belonging to 'a generation of advocates who were pre-eminent in the strategy and tactics of the courtroom and who brought to the conduct of the case a great deal of personality and wit'. Another observer noted that Windeyer's clients in criminal cases owed 'much to the emotional appeal of his advocacy'; some likened him to the English barrister Marshall Hall.

A staunch supporter of (Sir) Edmund Barton [q.v.7], Windeyer toiled to attain Australian Federation and throughout his life actively proposed constitutional reform. He was interested in politics, but was considered 'too unpredictable to be a good party man or to gain party selection'. Eventually, in 1929 he stood for the Australian People's Party and nearly unseated (Sir) Robert Parkhill [q.v.11] for the Federal seat of Warringah.

Windeyer lectured at the University of Sydney (1935-44), served on its senate (1934-44) and helped to establish the university archives. As patron of the Sydney Repertory Theatre Society, he worked closely with Evelyn Tildesley [q.v.]. He was a fellow of the Royal Economic Society, London, councillor of the Prisoners' Aid Association of New South Wales and a committee-member for the Food for Britain Appeal. Managing Tomago, the family's country estate, he learned about farming and preferred 'growing vegetables to flowers' at his Lindfield home. His recreations were motoring and yachting, and he was vice-commodore of Royal Prince Alfred Yacht Club. He was a gifted conversationalist and relished congenial company. Of middle height, he had 'a face like wrinkled canvas, thin white hair which juts in front, a big mouth and eyes like a highly intelligent bird', with 'a rather harsh, high pitched inquisitional voice'.

His wife, who had served from 1914 with the Voluntary Aid Detachment in England, France and Belgium, petitioned for divorce on her return in 1919, but consented to a *modus vivendi*. Richard Windeyer died on 8 November 1959 at Gordon and was cremated with Anglican rites. Four sons and two daughters survived him; his eldest son Charles had been killed in action in World War I.

Articled to Robert Smith of Norton Smith & Co., solicitors, William Windeyer was admitted as a solicitor on 22 August 1896, began practice in Sydney on his own and eventually established a law firm that continues to bear his name. He came to have many large corporate clients, including insurance companies and newspaper publishers. On 4 October 1899 at Christ Church, Gladesville, he married Ruby Millicent, second daughter of John Le Gay Brereton [q.v.3]. On the night of 18 May 1902 Windeyer took the main part in rescuing young people from a rowing boat capsized in Fern Bay, near his Hunters Hill home, and was awarded a silver medal by the Royal Shipwreck Relief and Humane Society of New South Wales.

Elected an alderman of Hunters Hill Municipal Council in 1904, Windeyer served for twenty-three years and was mayor in 1915-24; the W. A. Windeyer Memorial Reserve was named after him. He was a director of Standard Life Association Ltd and Bain's White Ant Exterminator Co. Ltd, president of the Hunters Hill branch of the Liberal Association, a council-member of the Kindergarten Union of New South Wales, chairman of the Boy Scouts' Association from 1943, and director of and honorary solicitor to the Sydney Homoeopathic Hospital. He was appointed M.B.E. in 1920. His work for returned servicemen was recognized in 1936 by the Returned Sailors' and Soldiers' Imperial League of Australia.

As president of the Suburban and Country Golf Association, and secretary of the New South Wales Golf Council and of the New South Wales Golf Club, he pressed for uniform handicapping and wrote a booklet on the rules of golf. Like his brother, William enjoyed gardening, boating and fishing. He died in St Luke's Hospital, Darlinghurst, on 25 March 1943 and was cremated with Anglican rites. His wife, daughter and two sons survived him; his youngest son Henry had died in 1941 of wounds received at Tobruk, North Africa.

Cyclopedia of N.S.W. (Syd, 1907); Newspaper Cartoonists' Assn of NSW, *Sydneyites as we see 'em*

1913-15 (Syd, 1915?); G. E. Hall and A. Cousins (eds), *Book of remembrance of the University of Sydney in the war 1914-18* (Syd, 1939); I. Brodsky, *Hunters Hill 1861-1961* (Syd, 1961); J. M. Bennett (ed), *A history of the New South Wales Bar* (Syd, 1969) and *A history of solicitors in New South Wales* (Syd, 1984); L. F. Fitzhardinge, *The little digger* (Syd, 1979); Univ Syd, *Gazette*, Apr 1960, p 280; *SMH*, 16 Oct 1920, 29 May 1936, 26 Mar 1943, 10 Nov 1959; M. D. Hay, Some reminiscences of the N.S.W. Bar (ts, Law School, Univ Syd); Piddington *and* Windeyer papers (ML); Newspaper-cuttings (LaTL); Roy Humane Soc of NSW records; information from Messrs H. C. and W. V. Windeyer, Syd.

J. M. BENNETT

WINN, ROY COUPLAND (1890-1963), psychoanalyst, was born on 26 June 1890 at Newcastle, New South Wales, fifth son of William Winn, draper, and his wife Janet, née Shade, both native-born. Educated at Sydney Grammar School and the University of Sydney (M.B., Ch.M., 1915), Roy was appointed junior resident medical officer at Royal Prince Alfred Hospital.

Although his parents were strict Methodists and Winn wanted to be a medical missionary, he enlisted in the Australian Imperial Force and was commissioned on 27 July 1915 as a captain in the Australian Army Medical Corps. He was posted to the 1st Australian General Hospital, Heliopolis, before becoming regimental medical officer for the 14th Battalion at Gallipoli, and later in Egypt and France. Appointed bearer captain, 4th Australian Field Ambulance, in December 1916, he was mentioned in dispatches next January. He devised new treatments for trench foot and gained experience in treating shell-shock, but was seriously wounded in the battle of Messines in June 1917: his right foot was amputated and he was evacuated to England. In August he was promoted major and awarded the Military Cross. On 23 January 1918 he married Bertha Elizabeth Browne (d. 1942) at Christ Church, West Green, Middlesex. He returned to Australia in May and his A.I.F. appointment terminated on 24 August.

After a term as junior resident medical officer at Sydney Hospital, Winn went to England in 1920 to train under R. M. Riggall of the British Psycho-analytical Society; he also gained experience at University College and Maudsley hospitals, London, and worked as a resident assistant physician at West London Hospital. Back in Sydney in 1922, he found little call for his psychoanalytic training and, while honorary assistant physician at Sydney Hospital (1924-34), became interested in the treatment of diabetes.

Courageously deciding in 1931 to begin private practice as a psychoanalyst, Winn sold his home to buy rooms in Macquarie Street.

He faced considerable antagonism from sections of the medical profession and his offer to serve as honorary psychoanalyst at Sydney Hospital was rejected. Publishing two articles on psychoanalysis in the *Medical Journal of Australia*, he corresponded with Sigmund Freud and studied the work of Melanie Klein. With Paul Dane, in the late 1930s Winn endeavoured to bring a training analyst to Australia and in 1940 was a foundation board member of the Institute for Psycho-analysis, Melbourne, which offered training by Clara Lazar Geroe from Hungary. In 1952 he provided an endowment to establish a similar institute in Sydney.

Clean shaven, broad shouldered and handsome, Winn had a keen sense of humour and was respected for his kindness and tolerance. He loved swimming and deep-sea fishing. On 10 January 1945 he had married Nell Birkenhead Gale at St Mark's Anglican Church, Darling Point. A foundation member (1946) of the Australasian Association of Psychiatrists, he also belonged to the Australasian Association of Psychology and Philosophy, the Institute of Psycho-analysis, London, the State branch of the British Medical Association, the Anthropological Society of New South Wales and the Royal Australian Historical Society. Survived by his wife, and by the daughter and two sons of his first marriage, he died at Concord on 17 August 1963 and was cremated.

A. G. Butler (ed), *Official history of the Australian Army Medical Services in the war of 1914-1918*, 2-3 (Canb, 1940, 1943); *MJA*, 29 Feb 1964; *Meanjin Q*, 1982, no 3; AIF service record (AWM); information from Mrs B. J. Ferguson, Turramurra, Dr R. W. Winn, Church Point, Assoc Prof M. M. Winn, Longueville, and Mrs N. B. Winn, Manly, Syd.   STEPHEN GARTON

WINNEKE, HENRY CHRISTIAN (1874-1943), judge, was born on 23 April 1874 at Talbot, Victoria, youngest son of Christian Winneke, miner, and his wife Auguste, late Müller, née Runge, both from Hanover, Germany. Educated locally at Prince Alfred State School, Henry won scholarships to Dookie Agricultural College, and Scotch College, Melbourne, where he excelled at football and rowing, and was dux in 1892 and 1893. Entering Ormond College, University of Melbourne (B.A., 1897; LL.B., 1898; LL.M., 1899), with a scholarship in 1894, he was awarded first-class honours in classics, philosophy and law, as well as the Supreme Court prize.

He was articled to Walter Rylah in 1900, admitted to the Victorian Bar in 1902 and commenced practice in Selborne Chambers. For some years Winneke continued to play football for the Fitzroy Seconds and was an active member of the Clifton Parliamentary Debating Society. On 2 July 1907 at St Paul's Independent Church, North Fitzroy, he married Ethel Janet O'Neill. They settled at Fitzroy where Winneke was elected to the municipal council in 1912. He represented the council on the Melbourne Tramways Trust.

At the Bar Winneke gradually developed a wide general practice. His reputation was established by his appearance as counsel at the long inquiry into the Sunshine railway accident of 1908 and by his subsequent successful defence of the engine driver in the Richmond rail disaster of 1910. While his colleagues predicted eventual elevation to the Supreme Court bench, Winneke accepted appointment to the Victorian County Court and Court of Mines in June 1913. An early pioneer in using the motor car, he frequently drove from Ballarat, where he was located, to sit at other circuit towns in western and north-western Victoria. In 1919 he returned to Melbourne to sit as a county court judge and as chairman of the Railways Classification Board and the State Coal Mine Industrial Tribunal.

As a judge, Winneke was well liked and widely respected, though the manner in which he conducted proceedings was initially regarded as a little unorthodox. He was a cultured man of considerable personal charm who combined the common sense of his rural background with legal knowledge and judicial wisdom. Goodnatured and friendly, with a dry wit, he encouraged barristers to argue the issues fully before him. While shrewd in his judgements of people, he demonstrated an affinity with most litigants. Winneke's sentences were never harsh and he was more willing than his brother judges to release the accused on a good behaviour bond. Some of his witticisms passed into legal lore. A witness who proclaimed virtuously that he did not drink, smoke or go to the races was asked by His Honour: 'Do you eat grass?' When the witness replied 'No', Winneke commented that he did not seem to be 'fit company for either man or beast'.

In his later judicial years much of Winneke's time was spent in the industrial field where he gained the respect both of the railways' commissioners and of the unions. During the Depression the relative freedom of the Victorian coal industry from industrial unrest was largely due to his fairness, tact and geniality. Survived by his wife and two sons, Winneke died of cancer on 9 December 1943 in East Melbourne and was cremated. His estate was sworn for probate at £13 057.

A. Dean, *A multitude of counsellors* (Melb, 1968); R. Coleman, *Above renown* (Melb, 1988); *Aust Law*

J, 21 Jan 1944; *Argus,* 11, 14 Dec 1943; *Herald* (Melb), 13 Dec 1943.   CHARLES FRANCIS

WINSPEAR, WILLIAM ROBERT (1859-1944), socialist and journalist, was born on 16 February 1859 at Ferryhill, Durham, England, son of John Winspear, coalminer, and his wife Elizabeth, née Robson. Having migrated to New South Wales about 1874, Bob worked in the New Lambton coalmines where he developed radical ideas. At the Newcastle registrar's office he married Alice Maud Drake on Christmas eve 1885. A small inheritance enabled him to stop working as a miner and on 12 March 1887, with Alice's help, he published the first issue of the *Radical* from his home at Hamilton, near Newcastle; in August it became the mouthpiece of the Australian Socialist League. Renamed the *Australian Radical* in March 1888, the paper ceased publication in April 1890 after Winspear had differences with the league because of its growing support for state socialism: he believed that socialism marked 'the progress of mankind towards freedom' where authority and control should be decentralized.

In the depressed 1890s Winspear was forced to sell his printing plant and move his family to Sydney; there he was unable to support them. According to contemporary newspapers, he was imprisoned for housebreaking in a desperate attempt to provide food. After being refused help by several charities, 32-year-old Alice hanged herself on 30 October 1898, apparently in the hope that the government would be forced to provide for their five children. The children were dispatched to live with different relations while Winspear served his sentence. He eventually found work as a clerk and in 1910 published a volume, *Poems.*

Full-time treasurer of the Australian Socialist Party (1912-16), he often edited its newspaper, the *International Socialist,* to which he frequently contributed poetry, articles and 'socialist fables', sometimes as 'W.R.W.' In 1914 he analysed the inadequacies of recent Labor governments in his lengthy pamphlet, *Economic warfare,* in which he argued that the working class was worse off than in 1910 and that Labor's nationalization proposals were 'state capitalist' rather than socialist. With his comrade Harry Holland [q.v.9], he wrote the party's 'Open Letter to the Conscript Boys of Australia', advocating resistance to the Labor government's 'compulsory militarism' for 'voteless lads'. Ironically, Winspear is best known for a poem he did not write: the 'Blood Vote', which became famous as anti-conscription propaganda, was written by E. J. Dempsey, a leader-writer on the pro-conscription *Evening News,* who asked Winspear to sign the poem.

After the war Winspear worked for the *Torch,* the local newspaper at Bankstown. He remained apart from all political parties, but in 1939 wrote and published a three-volume pamphlet, *Essays and rhymes of the system,* which showed that he had retained libertarian socialist convictions. Survived by two sons and a daughter, he died on 20 February 1944 at Bankstown and was buried in the Presbyterian section of Rookwood cemetery.

ALP, Golden Jubilee Cttee, *50 years of Labor* (Syd, 1940); V. Burgmann, 'The mightier pen: William Robert Winspear' in E. C. Fry (ed), *Rebels and radicals* (Syd, 1983), and *'In our time'* (Syd, 1985); B. James, *Anarchism and State violence in Sydney and Melbourne, 1886-1896* (Newcastle, 1986); *International Socialist Review* (Syd), Apr 1910-Sept 1916; *Communist Review,* 1 July 1937, p 51; *People and Collectivist,* 5, 26 Nov 1898; *Daily Telegraph* (Syd), 31 Oct, 1 Nov 1898; *SMH,* 1 Nov 1898.   VERITY BURGMANN

WINTER, ANTHONY WILLIAM (1894-1955), athlete, was born on 25 August 1894 at Brocklesby, New South Wales, second child of Anthony Winter, fettler, and his wife Sarah Ann, née Boyton, both native-born. Known as 'Nick', he attended the local public school and worked as a labourer before enlisting in the Australian Imperial Force on 31 July 1915. He embarked for Egypt with reinforcements for the 7th Light Horse Regiment in October and was posted to the Australian Army Service Corps as a driver in January 1916; arriving in France in June, he was employed mainly in depot duties. His A.I.F. appointment ended soon after he returned to Australia in June 1919.

Next December Winter became a fireman under the Board of Fire Commissioners of New South Wales and was later stationed at Manly. On 2 July 1921 he married Minnie Pearl Josland at the Methodist Church, Helensburgh. Tall and slender, with blue eyes and a dark complexion, he was muscular, ambidextrous and double-jointed. He loved any sport which required 'nerve, skill, speed, stamina, strength and determination', and played football, cricket, tennis and golf. He also enjoyed wrestling, single tug-of-war and cycling backwards, but the leaping events were his forte. As a member of Botany Harriers, and then of South Sydney and Western Suburbs amateur athletic clubs, he competed successfully in the high jump and hurdles, but excelled in the running hop, step and jump (triple jump). At the Dunn Shield competition in December 1919 he had set a new Australasian record of 47 ft. 7 ins. (14.503 m) and by

1924 held the Australasian record of 49 ft. 8½ ins. (15.15 m).

In the 1924 Olympic Games in Paris Winter realized his 'life's ambition' when he cleared 15.525 metres (50 ft. 11¼ ins.), setting a new Olympic record and breaking the world record which had stood since 1911. Described as a 'devil-may-care Australian', he was given an enthusiastic reception on coming home to Sydney with fellow gold medallists Andrew Charlton [q.v.7] and Richmond Eve. After a special trial, in 1928 Winter was included in the team for the Amsterdam Olympic Games, but did not qualify for the final of the triple jump. In January 1930 he won the event at the national championships in Sydney, clearing only 47 ft. 3 ins. (14.4 m); he took second place in 1932, shortly before retiring from competition.

Having practised on the fire station's billiard-table, Winter became a skilled '200-break' player. He was 'more interested in setting himself challenges than in playing the orthodox game', but finished runner-up in the State championships in July 1927. He revelled in trick shots; even Walter Lindrum [q.v.10] could not execute one of Nick's *massé* strokes. Leaving the fire service in December 1927, Winter ran a billiard-saloon in George Street, while conducting a hairdressing and tobacconist business. In the 1940s he managed a billiard-room in Pitt Street and later worked as a clerk. A heavy drinker for several years, he died from carbon monoxide poisoning at his Pagewood home on or about 6 May 1955; the coroner returned an open finding. Survived by his wife, son and daughter, Winter was cremated with Anglican rites.

A. Ricketts, *Walter Lindrum* (Canb, 1982); G. Lester, *Australians at the Olympics* (Syd, 1984); Amateur Athletics Assn of NSW, *100 years of the NSW AAA* (Syd, 1987); R. and M. Howell, *Aussie gold* (Brisb, 1988); *SMH*, 15 July 1919, 14 July 1924, 28 July 1927, 27 Apr 1928, 28 Jan 1930, 8 May, 11 June, 2 July 1955; *Sporting Globe*, 7 May, 16 July 1924; *Referee*, 16 July, 8 Oct 1924; *Sydney Mail*, 8 Oct 1924; *Daily Telegraph* (Syd), 3 Aug 1928; information from Mr A. Winter, Caringbah, and Mrs S. Harris, Kogarah, Syd.

IAN F. JOBLING

WINTER, JOSEPH (1853-1896), journalist and politician, was born on 29 November 1853 at Prahran, Melbourne, son of George Winter, shoemaker, and his wife Eliza, née Hillman. George, a sociable and successful man, founded the local cricket club and established a boot repair shop in Bourke Street. His death in 1858 signalled a decline in the family's fortunes and they moved to cheaper premises at Richmond where Joseph attended a number of denominational schools. At 13, he was employed as a 'printer's devil' by a city firm. He gradually progressed in the printing trade, becoming an apprentice back-ruler for Sands [q.v.6] & MacDougall and working as a journeyman, before opening a stationery and book store in 1899 in Swan Street, Richmond.

He spent his spare time in self-improvement. At the age of 8 he had read Macaulay's *History of England*; in his teens he joined the Australian Natives' Association and the Young Men's Mutual Improvement Society. Of middle height and medium build, bespectacled and moustached, with a 'full, grave face', Winter underwent a 'severe mental training', read widely, debated earnestly and became president of the South Melbourne branch of the A.N.A. Throughout the 1880s he was elected to a number of executive positions in the Bookbinders' and Paper Rulers' Society; as its delegate to the Intercolonial Trade Union Congress, Winter was among the first to advocate independent labour representation in parliament. Elected vice-president and president of the Trades Hall Council in the early 1890s, he chaired the Labor Convention which oversaw the creation of Progressive Political Leagues. Moving to South Melbourne, he was selected in March 1892 as Labor's candidate for that electorate in the Legislative Assembly. At this time he was editing the labour paper, *Commonweal and Workers' Advocate*: independent of both the Labor Party and the trade unions, it was a forum for radical and progressive opinion until it folded in 1893, a casualty of the depression. His brief journalistic career should not be confused with that of his namesake, editor of the Catholic *Advocate*.

Elected in April 1892 and returned with an increased majority in 1894, Winter proved an able exponent of the Liberal and Labor alliance which supported an increased protective tariff, industrial legislation and a medley of social reforms. Though he sometimes styled himself a radical, his politics were cautious and moderate. He believed that Labor's mission was to promote legislation for all classes and advocated Federation as fervently as he did industrial legislation. Despite his habit of wearing a bell-topper to the House, Winter never lost touch with his predominantly working-class electorate and argued tirelessly for relief work for the unemployed. He served on several parliamentary committees, including the royal commission on state banking which he chaired in 1894.

Winter died of heart disease on 2 May 1896 at South Melbourne and was buried in Boroondara cemetery. He was survived by his wife, Emma Florence, née Thomas, whom he had married at Richmond on 21 August 1884 with Wesleyan forms, and by their son and three daughters. His estate was sworn for probate at £30.

Hist Studies, 4, no 16, May 1951, p 241, 21, no 83, Oct 1984, p 174; *Table Talk*, 11 Jan 1895; *Age* and *Argus*, 4 May 1896; *Weekly Times* (Melb), 9 May 1896; S. M. Ingham, Some aspects of Victorian liberalism 1880-1900 (M.A. thesis, Univ Melb, 1950); M. G. Finlayson, Victorian politics 1889-94 (M.A. thesis, Univ Melb, 1964); B. C. Scates, 'Faddists and extremists': radicalism and the labour movement in south-eastern Australia, 1886-1898 (Ph.D. thesis, Monash Univ, 1987); Australian Bookbinders and Paper Rulers Consolidated Trade Union, Minutes of Meetings, 1884-1896 (Printing and Kindred Industries Employees Union, Melb); Trades Hall Council, Minutes of Meetings (LaTL).   BRUCE SCATES

WIRTH, MAY EMMELINE (1894-1978), circus rider, was born on 6 June 1894 at Bundaberg, Queensland, daughter of John Edward Zinga, a circus artist from France whose real name was Despoges, and his native-born second wife Dezeppo Marie, née Beaumont. After her parents separated, May was adopted in 1901 by MARY ELIZABETH VICTORIA ('MARIZLES') WIRTH (1868-1948), equestrienne and sister of Philip and George Wirth [qq.v.]. Born on 7 December 1868 at Dalby, Queensland, Marizles had married John Augustin Martin (d. 1907), circus musician, on 9 February 1891 at St Andrew's Anglican Cathedral, Sydney. With their only daughter Stella (b. 1892), they toured overseas with Wirth Brothers' Circus in 1893-1900.

Having been taught by her father to do the 'flip-flap', May soon featured in balancing and tumbling acts, and as a tightwire performer and contortionist. From Philip and Marizles she learned equestrian skills and from ringmaster John Cooke the feet-to-feet forward somersault on a bareback horse. At the age of 10 she was a 'real trick rider' and began appearing in acts with Stella and Marizles. In Melbourne in 1906 she was billed as 'May Ringling', the 'American fearless hurricane hurdle rider'. A 'remarkably pretty girl', she grew to only 4 ft. 11 ins. (149.9 cm) tall.

After starring in Sydney in April 1911, when she 'rode and drove eight ponies, and turned somersaults on a cantering grey', May visited the United States of America with her mother and sister. Engaged by John Ringling for two seasons to tour with his Barnum & Bailey circus, she was billed as 'the world's greatest bareback rider' and given a conspicuous place on the programme at their opening show in New York on 21 March 1912. The elegantly gowned Marizles was ringmistress and Stella also performed. An immediate success, May developed her act by somersaulting backwards through rings and by leaping from the ground to the back of her galloping horse with her feet encased in baskets. Although

seriously injured in a fall during a performance in April 1913, she appeared with Carl Hagenbeck's Wonder Zoo and Circus at London's Olympia next December. In 1914 Marizles, May and Stella appeared with two male riders in vaudeville in England and France.

As the 'Royal Wirth Family', the troupe toured Australasia with Wirth Bros Ltd Circus in 1915-16, performing vaudeville, burlesque and equestrian items. May was dainty, 'like a butterfly in flight . . . alive, alert' and delighted Sydney audiences. In 1917 the troupe toured North America with Ringling Brothers. As the 'May Wirth Troupe', they were joined by Philip Vincent Jones, known as St Leon, who later married Stella. May remained the star equestrienne when the Ringling Brothers and Barnum & Bailey circuses amalgamated in 1919. At the Church of the Transfiguration ('The Little Church around the Corner'), New York, on 27 November that year, she married her manager Frank White who also adopted the professional name of Wirth; they were to remain childless.

May and her troupe toured with the Walter L. Main circus in the 1921 and 1923 seasons, performing in 1922 at the Coliseum, London; in the winter months they played in vaudeville in Europe. She again starred in Ringling Brothers and Barnum & Bailey combined shows in 1924, but left in 1927 to tour country fairs and indoor circuses. In the winter of 1931 her troupe was featured as the St Leon Indoor Circus and in March next year she performed the live circus scenes in the operetta, *The blue mask*, at Chicago.

Retiring at the peak of her career in 1937, May Wirth settled in New York; Marizles died there on 30 March 1948. May moved to Sarasota, Florida, where her name was added to the Circus Hall of Fame in 1964. A gracious, gentle woman, with 'merry brown eyes', she remained 'sprightly' and enjoyed sharing her circus memories. Predeceased by her husband, she died on 18 October 1978 at Sarasota and was cremated.

M. V. St Leon, *Spangles and sawdust* (Melb, 1983) and (comp), *Australian circus reminiscences* (priv print, Syd, 1984); Circus Fans of America Inc, *White Tops*, Mar-Apr 1979; *This Australia*, Spring 1983; *New York Clipper*, 30 Mar 1912; *Argus*, 13 Oct 1906, 25 Oct 1915; *New York Times*, 23 Apr 1913, 30 Mar, 28 Nov 1919, 4 Apr 1920; *Chicago Daily Tribune*, 29 Mar 1932; information from Mr and Mrs E. L. Zinga, Lindfield, Syd, and Mrs M. G. Black, Sarasota, Florida, US.

MARK VALENTINE ST LEON

WIRTH, PHILIP PETER JACOB (1864-1937) and GEORGE (1867-1941), bandsmen and circus proprietors, were born on 29 June 1864 at Beechworth, Victoria, and 30 July 1867 in Sydney, sons of John Wirth (1834-1880), a musician from Bavaria, and his English wife Sarah, née Phillips. Having arrived in Victoria in 1855, John and his brothers travelled the eastern colonies as itinerant musicians; in 1858 'Werth's band' was engaged with Jones's National Circus. About 1867 John bought land at Dalby, Queensland, and erected a hall where he gave music and dance lessons. Ashton's [q.v.7] Circus passed through Dalby in 1870 and engaged him as a bandsman. He was joined by his sons John and Harry, and later the younger Philip and George. Sarah and the daughters eventually settled in Sydney. In 1878 the band played for the opening of the railway at Tamworth, New South Wales; it also performed in processions, at bush and city balls, and at parties; by 1879 its members were again in Queensland with Ridge's Royal Tycoon Circus where they probably learned their first performing stunts.

About 1881 the brothers joined Ashton's Circus as Wirth's Tourist Band. Next year they set up their own troupe. John played the cornet, Harry the bass, Philip the trombone and George the tenor horn, each alternating with ring performances that included tumbling, horizontal bars, contortion, club-swinging and trapeze. Buying wagons and horses, they began travelling as a small circus. By 1887 it was the largest in Australia. While touring Victoria in 1889, they adopted rail transport. Thenceforth crowds flocked to see the arrival and unloading of the circus train wherever it went. In 1888 the Wirths visited New Caledonia and in 1890 New Zealand. There, on 28 September, Philip married Sarah Jane Hodgson (d. 1929) at St Mary's Church, Parnell, Auckland. George was an agile clown and 'jockey rider', but, following an accident, became business manager in 1889.

With the onset of the depression, in 1893 the Wirths decided to tour South Africa where, on 9 October 1894, George married Margaret Bain at the Church of St John the Evangelist, East London; they were to remain childless. A seven-year odyssey took the circus to South America, England, South Africa again, India and Java, before it returned to Perth in August 1900. The deaths of John junior in 1894 and Harry in 1895 left control to Philip and George, and their sister Marizles [q.v. May Wirth]. A spirited and sometimes bitter struggle ensued with Dan and Tom Fitzgerald, who had become Australia's leading circus proprietors, until their deaths in 1906 when the Wirths largely absorbed the rival company. The Fitzgeralds' management innovations—and their customary presentation of a gold-mounted whip to the Melbourne Cup winning jockey—were continued. In 1907 the Wirths leased the Olympia building in Melbourne (now the site of the Victorian Arts Centre); by then, elephants had been added to the circus menagerie.

Wirth Bros Ltd Circus was incorporated in 1913; in that year the brothers inherited a fortune from an American uncle. George, 'a small man, brown and wiry', sported a toothbrush moustache. Philip, whose moustache in early life was a flourishing handlebar, towered over him. Each year they, or their trusted lieutenants, searched for fresh acts and brought such artists as the Flying Codonas from the principal circuses of Europe and North America; by contrast, local talent was seldom engaged or developed, although Philip was an excellent trainer of horses and somersault equestrians. Both brothers acted as ringmasters. Built for £40 000 by the Sydney Municipal Council and leased to the brothers, Wirth's Hippodrome opened in April 1916. Rebuilt in 1927, it became the Capitol Theatre.

Apart from an unsuccessful tour to Java in 1935, Wirth's Circus confined its operations after 1900 to Australasia. George and Philip published autobiographies, *Round the world with a circus* (1925) and *The life of Philip Wirth* (1934). They belonged to the Australian Jockey and the Victoria Racing clubs; George was also a member of the Victoria Amateur Turf Club and the Royal Automobile Club of Australia; Philip was a Freemason and a member of the Royal Agricultural Society of New South Wales. On 5 March 1929 he married Alice Maud Willis at St Aidan's Church, Berrigan, New South Wales. Survived by his wife, their five daughters and two sons, and by a daughter of his first marriage, he died at his Coogee home on 29 August 1937 and was buried in the Anglican section of North Adelaide cemetery. His estate was sworn for probate at £33 379. George had retired in 1930, but in 1936 became a director of National [film] Studios Ltd, Pagewood. He died in Sydney on 16 October 1941, leaving an estate sworn at £49 126. His wife survived him. Australia's most outstanding circus continued to be run by Philip's family and was the only one permitted to travel in Australia during World War II, albeit on a reduced scale and with its itinerary limited by petrol rationing. Wirth's Circus flourished after the war, declined with the advent of television, and in 1963 disbanded.

M. V. St Leon, *Australian circus reminiscences* (Syd, priv print, 1984); *Table Talk*, 18 Nov 1926; *Age*, 30 Oct 1937; *SMH*, 30 Aug 1937, 17 Oct 1941; collection of historical circus material (held by author, Glebe, Syd); information from Mrs M. Wright, Springwood, NSW.

MARK VALENTINE ST LEON

WISDOM, EVAN ALEXANDER (1869-1945), businessman, soldier and administrator, was born on 29 September 1869 at Inverness, Scotland, son of Francis William Wisdom, music-seller, and his wife Mary, née Cameron. He was educated at Inverness and in Edinburgh. As a young man he served in the militia, first in an infantry battalion and then in the Midlothian Coast Artillery.

At the age of 22 he migrated to Western Australia and went as a prospector to Southern Cross on the Yilgarn goldfield. In 1892, as soon as news came of the gold discovery at Coolgardie, Wisdom joined the rush and was one of the first to arrive on the field. He did well, and opened a store. Within a year he joined the rush to Kalgoorlie; there, too, he prospered, acquiring extensive mining interests and establishing the Exchange Hotel. Late in 1894 he went to Scotland where, on 16 April 1895, he married Agnes Bell Jackson in Edinburgh with Presbyterian Free Church forms. They travelled to Western Australia and settled at Claremont, Perth. Wisdom retained his business links with the goldfields.

In October 1901 Wisdom was appointed lieutenant in the Western Australian Mounted Infantry; given command of the Cannington troop, he was promoted captain in 1903; next year he was posted to militia headquarters in Perth. He was brigade major of the Western Australian Infantry Brigade in 1908 and, in spite of militia commitments and business ties, found time for politics. He was mayor of Cottesloe in 1908-13 and member for Claremont in the Legislative Assembly in 1911-17.

On the outbreak of war in 1914 Wisdom had been placed in charge of the Karrakatta training camp. In March 1915 he transferred to the Australian Imperial Force as brigade major of the 5th Infantry Brigade. He served with it throughout most of the Gallipoli campaign. In February 1916, as a lieut-colonel, he took command of the 18th Battalion. In June he was awarded the Distinguished Service Order. Late that year his battalion was in the bloody battles of Pozières Heights and Flers, France. In December he was promoted brigadier general commanding the 7th Brigade which fought at Lagnicourt in March 1917 and in the 2nd battle of Bullecourt in May. Wisdom was appointed C.B. in June. Late in 1917 the brigade was in Flanders at the battles of Menin Road, Broodseinde and Passchendaele. Meanwhile, his wife had moved to London to do charity work.

In 1918 the 7th Brigade was at Morlancourt in June and at Hamel in July, and took part in the battle of Amiens, the storming of Mont St Quentin and the fighting for the Beaurevoir Line. Wisdom was appointed C.M.G. in January 1919. During the war he had been mentioned in dispatches six times. He spent most of 1919 in England with the Repatriation and Demobilization Department, A.I.F. Returning to Australia in December, he was appointed to the chairmanship of the Central War Gratuities Board in May 1920. A few months later he successfully applied for the post of administrator of the Mandated Territory of New Guinea.

Taking over at Rabaul from Thomas Griffiths [q.v.9] on 21 March 1921, during the next few years Wisdom converted the improvised military administration into a professional public service. In accordance with the terms of the League of Nations mandate he did his best to advance the welfare of the native population. He was handicapped at first by attitudes inherited from the German colonial period, and, after 1926, by owners of the expropriated plantations and by German missionaries. Like later administrators, he was troubled by the intransigence of the planters, their occasional maltreatment of workers, and their influence in Australian political circles. In 1930 the fall in copra prices and gold production compelled him to reduce government activities.

Late in 1931 Wisdom took leave to accompany his wife to Sydney where she died in November. Resuming duty early in 1932, he formally opened the Bulolo Gold Dredging Co. in March; gold production rose again and fiscal troubles receded. Wisdom, however, was not to see the benefit: tired and lonely, after eleven years in office he applied for furlough. He left Rabaul in June 1932 and retired in June 1933. Resuming his earlier interests, he became involved in new mining ventures in Western Australia and alternated between the Melbourne Club and Perth where he kept in close touch with old friends on the goldfields. He died without issue on 7 December 1945 in Melbourne and was cremated.

C. E. W. Bean [q.v.7] described Wisdom in wartime as 'a level-headed, cautious, experienced leader'. People who knew him in New Guinea saw him as honest, discreet, temperate, shrewd and hardworking, with a sly sense of humour. He will be remembered as a very competent commander in World War I and as an intelligent, just and able administrator during eleven difficult years in New Guinea.

J. S. Battye (ed), *Cyclopedia of Western Australia*, 2 (Adel, 1913); C. E. W. Bean, *The story of Anzac*, 1, 2 (Syd, 1921, 1924), and *The A.I.F. in France*, 1916-18 (Syd, 1929, 1933, 1937, 1942); P. Ryan (ed), *Encyclopaedia of Papua and New Guinea* (Melb, 1972); *Kalgoorlie Miner*, 8 Jan 1946.

RONALD McNICOLL

WISE, BERNHARD RINGROSE (1858-1916), barrister, politician and Federationist, was born on 10 February 1858 at Petersham, Sydney, second son of Edward Wise [q.v.6], barrister, and his wife Maria Bate, née Smith, both English born. After Edward's death in 1865, the family returned to England. Bernhard and his brothers attended a grammar school at Leeds where, he recalled, 'our homemade clothes exposed us to ridicule and bullying'. To qualify her sons to attend Rugby School and satisfy a family tradition, Maria took employment in the town. Bernhard's seven years at Rugby as a 'Townie' and a 'Foundationer' were subject to exclusion and persecution, but he excelled in his studies, and as a debater and athlete. In 1876 he entered The Queen's College, Oxford, on a Rugby presentation worth £90 a year. He graduated brilliantly in jurisprudence (B.A., 1881), carried off both the university and British amateur mile championships, emerged as a radical Gladstonian Liberal and was president (1881) of the Oxford Union. Sidney Low considered that, of all his illustrious contemporaries at Oxford, 'Bernhard Wise was in some respects the most gifted and brilliant, with a charm of personality that cannot easily be surpassed'.

After Oxford, Wise spent a year in London during which he narrowly missed election to an All Souls fellowship. Contacts with such sponsors as George Meredith and his election as president of the Amateur Athletic Association opened opportunities for a career, but, together with Alfred Milner and other Oxford contemporaries, Wise became associated with the social reformer Arnold Toynbee and worked closely with him. Called to the Bar at the Middle Temple on 18 April 1883, he was attracted by the prospect of some form of public life and set his sights on his native Sydney. His fiancée Lilian Margaret Baird, who was related to eminent people in university, journalistic and theatrical circles, agreed to follow him.

All in all, it was a young man 'favoured by the Gods' who landed in Sydney in August 1883, 'eager, confident and confiding, not realizing I was coming among men who viewed life through different eyes'. Admitted to the New South Wales Bar on 28 August, he married Lilian at St Paul's Anglican Church, Melbourne, on 1 April 1884: Alfred Barry [q.v.3], bishop of Sydney and primate of Australia, officiated. Wise was an agnostic. Although he was not financially established (he had to borrow money for his wedding), the lure of the parliamentary life was strong. Enticement came from Sir Henry Parkes [q.v.5] who had met Wise in London. As a Parkes free trader, Wise surprised many of his associates in 1887 by nominating for the working-class constituency of South Sydney. There on the pub balconies and street corners of Surry Hills and Haymarket, he nightly took

on opponents such as A. J. Riley, the mayor of Sydney, James Toohey [qq.v.6], the Irish-supported brewer, and Mick Simmons, a local sporting identity. The stylishly-dressed young patrician, talking social reform with an Oxford accent, was a startling new phenomenon in colonial politics: those who listened found him ready with an advanced reform policy of direct taxation, payment of members and an eight-hour day. He held his ground and was elected.

Wise was appointed attorney-general (May 1887) in Parkes's administration, but inexperience and financial quicksands forced him to resign in February 1888 and he lost his seat in the 1889 election. With Toynbee as his exemplar, he continued to try to influence opinion by writing pamphlets and giving public addresses. As president of the Free Trade Association, he took a leading role in formulating a policy of social reform that extended beyond the narrow fiscal issue and liberal attachment to individualism and *laissez-faire*. He claimed later that his published lecture, *Free trade and wages* (Sydney, 1884), revealed 'at what early date I had formed those "labour views" to which in after years I have tried consistently to give effect'. His ideas were fully developed in *Industrial freedom* (London, 1892), published by the Cobden Club, and remained the ideological pivot of his whole political career.

Amid the industrial and class tensions engendered by the 1890 maritime strike, Wise stood 'the political hairs of many of his associates on end' by publicly opposing the 'freedom of contract' principle and claiming a contrary *freedom* to refuse labour, union preference and a common wage. He argued quixotically that there could be no freedom without equality, which the very concept of freedom of contract denied to the worker. Wise was 'entirely unprepared' for the social and professional storm which burst upon him, and later assessed this crisis as the turning-point in his career. Though many in the embryonic labour movement still found it hard to separate his views from his background and education, he was returned to the Legislative Assembly in 1891 as a member for South Sydney.

When Parkes stood down from leadership of the party in October, Wise proposed (Sir) George Reid [q.v.11] as his successor. Committed to the fiscal and tax reforms of Wise's Free Trade, Land and Reform League, Reid achieved office in 1894. After Parkes made another bid for leadership that year with the Federation issue, Wise faced a complicated conflict of loyalties: to party and leader, to his espoused principles and free trade associations, to his patron Parkes and national unity. He withheld his vote when Parkes made his 'unholy alliance' with his former enemy Sir George Dibbs [q.v.4] over a censure motion: the defeat of the motion left Wise isolated, reaping the scorn and bitterness reserved for the political apostate. Along with Parkes, he lost his seat at the 1895 election and left the Free Trade Party.

Wise then became an energetic advocate of Federation, speaking, travelling and writing as an editorial committee-member of the *Australian Federalist*. He was a delegate to the Australasian Federal Convention of 1897-98 where his liberal instinct, constitutional training and persuasive advocacy made a valuable contribution. Strongly supporting equal State representation in the Senate, he suggested the double dissolution proposal for the breaking of deadlocks between the Houses. Deakin [q.v.8] placed him in 'the first rank of men of influence in the Convention'. Wise was, however, to be unsuccessful in his attempt to enter the first Federal parliament when he failed in 1901 to win the country seat of Canobolas. There he encountered the same antagonism to the 'city' barrister as he had met in 1889 when, at Parkes's urging, he had taken on 'Paddy' Crick [q.v.8] in West Macquarie.

In 1898 Wise had won the Legislative Assembly seat of Ashfield as a member of (Sir) William Lyne's [q.v.10] Progressive Party. He was appointed Q.C. the same year. After Reid's defeat, Wise was attorney-general (September 1899-June 1904) and minister of justice (July 1901-June 1904) in the Lyne ministry and in the subsequent government of Sir John See [q.v.11]. Wise attained his highest office as acting premier for two short periods in 1904. Now stabled in a ministry of former Protectionist leaders (but with the fiscal issue removed to the Federal arena), he found himself allied with such democrats as Crick, E. W. O'Sullivan and J. L. Fegan [qq.v.11,8], and co-operating with Labor's W. A. Holman [q.v.9]. He found this period the 'best and happiest of my political life', and took a leading part in the framing and passage of social reform legislation, among it the Early Closing Act (1899), Old-age Pensions Act (1900) and the Women's Franchise Act (1902). Having helped to form the Prisoners' Aid Association, as minister of justice he turned to the prison system, incorporating measures for the health and education of prisoners and a reformatory release system in his Crimes Amendment Act (1905). Working closely with child-welfare reformers Frederick Neitenstein, (Sir) Charles Mackellar and Rose Scott [qq.v.10,11], he framed and introduced the state children's bill (1902) which, though defeated, hardly differed from the Neglected Children and Juvenile Offenders Act (1905) to be passed by (Sir) Charles Wade's [q.v.] government. It was Wise who chaired Catherine Helen Spence's [q.v.6] meeting in Sydney to support the child welfare movement.

The legislation with which Wise was most closely associated, and his crowning achievement, was the Industrial Arbitration Act of 1901. It was the culmination of the ideas first set out in his address to the 1885 Trades Union Conference and later in *Industrial freedom*—the responsibility of the state to establish conditions of justice and equality within the industrial society of capital and labour. Though it was, by then, a position close to the ideas of the Fabians (whose influence is often seen as decisive), it was Wise who framed, advocated, explained and defended the legislation, and who finally took a seat in the Legislative Council in 1900 to pilot the bill through the Upper House.

Despite the recognition and support he received from many in his own party and from Labor, conservative members feared where Wise would carry the party if he succeeded See as leader. Wise felt slighted when Governor Sir Harry Rawson [q.v.11] called on Thomas Waddell [q.v.] in June 1904 to form a government. Waddell refused to promote the local government extension bill (incorporating reforms of 'paramount urgency' which Wise had already prepared and committed) and Wise refused to serve under him.

One of the last to have kept up his practice while attorney-general, in 1904 a tired Wise took leave to visit England. Next year in South America he contracted malaria and seriously impaired his health. Never financially secure, he resumed practice at the English Bar in 1906. He contributed to journals and wrote *Australia and its critics* (London, 1905) and *The Commonwealth of Australia* (London, 1909). His illness prevented lengthy travel until 1908. When he returned to Sydney that year, his Legislative Council seat had been declared vacant and he found it difficult to regain his legal or political standing. He resumed legal work and published *The making of the Australian Commonwealth 1889-1900* (London, 1913) and *The war of nations* (Melbourne, 1914). Described by Deakin as a 'man of letters, all his tastes are literary', Wise was closely involved in Australian cultural life. A great supporter of artists, he corresponded with a circle of literary friends including (Sir) Mungo MacCallum and John Le Gay Brereton [qq.v.10,7]. He entertained Robert Louis Stevenson on his visit to Sydney, and Wise's family connexion with Henry Brodribb Irving kept him in touch with the theatrical world. A trustee of the National Art Gallery of New South Wales, he was also able to fulfil his father's wish to have land set aside in the Domain for a free public library. Wise was a member of the Athenaeum and Union clubs, president of the French Club and a patron of the Harriers Athletic Club.

Holman, a long-time friend and admirer, appointed Wise chairman of the royal commission on the mining industry at Broken Hill (1914-15); and as premier in 1914, Holman appointed him New South Wales agent-general in London. Wise threw all his energies into his wartime position, straining his weakened health. After visiting Australian troops at Salisbury, he died suddenly on 19 September 1916 at his Kensington home and was buried at Brookwood, Surrey. His wife and son survived him.

Of a career generally assessed as one of unfulfilled promise, Wise himself had concluded:

My failure in Sydney has been so complete— my qualities those which Australia does not recognise, my defects those which Australians dislike most.

Some have analysed a failure of character— restless inconsistency, inconstancy, insincerity—while others have painted a man unscrupulous, disloyal and scheming, guilty of the great sin of Australian politics, betrayal of his party. Another view, however, can contemplate a committed and principled politician, bringing with him the philosophy of T. H. Green's New Liberalism, the ethos of Arnold Toynbee and an English concept of political party life. Deeply committed to Australia, Wise entered its political life at a time when radical-conservative and nationalist-Imperial divisions were settling into loose fiscal party formations and into an emerging, class-based labour movement; his perpetual isolation might well be considered a political tragedy, rather than a personal failure. His own aspirations for a better society, implemented through parliament, were an influence acknowledged by many of his contemporaries. In 1916 Holman declared that: 'There is hardly anything in our public life which we have to consider to-day that cannot be traced back to his brilliant mind and clear foresight ... [Wise] held undisputed supremacy as the foremost debater, foremost thinker and foremost public man in the life of New South Wales'.

H. Parkes, *Fifty years in the making of Australian history* (Lond, 1892); A. Milner, *Arnold Toynbee* (Lond, 1895); National A'sian Convention/A'sian Federal Convention, *Official report* (and *record*) of the debates (Adel, Syd, 1897, Melb, 1898); H. V. Evatt, *Australian Labour leader* (Syd, 1942); A. Deakin, *The Federal story* (Melb, 1944); B. E. Mansfield, *Australian democrat* (Syd, 1965); B. Nairn, *Civilising capitalism* (Canb, 1973); J. Rickard, *Class and politics* (Canb, 1975); A. W. Martin, *Henry Parkes* (Melb, 1980); *SMH*, 21 Sept 1916; J. A. Ryan, B. R. Wise (M.A. thesis, Univ Syd, 1966); Parkes correspondence *and* Wise correspondence and news-cuttings (ML); NSW Agent-General correspondence and despatches, 1916 (CO 418/151-

52, AJCP microfilm, NL); B. R. Wise, Reverie and reminiscence. A personal memoir (ms, 1914, copy held by author).   J. A. RYAN

WISE, GEORGE HENRY (1853-1950), politician and solicitor, was born on 1 July 1853 in Melbourne, eldest child of James Wise, hairdresser, and his wife Mary, née McIntosh, both from Edinburgh. A slight, wiry child, George was sent as a 5-year-old to Scotch College, Melbourne, where he remained until matriculating in 1868, failing to excel in anything the school then considered important. He studied law as an articled clerk, was admitted to the Bar on 19 September 1874, worked at Sale as a managing clerk in a solicitor's office and started his own practice in 1877.

As a teenager Wise had frequently visited the galleries of the Victorian parliament, nurturing his dream of entering politics. He was elected to the Sale Borough Council in 1880, held his seat for twenty-four years and was mayor on six occasions. In 1886 Wise founded the Sale branch of the Australian Natives' Association. He joined the Victorian board of directors in 1887, became vice-president in 1888 and was elected chief president in 1891. A leading campaigner in Victoria for Federation, he also stood, unsuccessfully, for the Legislative Assembly in 1892, 1894 and 1904, and for the Senate in 1901 and 1903. In December 1906 he was surprisingly elected for the Federal seat of Gippsland, defeating Allan McLean [q.v.10] by 97 votes after a campaign underscored by sectarian murmurings.

This small man, 'with a picturesquely bald head, two bright and restless eyes and a mouth with a distinctly humourous twist', described himself in 1909 as a 'Liberal and Progressive from my boyhood'. He sat behind Deakin [q.v.8], urging his party to support full tariff protection, social reform and a strong national defence. An opponent of State rights, Wise repeatedly denounced those who did not take 'an Australian point of view' and called on the Federal government to assume all responsibilities permitted under the Constitution.

Wise was shocked by the Fusion of 1909. Unlike other Victorian Liberals, he was not seriously threatened by Labor in Gippsland and did not need an electoral alliance with conservatives. He was, however, genuinely upset that his colleagues had handed themselves over 'body and soul, to their enemies'. Wise insisted that there were just two positions in Australian politics—liberal and conservative—and that Labor and the Deakinites were natural allies against the forces of reaction. Disappointed, rather than bitter, he could not condemn Deakin with the ferocity of Sir William Lyne [q.v.10], but he deplored his leader's sacrifice of principle for the sake of political survival.

Standing as an Independent in the 1910 elections and opposed only by a Fusionist, Wise retained his seat with 62 per cent of the vote. Although he often supported Labor after 1909, Wise never joined the caucus. Suspicious of extra-parliamentary discipline, angered by attempts to give preference to unionists in government employment and by claims of 'a right to strike', he was too independent to commit himself to Labor. He was also proud of his adherence to the liberal-nationalist tradition which, in his view, had been deserted by the self-servers and undermined by the party machines.

The Liberals defeated him in Gippsland in 1913; he scraped back in 1914, won easily in the Nationalist landslide in 1917 and held off a challenger from the Victorian Farmers' Union in 1919. Following the Labor split in 1916, Wise was involved in the negotiations between W. M. Hughes and (Sir) Joseph Cook [qq.v.9,8]: while he did not then join the Nationalists, he was regarded as a Hughes supporter. Modestly and sensibly, he quashed suggestions that he might succeed Hughes after the defeat of the second conscription referendum in December 1917. Instead, he supported the prime minister, regarding him as the one man capable of uniting the non-Labor factions in pursuit of winning the war. He was rewarded with two ministerial posts: honorary minister (March 1918-February 1920) assisting and representing Senator (Sir) George Pearce [q.v.11], the minister for defence; and postmaster-general (February 1920-December 1921). Wise lost his portfolio in the 1921 reshuffle, a casualty perhaps of the move to bring S. M. (Viscount) Bruce [q.v.7] into the cabinet and certainly of his breach with Hughes over the transfer of wireless services to Amalgamated Wireless (Australasia) Ltd.

Defeated by the Country Party in the 1922 elections, Wise stood as an Independent Nationalist in 1925, finishing third behind the Country Party and Labor. In 1928, at 75, he stood as Independent Labor and was well beaten by the Country Party. The old man then retired from active politics, but retained his links with the A.N.A. and continued to practise as a solicitor at Sale until the end of 1948. He died there on 31 July 1950 and was buried in the local cemetery. He was predeceased by his wife Mary Thornton, née Smith, whom he had married at Sale on 14 April 1880 with Presbyterian forms. Three daughters and a son survived him.

History of Scotch College, Melbourne, 1851-1925 (Melb, 1926); J. A. La Nauze, *Alfred Deakin* (Melb, 1965); L. F. Fitzhardinge, *The little digger 1914-1952* (Syd, 1979); C. H. M. Clark, *A history of Australia,* 5 (Melb, 1981); *Punch* (Melb), 18 July 1907; *Age,* 1 Aug 1950; Deakin *and* Hughes papers (NL).
                                                        I. R. HANCOCK

WISE, PERCY WILLIAM CHARLTON (1870-1950), Anglican priest, was born on 15 January 1870 at Stoke Damerel, Devonshire, England, son of David Woodifield Wise, assistant paymaster, R.N., and his wife Harriet Blanche, née Sheppard. Percy was educated at Clewer House School, near Windsor, and at Corpus Christi College, Cambridge (B.A., 1893; M.A., 1902) where he came under the influence of J. R. Harmer [q.v.9], later bishop of Adelaide. After leaving the Clergy Training School, Cambridge, Wise was made deacon in 1893 and ordained priest in 1894. He then took up a curacy at Oundle, Northamptonshire. On 16 July 1895 he married Caroline Louisa Lyon (d. 1900) at St Michael's parish church, Ilsington, Devonshire; they were to remain childless. That year he accepted a curacy at Christ Church, North Adelaide.

In 1897 he became rector of Crafers where his energy led to the completion of the Church of the Epiphany two years later. Having visited England, Wise returned to Adelaide late in 1900 to take the pastoral charge of Goodwood, a parish in a poor state, with a small church and very few worshippers. Instituted rector on 14 December, he flung himself into the work and completed St James's Church, West Adelaide, in 1902, when it became a separate charge. In September 1903 the new Church of St George was consecrated: it was designed by his brother-in-law, the English architect T. H. Lyon, and much of the cost was met by Mrs Priscilla Bickford, a wealthy admirer of Wise. His preaching and practice won many to worship at St George's and he soon became the acknowledged leader of the Anglo-Catholic movement in South Australia. In 1902 he had been appointed special preacher at St Peter's Cathedral, Adelaide, where he was an honorary canon from 1904.

With Harmer's departure in 1905, Wise's course became troubled. The new bishop of Adelaide, Dr A. N. Thomas [q.v.], was concerned by some of Wise's controversial observances, including the offering of the requiem Mass on All Souls Day; in 1911 St George's was put under discipline. In 1918 Wise issued his *St George's Mass book for lay folk*; Thomas believed it contained 'grave errors of teaching and of practice'. When Wise refused to withdraw it, Thomas issued a public admonition in 1919 which led to Wise being charged in the ecclesiastical courts with 'breach of ritual'. Wise defended himself ably and, though the charges were not formally withdrawn, the case was dropped. Yet the stigma of disloyalty remained. During the 1920s, while remaining critical of episcopal policies, Wise withdrew from involvement in diocesan affairs, devoted himself to his work as a parish priest and gained a high reputation among Anglo-Catholics as a spiritual adviser. Between 1907 and 1937 he published a collection of addresses and several pamphlets.

With a lively sense of humour and a command of repartee, Wise had great charm of manner. His writing, like his preaching, was graceful, persuasive and memorable. He loved sport, especially golf and cricket. Following severe illness, he resigned his parish on 1 October 1940, one day after the resignation of Bishop Thomas. Wise died on 13 August 1950 at Highgate, Adelaide, and was cremated; his ashes were taken to England and buried in Ilsington churchyard beside those of his wife.

L. E. W. Renfrey, *Father Wise, rector of St George's, Goodwood* (Adel, 1951) and *Arthur Nutter Thomas* (Adel, 1988); H. J. Harrison and J. M. Truran, *St George's, Goodwood, 1880-1980* (Adel, 1980); D. Hilliard, *Godliness and good order* (Adel, 1986); *St George's Messenger*, 1902-40.

LIONEL E. W. RENFREY

WISEMAN, THOMAS (1847-1941), trader, publican and transport operator, was born on 12 September 1847 at Launceston, Van Diemen's Land, eldest son of Thomas Wiseman, shipwright, and his wife Harriet, née Rogers. From 1854 his parents bought and ran hotels at Emu Bay (Burnie), but Thomas senior continued shipbuilding and became a trader. Young Thomas was educated privately and went to school at Stanley. On 30 January 1868 he married Margaret Castles (d. 1920) at Wynyard with Anglican rites; they were to have eleven children. Having entered the hotel business, he was attracted by the boom conditions which followed the discovery of tin at Mount Bischoff. He returned to Burnie in 1873 and, with his brother Jesse, contracted to cart ore from the mine by bullock-teams. Performed under shocking conditions, the enterprise was profitable and lasted until 1878 when the brothers went into storekeeping and butchering at Waratah.

In 1882 Thomas sold out and moved back to Burnie where he built the Wiseman's Family Hotel. Selling it within a year, he bought Jones's Hotel which he renamed the Bay View Hotel. In 1890 he took over Jesse's mail contract and coach service, running it until the railway links to the West Coast and to Launceston were completed in 1901. He also acquired a large 'bait and livery stable' where horses and jinkers could be hired. Fire destroyed the Bay View Hotel in January 1897,

but it was rebuilt on a grander scale with sixty-five rooms.

Retiring from hotel-keeping in 1912, Wiseman moved to nearby Kandarah, a large house he had built for his family. Photographs show him in middle age as large framed, with receding hair, kind eyes and a well-groomed beard. He became a major property owner in the Burnie town centre and financed his sons in various enterprises, particularly the hotel trade and farming.

As he prospered, Wiseman had begun to play a leading role in community affairs. He was a foundation trustee of the Burnie Institute which built the Town Hall (1888), and the Burnie Theatre (1913) was erected largely through his backing. A member (1874-1907) of the local road trust, when Burnie became a municipal district in 1898 he became treasurer of the town board and was elected its chairman in 1903; first warden of the elected municipal council in 1906, he held a seat on that body until 1918. He was also a warden (1907-11) of the local marine board, chairman of the board of health (1903-07), the cemetery trust and the fire brigade (1901-15), and first vice-president of the Burnie Agricultural and Pastoral Society in 1913. Survived by two sons and five daughters, Wiseman died at Burnie on 1 August 1941; his estate was sworn for probate at £35 309.

Cyclopedia of Tasmania, 2 (Hob, 1900); P. G. Mercer, *Gateway to progress* (Burnie, Tas, 1969) and 'Hotels and banks of Burnie', *Arts Council Bulletin*, 8, no 9, Dec 1964, p 62; W. Winter, *Burnie Inn 1847-1901* (Burnie, 1974) and *Burnie Fire Brigade* (Burnie, 1974) and *Onward—Burnie historical highlights in a biography of Capt. William Jones* (Burnie, 1975); R. Pike, *Pioneers of Burnie* (Burnie, 1977); A. Ebdon, *Defying the odds* (Burnie, 1987); *Zeehan and Dundas Herald*, 5 July 1911; *Advocate* (Burnie), 2 Aug 1941.

PETER MERCER

WITHERS, WALTER HERBERT (1854-1914), artist and teacher, was born on 22 October 1854 at Aston Manor, Warwickshire, England, son of Edwin Withers, roper, and his wife Sarah, née Welch. Sent to school at Sutton Coldfield, Walter later attended art classes at the Royal Academy of Arts, London, and South Kensington schools before embarking for Australia at the behest of his father who opposed an artistic career. Breaking his journey at Port Said, he arrived in Melbourne on 1 January 1883.

After working on several country properties as a jackaroo for eighteen months, he moved to Melbourne where he enrolled in evening art classes at the Melbourne National Gallery school of painting under G. F. Folingsby [q.v.4]. Withers began to paint 9 by 7 ins. (23 by 18 cm) oil sketches, and also sought black-and-white work. Employed as a draughtsman by William Inglis & Co., and next by Ferguson & Mitchell, lithographic printers, he produced portraits in black and white for several periodicals. His work was accepted for exhibition in the Old Academy, Melbourne. At this time he met Frederick McCubbin, Tom Roberts [qq.v.10,11] and Louis Abrahams who became lifelong friends.

Encouraged by Roberts to travel overseas, Withers left Melbourne for London in May 1887; having journeyed overland from Naples, via Paris, he arrived in June. On 11 October 1887 he married Fanny Flinn in the parish church, Handsworth-with-Soho, Staffordshire. Soon after, they departed for Paris, settling for six months in a flat in Rue Tronchet. He studied with Australian artists E. Phillips Fox [q.v.8], Tudor St George Tucker [q.v.] and John Longstaff [q.v.10] at the Académie Julian where he drew from life under the supervision of Adolphe William Bouguereau and Joseph Nicolas Robert-Fleury. On the weekends he toured Paris, visiting major galleries where he was impressed and influenced by the works of Bastien LePage, Monet, Manet and Anton Mauve.

Commissioned by Ferguson & Mitchell to illustrate with pen and ink *The chronicles of early Melbourne* by Edmund Finn [q.v.1], Withers and his wife went to England to farewell relations and friends, travelled to Italy and returned to Melbourne on 11 June 1888. They rented a cottage at Kew where Withers established a studio and met the artists Arthur Streeton [q.v.], Charles Conder, Artur Loureiro and George Rossi Ashton [qq.v.3,5,7]. While his wife revisited England in 1889, Withers shared with Roberts and Streeton the home of Charles Davies at Eaglemont. His attempts to organize his fellow artists earned him the nickname 'Colonel'. In 1890 the Withers family moved into the mansion, Charterisville, at Heidelberg, where Withers established a studio and sub-let cottages to other artists. In April 1891 he also established a city studio in Collins Street, took private pupils and in May held a successful major exhibition there. With the onset of the 1890s depression, black-and-white work became scarce and Withers contemplated returning to England. He decided to stay when McCubbin found him teaching positions at three schools.

In 1893 Withers taught at Creswick, giving day classes *en plein air* and evening drawing classes at the School of Mines; among his students were Percy and Norman Lindsay [qq.v.10]. Next year he rented a house in Cape Street, Heidelberg, and produced some of his finest work: 'A Bright Winter's Morning' (1894), 'Tranquil Winter' (1895)

and 'The Storm' (1896) which won the first Wynne prize for landscape painting in 1897. He again won the prize in 1900 with 'Still Autumn'. 'Tranquil Winter' was exhibited in the colonial art exhibition held in London in 1898. That year he moved into a home that he had helped to design at Heidelberg.

Withers then rekindled friendships with pastoralists Edmund Smith and W. T. Manifold [q.v.10]. Smith invited him to paint at his properties at Point Henry and Cowes, while Manifold commissioned him to produce six large, historic, Art Nouveau panels as a mural for Purrumbete. Payment for this commission, completed in 1902, provided Withers with the means to buy Southernwood, a house on 2½ acres (1.01 ha) at Eltham, to which he added a studio. Because of ill health, he lived during the week at his studio in Oxford Chambers, Melbourne, and on weekends and holidays with his family at Eltham.

In 1904-05 Withers was president of the Victorian Artists' Society. Becoming dissatisfied with that body, he joined a group of fellow professional artists who formed the Australian Art Association in 1912. He was one of the judges of the work of the National Gallery students for fourteen years and in 1912-14 was a trustee of the Public Library, museums and National Gallery of Victoria. Withers' daughter remembered him as six feet (182.9 cm) tall and solidly built, with brown hair slightly curling at the sides, big, soft, hazel eyes and a large, bushy moustache. Plagued by rheumatism and in later life by heart and lung disease, he died of cerebral thrombosis on 13 October 1914 at Eltham and was buried nearby in the Anglican churchyard at St Helena. His wife, four daughters and a son survived him.

In his art Withers developed his own distinctive, poetic style, capturing nature in all her moods, and reflecting his early interest in the works of the English water-colour artists Peter De Wint and David Cox. Critics have discerned the influence of Constable in Withers' sombre, low-toned, lyrical landscapes, and of the Impressionists in his use of broken colour, his preoccupation with light and his interest in the momentary and the commonplace. He is represented in national, State and regional galleries, and in many private collections in Australia and abroad. An exhibition of his paintings was held in Collins House, Melbourne, in 1915, an Art Union of his paintings and those of his son Charles Meynell was held in May 1926, and a major retrospective exhibition of Withers' works was held in 1975 at the Geelong Art Gallery.

A. McCubbin, *The life and art of Walter Withers* (Melb, nd, c1920); C. B. Christesen (ed), *The gallery on Eastern Hill* (Melb, 1970); M. Rich, *Walter*

Withers: a survey, exhibition cat (Geelong, 1975); J. Clark and B. Whitelaw, *Golden summers* (Syd, 1985); A. Mackenzie, *Walter Withers: the forgotten manuscripts* (Melb, 1987) *and* Walter Withers, 1854–1914: a biographical sketch (ms, 1989, held by author, Lilydale, Melb); National Trust of Aust, *Trust News*, Sept 1987; *Age*, 26 July 1958, 21 July 1987; Withers papers *and* R. McCann papers (LaTL); personal information.

ANDREW MACKENZIE

WITTENOOM, SIR EDWARD CHARLES (HORNE) (1854-1936), pastoralist, politician and company director, and FREDERICK FRANCIS BURDETT (1855-1939), pastoralist, mine and business manager, were born on 12 February 1854 at Fremantle and 17 December 1855 at Gwambygine, near York, Western Australia, sons of Charles Wittenoom (d. 1866), grazier and bank director, and his wife Sarah Elizabeth (d. 1861), née Harding, and grandsons of John Burdett Wittenoom [q.v.2]. Both boys were educated at Bishop Hale's [q.v.4] school. At 15, Edward went jackarooing on Bowes station and Frank joined him in 1874 after working in the Western Australia Bank.

Together they leased Yuin station and lived rough while they explored and opened up the Murchison, east along the Roderick and Sandford rivers, to Nookawarra. Eventually they acquired over two million acres (809 380 ha) in crown leases and set up Murgoo, Boolardy, Nookawarra, Mileura and Belele stations. They trained Aboriginal shepherds and kept vigilance for stock thieves. Having collared, weighted and chained one offender before walking him 125 miles (201.2 km) to the Bowes lock-up, at the age of 22 Frank submitted to Commissioner Fairbairn that settlers should be allowed to deal with Aborigines 'in their own way'. On 23 August 1878 at St George's Anglican Cathedral, Perth, Edward married Laura Habgood. In 1881 he acquired White Peak station where he produced fine wool and established a notable sheep stud; five years later the brothers formed a stock and station agency at Geraldton and then added Day Dawn to their holdings. Their Murchison properties were dispersed after 1891 to meet debts of £25 000 due to drought and to a pastoral and pearling folly at La Grange, but Frank retained Boolardy and Nookawarra.

Already involved in local government, Edward was elected to the Legislative Council for Geraldton in 1883. Next year he went to England, but served again in 1885-86. Elected under responsible government as council-member for Central Province, in December 1894 he unexpectedly entered Sir John Forrest's [q.v.8] ministry as government spokesman in the council and minister for mines and education; he also had charge of posts and telegraphs. All these facilities were under strain because of gold-rush expansion, public service reorganization and technological changes in telegraphy; as 'a man of considerable independence of character ... accustomed to having his own way', he left a distinctive, autocratic mark on each. Although he survived criticisms about the telegraph service, he lost the education ministry in May 1897 following a head-on clash with the inspector-general of schools (Sir) Cyril Jackson [q.v.9]. In 1897 Wittenoom was a competent acting premier during Forrest's absence. Next year 'Ten Foot Ned's' unpopular dual-title mining regulations, allowing alluvial and reef mining on the same ground, were defied. Some miners were gaoled, but, after Wittenoom's effigy was paraded and Premier Forrest was mobbed at Kalgoorlie, the regulations were rescinded. Wittenoom resigned to become agent-general (1898-1901) in London.

In England he blossomed into Edwardian elegance: he gave parties, entertained at Henley and was knighted in 1900—the last K.C.M.G. to be personally invested by Queen Victoria at Osborne on the Isle of Wight. Back in Perth in 1901, he succeeded Frank as local managing director of Dalgety [q.v.4] & Co. and accepted directorships with Millars Karri & Jarrah Co. Ltd, Western Australia Bank (president 1917-27), Commercial Union Assurance Co., Amalgamated Collieries, the West Australian Trustee, Executor & Agency Co. Ltd and Bovril Australian Estates. He was president (1912-15, 1917) and chairman (1931) of the State Pastoralists' Association; he was also consul for France. Wittenoom had re-entered the Legislative Council in 1902 for North Province and, after an unsuccessful bid in 1906 for the Senate, returned to the council in 1910. President (1922-26), he remained there as the doyen of colonial conservatism until his retirement in 1934. During the Depression, Wittenoom was smartly lampooned by (Sir) Walter Murdoch [q.v.10] for advocating the closure of government high schools.

Sir Edward was of medium build, with a heart-shaped face and dark, curly hair which, as it greyed, gave him a distinguished demeanour. He dressed well. Wealth enabled him to live 'at ease'; when 'his bump of self esteem was not crossed', he was affable and hospitable. He enjoyed reading, horse-riding, cycling, bowls, motoring and the Weld Club. Widowed in 1923, he married 28-year-old Isabel du Boulay on 22 December 1924 in the Anglican archbishop's chapel, Perth. Survived by his wife and two daughters, and by a son and two daughters of his first marriage, he died in West Perth on 5 March 1936 and was buried in Karrakatta cemetery. His estate was sworn for probate at £36 735.

Frederick Francis Burdett Wittenoom, named after his grandfather and Murchison explorer F. T. Gregory [q.v.4], was a good bushman and a shrewd, versatile investor who survived in the outback and socialized in style. He visited England in 1887 to solicit funds for the Midland railway scheme and returned with several commercial commissions, including the local management of Dalgety's, on whose account he toured fifty-four stations in the north-west in 1888. Afterwards he embarked on a world trip. In the mid-1890s he settled in a bush camp at Boulder where he was engaged by Z. B. Lane [q.v.9] as joint general manager of Great Boulder, Perseverance and Great Boulder South mines. Wittenoom was simultaneously involved with activities as diverse as sawmilling, quarrying, stockbroking, the Boulder Progress Association and the Kalgoorlie race club. Fraternal contact was provided by the first telephone connexion between Boulder and Kalgoorlie which Frank installed in 1896.

Heavier in the jowls, he was more thick-set and portly than Edward. An inveterate traveller who belonged to the New York Circumnavigators Club, Frank was gregarious and entertaining. When abroad, he enjoyed shooting parties and social gatherings; when later afflicted by gout, he took thermal baths at Piest'any, Austria (Czechoslovakia). By 1903 he was living in Mount Street, Perth, where he grew prize carnations. Colonial director for mining companies like Fingal and Wallal, and a partner in three pastoral runs, he developed Cranmore Park, some 10 000 acres (4047 ha) at Walebing, for agriculture and stock-breeding. He was a committee-member of the Western Australian Pastoralists' Association for thirty-four years and presided over complex negotiations with shearers in 1917. A keen photographer and motorist, he was a founder of horse-racing clubs at Murchison and Kalgoorlie, and a committee-member (1910-39) of the West Australian Turf Club. Wittenoom died, unmarried, on 11 September 1939 in Perth and was buried with Anglican rites in Karrakatta cemetery. His portrait hangs in the Wittenoom room in the Weld Club over which he presided in 1919-20. Through a legacy, he is commemorated by a floral clock in Kings Park. His estate was sworn for probate at £204 170.

'Truthful Thomas', *Through the spy-glass* (Perth, 1905); J. S. Battye (ed), *Cyclopedia of Western Australia*, 2 (Adel, 1913); F. K. Crowley, *Australia's western third* (Melb, 1960); C. W. M. Cameron, *Frederick Francis Burdett Wittenoom, pastoral pioneer and explorer 1855-1939* (Perth, 1979); *PP* (LC WA), 1882 (3); *PD* (LC WA), 31 Aug 1881; *Dalgety's Review* (A'sia), Oct 1936; *West Australian*, 9 Nov, 9 Dec 1887, 18, 26 April 1890, 5, 20 Jan 1910, 12 Feb 1922, 6 Mar 1936, 12 Sept 1939; F. F. B. Wittenoom, Reminiscences: 1855-1939 (BL).

G. C. BOLTON
WENDY BIRMAN

WOLFE, HERBERT AUSTIN (1897-1968), turf journalist, was born on 19 July 1897 at Maitland, New South Wales, son of Herbert Austin Wolfe, accountant, and his wife Rebecca Thwaites, née Mayo, both native-born. He was educated at Homeville Public School, at Winchester, England, and at Fort Street Model School, Sydney, but, according to Harry Gordon, he was 'reared among horses'. Wolfe took his famous by-line, 'Cardigan', from the 1903 Melbourne Cup winner Lord Cardigan which his grandfather John Mayo bred at Heatherbrae, north of Maitland; Wolfe was present at the foaling of Lord Nolan, another of his grandfather's horses, which won the cup in 1908.

Enlisting in the Australian Imperial Force in September 1916, Wolfe served with the 6th Field Artillery Brigade in France in 1917-18. After the war he commenced veterinary studies, but abandoned them when his grandfather persuaded the sporting editor of the Sydney *Daily Telegraph* to take him on as a racing assistant. By 1923 Wolfe was racing editor of the Sydney *Referee*; he spent the next four years as sports editor of the Melbourne *Argus*. In 1927 he left journalism to become chairman of the stipendiary stewards of the Queensland Turf Club. Three years later he resumed his career as a journalist, writing for several Sydney newspapers until Sir Keith Murdoch [q.v.10], owner of the Melbourne *Herald*, told him that he wanted 'the best racing writer in Australia'. 'You're looking at him', was the reply. As turf editor from 1933, Wolfe covered twenty-one Melbourne Cups for the *Herald*. At the end of each cup he secured a phone and, within an hour, dictated 4000 words of copy from a few shorthand jottings in his racebook.

In 1932 he had accompanied Phar Lap to Mexico where the horse won the Agua Caliente Handicap. Wolfe obtained permission to land an aeroplane at the course so that he could fly to San Diego, California, to cable the story home. A fortnight later he was present when the gelding died; he attended the post-mortem and resolutely believed thereafter that Phar Lap had been poisoned. In 1934 Wolfe exposed a notorious fraud. Racing under different names in three States, the Sydney horse Erbie (as Redlock) landed heavy betting plunges. Wolfe travelled to Kadina, South Australia, saw the horse win and announced in the *Herald* that 'Redlock is a ring-in'.

'Cardigan' was recognized as Australia's leading turf writer. His renowned instincts for horses of quality led to a commission to buy brood-mares for Sol Green [q.v.9] in England in 1938. Stoutly built, Wolfe was described as 'an amiable, double-breasted kind of man who looked like a tidier, sleeker W. C. Fields'. Sir Ross Grey-Smith, chairman of the Victoria Racing Club, occasionally clashed with him, but praised his 'fearless and sometimes ruthless criticism'. Wolfe was 'much more than a wonderfully skilled reporter . . . He had a detective instinct'.

After a nine-month absence due to ill health in 1955, Wolfe returned to the *Herald* and continued to write for it until 1963. On 1 November 1962 at Wesley Church, Melbourne, he had married a divorcee Elsie Ross Robertson, née Weekes. He died at their Woollahra home, Sydney, on 6 April 1968 and was cremated. His wife survived him, as did the son of his first wife Winifred Annie Lyons.

H. Gordon, *An eyewitness history of Australia* (Melb, 1976); *People* (Syd), 23 Feb 1955; *Sun News-Pictorial*, 8 Apr 1968; *Herald* (Melb), 8, 9 Apr 1968; *Sporting Globe*, 10 Apr 1968; unpublished obituary, files, Herald Lib (Melb).

PETER PIERCE

WOLLASTON, SIR HARRY NEWTON PHILLIPS (1846–1921), barrister and public servant, was born on 17 January 1846 at Mokine, Western Australia, only son of Henry Newton Wollaston, clergyman, and his wife Susannah, née Sewell. In 1854 the family moved to New Zealand and later to Melbourne. Wollaston was educated at St John's College, Auckland, Nelson College, New Zealand, and the University of Melbourne (LL.B. Hons, 1885; LL.M., 1887; LL.D., 1890). Called to the Victorian Bar in 1885, he was standing counsel (1886-1901) to the Victoria Marine Board.

In July 1863, after having completed the civil service entrance examination, he had joined the Victorian Department of Trade and Customs where his career followed a traditional path of clerk, tide-surveyor and landing waiter. In 1888 he was promoted chief clerk and in 1891 collector of customs and secretary of the department. He was widely acknowledged as being a competent administrator and an authority on customs and marine legislation. In 1891, at the request of Sir John Forrest [q.v.8], he reviewed the Western Australian Department of Customs, recommended major restructuring and prepared draft legislation.

Wollaston next reviewed and consolidated Victoria's multifarious customs Acts and ordinances. He was the author of *The customs handbook and merchants' and importers' guide* (1887), *Trade customs and marine law administered by the department of trade and customs* (1892) and *Customs law and regulations with notes and references* (1904) which was long respected as a textbook. (Sir) George Turner [q.v.] made him a member of the civil service retrenchment committee, and in 1897 he was chairman of a committee to advise Turner on the financial clauses of the Commonwealth of Australia Constitution bill.

Appointed comptroller-general of customs and secretary of the Commonwealth Department of Trade and Customs in 1901, Wollaston worked closely with C. C. Kingston [q.v.9] in drafting legislation and the first Commonwealth customs tariff. Next year Kingston entrusted him with the task of drafting a navigation bill which, although praised by Kingston, was rejected by Sir Edmund Barton [q.v.7] as being in conflict with government policy. In 1903 Wollaston investigated allegations of irregularities in the distribution of votes in the Queensland electoral division. Having accompanied Sir William Lyne [q.v.10] to the 1907 Imperial Shipping Conference, London, Wollaston retired on 6 January 1911 and was succeeded by his son-in-law (Sir) Nicholas C. Lockyer [q.v.10]. In 1917-19 Wollaston chaired the Commonwealth Film Censorship Board.

Energetic and hard-working, he was highly regarded for his patience in having 'nursed Ministers through tight places when he knew they had erred'. Aware of the problems confronting Victorian manufacturers, he had interpreted the colony's protectionist tariff with sympathetic understanding, while being critical of 'Border Barbarisms' practised elsewhere. He brought a similar attitude to the administration of Commonwealth customs, although his legalistic interpretation of the tariff created many problems for importers and departmental officers during the early years of Federation. For all that, Melbourne *Punch* praised him as 'a keen, right-to-the-point, matter-of-fact man of the world' and the *Evening Standard* avowed that he was able 'to see smuggled opium through a stone wall, or concealed behind a bank of preserved ginger'.

Wollaston was awarded the I.S.O. (1903), and appointed C.M.G. (1907) and K.C.M.G. (1912). On 12 May 1868 he had married with Anglican rites Mary Annie Harker (d. 1911) at Trinity Church, East Melbourne; on 30 July 1914 he married Mary Henrietta Havard Price-Dent at St Saviour's parish church, Pimlico, London. Wollaston died on 11 February 1921 at Malvern, Melbourne, and was buried in Boroondara cemetery. His wife, and the son and three daughters of his first marriage, survived him.

J. Smith (ed), *Cyclopedia of Victoria*, 1 (Melb, 1903); I. Bertrand, *Film censorship in Australia* (Brisb, 1978); D. I. McDonald, 'The former customs clerks: Wollaston and Lockyer', *Canb Hist J*, no 20, Sept 1987, p 32, and for bibliog; *Evening Standard*, 28 July 1894; *Punch* (Melb), 24 Jan 1907, 25 June 1908; *SMH*, 14 Feb 1921; *Argus*, 15 June 1912.

D. I. McDonald

WOLLASTON, TULLIE CORNTHWAITE (1863-1931), opal dealer, was born on 17 May 1863 at Port Lincoln, South Australia, fourth child of George Gledstanes Wollaston, sheep farmer, and his wife Mary Glover, née MacGowan, both English born, and grandson of Archdeacon Wollaston [q.v.2]. Registered at birth as Henry Herbert, next year he was baptized Tullie Cornthwaite; he was always known by that name. He grew up on his father's station at Lake Hamilton where he acquired a lifelong appreciation of the land and its flora and fauna. After boarding at the Collegiate School of St Peter, Adelaide, where he proved a capable athlete, in 1881 he entered the public service. On 30 December 1886 in the Glenelg Congregational Church he married Emma Sarah Manthorpe; they were to have eleven children. Resigning from the Survey Office, he worked as a private surveyor and draughtsman before becoming involved in mining and marketing sapphires and the gems found by David Lindsay [q.v.10].

During 1888 Wollaston learned of an opal discovery in the Kyabra Hills, Queensland. Backed by Adelaide investors, on 21 November he set out by rail with the surveyor Herbert Buttfield; from the State's north, they used camels to cross harsh terrain. They arrived early next year, inspected the opal strike, bought specimens and obtained leases. Wollaston then sailed for London only to find that dealers were suspicious of the superior Australian stone. Having sold a little which was worked by lapidarists and sent to the United States of America, he came back to Adelaide and formed a partnership with the solicitor David Morton Tweedie. Late in 1889 Wollaston examined opal specimens sent to him from White Cliffs, near Wilcannia, New South Wales. Visiting the new find, he met Edmund Francis Murphy who subsequently became his agent. Wollaston sold White Cliffs opal to European and American buyers in London; in 1897-99 he annually spent about £50 000 buying stones for sale abroad. His generous valuations caused Tweedie to break their partnership.

In 1905 Murphy began buying for him on the field at Lightning Ridge, New South Wales. Taking specimens of the 'black opal' to the world market in 1906-08, Wollaston again encountered scepticism; by 1911 he had more than he could sell. He was next engaged in an unsuccessful pearling venture off Broome, Western Australia. When opal was found early in 1915 at Stuart Range (later Coober Pedy), South Australia, Wollaston bought the first parcel; he took specimens to America in 1916 and sold a significant quantity to a firm in Paris in 1919. In the mid-1920s he backed efforts to develop the Uley graphite and limestone deposits near Port Lincoln. As a director of Graphite Ltd, he visited London in December 1929, but failed to attract interest in the company's mine which closed after his return in 1930.

From 1881 Wollaston had transacted numerous land deals in Adelaide and on Eyre Peninsula. He bought land in 1904 at Bridgewater in the Adelaide Hills where he established Raywood, planting many exotic and native trees and shrubs, and propagating the popular claret ash; nearby, about 1925, he also set up Ray Nursery to encourage the planting of native flora. Raywood was later sold to (Sir) Alexander Downer and named Arbury Park; in 1965 it was transferred to the State government and again called Raywood. Wollaston's love of Australia's natural beauty shone through his publications, *The spirit of the child* (1914) and *Our wattles* (1916). To accompany his display of opals at the British Empire Exhibition at Wembley, London, he wrote the semi-autobiographical *Opal: the gem of the Never-Never* (1924).

Slim and dapper in appearance, Wollaston was a cultured, humane and religious man who loved children. He was hardy and resourceful in outback travel and 'fair and square' in business. Survived by his wife, three sons and six daughters, he died of cancer on 17 July 1931 at his Lower Mitcham home and was buried in St Jude's Anglican churchyard, Brighton, Adelaide. His estate was sworn for probate at £17 719.

E. F. Murphy, *They struck opal* (Syd, 1948); P. V. Wake, *Opal men* (Syd, 1969); D. H. Wollaston, *From now to domesday with the Wollastons* (Adel, 1975); *Advertiser* (Adel), 1 Feb 1888, 20 July 1931; information from Mrs A. Monro, Myrtle Bank, and Mrs E. Gardiner, Skye, Adel.

Bernard O'Neil

WOLSTENHOLME, MAYBANKE; *see* Anderson, Maybanke Susannah

WOOD, GEORGE ARNOLD (1865-1928), historian, was born on 7 June 1865 at Salford, Lancashire, England, eldest child of George Stanley Wood, cotton merchant, and his first wife Martha ('Pattie') Pickering (d. 1871), née Alliott. Belonging to a family active in Chapel and in Liberal Party affairs, Arnold inherited through his mother a proud tradition of Nonconformity dating back to the seventeenth century. After secondary schooling at Bowdon College, Cheshire, he went in 1882 to Owens College, Manchester (B.A., 1885), and in October 1885 to Balliol College, Oxford (B.A., 1888; M.A., 1890), where he read history.

His Oxford years were of profound importance in his development. Benjamin Jowett's Balliol attracted young men of bright intelligence, and the closest of Wood's wide circle of friends were all to achieve distinction. In such company his mind was broadened, his imagination stirred and his growth in maturity was remarkable. Jowett's college could enrich and liberalize the sense of calling derived from Wood's Nonconformist upbringing without threatening it.

In 1886 Wood shared the Brackenbury scholarship and in 1888 was awarded firstclass honours. In October he entered Mansfield College, the new Congregational foundation, on a scholarship to study theology. Study of scriptural sources stirred religious doubts, which he openly avowed, but he was persuaded to continue. In time he would become a reluctant agnostic. After winning the Stanhope prize for a brilliant essay on Wallenstein in 1889, Wood could have waited for a British university post, but was persuaded in 1890 to accept the new Challis [q.v.3] chair of history at the University of Sydney. He arrived in February 1891.

His inaugural public lecture in May on 'The study of history' showed him to be an original thinker with a passionate belief in the value of his subject. A student of the 1890s wrote of 'the revolution which he wrought . . . With life as he described it, one could not help feeling concerned'. Wood did his best to reproduce in Sydney the Oxford of his experience, sharing with unassuming friendliness in his students' talk, their societies and their games. With Walter Scott and (Sir) Mungo MacCallum [qq.v.11,10], he was a founder of the Teachers' Guild of New South Wales and was president of the Teachers' Association of New South Wales. On 27 December 1898 at Marrickville he married with Congregational forms Eleanor Madeline, sister of Hubert Whitfeld [q.v.].

Wood was greatly disturbed by the outbreak of the South African War, which he believed to be unjust, and stated his views in letters to the *Daily Telegraph* from November 1899. He was answered by MacCallum, his colleague, friend and precise opposite in all opinions about the war. After this hard-hitting but courteous exchange, Wood remained silent until reports of mounting infant mortality in the concentration camps drove him into an anguished protest against 'a policy that is bringing everlasting infamy upon the English

name'. Again he was answered by MacCallum.

In January 1902, with W. A. Holman [q.v.9] and others, Wood formed the Australian Anti-War League which advocated a negotiated peace on liberal terms. At a time of mounting hysteria, as its president Wood became a main target of attack; under pressure from the newspapers and some prominent men, on 3 February the university senate censured him. He had written a careful analysis of Australian opinion about the war for the *Manchester Guardian*. A garbled report of his article stirred a frenzy of demands that he should be dismissed; peace negotiations were well advanced when the full text of his article reached Sydney, and the attack fizzled out.

The irony was that Wood was as fervently loyal to the British Empire as any of his accusers, but his loyalty was to the Gladstonian view of an empire committed to liberty and justice. His public statements during the South African War, his articles for the *Manchester Guardian* in 1903-04 and a searching essay, 'Australia and Imperial Politics', in Meredith Atkinson's [q.v.7] *Australia* (Melbourne, 1920) consistently pleaded for a return to Gladstone's vision.

Meanwhile, Wood continued to widen the range of his university courses, particularly in the field of maritime discovery. Although he had no assistant until 1916, he managed to find time for a number of extension courses, including one on 'Industry in England, 1770-1875', the first series ever given at the Trades Hall by a Sydney university professor. Honorary secretary of the University Extension Board since 1902, he was an active member of the Workers' Educational Association central committee from 1914.

With the outbreak of World War I Wood studied the published diplomatic documents which convinced him that the German government had willed the war and should bear 'the immediate responsibility'. Yet he also sought in a lecture course of 1916 to understand 'the guilt of others'. He knew, too, that 'Prussianism' was not confined to Germany and from the outset feared that the sacrifice of young lives would be betrayed by those who believed that force could solve the problems of peace. He supported the war-effort in the ways open to him, while sharing MacCallum's dislike of hysterical anti-Germanism.

A post-war product of pre-war studies, his *The discovery of Australia* (London, 1922) was 'an excitement and a stimulus' to later scholars. In 1921 he had also sent the manuscript of 'The foundation of New South Wales' to his publishers, but it appeared only as scattered articles which obscured its characteristic theme that even people warped by an evil society could blossom, given hope and opportunity. Long overdue leave in 1924 enabled

Wood to prepare a lecture course on early New South Wales (given next year) and to write *The voyage of the Endeavour* (Melbourne, 1925). His prose was vigorous, enlivened by humour and a happy turn of phrase, and he enjoyed the detective work of the historian; but, above all, he was a teacher to whom publication was an acceptable by-product.

Progress was set against a measure of defeat. A post-war increase in student numbers made the personal teaching of his Oxford experience impossible—two men could not teach 350 students to their own satisfaction. 'The personal touch of mind and mind is necessary to education', he wrote in 1927 in an unsuccessful appeal for two tutor-lecturers. Recurrent eye-trouble added to the burden of marking far too many essays, examination papers and theses. Nevertheless, Wood began 1928 in good cheer, but ended the first term suffering from shingles in its severest form. After months of mind-breaking torment, he died by his own hand on 14 October 1928 at Randwick and was cremated. His wife, three sons and a daughter survived him.

Set against his life, the manner of his death was irrelevant. If anything rivalled his simple courtesy and integrity of mind, it was his jovial good-humour. Fortunate in the attachment of his family and in the unbroken respect and liking of his students, he knew that his life, as a whole life, had been happy. The slim young man of 1891 had added four stone to his ten by 1914. It was equally natural that the exuberant expectations of the 1890s should mellow into the tempered optimism of the older man. A verse in *Hermes* (November 1921) caught the general view: ·

Then come where tolerance and cheerful
   sanity
Temper the Ideal in Professor W . . .

Although he feared the capacity of the press to manipulate opinion and understood the obstinate persistence of poverty and social injustice, Wood discerned in English history a growth in liberty and social conscience which could be carried further by those who understood Milton's message of strenuous liberty. So he set before his students a portrait gallery of those democrats who had dared to rise to the challenges of their times, whether on a wider stage or in the isolation of Botany Bay. The true utility of history was to inspire the vision and steel the will. His own outlook was tempered by a salty enough understanding of human nature; still more, he believed in the capacity of ordinary men and women in favourable circumstances to grow in stature, and to free that capacity was his test of progress.

R. M. Crawford, '*A bit of a rebel*'(Syd, 1975), and for references; *Hermes*(Syd), 21, no 2, Aug 1915, p 48; *SMH*, 23 May 1891, 29 May 1902, 16, 17 Oct 1928; *Daily Telegraph* (Syd), 19 Oct, 11, 22, 30 Nov, 6 Dec 1899, 16 Dec 1901; *Manchester Guardian*, 22 Apr 1902, 16 Oct 1903, 13 May 1904; Wood papers (Univ Syd Archives); family information.

R. M. CRAWFORD

WOOD, THOMAS (1892-1950), composer and author, was born on 28 November 1892 at Chorley, Lancashire, England, only child of Thomas Wood, master mariner, and his wife Hannah, née Lee. Tommy later believed that his formal education had been immeasurably enriched by boyhood voyages with his father. Despite congenitally poor vision due to cataracts in both eyes, in 1913 he completed an external bachelor's degree in music through the University of Oxford. That year he entered Christ Church, Oxford, and moved in 1916 to Exeter College with which he was to remain associated. Rejected seven times as unfit for the navy during World War I, he joined a department of the Admiralty in 1917. After graduating from Oxford (B.A., 1918; M.A., 1920), he studied under Sir Charles Stanford at the Royal College of Music (D.Mus., 1920).

In 1921 Wood was appointed director of music at Tonbridge School, Kent, where one of his students recalled him as a 'bespectacled, untidy, little man'. Wood returned to Exeter College where he was a lecturer in 1924-27. In both posts he won golden opinions and began to compose choral and orchestral works, some of which subsequently received acclaim. On 2 July 1924 at the parish church, Wormingford, Essex, he had married St Osyth Mahala Eustace-Smith.

Apart from music, the prevailing passions of Wood's life were the British Empire, foreign travel and the sea; his writing is instinct with a fervent Imperial sentiment. He came to Australia in 1930 to conduct examinations for the Associated Board of the Royal Schools of Music and spent some two years travelling across the country. On his return to England, he wrote *Cobbers* (London, 1934), still the most perceptive and captivating characterization of Australia and its people ever written by a visitor. Wood revelled in the company of 'hard boiled citizens' and in the ways of ordinary men and women, but a deep sense of beauty and poetry combined with affectionate humour to produce his memorable descriptions, particularly of regional differences. As a collector of folk songs, he was so impressed by *Waltzing Matilda*—which he thought good enough 'to be the unofficial national anthem of Australia'—that he included its words and music in *Cobbers*.

In May 1936 Wood joined the British Ministry of Information. That year he published an excellent, 'modest but finely wrought', autobiography, *True Thomas*. He visited Canada in the late 1930s and then wrote *Cobbers campaigning* (London, 1940) in tribute to Australia's part in World War II. In the latter book he wrote: 'There is no turning back. I am now part of Australia, and—for ever—Australia is part of me'. Sponsored by the British government, in 1944 he returned to Australia to give a series of popular talks and broadcasts about wartime Britain. He was a committee-member of the Royal Philharmonic Society and chairman (1949) of the music panel of the British Arts Council. Survived by his wife, Wood died of coronary thrombosis on 19 November 1950 at his home at Bures, Suffolk, and was cremated. His estate was sworn for probate at £118 868.

DNB, 1941-50; *SMH*, 11, 30 Oct 1939, 29 Apr 1944, 20, 21 Nov 1950; *The Times*, 20, 24 Nov 1950, 24 Apr 1951.   RUSSEL WARD

WOODCOCK, LUCY GODIVA (1889-1968), teacher and trade union leader, was born on 23 February 1889 at Granville, Sydney, daughter of Thomas Woodcock, a railway surveyor from Jersey, Channel Islands, and his native-born wife Janet, née Howieson. Appointed to Pitt Town Public School as a pupil-teacher in October 1900, Lucy was transferred in May 1907 to Parramatta South where she completed the four-year training and teaching period. As a qualified primary teacher, she taught at Eden (1910-11), Coledale (1912), Lidcombe (1913-20) and Darlington (1921-27). She completed by evening study two degrees at the University of Sydney (B.A., 1922; B.Ec., 1924) where she was influenced by Professor R. F. Irvine [q.v.9] who broadened her feminism into a more general radicalism. Late in 1927 she went to London for a years exchange teaching. On her return in 1929, she was promoted to first assistant at Arncliffe and then Cessnock, and later to mistress at Grafton (1930), Abbotsford (1931) and finally Erskineville (1933) where she remained until her retirement in 1953. During the Depression she organized food and clothing for local children.

Throughout her career Lucy Woodcock was actively involved in the Teachers' Association of New South Wales, and from 1918 the New South Wales Teachers' Federation of which she was a long-standing member of the executive (1924-27, 1931-53); in 1934-53 she was senior vice-president. A tireless campaigner for the rights of women teachers, she opposed the Married Women (Lecturers and Teachers) Dismissal Act of 1932 (repealed 1947) and was prominent in campaigns to achieve salary restoration, a teachers' certificate, and equal pay and opportunities for female teachers. She was an author of *Justice versus tradition* (1925), produced by women teachers for the equal pay campaign, and jointly chaired with Muriel Heagney [q.v.9] the Council of Action for Equal Pay, founded in 1937. When the federation affiliated in 1942 with the Labor Council of New South Wales and the Australasian Council of Trade Unions, she was one of the first delegates to both bodies. In 1942-44 she was a member of the senate of the University of Sydney.

Her twenty years in the union's second highest elected position was a tribute to her personal popularity and to her ability to remain above factional struggles. Miss Woodcock served beside the long-term president Arthur McGuinness [q.v.10] and with the communist Sam Lewis. She retained her position when a vigorous anti-communist movement helped Harry Heath to defeat Lewis in 1952. In her retirement she was prominent in the civil rights case over the apparent victimization of Lewis by the Public Service Board, to which Heath had been appointed. Her pamphlet, *The Lewis case and you* (1956), trenchantly analysed the case and its political ramifications.

A strong-faced woman, with her hair pulled back severely above emphatic brows and alert eyes, Woodcock carried her crusades for equality, justice and peace beyond her profession. In campaigning against the dismissal of married teachers she had been supported by the United Associations of Women, of which she became vice-president after retiring from teaching and president in 1957-68. A foundation member (1937) of the New Education Fellowship (World Education Fellowship), she was its second president, then a vice-president until her death. Prominent in the Australian peace movement, she provoked controversy by attending the Stockholm peace meeting as an observer in 1954 and next year attended the World Peace Congress in Helsinki. She twice visited China as a delegate of the Australian Peace Council and helped to found the Australia-China Society. The Australian Aborigines Evangelical Fellowship was set up at a meeting at her Enfield flat in 1956. Lucy Woodcock died on 29 February 1968 at Ashfield, Sydney, and was cremated.

B. A. Mitchell, *Teachers, education, and politics* (Brisb, 1975); W. Mitchell, *50 years of feminist achievement* (Syd, 1979); G. Phelan, *Women in action in the Federation* (Syd, 1981); NSW Teachers' Federation, *Education* (Syd), Feb 1954; *SMH*, 1 Mar 1968; Dept of Education (NSW) records (Syd).   BRUCE MITCHELL

WOODD, HENRY ALEXANDER (1865-1954), Anglican clergyman, was born on 6 June 1865 at Denham Court, near Liverpool, New South Wales, sixteenth child and youngest son of Rev. George Napoleon Woodd and his wife Caroline, née Rust, both of whom had come from England to Sydney in 1837. A delicate child, Henry did not follow his brothers to The King's School, Parramatta, but was educated privately. He attended the University of Sydney (B.A., 1887), residing at St Paul's College, and was one of several college men inspired to enter the ministry by the warden Hey Sharp [q.v.11] and the liberal Bishop Barry [q.v.3]. Woodd was made deacon on 8 July 1888 and ordained priest on 22 December 1889 by Bishop Thomas [q.v.6] of Goulburn.

Woodd's first curacy was All Saints, Woollahra, where his father was living in retirement. In 1892 he was invited to serve in the diocese of Newcastle; to Woodd, the new bishop G. H. Stanton [q.v.6] was an inspiring figure with a congenial standard of churchmanship. After serving briefly as curate of Scone, Woodd became rector of Gundy (1893-95) and Murrurundi (1895-1901) where he met and, on 15 July 1902, married Dorothy Mabel Wilson. Meanwhile, Stanton had moved him to Morpeth, near the episcopal residence, and made him examining chaplain. His successor Bishop Stretch [q.v.] appointed Woodd registrar and archdeacon of Gloucester and, in 1910, of Durham. That year Woodd was made rector of Muswellbrook and a cathedral canon. Stretch moved the centre of the see to Newcastle, leaving Woodd to administer rural affairs. It was an area of work to which he was well suited.

In 1919 Reginald Stephen [q.v.], bishop of Tasmania, was translated to Newcastle. At once he made Woodd full-time archdeacon of the Hunter (Newcastle, 1921) with a salary as Stanton chaplain and vicar-general from 1922. Henceforward, Woodd assumed responsibilities across the whole diocese. He presided over the elections of Bishops Long and Batty [qq.v.10,7]. These prelates took an active interest in the affairs of church and state, so it fell increasingly to Woodd to cope with the domestic problems of the diocese. Although technically superannuated in 1935, he retained his principal offices until 1949. He lived in retirement at Merewether. Survived by his wife and three daughters, he died on 6 November 1954 at Merewether and was cremated. A memorial to him was placed in Christ Church Cathedral, Newcastle.

Handsome, affable and dignified, with an extraordinary knowledge of the diocese and region, Woodd had been an impressive figure at Newcastle. Although he sat in the Provincial and General synods and was a fellow (from 1926) of his beloved St Paul's College, Woodd was a Newcastle man first and foremost, content to hold the diocese together while his superiors pursued grander objects.

A. P. Elkin, *The diocese of Newcastle* (Syd, 1955); *Newcastle Morning Herald* and *SMH*, 8 Nov 1954; *Anglican*, 12 Nov 1954.   K. J. CABLE

WOODFULL, WILLIAM MALDON (1897-1965), cricketer and schoolteacher, was born on 22 August 1897 at Maldon, Victoria, third son of Thomas Staines Brittingham Woodfull, Methodist minister, and his wife Gertrude Lily, née Abey, both Australian born. Thomas (d. 1941) was to become secretary of the Methodist Conference in 1922 and president in 1923. Educated at Bendigo and Melbourne high schools, Bill graduated (B.A.; Dip.Ed., 1924) from the University of Melbourne where he played for the second XI.

After progressing through the conventional club teams, Woodfull played for the Victorian Colts and the State second XI, eventually entering the first-class ranks when he was chosen to play for the Victorian Sheffield Shield side in Adelaide in February 1922. An inauspicious 17 not out, going in at number 8, was followed in subsequent matches by exhibitions of concentration and impregnable defence which brought about his selection in Herbie Collins's [q.v.8] 1926 Australian team for England. Starting the tour with a score of 201 against Essex, followed by 118 against Surrey, Woodfull continued in such fine form that he headed the Australian first-class batting figures with 1672 runs at an average of 57.65 (eight centuries) and was named one of Wisden's five cricketers of the year. No Australian had previously averaged 50 on his first tour of England.

In 1928-29 Woodfull played in the Test series against England under Jack Ryder [q.v.11]; when the latter was surprisingly omitted from the Australian team for England in 1930, Woodfull was accorded the captaincy over the more highly fancied and colorful Vic Richardson [q.v.11] who became his deputy. Setting an example with his exemplary, teetotal style of living, Woodfull generated remarkable loyalty from a dedicated team and the Ashes were recaptured. His quiet, unassuming leadership and splendid after-dinner speeches made a great impression. As an opening batsman, in partnership with his fellow Victorian Bill Ponsford (they were affectionately known as Mutt and Jeff), Woodfull made an outstanding personal contribution.

In 1932-33 Woodfull's character received a gruelling test when he was Australian captain against Douglas Jardine's 'bodyline' tactics. Despite grave personal injury and severe provocation, Woodfull refused to retaliate on the grounds that it would be detrimental to the game of cricket. His only public reaction was his alleged eloquent rebuke to (Sir) Pelham (Plum) Warner: 'There are two teams out there but only one of them is playing cricket'. That Test series was a great strain, and no doubt hastened Woodfull's retirement after he had taken one more Australian team to England in 1934. A grateful public subscribed handsomely to a joint testimonial for Woodfull and Ponsford at the end of the tour; fittingly, Woodfull scored a century in the match.

In all, Woodfull played 35 Tests for Australia, was captain in 25, and made 2300 runs (including seven centuries) at an average of 46. His 174 first-class games brought him 13 392 runs at an average of 65 (with 49 centuries). His batting was characterized by a stolid defence which brought him the title of 'the unbowlable'; his style was rather stiff-armed, and lacked the grace and wristiness of that embodied by Alan Kippax [q.v.9], but its effectiveness was beyond question. Woodfull set a record in carrying his bat through an innings four times against English teams, first for the Australians against an English XI at Blackpool (1926), then for Victoria against the Marylebone Cricket Club (1928) and twice in Test matches (1928 and 1933), the latter feat not having been achieved by any player more than once during the first hundred years of Anglo-Australian Tests.

For forty-six years Woodfull taught with the Victorian Education Department. Much of his career was spent at Melbourne High School where he was assistant master (1927-40), vice-principal (1948-53) and principal (1956-62). He was also principal at Upwey (1945-47) and Box Hill (1954-56) high schools. His contribution to education was recognized in 1963 when he was appointed O.B.E. Woodfull died suddenly of coronary vascular disease on 11 August 1965 at Tweed Heads, New South Wales. Survived by his wife Gwenda Muriel, née King, whom he had married on 12 January 1927 at the Methodist Church, Albert Park, Melbourne, their daughter and two sons, he was cremated. Woodfull's brother, Howard Thomas Colin (1908-76), was director of the Royal Agricultural Society, Victoria.

G. Tebbutt, *With the 1930 Australians* (Lond, 1930); Education Dept (Vic), *Vision and realisation*, 2, L. J. Blake ed (Melb, 1973); A. Inch, *Honour the work* (Melb, 1977); C. Martin-Jenkins, *The complete who's who of test cricketers* (Adel, 1980); J. Pollard, *Australian cricket* (Syd, 1982); W. J. O'Reilly, *Tiger, 60 years of cricket* (Syd, 1985); *Table Talk*, 16 June 1926; *Age*, 23 Oct 1955, 22 May 1962, 1 Jan 1963, 12, 13 Aug 1965; *The Times* and *Herald* (Melb) and *Sun News-Pictorial*, 12 Aug 1965; personal information.

DONALD BRADMAN

WOODHOUSE, WILLIAM JOHN (1866-1937), classical scholar, was born on 7 November 1866 at Clifton, Westmorland, England, eldest son of Richard Woodhouse, station master, and his wife Mary, née Titterington. At Sedbergh School, Yorkshire, he received a 'sound and thorough training in the classical languages as such', but with 'a strange lack of contact with the realities of life, both modern and ancient'. In 1885 he won an exhibition to The Queen's College, Oxford (B.A., 1889; M.A., 1895), where he took first-class honours in both moderations and greats. In 1890, as a Newton student of the British School of Archaeology in Athens, he took part in the excavation of Megalopolis. Most of 1892 and 1893 was spent in Greece as a Craven fellow in a thorough topographical exploration of the rugged and little known region of Aetolia, north of the Gulf of Corinth. His preliminary report was awarded the triennial Conington prize in 1894. He published the results of his field-work in the *Journal of Hellenic Studies* from 1892 and, in 1897, a substantial book, *Aetolia*.

That year Woodhouse was appointed lecturer in classics at University College of North Wales, Bangor, and on 28 March at the parish church, Sedbergh, Yorkshire, married Eleanor Emma Jackson. Between 1898 and 1906 he produced school editions of Greek and Latin authors. His *Tutorial history of Greece* (1904), a deceptively modest book, was advanced in its use of archaeology and its robust common sense. He also contributed to Hasting's *Encyclopaedia of religion and ethics* and to the *Encyclopedia biblica*.

Before taking up a lectureship at the University of St Andrew's, Scotland, in 1900 Woodhouse was chosen to succeed Walter Scott [q.v.11] in the chair of Greek at the University of Sydney. By this move he cut himself off from the revolution then being brought about in classical studies by advances in archaeology and topography in which he might otherwise have played a notable part, though he remained a keen and sometimes critical spectator. He was to revisit Greece three times: in 1908 when he laid the foundation for a collection of casts of sculpture for the Nicholson [q.v.5] Museum of Antiquities, in 1921 when returning from the Congress of the Universities of the Empire at Oxford, and in 1935 near the end of his life, but his recollections remained strong and enabled him to convey to his students a vivid sense of the Greek countryside and people.

Whatever his regrets, Woodhouse threw himself energetically into his new life. Throughout his tenure he gave all the lectures in the whole Greek course, while occasionally also filling in for Latin. He established a family home in the Blue Mountains, living during the week in hotels and boarding houses around Sydney, but in 1922 he moved to Gordon, a fairly remote northern suburb. He occupied the long train journeys by teaching himself Albanian, Bulgarian and Hebrew. His lectures began on most mornings at 9; he invariably arrived before his students and sometimes started the lecture without them. In his earlier years he lectured for the University Extension Board and served on its joint committee with the Workers' Educational Association; as the curator of the Nicholson Museum from 1903, he 'laboured untiringly to strengthen and increase the collection'; he helped to reorganize the university union and to establish courses in divinity. Dean of the faculty of arts (1926-29) and a fellow of the senate (1925-29), he was for many years a member of the Bursary Endowment Board and a trustee of the Public Library of New South Wales.

It is small wonder that in thirty years he published only two articles: in 1912 'The scenic arrangements of the *Philoktetes* of Sophokles' (*J.H.S.*, XXXII) and in 1918 'The campaign and battle of Mantineia (*Annual of the British School at Athens*, No 22). In his later years, however, he withdrew somewhat from university affairs and garnered the fruit of his scholarship in three books which established his international reputation: *The composition of Homer's Odyssey* (Oxford, 1930, reprinted 1969), *King Agis of Sparta and his campaign in Arkadia in 418 B.C.* (Oxford, 1931, reprinted 1977) and *Solon the liberator*, published posthumously in 1938 (reprinted 1965). Other books were left unfinished.

As a teacher, Woodhouse was unorthodox but highly effective. Seldom sticking close to the text or appearing to notice his class, he conveyed his enthusiasm, critical approach and genial humanity in apparently rambling soliloquies seasoned with a chain of anecdotes and a puckish humour. It was impossible to take notes, but at the end of the year students found that they had acquired, almost unconsciously, much general wisdom and a fund of exact knowledge—even about the set book. His influence was carried by his students into the professions, schools and universities throughout Australia and abroad.

A sound linguistic scholar, Woodhouse was no pedant or narrow specialist. Before World War I he had outlined in an *Open letter addressed to the fellows of the University of Sydney* a proposal for a broadly based department of ancient history for non-classical students. His strength lay in his humanity and in his conception of the unity and universality of the Greek achievement. 'It's all in father Homer' was a favourite saying. His tastes were essentially simple: his favourite books were the *Odyssey*, the *Acts of the apostles* and *The pilgrim's progress*, all in a sense travel books, yet he was moved deeply by the poetry of Homer and the tragedians. In his own work he liked (as he was fond of saying of the Greeks) to 'keep his eye on the object', to study the text before him rather than what others said about it, on which he could sometimes be very amusing.

Survived by his wife, son and daughter, Woodhouse died of cancer on 26 October 1937 at Gordon and was cremated after an Anglican service. His estate was sworn for probate at £17 997. A memorial fund was used to buy Greek vases for the Nicholson Museum.

Honi Soit, 3 Nov 1937; Univ Syd Union, *Union Recorder*, 4 Nov 1937; *Aust Q*, 9, Dec 1937, 27, Dec 1955; *SMH*, 27, 28 Oct 1937; *The Times*, 28 Oct 1937; Univ Syd Archives; family information.

L. F. FITZHARDINGE

WOODRUFF, HAROLD ADDISON (1877-1966), veterinary pathologist and bacteriologist, was born on 10 July 1877 at Sheffield, Yorkshire, England, son of Herbert Woodruff, engineering draftsman, and his wife Mary, née Addison. Educated at Wesley College, Sheffield, Harold graduated at the Royal Veterinary College, London (M.R.C.V.S., 1898), and tutored in surgery there in 1898-99. After a short term as professor of veterinary science and bacteriology at the Royal Agricultural College, Cirencester, he returned in 1900 to the Royal Veterinary College as professor of materia medica and hygiene. He ran the extensive outpatients clinic from 1900 until 1908 when he was appointed to the chair of veterinary medicine. In 1912 he graduated M.R.C.S., L.R.C.P. (London).

Next year Woodruff came to Australia as professor of veterinary pathology and director of the veterinary institute at the University of Melbourne. In October 1915 he joined the Australian Imperial Force and served in Egypt and France as a major in the Australian Army Veterinary Corps (A.D.V.S. 3rd Division). Because the decline of the veterinary school was troubling the university council, he was permitted to return to Melbourne in 1917. President of the Veterinary Association of Victoria (1920-22) and of the Australian Veterinary Association (1922-23), he gave the presidential address to Section L of the Australasian Association for the Advancement of Science in 1920 and 1922.

On the closure of the veterinary school in 1928, Woodruff was offered the post of director of the bacteriology department; he was promoted professor in 1935. Under his somewhat rigorous régime the department steadily expanded and the teaching of bacteriology was given a firm foundation. Apart from his influence on the careers of several famous scientists, Woodruff's most notable success was to establish the Public Health Laboratories (now the Diagnostic Unit) within the bounds of the university. Throughout his career he published monographs, pamphlets and articles on veterinary, medical and theological issues.

Raised in the tradition of the Methodist Church, on his arrival in Victoria Woodruff was at once involved in many aspects of its work. He held a weekly prayer-meeting for students and in 1931 acquired land from Professor Henry Payne [q.v.11] at Healesville to build a Student Christian Movement camp. At conferences of the Australian S.C.M. (of which he was State and national chairman) he proved a popular group leader. A councillor of Queen's College, University of Melbourne, he served as acting master in 1928. Concerned for world peace, he spoke on the issue on radio and belonged to the League of Nations Union (president, 1938) and the Women's International League for Peace and Freedom. He felt so strongly about the dangers of Fascism that he toured the mining towns of Gippsland in 1934 to warn against racial discrimination. In 1946 he urged the abolition of the White Australia policy.

Requested to remain at his post, he delayed his retirement until 1944. In 1948 the university purchased his portrait (by Malcolm Hone) which was hung in the foyer of the lecture theatre named in Woodruff's honour in the new microbiology building. He maintained his interests in the church, the peace movement and music, and was elected chairman (1946) of the Zoological Board of Victoria; he was also able to give more time to his garden and to walking with the Wallaby Club. A firm believer in outdoor activities, he had ridden his horse to work from Kew until 1927. He was about 5 ft. 10 ins. (177.8 cm) tall, with a fair complexion, grey eyes and a direct gaze. His manner was energetic and firm, his opinions forthright: both indicated the extent to which he was imbued with the Methodist doctrine of assurance.

When Woodruff arrived in Australia he was accompanied by his wife Margaret Ada, née Cooper (d. 1916) whom he had married at Finchley, Middlesex, England, on 11 July 1908. On 24 June 1919 he married Isabella Scott Scoular Glaister at Queen's College. A founder of the Invergowrie Homecraft Hostel and its chief examiner in 1928-49, she was a founder and councillor of the Emily McPherson College of Domestic Economy and president (1931-33) of the Lyceum Club. After her death on 3 March 1954, Woodruff returned to Britain. He died in Edinburgh on 1 May 1966, survived by two sons of his first marriage who became eminent medical practitioners.

J. M. Gillison, *A history of the Lyceum Club* (Melb, 1975); *MJA*, 4 Mar 1967; *Pastoral Review*, 19 July 1966; *Herald* (Melb), 23 Apr 1925, 30 Jan 1946; *Argus*, 4 Dec 1934, 8 Dec 1949; Faculty of Veterinary Science, Minutes, 1906-69 *and* Registrar's correspondence (Univ Melb Archives); information from Dr P. S. Woodruff, Stirling, Adel, Rev F. Engles, Parkville, and Prof R. D. Wright*, Toorak, Melb.   NORAH L. KILLIP

WOODS, JAMES (1893-1975), aviator, was born on 14 November 1893 at Udny, Aberdeenshire, Scotland, fourth son of Charles Wood, journeyman shoemaker, and his wife Elizabeth, née Anderson. Educated at the local village school and at Robert Gordon's College, Aberdeen, at 14 Jimmy was apprenticed with a firm of automotive engineers and later became a chauffeur. He migrated in 1914 to New Zealand where he learned to fly. In England in 1918, he was commissioned in the Royal Air Force as an observer officer. He then worked in New Zealand and Scotland before joining Western Australian Airways in 1924. He flew passengers and cargo between Perth and the northwest ports. Well-groomed, genial, painstaking and imperturbable in a crisis, 'Woodsie' was seldom seen without his pipe, though it was rarely lit. On 5 June 1928 he married Mary (Mollie) Elizabeth Hadwiger at the registry office, Port Hedland; they were to remain childless.

Flying *The Spirit of Western Australia,* a De Havilland 60 Moth with a Gypsy II engine, in 1933 Woods—as he had long styled himself —attempted to break J. A. Mollison's record eight-day flight from Australia to England. Fierce monsoons and a damaged aircraft delayed his progress, causing him to take more than six weeks to complete the journey. Upon landing in England, he said: 'My name is Woods and I've just flown from Australia'. Next year he entered the Melbourne centenary air race: with D. C. Bennett, he flew a Lockheed Vega for London, but crash-landed at Aleppo, Syria. Returning home in November 1934, Woods became route manager for MacRobertson [q.v.11 Robertson]-Miller [q.v.10] Aviation Co. Ltd.

Responsible for several remarkable rescue operations, in 1942 he air-lifted survivors of the Japanese bombing at Broome and later rescued the passengers and crew of a beached Dutch Navy plane. Woods was appointed chevalier to the Order of Orange-Nassau (1943). On 1 January 1944 he was attached to the Royal Australian Air Force Reserve as a temporary squadron leader. An original 'seat of the pants' airman, he was happiest flying small planes by backing his own judgement and even effected repairs to his aircraft in flight. Increasing instrumentation, however, made his methods outmoded. In 1946, while taking off in a Lockheed Electra from Broome in fog, he crashed into mangroves. No one was seriously injured, but the plane was irreparably damaged. Woods's licence was suspended and his services with M.M.A. were terminated.

In 1948 he began the Woods Airways service which provided regular flights in two Avro Ansons from Perth to Rottnest Island: 'It's just a hop'. In constant conflict with the Department of Civil Aviation over minor infringements of regulations, Woods Airways was wound up in 1962 when Ansons were declared unsafe for carrying passengers and for flights over water. Woods was appointed M.B.E. in 1963. The Jimmy Woods [Air] Terminal at Rottnest Island was later named after him. At 70, he began Woods Helicopters Pty Ltd which undertook aerial spraying operations, charter flights for oil and mineral companies, advertising and joy rides. He sold the business in 1971 and returned to Albany. Survived by his wife, he died there on 9 May 1975 and was cremated with Presbyterian forms.

E. P. Wixted, *The north-west aerial frontier 1919-1934* (Brisb, 1985); J. Lewis, *Jimmy Woods, flying pioneer* (Perth, 1989), and for bibliog.

JULIE LEWIS

WOODS, JAMES PARK (1886-1963), soldier and orchardist, was born on 4 January 1886 at Two Wells, South Australia, son of James Woods, blacksmith, and his wife Ester, née Johnson. After his parents' death James was reared by a stepsister and, with his brothers, worked on a vineyard.

Soon after war broke out in 1914 Woods tried to enlist in Adelaide, but was rejected because of his height (5 ft. 4 ins., 163 cm). He travelled to Western Australia with his brother Will, and carted timber and fenced in the Katanning area before becoming a vigneron at Caversham. Following further unsuccessful attempts, James eventually enlisted in the Australian Imperial Force on 29 September 1916 when the height requirements had been lowered. He left Australia in December as a reinforcement for the 48th Battalion.

Having spent two periods in hospital in Britain, he reached France in September 1917, only to be invalided on and off until August 1918. On 18 September the 48th Battalion attacked the Hindenburg outpost line near Le Verguier, north-west of St Quentin. It took its objective, but British troops on the Australian flank were held up and a company of the 48th was sent in support. Ordered on patrol, Woods and two companions discov-

ered a German post comprising six machine-guns and over thirty troops. Without waiting for the force which was being organized to assault the strong-point, Woods led his small party against it. One German was wounded, another was captured and the rest of the garrison fled. The Germans then counter-attacked. Despite heavy fire, Woods climbed onto the parapet and, while lying there, held off successive attacks by throwing bombs handed to him by his companions. So effective was his defence that, when Australian reinforcements arrived, they were easily able to secure the post. Woods was awarded the Victoria Cross for his part in the action.

Returning to Australia in August 1919, he took up a small vineyard and orchard in the Swan Valley. On 30 April 1921 at the Caversham Methodist Church, Perth, he married Olive Adeline Wilson. Like many veterans of the A.I.F., Woods did not return home unscathed: he was plagued with ill health as a result of gassing and chest infections in the trenches. In 1937 he was granted a full pension and, although given only a few years to live, enjoyed a quiet retirement for the next twenty-six years. A keen cricketer when younger, Woods now took up fishing as a hobby. For a time he was president of the Caversham sub-branch of the Returned Sailors', Soldiers' and Airmen's Imperial League of Australia. In 1956 he joined other Australian V.C. winners in attending the V.C. centenary celebrations in London.

His sons Gordon and Norman served in the Royal Australian Air Force during World War II; Gordon (the first-born) was killed in October 1943. Late in life Woods lived at Claremont, Perth. Survived by his wife, three sons and three daughters, he died on 18 January 1963 in Hollywood Repatriation Hospital and was buried in Karrakatta cemetery.

C. E. W. Bean, *The A.I.F. in France*, 1918 (Syd, 1942); W. Devine, *The story of a battalion* (Melb, 1919); L. Wigmore (ed), *They dared mightily*, revised and condensed by J. Williams and A. Staunton (Canb, 1986); *Reveille* (Syd), 1 Mar 1963; *Advertiser* and *West Australian*, 21 Jan 1963; Nominal roll, 48th Battalion, AIF, *and* Honours and awards, 1914-18 war, Aust Army, *and* Official historian's biog cards (AWM); information from Mr N. Woods, Perth.

MATTHEW HIGGINS

WOODS, PERCY WILLIAM (1885-1937), soldier and manufacturer, was born on 8 November 1885 in Sydney, third child of Frederick Woods, a decorator from London, and his Melbourne-born wife Isabel, née England. After leaving school he was employed by James Sandy & Co. Ltd as a decorator. Slightly below average height, Woods was thickset, muscular and strong; as a young man he was a prominent amateur wrestler.

Commissioned lieutenant in the Senior Cadets, New South Wales, in 1911, Woods enlisted on 4 September 1914 in the Australian Imperial Force as a private and was allotted to the 3rd Battalion. He was a sergeant when the unit embarked for Egypt in October and landed on Gallipoli on 25 April 1915. Commissioned on 19 May and promoted lieutenant on 7 August, Woods was a platoon commander in the attack on Lone Pine in August. It was said that the strain of that operation turned his dark brown hair quite grey. He was mentioned in dispatches for his work on Gallipoli where he served until the evacuation.

On the formation of the 5th Division, A.I.F., in Egypt, Woods was transferred to the 55th Battalion in February 1916 and promoted captain on 12 March. After operations with the Egyptian Expeditionary Force, the battalion moved to the Western Front in June. For his courage and initiative in the battalion's first major action, at the battle of Fromelles on 19-20 July, Woods was awarded the Military Cross. As a major—with temporary rank from 1 January 1917, confirmed on 14 April—he led the battalion in the capture of Doignies, France, in the Hindenburg line operations in April, in the 2nd battle of Bullecourt in May and other front-line service (in the absences of the commanding officer) to 1 June. Woods took over command on 19 June as lieut-colonel. He received the Distinguished Service Order for the praiseworthy manner of his command and his direction of the battalion at Doignies.

In further service in France and Belgium during 1917 Woods fought in the actions at Polygon Wood and Wytschaete Ridge. In 1918 he took part in the major engagements of Villers-Bretonneux in April, and Péronne and the breaching of the Hindenburg line in September. He was awarded a Bar to his D.S.O. for conspicuous gallantry and able handling of his battalion at Péronne, and was thrice mentioned in dispatches for service on the Western Front. As battalion commander, he always sited his headquarters near his troops and frequently visited the front line. He was particular about his own appearance, and also insisted on smartness in all ranks and efficiency in all aspects of military operations.

Woods returned to Australia in December 1918 and maintained his concern for his men's welfare as patron of the 55th Battalion's Veterans' Association. Continuing his interest in the army, in 1921-25 he commanded the 55th Battalion, Australian Military Forces; he retired in 1926. On 24 January 1914 Woods had married Ethel Elizabeth Cook with Anglican rites at Christ Church St Laurence, Sydney. Divorced on 6 March 1928, he married Annie Donohoe at Dulwich Hill, Sydney, on the 31st. There were no children of either marriage. After the war Woods set up in business as a clothing manufacturer, working chiefly as a sales representative.

His application in 1932 for disability benefits was rejected by the Repatriation Commission on the ground that his ill health was not due to war service. Appealing against this decision, Woods was supported by wartime associates, including his batman and orderly-room sergeant; they testified that Woods had refused evacuation from the front line, despite being gassed on three occasions. On review, his pulmonary fibrositis was accepted as being war-related and a pension was granted. It was increased in 1933 when Woods stated that he was totally incapacitated. Survived by his wife, he died of cerebro-vascular disease on 5 January 1937 in Sydney Hospital and was cremated. Forty-two wartime members of the 55th Battalion were among the mourners at the service.

C. E. W. Bean, *The story of Anzac*, 2 (Syd, 1924), and *The A.I.F. in France* 1916-18 (Syd, 1929, 1933, 1942); E. Wren, *Randwick to Hargicourt* (Syd, 1935); *London Gazette*, 28 Jan 1916, 1 Jan, 28 Dec 1917, 1 Jan, 24 May 1918, 1 Feb, 11 July 1919; *Reveille* (Syd), Feb, Mar 1933, Feb 1937; *SMH*, 25 Dec 1918, 7, 8 Jan 1937; *Sydney Mail*, 13 Aug 1919; Records, Dept of Veterans' Affairs, Canb.

J. B. HOPLEY

WOODS, WALTER ALAN (1861-1939), journalist and politician, was born on 28 December 1861 at Mulgrave, Victoria, and registered as Walter William, eldest of twelve children of William Head, a native-born storekeeper, and his English wife Ann Margaret, née Priest, both strict Methodists. Walter was educated in state schools at Oakleigh and Brighton. On 30 May 1883 at St Jude's Anglican Church, Carlton, he married Caroline Riley (d. 1908); they were to have seven children. As a young man, he travelled through the Riverina, New South Wales, searching for work as a shearer, an experience which he commemorated in verse using the pseudonym 'John Drayman'. He quickly made a name for himself as a labour organizer and journalist. While secretary of the Wagga Wagga branch of the Amalgamated Shearers' Union in 1891, he helped to found and edit the *Hummer* which amalgamated with the Queensland *Worker* on 24 September 1892. Two months later he began editing *New Australia*, the journal of William Lane's [q.v.9] New Australia Co-operative Settlement Association, of which Head became Sydney secretary; he resigned as editor of the *Worker* in November 1893.

A friend of Arthur Rae, J. F. Archibald, (Dame) Mary Gilmore and Henry Lawson [qq.v.11,3,9,10], and one of Lawson's numerous creditors, Head published stories and verse (as 'John Drayman') in the *Bulletin*, the *Critic* and the *Worker*. With his wife and children, he intended to accompany members of the New Australia movement to Paraguay. His plan was tragically terminated in 1893 by the loss and presumed death of his son Rowland in the Gippsland bush, Victoria. His eldest son Walter left for Paraguay in the *Royal Tar* and never returned. Blighted by these events and by the false suspicion that Head had embezzled New Australia funds (he was probably liable for financial mismanagement), his marriage crumbled. He left Sydney for New Zealand about 1894.

Arriving at Launceston, Tasmania, in 1895, as Walter Ashe Woods he took over the editorship of the *Tasmanian Democrat*; next year he moved to Hobart and, as Walter Alan Ashe Woods, began working with James Paton, a Christian socialist and editor of the *Clipper*. Woods subsequently applied his talent for invention to marketing new products through his and Paton's Infallible Remedy Co. In 1901 they applied for a patent for 'An Improved method of removing marine growth from ship hulls while afloat'.

In 1903, as Walter Alan Woods, he became editor and part-owner of the *Clipper*, a post he held until 1909 when the journal was incorporated in the *Daily Post*. The *Clipper* was a Labor publication committed to the style of journalism made popular by the *Bulletin*. Literary competitions encouraged readers' contributions in verse and story. Woods saw his mission as educative, to inform readers about the 'truths' of socialism as espoused by such diverse authorities as Robert Blatchford and John Milton. He believed in the power of the word—to stimulate 'discussion preparatory to action'—and in the certainty of progress. Like a number of his contemporaries, Woods thought that the inevitable 'evolution of humanity' would lead to the 'glorious sunrise of socialism'.

Insisting that hard work was essential to inaugurate the new era, Woods exhorted workers to be 'earnest for reform'. His own efforts set a good example. When he took over the editorship of the *Clipper*, with David Balchen he convened the first meeting of the Workers' Political League, the forerunner of the Tasmanian Labor Party. Convinced by his experience in New South Wales that trade unionism was the backbone of the Labor movement, Woods organized workers into trade unions and lobbied for the reestablishment of a trades and labour council. In 1906 he won the seat of Hobart North

(later Denison) in the House of Assembly. He was returned in elections in 1909, 1912, 1913 and 1916. In 1917 he resigned Denison to contest the Senate, but was defeated in that year of Nationalist triumph. He was elected again to the assembly in 1925 and 1928, but lost the seat in 1931. While never a minister, he was chairman of committees (1925-26) and Speaker (1914-16, 1926-28).

Woods had married Jemima Gourlay Watkins on 14 September 1910 in Hobart with Presbyterian forms. She was a strong and capable woman whose work of child-rearing made possible both her husband's parliamentary career and their children's academic successes. A well-groomed, dapper, stout, jovial and impish man, Woods readily joined in children's games at W.P.L. picnics. His almost bald pate became a target for detractors, some of whom jibed at 'Father Woods' and his patriarchal association with the Tasmanian Labor Party. Admirers were impressed by his uncompromising opposition to exploitation, profiteering, sectarianism and absurd class distinctions. Though talkative, Woods rarely spoke about himself. He maintained close links with many Tasmanian writers and enjoyed a valued friendship with Edmund Morris Miller [q.v.10], with whose assistance he helped to endow Tasmanian libraries.

In parliament Woods had focused on land reform ('the Labor movement must become the land Restoration movement') and on the abolition of the Legislative Council. Identifying the Upper House as the chief obstacle in the path of progress, in November 1908 he had moved for the abolition of the council; his motion was defeated. Between 1906 and 1909 Labor's vote in the State elections doubled and the first Labor government in Tasmania took office under John Earle [q.v.8] on 20 October 1909. While Woods's dream of establishing a 'Cooperative Commonwealth' remained elusive, the Labor Party had, in the years of his association with the *Clipper*, established itself as a major political force. To Woods must go a large share of the credit. He died on 28 February 1939 at St Helen's Hospital, Hobart, and was cremated. He was survived by a son and daughter of his first marriage, and by his wife and their daughter and son who was a Rhodes Scholar (1934).

G. Souter, *A peculiar people* (Syd, 1968); D. J. Murphy (ed), *Labor in politics* (Brisb, 1975); W. H. Wilde, *Courage a grace* (Melb, 1988); *Meanjin Q*, Mar 1966; M. Lake, W. A. Woods and the *Clipper* 1903-09 (B.A. Hons thesis, Univ Tas, 1968); Woods papers (TA).   MARILYN LAKE

WOODS, WILLIAM MAITLAND (1864-1927), Anglican clergyman and military chaplain, was born on 4 January 1864 at Mayfair, London, son of Alfred Woods, master draper, and his wife Jane, née Damerel. Educated at the City of London School and St Mary Hall, Oxford, William graduated B.A. in 1889. That year he was made deacon and arrived in North Queensland to be curate of St James's Pro-Cathedral, Townsville. Appointed curate-in-charge, Thursday Island, in 1890, he was ordained priest on 11 April 1892. He married Ina Alice Mary Games on 3 January 1893 in the island's registry office. As the first rector of Thursday Island, he displayed 'a strong sense of missionary vocation' and saw the *Quetta* Memorial Church built before he moved in 1897 to Cairns. Woods then worked in parishes at Dalby (1899-1903), Kangaroo Point, Brisbane (1903-13), and Ariah Park, New South Wales (1913-15).

Having been appointed chaplain in the Queensland Land Forces in 1893, Woods had continued to serve in the Australian Military Forces. He transferred to the Australian Imperial Force on 9 August 1915. Two months later he was at Gallipoli, attached briefly to the 2nd Brigade, then to the 7th Light Horse Regiment with which he remained after the evacuation in December. Senior chaplain from 31 July 1916, he joined the staff of Major General (Sir) Harry Chauvel's [q.v.7] Anzac Mounted Division in September. During the advance through Sinai and Palestine, with its intermittent long periods of inaction, Woods lectured on the Holy Land. Grateful for his ministrations and aware of his interest in archaeology, the soldiers reported a number of finds they had uncovered. He learned of the discovery—made on 17 April 1917 by troops engaged at Shellal in the second battle of Gaza—of an exquisite church-floor mosaic. With the aid of expert advice and materials from Cairo, he supervised the removal and packing of the damaged mosaic which was later mounted in the Australian War Memorial, Canberra. Professor A. D. Trendall later dated the Shellal mosaic to A.D. 561-62 and assessed it as being worthy of 'a place of honour in the history of Byzantine art'.

Described as 'brilliant and witty', Woods was a strict Anglo-Catholic. George Lambert's [q.v.9] pencil-portrait (*c.*1918, now held by the A.W.M.) depicted him as bespectacled and balding, with prominent brows and gentle features. In 1919 Woods was appointed O.B.E. and mentioned in dispatches. He returned to Australia and his A.I.F. appointment terminated on 16 June; he immediately sailed to join his wife in Fiji where she had nursed during the war. They moved to Honolulu. Headmaster of Iolani College for a year and rector of St Clement's Episcopal Church from 1923, Woods gained the affection of his parishioners. He died of a cerebral

tumour on 6 February 1927 in Queen's Hospital, Honolulu, and was cremated. His wife, son and daughter survived him.

H. S. Gullett, *The Australian Imperial Force in Sinai and Palestine* (Syd, 1938); A. D. Trendall, *The Shellal mosaic* (Canb, 1942); J. Bayton, *Cross over Carpentaria* (Brisb, 1965); G. F. and E. M. Langley, *Sand, sweat and camels* (Kilmore, Vic, 1976); *Brisb Church Chronicle*, 1 Dec 1899, p 70, 1 Feb 1904, p 102, 1 Aug 1905, p 6; *Herald* (Melb), 4 Apr 1923; *Queenslander*, 12 Mar 1927; *Bulletin*, 19 June 1927; St Andrew's Cathedral, Honolulu, records; information from Assoc Prof K. J. Cable, Dept of Hist, Univ Syd.

J. P. HALDANE-STEVENSON

WOODWARD, BERNARD HENRY (1846-1916), museum director, was born on 31 January 1846 at Islington, London, son of Samuel Pickworth Woodward, professor of botany, and his wife Elizabeth, née Tenlon. Samuel was employed as an assistant in the department of geology and mineralogy at the British Museum (Natural History) from 1848. Little is known of Bernard's early life, but he gave his occupation as wine merchant when he married Emma Bertha Ayton at the parish church of Stoke Newington, Middlesex, on 24 August 1875. Suffering from bronchial disease, he came to Western Australia in September 1889 and in 1889-95 was government analyst, responsible for almost all assaying in the State. In 1893 he was also appointed inspector of mineral oils, in 1894 he was retained by the government to examine problems in flour and in 1896 he became assistant examiner in patents.

Furthermore, in 1889 Woodward had been made curator of the Geological Museum, Perth. Incorporating several individual collections previously maintained by his cousin H. P. Woodward [q.v.], the museum was opened to the public in 1891. Next year, when the government added a mixed historical and ethnographic collection to its holdings, the adjective 'geological' was dropped from its name. In 1897, shortly after a fine arts collection was started, the institution became the Western Australian Museum and Art Gallery, and Woodward was appointed its director. Slight, bespectacled and bearded, he filled the role admirably.

Seeking to illustrate good taste, he acquired examples of the classical cultures (Greece, Rome, Egypt) and displayed raw materials adjacent to artistic items. According to his *Guide* (1900), 'The first function of a museum is to give an example of perfect order and perfect elegance'. Woodward compiled catalogues, wrote papers for scientific journals and from 1910 edited the museum's serial, *Records*. He acquired grants to pursue research, and the series of free lectures which he first organized in 1905 persisted until the 1960s. A 'prominent figure in the public life of the State', he used the museum and gallery as a centre for culture. He retired officially in 1916.

In 1889 Woodward had promoted the Wilgie Sketching Club (whose members included James Linton and George Poole [qq.v.10,11]) and acted as its secretary. Foundation president (1896, 1914) of the Society of Arts, in 1890 he founded the Western Australia Natural History Society (the Royal Society from 1912) and was its honorary secretary. President (1893-98) of the Toodyay Vine and Fruit-growers' Association, he lived on his orangery at Harvey and in the face of indifference advocated protective reserves for indigenous flora and fauna. Woodward died of respiratory disease on 14 October 1916 at Harvey and was buried in the local cemetery. Woodward Park reserve was named after him.

J. S. Battye (ed), *Cyclopedia of Western Australia*, 1 (Adel, 1912); *British A'sian*, 30 Nov 1916; *Western Mail*, 3 July 1914, 13 Oct, 15 Dec 1916; *West Australian*, 10 July, 11 Oct 1916.

IAN M. CRAWFORD

WOODWARD, FRANK LEE (1871-1952), headmaster and Buddhist scholar, was born on 13 April 1871 at Saham Toney, Norfolk, England, third son of William Woodward, a country parson, and his wife Elizabeth Mary Ann, née Lee. Educated by his father, Frank entered Christ's Hospital (the Bluecoat School), London. After winning distinction as a classical scholar, sportsman and organist at Sidney Sussex College, Cambridge (B.A., 1893; M.A., 1902), he taught in several English public schools and regarded his profession as 'the noblest of them all', as 'a means of learning' and as 'a means of service'.

While at Stamford School, Lincolnshire, Woodward began studying Western and Eastern philosophy. In 1902 he joined the Theosophical Society, 'the most important event' in his life. Inspired to accept Buddha's teachings, he became a friend of Colonel H. S. Olcott, co-founder and president of the society and a pioneer of Buddhist education in Ceylon (Sri Lanka). In 1903 Woodward was invited to become principal of Mahinda Buddhist College, Galle, on the south-western coast of the island.

There Woodward set 'a very high tone'. A strict disciplinarian, he knew every pupil in the school, each of whom he nicknamed after a character in Shakespeare's plays. He lived frugally, like a Buddhist monk, and was respected for his experience, academic ability

and lack of ostentation. The school grew rapidly and had to be relocated. He contributed generously from his monetary inheritance, and designed, supervised and assisted with new buildings which included a science laboratory. The teaching of the Buddha dharma and Sinhalese language and history were important in the school: Woodward had Sinhalese accepted as a subject for the Cambridge local examinations. He advised the director of education in Ceylon and was actively associated with the movement for establishing a university.

By 1919 he was looking for peace and seclusion in which to continue his translations of the Buddhist scriptures for the Pali Text Society. Woodward settled near Launceston, Tasmania, and about 1927 bought a house in a neglected orchard in the Rowella district on the western bank of the Tamar River. A vegetarian, a mystic and a man of whimsy, he practised yoga, wore a turban and lived alone, surrounded by Buddhist scriptures on thousands of palm-leaves. Maintaining an extensive correspondence, he recorded the scores in every match played by the Bluecoat School's Old Blues Rugby XV.

Among scholars, Woodward is revered for translating eighteen of the forty-two volumes of the Pali texts into English and for compiling the vast concordance of the Pali canon which occupied the last fifteen years of his life. At the popular level, his volume, *Some sayings of the Buddha* (Oxford, 1925, 1939), has contributed to a wider understanding of Buddhism. Reduced to near poverty, Woodward died on 27 May 1952 at Beaconsfield Hospital, West Tamar, and was buried in Carr Villa cemetery, Launceston. A former associate Sir Ponnambalam Arunáchalam viewed him as a great apostle of Mahayana Buddhism who had 'combined in a rare degree . . . the active spirit of the West with the mysticism of the East'.

D. H. P. Gunawardena, *F. L. Woodward* (Colombo, Ceylon, nd); I. P. Oliver, *Buddhism in Britain* (Lond, 1979); L. McIntyre et al, *Rowella—Kayena (West Bay—Richmond Hill) from 1805* (Launc, 1987); P. Croucher, *Buddhism in Australia 1848-1988* (Syd, 1989); *Platypus* (Univ Tas Literary Mag), 1952; *Examiner* (Launc), 10 Aug 1983; N. J. Heyward, A Buddhist scholar (ms, 1954, held by ADB).

NIGEL HEYWARD

WOODWARD, HENRY PAGE (1858-1917), geologist, was born on 16 May 1858 at Norwich, Norfolk, England, eldest son of Dr Henry Woodward, geologist and later keeper of geology (1880-1901) at the British Museum (Natural History), and his wife Ellen Sophia, née Page. B. H. Woodward [q.v.] was his cousin. Educated at University College School and the Royal School of Mines, London, Harry gained field experience with the Geological Survey of England and Wales. In 1883-86 he was assistant government geologist in South Australia. He returned to London, intending to compete in the Indian geological survey examination; after a year at the Royal College of Science, in 1887 he was appointed government geologist for Western Australia.

His arrival in Perth in 1888 coincided with the early gold rushes. He reported almost immediately on the Northam fields and was to visit every goldfield in the colony, acquiring a store of anecdotes of adventures and incidents from his travels. Woodward's training was of immense practical value: his annual report for 1890, containing a general description of the geology of the region—republished as a *Mining handbook to the colony of Western Australia* (1894)—together with his related geological sketch map, was essential reading for miners and prospectors. He eventually published twenty-one reports and six geological maps. In the face of opposition, he induced the government to sink its first artesian bore at Guildford in 1894 and subsequently indicated other areas from which essential water was obtained. On 31 December 1890 at the parish church, Albany, he had married with Anglican rites Ellen Maude, daughter of J. F. T. Hassell [q.v.4].

Having resigned in 1895 (though remaining a government consultant), Woodward joined Bewick, Morcing & Co. of London and Coolgardie as local partner and manager of their mining and consulting business on the eastern goldfields. By 1897 he had begun to practise on his own account as a mining engineer. His investigations substantiated the viability of coal seams at Collie and he became a mine-owner himself. In April 1905 he rejoined the public service as assistant government geologist.

A fellow of the Geological Society, the Royal Geographical Society and the Imperial Institute, and an associate of the Institute of Civil Engineers, London, he was president (1896) of the Western Australian Institute of Mining and Mechanical Engineers, and a member of the Institute of Mines and Metallurgy, London. Survived by his wife and three sons, Harry Woodward died of cancer on 8 February 1917 at St Omer Hospital, West Perth, and was buried in Karrakatta cemetery.

W. B. Kimberly, *History of West Australia* (Melb, 1897); J. S. Battye (ed), *Cyclopedia of Western Australia*, 1 (Adel, 1912); *British A'sian*, 1 July 1897; *Morning Herald* (Perth), 16 Jan, 15 Feb 1896; *Western Mail* (Perth), 16 Feb 1917.

IAN M. CRAWFORD

WOODWARD, OLIVER HOLMES (1885-1966), mining engineer, metallurgist and soldier, was born on 8 October 1885 at Tenterfield, New South Wales, son of native-born parents Sydney Arthur Woodward, storekeeper, and his wife Jemima Johnstone, née Reid. He was educated at public schools and for two years at Newington College, Sydney. Early practical mining experience at Irvinebank, North Queensland, was followed by three years at Charters Towers where he worked underground and studied part time at the School of Mines. In 1909 he was awarded the W. H. Browne [q.v.7] medal for mining and in 1910 the medal for metallurgy. Further experience underground qualified him as a mine-manager. As such he went in 1913 to Mount Morgan and then to Papua where he assisted the geologist (Sir) Colin Fraser [q.v.8] at the Laloki and other mines. Late in 1914 Woodward returned to Mount Morgan to recover from malaria.

In August 1915 he enlisted in the Australian Imperial Force; he was commissioned and posted to No.1 Company of the newly raised Mining Battalion. He sailed for France in March 1916. On its arrival in Flanders the battalion was broken up and the 1st Tunnelling Company became an independent engineer unit. Deployed in the Armentières sector, France, the company fought on the surface as well as underground and in June 1916 Woodward won the Military Cross for blowing up a snipers' post in no man's land.

Early in 1917 the company took over mining operations in a sector south-east of Ypres, Belgium, which included deep galleries under the German lines; these led to two mines, one charged with 53 000 lb. (24 041 kg) of explosives and the other with 70 000 lb. (31 752 kg). For months the company protected these mines, using listening posts and countermines, until the opening of the battle of Messines when they were fired with devastating effect. Woodward, by this time a captain, headed the team in charge and personally fired the mines.

From August 1918 the tunnelling companies were employed on the surface as field engineers. On 29 September at Bony, east of Amiens, France, Woodward was in charge of three sections of the 1st Tunnelling Company which were employed on road maintenance and came under enemy fire; he once more distinguished himself by his courage and resourcefulness, and was awarded a Bar to his Military Cross. In the last weeks of the war his section was attached to the 1st British Division for its advance to the Rhine. For the crossing of the Sambre-Oise Canal east of Le Cateau, his men—under heavy fire—built a tank bridge spanning the walls of a lock; Woodward received a second Bar to his Military Cross, an extremely rare distinction.

Returning to Australia in May 1919, he went to the Mount Morgan Gold Mining Co. before taking up an appointment at Port Pirie, South Australia, as a general metallurgist with Broken Hill Associated Smelters, of which Fraser was joint managing director. On 3 September 1920 Woodward married Marjorie Moffat Waddell at St John's Anglican Cathedral, Brisbane. Soon afterwards he became plant superintendent at Port Pirie. In 1926 he was promoted to general superintendent. Over the nine years he held this position there was extensive rebuilding to accommodate metallurgical developments such as the continuous process for refining lead bullion. There was also a steady improvement in living and working conditions for employees.

With the support of Fraser and W. S. Robinson [q.v.11], in November 1934 Woodward became general manager of North Broken Hill Ltd. His thirteen years at Broken Hill witnessed an active rebuilding and a modernizing of surface plant: the British Broken Hill mine, idle since 1930, was re-opened; a new mill using gravity concentration followed by flotation was built and commissioned; ore haulage and hoisting practices were improved.

In 1940 Woodward became president of the Australasian Institute of Mining and Metallurgy. He joined the board of directors of North Broken Hill Ltd in December 1944 and remained on the board after retiring from general managership at the North Mine on 8 October 1947. He had also been a director of Broken Hill Associated Smelters and the associated Electrolytic Refining & Smelting Co. President of the Australian Mining and Metals Association (1952-54), he was appointed C.M.G. in 1956.

Woodward had written an autobiography and accounts of his wartime experiences and of the Broken Hill mining industry. From his small country property near Adelaide, in 1952 he moved to Hobart. Survived by his wife, a daughter and two sons, he died there on 24 August 1966 and was cremated.

A review of the Broken Hill lead-silver-zinc industry (Melb, 1950); Bd minutes, 26 Jan, 23 Nov 1961 (Nth Broken Hill Ltd); Woodward papers (Univ Melb Archives); personal information.

RONALD McNICOLL

WOOLCOCK, JOHN LASKEY (1861-1929), parliamentary counsel, was born on 7 November 1861 at St Clement, Cornwall, England, son of Rev. William Woolcock and his wife Elizabeth, née White. Intending to establish a mission of Bible Christians, William migrated with his family and reached Brisbane in 1866. John attended the Normal School and Brisbane Grammar School (1875-80), and won a State exhibition to the University of Sydney where he excelled in humanities and sciences (B.A., 1883). He then taught at Brisbane Grammar before being appointed private secretary to the premier (Sir) Samuel Griffith [q.v.9].

Reading law in Griffith's chambers, Woolcock learned the skills of drafting legislation, beginning with the introduction, notes and index to the Justices Act of 1886. He attended Griffith at conferences on Federation and Imperial policy in Sydney (1883), Hobart (1886) and London (1887) which prepared him for work on the executive of the Queensland Federation League in 1899. Called to the Bar on 6 December 1887, Woolcock became prominent in equity, constitutional and municipal law. In 1896 he served on the royal commission into local government; two years later he was secretary to the royal commission on the criminal code.

Appointed parliamentary counsel in 1899, Woolcock held the position until 1927, with the right of private practice. His knowledge of Queensland legislation had already been established in 1899 by his compilation with Alfred Pain of the five-volume *The Queensland statutes*. In 1911 he published a six-volume consolidation with Marcus Hertzberg. Some of his most important drafting was in the field of local government, such as the Local Authorities Act of 1902; other useful, annotated compendia related to the Mining Act of 1898 and its regulations (1900), the Health Act of 1900, and liquor legislation. A number of his major court appearances involved land issues, as in *R.* v. *Hopkins* (1915). In 1923 he appeared for the Brisbane Tramways Trust Co. Ltd when it was being taken over by the Brisbane Tramway Trust.

Although Woolcock had been steeped in Griffith's liberalism, Premier T. J. Ryan [q.v.11] experienced no difficulty after 1915 when he drew upon Woolcock's legal opinion on workers' compensation and on the abolition of the Legislative Council; Woolcock also appeared with Ryan in key actions like the Mooraberrie (meat acquisition) case.

A lover of books, especially of English literature and the classics, Woolcock had a well-stocked library in his home, Halwyn. In 1891 he was a member of the royal commission into the establishment of a university and, two years later, was largely responsible for inaugurating the university extension movement. He sat on the University of Queensland senate (1910-16) and chaired the education committee. Woolcock was a trustee of the Brisbane Grammar schools from 1899 and was the first old boy to be chairman of trustees (1906-29). In 1895 he helped to found the Queensland Public Library. He was twice married: on 17 June 1891 to Gertrude Mary Harpur (d. 1912) at St Andrew's Anglican Church, Summer Hill, Sydney, and on 27 May 1914 to Ida Hague Withrington at St John's Cathedral, Brisbane.

In declining health Woolcock was appointed a judge of the Supreme Court on 1 February 1927, but died of endocarditis on 18 January 1929 at Red Hill, Brisbane, and was buried in Toowong cemetery. Accorded a state funeral, he was praised as a jurist and a scholar who had 'done the State some service'. He was survived by his wife, and by a son and daughter of each of his marriages.

S. Stephenson (comp), *Annals of the Brisbane Grammar School, 1869-1922* (Brisb, 1923); R. Johnston, *History of the Queensland Bar* (Brisb, 1979); *Daily Mail* (Brisb), 19, 21 Jan 1929; Woolcock notebooks (his legal cases) (QA); information from Dr W. J. P. Woolcock, New Farm, Brisb.

W. ROSS JOHNSTON

WOOLLARD, HERBERT HENRY (1889-1939), professor of anatomy, was born on 2 August 1889 at Horsham, Victoria, son of Charles Woollard, salesman, and his wife Mary, née Smith, both Victorian born. At Queen's College, University of Melbourne, he studied medicine (M.B., B.S., 1910; M.D., 1912). Enlisting in the Australian Army Medical Corps, Australian Imperial Force, in September 1914, he was regimental medical officer to the 2nd Field Artillery Brigade at Gallipoli. Later, as a major, he served with distinction in France with the A.A.M.C. and was wounded at Pozières. Woollard saw continual front-line service, was mentioned in dispatches and awarded the French Croix de Guerre.

Demobilized in England, he studied for the primary examination of the Royal College of Surgeons. Course work in anatomy at University College, London, brought him into contact with (Sir) Grafton Elliot Smith [q.v.11]. Like his compatriots J. Shellshear and R. A. Dart who aspired to study surgery, Woollard decided to become an anatomist. He was appointed as an anatomy demonstrator at University College and in 1921 a Rockefeller fellowship enabled him to go to the Johns Hopkins Medical School, Baltimore, United States of America, to pursue experimental studies. The results of his work, published after his return to Britain, included an important paper on the factors involved in the establishment of vascular patterns, another on the phagocytic activity of haemal lymph glands and a third on the macrophage activity of the leptomeninges. He also contributed a monograph on the anatomy of *Tarsius spectrum* and papers on primate neuroanatomy. In

1925 Woollard began the programme of studies on peripheral innervation for which he is best remembered. Queen's University of Belfast awarded him the Symington memorial prize (1926) for the best original work published by a junior member of the Anatomical Society of Great Britain and Ireland during the preceding three years. Woollard's mastery of the current literature in his subject was reflected in his *Recent advances in anatomy* (London, 1927) which pointed to the vitality of the science of anatomy in other countries; its effect on anatomical research in Britain was profound and continuing.

From 1923 to 1927 Woollard was assistant professor of anatomy at University College, London. He returned to Australia to take up the chair of anatomy and histology (1928-29) at the University of Adelaide in succession to F. W. Jones [q.v.9]. Together with his mentor Elliot Smith, W. E. Le Gros Clark and J. I. Hunter [q.v.9], Woollard pioneered the use of a new style in British anatomical research designed to elucidate the functional implications of structure: it depended upon experimental, as opposed to static, descriptive techniques. He was also among those who advocated a reintegration of the teaching of histology with anatomy following the artificial separation of the two which had developed in British and Australian medical schools. His passionate wish to advance the scientific basis of medicine found yet another outlet in his active promotion of the teaching of radiological anatomy. Woollard returned to London to the chair of anatomy (1929-36) at the medical school of St Bartholomew's Hospital. There he was a guiding influence in planning a new medical college and developing within it an active and progressive anatomy department.

Succeeding Elliot Smith in 1936 as professor of anatomy at University College, London, Woollard won high regard for his research and leadership. He had been a member of the editorial committee of the *Journal of Anatomy* since 1931, but his inceptive insights found greater scope after he became its editor in 1936. Five ft. 4 ins. (162.6 cm) tall, Woollard was a vigorous, dedicated, idealistic enthusiast throughout his career. He had a personality full of colour and force, combining warmth and generosity to his friends and colleagues with uncompromising criticism and intolerance of whatever he saw as slipshod or insincere. In 1938 he was elected a fellow of the Royal Society.

During the last years of his career he was incapacitated by anginal attacks which he attempted to ignore: on 18 January 1939 Woollard collapsed and died at his work at University College hospital. He had married Mary Wilson Howard at Christ Church, Hampstead, on 29 October 1915. She and their two sons survived him.

E. Barclay-Smith, *The Anatomical Society of Great Britain and Ireland, a retrospect* (Lond, 1937); *Reveille* (Syd), Mar 1933, May 1938, May 1939; *British Medical J*, 1, 28 Jan 1939, p 193; *Lancet*, 1, 28 Jan 1939, p 239; *St Bartholomew's Hospital J*, 46, Mar 1939, p 119; *Science*, 89, 5 May 1939, p 404; *J of Anatomy* (Lond), 73, 1939, p 504; *Obituary Notices of Fellows of the Roy Soc*, 2 (1940), p 11; *The Times*, 19 Jan 1939.   MICHAEL J. BLUNT

WOOLLEY, EMMELINE MARY DOGHERTY (1843-1908), musician, was baptized on 16 June 1843 in Hereford Cathedral, England, eldest of seven children of Rev. John Woolley [q.v.6], headmaster, and his wife Mary Margaret, née Turner. Emmeline spent her early years at Norwich. Appointed principal of the University of Sydney in 1852, her father reached Port Jackson with his family on 9 July. Emmeline was educated at home with her four sisters and went to Italy at the age of 15. She spent two years at Florence where she studied the pianoforte, theory and composition under the elder Alessandro Kraus and acquired 'a highly finished cantabile in playing' from Pietro Romani. Profoundly affected by her memories of the services in Norwich Cathedral, she haunted churches and became familiar with the masses of Palestrina, Pergolesi and Cherubini. At Munich, Bavaria, she was taught the pianoforte by Julius von Kolb. She returned to Sydney, fluent in Italian and German, after an absence of five years.

Her father's death in 1866 left the family impoverished. Disliking public appearances, Miss Woolley confined her professional work to teaching music. She also officiated as organist at St John's Anglican Church, Darlinghurst, for ten years and succeeded in having its old organ replaced. With Ethel Pedley [q.v.11], a close friend who shared her house, Emmeline formed the St Cecilia Choir for female voices in 1884.

Visiting Europe next year, Miss Woolley inspected conservatories in Berlin and Brussels, met many musicians and attended a reception given for Liszt in London. With Miss Pedley, she organized some concerts for her pupils, and others to benefit such causes as the Women's Industries Exhibition and Centenary Fair (1888) and the Thirlmere Home for Consumptives, raising over £1200 by 1895. She introduced many new works, including selections from Gounod's *Redemption*, Sainton-Dolby's *St Dorothea* and chamber music by Clara Schumann and Grieg, as well as her own compositions, some of which were published.

Described by the chancellor as 'a daughter of the university', in 1889 Emmeline Woolley joined a ladies' committee to raise funds for a women's college at the University of Sydney. She was a foundation member of Women's College council (1891-1908) and in 1895 declined Louisa Macdonald's [q.v.10] request to act as principal because of her own impending visit to England.

As a composer, Miss Woolley was 'capable of considerable melodic inspiration'. Her triumph was *The captive soul*, written for Ethel Pedley's libretto. Scored for a chamber music ensemble, organ, two pianofortes, female choir and soloists, the cantata was performed on 11 June 1895; the choral dirge, 'Hush the spindle, hush the loom', made a deep impression and the manuscript was purchased by Novello & Co. Ltd, London. The cantata was performed in England and in 1906 by students at the Elder [q.v.4] Conservatorium of Music, Adelaide.

During her professional career, Miss Woolley was recognized as 'a pianist with a style at once scholarly and sparkling'. Dark, with strong features and hair severely drawn back, she 'ardently supported' Roberto Hazon's [q.v.9] efforts to found the Sydney Amateur Orchestral Society and remained on its committee until 1908. After Miss Pedley's death Emmeline conducted the St Cecilians in 1898-1907. She died of cancer on 18 March 1908 at her Darlinghurst home and was buried in the Anglican section of Waverley cemetery. She left £2000 to her niece Freda du Faur [q.v.8], the mountaineer.

A'sian Performing Right Assn, *APRA J*, Jan 1971, p 12; *Bulletin*, 8 July 1882; *SMH*, 12 June 1895, 19 Mar 1908, 28 May 1921; *Sydney Mail*, 22, 29 June 1895, 4 Sept 1907; Minutes of Council meetings (Women's College Archives); Louisa Macdonald letters (ML).   MARTHA RUTLEDGE

WOOLNOUGH, WALTER GEORGE (1876-1958), geologist, was born on 15 January 1876 at Brushgrove, Grafton, New South Wales, son of English-born Rev. James Woolnough, Wesleyan clergyman, and his American wife Phoebe Esther, née Hawke. He was educated at Sydney Boys' High School, Newington College—where he came under the influence of A. H. S. Lucas [q.v.10]—and the University of Sydney (B.Sc., 1898). Attracted by the personality and teaching of (Sir) Edgeworth David [q.v.8], as an undergraduate Woolnough accompanied David's expedition to Funafuti Atoll in 1897 to test Charles Darwin's [q.v.1] theory of coral reef formation. Having graduated with honours, Woolnough was appointed demonstrator in geology under David, and was lecturer in mineralogy and petrology at the University of

Adelaide in 1901-04. The surveys he carried out in Fiji in 1901 and 1905, with the support of the Royal Society, London, earned him D.Sc. degrees from the universities of Sydney (1904) and Adelaide (1905). His first visit to Fiji left a legacy of recurrent thrombosis; his physical disabilities lost him a place on Scott's 1910 polar expedition and would result in his rejection for military service in World War I, but in 1911 he was able to join J. A. Gilruth's [q.v.9] expedition to the Northern Territory.

In 1905-11 Woolnough was lecturer in geology at the University of Sydney, and acting professor during David's absences in 1906 and 1908-09. Woolnough was foundation professor (1913-19) of geology at the University of Western Australia where, with limited facilities and in makeshift quarters, he enthusiastically taught a wide range of geological topics. In 1913 the university awarded him an honorary D.Sc. A visit to Britain in 1919 to study salt deposits familiarized him with new aspects of economic geology; he joined Brunner Mond Alkali Co. which offered him the opportunity to travel widely in Australia. Reputed to have once walked 1000 miles (1609 km) in seven weeks, Woolnough used bicycle, horse, camel and car in his unsuccessful searches for productive salt deposits. In 1927 he became geological adviser to the Commonwealth of Australia, a 'temporary' post which he held until 1941. Having visited North American and Argentinian oilfields in 1930, Woolnough encouraged the use of aerial surveys and photography in the search for oil which he believed would be found in Australia and New Guinea in commercial quantities. In 1932 he recorded from the air the dome structures near Exmouth Gulf, Western Australia, where oil was subsequently discovered in 1953. Following his report on Commonwealth iron deposits, in 1940 the government placed an embargo on the export of iron ore and retained it until 1960.

After retiring in 1941 without a pension, Woolnough briefly turned to consulting and in 1942 began bibliographic and translating work. Forced by ill health to retire again in 1951 when aged 75, he continued to support himself by translating scientific articles from over a dozen languages often learned almost in the process of translation.

Woolnough's papers on the lateritic duricrust and on sedimentation in barred basins were major contributions to geomorphology and the theory of oil accumulation, but he published widely on a variety of geological topics. His periods of relaxation in Canberra were often spent with a geological hammer, looking for fossils. Bald in his later years, with a white goatee and small, twinkling eyes, he was described by a contemporary as 'one of the most

likable of men', 'full of interesting stories'. Woolnough's daughter, however, remembered the fanatical honesty and sense of responsibility that had contributed to her father's 'lifelong sense of insecurity and unworthiness which stalked even his most successful and affluent years'. He was president (1926) of the Royal Society of New South Wales, (W. B.) Clarke [q.v.3] medallist (1933), Clarke memorial lecturer (1936) and the Royal Society's medallist (1955); he was also an honorary member (1941) of the American Association of Petroleum Geologists, a rare distinction, and of the Geological Society of Australia (1957).

Virtually incapacitated from 1954, Woolnough died on 28 September 1958 at his home at Northbridge, Sydney, and was cremated. On 19 February 1902 at Croydon, Sydney, he had married Margaret Ilma Wilson with Wesleyan forms. His wife, a son and a daughter survived him. A small seamount south-east of Sydney, a library at the University of New England, Armidale, a reserve in Darwin and the Woolnough Hills, Western Australia, are all named after him.

Aust J of Science, 21 (1958-59), p 136; Linnean Soc NSW, *Procs*, 84 (1959), p 3; American Assn of Petroleum Geologists, *Bulletin*, Oct 1941, p 1954, Aug 1959, p 2035; *J of Geological Soc of Aust*, 6, no 1, 1958, p 54; *SMH*, 29 Sept 1958; *Sydney Mail*, 12 Mar 1930; Woolnough papers (NL).

D. F. BRANAGAN

WORMALD, JOSEPH DAWSON (1863-1921) and **HENRY PERCY** (1874-1932), fire engineers and manufacturers, were born on 3 January 1863 and 26 April 1874 in Edinburgh, sons of Joseph Dawson Wormald, writer to the signet, and his wife Mary Millar, née Anderson. Arriving in Australia in 1889, young Joseph entered into partnership with Stanley Russell to manufacture and import fire appliances. Living alternately in Sydney and Melbourne, the partners operated an agency from the Manchester engineering firm of Mather & Platt Ltd for the Grinnell sprinkler and Simplex fire extinguishers and fire door, as well as for the Palatine Insurance Co. Ltd of Manchester. Russell retired in 1896.

Harry was educated at Manchester Grammar School. After working for Agnew Bros at Manchester in 1888, he joined Dowson, Taylor & Co. (later Mather & Platt Ltd). He reached Sydney in 1890 and in 1891-98 was accountant cashier for the Scottish Union & National Insurance Co. In 1898 he became sub-manager for Russell & Wormald and in 1900 was admitted into partnership when the name was changed to Wormald Bros.

On 5 October 1904 at St Paul's Anglican Church, Burwood, he married Mildred Clive Chalmers.

By 1907, with its factory and store at 7 Deans Place and its office at 17 Bond Street, Sydney, Wormald Bros had agents throughout Australasia. With engineer W. E. L. Wears, in 1909 the brothers set up Embosteel Ltd to manufacture steel ceilings and embossed metal fittings, but within four years sold to Wunderlich [qq.v.] Ltd. On 21 December 1910 Wormald Bros Ltd was registered with a nominal capital of £25 000 in £1 shares. The original works to make Simplex equipment were moved to Surry Hills and then in 1912 to Young Street, Waterloo, where rolling shutters and hollow metal windows were made in 1913 and steel shelving three years later. In 1916 a branch was opened in Brisbane and in 1919 a factory was set up in Bay Street, Port Melbourne.

After severing his links with the Palatine Insurance Co., Joseph Wormald became chairman of the local board of the Union Assurance Society Ltd and a director of Anderson & Co., seed merchants. Upright, goodhearted and popular, he was an enthusiastic member of the Australian Golf and New South Wales clubs and of the Highland Society of New South Wales. He retired from active business with Wormald in 1918. In failing health, he left Sydney in March 1921 for a motoring holiday in Britain; he died of hepatic cirrhosis on 10 December 1921 in London.

A director of Wunderlich Ltd, Harry became managing director of Wormald Bros in 1918 when the company's capital was increased to £75 000. Reconstructed in 1920 with a nominal capital of £130 000, the firm expanded in the 1920s, building works in Brisbane and Adelaide, and renting them in Perth. A member of the New South Wales and Australian Jockey clubs, Harry belonged to the Australian, Royal Sydney and Leura golf clubs; his other recreations were motoring and gardening. In 1932 old links with Manchester were celebrated when an elder brother Sir John Wormald, for many years managing director of Mather & Platt, visited Australia. Survived by his wife, two sons and two daughters, Harry Wormald died of coronary thrombosis on 14 October 1932 at his Woollahra home and was cremated. His estate was sworn for probate in New South Wales at £25 518. A century after its foundation Wormald International Ltd was a world leader in the fire protection and security industry.

Cyclopedia of N.S.W. (Syd, 1907); Wormald Brothers Limited, *The story of Wormald Brothers* (Syd, 1952); *A'sian Insurance and Banking Record*, 21 Dec 1921; *SMH*, 13 Dec 1921, 15 Oct 1932.

G. P. WALSH

WORRALL, HENRY (1862-1940), Methodist minister and social reformer, was born on 26 February 1862 at Hartshead, Lancashire, England, son of James Worrall, cotton-mill manager, and his wife Charity, née Wood. Migrating to Australia, the family settled in Sydney where Henry attended a public school and in 1884 entered Newington College, the theological college of the Wesleyan Church. In 1886 he became a candidate for the ministry and, after marrying Elizabeth Ann Hodges (d. 1918) at the Wesleyan Church, Goulburn, on 23 February, sailed for Fiji.

Stationed at Ovalau and superintendent (from 1889) of the large circuit at Rewa, Worrall initiated missionary work among Indian immigrants and became renowned for his stamina, preaching, evangelism and opposition to Catholicism. After returning for deputation work in 1898, he remained in Australia because of his family's health. With characteristic modesty, he described his posting to the small Tasmanian circuit of Latrobe in 1899 as akin to 'putting a Dreadnought battleship in a duck-pond'. Ordained in 1890, he served in Hobart (1901) and in Victoria at Sale (1905), Bendigo (1906), Brunswick (1910), Prahran (1914), Kew (1920) and Ballarat (1925). The heathen-vanquishing missionary abroad was transformed into the social reformer confronting paganism at home. In Tasmania he had denounced Tattersall's lottery; at Bendigo his exposure of gold-thieving by mine employees created a furore. His campaigns against the evils of gambling and drink goaded the *Bulletin* and John Norton's [q.v.11] *Truth* to dub him 'wowser Worrall' and 'Worry-all', the meddling minister.

Impatient with the Bent [q.v.3] government's dilatory progress with its gambling and licensing reforms, Worrall attacked prominent politicians, including Sir Philip Fysh [q.v.8], a former partner in Tattersall's. When a young bookmaker fled from a mob of irate punters at Flemington and fell and broke his neck, Worrall depicted him as a simple country boy contaminated by city influences: on 22 July 1906 he preached a sermon, 'Who slaughtered the body and murdered the soul of Donald McLeod', which impeached 'in God's name' Victorian politicians, especially Sir Samuel Gillott [q.v.9], the chief secretary. Sir Thomas Bent moved that Worrall be called before the Bar of the Legislative Assembly. Upright and intransigent, Worrall composed himself for martyrdom, but found himself acting the only straight part in a farce which exposed the premier, his government and parliament to ridicule. The Speaker (Sir) Frank Madden [q.v.10] lightly reprimanded Worrall who had become a hero.

At the outbreak of World War I, Worrall

declared that he would preach every eligible man from his congregation into enlisting; among the 190 names on the honour roll at his Prahran church in 1919 were those of his three sons, one of whom was killed in action, another twice-wounded at Gallipoli, while the third won the French Croix de Guerre and the Distinguished Service Cross and Bar. Their service and sacrifice imparted a passion to the war which Worrall waged on the home front against shirkers, disloyalists, timid politicians and, above all, Dr Daniel Mannix [q.v.10]. Worrall's pursuit of the Victorian parliamentarian Alfred Farthing, spokesman for the Licensed Victuallers' Association, whose election Worrall attributed to 'rascality, rum and Rome', brought an unsuccessful action for libel in 1916. In his retiring address as president (1918-19) of the Methodist Conference of Victoria and Tasmania, Worrall made a rousing call for Protestant unity to protect the dawning heroic age from the menace of Catholicism. After the war he dedicated himself to the creation of 'a cleaner and brighter Australia' for the returning warriors. He found a public platform as president (thrice) of the Victorian Council of Churches and campaigned for prohibition in Britain (1922) and Australia (1924).

Worrall soldiered on as a supernumerary from 1928. He was grand master of the Loyal Orange Lodge of Victoria in 1931-33. His censorious attitude to the 'modern' evils of dancing, cards and the raffle progressively isolated him from his sons and their children. A widower, he married May Isabel Howell on 25 May 1927 in Wesley's Chapel, Holborn, London. Survived by his wife, and by two sons and three daughters of his first marriage, Worrall died at Canterbury, Melbourne, on 26 May 1940 and was buried in Burwood cemetery. Detested by his enemies as sanctimonious, overbearing and judgemental, disowned by some colleagues for his theatricality and vitriolic language, and rejected by members of his family for his bigotry and narrow-mindedness, he was lauded by militant Protestants, and Orangemen, as a courageous upholder of truth and liberty.

A. H. Wood, *Overseas missions of the Australian Methodist Church*, 2, *Fiji* (Melb, 1978); E. H. Buggy, *The real John Wren* (Melb, 1977); *J of Religious Hist*, June 1978; *Age*, 23 July-3 Aug 1906, 1 Mar 1918, 27 May 1940; *Argus*, 23 July-3 Aug 1906, 16, 17 June, 4 Sept 1916, 12 Mar, 30 Apr 1917, 1, 18 Mar 1918, 20 Mar 1919, 27 May 1940; *Bulletin*, 26 July, 2 Aug 1906; *Punch* (Melb), 27 July 1906, 27 Feb 1919; *Truth* (Melb), 28 July 1906; *Spectator* (Melb), 3, 10 Aug 1906, 5 Mar, 17 Sept 1915, 6 Mar 1918, 26 Mar 1919, 5 June 1940; Uniting Church in Aust, Synod of Vic, Archives, Melb; information from Mr G. Worrall *and* Mr and Mrs J. Johnson, Melb.　　　　JOHN LACK

WORRALL, JOHN (1861-1937), footballer, cricketer and journalist, was born on 21 June 1861 at Chinamans Flat, Maryborough, Victoria, seventh child of Joseph Worrall, miner, and his wife Ann, née Gaynor, both Irish born. Having attended the local state school, John went to Ballarat where he impressed the secretary of the Fitzroy club in the Victorian Football Association who induced him to move to Melbourne and to join the 'Maroons' in 1884. In his nine seasons until 1892 Worrall captained Fitzroy for seven years, represented Victoria in intercolonial matches and was named 'champion of the colony' in 1887 and 1890. A nuggetty and determined rover, he could soar for marks and kick accurately with either foot. Idolized by his supporters, he was commonly regarded as one of the three best Australian Rules footballers in the country.

Throughout summer he played cricket. In a career that totalled 140 first-class matches between 1883 and 1902, he scored 4660 runs (including seven centuries) at an average of 20.99, took 105 wickets at 23.10 (best figures 5 for 20) and held 101 catches. In 1896 for Carlton he hit an Australian record of 417 not out. He represented Victoria on 65 occasions, having 121 innings for 2407 runs at 20.93 (highest score 109), capturing 74 wickets at 22.09 and captaining the colony/State in sixteen games. He played eleven Test matches against England (1885-99), touring twice (1888 and 1899), for figures of 478 runs at 25.15, one wicket for 127 runs, and 13 catches. A right-handed opening bat whose belligerent drives could tear apart an attack, Worrall had tenacity on sticky wickets: in the 1899 Test at Headingley he made 76 of Australia's first innings total of 172. While on tour in July 1902 the Australian skipper, Joe Darling [q.v.8], contacted the Victorian Cricketers' Association, complaining that Worrall had informed an English umpire that two Australian Test bowlers—J. V. Saunders and M. A. Noble [qq.v.11]—were 'chuckers' who should be 'no-balled out of every game'. The V.C.A. delegates summarily banned Worrall from playing first-class cricket. He accepted the decision without demur and in 1909 was sufficiently reinstated to be appointed coach of the State's Colts.

Having assisted in founding the Victorian Football League in 1896, Worrall had joined Carlton as secretary/manager in 1902 and taken over the coaching of a club which in the previous five years had finished no higher than second last on the V.F.L. ladder. He began to rebuild the side by moulding young recruits—fast moving, high marking, big men —into a team that would develop a direct, long kicking game. As coach, he donned togs at training sessions, organized strict schedules, demanded unflinching courage and imposed stern discipline: 'Boys, booze and football don't mix'. Under Worrall, Carlton rose to dominance, reaching the finals in 1903-05 and winning triple premierships in 1906-08. With the triumphs came strife. In 1904 he survived a move to unseat him as secretary on allegations of mishandled gate-takings. In July 1909, after the players demanded to be paid more than 30 shillings a week and expressed resentment at his spartan constraints, Worrall resigned as coach. The feuding continued into 1910. He was accused of ballot-rigging and dumped as secretary when a 'reform' group swept to power on 20 March. Wounded by such treatment, he went to Essendon and coached the 'Same Old' to successive flags in 1911-12. When the Australian Football Council was formed in November 1905, Worrall was one of its two elected V.F.L. delegates. He was later made a life member of the A.F.C., as well as of the V.F.L. and the Fitzroy Football Club, but never of Carlton.

Already writing for the Sydney *Referee*, in 1916 Worrall joined the weekly *Australasian*. His knowledge, experience and judgement of football and cricket made him a respected authority on both codes. For over twenty years his columns were characterized by poised sentences and rich vocabulary; for all its partisanship, his direct prose was spiced with comparison, reminiscence and prediction, and conveyed a sense of drama. As early as 19 November 1932 Worrall saw menace in the English fast bowlers; by the 26th he wrote of their 'body attack', by 3 December of their intimidatory deliveries. He probably discussed the tourists' tactics with R. W. E. Wilmot and E. H. Buggy [q.v.7]; whichever of them coined the term 'bodyline', Worrall published it on 10 December thereby establishing the word in sporting idiom.

Short and stocky, broad shouldered and clean-shaven, Worrall had jowls in later life, but his intense eyes retained their twinkle. Tough and stubborn, passionately fond of sport without the sideshows, he did not make friends easily. With little time for backslappers, Jack counselled young players and did what he could to assist aspiring sports writers. He proved an inimitable raconteur about Dr W. G. Grace and the demon Spofforth [q.v.6]; while respecting (Sir) Donald Bradman, he remained convinced that Victor Trumper [q.v.] was Australia's greatest batsman. Worrall died at Fairfield on 17 November 1937. His wife Agnes Mary, née McCullum, whom he had married at Fitzroy with Victorian Free Church forms on 22 August 1893, survived him; there were no children. Champions turned out to his funeral at Heidelberg cemetery and flags at the Melbourne Cricket Ground flew at half-mast.

H. Buggy and H. Bell, *The Carlton story* (Melb, 1958); H. Larwood and K. Perkins, *The Larwood story* (Lond, 1965); B. Frindall (comp), *The Wisden book of Test cricket 1876-77 to 1977-78* (Lond, 1979); M. Sutherland et al, *The first one hundred seasons* (Melb, 1983); E. W. Swanton, *Gubby Allen* (Lond, 1985); J. Pollard, *The turbulent years of Australian cricket, 1893-1917* (Syd, 1987); C. Martin-Jenkins, *The complete who's who of Test cricketers* (Melb, 1987); W. S. Ramson (ed), *Australian National Dictionary* (Melb, 1988); *Australasian*, 19, 26 Nov, 3, 10, 17 Dec 1932, 7, 21 Jan, 27 May 1933, 27 Nov 1937.   JOHN RITCHIE

WRAGGE, CLEMENT LINDLEY (1852-1922), meteorologist, was born on 18 September 1852 at Stourbridge, Worcestershire, England, only child of Clement Ingleby Wragge, solicitor, and his wife Anna Maria, née Downing. Orphaned in early childhood, Clement was educated at Uttoxeter Grammar School, Staffordshire, and articled to a London solicitor. He went to sea, visited Sydney and in 1876 joined the South Australian surveyor-general's department. Wragge studied meteorology and in 1878 returned to Britain where he established weather observation stations, including one on Ben Nevis, Scotland, for which he received the gold medal of the Scottish Meteorological Society. Back in South Australia he set up similar stations at Walkerville and Mount Lofty in 1884, and founded the Meteorological Society of Australasia in 1886.

After reporting on Queensland's weather service, in January 1887 he was appointed meteorological observer in that colony's post and telegraph department. Wragge expanded the observation network, issued forecasts, pioneered research into tropical revolving storms in the south-west Pacific, lectured extensively and built an observatory at his Taringa home. He attended the world meteorology conference at Munich, Germany, in 1891 and was impressed by Brückner's ideas of planetary effects on climate; he also adopted current theory on the effects of sunspots on the weather and experimented with explosives to bring rain. When the Noumea-Queensland cable was completed in 1893, he brought New Caledonia into his network. By 1898 he had established weather stations in Tasmania (Mount Wellington and Hobart) and in New South Wales (Mount Kosciusko and Merimbula). He became involved in disputes with the New South Wales government over the cost of his projects, antagonized his colonial counterparts by issuing forecasts from the 'Chief Weather Bureau, Brisbane', and quarrelled with the premier (Sir) Robert Philp [q.v.11]. Wragge resigned and his bureau closed in June 1903.

A fellow of the Royal Geographical and

Royal Meteorological societies, Wragge published an *Australian weather guide and almanac* (1898), a short-lived serial called *Wragge: a meteorological, geographical and popular scientific gazette of the southern hemisphere* (1902), and *Romance of the South Seas* (1906). He was a fitness enthusiast and co-founder of the Brisbane Canoe Club; he turned to theosophy early and took up yoga and the occult in later life; he loved animals and was an ardent conservationist. His collection of ethnography, geology and natural history was donated to the city of Stafford, England.

Tall and thin, Wragge had an iron constitution and a 'mop of flaming red hair and explosive temper to match': his staff and opponents well knew that he posssessed the 'adjectival luxuriance of a bullocky'. In the professional field he was his own worst enemy, but he did encourage followers like Inigo Jones [q.v.9]. Credited with originating the use of classical, biblical and personal names for weather systems, he was nicknamed 'Inclement Wragge' for his rainfall forecasts.

Having advocated the creation of a national weather bureau, he was bitterly disappointed in 1907 when H. A. Hunt [q.v.9] became head of the Commonwealth Meteorological Bureau. Wragge went to Auckland, New Zealand, where he built an observatory. He revisited Queensland in 1913, but failed to win support for his proposed tropical cyclone research centre. Suffering a stroke, he died at his Birkenhead home, New Zealand, on 10 December 1922 and was buried nearby in the cemetery of the Church of Our Father. His wife and son survived him. Wragge exercised a significant influence on the foundations of Australian meteorology, even if his tempestuous career followed the growth, turbulence and eventual decay characteristic of the Coral Sea tropical revolving storms which so fascinated him.

W. J. Gibbs, *The origins of Australian meteorology* (Canb, 1975); *PD* (Qld), 1887, p 1958, 1892, p 624; *Qld Geog J*, 54, 1949-52, p 43; *Canb Hist J*, no 20, Sept 1987; *Telegraph* (Brisb), 1 July 1903; Wragge cuttings (RHSQ, Brisb).   PAUL D. WILSON

WRAY, FREDERICK WILLIAM (1864-1943), Anglican clergyman and military chaplain, was born on 29 September 1864 at Taradale, Victoria, sixth son of English-born Robert Mackie Wray, clerk, and his Irish wife Anne Rebecca, née Bury. Educated near Castlemaine, at 14 Fred joined the Victorian Volunteer Force and later the militia, serving a total of seven years. He was an undergraduate at Trinity College, University of Melbourne, in 1889-90 and decided to study for the Anglican ministry. Made deacon in 1894 and ordained priest on 22 December 1895 by Bishop F. F. Goe [q.v.9], Wray was minister at Dookie (1894-96) and Euroa (1896-1900). On 4 June 1897 he was appointed chaplain in the Victorian Military Forces.

An accomplished rower, marksman and Australian Rules footballer, the 'sporting parson'—nearly six feet (182.9 cm) tall, weighing 15 stone (95.3 kg) and 'a splendid type of a muscular Christian'—sailed as chaplain with Victoria's 2nd (Mounted Rifles) Contingent and arrived in South Africa on 5 February 1900. The contingent saw action in the Cape Colony, Orange River Colony and the Transvaal, then returned to Melbourne in December. Two bouts of enteric fever delayed Wray's repatriation until mid-1901. On 3 April 1902 he married Henrietta Olive Elizabeth Catford at Christ Church, Hawthorn. He resumed parish work, first at Yarrawonga (1902-13) and then at Rushworth, retaining his military appointment and gaining promotion to chaplain 2nd class in 1912.

On 1 December 1914 he joined the Australian Imperial Force and sailed for Egypt three weeks later. Allotted to the 4th Brigade, with particular responsibility for the 13th Battalion, he 'slipped ashore' at Gallipoli early on 26 April 1915 despite orders forbidding non-combatants from so doing. He became a familiar figure at the front line and earned the soldiers' gratitude. A fellow chaplain described him 'moving about in full view of the enemy' with 'a notebook and pencil in his hand . . . busy with the work of keeping a check on the names of the dead and a list of their personal effects'. On 3 May, after the 4th Brigade had suffered heavy losses, Wray described his duties: 'During the day I did field dressing, stretcher bearing, grave digging and filling and putting the bodies in'. Suffering from enteritis in August, he was successively taken to Malta, England and finally to Rushworth. For his service at Gallipoli he was mentioned in dispatches and appointed C.M.G.

Rejoining the 4th Brigade in Egypt in March 1916, Wray accompanied the 13th Battalion on operations in the desert and was again mentioned in dispatches. In June the brigade transferred to the Western Front, taking part in the battles of Pozières and Mouquet Farm in August. As at Gallipoli, Wray moved among the troops, giving spiritual and practical support; once more his work included assistance at dressing stations, burying the dead, sorting effects such as identity discs and pay books, and writing to the bereaved. On 14 October he wrote a letter critical of his Church for not providing as chaplains 'those specially fitted for work among men'. Posted in December as staff chaplain to Administrative Headquarters, A.I.F., London, he became senior chaplain early in 1917. Until his overseas service ended in August 1919, he administered chaplaincy affairs from London, making periodic visits to France. He was appointed C.B.E. in June.

Returning to civilian life, in 1920 Wray was appointed canon of Holy Trinity Cathedral, Wangaratta, and in 1928 rector of that parish. Erect and square-shouldered, he kept his soldierly bearing and traversed the Wangaratta area on foot or on a bicycle, never having learned to drive a motor car. He retained his interest in sport, and was active in the affairs of returned servicemen and in Freemasonry. Wray retired in 1935. Predeceased by his wife, he died on 18 November 1943 at his home in Sandringham, Melbourne, and was buried in the new Cheltenham cemetery. Two sons and three daughters survived him.

Aust Defence Dept, *Official records of the Australian military contingents to the war in South Africa*, P. L. Murray ed (Melb, 1911); C. E. W. Bean, *The story of Anzac*, 2 (Syd, 1924); T. A. White, *The fighting Thirteenth* (Syd, 1924); M. McKernan, *Padre* (Syd, 1986); *C of E Messenger* (Vic), 2 Dec 1901; *Church Standard*, 1 Dec 1916; *Australasian*, 20 Jan 1900; *Herald* (Melb), 19 Nov 1943; *Age*, 20, 22 Nov 1943; Wray war diary and letters from Sth African War *and* war diaries from World War I *and* undated contemporary press clippings (held by Mrs D. Lamont, Koonda, Vic).

DAVID DEXTER

WRAY, LEONORA (1886-1979), golfer, was born on 2 July 1886 at East Maitland, New South Wales, third child of Kenneth Mackenzie Wray, a sheriff's officer from Ireland, and his native-born wife Grace, née Edwards. When her family moved to Goulburn, Leonora saw the opening of the local golf club and began using a stick to hit a rubber ball 'golf style'. She attended Sydney Church of England Grammar School for Girls where Emmeline Du Faur and Olive King [qq.v.8,9] were fellow pupils; although golf was not a school sport, a cousin gave her a putter, her first club.

Living with her family in Sydney, Miss Wray became an associate member of the Australian Golf Club in 1904 and a council-member of the New South Wales Ladies' Golf Union. She was coached by a professional and rapidly developed into a cautious, deliberate player: 'never a chance thrown away, or a single shot played without a definite object'. Wearing a blouse with a stiff linen collar, a waisted jacket and an ankle-length skirt, and using only five clubs, she thrice won the State ladies' amateur championship in 1906-08, and the Australian title twice in 1907-08. She contracted typhoid fever in 1909 and did not play for the next decade.

Gradually recovering, Leo regained the national title in 1929 and the New South

Wales championship in 1930; her other titles included the western open (1931) and the northern open (1931-32). In 1929 she had partnered F. G. Murdoch to take the mixed foursomes championship. With a handicap of four in 1934, she continued to play with 'ease and accuracy' and maintained that a 'correct swing' was 'the secret of consistent golf'. She was champion woman player of the Australian club ten times between 1907 and 1938, and five times champion of the Royal Sydney Golf Club between 1924 and 1933.

A delegate to the inaugural meeting of the Australian Ladies' Golf Union in 1921, Miss Wray served as its secretary until 1923. She helped to establish the Tasman Cup competition with New Zealand in 1933 and was captain-manager of the touring team in 1937; she also managed the women's team that toured Great Britain in 1950. As president of the A.L.G.U. in 1954-59 and of the N.S.W.L.G.U. in 1957-65, she enthusiastically promoted junior golf. She was long-time associates' president of the Australian Golf Club and in World War II had worked for the Anzac Buffet Ladies' Auxiliary.

Commanding in 'stature and mien', Leo Wray had 'sharp eyes' and a deep, booming voice. An able raconteur who was known as the 'grand old lady' and the 'mother' of Australian golf, she inspired in younger players 'a mixture of fear and awe, respect and affection'. For many years she lived at Woollahra. Appointed M.B.E. in 1968, she died at Waverley on 4 April 1979 and was cremated with Anglican rites; her estate was sworn for probate at $174 143. Henry Hanke's portrait of Wray is held by the Australian Golf Club.

Aust Ladies' Golf Union golden jubilee championship, *Souvenir programme* (Syd, 1971); P. Perry (comp), *From green to gold* (Syd, 1975); *Syd Mail*, 22 Aug 1906, 21 Aug, 9 Oct 1907, 29 July 1908; *SMH*, 26 Nov 1929, 21 Oct 1937, 3 June 1938, 20 Feb 1940, 6 May 1950; *Sun News-ictorial*, 6 Dec 1965, 8 Jan 1968.

GILLIAN FULLOON

WREFORD, SIR ERNEST HENRY (1866-1938), banker, was born on 17 December 1866 in Adelaide, son of Henry Wreford, draper, and his wife Eliza, née Franklin. Educated at various preparatory schools and North Adelaide Grammar School, Wreford left at 16, with his wish to study law or literature thwarted, and joined the National Bank of Australasia, Adelaide, in 1882. After a series of postings to city and suburban branches, he found favour with J. G. Addison, the Adelaide assistant manager, who was impressed with his ability and mapped his subsequent career. In 1896-1906 Wreford was manager at Coolgardie on the Western

Australian goldfields before being sent in 1907 to the London office as secretary; in 1909 he was appointed acting assistant chief manager in Melbourne and succeeded Addison as chief manager (1912-35); he was elected a director immediately upon retiring in April 1935 and knighted that year.

The National increased its share of business under Wreford's steady stewardship, largely through mergers with the Colonial Bank of Australia in 1918 and the Bank of Queensland in 1920. He adhered to the banks' cartel agreements limiting competition for customers. Wary of the possibility of 'unfair' competition from the Commonwealth Bank of Australia, he resented the more aggressive practices of the Bank of New South Wales under its dynamnic general manager (Sir) Alfred Davidson [q.v.8]. Wreford prized his bank's reputation for soundness above fast growth and high profits. Yet, significant innovations were made, such as missions to the East and America to boost foreign business, a travel department and a safe deposit; women customers were wooed with their own banking section in the new Melbourne office. Like most bankers of his generation, Wreford resisted the growing influence of governments in matters of finance and banking, but, even as chairman of the Associated Banks of Victoria for various terms from World War I to the Depression, he was powerless to counter the rising tide. Known as 'The Chief' within the National Bank, Wreford was unpopular with his staff, despite doing much to improve their welfare particularly through the bank's provident funds. The establishment of a bank employees' union offended him.

Success and good looks sustained his considerable pride and vanity. Some 6 ft. 4 ins. (193 cm) tall, he used his commanding physical presence to good effect. A controlled person and sometime youthful preacher, he lived by a strict code of conservative values. He was a foundation member of the Australian national committee of the International Chamber of Commerce and a delegate to its 1925 conference in Brussels, and a member of the Melbourne Chamber of Commerce, the Royal Colonial Institute, various Victorian war loan committees and the Australian Red Cross Society, as well as chairman of the Australian committee of the Lady Northcote Child Emigration Funds. Literature, tennis, swimming and walking with the Wallaby Club provided his recreations. On 15 August 1903 he had married Louisa Nellie Estelle Fraser at St George's Anglican Cathedral, Perth. Wreford died on 10 May 1938 at Mount Eliza, Victoria, and was cremated. His wife, two sons and three daughters survived him. A portrait by W. B. McInnes [q.v.10] is held by the National Australia Bank, Melbourne.

G. Blainey, *Gold and paper* (Melb, 1958); R. F. Holder, *Bank of New South Wales*, 2 (Syd, 1970); C. B. Schedvin, *Australia and the great Depression* (Syd, 1970); Select cttee of the Senate appointed to consider and report upon the Central Reserve Bank bill, Evidence, *PP*(Cwlth Senate), 1929-31, 1, p 24; *A'sian Insurance and Banking Record*, Feb 1932, p 115, May 1935, p 388, June 1935, p 489; National Bank Staff Club, *National Bulletin*, May 1935, pp 1, 4; *Argus*, 11 May 1938; Wreford file (held by central records dept of National Aust Bank, Melb).

D. T. MERRETT

WREN, CHARLES WILLIAM (1856-1934), banker, was born on 15 November 1856 in North Adelaide, son of William John Wren, articled clerk, and his wife Mary Brodie, née Spence. Charles joined the English, Scottish and Australian Chartered Bank as exchange clerk in Adelaide in January 1872, rising rapidly to the joint position of accountant and branch inspector for South Australia in 1881. He moved to Melbourne in 1888 as inspector's accountant and on 6 March 1889 married Eleanor Dora Hall at St Stephen's Anglican Church, Elsternwick. Appointed resident inspector in New South Wales in 1901, Wren became the bank's Australasian general manager on 1 July 1909.

Three mergers with other banks during Wren's managership doubled business and branch numbers, and significantly improved the E.S.& A.'s position in relation to other trading banks. Wren was three times chairman of the Associated Banks of Victoria. He refused the first governorship of the Commonwealth Bank of Australia when it was offered to him by Prime Minister Andrew Fisher [q.v.8] in 1912; Wren recommended (Sir) Denison Miller [q.v.10] in his stead. Wren had an intimate knowledge of the E.S.&A. bank's affairs and served it with dedication and selflessness: on occasion, he would return to assist junior officers in balancing the ledgers. He was a 'valuable but over-constant letter writer' whose crabbed hand reflected his speed of thought. The London board came to know him well through his correspondence and through four visits he made while general manager. Its directors held him in high regard, but he strongly resented any interference by them in his management.

Wren's advancing age, coupled with its desire to retain his experience, caused the board to appoint E. E. L. O'Sullivan as a joint general manager in January 1928. While he did not favour a shared administration, O'Sullivan regarded Wren as the 'master' and as a 'valuable, close and personal friend'. In 1932 Wren's contract was extended by one year; he retired on 31 December 1933 after sixty-two years service, still 'remarkably well-preserved'.

A warm, affectionate and generous friend,

but a stern master, Wren was feared by customers and thought by some to be tactless and inclined to gossip. He dressed for dinner each night. Deeply interested in the theatre, he sometimes attended up to four performances a week. He was a passionate croquet player who was variously committeeman, patron, referee and umpire of the Victorian Croquet Association. Though a member of the Australian Club, Wren had been excluded from the Melbourne Club by the intervention of his predecessor Alexander Urquhart who had allegedly 'queered his pitch' there. On his retirement, Wren left for London by way of Europe. While in Italy an aneurysm necessitated the emergency amputation of his leg; he died on 19 April 1934 at the Clinica Bastianelli and was buried in Rome. His wife and daughter survived him. His estate was sworn for probate at some £58 000.

D. T. Merrett, *ANZ Bank* (Syd, 1985); *A'sian Insurance and Banking Record*, 21 Nov 1933, 21 May 1934; Aust and NZ Banking Group Ltd Archives, Melb.   T. J. HART

WREN, JOHN (1871-1953), entrepreneur, was born on 3 April 1871 at Collingwood, Melbourne, third son of illiterate though not indigent Irish immigrants John Wren, labourer, and his wife Margaret, née Nester. Leaving school at 12 to work in a wood-yard and then as a boot clicker, Wren supplemented his 7s. 6d. weekly wage by circulating betting cards, bookmaking and small-scale usury. Although short and 'bandy' from an ill-set fracture, he was a feisty 'scrapper', handy cricketer and prospective Collingwood footballer. Laid off work during the 1890s depression, Wren launched his Johnston Street totalizator in 1893 with a stake bolstered, so he boasted, by Carbine's 1890 Melbourne Cup victory and subsequent gambling coups. The 'tote' was later to net him £20 000 per annum. It was popular for its unique defences and scrupulous dealing in a suburb mistrustful of police and enthusiastic about betting. His demotic City Tattersalls Club (1903) drew attention to similarly illicit, though tolerated, punting in elite venues. Senator Andrew Dawson [q.v.8], formerly 'the world's first Labor premier', lectured there on 'theoretical socialism' with Wren in the chair.

That Wren became a local hero, generous to the needy—and the Catholic Church—enraged wowsers like W. H. Judkins [q.v.9] and Henry Worrall [q.v.]. The *Lone Hand* denounced this 'pestilent citizen' who drained the wages of 'infatuated workers', while Judkins condemned a 'Vesuvius of carnality ... greed ... animalism'. Undoubtedly Wren employed ex-criminals as henchmen, pun-

ished 'narks' and, under the lax police commissioner T. O'Callaghan [q.v.11], 'fixed' witnesses in gaming cases, though no one ever 'shelfed' him. Allegations that he corrupted Chief Secretary Sir Samuel Gillott and Judge Neighbour [qq.v.9,10] lacked foundation.

Action against 'totes' was also foiled by defective legislation which (Sir) Isaac Isaacs's [q.v.9] anti-gambling bill (1898) failed by one vote to repair. A nine-week police occupation of the 'tote' from the eve of the 1903 Melbourne Cup ended farcically with the last sentinels being bundled out as trespassers. Rumours that Wren must have been involved in the notorious bombing of David O'Donnell's [q.v.11] home were repudiated by the detective himself. Characteristically, however, when under personal attack, Wren led roughs to Hawthorn in 1905 to break up a George Swinburne [q.v.] election meeting. The latter's, and Judkins's, triumph came with (Sir) Thomas Bent's [q.v.3] Lotteries, Gaming and Betting Act (1906) which was passed after stonewalling by Frank Anstey [q.v.7] and Wren's lawyer David Gaunson [q.v.4]. By then a millionaire, Wren easily retreated to other diversifying interests. When Judkins died in 1912, Wren was 'the most generous donor' to a testimonial for this propagator of 'homely virtues'.

A sleazy reputation clung to Wren. While it is credible that he fixed the ageing 'Plugger' Martin's victory in the 1901 Austral Wheel Race, a similar charge about his £50 000 coup in Murmur's 1904 Caulfield Cup win is fanciful. The Victoria Racing Club's temporary refusal to accept Wren's nominations was based on competition for gamblers' shillings and distaste for his origin, associations and success. Wren's response was to buy into Richmond, Fitzroy and Ascot pony courses which he personally controlled and cleansed. His use of professional stewards was an innovation. There is no evidence that he had associations with the murderous tout 'Squizzy' Taylor [q.v.].

In 1910 Wren established the Victorian Trotting Association to reform a stagnant and corrupt sport, long before other States did the same. A typically audacious coup was to stage an 'Ascot Thousand' to replace the postponed Melbourne Cup in 1916. To stall the campaign against proprietary racing, he sold his Victorian interests in 1920 to the Victorian Racing and Trotting Association with (Sir) Gilbert Dyett [q.v.8] as secretary, but a select committee suggested that this action was a subterfuge. To Wren's chagrin, Premier Cain in 1947 established an independent control board. In Brisbane-Ipswich Wren owned six racecourses, including Doomben. A Queensland inquiry under a non-Labor government found in 1930 that, because proprietary racing was controlled by Wren, it was inherently corrupt. In 1948 Wren told a Commonwealth royal commission that he had bought Albion Park for £31 000, sold it for £450 000 and earned £300 000 from it. Wren owned the Belmont Park track in Western Australia, but it is unclear how involved he was in Sydney with J. J. Donohoe and Sir James Joynton Smith [qq.v.8,11]. After Murmur, Wren's own horses, carrying the Collingwood Football Club's magpie colours, were moderately successful. Garlin won the 1915 Doncaster, Pandect the 1940 Australian Jockey Club's Derby, Pure Fire the 1952 Victoria Racing Club and A.J.C. Sires' Produce stakes, but his Australian Cup winner, The Rover, failed by less than a length to win the 1921 Melbourne Cup and a plunge for £300 000. Wren was a cool loser.

He had entered boxing promotion in 1905. His Stadiums Ltd acquired R. L. Baker's [q.v.7] interests in 1915 and a near monopoly in eastern Australia. Under its enduring, loyal manager Richard Lean, who also ran Wren's cycling venue in Melbourne, the stadium was 'a harsh unimaginative enterprise' without statutory control. It dictated terms to boxers and repressed unionism, although there were handouts for derelicts like Ron Richards [q.v.11]. Locals were discouraged from seeking world titles abroad, but Wren had no part in Les Darcy's [q.v.8] nemesis. Stadiums Ltd's profits remained unknown, but boxing was not, as in the United States of America, run by gangsters. Wrestling, as elsewhere, degenerated into farce.

Wren's miscellaneous businesses, spread over thirty-one companies, nearly always using his associates' names rather than his own, had no corporate organization. His partners did not doubt his integrity. In 1904, with Sir Rupert Clarke [q.v.8], he joined the proprietors of the renovated Theatre Royal, Melbourne, and acquired freehold of the Criterion theatre and hotel, Sydney, receiving eventually £267 000 for their demolition. In addition to owning three suburban cinemas, he constructed with E. J. Carroll [q.v.7] and Frank Talbot the Melbourne Athenaeum Theatre. He purchased Morocco East, a grazing property in the Riverina, and, in the 1920s, two runs in Western Australia. One, Bidgemia, of 1 200 000 acres (485 628 ha), was sold lucklessly at the end of a nine-year drought. Wren speculated patiently and profitably in large tracts of marginal land in Sydney and Melbourne. He partnered E. G. Theodore [q.v.], Patrick Cody and Frank Packer in three lucrative Fiji gold-mines. Great Boulder Mines (Western Australia), Golden Plateau (Queensland) and a colliery at Newcastle were also successful, though not Roma oilfields with his friend Archbishop (Sir)

James Duhig [q.v.8], nor Watut goldfields in New Guinea.

Wren bought the Brisbane *Daily Mail* with Benjamin Nathan in 1915 and merged it with Sir Keith Murdoch's [q.v.10] *Courier* in 1933 as the *Courier-Mail*. On behalf of his and Cody's United Distillers Ltd, he lobbied 'patriotically' and successfully with James Scullin's [q.v.11] government for duties on fiercely competitive Scotch whisky. Australian Food Exporters Ltd (AFEX) and Barrett/Rowlands soft drink company were 'disasters'; Effron Yeast Pty Ltd was not. His Criterion restaurant opposite St Paul's Cathedral, Melbourne, yielded his estate £120 000 for freehold. He had a frock shop in Sydney and the franchise for Marigny Cold Wave cosmetics. Ultimately Wren's empire was 'hopelessly confused', partly because, according to his eldest son, he 'soft-heartedly stuck to too many drones as managers'. In Victoria his probate was to be valued at £1 003 946; in Queensland at £70 666. It took two and a half years to wind up his affairs.

Jack Lang [q.v.9], no friend of Wren (or of his associate Theodore), called him 'a champion wire-puller', but the extent of his political manipulations is impossible to gauge. Written evidence of them scarcely exists. The *Lone Hand* claimed knowledge of 'parasitism' from 1901 when Anstey allegedly became a 'client'. Wren was supposed to have influenced J. C. Watson's [q.v.] government of which Dawson was a member. Ultimately, in 1927 Anstey—evidently influenced by Theodore's election—resigned as deputy Federal parliamentary leader before accepting shares in Wren's New Guinea gold-mine. A royal commission in 1928 examined Wren (and others) to no effect in relation to a bribe paid to William Mahony to resign his Commonwealth parliament seat to make way for Theodore. Lang thought Scullin was 'a Wren man', but Scullin's biographer disdains such an idea—as did Tom Ryan's [q.v.11]. A. A. Calwell, an admirer of Wren, linked even the highly respected George Prendergast with Ned Hogan [qq.v.11,9] and Tom Tunnecliffe [q.v.] as 'Wren's man'. Justice Evatt was prepared to be seen at the football with him; (Sir) Robert Menzies appeared for him in litigation in 1947. Wren could telephone Prime Minister John Curtin to protest against wartime taxation, but got nowhere. His contributions to the electoral expenses of the idealistic Frank Brennan [q.v.7], for example, must have been routine, without any surety of reciprocal favours. Yet there is no doubt that Wren was co-broker in forming the Labor-supported Dunstan [q.v.8] government of 1935. Clearly some Labor and Country Party parliamentarians accepted favours and espoused his liquor and gambling interests, but his sanctions were limited. John Cain won party leadership despite eschewing Wren influence.

Wren's control over Melbourne's inner suburban politics was far from thorough, although branch stacking, rigged ballots, bogus trade unions, intimidation and jobbery were endemic. A mayor of Collingwood, Robert 'Sugar' Roberts, who reported to Wren on Sundays, was expelled from the Labor Party in 1925 for attempting to subvert Maurice Blackburn's [q.v.7] preselection for Fitzroy and for paying bribes to others to smear him as a 'communist'. Brennan was able to support Blackburn with impunity. Readmitted in 1929 and precipitately made Collingwood branch president, Roberts was still refused endorsement for municipal elections in 1935. Nothing comparable with Tammany Hall operated in Australia. Aside from protecting his own interests, Wren obviously enjoyed political fixing, as he did his popularity with sections of the working class. An eight-hour day procession gave 'Three Cheers for Jack Wren' as it passed City Tattersalls. He was often generous to strikers and gave £1000 to the waterside workers in 1928.

Enthusiastically supporting World War I, in 1915 Wren awarded £500 to Albert Jacka [q.v.9] as Australia's first Victoria Cross winner in that war and subsequently staked him in business. At 44, Wren joined the Australian Imperial Force, urged other sportsmen to do likewise, and became a corporal. He harangued his comrades against vice, set up a loan fund for them and improved their amenities before being discharged unfit in November 1915. He supported conscription, but spoke cogently on Irish independence, organizing the 1919 Irish Race Conference and fourteen Victoria Cross winners on white chargers for the triumphant 1920 St Patrick's Day march for Archbishop Mannix [q.v.10]; he had the event filmed and exhibited. Hibernians gave Wren an armchair embossed with *RUBHIN ABU* ('Wren to Victory'). His framed photograph hung in a back room at Raheen which Wren had offered to help to purchase for Mannix. Wren told Fr Hackett [q.v.9] that he had given £2 million to charitable causes, mainly Catholic. Donations were often anonymous. Because of his prejudice against higher learning, however, he did not contribute to the foundation of Newman College or to Hackett's Central Catholic Library. Wren's association with Mannix fanned the sectarian fears of Empire loyalists like Herbert Brookes and T. E. Ruth [qq.v.7,11] to new heights in 1917-22. 'Shall Wren be Crowned King?' asked one *Vigilant* headline. In the early 1940s Wren was persuaded to make an initial contribution to the Catholic Social Studies Movement, organized by B. A.

Santamaria, but withdrew support when he feared sectarianism would 'wreck the Labor Party he knew'. In 1948 the Catholic industrial grouper S. M. Keon excoriated Wren in the Victorian parliament in terms which would have delighted Judkins. Wren's Labor sympathies finally soured.

The Wrens had been disgraced in 1889 by the sentencing of an elder brother, Arthur, to flogging and imprisonment, in commutation of a death sentence, for aiding and abetting rape—unjustly, thought his family. The eldest brother, Joseph, went on binges. John was neither to drink, smoke, tolerate profanity, womanize, nor disown his brothers, who acquired substantial assets. Arthur's obituary in the *Argus* described him as philanthropic, popular and 'beloved by the poor of Collingwood'.

On 31 December 1901 at St Patrick's Catholic Cathedral, Melbourne, Wren married Ellen Mahon (d. 1968), a police constable's convent-educated daughter. After a honeymoon in New Zealand, his only trip abroad, he took her to a reconstructed Studley Hall, across the River Yarra, overlooking Collingwood, where they reared seven children (two others died in infancy) on an almost self-contained farmlet. Wren bedded in a sleep-out, showered at 6.30 a.m. in hot, then cold, water, and allowed the air to dry him. He ate spare, near-vegetarian meals, entertained infrequently and avoided business lunches, snapshots and publicity. He prayed daily on his knees, but did not formally practise Catholicism until his last years when he attended morning Mass. He wore suits purchased three at a time off-the-rack, and, disliking automobiles, usually walked to the city, occasionally meeting *en route* his neighbour Mannix. Wren's manner and speech remained those of his Collingwood past, but his sons attended Xavier College, Kew, and his four daughters Sacré Coeur Convent, Malvern. In spite of his stern patriarchy, theirs was, apparently, a contented home, though, according to his son, Wren 'never understood women'. Three daughters married in Europe; one notoriously associated with 'communists'. His eldest daughter Margaret studied violin overseas which led Wren to sponsor Fritz Kreisler's tour in 1925. Wren was more comfortable with his football club where, from World War I, he was premier patron but not, as believed, the virtual owner.

Self-made rather than self-educated, Wren pursued wealth and influence while retaining the values of the alienated rather than the 'improving' working class. Conspiratorial, aloof, taciturn, contemptuous of 'establishment opinion' and with a masterful grey-eyed stare, he was an apt subject for ethno-sectarian apocrypha. It was sensationally exploited in communist Frank Hardy's best-seller, *Power without glory* (1950), and its Australian Broadcasting Commission telecast (1976) in which even murders are imputed to him. Wren threw his copy into the wastepaper basket, but his sons chose, on gauche legal advice, to press an obsolescent criminal libel charge in respect of their mother's identification with Nellie West who seduces a tradesman, bears an illegitimate son, Xavier, the same name as Ellen's deceased infant, and is ostracized by her husband. Smartly defended, the case foundered on the prosecution's unwillingness to contest that West was Wren and therefore that Ellen was characterized. The jury supported the underdog, though the identifications were clear. Decades later, Hardy admitted that 'on balance' he did not think that Ellen was an adultress. The irreproachably pious and retiring Ellen was not upset by a verdict she foresaw. To a reporter, Wren simply mused: 'Not guilty! . . . Extraordinary'.

Wren and his cobber 'Jock' McHale [q.v.10], Collingwood's renowned coach, both suffered coronary occlusions following his 1953 premiership. Wren had bustled to get behind the Magpie goalposts for the last quarter. Survived by his wife, three daughters and two sons, he died in Mount St Evins hospital, Fitzroy, on 26 October. With Mannix presiding, the administrator of St Patrick's Cathedral celebrated Mass in hopeful white (not requiem black) vestments because it was the anniversary of the cathedral's consecration. Coadjutor-Archbishop Simonds and thirty priests assisted. Boys from Xavier preparatory school formed a guard of honour before the cortège proceeded to Boroondara cemetery. The diocesan *Advocate* praised Wren's charity, modesty and concern for freedom, citing his efforts on behalf of Fr Jerger [q.v.9]. At Wesley Church's Pleasant Sunday Afternoon, Rev. Irving Benson recalled Judkins's 'valiant fight for righteousness' and the 'crack of . . . [Wren's] whip in the corridors of parliament'. Calwell, a pallbearer at Wren's funeral, later wrote that Wren 'was a better Australian than his detractors' and had simply observed 'the principles of commercial morality'.

E. H. Sugden and F. W. Eggleston, *George Swinburne* (Syd, 1931); J. T. Lang, *I remember* (Syd, 1956); F. Hardy, *The hard way* (Lond, 1961); N. Brennan, *John Wren* (Melb, 1971); A. A. Calwell, *Be just and fear not* (Melb, 1972); M. Cavanough, *The Caulfield Cup* (Syd, 1976); E. H. Buggy, *The real John Wren* (Melb, 1977); P. Corris, *Lords of the ring* (Melb, 1980); R. Stremski, *Kill for Collingwood* (Syd, 1986); J. O'Hara, *A mug's game* (Syd, 1987); *PD* (LA Vic), 16 Dec 1898, 13, 25-27 Sept 1906, 28 July 1948; *PP* (Cwlth), 1926-28, 4, p 1235; *PP* (Qld), 1929-30, 2nd S, 2, p 1289; *Lone Hand*, May 1907; *Labour Hist*, May 1981; *J of Religious Hist*, June 1978; *Advocate* (Melb), 18 Nov 1893, 6 May 1899, 8 Dec 1900, 9 June 1906, 8 Sept 1919, 29 Oct 1953; *Argus*, 26 Feb, 8 Mar 1889, 27 July 1935, 3 June 1947, 28, 29 July 1948, 27 Oct 1953; *Bulletin*, 27 Oct, 1 Dec 1904, 4 Oct 1906, 26 May 1948; *Vigilant*, 1 July 1920; *SMH*, 29 Sept 1921, 24, 26 Dec 1983; D. W. Rawson, The organisation of the Australian Labor Party 1916-41 (Ph.D. thesis, Univ Melb, 1954); Hackett papers (Society of Jesus Provincial Archives, Hawthorn, Melb); *Power without glory*: scrap-book of news-clippings re libel charge (LaTL); research papers of G. Browne, Windsor, Melb; information from Messrs S. M. Keon*, J. P. Loughnan, Richmond, J. F. Wren, Jolimont, and L. McCarthy, MDHC Archives, Melb.

JAMES GRIFFIN

WRIGHT, COLIN WILLIAM (1867-1952), studmaster, was born on 10 October 1867 at Oxley, near Brisbane, son of John Wright, a Cornish-born farmer, and his wife Ellen, née McColl, from Scotland. Colin spent his early life on his father's dairy farm at Caboolture; later, with his brother James, he successfully dealt in cattle at Kilcoy. Switching to cattle-breeding, he bought Jellinbah station (695 square miles, 1800 km²) on the Mackenzie River, near Blackwater. Having sold it in 1911, he bought and sold Nottingham Downs, a sheep-property near Hughenden. After a world tour, in 1914 Wright took up Waverley, a 50 000-acre (20 235 ha) holding near St Lawrence, 125 miles (200 km) north of Rockhampton. Adding neighbouring properties, he trebled Waverley's area and made it capable of carrying 10 000 cattle.

When drought destroyed half his Hereford herd in 1926, Wright decided to seek a breed better adapted to the region. He became interested in the characteristics exhibited by beasts of Zebu (Brahman) or *Bos indicus* blood —especially their resistance to drought and tick, and their ability to exist and even thrive on poor quality pasture—and experimented with several part-Zebu animals which he brought from New South Wales. By the time these cattle had produced award-winning offspring, Wright had already made his decision. With a syndicate in 1933 he imported nineteen Zebus, chosen in the United States of America by Dr R. B. Kelley of the Council for Scientific and Industrial Research. He used the animals to produce pure Zebus, as well as mating them with Herefords.

Many cattlemen, like J. L. Wilson [q.v.], were at first sceptical and angry: they feared that Zebu crossbreeding would 'fill the country with mongrels and . . . do great damage to the cattle industry of Australia'. As late as 1939, after Wright's Waverley steers had won prizes for their carcasses, the Queensland minister for agriculture, F. W. Bulcock, said that 'the best things to do with our Zebus was to round them up and shoot them'. Other cattle-breeders, however, followed Wright's example and he lived to see central Queensland's cattle industry accept new animals for an unchangeable environment, rather than forcing existing ones to endure inimical conditions. Fittingly, in 1946 Wright became the first patron of the Australian Zebu Society.

A Broadsound Shire councillor for twenty-three years, Wright served three terms as its chairman. He was a generous benefactor to charities and was valued as a sincere man of firm convictions and good sense. He died, unmarried, at Rockhampton on 14 December 1952 and was cremated. His estate was sworn for probate at £162 636. The Colin Wright Laboratory at the University of Queensland school of veterinary science was opened in 1963.

I. Gibson, *Australian tropical beef cattle* (Townsville, 1963); L. McDonald, *Cattle country* (Brisb, 1988); *Qld Country Life*, 24 Dec 1952; *Procs of Roy Soc Qld*, 98 (1987), p 1; *Rockhampton Morning Bulletin*, 17 Dec 1952.   BRIAN F. STEVENSON

WRIGHT, DAVID McKEE (1869-1928), poet and journalist, was born on 6 August 1869 at Ballynaskeagh, Down, Ireland, second son of Rev. William Wright (d. 1899), a missionary working in Damascus, and his wife Ann (d. 1877), née McKee. David was educated locally at Glascar School, and from 1876 in England at Mr Pope's School and the Crystal Palace School of Practical Engineering, London. Migrating to New Zealand in 1887, he worked as a rabbiter on stations in Central Otago, and wrote prose and verse about station life for major provincial newspapers. He began divinity studies in 1896 at the University of Otago and next year was awarded a Stuart prize for poetry.

In charge of the Emmanuel Church, Oamaru, from April 1898, Wright married Elizabeth Couper at Dunedin on 3 August 1899; their son David was born in 1900, but the marriage did not last. Wright's pro-Boer sermons lost him patronage and he resigned as minister. Appointed in May to Newtown Congregational Church, Wellington, in 1901 he became minister of the Congregational Church at Nelson, but resigned on an issue of conscience in June 1905 and soon after was declared bankrupt. His journal, *Te Rauparaha, or the Nelson Times*, continued irregularly from 1905 until he joined the *New Zealand Mail* in 1907 as parliamentary reporter. Between 1896 and 1900 he had published four collections of ballads; from 1906 he contributed to New Zealand journals and to the Sydney *Bulletin*.

He moved to Sydney in May 1910 and wrote for the *Sun, Bulletin* and (*Australian*) *Worker*. As 'Maori Mac', Wright contributed numerous stories (many on Maori-Pakeha themes) and plays to the *Bulletin, Lone Hand* and other magazines; for the *Worker*, he chiefly wrote as 'Glen', 'Historicus' and 'W'. Under such pseudonyms as 'George Street', 'Pat O'Maori', 'Mary McCommonwealth' and 'Curse o' Moses', he published some 1600 poems in the *Bulletin* between 1906 and 1927. From emphasizing back-blocks themes, he came to represent social and political issues.

After 1913 Wright also wrote on Irish themes; some of his work was collected in *An Irish heart* (1918), on which his Australian reputation long rested. During World War I he defended Ireland and contributed pro-conscription editorials to the *Bulletin*. He edited its 'Red Page' from 1916 until 1926 when he fell out with S. H. Prior [q.v.11]. Wright's writing contained much that is facetious, satiric and elegiac. As an editorial consultant for Angus and Robertson [qq.v.7,11], he controversially edited Henry Lawson's [q.v.10] selected (1918) and collected poems (1925). Wright clashed with Jack Linsday in 1920-25 over the Lindsays' [qq.v.10] interpretation of Shakespeare and the ancient Greeks.

A friend of Christopher Brennan, Randolph Bedford, Frank Morton [qq.v.7,10] and Lawson, Wright was a 'charming, elongated Irishman with long grey bishop-like hair; perpetually reciting poetry and waving long arms and lean fingers'. In 1912-18 he lived with the writer 'Margaret Fane' (Beatrice Florence Osborne, d. 1962) in Sydney; they had four sons. From 1918 Wright lived with Zora Cross [q.v.8] in Greeanawn, a house at Glenbrook, Blue Mountains. He grew roses, and collected gems, china, books and postage stamps.

Suffering from angina pectoris, Wright died suddenly on 5 February 1928 at Glenbrook and was buried with Anglican rites in Emu Plains cemetery. He was survived by Zora, their two daughters, and his sons. His novel 'Luta of Lutetia' was serialized in the *Sydney Morning Herald* in 1930. A gifted speaker, Wright was remembered for his truthfulness and outstanding generosity to fellow writers. Harold Mercer believed that 'something of the parson always clung' to him.

DNB, vol 21; U. Wright, *The Rev. Dr. William Wright of Damascus* (Belfast, Nth Ireland, 1986); *NZ Life*, 10 Feb 1928, p 21; *New Triad* (Syd), Mar 1928, p 52; *Bulletin*, 12 May 1910, 15, 29 Feb 1928; *Worker* (Brisb), 3 Oct 1910; Z. Cross, unpublished letter to W. P. Hurst, 25 May 1928 (LaTL); information from Mrs A. Hersey, Glenbrook and Mr U. McK. Wright, Tregear, NSW, Mr K. E. McK. Wright, Papakura, NZ, Mr U. S. D. Wright,

Rathfriland, Nth Ireland, Mrs D. Newman, Holt, Norfolk, and Mrs D. Bramwell, Stratford-on-Avon, Warwickshire, Eng.   MICHAEL SHARKEY

WRIGHT, EMILY HILDA RIX; see NICHOLAS, EMILY

WRIGHT, JOHN ARTHUR (1841-1920), engineer and railway commissioner, was born on 25 November 1841 at Dover, Kent, England, son of John Wright, civil engineer, and his wife Mary Boylan, née Holahan. Educated at Queen Elizabeth School, Cranbrook, and at Clapham Grammar School, he was articled to Joseph Cubitt. Completing his indentures, Wright embarked on an engineering practice in Wales and then worked in Russia, Spain and France, mainly on railway and bridge construction projects. On 28 January 1870 he married Katherine Whitington at the parish church, Tuxford, Nottinghamshire.

Declining the post of engineer-in-chief in Brazil, in 1885 he was appointed director of public works, engineer-in-chief and commissioner of railways in Western Australia; he arrived in the *Penola* with his wife, children and servants in June. His appointment as commissioner carried with it a seat on the Executive Council in which he served from July 1885 to December 1890. Throughout his extended term of four and a half years he was responsible for an extensive construction programme which included the Great Southern Railway and work at the mouth of the Swan River (later Fremantle harbour). Wright retired on 31 December 1889 with a reputation for ability, energy and thoroughness. Following the introduction of responsible government in 1890, he was nominated to the Legislative Council; a member of that House from December 1890 to June 1894, he was a Western Australian representative at the National Australasian Convention in Sydney in 1891.

Having moved to Albany, Wright was associated with a printing firm which first published the Albany *Observer* in May 1890. In that year he was appointed manager of the West Australian Land Co. which, in return for large land grants, had contracted with the government in 1884 to construct and maintain a railway from Beverley to Albany and to introduce migrants. In 1897 the company sold its assets to the state. Wright had been retained in 1890 by the government as a consulting engineer; he took a further part in the construction of the G.S.R. and named the railway townships of Cranbrook and Tenterden after places in the county of his birth.

From 1896 he was acting resident magistrate at Albany and permanent resident magistrate in 1899-1908. Although, as commissioner, he had aroused hostility in Albany (being burnt in effigy during the citizens' acrimonious level-crossing dispute with the land company), he was a popular magistrate. Wright and his family participated in local functions and the residency became the focal point of the town's social life. A prominent Freemason, he was president of the Albany Turf Club and inaugurated its race week which grew into a traditional event. Survived by his wife, daughter and two sons, he died on 24 February 1920 at Albany and was buried in the local cemetery with Anglican rites.

D. S. Garden, *Albany* (Melb, 1977); *Herald* (Melb), 13 June 1885; *Possum*, 19 Nov 1887; *West Australian*, 1 Nov, 20 Dec 1889; *Inquirer*, 6 Nov 1889; personal information.   PAT BUNNY

WRIGHT, JOHN CHARLES (1861-1933), Anglican archbishop, was born on 19 August 1861 at Bolton, Lancashire, England, son of Rev. Joseph Farrall Wright, vicar of Christ Church, Bolton, and his wife Harriet, née Swallow. John was educated at Manchester Grammar School before proceeding as a scholar to Merton College, Oxford (B.A., 1884; M.A., 1887; D.D., 1909). Made deacon on 31 May 1885, he was ordained priest on 20 June 1886.

His tutor at Merton was E. A. Knox, a leading conservative Evangelical. Wright exhibited loyalty to his mentor at Merton and as Knox's curate (1885-88) at the Leicestershire parish of Kibworth Beauchamp. He strongly supported Knox's enforcement of ecclesiastical law and order, a characteristic that was to be shown later in his own career. After a curacy (1888-93) in the parish of Bradford, Wright was incumbent (1893-95) of Ulverston, Lancashire. On 5 October 1893 in St Peter's Church, Bournemouth, Hampshire, he married Dorothy Margaret Isabel, daughter of Colonel the Honourable Ivo de Vesci Fiennes and granddaughter of the 16th Baron Saye and Sele.

As an able Evangelical, Wright served at St George's Church, Leeds, from 1895 until Knox (then bishop of Manchester) appointed him in 1904 residentiary canon of Manchester, his personal chaplain and rector of St George's, Hulme. Promoted archdeacon early in 1909, he endorsed Knox's theological conservatism, but shared with other younger Evangelicals a wish to embrace modern scholarship. He chaired the 'Group Brotherhood' (later Anglican Evangelical Group Movement) which had been founded in 1906 to establish prayer and study groups for considering pressing social and theological issues. Wright published *Thoughts on modern Church life and work* (London, 1909).

Impressed by Wright's acquaintance with the needs of a large city, by his progressive outlook and by his strong Evangelical connexions, in 1909 the synod of the diocese of Sydney elected him to succeed Archbishop Saumarez Smith [q.v.11]. Wright promptly accepted, was consecrated bishop in St Paul's Cathedral, London, on 24 August and reached Sydney on 13 November. He immediately impressed people with his dignity. Encountering him in episcopal garb, the poet Kenneth Slessor described Wright: 'his face had a rosy Friesian serenity, his hair was a nimbus of saintly silver and his voice was as rich as pomegranates'.

Soon demonstrating that, while a convinced Evangelical, he believed in a much wider spectrum of opinion in the Anglican Church, Wright showed that he would be a bishop of all. In 1910 he appointed men who endorsed his own moderate views as dean of Sydney (Albert Talbot [q.v.]) and as principal of Moore Theological College (David Davies). Wright's pluralism was no invitation to license. He was foremost a constitutional administrator who saw his role as being to administer and enforce the laws of the Church, not to make them. That year he refused to licence a clergyman to the vacant rectorship of St James's, King Street, unless he agreed not to wear the chasuble. To many, this was an issue of doctrine, not dress; to Wright, it was a question of church law. Amid much acrimony, he prevailed and the chasuble disappeared from St James's. His stance changed the churchmanship of Sydney diocese by scuttling the influence of Anglo-Catholicism. From 1910 he required all clergy licensed in Sydney to agree not to wear the chasuble; only one clergyman in Sydney was later to wear it. Wright had ensured an Evangelical future for his diocese.

His style was to oversee rather than direct the rapidly expanding diocese; he sought to be chief pastor, not the Church's managing director, and to make churchmen individually, and the diocese as a whole, assume responsibility for their own situations. Not all appreciated the wisdom of such leadership.

Wright's widespread pastoral care was most evident during World War I when, without fanfare, he made pre-dawn walks to the wharfs to farewell every troop-ship; he wrote letters of welcome to all soldiers who returned. Regarding the war as holy, he spoke out in favour of conscription during the referenda, seeing it as a moral rather than a political issue. He contracted pneumonic influenza in 1919 and suffered bouts of respiratory illness for the rest of his life which often forced him to retreat from Sydney's humidity.

Renowned for his even temper, kindness, tolerance and charitable tongue, Wright was provoked to passionate anger by the Royal Easter Show opening on Good Friday; he conducted annual public protests to (Sir) Samuel Hordern [q.v.9], chairman of the Royal Agricultural Society of New South Wales. The show continued to open on that day.

Having been elected primate of Australia in 1910 by his fellow bishops, Wright demonstrated his capacity for holding together people of diverse views and persuading them to co-operate as the Australian Church earnestly sought a new constitution that would bring with it autonomy from England. Twice, in 1926 and 1932, it seemed that agreement had been reached, but to no avail. After the 1932 constitutional convention of the Church, a 'dead-tired' Wright believed that a new constitution was only months away. Now, he told Archbishop Lang of Canterbury, 'I can sing my Nunc Dimittis'. On 24 February 1933 Wright died while visiting his daughter at Christchurch, New Zealand; survived by his wife, son and three daughters, he was buried in South Head cemetery, Sydney. His portrait by Charles Gundall is in St Andrew's Cathedral chapter house and another by Ethel Stephens at Bishopscourt, Sydney.

E. A. Knox, *Reminiscences of an Octogenarian* (Lond, 1934); K. Slessor, *Bread and wine* (Syd, 1970); S. Judd and K. Cable, *Sydney Anglicans* (Syd, 1987); *Syd Diocesan Mag*, 1 Apr 1933, p 11; *Aust Church Record*, 2, 16 Mar 1933; *Church Standard* (Syd), 3 Mar 1933; *Church Times* (Lond) and *Church Record* (Eng), 3 Mar 1933; *Daily Telegraph* (Syd), 19 May 1915; *SMH*, 26 Oct 1916, 25 Feb 1933; S. Judd, Defenders of their faith: power and party in the Anglican diocese of Sydney, 1909-1938 (Ph.D. thesis, Univ Syd, 1984); Davidson *and* Lang papers (Lambeth Palace Lib, Lond).

STEPHEN E. JUDD

WRIGLEY, LESLIE JAMES (1875-1933), educationist, was born on 22 July 1875 at Richmond, Melbourne, son of James Wrigley, bookbinder, and his wife Sarah Jane, née Bedggood, both English born. Educated at the local primary school and at Wesley College, where he was dux in 1892, Wrigley graduated with honours from the University of Melbourne (B.A., 1894; M.A., 1896). After teaching at several private schools in Victoria, he studied at the London Day Training College (diploma of pedagogy, 1904) and at the University of Jena, Germany. He lectured at the former institution and at Bangor College, Wales, before returning to Melbourne in 1907 as senior master of modern languages at Wesley College. There he introduced a teacher-training scheme. On 4 April 1908 he married English-born Florence Adelaide

Willmoth at Elsternwick with Methodist forms. She was later a foundation member, honorary secretary (1915-18) and honorary treasurer (1923-24) of the Lyceum Club.

Having joined the Education Department in 1909, Wrigley was appointed principal of the University Practising School which opened next year and admitted twenty-seven diploma of education students. He required trainees to take classes and attend demonstration lessons. The school won esteem for its standards and innovative teaching. Wrigley was also vice-principal of the Melbourne Training College and chief lecturer in education at the university. In 1913 he extended the diploma course to a third year of academic training, thereby enabling participants to graduate in arts or science.

In December 1914 Wrigley resigned from University High School (as the practising school was known after 1913) to become an inspector of secondary schools. From 1915, as senior inspector, he assisted M. P. Hansen [q.v.9], the chief inspector. As chairman of the schools board's modern languages committee, Wrigley framed the intermediate and leaving certificate courses in ancient and modern languages and in history.

Appointed to the faculty of education in 1923, he took over as principal of the Melbourne Teachers' College in February 1927; following the death of John Smyth [q.v.], in November Wrigley became professor and dean of education. Unassuming and kindly, though 'alarmingly rapid in speech', he was tall, fair and very thin: his wiry frame embodied energy and a tremendous capacity for work; his rimless pince-nez enhanced his reserved, scholarly appearance.

While the quiet industriousness with which Wrigley guided the college through the Depression years silenced those who had questioned his suitability for the post, he was realistic enough to acknowledge that economic stringencies had driven his 'dream of a new training college building to the limbo of empty visions'. He remodelled the diploma of education course, and also acted as chairman of the schools board and censor of films.

Worn down by his many responsibilities, early in 1932 Wrigley sailed with his wife to England. On 24 July he was seriously injured when his thigh-bone was fractured in a car accident. A long convalescence delayed his return until March 1933 and he insisted on paying the salaries of lecturers who took his classes in his absence. Despite continuing discomfort, he came back to work and accepted membership of the professorial board in April. At Bethesda private hospital, Richmond, on 12 July 1933 Wrigley died of postoperative pneumonia. After a service in Queen's College chapel, he was buried in Springvale cemetery. A plaque to his memory

was placed in the music room at the college. His wife survived him; they had no children.

E. Sweetman, *A history of the Melbourne Teachers' College and its predecessors* (Melb, 1939); A. Hoy, *A city built to music* (Melb, 1961); Education Dept (Vic), *Vision and realisation*, L. J. Blake ed, 1 (Melb, 1973); J. M. Gillison, *A history of the Lyceum Club* (Melb, 1975); D. S. Garden, *The Melbourne teacher training colleges* (Melb, 1982); *PP* (Vic), 1910, 2, p 93; *Univ High School Record*, (nd, 1911?), Christmas 1912, 6, Christmas 1914, 7, June 1915; Melb Teachers' College, *Trainee*, Nov 1930; *Education Gazette and Teachers' Aid* (Vic), 24 Aug 1933; *Argus*, 4 Oct 1911, 13 July 1933; *Age*, 13 July 1933; G. A. Reid, The origins and early history of the state secondary school teachers in Victoria, 1872-1926 (M.Ed. thesis, Univ Melb, 1968); Univ Melb Archives.   JEFFREY ROBINSON

WUNDERLICH, ERNEST (HENRY CHARLES) JULIUS (1859-1945), FREDERICK OTTO (1861-1951), and ALFRED (1865-1966), manufacturers, were born on 16 May 1859, 28 June 1861 and 8 July 1865 at Islington, London, sons of Charles Frederick Wunderlich, clerk and later indigo merchant, and his German wife Caroline, née Schmedes. Ernest began his education at Percy House College, London, and the Bender Institute, Weinheim, Germany. In the early 1870s the family moved to Vevey, Switzerland, where the brothers attended the public school and went mountaineering—Otto later climbed the Matterhorn.

From the age of 16 Ernest studied architectural and mechanical drawing at the École Polytechnique, Lausanne. After being apprenticed to an engineer at Vevey, in 1878 he became a clerk and travelling salesman for a London firm and indulged his love of music and theatre. To benefit his health, in 1881 he went to South Africa with agencies for pianos, but economic setbacks and the loss of his wares in a fire forced him to return to London in 1884. Otto, a graduate of the Université de Lausanne (Bach. es Lettres, 1880), came to London to study medicine at St Bartholomew's Hospital (L.R.C.P., M.R.C.S., 1885; Dip.Pub. Health R.C.P.S., 1889) and practised in that city.

In London Ernest met Fanny Amalia Hoesch (d. 1942), a talented pianist and graduate of the Conservatorium of Music, Cologne, and married her at Burtscheid, Germany, on 15 May 1885. They arrived in Sydney in July. He worked as a manufacturers' agent, advertising for a time as a wine and spirit merchant. Having imported stamped zinc mansard windows for a Sydney builder, he turned to German stamped metal ceilings and erected some of his earliest imports in Sydney Town Hall and in the piano showrooms of O. C. Beale and W. H. Paling [qq.v.7,5].

Joined by his brother Alfred in 1887, Ernest took out his first patent for 'an improved ceiling' in April 1888. They sold their patents in December 1889 to W. H. Rocke & Co. of Melbourne who had established a ceiling factory at Redfern, Sydney; Ernest became manager in Melbourne and Alfred in Sydney. Late in 1892 the Sydney branch became insolvent: the brothers redeemed their patents, raised £10 000 and formed the Wunderlich Patent Ceiling & Roofing Co. Ltd (incorporated in 1904). By 1897 Wunderlichs advertised as sole agent for imported Marseilles tiles. On 27 March that year in Sydney Alfred married with German Lutheran forms Blanche Marguerite Guex, daughter of a Swiss banker.

Otto, 'The Doctor', reached Sydney in 1900. A formidable man, he specialized in the administrative, technical and scientific aspects of the company. He set up an improved costing system, remodelled the works, standardized manufacture, introduced better selling methods and deputed many tasks that had previously devolved on the principals. In June 1908 the Wunderlichs and Rocke united to form Wunderlich Ltd with nominal capital of £200 000; the three brothers became directors for life; W. L. Baillieu and Theodore Fink [qq.v.7,8] were among the Melbourne board-members. That year Wunderlich claimed to be the first Australian firm to introduce a 44-hour week without a pay reduction. The company opened branches in all States and in Wellington, New Zealand. Though terracotta products continued to be imported, from 1910 they were also produced at the Wunderlich works at Brunswick, Melbourne. In 1913 Embosteel Ltd was absorbed. In addition to starting a profit-sharing scheme for employees in 1914, Otto instigated other improvements for the health and betterment of the staff. In the early years, however, the firm preferred to employ boys from private schools and discriminated against Catholics.

Ernest, 'The Chief', remained chairman until 1945, but was content to leave the everyday running of the business to his brothers while he pursued cultural interests. An enthusiastic musician and composer, he criticized Percy Grainger's [q.v.9] 'free' music and published an album of songs and numerous piano pieces, some showing the influence of J. S. Bach. Ernest helped to establish the New South Wales State Conservatorium of Music and endowed exhibitions there; his friends included Henri Verbrugghen [q.v.], Joseph Bradley and W. A. Orchard [qq.v.7,11].

As a trustee and president (1926), Ernest tried to modernize the Australian Museum, Sydney, and founded its magazine in 1921; he donated a group of Aboriginal figures executed by Rayner Hoff [q.v.9] and a number of Egyptian artefacts, and in 1939 gave the museum his library of books on archaeology and anthropology. An able amateur astronomer and a fellow of the Royal Astronomical Society, London, he set up an observatory at his holiday home at Gunnamatta Bay, Port Hacking, which in 1924 he placed in trust for the New South Wales branch of the British Astronomical Association, of which he was president. He belonged to the Athenaeum and New South Wales clubs. His other recreations comprised boating, deep-sea fishing and entertaining international visitors (including the singer Lotte Lehmann and tennis player Jean Barotra). Like his brothers, he travelled extensively overseas. His autobiography, *All my yesterdays*, with a foreword by Neville Cardus, was published in 1945. Survived by his only son, Ernest died on 11 April 1945 at Bondi Junction and was cremated without a service. His estate was sworn for probate at £27 597.

Despite having to contend with anti-German hysteria, the Wunderlichs had survived World War I, building a new tile factory at Rosehill and a ceiling factory at Cabarita to make asbestos cement sheets from the company's mines at Barraba and Beaconsfield, Tasmania. Strong promotion was a feature of the firm's expansion in the 1920s: attractive catalogues and booklets were produced by artists and designers, notably William Dobell. During World War II the firm produced Wirraway cowlings, food cans and service badges for the war effort; Wunderlich also supplied building materials for post-war reconstruction.

On 31 December 1904 Otto had married Eva Francie Marion Ladd at the manse of St Luke's Presbyterian Church, Redfern; they were to have three sons and a daughter before she divorced him in April 1917. He later married Nance Annie Kaganski. Otto published *Accountancy in modern business* (1927), a *Technological guide to the private exhibition of arts and crafts in the Wunderlich showroom* (1932) and, privately, a translation in verse of the mediaeval French epic, *La chanson de Roland*. Survived by his wife, and by a son of his first marriage, he died on 12 May 1951 in Sydney and was cremated.

Alfred was probably the most accessible and least forbidding of the brothers. Meticulous in his actions, he had wide business interests: chairman of Wunderlich Ltd from 1945, he was a director of Meggit Ltd, Manufacturers' Mutual Insurance Ltd, Federal Match Co. Ltd, Michael Nairn & Co. (Aust.) Pty Ltd and Linoleum Holdings Ltd, and president of the New South Wales Chamber of Manufactures and the Associated Chambers of Manufactures of Australia (1911-12).

He belonged to the New South Wales Club and the Athenaeum, Melbourne, enjoyed dominoes, fencing and swimming, and sculled on Sydney Harbour until he was 80. President (from 1922) of the Royal Philharmonic Society of Sydney, he had a fine bass voice and sang regularly in its chorus as well as solo. Alfred loved French culture and worked devotedly for the Alliance Française in Sydney; in 1933 he received the gold medal of its Parisian headquarters and next year was appointed chevalier of the Légion d'honneur. For all but the last few years he went regularly to the Redfern works. At the age of 101 he died at his Centennial Park home on 12 July 1966 and was cremated with Anglican rites. His daughter and two of his three sons survived him.

Wunderlich's success owed much to the brothers' paternalistic attitude to their workforce which was rewarded by loyalty, a tradition of quality work and long service. The firm's products enhanced the interiors of many homes and public buildings, and its red roofing tiles and fibro sheets transformed the cultural landscape of suburban Australia. James Hardie (Asbestos) Ltd took over Wunderlich Humes Asbestos Pipes Pty Ltd in 1964; in 1969 Wunderlich Ltd was taken over by the Colonial Sugar Refining Co. Many records and artefacts from the old Redfern works are preserved in the Power House Museum, Sydney.

G. Forbes, *History of Sydney* (Syd, 1926); Wunderlich Ltd, *Forty years of Wunderlich industry, 1887-1927* (Syd, 1927), and published trade catalogues on building materials (Syd, 1922-50); F. Clune, *Saga of Sydney* (Syd, 1961); R. Strahan, *Rare and curious specimens* (Syd, 1979); S. Bures, *The House of Wunderlich* (Syd, 1987); *Aust Museum Mag*, 16 Apr 1935, p 340; *Australasian*, 16 Mar 1912, p 616; *SMH*, 28 May, 16 Sept 1921, 6 Apr 1922, 9 Jan, 27 June 1924, 14 Jan, 28 Mar 1929, 9 Feb 1934, 7 Mar 1935, 16 Jan 1936, 17, 22 May 1939, 25 Apr 1940, 14 Apr 1945, 11 May 1963, 14 July 1966; *Canb Times*, 8 July 1965; Wunderlich records (Univ Melb Archives).   G. P. WALSH

WYLLY, GUY GEORGE EGERTON (1880-1962), army officer, was born on 17 February 1880 in Hobart, son of Edward Arthur Egerton Wylly, an Indian Army officer, and his wife Henrietta Mary, née Clerk. As an infant Guy went to India with his parents. In 1885 the family settled at Sandy Bay, Hobart, where he attended The Hutchins School before completing his education at the Collegiate School of St Peter, Adelaide.

On 26 April 1900 Wylly embarked from Hobart as a lieutenant with the 3rd (1st Tasmanian Imperial) Contingent. After its arrival in South Africa, the unit was absorbed into the 4th Imperial Bushmen which by August was constantly under enemy fire in small engagements. On 1 September he had command of a troop of bushmen escorting a foraging party near Warmbad, Transvaal. Scouting ahead, he and seven others rode into an ambush in a narrow gorge: six men were wounded, including Wylly. Corporal E. S. Brown was hit in the leg and unhorsed. Wylly went to his aid, gave him his horse, then opened fire from behind a rock, enabling Brown and other men to withdraw, before he made his own escape. For his gallantry Wylly was awarded the Victoria Cross. Trooper J. H. Bisdee [q.v.7] won the V.C. during the same action.

Transferring to the British Army on 5 December 1900, Wylly was gazetted second lieutenant in the South Lancashire Regiment and joined its 2nd Battalion in India. On 1 October 1902 he obtained a transfer to the Indian Army, serving in the 46th Punjabis (1902-04) and the Queen's Own Corps of Guides, infantry (1904-06); he then joined the cavalry in the Q.O.C.G. From January 1906 to September 1909 he was aide-de-camp to Lord Kitchener, the commander-in-chief, East Indies.

Having qualified at the Staff College, Quetta, on 14 December 1914 Wylly was posted as staff captain in the Mhow Cavalry Brigade, serving with the British Expeditionary Force in France. Wounded in action in August 1915, he returned to his unit as brigade major following his promotion on 1 September. In June 1916 he was posted briefly to the staff of the British 4th Division and next month joined the staff of the 3rd Australian Division which was forming in England. From 24 February to 26 July 1917 he was on the staff of I Anzac Corps, his final appointment before returning to India. For his service in France and Belgium he was thrice mentioned in dispatches and was awarded the Distinguished Service Order in January 1918.

Between 1919 and 1933 Wylly took part in several operations on the North-West Frontier, earning four further mentions in dispatches. A lieut-colonel from 26 April 1926, he was given command of the 6th Duke of Connaught's Own Lancers. Promotion to colonel followed in April 1930. He was also an aide-de-camp to King George V in 1926-33. Appointed C.B. in 1933, he retired to Camberley, Surrey, England, where he died, unmarried, on 9 January 1962 and was cremated.

Aust Defence Dept, *Official records of the Australian military contingents to the war in South Africa*, P. L. Murray ed (Melb, 1911); L. Wigmore (ed), *They dared mightily* (Canb, 1963); R. L.

Wallace, *The Australians at the Boer War* (Canb, 1976); records (AWM).   A. J. SWEETING

WYMARK, FREDERICK VICTOR GREY (1872-1942), bookseller, was born on 6 October 1872 at Stawell, Victoria, son of Frederick George Wymark, a schoolmaster from England, and his Victorian wife Ann, née Sykes. Brought to Sydney as a child, Fred grew up at Woolloomooloo. When David Mackenzie Angus [q.v.7] established a book-selling business in Market Street in 1884, Fred became his first assistant, after fighting another boy for the job. George Robertson [q.v.11] joined Angus in 1886. With James Tyrrell [q.v.], Wymark delivered orders in a billycart; he was formally apprenticed to Angus in 1890. At the Castlereagh Street Congregational Church, Sydney, on 17 October 1894 he married Emily Sophia McCure.

Already in charge of the second-hand department, Wymark took over the expanding Australian section as Robertson's interest in buying and selling these books waned. On Angus's retirement in 1899, Wymark bought many of his shares and in 1907 became a director when Angus & Robertson Ltd was formed as a public company. In 1905 Robertson and Wymark had petitioned the Commonwealth parliament, seeking the amendment of copyright laws to protect Australian books from piracy in the United States of America.

'Tall, fair, blue of eye, big boned, quick-minded and quick-moving', Wymark combined 'the heart of a child' with a business-man's 'faculty of seeing instantly and clearly'. He persuaded his fellow directors to purchase the freehold of the Castlereagh Street shop and the adjoining building. In 1909 he instituted the firm's art gallery where his son Charles later worked.

Becoming an authority on books, prints, pictures, journals, letters and manuscripts relating to Australia and the Pacific, Wymark searched for treasures for David Scott Mitchell and later (Sir) William Dixson [qq.v.5,8] who freely acknowledged their indebtedness to him in building up their collections. He 'could sense an Australian rarity anywhere between Peru and Kamchatka, and knew its history, its value and its probable purchaser'. On his only business trip to Britain he persuaded many notable second-hand booksellers to give him first offer of rare items on Australasia and Oceania before the publication of their catalogues; he also dealt with European booksellers such as Mullers of Amsterdam. Norman Lindsay [q.v.10] told Robertson that he always regarded Wymark's 'genius for barter, the prerogative of Phoenician piracy, with profound respect'.

Wymark's insistence on investigating any offer enabled him to secure such choice items as the original drawings in colour for John Gould's [q.v.1] *The Birds of Australia* and James Cook's [q.v.1] letter on naming the east coast 'New South Wales'. Wymark purchased some important libraries, including that of James Norton [q.v.5] and the Colenso library from New Zealand for which he bid in person; among other rarities he obtained for the Mitchell and Dixson libraries were maps, charts, manuscripts, signed letters, pictures, portraits, coins, medals and stamps.

An 'alert genius', Wymark loved old books and playing bowls. Survived by his wife, son and daughter, he died at Church Point on 19 October 1942 and was cremated.

J. R. Tyrrell, *Old books, old friends, old Sydney* (Syd, 1952); A. H. Spencer, *The Hill of Content* (Syd, 1959); Aust Booksellers Assn, *The early Australian booksellers* (Adel, 1980); A. W. Barker, *Dear Robertson* (Syd, 1982); *Biblionews*, June 1976, p 27.   MARJORIE WYMARK*

WYNN, SAMUEL (1891-1982), wine merchant and Zionist, was born on 4 April 1891 at Ushimow, near Łódz, Russia (Poland), and named Shlomo ben David, son of Michael David Weintraub and his wife Rivkah, née Feigenbaum. Michael died when Shlomo was a child and he was brought up by his mother and two sisters. He received a religious education in the village and at a yeshiva at Nova Minsk to which he had run away, aged 11. His elder brother, a militant socialist, was imprisoned during the abortive 1905 revolution. At 14 Shlomo committed his own act of revolt against his orthodox religion by smoking a cigarette on the Sabbath. He began to read liberal and radical writers, especially Tolstoy. Soon afterwards he joined the family raisin wine business at Lodz where, in 1912, he married Chava (later Eva) Silman. To escape military service, he migrated with his wife from the German port of Bremen.

Arriving in Melbourne on 12 November 1913, Shlomo anglicised his name and obtained work on a farm near Stawell and at All Saints vineyard, Wahgunyah. He returned to Melbourne where he worked in a cork factory and as a cellarman. Recently naturalized, in 1918 Wynn purchased on time-payment a shop in Bourke Street licensed to sell 'colonial wine'. Nearby institutions provided a steady source of customers, ranging from the derelicts of Gordon House to public servants, politicians and the patrons of the Café Denat in Exhibition Street. Wynn bought the Café Denat in 1920 and formed a partnership with the restaurant's head waiter George Hildebrandt who became manager in 1924 of one of Wynn's three new retail wine stores. Wynn transferred the Café Denat to the rooms above the Bourke Street shop which had previously been his family home; in 1928 Rinaldo Massoni took over the restaurant and changed its name to the Florentino.

A wholesaler since 1922, with cellars in Little Bourke Street, Wynn had made regular buying trips to South Australia. In 1925 he began to sell his own vermouth under the 'Boronia' trademark. That year he invested in a winery at Magill, Adelaide, which collapsed in 1927. From the ruins, Wynn (the majority shareholder) and other creditors established Australian Wines Ltd. In 1933 he visited London and in 1939 exported 2000 hogsheads to Britain. By 1944 the company was producing 10 000 bottles of sparkling wine. After the war Samuel remained titular head, but managerial control of his expanding company passed to his eldest son David who in 1950 purchased Chateau Comaum (Coonawarra). In 1970 Wynn Estate Pty Ltd became a public company, Wynn Winegrowers Ltd, which was sold to Allied Breweries Ltd and Tooheys [q.v.6] Ltd in 1972.

In 1922 Wynn had been active in establishing the Jewish Welcome Society of Victoria; he was to be president (twelve times) of the Kadimah (Jewish National Library) in Melbourne. A dedicated worker for the Zionist cause, he was president of the State Zionist Council of Victoria during World War II and twice president of the Zionist Federation of Australia. He made ten visits to Palestine, carrying small arms into the country until 1948 at considerable personal risk, and opposed British restrictions on Jewish immigration and settlement in Palestine. All sixty-seven members of his extended family had been annihilated in Europe.

Only 5 ft. 1 in. (154.9 cm) tall with a large head, Sammy Wynn dressed well. He had a keen sense of humour and enjoyed talented company, but was himself reserved, and at times an anxious and driven man. Despite the strict orthodoxy of his upbringing, he was not religious, but in defence of his Jewish culture and the Zionist cause he was tenacious, even courageous, as he was in his approach to business.

Samuel was thrice married. His first wife Eva died in 1939. On 25 May 1940 at Auckland, New Zealand, he married a Canadian-born widow Ida Bension, née Siegler. IDA WYNN (1896?-1948) was a leader of international Zionism and a source of inspiration to many people. She had visited Australia in 1937 and 1939 on behalf of the Women's International Zionist Organisation to raise funds for Jewish children in Europe. A writer and philosopher, she was a friend of Martin Buber and of the poet Richard Beer-Hofmann whose work she translated. President of the W.I.Z.O. Federation of Australia, she was described by the State Zionist Council of Victoria as 'the most outstanding woman in the history of Australian Zionism.' A children's centre at Mount Carmel, Israel, was named after her. She died of heart disease on 1 August 1948 in East Melbourne. On 21 September 1950 at Caulfield, Melbourne, Wynn married Marguerite Herzfeld with Jewish rites. Survived by three sons of his first marriage, he died on 17 June 1982 and was buried in Melbourne general cemetery. His estate was sworn for probate at $325 867.

A. Wynn, *The fortunes of Samuel Wynn* (Melb, 1968); W. D. Rubinstein (ed), *Jews in the sixth continent* (Syd, 1987); S. D. Rutland, *Edge of the diaspora* (Syd, 1988); *People* (Syd), 30 Dec 1953; *Age*, 3 Aug 1948, 23 June, 17 Aug 1982; *Aust Jewish Herald*, 6 Aug 1948; *Aust Jewish News*, 25 June 1982.   DAVID DUNSTAN

WYNNE, AGAR (1850-1934), politician, was born on 15 July 1850 in London, son of Edward Agar Wynne, builder, and his wife Sarah Maria, née Palmer. The family migrated to Victoria in his boyhood. Educated at Melbourne Church of England Grammar School, Agar represented the school in football and matriculated in 1868. Having completed the articled clerk's course at the University of Melbourne, he was admitted as an attorney on 7 July 1874 and entered a succession of legal partnerships, initially with (Sir) Henry Cuthbert [q.v.3]. In Melbourne on 10 November 1886 he married with Australian Church forms a widow with two children, Mary Jane Robertson, née Smith (d. 1889). On 21 February 1896 at the Collins Street Independent Church he married a widow with three children, Annie Dudgeon, née Samuel.

Both a 'country-man and city man', in politics Wynne was not exactly a tory and not exactly a liberal. In 1888 he was elected to the Victorian Legislative Council as a member for Western Province. He held this seat until he resigned in 1903, serving as postmaster-general and solicitor-general in 1893-94 in (Sir) James Patterson's [q.v.5] administration, and as solicitor-general in 1900-02 in Sir George Turner's [q.v.] and (Sir) Alexander Peacock's [q.v.11] ministries. Wynne's outlook changed little: his early commitment to small government, national development, decentralization, and the promotion and proper regulation of business and industry remained prominent themes in his parliamentary speeches; more liberal in complexion were his support for old-age pensions and his advocacy of women's suffrage.

In 1906 Wynne won the Federal seat of Balaclava as an Independent Protectionist.

He gave most of his attention in the House to issues involving commerce and economic development, often citing his legal and business experience in support of his arguments. Swept up in the Fusion of 1909, he became postmaster-general (June 1913-September 1914) in (Sir) Joseph Cook's [q.v.8] ministry, but, by mid-1914, had decided to retire. Melbourne *Punch* attributed his decision to frustration with his inability to make his department run on sound business lines.

For Wynne, another three years out of parliament was enough. In 1917 he stood successfully for the Victorian Legislative Assembly seat of St Kilda. Once more, his energy and competence elevated him to ministerial rank, but no further. Reputed to have been a contender for the premiership, he was attorney-general, solicitor-general, minister of railways and a vice-president of the Board of Land and Works during the four months in office (November 1917-March 1918) of (Sir) John Bowser's [q.v.7] 'economy' government. The need for restraint in public spending exercised Wynne's mind more as he aged; before his final retirement from politics in 1920, he warned of dark days ahead.

His long-standing commitment to breaking up the great estates and seeing 'bone and sinew settled on the country' did not prevent Wynne from acquiring Nerrin Nerrin, a 7297-acre (2953 ha) property near Streatham. There he established his country home, ran merinos, raised thoroughbreds and created a sanctuary for wildlife. He had other pastoral interests in Victoria and Queensland. In the city he was a founder of the Argus and the National building societies, chairman of the Colonial Mutual Fire Insurance Co. Ltd, Dennys Lascelles Ltd and Melbourne Electric Supply Co., and had interests in mining and real estate. He had practised law until 1910.

Some 5 ft. 6 ins. (167.6 cm) tall, fine-featured and balding, Wynne sported a bushy moustache, kept dark at the tips by cigar smoke. Occasionally severe in manner, he was a tolerant Anglican who valued friendship and enjoyed life to the full. His first love was racing and from 1905 he was a committee-member of the Victoria Racing Club. His horses won the Australian Cup in 1903 and 1908, but his hope for a Derby winner at Flemington was never realized. He was sometime president of the Melbourne Swimming and St Kilda Yacht clubs, and of the Melbourne and Athenaeum clubs.

Late in life a series of strokes robbed Wynne 'of the power to move or speak'. He died on 12 May 1934 at Nerrin Nerrin and was buried in Camperdown cemetery. The daughter of his first marriage survived him and was the principal beneficiary of his estate, sworn for probate at £105 803. His portrait

by W. B. McInnes [q.v.10] is in the Athenaeum Club, Melbourne.

P. Loveday et al (eds), *The emergence of the Australian party system* (Syd, 1977); *PD* (Cwlth), 1934, p 18; *Punch* (Melb), 2 Nov 1911, 2 July 1914; *Age* and *Argus*, 14 May 1934; *Smith's Weekly* (Syd), 14 Oct 1933; G. A. Richardson, Personal reminiscences (notes on ADB file). DARRYL BENNET

WYNNE, WATKIN (1844-1921), newspaper manager, was born on 11 May 1844 at Black Notley, Essex, England, third child of William Wynne, yeoman, and his wife Sarah, née Davey. In 1852 Watkin migrated to Victoria with his widowed mother and three sisters. He attended the Free Church School at Geelong, was apprenticed to a printer with the *Ballarat Times* until 1861, worked as a journeyman on several regional papers and, after studying shorthand, joined the Ballarat *Evening Post* as a reporter. On 31 October 1866 at Ballarat he was married to Eleanor Sophie Picton (d. 1919) by her father, the local pastor of the Disciples of Christ.

Having formed a company among fellow employees to take over the *Post* and to buy its rival in 1872, Wynne went to Melbourne in 1876 as sub-editor of the *Daily Telegraph*. In 1879 he joined a syndicate—with three Victorian politicians J. J. Casey, J. G. Francis and Angus Mackay [qq.v.3,4,5] and two Sydney investors J. R. Carey [q.v.7] and Robert Sands—to found a second morning daily in Sydney. Moving there, Wynne became sub-editor of the new paper, the *Sydney Daily Telegraph*, which appeared on 1 July.

The *Telegraph* was not an immediate success. Following several resignations and threatened closure in 1883, Wynne became general manager next year and fundamentallly reorganized the paper. The syndicate became a limited liability company; Wynne recruited F. W. Ward [q.v.] as editor, L. J. Brient as news editor and Henry Gullett [qq.v.7,9] as associate editor. Appearing as the *Daily Telegraph* from 1884, the paper was described as 'sensationalist', 'liberal' and 'modern'. Improved cable services meant that in December 1884 the *Telegraph* 'scooped' the German annexation of New Guinea.

Daring, 'original, courageous, swift to decide and to act, unshackled by a single convention', Wynne gave the *Telegraph* anchorage through several changes of editor. He was mechanically minded and pioneered new technical processes in Australia. Touring England and the United States of America in 1893 to survey advances in typesetting, he purchased twelve Mergenthaler linotype machines which made production more efficient and allowed greater flexibility in layout.

He held patents for improvements to linotype printing, and also introduced zinc-etching to produce half-tone illustrations.

By 1887 the paper had increased circulation by 25 per cent and had begun to pay steady dividends. Wynne's management was characterized by shrewd business sense and strict discipline. Active in arbitration proceedings, he opposed closed-shop unionism, yet scrupulously observed prescribed conditions; he tried, as well, to modernize office design.

An avid sportsman and champion swimmer, Wynne was a founder of the Port Jackson Swimming, the Sydney Football and the Waverley Bowling and Recreation clubs. He imported one of the first motor cars to Australia. An alderman (1896-1901) on Waverley Municipal Council, he served as mayor in 1898-99; as a Freemason, he was a founder in 1888 (and later past grand warden) of the United Grand Lodge of New South Wales.

Wynne had a talent for anecdotes, a 'silver tongue' and a streak of whimsical generosity.

Of middle height, thickset but 'trained fine', he had very keen eyes which strongly contradicted any impression given by his whitening hair. He was consulted on the amalgamation of Melbourne evening papers in 1894 and on the reorganization of the London *Daily Telegraph* in 1906. Survived by six daughters and five sons, he died at Waverley on 8 July 1921 and was buried with Anglican rites in the local cemetery. His estate was sworn for probate at £265 113. Wynne's portrait by William Macleod [q.v.10] is held by the Waverley club.

B. T. Dowd, *The history of the Waverley municipal district* (Syd, 1959); H. Mayer, *The press in Australia* (Melb, 1964); R. B. Walker, *The newspaper press in New South Wales, 1803-1920* (Syd, 1976); *Cosmos Mag,* 30 Sept 1894, p 3; *A'sian Art Review,* 5 Oct 1899, p 20; *Newspaper News* (Syd), 1 Aug 1928, p 12, 1 Sept 1928, p 8; *Bulletin,* 2 Aug 1884; *Sun* (Syd), 8 July 1921; *Daily Telegraph* (Syd), 9 July 1921; P. Daly, Watkin Wynne (paper to the Waverley Hist Soc, 1986, held by its author, Paddington, Syd).   NICHOLAS BROWN

Y

'YABBA'; *see* GASCOIGNE

YENCKEN, EDWARD LOWENSTEIN (1854-1932), merchant, was born on 13 February 1854 at Brixton, Surrey, England, son of Edward Ferdinand Yencken, merchant, and his wife Ellen, née Druce. Young Edward attended school at Shrewsbury and, after his family arrived in Victoria, completed his education at Melbourne Church of England Grammar School. In 1871 he joined the Melbourne branch of the Bank of New South Wales, but next year removed to Brooks, Robinson & Co., wholesale oil, colour and glass merchants and importers of painters' and decorators' supplies, thus entering the trade he would eventually dominate. On 24 January 1882 at All Saints Anglican Church, St Kilda, he married English-born Florence Orr. That year, after reaching managerial level at Brooks Robinson, he decided to found his own business: he returned to England for ten months to establish connexions with British and European manufacturers, and to establish a buying office at 9 New Broad Street, London.

In January 1883 E. L. Yencken & Co., wholesale importers and general indent merchants, opened for business at 3 Flinders Street, Melbourne, sharing 'a handsome building on a bluestone foundation, having cellars and three floors above' with the tea merchants, Griffiths Bros. Unlike many of his older competitors, Yencken was reputed to have begun with 'a large capital'. His business expanded rapidly and survived the loss in May 1885 of goods worth £70 000 in a sensational fire. By 1888 the firm had two adjoining city warehouses and a large store by the Yarra River. Its warehouses were equipped with 'every modern labour-saving applicance', including hydraulic lifts connecting with an iron tramway which delivered goods to their entrances.

Yencken gradually absorbed the business of his main competitors, including that of Brooks Robinson. In 1892 the firm became a limited liability company and by the turn of the century Yencken was honoured as 'father' of the Melbourne trade. The business moved to Little Collins Street in 1904 and shifted from the city to South Melbourne after World War II. A noted member of the Yorick Club from 1903, Yencken enjoyed golf and gardening. Survived by his wife, two sons and two daughters, he died on 7 September 1932 at his Toorak home and was buried in St Kilda cemetery; his estate was sworn for probate at £11 863.

His younger son ARTHUR FERDINAND (1894-1944) was educated at Melbourne Church of England Grammar School and Corpus Christi College, Cambridge (B.A., 1919). Enlisting in the British Army in August 1914, he became a major in the artillery and was awarded the Military Cross. After World War I he joined the Foreign Office and rose to be British minister in Madrid. In 1941 he was appointed C.M.G. Arthur Yencken died on 18 May 1944 in an air crash south of Barcelona, Spain.

A. Sutherland, *Victoria and its metropolis*, 2 (Melb, 1888); T. Carrington and D. Watterson, *The Yorick Club* (Melb, 1911); *Aust Storekeepers and Traders J*, 23 Dec 1910, 31 Jan 1911; *Argus*, 8 Sept 1932; *The Times*, 20 May 1944.

STUART SAYERS

YEWEN, ALFRED GREGORY (1867-1923), journalist, was born on 16 May 1867 at Croydon, Surrey, England, fourth son of Charles Yewen, a canteen-keeper and former army bandmaster, and his wife Sarah Margaret, née Roberts. Gregory worked as a stonemason and gained his real education from the nascent socialist movement. In 1884 he helped William Morris to form the Socialist League, London. Morris presented him with the 1887 English translation of Karl Marx's *Capital* which he read thoroughly and kept all his life.

His lungs affected by his work, in 1888 Yewen migrated to Queensland, bringing an introduction from Morris to William Lane [q.v.9]. Moving to Sydney, he became active in the Australian Socialist League with W. H. T. McNamara [q.v.10]. Yewen's *A refutation of the single tax theory* (1890) was a historical critique of Henry George [q.v.4] whom he derided for apparent ignorance of Marx. Returning north in 1891, Yewen worked on Gresley Lukin's [q.v.5] *Boomerang* and joined Lane's *Worker*. When he left in September 1893, the *Worker* eulogized him as 'sternly uncompromising' and 'a most caustic and severe critic'.

Back in Sydney, Yewen threw in his lot with W. M. Hughes [q.v.9]. Between April and September 1894 they collaborated on the *New Order*, which Yewen edited. 'He ruled with a rod of iron', Hughes recalled. 'He was never known to smile. He never went out. He had no

594

recreations and only one shirt'. Yewen's paper was a weekly, eight-page political scattergun and featured a collection of paragraphs alongside topical verse by W. A. Holman [q.v.9]. Anti-Semitic, racist and republican, it pilloried Lane as the dictator of 'New Australia'.

Labor failed to win the 1894 election, although Hughes gained a seat. Soon, however, Yewen detected the new member backsliding on socialism and was so sickened that he abandoned politics. Thereafter, when they met in the street, Yewen would shout, 'Hughes, you rat!' Hughes retaliated by writing of him: 'I lived to see him sleek and opulent, arrayed in the favourite livery of capitalism—bell-topper and frock-coat and stiff collar'.

Sometime sub-editor on the *Stock and Station Journal*, in 1899 Yewen took a reporter's job on the *Sydney Morning Herald* where for fourteen years he covered the fat stock sales at Homebush. He wrote a weekly article on wool for the *Herald* and was the major contributor to *Dalgety's Review*. In 1900 he published *Yewen's directory of the landholders of New South Wales*. With Francis Gellatly [q.v.8], in 1901 he founded the periodical, *A.A.A., All About Australians*.

At North Sydney on 8 November 1900 Yewen married with Presbyterian forms Margaret Alice Scott, a former secretary of Sir Henry Parkes [q.v.5]; Holman was a witness. On a wide headland at Newport, north of Sydney, Yewen built with his own hands a stone house, Bungania. Unceiled roofs, open fires and split levels, complemented by coastal views, cows and an orchard, gave it an odd charm. Spending weekends there, Lane's brother Ernest noticed that Yewen never spoke about socialism. Survived by his wife and two sons, Yewen died at his home on 11 June 1923 of tuberculosis and was buried in the Anglican section of Manly cemetery.

E. H. Lane, *Dawn to dusk* (Brisb, 1939); W. M. Hughes, *Crusts and crusades* (Syd, 1947); B. James, *Anarchism and state violence in Sydney and Melbourne, 1886-1896*, (Newcastle, 1986); *Aust Standard*, 7 Sept 1889; Aust Journalists' Assn, *Copy*, 1 Dec 1913; *Worker* (Brisb), 2 Sept 1893; *SMH*, 13 June 1923; Yewen papers (held by Narrabeen Community Learning Centre and by Mrs W. Bale, Newport Beach, Syd). EDMUND CAMPION

YOUL, ALFRED (1849-1921), farmer and politician, was born on 23 August 1849 at Symmons Plains, near Perth, Tasmania, third son of (Sir) James Arndell Youl [q.v.6], pastoralist, and his wife Eliza, née Cox. In 1854 the family left to live at Clapham Park, Surrey, England. Educated at St Aubin's School, Jersey, and at Uppingham School, Leicestershire, Alfred worked in a lawyer's office and later on a sheep-farm in Shropshire. On 2 September 1875 at the parish church, Ercall Magna, he married Margaret Mansell (d. 1888), a farmer's daughter, and returned with her to Elsdon, Tasmania. Acquiring Leighlands, an adjacent pastoral property, he held some 2800 acres (1133 ha) of good pasture with a mile-long (1.6 km) frontage on the South Esk River. The Youls were to have three sons and four daughters, and lived in a large home at Leighlands.

His involvement in civic affairs provided a grounding for State politics. Youl served on the Evandale (1884-98) and Longford (1898-1916) municipal councils; he was a member of the board of health of the one and of the licensing bench and rabbit board of the latter; he was also chairman of the Perth main roads board and a member of the Northern Agricultural and Pastoral Association. District coroner from 1889 and chairman of the Longford Court of General Sessions, he was appointed a justice of the peace in 1893. He had married Annette Frances Wigan, a local farmer's daughter, on 9 February 1891 at St John's Anglican Church, Launceston. Sharing her husband's commitment to serve the community, Annette was active in several women's and charitable organizations. She was an able sportswoman who played competition croquet and golf.

Broad shouldered, Youl had rugged features and a luxuriant moustache. Elected to the Tasmanian House of Assembly as a Ministerialist in May 1903, he held the seat of Longford until April 1909, then represented Macquarie in the Legislative Council until 1920. Mrs Youl failed to win Wilmot when she stood for the assembly on a platform of women's issues in 1922.

Youl died at Leighlands on 3 February 1921 and was buried in Perth cemetery. He was survived by his wife (d. 1937) and one of their two sons, and by a son and three daughters of his first marriage. His estate was sworn for probate at £16 018. Several of his children had careers of note. Francis Victor Mansell (1886-1972) became an expert on pasture improvement and established Elsdon's famous Polworth stud. Geoffrey Arthur Douglas (1892-1971), a major in the Royal Field Artillery, was awarded the Military Cross and the Belgian Croix de Guerre in World War I; he commanded the 2nd/40th Battalion in the Northern Territory in World War II when the Japanese attacked Darwin. John Beresford Osmond (1894-1917), a lieutenant in the Australian Imperial Force, was killed at Bullecourt, France.

M. McArthur (ed), *Prominent Tasmanians* (Hob, 1924); *Cyclopedia of Tasmania* (Hob, 1931); *Tas*

Mail, 16 Dec 1920, 3 Feb 1921; *Mercury*, 4 Feb 1921, 23 Mar 1955; *Australasian*, 12 Feb 1921; *Examiner* (Launc), 7 Sept 1937.

G. H. STANCOMBE

YOUNG, FLORENCE MAUDE (1870-1920), actress and singer, was born on 2 October 1870 in Melbourne, daughter of Henry Henrard Young, jeweller, and his wife Elizabeth, née Tonkin, both English born. Florence attended Fitzroy Ladies' College. Her ambition for a stage career was thwarted by parental opposition until her father's Collins Street business failed during the land boom.

After an appearance with the Melbourne Liedertafel, she made her debut on 14 June 1890 as Beatrice in the Nellie Stewart [q.v.] Opera Co.'s production of *Boccaccio*. Miss Young then auditioned for J. C. Williamson [q.v.6] and on 25 October played Casilda in the first Australian production of *The gondoliers*. Although at this time her voice was untrained, her performance began a long line of successes in comic operas. She played Corisandre and Rosette in *Ma mie Rosette*, Yvonne and Paul in *Paul Jones*, Bettina and Fiametta in *La mascotte*, and Dorothy Bantam and Lydia Hawthorne in *Dorothy*. Her Gilbert and Sullivan roles ranged from Patience and Elsie Maynard to Katisha. In 1895 she took the first of several principal boy roles—in Williamson's production of the pantomime *Djin Djin*—for which her figure, acting and singing made her an obvious choice.

On 8 February 1897 at St Peter's Anglican Church, Melbourne, Florence married Robert Campbell Rivington. That year they went to London, where she appeared with George Musgrove's [q.v.5] company at the Shaftesbury Theatre, and next to South Africa where she was prima donna in Lockwood and Leville's company. Returning to London to play Dick Whittington in pantomime at the Fulham Grand Theatre (1898-99), she later toured England with a company performing *Falka*. Following these engagements, she became a pupil of Mme Marchesi in Paris. Enthusiastic about her dramatic soprano voice, Marchesi was annoyed when, within a year, Florence accepted Williamson's offer of an engagement in Australia rather than training for grand opera. Florence Young also visited the United States of America where she saw the natural performances of popular American actresses and subsequently adopted their approach.

Back in Australia in 1901, she appeared for Williamson as Poppy in *San Toy*. In 1904 she separated from her husband who was granted a divorce in 1912 on the grounds of his wife's desertion. As comic opera gradually gave way to musical comedy, she shone in productions such as *The country girl*, *The geisha* and *The girl in the train*; her best dramatic roles were in *The duchess of Dantzic* and *The climax*.

Recognized as the unofficial star of the Royal Comic Opera Co., Florence Young became one of the great favourites of Australian audiences: her first-night appearances elicited rapturous demonstrations. She seldom missed a performance and was noted for her generosity towards colleagues. In her later career she appeared in *The pink lady*, *The cinema star*, *Katinka*, *Theodore and Co.* and *Maytime*. Both her sisters—one of whom married (Sir) George Tallis [q.v.]—and two of her brothers appeared on the Australian stage. Florence Young died in Melbourne on 11 November 1920 of a cerebral haemorrhage and was buried in Melbourne general cemetery.

T. D. M. de Warre, *Through the opera glasses* (Syd, 1908); *Australasian*, 3 June 1893, 25 May, 10 Aug 1912; *Punch* (Melb), 28 May 1908; *Age, Argus* and *SMH*, 12 Nov 1920.   JOAN MASLEN

YOUNG, FLORENCE SELINA HARRIET (1856-1940), missionary, was born on 10 October 1856 at Motueka, near Nelson, New Zealand, fifth child of Henry Young, farmer, and his wife Catherine Anne, née Eccles, both Plymouth Brethren from England. Educated at home and for two years at a boarding school in England, at the age of 18 Florence experienced 'a crisis' during a prayer meeting at Dunedin: perceiving God's powers of forgiveness, she asked to be baptized.

Settling in Sydney in 1878, after the death of her parents Florence moved in 1882 to Fairymead, a sugar plantation near Bundaberg, Queensland, run by two of her brothers. With timidity, she began to hold prayer meetings for planters' families and, with one assistant, established the Young People's Scriptural Union which eventually attracted 4000 members. Her attentions were increasingly devoted to the Melanesian sugarworkers whose responsiveness to kindness she applauded and whose 'heathen' customs and 'addictions' to 'white men's vices' she abhorred. Asking that God instruct 'the teacher and the scholars', she conducted classes in pidgin English, using pictures, rote biblical phrases and a chrysalis to explain the resurrection.

Under Miss Young's guidance, the Queensland Kanaka Mission was formally established at Fairymead in 1886 as an evangelical, non-denominational church. Relying on unsolicited subscriptions and stressing 'salvation before education or civilization', it spread to other plantations and won considerable approval. The Q.K.M. aimed to prepare the Melanesians for membership of established

Christian churches after their repatriation and employed paid missionaries and members of Florence's extended family. Reassuring in its message of hope, its open-air hymn singing and its mass baptisms in local rivers, at its height in 1904-05 the Q.K.M. engaged nineteen missionaries and 118 unpaid 'native teachers', and claimed 2150 conversions. As she embraced departing converts, Florence exhorted them: 'No forget 'im Jesus'.

Tall and slender, with her hair worn austerely, the clear-eyed evangelist dressed in well-cut suits and bore herself confidently. Between 1891 and 1900 she had spent six precarious years with the China Inland Mission. Despite a nervous breakdown, she recognized her work as a preparation for the South Sea Evangelical Mission which became a branch of the Q.K.M. in 1904 in response to appeals for help from repatriated Q.K.M. teachers. That year, singing hymns during the crossing, she helped to settle White missionaries on Malaita in the Solomon Islands in the hope of nurturing an indigenous church.

Miss Young administered and dominated the expanding S.S.E.M. from Sydney and Katoomba, New South Wales, and made lengthy annual visits to the islands until 1926 when her modest autobiography, *Pearls from the Pacific*, was published in London. She regarded universities as 'hot-beds of infidelity' and was opposed to women entering them. Inflexible though serene in later years, she died on 28 May 1940 at Killara, Sydney, and was buried in Gore Hill cemetery with Presbyterian forms. By then, the S.S.E.M. had recorded over 7900 conversions.

H. I. Hogbin, *Experiments in civilization* (Lond, 1939); A. R. Tippett, *Solomon Islands Christianity* (Lond, 1967); P. Corris, *Passage, port and plantation* (Melb, 1973); D. Hilliard, *God's gentlemen* (Brisb, 1978); R. M. Keesing and P. Corris, *Lightning meets the west wind* (Melb, 1980); QKM and SSEM, *Not in Vain* (Annual Report), 1887-1940; *PIM*, 15 June 1940, p 70; *J of Pacific Hist*, 4, 1969, p 4; family information.   HELGA M. GRIFFIN

YOUNG, SIR FREDERICK WILLIAM (1876-1948), politician, was born on 5 January 1876 at Blyth, South Australia, son of John Young, storekeeper and later pastoralist, and his wife Isabella, née Russell. His elder brother was (Sir) Walter James Young [q.v.]. Frederick attended Prince Alfred College in 1889-92. Articled to the solicitor William Pope in 1893, next year he entered the University of Adelaide (LL.B., 1897) and was Stow [q.v.6] scholar. He was admitted to the Bar in 1898 and became a senior partner in the firm of Young & Newland. On 7 December 1904 at the Flinders Street Baptist Church, Adelaide, he married Florence (d.

1947), daughter of the 'Wheat King' John Darling [q.v.4].

Tall, spare, though well-built, with a quiet, deliberate manner of speaking that was relieved by humour and a winning address, Young was member for Stanley in the South Australian House of Assembly in 1902-05 and for Wooroora in 1909-15. In the Peake [q.v.11] Liberal ministry he was commissioner of crown lands and immigration in 1912-14. Young supported the expansion of railways as part of his policy to open up areas for settlement along the Murray River and Eyre Peninsula. An early protagonist of the State's sponsorship of the immigration of British youths to work on the land, he initiated the Immigration Act (1913), eventually implemented in the 1920s.

In 1915-18 Young was South Australian agent-general in London. Knighted in January 1918, he was appointed commander of the Order of the Crown of Belgium in 1919 for services during World War I. In December 1918 he was elected to the House of Commons as a Coalition Unionist for Swindon (Wiltshire); he did not seek re-election in 1922. Young remained in England directing British and Australian banking and pastoral interests, but occasionally visited Australia. He became a director of the English, Scottish and Australian Bank in 1919 and chairman in 1946; a board-member of the Australian Estates and Mortgage Co. in 1924, he was its chairman in 1937. Following the Depression, in the late 1930s he encouraged the expansion of Australian primary exports and the development of Australian secondary industry; he also advocated increasing the Australian population through immigration, especially from Britain, and from Europe. He had stressed the need for Imperial preference in trade and for committed membership of the British Empire to guarantee Australia's defence. Survived by his only son, Sir Frederick died at Buckingham Gate, London, on 26 August 1948. His estate was sworn for probate in England at £12 525.

British A'sian, 21 May 1914, 11 Mar 1915; *J of Hist Soc of SA*, no 14, 1986, p 137; *Mail* (Adel), 30 Nov 1912, 30 Jan 1915; *SMH*, 2 Jan, 21, 30 Dec 1918, 30 May 1919, 28 Nov 1934, 25 July 1935, 23 July 1936, 29 Jan 1937, 26 Dec 1938, 9 Dec 1947; *Advertiser* (Adel) and *The Times*, 27 Aug 1948.
R. E. NORTHEY

YOUNG, SARAH JANE (JEANNE) (1866-1955), political reformer, was born on 1 July 1866 at Unley, Adelaide, eighth daughter of John Forster, smith, and his wife Sarah Jane, née Jervis. Educated privately, she received coaching in mathematics and enjoyed music. Sarah was later a governess and piano teacher, and attempted freelance journalism. She lost the sight in one eye in a horse and trap accident. On 23 January 1889 in her father's East Adelaide home she married with Wesleyan Methodist forms Alfred Howard Young, a journalist; they were to have a daughter and three sons.

Inspired by Catherine Spence [q.v.6], she became secretary (1897) of the Effective Voting League. Styling herself Jeanne Forster Young, she was a forceful woman with finely chiselled features; she wrote and delivered authoritative lectures about proportional representation, illustrating them with lantern slides. In 1900 she and Spence campaigned in Sydney for eight weeks to have the Hare-Spence method adopted in Federal elections; they stayed there with Rose Scott [q.v.11]. After Catherine's death, in 1910 Jeanne completed and published her mentor's unfinished autobiography—precluding Spence's niece Lucy Morice [q.v.10] from so doing—and became prominent in the Spence Memorial and the Catherine Helen Spence scholarship committees.

During World War I Young joined the Australian Red Cross Society, the South Australian Soldiers' Fund and the Wattle Day League committees. As secretary of the league's motor ambulance committee which raised £8000, she directed a spectacular three-day exhibition and fair in 1916. She also contributed to the *Register*. Her jingoism alienated her husband, whom she left in 1917, though he continued to support her. That year she became a justice of the peace and in 1918 was secretary of the Women's Representation League. In 1916 she had been the first woman appointed to the Public Library, Museum and Art Gallery board, under (Sir) William Sowden's [q.v.] chairmanship; she contributed actively and argumentatively to its meetings until 1926; she resigned in 1928, by which time she was almost blind. Adjusting to her affliction, she developed an excellent memory for voices. She founded the Proportional Representation Group in 1930.

Jeanne returned to Alfred: in 1932 they spent eight months abroad, vainly seeking a cure in Switzerland for her blindness. In England she addressed proportional representation functions and attended a Commonwealth League conference as a delegate from South Australia's Women's Non-Party Association, of which she had been a foundation member (1909). After her husband's death in 1936, she completed her discursive *Catherine Helen Spence* (Melbourne, 1937). She had also written two unpublished novels, and become vice-president of the Writers' Fellowship of South Australia. As an Independent advocating proportional representation, she had campaigned unsuccessfully for the House of Assembly (Sturt, 1918; Burnside,

1938) and for the Senate (1937). President of the Democratic Women's Association (1937), she was appointed O.B.E. in 1938. She published her last cogent brochure, *Proportional representation in a nutshell*, in 1945. Survived by her daughter and a son, Mrs Young died at Rose Park on 11 April 1955 and was buried in North Road cemetery.

Annual Report of the Public Library, Museum and Art Gallery, *PP* (SA), 1917 (13); *Red Cross Record* (Adel), Sept 1916, Oct 1917; H. Jones, 'A postscript to the life of Catherine Helen Spence', *J of Hist Soc of SA*, 15, 1987, *also* 16, 1988, p 165; *Advertiser* (Adel), 31 Aug 1916, 9 June 1938, 14 Apr 1955; *Observer* (Adel), 9 Sept 1916; Electoral Reform Soc of SA, Records, 1910-75, *and* SA Soldiers' Fund, Minutes, 2 July 1915, 4 June 1925 (Mortlock Lib); Rose Scott correspondence (ML); information from Mr C. Young*, Mrs H. E. Young, West Beach, and Mrs T. Young, Belair, Adel.

HELEN JONES

YOUNG, Sir WALTER JAMES (1872-1940), businessman, was born on 2 April 1872 at Moonta, South Australia, son of John Young, storekeeper and later pastoralist, and his wife Isabella, née Russell. His younger brother was (Sir) Frederick William Young [q.v.]. Educated at Whinham College, North Adelaide, in 1887 Walter joined Elder Smith [qq.v.4,6] & Co., Adelaide. He made his first overseas tour for Elders in 1897, to England, America and Japan. Rising steadily, he became the firm's assistant manager (1906), general manager (1912) and managing director (1929). With Elders, he demonstrated a stability of judgement which largely accounted for his influence during and after World War I when, from the centre of Adelaide's business world, he advised and was consulted by State and Federal governments.

A member (1914-19) of the Commonwealth Shipping Board and an expert in the international commodity market, Young was sent early in 1917 on a mission to the United States of America on behalf of the Australian government. In 1918 he was appointed C.B.E. He took a central role in the promotion of orderly marketing arrangements for Australian produce in the trade turmoil at the end of World War I. Vice-chairman (from 1916) of the Commonwealth Central Wool Committee, he was chairman (1920) of its committee in London which negotiated post-war wool sales to the British government. He was also a member of the advisory committee of the Australian Wheat Board. In 1923 he again went to London for the Imperial Conference as one of Prime Minister S. M. (Viscount) Bruce's [q.v.7] most valued commercial advisers and a representative on the committee on intra-Imperial exchanges at the Economic Conference.

Described as a quiet, modest, kindly man, handicapped by a speech impediment and recurrent ill health, Young shunned publicity, but was excellently connected. A bachelor, he was prominent in the affairs of the Adelaide Club where he lived for lengthy periods.

Chairman (1927) of a special committee established by Premier (Sir) Richard Butler [q.v.7] to examine the State's finances, Young was associated with investigations into railway expenditure, the amalgamation of government departments and the general condition of the South Australian economy. His committee recommended increases in railway freight charges and fares, and in a wide range of government services. Young's impact was greatest during the Depression. In June 1930 he was appointed chairman of the government's advisory committee on finance, composed of some of the most powerful and respected advisers of the day— (Sir) Leslie Melville, R. R. Stuckey, L. C. Hunkin and J. W. Wainwright [q.v.]. After months of frenetic work, they submitted a report, 'The disabilities of South Australia under Federation', which argued the case for additional funds from the Commonwealth. Young played an influential role in persuading Premier L. L. Hill [q.v.9] to accept the Premiers' Plan of June 1931; he was active behind the scenes in the Emergency Committee of South Australia which organized an anti-Labor campaign in the Federal election in December that year. In 1932 he was appointed K.B.E.

Young was one of the original members of the Round Table group in Adelaide, chairman of the State branch of the Council for Scientific and Industrial Research, and a councillor (1924-37) of the University of Adelaide. As chairman of its finance committee, he helped to guide the university's expansion, particularly through large benefactions. His business responsibilities were wide: he was chairman of Imperial Chemical Industries (Australia and New Zealand) Ltd, as well as a director of Mutooroo, Beltana and Milo pastoral companies, and of Elder, Shenton [q.v.6] & Co. Ltd, Western Australia. He had interests in pastoral property in New South Wales and was a frequent visitor to other States.

Dogged by poor health after 1932, Sir Walter often retreated to St Magnus, his country property at Mount Pleasant, where he treasured his books, his gardens and his stock. Content to play the part of the modest businessman, he aspired to no more spectacular role than that of 'the quiet man who went on with the job'. After a long illness he died of hypertensive heart disease on 5 January 1940 at his North Walkerville home and was buried in North Road cemetery.

Elder Smith and Co. Ltd, *The first hundred years* (Adel, nd); H. T. Burgess (ed), *Cyclopedia of South Australia*, 2 (Adel, 1909); *Old Scholars Union, Whinham College* (priv print, Adel, 1928); *The Mutooroo Pastoral Company Limited after fifty years* (Adel, 1951); E. J. R. Morgan, *The Adelaide Club 1863-1963* (Adel, 1963); K. Sharp, *A history of Milo and Ambathala* (Adel, 1963); L. Dumas, *The story of a full life* (Melb, 1969); *PP* (SA), 1927, 2 (75, 76, 76A); T. Hytten, 'The finances of South Australia', *Economic Record*, 7, May 1931; *South Australiana*, 17, no 1, Mar 1978; *Advertiser* (Adel), 6 Jan 1940; M. J. Thompson, Government and Depression in South Australia, 1927-1934 (M.Ec. thesis, Flinders Univ, 1972).   ERIC RICHARDS

YOUNG, WILLIAM BLAMIRE (1862-1935), artist, was born on 9 August 1862 at Londesborough, Yorkshire, England, son of Lieut-Colonel Thomas Young, land agent, and his wife Mary, née Bowser. William was educated at Forest School, Walthamstow, Essex, and Pembroke College, Cambridge (B.A., 1884; M.A., 1897). In 1885 he was appointed mathematics master at Katoomba College, New South Wales. Enthusiastic, 6 ft. 3 ins. (190.5 cm) 'long . . . strong and healthy and very fond of cricket', he was active in the local community and established a friendship with the cartoonist Phil May [q.v.5].

In 1893 Young went back to England. After a short period at Herkomer's art school at Bushey, Hertfordshire, he became involved with the innovative poster work of James and William Beggarstaff. On 1 July 1895 at St Peter's parish church, Bushey, he married Mabel Ellen Sawyer, an accomplished woodcarver whose work contributed to their support. He returned to Australia and in 1895-98 was art advertising manager to the Austral Cycle Agency, Melbourne, whose advertisements appeared in *Cycling News, Sportsman,* the *Bulletin* and other popular magazines. Briefly engaged in producing posters with Norman and Lionel Lindsay [qq.v.10] and Harry Weston, Young became prominent as a poster artist. He next began to paint large water-colour scenes of Melbourne's pioneering days, among them the printing of the first newspaper, the first christening and Lady Franklin's [q.v.1] reception at Fawkner's hotel. Abandoning such work about 1906, he then attempted to communicate his reaction to the Australian landscape in an imaginative way, for he believed the gulf between the European artist and his Australian subject to be so great that to depict the landscape realistically was an empty exercise.

His first one-man show in Melbourne in 1910 was followed by others in Adelaide and Melbourne (1911), and Sydney and Melbourne (1912). When he left for England in December 1912, Young was well known in the Australian art world: his water-colours hung in several State galleries and he had exhibited with the Victorian Artists' Society, the Society of Artists, Sydney, the Royal Art Society of New South Wales and the Royal South Australian Society of Arts. A member of the T-Square Club, he had attended meetings of the Royal Victorian Institute of Architects and designed layouts for its *Journal*.

After eighteen months in Sussex preparing for an exhibition which was cancelled by the outbreak of World War I, early in 1915 Young joined the British Army as an instructor in musketry; in 1917 he completed *Landscape target practises for miniature rifle shooting*. He exhibited with the Royal Academy of Arts, Royal Society of British Artists, Royal Institute of Painters in Water Colours and other groups. In 1920 he held a large exhibition in London and was invited to provide miniatures for Queen Mary's dolls' house. Having maintained contact through several exhibitions held in Melbourne in 1920-21, Young returned there in 1923. *The art of Blamire Young* had been published as a special number of *Art in Australia* (1921), its text echoing his articles in *Drawing and Design* (London, 1919-20) and his unpublished 'Autobiographical Sketch' written in 1920. Securely established, 'he was recognized everywhere as one of the leading artists in water colour in Australia'. He showed regularly in most capital cities and was in demand for lectures and after-dinner speeches; a connoisseur of wine, he was also a member of the National Rose Society of Victoria.

Young was a voluminous writer and an astute critic: he had contributed to the *Argus* in 1904-12 and sent articles and drawings to journals such as the *Lone Hand*. One of his plays, *The children's bread*, was performed in Melbourne in December 1911. He published *The proverbs of Goya* in 1923 and produced 'Adventures in paint', a hand-written book with twenty-seven original water-colours in 1924. As art critic for the Melbourne *Herald* in 1929-34, he wrote over 400 articles. Young cannot be identified with either the modernist developments or the conservative academic establishment of the 1920s and 1930s in Melbourne: responsive to a range of art, he campaigned for what he considered 'modern art', but remained friendly with conservatives like R. H. Croll, Harold Herbert, Hans Heysen [qq.v.8,9] and Lionel Lindsay. While reviewing traditional artists appreciatively, he remained critical of attempts to emulate the early works of Streeton [q.v.] and Roberts [q.v.11], and deplored the effect on students of Bernard Hall and Max Meldrum [qq.v.9,10]. He welcomed the work of Margaret Preston, Arnold Shore, Rah Fizelle, Ola Cohn [qq.v.11,8], Eric Thake, Ethel Spowers and J. K. Moore, yet warned against sacrificing conviction for fashion.

Blamire Young died on 14 January 1935 at his Lilydale home and was buried in the local cemetery. His wife and two daughters survived him.

J. F. Bruce, *The art of Blamire Young*, special no of *Art in Aust* (Syd, 1921); Bernard Smith, *Australian painting 1788-1960* (Melb, 1971); E. Fink, *The art of Blamire Young* (Syd, 1983); E. L. Fink, The art of Blamire Young (M.A. thesis, Univ Melb, 1978).

ELLY FINK

YOUNG, WILLIAM JOHN (1850-1931), pastoralist, was born on 20 October 1850 in Belfast, Ireland, son of Charles Young, ship's captain, and his wife Annie, née Lyle. With his mother and brother James, he arrived in Victoria probably in 1854 and lived at Kyneton with his father who had migrated earlier and was to represent Kyneton in the Legislative Assembly (1874-92). Aged 17, William left school at Geelong and joined James in trading and farming ventures on the west coast of New Zealand for three years; he then grew cotton on Taveuni in the Fiji Islands until 1875 when he returned to Victoria.

In 1877 William was a jackaroo and later an overseer at Lansdowne station in the Tambo district, Queensland. He was appointed manager of Evesham near Longreach in 1883 and of Lansdowne in 1889, at an annual salary of £500. During the 1891 shearers' strike his employers paid him a bonus of £150; on his recommendation the men were given a wage increase of 25 per cent. The Lansdowne Pastoral Co. was deep in debt, but, without sparing himself or his men, Young virtually cleared the mortgage.

He moved in October 1898 to Noondoo station, Dirranbandi, as general manager of the London-based Australian Pastoral Co. His greatest contribution to the pastoral industry was to stabilize this company, whose holdings extended over southern and western Queensland and into New South Wales, despite overstocking, depressed prices and drought: during the 1902 drought, its sheep losses exceeded 137 000. Young concentrated on land improvement, especially artesian bores, and significantly increased meat sales to exporters, obtaining record prices during World War I. Appreciating his business acumen and foresight, the company appointed him general superintendent in 1920. From his base in Sydney he ensured the company's investment in the British Australian Wool Realisation Association Pty Ltd which benefited participating wool-growers in the postwar period.

Legends surrounded this tough, self-reliant bushman who was small and lean with a 'tigerish ferocity' for work and a remarkable recuperative capacity. A dawn-to-dusk working stint became known as a 'Billy Young day' and his marking of 8400 lambs in a day was claimed as a world record. Renowned for his quickness with figures, he was a popular member of the Queensland Club who was respected by pastoralists and business associates. He aimed, quite simply, to further the fortunes of his employers and had no other major interests.

On 4 December 1883 he had married Sydney-born Anne McNicoll (d. 1922) with Anglican rites at Christ Church, Daylesford, Victoria. Survived by their four sons and three daughters, Young died on 1 June 1931 at Darling Point, Sydney, and was buried in the Presbyterian section of South Head cemetery. His estate was sworn for probate at £15 314.

G. W. Lilley, *Story of Lansdowne* (Melb, 1973); *Pastoral Review*, 15 Aug 1907, p 487, 16 June 1931, p 561; *Graziers' Review*, 16 July 1931, p 269; J. L. Young, Private journal, 1875-1881 (microfilm, Univ Qld); Aust Pastoral Co. papers (OL).

BETTY CROUCHLEY

YOUNG, WILLIAM JOHN (1878-1942), biochemist, was born on 26 January 1878 at Withington, Manchester, Lancashire, England, son of William John Bristow Young, clerk, and his wife Hannah, née Bury. Educated locally at Hulme Grammar School, he graduated (B.Sc., 1898; M.Sc., 1902) at the Owens College, Manchester, and was awarded the Levinstein (1899-1900) and Dalton (1900-01) research exhibitions. On 30 July 1903 he married Janet Taylor at St Margaret's parish church, Whalley Range.

In 1900-12 Young was assistant biochemist to the Lister Institute of Preventive Medicine, London, where he collaborated with (Sir) Arthur Harden in a series of investigations of alcoholic fermentations by yeast that laid the foundations for subsequent understandings of the process. Through this pioneering work, Young contributed to the birth of the new science of biochemistry. He was awarded a D.Sc. by the University of London in 1910.

Appointed biochemist at the Australian Institute of Tropical Medicine, Townsville, Young migrated with his family to Queensland in 1913; his principal research there was on the metabolism of Whites living in the tropics. In 1920 W. A. Osborne [q.v.11], professor of physiology at the University of Melbourne, obtained Young's services as lecturer in physiology and biochemistry. As director of the department of biochemistry, Young was appointed associate-professor in 1924 and became foundation professor in 1938. Soon after arriving in Melbourne, he developed an interest in the applied biochemistry of food

preservation and transport, and subsequently became the leading Australian expert and innovator in this field: he solved problems associated with the conveyance of chilled meat and the preservation of citrus fruits, and devised the methods still used in the marketing of ripening bananas.

In 1926 (Sir) Albert Rivett [q.v.11] persuaded the university to allow Young leave to help the Council for Scientific and Industrial Research (with which he had worked closely) to establish laboratory and field studies into the biochemical problems of the cold storage of food. Despite Rivett's hopes of recruiting him, in 1928 Young returned to his teaching duties which included lecturing to agricultural, dental, medical and science students. He remained a consultant to the C.S.I.R. and his recommendations led to the formation of the section of food preservation and transport in 1931. His research career seems to have been unusually polarized between theory and practice, commencing with seminal theoretical studies and ending in cogent practicality.

A 'small, sharp-featured man with a sprightly step', Young was an enthusiastic bushwalker and president of the Wallaby Club (1925-26); he was also an amateur craftsman who described himself as a carpenter and tinkerer. Contemporaries spoke of him as an indefatigable worker and a charming companion. Gentle and modest, he had an uncommon sense of social involvement: he was a fellow of numerous professional associations and served on such public bodies as the Australian College of Dentistry (chairman, 1931-38) and the Victorian branch of the Australian Chemical Institute (president, 1938-39). Survived by his wife and daughter, Young died of a perforated gastric ulcer on 14 May 1942 in East Melbourne and was cremated. His portrait by Charles Wheeler [q.v.] is in the department of biochemistry, University of Melbourne.

C. A. Grant, *500 Victorians* (Melb, 1934); *J of the Chemical Soc* (Lond), 1943, p 44; *Food technology in Aust*, 38, 1986, p 158; Central Registry files (Univ Melb).

MAX MARGINSON

YOUNG, WILLIAM RAMSAY (1894-1965), soldier and butcher, was born on 13 July 1894 at Coatbridge, Lanarkshire, Scotland, son of David Young, wine merchant, and his wife Agnes, née Ramsay. The family migrated to Australia and settled in North Adelaide. Young was educated there and became a chorister at St Peter's Anglican Cathedral and a member of the South Australian Caledonian Society Pipe Band.

After completing his apprenticeship to a butcher, Young enlisted as a private in the Australian Imperial Force on 3 May 1915 and embarked for Egypt with the 2nd Reinforcements for the 27th Battalion in June. Service on Gallipoli brought promotion to lance corporal. The battalion reached France in March 1916. Young was promoted corporal on 1 September and awarded the Distinguished Conduct Medal later that month. The recommendation for the D.C.M. referred to his deeds on three occasions: on the night of 5-6 May two soldiers had been wounded in no man's land, Armentières, near the enemy's wire. Privates Young and Schenscher went 300 yards out to bring them back under heavy machine-gun fire. On the night of 29-30 June at Messines both men were engaged all night carrying wounded from the trenches under considerable artillery fire. Although their stretcher was broken by a shell, they procured another and continued to work. On the night of 4-5 August during the attack on Pozières Ridge both men again behaved with considerable bravery as stretcher-bearers for eighteen uninterrupted hours.

On 6 November Young was promoted sergeant and soon afterwards was awarded the Military Medal for working incessantly for forty hours during an attack on German trenches on 5 November. He 'showed a dogged determination in continuing his work, organising parties, and getting them down to the Regimental Aid Post' and searched no man's land under heavy shell- and machine-gun fire.

In November 1917 he was sent to the 6th Training Battalion in England, rejoining his unit in France in January 1918. During the advance at Morlancourt on 10 June he was wounded and won a Bar to his M.M. He was promoted warrant officer, class 2, and company sergeant major. His two brothers, Lance Corporal Alexander Young, M.M., 50th Battalion, and Private Thomas Young, 27th Battalion, also served with the A.I.F.

Coming home in 1919, Young married Caroline Ivy Freeman (d. 1971) in Adelaide on 21 May 1921; they had two children, then shifted to a butchering business at Minlaton. The Depression brought failure. The family moved to Keith where Young worked as a labourer before obtaining positions with the South Australian Railways at Brimbago and Wirrega. In 1935 he returned to Adelaide to a job at the Islington Railway Workshops. In World War II Young served from July 1940 with the 3rd Training Battalion and in May 1941 was promoted sergeant while stationed at the Loveday Prisoner-of-War Camp; from September he was a warrant officer. He was discharged medically unfit in October 1942. Back at Islington he eventually became supervisor of a hostel for migrant workers until retiring in 1954.

A Freemason and a fervent supporter of the Returned Sailors', Soldiers' and Airmen's Imperial League of Australia, Young was a

gregarious and generous man whose loud voice gave rise to his nickname, 'The Brompton Bull'. Survived by his wife, son and daughter, he died of cerebral thrombosis on 9 January 1965 in the Repatriation Hospital, Daw Park, Adelaide, and was cremated.

London Gazette, 29 Dec 1916, 19 Jan 1917, 21 Oct 1918; recommendation files for honours and awards 1914-18 War, AIF, 2nd Australian Division (AWM); information from Mrs A. E. Eaton, Campbelltown, Adel, and Mr R. W. Young, Brompton, Adel.
                                    R. R. FREEMAN

YOUNG WAI, JOHN (1847?-1930), Presbyterian minister, was born in Canton, China, and came to the Victorian goldfields in 1867. After spending three years mining with no particular success, he devoted his life to the Presbyterian Church. Realizing his inadequacies, in 1875 he began full-time training for the ministry at the Presbyterian Church of Victoria's new Chinese Mission Seminary at Fitzroy, Melbourne.

Before he completed his training the seminary was closed in 1877 because of 'student unrest' allegedly orchestrated by an instructor C. H. Cheong [q.v.3]. Young Wai next worked among Chinese communities in Victorian towns. In 1880 he was asked by the Presbyterian Mission to the Heathen to mediate a dispute between the American superintendent of the Chinese Mission in Melbourne and a Chinese mission worker. His efforts resulted in the departure of the American. Having declined an invitation to take over his post, Young Wai accepted a call to Sydney in 1882 where the Presbyterian Church's work among the Chinese had met with little success because of language difficulties. An eloquent preacher, he conducted his mission from the Scots Church. Following custom, he returned to China to seek a wife and married Sarah Ti See Man on 27 January 1886 at the German Church, Hong Kong. He brought his bride to Australia to share his work, especially among old people; he was also later assisted by his children.

His congregation having outgrown the schoolroom in the Scots Church, in 1893 Young Wai established a Chinese Presbyterian Church in Forster Street. He was ordained in October. His mission flourished and he established another church at Waterloo in 1897. He was inducted at Forster Street on 22 October 1898. At both churches he supervised the teaching of English to Chinese four nights a week. From the Moody and Sankey hymnal he translated 302 hymns into Chinese which were used throughout Australasia. He also helped to establish churches at Newcastle and Wollongong. On 20 July 1905 Young Wai was elected moderator of the General Assembly of the Presbyterian Church of New South Wales; he declined the honour because he considered himself an unworthy successor to Rev. Dill Macky [q.v.8].

Greatly respected in the Chinese community, Young Wai candidly supported the republican cause during and after the Chinese revolution in 1911. He had been involved in the Chinese anti-opium crusade (1905) and later campaigns to press for relaxation of the Immigration Restriction Act. Planning to retire in 1919, he learned that his replacement from Hong Kong had been refused an entry permit and stayed on while the moderator successfully petitioned the prime minister W. M. Hughes [q.v.9] for special dispensation.

Although Young Wai retired in 1920, he continued intermittently to help his Church and its congregations. Some of his flock went to Hong Kong and China, among them Harr Chan and Kwok Bew [q.v.9]. They set up businesses there and also established Presbyterian churches in Hong Kong and in their ancestral villages in China. Survived by his wife, three daughters and three sons, Young Wai died at Summer Hill, Sydney, on 21 June 1930 and was buried in Rookwood cemetery.

A. J. Campbell, *Fifty years of Presbyterianism in Victoria* (Melb, 1889); J. H. Terras, *The mission of the Presbyterian Church of New South Wales* (Syd, 1928); J. Cameron, *Centenary history of the Presbyterian Church in New South Wales* (Syd, 1905); C. A. White, *The challenge of the years* (Syd, 1951); C. F. Yong, *The new gold mountain* (Adel, 1977); *SMH*, 23, 24 June 1930; J. A. Welch, Pariahs and outcasts: Christian missions to the Chinese in Victoria in the nineteenth century (M.A. thesis, Univ Monash, 1980).   ADRIAN CHAN

YUILL, WILLIAM JOHN (1885-1960), dairyman, was born on 10 October 1885 at Sebastian, Sandhurst (Bendigo), Victoria, son of Victorian-born parents John Yuill, miner, and his wife Agnes Jane, née Cowie. William left school at 10 and at 16 became the breadwinner for his widowed mother and her six younger children. His interest in dairying arose from frequent visits to grandmother Yuill's farm-store farther out in the district. On 19 December 1911 at California Gully, Bendigo, he married Maude Stewart Prowse with Methodist forms.

After completing an examination, in 1917 Yuill was accepted as a dairy supervisor by the Victorian Department of Agriculture and appointed to Mirboo North where he campaigned against measuring the value of dairy herds only by breed and appearance. Persuaded by his arguments and his enthusiasm, district farmers established the Yinnar Herd

Testing Association in 1920. Yuill accompanied an official on his rounds through the pioneering settlements in an open buggy, helping with the Babcock test on which his claims for herd improvement were based. From these practices there developed the Gippsland United Cow Testing Association, later the Victorian United Cow Testing Association and later still the Victorian Herd Improvement Association.

A self-made man, Bill Yuill believed that work was the means of salvation; his outgoing, irrepressible personality, tolerant attitudes and flair for language and public speaking made him a popular figure wherever he spread his gospel. In 1921 he introduced the first Young Farmers' Club: he was to remain on the central council of the State-wide organization for many years. In 1925 he travelled Victoria with the Better Farming Train, forming herd test associations at stops on the way. He was an originator in 1930 of the Dairy Farm Competition which held annual educative field days and was an early contributor to radio broadcasts for farmers. Under the pen name 'S. C. Macarthur' he wrote for a variety of newspapers and contributed to the Victorian *Journal of Agriculture*.

Yuill kept in touch with the progress of dairy-farming abroad, particularly in America and New Zealand. As the struggle to introduce herd testing was won, he broadened his view of dairy improvement, adopting and popularizing the slogan of 'Breed, Weed and Feed'. His drive for testing the progeny of sires brought him into conflict with established breed societies, but his integrity and dedication enabled him to achieve his goals without losing their respect.

Despite his minimal education, Yuill progressed within the Department of Agriculture to become supervisor of herd testing for Victoria in 1937. Feeling the strains of intense commitment and constant travel, he retired in 1948 to join the Australian Jersey Herd Book Society as publicity officer. He was recognized as 'the father of dairy herd testing' and published a memoir in 1958. Apart from attending his local Presbyterian church and growing dahlias, Yuill made his work his life. He died on 5 October 1960 at Parkville, Melbourne, and was cremated. His wife, son and four daughters survived him.

K. Sillcock, *Three lifetimes of dairying in Victoria* (Melb, 1972); *J of Agr* (Vic), Apr 1923, Aug 1928, Nov 1960; *Age*, 6 Oct 1960; *Weekly Times* (Melb), 12 Oct 1960; letters from E. P. Prentice (USA), 10 Dec 1936, 2 Dec 1939, 25 Apr 1942 (held by Mr I. W. Yuill, Burwood, Melb); information from Mrs E. A. Black, Richmond, Mrs J. M. Watson, Burwood, and Mrs J. Down, Murrumbeena, Melb.   L. LOMAS

Z

ZADOW, CHRISTIANE SUSANNE AUGUSTINE (1846-1896), trade unionist and factory inspector, was born on 27 August 1846 at Runkel, Duchy of Nassau, daughter of Elizabethe Hemming and Johann Georg Hofmeyer, gardener, who were married next year. Educated at Wiesbaden and, on a scholarship, at the Ladies' Seminary, Biebrich-on-Rhine, she became a companion and governess, travelling through Germany, France, Russia, Siberia and England. Just over four feet (121.9 cm) tall, she was warm-hearted, alert and fluent in several languages. Having seen women reduced to 'veritable beasts of burden', on settling in London in 1868 she worked as a tailoress and helped oppressed female clothing workers in the East End.

At the register office, Westminster, on 30 May 1871 Augusta (as she now styled herself) married Heinrich Christian Wilhelm Zadow, a tailor and a political refugee from Germany. Seeking a just society, they embarked with their 3-year-old son in the *Robert Lees* as assisted migrants bound for Adelaide. Arriving in 1877, they lived at Goodwood. Augusta laboured tirelessly to assist the increasing number of Adelaide's female workers in the newly-mechanized clothing trades. To overcome the injustice of their penurious wages, she planned for structural change. Although a proposed women's co-operative clothing factory was not achieved in her lifetime, she was the major force in establishing the Working Women's Trades Union in 1890: she was its foundation treasurer and, from late 1891, a delegate to the United Trades and Labor Council. With Mary Lee and David Charleston [qq.v.10,7], she drew up a log of wages and prices for use in Adelaide. She investigated complaints about women's wages, work safety and sanitary conditions, and gathered evidence for a council sub-committee on sweating.

In 1893, during the depression, Mrs Zadow established the Co-operative White Workers' Association, supplying donated materials to shirt and underwear makers and paying fair wages from garment sales. She found employment for women as domestics; she also managed the Distressed Women and Children's Fund, her earnest appeals gaining colony-wide response in cash and kind. Using 'simple eloquence' and conviction, Augusta drew widespread support for female suffrage; after women in South Australia were enfranchised in 1894, Charles Kingston's [q.v.9] government appointed her an inspector of factories in February 1895. She resigned from the union and was naturalized in September. With

temporary premises and a minimal salary, she walked to inspect city and suburban factories, workshops and dressmaking establishments, and supervised the safety and working conditions of women and minors. When she encountered 'opposition and rudeness' from some employers, she continued undeterred. Her precise, practical reports and recommendations, written in copperplate, often at night, were adopted and set standards. She took no leave.

Augusta was compiling a report on the 1894 Factories Act when she contracted influenza; she died of haematemesis on 7 July 1896 in Adelaide. Mourners at her funeral, conducted with Anglican rites, included Kingston, twenty parliamentarians and many factory women. The Trades and Labor Council collected nearly 1000 threepenny subscriptions for her tombstone at West Terrace cemetery which honoured her 'Self-denying Efforts on Behalf of the Struggling and Oppressed'. Her husband and son survived her.

H. Jones, *Nothing seemed impossible* (Brisb, 1985) and *In her own name* (Adel, 1986); Report of inspector of factories, *PP* (SA), 1896 (87); *Voice* (Adel), 14 July 1893; *Advertiser* (Adel), 9 July 1896; *Register* (Adel), 11 July 1896; *Weekly Herald* (Adel), 17 July 1896; *Daily Herald* (Adel), 14 June 1913; United Trades and Labor Council of SA, Minutes, Dec 1889-Dec 1896, and Letter-book, 12 July 1896 (Mortlock Lib); Factories letter-book, 26 June, 27 Sept 1895, 21 Jan, 29 May, 8, 10 June, 6, 7, 8 July 1896 (PRO, SA). HELEN JONES

ZAHEL, ETHEL MAY ELIZA (1877-1951), teacher and administrator, was born on 3 February 1877 at Mackay, Queensland, fifth child of Joseph Priestley Kemp, a bookseller from England, and his native-born wife Sarah Edith, née Morton. On 6 November 1895, at Mackay, Ethel married with Catholic rites Mark Charles Zahel, a 40-year-old solicitor. After practising at Cairns and Cooktown, in August 1905 her husband took her to Thursday Island where he died on 4 June 1907. In that month Mrs Zahel accepted a temporary post as head teacher at the government school on the small and isolated Yam Island in Torres Strait, but resigned in November. Her permanent appointment to the Torres Strait Islands teaching service dated from 15 June 1909 when, accompanied by her only child, 13-year-old Ethel Lorenza, she returned to Yam. Her daughter died of malaria on 24 July. Posted on 19 August to Badu (Mulgrave Island), Mrs Zahel opened school on 18 October. She lived in the household of Frederick Walker, a former missionary who managed Papuan Industries Ltd.

Under the system of administration introduced to the Torres Strait Islands in 1898 by John Douglas [q.v.4], the government resident on Thursday Island, European teachers had to perform many duties unrelated to classrooms. Mrs Zahel was clerk and treasurer of the Badu court, and registrar of births, deaths and marriages; she also dispensed medicine. In 1915 she was given control of the 'company boats', owned by Islanders who dealt with Papuan Industries: she signed authorizations for provisioning the vessels and determined advance payments made for pearl-shell and trochus brought back to Badu. From 1911 (until the appointment of a European teacher in 1928) she paid monthly visits by dinghy to Adam (later Poid) village on Moa to assist the councillors and, after 1915, to supervise the mission-trained native teacher.

Visitors commented favourably on her work. Although Ethel was an untrained teacher, in 1911 Governor Sir William Mac-Gregor [q.v.5] praised the tone and scholastic attainments of her school; in 1924 Inspector Clement Fox described her as 'a bright vigorous woman, intelligent and forceful, of good address and of a genial disposition'; in 1927 the under secretary for public instruction Bernard McKenna [q.v.10] found her 'eminently fitted to discharge the many and diversified duties associated with her position'. Governor Sir Leslie Wilson [q.v.] recommended in 1933 that European teachers on the islands be denominated 'Superintendents . . . whose decisions, in all matters, shall be final—subject, of course, to appeal to the Chief Protector'. A strike by 'company boat' captains and crews in 1936, however, led to a reorganization of the Torres Strait administration and to increased responsibilities for indigenous councillors.

Evacuated from Torres Strait on 29 January 1942 after Australia had declared war with Japan, Mrs Zahel retired from the public service that year. From 1943 she lived in Brisbane. She died there on 9 April 1951 and was cremated with Anglican rites.

Queensland, *Report of the government resident at Thursday Island for 1898* (Brisb, 1899); C. M. Yonge, *A year on the great barrier reef* (Lond, 1930); Chief Protector of Aboriginals (Qld), *Annual Report*, 1907, 1909, 1911; *Cummins & Campbell's Mthly Mag*, July 1935; *Walkabout*, 1 July 1938; Chief Protector of Aboriginals Office, Correspondence 1907-1918 and file marked Isles Torres Strait, 1 Nov 1933 *and* Home Office, Correspondence, COL/B53, inward (Chief Protector of Aboriginals) items 6686, 13 June 1907, 12324, 20 Nov 1907 *and* GOV/53, Despatch no 41 of 1911 *and* Home Secretary's Office, Correspondence, 21 Jan 1924 *and* EDU/Mission Schools, in-letters 46438 of 1924, 26478 of 1927 (QA); information from Dept of Community Services, Qld.

MARGARET LAWRIE

ZEAL, SIR WILLIAM AUSTIN (1830-1912), engineer, businessman and politician, was born on 5 December 1830 at Westbury, Wiltshire, England, son of Thomas Zeal, wine merchant, and his wife Ann, née Greenland. Educated at private schools at Westbury and at Windsor, William obtained a diploma as surveyor and engineer in 1851. He arrived in Melbourne late in 1852 and spent two years on the Forest Creek (Castlemaine) goldfields. After his importing venture failed, he moved to Melbourne where he worked briefly for an architectural firm before joining the Melbourne, Mount Alexander and Murray River Railway Co. When the company was bought out by the Victorian government in 1856, Zeal remained as a government surveyor and railway engineer, supervising construction between Footscray and Sunbury. He then became general manager and attorney (1859-64) for Cornish & Bruce, contractors for the Melbourne-Sandhurst (Bendigo) line.

In 1864-65 Zeal represented Castlemaine in the Legislative Assembly. During his 1864 election campaign he attacked the competence of the Victorian railways engineer-in-chief Thomas Higinbotham [q.v.4]. The following year Zeal was exonerated by a select committee which investigated Higinbotham's implied allegation that Zeal had acted dishonestly while employed by the railways department. From 1866 Zeal partnered (Sir) William Mitchell [q.v.5] in Riverina pastoral ventures which were ruined by drought. Returning to Melbourne in 1869, Zeal subsequently designed the Moama-Deniliquin railway.

He again represented Castlemaine in 1871-74. Having unsuccessfully contested the Legislative Council seat of South Western Province in 1876, he won North Western Province (North Central from November 1882) in May 1882. A 'diehard' conservative, Zeal believed that the 'thrifty' classes with 'a stake in the colony' should be protected by the maintenance of Upper House powers. Rightly critical of the 1880s railway construction follies, he coined the word 'circumbendibus' to describe the worst examples. He had some liberal instincts and supported divorce law reform in 1889. Postmaster-general in the Shiels [q.v.11] ministry in 1892, he served on ten inquiries and was a member (1890-92) of the standing committee on railways.

Zeal's parliamentary career was crowned by presidency of the council in 1892-1901. Relishing the role of 'genial autocrat' and 'stern disciplinarian', he gave no ground in a clash with the Speaker of the Legislative Assembly (Sir) Thomas Bent [q.v.3] over control of a committee-room. Zeal was respected for his 'exquisite courtesy' and his bachelor status in no way impeded his social performance: his 'little dinners' were acknowledged as 'the most charming of feasts'. Appointed K.C.M.G. in 1895, he was a delegate to the Australasian Federal Convention of 1897-98. Sir William resigned his presidency in 1901 after successfully standing for the Senate, but was never at home in Federal parliament. Expecting to be chosen as president of the Senate, he was disappointed when Sir Richard Baker [q.v.7] was appointed. Zeal's complaints of government extravagance were given rough treatment by Labor senators and in 1906 he retired from politics. In 1908 he published a pamphlet attacking the board of works.

Tenacity and business sense had served him well: 'no Melburnian had a finger in more financial pies'. By the 1880s he was a 'considerable' mining investor and, at the turn of the century, held several directorships: he was chairman (1897-1912) of Goldsbrough, Mort [qq.v.4,5] & Co. Ltd, the Australian Mutual Provident Society's Victorian branch (1899-1912), the Perpetual Executors & Trustee Association (1895-1912) and the London Guarantee & Accident Co. Ltd. As one of the auditors of the National Bank, in 1870 Zeal had resisted pressure to temper criticism of management; later, as a director (1883-1912), he helped to devise a reconstruction scheme which kept the bank from going under in the crash of 1893. He was a member of the Institution of Civil Engineers, London, and a Prahran city councillor (1879-82).

A dapper little figure with sandy hair and beard, Zeal delivered peppery speeches, sprinkled with 'sharp, staccato rebukes', in a 'pleasant and musical tenor'. Although known for acts of private generosity, he was intensely self-contained and had few intimates. His recreations were solitary: walking and collecting art. Melbourne *Punch* characterized him in 1905 as living 'in a shell detached from the rest of mankind'. Zeal died at his Toorak home on 11 March 1912 and was buried in Melbourne general cemetery. His estate was sworn for probate at £74 804. He left his art collection to the Bendigo Art Gallery and made provision for a charitable trust.

J. Smith (ed), *Cyclopedia of Victoria*, 1 (Melb, 1903); G. Blainey, *Gold and paper* (Melb, 1958); *V&P* (LA Vic), 1864-65, 2 (D20); *Table Talk*, 6 May 1892, 14 Mar 1912; *Australasian*, 19 Aug 1893, 8 June 1895; *Punch* (Melb), 14 Dec 1905; *Age* and *Argus*, 12 Mar 1912; *Bulletin*, 21 Mar 1912.   GEOFF BROWNE

ZELMAN, SAMUEL VICTOR ALBERT (ALBERTO) (1874-1927), conductor, violinist and teacher, was born on 15 November 1874 in North Melbourne, eldest son of Alberto Zelman [q.v.6], a musician from Austria, and his English wife Harriott Eliza (Emily), née Hodgkinson. Alberto junior was a violin prodigy, making his first public appearance aged 6. His early teachers were his father, Roberto Bima, an Italian viola player with the Lyster [q.v.5] Opera Company, and Henry Curtis, a violinist and family friend. Educated at King's College, Fitzroy, and Hawthorn State School, in his adolescence he formed an orchestra which rehearsed in the homes of wealthy patrons; compelled by the need to understand his work as a conductor, he learned to play all the standard orchestral instruments.

At 17 Zelman toured Tasmania and New Zealand with the soprano Amy Sherwin [q.v.6]. When several influential Melbourne patrons attempted to raise funds to further his education abroad, his father opposed the move, thereby preventing his son from acquiring a conventional musical education, but encouraging in its place self-help which produced an independence of mind and an original concept of musical values.

A member of the orchestra founded by G. W. L. Marshall-Hall [q.v.10] in 1892, Zelman led the second violins from 1900. He left in 1910 to join the rival but short-lived Professional Orchestra, becoming its first conductor. In 1901-10 he taught violin at the Marshall-Hall Conservatorium (later known as the Albert Street and later still as the Melba [q.v.10] Conservatorium) and thereafter at the conservatorium of the University of Melbourne. He was a member of the university's board of examiners in music from 1906. Zelman resigned his university post when Marshall-Hall was reinstated as Ormond [q.v.5] professor of music in 1915. A long-standing quarrel between the two, of considerable importance to Zelman's career, was left unresolved when Marshall-Hall died that year.

In his early twenties Zelman had directed light opera for George Musgrove [q.v.5], but refused subsequent offers to conduct in the United States of America: the prospect of such a career was unattractive to his nature and temperament. He formed the Melbourne Symphony Orchestra in 1906 which remained a largely amateur body until it was supplemented by professionals following World War I. In 1905 he had founded the Melbourne String Quartette and after 1918 established the British Music Society Quartette. Choirmaster of the Independent Church, Collins Street, he was also conductor (1911-27) of the Royal Melbourne Philharmonic Society, for which his own orchestra played. He founded the Orchestral League in 1922 and was at various times a member of the executives of the Musical Society of Victoria, the British Music Society and the Savage Club.

On 6 April 1912, at Hawthorn, Zelman had married with Australian Church forms the soprano Maude Harrington Jenkins. They remained childless and lived in a rented flat at Hawthorn. In 1922 they spent several months in Europe where Zelman conducted the Berlin Philharmonic and the London Symphony orchestras, with Maude as soloist. He was enthusiastically received in Berlin and, although London was not impressed by his performances, returned to Australia with an enhanced reputation which increased the demand for his services.

Small, slight and never robust, Zelman rapidly exhausted himself. He died of complicated gastroenteritis on 3 March 1927 at Hawthorn and was buried in Box Hill cemetery. There is a tablet to his memory in St Paul's Cathedral, Melbourne, and at the Savage Club a light burns in his honour. Ranked at the time of his death as the country's foremost violinist and conductor, he was described by a contemporary Isabelle Moresby as 'an unselfish pioneer' who had 'none of the tricks and eccentricities often associated with genius'. Students and players left lavish testimonials to a teacher and friend who was personally unambitious, but evoked enduring devotion. The Zelman Memorial Symphony Orchestra was founded by his followers in 1933.

D. M. Dow, *Melbourne Savages* (Melb, 1947); I. Moresby, *Australia makes music* (Melb, 1948); W. A. Carne, *A century of harmony* (Melb, 1954); T. Radic, *G. W. L. Marshall-Hall*, music monograph 5, Univ WA (Perth, 1982); D. Fairweather, *Your friend Alberto Zelman* (Melb, 1984); M. T. Radic, Some historical aspects of musical associations in Melbourne, 1888-1915 (Ph.D. thesis, Univ Melb, 1977); letter from E. Rofe, 2 Dec 1974, to author, Malvern, Melb; Zelman collection (LaTL).

MAUREEN THERESE RADIC

ZERCHO, CHARLES HENRY (1866-1962) and FREDERICK WILLIAM (1867-1953), educationists, were born on 15 April 1866 and 16 August 1867 at Barkers Creek, Victoria, sons of a Saxon migrant Henry Zercho, stonemason, and his Scottish-born wife Agnes, née Nicol. Although of Lutheran descent on their father's side, the brothers were baptized as Anglicans at Castlemaine where they were educated.

Charles's career combined schoolmastering and ministering to a parish. In 1891-92 and again in 1911-13 he was chaplain and resident master at Brighton Grammar School. Made deacon in 1896 and ordained priest in 1897, he was minister of the parishes of Mitiamo (1896), Dookie (1897-98), Malmsbury (1898-1902) and St Peter's, Eaglehawk (1902-04). In 1904-10 he was minister of All Saints Church, Tatura, and principal of the Anglican high school. He was permitted to officiate in 1910-26 in the diocese of Melbourne.

In 1913 he was appointed headmaster of All Saints Grammar School, East St Kilda, a small, declining parish school. He graduated from the University of Melbourne (B.A., 1917). Zercho was a strict disciplinarian and a man of drive and vision who quickly gained the confidence of the parents. Tall and athletic, he had played football for Essendon in 1890 and strove to improve his school's sporting reputation. Under Zercho the school expanded from 70 to 190 pupils and outgrew its limited accommodation. The school council approved his plan to purchase a nearby property, but feared that he would open a school of his own and forced him to resign in 1919.

In 1920 Zercho became headmaster of Berwick Grammar School. His dynamic personality assisted its development, student numbers trebling within a year. He again fell foul of a parsimonious council which in 1921 terminated his services. He then went to Box Hill Grammar School as headmaster; once more, lack of financial support inhibited progress and in 1925 he left in despair. Thereafter he devoted himself to ministering to various parishes: Surrey Hills (1926-28), Healesville (1928-30) and, from 1930, St Oswald's, Glen Iris. In 1948 he retired to Queensland where he published two devotional works. Predeceased by his wife Margaret Emma, née Clark, whom he had married on 17 April 1900 at St Paul's Church, Bendigo, Zercho died at Murwillumbah, New South Wales, on 30 March 1962 and was cremated. A daughter survived him.

At the age of 14 Frederick began an apprenticeship at Thompson's [q.v.] engineering works, Castlemaine; he later qualified as a licensed shorthand writer, winning distinction at the law courts examination. In 1895 he became manager of Stott and Hoare's Business College, Melbourne, where he taught shorthand, typing, book-keeping and English. Next year he joined the United Typewriter Co. as head teacher at its Central Business College which topped the Melbourne law courts' shorthand examination in 1896-1902.

In 1906 Zercho resigned from the college and, with his former assistant Andrew MacDougall as co-proprietor, set up Zercho's Business College, first in Flinders Street and from 1911 in Collins Street. It became the largest business college in Australia. MacDougall sold out in 1909 to the Chartres family who took up a majority interest in the college. Zercho retained one hundred shares and the position of headmaster, while becoming a director of Chartres Pty Ltd.

Frederick Zercho had married Nellie Branford Grenfell (d. 1903) at Christ Church, Castlemaine, on 5 September 1893; on 21 October 1909 at Christ Church, St Kilda, he married Beatrice Maud Bentley. Survived by his wife and daughter, and by the son and daughter of his first marriage, he died on 15 April 1953 at Kew and was buried in Melbourne general cemetery. In 1968 the college was sold to Stott's Business College.

J. Hetherington, *The morning was shining* (Lond, 1971); *St Oswald's Anglican Church, Glen Iris* (Melb, 1976); *All Saints' Grammarian*, 1913-19; *Review of Reviews* (Melb), 20 Apr 1902; *Berwick County Times*, 19 Dec 1919, 22 Oct, 24 Dec 1920, 24 Mar, 23 Dec 1921, 6 Jan 1922; *Punch* (Melb), 10 Mar 1921; *Box Hill Reporter*, 9 Feb, 21 Dec 1923, 19 Dec 1924, 18 Dec 1925, 29 Jan 1926; M. E. Humphries, A school that has passed: All Saints' Grammar School, East St Kilda, 1871-1937 (M.Ed. thesis, Univ Melb, 1985); All Saints' Church, East St Kilda, *Annual Reports of Vestry*, 1913-19, *and* Minutes of Vestry, 1913-37; Univ Melb Archives.

MICHAEL E. HUMPHRIES

ZIESEMER, FRIEDRICH WILHELM ERNST (1897-1972) and THEODOR MARTIN PETER (1899-1961), wheat-growers, were born on 8 August 1897 and 26 May 1899 at Pittsworth, Queensland, sons of August Friedrich Wilhelm Ziesemer, farmer, and his wife Wilhelmina, née Mundt, both German born. Reared on a dairy farm at Rosevale, near Dalby, as young men they went north, cutting cane to finance their first farm; Friedrich also worked as a drover and horse-breaker.

Forming a partnership, in 1921 they bought 640 acres (259 ha) of rich black soil at Bongeen, near Pittsworth, for £1920. The land was considered suitable only for grazing, but the brothers broke up 120 acres (48.6 ha) during their first year of operation and planted wheat, a crop that had previously been restricted on the Darling Downs to small-farming. Breaking up another 350 acres (141.6 ha) for wheat in their second year, they doubled their property's size in 1923 by purchasing an adjoining block. The Ziesemers' successful example attracted other wheat-growers to the district.

Prepared to experiment with mechanized farming, in 1923 Ziesemer Bros bought their first tractor. In 1931 their 2800-acre (1133 ha) Bongeen holding was serviced by a plant of three Twin-City tractors, six headers and —the pride of their fleet—a Sunshine auto-header (named White Nose after the 1931 Melbourne Cup winner). By 1935 they owned ten Sunshines: it was claimed that no wheat farm in Australia was as well equipped. At their peak, Ziesemer Bros had 4000 acres (1618.8 ha) under cultivation and chartered special trains to carry their harvest. In the late 1920s they branched into dairy-farming. Purchasing Tosari, a 2000-acre (809.4 ha) farm at Yandilla, they used the first electric milking machines in the district and developed the property into a model dairy-farm.

The brothers had married sisters: on 4 October 1922 Theodor married with Anglican rites Elsie Elizabeth Naumann at St Andrew's Church, Pittsworth; on 30 December 1926 Friedrich married Grace May Naumann at the Lutheran parsonage, Toowoomba. The fruitful partnership was dissolved in the 1940s and the brothers then helped to establish their respective sons on the land. Friedrich bought Khamoo in the Condamine district, partially clearing and cultivating it before disposing of it in 1963; he later jointly purchased a Taroom cattle property with a son. Theodor retired in 1951, but in 1955 he and his sons bought 1250 acres (505.9 ha) of virgin brigalow country in the Condamine, on which they produced wheat that won awards at Toowoomba only two years later.

Survived by his wife, two daughters and two sons, Ted died of uraemia and cancer on 28 November 1961 at St Vincent's Hospital, Toowoomba, and was cremated; his estate was sworn for probate at £59 464. Fred died at Toowoomba on 3 October 1972 and was cremated with Anglican rites; he was survived by his wife and three sons; his estate was valued at $116 109. As agricultural entrepreneurs the Ziesemers had experimented with crops and equipment, and played a significant part in developing the Darling Downs into the granary of Queensland.

Pittsworth Sentinel, 30 Nov 1961, 12 Oct 1972; History—wheat development—Ziesemer family (ts from newspaper-cuttings, OL).

BRIAN F. STEVENSON

ZIMPEL, WILLIAM JAMES (1859-1923), furniture-maker and merchant, was born in Pesth, Hungary, on 25 February 1859, son of David Zimpel, stationer, and his wife Anna. When William was aged 5 the family migrated to Turkey and for twelve years lived in Constantinople where he learned the rudiments of the furniture trade. After the death of his parents, he went to England with his sister Klara and brother Adolf, and was apprenticed to John Stringer, an art furniture manufacturer in London. Stringer later described him as 'one of the most respectable, steady and worthy men I have ever had in my employ'. In 1884 Zimpel was chosen as one of a hundred men to be brought to Western Australia by

James Grave to work in his Federal Furniture Factory in Perth. Pronounced 'a thoroughly practical cabinet maker' who 'has made all kinds of high class work' and whose 'jobs have been exhibited in the Great Exhibitions', Zimpel arrived at Fremantle in June 1884 in the *Bonnington*. On 3 February 1886 he married Frances Nellie Harland at St George's Anglican Cathedral, Perth; they were to have eight children.

Concurrently with his employment Zimpel had begun working on his own, establishing a furniture factory and later shops at 797-807 Hay Street. The business built up a reputation for being able to supply all levels of the community and secured many government contracts. It also profited by Zimpel's astute move to establish a country order department. He ran a wholesale trade in mattresses in the coastal and goldfields districts, and had 'constantly in stock from 30 to 40 different varieties of perambulator'. Zimpels grew into the largest wholesale and retail furniture business in Western Australia; by the turn of the century it employed about forty factory hands; the company's staff subsequently grew to over one hundred.

Zimpel had become a naturalized British subject in 1888. Quiet and reserved, he was highly regarded as one of Western Australia's leading businessmen. He gave evidence before the commission of the Legislative Assembly appointed to inquire into the operation of the customs tariffs in the colony (1893) and before the joint select committee which considered the draft Commonwealth bill (1899). A local municipal councillor, he built his house, Pine Lodge, in John Street, Cottesloe, where he was among the first to plant the renowned avenue of Norfolk Island pines which were nurtured with water from his well. Survived by his wife, six daughters and a son, he died on 3 December 1923 at Cottesloe and was buried in Karrakatta cemetery. His son Cecil Edward William became managing director of Zimpels: after nearly a century of unbroken ownership by the family of its Hungarian founder, the company was sold in 1981 to Parrys Esplanade Ltd who retained the name Zimpels.

E. F. Kunz, *Blood and gold* (Melb, 1969) and *The Hungarians in Australia* (Melb, 1985); R. M. James, *Heritage of pines* (Perth, 1977); *V&P* (LA WA), 1893 (22), p 34, 1899, 3 (A10), p 188.

E. F. KUNZ

ZWAR, ALBERT MICHAEL (1863-1935) and HENRY PETER (1873-1959), tanners and politicians, were born on 17 July 1863 and 2 December 1873 at Broadford, Victoria, two of eleven children of Michael Zwar, farmer,

and his wife Agnes, née Zimmer, both Sorbs from Saxony. Their cousin was T. B. Zwar [q.v.]. Educated at the local state school, Albert joined Eliza Tinsley & Co. (England) at Melbourne as a clerk before opening a small business at Yarrawonga. In 1888, with his brother William and Leonard Lloyd, he purchased the Ovens Tannery near Beechworth. Albert married Harriet Augusta Lawrence on 10 May 1893 at Beechworth with Presbyterian forms.

Forceful and enterprising, Albert became 'the uncrowned king of Beechworth'. When the tannery was destroyed by fire in 1915, he resisted economic inducements to move to Melbourne and rebuilt on a larger scale; by 1919 the firm's exports to London were valued at £72 714. As chairman and managing director, he incorporated the tannery in 1920 as Zwar Bros Pty Ltd. Next year he increased the tannery's supply of pure water by purchasing from the Rocky Mountain Extended Gold Sluicing Co. Ltd a tunnel which ran under Beechworth and was fed by springs. He travelled overseas in 1922 and bought the latest machinery for processing high quality leather. In 1925 fuel-oil engines were installed to generate electricity and Zwar contracted with the shire council to supply Beechworth with electricity. Between 1930 and 1931 the company took over two major customers in Melbourne, Goldings Pty Ltd, Canterbury, and Robert S. Don, Brunswick. The tannery, employing nearly two hundred people by 1935, was Beechworth's main industry.

Belonging to the Victorian Farmers' Union and the Country Party, Zwar was member for North Eastern Province in the Victorian Legislative Council in 1922-35. Formidable, conservative and a staunch Anglican, he was president of the Beechworth Technical School Board, the Ovens District Hospital, and the local bowling and rifle clubs. He died on 23 February 1935 at Beechworth and was buried in the local cemetery. His wife, three sons and a daughter survived him; his estate was sworn for probate at £43 718.

Henry Zwar attended Melbourne Church of England Grammar School on a scholarship, but left at 15 to work on his father's farm. Later apprenticed to his brothers, he was admitted to the partnership in 1901 after William withdrew to buy the Parkside Tannery at Preston. On 28 March 1899 Henry had married Jane Frier Cunningham at Beechworth with Congregational forms. With Albert, he bought the Parkside tannery from William. Lloyd sold out of the Beechworth partnership in 1914 and Henry became the sole owner of Parkside in 1919, having relinquished his share in the Beechworth tannery. As managing director of Henry P. Zwar Pty Ltd, he employed over one hundred men at his premises in Cramer Street, Preston, producing leather, mainly for automobile and furniture upholstery. A member of the Commonwealth Leather Board during World War I, and of the Tanners' Wages Board of Victoria, he was sometime president of the Federated Master Tanners' Association of Australia and of its Victorian branch. Known locally as 'H.P.' or 'Dick', Zwar was also a member (1929-35) of the Preston City Council and mayor in 1933-34.

He was president of the local branch of the National Federation in 1927 when he unsuccessfully contested the Legislative Assembly seat of Heidelberg. Winning it in 1932 for the United Australia Party, he held the seat until its abolition in 1945, increasing his vote in the Labor stronghold of Preston to a large majority. In parliament Zwar voted independently, claiming 'conscience as the final court of appeal'. His overriding concerns were for the unemployed and for the plight of widows and deserted wives: as president (1929-32) of the Preston unemployment relief committee, he had helped many people and was able to draw on this experience to advocate more humane government policies. Zwar stressed the value of secondary industries and heaped contempt on Labor's alliance with the Dunstan [q.v.8] Country Party government in 1935-43, arguing that it had led Labor members to betray their responsibilities for social welfare. In 1945 as an Independent Liberal he unsuccessfully contested the new seat of Preston.

Tall and dignified, with a brush moustache, Henry was gregarious and philanthropic. A life governor of several Melbourne hospitals, he was also tireless in his efforts to assist returned servicemen: the Returned Sailors' and Soldiers' Imperial League of Australia honoured him repeatedly (awarding him their gold medal of merit) and the Limbless Soldiers' Association presented him with their silver medal. President (1944-47) of the Victorian Football Association and a trustee of the Melbourne Cricket Ground, he was associated, usually as president, with numerous Preston sporting and athletic clubs. An Anglican and a member of the local branch of the Australian Natives' Association, he was involved with Preston's school boards, citizens' band and horticultural society. Zwar was chairman of H. H. Webb & Co. Pty Ltd, importers and merchants, and a director of the Bendigo Certified Milk Co. He was appointed O.B.E. in 1950. The tannery was sold by the family in 1957. Survived by two daughters and a son, Henry Zwar died on 12 January 1959 at Kew, Melbourne, and was buried in Preston cemetery. His Victorian estate was sworn for probate at £50 590. A local sports reserve, and a fountain at the Preston and Northcote Community Hospital,

commemorate him. His portrait is in the Preston City Library.

A. Kenyon, *The story of Australia* (Melb, 1936); M. Fiddian, *The Bullants* (Melb, 1983); C. Woods, *Beechworth* (Melb, 1985); R. Wuchatsch, *Westgarthtown* (Melb, 1985); *Ovens and Murray Advertiser*, 25 Apr 1928, 27 Feb 1935; *Preston Post*, 14 Jan 1959; J. J. Macaulay, The Beechworth Tannery, 1888-1961 (two mss, 1971, Univ Melb Archives); information from Pastor K. Zwar, Croydon, Melb.

CAROLE WOODS

ZWAR, TRAUGOTT BERNHARD (1876-1947), surgeon, was born on 20 June 1876 at Kapunda, South Australia, son of John Zwar, homoeopathic doctor, and his wife Anna, née Kaiser, Lutherans who had left Saxony in 1849 to avoid religious persecution. Albert and Henry Zwar [qq.v.] were his cousins. Educated at Prince Alfred College, Adelaide, Bernard commenced medical studies at the University of Adelaide; after the temporary closure of the clinical school in 1898, he continued his course at the University of Melbourne (M.B., 1899; Ch.B., 1901; M.D., 1902) where he graduated with first-class honours and the exhibition in medicine.

After serving as senior resident surgeon at the Melbourne Hospital (1900-01) and resident medical officer at the Austin Hospital (1901-04), Zwar travelled to England and Germany for postgraduate study. Returning to the University of Melbourne, he graduated M.S. (1908), joined the staff of St Vincent's Hospital as honorary anaesthetist and became surgeon to out-patients; from 1911 he worked in the latter capacity at the Melbourne Hospital. In private practice he shared rooms in Collins Street and worked in close association with Dr Leslie Scott Latham, brother of (Sir) John Latham [q.v.10].

A captain in the Australian Army Medical Corps from 1912, Zwar was appointed major in the Australian Imperial Force in October 1914 and allotted to the 2nd Australian Stationary Hospital. He tended the wounded at the Gallipoli landing and later served in Egypt. Invalided home in February 1916, on 4 May at Hawthorn he married with Presbyterian forms Essy Craig, a nurse.

At the Melbourne Hospital, Zwar was honorary surgeon to in-patients from 1919 and honorary consulting surgeon from 1935; he was also a member of the committee of management from 1925 and president in 1937-45. He won acceptance for and implemented the move of the hospital to its site in Parkville. Lecturer in surgery at the university in 1924-35, he was elected to its council in 1935 and served as deputy chancellor in 1943-44.

In the wider medical community Zwar undertook myriad responsiblities. A councillor (1922-37) of the Victorian branch of the British Medical Association, he was president in 1929. He served, as well, as president of the Melbourne Medical Asociation (1922-23), and as chairman of the Nurses' Board of Victoria (1924-27) and the Walter and Eliza Hall [qq.v.9] Institute of Research in Pathology and Medicine (1937-47). A founder of the College of Surgeons of Australasia (1927), he belonged to the Medical Board of Victoria, the advisory committee of the Repatriation Commission, and the Anti-Cancer Council. He was appointed C.M.G. in 1941.

Gruff, sincere and lovable, 'Zeddie'—as he was affectionately nicknamed—was a keen golf, tennis and bridge player, an active member of the Wallaby Club and a voracious reader. He created a beautiful garden at his Malvern home. Although students joked about his quaint, formal and rather stiff ways, colleagues respected his honesty and purpose, straightforwardness and loyalty. Survived by his wife and son, Zwar died at his home on 16 January 1947 and was buried in Melbourne general cemetery. His estate was sworn for probate at £15 633; his portrait by Charles Wheeler [q.v.] is held by the Royal Melbourne Hospital.

P. Kenny (ed), *The founders of the Royal Australasian College of Surgeons* (Melb, 1984); *MJA*, 26 Apr 1947.   BENJAMIN RANK